1 MONTH OF
FREE
READING

at

www.ForgottenBooks.com

By purchasing this book you are eligible for one month membership to ForgottenBooks.com, giving you unlimited access to our entire collection of over 1,000,000 titles via our web site and mobile apps.

To claim your free month visit:

www.forgottenbooks.com/free1235599

ISBN 978-0-332-73605-1
PIBN 11235599

THE

APOCALYPSE EXPLAINED

ACCORDING TO

THE SPIRITUAL SENSE;

IN WHICH ARE REVEALED

.

THE ARCANA WHICH ARE THERE PREDICTED, AND HAVE
BEEN HITHERTO DEEPLY CONCEALED.

FROM A LATIN POSTHUMOUS WORK

OF

EMANUEL SWEDENBORG.

FIRST AMERICAN, FROM THE LAST LONDON EDITION

IN FIVE VOLUMES.

— VOL. III. —

Boston:

PUBLISHED BY OTIS CLAPP,

No. 1 BEACON STREET.

1859.

THE

APOCALYPSE EXPLAINED.

CHAPTER IX.

1. And the fifth angel sounded, and I saw a star fall from heaven unto the earth; and to him was given the key of the bottomless pit.

2. And he opened the bottomless pit; and there arose a smoke out of the pit, as the smoke of a great furnace : and the sun and the air were darkened by reason of the smoke of the pit.

3. And there came out of the smoke locusts upon the earth; and unto them was given power, as the scorpions of the earth have power.

4. And it was commanded them that they should not hurt the grass of the earth, neither any green thing, neither any tree ; but only those men who have not the seal of God in their foreheads.

5. And to them it was given that they should not kill them, but that they should be tormented five months; and their torment was as the torment of a scorpion, when he striketh a man.

6. And in those days shall men seek death, and shall not find it; and shall desire to die, and death shall flee from them.

7. And the shapes of the locusts were like unto horses prepared unto battle; and on their heads were as it were crowns like gold, and their faces were as the faces of men.

8. And they had hair as the hair of women, and their teeth were as the teeth of lions.

9. And they had breastplates, as it were breastplates of iron ; and the sound of their wings was as the sound of chariots of many horses running to battle.

10. And they had tails like unto scorpions; and there were stings in their tails ; and their power was to hurt men five months.

11. And they had a king over them, the angel of the bottomless pit; whose name in the Hebrew tongue is Abaddon, but in the Greek tongue he hath his name Apollyon.

12. One woe is past; behold, there comes two woes more hereafter.

13. And the sixth angel sounded, and I heard a voice from the four horns of the golden altar which is before God.

14. Saying to the sixth angel, who had the trumpet, Loose the four angels that are bound at the great river Euphrates.

15. And the four angels were loosed, who were prepared for an hour, and a day, and a month, and a year, to slay the third part of men.

16. And the number of the armies of horsemen was two myriads of myriads; and I heard the number of them.

17. And thus I saw the horses in the vision, and them that sat on them, having breastplates of fire, and of jacinth, and brimstone: and the heads of the horses were as the heads of lions; and out of their mouths issued fire, and smoke, and brimstone.

18. By these three was the third part of men killed, by the fire, and by the smoke, and by the brimstone, which issued out of their mouths.

19. For their power is in their mouth, and in their tails: for their tails were like unto serpents, and had heads, and with them they do hurt.

20. And the rest of men who were not killed by these plagues, yet repented not of the works of their hands, that they should not worship devils, and idols of gold, and silver, and brass, and stone, and of wood, which neither can see, nor hear, nor walk:

21. Neither repented they of their murders, nor of their sorceries, nor of their fornications, nor of their thefts.

EXPLICATION.

533. Verses 1, 2. "And the fifth angel sounded, and I saw a star fall from heaven unto the earth: and to him was given the key of the bottomless pit. And he opened the bottomless pit; and there arose a smoke out of the pit, as the smoke of a great furnace; and the sun and the air were darkened by reason of the smoke of the pit."—"And the fifth angel sounded," signifies the influx out of heaven manifesting the state of the church, that it was absolutely changed; "and I saw a star fall from heaven unto the earth," signifies the knowledges of truth falsified, and thus turned into falsities; "and to him was given the key of the bottomless pit," signifies communication and conjunction with the hells: "and he opened the bottomless pit," signifies communication and conjunction with the hells, where and whence such falsities are: "and there arose a smoke out of the pit, as the smoke of a great furnace," signifies dense falsities thence, originating in the evils of earthly and corporeal loves: "and the sun and the air were darkened by reason of the smoke of the pit," signifies that the light of truth from the Lord was made thick darkness by infernal falsities.

534. "And the fifth angel sounded"—That these words signify influx out of heaven manifesting the state of the church, that it was absolutely changed, appears from the signification of sounding with

a trumpet, as denoting influx out of heaven, and a change of the state of the church, concerning which, see above, n. 502 : in this case, that the state of the church was absolutely changed, because it was said just above, concerning the three last times of the angel sounding, " woe, woe, woe, to the inhabiters of the earth, by reason of the other voices of the trumpet of the three angels which are yet to sound ;" the change which is described in what now follows, is, that all truth was destroyed, and that the falsity, which was in the place of it, opened the hells, whence falsities issued out.

535. " And I saw a star fall from heaven unto the earth"—That hereby are signified the knowledges of truth falsified, and thus turned into falsities, appears from the signification of stars, as denoting the knowledges of good and truth, concerning which, see above, n. 72, 402; and from the signification of falling from heaven, as denoting to perish, which is the case with the knowledges of truth when they are denied, and when they are falsified; in this case, when they are falsified ; for this book does not treat of those who deny truths, but of those who falsify them ; for they who deny truths are not amongst those who are in the former heaven, and are cast down thence into hell at the day of the last judgment, for these are cast thither immediately after death ; but it is they who falsify truths from various causes who are treated of in this book, inasmuch as they made to themselvs a heaven which was afterwards destroyed. The knowledges of good and truth from the Word, are falsified by those, who acknowledge the Word, but apply it to favor their own loves, and the principles which are from self-derived intelligence, for thus they turn the truths of the Word into falsities, and thus the knowledges of good and truth with them perish : from these considerations it may appear that by the star falling from heaven unto the earth, is signified that the knowledges of truth were falsified, and thus turned into falsities, see above, n. 517.   That to fall down, or to fall from heaven to the earth, signifies to perish, that is, not to have any more a place in heaven, but to be cast down thence, and conjoined with hell, is evident from what follows, where it is said, " And to him was given the key of the bottomless pit," the bottomless pit denoting the hell where and whence are the falsities of evil. The same is signified by falling from heaven unto the earth, where it is said in the Revelations : " And the stars of heaven fell unto the earth" (vi. 13).   And again : " And his tail drew the third part of the stars of heaven, and did cast them to the earth" (xii. 4).   And in Daniel : " And it waxed great, even to the host of heaven ; and it cast down some of the host, and of the stars to the ground, and stamped upon them" (viii. 10).   And in Matthew : " Immediately after the tribulation of those days shall the sun be darkened, and the moon shall not give her light, and the stars shall fall from heaven, and the powers of the heavens shall be shaken" (xxiv. 29).   The same is also signified by the words of the Lord in Luke : " And he said unto them, I beheld Satan as lightning fall from heaven" (x. 18).   Here by Satan is understood all the falsity which destroys truth, for the hells where such falsities are, and whence they arise,

are called Satan, and the hells where and whence the evils are which destroy goods, are called the Devil, wherefore by Satan as lightning falling from heaven, is understood, that all the falsity which destroyed the truth of the Word, was cast down out of heaven. The same is also signified by the following words in the Revelations: "And the great dragon was cast out, that old serpent called the Devil, and Satan, which deceiveth the whole world: he was cast out into the earth, and his angels were cast out with him" (xii. 9). From these considerations it may appear that by falling, and being cast down out of heaven to the earth, is signified, to have no more place in heaven, but in hell, consequently to perish; by the earth, here, is also signified what is cursed, as was shown above, n. 304 at the end. The reason why they who falsify the truths of the Word by interpretations to confirm evils of the life, avert themselves from heaven and convert themselves to hell, is, because the conjunction of heaven with man is by the Word, for heaven is in the spiritual sense of the Word, and man is in its natural sense, wherefore the conjunction of heaven with the world is by the Word; on this account, also, the Word is called a covenant, and a covenant denotes conjunction: it is from this ground, that they who apply the Word to evils of the life, and to false principles which are from self-derived intelligence, cannot be conjoined with heaven; and they who are not conjoined with heaven are conjoined with hell; for man must of necessity be either in heaven or in hell, as it is not allowed him to hang between both. But they who apply the Word to falsities which do not disagree with good of life, such as are with the upright Gentiles who have not the Word, and with the simple in the church who believe in the Lord, and lead a good life, inasmuch as from their falsities they have respect to good, the Lord also applies them to good, and turns them to heaven; for the essential principle in heaven is the good of life, which is the same thing with the good of love to the Lord, and with the good of love towards the neighbor, or charity; for according to this good, every one there has perception of truth, intelligence, and wisdom. Hence, then, it may appear what is understood by the falsification of truth from the Word, which is here signified by the star falling from heaven unto the earth.

536. "And to him was given the key of the bottomless pit"— That hereby is signified communication and conjunction with the hells, appears from the signification of a key, as denoting opening, concerning which we shall speak presently; and from the signification of the bottomless pit, as denoting the hells where and whence are the falsities of evils, of which we shall speak in the following articles. The reason why it is said, that the key of the bottomless pit was given to the star falling from heaven unto the earth, is, because by the star, in this case, are signified the knowledges of truth from the Word falsified by applications to evils and the falsities thence derived; and evils of falsities, and falsities of evils, with man, open the hells where similar evils and falsities exist. But what is understood by opening the hells, will also be explained in,

the following article, where it is said : "And he opened the bottom-less pit." That a key signifies opening, is from appearance in the spiritual world ; for in that world there are houses and chambers, also doors by which they enter, and locks and keys by which they are opened, and they all signify such things as are in man ; the house itself corresponds to the interiors of the spiritual and natural mind ; in like manner the chambers ; and the doors correspond to the communications which are between the interiors of the spiritual and natural mind ; and the key corresponds to admission and open-ing from one part into the other ; in a word, the most minute things belonging to the house in which spirits and angels dwell, correspond to similar things in them. Few of the spirits know this, because few think anything of correspondences, for being in them, they do not reflect upon them : the case herein is as with man in the world, few know the qualities of their affections and thoughts, because they are in them, and hence do not reflect upon them, when notwith-standing they are innumerable, as may appear from analytical par-ticulars which have been discovered by many of the learned, all which are operations of the mind. From what has been said above it may be known, whence it is that a key is here mentioned, and that it signifies admission and opening. It has the like signification in other passages in the Word ; thus in Matthew : "And I will give unto thee the keys of the kingdom of heaven" (xvi. 19).* Again, in the Revelation : "I am he that liveth, and was dead ; and, be-hold, I am alive for ever more, amen ; and have the keys of hell and of death" (i. 18). And again : "These things saith he that is holy, he that is true, he that hath the key of David, he that openeth, and no man shutteth ; and shutteth, and no man openeth" (iii. 7) ; see above, n. 206. And again : "And I saw an angel come down from heaven, having the key of the bottomless pit, and a great chain was in his hand. And he laid hold on the dragon, that old serpent, which is the devil, and Satan, and bound him a thousand years" (xx. 1, 2). This passage will be explained in its proper place. So again, in Luke : "Woe unto you, lawyers ! for ye have taken away the key of knowledge ; ye enter not in yourselves, and them that were entering in ye hindered" (xi. 52). They were called lawyers, who searched the scriptures, and taught how they were to be under-stood ; and inasmuch as the sacred scripture, or the Word, is the ground of communication, and thence of conjunction with heaven, as was said in the article above, and truths are what open the com-munication, and the goods of truths are what constitute conjunction, whereas truths falsified, which in themselves are falsities of evil, are what cause disjunction, therefore it is said that they had taken away the key of knowledge, that is, that by means of truths they could have opened communication with heaven to those whom they taught ; but because they perverted the Word by applications to their own loves, and thence to false principles, it is therefore said :

---

* Which may be seen explained above, n. 206 ; also in Isaiah, chap. xxii. 21, 22, where the same is said concerning Eliakim, as may also be seen explained above, n. 206.

"Ye enter not in yourselves, and them that were entering in ye hindered." From these considerations also it may appear, that the key which opened the pit, signifies communication and conjunction with the hells by the falsities into which the truths of the Word are turned by those who falsify them in applying them to evils of the life, and to the false principles thence derived.

537. "And he opened the bottomless pit"—That hereby are signified communication and conjunction with the hells, where and whence such falsities are, appears from the signification of opening, as here denoting to communicate and conjoin, concerning which we shall speak presently; and from the signification of the bottomless pit, as denoting the hell where and whence such falsities are. The reason why these hells are called in the Word pits, bottomless pits, and wells, is because a well signifies the Word in the sense of the letter, and the truth of doctrine thence derived, but in the opposite sense, the Word falsified, and the false doctrine thence derived; and the abyss or deep of the sea signifies hell. The reason why it signifies the hell where they are, who falsified the Word by applying its truths to evils of the life, is, because those hells appear to them who are above, as seas, and those who are there as in the bottom of them. It has been also granted me to see those seas or hells, and those who are in the bottom of them, whence they have also spoken with me, and said that they were not in waters, but on dry ground; hence it was also evident, that the waters of those seas are appearances corresponding to the falsities in which the inhabitants are principled; moreover, the waters of those seas are grosser and denser according to the falsifications, and the depths are also various according to the evils from which they are falsified. But concerning the signification of abyss in the Word more will be seen below. The reason why the opening of the bottomless pit signifies communication and conjunction with such hells, is, because the hells are not opened except when evil spirits enter, which takes place when they have passed their time in the world of spirits; for it is not allowed to any evil spirit to go out from hell, after he has been once cast thither, and if he do go out he presently falls back thither. But every man is conjoined with spirits who are in the world of spirits, and with spirits of a quality agreeing with his own; wherefore the man who falsifies the Word, in applying it to evils of life, and to falsities confirming those evils, is conjoined with similar spirits, and by them with the hells, which are in similar falsities. Every man after death becomes a spirit, and is then immediately tied or bound either to infernal, or to heavenly societies, according to his life in the world; and all spirits, before they are cast down into hell, or elevated into heaven, are first in the world of spirits, and at that time with men who live in the world, the evil spirits with the evil, and the good with the good, and by these man has communication and conjunction either with the hells or with the heavens. Hence it is evident, that by opening the pit is not signified to open hell, but communcation, and by communication to have conjunction with hell. From all the hells, also, there exhale falsities of evil in great abundance, in which the spirits are who are

in the world of spirits, and together with them, the men who are in similar falsities in our world : neither spirit nor man can be any where else, than where the love of his life is, for what a man loves, that he wills, thinks, and breathes; concerning the nature of the world of spirits, see the work concerning H. & H. n. 421–431.

The reason why a pit or a well signifies the Word and the truth of doctrine, and, in the opposite sense, the Word falsified, and thence the falsity of doctrine, is, because wells contain waters, and waters signify truths, and, in the opposite sense, falsities, as shown above, n. 71, 483, 518.   That a well signifies both the latter and the former, appears from the following passages in the Word ; thus in Moses : "And from thence they went to Beer ; that is the well whereof Jehovah spake unto Moses, Gather the people together, and I will give them water.   Then Israel sang this song, Spring up, O well ; sing ye unto it : the princes digged the well, the nobles of the people digged it, by the direction of the lawgiver, with their staves" (Numb. xxi. 16, 17, 18).   That a well here signifies the truth of doctrine from the Word, may appear from the song which Israel sang concerning it ; by, "Spring up, O well, sing ye unto it," is sig- nified, that doctrine from the Word should teach truth, and that they should receive it, the calling forth of truth is signified by, spring up, O well, and reception and instruction by, sing ye unto it ; "The princes digged the well, the nobles of the people digged it, by the direction of the lawgiver, with their staves," signifies that they who are in truths and in the goods of truths are enlightened by the Lord, and search out and collect doctrine by the Word from him ; princes denote those who are in truths ; nobles of the people, those who are in the goods of truth ; and to dig denotes to search out and collect ; lawgiver signifies the Lord as to the Word, and as to doctrine from the Word, and staves signify power and strength of mind, in this case, by the Lord, from the Word, because it is said, by direction of the lawgiver ; hence it is evident, what the well here signifies.   The reason why Israel sung a song concerning this well, was, because Beer, in the original tongue, signifies a well, and a well, in the spi- ritual sense, signifies the Word and doctrine from the Word ; in like manner as Beersheba, which is frequently mentioned in the histori- cal parts of the Word.   The same is meant by Jacob's well at which the Lord sat, and conversed with the women of Samaria, to whom he said ; "If thou knowest the gift of God, and who it is that saith to thee, Give me to drink ; thou wouldst have asked of him, and he would have given thee living water.   Whosoever drinketh of the water that I shall give him shall never thirst ; but the water that I shall give him shall be in him a well of water springing up into ever- lasting life" (John iv. 6–14).   The reason why the Lord spake with the woman of Samaria at that well, was, because by the woman of Samaria was understood the church to be established with the Gen- tiles, and by the Samaritans, who are also mentioned in other pass- ages, were understood the gentiles or nations which would receive doctrine from him, and concerning him ; by that well was signified doctrine from the Word ; by the water, the truth of doctrine ; and by the Lord sitting at the well, the Word or divine truth.   That salvation is from the Lord by means of divine truth from the Word, is signified by the water which he would give becoming a well of water springing up into everlasting life.   The same is meant by the wells which the servants of Abraham and the servants of Isaac dug, and concerning which they strove with the servants of Abimelech (Gen. xxi. 25 ; xxvi. 15, 18–22, 25, 32).   By the wells which the servants of Abraham and the servants of Isaac dug, are signified truths of doctrine, because by Abraham, Isaac, and Jacob, in the Word, is understood the Lord ; but by Abimelech king of Gerar, or of the Philistines, are understood those who place salvation in truths alone without the good of life, as they who are in faith alone do at this day ; and inasmuch as all truth is from good, or the all of faith from charity, and they who separate and exclude good from truth, or charity from faith, cannot possess any genuine truth of doctrine, but all the truth of the Word is with them as a mere sense of the words without any perception of the thing, thus as a shell without a kernel, therefore they strive or quarrel concerning the truths of faith.   This was represented and signified by the strife of the servants of Abimelech with the servants of Abraham and of Isaac concerning the wells.   There is an internal spiritual sense in the historical parts of the Word, as well as in the prophetical parts of it, as may appear from the A. C., where the historical circumstances which are contained in Genesis and Exodus are explained as to their internal spiritual sense, as also the circumstances related concerning the wells of Abraham and Isaac, which may be seen in the other historical relations concerning wells in the Word. As in Luke : " Which of you shall have an ass or an ox fallen into a pit, and will not straightway pull him out on the sabbath day ?" (xiv. 5.)   The reason why there was a statute to this purpose enjoined on the Israelites and Jewish nation, was, on account of the spiritual sense contained in it ; for all the statutes, judgments, and precepts, given to the children of Israel, signified spiritual things pertaining to heaven and to the church ; this statute therefore signified, that if any one shall fall into what is false and evil, he is to be brought out of it by the truth which is taught from the Lord on the sabbath day.   By a pit or well, in the above passage, falsity and its evil are understood ; by an ass and an ox are signified the truth and good of the natural man ; by falling into the pit is signified falling into falsity and its evil : by being drawn out on the sabbath day, is signified to be instructed and thereby led out of them ; for the sabbath day signifies the Lord as to instruction and doctrine, wherefore he calls himself Lord of the sabbath.*

Nearly similar is the spiritual sense contained in these words of Moses : " And if a man shall open a pit, or if a man shall dig a pit, and not cover it, and an ox or an ass fall therein ; the owner of the pit shall make it good, and give money unto the owner of them ; and the dead beast shall be his " (Exod. xxi. 33, 34).   Here, by a man opening a pit is signified the propagation of any falsity pertaining to

---

* That ass signifies the truth of the natural man, may be seen in the A. C. n. 2781, 5741 ; and that ox signifies the good of the natural man, n. 2180, 2566, 9135, in the same.

himself; " or if a man shall dig a pit," signifies if he shall frame or hatch what is false; "and an ox or an ass fall therein, " signifies the perversion of good and truth in the natural principle pertaining to another. " The owner of the pit shall make it good," signifies, that he with whom the falsity originates, shall amend it: "and give money to the owner of them," signifies that he shall do so by truth pertaining to him, whose g d and truth in the natural principle was perverted: "and the dead beast shall be his" signifies, that the evil, or the falsity, remains with him.* Thus also in Matthew: "Let them alone: they be blind leaders of the blind. And if the blind lead the blind, both shall fall into the ditch " (xv. 14; Luke vi. 39). This the Lord said to the scribes and pharisees, who, although they had the Word, in which are all divine truths, yet understood nothing of truth; and inasmuch as they taught falsities, and their falsities were also believed by the people, they are therefore called blind leaders of the blind; the blind in the Word denoting those who do not understand truth; and because a pit or ditch signifies what is false, it is said that they shall both fall into it. So in David: " Deliver me out of the mire, and let me not sink: let me be delivered from them that hate me, and out of the deep waters. Let not the waterflood overflow me, neither let the deep swallow me up, and let not the pit shut her mouth upon me" (Psalm lxix. 15, 16). That pit here signifies the hell where and whence are falsities, is manifest, for it is said, "let not the pit shut her mouth upon me, " that is, let not the hell whence are falsities, or the falsities from hell, wholly possess me, so that I may not escape; the mire, out of which it is said, "deliver me, and let me not sink," denotes the evil of what is false, and to sink denotes to perish thereby; " let me be delivered from them that hate me, and out of the deep waters, " signifies to be liberated from the evils and falsities which are from the hells, haters denoting evils thence derived, and deep waters denoting fals.ties thence derived: neither let the deep swallow me up," signifies, the hell where are the falsities of evil, or the falsities of evil from hell. So again: " The words of his mouth were smoother than butter, but war was in his heart; his words were softer than oil, yet were they drawn swords But thou, O God, shalt bring them down into the pit of destruction " (Ps. lv. 21, 23). These things are said of those who make a pretence to good affections whilst they speak falsities by which they seduce; by the words of their mouth being smoother than butter, is signified, good pretended by the affections, butter denoting the good of external affection; their words being softer than oil, signifies things similar, oil denoting the good of internal affection; " yet were they drawn swords, " signifies when notwithstanding they are falsities destroying good and truth, drawn swords denoting falsities destroying; "but thou, O God, shalt cast them down into the pit," signifies into the hell where the destructive falsities of that kind prevail. Inasmuch as pits in the Word signify nearly the same as wells, it may be expedient to adduce also some passages concerning pits. Thus in Jeremiah: " And their nobles have sent their little ones to the waters: they came to the pits, and found no water; they returned

* These things may be seen more fully explained in the A. C. n. 9084-9089 .

with their vessels empty" (xiv. 3). Here, by nobles are signified those who lead and teach others; by little ones, those who are led and taught; and by waters, truths; hence it is evident what is signified by their nobles sending the little ones to the waters. By the pits in which there was no water are signified doctrinals in which there were no truths, whence it may also appear what is signified by their coming to the pits and finding no water; that they had no science or understanding of truth, is signified by their returning with their vessels empty, vessels in the Word denoting things recipient of truth, consequently scientific and intellectual things. So in Zechariah: "As for thee also, by the blood of thy covenant I have sent forth thy prisoners out of the pit wherein is no water" (ix. 11). This is spoken respecting the liberation of the faithful by the Lord, who were detained in the inferior or lower earth until his advent; and also concerning the enlightening of the Gentiles who were in falsities from ignorance; by the blood of thy covenant is signified the divine truth proceeding from the Lord, consequently the Word, which is called a covenant, because thereby conjunction is effected, a covenant denoting conjunction: by the prisoners in the pit in which there is no water, are understood those who are in falsities from ignorance; pit here denoting a doctrine not of truth, and also the inferior earth where they who were in falses from ignorance were detained until the coming of the Lord; "wherein is no water," denotes where there is no truth; they are called prisoners, because they could not be liberated from falsities but by the Lord. Again in Jeremiah: "For my people have committed two evils; they have forsaken me the fountain of living waters; and have hewed them out cisterns, broken cisterns, that can hold no water" (ii. 13). By hewing them out cisterns, broken cisterns, that can hold no water, is signified to hatch doctrines from self-derived intelligence, which, inasmuch as they are from man's proprium, are falsities, for the proprium of man is nothing but evil, and being evil it also produces falsity for evil cannot produce anything else but falsity; this passage may be seen explained above, n. 483. Again in the same prophet: "Neither said they, where is Jehovah that brought us up out of the land of Egypt, that led us through the wilderness, through a land of deserts and of pits, through a land of drought and of the shadow of death, through a land that no man passed through, and where no man dwelt?" (ii.6.) That by the wilderness in which the children of Israel were led, was represented and signified the first state of the church to be established with those who are in mere ignorance of good and truth, has been shown in the A. C. in which the book of Exodus is explained; and inasmuch as that state was represented and signified by their wandering in the wilderness, therefore it is said that Jehovah led them through a land of deserts and of pits, a land of drought and of the shadow of death; by the land of deserts and of drought is understood here, as elsewhere in the Word, a state of non-perception of good, and by a land of pits and of the shadow of death, is understood a state of ignorance of truth, and thence a state of falsity; by no man passing through, and no man dwelling therein, is signified no understanding of truth, nor perception of good, man (vir) in the Word denoting the understanding of truth, and man (homo) the perception of good, and by there being neither one nor the other, is signified no church, either as to truth or as to good. Again, in Isaiah: "The captive exile hasteneth that he may be loosed, and that he should not die in the pit, nor that his bread should fail" (li. 14). This is said concerning the Lord, His advent is understood by "the captive exile hasteneth," liberation from the falsities of ignorance, by not dying in the pit, wherefore the same is here signified by pit, as by the pit mentioned above in which were the prisoners; supply of spiritual instruction and nourishment, is signified by his bread not failing, for by bread is understood all spiritual food, and by spiritual food is understood instruction in truths and goods, whence come intelligence and wisdom. So in Ezekiel: "Behold, therefore I will bring strangers upon thee, the terrible of the nations: and they shall draw their swords against the beauty if thy wisdom, and they shall defile thy brightness. They shall bring thee down to the pit, and thou shalt die the deaths of them that are slain in the midst of the seas" (xxviii. 7, 8). These things are spoken concerning the prince of Tyrus, by whom are understood those who from self-derived intelligence hatch falsities, by which the knowledges of truth and good are destroyed; their ruin, by their own falsities is signified by, "Behold, therefore I will bring strangers upon thee, the terrible of the nations," strangers denoting falsities which destroy truths, and the terrible of the nations, evils which destroy goods; that they shall be destroyed by their own falsities originating in self-derived intelligence, is signified by "And they shall draw their swords against the beauty of thy wisdom, and they shall defile thy brightness," swords denoting falsities destroying truths; the pit into which they shall be brought down, signifies infernal falsity; and by them that are slain in the midst of the seas, are signified those who perish by falsities, the midst of the seas signifying the hell where and whence falsities are, in like manner as the abyss. And in Jeremiah: "Then took they Jeremiah, and cast him into the dungeon of Malachia the son of Hammelech, that was in the court of the prison: and they let down Jeremiah with cords. And in the dungeon there was no water, but mire, so Jeremiah sunk in the mire. Then the king commanded Ebed-melech the Ethiopian, saying, Take from hence thirty men with thee, and take up Jeremiah the prophet out of the dungeon before he die. So Ebed-melech took the men with him, and went into the house of the king under the treasury, and took thence old cast clouts and old rotten rags, and let them down by cords into the dungeon to Jeremiah. So they drew up Jeremiah with cords, and took him up out of the dungeon" (xxxviii. 6–13). By these things is signified the truth of doctrine falsified, the prophet signifying the truth of doctrine, and his being cast into the dungeon, signifying the falsification thereof; by the old cast clouts and the rotten rags with which they drew him out, is signified the vindication of the truth of doctrine, and restitution, by such goods and truths of the literal sense of the

Word, as were not perceived and understood, and therefore were neglected and rejected; these things are signified by those rags; to what purpose else would it be to mention in the divine Word, that the prophet was drawn out by such things. From these few passages it may appear, what is signified by a well and by a pit in the Word, namely, the Word and the truth of doctrine, and, in the opposite sense, the Word falsified, and thence the falsity of doctrine. In some passages also by a well and pit, is signified the same as by a fountain, concerning the signification of which in both senses see above, n. 483.

538. It was said above that the bottomless pit signifies the hells where and whence falsities are : the reason of this signification is, because those hells, where the falsities of evil have rule, appear as seas, in the depths of which are the infernal crew, who are principled in the falsities of evil ; the reason of their appearing as seas is, because falsities continually flow out from them and appear as waters, wherefore waters in the Word also signify falsities ; from the waters themselves also the quality of the falsity is known, for falsities are of various kinds, namely, as many as there are evils ; the falsities which are from grievous evils appear over those hells as gross and black waters, and falsities from the evil of the love of self, as red waters, the quality of the genus of the falsity being distinguishable from the grossness and color. It is to be remembered that in the spiritual world, truths also appear as waters, but as waters of a thin and pure quality ; the reason is, because there are three degrees of the life of man, as there are three heavens ; they in whom the third degree is opened are in an atmosphere pure as ether, in such atmosphere as they who dwell in the third or inmost heaven ; but they, in whom only the second degree is opened, are in an atmosphere of an aerial appearance, in such are they of the second or middle heavens ; but they in whom the first degree only is opened, are in an atmosphere of a watery appearance, but thin and pure, in such are they of the first or ultimate heaven ; the reason of which is, because interior perceptions and thoughts, as being more perfect, correspond to a like purity of the atmosphere, in which they are, for they diffuse themselves from every angel, and still more from every angelic society, and present a corresponding sphere, which sphere appears in a like purity to that of the perceptions and thoughts of the angels, or of their intelligence and wisdom. This sphere appears as an atmosphere, as an etherial atmosphere in the inmost heaven, as an aerial atmosphere in the middle heaven, and as a thin watery atmosphere in the ultimate heaven, as was said above ; hence it is evident that an atmosphere of a watery appearance corresponds to natural thought and perception, but that an atmosphere which is as it were thinly watery, corresponds to spiritual natural thought and perception, in which are the angels of the ultimate heaven ; but the atmosphere which is of a gross watery nature, verging either to black or to red, corresponds to natural thought in which there is nothing spiritual ; and such natural thought pertains to those who are in the hells where falsities have rule ; for

all who are there are merely natural and sensual.* From these considerations it may appear, whence it is that the hells of falsities are in the Word called seas and pits, seas, because they appear as seas, and pits from their depth.

The same falsities are plainly meant in the following passages of the Word: thus in Moses: "Pharaoh's chariots and his host hath he cast into the sea: his chosen captains also are drowned in the Red Sea. The depths have covered them: they sank into the bottom as a stone. And with the blast of thy nostrils the waters were gathered together, the floods stood upright as a heap, and the depths were congealed in the heart of the sea" (Exod. xv. 4, 5, 8); these words form part of the song of Moses concerning Pharoah and his host after they were drowned in the Red Sea. By Pharaoh and his host are signified those who are in the falsities of evil, and by the Red Sea, is signified the hell where those falsities are; hence it is evident that by the depths which covered them, the hells are signified.† Again, in David: "He rebuked the Red Sea also, and it was dried up: so he led them through the depths as through the wilderness" (Psalm cvi. 9). And in Isaiah: "Art thou not it which hath dried the sea, the waters of the great deep; that hath made the depths of the sea a way for the ransomed to pass over?" (li. 10–15.) Again, in the same prophet: "Then he remembered the days of old, Moses, and his people, saying, Where is he that brought them up out of the sea with the shepherd of his flock? where is he that put his holy spirit within him? That led them by the right hand of Moses with his glorious arm, dividing the water before them, to make himself an everlasting name? That led them through the deep as a horse in the wilderness, that they should not stumble" (lxiii. 11, 12, 13). Here by the children of Israel before whom the Red Sea was dried up that they might pass safely through, are understood all who are in truths from good, whom the Lord defends, lest the falsities of evil which ascend continually from the hells should injure them; this is what is understood by drying up the sea, the waters of the great deep, and by making the depths thereof a way for the ransomed to pass over; likewise by leading them through the depths; for the falsities exhaled from the hells continually cling to man, consequently the hells, for whether we speak of falsities from the hells, or of the hells themselves, it is the same thing; but the Lord continually dissipates them with those who are in truths originating in good from himself; this then is what is signified by drying up the sea, and leading them through the depths. They who are in truths grounded in good from the Lord, are understood by the ransomed. The same is signified by the following passages in Isaiah: "That confirmeth the word of his servant, and performeth the counsel of his messengers; that saith to Jerusalem, Thou shalt be inhabited; and to the cities of Judah, Ye shall be

---

* That man has three degrees of life as the three heavens, and that they differ in purity, may be seen in the work concerning H. & H. n. 33, 34, 208, 209, 211.

† But the whole passage may be seen explained in the A. C. n. 8272–8279, and 8286–8289.

built, and I will raise up the decayed places thereof: That saith to the deep, be dry, and I will dry up thy rivers" (xliv. 26, 27). By Jerusalem is signified the church of the Lord, and by the cities of Judah are signified the goods and truths of doctrine; the restoration of the church and of doctrine is signified by being inhabited and built; the dissipation of the evils and falsities which are from the hells, and protection from them, are signified by drying up the deep and making dry the rivers. The same thing is signified by those words in Zechariah: "And he shall pass through the sea with affliction, and shall smite the waves in the sea, and all the deeps of the rivers shall dry up: and the pride of Assyria shall be brought down, and the sceptre of Egypt depart away" (x. 11). That they who live in truths from good are defended by the Lord, although falsities from the hells encompass them, is signified by Israel passing through the sea, and smiting the waves in the sea, and all the deeps of the river being dried up; for by Israel are understood those who are in truths from good; by the sea is understood hell and all the falsity thence derived; by the waves of the sea are signified reasonings from falsities against truths; by drying up all the deeps of the rivers is signified to dissipate all the falsities of evil, even those which are more deep or profound; the river Nile denoting the false scientific principle; wherefore it follows, "And the pride of Assyria shall be brought down, and the sceptre of Egypt shall depart away;" by Assyria is signified reasoning from falsities against truths, and by Egypt, the scientific principle applied to confirm falsities; the pride of Assyria which shall be cast down, signifies self-derived intelligence from which reasoning proceeds, and the sceptre of Egypt, which shall depart away, signifies the power which accedes to reasoning by scientifics which are applied for confirmation. So in Ezekiel: "Thus saith Jehovah God; In the day when he went down to the grave I caused a mourning: I covered the deep for him, and I restrained the floods thereof, and the great waters were stayed" (xxxi. 15). This is said of Pharaoh and Assyria; and by Pharaoh is signified the same as by Egypt, namely, the scientific principle destroying the truth of the church by application to falsities; and by Assyria is signified reasoning from falsities; that they who are such are cast down into hell, where such falsities, and reasonings, from them are, is signified by his going down into hell, and by the deep being covered for him; hence also it is evident that the deep denotes where and whence are the falsities of evil. So in Micah: "He will turn again, he will have compassion upon us; he will subdue our iniquities; and thou wilt cast all their sins into the depths of the sea" (vii. 19). Inasmuch as the depths of the sea, denote the hells where and whence are evils and falsities, therefore it is said that he shall cast all their sins into the depths of the sea. Again, in Ezekiel: "For thus saith the Lord Jehovah; When I shall make thee a desolate city like the cities that are not inhabited; when I shall bring up the deep upon thee, and great waters shall cover thee; when I shall bring thee down with them that descend into the pit, with the people of old time, and shall set thee in the low parts of the earth, in places desolate of old, with them that go down to the pit, that thou be not inhabited ; and I shall set glory in the land of the living" (xxvi. 19, 20). This is said of Tyrus, by which is signified the church as to the knowledges of truth and good, or as to the truths of the natural man, for the truths of the natural man are the knowledges of truth and good ; the vastation of the church as to these things is here treated of ; to make Tyrus a desolated city, as cities that are not inhabited, signifies the doctrine of the church without truths, and as doctrines which are without good, for the truths of doctrine without good are not truths, inasmuch as all truths are of good ; by bringing up the deep upon Tyrus, and causing great waters to cover her, is signified immersion in falsities from hell in much abundance, the deep denoting hell, and great waters denoting falsities in much abundance ; " with them that descend into the pit, with the people of old time," signifies unto those in hell who were there from the most ancient church just before the deluge, who are called the people of old time, as being from ancient time, and were, above all others, in falsities of a direful nature. Hence it is evident, what is signified by making Tyrus a desolate city, like the cities that are not inhabited, bringing her down with them that descend into the pit, with the people of old time, and setting her in the low parts of the earth, that she should not be inhabited : not to be inhabited denotes here not to be in any truths, because not in good, for such persons do not dwell in houses but in pits.   Similar things are signified by the following passage in Zechariah : " Behold, Jehovah will cast her out, and he will smite her power in the sea ; and she shall be devoured with fire" (ix. 4). This also is said of Tyrus, and by casting her out, smiting her power in the sea, and devouring her with fire, is signified to cast the falsities into hell, the sea denoting the hell in which are the falsities of evil, and her power or wealth denoting those falsities themselves. So again, in Ezekiel : " Thy rowers have brought thee into great waters ; the east wind hath broken thee in the midst of the seas. Thy riches, and thy fairs, thy merchandize, thy mariners, and thy pilots, thy calkers, and the occupiers of thy merchandize, and all thy men of war, that are in thee, and in all thy company which is in the midst of thee, shall fall into the midst of the seas in the day of thy ruin" (xxvii. 26, 27). These things also are said concerning Tyrus and her ships, by which are signified the knowledges of good and truth, or the truths of the natural man, which they procure for themselves, and which they sell, but in the present case they denote falsities ; by the midst of the seas, in which it is said the east wind hath broken her, and into which she shall fall in the day of her ruin, is signified the same as by the deep, namely, the hell whence are falsities of doctrine ; the east wind denotes influx out of heaven, and the day of her ruin, the last judgment ; by her riches are signified falsities ; by her fairs and merchandize are signified the acquisitions and communications thereof ; by her mariners, the ministers, and by the pilots, the prelates who lead and teach ; by the men of war, those who defend, and by the company, false doctrines. So in Jo-

nah: "Then Jonah prayed unto Jehovah his God out of the fish's bell:
and said, I cried by reason of mine affliction unto Jehovah, and I
heard me; out of the belly of hell cried I, and thou heardest my voice
For thou hadst cast me into the deep, in the midst of the seas; an
the floods compassed me about; all thy billows and thy wave
passed over me. Then I said, I am cast out of thy sight; yet
will look again toward thy holy temple. The waters compasse
me about, even to the soul; the depth closed me round about, th
weeds were wrapped about my head. I went down to the bottom
of the mountains; the earth with her bars was about me for ever
yet hast thou brought up my life from corruption, O Jehovah, m
God" (ii. 1–6). That by Jonah's being in the belly of the whal
three days and three nights, was represented that the Lord woul
so be in the heart of the earth, the Lord himself teaches in Matthe'
(xii. 39, 40; xvi. 4; Luke xi. 29, 30); and by these words of Jo
nah are described the dire temptations of the Lord; and inasmuc
as temptations exist by inundations of evils and falsities, which as
cend from hell, and as it were overwhelm, it is said, that he crie
out from the belly of hell, and that he was cast into the deep, eve
into the midst of the seas, by which also is signified hell; by th
floods, and by the waters, which compassed him about, and by th
waves and billows which passed over him, are signified evils an
falsities thence derived; by the depth which closed him round about
are signified the hells where and whence falsities are; by the bot
toms of the mountains to which he went down, are signified th
hells where and whence are evils; that he was as it were bound b
them, is signified by the weeds wrapping his head, and by the bar
of the earth being upon him, weeds denoting falsities, and the bar
of the earth, evils; victory over them from his own proper power, i
signified by, "Yet hast thou brought up my life from corruption, (
Jehovah, my God:" it is said, thou hast brought up my life from
corruption, but by this, when predicated of the Lord, is meant tha
he brought up himself from corruption, by virtue of his own divin
principle, thus by his own proper power. Similar things are signi
fied by the following passages in David: "Deep calleth unto dee
at the noise of thy water-spouts; all thy waves and thy billows ar
gone over me" (Psalm xlii. 7). So again: "Save me, O God, fc
the waters are come in unto my soul. I sink in deep mire wher
there is no standing; I am come into deep waters, where the flood
overflow me. Deliver me out of the mire, and let me not sink: le
me be delivered from them that hate me, and out of the deep wa
ters. Let not the water-flood overflow me, neither let the pit shu
her mouth upon me" (Psalm lxix. 1, 2, 14, 15). Again: "Tho
which hast showed me great and sore troubles, shalt quicken m
again, and shalt bring me up again from the depths of the earth
(Psalm lxxi. 20). And again: "I am counted with them that g
down into the pit; I am as a man that hath no strength: Fre
among the dead, like the slain that lie in the grave, whom thou re
memberest no more, and they are cut off from thy hand. Thou ha
laid me in the lowest pit, in darkness, in the deeps" (Psalm lxxxvii

4, 5, 6). In these passages also the temptations of the Lord, by which he subjugated the hells, and glorified his humanity, whilst in the world, are described; by waves and billows, are signified evils and falsities, and by deeps the depths of the earth and sea, and likewise by the pit and the deepest or lowest pit, are signified the hells where and whence those evils and falsities are; for as was said above, temptations are as it were immersions into the hells, and obsessions by evils and falsities. These things are signified by the lamentations in David in many places, and also in the prophets; for in the spiritual sense of the Word the temptations of the Lord are much treated of, by which he subjugated the hells, and disposed all things to order in the heavens and in the hells, and by which he glorified his human principle; they are especially understood by the things predicted in the prophets and in the Psalms concerning the Lord, and by the things fulfilled by him, as mentioned in Luke (xxiv. 44).

By the deep, and by the sea and the depths thereof, are also signified the hells, in the following passages; as in Jeremiah: "Flee ye, turn back, dwell deep, O inhabitants of Dedan, and Hazor (xlix. 8, 30). Again: "The sea is come up upon Babylon; she is covered with the multitude of the waves thereof" (li. 42). And in Amos: "Thus hath the Lord Jehovah showed unto me; and behold, the Lord Jehovah called to contend by fire, and it devoured the great deep" (vii. 4). And in David: "The waters saw thee, O God, the waters saw thee; they were afraid; the depths also were troubled" (Psalm lxxvii. 16). And again: "Therefore will not we fear, though the earth be removed, and though the mountains be carried into the midst of the sea; though the waters thereof roar and be troubled" (Psalm xlvi. 2, 3). And in Moses: "In the same day were all the fountains of the great deep broken up, and the windows of heaven were opened" (Gen. vii. 11). And again: "The fountains also of the deep, and the windows of heaven were stopped" (Gen. viii. 2). So in Job: "But where shall wisdom be found? and where is the place of understanding? Man knoweth not the price thereof. The depth saith, It is not in me; and the sea saith, It is not with me" (xxviii. 12, 13, 14). And again: "Hast thou entered into the springs of the sea? or hast thou walked in the search of the depth? Have the gates of death been opened unto thee? or hast thou seen the doors of the shadow of death?" (xxxviii. 16, 17.) So in the Evangelists: "But whoso shall offend one of these little ones which believe in me, it were better for him that a millstone were hanged about his neck, and that he were drowned in the depth of the sea" (Matt. xviii. 6; Mark ix. 42; Luke xvii. 2). And again: "The devils who obsessed the man besought Jesus that he would not command them to go into the deep, therefore he suffered them to enter into the herd of swine" (Matt. viii. 31, 32; Luke viii. 31, 32, 33). And also in the following passages in the Revelation: "And when they shall have finished their testimony, the beast that ascendeth out of the bottomless pit shall make war against them, and shall overcome them, and kill them" (xi. 7). And again: " The beast that thou sawest was, and is not; and shall ascend out of the bottomless pit, and go into perdition" (xvii. 8). And again: " And I saw an angel come down from heaven, having the key of the bottomless pit and a great chain in his hand. And he laid hold on the dragon, and bound him a thousand years; and cast him into the bottomless pit" (xx. 1, 2, 3). In these passages also, by the depth of the sea and by the deep, is signified the hell where are the falsities of evil, and whence they arise; the reason of which is, because the evil spirits who are there, and who, whilst they lived as men in the world, were in the falsities of evil, appear to dwell as in the bottom of the seas, and this the more deeply according to the grievousness of the evil from which the falsity was derived. As depths signify the hells, where and whence are falsities, so they likewise signify the ultimates of heaven, where and whence are the knowledges of truth, which are the truths of the natural man; the reason is, because the ultimates of heaven also appear as in waters, but such as are thin and clear; for, as was said above, the atmosphere of the supreme heaven is as an ethereal atmosphere, the atmosphere of the middle heaven as aerial, and the atmosphere of the ultimate heaven as it were watery. The reason why this latter atmosphere so appears, is, because the truths pertaining to those who are in it, are truths of the natural man, and the atmosphere of the natural man is as it were watery; hence also are the appearances of rivers, lakes, and seas, in the spiritual world: wherefore by seas are also signified knowledges and scientifics in common or in every aggregate; concerning which, see above. n. 275, 342. Similar things are also signified by depths in the following passages; as in Moses: " For Jehovah, thy God, bringeth thee into a good land, a land of brooks of water, of fountains and depths that spring out of the valleys and hills" (Deut. viii. 7); this passage may be seen explained above, n. 578. So again: " The God of thy father who shall bless thee with blessings of heaven above, blessings of the deep that lieth under" (Gen. xlix. 25; Deut. xxxiii. 13); see above, n. 448. So in David: " By the word of Jehovah were the heavens made; and all the host of them by the breath of his mouth. He gathereth the waters of the sea together as a heap; he layeth up the depth in store houses" (Psalm xxxiii. 7); see also above, n. 275. Again : " Thou coveredst it with the deep as with a garment; the waters stood above the mountains" (Psalm civ. 6); see also above, n. 275. Again: " Praise Jehovah from the earth, ye dragons and all deeps" (Psalm cxlviii. 7). By deeps in these passages are signified the ultimates of heaven, in which are the spiritual-natural angels. So again, in Ezekiel: " The waters made him great, the deep set him up on high" (xxxi. 4); see above, n. 518. Moreover by depths are also signified divine truths in abundance, and the arcana of divine wisdom. Thus in David: " He clave the rocks in the wilderness, and gave them drink as out of the great depths" (Psalm lxxviii. 15). And again: " Thy judgments are a great deep. O Jehovah, thou preservest man and beast" (xxxvi. 6). The same may be seen in numerous other passages of the Word.

539. " And there arose smoke out of the pit, as the smoke of a great furnace"—That hereby are signified dense falsities from the evils of earthly and corpòreal loves, appears from the signification of smoke, as denoting the falsity of evil, concerning which we shall speak presently ; and from the signification of the pit, as denoting the hell where they are who have falsified the Word, concerning which see above, n. 537 ; and from the signification of a great furnace, as denoting the evils of earthly and corporeal loves, from which such falsities break forth, of which we shall speak in the following article.　The reason why smoke signifies the falsity of evil, is, because it proceeds from fire, and fire signifies the loves of self and the world, and thence all evils ; wherefore also the hells which are in falsities from the evils of those loves, and more so where they are who have falsified the Word by applying it in favor of those loves, appear in a fire as of a great furnace, from which a dense smoke mixed with fire ascends.　It has been also granted me to see those hells, and it was evident that the loves of those who were in them caused the appearance of such a fire, and that the falsities thence issuing presented the appearance of a fiery smoke ; such things, however, do not appear to those who are therein, their life being in those loves, and in the falsities thence derived ; by these they are tormented in various manners, and not from material fire and smoke, such as are in the natural world.*　That smoke signifies the dense falsity issuing from evil, may appear from the following passages. Thus in Moses : "And Abraham looked towards Sodom and Gomorrah, and toward all the land of the plain, and behold, and lo, the smoke of the country went up as the smoke of a furnace" (Gen. xix. 28).　By Sodom and Gomorrah, in the spiritual sense, are understood those who are altogether in the loves of self, hence by the smoke, which was seen by Abraham to arise after the burning of those cities, is signified the dense falsity pertaining to those who are altogether in that love : for they who love themselves above all things, are in the greatest darkness as to things spiritual and celestial, being merely natural and sensual, and altogether separated from heaven ; and in such case they not only deny things divine, but also contrive falsities, by which they destroy them ; these falsities are what are signified by the smoke seen rising from Sodom and Gomorrah.　Again, it is written : " And when the sun went down, and thick darkness arose, behold a smoking furnace, and a burning lamp that passed between those pieces" (Gen. xv. 17).　These things are said concerning the posterity of Abraham from Jacob, as may appear from what precedes in that chapter ; the sun going down signifies the last time, when consummation takes place : and thick darkness arising signifies evil in the place of good, and falsity in the place of truth : "behold a smoking furnace," signifies the most dense falsity originating in evils : the burning lamp signifies the burning of cupidities ; its passing between the pieces, signifies,

* As may better appear from the article in the work concerning H. & H. n. 566–575, where is explained what is meant by infernal fire, and by gnashing of teeth.

which separated them from the Lord.* Again, in Moses : "And Moses brought forth the people out of the camp to meet with God; and they stood at the nether part of the mount. And mount Sinai was altogether on a smoke, because Jehovah descended upon it in fire; and the smoke thereof ascended as the smoke of a furnace, and the whole mount quaked greatly" (Exod. xix. 17, 18). And afterwards it is said : "And all the people saw the thunderings, and the lightnings, and the noise of the trumpet, and the mountain smoking; and when the people saw it, they removed, and stood afar off. And they said unto Moses, Speak thou with us, and we will hear; but let not God speak with us lest we die" (Exod. xx. 18, 19). These things represented the nature and quality of the Jewish people, for Jehovah, that is, the Lord, appears to every one according to his quality. Thus to those who are in truths derived from good, he appears as a serene light, but to those who are in falsities from evil, as smoke from a fire; and inasmuch as that people were in earthly and corporeal loves, and thence in the falsities of evil, therefore the Lord from mount Sinai appeared to them as a devouring fire, and as the smoke of a furnace.† The same is signified by smoke and fire in the following passages in David : "Because he was wroth, there went up a smoke out of his nostrils, and fire out of his mouth devoured : coals were kindled by it. He bowed the heavens also, and came down; and darkness was under his feet" (Psalm xviii. 7, 8, 9; 2 Sam. xxii. 8, 9, 10). In these passages it is not meant that a smoke and a devouring fire ascended from Jehovah, for there is no wrath in him; but it is thus said, because the Lord appears thus to those who are in falsities and evils, for they view him from their own falsities and evils. So again; "He looketh on the earth, and it trembleth; he toucheth the hills and they smoke" (Psalm civ. 32). And again : "Bow thy heavens, O Jehovah, and come down; touch the mountains, and they shall smoke" (Psalm cxliv. 5). And in Isaiah : "Howl, O gate; cry, O city; thou whole Palestina, art dissolved : for there shall come from the north a smoke" (xiv. 31). By the gate here mentioned, is signified the introductory truth of the church; by city is signified doctrine; by "thou whole Palestina" is signified faith; hence by "howl, O gate, cry, O city, thou whole Palestina, art dissolved," is signified the vastation of the church as to the truth of doctrine, and thence as to faith; by the north is signified the hell where and whence are the falsities of doctrine and the falsities of faith; and by the smoke those falsities themselves are signified; hence by a smoke coming from the north is signified falsity devastating from the hells. So in Nahum : "Behold, I will burn her chariots in the smoke, and the sword shall devour thy

---

* These things also may be seen more fully explained in the A. C. n. 1858–1862.

† That the sons of Jacob were of such a nature and quality is shown in many places in the A. C. from which see what is collected in the D. of the N. J. n. 248; and that the Lord appears to every one according to his quality, as a vivifying and recreating fire to those who are in good, and as a consuming fire to those who are in evil, may be seen in the A. C. n. 934, 1861, 6832, 8814, 8819, 9434, 10,551; what the other particulars signify in the passages above adduced, may also be seen in the same work, where the book of Exodus is explained.

young lions" (ii. 13). The subject here treated of is the devastation of the church; by burning the chariots in the smoke is signified the perversion of all the truths of doctrine into falsities, smoke signifying falsity, and chariots denoting doctrine; and by the sword devouring the young lions, is signified that falsities will destroy the principal truths of the church, young lions denoting the principal and defensive truths of the church, and sword denoting falsity destroying truth. So in Joel: "And I will show wonders in the heavens and in the earth, blood and fire, and pillars of smoke" (ii. 30). The subject here treated of is the last judgment, and by blood, fire, and pillars of smoke, are signified the truth of the Word falsified, the good thereof adulterated, and the mere falsities which arise in the church; blood denotes the truth of the Word falsified, fire, the good thereof adulterated, and pillars of smoke, denote the mere and dense falsities thence arising. Again, in David: "But the wicked shall perish, and the enemies of Jehovah as the fat of lambs shall be consumed; into smoke shall they consume away" (Psalm xxxvii. 20). Here, by the wicked perishing, and the enemies of Jehovah being consumed into smoke, is signified that they shall perish by the falsities of evil; they are called wicked who are in falsities, and enemies who are in evils, and smoke denotes the falsity of evil. Again: "As smoke is driven away, so drive them away; as wax melteth before the fire, so let the wicked perish in the presence of God" (Psalm lxviii. 2). The destruction of the wicked is here compared to smoke driven away by the wind, and to wax which melts before the fire, because smoke signifies falsities, and fire, evils. So in Isaiah: "The heavens shall vanish away like smoke, and the earth shall wax old like a garment" (li. 6). Here also by smoke is signified falsity, in which they should perish who were in the former heaven; and by the garment waxing old is signified truth destroyed by the falsities of evil. Comparison is made with smoke vanishing away, and with a garment waxing old, because comparisons in the Word are also correspondences, and are alike significative. So in Hosea: "And now they sin more and more, and have made them molten images of their silver, and idols according to their own understanding, all of it the work of the craftsmen: Therefore they shall be as the morning cloud, and as the early dew that passeth away, as the chaff that is driven with the whirlwind out of the floor, and as the smoke out of the chimney" (xiii. 2, 3). By these words are described the doctrines which are from self-derived intelligence, in which are evils of falsity, and falsities of evil: such doctrines are signified by the molten images of silver, and by idols: their silver, and the work of the craftsmen, signify what is from self-derived intelligence; hence it is also said, that they have made them molten images of their silver, and idols according to their own understanding, all of it the work of the craftsmen; that those doctrines, being falsities, would pass away, is signified by their being as smoke out of the chimney. The reason why they are said to be as the morning cloud, and as the early dew that passeth away, and as the chaff that is driven with the whirlwind out of the floor, is, because the church in its beginning is as the morning cloud, as the early dew, and as chaff that is driven with the whirlwind out of the floor, by which are signified truths of good and goods of truths, which nevertheless successively pass away, and are changed into falsities of evil, and into evils of falsity. By smoke is also signified falsity in other passages in the Revelation; as in the following: " And out of the horses' mouths issued fire and smoke and brimstone. By these three was the third part of men killed, by the fire, and by the smoke, and by the brimstone" (ix. 17, 18). Again: " And the smoke of their torment ascendeth up for ever and ever" (xiv. 11). And again: "And again they said, Alleluia. And her smoke rose up for ever and ever" (xix. 3). Inasmuch as fire signifies love in both senses, as well celestial love as infernal love, and hence smoke signifies what flows from love, both the falsity which is from infernal love, and the truth which is from celestial love, therefore smoke also, in a good sense, signifies the holy principle of truth, as may be seen above, n. 494. So again, in the following passages: " And Jehovah will create upon every dwelling-place of mount Zion, and upon her assemblies, a cloud and smoke by day, and the shining of a flaming fire by night: for upon all the glory shall be a defence" (Isaiah iv. 5); this passage may be seen explained above, n. 294, 475, 504. Again, in the same prophet: " And the posts of the door moved at the voice of him that cried, and the house was filled with smoke" (vi. 4). And in the Revelation it is written: " And the temple was filled with smoke from the glory of God, and from his power" (xv. 8). And again: "And the smoke of the incense, which came with the prayers of the saints, ascended up before God out of the angel's hand " (viii. 4).

540. Now, since it is said, that the smoke arose out of the pit as the smoke of a great furnace, and hitherto it has been shown that smoke signifies dense falsity, it is of importance also to show that a furnace signifies the evils of earthly and corporeal loves, and thus that smoke, as the smoke of a great furnace, signifies dense falsities originating in those loves. This signification of a furnace is also grounded in appearances in the spiritual world; for the hells in which those loves reign, when they are looked into, appear as furnaces glowing with fire, and over them appears smoke, such as ascends from furnaces, and from places on fire; hence it is that, in the Word, furnaces signify either the hells, or a company of men, or man himself, in whom such loves and cupidities reign, or what amounts to the same, where the evils are which flow from them. These things are signified by furnaces, chimneys, and ovens of fire in the following passages; thus in Matthew: " The Son of man shall send forth his angels, and they shall gather out of his kingdom all things that offend, and them which do iniquity; and shall cast them into a furnace (or chimney) of fire. At the end of the world, the angels shall come forth, and sever the wicked from among the just, and shall cast them into a furnace (or chimney) of fire; there shall be wailing and gnashing of teeth" (xiii. 41, 42, 49, 50). That by a furnace or chimney of fire, men-

tioned in these passages are understood the hells is evident; the end of the world signifies the last time of the church, when judgment takes place; that the evil are then to be separated from the good and to be cast into hell, is signified by the angels shall gather all things that offend, and them who do iniquity, and shall separate the evil from among the just, and shall cast them into a furnace of fire; hell is called a furnace of fire, because it appears fiery from the love of self and of the world; that the torment arising from these loves is understood by internal fire, may be seen in the work concerning H. & H. n. 566–575. So in Malachi: "Behold, the day cometh that shall burn as an oven; and all the proud, yea, and all that do wickedly, shall be stubble: and the day that cometh shall burn them up" (iv. 1). This also is said respecting the last time of the church, and the last judgment then to take place, both which are signified by the day that cometh; by an oven is also understood the hell where they are, who by doctrine confirm themselves in falsities, and by life in evils originating in earthly and corporeal loves; that they will perish from their own loves, is understood by all the proud, yea, and all that do wickedly shall be stubble, and the day that cometh burneth them up: all the proud here mentioned, are they who, by doctrine, confirm themselves in falsities, and all that do wickedly, signifies those who by life confirm themselves in evil. So in Hosea: "They make the king glad with their wickedness, and the princes with their lies. They are all adulterers, as an oven heated by the baker, who ceaseth from raising after he hath kneaded the dough until it be leavened. For they have made ready their heart like an oven while they lie in wait; their baker sleepeth all the night; in the morning it burneth as a flaming fire. They are all hot as an oven, and have devoured their judges; all their kings are fallen; there is none among them that calleth unto me. Ephraim is a cake not turned" (vii. 3–8). By these words in the spiritual sense, are described the sons of Jacob, and that from the loves of self and of the world they perverted all good into evil, and thence all truth into falsity; by the king whom they make glad by their wickedness, is signified all the falsity from evil, for a king signifies truth from good, and in the opposite sense, falsity from evil, by the princes whom they make glad with lies are signified the principal falsities. That from their loves they perverted goods and truths, is signified by, "They are all adulterers as an oven heated by the baker," to adulterate denotes to pervert good and thence truth, which is compared to an oven heated by the baker, because they compact falsities as into a mass or dough, to favor their loves; and inasmuch as evils and falsities are not separated from the goods and truths which are derived from the literal sense of the Word, but cohere, it is said, "who ceaseth from raising after he hath kneaded the dough until it be leavened," fermentation or leavening denoting separation, but here non-separation is denoted by its being said, "he ceaseth to knead the dough until it be leavened." The same is signified by Ephraim being a cake not turned, Ephraim denoting the understanding of truth; that hence there remain nothing but the evils pertaining to those loves which falsities favor, is signified by, "their baker sleepeth all the night; in the morning it burneth as a flaming fire, they are all hot as an oven." This comparison is made, because they compact doctrines from falsities, just as a baker makes bread and cakes in his oven; that thus they destroy all the goods and truths which they derive from the Word, is signified by, "and have devoured their judges; all their kings are fallen," judges denoting the goods of truth, and kings, the truths themselves; that this is the consequence of their desiring to be wise of themselves, and not from the Lord, is signified by "there is none among them that calleth unto me;" that these words are to be understood spiritually, may be seen only from common intuition, but that the particulars signify and describe such things as are here mentioned, thus what is understood by kings, princes, judges, adulterers, likewise by an oven and a baker, can only be seen from the internal sense; moreover, they who compact truths or falsities so as to cohere, appear in the spiritual world as bakers kneading a mass or dough, near whom also there is an oven. So in Lamentations: "Our skin was black like an oven because of the terrible famine" (v. 10). These words contain a lamentation over the deprivation of truth, and the inundation of falsity; famine signifies the want and deprivation of truth, as may be seen above, n. 386; and the terrible famine, extreme want, and also the inundation of falsities, for where there are no truths there will be falsities, and terrible famine or storms of famine in the Word have the same signification as inundation. "Our skin was black like an oven," signifies that the natural man is without the light of truth, and thence in the darkness of falsity; here also an oven signifies the fabrication of doctrine from falsities and not from truths; but concerning this, see above, n. 386, where it is more fully explained. So in Ezekiel: "Son of man, the house of Israel is to me become dross; all they are brass, and tin, and iron, and lead, in the midst of the furnace; they are even the dross of silver. Behold, therefore, I will gather you into the midst of Jerusalem. As they gather silver, and brass, and iron, and lead, and tin, into the midst of the furnace, to blow the fire upon it, to melt it; so will I gather you in mine anger and in my fury, and I will leave you there, and melt you. As silver is melted in the midst of the furnace, so shall ye be melted in the midst thereof" (xxii. 18–22). By these words are described the false doctrines which the Jews and Israelites compacted from the literal sense of the Word, which they applied to themselves, and to their own loves only: such doctrines are called the dross of silver, because silver signifies the truth of the Word, and dross, nothing of truth, or what is abstracted from truth, which is rejected. The things which are of the literal sense of the Word, are signified by brass, iron, tin, and lead, because these things signify the goods and truths of the natural man, for whom the literal sense of the Word is given; and whereas from this sense they compacted their false doctrines, which were traditions, it is said that they shall be melted together; and whereas they were applied to their loves, which were the loves of self and of the world, it is said that Jehovah would gather them into the midst of the furnace, to blow the fire upon it, to melt it, fire signifying those loves; and whereas also their doctrines are understood, it is said that they should be gathered together into the midst of Jerusalem, Jerusalem signifying the church as to doctrine, thus also the doctrine of the church. So again, in Moses: "And it came to pass, that when the sun went down, and it was dark, behold a smoking furnace, and a burning lamp that passed between those pieces" (Gen. xv. 17). That the falsities of evil, and the evils of falsity, bursting from the filthy loves of the Jewish and Israelitish nation, are here meant by the smoking furnace, and by the burning lamp which passed between the pieces, may be seen in the article above; for Abraham desired that his posterity might rule over the whole land of Canaan, and because the Lord foresaw that the church would be instituted with that nation, therefore he made a covenant with Abraham. Nevertheless what their quality would be, is predicted in that vision. So in Nahum: " Draw thee waters for the siege, fortify thy strong holds, go into clay, and tread the mortar, make strong the brick kiln. There shall the fire devour thee, the sword shall cut thee off" (iii. 14, 15). By these words is described the destruction of truth by the falsities of evil; the waters for the siege denote the falsities by which they endeavor to destroy truths; by fortifying the strong holds, is signified to fortify them by such things as appear as truths; by going into the clay, and treading the mortar, is signified to make them appear to cohere, mortar denoting falsity from evil conjoining; by making strong the brick kiln is signified to repair the doctrine compacted of falsified truths and fictions, for bricks signify the falsities which are invented and do not cohere with truths; by " the fire shall devour thee," is signified that they shall perish by the evils of their own loves, and by " the sword shall cut thee off," is signified that they shall perish by falsities. Again, in Jeremiah: " Take great stones in thy hand, and hide them in the clay in the brick kiln, which is at the entry of Pharaoh's house. Behold, I will send and take the king of Babylon, and will set his throne upon these stones that I have hid. And when he cometh, he shall smite the land of Egypt. And I will kindle a fire in the houses of the gods of Egypt; and he shall array himself with the land of Egypt, as a shepherd putteth on his garment" (xliii. 9–12). By these things was represented the profanation of truth by reasonings from scientifics falsely applied; by the great stones hidden in the brick kiln are signified the truths of the Word falsified by fictions originating in self-derived intelligence, stones denoting the truths of the Word, and the brick kiln, doctrine compacted from things fictitious; by the house of Pharaoh is signified the natural man as to scientifics; the door denotes the scientific sensual principle, by which there is entrance into the natural man, and by which falsifications are made; by the king of Babylon is signified the profanation of truth; by his throne being set upon those stones, and by his smiting the land of Egypt, and kindling a fire in the houses thereof, is signified, that by the scientifics of the the natural man he would pervert all the truths of doctrine, and profane them; that he would subject to himself the natural man as to all things therein, which is done by confirmations of falsities from scientifics, is signified by his arraying himself with the land of Egypt, as a shepherd putteth on his garment; that thus all things of the natural man would perish by the evils of earthly and corporeal loves, is signified by, " I will kindle a fire in the house of the gods of Egypt." Inasmuch as by Egypt is signified the natural man as to the scientific principle there, and likewise by a furnace of iron, therefore, in the Word, Egypt is called an iron furnace; as in Jeremiah: " In the day that I brought them forth out of the land of Egypt, from the iron furnace" (xi. 3, 4). And in Moses: " But Jehovah hath taken you, and brought you forth out of the iron furnace, even out of Egypt" (Deut. iv. 20). Again, in the 1st Book of Kings: " Which thou broughtest forth out of Egypt, from the midst of the furnace of iron" (viii. 51). And in David: " I removed his shoulder from the burden: his hands were delivered from the pots" (lxxxi. 6). The natural man as to what is scientific is signified by the iron furnace, the furnace denoting the natural man, and iron, what is scientific, in this case, scientific falsity, because it is said, that they were brought out of it; for the natural man unless he be led by the spiritual man, is in falsities and evils, by reason that he has not any light from heaven, for light from heaven flows through the spiritual man into the natural, and enlightens, teaches, and leads; the case is altogether otherwise, when the natural man does not think and act under the auspices of the spiritual man; man in such case is in a state of servitude, for he thinks and acts from falsities and evils which are from hell, and therefore in treating of the deliverance of the Israelites out of Egypt, it is also said that they were brought out of the house of bondage; for all freedom of thinking and acting is from the spiritual man, inasmuch as this man thinks and wills from the Lord out of heaven, and to be led of the Lord is freedom. From these considerations it may appear whence it is that Egypt is called an iron furnace, and also a house of bondage, which bondage is likewise signified by the burden of Egypt, from which the shoulder of Israel is said to be removed; that iron signifies what is scientific pertaining to the natural man, may be seen above, n. 176.

As most things in the Word have also an opposite sense, so also has an oven; thus in Isaiah: "Saith Jehovah, whose fire is in Zion, and his furnace in Jerusalem" (xxxi. 9). Here by the fire is signified the good of love, and by an oven or furnace, truth from that good, thus the truth of doctrine; similar things are also signified by Zion and Jerusalem, by Zion is signified the church as to the good of love, and by Jerusalem the church as to the truth of doctrine. So in Moses, speaking of the meat offering, as " Baken in the oven, baken in a pan, and baken in the frying pan" (Lev. ii. 4–7), which things are explained in the A. C. Thus also in the Revelation: " And his feet like unto fine brass, as if they burned in a furnace" (i. 15); concerning which see above, n. 69.

541. " And the sun and the air were darkened by reason of the smoke of the pit"—That hereby is signified that the light of truth

from the Lord was made thick darkness by infernal falsities, appears from the signification of the sun and the air being darkened, as denoting the light of truth from the Lord becoming thick darkness, concerning which we shall speak presently; and from the signification of by the smoke of the pit, as denoting by dense falsities which are from hell, thus by infernal falsities.* The reason why the sun and the air being darkened, signifies the light of truth from the Lord becoming thick darkness, is, because the Lord in the angelic heaven is a sun, and the divine truth proceeding from the Lord as a sun, presents all the light there, and illuminates both the sight and understanding of the angels, wherefore when that sun is there obscured, the light of truth which is from the Lord, becomes thick darkness; falsities from hell are what cause the obscuration. From the light of heaven made thick darkness by the falsities of evil, comes all denial of the divine principle and of divine things by those who are merely natural; for they view divine things in thick darkness, and thence see them as thick darkness, wherefore they deny them; the light of heaven also, when it flows into those who are in the falsities of evil, actually becomes thick darkness in the spiritual world. Hence, therefore, it is, that the evil not only do not see and understand spiritual things, that is, the things which are of heaven and the church, but also in heart deny them.† The reason why it is said that the air also was obscured, is because the light of truth is thereby understood, for the air gives light from the sun. The same is signified by the term clouds, or ethers, in David: "Thy mercy, O Jehovah, is in the heavens; and thy truth reacheth unto the clouds" (Psalm xxxiv. 5; lvii. 10; cviii. 4). In these passages mercy signifies the divine good of the divine love, and truth the divine truth, and inasmuch as divine truth is the light of heaven, as was just said, therefore it is said, "Thy truth reacheth to the clouds;" by which is signified the divide light even to the supreme heaven, where it is in the highest degree. The same is signified in Psalm lxxvii. 18; Psalm lxxviii. 23, 24.

542. Verses 3, 4, 5, 6, 7, 8, 9, 10, 11, 12. "And there came out of the smoke locusts upon the earth: and unto them was given power, as the scorpions of the earth have power. And it was commanded them that they should not hurt the grass of the earth, neither any green thing, neither any tree; but only those men which have not the seal of God in their foreheads. And to them it was given that they should not kill them, but that they should be tormented five months: and their torment was as the torment of a scorpion, when he striketh a man. And in those days shall men seek death, and shall not find it; and shall desire to die, and death shall flee from them. And the shapes of the locusts were like unto horses prepared unto battle; and on their heads were as it were

---

* That smoke signifies dense falsities, and that the bottomless pit signifies the hells where and whence they are, may be seen above, n. 536–530. •

† That the Lord in the angelic heaven appears as a sun, and that the divine truth, proceeding from the Lord as a sun, presents all the light of heaven, thus all the intelligence and wisdom which the angels have, may be seen in the work concerning H. &. H. n. 116–125, and n. 126–140.

crowns like gold, and their faces were as the faces of men. And they had hair as the hair of women, and their teeth were as the teeth of lions. And they had breastplates, as it were breastplates of iron ; and the sound of their wings was as the sound of chariots of many horses running to battle. And they had tails like unto scorpions, and there were stings in their tails : and their power was to hurt men five months. And they had a king over them, which is the angel of the bottomless pit, whose name in the Hebrew tongue is Abaddon, but in the Greek tongue hath his name Apollyon. One woe is past ; and, behold, there come two woes more hereafter."— "And there came out of the smoke locusts upon the earth," signi- fies, that from infernal falsities they became corporeal sensual in the church ; "and unto them was given power as the scorpions of the earth have power," signifies their persuasive faculty, and the effect and power thereof; "And it was commanded them that they should not hurt the grass of the earth, neither any green thing, neither any tree," signifies, that they should not hurt any scientific that is true and alive from the literal sense of the Word, nor any knowledges of truth and good therein ; "but only those men which have not the seal of God in their foreheads," signifies, but only the understand- ing of truth and perception of good with those who are not in truths derived from good from the Lord. "And to them it was given that they should not kill them," signifies, that they should not be de- prived of the faculty of understanding truth and of perceiving good : "but that they should be tormented five months," signifies, that by the falsities of evil the understanding should be darkened and drawn away from seeing the truth so long as they are in that state : "and their torment was as the torment of a scorpion, when he striketh a man," signifies that the darkening and hindrance from seeing the truth is from the persuasion with which the mind is infatuated. "And in those days shall men seek death, and shall not find it," signifies, that in such case they are willing to destroy the faculty of understanding truth, but that nevertheless they cannot : "and shall desire to die, and death shall flee from them," signifies that they are willing to destroy the faculty of perceiving good, which is of spiritual life, but in vain. "And the shapes of the locusts were like unto horses prepared unto battle," signifies that the sensual man became a man of reasoning, as from the understanding of truth : "and on their heads were as it were crowns like gold," signifies that they appear to themselves, when they reason, as wise and vic- torious : "and their faces were as the faces of men," signifies that they appear to themselves as spiritual affections of truth. "And they had hair as the hair of women," signifies that they also appear to themselves as affections of natural truth : "and their teeth were as the teeth of lions," signifies that sensual things, which are the ultimates of the intellectual life, are to them apparently as in power over all things. "And they had breast-plates as it were breast- plates of iron," signifies the persuasions with which they gird them- selves for combats, against which the truths of the spiritual rational man do not prevail : "and the sound of their wings was as the sound of chariots of many horses running to battle," signifies reasonings as from truths of doctrine understood from the Word, for which they must fight ardently. "And they had tails like unto scorpions," signifies sensual scientifics which are persuasive: "and there were stings in their tails," signifies the craftiness of deceiving by them: "and their power was to hurt men five months," signifies that they would induce a stupor as to the understanding of truth, and the perception of good, so long as they are in that state. "And they had a king over them, which is the angel of the bottomless pit," signifies that they received influx from the hell where they are who are in the falsities of evil and merely sensual: "whose name in the Hebrew tongue is Abaddon, but in the Greek tongue hath his name Apollyon," signifies the quality thereof as being destructive of all truth and good. "One woe is past; and, behold, there came two woes more hereafter," signifies one lamentation over the devastation of the church, and that lamentation over the further devastation . thereof follows.

543. "And there came out of the smoke locusts upon the earth"—That hereby is signified that from infernal falsities they became corporeal sensual in the church, appears from the signification of smoke, as denoting infernal falsity, concerning which see above, n. 539, where it is shown, that by the bottomless pit, out of which the smoke ascended, is signified the hell where and whence are the falsities of evil which falsify the truths of the Word, and that, consequently, smoke signifies infernal falsity; and from the signification of locusts, as denoting the ultimate sensual principle of man which is in the falsity of evil, concerning which we shall speak presently; and from the signification of coming out upon the earth, as denoting upon the church, for the earth signifies the church; the things also, which are contained in the Revelation are predicted concerning the church and its state.

That locusts signify the ultimate sensual principle of man, which is in the falsity of evil, may appear from all and singular of the things related in this chapter to verse 12, from the explication of which it may be manifest that nothing else is understood by locusts; but it may be expedient first to explain what is meant by the ultimate sensual principle of man. It is not the sensual principle of sight, hearing, smell, taste, and touch, which is here meant, for these things are proper to the body, but it is the ultimate or lowest principle of thought and affection, which is first opened with infants, and which is of such a nature, that they do not think anything else, nor are affected with any other objects, than what make one with the senses above mentioned; for infants learn to think by means of the senses, and to be affected with objects according to the things which have pleased the senses; wherefore the first internal principle, which is opened in them, is the sensual, which is called the ultimate sensual principle of man, and also corporeal sensual: but afterwards, as the infant advances in age, and becomes a boy, the sensual principle is opened more interiorly, from which he thinks naturally, and is also affected naturally: at length, when he becomes a youth and young man, his sensual principle is opened still more interiorly, from which he thinks rationally, and if he is in the good of charity and faith, spiritually, and also is affected rationally and spiritually; this thought and affection is what is called the rational and spiritual man, whereas the former is called the natural man, and the first, the sensual man. With every man, the interiors which are of his thought and affection, are opened successively, and this by continual influx out of heaven from the Lord: by this influx is first formed the sensual principle proximately adhering to the body, whence man becomes sensual: afterwards the natural whence he becomes natural; and after this the rational and therewith the spiritual, whence he becomes a rational and spiritual man; but this is formed and perfected only in proportion as man thinks concerning God, and concerning the divine things which are from God, and in proportion as he is affected with them, that is, in proportion as he wills and lives according to them; for if he does not do this, then the spiritual man is opened in a common or general manner, but is not formed, much less perfected. By the common or general opening of the spiritual man, man has the faculty of thinking, and of speaking, rationally from his thought, for this is the common effect of the influx of heaven with every man. Hence it may appear, that there are given to man thoughts and affections both spiritual, natural, and also sensual, and that spiritual thoughts and affections are given to those who think from God concerning God, and concerning things divine; but that only natural thoughts and affections are given to those who do not think from God concerning God, and concerning things divine, but only from themselves, or from the world concerning themselves or concerning the world; but, it is to be observed, that to think from self or from the world, it is in reality to think from hell, for whosoever does not think from God thinks from hell, it being impossible for any one to think from both at the same time. But they who deny God, and thence the divine things of heaven and the church, and confirm themselves against them, become all sensual men more or less, according to confirmations: when their minds are engaged upon spiritual things they think only on falsities, and are affected with evils; and if they think on any truths, whether they be spiritual, moral, or civil, it is only from the science of such things as are in the memory, and they see nothing beyond proximate causes, which they are also able to confirm; and if they are affected with goods, it is only from a delight which is for the sake of themselves or of the world, thus from some cupidity originating in the love of self, or in the love of the world. The thought of the sensual man is what is called material thought, and his affection is what is called corporeal affection, which is cupidity. Moreover it is to be observed, that all the evils which man derives from his parents, which are called hereditary evils, reside in his natural and sensual man, but not in the spiritual; hence it is that the natural man, and most especially the sensual man is opposed to the spiritual; for the spiritual man from infancy, is closed, and is only opened and formed by divine truths received in the understanding and will; and in proportion as the spiritual man is opened and formed, and according to the quality thereof, in the same proportion are the evils of the natural and sensual man removed, and goods implanted in their place. Since all evils reside in the natural and sensual man, it follows, that falsities reside there also, because all falsities are of evil; for whilst man lusts, and wills from evil, he thinks and speaks from falsity; for the evil of the will, when it forms itself in the thought, so as to be manifested to others, or to itself, as to its quality, is called falsity, wherefore falsity is the form of evil, as truth is the form of good. From these considerations it may appear what is the nature and quality of the man who is called a sensual man, and that a man becomes sensual, when the evils into which he is born are pursued in act, and more superadded to them from himself. So far as this is the case, and man confirms himself therein, so far the spiritual man is kept closed; in which case the natural and sensual man denies things divine which pertain to heaven and the church, and only acknowledges such things as pertain to the world and nature; yea, the sensual man in this case, is so blind as to believe nothing but what he sees with his eyes and touches with his hands. In this state are many of the learned, how wise and intelligent soever they may be supposed to be from their ability in speaking from the sciences which are in the memory, and this apparently as of the rational man; because their spiritual mind is opened, as is the case with every man, in a common or general manner, according to what was shown above. Inasmuch as in what follows in this chapter much is said concerning the locust, and as by the locust is signified the sensual principle, which is the ultimate or extreme of the natural man, it is of importance that the nature and quality of this sensual principle be fully known, and hence also the nature and quality of the sensual man: we shall, therefore, here adduce what is stated in the A. C. on this subject under the following heads.* That no-

* That the sensual is the ultimate principle of the life of man, adhering and inhering to his corporeal principle, n. 5077, 5767, 9121, 9216, 9331, 9730. That he is called a sensual man, who judges all things from the senses of the body, and who believes nothing but what he can see with his eyes and touch with his hands, saying that this is something, and rejecting everything else, n. 5094, 7693. That such a man thinks in extreme things or principles, and not interiorly from any spiritual light, n. 5089, 5094, 6564, 7693. That the interiors of his mind, who sees from the light of heaven, are closed, so that he can see therein nothing of the truth pertaining to heaven and the church, n. 6564, 6844, 6845. In a word, that he is in a gross natural light, and thus perceives nothing which is from the light of heaven, n. 6201, 6310, 6564, 6844, 6845, 6598, 6612, 6614, 6622, 6624. That hence he is interiorly against the things of heaven and the church, n. 6021, 6316, 6844, 6845, 6948, 6949. That the learned, who have confirmed themselves against the truths of the church, are sensual, n. 6316. That sensual men reason with acuteness and readiness, because their thought is near their speech, so as to be almost in it, and because they place all intelligence in discoursing from the memory alone, n. 195, 196, 5700, 10,236; but that they reason from the fallacies of the senses, with which the vulgar are captivated, n. 5084, 6948, 6949, 7693. That sensual men are crafty and malicious above all others, n. 7693, 10,236. That the covetous, adulterers, the voluptuous, and the deceitful, are especially sensual, n. 6310; that their interiors are unclean and filthy, n. 6201: that thereby they communicate with the hells, n. 6311. That they who are in the hells are sensual; and the more so the more deep their hells, n. 4623, 6311. That the sphere of infernal spirits conjoins itself with the sensual principle of man from behind, n 6312. That they who reasoned from the sen-

thing else is signified by the locust than the sensual principle of man which has now been described, may appear also from other passages in the Word where the locust is mentioned.   Thus in Moses: "Behold, I will bring the locust into thy coast.   And they shall fill thy houses, and the houses of all thy servants, and the houses of all the Egyptians.   And Moses stretched forth his rod over the land of Egypt, and Jehovah brought an east wind upon the land all that day, and all that night; and when it was morning, the east wind brought the locusts.   And the locusts went up over all the land of Egypt, and rested in all the coasts of Egypt: very grievous were they, before them there were no such locusts as they, neither after them shall there be such.   For they covered the face of the whole earth, so that the land was darkened; and they did eat every herb of the land, and all the fruit of the trees which the hail had left; and there remained not any green thing in the trees, or in the herbs of the field, through all the land of Egypt" (Exod. x. 4, 6, 13–15). All the miracles in Egypt, as well as all the other miracles recorded in the Word, involve and signify spiritual things pertaining to heaven and the church, consequently the plagues of Egypt signify spiritual plagues; this plague of the locusts denotes the destruction of the whole natural man by the irruption of evil and falsity from the sensual principle ; by Egypt is signified the natural man as to what is scientific and pleasurable therein, and by locust the falsity and evil of the sensual man vastating the natural man, that is, expelling

_____

sual principle, and thence against the genuine truths of faith, were called by the ancients serpents of the tree of science, n. 195, 196, 197, 6398, 6949, 10,313.   The sensual principle of man, and the sensual man are further described, n. 10,236 ; and the extension of the sensual principle in man, n. 9731.   That sensual things ought to be in the last place, and not in the first, and that, with a wise and intelligent man, they are in the last place, and subject to things interior, but that, with an unwise man, they are in the first place, and have rule, and that these are they who are properly called sensual, n. 5077, 5125, 5128, 7645.   That if sensual things are in the last place a way is opened by them to the understanding, and truths are polished by a mode of extraction, n. 5580.   That the sensual things of man are proximately extant to the world, and admit the things which flow to them from the world, and as it were sift them, n. 9726.   That the external or natural man communicates by those things with the world, but by rational things with heaven, n. 4009.   That sensuals thus subminister such things as are serviceable to the interiors of the mind, n. 5077, 5081.   That there are sensual things which subminister to the intellectual part, and others which subminister to the will part, n. 5077. That unless the thought be elevated from sensual things, man can attain but little wisdom, n. 5089.   That a wise man thinks above the sensual principle, n. 5089, 5094.   That man, when his thought is elevated above sensual things, comes into a clearer light, and at length into heavenly light, n. 6183, 6313, 6315, 9407, 9730, 9922.   That elevation above things sensual, and abstraction from them, were known to the ancients, n. 6313.   That man in his spirit may see things which are in the spiritual world, if he could be drawn from the sensual things of the body, and be elevated into the light of heaven by the Lord, n. 4622; the reason of which is, because it is not the body which thinks, but the spirit of man in the body, and in proportion as he thinks in the body, in the same proportion he thinks grossly and obscurely, thus in darkness, but in proportion as he thinks not in the body, he thinks clearly and in the light, n. 4622, 6614, 6622.   That the ultimate of the understanding is the sensual scientific principle, and that the ultimate of the will is sensual delight, n. 9996.   What is the difference between the sensual things which are common with the beasts, and those which are not common with them, n. 10,236. That there are sensual persons not evil, because their interiors are not shut in the manner above described, concerning whose state in the other life, see n. 6311.

thence and destroying all the truth and good of the church; therefore it is said, " And the locusts went over all the land of Egypt, and rested in all the coasts of Egypt." By the land of Egypt is signified the natural principle of the men of the church, and by the coasts of Egypt is signified their sensual principle, for the sensual principle is the ultimate or extreme of the natural, wherefore it is its coast or border, and the locust is the falsity and evil therein. Inasmuch as the falsity and the evil of the sensual man are the most grievous of all, being corporeal and earthly, therefore it is said that the locusts were very grievous, and that before them there were no such locusts as they were, and that there should be none such after them. The reason of this was, that the Egyptians were skilled in the science of correspondences, and thence were acquainted with the spiritual things of heaven, which they turned into magic. Inasmuch as the falsity and the evil of the sensual man, when they break into the natural man, depopulate it entirely, by destroying every truth and every good therein, therefore it is said, that the locusts covered the face of the whole earth, so that the land was darkened, and that they did eat every herb of the land, and all the fruit of the trees; the land of Egypt, as was said, denoting the natural principle of the men of the church, the herb of the land denoting the truth in that principle, and the fruit of the trees the good thereof. The same is also understood by the locusts filling the house of Pharaoh, and of his servants, and of all the Egyptians, for by them is signified the natural mind in its whole extension; for house in the Word signifies the interior things of man which are of his spiritual and natural mind, and in this case the things which are of his natural mind. It is said that by the locusts here mentioned, going up over all the land of Egypt, is signified the irruption of falsity and evil out of the sensual man into the natural, when, notwithstanding, the natural man is interior and the sensual exterior, and irruption or influx proceeds not from the exteriors into the interior, but from the interior into the exterior; it is therefore necessary to be observed, that by the irruption or influx of the sensual man into the natural, is meant the closing up of the natural man until it becomes like the sensual, whence the extension of the evil and falsity is greater, and both in like manner become corporeal and earthly. In other cases however, man, from his infancy, learns to separate the sensual man from the natural, by speaking truth and doing good, although from the sensual man he thinks what is false, and wills evils, and this he does until they are altogether separated, which is done when man is reformed and regenerated by the Lord; but if they are not separated, man cannot do otherwise than think and will insanely, and thence speak and act insanely.

Inasmuch as by locusts is signified the sensual principle as to falsity and evil, or what is the same thing, the falsity and evil of the sensual man, therefore the same is signified by the caterpillar and the locust, as mentioned in David: "He sent divers sorts of flies among them, which devoured them; and frogs which destroyed them. He gave also their increase unto the caterpillar, and their labor unto

the locust" (Psalm lxxviii. 45, 46). And again: "He spake, and
the locusts came and caterpillars, and that without number. And
did eat up all the herbs in their land, and devoured the fruit of their
ground" (Psalm cv. 34, 35). In these passages by locusts is signified the falsity pertaining to the sensual man, and by the caterpillars
is signified the evil of the same, or the falsity and evil which are
in the sensual man and from it. The reason why the latter are signified by the caterpillars, and the former by the locusts, is, because
the caterpillar is also a species of locust, which is evident from this
circumstance, that what is here said by David is concerning the locusts in Egypt, and yet in Moses the locust only is mentioned, and
not the caterpillar. The same things are signified by the locust
and the caterpillar in Joel: "That which the palmer-worm hath
left hath the locust eaten; and that which the locust hath left hath
the cankerworm eaten; and that which the cankerworm hath left
hath the caterpillar eaten. Awake, ye drunkards, and weep; and
howl, all ye drinkers of wine, because of the new wine; for it is
cut off from your mouth" (i. 4, 5). So again, in the same prophet:
"And the floors shall be full of wheat, and the fats shall overflow
with wine and oil. And I will restore to you the years that the locust hath eaten, the cankerworm, and the caterpillar, and the palm-
erworm, my great army which I sent among you" (ii. 24, 25). That
by the noxious animalcula here mentioned are signified falsities and
evils vastating and consuming the truths and goods of the man of
the church, is evident, since it is said, that all who drink wine should
howl for the new wine which is cut off from their mouth, and by
wine and new wine is signified the truth of the church; likewise
from its being said that their floors should be full of wheat, and that
their fats should overflow with wine and oil, for by the floor is signified the doctrine of the church, by the wheat and the oil are signified the goods thereof, and by the new wine, the truths thereof.
So in Nahum: "There shall the fire devour thee; the sword shall
cut the off, it shall eat thee up like the cankerworm: make thyself
many as the cankerworm: make thyself many as the locusts. Thou
hast multiplied thy merchants above the stars of heaven: the cankerworm spoileth, and fleeth away. Thy crowned are as the locusts,
and thy captains as the great grasshoppers, which camp in the
hedges in the cold day, but when the sun ariseth they flee away, and
their place is not known where they are" (iii. 15, 17). These things
are said concerning the "bloody city," by which is signified doctrine composed of falsified truths, thus doctrine from falsities; the
destruction of those who are in a faith and life according to that doctrine, is signified by "There shall the fire devour thee; the sword
shall cut thee off." By fire which shall devour, is signified evil
destroying good, and by the sword, falsity destroying the truth; and
since the evil and falsity from the sensual man are understood, it is
therefore said, "it shall eat thee up as the cankerworm; make thyself many as the cankerworm; make thyself many as the locust.
Thou hast multiplied thy merchants above the stars of heaven."
The reason this multiplication is mentioned as being like that of the

cankerworm, and of the locust, is, because falsifications of the Word are made in the greatest abundance by those who are sensual, thus by the sensual man, for the sensual man is signified by the cater-pillar and locust, as was shown above. The reason why the sensual man falsifies the Word above others, is, because the ultimate sense of the Word, which is the literal sense, is for the natural and sensual man, but the interior sense for the spiritual man; hence it is that man, when he is not a spiritual man, but only natural and sensual, who is in evil, and thence in falsities, does not see the goods and truths which are in the Word, but applies the ultimate sense thereof to confirm his falsities and evils: merchants signify those who falsify, and communicate, and vend. " Thy crowned are as the locusts, and thy captains as the great grasshoppers," signifies that the primary and principal things of doctrine of the bloody city are falsities of evil, and that from them also those falsities proceed. " Which camp in the hedges in the cold day," signifies in the truths of the Word, which do not appear as truths, because they are falsi-fied, and because they are from evil, hedges denoting truths not ap-pearing, because falsified, and the cold day denoting the state of the love of evil. "But when the sun ariseth they flee away, and their place is not known where they are," signifies that they consume all truth and good, so that there are no remains. The same as is here signified by multiplying as the locust, is signified in Jeremiah xlvi. 20, 22, 23: likewise in the book of Judges, vi. 5; vii. 12. Falsity in the extremes, as the most dense falsity, is also signified by the locust in the following passage in Moses: " Thou shalt carry much seed into the field, and shall gather but little in; for the locust shall consume it" (Deut. xxviii. 38). This was one of the curses with which the Israelites were threatened if they did not observe and do the commandments of Jehovah. By the seed of the field is under-stood the Word, and by the locust, the dense falsity from the sen-sual man consuming and destroying it. The same is signified by locust in Isaiah xxxiii. 3, 4: and in David, Psalm cix. 22, 23.

Since the sensual is the ultimate and lowest principle of the life of man's thought and affection, as was said above, and as the lowest principle, when viewed from the others, which are in a superior and more eminent place, is little, it is therefore compared to locusts, as in the following passages in Isaiah: " It is he that sitteth upon the circle of the earth, and the inhabitants thereof as locusts" (xl. 22). By these words is signified that men as to intelligence, are in the lowest principles, and the Lord in the supreme. In like manner, men, viewed by those who are in persuasion of their own eminence above others, are compared to locusts or grasshoppers, in Moses: " And there we saw the giants; the sons of Anak, which come of the giants: and we were in our own sight as grasshoppers, and so we were in their sight" (Numb. xiii. 33). By the giants (Naphalim) and the Anakim (sons of Anak) are signified in the Word those who are in the greatest persuasion of their own innocence, and, in the abstract sense, the most dire persuasions; this may be seen in the A. C. n. 311, 581, 567, 1268, 1270, 1271, 1673, 3686, 7686. Their being in their own eyes as grasshoppers, and appearing as such in the sight of others, is agreeable to appearances in the spiritual world, for there, when they who are in a persuasion of their own eminence look at others, they see them as little and vile, and these also then appear such to themselves.

Forasmuch as by the locust is signified the sensual principle, which is the ultimate principle of the life of man's thought, or the ultimate principle in which the understanding closes, and upon which it subsists, hence this ultimate principle is as the basis and foundation upon which the interior or superior things stand, pertaining to the understanding and will of man; as likewise the interior and superior things, which are called in the Word spiritual and celestial; and as all things must have a foundation in order to their consistence and subsistence, therefore the literal sense of the Word, which is the ultimate sense and the basis, is natural and sensual, and is also understood, in a good sense, by the locust, consequently also the truth and good thereof; hence it is, that John the Baptist, did eat locusts, and that the children of Israel were allowed to eat them. Hence also it is said concerning John the Baptist: "And the same John had his raiment of camel's hair, and a leathern girdle about his loins; and his meat was locusts and wild honey" (Matt. iii. 4; Mark i. 6). The reason why John the Baptist was thus clothed, was, because, like Elias, he represented the Word, and by raiment of camel's hair, by a leathern girdle, and by eating locusts and wild honey, he represented the ultimate sense of the Word, which, as was said, is natural-sensual, because it is for the natural-sensual man; by raiment is signified truth clothing good; by camel's hair is signified the ultimate principle of the natural man, which is sensual; by locusts and wild honey is also signified the same as to appropriation; by the locust the sensual principle as to truth; by wild honey, the sensual principle as to good; and by eating, the appropriation thereof. It is to be observed that in ancient times, when churches were representative churches, all who were in ministeries were clothed according to their representations, and also did eat according thereto. That it was allowed to the children of Israel to eat the locust, appears from these words in Moses: "All fowls that creep, going upon all four, shall be an abomination unto you. Yet these may ye eat, of every flying creeping thing that goeth upon all four, which hath legs above their feet, to leap withal upon the earth; the locust after his kind" (Lev. xi. 20, 21, 22). The reason why the Israelites were allowed to eat locusts because of their having legs above their feet to leap with, was, because legs signify natural good conjoined to spiritual good, and feet, natural truth derived from that good; and all truth which is from good ought to be appropriated and conjoined to man, but not the truth which is not from good, for this latter truth is conjoined with some evil; wherefore it is said that "All fowls that creep, going upon all four, shall be an abomination unto you." It is said also to leap upon the earth, because by leaping, when predicated of birds, is signified to live, the same as by walking when predicated of the animals of the earth;

and the spiritual life is from truths which are derived from good, which are signified by leaping with the feet upon which are legs; but spiritual death is from truths conjoined to evil, which is signified by going upon four feet upon which are no legs, wherefore it is said to be abomination to eat such things.

Inasmuch as by a horse is signified the intellectual principle, and by a locust the sensual, which is the ultimate of the intellectual, and the intellect lives whilst it is in its ultimate, therefore the ancients spake of horses leaping and jumping as the locust. Thus in Job: "Hast thou given the horse strength? hast thou clothed his neck with thunder? Canst thou make him leap as a grasshopper? the glory of his nostrils is terrible" (xxxix. 19, 20). The quality of the intellect is here described by a horse, as being robust, moving out and curving in the neck, and walking by leaps; and as the ultimate of the intellect is the sensual principle, and this is signified by the locusts or grasshopper, and the life of the intellect in this ultimate by jumping and walking by leaps, therefore it is said that the horse leaps as the locust. The most ancient books, amongst which is the book of Job, were written by mere correspondences; for the science of correspondences was then the science of sciences, and they were esteemed above all others, who could compose books most abounding in the most significant correspondences: the book of Job is of this nature; but the spiritual sense therein collected from correspondences does not treat concerning the holy things of heaven and the church, like the spiritual sense in the prophets, wherefore it is not amongst the books of the Word; nevertheless passages are adduced from it on account of the correspondences of which it is full.

544. "And unto them was given power, as the scorpions of the earth have power"—That hereby is signified their persuasive faculty, and the effect and potency thereof, appears from the signification of a scorpion, as denoting the persuasive principle, which is of an infatuating and suffocating nature, concerning which we shall speak presently; and from the signification of power, as denoting potency and effect, in this case, the potency of the sensual man from the faculty of persuasion, and the effect, which is infatuating and suffocating. The nature and quality of the persuasive principle, signified by the scorpion, are as yet scarcely known to any one in the world, because that it is the persuasive principle of the spirit of the sensual man, in which he is when he becomes a spirit, but not whilst he lives as a man in the world; the reason is, because a man in the world rarely speaks out what his spirit thinks and intimately loves, for he is taught from infancy to converse about such things as pertain to civil and moral life, and even such as pertain to spiritual life, although his spirit, which thinks and wills inwardly, is differently inclined: the spirit of man, whilst it resides in the body, makes a show of such things before the world, because otherwise he cannot secure favor, so as to obtain the ends which his spirit aims at, which are principally honors and gains, and a name and fame on account of them. This is the reason why the nature and quality of

the infatuating and suffocating persuasive principle, which is signified by the scorpion, are not known in the world; such, however,
is its nature with the spirits in whom it is operative, that it infuses
itself into the soul and spirit of another, and lays asleep, and almost
extinguishes, his rational and intellectual faculties, whence he cannot possibly know otherwise, than that which is spoken is the truth,
although it should be most false. They who are in such a persuasive principle, do not speak from any reason, but from a blind faith
without reason, because from the ultimate sensual principle, in which
no reason exists, but only a persuasive faith grounded in such things
as ascend from the body, and flow in from the world, inflated by
the fire of self-love, which inflates, draws out, and infuses into another; wherefore they are more especially in this persuasive principle, who have imbued falsities from the love of self, and believe
themselves to be wiser than others. This persuasive principle is
said to be infatuating, because it induces a stupor upon the understanding; and it is called suffocating, because it takes away the free
respiration of another; for every one respires conformably to the
thought of his mind. But whereas such a persuasive principle is
most noxious and pernicious, because it induces as it were a swooning in the mind of another, so that he cannot see anything rationally,
therefore spirits are severely prohibited from using it; and they who
do use it are separated from others, and are either chastised or sent
down into hell; for in the spiritual world every one is allowed to
confirm the sentiments of his mind, whether they be true or false,
by things rational and intellectual, but not by any persuasive fas-
cination.* The reason why such a deadly persuasive principle is
signified by the scorpion, is, because the scorpion, when it stings a
man, induces a similar swooning upon his mind, and thence death,
if it is not healed.

Murderous persuasions are also signified by scorpions, in the following passages: Thus in Luke: "And he said unto them, I beheld
Satan as lightning fall from heaven. Behold, I give unto you power
to tread on serpents and scorpions, and over all the power of the
enemy; and nothing shall by any means hurt you" (x. 18, 19).
That by serpents and scorpions here mentioned, are not understood
serpents and scorpions, is evident, for the Lord says, that he saw
Satan as lightning fall from heaven, and that he gives them power
over all the potency of the enemy; wherefore by serpents and scor-

---

* But more concerning this persuasive principle may be seen in the A. C ; as,
that they who are affected by it are inwardly bound, n. 5096; that they who make
use of it shut up the rational principle of others, and, as it were, to suffocate them, n.
3895, 5128: that the Nephilim, or Giants, Anakim, and Rephaim, mentioned in
the Word, were, above all others, in direful persuasions of falsity, n. 581, 1268, 1270.
1271, 1673, 7686; that before the advent of the Lord, they infested all in the other
life by their direful persuasions, and almost extinguished their spiritual life, n. 7686;
that they were cast into hell by the Lord, when he was in the world, and that that
hell still appears as under a misty rock, and they who approach near it fall into a
swoon, n. 311, 581, 1268, 1270, 7686; what has been experienced from some of the
devils from that hell, to whom it was permitted to assault me with their influences,
n. 1268, 1269, 1270, 1271; concerning the mischief arising from the persuasions of
falsity. n 794, 806; that there are many kinds of persuasions of falsity, n 1673.
1675

pions, in the internal sense, are signified the crew of Satan, who had been in subtle and direful persuasions of falsity, by which men are spiritually murdered after death, unless they are defended by the Lord : the antediluvians, who were called the Nephilim, were in such persuasions above all others, and, unless the Lord, when he was in the world, had subjugated and cast them into hell, and shut their hell, no mortal could have been saved; for they infested, and almost murdered, whomsoever they met in the spiritual world. That the Lord liberated the spiritual world from these and such like spirits, is understood by his seeing Satan falling from heaven, and by his giving to those who are in truths from good derived from him, the power of treading upon serpents and scorpions. This direful persuasive principle is also signified by scorpions, in the following passage of Ezekiel : "And thou, son of man, be not afraid of them, neither be afraid of their words, though briars and thorns be with thee, and though thou dost dwell among scorpions; be not afraid of their words, nor be dismayed at their looks. For they are hard in face, and obdurate in heart " (ii. 6. 7). Here, by dwelling among scorpions is understood, among those who had persuaded themselves, and resolutely persuade others, to admit falsities, and who admit not any truth, wherefore they are called refractory and thorny, likewise hard in face and obdurate in heart; the interiors also of the rational mind, with those who are in a strong persuasion of what is false, are shut, and therefore they think and speak only from the ultimate sensual principle, which, when it is enkindled from the fire of self love, is hard and obdurate, and also hardens and renders obdurate the interiors of others to whom it addresses itself: for in the spiritual world, there is a communication of minds, that is, of thoughts and affections, and from those who are in such persuasive principles, infusion ; hence are the effects above mentioned. So in Moses : "Who led thee through that great and terrible wilderness, wherein were fiery serpents and scorpions " (Deut. viii. 15). By the journeyings and wanderings of the children of Israel in the wilderness forty years, were represented and signified the temptations of the faithful, and as these are effected by the injections and persuasions of falsities from evil spirits, it is said, that they were led through a wilderness great and terrible, wherein were fiery serpents and scorpions. Moreover, by serpents in general is signified the ultimate sensual principle of man, and by the various species of serpents are signified the various states of that principle, as to evils and falsities : for sensual men are, above all others, crafty and malicious, and believe themselves, and induce others to believe, that they excel in ingenuity, intellect, and judgment; but I can assert, that they have nothing of understanding and judgment, but that they are in the same proportion stupid, with respect to such things as are essential to faith and life, as they are ingenious in contriving evils and persuading falsities ; and wickedness, as is well known, is not wisdom, for wisdom is of truth from good, whereas wickedness is of falsity from evil, which destroys the truth which is from good, because they are opposites, and what is opposite destroys.

545. "And it was commanded them, that they should not hurt the grass of the earth, neither any green thing, neither any tree "— That hereby is signified that they should do no injury to any scientific that is true and alive from the literal sense of the Word, nor to any knowledges of truth and good therein, appears from the signification of not hurting as denoting not to do injury; and from the signification of grass as denoting the scientific which is true; and from the signification of green thing, as denoting the scientific which is alive, concerning which see above, n. 507; and as every scientific is true and alive from the Word, hence by not hurting the grass of the earth nor any green thing, is signified, not to do injury to any scientific that is true and alive from the Word; and from the signification of trees, as denoting the knowledges of truth and good, also from the Word, concerning which see above, n. 109, 420. By scientifics from the Word are understood all things of the literal sense thereof, in which there does not appear any things doctrinal; but by the knowledges of truth and good are understood all things of the literal sense of the Word, in which and from which doctrinal things are: by this, therefore, namely, that they should not hurt any scientific that is true and alive, nor the knowledge of truth and good from the Word, is understood, that the sensual man, by his persuasive principle, shall not pervert any sense of the letter of the Word, by denying it to be true, for if he does this, all is lost with him, since there is then no hope of his reformation, nor any faculty of understanding the truth of the church; for he who denies the Word to be divine throughout the entire sense of the letter, breaks off his connection with heaven, since the conjunction of man with heaven is by the Word, as may be seen in the work concerning H. & H. n. 303–310. The state here described is that of the man of the church when near its end, namely, that from internal or spiritual he becomes external and sensual; but still, lest he should altogether perish, it is provided, and care is taken, by the Lord, that he may not do injury to anything in the literal sense of the Word by denying it to be true and alive, that is, divine, although by the sense of the letter he confirms his falsities and evils; for so long as he does not deny the divine principle in the Word, he still hears or reads it, and thereby is in some conjunction with heaven. Hence it is evident, that by these words is signified, that this principle of the church should still remain; but by what follows, namely, that they should hurt those men only who have not the seal of God in their forehead, is signified that the ultimate sensual principle here treated of, should only do injury to the understanding of truth with those who are not in truths originating in good from the Lord.

546. "But only those men which have not the seal of God in their foreheads "—That hereby is signified that they should hurt only the understanding of truth and the perception of good, with those who are not in truths originating in good from the Lord, appears from the signification of man, as denoting the affection of truth and thence intelligence and wisdom, concerning which see above, n. 280; but in the present case, the understanding of truth

and the perception of good, of which we shall speak presently; and from the signification of having the seal of God in their forehead, as denoting to be in truths originating in good from the Lord, concerning which see above, n. 427. The reason why by man is signified the understanding of truth and perception of good, is, because it is by virtue of these that man is man, wherefore when man is mentioned in the Word, in the spiritual sense is understood that, by virtue of which man is man, for this is his spiritual principle. Man has two faculties in which all his life consists, namely, understanding and will; acccording to the quality, therefore, of the understanding and will, such is the man; if he has the understanding of truth and the will of good, he is truly man, for truth and good are from the Lord, and it is from the Lord alone that man is man, as may appear from what is said, and shown in the work concerning H. & H. n. 59–102; but if he has not the understanding of truth and the will of good, but in the place of truth, what is false, and in the place of good, evil, then indeed he is called man, but still he is not man, except from this circumstance only, that he has the faculty of understanding truth, and of perceiving good; concerning which faculty we shall speak in the following article. From these considerations it may appear, that by men, in the Word, are understood such things as constitute men, and, in the present case, the understanding of truth and the perception of good. That these things are here understood by men, may also appear from this consideration, that it is said concerning the locusts, that they should hurt men, but not the grass of the earth, the green things, and the trees; and by the locust is signified the ultimate principle of the life of man, which is called sensual; and this principle, when it is in the persuasion of what is false, and reads or hears the Word, still does not hurt or injure anything of the Word in the sense of the letter, this sense being for the natural sensual man, which he therefore believes, although he applies it to confirm his falsities; but it hurts and injures the understanding of truth and the perception of good; for the sensual man cannot elevate his thought above the sense of the letter of the Word, and if he attempt to elevate it, he either falls into what is false, or his persuasive faith concerning the Word perishes. From what has been adduced, it may now be known, what is understood by the locusts being commanded not to hurt the grass of the earth, nor any green thing, neither any tree, but only those men who had not the seal of God in their foreheads.

547. "And to them it was given that they should not kill them"— That hereby is signified, that they should not be deprived of the faculty of understanding truth and of perceiving good, appears from the signification of men, as denoting the understanding of truth and the perception of good; see above, n. 546; and from the signification of killing them, as denoting to destroy as to spiritual life, concerning which see above, n. 315; but in the present case, to deprive of the faculty of understanding truth and perceiving good. The reason why this is here signified by killing men, is, because every man is born into the faculty of understanding truth and perceiving good;

for this faculty is the very spiritual principle by which every man is distinguished from beasts : this faculty man never destroys, for if he should destroy it, he would be no longer a man but a beast : it appears indeed as if the sensual man, who is in the falsities of evil, had destroyed it, because he neither understands truth nor perceives good when reading the Word or when hearing it from others, but still he has not destroyed the faculty itself of understanding and perceiving, but only the understanding of truth and the perception of good, so long as he is in the falsities in which he has confirmed himself from evil; for whilst he is averse from hearing truth, there appears a want of ability to understand ; but if the persuasion of the falsity which thus hinders be removed, he then understands and perceives that truth is truth, and that good is good, as a spiritual-rational man.   That this is the case, has been given me to know by much experience ; for there were many of the infernal crew, who had confirmed themselves in falsities against truths, and in evils against goods, who thence became such, that they desired not to hear anything of truth, much less to understand it, concerning whom therefore others conceived an opinion that they could not understand truth ; but the same spirits, when the persuasion of the falsity was removed from them, came into the power and faculty of understanding what was true, equally with those who were in the understanding of truth and in the perception of good ; but presently, when they relapsed into their former state, they appeared again as if they could not understand truth, yea, were exceedingly indignant at having understood, saying then, that nevertheless it was not truth : for affection which is of the will causes all the understanding pertaining to man, the very life of the understanding being thence derived : let it be considered, whether any one can think without affection, and whether the affection be not the very life of the thought, consequently of the understanding ; by affection is meant the affection of love, or love in its continuity. From these considerations it is evident that man can indeed destroy the understanding of truth and the perception of good, which is effected by the falsities of evil, but that still he does not, on that account, destroy the faculty of understanding truth and of perceiving good, since, if he did, he would no longer be a man, the human principle itself consisting in this faculty.   It is by virtue of this faculty, that man lives after death, and then appears as a man, for the divine principle is therewith conjoined.   Hence it is, that although man, as to his two lives, which are the life of his understanding and the life of his will, be averse from the divine principle, yet by virtue of his ability to understand truth and to perceive good, he has conjunction with the divine principle, and thence lives to eternity.   From what has been observed, then, it may be seen, that by its being given to the locusts not to kill men, is signified, that still they should not be deprived of the faculty of understanding truth and of perceiving good.

548. "But that they should be tormented five months"—That hereby is signified that the understanding should be darkened by the falsities of evil, and be drawn away from seeing truth, so long as

they remained in that state, appears from the signification of tormenting, as denoting to darken as to the understanding, and to be withdrawn from seeing truth, of which we shall treat presently; and from the signification of five months, as denoting so long as they remain in that state. The reason why to torment here signifies to darken as to the understanding, and to be drawn away from seeing truth, is, because it is said concerning the locusts, and their power of hurting as scorpions, and by the locust is understood the ultimate principle of the life of man, which is called the sensual, and by the power of hurting as scorpions is signified the persuasive faculty, which is of such a nature, as to take away from the understanding the light of truth, and induce infernal darkness; wherefore it now follows, that their torment was as the torment of a scorpion when he strikes a man, for by the scorpion is signified such a persuasive principle; as may be seen above, n. 544. This is said to torment, because it is said above, that the locusts should hurt men, but should not kill them; and to hurt and not to kill is to torment. The persuasive principle also, of the sensual man, who is in the falsities of evil, hurts the understanding by darkening and drawing it away from seeing truth, although it does not deprive it of the faculty of understanding and perceiving; and because it is compared with the pain arising from the stroke of a scorpion, it is said to torment. The reason why five months signify so long as men are in that state, is, because a month signifies a state, and the number five signifies some or somewhat, and hence also, so long as. The reason why months signify states, is, because all times, in the Word, as ages, years, weeks, days, and hours, signify states of life, as may be seen in the work concerning H. & H. n. 162–169; hence also months have the same signification. That five signify some, or somewhat, may appear from those passages in the Word, where that number occurs; for the numbers 10, 100, 1000, signify much and all, hence five signify some and somewhat; for those numbers which signify much, arise from the number five, which signifies some, and the numbers which are compounded and derived, draw their signification from the simple numbers, from which, by multiplication, they are compounded and derived, as may be seen above, n. 429, 430; the reason why the number five also signifies so long as, is, because it is said, five months, and by five months is there signified a state of duration. This signification of five months appears remote, from this circumstance, that man, so long as he lives in the world, is in natural thought, and natural thought derives its ideas from spaces and times, and also from numbers and measures; for these things are proper to nature, because all things in nature are determined by them; but spiritual thought is without any determinate idea of space, time, number, and measure; hence it is, that it appears as remote and strange to man in the world, that five months should signify so long as that state continues, that is, the state of persuasion of what is false, for so long the understanding is darkened and drawn away from seeing the truth; but when the persuasion, of what is false is removed, man comes into the faculty of seeing truth, if he desire to see it, which faculty is given to every man.

That five, in the Word, signify somewhat and some, likewise all of such quality, and things similar, may appear from the following passages : " Then shall the kingdom of heaven be likened unto ten virgins. And five of them were wise and five were foolish" (Matt. xxv. 1, 2). The reason why the Lord compared the kingdom of the heavens to ten virgins, is, because the kingdom of the heavens signifies the church, as does also a virgin ; and ten virgins signify all who are of the church ; the reason of its being said, that five were wise and five foolish, was, because five signify some of them, or all who are of such a quality on one part ; that a virgin signifies the church, may appear from many passages in the Word, where mention is made of the virgin of Zion, the virgin of Jerusalem, the virgin of Israel, by whom the church is signified. The same is signified by ten, and by five, in the parable which the Lord spake concerning the nobleman who "to his ten servants delivered ten pounds. Then came the first, saying, Lord, thy pound hath gained ten pounds. And he said unto him, Have thou authority over ten cities. And the second came, saying, Lord, thy pound hath gained five pounds. And he said to him, Be thou also over five cities" (Luke xix. 12–19). The numbers ten and five are mentioned by the Lord, because ten signify much, and five, some ; but by their trading is signified the acquisition and provision of heavenly intelligence ; and by their having authority over cities, is signified intelligence or wisdom, for a city, in the Word, signifies doctrine, and to have authority over it signifies to be intelligent or wise ; and to have authority over ten cities, signifies much, and over five signifies some. Some also, and all who are of such a quality, are signified by the number five in the parable of the Lord concerning the rich man and Lazarus, in which it is said that the rich man entreated Abraham to send Lazarus to his five brethren who were yet alive. So again, in the parable of the great supper, one of those who were invited excused himself on the ground that he had bought five yoke of oxen, and must go to prove them (Luke xvi. 27, 28 ; xiv. 19). By oxen in the Word are signified the natural affections, and by five yoke of oxen are signified all those affections or cupidities which lead away from heaven ; heaven and the church, as to spiritual nourishment or instruction, are signified by the great supper to which they were invited ; who cannot see that the number five in these four parables involves some arcanum, because it is spoken by the Lord ? So again, in Isaiah : " In that day shall five cities in the land of Egypt speak the language of Canaan, and swear to Jehovah of hosts. In that day shall there be an altar to Jehovah in the midst of the land of Egypt" (xix. 18, 19). In that day, signifies the advent of the Lord ; five cities in the land of Egypt speaking the language of Canaan, signifies, that then some who are natural shall become spiritual, and shall acknowledge the truths of genuine doctrine, and shall worship the Lord from the good of charity ; these things may be seen particularly explained above, n. 223. Here, therefore, mention is made of five cities, that some at that time may be understood, and likewise some truths of doctrine. So again: "Yet gleaning grapes shall be left in it, as the shaking of an olive tree, two or three berries in the top of the uppermost bough, four or five in the outmost fruitful branches thereof" (xvii. 6). And in Luke: "For from henceforth there shall be five in one house divided, three against two, and two against three" (xii. 52). That in these passages also five signify some, and all of such a quality, may be seen above, n. 532, where they are explained. So again, there was a law given to the Israelites in these words; "If a man shall steal an ox, and kill it, or sell it, he shall restore five oxen" (Exod. xxii. 1). Here by an ox, in the spiritual sense, is understood the good of the natural man; by restoring five oxen for an ox, is signified that he shall sufficiently amend what he had perverted and extinguished; to steal is to take away, to kill is to extinguish, and to sell is to pervert. By the fifth part is also signified as much as is sufficient in the following passages: Lev. v. 16; xxii. 14; xxvii. 13, 15, 19, 27, 31; Numb. v. 7. The same is also signified by the fifth part of the produce of the land of Egypt which the officers of Pharaoh were commanded to take up and lay in store during the seven years of plenty (Gen. xli. 34; xlvii. 24). Again, the same is signified by Abner's smiting Asahel with the hinder end of his spear under the fifth rib (2 Sam. ii. 23). Under the fifth rib signified as much as was sufficient for death; for the same number which signifies somewhat, and all which is on one part, also signifies as much as is sufficient when it is predicated of quantity, and so long as is sufficient when it is predicated of time.

Forasmuch as this number signifies somewhat, and the all of one part, hence it also signifies little and few, when a great quantity, which is also marked by numbers, follows or precedes; for in this case the all of one part is respectively few. Thus in Isaiah: "One thousand shall flee at the rebuke of one; at the rebuke of five shall ye flee" (xxx. 17). And in Moses: "And five of you shall chase a hundred, and a hundred of you shall put ten thousand to flight" (Lev. xxvi. 8). Again, in the evangelists it is stated that the Lord fed five thousand men with five loaves and two fishes (Matt. xiv. 15–21; Mark vi. 38–43; Luke ix. 13–17; John vi. 9–13). On this occasion it is said that they took up twelve baskets of the fragments which remained, by which is signified fulness, thus fulness of instruction, and also full benediction. So in Luke, by five are signified few, where it is said, "Are not five sparrows sold for two farthings, and not one of them is forgotten before God? Fear not therefore: ye are of more value than many sparrows" (xii. 6, 7). Here the reason why five sparrows are mentioned, is, because five denote what are few and of little value respectively as to man, hence it is afterwards said, "ye are of more value than many sparrows." Any one may readily perceive that this number would not have been mentioned by the Lord unless it had been significative. So again, in consequence of this meaning of the number five, it was commanded that the tabernacle should be made with ten curtains, the five

curtains to be coupled together one to another, and the other five
curtains to be coupled one to another (Exod. xxvi. 1, 2, 3).*

549. " And their torment was as the torment of a scorpion when
he striketh a man"—That hereby are signified that the darkening
and withdrawing the mind from perceiving truth, are from the persuasion with which it is infatuated, appear from the signification of
torment, as denoting the darkening of the mind, and withdrawing it
from seeing truth; see above, n. 548. And from the signification
of a scorpion, as denoting the persuasive principle infatuating and
suffocating, concerning which see also above, n. 544. Wherefore
by their torment being as the torment of a scorpion when he striketh
a man, are signified that the darkening and withdrawing the mind from
perceiving truth, are from the persuasion with which it is infatuated.†
The reason why that persuasive principle is said to be infatuating,
is, because it takes away the use of reason, insomuch that reason,
or the rational mind, sees nothing but what he who is in such a persuasive principle speaks; for it excites in a moment everything
which consents, and covers everything which dissents, whence the
mind becomes infatuated, in consequence of being darkened and
drawn away from seeing the truth. The reason why it is also said
to be suffocating, is, because it deprives the understanding of the
faculty of thinking freely, and of extending the sight in every direction, as is done by every rational man, and when this is the case the
respiration labors ; for the voluntary respiration derives its all from
the understanding, hence it also accommodates itself to the thought
thereof, as the motion of the heart derives its all from the will, and
accommodates itself to the affection thereof.‡ That a strong persuasive principle has not only the power of infatuating, but also of
suffocating, has been given me to know by real experience.

550. " And in those days shall men seek death, and shall not find
it"—That hereby is signified, that they will then desire to destroy
the faculty of understanding truth, but that still this cannot be done,
appears from the signification of "in those days," as denoting then,
namely, when the man of the church from internal becomes external,
or when from rational he becomes sensual ; and from the signification of seeking death, as denoting a desire to destroy the faculty of
understanding truth, concerning which we shall speak presently ;
and from the signification of not finding it, as denoting not to be able
to destroy. That by seeking death is here signified a desire to destroy the faculty of understanding truth, is evident from what precedes, because it is consequent upon it; for it was said, that the
locusts should hurt only the men who had not the seal of God in
their foreheads, and afterwards, that to them it was given that they

---

* That ten signify all in the aggregate, and five the all of one and of the other part,
may be seen in the A. C. n. 9595, 9604.

† Concerning the quality and origin of the persuasive principle, which infatuates,
and as it were suffocates, see above, n 543.

‡ That the respiration of the lungs corresponds to the understanding and its
thought, and the motion of the heart to the will and its affection, may be seen in
the A. C. n. 1119, 3883–3896, 9281.

should not kill them, but that they should torment them, by which is signified, that they should only injure the understanding of truth and the perception of good with those who are not in truths from good derived from the Lord, but that still they should not deprive them of the faculty of understanding truth, and of perceiving good, as may be seen above, n. 546, 547.   Hence then it follows, that by the death which they seek, and which they desire, is signified the privation of the faculty of understanding truth and perceiving good, to destroy these being to destroy the life which is properly human; for in this case man would be no longer man, but a beast, as was said above; and hence it is evident, that the privation of this life is what is signified by death.   The reason why it is said that they desire to destroy the two faculties of the life truly human, is, because sensual men, from the persuasion concerning the falsities of evil in which they are, do not desire to understand truth and to perceive good, for they are delighted with their own falsities of evil, and hence with thinking from the delight of falsity, and with willing from the delight of evil, wherefore they avert themselves from good and truth, because they are opposites; some are sad at them, some nauseate them, and some reject them with anger, every one according to the quantity and quality of the falsity in which he persuades himself: in a word, such a sensual man does not admit reasons from the understanding against the falsities of evil in which he is, thus he does not will to understand and become rational, although he has the power of becoming so, because he is a man.   This, therefore, is what is signified by, " they shall seek death, and shall not find it."

551. " And shall desire to die, and death shall flee from them"— That hereby is signified that they are willing to destroy the faculty of perceiving the good which is of spiritual life, but in vain, appears from the signification of dying, as here denoting to destroy the faculty of perceiving good, concerning which we shall speak presently, and from the signification of "death shall flee from them," as denoting that they cannot destroy, thus that they desire in vain.   The reason why by dying is here signified to destroy the faculty of perceiving good, and why by dying mentioned above is signified to destroy the faculty of understanding truth, is, because every man has two lives, the life of the understanding, and the life of the will; the life of the understanding is the faculty of understanding truth, and the life of the will is the faculty of perceiving good; hence death is the deprivation of both the one and the other.   The reason why death in the first place signifies the deprivation of the faculty of understanding truth, and in the second place, the deprivation of the faculty of perceiving good, is, because in what precedes both these lives are treated of, and because, in the Word, where truth is treated of, good is also treated of, on account of the marriage of good and truth in every part of the Word; concerning which see above, n. 238, 288, 484.   Hence it may appear that by the death here mentioned, is signified the deprivation of the faculty of perceiving good; from this cause it is, that two expressions nearly similar are mentioned together, and also that to seek death is predicated of what pertains to

the understanding, and to desire death of what pertains to the will. For since the spiritual life proper to man consists in these faculties, therefore their willingness to destroy spiritual life is also signified. To every man also is given the faculty of perceiving good, as well as the faculty of understanding truth ; for truth loves good, and good loves truth, and therefore they continually desire to be conjoined, and they are conjoined, as will and understanding, or as affection and thought; when this conjunction takes place, then the understanding thinks truth from the affection of thinking it, and in this case the understanding also sees it, and the will perceives it ; to perceive truth from the affection of the will is to perceive good, for truth is turned into good, whilst man wills or is affected by it, that is, whilst he loves it ; from this cause everything which is loved is called good.

552. " And the shapes of the locusts were like unto horses prepared unto battle"—That hereby is signified that the sensual man became a man of reasoning as from the understanding of truth, appears from the signification of the locusts, as denoting the men of the church become sensual by the falsities which are from evil, concerning which see above, n. 543 ; and from the signification of horses prepared unto battle, as denoting reasonings, in this case, as from the understanding of truth, because it is said, that they were like unto them ; that by horses is signified the understanding, may be seen above, n. 355, 364 ; and all understanding is of truth ; and inasmuch as by war, in the Word, is signified spiritual combat, which is that of falsity against truth, and of truth against falsity, therefore by horses prepared unto battle are signified reasonings, in this case, as from the understanding of truth, for by reasonings spiritual combats are maintained. In what now follows to verse 12, the subject treated of is the sensual man who is in falsities from evil, as to his quality in respect to understanding and will, and he is described by locusts and their various appearances ; for all the affections, and thence the thoughts of man, are represented in the spiritual world by various beasts of the earth, and by birds, and they are also presented to view in such forms as correspond ; and the beasts there represented, according to the affections of the spirits from which they are, appear like the beasts of our world, but sometimes with successive changing and variety approximating to forms composed of different beasts, besides that they are also clothed and decorated with various insignia as to their heads and their bodies ; such things have been frequently seen by me, and the qualities of the affections and inclinations of those who were represented were thence made manifest. It is from this representation of affections and thoughts in the spiritual world, that beasts and birds, in the Word, derive their significations. That sensual men, who are in falsities from evil, are represented, and thence signified by locusts, was shown above, n. 543 ; their quality is now described by their various forms, and by various insignia ; as that they were like unto horses prepared unto battle ; and on their heads were as it were crowns like gold ; that their faces were as the faces of men ; and that they had hair, as the

hair of women, and teeth as the teeth of lions; also that they had breast plates, and various other things; all of which are representatives, such as exist in the spiritual world, corresponding to falsities from evil, and to the persuasive principle of the sensual man; it would not, however, be possible for any one to know what such things represent and signify, without the knowledge of correspondences; neither could the quality of the sensual man be known, and the quality of his persuasive principle. The reason why the sensual man, who is in falsities from evil, reasons as from the understanding of truth, is, because he is in the persuasion that falsity is truth, and that evil is good; and so long as he is in this persuasion he cannot see anything rationally and intellectually, but what he has persuaded himself in, he believes to be of the highest reason, and of eminent understanding; for his rational and intellectual principle is shut, and hence he is in a persuasive faith concerning the things which he thinks and speaks.*

553. " And on their heads were as it were crowns like gold "— That hereby is signified, that they appear to themselves, when they reason, as wise and conquerors, appears from the signification of head as denoting wisdom and intelligence, concerning which we shall speak presently; and from the signification of a crown of gold as denoting a reward of victory; concerning which see above, n. 358. The reason of this signification is, because kings, in ancient times, when they were in combats with their enemies, wore crowns of gold upon their heads, besides various other insignia which then belonged to kings; the reason was, because kings represented the Lord as to divine truth, and divine truth combats from divine good; this therefore was represented by a crown of gold, and wisdom and intelligence itself by the head upon which the crown was; hence crowns were assigned to martyrs for they combated from divine truth against falsities from evil which are from hell, and came off conquerors, because they maintained the combat even unto death which they feared not. From these considerations it may appear that by the locusts having upon their heads as it were crowns like gold, is signified, that they who are sensual men, from the persuasion of the falsity in which they are principled, appear to themselves as wise and conquerors. Since the locusts are described as to their heads, their faces, their breasts, upon which were breast plates, and as to their tails, their hair and teeth, it is of importance that it be here known, what is signified by their heads, and afterwards what by the other parts. By head, in the Word, is signified wisdom and intelligence, because these principles reside in the head; but when they are treated of who are not in any wisdom and intelligence, because in falsities from evil, then by head are signified folly and insanity, because falsities from evil are there and thence: but in the present case, as the subject treated of respects those who are sensual, and in the persua-

* That the sensual man reasons acutely and with readiness, because his thought is so near his speech as to be almost in it, and because he places all intelligence in discoursing from the memory alone, may be seen in the A. C. n. 195, 196, 5700, 10,236.

sion of falsity, by the head is properly signified folly and insanity, for they see falsities as truths, and evils as goods, being perpetually in visions from fallacies : hence it is, that it is said of them, that " on their heads were as it were crowns like gold, and their faces as the faces of men," with other things of a like nature, all which were appearances originating in their fantasy, wherefore it is said as it were crowns, and like gold, whence it is evident that those appearances were not real, but fallacious appearances : for all the appearances which exist in the heavens, are real, because they are correspondences ; for the interior things pertaining to the affections and thence thoughts of the angels, when they pass to the sight of their eyes, are clothed in forms such as appear in the heavens, and as they are visible, they are called appearances, and are said to be correspondences, and are real because from creation : but the case is otherwise with respect to the appearances in some of the hells, where they are who are in false persuasions from evil ; from these persuasions exist fantastic visions, in which there is inwardly nothing real, wherefore they also vanish away upon the influx of only a single ray from the light of heaven : of such a nature are the appearances which are here related concerning the locusts.*

554. " And their faces were as the faces of men"—That hereby is signified that they appear to themselves as spiritual affections of truth, appears from the signification of faces, as denoting the interiors of the mind and affection ; concerning which see above, n. 412 ; and from the signification of man, as denoting the spiritual affection of truth, and thence intelligence and wisdom ; concerning which also see above, n. 280 ; and inasmuch as faces are types of the interiors of man, hence they signify the same as men themselves, namely, affections of truth, but in the present case that they appear to themselves as affections of truth ; and thence intelligent and wise, because it is said of the locusts, that their faces were seen as the faces of men. The locusts appearing with such faces, is because of the strong persuasive principle in which sensual men are who are in falsities from evil, who are signified by the locusts, the persuasive principle itself presenting such appearance but this only before themselves and before others who are also in falsities from evil, but not before the angels of heaven ; the reason is because the angels are in the light of heaven, and whatsoever they see they see from that light, and the light of heaven, inasmuch as it is divine truth, dissipates everything fantastic originating in the persuasive principle. The reason why sensual men thus appear to themselves, is, because sensual men persuade themselves that they are in truths from good above all others although they are in falsities from evil ; for they cannot view anything inwardly from heaven, but only outwardly from the world, and they who see from the world alone, see only from an infatuated light, from which they suppose themselves to be more intelligent and wiser than others, not knowing wherein intelligence and wisdom

* But concerning appearances in the spiritual world, as well real as not real, more may be seen in the work concerning H. & H. n. 170–176, 369 ; as also above in the explication, n. 395.

consist, or whence they come : from this persuasive faith it is, that they believe themselves to be in the spiritual affection of truth, and this is signified by the faces of the locusts appearing as the faces of men.   But it may be expedient to illustrate these things by experience from the spiritual world.   All who are in the heavens, are men as to their faces and the other parts of the body, for they are in the spiritual affection of truth, and the spiritual affection of truth is itself in form a man, because this affection is from the Lord, who is the only man, and because from him the universal heaven conspires to the human form ; hence it is that the angels are the forms of their own affections, which also appear from their faces ; but these things are amply expounded in the work concerning H. & H. n. 59–102. But in hell, where all are external and sensual, because in falsities from evil, they also appear to themselves as men, even as to their faces, but only amongst their own ; but when they are beheld in the light of heaven, they appear as monsters, with a direful face, and sometimes instead of the face only what is hairy, or with a horrible grate of teeth, and sometimes lurid, as dead, in which there is not any living human principle, for they are forms of hatred, revenge, and cruelties, in which is spiritual death, because in opposition to the life which is from the Lord.   That they appear amongst themselves in face as men, is from fantasy, and persuasion thence derived; but concerning these appearances see also in the work concerning H. & H. n. 553.

555. " And they had hair as the hair of women"—That hereby is signified that they also appear to themselves natural affections of truth, appears from the signification of hair, as denoting things pertaining to the natural man, and specifically the scientific truths therein ; concerning which see above, n. 66 ; and from the signification of women, as denoting affections, concerning which we shall speak presently.   The reason why hair signifies what pertains to the natural man is, because the head signifies what pertains to the spiritual man, and all things of the natural man invest all things of the spiritual man, as the hair invests the head ; the head also corresponds to things spiritual, and the hair to things natural, whence they are likewise significative.   It is from this correspondence that the angels appear adorned with beautiful hair, and that, according to its ordinate arrangement, gracefulness, and neatness, may be known the quality of the correspondence of their natural man with the spiritual.   Now since women signify affections, it may appear that by the locusts having hair as the hair of women, is signified that they who are meant by the locusts appear to themselves as natural affections of truth : this is also evident from the series of things treated of ; for by their faces being as the faces of men, is signified the appearance as if they were spiritual affections of truth, whence it now follows, that by their hair being as the hair of women, is signified the appearance as if they were natural affections of truth ; presently also it is said of their teeth, that they were as the teeth of lions, and by them are signified the ultimates of the natural man as to science and as to potency.   In the prophetic

Word mention is frequently made of a woman and also of daughter and virgin. But heretofore it has been unknown what is signified by them: that a woman, daughter, and virgin, are not meant, is very evident, for they are mentioned where the church is treated of; but what they spiritually signify may be seen from the series of the things treated of in the internal sense.

That by a woman is signified the church as to the affection of truth, and thence the affection of truth pertaining to the church, may appear from the following passages in the Word. Thus in Jeremiah: "Wherefore commit ye this great evil against your souls, to cut off from you man and woman, child and suckling, out of Judah, to leave you none to remain!" (xliv. 7.) Again, in the same prophet: "I will break in pieces man and woman; old and young, the young man and the maid" (li. 22). So in Ezekiel: "Slay utterly old and young, both maids and little children, and women" (ix. 6). And in Lamentations: "They ravished the women in Zion, and the maids in the cities of Judah. Princes are hanged up by their hand: the faces of elders were not honored" (v. 11, 12). In these passages, by man and woman, old man and infant, youth, and virgin, are not understood man, woman, old man, infant, youth, and virgin, but all things pertaining to the church; by man and woman are signified truth and the affection thereof, by old man and infant, wisdom and innocence, by youth and virgin, the understanding of truth and the affection of good: that such things as pertain to the church are signified by these names, appears from the subjects treated of in these chapters, which are the church, and the desolation thereof as to truth and good; for the Word is inwardly spiritual, because it is divine, wherefore if nothing more were meant than what appears in the literal expressions above mentioned, it would be natural and not spiritual; but when by man and woman is understood the church as to truth and the affection thereof, by old man and infant, the church as to wisdom and innocence, and by young man and virgin, the church as to intelligence and the affection thereof, then it is made spiritual; man also is man, by virtue of the church being in him, and where the church is, there is heaven. Wherefore when mention is made of an old man, a young man, an infant, a man, a woman, and a virgin, the expressions signify whatever pertains to the church, corresponding to the age, sex, inclination, affection, intelligence, and wisdom. That by woman is signified the church as to the affection of truth, or the affection of truth pertaining to the church, may also appear from these words in Isaiah: "And in that day seven women shall take hold of one man, saying, We will eat our own bread, and wear our own apparel: only let us be called by thy name, to take away our reproach" (iv. 1). The subject there treated of is the end of the church, when there is no longer any truth for these words precede: "Thy men shall fall by the sword, and thy mighty in the war;" by which is signified that the understanding of truth would be destroyed by falsities, so that there would be no longer resistance in combats. Hence it is afterwards said: "In that day shall the branch of Jehovah be beautiful and glorious" (iv. 2). This is said concerning the Lord's advent, and signifies that truth should spring up anew in the church; by seven women taking hold of one man, is signified that from affection they would desire and seek truth, but would not find it, man denoting truth, women affections or desires for truth, and seven denoting what is holy; that they would not find instructions in genuine truths, and thereby spiritual nourishment, is signified by their saying, "We will eat our own bread, and wear our own apparel," bread denoting instruction and spiritual nourishment, and apparel truth clothing good; that it is only truth which can be applied, and by application conjoined, is signified by, "only let us be called by thy name;" and inasmuch as all honor is from the spiritual affection of truth and the conjunction thence derived, and otherwise there is no honor, therefore it is added, "to take away our reproach." So in Jeremiah: "Turn again, O virgin of Israel, turn again to these thy cities. How long wilt thou go about, O thou backsliding daughter? for Jehovah hath created a new thing in the earth, A woman shall compass a man" (xxxi. 21, 22). The subject here treated of is the spiritual captivity in which the church was before the advent of the Lord. The church is said to be in spiritual captivity, when there is no truth, and yet truth is desired; in such captivity were the Gentiles, with whom the church was established. "Turn again, O virgin of Israel, turn again to these thy cities," signifies, that they should return to the truths of doctrine, the virgin of Israel denoting the church, and her cities denoting truths of doctrine; "for Jehovah hath created a new thing in the earth, a woman shall compass a man," signifies the establishment of a new church, in which truth should be conjoined to its affection; to create a new thing in the earth denotes to establish that new thing, woman denotes the church as to the affection of truth, man denotes truth, and to compass denotes to be conjoined. And in Isaiah: "As a woman forsaken and grieved in spirit, and a wife of youth, when thou wast refused, saith thy God. For a small moment have I forsaken thee; but with great mercies will I gather thee" (liv. 6, 7). Here by a woman forsaken and grieved in spirit, is understood the church, which is not in truths, but still in the affection or desire for them, woman denoting the church, which is said to be forsaken when it is not in truths, and grieved in spirit, when in grief from the affection or desire for truths; by a wife of youth is understood the ancient church, which was in truths from affection; and by the same when refused, is understood the Jewish church, which was not in truths from any spiritual affection; the establishment of a new church by the Lord, and liberation from spiritual captivity, are understood, "for a small moment have I forsaken thee; but with great mercies will I gather thee." And in Jeremiah: "Yet hear the word of Jehovah, O ye women, and let your ear receive the word of his mouth, and teach your daughters wailing, and every one her neighbor lamentation. For death is come up into our windows, and is entered into our palaces, to cut off the children from without, and the young men from the streets" (ix. 17–21). The reason why it was said to the woman, " Yet hear the word of Jehovah, and let your ear receive the word of his mouth," was, because by them was signified the church from the affection and reception of truth; by those who were to be taught wailing and lamentation, are signified all who are of the church; mourning and lamentation signifying that these things were to be done on account of the vastation of the church, as to its truths and goods; by " death is come up into our windows, and is entered into our palaces," is signified the entrance of infernal falsity, into the understanding, and thence into all things of thought and affection, windows denoting the understanding, and palaces, all things of thought and affection; " to cut off the children from without, and the young men from the streets," signifies the vastation of truth in the birth, and of the truth that is born, children from without denoting truth springing up, or in the birth, and young men from the streets denoting the truth that is born. So in Ezekiel : " Son of man, there were two women, the daughters of one mother, and they committed whoredoms in Egypt; they committed whoredoms in their youth : and the names of them were Aholah the elder, and Aholibah her sister; and they bare sons and daughters. Samaria is Aholah, and Jerusalem Aholibah " (xxiii. 2, 3, 4). Inasmuch as by Samaria, the metropolis of the Israelites, is signified, in the Word, the spiritual church, and by Jerusalem, the metropolis of the Jews, the celestial church, each as to doctrine, therefore they are called women; and, because both of those churches act as one, they are therefore called the daughters of one mother, mother also signifying the church, as likewise do Aholah and Aholibah, or the tent or habitation of God, for this signifies heaven where divine truth and divine good are, consequently, also, where the church is, the church being the heaven of the Lord on earth; by their committing whoredom in Egypt in their youth, is signified, that they were then in no truths but in falsities, for in Egypt they had not the Word; for this which was written by Moses and the prophets, was afterwards given them, and whereby a church was instituted among them; to commit whoredom in Egypt, signifies, to falsify truths by scientifics pertaining to the natural man, and to falsify truths there, denotes to turn holy things into magic, as was the case with the Egyptians; the sons and daughters whom they brought forth, signify the falsities and evils of the church. So in Micah : " Even of late my people is risen up as an enemy : ye pull off the robe with the garment from them that pass by securely as men averse from war. The women of my people have ye cast out from their pleasant houses; from their children have ye taken away my glory for ever " (ii. 8, 9). Here, by pulling off the robe, with the garment, from them that pass by securely as men averse from war, is signified to deprive of truths all who are in truths, and who have combated against falsities; they who pass by securely denote all who are in truths, men averse, or returning from war, denote those who have been in temptations, and have combated against falsities; by casting out from their pleasant houses the women of

Jehovah's people, signifies to destroy the affections of truth, and thereby the pleasures and happiness of heaven; the women denoting the affections of truth, and their pleasant houses denoting the pleasures and happiness of heaven, for these are the affections of good and truth. So in Zechariah: "For I will gather all nations against Jerusalem to battle; and the city shall be taken, and the houses rifled, and the women ravished" (xiv. 2). Here by all nations are signified evils and falsities of every kind; by Jerusalem is signified the church; by city, doctrine; by houses, all that is holy of the church; by women are signified the affections of truth, and by their being ravished is signified that truth shall be perverted, and that thence the affections of truth will perish. So again, in the same prophet: "In that day shall there be a great mourning in Jerusalem, and the land shall mourn every family apart; the family of the house of David apart, and their wives apart; the family of the house of Nathan apart, and their wives apart; the family of the house of Levi apart, and their wives apart; the family of Shimei apart, and their wives apart; all the families that remain, every family apart, and their wives apart" (xii. 11–14). What is signified by David and his house, likewise by Nathan, Levi, and Shimei, and their houses, has been already shown in the explications above; namely, that by David is signified the divine truth, by Nathan, the doctrine of truth, by Levi, the good of charity, and by Shimei are meant truth and good as to perception and obedience. The reason why it is said that the families shall mourn apart, and their wives apart, is, because by families are signified the truths of the church, and by women, the affections of truth, which mourn apart when truth mourns that there is no affection for it, and affection that there is no truth for it. These things are said concerning the mourning over all and everything pertaining to the church as being vastated and destroyed, for all and singular the things of the church are signified by all the families that remain, by which are meant the tribes; that by the twelve tribes, are signified all things of the church in the aggregate, may be seen above, n. 430, 431. Jerusalem signifies the church and its doctrine. Thus also in Matthew: "Then shall two be in the field, the one shall be taken, and the other left. Two women shall be grinding at the mill, the one shall be taken, and the other left" (xxiv. 40, 41). By the first two here mentioned are understood men, and by the last two, women; and by men are signified those who are in truths, and by women those who are in good from the affection of truth: in this case also by men are signified those who are in falsities, and by women, those who are in evils from the affection of what is false; because it is said that one shall be taken, and the other shall be left; that is, that they shall be saved who are in truths from affection, and they shall be condemned who are in evils from affection; field signifies the church; to grind at the mill, signifies to procure for themselves the truths of doctrine from the Word; and they who apply them to good are signified by those who shall be taken, and they who apply them to evil are signified by those who shall be left; but this passage may be seen further explained in the A. C. n. 4334, 4335. So in Moses: " And when I have broken the staff of your bread, ten women shall bake your bread in one oven, and they shall deliver you your bread again by weight; and ye shall eat and not be satisfied " (Levit. xxvi. 26). By these words, in the spiritual sense, is understood that truth from good, by which men are spiritually nourished, shall fail ; for bread signifies all spiritual food, which is for the nourishment of the man of the church. By women are signified those of the church who are in the affection of truth. By ten women baking bread in one oven, is signified, that they shall search for truth which may be conjoined to good, but shall only find a very little ; for to bake signifies to prepare and conjoin so as to serve for the use of life. To deliver the bread by weight, signifies its being rare ; and to eat and not be satisfied, signifies, because truth from good is so scanty and rare, as scarcely to yield any spiritual nourishment for the soul. Again, in Moses: " The woman shall not wear that which pertaineth unto a man, neither shall a man put on a woman's garment ; for all that do so are abomination unto Jehovah thy God " (Deut. xxii. 5). Here by a man and his raiment is signified truth, and by a woman and her garment is signified the affection of truth. These principles are distinct in every man, as understanding and will, or as thought which is of the understanding, and affection which is of the will, and unless they were distinct, the sexes would be confounded, and no marriage would be effected, in which the man is the truth of the thought, and the woman the affection thereof. That both, namely, man and woman, were so created as that they may be two and yet one, appears from the book of Genesis, in which it is said concerning their creation, " So God created man in his own image, in the image of God created he him ; male and female created he them " (Gen. i. 27). And it is afterwards said, " And Adam said, This is now bone of my bones, and flesh of my flesh : she shall be called Woman, because she was taken out of man. Therefore shall a man leave his father and his mother, and shall cleave unto his wife : and they shall be one flesh " (Gen. ii. 23, 24 ; Mark x. 6-9). Here, by man is understood the church in general and in particular. The church in particular is a man of the church, or the man in whom the church is. By God creating man in his own image, is signified in the image of heaven ; for by God, or Elohim, in the plural, is signified the Divine proceeding which constitutes heaven, and the man who is a church, or in whom the church is, is a heaven in the least form, for he corresponds with all things of heaven ; as may be seen in the work concerning H. & H. n. 7-12, 51-58. By male is signified here, as above, the truth of the understanding, and by female, the good of the will ; the wife being said to be bone of the bones, and flesh of the flesh of the man, signifies that the good, which is the wife, is from the truth which is the man, bone signifying truth before it is vivified, that is, conjoined to good, such as is the truth of the memory with man ; and since all good is formed from truths, it is said, " because she was taken out of man." That a man shall leave his father and mother, and shall cleave to his wife, signifies that truth shall be of good, and that hence both shall become one good, which is signified by their being one flesh, flesh signifying good and also man.   These things, however, can be comprehended only by few, as not entering the understanding of man, unless it be known that the subject treated of in the two first chapters of Genesis is the new creation, or regeneration of the men of the church; in the first chapter their regeneration is treated of, the second chapter treats of their intelligence and wisdom; and by male and female, or by man and wife, is understood, in the spiritual sense, the conjunction of truth and good, which is called the heavenly marriage, into which marriage man comes when he is regenerated and becomes a church; and man is regenerated and made a church when he is in good and thence in truths, which is understood by his leaving father and mother, and cleaving to his wife, and their being one flesh.[*]

Since by man and woman is signified the conjunction of truth and good, therefore Moses, when he saw that the children of Israel took to themselves the female captives of the Midianites, said, "Now, therefore, kill every male among the little ones, and kill every woman that hath known man by lying with him.   But all the women children, that have not known man by lying with him, keep alive for yourselves" (Numb. xxxi. 17, 18).   The reason why these things were commanded was, because a woman not conjoined to a man signified the church as to the affection for truth, or for conjunction with truth; but a woman conjoined to a Midianitish man, signified good adulterated; for the Midianites represented, and thence signified, the truth which is not truth because not from good, consequently falsity; and hence it was that the women were to be slain who had known man, and that those who had not known man were to be preserved alive.   That the Midianitish women signified the defilement of good by falsities, and thence good adulterated and profaned, which is filthy adultery, appears from the circumstances related concerning the whoredom of the children of Israel with the women of the Midianites (Numbers xxv).

He who does not know that a woman signifies the spiritual affection of truth, likewise, that the evils and falsities which every one has are in the natural man, and not any in the spiritual man, cannot know what is signified by what is written concerning a female captive, in the following passage in Moses: "And seest among the captives a beautiful woman, and hast a desire unto her, that thou wouldest have her to thy wife; then thou shalt bring her home to thy house; and she shall shave her head and pare her nails; and she shall put the raiment of her captivity from off her, and shall remain in thy house, and bewail her father and her mother a full month: and after that thou shalt go in unto her, and be her husband, and she shall be thy wife" (Deut. xxi. 10–13).   Here also by a

---

[*] But a still clearer idea may be obtained, upon this subject, from what is said in the D. of the N. J. concerning good and truth, n. 11–19; concerning the will and understanding, n. 28–33; concerning regeneration, n. 173–182; likewise concerning good from which truths are derived, n. 24.

woman, is signified the church as to the spiritual affection of truth, or the spiritual affection of truth pertaining to the man of the church, but by a beautiful captive woman is signified the religious principle with the gentiles in whom is the desire or affection of truth; by her being brought home into the house, shaving her head, paring her nails, and putting the raiment of her captivity from off her, is signified her being led into the interior or spiritual things of the church, and thereby rejecting the evils and falsities of the natural and sensual man; the house signifies things interior, which are things spiritual; the hair of the head, which was to be shaved, signifies the falsities and evils of the natural man; the nails which were to be paired, signified the falsities and evils of the sensual man; and the raiment of captivity signifies the false principle of religion in which he is as it were held captive, who desires truth from affection; the latter things and the former therefore he will reject, because they are in the natural and sensual man, as was said above; that the captive woman should bewail her father and her mother a full month, signifies that the evils and falsities of the former religion should be buried in oblivion; that the man should afterwards go in unto her, and be her husband, and that she should be his wife, signifies that thus truth, which is signified by the man, should be conjoined with its affection, which is signified by the wife. The reason why this statute was given, no one can know, unless he understand, from the spiritual sense, what is signified by a beautiful woman taken captive from the enemy, what by bringing her home to the house, what by the hair of her head, which was to be shaven, what by the nails, and the raiment of captivity, and unless he know something concerning the conjunction of truth and good, for on this conjunction are founded all the precepts in the Word concerning marriages. The church as to the affection of truth is also signified by the woman clothed with the sun, laboring to bring forth a child, and before whom stood the dragon ready to devour her child as soon as it was born, and who fled into the wilderness (Rev. xii. 1, 4, 6). That by the woman, here, is signified the church, and by the man child whom she brought forth, the doctrine of truth, will be seen in the explication of that chapter.

Forasmuch as woman signifies the church as to the affection of truth from good, or the affection of truth from good pertaining to the man of the church, in the opposite sense also by woman is signified the cupidity of falsity from evil; for most things in the Word have also an opposite signification. This is also signified in the following passage, by woman and women. Thus in Jeremiah: "Seest thou not what they do in the cities of Judah and in the streets of Jerusalem? The children gather wood, and the fathers kindle the fire, and the women knead their dough, to make cakes to the queen of heaven, and to pour out drink offerings unto other gods" (vii. 17, 18). What these prophecies involve, cannot possibly be known, unless it be known what is signified by the cities of Judah, the streets of Jerusalem, the children, the fathers, and the women, also what is signified by gathering wood, by kindling a fire, by kneading the dough, and what by cakes, by the queen of heaven, and by drink offerings; but when the signification of such things are known, and these are assumed in their place, the spiritual sense thence results which these prophecies involve. By the cities of Judah are signified the doctrines of the church; by the streets of Jerusalem, the truths thereof, and, in the present case, falsities; children denote those who are in truths of doctrine, in this case, those who are in falsities, who are said to gather wood when they procure for themselves falsities from evils; fathers denote those who are in the goods of the church, in this case, those who are in evils, who are said to kindle a fire when they approve and excite from the love of evil; women denote the affections of truth from good, in this case, the cupidities of falsity from evil, they are said to knead the dough, when they fabricate doctrine from cupidities and according to them; to make cakes to the queen of heaven, signifies to worship infernal evils of every kind, to make cakes denoting to worship from evils, and the queen of heaven, denoting all evils in the aggregate, for the queen of heaven signifies the same as the host of heaven; to pour out drink-offerings unto other gods signifies to worship from falsities, other gods denoting infernal falsities; for God, in a good sense, signifies divine truth proceeding, but other gods signify infernal falsities, which are falsities from evil. So in Isaiah: "As for my people, children are their oppressors, and women rule over them. O my people, they which lead thee cause thee to err, and destroy the way of thy paths" (iii. 12). Here by oppressors, children, and women, are signified those who violate, are ignorant of, and pervert, truths; by oppressors are meant those who violate truths; by children, those who are ignorant of them, and by women, the cupidities which pervert them; the leaders who cause them to err, signify those who teach; to destroy the way of their paths, signifies ignorance of the leading truth. Again, in the same prophet: "When the boughs thereof are withered, they shall be broken off: the women come, and set them on fire: for it is a people of no understanding" (xxvii. 11). This is said concerning the church vastated; by the boughs being withered, are signified the truths of good destroyed by evil loves; by the women who set them on fire, are signified the cupidities of falsity, which altogether consume. So again: "Rise up, ye women that are at ease; hear my voice, ye careless daughters; give ear unto my speech, for the vintage shall fail, the gathering shall not come (xxxii. 9, 10). In this passage by the women who are at ease are meant the cupidities of those who have no concern for the vastation of the church; by the careless daughters are signified the falsities of those who trust in self-derived intelligence, for women and daughters signify all who are such in the church, whether they be men or women; by the vintage which shall fail, and by the gathering which shall not come, is signified, that the truth of the church shall be no more, for the same is signified by vintage as by wine, namely, the truth of the church, whence it is evident, what is signified by the gathering thereof. Again, in Ezekiel: "But if a man be just, and hath not eaten upon the mountains, neither hath lifted up his eyes to the idols of the house of Israel, neither hath defiled his neighbor's wife, neither hath come near to menstruous woman " (xviii. 5, 6). Here the man who has not eaten upon the mountains, is said to be just, by which is signified, that the worship of such a man is not from infernal loves, for this is signified in the Word by sacrificing, and eating of the sacrifice upon mountains; " neither hath lifted up his eyes to the idols of the house of Israel," signifies, whose worship is not from the falsities of doctrine, for idols signify those falsities, and the house of Israel signifies the perverted church in which they are found to exist; " neither hath defiled his neighbor's wife," signifies, who has not adulterated the good of the church and of the Word ; " neither hath come near to a menstruous woman," signifies, who has not defiled truths by the cupidities of falsity. So in Lamentations : " The hands of the pitiful women have sodden their own children ; they were their meat in the destruction of the daughter of my people " (iv. 10). By these words is signified the destruction of the truth and good of doctrine drawn from the Word, by falsities, and the appropriation of those falsities, with the consequent vastation of the church : by the pitiful women are signified the affections of falsity, in the opposite sense, the affections of truth ; by their having sodden their children, is signified their having destroyed by falsities the truths and goods of doctrine from the Word ; by their being meat for them, is signified the appropriation of falsities ; and by the destruction of the daughter of my people is signified the vastation of the church. By women are also signified evil desires, as in the following passages in the Revelation (xiv. 4 ; xvii. 3) ; concerning which we shall treat hereafter.

556. " And their teeth were as the teeth of lions"—That hereby is signified that things sensual, which are the ultimates of the intellectual life, are, apparently, to them as in potency over all things, appears from the signification of teeth, as denoting things sensual, which are the ultimates of the natural life as to the understanding, concerning which we shall speak presently ; and from the signification of lions, as denoting the truths of the church as to potency, but in this case, as denoting falsities destroying truths, thus also as to potency, concerning which see above, n. 278. The reason why falsities are here denoted, is, because by the locusts are signified the corporeal sensual who are in the falsities of evil. The reason why they appear to themselves to be in understanding, and thence in potency over all things, is, because the persuasive principle itself, which has been treated of above, resides in the sensual principle, which is the ultimate of the natural life ; for this sensual principle, or the sensual man, is in the confidence of self, and in the faith that he is wiser than all others, for he cannot weigh and explore himself, because he does not think interiorly ; and when he has persuaded himself of this, then in all things which he speaks, there are this confidence and faith. Hence the speech of the sensual man, inasmuch as its sound is derived from his confidence and faith, fascinates and infatuates the minds of others, for it produces such an

effect, which especially manifests itself in the spiritual world, where man speaks from his spirit; for the affection of self-confidence, and of the faith thence derived that a thing is so, is in the spirit of man, and the spirit of man speaks from the affection; it is otherwise in the natural world, in which the spirit of man discourses by the body, and, on account of the world, produces such things as are not of the affection of his spirit, which he rarely propagates, lest the quality thereof should be known.   Hence also it is, that it is not known in the world, that there exists a persuasive principle of such an infatuating and suffocating quality as is in the spirit of the sensual man, who believes himself to be wise above others.   From these considerations it may appear, whence it is that by their teeth being as the teeth of lions, is signified, that sensual men appear to themselves as being in understanding, and thence in potency over all things.* This is also evident from numerous passages of the Word; as in David: "My soul is among lions: whose teeth are spears and arrows, and their tongue a sharp sword" (Psalm lvii. 4).   Here, by lions are signified those who by means of falsities destroy the truths of the church; their teeth, which are said to be spears and arrows, signify the scientifics which they apply to confirm falsities and evils, and so to destroy the truths and goods of the church; "their tongue a sharp sword," signifies crafty reasons from falsities, which are called a sharp sword, because a sword signifies falsity destroying truth. Again: "Break their teeth, O God, in their mouth; break out the great teeth of the young lions" (Psalm lviii. 6).   By their teeth in their mouth are signified the scientifics from which they produce falsities; the great teeth of the young lions signify the truths of the Word falsified, which in themselves are falsities, and by which they especially prevail in effecting the destruction of the truths of the church.   So in Joel: "For a nation is come up upon my land, strong, and without number, whose teeth are teeth of a lion, and he hath the cheek teeth of a great lion.   He hath laid my vine waste, and barked my fig-tree" (i. 6, 7).   By a nation coming up upon the land is here signified evil devastating the church, a nation denoting evil, and land denoting the church; by their being strong and without number, is meant that they are potent and manifold, the term strong is predicated of the potency of evil, and without number, is predicated of the potency of falsity; "whose teeth are the teeth of a lion," signifies destruction by falsities; the cheek teeth of a great lion, signify truths falsified; by laying the vine waste, and barking the fig-tree, is signified the destruction of truths spiritual and truths natural, truths spiritual are those which pertain to the spiritual sense of the Word, and truths natural are those which pertain to the sense of the letter; see also above, n. 403, where this is explained; by the teeth of lions in these passages, are signified the same things that are signified by the words under consideration.   By teeth are properly signified those things which are only in the

* That teeth signify things sensual, which are the ultimates of the natural life as to science, appears from the correspondence of teeth, concerning which see the work concerning H. & H. n. 575; and in the A. C. n. 5565–5568.

memory, and are thence brought forth, for the things which are in the memory of the sensual man correspond to the bones and teeth. Again, in Daniel : " And behold another beast, a second like to a bear, and it had three ribs in the mouth of it between the teeth of it ; and they said thus unto it, Arise, devour much flesh. After this, behold a fourth beast, dreadful and terrible, and strong exceedingly ; and it had great iron teeth ; it devoured and brake in pieces, and stamped the residue with the feet of it" (vii. 5, 7). By the beast which came up from the sea, is understood the love of dominion to which holy things serve as means, and by the four beasts are signified the successive increasings thereof; by this second beast, which was like to a bear, is signified the second state, when such dominion is confirmed by the Word ; they who do this also appear in the spiritual world like bears ; the three ribs in the mouth between the teeth, signify all things of the Word, which they apply, and which they understand only, according to the letter, the three ribs denote all things of the Word, " in the mouth," denotes, which they apply in teaching, "between the teeth of it," denotes, which they only understand as to the letter, that is, according to the quality of the sensual man ; by its being said to the beast, " Arise, devour much flesh," is signified, that they applied many things, and thereby destroyed the genuine sense of the Word. By the fourth beast which came up from the sea, dreadful and terrible, and strong exceedingly, is signified the fourth and last state of the church, when, by the holy things, which they have used as means, they have established for themselves a dominion over heaven and earth, which state being profane, and of a prevailing nature, is called dreadful and terrible, and strong exceedingly : great iron teeth signify falsities from the sensual man, which are hard against the truths and goods of the church ; by devouring and breaking in pieces, is signified, that they perverted and destroyed ; by stamping the residue with the feet, is signified, that what they could not pervert and destroy they defiled and blotted out by the evils of natural and corporeal loves. The other particulars concerning these beasts, may be seen explained above, n. 316. Again, in Moses : " I will also send the teeth of beasts upon them, with the poison of serpents of the dust" (Deut. xxxii. 24). These, among other evils, were denounced upon the Israelitish and Jewish people, if they should not keep the commandments and statutes, and judgments of Jehovah ; by the teeth of beasts are signified falsities arising from evils of every kind : and by the poison of serpents of the dust, are signified those who kill, and altogether destroy the spiritual life of man ; by beasts, in the Word, are signified such things as belong to the natural man, and by serpents of the dust, the things belonging to the sensual man, and when these are separated from the spiritual man, they are mere falsities from evils, inasmuch as they are things of the body only, to which they adhere, and of the world to which they are proximately extant, and from the body and the world arises all thick darkness in things of a spiritual nature. Again, in David : " Arise, O Jehovah ; save me, O my God ; for thou hast smitten all mine enemies upon the cheek bone; thou hast broken the teeth of the ungodly" (Psalm iii. 7)· Here, by smiting the enemies on the cheek bone, is signified the destruction of the interior falsities of those who are against the goods and truths of the church, such persons, with the falsities of their evils, being understood by enemies in the Word. To break the teeth of the ungodly signifies to destroy exterior falsities, which are such as have their foundation in the fallacies of the senses, and are thence confirmed. From what is said in David concerning smiting the cheek bone, and breaking the teeth, as denoting to destroy interior and exterior falsities, it may appear what is understood by the following words of the Lord, in Matthew: "Ye have heard that it hath been said, An eye for an eye, and a tooth for a tooth: but I say unto you, That ye resist not evil: but, whosoever shall smite thee on thy right cheek, turn to him the other also. And if any man will sue thee at the law, and take away thy coat, let him have thy cloak also; and, whosoever shall compel thee to go a mile, go with him twain. Give to him that asketh thee, and from him that would borrow of thee turn not thou away" (v. 38–42). That these words are not to be understood according to the letter, must be obvious to every one; for who considers himself held by Christian love, to turn the left cheek to him who smites the right, and to give the cloak also to him who would take away the coat? in a word, who is there to whom it is not allowable to resist evil? but inasmuch as all things which the Lord spake, were in themselves divine celestial, it may appear that these words, as well as the others which the Lord spake contain a celestial sense. The reason why such a law was given to the children of Israel, as that they should give an eye for an eye, and a tooth for a tooth (Exod. xxi. 23, 24; Lev. xxiv. 20; Deut. xix. 21), was, because they were external men, and thence were only in the representatives of things celestial, and not in celestial things themselves, hence neither were they in charity, in mercy, in patience, or in any spiritual good, and therefore they were in the law of retaliation; for the celestial law, and consequently the Christian law, which the Lord taught in the Evangelists, is: "Therefore all things whatsoever ye would that men should do to you, do ye even so to them; for this is the law and the prophets" (Matthew vii. 12; Luke vi. 31). Inasmuch as this is the law in heaven, and from heaven in the church, hence also every evil has with itself a corresponding punishment, which is called the punishment of evil, being in the evil, and as it were conjoined with it, and from this flows the punishment of retaliation, which was dictated to the children of Israel, because they were external men, and not internal. Internal men, such as are the angels of heaven, do not desire retaliation of evil for evil, but from celestial charity forgive freely, for they know that the Lord defends all who are in good against the evil, and that he defends according to the good pertaining to them, and that he would not defend, if, on account of the evil done to them, they should suffer enmity, hatred, and revenge, to be enkindled, for these things avert protection. These are the things, therefore, involved in the above words of the

Lord, but their signification shall be given in order: "An eye for an eye, and a tooth for a tooth," signifies, that so far as any one takes away from another the understanding of truth, and the sense of truth, so far they are taken away from himself, the eye signifying the understanding of truth, and a tooth, the sense of truth, for the tooth denotes either what is true or false, such as pertains to the sensual man; that he who is in Christian-good, will permit an evil person to take those things away as far as he can, is described by what the Lord replies upon the same subject; the precept not to resist evil, signifies, that it is not to be fought against in return, nor recompensed, for the angels do not fight with the evil, much less do they recompense evil for evil, but they permit them to do it, because they are defended by the Lord, and hence no evil from hell can possibly hurt them: "But whosoever shall smite thee on thy right cheek, turn to him the other also," signifies, if any one shall desire to injure the perception and understanding of interior truth, it should be permitted so far as he makes the attempt, the cheek signifying the perception and understanding of interior truth, the right cheek the affection, and thence perception thereof, and the left, the understanding thereof, and because mention is made of the cheek, mention is also made of smiting, by which is meant to do hurt; for all things about the mouth, as the throat, the mouth itself, the lips, the cheek bones, the teeth, signify such things as belong to the perception and understanding of truth, because they correspond to them, wherefore they are used to express such things in the literal sense of the Word, which consists of mere correspondences: "And if any man will sue thee at the law, and take away thy coat, let him have thy cloak also," signifies, if any one desire to take away the truth which is within, or interior, that he shall be allowed also to take away that which is without or exterior, the coat signifying truth interior, and the cloak, truth exterior; this also the angels do when they are with the evil, for the evil cannot take away anything of good and truth from the angels, but they can from those, who on that account burn with enmity, hatred and revenge, for these evils avert and reject the protection which is from the Lord: "And whosoever shall compel thee to go a mile, go with him twain," signifies, if any one desire to lead thee away from what is true to what is false, and from good to evil, that he shall not be opposed, because he cannot do it, a mile signifying the same as a way, namely, that which leads away and leads: "Give to him that asketh thee," signifies that it should be permitted; "and from him that would borrow of thee turn thou not away," signifies to instruct, if any one desire to be instructed, for the evil desire this in order that they may pervert and deprive, which, however, they cannot do. This is the spiritual sense of the above words, in which are stored up the things which have been now said, which are more especially for the angels, who perceive the Word only according to its spiritual sense; they are also for men in the world, who are principled in good, when the evil try to seduce them. That the opposition of the evil against those whom the Lord defends is of such a nature, has been given me to know by much experience; for they have continually laboured with all their might, and in every possible way, to deprive me of truths and goods, but in vain.

From what has been adduced, it may in some degree appear, that by a tooth is signified what is true or what is false in the sensual principle, which is the ultimate of the intellectual life of man; that this is signified by a tooth, is evident from the Lord's reply, in which the perception and understanding of truth are treated of, which the evil intend to take away from the good. The same may yet further appear from the following passages; as in Jeremiah: "In those days they shall say no more, the fathers have eaten a sour grape, and the children's teeth are set on edge. But every one shall die for his own iniquity: every man that eateth the sour grapes, his teeth shall be set on edge" (xxxi. 29, 30; Ezek. xviii. 2, 3, 4). That this involves that the sons and posterity shall not incur punishment on account of the evils of their parents, but every one on account of his own evil, is evident; by eating sour grapes is signified to appropriate to themselves the falsity of evil, for a sour grape, which is a bitter and bad grape, denotes the falsity of evil, and to eat, signifies to appropriate; and by their teeth being set on edge, is signified to be thence in the falsity of evil, for the teeth here, as above, signify falsities in ultimates, or in the sensual man, in which the evils of the parents, which are called hereditary evils, principally lie concealed with the children, and to be set on edge, signifies the appropriation of falsity from evil; for man is not punished on account of hereditary evils, but on account of his own, and only on account of what are hereditary so far as he makes them actual in himself, wherefore it is said, "But every man shall die for his own iniquity; every man that eateth the sour grape, his teeth shall be set on edge." So in Job: "All my inward friends abhorred me; my bone cleaveth to my skin and to my flesh, and I am escaped with the skin of my teeth" (xix. 19, 20). By these words, in the literal sense, is understood, that he became both lank and lean; but in the spiritual sense, is signified, that temptations so suppressed the interiors of his mind, that he became sensual, and only thought in extreme principles; but still that he did not think falsities but truths; this is signified by escaping with the skin of his teeth, teeth without skin denoting falsities, but with skin, not absolute falsities, because still in some degree clothed. So in Amos: "And I also have given cleanness of teeth in all your cities, and want of bread in all your places" (iv. 6). Here, by cleanness of teeth is denoted a scarcity of truth in doctrines; and by want of bread, a scarcity of good derived from doctrines in the life. So in Zechariah: "And I will take away his blood out of his mouth, and his abominations from between his teeth" (ix. 7). This is spoken concerning Tyre and Zidon, by which are signified the knowledges of truth and good, in the present case, those knowledges falsified; by taking away blood from the mouth is signified the falsifications of the knowledges of truths; and by abominations from between the teeth, are signified the adulterations of the knowledges of good; the knowledges of good are also truths, for to know goods is an effect of the understanding, and the understanding is of truth. So in David : "Then the waters had overwhelmed us, the proud waters had gone over our soul. Blessed be Jehovah, who hath not given us a prey to their teeth" (Psalm cxxiv. 4, 5, 6). By waters overwhelming, are signified the falsities which inundate and, as it were, overwhelm man when he is in temptations; hence, it is said, "Blessed be Jehovah, who hath not given us a prey to their teeth," that is, to the hells which, by falsities, destroy truths, thus to destroying falsities. Again, in Job : "And I brake the jaws of the wicked, and plucked the spoil out of his teeth" (xxix. 17). These words of Job are spoken concerning himself, and by his saying, "I brake the jaws of the wicked," is signified that he combated against falsities, and conquered them, the jaws of the wicked signifying scientifics derived from the literal sense of the Word, and applied to confirm falsities for the purpose of destroying truths ; his delivering others from falsities by instructing them, is meant by, "I plucked the spoil out of his teeth." Inasmuch as the teeth signify falsities in the extremes, by gnashing of teeth is signified, to combat with vehemence and anger from falsities against truths in the following passages. Thus in Job : "He teareth me in his wrath, who hateth me : he gnasheth upon me with his teeth, mine enemy sharpeneth his eyes upon me" (xvi. 9). And in David : "But in mine adversity they rejoiced and gathered themselves together against me, and I knew it not; they did tear me, and ceased not. They gnashed upon me with their teeth" (Psalm xxxv. 15, 16). Again : "The wicked plotteth against the just, and gnasheth upon him with his teeth" (Psalm xxxvii. 12). Again : "The wicked shall see it, and be grieved ; he shall gnash with his teeth" (Psalm cxii. 10). And in Micah : "Thus saith Jehovah concerning the prophets that make my people err, that bite with their teeth" (iii. 5). And in Lamentations : "All thine enemies have opened their mouth against thee : they hiss and gnash the teeth" (ii. 16). And in Mark : "And one of the multitude answered and said, Master, I have brought unto thee my son, which hath a dumb spirit ; and wheresoever he taketh him, he teareth him : and he foameth and gnasheth with his teeth, and pineth away : and I spake to thy disciples that they should cast him out; and they could not. Jesus rebuked the foul spirit, saying unto him, Thou dumb and deaf spirit, I charge thee, come out of him, and enter no more into him" (ix. 17–25). He who knows not the spiritual sense of the Word, may suppose that in the above passages mention is made of the gnashing of teeth, merely because when men gnash their teeth they are angry and intend evil, but the true reason is that by gnashing of teeth are understood the effort and act of destroying truths by falsities, for the teeth signify falsities in the extremes, and gnashing signifies the vehemence of combating for them ; this effort and act are also from correspondence : such also was the deaf and dumb spirit which the Lord cast out; for all spirits are from the human race, and this spirit was from that kind of men, who had combated vehemently for falsities against truths ; hence it is, that he who was obsessed by him foamed, and gnashed with his teeth. He is called by the Lord deaf and dumb, because he was not willing to perceive and understand truth, for such are signified by the deaf and dumb; and inasmuch as he was resolute and obstinate against truths, and confirmed himself in falsities, therefore he could not be cast out by the disciples, for the falsities for which he had combated could not be shaken off by them, as they had not yet arrived at a proper state, wherefore also the disciples were rebuked on that account by the Lord. That this spirit was of such a nature, but not he who was obsessed by him, is signified by the spirit tearing him, and by the obsessed pining away; also by the Lord commanding the spirit to enter no more into him. From these considerations it may also appear what is signified by the gnashing of teeth, mentioned in Matthew viii. 12; xiii. 42, 50; xxii. 13; xxiv. 51; xxv. 30; Luke xlii. 28. By gnashing of teeth in the hells is understood the continual disputation and combating of falsities amongst themselves, and against truths, consequently of those who are in falsities, conjoined with contempt of others, enmity, mocking or derision, scorning, blaspheming, which also burst forth into attempts to tear each other in pieces, for every one fights for his own falsity from the love of self, of erudition, and of fame. These disputations and combats are heard out of those hells as gnashings of teeth, and are also turned into gnashings of teeth when truths flow in thither out of heaven. More may be seen upon this subject in the work concerning H. & H. n. 575. It is from this circumstance of the teeth of the evil corresponding to the falsities of the ultimates of their intellectual life, and which are called corporeal sensual, that the spirits who are of such a nature appear deformed in the face, of which the teeth form a prominent part, standing out and being extended like a grating, in a kind of a gaping grin, and this because such grinning of teeth corresponds to the love and cupidity of combating for falsities against truth. Inasmuch as teeth correspond to the ultimates of the intellectual life of man, which are called sensual, and these are in the falsities of evil when they are separated from the truths of the interior understanding, which are called spiritual, but the same correspond to truths of good in the sensual principle when they are not separated; hence it is that teeth, in the Word, also signify ultimate truth; as in Job xix. 19, 20; Amos iv. 6, which may be seen explained above. And inasmuch as the Lord glorified his whole humanity, that is, made it divine, therefore it is said concerning him, in Moses, "His eyes shall be red with wine, and his teeth white with milk" (Gen. xlix. 12). By his eyes being red with wine, is signified that his intellectual principle was divine truth derived from divine good; and by his teeth being white with milk, is signified that his sensual principle in like manner was divine truth from divine good; for by Shiloh in that chapter is understood the Lord. Because teeth correspond to the ultimates of the intellectual life, which are called sensual, therefore good spirits and angels enjoy teeth equally as men, but with them they correspond to truths in the ultimate sensual principle, for the sensual principle, with them, is not separated from the truths of the interior understanding which are called spiritual.

557. " And they had breast-plates, as it were breast-plates of iron "—That hereby are signified the persuasions with which they gird themselves for combats, against which the truths of the spiritual rational man do not prevail, appears from the signification of breast plates, or coats of mail, as denoting defences against evils and falsities in combats, but in this case defences of evils and falsities against goods and truths, because the subject treated of has respect to those who are in falsities of evil against truths. The reason why persuasions are what are here signified by breast-plates, is, because sensual men, who are in the falsities of evil, and who are here described, do not combat from reason against truths, for they do not see truths but only falsities, and hence are in the persuasion that falsities are truths, wherefore they combat solely from the persuasion of falsity, and this persuasion with them is of such a nature, that the truths which the spiritual-rational man produces are of no avail, for they are repelled as a sword from a breast-plate or coat of mail: hence by breast-plates as it were breast-plates of iron, are signified persuasions against which truths do not prevail.* Moreover, breast-plates, or coats of mail, cover that part of the body called the breast, or thorax, by which is signified the spiritual affection of truth. All affection also is contained in the tone of the voice, which is emitted together with the speech from the breast ; but they who are here signified by locusts, and who are sensual men who are in falsities, have no other affection than that of the love of self, which being full of self-confidence and of the persuasion that their falsity is the truth, and this being in the tone of the voice emitted together with the speech from the breast, therefore the locusts appeared in breast-plates which were as breast-plates of iron ; iron also signifies truth in ultimates, and likewise falsity there, and at the same time the hard and persuasive principle therein, which causes the falsity to be so hard that the truths opposed to it rebound, as if they were of no account or avail. Whereas the persuasion of sensual men, who are in falsities grounded in self-confidence, is of such a nature, and with spirits is so potent, as to suffocate and extinguish the rational principle of other spirits with whom they converse, therefore in the world of spirits it is severely prohibited, and they who make use of it are sent where they are vexed even to swooning by persuasions still stronger from other spirits, and this until they desist.

Since breast-plates, or coats of mail, were in use in wars, and to put them on signified to gird themselves for war and thus to fight, therefore, in the Word, they who were girt for battle are said to put on coats of mail. Thus in Jeremiah : " Harness the horses ; and get up, ye horsemen ; and stand forth with your helmets ; furbish the spears, and put on coats of mail " (xlvi. 4). By these words is

---

* * That the persuasive principle with sensual men is of such an infatuating and suffocating nature, that the spiritual-rational principle cannot prevail against it, may be seen above, n. 544, 549, 556.

not understood the combat of one army against another, but the combat of the spiritual-rational man against the natural man, who, from scientifics falsely applied, combats against truths and goods; for the subject here treated of is the army of Pharaoh, king of Egypt, whom the king of Babylon smote, and by Pharaoh king of Egypt is understood the natural man, and by the king of Babylon near Euphrates is understood the spiritual-rational man, wherefore by "Harness the horses; and get up, ye horsemen, and stand forth with your helmets; furbish the spears, and put on the coats of mail," are signified such things as relate to the combat of the spiritual rational man against the natural man who is in falsities; horses denote things pertaining to the understanding, chariots, to which they are harnessed, things pertaining to doctrine, horsemen denote the intelligent, helmets denote things pertaining to reason, spears denote truths combating, and the coats of mail denote the might and strength of combating and resisting; the reason why these are denoted by the coats of mail, is, because they gird the breast, and from the breast, by means of the arms, is all the strength of combating and resisting. Again, in the same prophet: "Against him that bendeth let the archer bend his bow, and against him that lifteth himself up in his coat of mail" (li. 3). Here also the coat of mail is used to denote the power of combating and resisting. So in Isaiah: "For he put on righteousness as a coat of mail, and an helmet of salvation upon his head" (lix. 17). These words treat of the Lord, and of the subjugation of the hells by him; and by his putting on righteousness as a coat of mail, are signified his zeal of vindicating the faithful from hell, and the divine love of saving the human race; and since it was from the zeal of divine love, and power therein originating, that the Lord fought and conquered, therefore his righteousness is called a coat of mail; but by the helmet of salvation is signified the divine truth from the divine good, whence is salvation, for a helmet signifies the same as the head, because it is put on the head; that the head, when predicated of the Lord, signifies the divine truth and the divine wisdom, will be seen in the following pages.

558. "And the sound of their wings was as the sound of chariots of many horses running to battle"—That hereby are signified reasonings as from truths of doctrine derived from the Word and understood, for which they most ardently combat, appears from the signification of the sound of wings, as denoting reasonings, concerning which we shall speak presently; and from the signification of the sound of chariots, as denoting doctrines or truths of doctrine from the Word, concerning which also we shall speak presently; and from the signi   tion of horses, as denoting the understanding of the Word, concerning which see above, n. 335, 364, 372, 373, 381, 382; and from the signification of running to battle, as denoting the ardor of combating, for war signifies spiritual combats, and to run denotes ardor for it: from these considerations it may appear that by the sound of their wings being as the sound of chariots of many horses running to battle, are signified reasonings

as from truths of doctrines derived from the Word and understood, for which they most ardently combat. In order to the understanding of these things, it is to be observed, that spiritual combats, which are for truths against falsities, are maintained from the Word, and are confirmed by series of arguments and conclusions, whereby the mind being enlightened is fully convinced; this, therefore, is what is signified by the sound of their wings being as the sound of chariots of many horses running to battle. The reasonings of the sensual man from falsities and for falsities, appear altogether similar to those of the spiritual man, in the external form, but in the internal they are altogether dissimilar, for they have not any series of argumentations and conclusions, but only persuasions derived from sensual scientifics, with which the mind is infatuated but not convinced; the quality of these scientifics will be explained in the following article.*

559. " And they had tails like unto scorpions"—That hereby are signified sensual scientifics, which are of a persuasive nature, appears from the signification of tails, as denoting sensual scientifics, concerning which we shall speak presently; and from the signification of scorpions, as denoting things persuasive, infatuating and suffocating; concerning which see above, n. 544; hence tails like unto scorpions signify sensual scientifics, which are persuasive. The reason why tails signify sensual scientifics, is, because the tails which are attached to the animals of the earth, are continuations of the spine of the back, which is called the spinal marrow, and this is the continuation of the brain, and by the brain is signified intelligence and wisdom, in like manner as by the head, because intelligence and wisdom reside there in their principles or beginnings; and inasmuch as tails are the ultimates thereof, they signify sensual scientifics, for these are the ultimates of intelligence and wisdom. Sensual scientifics are those which enter from the world through the five senses of the body, and hence, viewed in themselves, are more material, corporeal, and worldly, than those which are more interior. All who are in the love of self, and have confirmed themselves against divine and spiritual things, are sensual men, and when they think in their spirit, as is the case when they are left to themselves, they think concerning things divine and spiritual from sensual scientifics, whence they reject things that are divine and spiritual as not to be believed, because they do not see them with their eyes, or touch them with their hands, and apply their own scientifics, which they have made sensual and material, to destroy them. Take, for example, the learned men of this kind who are skilled in natural history, anatomy, botany, and the other branches of human erudition; when such persons see the wonderful things that exist in the animal and vegetable kingdoms, they say in their hearts that all these things are from nature, and not from the divine being or principle, and for this

---

* That wings signify spiritual truths, and that hence the sound of wings signifies discussions from them, consequently reasonings, and in the supreme sense the divine spiritual principle, which is the divine truth, may be seen above, n. 283. But that chariots signify doctrines, or truths of doctrine, was shown above, n. 355; in treating of the signification of a horse, as denoting the intellectual principle, and, where the Word is treated of, as denoting the understanding of the Word.

reason, because they believe in nothing but what they can see with their eyes and touch with their hands, for they cannot elevate their minds, and thereby see those things from the light of heaven, for this light is mere darkness to them, but they detain their minds in things terrestrial, almost like the animals of the earth, with which they also compare themselves; in a word, with such persons, all the sciences become sensual: for according to the quality of the man himself, such are all things pertaining to his understanding and will; if the man is spiritual, all things become spiritual to him; if he is only natural, all things become natural and not spiritual; if he is sensual, all things become sensual, and this, however erudite and learned he may appear before the world: but since all men have the faculty of understanding truths and perceiving goods, they can speak, by virtue of this faculty, as if they were spiritual-rational, but still they are sensual as to the spirit, for when such speak before the world they do not speak from the spirit, but from the memory pertaining to the body. These observations are adduced, in order that it may be known what sensual scientifics are. The reason why these are what chiefly persuade, or are most persuasive is, because they are the ultimates of the understanding; for the understanding terminates therein, as in its ultimates, which captivate the vulgar, because they are appearances derived from such things as they see in the world by their eyes; and so long as the thought adheres in them, the mind cannot be disposed to think interiorly or above them, until they are removed; for the interior things of the mind all terminate in ultimates, and rest upon them as a house upon its foundation, hence ultimates, or sensual scientifics, are the things which chiefly persuade; but this is the case only with those whose minds cannot be elevated above things sensual: but with those who are in the light of heaven from the Lord, the mind is elevated above them, and the light of heaven dissipates them: hence spiritual men rarely think from things sensual, for they think from things rational and intellectual, whereas sensual men, who have confirmed themselves in falsities against things divine and spiritual, when they are left to themselves, cannot think but from things sensual.

That tails signify sensual scientifics, may appear from the following passages. Thus in Isaiah: " Therefore Jehovah will cut off from Israel head and tail, branch and rush, in one day. The ancient and honorable, he is the head; and the prophet that teacheth lies, he is the tail " (ix. 14, 15). By these words is understood, that all intelligence and wisdom are about to perish, and all the science of truth; by the head are signified intelligence and wisdom, wherefore it is said, " the ancient and honorable, he is the head," for the ancient signifies the intelligence of truth, and the honorable, the wisdom of good; but by the tail is signified the sensual scientific principle, which is the ultimate of intelligence and wisdom, and when this is not conjoined with spiritual intelligence, it becomes a false scientific principle, or the scientific principle applied to confirm falsities, which is the sensual scientific of the sensual man, who sees nothing from the understanding; hence it is that the prophet that

teacheth lies is called the tail, for by a prophet is signified the doctrine of truth, and hence the science of truth, but in this case the
doctrine is the science of what is false, for a lie signifies what is
false, and the teacher of a lie, him who teaches falsity, by applying
scientifics from the literal sense of the Word to the confirmation of
falsities.   Again, in the same prophet : " Neither shall there be any
work for Egypt, which the head or tail, branch or rush may do"
(xix. 15).   Here, by Egypt is signified science, the science of spiritual things as well as of natural ; by there being no work for it
which the head or tail, branch or rush may do, is signified that it
has no spiritual things, neither natural things, by which the spiritual
are confirmed, the head denoting the knowledges of things spiritual
by which comes intelligence, and the tail denoting natural scientifics, which are serviceable to things spiritual as means of intelligence ; similar things are signified by the branch and the rush, the
branch denoting spiritual truth, and the rush, the sensual scientific,
which is ultimate truth ; for if the former and the latter, or first and
ultimate principles, do not make one in man, then he has not the
head and the tail.   So in Moses : " And Jehovah shall make thee
the head, and not the tail ; and thou shalt be above only, and thou
shalt not be beneath, if that thou hearken unto the commandments
of Jehovah thy God, which I command thee this day, to observe and
to do them" (Deut. xxviii. 13).   In these words by Jehovah making
them the head is signified their being made spiritual and intelligent,
so as to be elevated out of the light of the world into the light of
heaven ; and to make them the tail, is to make them sensual and foolish, so as that they cannot look to heaven but to the world ; hence
it is said, " and thou shalt be above only, and thou shalt not be beneath," to be above, denoting to be elevated by the Lord, so as to
look to heaven, and to be beneath denoting not to be elevated by
the Lord, but from self, and man from himself looks only to the
world.   The reason of this is that the interiors of man's thought
and affection are elevated to heaven by the Lord, when he is in good
of life, and thence in truths of doctrine, but when he is in evil of
life, and thence in falsities, then his interior things look downwards,
thus only to his own body and to such things as are in the world,
and thus to hell, whence he puts off the nature truly human, and
puts on the beastly nature, for beasts look downwards, and to such
things only as they meet with in the world and upon the earth. Elevation into the light of heaven by the Lord is an actual elevation of
the interiors of man to the Lord ; and depression or dejection to
such things as are beneath and without the eyes is an actual depression and dejection of the interiors, and when this is the case, all the
thought of the spirit is then immersed in the ultimate sensual principle.   Again, in Moses : " The stranger that is within thee shall
get up above thee very high ; and thou shalt come down very low.
He shall lend to thee, and thou shalt not lend to him ; he shall be
the head, and thou shalt be the tail " (Deut. xxviii. 43, 44). These
words are to be understood in the same manner ; by being the head
is signified to be spiritual and intelligent, and by being the tail is

signified to be sensual and foolish; wherefore it is also said, "he shall lend to thee, but thou shalt not lend to him," by which is signified, he shall teach thee truths, but thou shalt not teach him. So in Isaiah: "And say unto him, Take heed, and be quiet; fear not, neither be faint-hearted for the two tails of these smoking fire-brands, for the fierce anger of Rezin with Syria, and of the son of Remaliah" (vi. 4). By Rezin and Syria is signified the rational principle perverted, and by the son of Remaliah the king of Israel, who is also called Ephraim, is signified the intellectual principle perverted; the intellectual principle, signified by Ephraim king of Israel, has relation to the Word, and the rational principle, signified by Rezin and Syria, has relation to sciences which confirm; for man, in order to have the understanding of the Word, must also have rationality, and when these two principles are perverted, they look only downwards to the earth, and outward to the world, as sensual men do who are in the falsities of evil; hence they are called tails; a smoking fire-brand signifies the concupiscence of falsity, and thence wrath against the truths and goods of the church. So again, in Moses: "And Jehovah said unto Moses, Put forth thy hand, and take the serpent by the tail. And he put forth his hand, and caught it, and it became a rod in his hand" (Exod. iv. 4).* Since by tails are signified the ultimates of intelligence and wisdom, which are sensual scientifics, and as all the processes of the sacrifices signified divine celestial and spiritual things, therefore also it was commanded that they should remove the tail near the spine of the back, and also should sacrifice it with other parts there mentioned (Lev. iii. 9; viii. 25; ix. 19; Exod. xxix. 22).† Because tails signify sensual scientifics, and these, when they are separated from the interiors which are spiritual, consequently when they do not, with the interiors, look inwards and upwards, but outwards and downwards, signify falsities confirmed by scientifics, therefore in the following parts of the Revelation, where falsities from that origin are treated of, it is said respecting the horses seen by John in the vision, that their power was in their mouth, and in their tails: for their tails were like unto serpents, and that they had heads with which they did hurt (ix. 19). And again, it is said respecting the great red dragon, that his tail drew the third part of the stars of heaven, and cast them to the earth (xii. 4). These things may be seen explained below.

560. "And there were stings in their tails"—That hereby is signified the craftiness of deceiving by them, appears from the signification of stings, as denoting craftiness and subtilties to persuade falsities, wherefore it follows, that in them was the power of hurting men, for he who deceives craftily and subtilly hurts most of all; the reason why stings were in their tails, is, because scientifics, sen-

* That here also by tail is understood the sensual principle, which is the ultimate of the natural, may be seen in the A. C. n. 6951–6955.
† That the burnt offerings and sacrifices signified divine celestial and spiritual things, which are the internals of the church, and from which true worship is performed, may be seen in the A. C. n. 2180, 2805, 2807, 2830, 3519, 6905, 8936.

sually perceived, whether from the Word or from the world, from which human erudition is derived, are what they deceive by ; they deceive by scientifics from the Word, by explaining it sensually according to the letter, and not according to its interior sense ; and by scientfics from the world, by using them for confirmation. It is to be observed, that sensual men are crafty and subtle above others, consequently acute in the art of deceiving ; for as intelligence and prudence belong to those who are spiritual men, so maliciousness and craftiness belong to those who are sensual and in falsities ; the reason is, because in evil resides all maliciousness, and in good, all intelligence. It is supposed in the world, that they who are crafty and subtle, are also prudent and intelligent ; but craftiness and maliciousness are not prudence and intelligence, but, viewed in themselves, are insanity and folly ; for such remove themselves from eternal happiness, and cast themselves into eternal misery, which is not to be prudent and intelligent, but insane and foolish : moreover all things pertaining to celestial and angelic wisdom are with them in dense darkness, and where wisdom is thick darkness, there of necessity is folly. That sensual men are crafty and subtle, is evident from those who are in the hells, where all are merely natural and sensual, who have so much craftiness and subtilty that it can scarcely be believed by any one.[*] That stings signify craftiness, may appear without confirmation from the Word, for in common discourse the crafty devices by which men are deceived are called stings, and the discourse itself is called acute, or sharp-pointed. But specifically by stings are signified interior falsities, which are such as cannot be shaken off, being derived from the scientifics and fallacies of the senses : that these falsities are signified by stings or sharp points, may appear from representatives in the spiritual world, where interior falsities are represented in various manners by things of a sharp nature, as by the sharp points of swords, by darts, and by things pointed in various forms, and this when they intend to do hurt ; for this reason it is also there forbidden to exhibit such things to view, for spirits, when they see them, become furious with a desire of hurting.

These falsities are signified by stings in Amos : "Jehovah God hath sworn by his holiness, that lo, the days shall come upon you, that he will take you away with stings, (or kicks) and your posterity with fishhooks" (iv. 2). By taking them away with stings is signified leading them away from truths by scientifics from the Word and from the world falsely applied ; and to draw away their posterity with fishing-hooks signifies effecting the same by the fallacies of the senses, from which the sensual man reasons. And in Moses : "But if ye will not drive out the inhabitants of the land from before you, then it shall come to pass, that those which ye let remain of them shall be thorns in your eyes, and stings in your sides, and shall vex you in the land wherein ye dwell" (Numb. xxxiii. 55). By the inhabitants of the land whom they should expel, are signified

---

[*] As may be seen in the work concerning H. & H. n. 576–581, where the maliciousness and wicked devices of the infernal spirits are treated of.

the evils and falsities of religion, and of doctrine; for these were signified in the abstract sense by the nations of the land of Canaan; hence by their being thorns in their eyes, is signified the hurt offered to the truths of the church by malicious falsities, and by their being stings in their sides, is signified the same with respect to the goods of the church; by eyes in the Word, is signified the understanding of truth, and by sides are signified the things of charity, consequently goods.

561. "And their power was to hurt men five months"—That hereby is signified that they induced a stupor upon the understanding of truth, and the perception of good, so long as the state continued, appears from the signification of hurting, as denoting to bring injury on anything, in the present case, to induce a stupor, concerning which we shall speak presently; and from the signification of men as denoting those who have the understanding of truth and the perception of good, and in the abstract, the understanding of truth and perception of good, because from these man is man, concerning which see above, n. 546; and from the signification of five months, as denoting so long as they are in that state, concerning which, also see above, n. 548. The reason why to hurt here signifies to induce a stupor, is, because it is said above, that their tails were like unto scorpions, and by scorpions is signified the persuasive principle infatuating and suffocating, consequently also inducing a stupor, for, as has been said above concerning that persuasive principle, it is of such a nature with spirits as to stupify the rational and intellectual principles, whence it also induces a stupor.

562. "And they had a king over them, which is the angel of the bottomless pit"—That hereby is signified, that they receive influx from the hell where those are who are in the falsities of evil, and merely sensual, appears from the signification of a king, as denoting truth from good, and in the opposite sense, as in this case, falsity from evil, concerning which, see above, n. 31; and from the signification of the angel of the bottomless pit, as denoting the hell in which the falsities of evil are; for by the angel here mentioned is not understood one angel, but the hell in which all such are; that by an angel in the Word is understood entire angelic societies which are in a similar good, may be seen above, n. 90, 302, 307; hence also by an angel in the opposite sense is signified infernal societies, which are in similar evil. That the hells where they are who are principled in the falsities of evil, and who are merely sensual, are here meant, is evident from the angel being styled the angel of the bottomless pit, the bottomless pit denoting the hell of such, concerning which, see above, n. 538; and from its being spoken concerning the locusts, by which are signified men who are become merely sensual by infernal falsities; see above, n. 543. The reason why having over them a king signifies to receive influx thence, is, because all evils, and the falsities thence derived, are from hell, and because all who are in evils and thence in falsities, are ruled and led of the hells, wherefore hell is to them as a king who rules over them, and to whom they yield obedience; inasmuch as this is effected by in-

flux when they live in the world, and the efflux thence is what leads ; by having a king over them is signified to receive influx.

563. " Whose name in the Hebrew tongue is Abaddon, but in the Greek tongue hath his name Apollyon"—That hereby is signified the quality thereof as destroying all truth and good, appears from the signification of name, as denoting the quality of state and the quality of a thing, concerning which, see above, n. 148 ; and from the signification of Abaddon in the Hebrew tongue as denoting perdition, in like manner as does Apollyon in the Greek tongue ; consequently the perdition of truth and g d, because this is the subject treated of. The reason why the sensual principle of man, which is the ultimate of the intellectual life, is destructive of all spiritual truth and good, which is the truth and good of the church, is, because that principle is proximately extant to the world, and proximately adheres to the body, whence both from the world and the body it has affections and thence thoughts, which, viewed in themselves, are diametrically opposed to spiritual affections and thoughts, which are from heaven ; for man, from that sensual principle, loves himself and the world above all things, and in proportion as these loves have rule, in the same proportion evils and the falsities therein originating have rule, for evils and falsities spring up and issue from these loves, as from their origins ; in these loves all are principled who become merely sensual by evils of life and the falsities thence derived. Any one may see that this is the case, by virtue of the faculty of understanding which is given to every man ; for if that principle rules which is proximately extant to the world, and proximately adheres to the body, it follows of consequence, that the world itself and the body itself, with all their voluptuousnesses and concupiscences, which are the pleasures of the eye and of the flesh, exercise dominion. Hence every one may also see, that man must be entirely withdrawn and elevated from these sensual things, and from the lust, in order that he may come into spiritual affections, and the thoughts thence derived. This withdrawing and elevation is effected by the Lord alone, when man suffers himself to be led of the Lord by the laws of order, which are the truths and goods of the church, to himself, and thus to heaven ; and when this is the case, man leaves this ultimate sensual principle, as often as he is in a spiritual state, and is kept elevated above it ; the reason also of this is, because this sensual principle is altogether destroyed with man, for therein is the proprium, into which every one is born, which in itself is nothing but evil. From these considerations it may appear, whence it is that this sensual principle is called perdition, or Abaddon and Apollyon. It is to be observed that there are three degrees of life in every man, an inmost, a middle, and an ultimate ; and that man becomes more perfect, that is, more wise, in proportion as he becomes more interior, because he thereby comes more interiorly into the light of heaven ; and that he becomes more imperfect, that is, less wise, in proportion as he becomes more exterior, because he thereby comes from the light of heaven nearer to the light of the world. Hence it may appear, what is the quality of the merely sen-

sual man, who sees nothing from the light of heaven, but solely from the light of the world, namely, that all things pertaining to the world, are to him in light and splendor, and all things pertaining to heaven, in darkness and thick darkness; and when these latter are in darkness and in thick darkness, and the former in light and splendor, it follows that the only fire of life, or love which enkindles and leads, is the love of self and thence the love of all evils, and that the only light of life, which strikes and instructs the sight of the thought, is what favors the evils which are loved, and these are the falsities of evil. From these considerations it may also be seen, what is the quality of the merely sensual man, who is the subject treated of hitherto in this chapter.

564. "One woe is past; and, behold, there come two more woes hereafter "—That hereby is signified one lamentation over the devastation of the church, and that lamentation over the further devastation thereof follows, appears from the signification of woe, as denoting lamentation over the evils and falsities thence derived, which vastate the church; concerning which, see above n. 532.

565. Verses 13, 14, 15, 16, 17, 18, 19. "And the sixth angel sounded, and I heard a voice from the four horns of the golden altar, which is before God, saying to the sixth angel who had the trumpet, Loose the four angels that are bound at the great river Euphrates. And the four angels were loosed, who were prepared for an hour, and a day, and a month, and a year, to slay the third part of men. And the number of the armies of horsemen were two myriads of myriads: and I heard the number of them. And thus I saw the horses in the vision, and them that sat on them, having breastplates of fire, and of jacinth, and of brimstone: and the heads of the horses were as the heads of lions: and out of their mouth issued fire, and smoke, and brimstone. By these three was the third part of men killed, by the fire, and by the smoke, and by the brimstone, which issued out of their mouths. For their power is in their mouth, and in their tails: for their tails were like unto serpents, and had heads, and with them they do hurt."—"And the sixth angel sounded," signifies influx out of heaven manifesting the state of the church in its end, as being absolutely perverted: "and I heard a voice from the four horns of the golden altar which is before God," signifies revelation from the Lord out of the spiritual heaven: "saying to the sixth angel who had the trumpet," signifies concerning the perverted state of the church in its very end: "Loose the four angels that are bound at the great river Euphrates," signifies reasonings from fallacies, pertaining to the sensual man, not received before: "And the four angels were loosed," signifies the license of reasoning from fallacies: "who were prepared for an hour, and a day, and a month, and a year," signifies continually in the state: "to slay the third part of men," signifies, of depriving themselves of all understanding of truth, and thence of spiritual life: "And the number of the armies of the horsemen was two myriads of myriads," signifies innumerable falsities of evil, from which and for which they reason, conspiring against the truths of good: "and

I heard the number of them," signifies their quality perceived: " And thus I saw the horses in the vision, and them that sat on them," signifies, the falsification of the Word by reasonings from fallacies : " having breast-plates of fire, and of jacinth, and brimstone," signifies, combating from the cupidities of the love of self and of the world, and from the falsities therein originating : "and the heads of the horses were as the heads of lions," signifies the science and thought thence derived destructive of truth : "and out of their mouths issued fire, and smoke and brimstone," signifies the things thought, and thence reasonings springing from the love of evil, from the love of falsity, and from the concupiscence of destroying truths and goods by the falsities of evil: " By these three was the third part of men killed, by the fire, and by the smoke, and by the brimstone, which issued out of their mouths," signifies, that all the understanding of truth, and the spiritual life thence derived were extinguished by them : " For their power is in their mouth, and in their tails," signifies, sensual thoughts and reasonings thence derived very much prevailing: "for their tails were like unto serpents, and had heads," signifies, that from sensual scientifics, which are fallacies, they reason craftily: "and with them they do hurt," signifies, that so they pervert the truths and goods of the church.

566. " And the sixth angel sounded "—That hereby is signified influx out of heaven, manifesting the state of the church in its end as being absolutely perverted, appears from the signification of sounding a trumpet, as denoting influx out of heaven, whence changes take place in the inferior parts, by which is manifested the quality of the state of the church, concerning which, see above, n. 502; in this case, its quality in its end, because it is the sounding of the sixth angel ; for the successive changes of the state of the church are described by the seven angels who sounded the trumpets, and in this case the change thereof about the end by the sixth angel sounding, for the end itself, which takes place when the last judgment is at hand, is described by the sounding of the seventh angel ; and because the state of the church in its end is absolutely perverted, this is also signified by these words.

567. " And I heard a voice from the four horns of the golden altar which is before God"—That hereby is signified revelation from the Lord out of the spiritual heaven, appears from the signification of hearing a voice, as denoting revelation, because what was revealed by that voice next follows; and from the signification of the golden altar which is before God, as denoting the divine spiritual principle, concerning which we shall speak presently ; and from the signification of the four horns of the altar, as denoting the divine spiritual in its ultimates ; for the horns were in the ultimates of both altars, as well the altar of burnt-offering as the altar of incense, which is the golden altar ; and inasmuch as the horns were the ultimates of those altars, therefore they signified the divine principle as to potency, for all potency is in ultimates, and hence it is, that the horns of the altars signified the divine principle, as to omnipotence ; concerning which signification, see above, n. 316. That the altar

of burnt-offering signified the divine celestial principle, which is the divine good, may be seen above, n. 391, 490, 496; but that the altar of incense, or the golden altar, represented and thence signified the divine spiritual principle, which is the divine truth proceeding from the Lord, appears from the description thereof, which will be adduced below. Something shall first be said to explain whence it was that the voice was heard from the four horns of the altar; the horns, which ultimately proceeded and stood out from the altars above mentioned, signified all things belonging thereto as to potency or power, as may appear from what has been said and shown above.* Hence, inasmuch as responses and revelations were made in ultimates, the reason is manifest, why the voice was heard from the four horns of the golden altar, namely, because the golden altar signifies the divine spiritual principle, which is the divine truth which reveals, and because the horns signify the ultimates thereof, by which revelation is made. The reason why the golden altar, upon which they offered incense, signifies the divine spiritual principle, which is divine truth proceeding from the Lord, is, because the incense which was offered upon that altar signified worship from spiritual good, and the hearing and reception thereof by the Lord; concerning which, see above, n. 324, 491, 492, 494.

That the altar of incense signified the divine spiritual principle, and that the offering of incense upon it signified worship from spiritual good, and acceptable hearing and reception by the Lord, appears from the construction of that altar, in which everything was representative and significative of that worship. The construction of the altar of incense is thus described in Moses : " And thou shalt make an altar to burn incense upon; of Shittim wood shalt thou make it. A cubit shall be the length thereof, and a cubit the breadth thereof; four square shall it be : and two cubits shall be the height thereof: the horns thereof shall be of the same. And thou shalt overlay it with pure gold, the top thereof, and the sides thereof round about, and the horns thereof; and thou shalt make unto it a crown of gold round about. And two golden rings shalt thou make to it, under the crown of it, by the two corners thereof, upon the two sides of it shalt thou make it; and they shall be for places for the staves to bear it withal. And thou shalt make the staves of Shittim wood, and overlay them with gold. And thou shalt put it before the veil that is by the ark of the testimony, before the mercy seat that is over the testimony, where I will meet with thee. And Aaron shall burn thereon sweet incense every morning : when he dresseth the lamps, he shall burn incense upon it. And when Aaron lighteth the lamps at even, he shall burn incense upon it, a perpetual incense before Jehovah throughout your generations. Ye

* N. 346, 417, and also from what has been said and shown concerning ultimates in the A. C. as, that interiors flow in successively into externals, even into the extremes or ultimates, and that there also they exist and subsist, n. 634, 6239, 6465, 9216, 9217 ; and that they not only flow in successively, but also form in the ultimate what is simultaneous, in what order, n. 5897, 6451, 8603, 10,099 : that hence strength and power are in ultimates, n. 9836 ; that hence responses and revelations were given in ultimates, n. 9905, 10,548.

shall offer no strange incense thereon, nor burnt-sacrifice, nor meat-offering: neither shall ye pour drink-offering thereon. And Aaron shall make an atonement upon the horns of it once in a year with the blood of the sin offering of atonement; once in the year shall he make atonement upon it throughout your generations: it is most holy unto Jehovah" (Exod. xxx. 1–10). That all these particulars concerning the altar of incense, signify, in the internal sense of the Word, worship from spiritual good, which is the good of charity towards our neighbor, and also acceptable hearing and reception by the Lord, may be seen in the A. C. n. 10,176–10,213; where they are explained in their series.

568. "Saying to the sixth angel who had the trumpet"—That hereby is signified concerning the perverted state of the church, in the very end thereof, appears from the signification of saying, as denoting those things which are revealed from heaven, and which now follow; and from the signification of the sixth angel having the trumpet, as denoting concerning the perverted state of the church in its very end; that these things are signified by the sixth angel sounding, may appear from what has been said, n. 566.

569. "Loose the four angels that are bound at the great river Euphrates"—That hereby are signified reasonings from fallacies pertaining to the sensual man, not received before, appears from the signification of the angels at the river Euphrates, as denoting reasonings from fallacies which are in the sensual man, concerning which we shall speak presently; and because reasonings from such fallacies were not received in the church before, therefore those angels are said to be bound at that river, and are said to be four because of the conjunction of what is false with evil, for this number, in the Word, signifies the conjunction of good and truth, and in the opposite sense, as in this case, the conjunction of evil and what is false; as may be seen above, n. 283, 384, 532. In the preceding verses the subjects treated of were the sensual man, who is principled in the falsities of evil, and the effect of the persuasions in which such a man is, wherefore in what now follows, reasoning from the sensual principle shall be treated of; and inasmuch as the sensual principle reasons only from such things as are extant in the world before the senses, it reasons from fallacies, which are called fallacies of the senses, when it reasons concerning spiritual things, that is concerning the things of heaven and the church, and hence it is here said, reasonings from fallacies pertaining to the sensual man; but concerning these fallacies and concerning reasoning from them, more will be said presently. The subject here treated of is the state of the church in its very end, which state takes place when the men of the church, becoming sensual, reason from the fallacies of the senses, and when they reason from these concerning the things of heaven and the church, then they absolutely believe nothing, because they understand nothing. It is a known thing in the church, that the natural man does not perceive the things of heaven, unless the Lord flows in and gives illumination, which is effected by means of the spiritual man; much less can the sensual man under-

stand and believe, because this is the ultimate of the natural, to whom the things of heaven, which are called spiritual things, are altogether in thick darkness. Genuine reasonings concerning things spiritual, exist from the influx of heaven into the spiritual man, and thence, by the rational, into the sciences and knowledges which are in the natural man, by which the spiritual man confirms himself: this way of reasoning concerning spiritual things is according to order: but the reasonings concerning spiritual things, which are effected from the natural man, and still more those which are effected from the sensual man, are altogether contrary to order, for the natural man, and especially the sensual man, cannot flow into the spiritual man, and from himself see anything there, for physical influx is not given; but the spiritual man can flow into the natural, and thence into the sensual, since spiritual influx is given; but upon this subject more may be seen in the D. of the N. J. n. 51, 277, 288. From these considerations it may be seen, what is understood by the things which now follow, namely that in the very end of the church man speaks and reasons concerning spiritual things, or concerning the things of heaven and the church, from the corporeal sensual' principle, and thus from the fallacies of the senses, consequently, that although man then speaks in favor of things divine, yet he does not think in favor of them; for man can speak, from the body, differently to what he thinks in his spirit, and the spirit which thinks from the corporeal sensual principle, cannot do otherwise than think against things divine, but still from the corporeal sensual principle man can speak in favor of them, and especially if they are the means of his acquiring honors and gain. Every man has two memories, namely, a natural memory and a spiritual memory, and he can think from both, from the natural memory when he speaks with men in the world, but from the spiritual memory, when he speaks from his spirit; this, however, man rarely does with another, but only with himself, which is to think. Sensual men cannot speak or think from their own spirit with themselves otherwise than in favor of nature, consequently in favor of things corporeal and worldly, because they think from the sensual principle, and not from the spiritual, they are even altogether ignorant of what the spiritual principle is, because they have shut their spiritual mind, into which heaven by virtue of its light flows.

But to proceed to the explication of what is signified by the voice which was heard from the horns of the golden altar, saying to the sixth angel, that he should loose the four angels that were bound at the river Euphrates. By the river Euphrates is signified the rational principle, and hence also reasoning; the reason of this signification of the river Euphrates, is, because it divided Assyria from the land of Canaan, and by Assyria, or Ashur, is signified the rational principle, and by the land of Canaan, the spiritual principle. There were three rivers which formed the boundaries of the land of Canaan, besides the sea, namely the river of Egypt, the river Euphrates, and the river Jordan: by the river of Egypt was signified the science of the natural man: by the river Euphrates was signified the rational

principle pertaining to man, and derived from sciences and knowledges; and by the river Jordon was signified entrance into the
internal or spiritual church: for by the regions on the other side
Jordon, where the tribes of Reuben and Gad, and the half tribe of
Manasseh, had allotted inheritances, was signified the external or
natural church, and inasmuch as that river was between those
regions and the land of Canaan, and afforded a passage, therefore
by it was signified entrance from the external church, which was
natural, into the internal church which was spiritual; this was
the reason that baptism was there instituted, for baptism represented the regeneration of man, whereby the natural man
is introduced into the church, and becomes spiritual.   From
these considerations it may be seen what those three rivers signify
in the Word: all the places also which were without the land of
Canaan, signified such things as pertain to the natural man, whereas
those which were within the land of Canaan signified such things
as pertain to the spiritual man, thus which pertain to heaven and
the church; the two rivers, therefore, namely, the river of Egypt or
the Nile, and the river of Assyria or Euphrates, signified the termi-
nations of the church, and also introductions into the church;
knowledges also and sciences, which are signified by the river of
Egypt, are what introduce, for without knowledges and sciences no
one can be introduced into the church, nor perceive the things
which pertain to the church; for the spiritual man, by means of the
rational, sees its spiritual things in sciences, as a man sees himself
in a mirror, and acknowledges itself in them, that is, its own truths
and goods, and moreover confirms its spiritual things by knowledges and scientifics, as well by those which are known from the
Word as by those which are known from the world.   But the river
of Assyria, or Euphrates, signified the rational principle, because by
this principle man is introduced into the church; by the rational
principle is meant the thought of the natural man from knowledges
and sciences, for a man who is imbued with sciences is able to see
things in a series, from first and mediate principles to the ultimate,
which is called the conclusion, consequently, he can analytically
dispose, weigh, separate, conjoin, and at length conclude things,
even to a further, and at length to the ultimate end, which is the
use he loves; this therefore is the rational principle, which is given
to every man according to uses, which are the ends which he loves.
Inasmuch as the rational principle of every one is according to the
uses of his love, therefore that principle is the interior thought of
the natural man from the influx of the light of heaven; and inasmuch as man by rational thought is introduced into spiritual thought,
and becomes a church, therefore by that river, namely the river
Euphrates, is signified the natural introducing principle.   It is one
thing to be rational, and another thing to be spiritual; every spiritual man is also rational, but the rational man is not always spiritual;
the reason is, because the rational principle, that is, the thought
thereof, is in the natural man, but the spiritual principle is above
the rational, and by the rational passes into the natural, thus into

the knowledges and scientifics of its memory. It is, however, to be observed, that the rational principle does not introduce any one into the spiritual, but it is so said, only because of its so appearing; for the spiritual principle flows into the natural by means of the rational, and so introduces; for the spiritual principle is the inflowing divine principle, for it is the light of heaven, which is the divine truth proceeding, and this, through the superior mind, which is called the spiritual mind, flows into the inferior mind, which is called the natural mind, and conjoins this to itself, and by that conjunction causes the natural mind to form a one with the spiritual; thus introduction is effected. Inasmuch as it is contrary to divine order for man by his rational principle to enter into the spiritual, therefore in the spiritual world there are angel guards to prevent this taking place; hence it is evident what is signified by the four angels bound at the river Euphrates, and afterwards what is meant by loosing them. By the angels bound at the river Euphrates, is signified guard lest the natural principle of man should enter into the spiritual things of heaven and the church, for hence there would be nothing but errors and heresies, and at length denial. In the spiritual world there are also ways which lead to hell, and ways which lead to heaven, likewise, ways which lead from spiritual things to natural, and thence to things sensual; and in those ways also there are guards placed, lest any one should go contrariwise, inasmuch as he would thence fall into heresies and errors, as was just said: those guards are placed by the Lord in the beginning of the establishment of the church, and are kept up lest the man of the church, from his own reason or understanding, should introduce himself into the divine things of the Word, and of the church: but in the end, when the men of the church are no longer spiritual, but natural, and many of them merely sensual, so that with them there does not exist any way from the spiritual man into the natural, then those guards are removed, and the ways are opened, and the ways being opened, they go in a contrary order, which is done by reasonings from fallacies; hence it comes to pass that the man of the church can speak in favor of divine things from the mouth, whilst in heart he thinks against them, or can speak for them from the body, and think against them from the spirit; for reasoning concerning divine things from the natural and sensual man produces this effect. Hence it may now appear what is signified by the four angels bound at the river Euphrates, and what by their being loosed.

That the river Euphrates signifies the rational principle, by which there is a way from the spiritual man into the natural, may be seen from the following passages in the Word. Thus in Moses; " In the same day Jehovah made a covenant with Abraham, saying, Unto thy seed have I given this land, from the river of Egypt unto the great river, the river Euphrates" (Gen. xv. 18). By these words, taken in the literal sense, is described the extension of the land of Canaan, but in the internal sense, the extension of the church from its first to its ultimate boundary; its first boundary is the scientific principle, which is of the natural man, the other boundary is the rational principle, which is of the thought; the former, namely, the scientific principle which is of the natural man, is signified by the river of Egypt,—the Nile, and the rational principle, which is of the thought, by the river of Assyria,—Euphrates; the spiritual church, which is signified by the land of Canaan, extends itself to both these, and in like manner the spiritual mind which is possessed by the man of the church: both these principles, the scientific and the rational, are in the natural man, of which man one end is what is scientific and of knowledge, and the other is what is intuitive and of thought, and into these ends the spiritual man flows whilst he flows into the natural man; the conjunction of the Lord with the church by these principles is signified by the covenant which Jehovah established with Abraham; but these things are signified by the above words in the internal sense, whereas in the supreme sense the union of the divine essence with the human of the Lord is understood; according to which sense those words are explained in the A. C. n. 1863–1867. So in Zechariah: " And his dominion shall be from sea even to sea, and from the river even to the ends of the earth" (ix. 10). And in David: (Psalm lxxii. 8). These things are said concerning the Lord, and concerning his dominion over heaven and earth; and by dominion from sea even to sea, is signified the extension of things natural, and by dominion from the river even to the ends of the earth, is signified the extension of things rational and spiritual; see also above, n. 518. So in Moses: "The land of the Canaanites, and unto Lebanon, unto the great river, the river Euphrates. Behold, I have set the land before you: go in and possess the land " (Deut. i. 7, 8). And again: " Every place whereon the soles of your feet shall tread shall be yours; from the wilderness and Lebanon, from the river, the river Euphrates, even unto the uttermost sea shall your coast be" (Deut. xi. 24). So in Joshua: " From the wilderness and this Lebanon, even unto the great river, the river Euphrates, all the land of the Hittites, and unto the great sea toward the going down of the sun, shall be your coast" (i. 4). In these passages the extension of the church is described from one boundary to the other; one of which is what pertains to knowledge and science, and is signified by Lebanon and the sea, and the other is that which pertains to intuition and thought, and is signified by the river Euphrates; the extension of the land of Canaan denotes the extension of the church, for by the land of Canaan, in the Word, is signified the church: the reason why the river is twice mentioned, namely, the great river, the river Euphrates, is, because by the great river is signified the influx of things spiritual into things rational, and by the river Euphrates, the influx of things rational into things natural, thus by both is signified the influx of things spiritual by the rational principle into things natural. So in Micah: " In that day he shall come even to thee from Assyria, and from the fortified cities, and from the fortress, even to the river, and from sea to sea, and from mountain to mountain" (vii. 12). In this passage the establishment of the church among the Gentiles by the Lord is described " that day" signifying the Lord's advent; the extension of the church from one boundary to the other, is signified by " he shall come even to thee from Assyria, and from the fortified cities, and from the fortresses, even to the river," the extension of truth to the same degree is signified by " and from sea to sea," and the extension of good by "from mountain to mountain." Again, in David : " Thou hast brought á vine out of Egypt : thou hast cast out the heathen and planted it. She sent out her boughs unto the sea, and her branches unto the river" (Psalm lxxx. 8–11). Here by the vine which God is said to have brought out of Egypt are meant the children of Israel and the church, for a vine signifies the spiritual church, which church was also signified by the children of Israel ; and inasmuch as the church is called a vine, it is said, " Thou hast cast out the heathen, and planted it. She sent her boughs unto the sea, and her branches unto the river," by which is described the extension of the spiritual things of the church, the sea denoting one extremity thereof, and the river, namely, the Euphrates, denoting the other. By the Euphrates, which was the fourth branch of the river that went out of Eden to water the garden (Gen. ii. 10, 14), is also signified the rational principle, for by the garden in Eden, or Paradise, is signified wisdom; the signification of the three other branches of this great river may be seen explained in the A. C. n. 107–121. Inasmuch as the river Euphrates signifies the rational principle, it signifies, in the opposite sense, reasoning ; by reasoning are here understood thought, and argumentation from fallacies and falsities, but by the rational principle are understood thought and argumentation from sciences and from truths ; for every rational principle is cultivated by sciences, and is formed by truths, wherefore he is called a rational man who is led by truths, or whom truths lead ; but it is possible for a man who is not rational to reason, for by various reasonings he can confirm falsities, and also induce the simple to believe them, which is principally done by the fallacies of the senses, concerning which more will be said below. This reasoning is signified by the river Euphrates in the following passages : " And now what hast thou to do in the way of Egypt, to drink the waters of Sihor? or what hast thou to do in the way of Assyria, to drink the waters of the river ?" (Jeremiah ii. 18.) By these words is signified that spiritual things are not to be investigated by the scientifics of the natural man, nor by reasons therein originating, but by the Word, thus out of heaven from the Lord ; for they who are in spiritual affection, and in thought thence derived, see the scientifics of the natural man, and the reasonings therein originating as below them, but no one can see spiritual things from the latter, for things inferior may be viewed on all sides from on high, but not vice versa ; to investigate spiritual things by the scientifics of the natural man, is signified by, " what hast thou to do in the way of Egypt, to drink the waters of Sihor ?" and by reasonings thence derived is signified by " what hast thou to do in the way of Assyria, to drink the waters of the river ?" Egypt and the river thereof signify scientifics of the natural man, and Assyria and its river signify reasonings from them. So again, in Isaiah : " In the same day shall the Lord shave with a razor that is hired, namely, by them beyond the river, by the king of Assyria, the head, and the hair of the feet: and it shall also consume the beard " (vii. 20). These words treat of the state of the church in its end, when the Lord was about to come; that reasonings grounded in falsities, would then deprive the men of the church of all wisdom and spiritual intelligence, is described by the above words: those reasonings are signified by " them beyond the river, by the king of Assyria," the river, denoting the Euphrates; the deprivation of spiritual wisdom, and of intelligence thence derived, is signified by the hair of the head and of the feet being shaved with a razor that is hired, and by the beard being consumed: for by hair are signified natural things in which spiritual things operate, and in which they close or terminate, hence in the Word, they signify the ultimates of wisdom and intelligence, the hair of the head signifies the ultimates of wisdom, the beard signifies the ultimates of intelligence, and the hair of the feet the ultimates of science; without these ultimates, things prior can no more exist than a column without a basis, or a house without a foundation.* Again, in the same prophet: " Now, therefore, behold, the Lord bringeth up upon them the waters of the river strong and many, even the king of Assyria, and all his glory: and he shall come up over all his channels, and go over all his banks: and he shall pass through Judah: he shall overflow and go over" (viii. 7, 8). These words signify the entire falsification of all things of the Word in the church by reasonings from fallacies and falsities; by the waters of the river, strong and many, even the king of Assyria, are signified reasonings from mere fallacies and falsities; by coming up over all his channels, and going over all his banks, is signified, the falsification thereby of all and singular things of the Word; by Judah, which he shall pass through, is signified the church where the Word is, thus the Word itself. So again, in Jeremiah: " Against Egypt, against the army of Pharaoh-necho, king of Egypt, which was by the river Euphrates in Carchemish, which Nebuchadrezzar, king of Babylon smote. They shall stumble and fall toward the north by the river Euphrates" (xlvi. 2, 6). By these words is signified the destruction of the church and its truths by false reasonings grounded in scientifics; by the river Euphrates are signified false reasonings; by Egypt and the army thereof are signified scientifics confirming; by the north where they should stumble and fall, is signified whence those falsities arise: this passage also may be seen more fully explained above, n. 518, at the end. Again, in the same prophet: " Thus saith the Lord Jehovah unto me, Go and get thee a linen girdle, and put it upon thy loins, and put it not in water. And arise, go to Euphrates, and hide it there in a hole of the rock. So I went and hid it by Euphrates, and it came to pass after many days, that Jehovah said unto me, Arise, go to Euphrates, and take the girdle from thence. Then I went to Euphrates, and took the girdle: and behold, the girdle was

* That they who have deprived themselves of intelligence by reasonings from fallacies and from falsities, appear in the spiritual world as bald, may be seen above, n. 66.

marred, it was profitable for nothing. For as the girdle cleaveth to the loins of a man, so have I caused to cleave unto me the whole house of Israel, and the whole house of Judah, saith Jehovah ; that they might be unto me for a people, and for a name, and for a praise, and for a glory; but they would not hear" (xiii. 1–11). By these circumstances were represented the quality of the Israelitish and Jewish church and its consequent state : by the girdle of linen which the prophet put upon his loins is signified the conjunction of the church with the Lord by the Word; for by a prophet is signified doctrine from the Word, and by the girdle upon the loins of the prophet is signified conjunction ; the falsifications of the Word by evils of life and falsities of doctrine, and the reasonings thence derived which favor them, are signified by the girdle being marred in the hole of the rock at Euphrates : for the conjunction of the Lord with the church is by the Word, and when this is perverted by reasonings which favor evils and falsities, then there is no longer conjunction, and this is understood by the girdle being profitable for nothing ; that this was the case with the Jews, appears from the Word both of the old and new testament, in the latter of which it is manifestly declared, that they perverted all things written in the Word concerning the Lord, and also all the essentials of the church, and that they falsified them by their traditions. So again, in Jeremiah : "And it shall be, when thou hast made an end of reading this book, that thou shalt bind a stone to it, and cast it into the midst of Euphrates : and thou shalt say, Thus shall Babylon sink, and shall not rise from the evil that I will bring upon her" (li. 63, 64). Here, by the book of prophecy which was read, is specifically understood that Word which was in that book, but in general, the whole Word; by his casting it into the midst of Euphrates, is signified, that the Word, in process of time, would be falsified through the reasonings which favor evils by those who are understood by Babylon, Babylon denoting those who adulterate the Word. Again, in Isaiah: "And Jehovah shall utterly destroy the tongue of the Egyptian sea ; and with his mighty wind shall he shake his hand over the river, and shall smite it in the seven streams, and make men go over dry shod. And there shall be a highway for the remnant of his people, which shall be left from Assyria ; like as it was to Israel in the day that he came up out of the land of Egypt" (xi. 15, 16). These words signify that all falsities, and all reasonings thence derived, shall be dissipated before those who are principled in truths originating in good from the Lord, and who, in other words, belong to the church, and that they shall, as it were, pass safely through the midst of them ; this is the case in the spiritual world with those whom the Lord defends. The same thing is here understood by the drying up of the Red Sea before the children of Israel; those who pass through under the protection of the Lord are signified by the remnant which shall be left from Assyria, Assyria denoting those who have not perished by reasonings from falsities. Similar also is the meaning of the following passage in the Revelation : "And the sixth angel poured out his vial upon the great river Euphrates, and

the water thereof was dried up, that the way of the kings of the
east might be prepared" (xvi. 12). These words will be explained
in their proper place. From all that has been adduced, it may now
appear, that by the river Euphrates is signified the rational principle,
by means of which the spiritual mind enters into the natural, and that,
in the opposite sense, it signifies reasoning from fallacies and from
falsities. It is however to be observed, that reasonings are in a like
degree with the thoughts, for they descend from them; consequently,
that there are reasonings from the spiritual man, which however
may rather be called conclusions from reason and from truths; that
there are reasonings from the natural man, and also from the spiritual man : reasonings from the spiritual man are rational, and, as was
observed, are rather to be called conclusions from reasons and from
truths, because they are from an interior principle, and from the light
of heaven; but reasonings from the natural man concerning spiritual
things are not rational, how much soever they may be so in things
moral and civil, which appear before the eyes, for they are from
natural light alone, but reasonings which are from the sensual man
concerning spiritual things are irrational, because they are derived
from fallacies, and thence from ideas which are false; these latter
are the reasonings which are treated of throughout the Revelation.

570. "And the four angels were loosed"—That hereby is signified liberty of reasoning from fallacies, appears from the signification of the four angels bound at the river Euphrates, as denoting
reasonings from fallacies pertaining to the sensual man, not received
before; concerning which, see above, n. 569; hence it follows, that
by their being loosed is signified the liberty now granted of reasoning from fallacies. The reason of this liberty being now given, or
of its taking place at this time, is, because the sensual man reasons
only from such things as are in the world, things that he can see
with his eyes, whilst he denies the existence of those things which
are within and above them, merely because he cannot see them;
hence it is that he denies, or does not believe in, the existence of
those things which belong to heaven and the church, because they
are above his thoughts, and that he ascribes all things to nature.
Thus does the sensual man think with himself, or in his spirit, but
he thinks otherwise before the world, for before the world he speaks
from his memory, also concerning spiritual things from the Word, or
from the doctrine of the church, and the things which he thus speaks
are the same in sound, as when the spiritual man speaks them : such
is the state of the men of the church in its end; and in this state,
with whatever elegance they may connect the words which they
speak or preach as from a spiritual origin, they nevertheless flow
from the ultimate sensual principle, in which their spirit is, which,
when left to itself, reasons against them, because it reasons from fallacies, consequently from falsities.

571. "Who were prepared for an hour, and a day, and a month,
and a year"—That hereby is denoted to be continually in a state,
appears from the signification of being prepared for an hour, and a
day, and a month, and a year, as denoting to be continually in a

state, namely, of depriving themselves of all understanding of truth and thence of spiritual life, which is signified by what follows, namely, that they might slay the third part of men; for by hours, days, months, and years, in the Word, are signified states of life in particular and in general, whence by being prepared for those times, is signified to be continually in that state. The reason why hours, days, months, and years, in the spiritual sense of the Word, do not signify hours, days, months, and years, is, because in the spiritual world times are not distinguished into such intervals, for the sun, from which the angelic heaven has its light and its heat, is not carried about, as the sun in the natural world is to appearance, wherefore it does not make either years, months, days, or hours; but times in the spiritual world, which still succeed as times in the natural world, are distinguished by states of life.* From these considerations it may appear, that by the angels being prepared for an hour, a day, a month, and a year, is signified to be continually in a state, which is treated of in what follows. That an hour signifies a state, and in like manner that a day, a month, and a year signify states, is evident from those passages of the Word in which they are mentioned, but to adduce them all here would be tedious; that such, however, is the case, may be seen from what is said and shown concerning time in the work concerning H. & H.; likewise in the A. C. where it is also shown, that times in the Word do not signify times but states of life, n. 2788, 2837, 3254, 3356, 4814, 4901, 4916, 7218, 8070, 10,133, 10,605. The reason why times signify states, is also, because in the spiritual world there are not stated times of the day, called morning, noon, evening, and night, nor stated times of the year, called spring, summer, autumn, and winter, neither changes of light and shade, of heat and cold, as in the natural world, but instead of these there are changes of state as to love and faith, from which there cannot be given any notion of the intervals into which our times are distinguished, although times have progression there as in the natural world; concerning which, see A. C. n. 1274, 1382, 3356, 4882, 6110, 7218. And as the sun of the angelic heaven, which is the Lord, is continually in its rising, and does not make circumvolutions as the sun of our world does in appearance, but there only exist changes of state with the angels and spirits according to their reception of the good of love, and of the truth of faith, therefore times correspond to states and signify them; A. C. n. 4901, 7381; and angels and spirits think without any idea of time, which is not possible with man, A. C. n. 3404.

572. "To slay the third part of men"—That hereby is signified, depriving themselves of all understanding of truth, and thence of spiritual life, appears from the signification of slaying as denoting to deprive of spiritual life, concerning which see above, n. 547; and from the signification of men, as denoting the understanding of

---

* What these are, may be seen explained in the work concerning H. & H. where the subject treated of is the sun in heaven, n. 116–125; concerning the changes of the states of the angels in heaven, n. 154–162; and concerning time in heaven, n. 162–169.

truth; see also above, n. 546, 547; that the third part, when predicated of truths, denotes all, may be seen above, n. 506; here,
therefore, by slaying the third part of men, is signified deprivation
of all the understanding of truth. The reason of its being said that
they deprive themselves, is, because they who become sensual by
evils of life and falsities of doctrine through reasonings from fallacies, deprive themselves of the understanding of truth, but they do
not so deprive others, except those who are also sensual: the reason why they thence deprive themselves of spiritual life, is, because
man acquires spiritual life by the understanding, for in proportion
as the understanding is opened and suffers itself to be enlightened
by truths, in the same proportion man becomes spiritual; but the
understanding is opened by truths from good, but not by truths without good; for in proportion as man lives in the good of love and
charity, in the same proportion he thinks truths; for truth is the
form of good, and all good with man is of his will, and all truth is
of his understanding, wherefore the good of the will presents its
form in the understanding, and the form itself is the thought from
the understanding, originating in the will.

573. "And the number of the armies of the horsemen was two
myriads of myriads"—That hereby are signified the falsities of evil
from which and for which are reasonings innumerable and conspiring against the truths of good, appears from the signification of armies, as denoting the falsities of evil, concerning which we shall
speak presently; and from the signification of horsemen, as denoting reasonings thence derived, for by horses, in the Word, is signified the understanding of truth, and in the opposite sense, the understanding perverted and destroyed, as may be seen above, n. 355,
364, 372, 373, 381, 382; hence by horsemen, in this sense, are signified reasonings from falsities, inasmuch as these are of the understanding perverted and destroyed, for truths constitute understanding,
but falsities destroy it; and from the signification of two myriads
of myriads, as denoting their being innumerable and conspiring
against the truths of good,* and it is said two myriads of myriads
because by these numbers are signified their being innumerable,
conjoined, and conspiring, for the number two signifies conjunction,
consent, and conspiracy, as may be seen above, n. 283, 384. The
reason why it is said, against the truths of good, is, because the
subject treated of in what follows is the destruction of truth by the
armies of those horsemen: from these considerations it may be seen,
that by the number of the armies of the horsemen being two myriads
of myriads, are signified the falsities of evil from which, and for
which are reasonings, and that they are innumerable and conspiring
against the truths of good. In the Word, frequent mention is made
of armies or hosts, and the Lord is also called Jehovah of Hosts or
Sabaoth, and by hosts or armies are there signified truths from
good combating against falsities derived from evil, and in the opposite sense, falsities derived from evil combating against truths de-

* That myriads signify innumerable, and are predicated of truths, may be seen
above, n. 336.

rived from good. The reason why such things are signified in the Word by armies, is, because by the wars there mentioned, both in the historical and prophetical parts, in the internal sense are signified spiritual wars, which are waged against hell and against the diabolic crew there, and such wars have relation to truths and goods combating against falsities and evils, and hence it is that armies signify all truths derived from good, and in the opposite sense, all falsities derived from evil. That in the Word armies signify all truths derived from good, is evident from this circumstance, that the sun, the moon, the stars, and also the angels, are called the armies of Jehovah, because they signify all truths derived from good in their whole compass; also that the children of Israel, because they signified the truths and goods of the church, are called armies; and inasmuch as all truths and goods are from the Lord, and the Lord alone combats for all in heaven, and for all in the church, against falsities and evils which are from hell, therefore he is called Jehovah Sabaoth, that is, Jehovah of armies.

That the sun, the moon, and the stars, are denominated armies in the Word, is plain from numerous passages. Thus in Moses: " Thus the heavens and the earth were finished, and all the host of them" (Gen. ii. 1). So in David: " By the word of Jehovah were the heavens made; and all the host of them by the breath of his mouth" (Psalm xxxiii. 6). Again: " Praise ye him, all his angels: praise ye him, all his hosts. Praise ye him, sun and moon: praise him, all ye stars of light" (Psalm cxlviii. 2, 3). And in Isaiah: " And all the host of heaven shall be dissolved, and the heavens shall be rolled together as a scroll: and all their host shall fall down, as the leaf falleth off from the vine, and as a falling fig from the fig-tree"(xxxiv. 4). And again, in the same prophet: " I have made the earth, and created man upon it: I, even my hands, have stretched out the heavens, and all their host have I commanded" (xlv. 12). And again: " Lift up your eyes on high, and behold who hath created these things, that bringeth out their host by number: he calleth them all by names" (xl. 26). So in Jeremiah: " As the host of heaven cannot be numbered, neither the sand of the sea measured" (xxxiii. 22). In these passages, the sun, the moon, and stars, are called an army, because by the sun is signified the good of love, by the moon, truth from good, and by the stars are signified the knowledges of truth and good, consequently they signify goods and truths in their whole compass, which are called an army, because they resist evils and falsities, and perpetually conquer them as enemies. So in Daniel: " And out of one of them came forth a little horn. And it waxed great, even to the host of heaven; and it cast down some of the host and of the stars to the ground, and stamped upon them. Yea, he magnified himself even to the prine of the host, and by him the daily sacrifice was taken away, and theplace of his sanctuary was cast down. And an host was given him against the daily sacrifice, and it cast down the truth to the ground; Then I heard one saint speaking, How long shall be the vision concerning the daily sacrifice, and the transgression of desolation, to give both the sanc-

tuary and the host to be trodden under foot? And he said unto me,
The vision of the evening and the morning is true" (viii. 9–14, 26).*
By the host of heaven, some of which he cast down to the earth, are
understood the truths and goods of heaven; for the subject here
treated of is the last state of the church, when the truths and goods
of heaven are esteemed as of no account, and rejected, which is signified by their being trodden under foot; hence it also follows, that
he cast down the truth to the earth: by the prince of the host is
understood the Lord, who is also called Jehovah God Sabaoth, or
of armies: that all worship from the good of love and the truths of
faith would perish, is signified by the daily sacrifice being taken away
from him, and the place of his sanctuary being cast down: that this
would come to pass in the end of the church, when the Lord would
come into the world, is signified by, "the evening and morning,"
the evening denoting the end of the old church, and the morning,
the commencement of the new church. That the angels are called
hosts or armies appears from the following passages. Thus in
Joel: "And Jehovah shall utter his voice before his army: for his
camp is very great" (ii. 11). And in Zechariah: "And I will
encamp about my house because of the army, because of him that
passeth by, and because of him that returneth: and no oppressor shall
pass through them any more" (ix. 8). And in David: "Bless ye Jehovah, all ye his hosts, ye ministers of his that do his pleasure" (ciii.
21). And in the 1st Book of Kings: "And he said, I saw Jehovah
sitting on his throne, and all the host of heaven standing by him on
his right hand and on his left. And one said on this manner, and
another said on that manner" (xxii. 19, 20). So in the Revelation:
"And the armies which were in heaven followed him upon white
horses, clothed in fine linen, white and clean" (xix. 14). And
again: "And I saw the beast, and the kings of the earth, and their
armies gathered together to make war against him that sat on the
horse, and against his army" (xix. 19). The reason why the
angels gathered together or consociated are called armies, is, because
by angels, in like manner as by armies, are signified divine truths and
goods, inasmuch as they are the recipients thereof from the Lord;
concerning which, see above, n. 130, 200, 302.

It is for the same reason, also, that the children of Israel, since by
them are signified the truths and goods of the church, are called
armies. Thus in Moses: "These are that Aaron and Moses, to
whom Jehovah said, Bring out the children of Israel from the land of
Egypt according to their armies" (Exod. vi. 26). Again: "That
I may bring forth mine armies, and my people the children of Israel,
out of the land of Egypt by great judgments" (Exod. vii. 4).
Again: "And it came to pass even the self same day, that all the
hosts of Jehovah went out from the land of Egypt" (xii. 41). And
again: "Thou and Aaron shall number them by their armies"
(Numb. i. 3). Again it is said: "Every man shall pitch by his own

---

* What is signified by the he-goat, here mentioned, by his horns, and by the little horn which waxed great even to the host of heaven, may be seen above, n. 316,
336, 504.

standard, about the tabernacle of the congregation—throughout their armies" (Numb. ii. 2, 3, 24). Again: "Take from among the sons of Levi, all that enter into the host to do the work in the tabernacle of the congregation" (Numb. iv. 2, 3, 30). The reason why the children of Israel were called the·armies of Jehovah was, because they represented the church, and signified all the truths and goods thereof.* The reason of their being called armies in the plural, is,·because each tribe was called an army, as may appear in Moses, where, when it was commanded him to make a computation of all according to their armies, they were computed according to their tribes (Numb. i. 3, and following verses): in like manner when the camp was pitched around the tent of assembly according to the tribes, it is said throughout their armies (Numb. ii. 3, 9, and following verses); the reason why the tribes were called armies, is, because the twelve tribes taken together represented all the truths and goods of the church, and each tribe some universal essential thereof; concerning which, see above, n. 431. From these considerations it may be seen, that the truths and goods of heaven and the church are understood by armies in the Word; from which it is manifestly evident whence it is that Jehovah is called in the Word, Jehovah Sabaoth, and Jehovah God Sabaoth, that is, of armies (as in Isaiah i. 9, 24; ii. 12; iii. 1, 15; v. 7, 9, 16, 24; vi. 3, 5; viii. 13, 18; xiv. 22, 23, 24, 27; xvii. 3; xxv. 6; xxviii. 5, 22, 29; xxix. 6; xxxi. 4, 5; xxxvii. 16; Jerem. v. 14; xxxviii. 17; xliv. 7; Amos v. 16; Haggai i. 9, 14; ii. 4, 8, 23; Zech. i. 3; Malachi ii. 12; and various other places).

From the above considerations it is now evident, that by armies are signified the truths and goods of heaven and the church in their whole compass; and inasmuch as most things in the Word have also an opposite sense, and as this is the case with respect to armies, therefore in that sense they signify falsities and evils in their whole compass. This will appear from the following passages of the Word. Thus in Jeremiah: "Because of all the houses upon whose roofs they have burned incense unto all the host of heaven, and have poured out drink offerings unto other gods" (xix. 13). And in Zephaniah: "And them that worship the host of heaven upon the house tops" (i. 5). And in Moses: "And lest thou lift up thine eyes unto heaven, and when thou seest the sun, and the moon, and the stars, even all the host of heaven, shouldest be driven to worship them, and serve them" (Deut. iv. 19; xvii. 3). And in Jeremiah: "They shall bring out the bones, and they shall spread them before the sun, and the moon, and all the host of heaven, whom they have loved, and whom they have served" (viii. 1, 2). Here by the army, or the host of heaven, are meant the sun, moon, and stars, because by these are signified all goods and truths in the aggregate, but, in this case, all evils and falsities; for by the sun, in the opposite sense, as here, is signified all evil flowing from the love of self, by

* As may seen in the A. C. n. 5414, 5801, 5803, 5806, 5812, 5817, 5819, 5826, 5833, 5879, 5951, 6637, 6962, 6868, 7035, 7062, 7198, 7201, 7215, 7223, 7   34, 8805, 9340.

the moon, the false principle of faith, and by the stars, falsities in general; that by the sun, moon, and stars, in the natural world, when they are worshiped instead of the sun and moon of the angelic heaven, are signified direful evils and falsities, may be seen in the work concerning H. & H. n. 122, 123; as also above, n. 401, 402, 524; and since truths derived from good, combat against falsities derived from evil, and, vice versa, falsities from evil against truths from good, therefore they are called armies; there is therefore continual combat; for evils and falsities continually exhale from the hells, and endeavor to destroy the truths from good which are in heaven, and from heaven, whilst the latter continually resist; for everywhere in the spiritual world there is an equilibrium between heaven and hell; and where there is an equilibrium, there two forces continually act against each other, one acting and the other reacting, and continual action and reaction is continual combat; but an equilibrium is always provided by the Lord; concerning which, see the work on H. & H. n. 589–596, and n. 597–603. And inasmuch as there is such a continual combat between heaven and hell, therefore, as all things of heaven are called armies, so also are all things of hell; all things of heaven have reference to goods and truths, and all things of hell, to evils and falsities. Hence it is that in the following passages armies signify the falsities of evil. Thus in Isaiah: "For the indignation of Jehovah is upon all nations, and his fury upon all their armies: he hath utterly destroyed them, he hath delivered them to the slaughter" (xxxiv. 2). Here by nations are signified evils, and by armies, falsities from evil: the total destruction of these is signified by their being delivered to the slaughter. Again: "The noise of a multitude in the mountains, like as of a great people; a tumultuous noise of the kingdoms of nations gathered together: Jehovah of hosts mustereth the host of the battle" (xiii. 4). Here by the noise of a multitude in the mountains, falsities originating in evils are signified, a multitude denoting falsities, and mountains denoting evils; "like as of a great people," signifies the appearance of truth originating in good, the words, "like as," denoting appearance, people denoting those who are in truths, thus, in the abstract, truths themselves, and great is predicated of good: by a tumultuous noise of the kingdoms of nations gathered together, is signified the dissension of the church arising from evils and the falsities thence derived, a tumultuous noise denoting dissension, kingdoms, the church as to truths and falsities, and nations gathered together signifying evils and the falsities thence derived conspiring against the goods and truths of the church: "Jehovah of hosts mustereth the host of the battle," signifies that it is effected by the Lord, for this is attributed to the Lord, as is plain from the verse immediately following, in which it is said, "They come from a far country, from the end of heaven, even Jehovah, and the weapons of his indignation, to destroy the whole land" (verse 5). This is attributed to Jehovah just as evil, the punishment of evil, and the destruction of the church are attributed to him in other passages of the Word, because such is the appearance of

things, and the literal sense of the Word is written according to appearances; but by such things in the spiritual sense, is understood
that they proceed from the man of the church himself. Again, in
Jeremiah: " And spare ye not her young men; destroy ye utterly
all her host" (li. 3).   The subject here treated of is Babylon; and
by not sparing her young men, is signified the destruction of confirmed falsities; by the utter destruction of her host, is signified the
total destruction of falsities originating in evil, thus the complete
destruction of Babylon.   The same is signified by the army of
Pharaoh, the army of the Chaldeans, and the host of Pharaoh,
mentioned in the following passages (Jer. xxxviii. 7–11); and
in Moses, by " The waters returned, and covered the chariots, and
the horsemen, and all the host of Pharaoh " (Exod. xiv. 28; xv.
4); these passages may be seen explained above, n. 355; and in
the A. C. n. 8230, 8275.   So in Daniel: " For the king of the
north shall return, and shall set forth a multitude greater than the
former, and shall certainly come after certain years with a great
army and with much riches.   And he shall stir up his power and
his courage against the king of the south with a great army; and
the king of the south shall be stirred up to battle with a very great
and mighty army; but he shall not stand " (xi. 13, 25).   Here the
subject treated of is the war between the king of the north and the
king of the south, and by the king of the north are understood those
within the church who are in the falsities of evil, and by the king of
the south, those within the church who are in the truths of good;
their collision and combat in the end of the church, are described by
their war, in the spiritual sense; wherefore by the army of the king
of the north are understood falsities of every kind, and by the army
of the king of the south are understood truths of every kind.   So in
Luke: " And when ye shall see Jerusalem compassed with armies,
then know that the desolation thereof is nigh " (xxi. 20).   In this
chapter the Lord speaks of the consummation of the age, by which
is signified the last time of the church; by Jerusalem is understood
the church as to doctrine; and by its being compassed with armies,
is understood its being occupied by falsities; that then is the destruction thereof, and presently the last judgment, is signified by
the desolation thereof being then nigh.   It is supposed that these
things are said concerning the destruction of Jerusalem by the Ro-
mans, but from the particulars of the chapter it is evident that it
treats of the destruction of the church in its end; as also in Matthew xxiv. from the first verse to the last, all things whereof are
explained in the A. C.   Nevertheless this forms no obstacle to the
literal sense having respect to the destruction of Jerusalem, but that
destruction represented and thence signified the destruction of the
church in its end; this is confirmed by everything contained in the
chapter, viewed in the spiritual sense.   Again, in David: " But
thou hast cast off, and put us to shame: and goest not forth with
our armies.   Thou makest us to turn back from the enemy " (Psalm
xliv. 9, 10).   Here by God not going forth with their armies, is signified that he did not defend them, because they were in falsities of

evil, for armies denote falsities of evil; hence it said that they were cast off, and put to shame, and made to turn back from the enemy, the enemy denoting evil, which is from hell. Again, in Joel: "And I will restore to you the years that the locust hath eaten, the canker-worm, and the caterpillar, and the palmer worm, my great army which I sent among you" (ii. 25). That by the great army here mentioned falsities and evils of every kind are signified, is evident from this consideration, that by those noxious animalcula,—the locust, the canker-worm, the cater-pillar, and the |palmer worm, are signified the falsities and evils which vastate or consume the truths and goods of the church.* From what has been adduced it is now evident what armies signify in the Word in both senses. The armies mentioned in the histori-cal parts of the Word have the same significations, for they contain a spiritual sense, as well as the prophetical parts, but it does not so clearly shine forth from them, because the mind being detained in the historical circumstances, can scarcely be elevated above worldly things so as to see the spiritual things which are stored up in them.

574. "And I heard the number of them"—That hereby is signi-fied the perception of their quality, appears from the signification of hearing, as denoting to perceive, see above, n. 14, 529; and from the signification of number, as denoting the quality of the thing treated of, concerning which, see above, n. 429; in this case, the quality of the falsities of evil conspiring against the truths of good, from which and for which are the reasonings of the sensual man, which are signified by the number of the armies of the horsemen, spoken of just above. The quality of these is further described in the next verse in these words: "And thus I saw the horses in the vision, and them that sat on them, having breast-plates of fire, and of jacinth, and of brimstone: and the heads of the horses were as the heads of lions; and out of their mouths issued fire and smoke and brimstone." These words are expressive of the quality which is here signified by their number. It may seem as if something of number were here understood by number, but in the spiritual world numbers are not known, for spaces and times there are not meas-ured and determined by numbers, as in the natural world, wherefore by all numbers, in the Word, are signified things, and by the num-ber itself is signified the quality of the thing treated of; concerning which, see above, n. 203, 336, 429, 430; and in the work concern-ing H. & H. n. 263.

575. "And thus I saw the horses in the vision, and them that sat on them"—That hereby are signified falsifications of the Word by reasonings from fallacies, appears from the signification of hor-ses, as denoting the understanding of the Word; concerning which, see above, n. 355, 364, 372, 373, 381, 382; in this case, the falsifi-cations thereof, because it is said, that he saw the horses in vision, concerning which we shall speak presently; and from the significa-tion of them that sat on them, as denoting those who are intelligent

* As may be seen above, n. 543, where this passage is explained, and it is shown that locusts and caterpillar signify the falsities of the sensual man.

in the Word, concerning which signification see also the passages above cited, but in this case, reasonings concerning the sense of the Word originating in fallacies, inasmuch as the subjects here treated of are the sensual man, and his reasonings from fallacies, as may be seen above, n. 569; and because it is said that he saw them in vision, and not, as before, in the spirit, to see in vision here signifies from fallacies. For visions, which, and from which, man, or the spirit of man, sees, are of a twofold kind: there are real visions, and visions that are not real: real visions are of such things as really appear in the spiritual world, altogether corresponding to the thoughts and affections of the angels, consequently they are real correspondences; such were the visions which appeared to the prophets who prophesied truths, and such also were the visions which appeared to John, and which are described throughout the Revelation; but visions that are not real are such as appear in the external form like those that are real, but not in the internal, being produced by spirits by means of fantasies; such were the visions which appeared to the prophets who prophesied vain things or lies, which being not real were fallacies, and therefore signified fallacies: and since the horses and them that sat on them were seen by John in such vision, therefore by them are signified reasonings from fallacies, and thence falsifications of the Word. Forasmuch as real visions appeared to the prophets, by whom the Word was written, and visions that were not real to others who were also called prophets, and the visions of these latter were vain, and are in the Word, also called lies, it is of importance that the nature and quality of visions should be known. It is to be observed, that all things which really appear in the spiritual world, are correspondences, for they correspond to the interiors of the minds of the angels, or of their affection and thought thence derived, wherefore they also signify such things; for the spiritual principle which is of the affection, and thence of the thought of the angels, clothes itself with forms such as those which appear in the three kingdoms of the natural world, namely, the animal, the vegetable, and the mineral, and all these forms are correspondences, such as were seen by the prophets, and which signified the things to which they corresponded. But there are also appearances in the spiritual world, which are not correspondences, which are produced from spirits, especially the evil, by means of fantasies, for by these those spirits can present to the view, palaces, and houses full of decorations, likewise ornamented garments, and can also induce upon themselves beautiful faces, with other things of a like nature; but as soon as the phantasy ceases, all the things which it has produced vanish, in consequence of their being merely external in which there is nothing internal: as such visions exist from from fantasies, they signify fallacies, because they deceive the senses, and fallaciously present to the view things similar to those which are real; since these are what are here signified, it is therefore said, "And thus I saw the horses in the vision." The subject now treated of being reasonings from fallacies, we shall here explain what fallacies are. Fallacies exist in

natural, in civil, in moral, and in spiritual things, and in each they
are of great variety; but as fallacies in spiritual things are what are
here understood, therefore the nature and quality of these shall be
illustrated by some examples. The sensual man is in fallacies, because all the ideas of his thought are derived from the world and
enter through his bodily senses, wherefore he also thinks and concludes from them concerning things spiritual; he is also ignorant as
to what the spiritual principle is, and believes that nothing can be
given above nature, and if anything be given, that it is natural and
material: he cannot at all apprehend, that in the spiritual world,
there exist objects like those in the natural world, namely, that
there can appear there paradises, shrubberies, beds of flowers, grass-
plats, palaces, houses; these things he calls fantasies, although he
knows that similar things were seen by the prophets when they
were in the spirit; the reason why sensual men do not believe such
things to have existence in the spiritual world is, because whatever
they do not see with their eyes, or perceive with some sense of the
body, they suppose to be nothing or a thing of nought. They who
judge from fallacies cannot at all apprehend, that man after death
is in a perfect human form, nor that the angels are in that form;
wherefore they deny that men after death are human forms, supposing them to be phantoms, without eyes, ears or mouth, consequently
without sight, hearing, or speech, flying about in the air, and wait-
ing for the resurrection of the body, that they may see, hear, and
speak; the reason is, because they think from the fallacies of the
bodily senses. They who reason and conclude from the fallacies
of the senses, attribute all things to nature, and scarcely anything to
the Divine Being; and if they attribute creation to the Divine Being,
they still suppose all things to be transferred into nature, and all the
effects which appear flow from nature alone, and nothing from the
spiritual world; as when they see the wonderful phenomena dis-
played in the changes through which the silk worm and the butter-
fly pass, in the economy of bees, and in the generation of animals
from eggs, and in innumerable other things of an equally wonderful
nature, they suppose nature to be the sole artificer of these things,
and cannot think anything of the spiritual world, and the influx
thereof into the natural, and of the existence and subsistence of
such admirable things being thence derived; when notwithstanding
the case is, that the divine principle flows in continually by the
spiritual world into the natural, and produces all such things, and
that nature was created to be serviceable in the clothing of those
things which proceed and flow in from the spiritual world. But to
enumerate all the fallacies in spiritual things pertaining to the sensual man of the church, would be tedious; some of them may be
seen enumerated in the D. of the N. J. n. 53.

676. " Having breast-plates of fire, and of jacinth, and of brimstone"—That hereby are signified reasonings combating from the
cupidities of the loves of self and of the world, and from the falsities
therein originating, appears from the signification of breast-plates, as
denoting armor for war, and specifically defences in combats, which

are treated of above, n. 557; and from the signification of fire or fiery, as denoting the cupidity of the love of self, and thence of all evil, concerning which, see above, n. 504; and from the signification of jacinth or blue, as denoting the cupidity of the love of the world and thence of everything false, concerning which we shall speak presently; and from the signification of brimstone or sulphureous, as denoting the concupiscence of destroying the goods and truths of the church by the falsities of evil, concerning which, see below, n. 578; in this case as denoting falsity burning from those two loves; from these considerations it may appear, that by breastplates of fire, and of jacinth, and of brimstone, are signified reasonings combating from the cupidities of the loves of self and of the world, and from the falsities therein originating. With respect to the jacinth or blue, it is to be observed that, in the spiritual sense, it signifies the celestial love of truth, but in the opposite sense, the diabolical love of falsity, and also the love of the world; this may appear from its being of a celestial color, and by that color is signified truth from a celestial origin, and thence, in the opposite sense, falsity from a diabolic origin. In the spiritual world there appear the most choice colors, which derive their origin from good and truth; the reason is that colors there are modifications of heavenly light, thus of the intelligence and wisdom of the angels in heaven. Hence it was, that in the curtains of the tabernacle and in the garments of Aaron were interwoven blue, purple, and scarlet, double-dyed; for by the tabernacle was represented the heaven of the Lord, and by the garments of Aaron, the divine truth pertaining to heaven and the church, and by those things of which the tabernacle was constructed, and which formed the contexture of the garments of Aaron, were represented celestial and spiritual things, which are of the divine good and divine truth. This will more fully appear from the following passages of the Word. Thus in Moses: "And thou shalt make a vail of blue, and purple, and scarlet, and fine twined linen of cunning work" (Exod. xxvi. 31). And again: "And thou shalt make a hanging for the door of the tent, of blue, and purple, and scarlet" (verse 36). Again: "And for the gate of the court shall be a hanging of twenty cubits of blue, and purple, and scarlet" (Exod. xxvii. 16). The loops also on the edge of the curtain of the tent were to be made of blue; the ephod was to be made of blue, and of purple, and of scarlet, and fine twined linen, with cunning work; the breast-plate of judgment was to be made with cunning work, after the work of the ephod, of gold, of blue, and of purple, and of scarlet; and when the camp went forward in the wilderness, Aaron and his sons were commanded to take down the covering vail, and to cover the ark of the testimony with it, to spread over it a cloth wholly of blue, to spread a cloth of blue over the table of shew bread, over the candlestick and the lamps, over the golden altar, and over all the vessels of the ministry (Exod. xxvi. 4; xxviii. 4, 5, 6, 16; Numb. iv. 5–12). The reason of these things was, because the divine truth proceeding from the divine love, which was signified by the cloth of blue, embraces and

defends all the holy things of heaven and the church, which things
represented. In consequence of the signification of blue, as denoting the celestial love of truth, Moses was commanded to speak
to the children of Israel, and order them to make a "fringe in the
borders of their garments throughout their generations, and to put
upon the fringe a ribband of blue, that they might look upon it, and
remember all the commandments of Jehovah, and do them" (Numb.
xv. 37–39); the ribband of blue being evidently declared to be for
the remembrance of the commandments of Jehovah, the signification thereof is obvious; the commandments of Jehovah are the essential truths of heaven and the church, and they alone remember
them who are in the celestial love of truth. That blue signifies the
love of truth, is plain from the following passages in Ezekiel:
"Fine linen with broidered work from Egypt was that which thou
spreadest forth to be thy sail; blue and purple from the isles of
Elisha was that which covered thee. These were thy merchants in
all sorts of things, in blue clothes, and broidered work, and in chests
of rich apparel" (xxvii. 7, 24). These things are said of Tyrus, by
which is signified the church as to the knowledges of truth, thus
also the knowledges of truth pertaining to the church, and by the
merchandise and tradings mentioned in that chapter is described the
procuring of intelligence by those knowledges; by broidered work
from Egypt is signified the science of such things as pertain to the
church, which being in an inferior place, and thus round about or
without, it is called spreading forth, and said to be for a sail: by
blue and purple from the isles of Elisha, is signified the spiritual
affection of truth and good; they are therefore said to be for a covering, a covering denoting truths: by blue clothes and broidered work,
are signified all truths spiritual and natural, which, together with
knowledges from the Word, are also understood by chests of rich
apparel.
     Inasmuch as blue signifies the celestial love of truth, therefore
also, in the opposite sense, it signifies the diabolic love of falsity;
in which sense it is also mentioned in the Word. Thus in Ezekiel
it is said: "Son of man, there were two women, the daughters of
one mother: And they committed whoredoms in Egypt; they committed whoredoms in their youth. And the names of them were
Aholah the elder, and Aholibah her sister: Samaria is Aholah, and
Jerusalem Aholibah. And Aholah played the harlot when she was
mine; and she doted on her lovers, on the Assyrians her neighbors,
which were clothed with blue; captains and rulers, all of them desirable young men, horsemen riding upon horses" (xxiii. 2–6).
Here by Samaria and Jerusalem is signified the church, by Samaria,
the spiritual church, and by Jerusalem, the celestial church, which
are called Aholah and Aholibah, because by those names is signified
a tent, and by a tent is signified the church as to worship; by
woman also, in the Word, is signified the church; by their commit-
ing whoredoms in Egypt, is signified that they falsified the truths
of the church by the scientifics of the natural man; by doting on
the Assyrians, is signified that they falsified by reasonings from

those scientifics, Ashur and Assyria denoting reasonings; they are said to be clothed in blue, by reason of fallacies and falsities, which in the external form appear as truths, because drawn from the literal sense of the Word perversely applied. And because of the same appearance they are also called rulers and captains, desirable young men, and horsemen riding upon horses, for they who reason from self-derived intelligence appear to themselves, and to others who are in a similar state, as intelligent and wise, and the things which they speak as the truths of intelligence and the goods of wisdom, when notwithstanding they are falsities, which they love because they are from their proprium; rulers and captains signify principal truths, and horsemen riding upon horses, those who are in intelligence. So in Jeremiah: " Silver spread into plates is brought from Tarshish, and gold from Uphaz, the work of the workman, and of the hands of the founder: blue and purple is their clothing: they are all the work of cunning men " (x. 9). The subject here treated of is the idols of the house of Israel, by which are signified false doctrines, because they are from self-derived intelligence, hence they are called the work of the workman, and of the hands of the founder, and all the work of cunning men, and this because of their appearing to themselves as truths and goods; silver from Tarshish, and gold from Uphaz, signify their appearing in the external form as truth and good, because from the literal sense of the Word. From these considerations it is evident that, in the above passages, blue signifies the love of what is false, because originating in the proprium, or in self-derived intelligence. The reason why blue also signifies the love of the world, is, because the love of the world corresponds to the love of what is false, as the love of self, which is signified by fire, corresponds to the love of evil; for from the love of self comes all evil, and from the love of the world originating in the love of self comes all that is false; for spiritual evil, which is signified by the love of the world, is, in its essence, falsity, as spiritual good is, in its essence, truth; as may be seen in the work concerning H. & H. n. 15.

577. "And the heads of the horses were as the heads of lions "— That hereby are signified science, and thought thence derived, destructive of truth, appears from the signification of the heads of the horses, as denoting science and the thought thence derived, as will be seen presently; and from the signification of the heads of lions, as denoting thence the destruction of truth. The reason why the heads of lions here signify the destruction of truth, is, because a lion, in the supreme sense, signifies the divine truth as to power, and, in the opposite sense, what is false destroying truth, consequently, the destruction of truth, and the head of a lion signifies the powers of the mind by which destruction is effected, and which are reasonings grounded in falsities; that a lion signifies the divine truth as to power, and, in the opposite sense, what is false destroying it, may be seen above, n. 278. The reason why the heads of the horses signify science and thought thence derived, is, because head signifies intelligence, and horse, the understanding; but whereas

the subjects here treated of are the sensual man and his reasonings from falsities, and the sensual man who reasons from falsities, has no intelligence, but only science and the thought thence derived, therefore these are here signified by the heads of the horses.* The reason why the head signifies intelligence, is, because the understanding and will of man reside in the interior parts of his head, and hence in the front part of the head, which is the face, are the senses of sight, hearing, smell, and taste, into which the understanding and will flow from the interior, vivifying them, and also causing them to enjoy their sensations; hence it is, that by head, in the Word, is signified intelligence. But whereas they alone are intelligent who receive influx from heaven, for all intelligence and wisdom flow in out of heaven from the Lord, it follows, that no intelligence can be given with those who are principled in the falsities of evil; for with them the superior and spiritual mind is shut, and only the inferior mind, which is called the natural mind, is open, and this mind, when the superior is shut, does not receive anything of truth and good, consequently no intelligence from heaven, but solely from the world, wherefore such persons, instead of intelligence, have only science, and thought grounded in science, from which proceeds reasoning, and thereby the confirmation of what is false and evil against truth and good.

That by head, in the Word, are signified intelligence and wisdom, and, in the opposite sense, science, and thence infatuated thought, is evident from the following passages in the Word. Thus in Ezekiel: "And I put a jewel on thy forehead, and earrings in thine ears, and a beautiful crown upon thy head" (xvi. 12). These things are said concerning Jerusalem, by which are signified the church and its quality at the beginning; by the jewel put on the forehead is signified the perception of truth from good, by earrings in the ears are signified hearing and obedience, and by a crown upon the head is signified wisdom, for intelligence which is from divine truth becomes wisdom from the good of love, which is signified by a crown of gold. So in the Revelation: "And there appeared a great wonder in heaven; a woman clothed with the sun, and the moon under her feet, and upon her head a crown of twelve stars" (xii. 1). That by the head in this passage is signified intelligence, will be seen in the explication of that chapter. By the Jews placing a crown of thorns upon the head of the Lord, and smiting his head (Matt. xxvii. 29, 30; Mark xv. 19; John xix. 2), was signified, the reproachful manner in which they treated divine truth, and divine wisdom itself; for they falsified the Word, which is divine truth, and contains the divine wisdom, and adulterated it by their traditions, and by applications to themselves, thus desiring a king who should raise them up above all the nations of the earth; and inasmuch as the kingdom of the Lord was not terrestrial but heavenly, therefore they perverted all things which were said concerning him in the Word, and mocked at what was predicted of him: this was what was represented by their placing a crown of

* That they who are principled in falsities have no intelligence, but instead of intelligence, only science, may be seen in the D. of the N. Jn 33.

thorns upon his head, and by their smiting him on the head. It is also said in Daniel, treating of the statue of Nebuchadnezzar seen in a dream: " This image's head was of fine gold, his breast and his arms of silver, his belly and his thighs of brass, his legs of iron, his feet part of iron and part of clay" (ii. 32, 33). By that statue were represented the successive states of the church; by the head being of gold was represented and signified the most ancient church, which was in celestial wisdom, and thence in intelligence above all the churches that followed, and this wisdom and intelligence are understood by the head being of gold.* And in David: "Thou broughtest us into the net: thou laidst affliction upon our loins. Thou hast caused men to ride over our heads" (Psalm lxvi. 11, 12). By causing men to ride over our heads is denoted that in the church there was then no intelligence. And in Moses: "The blessings of thy father, they shall be on the head of Joseph, and on the crown of the head of him that was separated from his brethren" (Gen. xlix. 26; Deut. xxi. 12). By the blessings here mentioned being on the head of Joseph, is signified that all those things previously mentioned, and which are the blessings of heaven, should take place in the interiors of his mind, which are the lives of his understanding and will, for these are the interiors of the mind; by their being on the crown of the head of him who was separate, or a Nazarite, from his brethren, is signified, that they should also take place in the exteriors of his natural mind, for the Nazariteship signifies the exteriors of the natural mind, since it signifies hairs, or the hair of the head.† Again : "Take you wise men, and understanding, and known among your tribes, and I will make them heads over you" (Deut. i. 13). The reason why it is here said, " I will make them heads over you," is, because wisdom and intelligence are understood, in which they should excel, hence it is said, "Take you wise men and understanding." So in Isaiah: "For Jehovah hath poured out upon you the spirit of deep sleep, and hath closed your eyes, the prophets; and your heads, the seers, hath he covered" (xxix. 10). Here by prophets are signified those who teach truths, and abstractedly the doctrine of truth and intelligence, wherefore it is said, " Jehovah hath closed your eyes, the prophets; and your heads, the seers, hath he covered," where the prophets are called eyes, and the seers, heads, because by the eyes is signified the understanding of truth as to doctrine, and by seers, intelligence, in like manner as by the head. Again: "Therefore Jehovah will cut off from Israel head and tail, branch and rush, in one day. The ancient and honorable, he is the head, and the prophet that teacheth lies, he is the tail" (ix. 14, 15). And again: "Neither shall there be any work for Egypt, which the head or tail, branch or rush, may do" (xix. 15).‡ Again, in the same prophet: "In the same day shall the Lord shave

* That the other parts of the statue signified the states of the churches following, may be seen above, n. 176, 411.
† But these words may be seen further explained above, n. 448; and in the A. C. n. 6437, 6438.
‡ That by these words is signified that all intelligence and science of truth should perish, may be seen above, n. 559, where they are more fully explained.

with a razor that is hired, namely by them beyond the river, by the king of Assyria, the head, and the hair of the feet: and it shall also consume the beard" (vii. 20). That by these words is signified that reasonings grounded in falsities would deprive the men of the church of all wisdom and spiritual intelligence, may be seen above, n. 569, where they are particularly explained; it is said, beyond the river, because by the river Euphrates is signified reasonings from falsities, here therefore is signified invasion thence into the truths of the church which are destroyed by reasonings from falsities. And in Ezekiel : " And thou, son of man, take thee a sharp knife, take thee a barber's razor, and cause it to pass upon thy head and upon thy beard. Thou shalt burn with fire a third part in the midst of the city, and thou shalt take a third part and smite about it with a knife, and a third part thou shalt scatter in the wind" (v. 1, 2). Here also by causing a razor to pass over the head, is signified, to deprive of all intelligence of truth ; the reason is, because unless there are the ultimates of intelligence, which are signified by the hairs of the head, which it is said he should shave with a razor, by causing it to pass over the head, intelligence perishes; for when the ultimates are taken away, it is as when the base is taken away from a column, or the foundation from a house; hence it is that in the Jewish church, which was a representative church, it was unlawful to shave the hair of the head, and to induce baldness, and in like manner the beard : wherefore also they who are without intelligence appear bald in the spiritual world. From these considerations it may appear what is signified by a bald head, or by baldness, in the following passages. Thus in Isaiah : " On all their heads shall be baldness, and every beard cut off" (xv. 2). These words also denote that there no longer existed with them any intelligence. And in Ezekiel : " And shame shall be upon all faces, and baldness upon all their heads" (vii. 18). And again, in the same prophet : " Every head was made bald, and every shoulder was peeled" (xxix. 18). These words denote the same thing as the preceding. Hence also it was that Aaron and his sons were forbidden to shave their heads and the corner of their beards; concerning which it is thus written in Moses : " And Moses said unto Aaron and unto his sons. Uncover not your heads, neither rend your clothes ; lest ye die, and lest wrath come upon all the people" (Levit. x. 6). And again : " They shall not make baldness upon their head, neither shall they shave off the corner of their beard" (xxi. 5). By beard is signified the ultimate of the rational man, and by not shaving the beard, is signified not to deprive themselves of the rational principle, by taking away the ultimate thereof; for, as was said above, when the ultimate is taken away, the interior also perishes.* Inasmuch as shame was represented by the hands upon the head, therefore it is said in Jeremiah : " Thou also shalt be ashamed of Egypt, as thou wast ashamed of Assyria. Yea, thou shalt go forth from him,

---

* What is understood by the woman taken captive from the enemy, shaving her head and dressing her nails, if she should be desired for a wife, may be seen explained above, n. 555.

and thy hands upon thy head" (ii. 36, 37).   Again, in the same prophet: "They were ashamed and confounded, and covered their
heads" (xiv. 3).   Because covering the head with the hands was
representative of shame, it is said of Tamar, after she had been dis-
graced by her brother Ammon, that she laid her hand on her head,
and went on crying; by which action was signified that there remained no longer any intelligence.   Grief also for sin in having
acted insanely and foolishly, was represented by sprinkling dust
upon the head, and by thrusting down the head even to the earth,
by which also was signified being accursed; as in Ezekiel: "And
they shall cast dust upon their heads, they shall wallow themselves
in ashes" (xxvii. 30).   And in Lamentations: "The elders of the
daughter of Zion sit upon the ground, and keep silence: they have
cast up dust upon their heads; they have girded themselves with
sackcloth: the virgins of Jerusalem hung down their heads to the
ground" (ii. 10).   But by the head, in the opposite sense, is signified
the craftiness pertaining to those who are in the love of ruling; this
is understood by the head in the following passages.   Thus in
Moses: "And I will put enmity between thee and the woman, and
between thy seed and her seed; it shall bruise thy head, and thou
shalt bruise his heel" (Gen. iii. 15).   And in David: "Jehovah at
thy right hand shall strike through kings in the day of his wrath.
He shall judge among the heathen, he shall fill the palaces with the
dead bodies; he shall wound the heads over many countries.   He
shall drink of the brook in the way: therefore shall he lift up his
head" (Psalm. cx. 5, 6, 7); this passage may be seen explained
above, n. 518.   And again: "But God shall wound the head
of his enemies, and the hairy scalp of such an one as goeth on
still in his trespasses" (Psalm. lxviii. 21).   That the craftiness by
which they intend and contrive evil for others returns upon themselves, is signified by, "recompensing their way upon their own
head," Ezek. ix. 10; xi. 21; xvi. 43; xvii. 19; xxii. 31; Joel. iii.
4–7.   But what is signified in the Revelation, by seven heads upon
which were seven diadems (xii. 3; xiii. 1, 3; xvii. 3, 7, 9), will be
seen in the following pages.   Moreover, by the head, as being the
supreme and primary part in man, are also signified various other
things; as the peak of a mountain, the top of anything, what is
primary, the beginning of a way, of a street, of a month, and the
like.

578.   And out of their mouths issued fire, and smoke, and brimstone"—That hereby are signified thoughts and reasonings thence
derived bursting forth from the love of evil, from the love of what is
false, and from the concupiscence of destroying truths and goods by
the falsities of evil, appears from the signification of the mouth, as
denoting thought and reasoning thence derived, of which we shall
speak in the explication of the 19th verse; and from the signification of fire, as denoting the love of self, and thence the love of evil;
concerning which, see above, n. 504, 539; and from the signification of smoke, as denoting the dense falsity issuing from the love of
evil; concerning which, also see above, p. 494, 539; and from the

signification of brimstone, as denoting the concupiscence of destroying the truths and goods of the church by the falsities of evil.

That this is the signification of brimstone, may appear from those passages of the Word where it is mentioned. "Then Jehovah rained upon Sodom and upon Gomorrah brimstone and fire" (Gen. xix. 24). And in Luke: "But the same day that Lot went out of Sodom, it rained fire and brimstone from heaven, and destroyed them all. Even thus shall it be in the day when the Son of man is revealed" (xvii. 29, 30). By the inhabitants of Sodom and Gomorrah, are meant those who are in the falsity of evil originating in the love of self; and since as the falsities of evil originating in that love destroyed them, therefore it rained brimstone and fire, brimstone, because of the concupiscence of destroying the church by the falsities of evil, and fire because that concupiscence burst forth from the love of self; that thus it should be when the Son of man should be revealed, signifies, that then also the falsities of evil originating in the love of self would destroy the church: such rain also appears in the spiritual world, when the evil, who are in falsities from that love, are cast down into hell. So again, in Moses: "So that the generation to come of your children that shall rise up after you, and of the stranger that shall come from a far land, shall say, when they see the plagues of that land, and the sicknesses which Jehovah hath laid upon it; and that the whole land thereof is brimstone, and salt, and burning, that it is not sown, nor beareth, nor any grass groweth thereon, like the overthrow of Sodom and Gomorrah, Admah and Zeboim" (Deut. xxix. 22, 23). These were the maledictions denounced upon the children of Israel, if they kept not the precepts and statutes commanded them, and if they worshiped the gods of the surrounding nations, because then the church would become vastated and destroyed by the falsities of evil, and the evils of falsity, hence it is said that the whole land should be brimstone, and salt, and burning, the land denoting the church: by its not being sown, nor bearing, nor any grass growing thereon, is signified, that there should be no more reception or production of any truth from good. Again, in Isaiah: "For Tophet is ordained of old: yea, for the king it is prepared; he hath made it deep and large: the pile thereof is fire and much wood; the breath of Jehovah, like a stream of brimstone doth kindle it" (xxx. 33). By Tophet is here signified the hell in which the direful and cruel love of destroying all the truths and goods of the church reigns, especially the cruel lust of destroying the goods of innocence; that direful hell originates in the falsities of evil, and is signified by, "he hath made it deep and large;" the king, for whom it is prepared, signifies the infernal falsity itself; "the pile thereof is fire and much wood," signify evils of every kind originating in that love; and because that hell burns from the concupiscence of destroying, it is said that the breath of Jehovah, like a stream of brimstone doth kindle it; for there, as soon as they hear from any one the truths of the church, and perceive the goods of the same, they are inflamed with the desire of destroying and extinguishing them. Again, in the same prophet:

"For it is the day of the vengeance of Jehovah, and the year of recompences for the controversy of Zion. And the stream thereof shall be turned into pitch, and the dust thereof into brimstone, and the land thereof shall become burning pitch. It shall not be quenched night nor day; the smoke thereof shall go up for ever" (xxxiv. 8, 9, 10). The day of the vengeance of Jehovah, and the year of recompences for the controversy of Zion, signify the Lord's advent, and the last judgment then accomplished by him; the stream being turned into pitch, and dust into brimstone, signify the hell into which they are cast, who are in the falsities of evil, and in the evils of falsity; the evil of infernal love, and its punishment, are signified by the land burning night and day, and not being quenched; and the dire falsity from that evil is signified by the smoke ascending for ever. Again in Ezekiel: "And I will plead against him with pestilence and with blood; and I will rain upon him, and upon his lands, and upon the many people that are with him, an overflowing rain, and great hailstones, fire and brimstone" (xxxviii. 22). This is spoken of Gog, by whom are understood those who place all worship in a holy and pious external, and not in what is internal, when notwithstanding the quality of external worship is according to the internal principle by which it is influenced; it is said that Jehovah shall rain upon them an overflowing rain, and great hailstones, fire, and brimstone, by which are signified falsities and evils destroying all the truths and goods of the church; fire and brimstone denote the evils of falsity, and the falsities of evil, which are both of a diabolical nature. Again in David: "Upon the wicked he shall rain snares, fire and brimstone, and an horrible tempest: this shall be the portion of their cup" (Psalm xi. 6). By these words is signified, that the impious are destroyed by their own evils originating in what is false, and by their own falsities originating in evil, which destroy in them all the truths of the church; snares, fire, and brimstone, denote the evils of falsity, and the falsities of evil; by the horrible tempest which shall be the portion of the cup of the wicked, is signified the total destruction of all truth with them: that it is not meant that Jehovah shall rain fire and brimstone upon the wicked is manifest, for it is also said that he shall rain snares upon them; by fire and brimstone therefore must be meant such things as are wholly destructive of the truths and goods of the church. In like manner in Job: "Brimstone shall be scattered upon his habitation" (xviii. 15). This is said of the wicked, and by brimstone is understood the falsity of evil, which is of such a nature as to destroy everything of the church in man; such is the falsity originating in the evil of the love of self, which was also prevalent in those who dwelt in Sodom and Gomorrah, concerning which it is said, not only that it overthrew the cities, the plain, and all the inhabitants, but also that it destroyed that which grew upon the ground, by which is signified the truth of the church springing up (Gen. xix. 25). Similar things are signified by fire and brimstone in the following passages in the Revelation: "If any man worship the beast and his image, he shall be tormented with fire and brimstone" (xiv. 9, 10). Again: "And the beast, and the false prophet were cast alive into a lake of fire burning with brimstone" (xix. 26). Again: "And the devil was cast into the lake of fire and brimstone, where the beast and the false prophet are" (xx. 10). And again: "But the fearful, and the unbelieving, and the abominable, and murderers, and whoremongers, and sorcerers, and idolators, and all liars, shall have their part in the lake which burneth with fire and brimstone" (xxi. 8).

579. "By these three was the third part of men killed, by the fire, and by the smoke, and by the brimstone, which issued out of their mouths"—That hereby is signified that all understanding of truth, and thence spiritual life, were extinguished by them, appears from the signification of the third part of men, as denoting all intelligence or all understanding of truth, and as spiritual life is thence derived, therefore this also is involved; and from the signification of being killed, as denoting to be extinguished, for when the understanding of truth is extinguished, man is spiritually killed;* and from the signification of fire, smoke, and brimstone, issuing out of their mouths, as denoting the thoughts and thence reasonings bursting from the love of evil, from the love of what is false, and from the concupiscence of destroying truths and goods by the falsities of evil; concerning which, see above, n. 578; from these considerations it may be seen what is signified by those words. These things are said concerning the horses seen in vision, namely, that out of their mouths issued fire, smoke, and brimstone; and as by the horses seen in vision are signified the falsifications of the Word by reasonings grounded in fallacies, it is evident that by the fire, smoke, and brimstone, are signified those things which plead in excuse, which are the loves of evil and of what is false, and the concupiscences of destroying the truths and goods of the church; and this is effected by thoughts and reasonings from fallacies concerning the sense and understanding of the Word; for when man thinks only from fallacies, he thinks solely from such things as appear at first sight in the sense of the letter, and not from any interior literal sense; hence he conceives the most gross and hard ideas concerning every doctrine derived from the Word; as that God is angry, that he punishes, casts men into hell, tempts them, that he repents himself, and many other things of a like nature; besides thinking also corporeally and materially of everything that he reads in the Word, and of nothing spiritually; whence his thought is merely sensual, and being merely sensual is solely from the love of self and of the world, and hence is altogether from evils and falsities; when such a man therefore is left to himself, and thinks from his own spirit, he thinks from the affection of those loves, which he conjoins to those things which are in the Word; and when the divine things of the Word are conjoined to such loves, then all things therein are adulterated and falsified, for the divine things of the Word can never be conjoined but with celestial love or with spiritual affection, in

* As may be seen above, n. 315; that the third part, when predicated of truths denotes all, see n. 506; and that man denotes the understanding of truth and the perception of good, n. 280, 546.

any other case the superior mind, which is called the spiritual mind, is closed, and the inferior mind only, which is called the natural mind, is opened; yea, with those who conjoin the truths of the Word with the affection of the love of self the natural mind is also closed, and the ultimate of this mind only is opened, which is called the sensual principle, which inheres next to the body and is extant next to the world; hence it is, that the spirit of man becomes corporeal, which can have no lot with angels, who are spiritual.

580. "For their power is in their mouth"—That these words signify sensual thoughts, and thence reasonings, with which they very greatly prevail, appears from the signification "of their power," as denoting to prevail, in this case to prevail very greatly; and from the signification of the mouth, as denoting sensual thought and thence reasonings, for by the mouth, and by the things pertaining to it, are signified such things as pertain to the understanding and thence to thought and speech, because these correspond to the mouth; for all the organs of speech which are employed in one expression are called the mouth, as the larynx, the glottis, the throat, the tongue, the palate, the lips, are organs serviceable to the understanding for enunciation and elocution; hence it is that by the mouth is signified the thought, and thence reasonings. But whereas the thought of man is interior and exterior, namely, spiritual, natural, and sensual, therefore the thought signified by the mouth is according to the quality of the subject treated of, in this case, sensual thought, because the subject treated of is man made sensual by the falsities of evil: sensual thought is the lowest thought of all, and is material, and corporeal; in this thought are all who are in evils as to life, and thence in falsities as to doctrine, how learned and erudite soever they may be supposed to be, and however they may dress out their falsities in a beautiful series, and embellish them with elegant and eloquent discourse. That the mouth, from correspondence, thus in the spiritual sense, signifies the thought, but in the natural sense, utterance or enunciation, may appear from the following passages. Thus in David: "The mouth of the righteous speaketh wisdom" (Psalm xxxvii. 30). By the mouth is here signified thought from the affection, for thence man meditates wisdom, and not from the mouth and its speech. So in Luke: "For I will give you a mouth and wisdom, which all your adversaries shall not be able to gainsay nor resist" (xxi. 15). Here the mouth is evidently put for speech from the understanding, thus for thought from which man speaks. So in Matthew: "Not that which goeth into the mouth defileth a man; but that which cometh out of the mouth, this defileth a man. Whatsoever entereth in at the mouth goeth into the belly, and is cast out into the draught. But those things which proceed out of the mouth come forth from the heart. For out of the heart proceed evil thoughts, murders, adulteries, fornications, thefts, false witness, blasphemies" (xv. 11, 17, 18, 19). By what enters into the mouth, in the literal sense, is understood food of every kind, which, after its use in the body, goes through the belly into the draught; but, in the spiritual sense, by the things which enter into

the mouth, are understood all things which enter into the thought from the memory, and also from the world, which things also correspond to food; and those things which enter into the thought, and not at the same time into the will, do not render a man unclean, for the memory, and the thought thence derived pertaining to man are only as the entrance to him, since the will is properly the man; the things also which enter the thought and proceed no further, are rejected as it were through the belly into the draught; the belly from correspondence signifies the world of spirits, whence thoughts flow in with man, and the draught signifies hell. It is to be observed, that man cannot be purified from evils, and thence from falsities, unless the unclean things which are in him emerge even into the thought, and are there seen, acknowledged, discerned, and rejected. From these considerations it is evident, that by what enters into the mouth, is signified, in the spiritual sense, what enters into the thought from the memory and from the world; but by what comes out of the mouth, in the spiritual sense, is signified thought from the will, or from the love; for by the heart, from which it comes out into the mouth, and from the mouth, is signified the will and love of man; and inasmuch as the love and will constitute the whole man, for the quality of man is according to his love, hence those things which thence proceed into the mouth, and out of the mouth, make the man unclean; that in the heart are evils of every kind, appears from the things enumerated: thus are these words of the Lord understood in the heavens; that the heart signifies the will and love, may be seen above, n. 167. So in Isaiah: "Then flew one of the seraphims unto me, having a live coal in his hand, taken from off the altar: And he laid it upon my mouth, and said, Lo, this hath touched thy lips; and thine iniquity is taken away, and thy sin purged" (vi. 6, 7). By one of the seraphim touching the mouth and lips of the prophet with a live coal from off the altar, is signified his interior purification, which is that of the understanding and will, and thence inauguration into the gift of teaching; by the live coal from off the altar is signified the divine love, from which is all purification, and by the mouth and lips are signified the thought and affection, or what amounts to the same, the understanding and the will, by which man is purified from iniquity and removed from sin, wherefore it is said, "and thine iniquity is taken away, and thy sin purged;" that iniquity is not taken away, and that sin cannot be purged by the application of a live coal to the mouth and lips, may be plain to every one.*

581. "For their tails were like unto serpents, and had heads"— That hereby is signified, that from sensual scientifics, which are fallacies, they reason craftily, appears from the signification of tails, in this case, of the tails of horses as denoting the scientifics which are called sensual, because they are the ultimates of the understanding,

---

* That the things pertaining to the mouth correspond to things intellectual, because from them the voice and speech proceed, may be seen in the A. C. n. 8068, 9384. That from the mouth and from the heart, denotes from the understanding and from the will, n. 3313, 8068, in the same.

concerning which see above, n. 559; and from the signification of a serpent, as denoting the craftiness of the sensual man, of which we shall speak further presently; and from the signification of having heads, as denoting to reason by those scientifics; for by the head is signified intelligence, whence by having a head, is signified to be intelligent; the reason why it denotes to reason by those scientifics, is, because by the head, when predicated of the sensual man, are signified science, and thence infatuated thought, as may be seen above, n. 576, consequently also reasoning by sensual scientifics; from these considerations it may appear, that by the tails of the horses being like serpents, and having heads, is signified, that from sensual scientifics, which are fallacies, they reason craftily. It is said, that they are fallacies, because sensual scientifics become fallacies when man reasons from them concerning spiritual things; as for example, that dignities and opulence are real blessings; that glory, such as belongs to the great in the world, is that in which heavenly beatitudes consist; and that the Lord desires adoration from man for the sake of his own glory; with other things of a like nature; which are fallacies, when they are applied to things spiritual; for the sensual man, not being endued with intelligence, thus thinks, for he cannot possibly know otherwise.

That serpents, in the Word, signify the sensual man as to craftiness or subtlety, and as to prudence, is evident from the following passages. Thus in Moses: "Now the serpent was more subtle than any beast of the field which Jehovah God had made" (Gen. iii. 1). By the serpent here mentioned, is not understood a serpent, but the sensual man, and in the general sense, the sensual principle itself, which is the ultimate of the human understanding; by Adam and his wife, mentioned in the same chapter, is signified the most ancient church, which fell away when they who composed it began to reason from sensual scientifics concerning divine things, which reasoning is signified by their eating of the tree of the knowledge of good and evil: their subtlety in reasoning concerning divine things from the sensual principle, is described by the reasoning of the serpent with the wife of Adam, by which they were deceived; the reason why the serpent is said to have been more subtle than any beast of the field, is, because of his having poison, and his bite being thence deadly, also from his hiding himself in lurking places; poison signifies craft and treachery, and thence the bite of the serpent, deadly hurt; and the lurking places from which he bites, and in which he conceals himself, signify subtleties. It is to be observed, that all beasts signify affections, such as pertain to man, and serpents signify the affections of the sensual man, by reason of their creeping on the belly upon the ground, in like manner as the sensual principle of man, for this is in the lowest place, and as it were creeps upon the ground under all other principles: sensual men also, in the spiritual world, dwell in the lower parts, for they cannot be elevated towards the superior, since they are in externals, and judge and conclude of everything from externals. The evil also, who are in the hells, are mostly sensual, and many of them subtle, wherefore when they are viewed from the light of heaven, they appear as serpents of various kinds, and hence it is, that the devil is called a serpent: the reason why the infernals are also crafty or subtle, is, because evil conceals in itself all subtlety and malice, as good does all prudence and wisdom; concerning this subject more may be seen in the work concerning H. & H. n. 576–581, where the malice and wicked arts of infernal spirits are treated of. Hence now it is that the devil or hell is called a serpent in the following passages. Thus in the Revelations: "And the great dragon was cast out, that old serpent called the Devil, and Satan, which deceiveth the whole world" (xii. 9, 14, 15). And in David: "They have sharpened their tongues like a serpent; adder's poison is under their lips" (Psalm cxl. 3). By these words is signified their subtle and treacherous deception. Again: "Their poison is like the poison of a serpent" (Psalm lviii. 4). And in Job: "He shall suck the poison of asps: the viper's tongue shall slay him" (xx. 16). And in Isaiah: "They hatch cockatrice eggs, and weave the spider's web: he that eateth of their eggs dieth, and that which is crushed breaketh out into a viper" (lix. 5). This is said concerning evil men, who by treachery and craft seduce others in spiritual affairs; the clandestine evils to which they allure by their craftiness, are signified by the eggs of the cockatrice, which they are said to hatch; their treacherous falsities are signified by the spider's web which they are said to weave; the deadly hurt which they effect, if they are received, is signified by "he that eateth of their eggs dieth, and that which is crushed breaketh out into a viper." Inasmuch as the Pharisees were of such a quality therefore they are called by the Lord, "serpents, a generation of vipers" (Matt. xxiii. 33). That the subtlety and malice of such could do no hurt to those whom the Lord protects, is signified by the following words in Isaiah: "And the sucking child shall play on the hole of the asp, and the weaned child shall put his hand on the cockatrice' den" (xi. 8). In these words, by the sucking child and the weaned child are signified those who are in the good of innocence, namely, those that are principled in love to the Lord; and by the hole of the asp and the den of the cockatrice, are understood the hells in which are the spirits who are distinguished for their treachery and subtlety, the entrances into which also appear as dark holes, and within, as dens. That the subtlety and malice of infernal spirits should not hurt those whom the Lord protects, is also signified by these words of the Lord to his disciples: "Behold, I give unto you power to tread on serpents and scorpions, and over all the power of the enemy" (Luke x. 19). And again: "They shall take up serpents; and if they drink any deadly thing, it shall not hurt them" (Mark xvi. 18). By their having power tread on serpents, is signified that they should be enabled to despise and make light of the treacheries, subtleties, and wicked arts, of the infernal crew, wherefore it is also said, "and over all the power of the enemy," the enemy denoting the infernal crew, and his power denoting craftiness. The malice and subtleties of the infernal spirits, who, taken together, are called the devil and satan, are also understood by serpents in the following passages. Thus in Moses : " Who led thee through that great and terrible wilderness, wherein were fiery serpents, and scorpions" (Deut. viii. 15). By the journeyings of the children of Israel in the wilderness, were represented, and thence signified, the temptations of the faithful; the infestations which then take place from the hells by evil spirits and genii, are signified by the serpents, fiery serpents and scorpions. Again in Isaiah: " Rejoice not thou, whole Palestina, because the rod of him that smote thee is broken: for out of the serpent's root shall come forth a cockatrice, and his fruit shall be a fiery flying serpent" (xiv. 29). By Palestina is here signified faith separate from charity; the seduction of many by the sophistries by which that faith is confirmed, is signified by " out of the serpent's root shall come forth a cockatrice, and his fruit shall be a flying fiery serpent." Again in Jeremiah : " For, behold, I will send serpents, cockatrices among you, which will not be charmed, and they shall bite you" (viii. 17). Again: " The voice thereof shall go like a serpent" (xlvi. 22). And in Amos: " And though they be hid from my sight in the bottom of the sea, thence will I command the serpent, and he shall bite them" (ix. 3). The subtleties here treated of are also signified in Isaiah by " Leviathan that crooked serpent" (xxvii. 1). That by serpents, in the Word, is signified subtlety, and also the prudence of the sensual man, is evident from the words of the Lord in Matthew: " Be ye wise as serpents and harmless as doves" (x. 16). They are called wise or prudent who are principled in good, and they are called subtle who are principled in evil, for prudence is of truth derived from good, and subtlety is of the falsity derived from evil ; and since these words were spoken to those who were in truths derived from good, therefore by serpents, as here mentioned, is understood prudence. Inasmuch as the subtleties of the evil are diabolical, they who are principled in them are said to eat the dust. Thus in Moses: " And Jehovah God said unto the serpent, Thou art cursed above all cattle, and above every beast of the field; upon thy belly shalt thou go, and dust shalt thou eat all the days of thy life" (Gen. iii. 14). And in Isaiah: " And dust shall be the serpent's meat" (lxv. 25). And in Micah: " They shall lick the dust like a serpent" (vii. 17). By dust is signified what is cursed ; and by walking upon the belly is signified the sensual principle, which is the ultimate of the life of man, and since it is the ultimate of the life, it is therefore in no intelligence and wisdom, but in subtlety and malice, which are contrary to intelligence and wisdom. Again, in Moses: " Dan shall be a serpent by the way, an adder in the path, that biteth the horse heels, so that his rider shall fall backwards" (Gen. xlix. 17). The signification of this prophecy concerning Dan cannot be known to any one unless he understand what is signified by a horse and his heels, likewise what by a serpent; by a horse is signified the understanding of truth, and by a rider intelligence ; by a serpent is signified the sensual principle, which is the ultimate of the intellectual life; by the heels of a horse are signified truths in the ultimates, which are sen-

sual scientifics; that the sensual principle, by reasonings from fallacies, hurts and seduces the understanding, is signified by the serpent biting the heels of the horse, and the horseman falling backwards: these things are said concerning Dan, because the tribe named
from him was the last of the tribes, and thence signified the ultimates
of truth and good, consequently the ultimates of the church, concerning which, see A. C. n. 1710, 3923, 6396, 10,335, where this prophecy is explained. The sensual principle, which is the ultimate
of the intellectual life, is also signified by the crooked serpent, in
Isaiah xxvii. 1; Job xxvi. 13; also by the serpent into which the
rod of Moses was turned (Exod. iv. 3, 4; vii. 9–12), as may be seen
in the A. C. n. 6949, 7293. The sensual things also, which are
the ultimates of the life of man, are signified by the fiery serpents
sent amongst the people, who desired to return to Egypt; but the
healing of the bite of such serpents by the divine sensual principle
of the Lord, is signified by the brazen serpent, placed upon a pole,
by looking at which they revived (Numb. xxi. 5–9): it is said the
divine sensual principle of the Lord, because the Lord, when he was
in the world, glorified, that is made divine, his whole humanity,
even to the ultimate thereof, as may appear from this circumstance,
that he left nothing in the sepulchre, and that he said unto his disciples, "A spirit hath not flesh and bones, as ye see me have" (Luke
xxiv. 39). The ultimate sensual principle, which the Lord also
glorified or made divine, is signified by the brazen serpent set upon
a pole, concerning which the Lord himself thus spake in John:
"And as Moses lifted up the serpent in the wilderness, even so must
the Son of man be lifted up: That whosoever believeth in him should
not perish, but have eternal life" (iii. 14, 15). The Lord was represented by this sign before the Israelitish and Jewish people, because they were merely sensual, and the sensual man cannot elevate
his thought, in looking to the Lord, beyond and above the sensual
principle; for every one looks at the Lord according to the elevation of his understanding, the spiritual man looks to the divine rational principle, and so on: from these considerations it is evident,
that by the brazen serpent is also signified the sensual principle, but
the glorified or divine sensual principle of the Lord.

582. "And with them they do hurt"—That hereby is signified
that thus they pervert the truths and goods of the church, appears
from the signification of hurting, as denoting to pervert the truths
and goods of the church by subtle reasonings from sensual scientifics
or fallacies; for by the horses seen in the vision, concerning whose
tails these things are said, are signified falsifications of the Word by
reasonings from fallacies, as may be seen above, n. 574. From the
horses thus seen by John in the vision, the nature and quality of
representative appearances in heaven may be readily understood,
namely, that affections there, when they are represented by animals,
are exhibited to view in the forms of such animals as appear in our
world, but still everywhere with variety as to their members, especially as to the countenance, the most minute particulars of which,
by virtue of correspondence, signify various things of the affection

thus represented; as, in the present case, that horses were seen, whose heads were as the heads of lions, and their tails like those of serpents, having heads, and that those who sat upon the horses, had breast-plates which were fiery, blue, and sulphureous. Animals continually appear in the spiritual world in various forms, and have also been frequently seen by me; and by the knowledge of correspondences, it is there known what they each signify: for all the affections which flow from angelic minds, are imaged before their eyes by animals of every kind which is on the earth, in the air and in the sea; likewise also by the subjects of all things which are in the vegetable kingdom of the earth, and by the subjects of all things which are in the mineral kingdom of the earth; hence it is, that such things in our world were made representative of celestial and spiritual things. The reason why such representatives exist in the spiritual world, is, because in that world there are spiritual things interior and exterior; interior spiritual things are those that relate to affection, and to thought thence derived, or to the intelligence of truth, and the wisdom of good; and exterior spiritual things are so created by the Lord, that they may clothe or invest interior spiritual things, and when these are clothed and invested, there then exists such forms as are in the natural world, in which, therefore, interior spiritual things ultimately terminate, and in which they ultimately exist.

583. Verses 20, 21. " And the rest of the men who were not killed by these plagues, yet repented not of the works of their hands, that they should not worship demons, and idols of gold, and silver, and brass, and stone, and of wood; which neither can see, nor hear, nor walk: Neither repented they of their murders, nor of their sorceries, nor of their fornications, nor of their thefts."—" And " And the rest of the men who were not killed by these plagues," signifies those who did not perish by the cupidities above mentioned: " yet repented not of the works of their hands," signifies, who have not actually averted themselves from such things as are of the proprium: " that they should not worship demons," signifies, that they should not worship their own cupidities: " and idols of gold, and silver, and brass, and stone, and wood," signifies false doctrines which are from self-derived intelligence, favoring the loves of the body and of the world, and the principles thence conceived: "which neither can see, nor hear, nor walk," signifies, in which and from which there is nothing of the understanding of truth and perception of good, and thus nothing of spiritual life; " Neither repented they of their murders," signifies, who have not actually averted themselves from extinguishing those things which pertain to the understanding of truth, to the will of good, and thence to spiritual life: " nor of their sorceries, nor of their fornications," signifies from perverting good, and falsifying truth: " nor of their thefts," signifies from taking away the knowledges of truth and good, and thereby the means of procuring for themselves spiritual life.

584. " And the rest of the men who were not killed by these plagues"—That hereby is signified, who have not perished from the

cupidities above mentioned, appears from the signification of the rest of the men who were not killed, as denoting all those who did not perish; that to be killed, in the Word, signifies to be spiritually killed, which is to perish in eternal death, may be seen above, n. 547, 572; and from the signification of these plagues, as denoting the cupidities above mentioned, namely, the cupidities arising from the love of evil, and the love of what is false, likewise the concupiscence of destroying the truths and goods of the church by the falsities of evil, all which are signified by the fire, smoke, and brimstone, issuing out of the mouth of the horses, as may be seen above, n. 578; these are called plagues, because by plagues in the Word, are signified such things as destroy spiritual life with men, and consequently the church, and, of course, the things which induce death, understood in a spiritual sense, which in general have reference to the cupidities arising from the loves of self and of the world; for these loves are the roots from which evils and falsities of every genus and species bud forth and are born.

Such things are also signified by plagues in the following passages in the Revelation: "These have power over waters to turn them to blood, and to smite the earth with all the plagues as often as they will" (xi. 6). So again: "And men blasphemed God because of the plague of the hail; for the plague thereof was exceeding great" (xvi. 21). And again: "Therefore shall her plagues come in one day, death, and mourning, and famine" (xviii. 8). And again: "And I saw seven angels having the seven last plagues; for in them is filled up the wrath of God" (xv. 1). That by plagues are understood such things as induce upon men spiritual death, consequently, which altogether destroy and devastate the church with man individually, and thus generally, will be seen in the places where plagues are mentioned in the following chapter, and especially where the seven last plagues are treated of. Similar things are understood by plagues in the following passages in the prophets. Thus in Isaiah: "Moreover the light of the moon shall be as the light of the sun, and the light of the sun shall be seven fold, as the light of seven days, in the day that Jehovah bindeth up the breach of his people, and healeth the stroke of their plague" (xxx. 26). And in Jeremiah: "For thus saith Jehovah, thy bruise is incurable, and thy plague is grievous. For I have wounded thee with the wound of an enemy. I will restore health unto thee, and I will heal thee of thy plagues" (xxx. 12, 14, 17). Again, in the same prophet: "Also Edom shall be a desolation: every one that goeth by it shall hiss at all the plagues thereof" (xlix. 17). Again: "Every one that goeth by Babylon shall hiss at all her plagues" (l. 13). And in Moses: If thou will not observe to do all the words of this law; then Jehovah will make thy plagues wonderful, even great plagues, and of long continuance and sore sickness, and of long continuance. Also every sickness, and every plague, which is not written in the book of this law, them will Jehovah bring upon thee, until thou be destroyed" (Deut. xxviii. 58–61). By the plagues here mentioned are signified spiritual plagues, which do not destroy the body, but the soul, and which are enumerated in the chapter whence the above passages are quoted (verse 20–68). What plagues signify in the spiritual sense, is thus described by corespondences in Zechariah: "And this shall be the plague wherewith Jehovah will smite all the people that have fought against Jerusalem; Their flesh shall consume away while they stand upon their feet, and their eyes shall consume away in their holes, and their tongue shall consume away in their mouth. And so shall be the plague of the horse, of the mule, of the camel, and of the ass, and of all the beasts that shall be in these tents, as this plague" (xiv. 12, 15). These things are said concerning those who endeavor to destroy the truths of the church by falsities; Jerusalem signifies the church as to the truths of doctrine, and to fight against it denotes to endeavor to destroy those truths by falsities; their flesh being consumed away while they stand on their feet, signifies, that with those who attempt this, all the will of good will perish, and that thus they shall become merely corporeal natural, for flesh signifies the will and its good or evil, and feet signify the things of the natural man, whence to stand upon the feet signifies to live from them alone: their eyes being consumed away in their holes signifies, that all understanding of truth shall perish, eyes signifying that understanding; and by their tongue being consumed away in their mouth, is signified, that all perception of truth and affection of good shall perish; this passage may be seen more fully explained above, n. 455. Things nearly similar are signified by the plague of the horse, the mule, the camel, the ass, and every beast, for by the plague of these is signified the loss of all understanding of truth, both spiritual and natural; and by the plague of the beast is signified the loss of all the affection of good. The same is evident from the miracles performed by Jesus when John sent two of his disciples to ask him if he was the promised Messiah: "In the same hour he cured many of their infirmities and plagues, and of evil spirits; and unto many that were blind he gave sight" (Luke vii. 21). By the plagues here mentioned are obviously to be understood obsessions, and calamitous states at that time inflicted upon men by evil spirits, which nevertheless all signified correspondent spiritual states; for all the healings of diseases performed by the Lord signified spiritual healings, and hence the miracles of the Lord were divine; as this, that he gave sight to many blind, which signified to give those who were in ignorance of truth to understand the truths of doctrine. So again, by the wounds, or plagues, which the thieves inflicted on the man who went down from Jerusalem to Jericho (Luke x. 30), are also signified spiritual plagues, which were the falsities and evils infused into sojourners and Gentiles by the scribes and pharisees, as may be seen above, n. 444, where this parable is explained as to the spiritual sense.

585. "Yet repented not of the works of their hands"—That hereby is signified who have not actually averted themselves from such things as are of the proprium, appears from the signification of repenting as denoting to turn away actually from evil, concerning which we shall speak presently; and from the signification of the

works of their hands, as denoting such things as man thinks, wills, and does, from the proprium; that those things are signified by the works of the hands, will appear from the passages in the Word, which will be adduced presently; also from this consideration, that works are those things which are of the will, and thence of the understanding, or which are of the love and thence of the faith; as may be seen explained above, n. 98; and that hands signify power, and their hands their own proper power, thus also whatever proceeds from the proprium of man. With respect to the proprium of man, it is to be observed, that it is nothing but evil, and what is false thence derived; the will proprium is evil, and the intellectual proprium thence derived is falsity; and this proprium man derives principally from parents, grandfathers, and great grandfathers, in a long series back, so that at length the hereditary nature, which is his proprium, is nothing but evil successively heaped together and condensed; for every man is born into two diabolical loves, namely, the love of self, and the love of the word, from which loves all evils and falsities flow, as from their own fountains; and inasmuch as man is born into those loves, he is also born into evils of every kind; concerning which more may be seen in the D. of the N. J. n. 65–83. Inasmuch as man, as to his proprium, is of such a nature, the Lord, in his divine mercy, has provided means by which he may be removed from it; these means are furnished in the Word; and when man acts in accordance with them, that is, when he thinks and speaks, wills and acts, from the divine Word, then he is kept by the Lord in things divine, and thus is withheld from his proprium; and as he perseveres in this, a new proprium as it were, as well voluntary as intellectual, is formed in him by the Lord, which is altogether separated from his own proprium; thus man is as it were created anew, and this is what is called his reformation and regeneration by truths from the Word, and by a life according to them; on this subject more may be seen in the D. of the N. J. in the article concerning remission of sins, n. 159–172, and concerning regeneration, n. 173–186. That to perform repentance is actually to avert oneself from evils, may be evident to any one, since the quality of every man is according to his life, and the life of man principally consists in willing and thence acting; from which it follows, that repentance, which is of the thought alone, and thence of the mouth, and not at the same time of the will and thence of the act, is not repentance, for in this case the life remains of the same quality afterwards as it was before; hence it is evident, that to perform repentence is actually to avert oneself from evils, and to enter upon a new life; concerning which, see the D. of the N. J. n. 159–172. That the works of the hand signify such things as a man thinks, wills, and does, from the proprium, may appear from the following passages in the Word: "Provoke me not to anger with the works of your hands; and I will do you no hurt. Yet ye have not hearkened unto me, saith Jehovah: that ye might provoke me to anger with the works of your hands to your own hurt. For many nations and great kings shall serve themselves of them also : and I will recompense them according to their deeds, and according to the works of their own hands" (Jeremiah xxv. 6, 7, 14). In these passages, by the work of their hands, and by their deeds, are understood, in a proximate sense, their molten images and idols, but, in the spiritual sense, by the work of their hands, are signified, all the evil and falsity which result from the love and intelligence originating in the proprium; by molten images and idols, which are called the works of their hands, the same things are also signified, as will be seen in what follows, when we come to treat of the signification of idols. Inasmuch as the proprium of man is nothing but evil, thus against the Divine Being, therefore it is said, "and provoke me not to anger with the works of your hands; and I will do you no hurt," to provoke God to anger signifying to be against him, whence man has evil; and since as all evils and falsities are from man's proprium, therefore it is said, "For many nations and great kings shall serve themselves of them," by which is signified, that evils from which are falsities, and falsities from which are evils, shall occupy them, many nations denoting evils from which falsities are derived, and great kings denoting falsities from which evils are derived. Again, in the same prophet: "For the children of Israel have only provoked me to anger with the work of their own hands" (xxxii. 30). And again : "In that ye provoke me unto wrath with the works of your own hands, burning incense unto other gods in the land of Egypt" (xliv. 8). By the works of their hands, in the spiritual sense, is here understood worship from falsities of doctrine, which are from self-derived intelligence, such worship being signified by burning incense to other gods in the land of Egypt, for to burn incense denotes worship, other gods denote falsities of doctrine, and the land of Egypt denotes the natural principle, in which the proprium of man resides, and consequently whence comes self-derived intelligence; thus is this passage of the Word understood in heaven. And again : "I will utter my judgments against them touching their wickedness who have forsaken me, and have burned incense unto other gods, and worshiped the works of their own hands" (i. 16). Here also by burning incense unto other gods, and worshiping them, is signified worship from falsities of doctrine, and by worshiping the works of their own hands, is signified worship from such things as are from self-derived intelligence; and that they are derived from the proprium, and not from the divine being, is signified by "who have forsaken me." Thus also in Isaiah : "At that day shall a man look to his Maker, and his eyes shall have respect to the Holy One of Israel. And he shall not look to the altars, the work of his hands, neither shall respect that which his fingers have made" (xvii. 7, 8). This is spoken concerning the advent of the Lord, and the new church to be then established; by his Maker, to whom it is said a man shall at that day look, is understood the Lord as to divine good, and by the Holy One of Israel, to whom his eyes shall have respect, is understood the Lord as to divine truth; by the altars, the work of his hands, to which it is said he shall not look, neither have

respect, is signified worship from evils, and thence from falsities of
doctrine originating in self-derived intelligence; hence by these
words is understood, that the all of doctrine shall be from the Lord,
and not from the proprium of man, which is the case when man is in
the spiritual affection of truth, that is, when he loves truth for its
own sake, and not from regard to his own reputation and name.
Again, in the same prophet: "O Jehovah, the kings of Assyria
have laid waste all the nations, and have cast their gods into the
fire: for they were no gods, but the work of men's hands, wood and
stone" (xxxvii. 18, 19). Here by the gods of the kings of Assyria
are signified reasonings from falsities and evils, which agree with
the proprium of man, and are therefore styled the work of his hands;
wood and stone, or idols of wood and stone, signify the evils and
falsities of religion, and of doctrine originating in the proprium.
Again: "In that day every man shall cast away his idols of silver,
and his idols of gold, which your own hands have made unto you
for a sin. Then shall the Assyrian fall" (xxxi. 7, 8). This passage
relates to the restoration of the church; and by the idols of silver,
and the idols of gold, which they shall in that day cast away, are
signified the falsities and evils of religion and of worship, which they
call truths and goods; and since the falsities and evils of religion
and of worship are from self-derived intelligence, therefore it is
said, which your hands have made unto you; that there shall then
be no reasonings from such things, is signified by "then shall the
Assyrian fall." Again, in Jeremiah: "Silver spread into plates is
brought from Tarshish, and gold from Uphaz, the work of the workman, and of the hands of the founder: blue and purple is their
clothing: they are all the work of cunning men" (x. 9). By these
words are described the falsity and evil of religion and of worship
which are confirmed from the literal sense of the Word; silver spread
into plates from Tarshish, signifies the truths of the Word in that
sense, and gold from Uphaz signifies the good of the Word in that
sense; and inasmuch as those falsities and evils are from self-derived
intelligence, they are called the work of the workman, and of the
hands of the founder; the truth of good also, and the good of truth,
from the literal sense of the Word, by which they confirm, and as it
were invest, the falsities of evil and the evils of what is false, which
are from self-derived intelligence, are signified by the blue and
purple of the raiment, all the work of cunning men. Moreover, by
the work of the smith, the artificer, and the workman, in the Word,
is also signified such a principle of doctrine, religion, and worship,
as originates in self-derived intelligence; hence it was, that the
altar, and also the temple, were, by command, built of entire stones,
and not hewn by any workman or artificer. Respecting the altar it
is thus commanded in Moses: "And if thou wilt make me an altar
of stone, thou shalt not build it of hewn stone: for if thou lift up thy
tool upon it, thou hast polluted it" (Exod. xx. 25). And in Joshua:
"Then Joshua built an altar unto Jehovah God of Israel in Mount
Ebal, an altar of whole stones, over which no man hath lift up any
iron" (viii. 30, 31). Again, concerning the temple of Jeru   ʓ

is said in the first book of Kings: "And the house was built of stone made ready before it was brought thither: so that there was neither hammer, nor axe, nor any tool of iron heard in the house while it was in building" (vi. 7). The altar, and afterwards the temple, were in an especial manner representative of the Lord as to divine good and divine truth, wherefore, by the stones of which they were built, were signified the truths of doctrine, of religion, and of worship, stones in the Word also denoting truths; that nothing of self-derived intelligence should accede to the truths of doctrine and worship thence derived, and consequently be therein, was represented by the stones being entire, and not hewn, of which the temple and the altar were built; for by the work of the workman, and of the artificer, was signified such intelligence; by the tools also, as the hammer and the axe, and by iron in general, is signified truth in its ultimate, and this is especially falsified by the proprium of man, for this truth is the same with the truth of the literal sense of the Word. These things are said concerning the signification of the works of the hands of man; but where works of the hands, in the Word, are attributed to Jehovah, that is, to the Lord, they signify the reformed or regenerate man, likewise the church, and, specifically, the doctrine of truth and good pertaining to the church. These things are signified by works of the hands in the following passages. Thus in David: "The works of his hands are verity and judgment" (Psalm cxi. 7). Again: "Jehovah will perfect that which concerneth me: thy mercy, O Jehovah, endureth for ever: forsake not the works of thine own hands" (Psalm cxxxviii. 8). And in Isaiah: "Thy people shall be all righteous: they shall inherit the land forever, the branch of my planting, the work of my hands, that I may be glorified" (lx. 21). Again, in the same prophet: "But now, O Jehovah, thou art our father: we are the clay, and thou our potter; and we all are the work of thy hand" (lxiv. 8). And again: "Woe unto him that striveth with his Maker! Let the potsherd strive with the potsherds of the earth. Shall the clay say to him that fashioneth it, What makest thou? or thy work, He hath no hands? Thus saith Jehovah, the Holy One of Israel, and his maker, Ask me of things to come concerning my sons, and concerning the work of my hands command ye me" (xlv. 9, 11). That by Jehovah the holy one of Israel, and his maker, the Lord is understood, is evident from what follows in verse 13; and by the work of his hands is understood the man who is regenerated by him, thus the man of the church. And again: "Whom Jehovah of hosts shall bless, saying, Blessed be Egypt my people, and Assyria the work of my hands, and Israel mine inheritance" (xix. 25). Egypt here signifies the natural principle, Assyria the rational, and Israel the spiritual; and Assyria is called the work of the hands of Jehovah, because this principle is what is reformed in man, for the rational is that which receives truths and goods, and from this the natural; the spiritual principle is what regenerates, that is, the Lord by spiritual influx; in a word, the rational is the medium between the spiritual and the natural, and the spiritual, which regenerates, flows in by the rational

into the natural, and thus the latter is regenerated. Again, in
Moses: "Bless, Jehovah, his substance, and accept the work of
his hands" (Deut. xxxiii. 11). This is spoken of Levi, by whom is
signified the good of charity, and, in the supreme sense, the Lord as
to that good; reformation thereby is understood by the work of his
hands.

586. "That they should not worship demons"—That hereby is
signified that they should not worship their own cupidities, appears
from the signification of worshiping, and from the signification of
demons, as denoting evil cupidities. The reason why demons denote evil cupidities, is, because by demons are understood infernal
spirits, and all spirits who are in the hells are nothing but evil cupidities; for all spirits who are in the hells and all the angels who
are in the heavens, are from the human race, and every man after
death becomes such as was the quality of his life in the world, consequently the quality of his affection; so that after death man is
altogether his own affection, the good man the affection of good and
truth, and the evil man the affection of evil and of what is false;
every man, also, after death, thinks, wills, speaks, and acts, according to his own affection: the affection of evil, and of what is false,
is what is called cupidity, and is signified by a demon. But what
is understood by worshiping demons, shall also briefly be explained:
every man is in consort with spirits, for without such consort and
conjunction no one can live, and the spirits attendant on man are in
accordance with the quality of his affections or cupidities; wherefore when man, in his worship, has not respect to the Lord or to
his neigbbor, but to himself and to the world, that is, when he worships God for the sole end of being exalted to honors, and of gain-
ing wealth, or that he may do injury to others, he worships demons,
for the Lord is not present in his worship, but infernal spirits are
present, who are consociated with him; with these spirits also such
madness prevails, that they believe themselves to be gods, and that
they are worshiped; for every spirit, as well as every man, who is
in the love of self, seeks to be worshiped as a god, and hence it
is that such mad cupidity resides with men after death, when they
become demon-spirits; this, therefore, is what is signified by worshiping demons.

This worship is also understood by sacrificing to devils. Thus
in Moses: "They provoked him to jealousy with strange gods,
with abominations provoked they him to anger. They sacrificed to
devils, not to God; to gods whom they knew not" (Deut. xxxii.
16, 17). Again: "And they shall no more offer their sacrifices unto devils, after whom they have gone a whoring" (Levit. xvii. 7).
The sacrifices which were offered at the door of the tent represented
the worship of the Lord, because the altar, and also the tabernacle,
represented heaven, where the Lord is present; but the sacrifices
which they offered elsewhere, represented worship where the Lord
is not present, thus the worship of demons: for all things at that
time were representative. So in David: "They sacrificed their
sons and their daughters unto devils" (Psalm cvi. 36, 37). This

was altogether infernal; but, in the spiritual sense, by sacrificing their sons and daughters, was signified, their evil cupidities to pervert and destroy the truths and goods of the church; for sons signify the truths of the church, and daughters, the goods thereof. So in Isaiah : " The wild beasts of the desert shall also meet with the wild beasts of the island, and the demon shall cry to his fellow; the screech owl shall also rest there, and find for herself a place of rest" (xxxiv. 14). Here the subject treated of is the total devastation of the church, by corporeal and merely natural concupiscences, from which flow forth evils and falsities of every kind; those concupiscences are signified by wild beasts of the desert, likewise by the owl and demon of the wood, or satyr. Again, in like manner: "But wild beasts of the desert shall lie there; and their houses shall be full of doleful creatures; and owls shall dwell there, and demons shall dance there" (xiii. 21). These things are spoken concerning Babylon; that such merely natural and corporeal concupiscences appertain to those who are understood by Babylon, and constitute the life of their mind, is signified by their houses being filled with such things, and by their dwelling and dancing there: by house is signified the mind of man, with the things therein contained; by owls are signified falsities, and by the demons or satyrs, cupidities merely corporeal. Similar language is used respecting Babylon in the Revelation : " Babylon is become the habitation of devils, and the hold of every foul spirit, and a cage of every unclean and hateful bird " (xviii. 2). By the demons cast out by the Lord, by which many were then obsessed, are signified falsities of every kind, with which the church was infested, and from which it was liberated by the Lord (as in Matt. viii. 16, 28; ix. 32, 33; x. 8; xii. 22; xv. 22; Mark i. 32, 34; Luke iv. 33, 36; viii. 2, 26, 40; ix. 1, 37, 42, 49; xiii. 32, and elsewhere).

587. " And idols of gold, and silver, and brass, and stone, and wood"—That hereby are signified false doctrines, which are from self-derived intelligence, favoring the loves of the body and of the world, and the principles thence conceived, appears from the signification of idols, as denoting falsities of doctrine, of religion, and of worship, which are from self-derived intelligence. But what idols of gold, silver, brass, stone, and wood, especially signify, will be seen from the signification of gold, silver brass, stone, and wood; by gold is signified spiritual good, by silver, spiritual truth, by brass, natural good, by stone, natural truth, and by wood, sensual good: all these goods and truths enter into genuine doctrine, because it is drawn both from the spiritual and natural sense of the Word. When a false doctrine is confirmed by the spiritual things of the Word, it then becomes an idol of gold and an idol of silver; but when it is confirmed by the natural things of the Word, namely, such as are in the sense of the letter, it then becomes an idol of brass and stone; and when it is confirmed by the mere sense of the letter, it becomes an idol of wood; for the sense of the Word, as well the interior or spiritual, as the exterior or natural, may be applied to confirm falsities, as is evident from the innumerable heresies which are all

thence confirmed. Confirmations of falsities take place in consequence of the genuine sense of the Word not being understood; and the reason of this is, because the loves of man's proprium bear rule, and thereby the principles thence conceived; and when these bear rule, man sees nothing from the light of heaven, but everything from the light of the world, separate from the light of heaven; and when the light of the world is separated from the light of heaven, then thick darkness takes place in things of a spiritual nature. It is to be observed, that the children of Israel brought with them from Egypt, and also from the nations, the filthy custom of worshiping idols; and as they were merely external men, they had that worship also implanted in them from natural inclination, as may appear from the idolatries of so many of the kings of Judah and Israel related in the Word, and also from the idolatry of Solomon himself, who was the wisest of those kings; but still the idols which they made for themselves, and which they worshiped, where they are mentioned in the Word signify, in the spiritual sense, false doctrines from self-derived intelligence, from which, and according to which worship is performed. This signification of idols also derives its cause from the spiritual world; for there the evil spirits, who frame for themselves false doctrines, appear as it were to form idols, and mark them with various characters, until they appear as in the human form; they also make selections from various representatives, and unite them so as to cohere, and thus produce a semblance of that form in things external. I have been permitted to see the formation of such idols by the leaders of the church, who have persuaded themselves that falsities were truths; and as they excelled in ingenuity, they knew how to connect, and afterwards to invest, the most minute particulars, which they do with great industry: such an idol I have seen made by the English, by which they represented faith alone to be essential to salvation, producing the goods of charity, without any co-operation of man. The reason why idols are formed in the spiritual world by those who are in false doctrines originating in self-derived intelligence, is, because divine truths, from which the genuine doctrine of the church is derived, induce upon angels the human form, wherefore also angels, in the Word, signify divine truths; hence it is, that false doctrines, which are confirmed from the Word, are exhibited as idols in the human form; the truths of the Word, which are falsified, and which they use for confirmations, induce that form, but inasmuch as the truths are falsified, an idol is exhibited, which has not any life.

That idols, graven and molten images, signify the falsities of doctrine, of religion, and of worship, is plain from numerous passages in the Word. Thus in Isaiah: "The workman melteth a graven image, and the goldsmith spreadeth it over with gold, and casteth silver chains. He that is so impoverished that he hath no oblation, chooseth a tree that will not rot; he seeketh unto him a cunning workman to prepare a graven image, that shall not be moved" (xl. 19, 20). By these words is described the manner in which doctrine is forged and compacted by falsities, thus by such things as are from self-derived intelligence, for they are all falsities; by the workman that melteth the image, the goldsmith that spreadeth it over with gold, and the cunning workman who prepares it, is understood one who feigns and forms such doctrine; that it may appear as good in the external form, is signified by covering it over with gold; that falsities may cohere and appear as truths, is signified by casting chains of silver; that so it may be acknowledged, and the falsity not be seen, is signified by choosing a tree that will not rot, and by preparing a graven image that shall not be moved. So in Jeremiah: " Every man is brutish in his knowledge; every founder is confounded by the graven image: for his molten image is falsehood, and there is no breath in them. They are vanity, and the work of errors: in the time of their visitation they shall perish" (x. 13, 14; li. 17, 18). Inasmuch as a graven image signifies the falsity of doctrine, of religion, and of worship, therefore it is said, " every man is brutish in his knowledge, every founder is confounded by the graven image," by the knowledge by which man becomes brutish is signified self-derived intelligence, and the falsity thence derived is signified by the graven image; the same falsity is also understood by the molten image being a falsehood, vanity, and the work of errors: that there is no spiritual life in falsities, or in those things which are from self-derived intelligence, is understood by there being no breath in them; for life is solely in divine truths, or in truths which are from the Lord, as he himself teaches when he says: " The words that I speak unto you, they are spirit, and they are life" (John vi. 63). Again, in Jeremiah: " For one cutteth a tree out of the forest, the work of the hands of the workman, with an axe. They deck it with silver and with gold; and fasten it with nails and with hammers, that it move not. They are upright as the palm-tree, but they speak not: they must needs be borne, because they cannot go. But they are altogether brutish and foolish: the stock is a doctrine of vanities. Silver spread into plates is brought from Tarshish, and gold from Uphaz, the work of the workman, and of the hands of the founder: blue and purple is their clothing: they are all the work of cunning men. But Jehovah is the true God, he is the living God, and an everlasting king" (x. 3–10). That by the graven image here treated of, is understood the falsity of doctrine, of religion, and of worship, ingeniously feigned and formed by self-derived intelligence, appears from everything contained in the description when viewed in the spiritual sense; thus self-derived intelligence, by which the image is cut out and formed, is signified by the work of the hands of the workman, with the axe, and the work of the workman, and the hands of the founder, also by the work of cunning men; that these things signify what is from self-derived intelligence, was shown in the preceding article: the falsities thence derived are signified by their being altogether brutish, and the stock a doctrine of vanities; that they have no life is signified by their being upright as the palm tree, and by their being able neither to speak nor to go, to speak and to go denoting to live, and to live signifying to live spiritually: confirmations from the Word are signified by silver spread into plates brought from Tarshish, and by gold from Uphaz, also by the clothing of blue and purple: by silver from Tarshish are signified the truths of the Word, and by gold from Uphaz the goods of the Word, both falsified, so in like manner the blue and the purple ; that all the truth of doctrine, of religion, and of worship, is from Jehovah, that is from the Lord, is understood by "Jehovah is the true God, he is the living God, and an everlasting king," for from divine truth the Lord is called God, also the living God, and a king.   Again, in Isaiah : " They that make a graven image are all of them vanity : and their delectable things shall not profit ; and they are their own witnesses; they see not, nor know.   Behold, all his fellows shall be ashamed : and the workman.   The smith with the tongs both worketh in the coals, and fashioneth it with hammers, and worketh it with the strength of his arms : yea, he is hungry, and his strength faileth : he drinketh no water, and is faint. The carpenter stretcheth out his rule : he marketh it out with a line ; he fitteth it with planes, and he marketh it out with the compass, and maketh it after the figure of a man, according to the beauty of a man ; that it may remain in the house.   He heweth him down cedars, and taketh the cypress and the oak.   Then shall it be for a man to burn : for he will take thereof, and warm himself; yea, he kindleth it, and baketh bread ; yea, he maketh a god, and worshipeth it ; he maketh it a graven image, and falleth down thereto. They have not known nor understood ; for he hath shut their eyes, that they cannot see ; and their hearts that they cannot understand. And none considereth in his heart, neither is there knowledge nor understanding to say, Is there not a lie in my right hand ?" (xliv. 9–20.)   By the whole of this description of the graven image is understood the formation of doctrine from self-derived intelligence, and the particulars of the description signify the particular parts of such formation ; to what purpose else would such a minute description of the formation alone of a graven image be given in the divine Word ? That there was, at that time, with the men of the church, nothing but what was false, because from self-derived intelligence, is understood by " they that make a graven image are all of them vanity ; and their delectable things shall not profit ;" also by " And none considereth in his heart, neither is there knowledge nor understanding to say, is there not a lie in my right hand ?"   The self-derived intelligence from which the falsity of doctrine is formed, is described by " The smith with the tongs both worketh in the coals and fashioneth it with hammers, and worketh it with the strength of his arms," these expressions denoting the production of falsities which favor the love of man's proprium : the conjoining of falsities to falsities by means of fallacies, by which they appear as truths, is described by " The carpenter stretcheth out his rule ; he marketh it out with a line ; he fitteth it with planes, and he marketh it out with the compass, and maketh it after the figure of a man, according to the beauty of a man ; that it may remain in the house ;" by the figure of a man is signified the appearance of truth, and by the beauty of a man, the appearance of intelligence thence derived, and by remaining in the house is signified the appearance of spiritual life thence derived. That thence there was no life of intelligence, or of the perception of truth and good, is signified by, "They have not known nor understood; for he hath shut their eyes that they cannot see; and their hearts, that they cannot understand." The particular exposition of every circumstance in this description would be tedious; enough has been said to show that something more interior and more wise is signified than the formation only of a graven image; let it be known, that such heavenly wisdom is contained in this description as is ineffable, in which wisdom are the angels when it is read by man, although man thinks of nothing but a graven image and its formation: for as many as are the expressions in the above passage, so many are the correspondences, and hence so many arcana of wisdom. So in Habakkuk: "What profiteth the graven image that the maker thereof hath graven it: the molten image, and a teacher of lies, that the maker of his work trusteth therein to make dumb idols? Woe unto him that saith to the wood, Awake, to the dumb stone, Arise, it shall teach! Behold, it is laid over with gold and silver, and there is no breath at all in the midst of it. But Jehovah is in his holy temple" (ii. 18, 19, 20). Inasmuch as by graven image is understood the falsity of doctrine, of religion, and of worship, in which there is no spiritual life, because it is from self-derived intelligence, therefore it is said, "What profiteth the graven image that the maker thereof hath graven it; the molten image, and a teacher of lies, that the maker of the work trusteth therein, to make dumb idols?" lies signifying what is false, and a teacher of lies signifying him who utters falsities; that there is no intelligence or life therein, or thence derived, is signified by making dumb idols, and by there being no breath at all in the midst of it; that all the truth of doctrine, of the church, and of worship, is from the Lord alone, is signified by "Jehovah is in his holy temple," the holy temple is heaven, where divine truth is, and whence it proceeds. Again, in David: "Their idols are silver and gold, the work of men's hands. They have mouths, but they speak not: eyes have they, but they see not" (Psalm cxv. 4, 5; cxxxv. 15, 16). Their idols being silver and gold, signifies external worship without internal, confirmed from the literal sense of the Word not understood, and also from the fallacies of the senses; the work of men's hands signifies from self-derived intelligence, as explained in the preceding article: "they have mouths, but they speak not, eyes have they, but they see not," signifies that thus they have neither thought, nor understanding of truth. The reason why nothing can come thence but what is false, is, because the proprium of man is nothing but evil, for it favors his own love and his own intelligence, wherefore he does not study truths for the sake of truths, but only for the sake of fame, of a name, glory, and gain, and when these bear rule, heaven cannot flow in with its light, and open the sight and enlighten, wherefore such persons see like owls, moles, and bats, in the dark. Again, in Isaiah: "In that day a man shall cast his idols of silver, and his idols of gold, which they made each man for himself to worship, to the moles and to the bats" (ii. 20). And in Jeremiah: "A draught is upon her waters; and they shall be dried up: for it is the land of graven images, and they are mad upon their idols. Therefore the wild beasts of the desert with the wild beasts of the islands shall dwell there, and the owl shall dwell therein" (l. 38, 39). By a draught upon her waters is signified a total destitution of truth; the wild beasts of the desert with the wild beasts of the islands, signify infernal falsities and evils, and by the owl is signified the affection of what is false. These things are said respecting the Chaldeans, and the inhabitants of Babylon, by whom are signified the profanations of truth and good by falsities favoring evils which they frame to themselves for the sake of dominion. So in Hosea: "And have made them molten images of their silver, and idols according to their own understanding, all of it the work of the craftsmen: they say of them, let the men that sacrifice kiss the calves" (xiii. 2). Inasmuch as a molten image signifies doctrines from self-derived intelligence, it is therefore here said, "they have made them molten images of their silver, and idols according to their own understanding, all of it the work of the craftsmen;" and because they thus destroy spiritual life, and assume what is merely natural, mention is made of their sacrificing, and of kissing the calves, to sacrifice denoting to destroy spiritual life, and to kiss the calves denoting to become merely natural. Again, in Isaiah: "Behold, they are all vanity, their works are nothing; their molten images are wind and confusion" (xli. 29). Here, by "they are all vanity, their works are nothing," are signified the evils of doctrine, of religion, and of worship; and the falsities thereof are signified by "their molten images are wind and confusion," wind and confusion being predicated in the Word of falsities originating in the proprium. And in Jeremiah: "Why have they provoked me to anger with their graven images, and with strange vanities?" (viii. 19.) The strange vanities here spoken of signify the falsities of religion, in like manner as graven images do, hence it is said, "with their graven images, and strange vanities." And in Ezekiel: "Every man of the house of Israel that setteth up his idols in his heart, and putteth the stumbling block of his iniquity before his face, and cometh to the prophet, I Jehovah will answer him that cometh according to the multitude of his idols" (xiv. 4). Here also idols denote the falsities of doctrine which are from self-derived intelligence, to receive which, and to acknowledge them, is signified by setting up idols in their heart; and to be affected with them, and live according to them, is signified by putting the stumbling block of their iniquity before their face; that the Lord cannot reveal genuine truths of doctrine to such persons, so long as they are in those falsities, is signified by their coming to the prophet, and by Jehovah answering him that cometh according to the multitude of his idols: by the prophet is here understood one who teaches truths, and in the abstract sense, the doctrine of genuine truth which is from the Lord; and by the multitude of idols are signified falsities in abundance, for from one falsity, assumed as a principle, flow falsities in abundance, besides those connected in a series, whence they are called, in the plural, idols, and a multitude of idols. Again in the same prophet: "Then will I sprinkle clean water upon you, and ye shall be clean: from all your filthiness, and from all your idols will I cleanse you" (xxxvi. 25). Inasmuch as by idols are signified falsities of doctrine, it is therefore said, "I will sprinkle clean water upon you," for by clean water are signified genuine truths, and by sprinkling it upon them, is signified to purify from falsities; those falsities are also called uncleannesses, because they are falsities from evil, and producing evils. So in Micah: "Therefore I will make Samaria as a heap of the field, and as plantings of a vineyard; and I will pour down the stones thereof into the valley, and I will discover the foundations thereof. And all the graven images thereof shall be beaten to pieces, and all the hires thereof shall be burned with the fire, and all the idols thereof will I lay desolate; for she gathered it of the hire of an harlot, and they shall return to the hire of an harlot" (i. 6, 7). By Samaria, after it became idolatrous, was represented the church vastated as to truths of doctrine and as to goods of life, or destroyed by falsities of doctrine and by evils of life; devastation as to all the truths of the church, is signified by, "I will make Samaria as a heap of the field, and as plantings of a vineyard; and I will pour down the stones thereof into the valley, and I will discover the foundations thereof;" the field denotes the church, the heap of the field denotes the devastation thereof, stones denote the truths of the church, and foundations, the natural truths upon which the church is founded; the total devastation of which is signified by the stones being poured down into the valley, and the foundations being discovered; the destruction of the church by falsities of doctrine, is signified by the graven images being beaten to pieces, and the idols laid desolate; by the hire of a harlot, which shall be burned with the fire, is signified the falsification of truth by applications to favor the loves of self and of the world. Similar things are signified by graven images, molten images, and idols, in the following passages. Thus in Isaiah: "As my hand hath found the kingdom of the idols, and whose graven images did excel them of Jerusalem and of Samaria; shall I not, as I have done unto Samaria and her idols, so do to Jerusalem and her idols?" (x. 10, 11.) Again: "Ye shall defile also the covering of thy graven images of silver, and the ornament of thy molten images of gold; thou shalt cast them away as a menstruous cloth; thou shalt say unto it, Get thee hence" (xxx. 22). And again: "For in that day every man shall cast away his idols of silver, and his idols of gold, which your own hands have made unto you for a sin" (xxxi. 7). And again: "Lest thou should say, Mine idol hath done them, and my graven image, and my molten image, hath commanded them" (xlviii. 5). And again: "They shall be turned back, they shall be greatly ashamed, that trust in graven images, that say to the molten images, Ye are our gods" (xlii. 17). So again: "Babylon is fallen, is fallen; and all the graven images of her gods he hath broken unto the ground" (xxi. 8, 9). And in Ezekiel: "And your altars shall be desolate, and your images shall be broken: and I will cast down your slain men before your idols. And I will lay the dead carcases of the children of Israel before their idols" (vi. 4, 5). And in Micah: "Thy graven images also will I cut off, and thy standing images out of the midst of thee; and thou shalt no more worship the work of thy hands," (v. 13). And in Moses: "And I will cast your carcases upon the carcases of your idols, and my soul shall abhor you" (Levit. xxvi. 30). Again: "The graven images of their gods shall ye burn with fire: thou shalt not desire the silver or gold that is on them, nor take it unto thee: for it is an abomination unto Jehovah thy God" (Deut. vii. 25). And again: "Cursed be the man that maketh any graven or molten image, an abomination unto Jehovah, the work of the hands of the craftsman, and putteth it in a secret place" (Deut. xxvii. 15). The same as is signified by idols of gold, silver, brass, stone, and wood, is also signified by the gods of gold, of silver, of brass, of iron, of wood, and of stone, which king Belshazzar praised, when, with his nobles and wives, he drank wine out of the vessels of gold and of silver, which were brought from the temple of Jerusalem; on account of which the hand writing appeared on the wall, (Dan. v. 1, and following verses). By the vessels of gold and silver of the temple of Jerusalem, were signified the holy goods and truths of the church; by the gods of gold, silver, brass, iron, wood, and stone, which the king of Babylon then praised, are meant the same as by idols made of such things, namely, the evils and falsities of doctrine and of worship, to praise denoting to worship; by drinking out of the vessels of the temple of Jerusalem and at the same time praising or worshiping the gods, is signified the profanation of good and truth by evils and falsities in worship; and inasmuch as every-thing spiritual pertaining to man perishes by profanation, and with-out spirituality man is not man, therefore for this cause his father Nebuchadnezzar was driven out from man, and became as a beast. Forasmuch as the external without the internal is not to be wor-shiped, but the external from the internal, thus the internal in the external, therefore it was forbidden to make any graven image in the likeness of anything living on the earth. Thus in Moses "Lest ye corrupt yourselves, and make you a graven image, the similitude of any figure, the likeness of male or female, the likeness of any beast that is on the earth, the likeness of any winged fowl that flieth in the air, the likeness of any thing that creepeth on the ground, the likeness of any fish that is in the waters beneath the earth" (Deut. iv. 15, 16; v. 8). The reason of this prohibition was, because the Jewish nation, above every other, was principled in externals without internals, and thence in the worship of all the external things which the Gentiles called holy; and to worship other external things, besides those which represented heavenly things, which were the altar, the sacrifice upon it, the tabernacle of the assembly, and the temple, was idolatrous; the latter things indeed, were also idolatrously worshiped by the Jews, but still, in consequence of there being with them a representative church, their worship was accepted on account of the representation, although an to their souls they were not affected by it ; as may appear from the various observations made concerning that nation in the A. C. from which see what is collected in the D. of the N. J. n. 248. And inasmuch as to worship the external elsewhere than where it was commanded, which was near the tabernacle in the wilderness, and near the temple and in the temple in Jerusalem, was to worship the representative itself without any intuition of the thing represented, thus what was earthly alone, without what was heavenly, therefore it was prohibited them, and even so far as that they should not make to themselves graven images of such things ; for of such a nature and quality was that nation, that as soon as they saw them made, they worshiped them.   The idolatrous worship of resemblances, not only of man, but also of various beasts, birds, and reptiles, which prevailed amongst the Gentiles, took its rise from the information, which they had from the ancients, that things celestial and spiritual were thereby signified; as that beasts signified affections, birds thought thence derived, and reptiles and fishes the same in the sensual natural man; hence it was, when they heard that the holy things of heaven and the church were signified by them, that they who were in external worship without any internal, began to worship those things ; as the Egyptians, and thence the Israelites in the wilderness, and afterwards in Samaria, worshiped calves, because calves with the ancients signified the good affections of the natural man.

588. " Which neither can see, nor hear, nor walk"—That hereby is signified in which, and from which there is nothing of the understanding of truth nor perception of good, and thus nothing of spiritual life, appears from the signification of seeing, as denoting to understand truth ; concerning which, see above, n. 11, 260, 529; and from the signification of hearing, as denoting to perceive and obey ; concerning which, also see above, n. 14, 249; and as denoting to have understanding to perceive, see n. 529; and from the signification of walking, as denoting to live spiritually, and when predicated of the Lord, as denoting life itself ; concerning which, also see above, n. 97.   Hence it may appear, that by neither seeing, hearing, nor walking, is signified, that there is no understanding of truth, no perception of good, and thence not any spiritual life. The reason why these things are not in them and from them, namely, idols, is, because by idols are signified falsities of doctrine, of religion, and of worship, and in falsities such things are not, but only in truths derived from good ; in the latter, and from the latter, are all understanding, perception from the will of good, and consequently spiritual life : it is said, consequently, because spiritual life consists in the understanding of truth, and in perception from the will of good ; for truths are in the light of heaven, insomuch that truths themselves give light in heaven, and this because the divine truth proceeding from the Lord makes all light in the spiritual world, and that light gives all intelligence and wisdom to the angels. Inasmuch then as truths themselves are of the light, it follows that falsities are of no light, for they extinguish it, wherefore falsities, in the Word, are called darkness ; as may be seen above, n. 526 : and inasmuch

as they are darkness, they are the shades of spiritual death. It is however to be observed, that the falsities of evil are such darkness, but not the falsities which are not from evil. The reason why to hear, signifies perception from the will of good, and thence obedience, is, because speech enters the ear together with sound, and the truths of speech enter the understanding and thence the thought, and the sounds enter the will and thence the affection. That in the spiritual world sounds present and produce affection which is of the will, and the expressions of the sound, the thought which is of the understanding, may be seen in the work concerning H. & H. n. 236, 241; and above, n. 323. Hence it may appear, whence it is that to hear and to hearken also signify to obey, and the ear and hearing, obedience.

589. " Neither repented they of their murders"—That hereby is signified, who have not actually averted themselves from extinguishing those things which are of the understanding of truth, of the will of good, and thence of spiritual life, appears from the signification of repenting, as denoting actually to avert one's self, as was shown above, n. 585; and from the signification of murders, as denoting the extinction of the understanding of truth, of the will of good, and thence of spiritual life; for by man are signified the understanding of truth, and wisdom, as may be seen above, n. 280, 546, 547: and by slaying is signified to extinguish spiritual life by the falsities of evil, see also above, n. 315, 547, 572. That murder or manslaughter signifies the extinction of spiritual life, may appear without confirmations from other passages of the Word, when it is considered that all the particulars here mentioned are to be spiritually understood, and to kill or slay spiritually is to extinguish spiritual life, which is done by the falsities of evil. Hence it is that the devil is called a murderer from the beginning, according to the words of the Lord in John: " Ye are of your father the devil, and the lusts of your father ye will do. He was a murderer from the beginning, and abode not in the truth, because there is no truth in him. When he speaketh a lie, he speaketh of his own: for he is a liar, and the father of it" (viii. 44). These things are said of the Jewish nation itself which by its idolatries and traditions, extinguished spiritual life by the falsities of evil: by the father of it, are understood their fathers; because of their thus extinguishing the spiritual life by falsities of evils, it is said, " the truth is not in him, when he speaketh a lie, he speaketh of his own, for he is a liar, and the father of it;" by a lie is signified, in the Word, the falsity of evil. The same is signified by murders, and by a lie, in the following passage of the Revelation : " For without are dogs, and sorcerers, and whoremongers, and murderers, and idolaters, and whosoever loveth and maketh a lie" (xxii. 15). Inasmuch as they who are understood by Babylon, in the Word, extinguish all divine truths by the falsities of evil, therefore Babylon is designated as an abominable branch, as the raiment of those that are slain, thrust through with the sword, because she has destroyed the land, and slain her people" (Isaiah xiv. 19, 20). Here they are said to be slain, thrust

through with the sword, who have perished by the falsities of evil; by the land which is destroyed is signified the church; and by slaying the people is signified to extinguish the truths of the church.

590. " Nor of their sorceries, nor of their fornications"—That hereby is signified, from perverting good and falsifying truth, appears from the signification of sorceries, as denoting the perversion of good, concerning which we shall speak presently; and from the signification of fornications, as denoting the falsifications of truth, concerning which, see above, n. 141, 161. That sorceries, in the spiritual sense, signify perversions of good, may appear from this consideration, that they are mentioned conjointly with fornications, and fornications signify the falsifications of truth, and, in the Word, where truth is treated of, good is also treated of, because of the divine celestial marriage in every part thereof; it is also said, that they repented not of their murders, sorceries, and fornications, and by murders are signified the extinctions of the affection of the good of the will, and of the perception of truth of the understanding; see above, n. 589; and the affection of the good of the will, is extinguished, when the good of the Word is perverted, and the perception of the truth of the understanding, when the truth of the Word is falsified; hence also it may appear what is here signified by sorceries. In ancient times, various kinds of infernal arts, called magic, were in use, of which some are recounted in the Word (as in Deut. xviii. 9, 10, 11); amongst them were also enchantments, whereby they induced affections and pleasures which another could not resist; this was affected by sounds and tacit voices, which they either produced or muttered, and which, by analogous correspondences, had communication with the will of another, and excited his affection, and fascinated him, to will, think, and act in a certain manner. Such enchantments the prophets were skilled in, and also used, by which they excited good affections, hearing, and obedience, and these enchantments are mentioned in a good sense in the Word (Isaiah iii. 1, 2, 3, 20; xxvi. 16; Jer. viii. 17; and in David, Psalm lviii. 4, 5). But inasmuch as by such speeches and mutterings, evil affections were excited by the evil, and thus enchantments were made magical, therefore they are also recounted among the magical arts, and severely prohibited (Deut. xviii. 9, 10, 11; Isaiah xlvii. 9, 12; Rev. xviii. 23; xxii. 15).

591. " Nor of their thefts"—That hereby is signified from taking away the knowledges of truth and good, and thereby the means of procuring for themselves spiritual life, appears from the signification of theft, and of stealing, as denoting to take away from any one the knowledges of good and truth, which may be serviceable as the means of procuring to himself spiritual life; concerning which, see above, n. 193. The reason of this signification of theft and of stealing, is, because by wealth, raiment, utensils, and other things which thieves take away, are signified the knowledges of truth and good, wherefore spiritual theft, or theft in the spiritual sense, denotes the taking away of the latter, as natural theft, or theft in the natural sense, denotes the taking away the former. That this is signified

by theft may appear from this consideration, that in this verse the subject especially treated of is the extinction of spiritual life with others, and spiritual life is extinguished by the perversions of good and the falsifications of truth, likewise, by deprivation of the knowledges of truth and good, by which spiritual life is procured; and both the former and the latter are what are signified by murders, enchantments, fornications, and thefts, as has been already shown.

CHAPTER X.

1. And I saw another mighty angel coming down from heaven clothed with a cloud; and a rainbow was over his head, and his face was as it were the sun, and his feet as pillars of fire.

2. And he had in his hand a little book open, and he set his right foot upon the sea, and his left foot upon the earth.

3. And he cried with a loud voice, as when a lion roareth. And when he had cried, seven thunders uttered their voices.

4. And when the seven thunders had uttered their voices, I was about to write; and I heard a voice from heaven, saying unto me, Seal up those things which the seven thunders uttered, and write them not.

5. And the angel whom I saw standing upon the sea and upon the earth, lifted up his hand to heaven.

6. And sware by him that liveth for ever and ever, who created heaven, and the things that therein are, and the earth, and the things that therein are, and the sea, and the things that are therein, that there should be time no longer.

7. But in the days of the voice of the seventh angel, when he shall begin to sound, the mystery of God should be finished, as he hath declared to his servants the prophets.

8. And the voice which I heard from heaven, spake unto me again, and said, Go, take the little book which is open in the hand of the angel who standeth upon the sea and upon the earth.

9. And I went unto the angel and said unto him, Give me the little book. And he said unto me, Take it, and eat it up; and it shall make thy belly bitter, but it shall be in thy mouth sweet as honey.

10. And I took the little book out of the angel's hand, and ate it up; and it was in my mouth sweet as honey: and as soon as I had eaten it, my belly was bitter.

11. And he said to me, Thou must prophecy again before many peoples, and nations, and tongues, and kings.

EXPLICATION.

592. Verse 1. "AND I saw another mighty angel coming down from heaven, clothed with a cloud; and a rainbow was upon his head, and his face was as it were the sun, and his feet as pillars of fire."—"And I saw another mighty angel coming down from heaven," signifies the Lord as to the Word, in this case, as to its ultimate sense, which is called the sense of the letter: "clothed with a cloud," signifies the ultimate of the Word: "and a rainbow was upon his head," signifies the interior things of the Word: "and his face was as it were. the sun," signifies the divine love of the Lord, from which is all divine truth, which in heaven, and in the church is the Word: "and his feet as pillars of fire," signifies divine truth, or the Word in ultimates, sustaining interior things therein, also full of the good of love.

593. "And I saw another mighty angel coming down from heaven"—That hereby is signified the Lord as to the Word, in this case, as to its ultimate sense, which is called the sense of the letter, appears from the signification of a mighty angel, as denoting the Lord as to the Word, concerning which we shall speak presently; the reason why it denotes the Lord as to the Word in its ultimate sense, which is called the sense of the letter, is, because from that sense the Lord is called mighty, for all the strength, and all the power of divine truth, exist and consist in its ultimate, consequently in the literal sense of the Word, concerning which also we shall speak presently. Inasmuch as the literal sense of the Word is here understood, therefore it is said of the angel that he was seen coming down from heaven, the same being said concerning the Word, which is divine truth; for this descends from the Lord through the heavens into the world, wherefore it is adapted to the wisdom of the angels who are in the three heavens, and is also adapted to men who are in the natural world. Hence also it is, that the Word in its first origin is altogether divine, afterwards celestial, then spiritual, and lastly natural; it is celestial for the angels of the inmost or third heaven, who are called celestial angels, spiritual for the angels of the second or middle heaven, who are called spiritual angels, and celestial and spiritual-natural for the angels of the ultimate or first heaven, who are called celestial and spiritual-natural angels, and natural for men in the world, for men, so long as they live in the material body, think and speak naturally; hence then it is, that the Word is given with the angels of each heaven, but with a difference according to the degree of their wisdom, intelligence and science; and although it differs as to the sense in each heaven, still it is the same Word. The Divine principle itself, which is in the Word from the Lord, when it descends to the inmost or third heaven, becomes divine celestial, when it thence descends to the middle or second heaven, it becomes divine spiritual, and when from this heaven it descends to the ultimate or first, it becomes divine celestial, or

spiritual-natural, and lastly, when it thence descends into the world, it becomes a divine natural Word, such as it is with us in the letter: these successive derivations of the divine truth proceeding from the Lord himself, exist by virtue of correspondences established from creation itself between things superior and inferior, concerning which, the Lord willing, more will be said hereafter. The reason why all strength, and all power are in the ultimates of divine truth, thus in the natural sense of the Word, which is the sense of the letter, is, because this sense is the continent of all the interior senses, namely, of the spiritual and celestial, spoken of above ; and since it is the continent, it is also the basis, and in the basis lies all strength ; for if things superior do not rest upon their basis, they fall down and are dissolved, as would be the case with the spiritual and celestial things of the Word if they did not rest upon the natural and literal sense, for this not only sustains the interior senses, but also contains them, wherefore the Word or divine truth, in this sense, is not only in its power, but also in its fulness.* From these considerations, it also follows, that the all of the doctrine of the church ought to be formed and confirmed from the literal sense of the Word, and that all the power of doctrine is thence derived, concerning which, also, see above, n. 356 ; for this reason it is that the angel coming down from heaven is called mighty. That by an angel in the Word, in the supreme sense, is understood the Lord in the respective sense, every recipient of divine truth from the Lord, and in the abstract sense, divine truth itself, may be seen above, n. 130, 302 ; here, therefore, by the angel is understood the Lord as to the Word, because the Word is divine truth itself. That the Lord himself is here meant by the angel, may appear from a similar representation of him, as to his face, and as to his feet, in the first chapter of this book, where, treating of the Son of man, who is the Lord, it is said : " His countenance was as the sun shineth in his strength ; and his feet like unto fine brass, as if they burned in a furnace" (verses 15, 16).

594. " Clothed with a cloud "—That hereby is signified the ultimate of the Word, appears from the signification of being clothed, as denoting to be from without him, for that which clothes is also without, since it is further in the circumference ; in this case therefore it denotes what is ultimate ; and from the signification of a cloud, as denoting divine truth in the ultimates, consequently the Word in the sense of the letter. This signification of cloud is evident from appearances in the spiritual world ; likewise from the Word, where clouds are mentioned. From appearances in the spiritual world, thus ; the universal angelic heaven consists solely of

* But upon this subject more may be seen above; namely, that strength is in the ultimate, because the Divine principle there is in its fulness, n. 346, 567 ; the same is also further explained in the A. C. viz. that interior things, successively flow into exteriors, even into the extreme or ultimate, and that therein they co-exist, n. 643, 6239, 6465, 9216, 9217: that they not only flow in successively, but also form in their ultimate what is simultaneous, in what order, n. 5897, 6451, 8603, 10,099: that hence strength and power is in the ultimates, n. 9836, that hence responses and revelations are given in ultimates, n. 9905, 10,548; that hence the ultimate is holy above the interiors, n. 9824.

the divine truth which proceeds from the Lord, the reception of which constitutes angels : in the supreme heaven this truth appears as the pure aura which is called ether; in the inferior heaven, as less pure, almost as the atmosphere, which is called air; in the lowest heaven it appears as a thin watery element, upon which is vapor like a cloud: such is the appearance of divine truth according to degrees in descent.   There is a similar appearance when the angels of the superior heavens speak concerning divine truths, their discourse, in such case, being presented to the view of those who are in the lowest heaven under the aspect of a cloud, which flies hither and thither, whilst the more intelligent amongst them know from its gilding, its brightness, and form, what the angels of the superior heavens are discoursing about with each other; hence it is evident, whence it is that a cloud signifies divine truth in ultimates. Inasmuch as the expressions in the Word are, for the most part, taken from appearances in the spiritual world, and hence signify things similar to what there exist, therefore this is the case also with respect to clouds.   That a cloud signifies the literal sense of the Word, which is divine truth in ultimates, appears in the Word from the following passages.   Thus in Matthew: "And Jesus taketh Peter, James, and John, and bringeth them up into a high mountain, and was transfigured before them : and his face did shine as the sun, and his raiment was white as the light.   And, behold, there appeared unto them Moses and Elias talking with him.   While he yet spake, behold, a bright cloud overshadowed them : and, behold, a voice out of the cloud, which said, This is my beloved Son, in whom I am well pleased; hear ye him" (xvii. 1-5; Mark ix. 1-7).   And in Luke: "While he thus spake, there came a cloud, and overshadowed them : and they feared as they entered the cloud. And there came a voice out of the cloud, saying, This is my beloved Son: hear him" (ix. 34, 35).   In this transfiguration the Lord also represented divine truth, which is the Word; for the Lord, when he was in the world, made his humanity divine truth, and when he departed out of the world, he made his humanity divine good by unition with the Divinity itself, which was in him from conception.*   Hence it is, that the particular things which were seen at the transfigura- of the Lord, were significative of divine truth proceeding from his divine good: the divine good of the divine love, which was in him, and from which was the divine truth in his humanity, was represented by his face shining as the sun, for the face represents the interiors, wherefore these shine forth through the face, and the sun signifies the divine love; as may be seen above, n. 401, 424.   The divine truth was represented by the Lord's raiment, which became white as the light; for garments in the Word signify truths, and the garments of the Lord the divine truth; as may be seen above, n. 64, 271, 395; on which account also they appeared white as the light; for divine truth makes the light in the angelic heaven, and is there-

* That the Lord made his humanity divine truth when he was in the world, and afterwards divine good, may be seen in the D. of the N. J. n. 303, 304, 305, 306 ; and that the Lord is the Word, n. 263.

fore signified by light in the Word; concerning which, more may
be seen in the work on H. & H. n. 126–140. Inasmuch as the
Word, which is the divine truth, was represented by the transfiguration of the Lord, therefore Moses and Elias were seen speaking with
him, Moses and Elias signifying the Word, Moses, the historical
Word, and Elias the prophetical : but the Word in the letter was
represented by the cloud which overshadowed the disciples, and into
which they entered ; for by disciples, in the Word, was represented
the church, which, at that time and afterwards, was only in truths
from the literal sense ; and because revelation and responses are
made by divine truth in the ultimates, as was said in the article
above, and this truth is such as is the truth of the literal sense of the
Word, therefore it was that a voice was heard out of the cloud,
saying, "This is my beloved son, hear him," denoting that he is
divine truth, or the Word. He who does not know that by clouds
in the spiritual sense of the Word is understood the Word in the
letter, cannot know the arcanum involved in these words : "And
then they shall see the Son of man coming in the clouds of heaven
with power and great glory" (Matt. xxiv. 30 ; Mark xiii. 26 ; xiv.
62 ; Luke xxi. 27). And in the Revelation : "Behold, he cometh
with clouds ; and every eye shall see him " (i. 7). And again :
" And I looked, and behold a white cloud, and upon the cloud one
sat like unto the Son of man " (xiv. 14). And in Daniel : " And I
saw in the night visions, and behold, one like the Son of man came
with the clouds of heaven " (vii. 13). He who is ignorant of the
spiritual signification of clouds, as denoting the truths in the literal
sense of the Word, cannot apprehend otherwise, than that in the
consummation of the age, that is, in the end of the church, the Lord
will come in the clouds of heaven, and manifest himself to the
world ; but it is well known that since the Word was given, the
Lord manifests himself by that alone, for the Word, which is divine
truth, is the Lord himself in heaven and in the church ; hence it
may now be evident, that the manifestation there predicted signifies
his manifestation in the Word ; and the manifestation of the Lord
in the Word was accomplished by his opening and revealing its
internal or spiritual sense, for in this sense is the divine truth itself,
such as it is in heaven, and the divine truth in heaven is the Lord
himself there ; hence then it is evident that by the Lord's coming
in the clouds of heaven with glory, is signified the revelation of him
in the literal sense of the Word, by virtue of its spiritual sense.*
That cloud signifies the divine truth in ultimates, consequently the
Word in the sense of the letter, may still further appear from the
following passages. Thus in Isaiah : " Behold, Jehovah rideth upon
a swift cloud, and shall come into Egypt : and the idols of Egypt
shall be moved at his presence, and the heart of Egypt shall melt in

---

* That the clouds of heaven signify the things which are of the literal sense, and
glory those which are of the spiritual sense, may be seen in the work concerning
H. & H. n. 1 ; and the revelation itself of the spiritual sense, in the small work concerning the W. H.; the Son of man also signifies the Lord as to divine truth, as
may be seen above, n. 63, 151.

the midst of it " (xix. 1).   In these words by Egypt is not meant Egypt, but the natural man separate from the spiritual, which is then in falsities and evils, and thereby perverts all the truths and goods of the church ; that those falsities and evils destroy him, when truth from good flows in from the Lord, is described by these words of the prophet understood in the internal sense ; Jehovah riding upon a swift cloud, signifies the Lord enlightening the understanding with truths, to ride, when predicated of Jehovah, or the Lord, denoting to enlighten the understanding, and a swift cloud denoting truth; that in such case the idols of Egypt are put in commotion and the heart of the Egyptian melts, signifies, that the evils and falsities of the natural man separate from the spiritual, then destroy him, idols denoting falsities, the heart denoting evils, and Egypt, the natural man.   So in Moses: "There is none like unto the God of Jeshurun, who rideth upon the heaven in thy help, and in his excellency on the sky.   The eternal God is thy refuge, and underneath are the everlasting arms " (Deut. xxxiii. 26, 27).   Here also by riding upon the heaven and on the sky or clouds, is signified to enlighten the understanding by the influx of spiritual truth into natural truth, which is the truth of the literal sense of the Word ; inasmuch as the divine truth in the heavens is spiritual, and the divine truth in the earth is natural, and the latter is illustrated by the former, therefore it is said, " and in his excellency on the sky ;" " the eternal God is thy refuge," denotes the divine truth with the angels, and " the everlasting arms " denote the same truth with men ; the truths of the literal sense of the Word are what are understood by the everlasting arms, for that sense is the very strength of divine truth, arms signifying strength ; that the strength of divine truth is in the literal sense of the Word may be seen in the article above.   So in David : " And he rode upon a cherub, and did fly : yea he did fly upon the wings of the wind.   He made darkness his secret place : his pavilion round about him were dark waters and thick clouds of the skies. At the brightness that was before him his thick clouds passed " (Psalm xviii. 10, 11, 12).   Here also is described the illustration of the Word, and thence the illumination of the men of the church ; illustration by the influx of divine truth from the heavens is signified by, " he rode upon a cherub, and did fly ;" divine truth in ultimates, which is illustrated, is signified by the wings of the wind, darkness, dark waters, and thick clouds of the skies ; the various degrees of the understanding receiving illumination are signified by those things ; that the obscurities of the ultimate or literal sense are thereby dissipated, is understood by, " at the brightness that was before him his thick clouds passed." So again : " Sing unto God, sing praises to his name : extol him that rideth upon the heavens " (Psalm lxviii. 4).   By him that rideth upon the heavens or upon clouds, is here also understood the Lord as to the illustration of the Word ; clouds denote truths in the ultimates, which are illustrated, and this is effected by the influx of light, which is divine truth, from the spiritual world or heaven.   So in Nahum : " Jehovah hath his way in the whirlwind and in the storm, and the clouds are the dust of his feet" (i. 3). Truth in the ultimates, which is the truth of the literal sense of the Word, is called the clouds, the dust of the feet of Jehovah, because it is the natural and lowest truth, in which the divine truth in heaven, which is spiritual, terminates, and upon which also it subsists; divine truth in the ultimates, inasmuch as it is but little understood unless it be illustrated from heaven, and is therefore a ground of disputation and controversy, is understood by the whirlwind and the storm, in which Jehovah hath his way, spiritual storm and tempest denoting disputation concerning the genuine sense of the Word, which nevertheless the Lord illustrates by influx with those who desire the truth. So in David: "His seed shall endure for ever, and his throne as the sun before me. It shall be established for ever as the moon, and as a faithful witness in the clouds" (lxxxix. 36, 37). These things are spoken concerning the Lord, and by the seed which shall endure for ever, is signified the divine truth which is from him: by his throne which shall be as the sun before him, and established for ever as the moon, are signified heaven and the church, as to the good of love, and as to the truth of faith; by, "as the sun," is signified as to the good of love, and by "as the moon," as to the truth of faith; a faithful witness in the clouds, signifies that he is the divine truth, for witness, when predicated of the Lord, signifies that which proceeds from him, and this being of him witnesses concerning him. Again: "Who layeth the beams of his chambers in the waters: who maketh the clouds his chariot: who walketh upon the wings of the wind" (Psalm civ. 3). These few words are descriptive of heaven and the church, and at the same time of doctrine from the Word. "Who layeth the beams of his chambers in the waters" signifies that the Lord forms heaven and the church from divine truths, waters signify divine truths, the beams of his chambers signify the heavens and the church, and to lay, signifies to form them: "who maketh the clouds his chariot" signifies doctrine from ultimate divine truths, clouds denoting ultimate divine truths, such as are in the literal sense of the Word, and a chariot denoting doctrine; this is said because all the doctrine of the church is to be drawn from, and confirmed by the literal sense of the Word. "Who walketh upon the wings of the wind," signifies life communicated to doctrine from spiritual influx, to walk signifying to live, and, when predicated of the Lord, life itself, the wings of the wind denoting the spiritual things of the Word; that waters signify truths, may be seen above, n. 71, 483, 518, 537, 538. So in Isaiah: "And I will lay it (my vineyard) waste: I will also command the clouds that they rain no rain upon it" (v. 5, 6). By these words is understood that then there shall be no understanding of divine truth or the Word in the church; the vineyard denotes the church, clouds denote the literal sense of the Word, and by their raining no rain, is meant that then there shall be no understanding of divine truth from the Word. Again, in David: "Who covereth the heavens with clouds, who prepareth rain for the earth, who maketh grass to grow upon the mountains" (Psalm cxlvii. 8). To cover the heavens with clouds, signifies to defend and keep together the spiritual things of the Word, which are in the heavens, by natural truths such as are in the literal sense of the Word; "who prepareth rain for the earth," signifies instruction thence for the church; "who maketh grass to grow upon the mountains," signifies nourishment thereby for those who are in the good of love.¹ The same is signified by the following words in Isaiah: "Drop down, ye heavens, from above, and let the skies pour down righteousness: let the earth open, and bring forth salvation" (xlv. 8). And in Judges: "Jehovah, when thou wentest out of Seir, when thou marchedest out of the field of Edom, the earth trembled, and the heavens dropped, the clouds also dropped water" (v. 4). Here by Jehovah going forth out of Seir, and marching out of the field of Edom, is signified the illumination of the Gentiles by the Lord, when he assumed the humanity : by the earth trembling, is signified the state of the church then thoroughly changed; by the heaven's dropping, and the clouds dropping water, are signified instruction, influx, and perception of divine truth; to drop signifies instruction and influx, water denotes truths, the heavens denote the interior things of truth, and clouds, the exterior, namely such as are in the literal sense of the Word. Again, in David: "The clouds poured out water: the skies sent out a sound: thine arrows also went abroad" (Psalm lxxxvii. 17). Here, by the clouds pouring out water, is signified that genuine truths are derived from the literal sense of the Word; by the skies sending out a sound is signified influx from the heavens; by, "thine arrows also went abroad" are signified divine truths thence derived. So in Job: "He bindeth up the waters in his thick clouds; and the cloud is not rent under them. He holdeth back the face of his throne, and spreadeth his cloud upon it" (xxvi. 8, 9). Here, also, clouds denote ultimate truths in order, and because these contain in themselves, and include, spiritual truths that they may not be dissipated, this is expressed and signified by God binding up the waters in his thick clouds, and the cloud not being rent under them; inasmuch as exterior truths which are called natural, also encompass and shut in interior truths, which are called spiritual, and are proper to the angels of the heavens, therefore this likewise is expressed and signified by, "He holdeth back the face of his throne, and spreadeth his cloud upon it." And in Isaiah : "Jehovah said unto me, I will take my rest, and I will consider in my dwelling place like a clear heat upon herbs, and like a cloud of dew in the heat of harvest" (xviii. 4); here a cloud of dew signifies truth from good fructifying. Again, in the same prophet: "And Jehovah will create upon every dwelling place of mount Zion, and upon all her assemblies, a cloud and smoke by day, and the shining of a flaming fire by night: for upon all the glory shall be a defence" (iv. 5). Here by the dwelling of mount Zion is signified the good of the celestial church, and by her assemblies are signified the truths of that good; the defence thereof lest it should be hurt from too much light or from too much shade, is signified by the cloud and smoke by day, and the shining of a flaming fire by night; and since all spiritual good and truth are preserved by natural good and truth, that they may not be hurt, therefore it is said that upon all the glory shall be a defence, glory denoting spiritual good and truth. The same is signified by, " For the cloud of Jehovah was upon the tabernacle by day, and the fire was on it by night " (Exod. xl. 34, 38; Numb. ix. 15–23; x. 11, 12, 34; xiv. 14; Deut. i. 33). So again, it is said: " And Jehovah went before them by day in a pillar of a cloud, and by night in a pillar of fire " (Exod. xiii. 21). And again: " And the pillar of the cloud came between the camp of the Egyptians and the camp of Israel " (Exod. xiv. 19, 20). And in David: " In the day time also he led them with a cloud, and all the night with a light of fire" (Psalm lxxviii. 14). And again: " Egypt was glad when they departed: for the fear of them fell upon them. He spread a cloud for a covering; and fire to give them light in the night " (Psalm cv. 38, 39). The reason why there was a cloud upon the tabernacle by day, and a fire by night, was, because the tabernacle represented heaven and the church, the cloud, the presence of the Lord by divine truth, and the fire, his presence by divine good, which is called the good of faith, each ultimate in order, whence they were as coverings for the tabernacle; on this account it is said in the passages adduced above from David and Isaiah: " For upon all the glory shall be a defence;" and, " he spread a cloud for a covering." The same is signified by the cloud which covered mount Horeb, and into which Moses entered; also by the cloud in which Jehovah descended on mount Sinai, and by the cloudy pillar which descended, and stood at the door of the tabernacle (Exod. xxiv. 15, 18; xix. 9; xxxiv. 5; xxxiii. 9, 10). Such also is the signification of the cloud mentioned in the following passages in Ezekiel: " And I looked, and, behold, a whirlwind came out of the north, a great cloud, and a fire infolding itself, and a brightness was about it " (i. 4). And again: " Now the cherubim stood on the right side of the house, when the man went in; and the cloud filled the inner court. Then the glory of Jehovah went up from the cherub, and stood over the threshold of the house; and the house was filled with the cloud, and the court was full of the brightness of Jehovah's glory " (x. 3, 4). By the cherubim here mentioned is signified the Lord's providence or guard, that he may not be approached otherwise than by the good of love; hence also by cherubim are signified the heavens, specifically, the inmost or third heaven is meant, because the angels of that heaven receive divine truth in the good of love, wherefore it is divine truth, which, in its essence, is the good of love, which defends: this divine truth, as it descends out of the inmost heaven into the inferior heavens, and at length into the world where men are, thus by degrees, from pure becomes more dense, and hence it is that in the lowest degree it appears as a cloud, by which therefore is signified the divine truth accommodated to the apprehension of the angels who are in the lowest heaven, who are spiritual-natural, and, lastly, to the apprehension of men in the natural world: and inasmuch as the divine truth in this degree is similar to the divine truth which is in the literal sense of the Word, therefore by a cloud is signified the Word as to the literal sense; this divine truth is what filled the court like a cloud, and lastly the house, at the right side of which stood the cherubim; and inasmuch as this divine truth is inwardly spiritual, and shines from celestial light, therefore it is called glory, and it is said that the court was filled with the brightness of the glory of Jehovah. Hence also it is said in Job: "Dost thou know where God disposed them, and caused the light of his cloud to shine?" (xxxvii. 15.)

Inasmuch as the superior heavens appear to the view of those who are in the inferior heavens as covered over with a light and bright cloud, because the inferior angels cannot otherwise behold the superior or interior divine principle than according to their quality, hence also the divine truth in the superior heavens, or what is the same thing, the superior heavens themselves, are in some passages of the Word understood by clouds; for whether we say divine truth, or the heavens, it is the same thing, forasmuch as the heavens are heavens, by virtue of divine truth, and the angels there are angels by virtue of the reception of it; in this sense clouds are mentioned in numerous passages of the Word. Thus in Isaiah: "I will ascend above the heights of the clouds; I will be like the Most High" (xiv. 14). And in Jeremiah: "We would have healed Babylon, but she is not healed; forsake her, and let us go every one into his own country: for her judgment reacheth unto heaven, and is lifted up even to the skies" (li. 9). And in David: "Ascribe ye strength unto God: his excellency is over Israel, and his strength is in the clouds" (Psalm lxviii. 34). In these passages the same thing is signified by clouds, as by the waters above the firmament (Gen. i. 7); and by the waters above the heavens (Psalm cxlviii. 4); for clouds are composed of water, and that water signifies divine truth, may be seen above, n. 7, 483, 518. Forasmuch as there are clouds that are of a thinner and brighter quality, and also such as are grosser and blacker, and the former appear beneath the heavens, but the latter about some of the hells, it is hence evident that, in the opposite sense, clouds also signify the falsities of evil, which are contrary to truths from good; as in the following passages. Thus in Ezekiel: "As for Egypt, a cloud shall cover her, and her daughters shall go into captivity" (xxx. 18). Again, in the same prophet: "So will I seek out my sheep, and will deliver them out of all places where they have been scattered in the cloudy and dark day" (xxxiv. 12). And again: "Thou shalt ascend, thou shalt be like a cloud to cover the land" (xxxviii. 9). Hence also it is that the last judgment, when they who are in falsities of evil perish, is called "A day of clouds and of thick darkness" (Joel ii. 2; Zephaniah i. 15). The same is signified by the clouds, and thick darkness, which appeared to the children of Israel over mount Sinai at the giving of the law (Deut. iv. 11; v. 22, 23); for although Jehovah, that is, the Lord, descended upon that mountain in a bright cloud, yet it appeared before the eyes of the people, who were in the falsities of evil, as a thick and dark cloud; concerning which, see the A. C. n. 1861, 6832, 8814, 8819, 9434, 10,551.

595. " And a rainbow was over his head"—That hereby are signified the interior things of the Word, appears from the signification
of a rainbow, as denoting the divine truth such as the Word is in the
spiritual sense, concerning which we shall speak presently; and
from the signification of being over the head, as denoting what is
interior; for what is above and superior signifies that which is within
and interior, as may appear from this consideration, that when mention is made of what is interior, then in heaven is understood what
is superior; for the heavens where the interior angels are, or those
who are interiorly wise, appear also above the heavens where the
exterior angels are, or those who are exteriorly wise; hence it is,
that the three heavens are distinguished from each other as to alti-
tude, the inmost or third heaven appearing over the middle or second
heaven, and this over the ultimate or first. The reason why what is
superior signifies what is interior, is, because when things superior
and inferior are together, that is, form what is simultaneous, as in
the head of man, they then co-exist in that order; so that those
things which stood above in successive order, are reposited within,
and those which stood below in successive order, are reposited without, hence it is that things superior signify things interior, and
things inferior signify things exterior. This may be illustrated to
the apprehension by the idea of a superficies, in the centre of which
are things purer, and in the peripheries such as are grosser; such a
superficies, also, do things superior and inferior form, when they let
themselves down into one, and constitute what is simultaneous:
from these observations, it may also appear what is signified by the
angel being clothed with a cloud, spoken of above, for to be clothed,
for the same reason, and hence the idea, denotes to be from without
and beneath. The reason why a rainbow signifies divine truth interior, such as the Word is in the spiritual sense, is, because the
light of heaven, in like manner as the light of the world, according
to its incidence into objects, and its modifications therein, presents
variegations of colors, and likewise rainbows, which also it has
been granted me to see occasionally in the angelic heaven, as may
be seen described in the A. C. n. 1623, 1624, 1625. The rainbows
which appear in the angelic heaven differ from the rainbows which
appear in the world in this, that the rainbows of heaven are from a
spiritual origin, whereas the rainbows of the world are from a natural origin; for the rainbows of heaven are from the light which has
its origin from the Lord as a sun, and inasmuch as that sun is in its
essence the divine love of the Lord, and the light thence derived is
divine truth, hence the variegations of light, which are presented as
rainbows, are variegations of intelligence and wisdom with the
angels; from this circumstance it is, that rainbows there signify the
form and beauty of divine truth spiritual; but the rainbows of the
world are from a natural origin, namely from the sun of the world
and its light, and hence are only modifications and thence variegations of light from the water falling from a cloud; and since there
are similar colored appearances in the spiritual world as in the natural world, and such appearances correspond, hence by the rainbows

of the world are signified the same as by the rainbows of heaven, namely, spiritual divine truths in their form and beauty; these truths are such as those of the Word in the spiritual sense.

Similar things are signified by the rainbow in the following passages in Ezekiel: " And above the firmament that was over their heads was the likeness of a throne, as the appearance of a sapphire stone; and upon the likeness of the throne was the likeness of the appearance of a man above upon it. And I saw as the color of amber, as the appearance of fire round about within it, from the appearance of his loins even upward, and from the appearance of his loins even downward, I saw as it were the appearance of fire, and it had brightness round about. As the appearance of the bow that is in the cloud in the day of rain, so was the appearance of the brightness round about. This was the appearance of the likeness of the glory of Jehovah" (i. 26, 27, 28). Inasmuch as by the cherubim, described in this chapter, are signified providence and guard lest the Lord should be approached otherwise than by the good of love, therefore there appeared a throne, and upon the throne the appearance of a man, and by the throne is signified the universal heaven, and by the man upon the throne, the Lord himself; by the color of amber, as the appearance of fire round about within it, from the appearance of his loins even upward, is signified celestial divine love, which reigns in the superior heavens, for the superior heavens are represented by the superior part of the body, from the loins upwards, to which they correspond, for they constitute that part in the grand man, which is heaven: " the color of amber, as the appearance of fire," signifies that love and in like manner the loins, for the loins correspond to the marriage of good and truth, in which they are who are in the superior heavens, whence it is that heaven is called a marriage, and that the Lord is called bridegroom and husband, and heaven and the church a bride and wife. By the appearance of his loins downward, having the appearance of fire, and brightness round about, as the appearance of the bow that is in the cloud in the day of rain, is signified divine love spiritual, which reigns in the inferior heavens, for the region of the body from the loins even to the soles of the feet corresponds to that love; and because that love proceeds from divine love celestial, it is called fire and brightness; divine truth from the divine good of love being what shines and presents the appearance of a rainbow; hence also it is evident, that the translucence of divine truth spiritual, through divine truth natural, presents that appearance in the heavens, and consequently is thereby signified, as was said above.*

The same also is signified by the bow in the cloud, or the rainbow, in the book of Genesis: " And God said, This is the token of the covenant which I make between me and you and every living crea-

---

* But these things may be more clearly understood from what is said in the treatise on H. & H. concerning heaven; as that from the divine human principle of the Lord it has reference to one man, n. 59–87; concerning the correspondence of all things of heaven with all things of man, n. 87–102; and in the A. C. concerning the correspondence of the loins, n. 3021, 4280, 4462, 5050–5062.

ture that is with you, for perpetual generations: I do set my bow in the cloud, and it shall be for a token of a covenant between me and the earth. And it shall come to pass, when I bring a cloud over the earth, that the bow shall be seen in the cloud : and I will remember my covenant, which is between me and you and every living creature of all flesh; and the waters shall no more become a flood to destroy all flesh. And the bow shall be in the cloud; and I will look upon it that I may remember the everlasting covenant between God and every living creature of all flesh that is upon the earth " (ix. 12–16). Here it is to be observed that unless it be known that there is a spiritual sense in every part of the Word, it may be supposed, that the bow in the cloud, which is called a rainbow, appears for a sign that the earth shall no more be destroyed by a flood, when notwithstanding that bow exists from natural causes, and is mediately reproduced when the rays of light from the sun strike upon the watery particles of the rain from a cloud, whence it is evident that similar rainbows also existed before the flood; by the rainbows, therefore, which are seen by men on earth, in consequence of the correspondence between things spiritual and things natural, are understood the rainbows seen by the angels in the spiritual world, all which exist from the light of heaven and the modification thereof in the spiritual-natural sphere of that world, consequently from divine truth spiritual, and the translucence thereof in divine truth natural, for all the light in heaven is spiritual, and is in its essence divine truth proceeding from the Lord; hence therefore it may appear that by the bow in the cloud, or rainbow, is signified divine truth spiritual, translucent through divine truth natural, which translucence has place with those who are reformed and regenerated by the Lord by means of divine truth and a life according to it; the translucence itself also appears in the heavens as a rainbow. By the sign of a covenant is signified the presence and conjunction of the Lord with man, for a covenant denotes conjunction; this sign was given, because the flood, which then destroyed the human race, signified the dire falsities of evil, by which the posterity of the most ancient church perished; the restitution and establishment of a new church, which is called the ancient church, by divine truth conjoined to spiritual g od, which in its essence is charity, is representatively exhibited by rainbows in heaven, and hence is signified by rainbows in the world. As these words involve more arcana than can be explained in a short compass, they may be seen particularly explained in the A. C. n. 1031–1060.

596. " And his face was as it were the sun"—That hereby is signified the divine love of the Lord, from which is all divine truth, which in heaven and in the church is the Word, appears from the signification of face, when predicated of the Lord, as denoting the divine love, the divine mercy, and every good, concerning which, see above, n. 74, 412 ; and from the signification of the sun, when predicated of the Lord, as denoting also the divine love, concerning which, see above, n. 401, 524, 527 ; and inasmuch as from the Lord as a sun, in the angelic heaven, proceeds all the light which

is there, and since the light there is divine truth, hence is also understood, from which is all divine truth, and inasmuch as the Word includes all divine truth, and as the same Word which is in the world is also in heaven, and since by the mighty angel coming down from heaven is understood the Lord as to the Word, as may be seen above, n. 593, therefore it is here said the divine truth, which in heaven and in the church is the Word; that the same Word which is in the world, is also in heaven, may be seen in the work concerning H. & H. n. 259, 261, 303–310.

597. " And his feet as pillars of fire"—That hereby is signified the divine truth or Word in ultimates, which is the natural principle sustaining the interior things therein, also full of the good of love, appears from the signification of feet, when predicated of the Lord, as denoting the divine good of the divine love natural, which is the ultimate in divine order, concerning which, see above, n. 65, 69; and from the signification of pillars, as denoting truths inferior which sustain the superior, concerning which see also above, n. 219; and from the signification of fire, when predicated of the Lord, as denoting the divine love, concerning which, see also above, n. 68, 496, 504; from these considerations it may appear, that by the feet of the angel which were seen as pillars of fire, is signified the divine truth, or the Word in its ultimates, which is the natural principle sustaining the interior things therein, also full of the good of love. By divine truth in the ultimates is understood the Word in the literal sense; and inasmuch as this sense is natural, and the natural principle is the ultimate of divine order, therefore it sustains the divine truth spiritual and celestial, altogether as pillars sustain a house, and as the feet sustain the body; for without the natural sense of the Word, the interior things, which are spiritual and celestial, would fall to ruin, as a house when its pillars are removed from under it. Hence therefore all things, even to the most minute particulars, which are in the ultimate of the Word, or in its natural sense, are perpetual correspondences, that is, they correspond to things spiritual and celestial which are in the heavens, and hence are also significative of them : from which considerations it may, in some degree, be manifest, how the divine truth natural, which is the Word in the world, sustains the divine truth spiritual and celestial, which is the divine truth in heaven, as pillars sustain a house : it may also hence appear, why the feet of the angel were seen as pillars of fire. That the Word also in its ultimate or natural sense is full of the good of love, may appear from these words of the Lord : " Thou shalt love the Lord thy God with all thy heart, and with all thy soul, and with all thy mind. This is the first and great commandment. And the second is like unto it, Thou shalt love thy neighbor as thyself. On these two commandments hang all the law and the prophets" (Matthew xxii. 37–40). Here by the law and the prophets is understood the Word in its whole compass, and in the most minute particulars ; consequently by these words is understood that everything in the Word hangs on the good of love to the Lord, and on the good of charity towards our neighbor.

598. Verses 2, 3, 4. "And he had in his hand a little book open, and he set his right foot upon the sea, and his left foot upon the earth. And cried with a 'loud voice as when a lion roareth; and when he had cried, seven thunders uttered their voices. And when the seven thunders had uttered their voices, I was about to write: and I heard a voice from heaven, saying unto me, Seal up those things which the seven thunders uttered, and write them not."— " And he had in his hand a little book open," signifies the Word manifested : "and he set his right foot upon the sea, and his left foot upon the earth," signifies the sense of the letter which is natural, in which are all things pertaining to heaven and the church : " and he cried with a loud voice as when a lion roareth," signifies testification of grievous lamentation on account of the desolation of divine truth in the church: "and when he had cried, seven thunders uttered their voices," signifies instruction from heaven, and perception concerning the last state of the church : " And when the seven thunders had uttered their voices, I was about to write," signifies that he was desirous to manifest that state : " and I heard ' a voice from heaven saying unto me, Seal up those things which the seven thunders uttered, and write them not" signifies a command from the Lord, that those things should be reserved, and not yet be manifested.

599. " And he had in his hand a little book open"—That hereby is signified the Word manifested, appears from the signification of a little book open, as denoting the Word manifested. That this is denoted by the little book open, may appear from this consideration, that by the mighty angel coming down from heaven, who had in his hand the little book, is represented the Lord as to the Word, and indeed as to its ultimate sense, which is called the sense of the letter, as may be seen above, n. 593; and inasmuch as the Word is manifested to angels as well as to men, therefore it is said, a little book open.

600. " And he set his right foot upon the sea, and his left foot upon the earth"—That hereby is signified the sense of the letter, which is natural, in which are all things of heaven and the church, appears from the signification of feet, when predicated of the angel, by whom is understood the Lord as to the Word, as denoting the divine truth in ultimates, or the Word in the natural sense, which is the sense of the letter ; concerning which, see above, n. 65, 69. By feet, in the general sense, are signified things natural, because man, from the head to the soles of the feet, corresponds to heaven, which in its whole compass has reference to one man ; the head corresponds to the inmost or third heaven, the angels of which are celestial ; the breast even to the loins corresponds to the middle or second heaven, the angels of which are called spiritual ; and the feet correspond to the ultimate or first heaven, the angels of which are celestial-natural and spiritual-natural ; but the soles of the feet corespond to the world, in which everything is natural : from these considerations it is manifest, whence it is that the feet signify things natural ; concerning which correspondence, more may be seen in

the work concerning H. & H. n. 59–86, and 87–102. Hence then it is evident, why the feet of the angel, by whom is represented the Lord as to the Word, signify the natural sense of the Word which is the sense of the letter, and from the signification of his right foot upon the sea, and his left foot upon the earth, as denoting all things of heaven and the church; for by the right are signified all things pertaining to good from which truth is derived, and by the left, all things pertaining to truth from good; and by the sea and the earth are signified all things pertaining to heaven and the church exterior and interior, by the sea, exterior things, and by the earth, interior things; and inasmuch as all things of heaven and the church have reference to good and to truth, likewise to things exterior and interior, therefore by these words are signified all things in general pertaining to heaven and the church.   The reason why the angel was seen to stand upon the sea, and upon the earth, is, because the outward appearance of things, in the spiritual world, is similar to that of things in the natural world, namely, as in the latter, so also in the former, there are seas, and likewise earths, seas round about, and earths between them; see above, n. 275, 342, 538; from which circumstance it is manifest, that by sea and earth are signified all things of heaven, and likewise of the church.   Inasmuch as the right and left are mentioned in the Word throughout, and in some places, the right alone, or the left alone is mentioned, it may be expedient to explain, in a few words, what is signified by each of them, and what by both together.   This may be known by the position of the quarters in the spiritual world, where to the right is the south, and to the left is the north, and in front is the east, and behind is the west; for an angel is perpetually turned to the Lord as a sun, wherefore before him is the Lord as the east, and behind him is the Lord as the west, and at his right hand is the south, and at his left hand the north: from this conversion it is, that the right signifies truth in the light, and the left, truth in the shade; or, what is the same thing, that the right signifies spiritual good, which is truth in the light, and the left signifies spiritual truth, which is truth in the shade; thus also the right signifies good from which truth is derived, and the left, truth from good: such things are signified by all the right and left parts of the body, and also of the head; as by the right and left eye, by the right and left hand, by the right and left foot, and so on, the signification proper to each member or part being still retained. From these few observations it may be known what is generally and specifically signified, in the Word of both the Old and New Testament, by the right and left.   Thus in Matthew : " But when thou doest thine alms, let not thy left hand know what thy right hand doeth : That thine alms may be in secret" (vi. 3, 4).   By these words is signified that good is to be done from good, and for the sake of good, and not for the sake of self and the world in order that it may appear; by alms is understood every good work; and by " let not thy left hand know what thy right hand doeth," is signified that good is to be done from good itself, and not without good, inasmuch as otherwise it is not good; by the right hand is signified good from which truth is derived, and by the left hand, truth from good, as was said above; these act as one with those who are in the good of love and charity, but not so with those who regard themselves and the world in the good things which they do, wherefore by the left hand are here understood, to know, and to act without good; "that thine alms may be in secret," signifies that it may not be for the sake of appearance. Again: "And he shall set the sheep on his right hand, but the goats on the left. Then shall the king say unto them on his right hand, Come ye blessed of my Father, inherit the kingdom prepared for you from the foundation of the world. Then shall he say unto them on the left hand, Depart from me, ye cursed, into everlasting fire, prepared for the devil and his angels" (xxv. 33, 34, 41). He who does not know the proper signification of sheep and of goats, may suppose, that by sheep are understood all the good, and by goats all the evil; but in the proper sense, by the sheep are understood those who are in the good of charity towards their neighbor, and thence in faith, and by the goats are understood those who are in faith separate from charity, thus all upon whom judgment takes place in the last time of the church; for all who were in the good of love to the Lord, and thence in the good of charity and faith, were taken up into heaven before the last judgment, and all who were in no good of charity, and thence in no faith, consequently all who were interiorly and at the same time exteriorly evil, were cast down into hell before the last judgment; but they who were inwardly good and not equally so outwardly, also they who were inwardly evil but outwardly in good, were all left to the last judgment, when they who were inwardly good were taken up into heaven, and they who were inwardly evil were cast down into hell; concerning this circumstance, see what is said, from things seen and heard, in the small tract concerning the L. J. From these considerations it may be plainly seen, that by goats are to be understood those who were principled in faith separate from charity, and this is also meant by the he-goat in Daniel (viii. 5–25); and in Ezekiel (xxxiv. 17). Hence then it is evident, that by the right hand, where the sheep are, is understood the good of charity and of faith thence derived, and by the left hand, where the goats are, is understood faith separate from charity: the reason why it is said to the sheep, that they should inherit the kingdom prepared for them from the foundation of the world, is, because, in the heavens, at the right hand is the south, where are all who are in truths from good, for in the southern part is the divine proceeding itself, of such a quality, which is meant by the kingdom prepared from the foundation of the world, hence also they are called the blessed of the Father, for by the Father is understood the divine good, from which are all things of heaven; but concerning the goats, who are at the left hand, it is not said, prepared from the foundation of the world, but it is called everlasting fire, prepared for the devil and his angels, because the evil prepare for themselves their own hell: they are called cursed, because by the cursed in the Word, are understood all who avert themselves from the Lord, for such reject charity and the faith of the church. What is signified by everlasting fire may be seen in the work concerning H. & H. n. 566–575. Similar things are meant, as by sheep and goats, by the two thieves who were crucified, one on the right, and the other on the left hand of the Lord; hence it was said by the Lord to the one who acknowledged him, "Verily I say unto thee, To-day shalt thou be with me in paradise" (Matt. xxvii. 38; Mark xv. 27; Luke xxiii. 39–43). And in John, Jesus said to his disciples who were fishing, "Cast the net on the right side of the ship, and ye shall find. They cast therefore, and now they were not able to draw it for the multitude of fishes" (xxi. 6). Here because by fishing, in the Word, are signified the instruction and conversion of men who are in external or natural good, in which good were most of the Gentiles at that time, for by fish are signified the things pertaining to the natural man, and by a ship is signified doctrine from the Word, therefore by the right side of the ship is signified the good of life; hence it may appear what is signified by the Lord's commanding them to cast the net on the right side of the ship, namely, that they should teach the good of life; that thus they would convert the Gentiles to the church, is signified by their finding in such abundance that they could not draw the net for the multitude of fishes; it must be obvious to every one, that the Lord would not have commanded them to cast the net on the right side of the ship, if the right side had not been significative of something spiritual. Again, in Matthew: "And if thy right eye offend thee, pluck it out, and cast it from thee. And if thy right hand offend thee, cut it off, and cast it from thee" (v. 29, 30). That by the right eye and the right hand the Lord did not here mean the right eye and the right hand, may be obvious to every one from this consideration, namely, that the eye was to be plucked out, and the hand to be cut off, if they offended; but inasmuch as by eye, in the spiritual sense is signified everything pertaining to the understanding and the thought thence derived, and by the right hand whatever pertains to the will and the affection thence derived, it is obvious that by plucking out the right eye, if it offended, is signified, that if evil be thought it ought to be rejected from the thought; and that by cutting off the right hand, if it offended, is signified, that if evil be willed, it is to be shaken off from the will; for the eye itself cannot offend, nor can the right hand, but the thought of the understanding and the affection of the will to which they correspond, can offend: the reason why the right eye and the right hand are mentioned, and not the left eye and the left hand, is, because by the right is signified good, and in the opposite sense evil, but by the left is signified truth, and, in the opposite sense what is false, and all offence is from evil, but not from what is false, unless indeed, that falsity be the falsity of evil. That these things are said concerning the internal man, whose part it is to think and to will, and not concerning the external, whose part it is only to see and to act, is evident also from the words immediately preceding, "But I say unto you, That whosoever looketh on a woman to lust after her hath committed adultery with her already in his heart."

Again: "Then came to him the mother of Zebedee's children with her sons, and saith unto him, Grant that these my two sons may sit, the one on thy right hand, and the other on the left, in thy kingdom. But Jesus answered and said, Ye know not what ye ask,—To sit on my right hand, and on my left, is not mine to give, but for whom it is prepared of my Father" (xx. 20–23; Mark x. 35, 40). The reason why the mother of Zebedee's children, James and John, made this request of the Lord was, that by mother is to be understood the church, by James, charity, and by John, the good of charity in act; these two principles, or they who are in them in heaven, are at the right hand and the left of the Lord; to the right hand there is the south, and to the left hand is the north, and in the south are those who are in the clear light of truth from good, and in the north are those who are in the obscure light of truth from good: the divine principle itself, proceeding from the Lord as a sun, produces such a divine sphere in those quarters, on which account none can possibly dwell there but those who are in such truths from good; this is signified by its being said, that to sit on the right hand, and on the left hand of the Lord, is only for those to whom it is given or prepared by the Father; by the Father is understood the divine good of the divine love, from which is heaven, and everything belonging to heaven; by these words of the Lord therefore is understood, that the Lord gives to those to sit on his right hand and on his left in the heavens, for whom it is prepared from the foundation of the world to be allotted as an inheritance in the south and in the north. That by the right hand is understood the south in the heavens, appears manifestly in David: "The heavens are thine, the earth also is thine: as for the world, and the fulness thereof, thou hast founded them. The north and the right hand (or the south) thou hast created them" (Psalm lxxxix. 11, 12). By the heavens and the earth are understood the superior and inferior heavens, in like manner the internal and external church; by the world, and the fulness thereof, are understood the heavens, and the church in general, as to good, and as to truth, by the world, heaven and the church as to good, and by the fulness thereof, heaven and the church as to truth; and inasmuch as these principles, or those who are in them, are in the north and in the south, and the south is at the right hand of the Lord, therefore it is said, the north and the right hand; and inasmuch as such is the quality of divine truth united to divine good in those quarters from the foundation of the world, as was said above, it is therefore said, "thou hast founded and thou hast created them." And in Isaiah: "And though the Lord give you the bread of adversity, and the water of affliction, yet shall not thy teachers be removed into a corner any more, but thine eyes shall see thy teachers: And thine ears shall hear the word, saying, This is the way, walk ye in it, when ye turn to the right hand, and when ye turn to the left" (xxx. 20, 21). These words treat of the state of those who are in temptations, and who, by means of temptations, and after they are past, admit and receive instruction in the truths of doctrine; the temptations themselves are signified by the bread of adversity,

and by the waters of affliction; by the bread of adversity are signified temptations as to the good of love, and by waters of affliction
are signified temptations as to the truths of faith; for temptations
are of two kinds, namely, as to good which is of love, and as to truth
which is of faith; bread signifies the good of love, and waters signify
the truths of faith, and adversity and affliction signify states of temptation; instruction in the truths of doctrine is signified by, "thine
eyes shall see thy teachers," eyes denoting understanding and faith,
and teachers denoting doctrine; the good of life according to truths
of doctrine is signified by, "thine ears shall hear the word," ears
denoting obedience, and whereas obedience is of the life, therefore
by hearing the word is signified a life according to the truths of doctrine; instruction and obedience are further described by, "saying,
This is the way, walk ye in it, when ye turn to the right, hand,
and when ye turn to the left;" by way is signified truth leading,
truth leading to the south in heaven is understood by turning to the
right, and truth leading to the north there is signified by turning to
the left.   Again, in the same prophet: "Enlarge the place of thy
tent, and let them stretch forth the curtains of thy habitations:
Spare not, lengthen thy cords, and strengthen thy stakes; For thou
shalt break forth on the right hand and on the left; and thy seed
shall inherit the Gentiles, and make the desolate cities to be inhabited " (liv. 2, 3).   The subject here treated of is the establishment
of the church among the Gentiles or nations; by, "Enlarge the
place of thy tent," are signified the increments of the church as to
worship originating in good; by, "let them stretch forth the curtains of thy habitations," are signified the increments of the church
as to truths of doctrine; by, "lengthen thy cords," is signified the
extension of those doctrines; by, "strengthen thy stakes," is signified confirmation from the Word; by breaking forth on the right
and on the left, is signified amplification as to the good of charity,
and as to the truth of faith, on the right denoting as to the good of
charity, and on the left, as to the truth of faith originating in that
good; by the seed which shall inherit the Gentiles, is signified
truth by which are goods, seed denoting truth, and nations denoting
goods; and by the desolate cities, which the nations shall make to
be inhabited, are signified truths originating in the goods of life;
desolate cities denoting truths of doctrine, where there were not
truths before, nations denoting the goods of life from which are
truths, and to dwell denoting to live. So again: "Through the
wrath of Jehovah of hosts is the land darkened, and the people shall be as the fuel of the fire: no man shall spare his
brother.   And he shall snatch on the right hand, and be hungry;
and he shall eat on the left hand, and they shall not be satisfied:
they shall eat every man the flesh of his own arm " (ix. 19, 20).
By these words is described the extinction of good by what is false,
and of truth by evil; the extinction of all good and truth, however
they may be inquired for, is signified by, " he shall snatch on the
right hand, and be hungry, and he shall eat on the left hand, and
they shall not be satisfied;" the right hand denotes good from which

comes truth; the left hand denotes truth derived from good; to snatch on the right hand, and to eat on the left, signify inquiry; to be still hungry and not satisfied, denotes their not being found, and if found, still not received; the remainder may be seen explained above, n. 386. And in Ezekiel: " As for the likeness of their faces, they four had the face of a man, and the face of a lion, on the right side : and they four had the face of an ox on the left side ; and they four had the face of an eagle " (i. 10); what is signified by the cherubim, and by their faces, which were as the faces of a man, of a lion, of an ox, and of an eagle, may be seen above, n. 277–281. The reason why the face of the man and of the lion were seen on the right side, is, because by man is signified divine truth in light and intelligence, and by the lion, divine truth thence in power, such as is in heaven in the south; and the face of the ox being seen on the left side, signifies the good of truth in obscurity, for by an ox is signified the good of the natural man, which is in obscurity with those who in heaven dwell to the north. So in Zechariah: " In that day will I make the governors of Judah like an hearth of fire among the wood, and like a torch of fire in a sheaf; and they shall devour all the people round about, on the right hand and on the left: and Jerusalem shall be inhabited again in her own place, even Jerusalem " (xii. 6). The subject here treated of is the establishment of the celestial church, or of the church which shall be principled in the good of love to the Lord, and is understood by the house of Judah: by her governors are understood the goods together with the truths of that church ; the dispersion of evils and falsities by them is signified by their being made like an hearth of fire among the wood, and like a torch of fire in a sheaf, and by their devouring all the people round about, on the right hand and on the left; the evils to be dispersed by that church are signified by, "like an hearth of fire among the wood, and like a torch of fire in a sheaf;" and the falsities to be dispersed, are signified by all the people round about, whom they shall devour or consume; that the church shall be safe from the infestation of evils and falsities, and shall live in the good of life according to truths of doctrine, is signified by, " Jerusalem shall be inhabited again in her own place, even in Jerusalem ;" to be inhabited is predicated of the good of life, and Jerusalem signifies the church as to the truths of doctrine. Again, in Ezekiel: " I have set the point of the sword against all their gates: ah! it is made bright, it is wrapped up for the slaughter. Go thee one way or other, either on the right hand, or on the left, whithersoever thy face is set " (xxi. 15, 16). By these words is described the destruction of truth by dire falsities ; by the sword is signified those falsities destroying truth, and the direfulness of such falsities is denoted by the sword being made bright and wrapped up for the slaughter; that they who are in such false principles are destitute of good and truth, how studiously soever they may inquire, is signified by, " Go thee one way or other, either on the right hand, or on the left, whithersoever thy face is set." And in Zechariah: " Woe to the idol shepherd that leaveth the flock ! the sword shall be upon his arm, and upon his right eye : his arm shall be clean dried up, and his right eye shall be utterly darkened " (xi. 17). Here by the idol shepherd that leaveth the flock, are understood those who do not teach truth and thereby lead to the good of life, and who are not concerned, whether what they teach be true or false; by the sword being upon his arm is signified what is false destroying all the good of the will, and by its being upon his right eye is signified falsity destroying every truth of the understanding; that they shall be deprived of all good and truth is signified by his arm being clean dried up, and his right eye utterly darkened; these words also may be seen further explained, n. 131, 152. Forasmuch as the right region of the body, and the members of the right region, signify good by which is truth, therefore when Aaron and his sons were inaugurated into the priesthood, it was commanded, that the blood of the ram should be taken, and put upon the tip of their right ear, upon the thumb of their right hand, and upon the great toe of their right foot, (Exod. xxix. 20); this was commanded, because blood signified divine truth, by which man has the good of love, for the latter was represented by Aaron, and the former by his sons; and inasmuch as all inauguration to represent the divine good of love is effected by divine truth, therefore blood was put upon the tip of the right ear, upon the thumb of the right hand, and upon the great toe of the right foot; by the tip of the right ear is signified obedience from perception; by the thumb of the right hand is signified good in the will; and by the great toe of the right foot is signified good in act. Inasmuch as by the leper is signified good consumed by falsities, the manner of the restitution thereof by divine means is described by the process of the cleansing of the leper, understood according to the spiritual sense, from which we shall adduce only a small part. Thus in Moses : " And the priest shall take some of the blood of the trespass-offering, and the priest shall put it upon the tip of the right ear of him that is to be cleansed, and upon the thumb of his right hand, and upon the great toe of his right foot : And the priest shall take some of the log of oil, and pour it upon the palm of his own left hand ; And the priest shall dip his right finger in the oil that is in his left hand, and shall sprinkle of the oil with his finger seven times before Jehovah "(Levit. xiv. 14–28). Similar things are here meant by the tip of the right ear, the thumb of the right hand, and the great toe of the right foot; the same is also signified by the blood, namely, divine truth, for divine truth purifies man from the falsities which consumed the goods belonging to him ; and when he is purified from these, good may be produced by truths, and the man thereby healed of his leprosy. From what has been adduced then it may be seen, that by the right and the left are signified good from which is truth, and truth from good, as was said above ; to what purpose else could it be, that the blood should be sprinkled upon the right part of those members, and that the oil should be poured into the left palm, and sprinkled with the right finger? So in Ezekiel : " Lie thou also upon thy left side, and lay the iniquity of the house of Israel upon it " (iv. 4). The reason of this command was, because a prophet signifies one who teaches, and, in the abstract sense, the doctrine of the church; by the left side is signified the doctrine of truth from good, and by truths from good man is purified from his iniquities. Again, respecting the situation of the ten brazen lavers of the temple, it is said, in the 1st Book of Kings, "And he put five bases on the right side of the house and five on the left side of the house: and he set the sea on the right side of the house eastward over against the south" (vii. 39). The reason of this was, because the house or temple represented heaven and the church, and the lavers represented purifications from falsities and evils, and preparations thereby for entrance into heaven and the church; the right side of the house is signified the south in the heavens, where divine truth is in its light, and the left side signified the north, where divine truth is in its shade; thus by the ten lavers were signified all things pertaining to purification, and all who are purified, and by five on the one side, and five on the other, were signified those, or that kind of men, with whom divine truth is in the light, and with whom it is in the shade, for ten signify all things and all, and five, one part or one kind; but the brazen sea represented the common or general purificatory, and the reason why this was placed on the right side of the house eastward over against the south, was, because divine truth, which purifies, proceeds from the divine love of the Lord, for the east is where the Lord appears as a sun, and the divine truth, which is the light of heaven from that sun, in the south is in its clearness and sunshine; this was the reason why the common purificatory was placed eastward over against the south. These arcana of the Word cannot be understood in the world, except from a knowledge of the quarters in heaven, which are differently circumstanced to what they are in the world; concerning the quarters in heaven, see what is said, from things seen and heard, in the work concerning H. &. H. n. 141–153. Forasmuch as, in the spiritual world, every one enters and walks in the ways which lead to those who are in a similar ruling love, and every one has liberty to go which way he wills, thus in that into which, and through which, his love leads him, and those ways to the right and the left tend to one or the other love, thus to that which is implanted, therefore also by the right and left is signified what is pleasant, free, and wished for. Thus in Moses: "And Abraham said unto Lot, Separate thyself, I pray thee, from me: if thou wilt take the left hand, then I will go to the right; or if thou depart to the right hand, then I will go to the left" (Gen. xiii. 8, 9). And again, when Abraham's servant asked Rebecca as a wife for Isaac, he said to Laban: "And now if ye will deal kindly and truly with my master, tell me: that I may turn to the right hand, or to the left" (Gen. xxiv. 49). By not declining, going, or turning to the right hand or to the left, is also signified not to go in any other way than that into which the Lord himself leads, and into which the good and truth of heaven and the church lead, thus not to walk erroneously, as "That they should not recede from the word of the priest and Levite, and of the judge, nor from the precepts of the Word, to the right hand or to the left"

(Deut. xvii. 11, 20; xxviii. 14; Joshua i. 7; 2 Sam. xiv. 19), "and that the children of Israel should not turn to the right hand or to the left, but should go by the king's high way when they passed through the land of Edom" (Numb. xx. 17); and also when they passed through the land of the king of Sihon (Deut. ii. 27); that the right hand signifies full power, and, when predicted of the Lord, the divine omnipotence, may be seen above, n. 298.

601. "And cried with a loud voice, as when a lion roareth"— That hereby is signified testification of grievous lamentation on account of the desolation of divine truth in the church, appears from the signification of crying with a loud voice, as denoting testification of grievous lamentation, concerning which we shall speak presently; and from the signification of, "as when a lion roareth," as denoting, on account of the desolation of divine truth in the church; for by a lion is signified divine truth in its power, as may be seen above, n. 278; and by roaring is signified the effect of grief, on account of the desolation thereof. This signification of these words may also appear from what follows in this chapter, in which the desolation of divine truth in the church is treated of; for by the mighty angel coming down from heaven, is understood the Lord as to the Word, which is divine truth, concerning whom it is afterwards said that he lifted up his hand to heaven, and swear by him that liveth for ever and ever, that there should be time no longer; by their being time no longer is signified, that there should be no longer any understanding of divine truth, nor, consequently, any state of the church: and it is afterwards said; "But in the days of the voice of the seventh angel, when he is about to sound, the mystery of God should be finished," by which is signified the last judgment, which takes place when there is no longer any faith of divine truth in consequence of their being no good of charity: from these considerations it is evident, that by crying with a loud voice as when a lion roareth, is signified testification of grievous lamentation on account of the desolation of divine truth in the church. Moreover, mention is frequently made of a lion in the Word; and by a lion, in the supreme sense, is signified the Lord as to divine truth, and likewise heaven and the church as to the same, from the Lord; whence a lion also signifies the divine truth as to power, concerning which signification, see above, n. 278; hence it is evident what is signified by roaring, or the roaring of a lion, namely, the ardent affection of defending heaven and the church, and thus of saving the angels of heaven and the men of the church, which is effected by destroying the falsities of evil by divine truth and its power; but in the opposite sense by roaring, and the roaring of a lion, is signified the ardent cupidity of destroying and devastating the church, which is effected by destroying divine truth by the falsities of evil; these things are signified by the roaring of a lion, because when a lion is hungry and seeks his prey, and when he is enraged against his enemy, he is wont to roar. That such things are signified by roaring, may appear from the following passages. Thus in Isaiah: "For thus hath Jehovah spoken unto me, Like as the lion and the young lion roaring on his prey,

when a multitude of shepherds is called forth against him, he will
not be afraid of their voice, nor abase himself for the noise of them :
so shall Jehovah of hosts come down to fight for mount Zion, and
for the hill thereof" (xxxi. 4). Jehovah is compared to a lion roaring, because by a lion is signified the Lord as to divine truth and its
power, and by roaring is signified the ardor of defending the church
against evils and falsities, wherefore it is said, " so shall Jehovah of
hosts come down to fight for mount Zion, and for the hill thereof;"
mount Zion denotes the celestial church, and the hill thereof, or
Jerusalem, denotes the spiritual church; the prey over which the
lion roareth, signifies liberation from hell. So in Joel : " Jehovah
shall also roar out of Zion, and utter his voice from Jerusalem ; and
the heavens and the earth shall shake : but Jehovah will be the hope
of his people, and the strength of the children of Israel " (iii. 16).
Here the defence of the faithful by the Lord, by divine truth, is
described by Jehovah roaring out of Zion, and uttering his voice
from Jerusalem; the vehement power of divine truth, and the terror
consequent thereon, are described by the heavens and the earth
shaking; and salvation and defence is described by Jehovah being
the hope of his people, and the strength of the children of Israel ;
the people of Jehovah and the children of Israel denote the faithful
who are of the church. And in Hosea : " I will not return to destroy
Ephraim. They shall walk after Jehovah : he shall roar like a lion :
when he shall roar, then the children shall tremble from the west.
They shall tremble as a bird out of Egypt, and as a dove out of the
land of Assyria : and I will place them in their houses, saith Jehovah " (xi. 9, 10, 11). Here by Ephraim is signified the church as
to the understanding of truth, concerning which therefore the following things are said ; to walk after Jehovah signifies to worship the
Lord, and to live from him; " he shall roar like a lion," signifies
their defence by divine truth ; " when he shall roar, then the children shall tremble from the west," signifies that they who are in
natural good shall draw near to the church ; " they shall tremble as
a bird out of Egypt," signifies their natural thought from scientific
truths, a bird denoting thought, and Egypt, the scientific principle,
which is natural truth ; " and as a dove out of the land of Assyria,"
signifies that they shall have rational good and truth, a dove denoting rational good, and the land of Assyria, the church as to rational
truth ; for to man belong both natural and rational good and truth,
the natural is inferior or exterior, having regard to the world, the
rational is superior or interior, conjoining the natural with the spiritual; the natural is signified by Egypt, the rational, by Assyria,
and the spiritual by Israel ; to place them in their houses, signifies
life from the will of good and from the understanding of truth ; the
human mind, which consists of those principles, is understood by
house, and to live is signified by location therein. Again, in Amos :
" Surely the Lord Jehovah will not do a word without revealing his
secret unto his servants the prophets. The lion hath roared, who
will not fear ? the Lord Jehovah hath spoken, who can but prophecy ?" (iii. 7, 8.) Here by the Lord Jehovah not doing a word

without revealing his secret to his servants the prophets, is signified, that the Lord opens the interior things of the Word and of doctrine to those who are in truths from good; by revealing his secret are signified the illustration and opening of the interior things of the Word; by his servants the prophets, are signified those who are in the truths of doctrine and who receive; "the lion hath roared, who will not fear?" signifies a powerful revelation and manifestation of divine truth; "the Lord Jehovih hath spoken, who can but prophecy?" signifies the reception thereof, and manifestation; the Lord is called Lord Jehovih, when the subject treated of is good. Again, in Zechariah: "There is the voice of the howling of the shepherds; for their glory is spoiled: a voice of the roaring of young lions; for the pride of Jordon is spoiled" (xi. 3). The voice of the howling of the shepherds because their glory is spoiled, signifies the grief of those who teach, on account of the good of the church perishing; they are called shepherds who teach truths and thereby lead to the good of life, and their glory denotes the good of the church; the voice of the roaring of the young lions because the pride of Jordan is spoiled, signifies grief on account of the desolation of divine truth in the church. They are called lions who are in divine truths; roaring signifies grief; the pride of Jordan which is spoiled, signifies the church as to divine truth which introduces. Thus also in Job: "After it a voice roareth: he thundereth with the voice of his excellency; and he will not stay them when his voice is heard. God thundereth marvellously with his voice" (xxxvii. 4, 5). Here, by roaring and thundering with the voice, is signified the power and efficacy of divine truth or the Word.

In the passages that have been adduced, in an extended sense, by roaring is signified the ardent affection of defending heaven and the church, or the angels of heaven and the men of the church, which is effected by destroying the falsities of evil by divine truth, and its power. But by roaring, in the opposite sense, is signified the ardent cupidity of ruining and destroying the church, which is done by destroying divine truth by the falsities of evil. In this sense to roar is mentioned in the following passages. Thus in Jeremiah: "And Babylon shall become heaps, a dwelling place for dragons, an astonishment, and an hissing, without an inhabitant. They shall roar together like lions: they shall yell as lions' whelps. In their heat I will make their feasts, and I will make them drunken, that they may rejoice, and sleep a perpetual sleep, and not awake, saith Jehovah" (li. 37, 38, 39). The destruction of Babylon, so that there shall be no longer any truth or any good found in her, is signified by, "Babylon shall become heaps, a dwelling place for dragons, an astonishment, and an hissing." Babylon signifies those who abuse holy things for the purpose of ruling by them: their ardent cupidity of destroying divine truth by the falsities of evil, is signified by, "they shall roar together like lions, they shall yell as lions whelps." The ardor of those consociated to effect this wickedness is signified by, "In their heat I will make their feasts;" that such shall be insane from the falsities of evil is signified by, "I will make them drunken that they may rejoice." That they will never understand anything of truth, and thence will not see life, is signified by, "that they may sleep a perpetual sleep, and not awake." Again, in the same prophet: "Is Israel a servant? Is he home born? Why is he spoiled? The young lions roared upon him, and yelled, and they made his land waste; his cities are burned, without inhabitant" (ii. 14, 15). By Israel being a servant, home-born, or a son of the house, is signified the church which had been in truths and goods, and that hitherto it is not. Israel signifies the church, servants, those who are in truths, home-born, or a son of the house, those who are in goods: "why then is he spoiled," signifies the devastation thereof; the young lions roared upon him and yelled, signifies the desolation of divine truth in the church by the falsities of evil: "they have made his land waste," signifies the destruction of that church by evils: "his cities are burned without inhabitant," signifies the destruction of the doctrines of the church also by evils, so that there is no good of the church left. And in Ezekiel: "And she brought up one of her whelps; it became a young lion, and it learned to catch the prey; it devoured men, and laid waste the cities, and the land was desolated, and the fulness thereof, by the noise of his roaring" (xix. 3–7). These things are said concerning the Jewish church, which is here understood by the mother of lions. By the young lion is signified the falsity of evil in the ardor of destroying the truth of the church: by catching the prey, is signified the destruction of the truth and good of the church. "He devoured men, and he defiled widows, and devastated the cities," signifies the destruction of all the understanding of truth, and of good desiring truth, likewise of doctrines; men signifying the understanding of truth, widows, the good desirous of truth, and cities, doctrines: "the land is desolated and the fulness thereof, by the noise of his roaring," signifies the devastation of the church, and the extinction of all truth from the Word, by the falsity of evil; the land denoting the church, the fulness denoting the truths thereof from the Word, and the noise of his roaring denoting the falsity of evil destroying. Again, in Jeremiah: "I will call for a sword upon all the inhabitants of the earth. Therefore say unto them, Jehovah shall roar from on high, and utter his voice from his holy habitation; he shall mightily roar upon his habitation. A noise shall come even to the ends of the earth; for Jehovah hath a controversy with the nations; he will plead with all flesh; he will give them that are wicked to the sword" (xxv. 29, 30, 31). Here the vastation of the church is attributed to Jehovah, although men themselves are the sole cause of it. "I will call for a sword upon all the inhabitants of the earth," signifies falsity destroying all the truth in the universal church. "Jehovah shall roar from on high, and utter his voice from his holy habitation," signifies testification of grief in heaven on account of the vastation of divine truth. "He shall mightily roar upon his habitation," signifies grievous sorrow and lamentation over all things of the church. "A noise shall come even to the ends of the earth," signifies the perturbation of all things from first to last pertaining to the church. "For Jehovah hath a controversy with the nations, he will plead with all flesh," signifies visitation and judgment on all who are in evil. "He will give them that are wicked to the sword," signifies their destruction from falsities. And in Amos: "Jehovah will roar from Zion, and utter his voice from Jerusalem; and the habitations of the shepherds shall mourn, and the top of Carmel shall wither" (i. 2). By Jehovah roaring from Zion, is here signified grievous sorrow, and by uttering his voice from Jerusalem is signified lamentation; the mourning of the habitations of the shepherds, and the withering of the top of Carmel, signify on account of the vastation of all the goods and truths of the church, the habitations of the shepherds signifying all the goods of the church, the top of Carmel signifying all the truths thereof, and the mourning and withering denoting vastation. The reason why the top of Carmel signifies the truths of the church is, because in Carmel there were vineyards, and the truth of the church is signified by wine. Again, in Isaiah: "Therefore is the anger of Jehovah kindled against his people, and hath smitten them. And he will lift up an ensign to the nations from far, and will hiss unto them from the end of the earth. His roaring is like the roaring of a lion, he roareth as the young lions; yea, he shall war and lay hold of the prey, and shall carry it away safe, and none shall deliver it. And he shall roar against them like the roaring of the sea; and if one look unto the land, behold darkness and sorrow, and the light is darkened in the ruins thereof" (v. 25–30). Here also the roaring like the roaring of a lion, and as of young lions, signifies grief and lamentation over the vastation of divine truth in the church by the falsities of evil. By laying hold of the prey and none delivering it, is signified the liberation and salvation of those who are in truths from good. The vastation itself is described by, "behold darkness and sorrow, and the light is darkened in the ruins thereof." Darkness denotes falsities, sorrow denotes evil, the darkening of the light denotes the evanescence of divine truth, and ruins signify total subversion. So in David: "The enemy hath done wickedly in the sanctuary. Thine enemies roar in the midst of thy feast" (Psalm lxxiv. 3, 4). The enemy here mentioned signifies evil from hell, the sanctuary signifies the church, and the feast, worship; hence it is evident what is signified by those words in a series. That roaring signifies grievous lamentation from grief of heart, appears from these passages in David: "When I kept silence, my bones waxed old through my roaring all the day long" (Psalm xxxii. 3). And again: "I am feeble and sore broken: I have roared by reason of the disquietness of my heart" (Psalm xxxviii. 8). And in Job: "My sighing cometh before I eat, and my roarings are poured out like the waters" (iii. 24).

602. "And when he had cried, seven thunders uttered their voices"—That hereby is signified instruction from heaven and perception concerning the last state of the church, appears from the signification of uttering voices, as denoting to instruct, in the present case to instruct from heaven, because it is said that the seven thunders uttered their voices; and from the signification of the seven thunders, as denoting the divine truth as to understanding

and perception, concerning which, see above, n. 273; the thunders are said to be seven, because the number seven signifies all, and what is full, and is' used when things holy are treated of; concerning which, see above, n. 20, 24, 257, 299. The reason why it relates to the last state of the church, concerning which John was instructed from heaven by voices as of thunders, is, because that state is treated of in the present chapter, as may appear from these words (in verse 7): "But in the days of the voice of the seventh angel, when he is about to sound, the mystery of God should be finished; as he hath declared to his servants the prophets;" and that it shall still be taught in the church, before that state, which is the end, shall come, is understood by the last words of this chapter, "Thou must prophesy again before many peoples, and nations, and tongues, and kings" (verse 11): hence then it may appear, that by the seven thunders uttering their voices is signified instruction from heaven, and perception, concerning the last state of the church.

603. "And when the seven thunders had uttered their voices, I was about to write"—That hereby is signified that he was desirous to manifest that state, appears from the signification of, when the seven thunders had uttered their voices, as denoting instruction from heaven, and perception, concerning the last state of the church, concerning which, see just above, n. 602; and from the signification of, "I was about to write," as denoting to be desirous to manifest; that to write denotes to manifest is evident.

604. "And I heard a voice from heaven saying unto me, Seal up those things which the seven thunders uttered, and write them not"— That hereby is signified a command from the Lord that those things should be reserved and not yet manifested, appears from the signification of hearing a voice from heaven, as denoting a command from the Lord, which is, "write them not;" and from the signification of sealing up those things which the seven thunders uttered, as denoting that they should be kept in silence and reserved, namely, those things in which he was instructed, and which he perceived, concerning the last state of the church; and from the signification of, "write them not," as denoting that they are not yet to be manifested; concerning which, see just above, n. 603. That to seal up denotes to keep in silence, and to reserve until another time, appears from what follows in this book where the middle state of the church is treated of, which intercedes between the sounding of the sixth and seventh angel, that is, between the state of the church which is almost last, and that which is the last, wherefore the things which are to take place in the last or ultimate state, are what are to be reserved, and not yet manifested.

605. Verses 5, 6, 7. "And the angel which I saw stand upon the sea and upon the earth lifted up his hand to heaven, and swear by him that liveth for ever and ever, who created heaven, and the things that therein are, and the earth, and the things that therein are, and the sea, and the things which are therein, that there should be time no longer: But in the days of the voice of the seventh angel, when he is about to sound, the mystery of God should be finished, as he

hath declared to his servants the prophets."—" And the angel which I saw stand upon the sea and upon the earth," signifies the Lord to whom all things of heaven and the church are subject: "lifted up his hand to heaven, " signifies attestation before the angels concerning the state of the church : " and sware by him that liveth for ever and ever, " signifies verity from his own Divine principle : " who created heaven, and the things that therein are, and the earth, and the things that therein are, and the sea, and the things which are therein," signifies the Lord as to all things of heaven and the church interior and exterior : " that there should be time no longer," signifies that there should be no longer any understanding of divine truth, and thence not any state of the church : " But in the days of the voice of the seventh angel, when he is about to sound," signifies the last state of the church, and then revelation of divine truth : " the mystery of God should be finished, as he hath declared to his servants the prophets," signifies prediction in the Word concerning the advent of the Lord to be fulfilled when the end of the church is at hand.

606. " And the angel which I saw stand upon the sea and upon the earth"—That hereby is signified the Lord, to whom all things of heaven and the church are subject, appears from the signification of an angel coming down from heaven, as denoting the Lord, concerning which, see above, n. 593 ; and from the signification of standing upon the sea and upon the earth, as denoting to whom all things of heaven and the church are subject, concerning which, also see above, n. 600 ; hence by standing upon them is signified their being subject to him.   Thus in David : " Thou madest him to have dominion over the works of thy hands ; thou hast put all things under his feet" (Psalm viii. 6).   This is spoken of the Lord, whose dominion over all things of heaven and the church, is understood by all things being put under his feet.   And in Isaiah : " And I will make the place of my feet glorious" (lx. 13).   By the place of the feet of the Lord, in the general sense, are understood all things of heaven and the church, inasmuch as the Lord as a sun is above the heavens ; but, in a particular sense, by the place of his feet is signified the church, for the church of the Lord is with men in the natural world, and the natural principle is the ultimate, in which the divine closes, and upon which it, as it were, subsists ; hence it is, that the church in the earths is also called the footstool of the Lord ; as in the same prophet : " Thus saith Jehovah, The earth is my footstool" (lvi. 1 ; Matthew v. 35).   Also in Lamentations : " How hath the Lord cast down from heaven unto the earth the beauty of Israel, and remembered not his footstool " (ii. 1).   And in David : " We will go into his tabernacle : we will worship at his footstool " (Psalm cxxxii. 7). This also is spoken of the Lord, and by his footstool is signified the church in the earths.   From these considerations it is evident that by standing upon the sea and upon the earth, when predicated of the Lord, is signified that all things of heaven and the church are subject to him ; but specifically by the sea and the earth, upon which he set his feet, are signified the ultimate heaven, and the church in the earths, as was just said ; for by the superior parts of the body of

the angel, are signified the superior heavens, because they correspond to them; for the inmost heaven corresponds to the head, and the middle heaven, to the breast even to the loins, and the ultimate heaven, to the feet, but the church in the earths, to the soles of the feet, whence it is that this latter is understood by his footstool. From this correspondence it may be concluded, what is represented generally and specifically by the angel standing upon the sea and upon the earth, by whom the Lord is understood, namely, that the universal heaven is represented, for the Lord is heaven, and his divine human principle forms it to his own image, hence it is, that the universal heaven, in the sight of the Lord, is as one man, and corresponds to all things of man, wherefore heaven is also called the grand man; concerning this subject, see what is said, in the work concerning H. & H. n. 59–102.

607. "Lifted up his hand to heaven"—That hereby is signified attestation before the angels concerning the state of the church, appears from the signification of lifting up the hand to heaven, as denoting attestation before angels; that this is concerning the state of the church is evident from what follows. That it is attestation before the angels which is here signified by lifting up the hand to heaven, may be concluded from this consideration, that attestations are effected by the raising of the hands to heaven, also from this circumstance, that he sware by him that liveth for ever and ever that there should be time no longer, as immediately follows, and to swear is an expression of attestation, and the time that should be no longer signifies the state of the church.

608. "And sware by him that liveth for ever and ever"—That hereby is signified verity from his own divine principle, appears from the signification of swearing, as denoting asseveration and confirmation, and when predicated of the Lord, as denoting verity, concerning which we shall speak presently; and from the signification of, "him that liveth for ever and ever," as denoting the Divine Being from eternity, who alone lives, and from whom is derived the life of all in the universe, both of angels and of men; that this is signified by him that liveth for ever and ever, may be seen above, n. 289, 291, 349. That to swear signifies asseveration and confirmation, but, in the present case, verity, as being from the angel, by whom is understood the Lord, may appear from this consideration, that to swear is to assert and confirm the reality of a thing, and when predicated of the Lord is divine verity; for oaths are taken only by those who are not interiorly in verity itself, that is, who are not interior but only exterior men; hence they can never be taken by the angels, and much less by the Lord; but the reason why he is said to swear in the Word, and why the Israelites were allowed to swear by God, was, because they were only exterior men, and because the asseveration and confirmation of the internal man, when it comes into the external, falls into swearing; and in the Israelitish church all things were external, which represented and signified things internal: the case is similar also with respect to the Word in the sense of the letter; hence it may appear that by the angel swear-

ing by him that liveth for ever and ever, it is not to be understood that he thus sware, but that he said in himself that it is verity, and that this falling into the natural sphere, according to corresponden-ces, was converted into swearing. Now inasmuch as to swear is only what is external corresponding to the confirmation of the mind of the internal man, and hence is significative thereof; therefore in the Word of the Old Testament it is said to be lawful to swear by God, and even God himself is said to swear. That this signifies confirmation, asseveration, and simply the verity of a thing, or that it is true, may appear from the following passages. Thus in Isaiah: "Jehovah hath sworn by his right hand, and by the arm of his strength" (lxii. 8). And in Jeremiah: "Jehovah of hosts hath sworn by himself" (li. 14; Amos vi. 8). And again, in Amos: "The Lord Jehovah hath sworn by his holiness" (iv. 2). And again, in the same prophet: "The Lord Jehovah hath sworn by the excellency of Jacob" (viii. 7). And in Jeremiah: "Behold, I have sworn by my great name" (xliv. 26). By Jehovah being said to swear by his right hand, by himself, by his holiness, and by his name, is signified, by the divine verity; for by the right hand of Jehovah, by the arm of his strength, by his holiness, by his name, and by himself, is understood the Lord as to divine truth, thus divine truth proceeding from the Lord; the same is signified also by the excellency of Jacob, for by the mighty one of Jacob is understood the Lord as to divine truth. That to swear, when predicated of Jehovah, signifies confirmation from himself, or from his own divine principle, is evident in Isaiah: "By myself have I sworn, the word is gone out of my mouth in righteousness, and shall not return" (xlv. 23). And in Jeremiah: "I swear by myself, saith Jehovah, that this house shall become a desolation" (xxii. 5). Inasmuch as by swearing, when predicated of Jehovah, is signified divine verity, therefore it is said in David, "Jehovah hath sworn in truth unto David; he will not turn from it" (Psalm cxxxii. 11). Jehovah God, or the Lord, never swears, for it is not suitable to God himself, or the divine verity, to swear; but when God, or the divine verity, wills to have anything confirmed before men, then that confirmation, in its descent into the natural sphere, falls into an oath, or into the form of an oath, as used in the world: hence it is evident, that although God never swears, yet in the literal sense of the Word, which is the natural sense, it may be said that he swears; this therefore is what is signified by swearing when predicated of Jehovah or the Lord in the preceding passages, and also in the following. Thus in Isaiah: "Jehovah of hosts hath sworn, saying, Surely as I have thought, so shall it come to pass" (xiv. 24). And in David: "I have made a covenant with my chosen, I have sworn unto David my servant. Jehovah, thou swearest unto David in thy truth" (Psalm lxxxix. 3, 49). And again: "Jehovah hath sworn, and will not repent" (Psalm cx. 4). And in Ezekiel: "Yea, I sware unto thee, and entered into a covenant with thee, saith the Lord Jehovih, and thou becamest mine" (xvi. 8). And in David: "Unto whom I sware in my wrath" (Psalm xcv. 11). And in

Isaiah: "I have sworn that the waters of Noah should no more go over the earth" (liv. 9). And in Luke: "To remember his holy covenant; the oath which he sware to our father Abraham" (i. 72, 73). And in David: "Which covenant he made with Abraham, and his oath unto Isaac" (Psalm cv. 8, 9). And in Jeremiah: "That I may perform the oath which I have sworn unto your fathers" (xi. 5; xxxii. 22; Deut. i. 34, 35; x. 11; xi. 9, 21; xxvi. 3, 15; xxxi. 20; xxxiv. 4). From these passages it may be seen what is understood by the angel lifting up his hand to heaven, and swearing by him that liveth for ever and ever. The same thing is also evident from the following passages in Daniel, namely that to swear, when predicted of Jehovah, signifies attestation before the angels concerning the state of the church, that what follows is divine verity: "And I heard the man clothed in linen, when he held up his right hand and his left hand unto heaven, and sware by him that liveth for ever and ever" (xii. 7). Inasmuch as the church instituted with the children of Israel was a representative church, in which all things that were commanded were natural things, which represented, and thence signified spiritual things, therefore it was permitted them to swear by Jehovah, and by his name, likewise by the holy things of the church, by which was represented, and thence signified, internal confirmation, and also verity. This will plainly appear from the following passages. Thus in Isaiah: "He who blesseth himself in the earth shall bless himself in the God of truth; and he that sweareth in the earth shall swear by the God of truth" (lxv. 16). And in Jeremiah: "And thou shalt swear Jehovah liveth, in truth, in judgment, and in righteousness" (iv. 2). And in Moses: "Thou shalt fear Jehovah thy God, and serve him, and shalt swear by his name" (Deut. vi. 13; x. 20). And in Isaiah: "In that day shall five cities in the land of Egypt, swear to Jehovah of hosts" (xix. 18). And in Jeremiah: "And if they will diligently learn the ways of my people, to swear by my name, Jehovah liveth" (xii. 16). And in David: "Every one that sweareth by him shall glory: but the mouth of them that speak lies shall be stopped" (Psalm lxiii. 11). Here, to swear by God, signifies to speak verity, for it follows, "but the mouth of them that speaketh lies shall be stopped:" that they sware by God, see also Gen. xxi. 23, 24, 31; Joshua ii. 12; ix. 20; Judges xxi. 7; 1 Kings i. 17. Since it was allowed to the ancients to swear by Jehovah God, it therefore follows that it is a most enormous evil to swear falsely or to a lie: as appears from these passages. Thus in Malachi: "And I will be a swift witness against the sorcerers, and against the adulterers, and against false swearers" (iii. 5). And in Moses: "Thou shalt not take the name of Jehovah thy God in vain; and ye shall not swear by my name falsely, neither shalt thou profane the name of thy God" (Exod. xx. 7; Deut. v. 7; Lev. xix. 12; Zech. v. 3). And in Jeremiah: "Run ye to and fro through the streets of Jerusalem, and see now, if ye can find a man, who saith, Jehovah liveth; surely they swear falsely. Thy children have forsaken me, and sworn by them that are no gods" (v. 1, 2, 7). And in Hosea:

"Come not ye unto Gilgal, nor swear Jehovah liveth" (iv. 15). And in Zephaniah: "And I will cut off man from off the land; and them that worship and swear by Jehovah, and that swear by Malcham; and them that are turned back from Jehovah" (i. 3, 5, 6). And in Zechariah: "And love no false oath" (viii. 7). And in Isaiah: "Hear ye this, O house of Jacob, which swear by the name of Jehovah, but not in truth, nor in righteousness" (xlviii. 1). And in David: "He that hath clean hands and a pure heart; who hath not lifted up his soul unto vanity, nor sworn deceitfully" (Psalm xxiv. 4). From these passages it may be seen, that to the ancients, who were in the representatives and significatives of the church, it was permitted to swear by Jehovah God, in order to testify verity, and thereby was signified that they thought what was true, and willed what was good: but it was more especially granted to the sons of Jacob, inasmuch as they were altogether natural and external men, and not internal and spiritual; and mere external or natural men are desirous of having the truth of a thing attested and confirmed by oaths, whereas internal or spiritual men are unwilling, yea, are averse from oaths, and account them horrible, especially those in which God is appealed to, and the holy things of heaven and the church, and are contented with saying, and with having it said, that a thing is so, or that it is true. Forasmuch as swearing is not for the internal or spiritual man, and the Lord, when he came into the world, taught men to be internal or spiritual, and for that end afterwards abrogated the external things of the church, and opened the internals thereof, therefore he also prohibited swearing by God and by the holy things of heaven and the church. This plainly appears from his own words as recorded in Matthew: "Again, ye have heard that it hath been said by them of old time, Thou shalt not forswear thyself, but shalt perform unto the Lord thine oaths: But I say unto you, Swear not at all; neither by heaven; for it is God's throne: neither by the earth; for it is his footstool: neither by Jerusalem, for it is the city of the great King. Neither shalt thou swear by thy head, because thou canst not make one hair white or black" (v. 33–36). In this passage the holy things which shall not be called upon in oaths are particularly mentioned, namely, heaven, the earth, Jerusalem, and the head; and by heaven is understood the angelic heaven, wherefore it is called the throne of God, and that by the throne of God is understood that heaven, may be seen above, n. 253, 462, 477; by the earth is understood the church, as may be seen above, n. 29, 304, 413, 417; wherefore it is called the footstool of God, concerning which, see above, n. 606; by Jerusalem is understood the doctrine of the church, wherefore it is called the city of the great king, and that a city denotes doctrine, may be seen above, n. 223; and by the head is understood intelligence thence derived, concerning which, see above, n. 553, 578; wherefore it is said, "thou canst not make one hair white or black," by which is signified, that man can understand nothing of himself. Again, in the same Evangelist: "Woe unto you, ye blind guides, which say, Whosoever shall swear by the temple, it is nothing; but whosoever shall swear by the gold of the temple, he is a debtor! Ye fools and blind: for whether is greater, the gold, or the temple that sanctifieth the gold? And whosoever shall swear by the altar, it is nothing; but whosoever sweareth by the gift that is upon it, he is guilty. Ye fools and blind: for whether is greater, the gift, or the altar that sanctifieth the gift? Whosoever therefore shall swear by the altar, sweareth by it, and by all things thereon. And whosoever shall swear by the temple, sweareth by it, and by Him that dwelleth therein. And he that shall swear by heaven, sweareth by the throne of God, and by Him that sitteth thereon " (xxiii. 16–22). The reason why they were not to swear by the temple and by the altar, is, because to swear by them, was to swear by the Lord, by heaven, and by the church; for by the temple, in the supreme sense, is understood the Lord as to divine truth, and, in the respective sense, heaven and the church as to that truth, likewise all worship from divine truth are understood, as may be seen above, n. 220; and by the altar is signified the Lord as to divine good, and, in the respective sense, heaven and the church as to that good, likewise all worship from divine good are understood, as may also be seen above, n. 391; and inasmuch as by the Lord are understood all divine things which proceed from him, for he himself is in them, and they are of him, therefore he who swears by him, swears by all things that are of him; in like manner, he who swears by heaven and the church, swears by all the holy things which pertain to them, for heaven is the aggregate and the continent thereof; and in like manner the church; wherefore it is said, that the temple is greater than the gold of the temple, because the temple sanctifies the gold, and that the altar is greater than the gift which is upon it, because the altar sanctifies the gift.

609. " Who created heaven, and the things that therein are, and the earth, and the things that therein are, and the sea, and the things which are therein "—That hereby is signified the Lord as to all things of heaven and the church, interior and exterior, appears from the signification of creating, as denoting not only to give a thing existence, but also to give it perpetual existence, holding it together and sustaining it by the Divine proceeding; for the heavens have existed, and do perpetually exist, that is subsist, by the Divine principle of the Lord, which is called the divine truth united to divine good, which being received by the angels constitutes heaven; hence it is that when heaven is mentioned, the Lord is understood, because heaven, where the angels are, is heaven from the Lord, that is from the Divine principle proceeding from him; this therefore is what is here signified by creating; that to create, when spoken concerning the church, and the men of the church, is to create anew, that is, to regenerate may be seen above, n. 4: and from the signification of heaven, the earth, and the sea, and the things which are in them, as denoting all things of heaven and the church, interior and exterior; by heaven, the earth, and the sea, are here signified specifically, the superior and inferior heavens, inasmuch as in the spiritual world the appearance of things is similar to what it is in the natural world,

consequently, there are mountains, earths, and seas, and the mountains there are the superior heavens, because the angels of those heavens dwell upon mountains, and the earth and sea there are the inferior heavens, for the angels of these heavens dwell upon the earths below the mountains, and as it were in seas, concerning which, see above, n. 594; hence it is, that the angel who spake these things, was seen to stand upon the earth and the sea. The reason why by the earth, and the sea, and the things which are in them, are also signified all things of the church, as well interior as exterior, is, because in the church there are things interior and exterior, as in the heavens there are things superior and inferior, and the former correspond to the latter; that by the sea and the earth is signified the church as to the exteriors and interiors thereof, may be seen above, n. 600. According to the sense of the letter, by heaven, the earth, and the sea, are understood the visible heaven, the habitable earth, and the navigable sea, and by the things therein are understood the birds, beasts, and fishes; but that these are not the things properly understood by those words, is evident from this circumstance, that the angel was seen by John, when he was in the spirit, to stand upon the sea and upon the earth, and what is seen in the spirit, is not seen in the natural world, but in the spiritual world, where also, as was said above, there are earths, and seas, and angels, and spirits in them; concerning the appearance of seas in that world, and concerning those who are therein, see above, n. 342.

610. "That there should be time no longer"—That hereby is signified that there shall be no longer any understanding of divine truth, and thence not any state of the church, appears from the signification of time, as here denoting the state of man as to the understanding of the Word, and thence the state of the church, because these are the subjects treated of in this chapter. The reason why time signifies state, is, because times in the spiritual world are no otherwise determined and distinguished than by states of life, particular and general; the reason of this is, because the sun in that world, which is the Lord, is constant and stationary in the same place of heaven, which there is the east, and does not make any revolution as the sun in the natural world appears to do. By the apparent revolution of this sun, times are determined, and so exist in general and in particular; in general, the year and its four seasons, which are called spring, summer, autumn, and winter; these four seasons of the year also are the four natural states thereof corresponding to so many states in the spiritual world, which are the general spiritual states thereof; in particular, within those common or general states in the natural world, there are determined and stated times, which are called months and weeks, but chiefly days, which are distinguished into four natural states, which are called morning, noon, evening, and night, to which also correspond four states in the spiritual world. In the spiritual world, inasmuch as the sun, as was said above, is not carried about, but remains constant and stationary in the east, time is not measured by years, months, weeks, days, and hours, consequently neither is there any deter-

mination by times, but only determination by states of life, general
and particular; hence it is, that in the spiritual world it is not
known what time is, but only what state is, for the determination of
a thing is what gives the notion of it, and it is named accordingly.
This then is the reason why it is not known, in the spiritual world,
what times are, although they succeed each other there, as in the
natural world, but instead of times there are states and their changes;
hence also it is, that times, where they are mentioned in the Word,
signify states.* Forasmuch as by time are understood the things
pertaining to time in the natural world, as those of the year, and of
the day, those of the year being seed time and harvest, and those of
the day being morning and evening, by these therefore, in the Word,
are also described the states of the church. By seed time is described and signified the establishment of the church; by harvest,
its fructification; by morning, the first time of the church; and by
noon to evening, its progression. These natural states also correspond to spiritual states, which are states of heaven and of the
church. As to what concerns the church, it passes through those
states in general, and so does every man of the church in particular.
Every man of the church is also inaugurated into those states from
his first age, but when the church is at its end, he can then no longer
be inaugurated, for divine truth is not received, but is either rejected
or perverted, whence there can be neither seed time nor harvest,
that is, no establishment nor any fructification, neither can there be
morning nor evening, that is, neither beginning nor progression,
which are the states understood and signified by times in the Word;
and inasmuch as in the end of the church those states cease with the
men of the church, therefore it is here said that there shall be time
no longer; by which is therefore signified, that there shall be no
longer any understanding of divine truth or the Word, consequently
not any state of the church.

The same is signified by time, in Ezekiel: "An evil, an only
evil, behold, is come. An end is come, the end is come; it watched
for thee; behold it is come. The morning is come unto thee, O
thou that dwellest in the land: the time is come" (vii. 5, 6, 7).
These things also are said concerning the state of the church: the
end of the former church is first described, and the establishment of
the new church afterwards: the end of the former church by these
words, an evil, one evil, behold, is come, an end is come, the end is
come; the establishment of the new church is described by these
words, "The morning is come unto thee, O thou that dwellest in
the land: the time is come." The morning signifies the state of a
new church, or the commencement of a church, and time, the progressive state of the same, consequently the same as seed time and
harvest, and morning and evening, mentioned above, and consequently also the state of the church as to the understanding of truth,
and the will of good. So in Daniel: speaking of the fourth beast, it is

* Concerning time, and times, in the spiritual world, more may be seen in the
work concerning H. & H. n. 162-169; and concerning the change of states with
the angels, n. 154-161.

said, " And he shall speak great words against the Most High, and shall wear out the saints of the Most High, and think to change times and laws : and they shall be given into his hand until a time and times, and part of a time" (vii. 25).   By the fourth beast is understood the evil which was about fully to vastate the church ; the falsities destroying the truths of the church are understood by the words which he shall speak against the Most High, and by which he will wear out the saints of the Most High ; the saints of the Most High, in the abstract sense, signifying divine truths. That the truths of the Word, and the goods thereof, will then be converted into falsities and evils, is signified by his changing the times and laws, or justice ; times denoting states of the church as to the understanding of truth : the duration of that state as to the end of the church, is signified by, " until a time, and times, and part of a time," by which is understood a full state of vastation. The same is signified by the following words in the same prophet : " And I heard the man clothed in linen, which was upon the waters of the river, when he held up his right hand and his left hand unto heaven, and swear by him that liveth for ever and ever, that it shall be for a time, times, and a half, and when he shall have accomplished to scatter the power of the holy people, all these things shall be finished " (xii. 7). By time is here signified state ; and by time, times, and a half, is signified a full state of vastation ; wherefore it is said, " when he shall have accomplished to scatter the power of the holy people," the holy people denoting those of the church who are in divine truth, and, abstractedly, divine truths themselves.   To the same purpose it is said in the Revelation, of the woman, that she should fly into the wilderness " for a time, and times, and half a time" (xii. 14).   Inasmuch as time signifies those things which appertain to time, as spring, summer, autumn, and winter, by which are signified states of a person about to be regenerated, and of a regenerate person : likewise such things as pertain to those times, namely, seed-time and harvest, by which is signified the state of the church as to the implantation of truth, and as to the fructification of good thence derived ; therefore similar things are also signified by the times of the day, which are morning, noon, evening, and night ; as in the following passages.   Thus in Genesis : " While the earth remaineth, seed-time and harvest, and cold and heat, and summer and winter, and day and night shall not cease" (viii. 22) ; these words may be seen explained in the A. C. n. 930–937.   So in David : " The day is thine, the night also is thine : thou hast prepared the light and the sun.   Thou hast set all the borders of the earth : thou hast made summer and winter" (Psalm lxxiv. 16, 17).   And in Jeremiah : " Thus saith Jehovah, which giveth the sun for a light by day, and the ordinances of the moon and of the stars for a light by night.   If those ordinances depart from before me, then the seed of Israel also shall cease from being a nation before me for ever" (xxxi. 35, 36).   And again, in the same prophet : " If my covenant be not with day and night, and if I have not appointed the ordinances of heaven and earth, then will I cast away the seed of Jacob,

and David my servant" (xxxiii. 25, 26).   Here by the ordinances
of the sun, of the moon, and of the stars, likewise by the covenant
of the day and of the night, and by the ordinances of heaven and
of the earth, are signified similar things as by times, inasmuch as
times exist from those ordinances.   That by seed time and harvest,
summer and winter, likewise by day and night, are signified similar
things as by times, was shown above.   Hence it follows that the
same things are signified by times in these words in Genesis : " And
God said, Let there be lights in the firmament of the heaven to
divide the day from the night; and let them be for signs and for
seasons, and for days and for years" (Gen. i. 14).   By these lumin-
aries, namely, the sun and the moon, are signified love and faith;
for in the spiritual sense of the chapter the new creation or regeneration of the man of the church is treated of, and by the things
there said concerning the sun and the moon, are signified those
things which principally regenerate man and constitute the church;
wherefore by those words and the following is described the process
by which regeneration is accomplished, and afterwards the states of
regeneration are described.   From these considerations it may now
be seen what is signified by there being time no longer.

611. " But in the days of the voice of the seventh angel, when he
shall begin to sound "—That hereby are signified the last state of
the church, and then revelation of divine truth, appears from the
signification of the days of the voice of the seventh angel, as denoting the ultimate or last state of the church; for the progressive
changes of the state of the church are desribed by the sounding of
the seven angels, whence the voice of the seventh angel signifies
the last state; and from the signification of, " when he shall
begin to sound," as denoting revelation then of divine truth.   That
by sounding a trumpet is signified the influx of divine truth, and its
revelation, may be seen above, n. 50.   That its revelation is here
signified, is evident, from the following part of this verse, where it is
said, " the mystery of God should be finished, as he hath declared
to his servants the prophets," by which is signified that the prediction concerning the advent of the Lord shall then be fulfilled : with
the advent of the Lord there is also revelation of divine truth.

612. " The mystery of God should be finished, as he hath declared
to his servants the prophets"--That hereby is signified prediction
in the Word concerning the advent of the Lord to be fulfilled when
the end of the church is at hand, appears from the signification of
being finished, as denoting to be fulfilled; and from the signification
of " the mystery of God which he hath declared," as denoting the
advent of the Lord, concerning which we shall speak presently;
and from the signification of " his servants the prophets," as denoting the truths of doctrine, and, in the present case, the Word.*   The
reason why the Word also is denoted, is, because the Word is the

---

* That they are called servants of the Lord who are in truths from good, may
be seen above, n. 6, 409; and that they are called prophets who teach doctrine,
and that in the abstract sense, doctrine itself is denoted by them, will be further
demonstrated below.

doctrine of divine truth, and because the Word was written by the prophets, likewise because the all of doctrine must be drawn from the Word. Hence it now follows, that by the " mystery of God should be finished, as he hath declared to his servants the prophets," is signified prediction in the Word concerning the advent of the Lord to be fulfilled when the end of the church is at hand. This signification of those words is also evident from what precedes and from what follows. In what precedes it is said, that this shall come to pass in the days of the voice of the seventh angel, by which is understood, that it shall come to pass when the end of the church is at hand; and in what follows after that the seventh angel had sounded, it is said, " the kingdoms of the world are become the kingdoms of the Lord and of his Christ;" and afterwards, that the temple of God was opened in heaven, and the ark of his covenant was seen in his temple (xi. 15–19). The same may also further appear from this consideration, that when the end of the church is at hand, the Word is opened, and a new church established. This also is understood by the advent of the Lord, for the Lord is the Word; wherefore when this is opened, the Lord appears.* The end of the church is also understood by evening, and the advent of the Lord by morning, in the following passage in Daniel : " Two thousand and three hundred. The vision of the evening and the morning which is told is true" (viii. 14, 26). Here the evening signifies the end of the former church, and the morning, the advent of the Lord and the beginning of a new church. The same is signified by morning in these words in Ezekiel: " An evil, behold is come. An end is come, the end is come : it watcheth for thee; behold, it is come. The morning is come unto thee, O thou that dwellest in the land, the time is come" (vii. 5, 6, 7). Here also by the end is signified the end of the church, and by the morning, the advent of the Lord and the beginning of a new church are signified. In like manner in Zechariah : " It shall be one day which shall be known to Jehovah, not day nor night; but it shall come to pass that at evening time it shall be light" (xiv. 7). By the one day which shall be known to Jehovah, is understood the advent of the Lord; by the time of evening is understood the end of the church, when all divine truth is obscured and falsified; and by light is signified the divine truth manifiested. This new light, or that morning which shall appear in the end of the church, is also here understood by the mystery of God which shall be finished, as he hath declared to his servants the prophets.

In the Word, mention is frequently made of evangelizing, and of the gospel [evangelium], and thereby is signified the advent of the Lord, as may appear from the following passages. Thus in Isaiah: " O Zion, that bringest good tidings, get thee up into the high moun-

---

* That the Word was opened when the Lord came into the world, is a known thing; that it is also now opened by the revelation of the spiritual sense thereof, may appear from the small treatise concerning the W. H. and in the work concerning H. & H. n. 1 ; and that now is the end of the church, may be seen in the work concerning the L. J. n. 33–39, and n. 45–52.

tain; O Jerusalem, that bringest good tidings, lift up thy voice with strength; say unto the cities of Judah, Behold your God. Behold, the Lord Jehovih will come with strong hand, and his arm shall rule for him. He shall feed his flock like a shepherd" (xl. 9, 10, 11). That these things are said concerning the advent of the Lord is fully evident, and hence it is that Zion and Jerusalem are called evangelizers, or bringers of good tidings. By Zion are understood all who are of the celestial church, who are those that are principled in love to the Lord, wherefore it is said, " get thee up into the high mountain," the high mountain denoting that love, as may be seen above, n. 405. By Jerusalem are understood all who are of the spiritual church, who are those that are principled in the doctrine of genuine truth, wherefore it is said, " lift up thy voice with strength;" by which is signified confession from genuine truths. By the cities of Judah, to which it is said, " Behold your God, behold the Lord Jehovih will come with strength," are signified doctrines from the Word; by cities, doctrines; and by Judah is signified the Word. That Zion and Jerusalem are called evangelizers, because the gospel [evangelium] signifies the advent of the Lord, is manifest, for it is said, " Behold your God, behold the Lord Jehovih will come with strength." That he will accomplish a judgment, and defend those who acknowledge him, is signified by, " his arm shall rule for him, he shall feed his flock like a shepherd." Again, in the same prophet: " How beautiful upon the mountains are the feet of him that bringeth good tidings, that publisheth peace, that bringeth good tidings of good, that publisheth salvation; that saith unto Zion, Thy God reigneth. For they shall see eye to eye, when Jehovah shall bring again Zion" (lii. 7, 8). These words also are spoken of the Lord's advent, who is evidently understood by, " thy God reigneth," and by, " they shall see eye to eye, when Jehovah shall bring again Zion." The same thing is evident from what follows in that chapter, hence it is that mention is made of evangelizing, or bringing good tidings; the rest of that verse may be seen explained above, n. 365. So in Nahum: " Behold upon the mountains the feet of him that bringeth good tidings, that publisheth peace. O Judah, keep thy solemn feasts" (i. 15). And in Isaiah: " The spirit of the Lord Jehovih is upon me; because Jehovah hath anointed me to preach good tidings unto the meek; he hath sent me to bind up the broken hearted, to proclaim liberty to the captives, and the opening of the prison to them that are bound; to proclaim the acceptable year of Jehovah, and the day of vengeance of our God; to comfort all that mourn" (lxi. 1, 2). That these things are said concerning the Lord and his advent, may be seen from what is said in Matthew v. 3; Luke iv. 16–22. The advent itself is understood by the acceptable year of Jehovah, and the day of vengeance of our God. By the meek, or the poor, the bound and the blind, to whom the Lord is said to preach the good tidings of good, are meant the gentiles, who are said to be poor, blind, and bound, because of their not having the Word, and thus being in ignorance of truth. The gentiles are also understood in the following passages of the Word. Thus in Matthew: "The poor have the gospel preached unto them" (xi. 4, 5). And in David: "Sing unto Jehovah, bless his name; show forth his salvation from day to day; for he cometh, for he cometh to judge the earth: he shall judge the world with righteousness, and the people with his truth" (Psalm xcvi. 2, 3, 12, 13). The acknowledgement and celebration of the Lord with joy of heart on account of his advent, is signified by "Sing unto Jehovah, bless his name; show forth his salvation from day to day." The advent itself is described by Jehovah cometh; and inasmuch as his advent is when the last judgment takes place, it is therefore said, "he cometh to judge the earth; he shall judge the world with righteousness, and the people with his truth." By the earth is understood the church; by the world are understood those in the church who are in the good of charity; and by the people, those who are in truths thence derived. That the advent of the Lord is when the last judgment takes place, was said above, for then the evil will be separated from the good, or the goats from the sheep, and the evil will be judged to hell, and the good to heaven, which is also signified by the words of Isaiah in the above passage, "to proclaim the day of vengeance of our God, to comfort all that mourn." This is the reason that where the last judgment is treated of, mention is also made of evangelizing. The same thing is mentioned in the following passage in the Revelation: "And I saw another angel fly in the midst of heaven, having the everlasting gospel to preach unto them that dwell on the earth, and to every nation, and tribe, and tongue, and people, saying with a loud voice, Fear God, and give glory to him, for the hour of his judgment is come" (xiv. 6, 7). That when the end of the church takes place, the advent of the Lord will be proclaimed, is predicted by the Lord himself in Matthew: "And this gospel of the kingdom shall be preached in all the world for a witness unto all nations; and then shall the end come" (xxiv. 14). That the advent of the Lord is understood by evangelization or the preaching of the gospel, is very evident from the following passages. Thus in Luke: "And the angel answering said unto him, I am Gabriel, that stand in the presence of God; and am sent to speak unto thee, and to show thee these glad tidings" (i. 19). And again, in the same Evangelist: "And the angel said unto them, Fear not, for behold, I bring unto you good tidings of great joy, which shall be to all people. For unto you is born this day in the city of David a Savior, which is Christ the Lord" (ii. 10, 11). And again, in the same, respecting the preaching of John, it is said: "And he came into all the countries about Jordan, preaching the baptism of repentance for the remission of sins. And many other things in his exhortation preached he unto the people" (iii. 3, 18). And again: "The law and the prophets were until John: since that time the kingdom of God is preached" (xvi. 16). So in Matthew it is said: "And Jesus went about all Galilee, teaching in their synagogues and preaching the gospel of the kingdom" (iv. 23; xi. 1; Mark i. 14, 15; Luke vii. 22; viii. 1; ix. 1–6). By the kingdom of God, in the above passages, are understood a new heaven and a new church from the

Lord. Inasmuch as to preach, or to evangelize, signifies to announce the advent of the Lord, hence by the gospel, in the supreme sense, is signified the Lord himself as to his advent, as to judgment, and as to the salvation of the faithful, in the following passages in Mark: " For whosoever will save his life shall lose it; but whosoever shall lose his life for my sake and the gospel's, the same shall save it" (viii. 35; x. 29, 30). And again, in the same Evangelist: "And he said unto them, Go ye into all the world, and preach the gospel to every creature" (xvi. 15).

613. Verses 8, 9, 10. " And the voice which I heard from heaven, spake unto me again, and said, Go, and take the little book, which is open in the hand of the angel which standeth upon the sea and upon the earth. And I went unto the angel, and said unto him, Give me the little book. And he said unto me, Take it, and eat it up; and it shall make thy belly bitter, but it shall be in thy mouth sweet as honey. And I took the little book out of the angel's hand, and ate it up; and it was in my mouth sweet as honey: and as soon as I had eaten it, my belly was bitter."—"And the voice which I heard from heaven spake unto me again, and said," signifies exploration of the men of the church, as to the quality of the understanding of the Word still remaining with them; " Go, take the little book which is open in the hand of the angel who standeth upon the sea and upon the earth," signifies the Word manifested by the Lord to heaven and the church. "And I went unto the angel, and said unto him, Give me the little book," signifies the faculty of perceiving from the Lord the quality of the Word: " And he said unto me, Take it, and eat it up," signifies, that he should read, perceive, and explore the Word, and the quality thereof, within and without: "and it shall make thy belly bitter," signifies that it was inwardly undelightful, because adulterated: "but it shall be in thy mouth sweet as honey," signifies that it was delightful outwardly: " And I took the little book out of the angel's hand, and ate it up," signifies exploration: " and it was in my mouth sweet as honey," signifies that the Word, as yet, as to its external or literal sense, was perceived as delightful, but this only because of its serving to confirm false principles, originating in the love of self and of the world: "and as soon as I had eaten it, my belly was bitter," signifies, that it was explored and perceived that the Word was inwardly undelightful, because of the truth of the literal sense thereof being adulterated.

614. " And the voice which I heard from heaven, spake unto me again, and said "—That hereby is signified exploration of the men of the church as to the quality of the understanding of the Word as yet remaining with them, appears from the things which precede, and from those which follow in this chapter, for the voice from heaven which spake with him and said, involves those things; in those which precede, the subject treated of is the understanding of divine truth or the Word, as appears from verses (2, 3, 4), where by the voice with which the mighty angel coming down from heaven cried, and by the voices of the seven thunders, is signified the manifesta-

tion of the quality of the state of the church as to the understanding of the Word, as may be seen above, n. 601, 602, 603, 604; in those which follow, the subject treated of is the understanding of the Word as yet remaining with the men of the church; for by the little book which the angel had in his hand, is signified the Word, and by eating it up is signified exploration, and by its being sweet in the mouth, and bitter in the belly, is signified that in the sense of the letter it was delightful, but in the internal sense, in which are real truths, unpleasant; this will further appear from what follows. These then being the things treated of above, and which are to be yet treated of, it is plain, that by the voice, which he heard from heaven speaking to him again, and saying, is signified the exploration of the men of the church, as to the quality of the understanding of the Word as yet remaining with them. It is to be observed, that the understanding of the Word perishes in the church by degrees, as the man of the church from internal becomes external, and from internal he becomes external as he recedes from charity, consequently as he recedes from the life of faith. When the man of the church is such, he may indeed be delighted with the reading of the Word, but still he is not delighted with the truth itself, which is the interior sense thereof, for the real life of faith, which is charity, is what produces the affection of interior truth, and thence the delightfulness thereof; wherefore the Word, as to the sense of the letter, may indeed be loved, but this only because it can be drawn over to confirm the false principles which originate in the love of self and of the world, for the Word, in the letter, is of such a quality : hence flows the consequence, that in the end of the church there remains scarcely any understanding of truth; truths from the Word are indeed spoken with the mouth, but without any idea of the real truth contained in them. That this is the case, I have been permitted to prove in the case of many in the spiritual world, and it was found, that although they spoke truths so far as they spoke from the Word, yet they had no understanding of them, so that they were as empty vessels, and as tinkling bells, sounding only from such things as they drew forth from the memory, and were entirely destitute of any perception of the understanding : when man is of such a quality he cannot inwardly possess anything celestial and spiritual, but only what is natural, from the body and the world, which, when separated from what is celestial and spiritual, becomes infernal. From these considerations also it may be seen, what is understood in what follows, by the little book given to John to eat being in his mouth sweet as honey, but making his belly bitter.

615. " Go, take the little book, which is open in the hand of the angel which standeth upon the sea and upon the earth "—That hereby is signified the Word manifested from the Lord to heaven and the church, appears from the signification of the little book open, as denoting the Word manifested, concerning which, see above, n. 599 : and from the signification of the angel who had the little book in his hand, as denoting the Lord as to the Word, concerning which, see above, n. 593; and from the signification of the sea and the

. earth, as denoting heaven and the church, concerning which, see
also above, n. 600; and from the signification of standing upon
them, as denoting the subjection of all things in them, concerning
which, see also above, n. 606. Hence it may appear, that by the
little book open in the hand of the angel who stood upon the sea
and upon the earth, is signified the Word manifested from the Lord
to heaven and the church; what is signified by taking it and eating
it up will be explained in what follows.

616. "And I went unto the angel, and said unto him, Give me
the little book "—That hereby is signified the faculty of perceiving
from the Lord the quality of the Word; appears from the signification of going to the angel and saying, give me the book, as denoting,
in the proximate sense, obedience to the command, because he was
commanded to go and take it; but, in a more remote sense, which
is also the interior sense, by those words is understood the faculty of
perceiving from the Lord the quality of the Word. The Lord gives
to every man the faculty of perceiving this, but still no one does perceive, unless he desire as it were of himself to perceive it; this
reciprocal principle is necessary on the part of man in order that he
may receive the faculty of perceiving the Word, and unless a man
desire and set himself to do this as of himself, there cannot be any
faculty appropriated to him; for it is necessary, in order to appropriation, that there be an active principle and a re-active; the active
is from the Lord, and also the re-active, but this appears as from
man, for the Lord himself gives this re-active principle, and hence
it is from the Lord and not from man; but inasmuch as man does
not know otherwise than that he lives from himself, consequently
that he thinks and wills from himself, hence he ought to use the re-
active principle as from the proprium of his life, and when he so
uses it, then first it is implanted in him, conjoined, and appropriated. He who believes that divine truths and goodnesses flow in,
without such a re-active or reciprocal principle, is much deceived,
for this would be to hang down the hands and wait for immediate
influx, as is the case with those who altogether separate faith from
charity, and say that the goods of charity, which are the goods of
life, flow in without any co-operation of the will of man, when notwithstanding the Lord teaches that he continually stands at the door
and knocks, and that man should open the door, and that he enters
in to him who opens (Rev. iii. 20). In fine, action and re-action
constitute all conjunction, and action and mere passion, none; for
an agent or active principle, when it flows in into a mere patient or
passive principle, passes through and is dissipated, for the passive
yields and recedes; but when an agent or active principle flows into
such a passive as is also a re-active principle, then they are applied,
and both remain conjoined; thus it is with the influx of divine good
and divine truth into the will or into the love of man; wherefore
when the Divine principle flows into the understanding alone, it
passes through and is dissipated, but when it flows into the will,
where the proprium of man resides, it then remains conjoined.
From these considerations it may be seen what arcanum is involved

in its being first said, " Go, take the little book, which is open in the hand of the angel which standeth upon the sea and upon the earth," and then that he " went unto the angel, and said unto him, Give me the little book," upon which the angel said unto him, " Take it, and eat it up," for thus is described the reactive and reciprocal principle ; hence then it is that by those words is signified the faculty of receiving and perceiving from the Lord the quality of the Word. The reception of the divine influx is also described in like manner in other passages of the Word.

617. " And he said unto me, Take it, and eat it up "—That hereby is signified that he should read, perceive, and explore the Word, as to its quality within and without, appears from the signification of saying, " take the little book," as denoting to give the faculty of perceiving the quality of the Word, that is, the quality of the understanding of the Word now in the church, concerning which see the preceding article, n. 616; and from the signification of eating up, as denoting to conjoin or appropriate to one's self, and inasmuch as the Word is conjoined to man by reading and perception, therefore here by eating up are signified reading and perception. The reason why eating up here also signifies to explore, is, because it is afterwards said that the little book would make his belly bitter, and would be in his mouth sweet as honey, by which is understood the exploration of the quality of the Word as to the understanding thereof within and without : its quality within is signified by the belly and its bitterness, and without, by the mouth in which it was perceived to be sweet as honey : from these considerations it is plain, that by these words, " And he said unto me, Take it, and eat it up," is signified, that he should read, perceive, and explore the Word, as to its quality within and without. In the Word, mention is frequently made of eating and drinking, and they who are unacquainted with the spiritual sense suppose that these expressions signify nothing more than natural eating and drinking ; whereas they signify spiritual nourishment, consequently, the appropriation of good and truth, eating signifying the appropriation of good, and drinking, the appropriation of truth : any one may know, who believes in the spirituality of the Word, that by eating and drinking, as by bread, food, wine, and drink, is signified spiritual nourishment, for otherwise the Word would be merely natural, and not at the same time spiritual, thus only for the natural man, and not for the spiritual man, much less for the angels. That by bread, food, wine, and drink, in the spiritual sense, is understood the nourishment of the mind, has been frequently shown above, and also that the Word every where is spiritual, although in the sense of the letter it is natural. To be spiritually nourished is to be instructed and imbued, consequently it is to know, to understand, and to be wise; unless man enjoys this nourishment together with the nourishment of the body, he is not a man, but a beast ; which is the reason that they who place all delight in feastings and banquetings, and daily indulge their palates, are stupid as to things spiritual, however they may be able to reason concerning the things of the world and of the body,

whence, after their departure from this world, they live rather a
beastly than a human life, for instead of intelligence and wisdom
they have insanity and folly. These things are mentioned, in order
that it may be known, that here, by eating up the little book, is
signified to read, to perceive, and to explore the Word, for by the
little book, which was in the hand of the angel coming down from
heaven, is understood the Word, as was said above : besides, no
one can eat or devour any book, so neither the Word, naturally
from which also it is evident, that by eating is here signified to be
spiritually nourished.

That by eating and drinking, in the Word, are also signified to
eat and drink spiritually, which is to be instructed, and by instruction both to imbue the life, and to appropriate to one's self good and
truth, consequently intelligence and wisdom, may further appear
from the following passages. Thus in Jeremiah : "Thy words
were found, and I did eat them; and thy word was unto me the joy
and rejoicing of my heart " (xv. 16). Here, by eating is evidently
denoted to eat spiritually, which is to know, to perceive, and to appropriate, for it is said that the prophet did eat the words of Jehovah, and that they became the joy and rejoicing of his heart; the
words of God are his precepts or divine truths. The same thing is
signified by what the Lord said to the tempter, as recorded in Matthew: "Man shall not live by bread alone, but by every word that
proceedeth out of the mouth of God " (iv. 4; Luke iv. 4; Deut.
viii. 3). And again : " Labor not for the meat which perisheth, but
for that meat which endureth unto everlasting life " (John vi. 27).
And in another place : " In the mean while his disciples prayed him,
saying, Master, eat. But he said unto them, I have meat to eat that
ye know not of. Therefore said the disciples one to another, Hath
any one brought him aught to eat? Jesus saith unto them, My
meat is to do the will of him that sent me, and to finish his work "
(John iv. 31–34). From these passages it is also evident, that to
eat, in the spiritual sense, signifies to receive in the will, and to do,
whence comes conjunction; for the Lord, by doing the divine will,
conjoined the divine principle which was in him with his human, so
that he appropriated the divinity to his humanity. It was for the
same reason also, that the Lord fed five thousand men, besides
women and children, with five loaves and two fishes, and after they
had eaten and were filled they took up twelve baskets of fragments
(Matthew xiv. 15–21 ; John vi. 5, 13, 23); And that he fed four
thousand men, from seven loaves and a few fishes (Matthew xv. 32,
and the following verses). This miracle was performed because the
Lord had before been teaching the people, and they received and
appropriated to themselves his doctrine ; this was what they spiritually ate, whence the natural eating followed, namely, flowed in
with them out of heaven, as the manna with the children of Israel,
unknown to themselves ; for at the will of the Lord, spiritual food,
which is also real food, but only for spirits and angels, is turned into
natural food, in like manner as it was turned into manna with the
children of Israel every morning. The same is signified in Luke by

eating bread in the kingdom of God, as in these words: "And I appoint unto you a kingdom; that ye may eat and drink at my table in my kingdom" (xxii. 28, 29, 30). In these words also by eating and drinking are signified to eat and drink spiritually, consequently to eat denotes to receive, perceive, and appropriate the good of heaven from the Lord, and to drink denotes to receive, perceive, and appropriate the truth of that good; for to eat is predicated of good, because bread signifies the good of love, and to drink is predicated of truth, because water and wine signify the truth of that good. So again, in Luke: "Blessed is he that shall eat bread in the kingdom of God" (xiv. 15). Hence also it was that the Lord likened the kingdom of God to a great supper, to which those who were invited did not come, and which was attended only by those who were brought in from the streets and the lanes of the city (verse 16–24). Spiritual eating, by which the soul is nourished, is also signified by eating in the following passages of the Word. Thus in Isaiah: "If ye be willing and obedient, ye shall eat the good of the land" (. 19). Here by eating the good of the land is signified spiritual good, hence it is said, "If ye be willing and obedient," that is, if ye do, for spiritual food is given, conjoined, and appropriated, to man, by willing and thence doing it. And in David: "Blessed is every one that feareth Jehovah; that walketh in his ways. For thou shalt eat the labor of thy hands: happy shalt thou be, and it shall be well with thee" (Psalm cxxviii. 1, 2). By eating the labor of his hands is signified the celestial good which man receives by a life according to divine truths from the Lord, and as it were acquires to himself by his own labor and study, wherefore it is said that he who feareth Jehovah and walketh in his ways shall eat the labor of his hands, that he shall be happy, and that it shall be well with him. Again, in Isaiah: "Say ye to the righteous, that it shall be well with him: for they shall eat the fruit of their doings" (iii. 10). By eating the fruit of their doings is signified the same as by eating the labor of their hands, mentioned above. So in Ezekiel: "Thou didst eat fine flour, and honey, and oil: and thou wast exceeding beautiful, and thou didst prosper into a kingdom" (xvi. 13). This was spoken of Jerusalem, by which the church is signified, in the present case, the ancient church, which was in truths and in spiritual good, and at the same time in natural good; by fine flour is signified truth, by honey, good natural or of the external man, and by oil, spiritual good or the good of the internal man; the reception, perception, and appropriation of this, is signified by eating fine flour, honey, and oil; that she became intelligent thence, is signified by, her becoming exceedingly beautiful, beauty denoting intelligence; that thence she became a church, is signified by her prospering into a kingdom, a kingdom denoting a church. Again, in Isaiah: "Behold, a virgin shall conceive, and bear a son, and shall call his name Immanuel. Butter and honey shall he eat, that he may know to refuse the evil, and choose the good. For before the child shall know to refuse the evil and choose the good, the land that thou abhorrest shall be forsaken of both her kings" (vii. 14, 15, 16). That the son whom the virgin should conceive and bring forth, and whose name should be called Immanuel, or God with us, is the Lord, as to his human principle, is manifest; the appropriation of divine good, spiritual and natural, as to the human principle, is understood by "butter and honey shall he eat," divine good spiritual, by butter, and divine good natural, by honey, and appropriation, by eating; and inasmuch as it is known how to refuse evil, and choose good, in proportion as divine good, spiritual and natural, is appropriated, therefore it is said, "that he may know to refuse the evil, and choose the good;" that the church was deserted and vastated as to all good and truth by scientifics falsely applied, and by reasonings thence derived, is signified by, "the land that thou abhorrest shall be forsaken of both her kings;" the land signifies the church; the desertion and vastation thereof are understood by its being abhorred and forsaken; and the two kings, who are the king of Egypt and the king of Assyria, signify scientifics ill applied, and reasonings thence derived, the king of Egypt, those scientifies, and the king of Assyria, those reasonings; that these are the kings who are here understood, is evident from what presently follows in the same chapter (verses 17, 18), where Egypt and Assyria are mentioned; these things also are what principally vastate the church. That the Lord came into the world when there was no longer any good and truth in the church, thus when there was nothing of the church remaining, has been occasionally shown above. Again, in the same prophet: "And it shall come to pass for the abundance of milk that they shall give that he shall eat butter: for butter and honey shall every one eat that is left in the land" (vii. 22). The subject here treated of is the new church to be established by the Lord; and by butter and honey is signified spiritual and natural good, and by eating is signified to appropriate, as above; by milk is signified what is spiritual from a celestial origin, from which those good are. So again: "Ho, every one that thirsteth, come ye to the waters, and he that hath no money; come ye, buy, and eat; yea, come, buy wine and milk without money and without price. Wherefore do ye spend money for that which is not bread? and your labor for that which satisfieth not? hearken diligently unto me, and eat ye that which is good, and let your soul delight itself in fatness" (lv. 1, 2). That to eat here signifies to appropriate to one's self from the Lord, is manifestly evident, for it is said, "Ho, every one that thirsteth, come ye to the waters, and he that hath no money; come ye, buy and eat;" by which is signified, that every one who desires truth, and who had not truth before, may procure and appropriate it to himself from the Lord; to thirst signifies to desire, water denotes truth, money, or silver, the truth of good, wherefore by him that hath no money is signified him that before had no truth of good; to come denotes to go to the Lord, to buy denotes to procure for himself, and to eat denotes to appropriate. "Come ye, buy wine and milk without money and without price," signifies to procure divine truth spiritual and divine truth natural without self-derived intelligence, wine denoting divine truth spiritual, and milk, divine truth spiritual-natural. "Wherefore do ye spend money for that which is not bread? and your labor for that which satisfieth not?" signifies, that it is in vain to endeavor from the proprium to procure the good of love, and that which nourishes the soul, money here denoting truth from the proprium, or self-derived intelligence, and in like manner labor. Bread denotes the good of love, and that which satisfies denotes that which nourishes the soul, in the present case, that which does not nourish. "Hearken diligently unto me," signifies, that those things are from the Lord alone, "and eat ye that which is good, and let your soul delight itself in fatness," signifies, that they may appropriate to themselves celestial good, from which is all delight of life, to delight in fatness denoting to be delighted from good, and soul signifying life. Again, in the same prophet: "For her merchandise shall be for them that dwell before Jehovah, to eat sufficiently, and for durable clothing" (xxiii. 18). This is spoken of Tyre, and by the merchandise of Tyre are signified the knowledges of good and truth of every kind. To dwell before Jehovah, signifies to live from the Lord; to eat sufficiently signifies to receive, perceive, and appropriate the knowledges of good sufficiently for the nourishment of the soul; "and for durable (or ancient) clothing," signifies to imbibe the knowledges of genuine truth; for to clothe, or cover, is predicated of truths, because garments signify truths, clothing, good, and durable, or ancient, is predicated of what is genuine, inasmuch as genuine truths were with the ancients. The same is signified by the following passages in Moses: "And your threshing shall reach unto the vintage, and the vintage shall reach unto the sowing time; and ye shall eat your bread to the full. And ye shall eat old store" (Levit. xxvi. 5, 10). Again: "And I will send grass in thy fields for thy cattle, that thou mayest eat and be full" (Deut. xi. 15). And again: "And ye shall eat, and not be satisfied" (Levit. xxvi. 26). And in Isaiah: "And they shall build houses, and inhabit them; and they shall plant vineyards, and eat the fruit of them. They shall not build, and another inhabit; they shall not plant, and another eat" (lxv. 21, 22). Every one knows what is signified by those words in the sense of the letter; but inasmuch as the Word in its interior is spiritual, spiritual things also are thereby understood, namely, such things as pertain to heaven and the church, for these are things spiritual. By building houses and inhabiting them, is signified to fill the interiors of the mind with the goods of heaven and the church, and thereby to enjoy celestial life, houses denoting the interiors of the mind, and to inhabit denoting celestial life thence derived. By planting vineyards and eating the fruit of them, is signified to enrich themselves with spiritual truths, and to appropriate to themselves the goods thence derived; vineyards denoting spiritual truths, fruit the goods thence derived, and to eat denoting to receive, perceive, and appropriate, for all good is appropriated to man by truths, namely, by a life according to them. Hence it is evident what is signified by, "they shall not build and another inhabit, they shall not plant and another eat." Another signifies the falsity and evil

which destroy truth and good; for when truths and goods perish
with man, falsities and evils enter.   Thus also in Jeremiah : "Build
ye houses, and dwell in them, and plant gardens, and eat the fruit
of them " (xxix. 5, 28).   These words are to be understood in the
same sense as the preceding.   Again, in Moses : " To give thee
great and goodly cities, which thou buildedst not, and houses full
of all good things, which thou filledst not, and wells digged, which
thou diggedst not, vineyards and olive trees, which thou plantedst
not: when thou shalt have eaten and be full " (Deut. vi. 10, 11).
By the natural man these things are understood only according to
the sense of the letter, but if there were not a spiritual sense contained in every particular, the Word would be merely natural, and
not spiritual, and thus it might be supposed that it is only worldly
opulence and abundance which are freely given to those who live
according to the divine precepts; but what would it profit a man if he
were to gain the whole world, and lose his own soul ?   Thus what
would it profit him if houses were given him full of every good,
likewise wells, olive trees, and vineyards, and to eat thereof to
satiety ?   But the case is, these worldly riches are mentioned to
denote spiritual riches, from which man has life eternal.   By the
great and goodly cities to be given to them, are signified doctrines
from genuine truths and goods ; by houses full of all good things,
are signified the interiors of the mind full of love and wisdom ;
by wells digged, are signified the interiors of the natural mind
full of the knowledges of good and truth; by vineyards and
olive trees, are signified all things both as to truths and goods pertaining to the church, vineyards denoting the church as to truths,
and olive trees the church as to goods ; for wine signifies truth, and
oil good : to eat to satiety, signifies plenary reception, perception,
and appropriation.   Again, in Isaiah : " Then shalt thou delight
thyself in Jehovah ; and I will cause thee to ride upon the high
places of the earth, and feed thee with the heritage of Jacob " (lviii.
14).   Here, by causing them to ride upon the high places of the
earth, is signified, to give them the understanding of superior or
interior truths concerning the things of the church and of heaven;
and by feeding them with the heritage of Jacob, is signified to gift
them with all things of heaven and the church ; for by the heritage
of Jacob is understood the land of Canaan, and by that land is understood the church, and in a superior sense, heaven.   Inasmuch as
eating signifies appropriation, it may readily be seen what is signified by the following words in the Revelation : " To him that overcometh will I give to eat of the tree of life, which is in the midst of
the paradise of God " (ii. 7); namely, the appropriation of celestial
life.   From the same may be seen also what is signified by eating
of the tree of the knowledge of good and evil mentioned in Genesis :
" And Jehovah God commanded the man, saying, Of every tree of
the garden thou mayest freely eat, but of the tree of the knowledge
of good and evil thou shalt not eat of it, for in the day that thou
eatest thereof thou shalt surely die " (ii. 16, 17).   By the tree of the
knowledge of good and evil, is signified the knowledge of things

natural, by which it is not allowable to enter into things celestial and spiritual which pertain to heaven and the church, for this is to enter from the natural man into the spiritual, which is an inverted way, and consequently does not lead to wisdom, but destroys it. By Adam and his wife is understood the most ancient church, which was a celestial church; the men of that church being principled in love to the Lord, had divine truths inscribed upon them, and thence knew from influx the things corresponding in the natural man, which are called scientifics; in a word, with the men of that church, spiritual influx had place, which is from the spiritual mind into the natural, and thus into the things which are therein, which things they saw according to their quality, as in a mirror, from correspondence. Spiritual things with them were altogether distinct from natural things, the former residing in their spiritual mind, and the latter in their natural mind, and hence they did not immerse anything spiritual in their natural mind, as is the case with men who are spiritual-natural; if therefore they had committed spiritual things to the natural memory, and in that manner had appropriated them to themselves, what was implanted with them would have perished, and they would have begun to reason from the natural man concerning spiritual subjects, and thence have formed their conclusions, which the celestial never do; this also would have been to desire to be wise from self-derived intelligence, and not from divine intelligence, as before, by which they would have extinguished all their celestial life, and have conceived natural ideas also concerning things spiritual. This therefore is what is signified by its being said, that they should not eat of the tree of the knowledge of good and evil, and if they did eat, that they should surely die. The case was similar with the most ancient people, who are understood by Adam, to what it is with those who are in the celestial kingdom of the Lord, who, if they imbue the natural man and its memory with the knowledges of spiritual truth and good, and desire to be wise from them, become stupid, although they are the most wise of all in heaven.* Again, it is said in David: "Yea, mine own familiar friend, which did eat of my bread, hath lifted up his heel against me" (Psalm xli. 9). This is spoken concerning the Jews, who were in possession of divine truths because they had the Word, as is evident from the following passage in John: "He that eateth bread with me hath lifted up his heel against me" (xiii. 18). From this application of the above words it is plain that by eating the bread of the Lord, is signified the appropriation of divine truth, but here the communication thereof, inasmuch as it could not be really appropriated to the Jews, the bread signifying the Word, from which spiritual nourishment is derived. To lift up the heel against him, signifies to pervert the literal sense of the Word even to the denial of the Lord, and to the falsification of every truth; for the divine truth is exhibited in an image as a man; whence heaven in its

* On this subject more may be seen in the work concerning H. & H. n. 20–28, where the two kingdoms, called celestial and spiritual, into which heaven is in general distinguished, are treated of.

whole compass is.called the grand man, and corresponds to all things pertaining to man ; for heaven is formed according to divine truth proceeding from the Lord; and inasmuch as the Word is divine truth, therefore this also, before the Lord, is in an image as a divine man; hence the ultimate sense thereof, which is the mere sense of the letter, corresponds to the heel. The perversion of the Word, or of the divine truth by the application of the sense of the letter to falsities, such as were the traditions of the Jews, is signified by lifting up the heel against the Lord.* Thus also in Luke : " Then shall ye begin to say, We have eaten and drunk in thy presence, and thou hast taught in our streets. But he shall say, I tell you, I know you not whence ye are ; depart from me, all ye workers of iniquity " (xiii. 26, 27). By their saying, when presented to judgment, that they had eaten and drunk in the presence of the Lord, is signified that they had read the Word, and imbibed thence the knowledges of good and truth, supposing that they should thereby be saved, wherefore it follows; "and thou hast taught in our streets," denoting that they were instructed in truths from the Word, thus from the Lord; but that to read the Word and be instructed from it could avail them nothing as to salvation, without a life according to it, is signified by the Lord's answer to them, "I tell you, I know you not whence ye are ; depart from me, all ye workers of iniquity ;" for it is of no avail to salvation to enrich the memory from the Word, and from the doctrines of the church, unless they are committed to life. Again, in Matthew : " Then shall the King say unto them on his right hand, I was an hungered, and ye gave me meat; I was thirsty, and ye gave me drink. Then shall he say also unto them on the left hand, I was an hungered, and ye gave me no meat; 'I was thirsty, and ye gave me no drink " (xxv. 34–42). By these words also are signified spiritual hunger and thirst, likewise, spiritual eating and drinking. Spiritual hunger and thirst are the affection and desire for good and truth, and spiritual eating and drinking are instruction, reception, and appropriation. It is here said concerning the Lord, that he hungered and thirsted, because from his divine love he desires the salvation of all ; and concerning men it is said that they gave him to eat and to drink; which is the case when, from affection, they receive and perceive good and truth from the Lord, and appropriate them to themselves by a life according to them. In like manner it will be said of the man who, from his heart, loves to instruct his fellow-men, and desires his salvation ; wherefore it is charity, or the spiritual affection of truth, which is described by these words and those which follow.

From what has been said it may now be seen what is signified by eating bread and drinking wine, in the spiritual sense, in the holy supper (Matthew xxvi. 26 ; Mark xiv. 22) ; where it is also said,

* That the universal heaven is in an image as a man, and thence corresponds to all things of man, and that heaven is such by reason of its being created and formed from the Lord by divine truth proceeding from him, which is the Word, from which all things were made (John i. 1, 2, 3), may be seen in the work concerning H. & H. n. 59, 102, likewise n. 200–212.

that the bread is the Lord's body, and the wine his blood.* That such things are signified by bread and wine, and by body and blood, as likewise by eating, may still more evidently appear from the following words of the Lord in John : " Your fathers did eat manna in the wilderness and are dead. This is the bread which cometh down from heaven : if any man eat of this bread, he shall live for ever ; and the bread that I will give is my flesh, which I will give for the life of the world. Verily, verily, I say unto you, Except ye eat the flesh of the Son of man, and drink his blood, ye have no life in you. Whoso eateth my flesh, and drinketh my blood, hath eternal life ; and I will raise him up at the last day. He that eateth my flesh, and drinketh my blood, dwelleth in me, and I in him. This is that bread which came down from heaven. He that eateth of this bread shall live for ever" (vi. 49–58.) That neither flesh and blood, nor bread and wine, are here meant, but the Divine proceeding from the Lord, must be evident to every one who enjoys the faculty of thinking inwardly ; for it is the Divine proceeding, which is divine good and divine truth, which gives eternal life to man, and causes the Lord to be in man, and man to abide in the Lord ; for the Lord is in man in his own divine principle, and not in the proprium of man, this being nothing but evil ; and the Lord is in man, and man in the Lord, when the divine proceeding is appropriated to man, by a right reception thereof. The appropriation itself is signified by eating, the divine good proceeding, by flesh and by bread, and the divine truth proceeding, by blood and by wine. In like manner as in the sacrifices, in which the flesh and the meat offering, which was bread, signified the good of love, and the blood and the wine, which were the drink offering, signified the truth from that good, both from the Lord. Since by flesh and bread is signified the divine good proceeding, and by blood and wine, the divine truth proceeding, therefore, by bread and flesh is understood the Lord himself as to divine good, and by blood and wine the Lord himself as to divine truth. The reason why the Lord himself is understood by those things, is, because the divine proceeding is the Lord himself in heaven and in the church ; wherefore the Lord says concerning himself, " This is the bread which cometh down from heaven ;" likewise, " He who eateth my flesh and drinketh my blood, dwelleth in me, and I in him." Forasmuch as bread signifies the Lord as to divine good, and to eat signifies appropriation and conjunction, therefore it is said when he manifested himself to his disciples, that ," it came to pass as he sat at meat with them, he took bread, and blessed it, and brake, and gave to them. And their eyes were opened, and they knew him" (Luke xxiv. 30, 31). From this circumstance it is also evident that to eat bread given by the Lord, signifies conjunction with him, by virtue of which the disciples, be-

* That by bread is there signified the good of love, and by wine the truth from that good, which is also the good of faith, and that the same is signified by flesh and blood, likewise that by eating are signified appropriation and conjunction with the Lord, may appear from what is said and shown in the D. of the N. J. n. 210–222.

ing enlightened, immediately knew him; for eyes in the Word correspond to the understanding, and thence signify it, and this is what is enlightened; hence it is said their eyes were opened: by breaking bread, in the Word, is signified to communicate good with anoother. The reason why the Lord ate with publicans and sinners, at which the Jews murmured and were offended (Mark ii. 15, 16; Luke v. 29, 30; vii. 33, 34, 35), was, because the gentiles, or nations, which are understood by the publicans and sinners, received the Lord, imbibed his precepts, and lived according to them whereby the Lord appropriated to them the good things of heaven, which is signified in the spiritual sense by eating with them. Inasmuch as by eating was signified to appropriate, therefore it was granted to the children of Israel to eat of the sanctified things, or of the sacrifices, for by the sacrifices were signified divine celestial and spiritual things, and hence by eating of them was signified the appropriation of them; hence various laws were given concerning what and where they should eat, and of what sacrifices. Thus it was commanded that Aaron and his sons should eat the flesh of the ram, and the bread that was in the basket, by the door of the tabernacle (Exod. xxix. 32, 33; Levit. vi. 9, 10, 11; vii. 6, 7; viii. 31, 32, 33; x. 13, 14, 15); that they should eat the shew bread in the holy place (Levit. xxiv. 9); that the daughter of a priest, being married to a stranger, should not eat of the holy things, but that the daughter of a priest, being a widow, or divorced, who had no offspring, but was returned to her father as in her youth, might eat of them (Lev. xxii. 12, 13); that certain descriptions of the people should eat (Numb. xviii. 10–19); that a stranger, a lodger or hired servant of a priest should not eat of them, but that he who was bought with money should eat (Levit. xxii. 10, 11, 12); that the unclean should not eat (Levit. vii. 19, 20, 21; xxi. 16 to end; xxii. 2–8); that they should not eat any part of the burnt-offerings, but of the eucharistic sacrifices, and should rejoice before Jehovah (Deut. xii. 27; xxvii. 7). In these and many other statutes and laws concerning the eating of things sanctified, are contained arcana concerning the appropriation of divine good and divine truth, and thence of conjunction with the Lord; but it is not necessary to unfold the particulars in this place, only that it may be known from the passages adduced, that to eat signifies to be appropriated and conjoined. Hence also it was that when the children of Israel were conjoined to the Lord by the blood of the covenant, and after Moses had read the book of the law before them, and they presently saw the God of Israel, it is said, "They did eat and drink" (Exod. xxiv. 6–11). That to eat flesh and drink blood signifies the appropriation of spiritual good and truth, may also be seen from the following passages in Ezekiel: " Thus saith the Lord Jehovih, Gather yourselves on every side to my sacrifice that I do sacrifice for you, even a great sacrifice upon the mountains of Israel, that ye may eat flesh and drink blood. Ye shall eat the flesh of the mighty, and drink the blood of the princes of the earth. And ye shall eat fat till ye be full, and drink blood till ye be drunken, of my sacrifice which I have sacrificed for you.

Thus ye shall be filled at my table with horses and chariots, with mighty men, and with all men of war. And I will set my glory among the heathen" (xxxix. 17–21). The subject here treated of is the convocation of all to the kingdom of the Lord, and specifically concerning the establishment of the church with the gentiles or nations, for it is said, " And I will set my glory among the heathen." By eating flesh and drinking blood, is understood that they should appropriate to themselves divine good and divine truth, flesh denoting the good of love, and blood the truth of that good : by the mighty, or oxen, are signified the affections of good ; by the princes of the earth, the affections of truth, and the plenary fruition thereof is signified by eating fat to satiety, and drinking blood to drunkenness. By fat are signified interior goods, and by blood, interior truths, which were manifested from the Lord when he came into the world, and appropriated by those who received him. Before the advent of the Lord, the Israelites were prohibited from eating fat, and from drinking blood, because they were only in externals, for they were natural sensual men, and not at all in things internal or spiritual, wherefore if it had been allowed them to eat fat and drink blood, by which the appropriation of interior goods and truths was signified, they would have profaned them, and therefore by eating those things was signified profanation. Similar things are signified by being filled at the table of the Lord with horses and chariots, with mighty men, and all men of war; by horse is signified the understanding of the Word, by chariot, doctrine from the Word, by the mighty and the man of war are meant, good and truth combating with evil and falsity, and destroying them; by the mountains of Israel, upon which they should eat, is signified the spiritual church, in which the good of charity is the essential principle. From these considerations it is manifest, that by eating is signified to appropriate, and that by flesh, blood, the mighty, the princes of the earth, the horse, the chariot, and the man of war, are signified things spiritual, which are to be appropriated, and by no means natural things, for to eat such things naturally would be wicked and diabolical. Similar things are signified in the Revelation by, " Come, that ye may eat the flesh of kings, and the flesh of captains, and the flesh of horses, and of them that sit on them, both free and bond " (xix. 17, 18). Forasmuch as most things in the Word have also an opposite sense, so likewise have eating and drinking, and in that sense they signify to appropriate what is evil and false, and thence to be conjoined to hell ; as may be seen from the following passages. Thus in Isaiah : " And in that day did the Lord Jehovih of hosts call to weeping, and to mourning, and to baldness, and to girding with sackcloth : and, behold, joy and gladness, slaying oxen, and killing sheep, eating flesh, and drinking wine : let us eat and drink, for to-morrow we shall die" (xxii 12, 13). The vastation of the church, and lamentation over it, are signified by being called in that day to weeping, mourning, baldness, and putting on sackcloth ; lamentation for the destruction of truth is signified by weeping, of good, by mourning, of all the affection of good, by baldness, and of all the affection of truth, by sackcloth ; by slaying the oxen and killing the sheep, is signified, to extinguish natural good and spiritual good ; by eating flesh and drinking wine, is signified to appropriate what is evil and false, flesh, in this place, denoting evil, and wine, the falsity of evil ; and to eat and drink thereof signify to appropriate them.   Again, in Ezekiel : And thy meat which thou shalt eat shall be by weight; thou shalt drink also water by measure.   And thou shalt eat it as barley cakes, and thou shalt bake it with dung.   Even thus shall the children of Israel eat their defiled bread among the Gentiles, whither I will drive them : and they shall eat bread by weight, and with care ; and they shall drink water by measure, and with astonishment : That they may want bread and water, and be astonished one with another, and consume away for their iniquity" (iv. 10–17). By these words in the prophet was represented the adulteration of divine truth, or the Word, in the Jewish nation ; the barley cakes made with dung signifies that adulteration, the barley cakes denoting good and truth natural, such as is the Word in the sense of the letter, and dung denoting infernal evil ; wherefore it is said, " Even thus shall the children of Israel eat their defiled bread," bread defiled denoting good defiled with evil, or adulterated : that they should want bread and water amongst the nations whither they were driven signifies, that they would no longer have any good and truth because of their being in evils and falsities, nations denoting evils and falsities, and to be driven thither denoting to be delivered up to them ; by their being astonished one with another, or being desolated, a man and his brother, are signified faith and charity, man denoting the truth of faith, and his brother, the good of charity, and to be desolated denoting the plenary extinction of both ; inasmuch as such things are signified by eating bread, and drinking water, therefore it is said that they shall consume away for their iniquity ; to consume away is predicated of spiritual life, when it perishes.   Forasmuch as beasts signify the affections, some of them good affections, and some evil affections, therefore laws were promulgated for the children of Israel, with whom was the representative church, what beasts should be eaten, and what should not be eaten (Levit. xi. 1–47) ; by which was signified what beasts represented good affections, which should be appropriated, and what evil affections, which should not be appropriated, inasmuch as good affections render a man clean, but evil affections render him unclean : all things contained in that chapter, as to the particular beasts and birds, and as to their hoofs, feet, and cud, by which the clean are distinguished from the unclean, are significative.   Again, in Isaiah : " And he shall snatch on the right hand, and be hungry, and he shall eat on the left hand, and they shall not be satisfied : they shall eat every man the flesh of his own arm : Manasseh, Ephraim ; and Ephraim, Manasseh" (ix. 20, 21).   By these words are described the extinction of good by falsity, and the extinction of truth by evil ; the extinction of all good and truth, however they may be inquired into, is signified by, " he shall snatch on the right hand, and be hungry, and he shall eat on the left hand, and they shall not be satisfied," to snatch and to eat here denoting to enquire, and to eat and not be satisfied, denoting their not being found, and if found, that still they cannot be received; "they shall eat every man the flesh of his own arm," signifies, that what is false shall consume the good, and that evil shall consume the truths in the natural man; Manasseh, Ephraim, and Ephraim, Manasseh, signifies, that the will of evil shall consume the understanding of truth, and that the understanding of what is false shall consume the will of good; this may be seen explained above, n. 386, 600. The consumption of all truth and of all good is signified by the following words in Moses : "And ye shall eat the flesh of your sons, and the flesh of your daughters shall ye eat" (Levit. xxvi. 29). And again, by those words in Ezekiel: "Therefore the fathers shall eat the sons, and the sons shall eat the fathers" (v. 10). Here the fathers signify the goods of the church, and in the opposite sense, the evils thereof; sons signify the truths of the church, and in the opposite sense, falsities; by daughters are signified the affections of truth and good, and in the opposite sense the cupidities of what is false and evil; their mutual consumption and extinction are signified by their eating each other; hence it is evident that these things are otherwise to be understood than according to the sense of the letter. Again, in Matthew: "For as in the days that were before the flood, they were eating and drinking, marrying and giving in marriage, until the day that Noah entered into the ark, and knew not until the flood came and took them all away; so shall also the coming of the Son of man be" (xxiv. 38, 39; Luke xvii. 26–30). These words are not to be understood literally, but spiritually; thus by eating is to be understood, the appropriation of evil, by drinking, the appropriarion of what is false; by marrying and giving in marriage, the conjunction of falsity with evils, and of evils with falsity; for the subject there treated of is the state of the church when the last judgment takes place; for this is signified by the coming of the Son of man; and it must be evident to every one, that there is nothing of evil in eating and drinking, and consequently, that both the good and the evil will then eat and drink, in like manner as before the deluge; hence it is not on account of these things that they perish, but on account of their appropriating to themselves evil and what is false, and conjoining them in themselves, which are the things there signified by eating and drinking, and by marrying and giving in marriage. Again, in Luke, the rich man in the parable is represented as thus speaking: "And I will say to my soul, Soul, thou hast much goods laid up for many years; take thine ease, eat, drink, and be merry" (xii. 19). And again: "But and if that servant say in his heart, My Lord delayeth his coming; and shall begin to beat the men servants and maidens, and to eat and drink, and to be drunken" (xii. 45). And again, in the same Evangelist, Jesus says: "And take heed to yourselves, lest at any time your hearts be overcharged with surfeiting and drunkenness" (xxi. 34). In these passages it appears as if by eating and drinking were understood luxury and intemperance in those who indulge their inclinations, but this is only the natural literal sense of the words, whereas, in the spiritual sense, they denote the appropriation of what is evil and false, as may appear from the passages above adduced, where eating and drinking have such a signification, also from this consideration, that the Word in the letter is natural, but inwardly spiritual, the latter sense being for angels, and the former for man.   Besides these, many other passages might be adduced from the Word, to testify and confirm the signification of eating, as denoting the reception, perception, and appropriation, of such things as serve for the nourishment of the soul; for, to eat spiritually is nothing else but to imbue the mind with its own food, which is the desire of knowing, understanding, and becoming wise in things pertaining to eternal life: this may also appear from the signification of bread and meat, of hunger and thirst, of wine and water, which have been treated of above in their proper places.   Forasmuch as to eat signifies to perceive the quality of a thing, and this is perceived by its savor, hence it is from correspondence, that in human language savor (sapor) is predicated of the perception of a thing, and thence also is derived the Word sapientia or wisdom.

618. "And it shall make thy belly bitter"—That hereby is signified that inwardly it was unpleasant, because outwardly adulterated, appears from the signification of being bitter, or of bitterness, as denoting unpleasantness from adulterated truth, of which we shall speak presently; and from the signification of the belly, as denoting what is interior.   The reason why the belly denotes what is interior, is, because it immediately follows these words, that in the mouth it shall be sweet as honey, and by the mouth is understood what is exterior, for what is taken in by the mouth, is masticated and passed into the belly, thus goes from the exterior to the interior, for it enters into the bowels of the man; but concerning the signification of belly, we shall speak further presently.   The reason why bitter or bitterness signifies what is unpleasant from adulterated truth, and that hence to make bitter signifies to render unpleasant, is, because what is sweet becomes bitter, and hence unpleasant, by mixture with anything foul or unpalatable, whence comes the bitterness of wormwood, gall, and myrrh; now inasmuch as sweet signifies what is delightful from the good of truth and the truth of good, hence bitter signifies what is unpleasant from adulterated truth.   This unpleasantness is not perceived and felt by any man in the natural world as bitter, but by spirits and angels in the spiritual world, for all good of truth adulterated, when it is turned with them into savor, is sensitively perceived as bitter; for spirits and angels have taste equally as men, but the taste of spirits and angels flow from a spiritual origin, whereas that of men is from a natural origin; the taste of bitterness with spirits, is from the truth of good adulterated, but, with men, it is from the commixture of a sweet quality with what is foul and unpalatable; the sensation of bitterness with John was also from a spiritual origin for he was then in the spirit, otherwise he could not have eaten the little book.   By truth adulterated is signified the truth of good applied to evil and commixed with its falsity, which is the case when the truths of the literal sense

of the Word are applied to filthy loves, and are thus commixed with evils : this is the unpleasantness which is here signified by the bitterness of the belly. It shall also be briefly explained, what is signified by what is interior in the Word, that is, by the interior things of the Word. The interior things of the Word are those which are contained in its internal or spiritual sense, and which are genuine truths : to these correspond the exterior truths of the Word, which are those in the external or natural sense, called the sense of the letter : when the exterior things of the Word, or the truths of the literal sense are falsified and adulterated, then the interior truths of the Word are falsified and adulterated ; wherefore when man applies the Word in the sense of the letter to the evils of his earthly loves, he causes it to be unpleasant to the angels who are in the internal or spiritual sense, and this unpleasantness, is as that of bitterness : from these considerations it may appear, that by its being said that the little book would make his belly bitter and did make it bitter, is signified that the Word was inwardly unpleasant. But the unpleasantness of which we have now treated is of a spiritual nature, whereas that which is merely spiritual-natural, and which is also here signified by bitterness, is that which arises from the truth of doctrine, which is connected inwardly from the literal sense of the Word, being unpleasant to those who are in the falsities of evil ; for the subject here treated of is the understanding of the Word by the men of the church at its end, when they are, for the most part in falsities from evil ; and in this case the falsities of evil, confirmed from the literal sense of the Word, are delightful to them, but truths confirmed from the same are undelightful ; this also is what is signified by the little book being in the mouth sweet as honey, but making the belly bitter.

That bitter signifies the truth of good adulterated, is evident from those parts of the Word in which it is mentioned. Thus in Isaiah : "Woe unto them that call evil good, and good evil ; that put darkness for light, and light for darkness ; that put bitter for sweet, and sweet for bitter ! Woe unto them that are mighty to drink wine, and men of strength to mingle strong drink" (v. 20, 22). That good and truth adulterated are here signified by bitter, is evident, for it is said, "Woe unto them that call evil good, and good evil ; that put darkness for light, and light for darkness," by which are signified the adulteration of good, and the falsification of truth ; for good is adulterated when good is called evil and evil good, and truth is falsified when darkness is put for light and light for darkness, darkness denoting falsities, and light denoting truths ; hence it is evident that similar things are signified by putting sweet for bitter and bitter for sweet, also by its being said, "Woe unto them that are mighty to drink wine, and men of strength to mingle strong drink ;" by them that are mighty to drink wine are signified those who adulterate the truth of the Word, and by men of strength to mingle strong drink, are signified those who falsify it, wine and strong drink denoting the truths of the Word, and mighty men, and men of str those who excel in ingenuity and subtlety in adulterati

Again, in the same prophet : " The new wine mourneth, the vine languisheth, all the merry hearted do sigh. They shall not drink wine with a song; strong drink shall be bitter to them that drink it" (xxiv. 7, 9). Here, by the new wine, which is said to mourn, and by the vine which is said to languish, is signified the truth of the Word of the church, which is destroyed, new wine denoting the truth of the Word, and vine, the truth of the doctrine of the church; by " all the merry hearted do sigh," and by, "they shall not drink wine with a song," are signified, that internal blessedness of mind, and felicity of heart will perish, because of the truth of spiritual good being destroyed; " strong drink shall be bitter to them that drink it" signifies, that the truth of good will be undelightful from the falsification and adulteration thereof. It is written also in Moses: " They could not drink of the waters of Marah, for they were bitter : and Jehovah showed him a tree, which when he had cast into the waters, the waters were made sweet " (Exod. xv. 24, 25). By the bitter waters of Marah were represented truths adulterated; for waters signify truths, and bitterness signifies adulteration. The healing of the waters by the tree which was cast into them, represented the good of love and of life shaking off what is false, and opening truth, and thus restoring it; for all truth is adulterated from evil of the life and love, wherefore by the good of love and of life it is opened and restored, because all truth is of good, and the good of love is like fire, from which truth appears in the light. The same thing was signified by the pottage into which the sons of the prophets cast bitter gourds, or grapes of the field, which Elisha healed by casting in fine flour (2 Kings iv. 38–41). By the pottage into which they cast bitter gourds, is signified the Word falsified; and by the fine flour which was cast in, by which it was healed, is signified truth from good; for truth which is from good dissipates the falsities which produce falsification. Forasmuch as the sons of Jacob perverted all the truths of the Word, and by application to themselves and to their earthly loves falsified and adulterated them, therefore it is said of them in the song of Moses, that their vine was as the vine of Sodom and of the fields of Gomorrah, and their grapes, grapes of gall, and clusters of bitterness (Deut. xxxii. 32). By a vine is signified the church as to truth, consequently also the truth of the church; and by grapes are signified goods thence derived, which are the goods of charity, and by clusters, the goods of faith; hence it is evident that by clusters of bitterness are signified the goods of faith adulterated. Again, mention is made in Moses of " the bitter waters that causeth the curse." This water was given by the priest to every woman accused by her husband of adultery. If the woman was guilty, the water entered into her and became bitter, causing her belly to swell, and her thigh to rot (Numb. v. 12–29). The reason of this law, which is called " the law of jealousies," was, that by the marriage of man and wife is signified the marriage of truth and good, for love truly conjugial descends from that spiritual marriage; hence by adultery is signified the conjunction of falsity and evil, and this was the reason why, in case of guilt, the water became bitter, by which is signified the adulteration of good; and whereas the belly signified conjugial love, in like manner as the womb, and also the thigh, hence it was that the belly swelled and the thigh rotted, by which, in the spiritual sense, was signified that the conjugial principle perished, or conjugial love itself spiritual and natural, the womb or belly signifying that love spiritual, and the thigh the same love natural. From these considerations it is evident that by bitter and bitterness, in general, are signified the falsification and adulteration of truth and good, and that the various species thereof are signified by gall, wormwood, myrrh, wild grapes, gourds, and the like.

619. " But it shall be in thy mouth sweet as honey"—That hereby is signified exterior delight, appears from the signification of the mouth, as denoting what is exterior; for the subjects here treated of are the little book, and the eating of it up. By the little book is signified the Word, and by eating it up are signified perception and exploration; whence by the mouth, which first receives, is understood the external of the Word; and from the signification of "sweet as honey," as denoting the delight of natural good. The reason that the external of the Word was sweet as honey, that is thus delightful, was, because the external of the Word is of such a nature that it can be applied to any love whatever, and to any principle thence conceived, which may also be thereby confirmed; the reason of this is, because in the external of the Word, which is the sense of the letter, many things are written according to appearances before the natural man, and many appearances, if they are not inwardly understood, are fallacies, such as are the fallacies of the senses; wherefore by those who love to live to the body and to the world, the external of the Word is drawn, by those appearances, to confirm evils of life and falsities of faith. This was especially the case with the sons of Jacob, who applied all things of the Word to themselves, and, from the sense of the letter, maintained it as a principle of their faith, which they also retain at this day, such as that they were elected in preference to others, and hence were a holy nation; also that their Jerusalem, the temple there, the ark, the altar, the sacrifices, with innumerable other things, were holy of themselves, not knowing or being willing to know, that the holiness of all those things consisted solely in their representing things divine proceeding from the Lord, which are called celestial and spiritual, and are the holy things of heaven and the church, and that to think them to be holy of themselves, and not from the divine things which they represented, was to adulterate and falsify the Word by applications thereof to themselves and their own loves. The case was similar with respect to their faith concerning the Messiah, which was, that he should be king of the world, and raise them above all the nations and people in the world; not to mention other things which they collected from the mere literal sense of the Word, and which to them were in the mouth sweet as honey. Hence it is, that those things which are in the spiritual sense of the Word, are undelightful, for in this sense are essential truths, which are not according to

appearances; as for instance, that that nation was not holy, but worse than every other nation, consequently that they were not elect; that the city of Jerusalem only signifies the church of the Lord, and doctrine concerning him and concerning the holy things of heaven and the church; and that the temple, the ark, the altar, and the sacrifices, represented the Lord and the holy things proceeding from him, and that hence, and from no other source, was their holiness derived.   These truths are those which are stored up inwardly in the literal sense of the Word, that is, in its internal spiritual sense, which truths they deny, in consequence, as was said, of their falsifying and adulterating the literal sense, and which therefore are to them undelightful as food that is bitter in the belly.   The reason of its being said that the little book should be in the mouth sweet as honey, is, because honey signifies the delight of natural good, which signification may appear from the following passages. Thus, in Ezekiel: "But thou, son of man, hear what I say unto thee; open thy mouth, and eat that I give thee.   And when I looked, behold, a hand was sent unto me; and lo, a roll of a book was therein.   And he spread it before me; and it was written within and without: and there was written therein lamentation, and mourning, and woe.   Moreover he said unto me, Son of man, eat this roll, and go speak unto the house of Israel.   So I opened my mouth, and he caused me to eat that roll.   And he said unto me, Cause thy belly to eat, and fill thy bowels with this roll that I give thee.   Then did I eat it; and it was in my mouth as honey for sweetness.   And he said unto me, Go, get thee unto the house of Israel, and speak with my words unto them" (ii. 8, 9, 10; iii. 1–4).   Similar things are involved in these words, as in those of which we are now treating in the Revelation.   The prophet Ezekiel's being commanded to eat the roll of the book, involves the same thing as John's being commanded to eat the little book, namely, exploration as to how the divine truth which is in the Word is as yet received, perceived, and appropriated, by those who are of the church; for by the prophet Ezekiel, and by John, are represented the doctrine of truth and the Word, hence exploration was made with them.   The reason why it was made by eating a book is, because to eat signifies to perceive, and thus to appropriate, as was shown above; and when this was explored, namely, in what manner the Word was as yet perceived, it is then said to the prophet Ezekiel, that he should go unto the house of Israel and speak the words of God unto them; also to the prophet John, that he must as yet prophecy, that is, teach the Word in the church; and this because the book was perceived to be in his mouth sweet as honey, that is, because the Word, as to the sense of the letter, is as yet delightful, though only so because this sense can be applied in favor of any false principles whatever, and of any loves of evil whatever, and thus may serve for confirming the delights of the natural life separate from the delights of the spiritual life, which, when they are separated, are merely delights of the loves of the body and of the world, whence arise principles of what is false originating in fallacies.   Again, in Isaiah:

"Behold, a virgin shall conceive, and bear a son, and shall call his name Emanuel. Butter and honey shall he eat, that he may know to refuse the evil, and choose the good " (vii. 14, 15). That these words are spoken of the Lord may be seen confirmed in Matt. i. 23. Any one may see that by butter and honey there mentioned are not meant butter and honey, but something divine corresponding to them, for it follows, " that he may know to refuse the evil and choose the good," which is not known by eating butter and honey; but by butter is signified the delight of spiritual good, and by honey, the delight of natural good, consequently the divine-spiritual and the divine-natural of the Lord are thereby signified, and thus his human principle interior and exterior. That the Lord's human principle is what is understood, may appear from its being said that a virgin shall conceive and bear a son; and that this son is divine, is evident from his name being called, God with us, name denoting quality, here therefore that it was divine. By butter and honey also is signified the delight of spiritual and natural good, in these words in the same chapter: " Butter and honey shall every one eat that is left in the land " (ver. 22). By them that are left in the land are understood those that are inwardly and also outwardly good from the Lord, consequently who receive the good proceeding from the Lord in truths; the blessedness thence of the internal or spiritual man, and likewise of the external or natural, is signified by butter and honey. Thus also in Job: " He shall suck the poison of asps: the viper's tongue shall slay him. He shall not see the rivers, the floods, the brooks of honey and butter " (xx. 16, 17). These things are said concerning hypocrites, who speak well and smoothly concerning God, concerning their neighbor, also concerning heaven and the church, when notwithstanding they think altogether otherwise, and because they can thus cunningly devise how to captivate the minds of others, while in their heart they harbor what is infernal, it is said, " He shall suck the poison of asps, the tongue of the viper shall slay him." That such possess not any delight of natural good nor of spiritual good, is understood by, " He shall not see the rivers, the floods, the brooks of honey and butter," rivers denoting those things that pertain to intelligence, and the floods, the brooks of honey and butter, the things pertaining thence to the affection and love, which are the very delights of heavenly life. All the delight of life which remains to eternity is the delight of spiritual good and truth, and of natural good and truth thence derived, whereas hypocritical delight is a natural delight separate from spiritual, but this delight, in another life, is turned into what is direfully infernal. That by butter and honey in this passage also are not understood butter and honey, is manifest, for in what part of the world are there found floods, and brooks of honey and butter? The same as is signified by butter and honey, is also signified by milk and honey. And inasmuch as by milk is signified the delight of spiritual good, and by honey, the delight of natural good, and these delights are given to those who are of the church of the Lord, therefore the land of Canaan, by which the church is signified, was called "a land flowing with milk and honey " (Exod. iii. 8, 17; Levit. xx. 24; Numb. xiii. 27; xiv. 8; Deut. vi. 3; xi. 9; xxvi. 9, 15; xxvii. 3; xxxi. 20; Joshua v. 6; Jerem. xi. 5; xxxii. 22; Ezek. xx. 6); that by the land of Canaan, in the Word, is understood the church, was shown above, n. 29, 304, 417. And the church is with those only who are in spiritual good and at the same time in natural good, for in these the church is formed by the Lord; for the church is in man, and not without him, consequently, not with those in whom those goods are not; these goods with their delights are signified by milk and honey. That in the land of Canaan there was also much honey at that time, on account of the church of the Lord being there, appears from the first book of Samuel, where it is said, "And all they of the land came to a wood, and there was honey upon the ground. Then said Jonathan, Mine eyes have been enlightened, because I tasted a little of this honey " (xxiv. 25, 29). The reason of Jonathan's eyes being enlightened by his tasting the honey was, because honey corresponds to natural good and its delight, and this good gives intelligence and enlightens, whence Jonathan knew that he had done evil. This is also agreeable to what is said in Isaiah, that the child should eat butter and honey, that he might know to refuse the evil and choose the good; for correspondences at that time exhibited their effects outwardly, inasmuch as all things of the Israelitish church existed from correspondences, by which were re-presented and signified things celestial and spiritual. The same as is signified by butter and honey is also signified by oil and honey in the following passages. Thus in Moses: " He made him to ride on the high places of the earth, that he might eat the increase of the fields; and he made him to suck honey out of the rock, and oil out of the flinty rock " (Deut. xxxii. 13). These words occur in the song of Moses, in which the subject treated of is the church in its beginning, and afterwards in its progression, and at length in its end; they who constituted the ancient church are described by these words, and not they who constituted the Israelitish church, for the latter were evil from the beginning even to the end, as is evident from their fathers in Egypt, and afterwards in the wilderness; but the ancient church, the men of which are understood by their fathers, was that which the Lord caused to ride upon the high places of the earth, and fed with the increase of the fields. That the good of na-tural love and the good of spiritual love, with their delights, were given to them by means of truths, from which their intelligence was derived, and according to which they lived, is signified by, he made him to suck honey out of the rock, and oil out of the flinty rock, honey denoting the delight of natural love, oil the delight of spirit-ual love, and the rock, and the flinty rock, truth from the Lord; that oil signifies the good of love and charity, may be seen above, n. 375, and that a rock signifies truth from the Lord, n. 443. So in David: " He should have fed them also with the fat of wheat, and with honey out of the rock should I have satisfied thee " (Psalm lxxxi. 16). Here by the fat of wheat is also signified the delight of spiritual good, and by honey out of the rock, the delight of natural good by truths from the Lord, as above. It is to be observed, that natural good is not good, unless it be also spiritual good; for all good flows in by the spiritual man or mind into the natural man or mind, and in proportion as the natural man or mind receives the good of the spiritual man or mind, in the same proportion he receives good; it is necessary that there be both, or in both principles, in order to constitute good; wherefore natural good separate from spiritual good is in itself evil, which nevertheless is perceived by man as good; inasmuch as the spiritual and natural must be together in order that there may be good, therefore in the passages which have been adduced, and in those still to be adduced, mention is made of butter and honey, milk and honey, fat and honey, likewise oil and honey; and by butter, milk, fat, and oil, is signified the good of spiritual love, and by honey, the good of natural love, together with their delights. Again, in Ezekiel: "Thus wast thou decked with gold and silver; and thy raiment was of fine linen and silk, and broidered work; thou didst eat fine flour, and honey, and oil: and thou wast exceeding beautiful, and thou didst prosper into a kingdom. My meat also which I gave thee, fine flour, and oil, and honey, wherewith I fed thee, thou hast even set it before them for sweet savor" (xvi. 13, 19). These things are said concerning Jerusalem by which is signified the church, first the ancient church, and afterwards the Israelitish church: concerning the ancient church, it is said, that she was decked with gold and silver, by which is signified, the love of good and truth with the men of the church; the raiment of fine linen, silk, and broidered work, signifies the knowledges of celestial, spiritual, and natural truth; fine linen signifies truth from a celestial origin, silk, truth from a spiritual origin, and broidered work, truth from a natural origin, which is called scientific truth. By eating fine flour, honey, and oil, are signified the perception of truth and good natural and spiritual, and the appropriation of the same; to eat, denoting to appropriate, fine flour denoting truth, honey, natural good, and oil, spiritual good, which were appropriated to them by a life according to the truths above mentioned. By becoming exceedingly beautiful and prospering into a kingdom, is signified, to become intelligent and wise, so as to constitute a church, beauty denoting intelligence and wisdom, and a kingdom signifying a church. But concerning the Israelitish church, which was only in externals without internals, whence the men of that church were idolatrous, it is said, that they set the fine flour, honey, and oil, before images of men, or idols, for a sweet savor, that is, that they perverted the truths and goods of the church into falsities and evils, and thus profaned them. Again, in the same prophet: "Judah, and the land of Israel, they were thy merchants: they traded in thy market wheat of Minnith, and Pannag, and honey, and oil, and balm" (xxvii. 17). This is spoken of Tyrus, by which is signified the church as to the knowledges of truth and good whence also by Tyrus are signified the knowledges of truth and good themselves pertaining to the church; by oil and honey are signified spiritual and natural good, as above. What is understood in the spiritual sense by Judah, and the land of Israel, likewise by wheat, Minnith, and Pannag, and by balsam, also by the tradings of Tyrus, may be seen explained above, n. 433. Again, in Moses: " A land of brooks of water, of fountains and depths that spring out of the valleys and hills ; a land of wheat and barley, and vines, and fig-trees, and pomegranates ; a land of oil olive, and honey " (Deut. viii. 7, 8). These things are said concerning the land of Canaan, by which is understood the church which is in celestial, spiritual, and natural good, and thence in truths ; but the particulars of this verse are explained above, n. 374, 403; where it is shown, that oil and honey signify the good of love in the internal or spiritual man and in the external or natural man. So in David : " The judgments of Jehovah are true and righteous altogether. More to be desired are they than gold, yea, than much fine gold : sweeter also than honey and the dropping of the honeycombs " (Psalm xix. 9, 10). By the judgments of Jehovah are signified the truths and goods of worship ; wherefore it is said, " the judgments of Jehovah are true, and righteous altogether;" righteousness, or justice, being predicated of the good of life and worship thence derived ; and as good is also signified by gold and fine gold, it is therefore said, that they are more desirable than gold and than much fine gold, gold denoting celestial good, fine gold, spiritual good, and desirable denoting what is of the affection and love ; inasmuch as the goods with which a man is affected are also delightful, therefore it is said, that they are sweeter than honey and the dropping of the honeycombs, sweet denoting what is delightful, honey, natural good, and the dropping of the honeycombs, natural truth. So again: " I have not departed from thy judgments : for thou hast taught me. How sweet are thy words to my taste! yea, sweeter than honey to my mouth " (Psalm cxix. 102, 103). Here the mouth denotes the external, the same as where it is said in the Revelation, that the little book was sweet as honey in the mouth. So in Luke : Jesus addressing his disciples, who were terrified on seeing him, and supposed that they had seen a spirit, said, " Behold, my hands and my feet, that it is I myself : handle me, and see ; for a spirit hath not flesh and bones, as ye see me have. And he said unto them, Have ye here any meat? And they gave him a piece of a broiled fish, and of a honeycomb. And he took it, and did eat before them " (xxiv. 39, 43). From the series of these words viewed in their spiritual sense it manifestly appears, that by honeycomb, or by honey, is signified natural good, for the Lord disclosed to his disciples that he had glorified or made divine his whole humanity, even as to the natural and sensual principle thereof ; this is signified by the hands and feet, and by the flesh and bones, which they saw and felt ; by the hands and feet, is signified the ultimate principle of man, which is called the natural, by the flesh, the good thereof, and by bones, the truth thereof ; for all things pertaining to the human body correspond to things spiritual, and the flesh corresponds to the good of the natural man, and the bones to the truths thereof ; concerning this correspondence more may be seen in the work concerning H. & H. n. 87–102. The

Lord also confirmed the same by eating before the disciples of a broiled fish and a honeycomb, the broiled fish signifying the truth of good of the natural and sensual man, and the honeycomb, the good of truth of the same, wherefore by eating of these things, and by the disciples feeling him, the Lord showed and confirmed that his whole humanity, even to the ultimates thereof, was glorified, that is, was made divine. Forasmuch as honey signifies the good of the natural man, therefore also it is said of John the Baptist, " And the same John had his raiment of camel's hair, and a leathern girdle about his loins; and his meat was locusts and wild honey " (Matt. iii. 4; Mark i. 6). The reason of this was, because John the Baptist represented the same as Elias, wherefore also it was said, that Elias should come, by whom was understood John ; Elias represented the Lord as to the Word, or the Word which is from the Lord, and in like manner did John ; and inasmuch as the Word teaches that the Messiah or the Lord was about to come, therefore John was sent before to preach concerning the advent of the Lord, according to the predictions of the Word: and inasmuch as John represented the Word, therefore the ultimates of the Word, which are natural, were represented by John, by his clothing, and also by his food, namely, by having his raiment of camel's hair, and the leathern girdle about his loins, the camel's hair signifying the ultimates of the natural man, such as are the exteriors of the Word, and the leathern girdle about his loins, the external bond or connexion thereof with the interior things of the Word, which are spiritual ; similar things are signified by locust and wild honey, by locust, is signified the truth of the natural man, and by wild honey, its good; whether we speak of the truth and good of the natural man, or of natural truth and good, such as the Word is in its ultimate sense, which is called the sense of the letter, or natural sense, it amounts to the same, for this was what John represented by his clothing and food. The reason why no leaven, nor any honey, should be used in the offerings made by fire to Jehovah (Levit. ii. 11), was, because leaven signifies the falsity of the natural man, and honey, the delight of the good of the natural man, and, in the opposite sense, the delight of his evil, which also is like leaven when it is mixed with such things as signify things of a holy and interior nature, for natural delight derives its all from the delights of the love of self and of the world ; and inasmuch as the Israelitish nation was in those delights more than other nations, therefore it was forbidden them to use honey in their sacrifices; concerning the signification of honey, as denoting the delight of the good of the natural man, more may be seen in the A. C. n. 5620, 6856, 8056, 10,137, 10,530. It is recorded of Sampson, that after he had rent the young lion, and returned to take a wife from the nation of the Philistines, " he turned aside to see the carcase of the lion : and, behold, there was a swarm of bees and honey in the carcase of the lion " (Judges xiv. 8, 9). By this circumstance was signified the dissipation of the faith which is separate from charity, which the Philistines represented ; it was on this account that the Philistines were called the uncircumcised, by which name is signified, that they were without spiritual love and charity, and only in natural love, which is the love of self and of the world; such faith, inasmuch as it destroys the good of charity, was represented by the young lion, which assaulted Sampson with intent to tear him in pieces, but Sampson, inasmuch as he was a Nazarite, and by his Nazariteship represented the Lord as to his ultimate natural principle, rent the lion in pieces, and afterwards found in his carcase a swarm of bees and honey, by which was signified, that after that faith is dissipated, the good of charity succeeds in its place. Similar things were represented and signified by the other circumstances related of Sampson in the book of Judges; for there is nothing written in the Word which does not represent and signify something pertaining to heaven and the church, which can only be known from the science of correspondences, and thence from the spiritual sense of the Word.

620. "And I took the little book out of the angel's hand, and ate it up"—That hereby is signified exploration, appears from those things which precede, namely, that by the little book is understood the Word, by the angel, the Lord as to the Word, and by eating it up, reception, perception, and appropriation thereof, consequently also exploration, in this case as to the quality of the understanding of the Word as yet remaining in the church, which exploration takes place from what is perceived, and according to perception; hence exploration took place with the prophet John, because by a prophet is signified the doctrine of the church, and in a universal sense the Word.

621. "And it was in my mouth sweet as honey"—That hereby is signified that the Word, as to its external or literal sense, was as yet perceived as the delight of good, but this only because of its serving to confirm false principles and loves of evil, or principles originating in the love of self and of the world, all which are falsities, as may be seen in what was said above.

622. "And as soon as I had eaten it, my belly was bitter"—That hereby is signified that it was perceived and explored that the Word was inwardly undelightful from the adulterated truth of the literal sense thereof, appears from those things which are explained above, n. 617, 618, where similar words occur. The reason why the belly here signifies the interiors of the Word, which are called spiritual, is, because exploration was represented by eating up the little book, by which is understood the Word, and by its savor, by which is understood perception; hence the first perception is signified by the savor in the mouth, where the little book was sweet as honey, and is the perception of the quality of the literal sense thereof, thus of the quality of the Word outwardly; but the other perception is signified by its savor when it comes into the belly, which is said to be made bitter, and this other perception is that of the quality of the spiritual sense thereof, thus of the quality of the Word inwardly: hence it is, that as by the mouth is signified the Word outwardly, therefore here by the belly, is signified the Word inwardly, because inwardly received and explored. The reason why

the belly signifies the interiors, is, because the belly stores up the food inwardly, and by food is signified everything which nourishes the soul, and because the belly, as well as the rest of the bowels, is within or in the midst of the body, hence it is that by the belly, and also by the bowels, in the Word, are signified the interiors. This will be still more evident from the following passages of the Word. Thus in Ezekiel : " Son of man, cause thy belly to eat, and fill thy bowels with this roll that I give thee" (iii. 3). By these words similar things are signified as are now explained in the Revelation ; for by the roll is signified the same as by the little book, namely, the Word, and by causing the belly to eat, and filling the bowels with the roll, is signified to explore how the Word is understood in the church, which is done by the reading and perception thereof. Again, in David : " Whose belly thou fillest with thy hid treasure ; they are full of children, and leave the rest of their substance to their babes" (Psalm xvii. 14). By the hid treasure here mentioned is signified the truth of the Word, by the belly, the interior understanding, whence by filling their belly with treasure is signified to instruct their interior understanding in the truths of the Word ; that they who are affected with truths and thence fully instructed, is signified by, " they are full of children," children denoting those who are in the affection of truth ; the babes of the children signify truths springing up, or in the birth, whence it is said that they leave the rest of their substance to their babes ;—it is here said, the interior understanding, for there is with man an exterior understanding and an interior ; the exterior understanding is of the natural mind, and the interior understanding is of the spiritual mind ; the interior is signified by the belly. Again, in John : " Jesus stood and cried, saying, If any man thirst, let him come unto me and drink. He that believeth on me, as the scripture hath said, out of his belly shall flow rivers of living water. But this spake he of the Spirit, which they that believe on him should receive" (vii. 37, 38, 39). After this manner the Lord describes the divine truth inwardly perceived by those who are in the spiritual affection of truth, who are understood by them that thirst, and come to the Lord and drink ; that with such there shall be understanding of divine truth, is signified by, " out of his belly shall flow rivers of water," rivers flowing out of the belly denoting the interior understanding or intelligence, and living water denoting divine truth from the Lord ; and inasmuch as by the holy spirit is signified the divine truth proceeding from the Lord, it is therefore added, " this spake he of the Spirit which they who believe on him should receive." Again, in Mark : " Whatsoever thing from without entereth into the man, it cannot defile him ; because it entereth not into his heart, but into the belly, and goeth out into the draught, purging all meats : That which cometh out of the man, that defileth the man. For from within, out of the heart of men, proceeds evil " (vii. 18–21 ; Matthew xv. 17–20). These words are to be understood thus, that all things, whether falsities or evils, which, either from the sight or hearing, flow into the thought of the understanding, and not into the affection of the will, do not affect or infect the man, inasmuch as the thought of the man, so far as it does not proceed from the affection of his will, is not in the man, but without him, wherefore it is not appropriated to him; the case is the same with respect to truth and good.   These things the Lord teaches by correspondences, when he says, that that which enters by the mouth into the belly does not render a man unclean, because it enters not into the heart, for that which enters into the belly is cast out into the draught; by which is understood, that whatever is from without, whether it be from objects of the sight, or from objects of the speech, or from objects of the memory, and enters the thought of the understanding of man, does not render him unclean, but that so far as it is not of his affection or will, it is separated and cast out, as what is taken into the belly is cast out into the draught.   These spiritual things the Lord expounded by natural things, inasmuch as the meats which are taken into the mouth, and thus passed into the belly, signify such things as man spiritually imbibes, and with which he nourishes his soul, and hence it is that the belly corresponds to the thought of the understanding, and is likewise significative of it. That the heart signifies the affection of the will of man was shown above; likewise, that that alone is appropriated to man which becomes of his affection or will.   That spiritual things, and not natural things, are understood, is evident, for the Lord declares that, from within, out of the heart of men proceed evil thoughts, adulteries, fornications, murders, thefts, and blasphemies.   Forasmuch as the falsities and evils which enter from without into the thoughts, enter from the hells, and, if they are not received by man in the affection of the will, are rejected into the hells, it is therefore said that they are cast out into the draught; for by the draught is signified hell, because in the hells all things are unclean, and they who are there are ejected out of heaven, which in form is as a man, whence it is called the grand man, and also corresponds to all things of man, whereas the hells correspond to the ejections from the belly of the grand man, or of heaven, whence it is that in the spiritual sense hell is understood by the draught.   The reason why the belly is said to purge all meats, is, because by the belly is signified the thought of the understanding, as was said above, and by meats are signified all spiritual nourishments, and the thought of the understanding is what separates the unclean from the clean, and so purges. Again, in Jeremiah: "Nebuchadnezzar the king of Babylon hath devoured me, he hath crushed me, he hath made me an empty vessel, he hath swallowed me up as a whale, he hath filled his belly with my delicacies, he hath cast me out" (li. 34). Here by Nebuchadnezzar the king of Babylon is signified the profanation of divine truth; and because they who profane it imbibe it more than others and apply it to filthy loves, especially to the love of rule, even to the transferring of all divine power to themselves, this is signified by its being said, "he hath swallowed me up as a whale, he hath filled his belly with my delicacies," the whale signifying the ultimate natural principle, in which they are who are in the love of self, and delicacies denoting the knowledges of truth and good from the Word, wherefore to fill the belly with them denotes here to imbibe and profane them.   Again, in David : " Have mercy upon me, O Jehovah, for I am in trouble : mine eye is consumed with grief, yea my soul and my belly" (Psalm xxxi. 9).   By the eye, the soul, and the belly, are here signified the understanding, and thence the thought of truth, interior and exterior ; thus by the belly are signified the interiors of the understanding, which are said to be consumed with grief when they perish by falsities.   Again : " For our soul is bowed down to the dust : our belly cleaveth unto the earth" (Psalm xliv. 25).   Here also by the soul and the belly in the spiritual sense is signified the thought of the understanding ; and by being bowed down to the dust, and cleaving to the earth, is signified the being imbued with falsities, for by dust and earth is here signified what is infernal and accursed.   The same is also signified by going upon the belly and by eating dust, as it was said to the serpent : "Thou art cursed above all cattle; and above every beast of the field ; upon thy belly shalt thou go, and dust shalt thou eat all the days of thy life" (Gen. iii. 14).   Hence also it was that it was altogether forbidden to eat, " whatsoever goeth upon the belly, for it was an abomination" (Levit. xi. 42).   The reason why by dust, and by the cleaving of the belly to the earth, is signified the infernal and accursed false principle, is, because the hells are under the earths in the spiritual world, and through the earths in that world falsities of evil are exhaled from the hells ; and because the belly from its correspondence signifies the interiors of the understanding and thought, which are infected and imbued with the falsities of evil if they adhere to those earths.   Hence also in the spiritual world no one lies with the belly upon the earth ; moreover to walk there upon the earth with the feet, denotes to touch and imbibe what is exhaled from the hells with the corporeal natural principle, which corresponds with the soles of the feet, and this part of the natural principle has no communication with the thoughts of the understanding, except with those who are in evils as to life and in falsities as to doctrine.   Again, in Job : " Their belly prepareth deceit" (xv. 35). And again, in the same : " For I am full of matter, the spirit within me constraineth me.   Behold, my belly is as wine which hath no vent" (xxxii. 18, 19).   By these words is meant that he could not open the thoughts of the understanding.   Again, in Jeremiah : " O Jerusalem, wash thy heart from wickedness, that thou mayest be saved.   How long shall thy vain thoughts abide in thy belly ?" (iv. 14.)   In these words thoughts are manifestly attributed to the belly, for it is said, " how long shall thy vain thoughts abide in thy belly?" wickedness also is attributed to the heart, because the heart corresponds to the will, in which wickedness resides.   And in David : " For there is no faithfulness in their mouth ; their belly is very wickedness ; their throat is an open sepulchre ; they flatter with their tongue" (Psalm v. 9).   Here also wickedness, or perditions, that is, evil thoughts, are attributed to the belly.   Again : " Both in the belly of a man and the deep heart" (Psalm lxiv. 6).   Here by the belly of a man are signified the thoughts of what is false, and by the deep heart, the affections of evil, the latter pertaining to the will, the former to the understanding. So in Habakkuk : "My belly trembled ; my lips quivered at the voice" (iii. 16). By the belly trembling is here signified grief of thought, wherefore it is also said, "my lips quivered at the voice," denoting a stammering thence of the speech. By the belly of the whale, in which Jonah was three days and three nights (Jonah ii. 1), are signified the hells where are the most dire falsities, with which he was encompassed, consequently grievous temptations, as may appear from the prophecy of Jonah in the same chapter, where it is said : "Out of the belly of hell cried I, and thou heardest my voice" (verse 2). That the bowels have a similar signification may be seen from the following passages. Thus in Isaiah : "Wherefore my bowels shall sound like a harp for Moab, and my inward parts for Kir-haresh" (xvi. 11). And in David : "Bless Jehovah, O my soul : and all my inward parts, bless his holy name" (Psalm ciii. 1). And again : "I delight to do thy will, O my God, yea thy law is in my bowels" (Psalm xl. 9). So in Ezekiel : "Their silver and their gold shall not be able to deliver them in the day of the wrath of Jehovah : they shall not satisfy their souls, neither fill their bowels" (vii. 19). By their silver and gold are signified the falsities and evils of the religion which is from self-intelligence and self-will ; that from these there is not any spiritual nourishment, or intelligence and affection of good, is signified by "they shall not satisfy their souls, neither fill their bowels." Inasmuch as by the bowels are signified the interiors of the thought, and these are what are affected with grief, therefore such grief is expressed in the Word by the moving of the bowels ; as in Isaiah, lxiii. 15 ; Jer. xxxi. 20 ; Lam. i. 20 ; Matt. ix. 36 ; Mark vi. 34 ; viii. 2 ; Luke i. 78 ; vii. 12, 13 ; x. 33, 34 ; xv. 20.

Whereas by the belly are signified the interiors of the thought or of the understanding, therefore by the fruit of the belly in the spiritual sense, are signified the goods of the understanding, and by sons the truths thereof. Thus in David : "Lo, sons are the heritage of Jehovah, and the fruit of the belly is his reward" (Psalm cxxvii. 3). And in Isaiah : "They shall have no pity on the fruit of the belly; their eye shall not spare the sons" (xiii. 18). And in Job : "I entreat for the sons of my belly" (xix. 17). And in Moses : "He will also bless the fruit of thy belly, and the fruit of thy land" (Deut. vii. 13). And in Hosea : "Yea, though they bring forth, yet will I slay the desires of their belly" (ix. 11, 16). The fruit of the belly, and the desires of the belly, signify in the literal sense natural offspring, but in the spiritual sense they signify spiritual offspring, which is science, intelligence, and wisdom, for into these man is re-born when he is regenerated ; hence it is that by births, by sons and daughters, and other names pertaining to nativity, are signified such things as pertain to spiritual nativity, that is to regeneration ; for the angels, who perceive the Word spiritually, are unacquainted with any other birth or fruit of the belly. Hence also it is, that by the womb and the belly are signified similar things in the following passages. Thus in Isaiah : "O that thou hadst harkened to my commandments! Thy seed had then been as the sand, and the off-spring of thy bowels like the gravel thereof" (xlviii. 18, 19). And in David: "I was cast upon thee from the womb: thou art my God from my mother's belly" (Psalm xxii. 10). And again: "For thou hast possessed my reins: thou hast covered me in my mother's belly" (Psalm cxxxix. 13). And again: "The wicked are estranged from the womb: they go astray from the belly, speaking lies" (Psalm lviii. 3). The same may be seen from numerous other passages of the Word. The reason why the belly or the bowels signify the interiors of the thought or of the understanding, is, because there are two lives with man, namely, the life of the understanding, and the life of the will; to those two fountains of life correspond all things of the body, wherefore also the latter are acted upon, and act at the disposal of the former, insomuch that whatever part of the body does not suffer itself to be actuated by the understanding and the will, is not alive; hence it is that the whole body is subject to the government of those two lives, for all things in the body which are moved, and so far as they are moved by the respiration of the lungs, are subject to the government of the life of the understanding, and all things in the body which are acted upon by the pulsation of the heart, and so far as they are acted upon, are subject to the government of the life of the will: it is hence that in the Word mention is frequently made of the soul and heart, and that the soul signifies the life of the understanding, likewise the life of faith, for the soul is predicated of respiration, and that the heart signifies the life of the will, likewise the life of the love: it is hence also that the belly and the bowels are predicated of thought which is of the understanding, and that the heart is predicated of affection which is of the will.

623. Verse 11. "And he said unto me, Thou must prophesy again before many peoples, and nations, and tongues, and kings."—"And he said unto me, Thou must prophesy again," signifies the divine command that the Word may as yet be taught; "before many peoples, and nations, and tongues, and kings," signifies with all who are in truths and goods as to life, and at the same time in goods and truths as to doctrine, consequently, that the Word may be taught as to goods of life, and as to truths of doctrine.

624. "And he said unto me, Thou must prophesy again"—That hereby is signified the divine command that the Word may as yet be taught, appears from the signification of saying, when by an angel, by whom in this chapter the Lord is represented as to the Word, as denoting command, for what the Lord says, the same is a command; and from the signification of prophesying, as denoting to teach the Word, concerning which we shall speak presently. The reason of its being said that he must as yet teach the Word, was, because the quality of the understanding of the Word as yet remaining in the church was explored, and it was found that the Word was delightful as to the sense of the letter, for this is signified by the little book being in the mouth sweet as honey, the little book denoting the Word. It was commanded that the Word should be

yet taught in the church, because the end thereof was not yet come, for the end of the church is described by the sounding of the seventh angel; but here the state proximately before the end is described by the sounding of the sixth angel, which state of the church is the subject now treated of. Moreover, before the end is fully come, the Word, when it is taught, is as yet delightful to some, but not so in the last state or end of the church, for then the Lord opens the interior things of the Word, which are undelightful, as was said above in treating concerning the eating up of the little book, and its making the belly bitter. The reason that the Word is still to be taught, although the interior truths thereof are undelightful, and that the last judgment does not take place before there is a consummation, that is, when there is no longer any good and truth remaining with the men of the church, is altogether unknown in the world, but is known in heaven, and is this; there are two kinds of men upon whom judgment takes place; one kind consists of those that are upright, and the other of those that are not upright: those that are upright are angels in the ultimate heaven, who, for the most part, are simple, because of their not having cultivated their understanding with interior truths, but only with exterior truths from the literal sense of the Word, according to which they have lived; hence it is that their spiritual mind, which is the interior mind, was not indeed shut, but neither was it opened, as with those who received interior truths in doctrine and in life, wherefore as to spiritual things they became simple, and are called the upright; but the non-upright are those, who have lived outwardly as Christians, but inwardly admitted evils of every kind into the thought and into the will, so that in the external form they appeared as angels although in the internal form they were devils. These, when they come into the other life, are, for the most part, consociated with the upright, that is, with the simple good who are in the ultimate heaven, for the exteriors consociate, and the simple good are such that they believe everything to be good which appears good in the external form, their thought not penetrating farther. But the non-upright are to be separated from the upright or simple good, before the coming of judgment, and after it, and this separation can only be effected successively. This therefore is the reason that before the time of the last judgment the Word is still to be taught, although inwardly it is undelightful, that is, as to its interior things, which therefore they do not receive, but only such things from the letter as favor their own loves, and the principles thence conceived, on account of which the Word, as to the literal sense, is still delightful to them: hence it may appear how the upright are separated from the non-upright. That on account of this reason the time is protracted after the last judgment before the new church is fully established, is an arcanum from heaven which at this day can only enter the understanding of a few ; and yet this is what the Lord teaches in the following passages in Matthew : " So the servants of the householder came and said unto him, " Sir, didst not thou sow good seed in thy field? from whence then hath it tares ? The servants said unto him, Wilt thou then that we go and gather them up? But he said, Nay; lest while ye gather up the tares, ye root up also the wheat with them. Let both grow together until the harvest: and at the time of the harvest I will say to the reapers, Gather ye together first the tares, and bind them in bundles to burn them; but gather the wheat into my barn. He that soweth the good seed is the Son of Man. The field is the world; the good seed are the children of the kingdom; the harvest is the end of the world. As therefore the tares are gathered and burned in the fire; so shall it be in the end of the world" (xiii. 27–30, 37–40). By the end of the world, or the consummation of the age, here mentioned, is signified the last time of the church; that before this the upright are not to be separated from the non-upright, because they are consociated by exteriors, is signified by not gathering the tares lest the wheat be rooted up with them. Concerning this circumstance see also what is said in the work concerning the L. J. n. 70. .

The reason why to prophesy signifies to teach the Word, is, because by a prophet, in the supreme sense, is understood the Lord as to the Word, and in the respective sense one who teaches the Word, but in the abstract sense are signified the Word itself, and also doctrine from the Word; these things being signified by a prophet, hence by prophesying is signified to teach the Word and doctrine from the Word. This signification may appear from the passages in the Word where prophets and prophesying are mentioned, when understood as to the spiritual sense. Thus in Matthew: "Many will say to me in that day, Lord, Lord, have we not prophesyed in thy name? and in thy name have cast out devils? and in thy name done many wonderful works? And then will I profess unto them, I never knew you: depart from me, ye that work iniquity" (vii. 22, 23). The subject here treated of is salvation, namely, that no one is saved by knowing the Word and teaching it, but by doing it; for in the verse preceding, it is said, that those only shall enter the kingdom of heaven who do the will of God (verse 21); and in the subsequent verses, that he who heareth the words of the Lord and doeth them is the wise man, but he who heareth and doeth them not is the foolish man (verses 24–27); hence it is evident, what is understood by the words of the Lord in the above passage; namely, that by, "Many will say to me in that day, Lord, Lord," is understood the worship of the Lord by prayers, and by words of the mouth only; by, "have we not prophesied in thy name," is understood to teach the Word, and doctrines from the Word, to prophesy denoting to teach, and the name of the Lord denoting according to doctrine from the Word; by casting out devils is signified to liberate from falsities of religion, devils denoting falsities of religion; by doing many wonderful works, is signified, to convert many; but inasmuch as they did these things not for the sake of the Lord, nor for the sake of truth and good, neither for the sake of the salvation of souls, but for the sake of themselves and the world, thus only that they might appear in the external form, therefore with respect to themselves, they did not do good but evil; this is understood by the

Lord's saying to them, "I never knew you: depart from me, ye that work iniquity;" it may seem as if they could not work iniquity in doing such things, but nevertheless all is iniquity which a man does for the sake of himself and of the world, inasmuch as there is not any love of the Lord and of his neighbor therein, but only the love of self and the world, and every one after death remains his own love. Again, speaking of the end of the world, or the consummation of the ages, Jesus saith: "And many false prophets shall rise, and shall deceive many. For there shall arise false Christs and false prophets, and shall show great signs and wonders; insomuch, that if it were possible, they shall deceive the very elect" (Matt. xxiv. 11, 24; Mark xiii. 22). In these passages, by false prophets and false Christs are not understood prophets, in the common acceptation of the term, but all those who pervert the Word and teach falsities; such are also false Christs, for Christ signifies the Lord as to divine truth, whence false Christs signify divine truths falsified; to show great signs and wonders, signifies the efficacy and power of falsities by confirmations from the literal sense of the Word, by these also signs and wonders are produced in the spiritual world, for the literal sense of the Word, however it may be falsified, has power, concerning which many wonderful circumstances might here be related, if it were needful; by the elect are signified those who are in spiritual good, that is, who are in the good of charity. Again: "He that receiveth a prophet in the name of a prophet, shall receive a prophet's reward; and he that receiveth a righteous man in the name of a righteous man, shall receive a righteous man's reward. And whosoever shall give to drink unto one of these little ones a cup of cold water only in the name of a disciple, verily I say unto you, He shall in no wise lose his reward" (Matt. x. 41, 42). No one can understand these things unless he know what is signified by a prophet, by a righteous man, by a disciple, and by the little ones, likewise what is meant by receiving them in their own name. By a prophet, in the abstract sense, is signified the truth of doctrine, by a disciple, the good of doctrine, by a righteous man, the good of life, and by receiving them in their own name is signified to receive those things from the love of them; thus by receiving a prophet in the name of a prophet, is signified, to love the truth of doctrine because it is truth, or to receive truth for its own sake; by receiving a righteous man in the name of a righteous man, is signified, to love good, and to do it because it is good, thus from the love or affection of the heart to receive it from the Lord; for he who loves truth and good for their own sakes, loves them from themselves, thus from the Lord, from whom they proceed, and inasmuch as he does not love them for the sake of self and the world, he loves them spiritually, and all spiritual love remains with man after death, and gives life eternal; to receive a reward signifies to bear in himself, or carry with him, that love, and thence to receive the blessing of heaven; to give to drink to one of the little ones a cup of cold water only in the name of a disciple, signifies, from innocence to love innocence, and by virtue thereof to love good and truth from the Word, and to teach them, to give to drink a cup of cold water signifying to love and teach from a small degree of innocence, little ones signifying the innocent, and, abstractedly, innocence itself, to give to drink a cup of cold water signifying to teach from a little innocence, and disciple signifying the good of doctrine from the Lord; hence by giving water to the little ones to drink, is signified, to teach truth from spiritual innocence, and also to instruct the innocent in truths. This is the spiritual interpretation of the above words, which, unless it be known, no one can understand what is signified by receiving a prophet and a righteous man in the name of a prophet and a righteous man, and that they should receive the reward of a prophet and a righteous man; reward signifies love with its delights enduring to eternity. Again, in the same Evangelist: " Many prophets and righteous men have desired to see those things which ye see, and have not seen them; and to hear those things which ye hear, and have not heard them" (xiii. 17). Here also by prophets and righteous men in the spiritual sense, are understood all who are in the truths of doctrine and in the good of life according to them; and by seeing and hearing are signified to understand and perceive, in this case, the interior truths proceeding from the Lord, for the understanding and perception of these reform man, when he also lives according to them. The reason why interior truths proceeding from the Lord, are here understood, is, because the Lord, when he was in the world, opened those truths. In the literal sense are understood to see and hear the Lord, but inasmuch as the Lord is the divine truth itself in heaven and in the church, consequently inasmuch as all divine truths are from the Lord, and the Lord himself taught them, and continually teaches them by the Word, therefore the understanding and perception thereof are signified by seeing and hearing the Lord. So in Joel: " I will pour out my spirit upon all flesh; and your sons and your daughters shall prophesy, your old men shall dream dreams, and your young men shall see visions " (ii. 28). These things are said concerning the advent of the Lord and the perception of divine truth by those who receive the Lord and believe in him: by the spirit which shall be poured out upon all flesh, is signified the divine truth proceeding from the Lord, for this is understood in the Word by the holy spirit; by prophesying are signified to understand and to teach the truths of doctrine; by dreaming dreams is signified to receive revelation, and by seeing visions is signified to perceive revelation; by sons and daughters are signified those who are in the spiritual affection of truth and good; by old men are signified those who are in wisdom, and by young men, those who are in intelligence. So in Amos: " Surely the Lord Jehovih will do nothing without revealing his secret unto his servants the prophets. The lion hath roared, who will not fear? The Lord Jehovih hath spoken, who can but prophesy?" (iii. 7, 8.) Here also by prophesying are signified to receive divine truth and to teach it; but this passage may be seen explained above; n. 601. Similar things are signified by prophesying, and by prophets, in the following passages in the Revelation: " And I will give unto my two witnesses, and they shall prophesy a thousand two hundred and sixty days, clothed in sackcloth " (xi. 3).   And again : " The time of the dead is come, that they should be judged, and that thou shouldest give reward unto thy servants the prophets " (xi. 18). Again : " The testimony of Jesus is the spirit of prophecy " (xix. 10).   And again : " Rejoice over her, O heaven, and ye holy apostles and prophets ; for God hath avenged you on her " (xviii. 20). That in these passages by prophets are understood those who are in truths of doctrine, and in the abstract sense, the truths of doctrine, and that by prophesying is understood to receive and teach them, especially to teach the Lord himself, will be seen when we come to explain them.   Again, in Amos : " Then answered Amos, and said to Amaziah, Jehovah took me as I followed the flock, and Jehovah said unto me, Go, prophesy unto my people Israel.   Thou sayest, Prophesy not against Israel, and drop not thy word against the house of Isaac.   Thy wife shall be a harlot in the city, and thy sons and thy daughters shall fall by the sword, and thy land shall be divided by line " (vii. 14–17).   By prophesying against Israel, and dropping a word against the house of Isaac, is signified, to reprove those of the church who are in the falsities of evil, to prophesy denoting to teach and reprove, and Israel and the house of Isaac denoting the church ; inasmuch as it is the falsities of evil for which they are reproved, therefore this is said to Amaziah, by whom the perverted church was represented ; that his wife shall be a harlot, signifies the falsification and adulteration of the Word ; that his sons and daughters shall fall by the sword, signifies, that the truths and goods of the church shall perish by the falsities of evil ; and that the land shall be divided by line, signifies, that the church, and everything belonging to it, shall be dissipated.   So in Hosea : " And by a prophet Jehovah brought Israel out of Egypt, and by a prophet was he preserved.   Ephraim provoked him to anger most·bitterly : therefore shall he leave his blood upon him " (xii. 13, 14).   By the prophet here mentioned, in the proximate sense, is understood Moses, by whom Israel was led out of Egypt, and afterwards guarded ; but, in the spiritual sense, by the prophet is understood the Lord as to the Word, and by Israel are understood all of the church who are in truths from good, and by Egypt is understood the natural man, which separate from the spiritual man, is damned. Hence by Jehovah bringing Israel out of Egypt by a prophet, is signified that the Lord leads out of damnation those who are in truths from good by means of divine truth which is the Word, and that by this he guards them ; by Ephraim provoking him to anger most bitterly, is signified that they perverted the Word as to the understanding thereof, Ephraim denoting the understanding of the Word, and bitterness denoting the perversions and thence falsities from which it becomes undelightful ; " therefore shall he leave his blood upon him," signifies damnation, on account of the adulteration of the truth which is in the Word.   Again, in the same prophet : " The days of visitation are come, the days of retribution are come ; Israel shall know it : the prophet is a fool, the man of spirit is mad, for the multitude of thine iniquity, and the great hatred. Ephraim is a watchman with my God, but the prophet is a snare of a fowler in all his ways, and hatred in the house of his God " (ix. 7, 8). Here, by the days of visitation and retribution, are signified the days of the last judgment, when the evil suffer punishment, which is signified by retribution, and is always preceded by visitation ; by Israel, the prophet, and the man of spirit, are not understood Israel, the prophet, and a man of spirit, but all those of the church who are in falsities of evil, and in evils of falsity, and who teach and confirm them from the literal sense of the Word ; the falsities of evil are signified by the multitude of iniquity, and the evils of falsity by great hatred ; by Ephraim, who is called a watchman with God, is signified the understanding of the Word, on which account he is so called ; but inasmuch as they who are in falsities of evil, and in evils of falsities pervert the understanding of the Word, and thus seduce craftily, therefore it is said, " the prophet is a snare of a fowler, and hatred in the house of his God." So in Ezekiel : "Son of man, prophesy against the prophets of Israel that prophesy, and say thou unto them that prophesy out of their own hearts, Hear ye the word of Jehovah ; Thus saith the Lord Jehovih, Woe unto the foolish prophets that follow their own spirit, and have seen nothing ! And my hand shall be upon the prophets that see vanity, and that divine lies " (xiii. 2, 3, 8). By the prophets mentioned here and in other parts of the Word, in the proximate sense, are understood prophets such as are mentioned in the Old Testament, and by whom the Lord spake ; but in the spiritual sense those prophets are not understood, but all who are led by the Lord ; for with them also the Lord flows in and reveals to them the arcana of the Word, whether they teach them or not, wherefore such are signified by prophets in the spiritual sense : but by the prophets who prophesy out of their own heart, and follow their own spirit, and who see vanity and divine lies, are understood all who are not taught and led by the Lord, but by themselves, whence they have the love of self instead of love for God, and the love of the world instead of love towards their neighbor, and consequently insanity instead of intelligence, and folly instead of wisdom, for from those loves falsities continually flow ; hence it is evident, what the above words signify in their series. So in Micah : " Therefore night shall be unto you for vision, and darkness shall arise unto you for divination ; and the sun shall go down upon the prophets, and the day shall be dark upon them " (iii. 6). Here, by " night shall be unto you for vision," is signified their having the understanding of what is false, instead of the understanding of truth ; darkness for divination, signifies falsities for revealed truths ; " the sun shall go down upon the prophets, and the day shall be dark upon them," signifies, that there shall be no more any light from the Lord, flowing in out of heaven and enlightening, but thick darkness from the hells darkening the understanding. Mention is made of prophets in many passages in the Word, and no other idea has hitherto been entertained concerning them than as of the prophets of the Old Testament, by whom the

Lord spake unto the people, and by whom he dictated the Word
but whereas the Word has in all its parts even in the most minute
a spiritual sense also, therefore, in this sense, by prophets are un
derstood all whom the Lord teaches, thus all who are in the spirit
ual affection of truth, that is, who love truth because it is truth, fo:
these, the Lord teaches, flows into their understanding, and enlight
ens; with such also this is more the case than it was with the pro
phets of the Old Testament, for they were not enlightened as to th
understanding, but only received by hearing the words which the:
were to say or write, neither did they at all understand their interio
spiritual sense.   From these considerations it may appear that b;
prophets, in the spiritual sense, are understood all who are wis
from the Lord, whether they also teach or not; and inasmuch a
every truly spiritual sense is abstracted from the idea of persons
places, and times, therefore by prophet is also signified, in the su
preme sense, the Lord as to the Word, and as to doctrine from th
Word, and likewise the Word itself, and doctrine: and in the oppo
site sense by prophets are signified the perversions and falsification
of the Word, and falsities of doctrine.   Such then being the signifi
cation of prophets in the Word, in both senses, we shall now adduc
a few passages wherein they are mentioned, from which it will b
more evident, that they signify all who receive and teach the Wor
and doctrine from it, and, in a sense separate from persons, th
Word itself and doctrine; and, in the opposite sense, those who per
vert the Word, and teach falsities of doctrine, and abstractedly, th
perversion of the Word and the falsities of doctrine.   Thus in Isaiah
" Therefore Jehovah will cut off from Israel head and tail in on
day.   The ancient and honorable, he is the head; and the prophe
that teacheth lies, he is the tail " (ix. 14, 15).   Again, in the sam;
prophet: " For Jehovah hath poured out upon you the spirit of dee;
sleep, and hath closed your eyes: the prophets and your rulers, th
seers hath he covered " (xxix. 10).   And in Jeremiah: " The;
have belied Jehovah, and said, It is not he: neither shall evil com
upon us; neither shall we see sword nor famine.   And the prophet
shall become wind, and the word is not in them " (v. 12, 13).   An;
again: " I have even sent unto you all my servants the prophets
daily rising up early and sending them " (vii. 25).   And again, i
the same prophet: " Therefore thus saith Jehovah of hosts concern
ing the prophets: Behold, I will feed them with wormwood, an
make them drink the water of gall: for from the prophets of Jerusa
lem is profaneness gone forth into all the land.   Hearken not unt
the words of the prophets that prophesy unto you: they make yo
vain: they make a vision of their own heart, and not out of th
mouth of Jehovah " (xxiii. 15, 16).   And again: " The prophet
that have been before me and before thee of old prophesied bot
against many countries, and against great kingdoms, of war, and (
evil, and of pestilence.   The prophet which prophesieth of peace
when the word of the prophet shall come to pass, then shall th
prophet be known, that Jehovah hath truly sent him " (xxviii. 8
9).   So in Matthew: " Woe unto you, Scribes and Pharisees, hypo

crites! because ye build the tombs of the prophets, and garnish the sepulchres of the righteous, and say, If we had been in the days of our fathers, we would not have been partakers with them in the blood of the prophets. Wherefore ye be witnesses unto yourselves, that ye are the children of them who killed the prophets. Wherefore, behold, I send unto you prophets, and wise men, and scribes: and some of them ye shall kill and crucify; That upon you may come all the righteous blood shed upon the earth, from the blood of righteous Abel unto the blood of Zecharias, son of Barachias, whom ye slew between the temple and the altar. O Jerusalem, Jerusalem, thou that killest the prophets, and stonest them which are sent unto thee" (xxiii. 29–37; Luke xi. 47–51). In these passages it appears as if by prophets were only understood the prophets by whom Jehovah, that is, the Lord, spake, when yet by killing the prophets the Lord did not understand the murdering of them only, but at the same time the slaughter and extinction of divine truth arising from the falsification and adulteration of the Word; for by a person and his function, in the spiritual sense, is understood the thing itself which the functionary performs or speaks, and thus by a prophet are understood divine truth or the Word, and doctrine thence derived; and inasmuch as the function of a person makes one in act with the person, therefore that thing in particular, which a prophet teaches, is understood by him: by shedding blood is also understood to adulterate the truths of the Word; and whereas this was done by the Jewish nation, therefore it is said, "O Jerusalem, Jerusalem, thou that killest the prophets, and stonest them which are sent unto thee;" by which words, in the spiritual sense, is understood, that they extinguish all divine truth which is with them from the Word. Inasmuch as by a prophet is understood the divine truth which is the Word, and which is from the Word in the church, and this cannot be extinguished except by those with whom divine truth or the Word is, therefore the Lord saith, "For it cannot be that a prophet perish out of Jerusalem" (Luke xiii. 33); for by Jerusalem is understood the church as to the doctrine of truth. In the Word also frequent mention is made of priest and prophet, and by priest is there understood one who leads to a life according to divine truth, and by prophet, he who teaches it. In this sense priest and prophet are mentioned in the following passages of the Word. Thus in Jeremiah: "For the law shall not perish from the priest, nor counsel from the wise, nor the word from the prophet" (xviii. 18). Again, in the same prophet: "And it shall come to pass at that day, that the heart of the king shall perish, and the heart of the princes; and the priests shall be astonished, and the prophets shall wonder" (iv. 9). So in Ezekiel: "Then shall they seek a vision of the prophet; but the law shall perish from the priest, and counsel from the ancients. The king shall mourn, and the prince shall be clothed with desolation" (vii. 26, 27). Here by a vision from the prophet is meant the understanding of the Word; by the law from the priest are meant the precepts of life; by counsel from the

ancients is meant wisdom thence derived; by the king and the prince
is meant intelligence by truths from good: this is the spiritual princi
ple of these words. And in Isaiah: " The priest and the prophe
have erred through strong drink, they are swallowed up of wine
they are out of the way through strong drink; they err in vision
they stumble in judgment " (xxviii. 7). Again, in Jeremiah: " 1
wonderful and horrible thing is committed in the land; the prophet
prophesy falsely, and the priests bear rule by their means; and m'
people love to have it so " (v. 30, 31). Again: " From the prophe
even unto the priest every one dealeth falsely " (viii. 10). And
again in the same prophet: " And when this people, or the prophet
or a priest, shall ask thee, saying, What is the burden of Jehovah'
thou shalt then say unto them, What burden? I will even forsaka
you, saith Jehovah, both the prophet, and the priest " (xxiii. 33, 34)
And in Zephaniah: "Her prophets are light and treacherous per
sons: her priests have polluted the sanctuary, they have done vio
lence to the law " (iii. 4). Again, in Jeremiah: " The priests saic
not, Where is Jehovah? and they that handle the law know me not
the prophet prophesied by Baal, and walked after things that do no
profit. The house of Israel is ashamed; they, their kings, thei
princes, and their priests, and their prophets " (ii. 8, 26). Beside
the above there are many other passages, where prophets and priest
are mentioned together, and by priests are understood those wh
teach life, and who lead to good, and by prophets, those who teac
truths by which they are to be led; but, in the abstract sense, b'
priests, and by the priesthood, is understood the good of love, con
sequently also the good of life, and by prophets is understood th
truth of doctrine, consequently, the truth which leads to good o
life: in a word, prophets are to teach, and priests to lead. Again
in Zechariah: "And it shall come to pass in that day, saith Jeho
vah of hosts, that I will cut off the names of the idols out of the land
and they shall no more be remembered: and also I will cause th
prophets and the unclean spirit to pass out of the land. And it shal
come to pass, that when any shall yet prophesy, then his father an
his mother that begat him shall say unto him, Thou shalt not live
for thou speakest lies in the name of Jehovah: and his father an
his mother that begat him shall thrust him through when he pro
phesieth. And it shall come to pass in that day, that the prophet
shall be ashamed every one of his vision, when he hath prophesied
neither shall they wear a rough garment to deceive. But he shall say,
am no prophet, I am a husbandman, for a man sold me from my boy
hood " (xiii. 2-5). The subjects here treated of are the advent of th
Lord into the world, and the abolition of representative worship, like
wise the falsities with which the doctrine of the church then abound
ed; for the Jewish nation, with which that church was, placed all wor
ship in externals, and nothing in internals, that is, they placed all in
sacrifices and such things as were external, and nothing in charity an
faith, which are things internal, whence their worship and doctrin
consisted of mere falsities, and the nation itself, viewed internally
was idolatrous. The abolition of such things by the Lord is describe

by these words of the prophet: thus by, " I will cut off the names of the idols out of the land, and they shall no more be remembered," is signified the abolition of idolatrous worship, that is, of worship merely external without being internal. By, "I will cause the prophets and the unclean spirit to pass out of the land," is signified the abolition of the falsities of doctrine; by, " when they shall yet prophesy, then his father and his mother that begat him shall say unto him, Thou shalt not live," is signified, that the church to be instituted by the Lord, which should be an internal church, should altogether extinguish the falsities of doctrine, if any one should teach them; by prophesying is signified to teach falsities of doctrine; by father and mother is signified the church as to good and as to truth; by father, the church as to good, and by mother, the church as to truth; and by, " thou shalt not live," is signified to extinguish; this is also signified by, " his father and his mother that begat him shall thrust him through." The abolition of the falsities of doctrine is also understood by, " the prophets shall be ashamed every one of his vision, when he hath prophesied; neither shall they wear a rough garment to deceive," the prophets and their vision denoting falsities of doctrine, and wearing a rough garment, or a coat of hair, to deceive, denoting to pervert the external things of the Word, such as are in its literal sense, for the coat of hair with the prophets represented the ultimate sense of the Word, in like manner as the clothing of John the Baptist, which was of camel's hair. By his saying, " I am a husbandman, for a man sold me from boyhood," is signified, that this is the case with them of the Jewish church, which was only external, not internal, because born therein, and consequently thereto addicted. So in Daniel : " Seventy weeks are determined upon thy people and upon thy holy city, to finish the transgression, and to make an end of sins, and to make reconciliation for iniquity, and to bring in everlasting righteousness, and to seal up the vision and prophesy, and to anoint the most holy " (ix. 24). These words are spoken concerning the advent of the Lord, when iniquity is consummated, or when there is no more any good and truth remaining in the church. " Upon thy people and upon thy holy city," signifies, upon the church and its doctrine, which are then altogether vastated and extinguished. " To finish transgression, and to make an end of sins," signifies, when all in the church are in falsities of doctrine, and in evils as to life, for, as was shown in what was premised to this article, the advent of the Lord and the last judgment do not take place until there is no longer any truth of doctrine and good of life remaining in the church, and this for the reason above mentioned, namely, that the upright may be separated from the non-upright. " To bring in everlasting righteousness," signifies the last judgment, when every one is rewarded according to his deeds. " To seal up the vision and the prophecy," signifies the end of the former church, and the beginning of a new church, or the end of the external church, which was representative of things spiritual, and the beginning of the internal church, which is itself spiritual, the vision and the prophecy denoting the falsities

of doctrine ; by the same words also is signified, that the Lor
would fulfil all things which were predicted of him in the Word
" to anoint the most Holy, or the holy of holies," signifies the glori
fication of the Lord's human principle by union with the essentia
divinity, and also all worship of him afterwards originating in lov
for him.   Thus also in Moses : "And Jehovah said unto Moses
See, I have made thee a god to Pharaoh : and Aaron thy brothe
shall be thy prophet " (Exod. vii. 1).   The reason why the Lor
said to Moses, " I have made thee a god to Pharaoh," was, becaus
Moses represented the law, by which is understood the divine truth
which is likewise signified by God in the spiritual sense ; for Mose
received from the mouth of the Lord the words which he was to sa·
unto Pharaoh, and he who thus receives is called god, whence it i
that the angels likewise are called gods, and hence also they signif
divine truths ; that Aaron should be his prophet, signifies, that h
should teach the truth received by Moses and declare it to Pharaoh
for by a prophet, as was said above, is signified one that teache
truth, and, abstractedly, the doctrine of truth ; these things may b
seen more fully explained in the A. C. n. 7268, 7269.   Hence it i
that the prophets of the Old Testament represented the Lord as t
the doctrine of divine truth, and that the chief of them represente
the Lord as to the Word itself from which the doctrine of divin
truth is derived, as Moses, Elias, Elisha, and John the Baptist ; an
whereas the Lord is the Word, that is, the divine truth, therefore h
himself, in the supreme sense of the Word, is called a prophet
Forasmuch as Moses, Elias, and John the Baptist, represented th
Lord as to the Word, therefore Moses and Elias appeared speakin
with the Lord, when he was transfigured (Matt. xvii. 3, 4 ; Mar
ix. 4, 5 ; Luke ix. 30) ; by Moses and Elias is there understood th
Word both historical and prophetical, by Moses, the historical Word
and by Elias, the prophetical, and this because the Lord, when h
was transfigured, presented himself in the form in which the divin
truth appears in heaven.   That Elias represented the Lord as to th
Word appears from the miracles recorded of him, which were als
significative of such things as pertain to divine truth or the Word
and whereas John the Baptist in like manner represented the Lor
as to the Word, therefore he was called Elias ; as appears in Mala
chi : " Behold, I will send you Elijah the prophet before the comin
of the great and dreadful day of Jehovah : and he shall turn th
hearts of the fathers to the children, and the heart of the children t
their fathers, lest I come and smite the earth with a curse " (iv. 5
6).   And it is plainly declared by the Lord himself that John wa
the Elias here spoken of (Matt. xi. 14 ; xvii. 10, 11, 12 ; Mark ix
11, 12, 13 ; not that he was Elias, but that he represented the sam
as Elias, namely the Word ; and inasmuch as the Word teaches tha
the Lord would come into the world, and in all its particulars, ever
the most minute, treats concerning him in the inmost sense, there
fore John was sent before him to teach concerning his advent, a
may be seen (Matt. xi. 9, 10 ; Luke i. 76 ; vii. 26).   From thes
considerations it may now be seen, whence it is that the Lord i

called a prophet, namely, because he was the Word, that is the divine truth itself, as may appear from John i. 1, 2, 14. That the Lord is called a prophet on account of his being the Word, appears also in Moses: "Jehovah thy God will raise up unto thee a prophet from the midst of thee, of thy brethren, like unto me; unto him ye shall hearken. I will put my words in his mouth; and he shall speak unto them all that I command him. And it shall come to pass, that whosoever will not hearken unto my words which he shall speak in my name, I will require it of him" (Deut. xviii. 15–19). The reason of its being said that Jehovah would raise up a prophet like unto Moses, was, because Moses represented the Lord as to the law, that is, as to the Word, as was said above, wherefore it is also said concerning Moses, that Jehovah would speak with him mouth to mouth, even apparently, and not in dark speeches (Numb. xii. 8); by which also the representative of the Lord by Moses is described; for the Lord spake with himself from Jehovah, that is, from the Essential Divine principle which was in him from conception, and this is what is understood, in the passage above cited, by, "I will put my words in his mouth; and he shall speak unto them all that I command him," and was also represented by Jehovah speaking with Moses mouth to mouth, and not as with the other prophets. Hence then it is that the Lord is also called a prophet in Matt. xxi. 11; Luke vii. 16; John vi. 40, 41; ix. 17.

625. "Before many peoples, and nations, and tongues, and kings" —That hereby is signified, with all who are in truths, and goods as to life, and at the same time in goods and truths as to doctrine according to every one's religion, consequently that the Word may be taught as to goods of life and as to truths of doctrine, appears from the signification of peoples and nations, as denoting those who are of the spiritual church, and those who are of the celestial church; they who are of the spiritual church are called in the Word people, but they who are of the celestial church are called nations. They who are of the spiritual church, and are called people, are those who are principled in truths as to doctrine and as to life; and they who are of the celestial church, and are called nations, are those who are principled in the good of love to the Lord, and thence in good as to life; concerning this signification of people and nations in the Word, see above, n. 175, 331: and from the signification of tongues, and many kings, as denoting those who are in goods and truths as to life and as to doctrine, but according to every one's religion; for tongues signify the goods of truth, and confession thereof, according to every one's religion; as may be seen above, n. 330, 455: and kings, signify truths which are from good, and many kings, various truths from good, but also according to every one's religion; concerning this signification of kings, see above, n. 31, 553. The reason why many kings signify various truths which are from good, is because the people and nations out of the church were, for the most part, in falsities as to doctrine, but still, inasmuch as they lived in love to God and in charity towards their neighbor, the falsities of their religion where accepted by the Lord as truths, be-

cause inwardly in their falsities there was the good of love, and the good of love qualifies all truth, and in such case qualifies the falsity which is believed by such to be truth ; the good also, which lies concealed within, causes such, when they come into the other life, to perceive genuine truths, and to receive them.   Moreover there are truths which are only appearances of truth, such as are those of the literal sense of the Word, which are also accepted by the Lord as genuine truths when there is in them the good of love to the Lord, and the good of love towards the neighbor, or charity ; in the other life also the good which is inwardly hid with them dissipates the appearances, and makes bare the spiritual or genuine truths.   From these considerations it may appear what is here understood by many kings ; concerning the falsities with the Gentiles or nations in which there may be good, see the D. of the N. J. n. 21.   From what has been said and shown in this and the preceding article, it is plain, that by its being said to John that he must prophecy again before many peoples, and nations, and tongues, and kings, is signified that the Word is as yet to be taught to those who are in goods and truths as to doctrine, and thence as to life ; but whereas it is said, "before many peoples, and nations, and tongues, and kings," therefore by those words is also signified, that the Word is to be taught as to goods of life and as to truths of doctrine, for these are the two essentials which the Word contains in its whole compass.   This then is the sense of those words abstracted from persons, which is the truly spiritual sense ; the sense of the letter in most places has respect to persons, and also mentions them, but the truly spiritual sense is altogether without respect to persons ; for the angels, who are in the spiritual sense of the Word, in everything which they think and speak, have not any idea of person or of place, inasmuch as the idea of person or of place limits and confines the thoughts, and thereby renders them natural ; but it is otherwise when the idea is abstracted from persons and places ; and hence it is that they have intelligence and wisdom, and that angelic intelligence and wisdom are ineffable ; for man, so long as he lives in the world, is in natural thought, and natural thought derives its ideas from persons, places, times, and things material, which, if they were taken away from man, his thought which comes to perception would perish, for he comprehends nothing without those things ; but angelic thought is without ideas derived from persons, places, times, and things material ; hence it is that angelic thought and speech is ineffable, and also incomprehensible to man.   The man, however, who has lived in the world a life of love to the Lord and of charity towards his neighbor, after his departure out of the world comes into that ineffable intelligence and wisdom, for his interior mind, which is the mind itself of his spirit, is then opened, and in such case the man, when he becomes an angel, thinks and speaks from that mind, and consequently thinks and speaks such things as he could not utter or comprehend in the world : every man has such a spiritual mind, which is like to the angelic mind : but in the world, inasmuch as he there speaks, sees, hears, and perceives by the material body, it lies hid within the natural mind, or lives above that mind, and what man therein thinks, he is altogether ignorant of; for the thought of that mind then flows into the natural mind, and there limits itself, closes, and presents itself to be seen and perceived. Man knows not, whilst he continues in the body in this world, that he possesses inwardly such a mind, in which are contained angelic wisdom and intelligence, because, as was said, all things which there engage attention flow into the natural mind, and thus become natural according to correspondences. These things are said in order that it may be known what is the quality of the Word in the spiritual sense, when that sense is altogether abstracted from persons and places, that is, from such things as derive their quality from what is material pertaining to the body and the world.

CHAPTER XI.

1. AND there was given to me a reed like to a staff; and the angel stood near, saying, Rise, and measure the temple of God, and the altar, and them that adore therein.

2. And the court which is without the temple, cast out abroad, and measure it not, because it is given to the nations, and the holy city shall they tread under foot forty and two months.

3. And I will give to my two witnesses, and they shall prophesy a thousand two hundred and sixty days, clothed in sacks.

4. These are the two olives, and the two candlesticks, which stand before the God of the earth.

5. And if any one shall be willing to hurt them, fire shall proceed out of their mouth, and shall devour their enemies ; and if any one shall be willing to hurt them, he must thus be killed.

6. These have power to shut heaven, that the rain rain not in the days of their prophecy ; and they have power over the waters to turn them into blood, and to smite the earth with every plague, as often as they will.

7. And when they shall have finished their testimony, the beast that cometh up out of the abyss shall make war with them, and shall conquer them, and kill them.

8. And their bodies shall lie on the street of the great city, which is spiritually called Sodom and Egypt, where also our Lord was crucified.

9. And they of the people and tribes and tongues and nations shall see their bodies three days and a half, and they shall not permit their bodies to be put into monuments.

10. And they that dwell upon the earth shall rejoice over them and shall be glad, and shall send gifts one to another, because those two prophets tormented them that dwell upon the earth.

11. And after three days and a half the spirit of life from God en-

tered into them, and they stood upon their feet; and great fear fell upon them that saw them.

12. And they heard a great voice out of heaven, saying to them, Ascend hither, and they ascended into heaven in a cloud, and their enemies saw them.

13. And in that hour there was a great earthquake, and the tenth part of the city fell, and there were slain in the earthquake, names of men, seven thousand; and the rest were affrighted, and gave glory to the God of heaven.

14. The second woe is past, behold the third woe cometh quickly.

15. And the seventh angel sounded, and there were great voices in heaven, saying, The kingdoms of the world are become our Lord's and His Christ's, and He shall reign unto the ages of ages.

16. And the twenty-four elders, who sat before God upon their thrones, fell upon their faces, and adored God.

17. Saying, We give Thee thanks, Lord God Almighty, Who art, and Who wast, and Who art to come, that thou hast assumed Thy great power, and hast entered upon the kingdom.

18. And the nations were angry, and Thy anger is come, and the time of the dead to be judged, and to give the reward to Thy servants the prophets and the saints, and to them that fear Thy name the small and the great; and to destroy them that destroy the earth.

19. And the temple of God was opened in heaven, and the ark of His covenant was seen in His temple: and there were lightnings, and voices, and thunders, and an earthquake, and great hail.

EXPLICATION.

626. Verses 1, 2. " And there was given to me a reed like to a staff; and the angel stood near, saying, Rise, and measure the temple of God, and the altar, and them that adore therein. And the court, which is without the temple, cast out abroad, and measure it not, because it is given to the nations, and the holy city shall they tread under foot forty and two months."—" And there was given to me a reed like to a staff," signifies, the mode of visitation, that is, of exploration of the quality of the church as to truth and good: " and the angel stood near, saying," signifies, the will of the Lord and command: " Rise, and measure the temple of God, and the altar, and them that adore therein," signifies, to explore the church, what its quality is as to the reception of divine truth and divine good, and thence as to the worship of the Lord: " and the court which is without the temple, cast out abroad, and measure it not," signifies, that the external of the Word, and thence of the church and worship, is not to be explored: " because it is given to the na-tions," signifies, inasmuch as it is perverted by evils of life and falses of doctrine: " and the holy city shall they tread under foot," signifies, that they will destroy all the doctrine of truth and good

from the Word : " forty and two months," signifies, even to the end of the old church, and the beginning of the new.

627. " And there was given to me a reed like to a staff "—That hereby is signified the mode of visitation, that is, of exploration of the quality of the church as to truth and as to good, appears from the signification of a reed, as denoting that by which quality is explored, for by measuring is signified to explore, and by measure, the quality of a thing ; hence by the reed, by which the temple and the altar were measured, as it follows, or by the reed of measure, is signified the mode of exploring quality : the reason why it denotes the mode of exploring the quality of the church as to truth and as to good, is, because it follows that the temple and the altar were measured, and them that adore therein, by which is signified the church as to truth and as to good, and thence as to worship.   The reason that the reed signifies also visitation, is, because visitation is the exploration of the quality of the men of the church, and because the visitation which precedes the last judgment, is what is afterwards treated of : the nature of that visitation or exploration, may appear from the visitation in Sodom, in that angels were first sent thither, and thereby visitation or exploration was made as to the quality of the reception of them, that is, as to the quality of the reception of divine good and divine truth, for those angels represent the Lord as to the divine proceeding ; and after it was explored that all in Sodom, except Lot, were not willing to receive them, but to offer injury to them, then their destruction came, by which is understood their last judgment.   The reason of the measuring being performed by a reed, is, because by a reed or cane is signified divine truth in the ultimate of order, and by a staff, which the reed was like, is signified power, and by truth in the ultimate of order, and its potency, all visitation or exploration is effected ; for all truths, even from the first, form what is simultaneous, or co-exist, in the ultimate, wherefore all things which are effected from the Divine [principle] are effected from first truths by ultimates ; in this case, therefore, visitation or exploration, which truth is signified by a reed or cane.   To the same purpose it is written, that, " One of the seven angels had a golden reed, with which he measured the city Jerusalem, and the gates thereof, and the wall thereof ; and he measured the city with a reed to twelve thousand furlongs" (Apoc. xxi. 15, 16) ; and in Ezekiel : " That in the hand of the angel there was a thread of flax and a measuring reed, and the reed was of six cubits, and that with it he measured the length, the breadth, and the height of the building, of the gate, of the porch, of the court, of the temple, and so on" (ch. xl. 3, 5, 6, 8, 11, 13, 17, and following ; ch. xli. 1 to 5, 13, 14, 22 ; ch. xlii. 1 to end) ; that by the measuring reed is here also understood the mode of exploring the church as to truth and as to good, may appear from this circumstance, that the angel measured everything of the temple, length, breadth, and height; and by length is signified good, by breadth, truth, and by height, the degrees of good and truth from supreme or inmost principles to the lowest or ultimate ; concerning this signification of length and breadth, see the work

concerning H. &. H. n. 197. That a reed signifies truth in ultimates, by which exploration is effected, may also appear from there
being likewise seen in the hand of the angel a thread of flax, whereby
is also signified truth ; likewise from the reed being of six cubits,
six denoting the same as the number three, viz. truths in the whole
complex, as may be seen above, n. 384, 532.   That to measure signifies to explore the quality of a thing will be seen in the following
article.   By ultimate truth, or truth in the ultimate of order, is meant
sensual truth, such as is in the literal sense of the Word, for those
who are merely sensual : divine truth in its descent proceedeth according to degrees, from the supreme or inmost to the lowest or ultimate : the divine truth in the supreme degree is such as the Divine
[principle] which proximately proceedeth from the Lord, thus such
as is the divine truth above the heavens, which, being infinite, cannot come to the perception of any angel; but the divine truth of the
first degree is what comes to the perception of the angels of the
third or inmost heaven, and is called divine truth celestial; from
this is derived the wisdom of those angels : the divine truth of the
second degree is what comes to the perception of the angels of the
second or middle heaven, and constitutes their wisdom and intelligence, and is called divine truth spiritual : the divine truth of the
third degree is what comes to the perception of the angels of the
ultimate or first heaven, and constitutes their intelligence and science, and is called divine truth celestial and spiritual natural ; but
the divine truth of the fourth degree is what comes to the perception
of the men of the church who are living in the world, and constitutes their intelligence and science ; this is called divine truth natural, and the ultimate of this is called divine truth sensual.   These
divine truths, according to their degrees in order, are in the Word,
and the divine truth in the ultimate degree, or in the ultimate of order, is such as is the divine truth in the literal sense of the Word,
which is for infants and for the simple, who are also sensual ; this
divine truth is what is signified by a reed or cane ; and inasmuch as
explorations with all are effected by this ultimate divine truth, as
was said above, therefore measurings and weighings, in the representative churches, were performed by reeds or canes, by which that
divine truth is signified ; that measurings were performed by reeds,
hath been just shown above ; that weighings were performed by the
same, appears in Isaiah, "They weigh silver with a reed" (xlvi. 6).
Forasmuch as reed signifies truth in the ultimates, such as is for the
simple and infants, who are not spiritual, but natural sensual, therefore it is also said in Isaiah, " A bruised reed he shall not break, and
smoking flax he shall not extinguish, and he shall bring forth verity
to judgment" (xlii. 3) ; treating concerning the Lord ; and by his
not breaking the bruised reed, is signified, that he will not hurt the
divine truth sensual with the simple and infants ; by not extinguishing the smoking flax, is signified, that he will not destroy the divine
truth which begins to live from a little good of love with the simple
and infants, flax denoting truth, and smoking denoting its living
from some little degree of love ; and inasmuch as both, viz. the reed

and the flax, are significative of truth, therefore it is also said concerning the Lord, that he will bring forth verity to judgment, by which is understood, that he will produce in them intelligence, judgment denoting intelligence. Reed also signifies the sensual or ultimate truth, such as hath place also with natural men, even the evil; as in the same prophet: " The dry place shall become a pool, and there shall be grass for the reed and rush" (xxxv. 7); speaking of the establishment of the church by the Lord; and that then they with whom there was not any before shall have intelligence by divine truth spiritual, is signified by, there shall be a dry place for a pool; and that then there shall be science by divine truth natural for those with whom before there was only sensual truth, is signified by grass instead of the reed and rush, grass denoting science from a spiritual origin, or by which spiritual truth is confirmed, and reed and rush denoting science from a sensual origin, or by which the fallacies of the senses are confirmed; this latter science, considered in itself, is only the lowest natural science, properly called material and corporeal, in which there is little or nothing of life. Again: " The streams shall recede, the rivers of Egypt shall be diminished and dried up, the reed and the flag shall wither" (xix. 6); by these words, in the spiritual sense, is understood, that all intelligence of divine truth should perish; the streams shall recede, signifies, that all things of spiritual intelligence shall depart; the rivers of Egypt shall be diminished and dried up, signifies, that all things of natural intelligence shall perish; the reed and the flag shall wither, signifies, that ultimate truth, which is called sensual, and is only scientific, shall vanish; streams and rivers denote the things appertaining to intelligence, Egypt denotes the natural principle, reed and flag denote scientific sensual truth or the sensual scientific principle; to recede, diminish, dry up, and wither, denote to perish and disappear. Again: " Thou hast confided upon the staff of this broken reed, upon Egypt, upon which, when a man leaneth, it entereth into his hand, and pierceth it; so is Pharaoh king of Egypt to all that confide upon him" (xxxvi. 6). By Egypt is signified the natural man separate from the spiritual, and the scientific thereof, which, when separate from the intelligence of the spiritual man, becomes foolish, and is applied to confirm evils of every kind, whence it also becomes false; this therefore is what is called the staff of a broken reed, reed, as was said, denoting truth in the ultimate of order, which is the scientific sensual; its being bruised signifies what is broken and not in coherence with any interior truth, which can alone cause consistency; staff denotes the power thence of perceiving and of reasoning concerning truths; hence it may appear, what is signified by, when a man leaneth upon it, it entereth into his hand, and pierceth it; to lean upon that staff, denotes, to confide in a self-derived power of perceiving truth, and of reasoning concerning it from proprium; and to enter into the hand and pierce it, signifies, to destroy all intellectual power, and to see and seize upon mere fables instead of truths; so is Pharaoh king of Egypt to all that confide upon him, signifies, that such is the natural man, separate from the spiritual, as to its scientifics, and intelligence thence derived, and reasoning from intelligence. So in Job: "Let my shoulder-blade fall from the shoulder, and mine arm be thence broken by a reed, because the dread of the destruction of God is upon me, and by reason of His Majesty I have no power. Have I made gold my hope, and said to pure gold, my confidence" (xxxi. 22, 23, 24): the subject here treated of is also concerning the confidence of self-derived intelligence, and by these words is described, in the spiritual sense, that from it nothing of truth can be seen, but what is merely false, which doth not cohere with any truth; no coherence is signified by the shoulder blade falling from the shoulder, and the arm being thence broken by a reed; the shoulder blade, the shoulder, and the arm, signify power, in this case, the power of understanding, and perceiving truth: to fall from the shoulder, and to be broken by a reed, signifies, to be separated from the spiritual power of perceiving truth, and thence to be deceived by the sensual corporeal man, and to perish by the false; reed denotes truth in the ultimate of order, which is called the scientific sensual, and which becomes merely false when it is of the natural man alone separate from the spiritual; the dread of the destruction of God, signifies, the loss of all the understanding of truth; by reason of his majesty to have no power, signifies, that nothing of the understanding and perception of truth is from the proprium of man, but all from God; to make gold a hope, and to say to pure gold, my confidence, signifies that he confided not in himself, in supposing anything of good to be from self. So in Ezekiel: "That all [the inhabitants of Egypt may know that I am Jehovah, because they were a staff of a reed to the house of Israel; when they took hold of thee by the hand thou wast broken in pieces, thou piercedst through all their shoulder; and when they leaned upon thee, thou wast broken, and hast made all their loins to be at a stand" (xxix. 6, 7): similar things are here said concerning Egypt as above, and by Egypt, here also is signified the natural man separate from the spiritual, and the scientific principle thereof, which, applied, to evils, is merely false; these things are said concerning those in the church who confide in self-derived intelligence; the sons of Israel signify those who are of the church; their confidence is signified by the staff of a reed; that all faculty of perceiving truth thence perished with them, is signified by, when they took hold of thee by the hand, thou brakest in pieces and piercedst through all their shoulder, the shoulder denoting the power or faculty of understanding truth; the loss thereof is signified by, when they leaned upon thee, thou brakest: that hence all the good of love and charity was destroyed and dissipated, is signified by, thou madest all their loins to be at a stand, loins denoting the marriage of truth and good, here therefore that truth was not conjoined to good; truth conjoined to good constitutes the good of love and charity, inasmuch as all the good of love and charity, is formed by truths. So in David: "Rebuke the wild beast of the reed [or cane], the congregation of the strong among the calves of the people; treading upon the plates of silver, he disperseth people, he desireth wars; the fat ones shall come out of Egypt, Ethiopia shall accelerate her gift to God" (Psalm lxviii. 31, 32): the subject here treated of is concerning the kingdom of the Lord : that heed should be taken of the false scientific, that is, of the scientific falsely applied from the natural man separate from the spiritual, is understood by, rebuke the wild beast of the reed [or cane]; inasmuch as those scientifics, being derived from the fallacies of the senses, strongly persuade, they are called the congregation of the strong; the calves of the people denote the goods of the church in the natural man; the plates of silver denote the truths of the church; to tread upon and disperse denotes to destroy and dissipate, which is done by those who are natural and sensual, and who think naturally and sensually, and not at the same time spiritually, thus who think from the natural and sensual man separate from the spiritual; this man is understood by the wild beast of the reed [or cane] : to desire wars, signifies, reasonings against truths; fat ones from Egypt and Ethiopia denote those who are in the science of things spiritual, and who are in the knowledges of truth and good, who will accede to the kingdom of the Lord, because they are in light from the spiritual man.   So in the first book of Kings : "Jehovah shall smite Israel as the reed noddeth in the waters, and he shall pluck away Israel out of the good land" (xiv. 15); the vastation of the church with the sons of Israel is compared to the nodding of the reed or cane in the waters, because by the reed or cane is signified the truth of the sensual man, which is ultimate truth, and when this truth is separated from the light of the spiritual man, it becomes false, for the sensual man derives all that it hath from appearances in the world, whence reasonings thence concerning things spiritual are mere fallacies, and from fallacies falses : what the fallacies of the senses are in things spiritual, and that falses are thence derived, may be seen in the D. of the N. J. n. 53; likewise in the explication above, n. 575; and that sensual scientifics are mere fallacies, when the sensual man reasons from them, n. 569, 581; likewise, what is the sensual principle, and the quality of the sensual man, may be seen in the D. of the N. J. n. 50.   It is written in the Evangelists, "That they placed a reed in the right hand of the Lord, and that afterwards they took the reed, and smote Him therewith on the head" (Matt. xxvii. 29, 30; Mark xv. 19); likewise, "That they put a spunge upon the reed and gave Him vinegar to drink" (Matt. xxvii. 48; Mark xv. 36): they who are unacquainted with the spiritual sense of the Word, may suppose that these and many other circumstances related concerning the passion of the Lord, involve nothing more than the common modes of derision; as that they set a crown of thorns upon His head; that they parted His garments among them but not the coat; that they bended the knee before Him for the sake of mocking Him; also the circumstance here adduced, that they placed a reed in His right hand, and afterwards smote His head therewith; likewise, that they filled a spunge with vinegar, or myrrhed wine, and set it upon a reed, and gave Him to drink : but it is to be observed, that all things which are related concerning the passion of the Lord, signify the mocking at divine truth, consequently the falsification and adulteration of the Word, inasmuch as the Lord, when He was in the world, was the divine truth itself, which, in the church, is the Word; and for this reason He permitted the Jews to treat Him altogether as they treated divine truth, or the Word, by the falsification and adulteration thereof; for they applied all things of the Word to their own loves, and derided every truth which was in disagreement with their loves; thus they derided the Messiah Himself, because He did not become king over the whole world, and exalt them above all people and nations, according to their explanation of the Word and religion thence derived : that all things related concerning the passion of the Lord signify such things, may be seen above, n. 64, 83, 195; but that their placing a reed in the hand of the Lord and afterwards smiting His head with it, signified that they falsified the divine truth or the Word, and altogether derided the understanding of truth and divine wisdom, is plain from this consideration, that by a reed is signified the false in extremes, as above, and by smiting the head is signified to reject and deride the understanding of truth, and divine wisdom, this being signified by the head of the Lord; and inasmuch as they represented the falsification of truth by giving the Lord vinegar to drink, therefore they also filled a spunge with it, and set it upon a reed, by which is signified the false in extremes, which is the false sustaining and subservient.

628. " And the angel stood near, saying"—That hereby is signified the will of the Lord, and command, appears from the signification of standing near, as here denoting will, concerning which we shall speak presently ; and from the signification of angel, as denoting the Lord as to the Word, concerning which see above, n. 593; and from the signification of saying, when from the Lord, as denoting command, for what the Lord saith is to be done, or that any one shall do, is command. The reason why the angel standing near in this passage denotes the will of the Lord, is, because in the spiritual world, when any one thinks of another with the intention and will of seeing him, speaking with him, and communicating to him a command, it causeth the other to be present, that is, to stand near ; for in that world there are not distances, which are constant and thence measurable, as in the natural world, but similitude of affection, and of thought thence derived, causeth presence, and dissimilitude causeth absence; all distances in that world are from this origin : this law of the spiritual world is derived from the universal principle, that the Lord is present with all according to their love for Him, and according to their love towards their neighbor, and the thoughts thence derived : from this universal principle exist all distances, that is, presence and absence, among angels and spirits; wherefore when any one desireth to speak with another, that is, thinks concerning him, from an intention or will of speaking with him, he becomes immediately present, or he himself is present with him; that this is the case, may also be seen in the work concerning H. & H. n. 191–199, where space in heaven is treated of. From these con-

siderations it may now appear, whence it is that the angel standing near signifies the will of the Lord; for to stand near is to be present.

629. "Rise, measure the temple of God, and the altar, and them that adore in it"—That hereby is signified to explore the quality of the church as to its reception of divine truth and divine good, and thence as to the worship of the Lord, appears from the signification of measuring, as denoting to explore the quality of a thing, concerning which we shall speak presently; and from the signification of temple, as denoting, in the supreme sense, the Divine Human [principle] of the Lord as to divine truth, and, in the respective sense, heaven and the church as to divine truth proceeding from the Lord, concerning which see above, n. 220; and from the signification of altar, as denoting, in the supreme sense, the Divine Human [principle] of the Lord as to divine good, and, in the respective sense, heaven and the church as to divine good proceeding from the Lord, concerning which also see above, n. 391, 490, 496; and from the signification of them that adore, as denoting worship; the reason why they that adore signify the worship of the Lord, is, because worship consists in adoration of the Lord, and because in the spiritual sense there is not anything of person understood, but only thing, abstracted from persons, concerning which see above, n. 99, 100, 270, 325, 625; hence it is, that by them that adore is signified adoration and worship: from these considerations it may appear, that by these words, Rise, and measure the temple of God, and the altar, and them that adore therein, is signified to explore the quality of the church as to its reception of divine truth and divine good proceeding from the Lord, and thence as to worship. That to measure, in the spiritual sense, does not signify to measure, may appear from this consideration, that it was commanded not only to measure the temple and the altar, but also them that adore therein; consequently to measure the temple and the altar must involve somewhat which is signified by their measures, thus, which is signified by the length, the breadth, and the height, for to measure them that adore in the temple, cannot be said, unless it signifies the exploration of their quality, or the quality of the thing signified. That to measure signifies to explore the quality of a thing, likewise to designate it, may appear from the passages in the Word where measuring and measures are mentioned; thus it is said in Ezekiel, "That the man who had the line of flax and the measuring reed in his hand, measured the building, likewise the threshold of the gate, the porch of the gate in the house, the porch of the gate from the house, the door of the gate, the gate from the roof of the bed chamber, and many other things, which he measured as to the length, the breadth, and the height" (xl. 3, 5, 6, 8, 11, 13, 17, and following verses): and afterwards, "that he measured the temple, the lintel over the door, the wall of the house, and the house itself, as to the breadth and the length" (xli. 1–5, 13, 14, 22); and again, "that he measured the inner court, and the things belonging to that court" (xlii); and lastly, "that he measured the altar, and the things belonging to the altar" (xliii. 13, and following verses): the measures were also de-

signated in numbers, namely, so many reeds, so many cubits, and
so many palms; from which it may appear, that by measuring those
things is not understood to measure them, but to designate the quality of the thing spiritually signified by each of the things measured,
namely, by the building, the gate, the porch, the temple, the upper
lintel, the wall, the court, and the altar : by the building, the house,
and the temple, is signified the church; by the door and the gate,
introductory truth; and by the porch and court, all things which
are without the church, but which still have respect thereto; these
are all things which appertain to the man of the church in his natural man; for the church itself appertaining to man is in his internal or spiritual man or mind, thus inwardly with him, but the things
which are in the external or natural man or mind, thus which reside
outwardly, all correspond to those things which are of the church
itself, which, as was said, are in the internal or spiritual man or
mind; these exterior things are what are signified by the porch
without the house and by the court; what the quality of these things
would be, is there designated by measures and numbers : for the subject treated of in those chapters is concerning the church of the Lord
which was to come, and which is called the internal church, and is
described as above: any one may see that such measurings would
be of no manner of account, unless they had been thus significative;
but what each mensuration signifies, may appear from the signification of the thing measured, and the quality thereof from the signification of the number by which the measure is expressed.   There are
only three things which are measurable, namely, breadth, length,
and height; and by breadth is signified the truth of the church, by
length, the good of the church, and by height, both as to degrees;
the degrees of truth and good are the quality of truth and good interiorly or superiorly, and exteriorly or inferiorly: the reason why
these things are signified by those three dimensions, is, because
breadth is predicated of heaven from the south to the north, and
length from the east to the west, and height from the third heaven,
which is in highest principles, to the first heaven, which is in lowest; and as they who dwell from south to north are principled in
the truths of doctrine, and they who dwell from east to west are
principled in the good of love, and they who dwell in the supreme
or third heaven are the most wise, and they who dwell in the first
or lowest heaven are respectively simple, therefore by breadth is
signified the truth of heaven or the church, by length the good,
and by height the wisdom and intelligence thereof as to degrees:
these things therefore are what are designated by mensuration in
general.   Again in the same prophet : " Son of man, show the house
to the house of Israel, that they may be ashamed for their iniquities;
and let them measure the form, when they have been ashamed for
all things which they have done; the form of the house and the disposition thereof, and the going out thereof, and the entrance thereof,
and all the forms thereof; teach them likewise all the statutes thereof,
and all the dispositions thereof, and all the laws thereof, and write
them in their eyes, that they may keep all the form thereof, and all

the statutes thereof, and do them " (xliii. 10, 11) : that by measuring the temple or the house, is signified to investigate and explore the quality of the church as to truth and as to good, may appear from its being said, that they should measure the form of the house, the going out thereof, and the entrance thereof; likewise, that they should keep all the form thereof; by which cannot be understood the form of the temple as to form only, but as to those things which are signified by the temple ; for it is added, that they may be ashamed for all their iniquities which they have done, by which is signified, that they may be ashamed for having departed from the laws and statutes of the church ; wherefore it is also said, that he may teach them all the statutes thereof, all the descriptions, and all the laws thereof; hence it is evident, that by temple is signified the church with its truths and goods, for these are the things, which are to be kept, and are signified by all the form of the house or the temple; by temple in the Word is signified the church as to truth, and by the house of God, the church as to good ; for the temple was built of stone, but the house of God, in ancient times, was of wood ; and stones signify truths, and wood, good. Again in Zechariah : " I lifted up mine eyes, and saw, and behold a man in whose hand was a measuring line : and I said, Whither goest thou ? and he said unto me, To measure Jerusalem, that I may see what is the breadth thereof, and what is the length thereof : and he said, Jerusalem shall inhabit the suburbs, by reason of the multitude of men and beasts in the midst thereof" (ii. 5, 6, 8) : these things are said concerning the advent of the Lord, and concerning the establishment of the New Church by Him, as may appear from verse 14 and 15, of the same chapter ; Jerusalem signifies that New Church, and to measure it signifies to explore and thence to know its quality and quantity ; breadth signifies the truth of its doctrine, and length the good of its love, as was shown above ; wherefore it is said, to measure Jerusalem, that I may see what is the breadth thereof, and what is the length thereof : that the church is there meant by Jerusalem, and not the city Jerusalem, is evident, for about the time of the advent of the Lord, Jerusalem was not of such quantity and quality as is there described, viz. that Jerusalem should inhabit the suburbs by reason of the multitude of men and beasts in the midst thereof, by which words is understood the multitude of the gentiles or nations that would accede to the church : by Jerusalem in the midst thereof is signified the church composed of those who would interiorly receive the Divine [principle] proceeding from the Lord, and by the suburbs, the church composed of those who would receive exteriorly ; the church of the Lord is internal and external ; in the internal church are those who are in intelligence and wisdom, and thence in the superior heavens, but in the external church are those who are principled in sciences and in the knowledges of truth and good from the Word, and not in any interior intelligence and wisdom, and thence are in the inferior heavens : these latter are called spiritual natural, but the former spiritual, and the spiritual are understood by those who are in the midst of Jerusalem, and the spiritual natural by those who are in the suburbs : by men and beasts are understood those who are in intelligence and thence in the good of life, by men those who are in intelligence, and by beasts those who are in the natural affection of good, and thence in the good of life. Similar things are signified by these words in the Apocalypse: "The angel who talked with me, had a golden reed, to measure the city of the New Jerusalem, the gates thereof, and the wall thereof: and he measured the wall, 144 cubits, which is the measure of a man, that is, of an angel " (xxi. 15, 17); where also by the New Jerusalem is understood the New Church, and by the city, the doctrine thereof: by its wall is signified the divine truth defending : by the number 144 are signified all truths and all good in the complex : this number is said to be the measure of a man, that is of an angel, which could not be said unless by measure was signified quality; but this will be explained hereafter.   Again in Ezekiel : " When the man went out towards the east, in whose hand was the measuring line, he measured a thousand by the cubit ; afterwards he made me to pass through the waters, the waters were of the ankles ; presently he measured a thousand, and made me to pass through the waters, the waters were of the knees ; and he measured a thousand, and made me to pass through the waters, the waters were of the loins ; again he measured a thousand, they were a river which I could not pass through, because the waters were very high, waters of swimming, a river which was not passed through ; and behold on the bank of the river were very many trees, on this side and on that side ; and every living soul which creepeth, and whithersoever the river cometh, shall live ; whence there shall be exceeding much fish " (xlvii. 3, 4, 5, 9): by these words is described how the intelligence which appertains to those who are of the church, increaseth by the reception of divine truth proceeding from the Lord; the divine truth proceeding from the Lord is signified by the waters issuing from under the threshold of the house towards the east, and descending from the right side of the house from the south of the altar, as is said in verse 1, of that chapter; by the east is signified love to the Lord, inasmuch as the east in heaven is where the Lord appeareth as a sun, and the right side thence is where divine truth is received in the greatest light, and that side is called the south, wherefore it is also said, from the south of the altar : how intelligence increaseth by the reception of divine truth proceeding from the Lord, is described by the waters which the prophet passed through, which first reached to the ankles, afterwards to the knees, then to the loins, and at length were so high that they could not be passed ; by the waters to the ankles is signified intelligence such as appertains to the sensual and natural man, for the ankles signify what is sensual and natural ; by the waters to the knees is signified intelligence such as appertains to the spiritual natural man, for the knees signify what is spiritual natural ; by the waters to the loins is signified intelligence such as appertains to the spiritual man, for the loins signify the marriage of truth and good, which is spiritual; by the waters which could not be passed, is signified celestial intelligence, which is called wisdom, such as appertains to the celestial man or to the angel of the third heaven, which, because it is ineffable, is said to be a river which could not be passed, and because it is far above the natural man, the waters are called waters of swimming; the river derived from those waters therefore signifies intelligence and wisdom; the knowledges of truth and good, likewise perceptions, are signified by the very many trees on the bank of the river on this side and on that side, trees denoting knowledges and perceptions; the life thence communicated to all things which are in the natural man, as well the knowledges as sciences thereof, is signified by, every living soul that creepeth, whithersoever the river cometh, shall live, likewise by there being exceeding much fish; soul that creepeth and fish signify those things which are in the natural man, which are called knowledges from the Word, also natural sciences, whereby spiritual things are confirmed; and to live signifies the influx of the Lord through the spiritual man and his intelligence into those knowledges and sciences; that waters signify the truths of doctrine from the Word, by which comes intelligence, may be seen above, n. 71, 483, 518. Thus also in Habakkuk; "He stood and measured the earth: he saw and dissipated the nations; for the mountains of eternity were dispersed, the hills of the age submitted themselves; his goings are of an age" (iii. 6); treating concerning the visitation and the last judgment, when the Lord should come into the world: by, He stood and measured the earth, is understood the exploration of the quality of the church at that time, to measure denoting to explore, and the earth denoting the church: by, He saw and dissipated the nations, is signified, the casting down of all into hell who are in evils and thence in falses, to dissipate denoting to cast into hell, and nations denoting those who are in evils and thence in falses; by the mountains of eternity were dispersed, is signified, that the celestial church, such as was with the most ancient people, who were principled in love to the Lord, perished, the mountains of eternity denoting that church and that love; by the hills of the age submitted themselves, is signified, that the spiritual church, such as was with the ancient people after the deluge, who were principled in love towards their neighbor, perished, the hills of the age denoting that church and that love; by His goings being of an age, is signified, according to the state of the church which then existed, and was perverted. Again in Isaiah: "Behold the Lord Jehovih cometh in strength, and His arm shall rule for Him; who hath measured the waters in the hollow of His hand, and meted out the heavens with a span, and comprehend the dust of the earth in a measure, and weighed the mountains in scales, and the hills in a balance" (xl. 10, 12); treating also concerning the Lord, and concerning divine truth, from which is heaven and the church and all wisdom: the advent of the Lord and arrangement of all things in the heavens by Him, from His own proper power, is signified by, behold the Lord Jehovih cometh in strength, and His arm shall rule for Him, His arm which shall rule denoting proper power; the arrangement thence of all things in the heavens by divine truth, is signified by, who hath measured the waters in the hollow of His hand, and meted

out the heavens with a span, and comprehend the dust of the earth
in a measure, and weighed the mountains in scales, and the hills in
a balance; by measuring the waters, is signified, to designate divine
truths; by meting out the heavens with a span, is signified, thence
to set in order or arrange the heavens; by comprehending the dust
of the earth in a measure, is signified the same with respect to things
inferior; by the hollow of the hand, the span, and the measure, is
signified the same as by measures and by the hand, namely, the
quality of a thing, and proper power; by weighing the mountains
in scales and the hills in a balance, is signified, to bring all things
into subordination and equilibrium, the scales and balance denoting
just equilibrium, and the mountains and hills the superior heavens,
the mountains those which are principled in love to the Lord, and
the hills those which are principled in charity towards the neighbor.
So in Job: "Where wast thou when I founded the earth? declare
if thou hast known intelligence, who laid the measures thereof, if
thou knowest, and who stretched out the line upon it, upon what
are its bases sunk, who laid the stone of its corner" (xxxviii. 4, 5
6): by the earth is here understood the church; by founding it, and
laying its measures, is signified to establish it and to designate its
quality, measure denoting the quality of a thing; by stretching out
upon it the line, is signified to contain in its quality: by sinking the
bases thereof and laying the corner stone, is signified, the foundation
thereof upon those things which are in the natural man, the corner
stone denoting the truth of the natural man, which is called scientific
truth, upon which the truth of the spiritual man, or spiritual truth
is founded.   Again in Jeremiah: "If these statutes shall depart
from before me, the seed of Israel also shall cease, that they may not
be a nation before me all the days; if the heavens shall be measured
upwards, and the foundations be searched through downwards, .
also will reprobate all the seed of Israel on account of all that they
have done" (xxxi. 36, 37): by statutes are there signified all the
things appertaining to the church, which were commanded the sons
of Israel, consequently, all things appertaining to worship; that if
they should not keep these, there would be no church with them, is
signified by, if these statutes shall depart from before me, the seed
of Israel shall cease, that they may not be a nation before me all the
days; by Israel is signified the church, and by the seed of Israel
the truth of the church; and that although a new heaven and new
church should be established, there would still be nothing of heaven
and the church with that nation, is signified by, if the heavens shall
be measured upwards, and the foundations shall be searched down
wards, I also will reprobate the seed of Israel on account of all that
they have done.   The reason why by meting and measuring is sig
nified to designate and determine the quality of a thing, and also to
explore it, is, because by measure is signified the quality of a thing
or quality in the abstract: that this is signified by measure, may ap
pear from the following passages: as in the Apocalypse: "The
angel measured the wall of the city New Jerusalem, 144 cubits
which is the measure of a man, that is, of an angel" (xxi. 17): the

the quality of what is understood by the wall of the city New Jerusalem is here meant by measure, is very evident, for what otherwise could be understood by the measure of a wall, 144 cubits, being the measure of a man, that is of an angel? So in Matthew: "Judge not that ye be not condemned, for with what judgment ye judge, ye shall be judged, and with what measure ye mete, it shall be measured to you " (vii. 1, 2): so in Luke: "Judge not that ye be not judged; condemn not that ye be not condemned; remit and it shall be remitted to you; give and it shall be given to you, good measure, pressed, shaken, and running over, shall they give into your bosom; for with what measure ye mete, it shall be measured to you again " (vi. 37, 38); these words may be seen explained in the work concerning H. & H. n. 349: thus also in Mark: "With what measure ye mete it shall be measured to you again; and to you that hear, more shall be given; whosoever hath, to him shall be given; but ' whosoever hath not, from him shall be taken even that which he hath " (iv. 24, 25): in these words is described charity towards our neighbor, or the spiritual affection of truth and good, viz. that in proportion as any one is principled in such charity or affection in the world, in the same proportion he comes into it after death: that evil is not to be thought concerning good and truth, is understood by, judge not that ye be not judged, condemn not that ye be not condemned; to think evil concerning what is evil and false is allowed to every one, but not concerning good and truth, for these in the spiritual sense, are understood by neighbor, and inasmuch as charity is thus understood, therefore it is also said, remit and it shall be remitted to you, give and it shall be given unto you; that the spiritual affection which is called charity shall remain after death according to the quantity and quality thereof, is understood by, with what measure ye mete it shall be measured to you again; and that the quantity and quality shall be replenished to eternity, is understood by, to you that have, more shall be given, also by, good measure, pressed, shaken, and running over, shall men give into your bosom, measure denoting the quantity and quality of affection or charity, which shall be increased to eternity within or according to the degree thereof opened in the world; see also the work concerning H. & H. as above, n. 349; that this shall come to pass with those who exercise charity, is understood by, to you that hear, more shall be given, to hear denoting to obey and do: that to love our neighbor, is to love what is true and good, likewise what is sincere and just, may be seen in the D. of the N. J. n. 84 to 106; that no other thought or judgment is here understood than concerning the spiritual life of another, may appear from this consideration, that it is allowable for every one to think concerning the moral and civil life of another, and also to judge concerning it, for without such thought and judgment concerning others no civil society could possibly subsist; wherefore by not judging and condemning is signified, not to think evil concerning our neighbor spiritually understood, viz. concerning his faith and love, which appertain to the spiritual life, for these lie concealed in the interiors, and hence are not known to any but to the Lord alone. Again, in John: " He whom the Father hath sent speaketh the words of God, for God hath not given the spirit by measure unto him" (iii. 24): by the spirit which God giveth is signified divine truth, and intelligence and wisdom thence derived; by not being given by measure, is signified, above all the quantity and quality of men, consequently what is infinite, for the infinity belonging to the Lord has no quantity and quality, these being properties of what is finite, for quantity and quality determine what is finite and terminate it, but what is without termination is infinite; hence also it follows that measure here signifies quality, for not from measure signifies without predication of quantity or quality. So in David: " Make known to me, Jehovah, my end, and the measure of my days what it is, that I may know how shortly I am ceasing; behold thou hast given my days as a handbreadth, and my time is as nothing before thee " (xxxix. 5, 6): it appears as if by these words the times of life only were understood, the end of which he desired to know, and that those times pass away quickly; but in the spiritual sense times are not understood, but instead thereof states of life; wherefore by, make known to me, Jehovah, my end, the measure of my days what it is, is signified, that he may know the state of his life and the quality thereof, thus what quality of life would remain with him; by, behold thou hast given my days as a hand- breadth, is signified, that the quality of the state of his life was of very little moment; and my time is as nothing before thee, signifies, that the state of his life was of no avail; for time and day, in the Word, signify states of life as to truth and as to good, and thence as to intelligence and wisdom, consequently it is here meant, that both the latter and the former, so far as they were from himself, were nothing worth : that such a sense is contained in these words, cannot be seen by those who think only naturally, because natural thought cannot be separated from the idea of time, but spiritual thought, such as is angelic thought, has nothing in common with time, neither with space or person. Forasmuch as measure signifies the quality of a thing, it may appear what is signified by the house of measures, Jer. xxxii. 14; by the portion of measures, Jer. xiii. 25; likewise by the men of measures, Isa. xlv. 14; where measures signify quality in every complex. Thus also in Moses: " Ye shall not do perversity in judgment, in measure, in weight, and in dimension; scales of justice, stones of justice, an ephah of justice, and a hin of justice, shall ye have " (Levit. xix. 35, 36): again : " There shall not be in thy bag divers stones, a great one and a little one; there shall not be in thy house divers ephahs, great and small; thou shalt have a perfect and a just stone, a per- fect and just ephah shalt thou have " (Deut. xxv. 13, 14, 15): and in Ezekiel : " Scales of justice, and an ephah of justice, and a bath of justice shall ye have" (xlv. 10); that by these measures and weights is signified estimation of a thing according to the quality of truth and good, may be seen above, n. 373.

630. " And the court which is without the temple cast out abroad, and measure it not"—That hereby is signified that the external of

the Word, and thence of the church and worship, is not to be explored, appears from the signification of the court, as denoting the external of the Word, and thence of the church and worship. The reason of this signification of the court is, because the temple signifies heaven and the church as to divine truth, as was said in the article above, and hence the court, which was without the temple, or before the front of the temple, signifies the first or ultimate heaven: for the temple, considered in itself, signifies the superior heavens; viz. the sacred place, where was the ark of the covenant, signified the inmost or third heaven, and the temple without the sacred place, the middle or second heaven, whence the court signified the ultimate or first heaven: and what signifies heaven, this also signifies the church, for the church is the Lord's heaven in the earths: and what signifies the church, this also signifies the Word, and also worship, for the Word is the divine truth, from which heaven and the church exists, and worship is according to divine truth which is the Word: hence it is, that the court signifies the external or ultimate of heaven and the church, and also the external or ultimate of the Word and of worship. The case is the same with respect to the Word and worship, as it is with respect to heaven and the church; for in the Word there are three distinct senses, as there are three heavens; the inmost sense, which is called the celestial sense, is for the inmost or third heaven, the middle sense, which is called the spiritual sense, is for the middle or second heaven, and the ultimate sense, which is called the celestial and spiritual-natural sense, is for the ultimate or first heaven; these three senses, besides the natural which is for the world, are in the Word and every particular thereof; and whereas the three heavens have the Word, and each heaven is in its own sense of the Word, and hence their heaven exists and also their worship, it therefore follows, that what signifies heaven, signifies also the Word and worship: from this circumstance then it is, that the court signifies the external of the Word, and thence the external of the church and of worship. Moreover it is to be observed, that there were two courts to the temple, one without the temple, and the other within, and by the court without the temple is signified the entrance itself into heaven and into the church, in which they are who are introducing into heaven; and by the court within the temple was represented the ultimate heaven: the case is the same with the church; as also with the Word and with worship; for by the court without the temple is signified the external of the Word, that is, the Word, such as it is in the natural sense, which is for the world, by which man is introduced into the spiritual sense thereof, in which the angels of heaven are principled: but what is properly signified by each court, the inward and the outward, will be said in what follows; likewise, what is signified by the court without the temple being cast out abroad, and not measured, will be shown in the following articles, in the explanation of what is signified by its being given to the nations. From what has been said, it may now in some degree be seen, what is signified by court and by courts in the Word; as in the following passages: as in Moses:

" Thou shalt make the court of the dwelling place to the corner of
the south towards the south, hangings for the court twenty pillars,
twenty bases, the hooks of the pillars and the fillets of silver : the
gate of the court with the vail; the length thereof shall be one hundred cubits from the south to the north, and the breadth thereof fifty
from the east to the west" (Exod. xxvii. 9, 18): this court was the
court of the tent of the assembly, by which in like manner was
represented and signified the ultimate or first heaven : for by the
tent of assembly was represented heaven; by the inmost thereof,
where the ark was, over which was the propitiatory, was represented
the inmost or third heaven; and by the law in the ark, the Lord
Himself as to divine truth or the Word ; and by the tent without the
vail, where the table was for the breads, the altar of incense, and
the candlestick, was represented the middle or second heaven ; and
by the court, the ultimate or first heaven; that the three heavens
were represented by that tent may be seen in the A. C. n. 3478,
9457, 9481, 9485; but what is specifically signified by the court,
and by all things appertaining thereto, may be seen n. 9741–9775.
Inasmuch as the court represented the ultimate heaven, and thence
also the external of the church, of the Word, and of worship, therefore " the residue of the meat-offerings and of the sacrifices for sin,
were eaten by Aaron and his sons in the court" (Levit. v. 9, 19);
by eating those sanctified things in the court, was signified to appropriate to themselves the goods of the church, which were signified
by the meat-offerings and sacrifices, and all appropriation of holy
things is effected by ultimates, for except by ultimates there can be
no appropriation of things interior and holy.   Concerning the temple also it is thus written in the 1st book of Kings : " Solomon made
a court before the front of the temple of the house, and afterwards he
built a court within, three orders of hewn stones, and an order of
hewn cedar" (vi. 3, 36): by the temple in like manner was represented heaven and the church : by the sacred place where the ark
was, was represented the inmost or third heaven, likewise the church
with those who are in inmost principles, which is called the celestial
church ; by the temple without the sacred place, was represented
the middle or second heaven, likewise the church with those who
are in similar principles, which is called the internal spiritual church;
by the inner court was represented the first or ultimate heaven,
likewise the church with those who are in ultimates, which is called
the internal natural church ; but by the outer court was represented
the entrance into heaven: and inasmuch as by the temple, in the
supreme sense, is signified the Lord as to His Divine Human [prin-
ple] likewise as to divine truth, hence it also signifies the divine
truth proceeding from the Lord, consequently the Word, for this is
the divine truth in the church ; that the Divine Human [principle]
of the Lord is signified by the temple, appears from the Lord's words
where He saith, "Dissolve this temple, and in three days I will
raise it up; and he spake of the temple of his body" (John ii. 18–
23); that by the temple is signified the church, appears from these
words of the Lord, " That there should not be left of the temple one

stone upon another which should not be dissolved " (Matt. xxiv. 1,
2; Luke xxi. 5, 6, 7); by which words is understood that all divine truth, consequently everything of the church, would perish;
for the end of the church is there treated of, which is called the consummation of the age.   That there were two courts built, an inner
and an outer, with little chambers, porticos or piazzas, &c. may appear from the description of them in Ezekiel : " The angel brought
me to the outer court, where behold were little chambers, and a
pavement made for the court round about, thirty little chambers upon
the pavement, which he measured as to the length and the breadth,
and he also measured the bed chambers, and the portico, and the
gate, everything as to length and breadth"(xl. 17–22, 31, 34, and following verses; chap. xlii. 1–14); and concerning the inner court in
the same prophet : " He measured the inner court, the gates thereof
towards the north, the east, and the south; the portico, the steps
with the ascents, the bed-chambers, the chambers of the singers, the
upper lintels," &c. (xl. 23–31, 44, and the following verses): and
in Jeremiah : " In the little chamber of Gamaliah the scribe, in the
superior court, at the door of the gate of the new house" (xxxvi.
10): in the prophet Ezekiel, from the xl. to xlviii. chapter, the
subject treated of is concerning a new city, a new temple, and a new
earth, whereby is signified the New Church which was to be established by the Lord; and by the chambers, the bed chambers, the
porticos, and the rest, are signified such things as appertain to the
church, its doctrine and worship; and by their dimensions, is signified the quality thereof, as was shown in the article above : but to
explain what is signified by each particular, does not belong to this
place, only that the courts signify the external things of heaven and
the church, and thence the externals of the Word and worship; this
may appear from this circumstance alone, that the temple in general
signifies heaven and the church, wherefore the three divisions of the
temple, viz. the courts, the temple itself, and the sacred place, signify the three heavens, according to their degrees; the nature and
quality of the three heavens, according to their degrees, may be seen
in the work concerning H. & H. n. 29–40.   That heaven and the
church are signified by the temple and the court, may more fully
appear from these words in Ezekiel : " The spirit lifted me up, and
introduced me into the inner court of the temple, when behold the
glory of Jehovah filled the house; and I heard one speaking unto me
out of the house, saying, Son of man, the place of my throne, and
the places of the soles of my feet, where I will dwell in the midst of
the sons of Israel for ever" (xliii. 4–7) : that by these courts is signified the ultimate heaven, or the external of the church, may appear from its being said, that he was introduced into the court, and
thence saw the house filled with the glory of Jehovah, the glory of
Jehovah denoting the divine truth, which constitutes heaven and
the church; also from its being afterwards said, that that house was
the place of the throne of Jehovah, and the place of the soles of His
feet, where He will dwell in the midst of the sons of Israel for ever :
that by the throne of Jehovah, is understood heaven, may be seen

above, n. 253, 297, 343, 460, 462, 477, 482; and that by the place
of the soles of the feet of Jehovah is understood the church, may
also be seen above, n. 606; by the sons of Israel are understood all
who are of the church of the Lord, consequently to dwell with them
for ever, signifies the perpetual presence of the Lord with them.
Again in the same prophet: "The glory of Jehovah lifted up itself
from upon the cherub upon the threshold of the house, and the house
was filled with a cloud, and the cloud filled the inner court, and the
court was full of the splendor of the glory of Jehovah; and the voice
of the wings of the cherubs was heard even to the outer court" (x.
3–6): by the cherubs seen by the prophet was represented the Lord
as to providence and guard that He may not be approached except
by the good of love; consequently by the cherubs are signified the
superior heavens, specifically the inmost heaven, for this is the heaven where that defence or guard is, as may be seen above, n. 277,
313, 322, 362, 370, 462; wherefore by the house which was filled
with the cloud, is signified heaven and the church; by the inner
court, which the cloud also filled, is signified the ultimate heaven,
and by the outer court, as far as which the voice of the wings of the
cherubs was heard, is signified the entrance into heaven, which specifically is in the natural world, and afterwards in the world of spirits; for by the church in the world, and afterwards by the world of
spirits, man enters into heaven; what the world of spirits is, may be
seen in the work concerning H. &. H. n. 421, 431, and following
paragraphs; but by the cloud, and by the splendor of the glory of
Jehovah is signified the divine truth proceeding from the Lord.
From these considerations it may now appear what is signified by
courts in the following passages; as in David: "Blessed [is the
man] whom thou choosest and causest to approach; he shall inhabit
thy courts; we shall be saturated with the good of thy house, with
the holiness of thy temple" (Psalm lxv. 5): by these words is signified, that they who are in charity, or in spiritual affection, shall
live in heaven, and be there in intelligence and wisdom from divine
truth and divine good; by the elect, or him whom thou choosest,
are signified those who are principled in love towards their neighbor
or in charity; by causing to approach, is signified spiritual love or
affection, for so far as man is in that love or in that affection, so far
he is with the Lord, for every one approaches Him according to that
love; by inhabiting the courts, is signified to live in heaven, to inhabit denoting to live, and the courts denoting heaven; by being
saturated with the good of the house, is signified to be in wisdom
from divine good; and by being saturated with the holiness of the
temple, is signified to be in intelligence from divine truth, and from
both to be in the fruition of heavenly joy; the house of God, signifies heaven and the church as to divine good, and the temple, heaven and the church as to divine truth, and holiness is predicated of
spiritual good, which is truth. Again: "A day in thy courts is
better than a thousand, I have chosen at the gate to stand in the
house of my God" (Psalm lxxxiv. 11): by the courts is there signified the first or ultimate heaven, by which is entrance into the supe-

nor heavens, wherefore it is added, I have chosen at the gate to stand in the house of my God. Again: "Give to Jehovah the glory of His name, bring an offering, and come into His courts" (Psalm xcvi. 8); so again: "Praise ye the name of Jehovah, praise, O ye servants of Jehovah, who stand in the house of Jehovah, in the courts of the house of our God" (Psalm cxxxv. 1, 2); again: "How amiable are thy dwellings, O Jehovah Zeboath, my soul hath desired, yea hath fainted, towards the courts of Jehovah" (Psalm lxxxiv. 2, 3); again: "Enter ye His gates in confession, His courts in praise, confess ye to Him, bless His name" (Psalm c. 4); again: "I will pay my vows to Jehovah before all His people, in the courts of the house of Jehovah, in the midst of thee, O Jerusalem" (Psalm xcvi. 14); and again: "The just shall flourish as the palm, he shall grow as the cedar in Libanus, they that are planted in the house of Jehovah shall germinate in the courts of our God" (Psalm xcii. 13, 14): that by the courts mentioned in these passages is understood heaven, specifically the ultimate heaven, and the church, may appear without explication. So likewise in the following passages; as in Isaiah: "They shall collect the corn and the must, they shall eat and shall praise Jehovah, and they who are gathered together shall drink it in the courts of my holiness" (lxii. 9): by collecting the corn and must, is signified instruction in the goods and truths of doctrine and of the church; by, they shall eat and shall praise Jehovah, is signified appropriation and the worship of the Lord; by, they who are gathered together shall drink it in the courts of my holiness, is signified the fruition of divine truth, and thence of felicity in the heavens. Again in Joel: "Between the court and the altar let the priests weep, the ministers of Jehovah, and let them say, spare thy people Jehovah" (ii. 17); by weeping between the court and the altar, is signified lamentation over the vastation of divine truth and divine good in the church; for by the court is signified the same as by the temple, viz. the church as to divine truth, and by the altar, the church as to divine good, whence by between the court and the altar, is signified the marriage of good and truth, which constitutes heaven and the church; and by weeping is signified lamentation over the vastation thereof. By courts are signified the ultimates of heaven, likewise the externals of the church, of the Word, and of Worship, also elsewhere in the Word; as in Isaiah i. 12; Zechar. iii. 7.

631. "Because it is given to the nations"—That hereby is signified, because it is perverted by evils of life and falses of doctrine, appears from the signification of the gentiles or nations, as denoting those who are in evils as to life, and thence in falses as to doctrine, and, in the abstract sense, evils of life and falses of doctrine: that evils and falses are signified by the nations may be seen above, n. 175, 331, 625. The reason why the external of the Word and thence of the church and worship is perverted by evils of life and by falses of doctrine, is, because the external of the Word, which is called the sense of the letter, is written according to appearances in the world, because it is for infants and the simple minded, who have

no perception of anything contrary to appearances, wherefore such by the sense of the letter, in which are appearances of truth, are introduced into interior truths, as they advance in age, and thus appearances are put off by degrees, and in the place thereof interior truths are implanted : this may be illustrated by numberless examples from the Word; as where it is written, that we should pray to God not to lead us into temptations, when notwithstanding God leads no one into temptations, but this is said because it so appears; in like manner it is said that God is angry, punisheth, casteth into hell, bringeth evil upon the wicked, and many other things of a similar nature, when notwithstanding God is never angry, never punisheth or casteth into hell, neither doth he at all do evil to any one, but these things belong to the wicked themselves, and are the consequences of their evils, for in the evils themselves are contained the evils of punishment; nevertheless these things are said in many passages in the Word, because it so appears : to take another example, it is said that "no one should call his father, Father; nor his master, Master" (Matt. xxiii. 8, 10), when notwithstanding it is proper so to call them; but it is so said because by Father is understood the Lord, who creates and begets us anew, and because He only teaches, and instructs; wherefore when man is in a spiritual idea, he will then think of the Lord alone as the Father and Master; but the case is otherwise when man is in a natural idea; moreover in the spiritual world or in heaven, no one knows any other father, teacher, or master, but the Lord, because from Him is all spiritual life; the case is the same in various other instances. From these considerations it may appear, that the external of the Word and thence the external of the church and worship, consists of apparent truths, wherefore they who are in evils as to life, apply it in favor of their own loves, and of the false principles thence conceived; and hence it is said, that the court, by which the external of the Word also is signified, is given to the nations, and afterwards, that they shall tread the holy city under foot. This comes to pass in the end of the church, when men are so far worldly, natural and corporeal, that interior truths, which are called spiritual truths, cannot be at all seen by them, whence it follows, that they then entirely pervert the Word as to the external or literal sense thereof: such a perversion of the literal sense of the Word took place also with the Jews at the end of the church with them, which is understood in the spiritual sense by the soldiers dividing the garments of the Lord, but not the coat, whereby is signified, that they who were of the church perverted all things of the Word as to the literal sense thereof, but not the Word as to the spiritual sense, because this they were unacquainted with; the particular explication of this may be seen above, n. 64. Similar is the case in the church at this day, because now is its end; for at this day the Word is not explained according to spiritual truths, but according to the appearances of the literal sense, which are not only applied to confirm evils of life, but also falses of doctrine; and inasmuch as interior or spiritual truths are not known nor received, it follows that the literal sense of the Word is perverted by evils of the will and falses of the thought thence derived; this therefore is what is signified by the court being given to the nations.

632. "And the holy city shall they tread under foot"—That hereby is signified, that they will destroy all the doctrine of good and truth from the Word, appears from the signification of the holy city, as denoting the doctrine of truth and good from the Word; in the literal sense by the holy city is understood Jerusalem, which, in the Word, is everywhere called the city, and the holy city, but by Jerusalem is understood the church, and by the city, doctrine of the church; that a city signifies doctrine, may be seen above, n. 223, whence the holy city signifies the doctrine of divine truth, for divine truth is what in the Word is called holy, n. 204; and from the signification of treading under foot, as denoting altogether to destroy, especially by things sensual and natural, consequently by fallacies, which are called the fallacies of the senses, from which, when not unfolded, mere falsities exist; the reason why such things are signified by treading under foot, is, because this is done by the soles of the feet, and the soles of the feet signify the sensual external things of man, and the feet his natural things: that this signification of the soles of the feet and of the feet is from correspondence, may be seen above, n. 65, 606; and in the work concerning H. & H. n. 96. It is said, that the nations shall tread under foot the holy city, by reason of its following after these words, "The court which is without the temple, cast out abroad, because it is given to the nations," and by the court is signified the external of the Word, of the church, and of worship, and the external of the Word is what is perverted, consequently adulterated and falsified by the nations, that is, by those who are in evils and falses; for, as was said in the preceding article, the external of the Word, which is called the literal sense thereof, is for infants and those that are simple, and therefore is written according to appearances, thus for those who are sensual and natural; for infants are first sensual, afterwards natural, and when they advance in age they become spiritual; but when man does not become spiritual, as is the case with every one who lives in evil, he cannot understand the Word spiritually, but merely naturally and sensually, and he who thus understands the Word, perverts it, and explains it according to the falses of his religion, and according to the evils of his life; hence it is that it is said, they shall tread it under foot: they who deny and contemn the truths of heaven and the church, also appear in the spiritual world to tread them under the soles of their feet, and this, as was said above, because the external sensual principle of man corresponds to the soles of the feet, by which treading under foot is effected: it is said that the external sensual principle of man does this, but this is only the case with the sensual principle of those who are merely sensual, who are those that deny the truths of heaven and the church, likewise who believe nothing but what they can see with their eyes and touch with their hands. Such persons are treated of in the following passages where mention is made of treading under foot; thus in Luke: "They shall fall by the edge of the sword, and they shall be

taken captive among all nations, and at length Jerusalem shall be trodden under foot of the nations, even till the times of the nations shall be fulfilled " (xxi. 24) : similar things are here signified as by the court being given to the nations, and the holy city trodden under foot forty and two months, which we are here now explaining in the Apocalypse ; for by, they shall fall by the edge of the sword, is signified, that they shall perish by falses ; by, they shall be taken captive among all nations, is signified, that evils will depredate the goods and truths of the church ; by Jerusalem being trodden under foot, is signified the destruction of the church as to doctrine, for Jerusalem signifies the church as to doctrine ; by its being trodden under foot by the nations, is signified the total destruction thereof by evils of life and by falses of doctrine ; even till the time of the nations be fulfilled, signifies until the evil is consummated, concerning which see above, n. 624 : this consummation is also signified by forty and two months ; the Lord also spake these words concerning the time proximately before the last judgment, which is here treated of in the Apocalypse. Again, in Ezekiel : " Is it a small thing to you that ye eat up the good pasture, but ye must tread down with your feet the residue of your pastures ; and that ye drink the sediment of the waters, but ye disturb the rest with your feet ; and so my flock feed upon what ye have trodden with your feet, and drink that which is disturbed by your feet" (xxxiv. 18, 19) : by the good pasture is signified all that which spiritually nourishes, especially the Word, and the knowledges of truth and good thence derived ; to eat it up, and to tread down the rest with the feet, signifies to destroy it so that it does not appear, also to destroy it that it may not be, which is done by reasonings from the corporeal sensual principle, and from the natural man separate from the spiritual ; this therefore is what is understood by treading under feet ; by the sediment of the waters are signified truths defiled by falses, for waters denote truths, and to drink thereof signifies to learn and to receive ; the rest of the waters disturbed by the feet, signifies truths not defiled by falses, but still confounded by reasonings from the natural man, the feet denoting the natural things with man : hence it may appear what is signified by my flock drinking what is trodden down and disturbed with the feet.   Again in Daniel : " The he-goat threw the ram to the ground, and trampled on him, nor was there any one to take the ram out of his hands ; afterwards one horn grew from a little one to the host of the heavens, and cast down of the host and of the stars to the earth, and trampled on them" (viii. 7, 10) : by the he-goat is there signified faith separate from charity, and by the ram is signified faith conjoined to charity, thus charity, the same as by the goats and sheep in Matthew, chap. xxv. 31–46 ; by the one horn which from a little one increased immensely, is signified justification by faith alone ; by the host of the heavens are signified all the truths and goods of heaven and the church, and by the stars are signified the knowledges of good and truth ; wherefore by treading under foot the ram and also the host of the heavens, is signified, altogether to destroy charity, and therewith all the truths and goods of heaven and the church, and this by the corporeal sensual principle; for they who are in faith separate from charity, that is, who believe that they shall be saved by faith alone, whatever their life may be, become corporeal sensual, and are consequently immersed in falses as to all things of the Word and of the church; for they have no perception of the Word, otherwise than according to the ultimate sense of the letter, nor do they see anything of that sense inwardly, and even if they speak truths from the Word, they still perceive them falsely; this therefore is what is signified by the he-goat casting down to the earth, of the host of the heavens and of the stars, and treading them under foot: that charity towards our neighbor, that is, the good of life is in like manner destroyed by them, is understood by the goat throwing the ram to the ground, and trampling upon him; for they who are in faith separate from charity, and who are understood by the he-goat, make faith the essential and charity not essential, wherefore they live to the body and the world, and are studious for themselves only, and not at all for their neighbor, and they who do this, cast down charity, which is understood by the ram, to the ground, and tread it under foot. Again, in Luke: "Other seed fell upon the way, which was trodden under foot, or the fowls of heaven devoured it" (viii. 5): by seed is signified divine truth, or the truth of the Word; by falling upon the way and being trodden under foot, is signified to be received only by the corporeal sensual principle, and not inwardly; for that which is received in the spirit and in the heart, is understood by the seed which fell into good ground; by the fowls of heaven which devoured the seed upon the way, are signified falses, for all evils and thence all falses reside in the corporeal sensual principle, wherefore unless man becomes spiritual, and thinks from a spiritual ground, he must think altogether from falses originating in evil: concerning the nature and quality of the corporeal sensual principle, and of sensual men, see the D. of the N. J. n. 50; also above in this work, n. 342, 543, 550, 552, 554, 556, 559, 563, 569, 570, 580. Again, in Isaiah: "I will make known to you what I will do to my vineyard; by removing the hedge thereof, it shall be to be eaten up, and by breaking through the wall thereof, it shall be to be trodden under foot" (v. 5): by the vineyard is there signified the church of the Lord, which is called the spiritual church; by removing the hedge, and breaking through the wall, is signified, to falsify and thus to destroy the truths that defend the church; the wall and the hedge about the vineyard denote the same as the wall and the bulwarks of Jerusalem; by eating up and treading under foot the vineyard, is signified, to vastate the church, so that no good and truth can spring up therein, and thus to destroy it. Again, in Jeremiah: "Many shepherds have destroyed my vineyard, they have trodden under foot my field, they have reduced the field of desire, into a wilderness of solitude" (xii. 10): by vineyard here also is signified the church of the Lord, in like manner by field; to destroy, to tread it under foot, and to reduce it into a wilderness of solitude, signifies so to destroy it as that nothing of the good and truth of the church is left remaining. Again, in Isaiah: "Our enemies have

trodden under foot our sanctuary" (lxiii. 18): by enemies are signified evils of life; by treading under foot the sanctuary, is signified
to destroy the truths of doctrine from the Word, and this also by the
corporeal sensual principle, for they who are in evils of life are all
corporeal sensual.   So in David: "The enemy persecuteth my soul,
and overtaketh and treadeth down my life to the earth, and maketh
my glory to dwell in the dust" (Psalm vii. 6): by enemy here also is
signified evil, in general the devil, that is, hell, whence evil comes,
and by treading down life to the earth and making glory to dwell in
the dust, is signified to destroy, by the corporeal sensual principle,
all the truths of heaven and the church, for these constitute spiritual
life, and are also signified by glory; dust is also predicated of the
corporeal sensual principle, which also is understood by walking
upon the belly and eating dust, as is every where said of the serpent.
Similar things are signified by treading under foot also in the following passages; as in Isaiah: "I will make the hypocritical nation
to be trodden down as the mire of the streets" (x. 6); and in Micah:
"The enemy of Jehovah shall be for a treading under foot, as the
dirt of the streets" (vii. 10); and in Zechariah: "They shall be as
mighty men treading down the mire of the streets in the war, they
shall fight in battle, because Jehovah is with them, and they shall
make them ashamed that ride upon horses" (x. 5); and in Malachi: "Then shalt thou tread the impious under foot, and they shall
be ashes under the soles of your feet, in the day when I shall do
[this]" (iv. 3); and in Isaiah: "The crown of pride, the drunkards
of Ephraim, shall be trodden under foot" (xxvii. 3); again: "I have
trodden down the people in my anger, and made them drunk in my
wrath, and I have made their victory to descend to the earth" (lxiii.
6); and in David: "By thee will we push our enemies, in thy name
will we tread them under that rise up against us" (Psalm xliv. 6);
again: "God shall tread down our enemies" (Psalm lx. 14; Ps. cviii.
14): by treading under foot in these passages is also signified to destroy, which is effected by those who are corporeal sensual, for they
who are of such a character tread under foot all things of heaven
and the church, for they are in lowest principles, neither can their
thoughts be elevated upwards by the Lord, for they themselves let
them down to the earth, and there they lick the dust; such are all
those that deny the Divine Being or [principle]; for the evils into
which man is born all reside in his natural and corporeal sensual
principles, wherefore unless he suffers himself to be elevated out of
them by the Lord, which is effected by divine means, which are the
truths and goods of faith and love, or truths and goods of doctrine
and life, he remains in his evils, which are implanted in his natural
and corporeal sensual principles, and then he treads under foot the
celestial and spiritual things appertaining to heaven and the church.
By treading upon the lion, the asp, serpents, and scorpions, are understood not only to destroy them, but also not to be hurt by them;
thus in David: "Thou shalt tread upon the lion and asp, the young
lion and the dragon shalt thou trample under foot" (Psalm xci. 13);
so in Luke: "Behold I give you power to tread upon serpents and

scorpions, and upon all the power of the enemy, so that nothing shall by any means hurt you" (x. 19): the reason why it is so expressed in the Word, is, because they who are in the hells appear before the eyes of good spirits and angels sometimes in the forms of various beasts and serpents, according to the species of evil and the false thence derived, in which they are principled; their thoughts themselves proceeding from the intention of their will are what present those appearances: the exhalations from their evils and falses continually exhale through the earths which are over those hells, or by which those hells are covered, wherefore to walk upon those places is dangerous to those who are only natural, and still more to those who are corporeal sensual, by reason of the exhalation thence arising and infecting them with its contagion; but they who are led by the Lord, may safely tread upon that earth without infection or infestation, the reason of which is, because the interiors of their mind, or of their thought and affection, are elevated by the Lord above their corporeal sensual principle, which corresponds to the soles of their feet: from these considerations it may appear, what is understood, in the proper sense, by treading upon the lion, the asp, serpents, and scorpions, without being hurt by them, as also why it is so said in the Word; but what is signified by lions, by serpents, scorpions, &c. has been shown elsewhere.

633. "Forty and two months"—That hereby is signified even to the end of the old church, and to the beginning of the new, appears from the signification of months, as denoting states, in this case the states of the church; for by times, whether they be hours, or days, or months, or years, or ages, are signified states, and those states are designated by the numbers by which those times are determined, as in this case by the number forty-two, concerning which, see above, n. 571, 610; and from the signification of forty-two as denoting the end of the former church and the beginning of the new; the reason of this signification of forty-two, is, because by that number are understood six weeks, and by six weeks is signified the same as by six days of one week, viz. a state of combat and labor, consequently the end, when the church is altogether vastated, or when evil is consummated; and by the seventh week, which then follows, is signified the beginning of the new church; for the number forty-two arises out of the multiplication of six into seven, whence it signifies the same as six weeks, and six weeks the same as six days of one week, viz. a state of combat and labor, as was said, and also a plenary state, in the present case, a plenary consummation of good and truth, that is, a plenary vastation of the church. In the Word mention is frequently made of forty, sometimes days, sometimes months, sometimes years, and by that number is there signified either a plenary vastation of the church, or a plenary state of temptation; this signification of the numbers forty and forty-two, may appear from the following passages; as in Ezekiel: "Egypt shall not be inhabited forty years; I will make Egypt a solitude in the midst of the lands that are desolate, and her cities in the midst of the cities that are devastated, they shall be a solitude forty years; and I will

disperse Egypt among the nations, and I will cast them down into
the lands; at the end of forty years I will gather together Egypt
from the people, whither they were dispersed, and I will bring back
the captivity of Egypt" (xxix. 11–14): by Egypt is signified the
church as to scientific truths, upon which doctrine is founded; the
scientific truths at that time were the sciences of correspondences
and representations, upon which the doctrine of their church was
founded; but inasmuch as the Egyptians turned those sciences into
magic, and thereby perverted the church, therefore the vastation
thereof is described, which is understood by forty years; this, therefore, is what is signified by Egypt not being inhabited forty years,
and the cities thereof being a solitude forty years : by Egypt's being
dispersed among the nations, and cast down into the lands, is signified that evils and falses would entirely occupy that church and pervert all the scientifics thereof; hence it is evident, that by forty
years is signified the state of the plenary vastation thereof, or even
to its end, when there would be no more any good and truth remaining; but the beginning of the new church, which is signified by the
end of forty years, is understood by these words, "at the end of
forty years I will gather together Egypt from the people whither
they were dispersed, and I will bring back the captivity of Egypt."
The like is signified in the same prophet, by "his lying on his right
side forty days, and laying siege to Jerusalem" of which it is said,
"that it shall want bread and water, and be desolated a man and
his brother, and they shall pine away for their iniquity" (v. 6, 7, 17):
the plenary vastation of the church is also signified by that number;
by Jerusalem is signified the church; by laying siege to it, is signified
to straighten it by evils and falses; by wanting bread and water, is signified to be vastated as to the good of love and as to the truth of doctrine; by being desolated man and brother, and by pining away for their
iniquity, are signified things of a similar nature, for man and brother
denote verity and charity, and to pine denotes to die away.   The
like is signified by the forty days of the deluge in Genesis : "For
yet seven days and I will cause it to rain upon the earth forty days
and forty nights, and I will destroy all substance, which I have
made, from upon the faces of the earth; and there was rain upon
the earth, forty days and forty nights; then after seven days, he
sent out a dove, which did not return unto him" (vii. 4, 12; chap.
viii. 6, 13): by the deluge is signified the devastation of the old
church, or of the most ancient church, likewise the last judgment
upon those who were of that church; by the reign of forty days is
signified the ruin thereof by the falses of evil; but the beginning of
a new church is signified by the drying up of the earth after those
forty days, and by its germinating anew; the dove which he sent
out signifies the good of charity, which was the essential of that
church; but concerning these things see the A. C. where they are
explained.   From this signification of the number originated the
law in Moses, "That the wicked man may be smitten with forty
stripes, and not more, lest thy brother seem vile in thine eyes"
(Deut. xxv. 3) : a plenary punishment is described by forty as well

as vastation, for punishment also is the consummation of evil; and whereas after punishment reformation succeeds, therefore it is said, that he shall not be smitten with any more stripes, lest thy brother should be vile in thine eyes : for by forty is signified the end of evil and also the beginning of good, wherefore if more stripes than forty were given, the beginning of good or reformation, would not be signified. The vastation of the church with the sons of Jacob by the servitude of four hundred years in Egypt, is signified by the words of Jehovah to Abraham : " Know thou that thy seed shall be a sojourner in a land not theirs, where they shall subject them to servitude four hundred years" (Gen. xv. 13) : by four hundred, is signified the same as by forty, in the same manner as by a thousand is signified the same as by a hundred, and by a hundred the same as by ten. The vastation of the church, and also plenary temptation, is also signified by the abiding of the sons of Israel forty years in the wilderness, concerning which it is written in the following passages : " Your sons shall be feeding in the wilderness forty years, and they shall bear your whoredoms, until your bodies shall be consumed in the wilderness" (Numb. xiv. 33, 34); " He made them to wander in the wilderness forty years, until all the generation was consumed which did evil in the eyes of Jehovah" (Numb. xxxii. 13); " Jehovah hath known thy walking through the great wilderness these forty years, Jehovah thy God was with thee, that thou shouldst not be destitute of anything" (Deut. ii. 7); " Thou shalt remember all the way which Jehovah thy God led thee these forty years in the wilderness, to afflict thee, and to tempt thee; he fed thee with manna to afflict thee, to tempt thee, and that he might do thee good at the last" (Deut. viii. 2, 3, 15, 16); " Your fathers tempted me, they proved me forty years, I was vexed in this generation, and I said, they are a people that err in their hearts, and the same have not known my ways" (Psalm xcv. 9, 10); " I have made you to ascend out of the land of Egypt, and I have led you in the wilderness these forty years to possess the land of the Amorites" (Amos ii. 10): from what has been adduced it may appear, that by forty years is not only signified the vastation of the church with the sons of Israel, but also a plenary state of temptation, likewise by the end of those years the beginning of a new church : the vastation of the church is described by these words, " that they should feed in the wilderness forty years, and should bear their whoredoms, until their bodies should be consumed ;" likewise by these, " until all this generation be consumed, which hath done evil in the eyes of Jehovah ;" likewise by these, " I have been vexed in this generation, and I said, they are a people that err in their heart, and the same have not known my ways ;" but the temptation which is also signified by forty years, is described by these words : " Jehovah thy God was with thee through the forty years, that thou shouldst not be destitute of anything ;" likewise by these, " Jehovah hath led thee these forty years in the wilderness, to afflict thee and to tempt thee, and he fed thee with· manna ;" likewise by these, " He led thee in the wilderness to tempt thee, and to do thee good at last :" the beginning of the new church, after the end of the forty years, is described by their introduction into the land of Canaan, which took place after those forty years; and is also understood by these words, " to do thee good at the last;" likewise by these, "I have led you in the wilderness forty years to possess the land of the Amorites." Plenary temptation is also signified by "Moses being upon Mount Sinai forty days and forty nights, during which he neither ate bread nor drank water" (Exod. xvi. 18; chap. xxxiv. 28; Deut. ix. 9, 11, 18, 25); in like manner, also, by " Jesus being in the wilderness, tempted by the devil, where He fasted forty days" (Matt. iv. 1, 2; Mark i. 13; Luke iv. 1). From these considerations it may appear, that the number forty in the Word, signifies plenary vastation and consummation, that is, when all the good of the church is vastated, and evil is consummated; likewise that by the same number is signified plenary temptation, as also the establishment of the church anew, or reformation. Hence it may be known what is signified by the holy city being trodden under foot by the nations forty and two months; as likewise by the following words in this book: " That to the beast coming up out of the sea was given a mouth speaking great things and blasphemies, and power was given to him forty and two months" (xiii. 15). Let not any one therefore suppose that by forty and two months are understood months, nor that any time is designated by the numbers mentioned here in the following pages.

634. Verses 3, 4. " And I will give to my two witnesses, and they shall prophesy a thousand two hundred and sixty days, clothed in sacks. These are the two olives, and the two candlesticks, which stand before the God of the earth."—" And I will give to my two witnesses," signifies the good of love and charity, and the truths of doctrine and faith, both from the Lord: "and they shall prophesy a thousand two hundred and sixty days," signifies that they shall teach, and what they shall teach, until the end of the old church, and the beginning of the new: "clothed in sacks," signifies in mourning on account of the non-reception of divine good and divine truth: "these are the two olives and the two candlesticks," signifies celestial good and spiritual good, or the good of love, and the truth of that good: " which stand before the God of the earth," signifies which are the divine things proceeding from the Lord, and are of Him in heaven and in the church.

635. "And I will give to my two witnesses"—That hereby is signified the good of love and charity, and the truth of doctrine and faith, both from the Lord, appears from the signification of witnesses, as denoting those who in heart and faith acknowledge and confess the Lord, His Divine [principle] in His Human, and His Divine Proceeding, for this is what essentially witnesses concerning the Lord, that is, acknowledges, and, from acknowledgment, confesses Him, concerning which signification of witness and testification, see above, n. 10, 27, 228, 392. The reason that the two witnesses here signify the good of love and charity, and the truth of doctrine and faith, is, because it follows, that the two witnesses are two olives and two candlesticks, and by two olives is signified the good of love

to God, and the good of charity towards our neighbor; and by the two candlesticks is signified the truth of doctrine, and the truth of faith, concerning which signification more will be said presently. The reason why those goods and truths are understood by witnesses, is, because those goods and truths, that is, all those who are principled therein, acknowledge and confess the Lord, for it is the Divine Proceeding, which is called divine good and divine truth, whence comes the good of love to God, and the good of charity towards our neighbor, and thence the truth of doctrine and truth of faith, which witness concerning Him; whence it follows, that they who are in them, likewise witness concerning the Lord, that is acknowledge and confess Him : for it is the Divine [principle] which witnesses concerning the Divine [principle], and not man from himself; consequently it is the Lord in the good of love, and in the truth of doctrine thence derived, which are with man, that does this. Inasmuch as all acknowledgement and confession of the Lord, and principally the acknowledgement and confession of the Divine [principle] in His Human, is from the Lord Himself, and inasmuch as to witness signifies to acknowledge and confess it, therefore witnessing is used to denote acknowledgement and confession from the Lord Himself concerning Himself, in the following passages : as in John : " Search the Scriptures, for they are they which witness of me " (v. 39): the Sacred Scriptures, or the Word, are the divine truth proceeding from the Lord, and the Divine Proceeding is the Lord Himself, in heaven and in the church, wherefore when it is said that the Scriptures witness concerning Him, it is understood that the Lord Himself witnesses of Himself. Again : " I am He that beareth witness of Myself, and My Father who sent Me, beareth witness of Me " (viii. 18): here it is openly declared that the Lord Himself, or the Divine in Him, witnesses concerning Him. So again : "Jesus said, when the Paraclete shall come, the spirit of verity, he shall testify concerning Me " (xv. 26, 27): by the Paraclete, the spirit of verity, is understood the Divine Proceeding from the Lord, which is the divine truth. And again : " Jesus said unto Pilate, Thou sayest because I am a king, for this came I into the world, that I might give testimony to the truth " (xviii. 37); to give testimony to the truth, signifies to cause the divine truth proceeding from Him to witness of Him; this divine truth also in the Word in signified by king. These things are adduced in order that it may be known, that to witness is to acknowledge and confess the Lord, and that this is from Him, consequently, that it denotes the good of love and charity and the truth of doctrine and faith, inasmuch as these are from the Lord and are of Him in man.

636. " And they shall prophesy a thousand two hundred and sixty days "—That hereby is signified that they shall teach, and what shall be taught, until the end of the old church, and the beginning of the new, appears from the signification of prophesying, as denoting to teach, concerning which see above, n. 624; in this case it signifies both to teach and to be taught, for it is said of the two witnesses, by whom are signified the good of love and charity and

the truth of doctrine and faith, for these with man are what teach, and what are also taught; for they who are in the goods of love, and in truths of doctrine, teach, and the goods of love and truths of doctrine are what are taught by them; and from the signification of a thousand two hundred and sixty days, as denoting even to the end of the old church, and the beginning of the new church, for by a thousand two hundred and sixty days is signified the same as by three and a half, inasmuch as a thousand two hundred and sixty days make three years and a half, computing three hundred and sixty days to the year, and by three and a half is signified the end of a former state and the beginning of a new one, in the present case, the end of the former church and the beginning of a new one, the last time of the church being the subject treated of: on account of this signification of that number, it is therefore said, in the 4th verse of this chapter, "They shall see their bodies three days and a half, and shall not permit them to be laid in sepulchres," and afterwards in verse 11 : "And after three days and a half the spirit of life from God entered into them;" in which passages by three days and a half, is signified the end of the old church, when the good of love and the truth of doctrine will not at all be received; and also the beginning of a new church when they will be received : the end of the former church is signified by the beast ascending out of the abyss to kill the witnesses, and the beginning of the new church is signified by the spirit of life from God entering into them.   The reason why the number a thousand two hundred and sixty signifies the same as three and a half, is, because in the Word ages, years, months, weeks, days, and hours, have a similar signification, for thereby times only are understood, and by times in general and in particular, or by times greater or less, are equally signified states, for a greater or less time designated by numbers does not change the signification of the thing, as was also shown above, n. 571, 633. The like is signified by the same number of days in the next chapter of the Apocalypse : "And the woman fled into the wilderness where she hath a place prepared by God, that there they may nourish her a thousand two hundred and sixty days " (xii. 6) : by the woman is there understood the church, by the wilderness, where she shall be nourished, is signified where there is no reception of good and truth, and by the accomplishment of those days is signified a new state of the church.

637. "Clothed with sacks"—That hereby is signified mourning on account of the non-reception of divine good and divine truth, appears from the signification of being clothed in sacks, as denoting mourning on account of the vastation and desolation of divine good and divine truth, in this case, on account of the non-reception thereof; for the witnesses were seen clothed in sacks, and by the witnesses are signified the divine good, from which is all the good of love and charity, and the divine truth, from which is all the truth of doctrine and faith, and these appear in mourning when they are not received, but in joy when they are received : it is in like manner said concerning the sun and moon, by which also are signified the good of love and truth of faith, "That the sun became black as a

sack of hair, and the moon became as blood " (Apocalypse vi. 12);
whereby is understood that all the good of love disappeared, and all
the truth of faith was falsified, as may be seen above, n. 401; not
that the sun in the angelic heaven, which is the Lord, ever becomes
black, but that it so appears to those who do not receive any light
from it.   In ancient times, when the externals of the church consisted of mere correspondences, and representatives of things spiritual therein originating, mourning was represented by various
things that were significative ; as by sitting and lying on the ground;
by rolling themselves in the dust ; by putting ashes on the head;
by rending the garments; and by putting on sacks : by rending the
garments and putting on sacks, was signified mourning on account
of the desolation of truth and good in the church, and on account of
the non-reception of them; for garments in general signified the
truths of the church, as may be seen above, n. 64, 65, 195, 271,
395, 475, 476, and hence the rending of the garments, signified grief
on account of the truths of the church being hurt, and as it were
rent asunder, by falses ; and the putting on of sacks signified mourning on account of the deprivation of good and truth, and consequent
vastation of the church : wherefore " When Hezekiah the king
heard the words of Tartan the captain of the king of Assyria, he
rent his garments, and covered himself with a sack, and came to the
house of Jehovah ; and he sent Eliakim who was over the house,
and Shebna the scribe, and the elders of the priests, clothed with
sacks to Isaiah " (2 Kings xix. 1, 2; Isaiah xxxvii. 1, 2): this was
done because by the king of Assyria is there signified the rational
principle perverted, or the rational principle which perverts the
truths and goods of the church and destroys them by falses, all the
words of Tartan, the captain of the king of Assyria, involving such
things ; and because the church was seen to be in imminent danger
of desolation and vastation, therefore, to testify mourning and grief
on account thereof, they rent their garments and covered themselves
with sacks.   In like manner when " Benhadad the king of Assyria
besieged Samaria, and there came a great famine, the king rent his
garments, and as he passed by upon the wall, the people saw, that
behold a sack was upon his flesh within " (2 Kings vi. 30): the same
is signified here as above, viz. imminent desolation and devastation
of the church, wherefore the king rent his garments, and had a sack
upon his flesh, which was a representative sign of mourning and
grief.   Mourning on similar occasions is likewise signified by what
is written in other places: as " That Jacob, when he believed that
Joseph was torn to pieces, rent his garments, and put a sack upon
his loins, and mourned over his son, many days" (Gen. xxvii. 34):
also, " That Ahab, after by the advice of Jezabel his wife he had
taken away the vineyard of Naboth, and heard the words of the
prophet concerning that cruel matter, rent his garments, and placed
a sack upon his flesh, and fasted, and lay in a sack, and went along
slowly " (1 Kings xxi. 27): likewise, " That the king of Ninevah,
after he had heard the words of Jonah, rose up from his throne, and
laid aside his robe from him, and covered himself with a sack, and

sat upon ashes, and proclaimed a fast, and that man and beast
should be covered with sacks " (Jonah iii. 5, 6, 8): also, " That
Daniel set his face to the Lord God, to seek supplication and prayer
in fasting, sack, and ashes " (Dan. ix. 3): and " That after Abner
was slain, David said to Joab and to all the people who were with
him, that they should rend their garments, and cover themselves
with sacks, and lament before Abner; and that David himself
walked behind the bier " (2 Sam. iii. 31): from these passages it is
evident, that in the Jewish and Israelitish church, mourning was
represented by the rending of the garments and putting on sacks;
and this because grief of mind and mourning of heart, which were
things interior, were at that time represented by things external,
which, by reason of their correspondence with spiritual things, were
significative. That the representative of mourning by sacks, principally signified mourning on account of the desolation of truth and
vastation of good in the church, and also, in particular, penitence,
and then mourning of heart on account of evils, may appear further
from the following passages: thus in Isaiah: " The Lord Jehovih
Zabaoth shall call in that day to weeping and to wailing and to
baldness, and to putting on a sack " (xxii. 12): the subject treated
of in that chapter is concerning the vastation of the church as to
divine truth, and the mourning on account thereof is described by
baldness and the putting on of a sack. And in Jeremiah: " The
lion cometh up out of a thicket, and the destroyer of the nations is on
his way, he hath gone forth out of his place to reduce the land to
wasteness; thy cities shall be destroyed, that there shall be no
inhabitant: for this gird ye with sacks, wail, howl " (iv. 7, 8): by
the lion out of the thicket is signified the false of evil destroying the
truths of the church, and by the destroyer of the nations is signified
the evil of the false destroying the good of the church; by the land
which they shall reduce to wasteness is signified the church, and by
the cities which shall be destroyed are signified the truths of doctrine; by girding with sacks is signified mourning on account
thereof, wherefore it is added, wail and howl. Again in the same
prophet: " O daughter of my people, gird thee with a sack, and roll
thee in ashes; make to thee the mourning of an only son, a wailing
of bitterness, for the vastator will come suddenly upon us " (vi. 26):
by the daughter of my people is understood the church; by girding
herself in a sack and rolling herself in ashes, is signified mourning
on account of the good and truth of the church being destroyed; the
perdition thereof, or vastation of the church is understood by the
vastator coming suddenly: that grievous mourning and grief on account of the destruction of good and truth is signified by girding
with a sack and rolling in ashes, is evident, for it is added, make to
thee the mourning of an only son, a wailing of bitterness. Again:
" Howl, O Heshbon, because Ai is devastated; cry out, O daughters of Rabbah; gird ye with sacks, wail, and wander among the
mounds; because their king is gone into exile, his priests and princes
together " (xlix. 3); treating concerning the sons of Ammon, by
whom are signified those who are in natural good and falsify the

truths of the church : they who are such in the church are described by the daughter of Rabbah ; mourning on account of the destruction of truth by falsification, is signified by, gird ye with sackcloth, wail, wander amongst the mounds, mounds denoting truths falsified ; that the truths of the church thence perished, is signified by their king being gone into exile, king denoting the truth of the church and to go into exile signifying to be destroyed; that the goods of the church also and the truths thence derived likewise perished, is signified by the priests and the princes together, priests denoting the goods of the church, and princes, the truths thence derived. Again in Lamentations : "They shall sit upon the earth, the elders of the daughter of Zion shall keep silence, they shall cast up the dust upon their head, they shall gird themselves with sacks ; the virgins of Jerusalem have made the head descend to the earth" (ii. 10): to sit upon the earth, to keep silence, to cast up the dust upon the head and to make the head descend to the earth, were all signs representative of mourning and grief on account of the church being vastated by evils and falses : the elders of the daughter of Zion signify those that are wise and intelligent in the church, and. abstractedly, wisdom and intelligence ; the daughters of Zion and the virgins of Jerusalem signify those in the church who are in the affections of good and truth, and, abstractedly, those affections themselves.   And in Ezekiel: "Thy pilots shall make themselves bald over thee, and shall gird themselves with sacks, and they shall weep over thee with bitterness of soul, with a bitter wailing" (xxvii. 31); treating of Tyre whereby is signified the church as to the knowledges of truth and good, consequently also the knowledges of truth and good appertaining to the church : in this case is described mourning on account of those knowledges being lost: the pilots signify all who bring and communicate those knowledges : to induce baldness, signifies mourning on account of all things of intelligence being destroyed ; to gird with sacks, signifies mourning on account of the knowledge of truth also being destroyed ; inasmuch as mourning is what is described, therefore it is added, they shall weep over thee with bitterness of soul, with bitter wailing.   And in the Evangelists: "Wo to thee, Chorazin, wo to thee, Bethsaida, for if the virtues had been done in Tyre and Sidon, which have been done in you, they would have repented long ago in sack and ashes" (Matt. xi. 21 ; Luke x. 13): to repent in sack and ashes is to grieve and mourn on account of the non-reception of divine truth, and on account of the falses and evils which hindered. Again in Joel: "Howl as a virgin girded with a sack over the bridegroom of her youth ; gird yourselves about and wail, ye priests, howl ye ministers of the altar ; come, pass the night in sacks, ye ministers of my God, because the meat-offering and the drink-offering are prohibited from the house of your God" (i. 8, 13): here also to be girded with sacks, and to pass the night in sacks, signifies mourning on account of the good and truth of the church being destroyed, for by the meat-offering is signified the good of the church, and by the drink offering the truth thereof.   And in Amos : "I will bring up upon all loins a sack, and upon every head baldness, and I will make it as the mourning of an only-begotten, and the last things as a bitter day " (viii. 10) : a sack upon the loins signifies mourning on account of the good of love being destroyed, for this is signified by the loins; and baldness upon the head signifies mourning on account of the understanding of truth being destroyed. Again in Isaiah : " Upon all heads of Moab shall be baldness, every beard shaven; in the streets thereof they have girded themselves with a sack; upon the roofs thereof, and in the streets thereof, he shall howl, coming down to weeping " (xv. 2, 3) : and in Jeremiah : " Every head baldness, and every beard shaven; upon all hands incisions, and upon the loins a sack ; upon all the roofs of Moab, and in the streets thereof, a mourning " (xlviii. 37, 38): by Moab are signified those who are in natural good and adulterate the goods of the church; that they have no understanding of truth, nor science of truth, is signified by baldness upon all the heads of Moab, and every beard shaven, like- wise by howling and mourning upon the roofs and in the streets; incisions upon all hands, signify things falsified ; mourning on ac- count thereof is signified by girding on a sack, likewise by howling and coming down to weeping.   Again in Isaiah : " It shall come to pass, in the place of an aromatic, shall be corruption, and in the place of a girdle, a rending, and in the place of platted work, baldness, and in the place of a robe, a girding of sack, burning in the place of beauty ; thy men shall fall by the sword, and thy strength in the war " (iii. 24, 25) : these things are said of the daughters of Zion, by whom the church is signified as to the affections of celestial good, consequently by the daughters of Zion are signified the affections of good appertaining to the celestial church : the loss and deprivation thereof through the pride of self- derived intelligence, is there described by the various things with which those daughters adorn themselves : the change of their affec- tions into such as are contrary and unbeautiful, is signified by, instead of an aromatic shall be corruption, instead of a girdle, a rent, instead of platted work, baldness, instead of a robe, a girding of sack, and instead of beauty, a burning ; by corruption is signified the vital principle perishing ; by the rent instead of a girdle, is sig- nified the dissipation of the perceptions of truth, instead of the con- nexion of them; by baldness instead of platted work, is signified infatuation instead of science; by burning instead of beauty, is sig- nified folly instead of intelligence, burning denoting the insanity which is from self-derived intelligence, which is foolishness, and beauty denoting intelligence; that the truths of the understanding would perish by falses, even till there would be no resistance against evils, is signified by, thy men shall fall by the sword, and thy strength in the war, the sword denoting the false destroying the truth.   Similar things are also signified by sack in the following pas- sages : as in Ezekiel : " All hands are let down, all knees go into waters, whence they shall gird themselves with sacks, and terror shall gather them, and upon all faces shall be shame, and upon all heads baldness " (vii. 17, 18) : and in David : " I, when they were sick, [made] a sack my garment, I afflicted my soul with hunger " (Psalm xxxv. 13) : again : " When I wept in the fast of my soul, it was turned to my reproach; when I made a sack my garment, I became a scoffing to them " (Psalm lxix. 11, 12) : and in Job : " I sewed a sack upon my skin, and made my horn in the dust ; my face was troubled through weeping " (xvi. 15, 16) : again in Isaiah : " I clothe the heavens with blackness, and I make a sack their covering " (l. 3) : and again in David : " Thou hast turned for me my mourning into dancing, thou hast opened my sack, and hast girded me with joy " (Psalm xxx. 12) : in these passages also sack signifies mourning ; and to gird a sack over the body instead of a garment, signifies mourning on account of the truth of the church being destroyed ; and to gird a sack upon the loins and upon the flesh signifies mourning on account of the good of the church being destroyed ; for a garment signifies the truth of the church, and the loins and flesh signify the good of the church. That to gird on a sack was only representative and thence significative of mourning and repentance, but did not itself constitute either mourning or repentance, appears from these words in Isaiah : " Is this the fast that I choose, a day for a man to afflict his soul, to bow down his head as a bulrush, and to lie down in a sack and ashes ; will ye call this a fast, and an acceptable day to Jehovah ? Is not this the fast, that I choose, to open the bonds of wickedness, to break thy bread to the hungry, and to bring the afflicted exile to thy house, and when thou seest the naked that thou cover him " (lviii. 5, 6, 7) : and in Joel : " Turn ye unto me with your whole heart, and in fasting and in weeping, and in wailing; and rend your heart, and not your garments " (ii. 13).

638. " These are the two olives and the two candlesticks "— That hereby is signified the good of love to the Lord and of charity towards our neighbor, and the truth of doctrine and of faith, from which are heaven and the church, appears from the signification of an olive yard, olive tree, and olive, as denoting, in an extensive sense, the celestial kingdom of the Lord and thence the celestial church, which is distinguished from other churches in this, that they of whom that church consists, are principled in love to the Lord and in love towards their neighbor; hence it is, that by an olive tree and olive each of those loves, or the good of each love, is signified, as will further appear in what follows :—and from the signification of a candlestick, as denoting, in an extensive sense, the spiritual kingdom of the Lord, and thence the spiritual church, and inasmuch as the principal thing of that church is the truth of doctrine and the truth of faith, therefore these also are understood by the candlesticks ; concerning this signification of a candlestick, see also above, n. 62. The reason why it is said that the two witnesses are the two olives, and the two candlesticks, which yet are four, is, because two signify conjunction and thence one : for there are two things which make one, namely good and truth : good is not good unless it be from truth, and truth is not truth, unless it be from good; wherefore when those two make one, then first they are and exist : this conjunction into one is called the heavenly marriage, and from

that marriage, is heaven and the church : the case is the same with celestial good, which is signified by the two olives, and with spiritual good, which is signified by the two candlesticks : for the good in the celestial kingdom of the Lord is the good of love to the Lord, and the truth of that good is called the good of brotherly and social love ; and the good in the spiritual kingdom of the Lord is the good of charity towards our neighbor, and the truth of that good is called the good of faith ; but it will be difficult to form a just idea of these things, unless it be known what is the quality of celestial good, and what is the quality of spiritual good ; also, what is the difference between them : from these considerations it may appear, whence it is that the two witnesses are called two olives and two candlesticks : that two signify conjunction into one, or the heavenly marriage, may be seen above, n, 532, at the end.   The reason why the olive tree signifies the celestial church, is, because by trees in general are signified perceptions and knowledges, and every church is a church by virtue of the knowledges of truth and good, and according to the perception of them ; and whereas oil signifies the good of love, as may be seen above, n. 375, therefore the olive yard and olive tree signify the church in which that good reigns.   There are three trees which principally signify the church, viz. the olive, the vine, and the fig tree, the olive signifying the celestial church, the vine the spiritual church, and the fig tree the external celestial and spiritual church.   Moreover, that such things as are here described are signified by the two olive trees and the two candlesticks, any one may see and conclude from this consideration, that they are called witnesses, consequently things which witness concerning the Lord, that is, acknowledge and confess Him ; likewise from what is afterwards said concerning them, viz. that the beast slew them, and afterwards that the spirit of life from God entered into them, which could not be said of olive-trees and candlesticks, unless they signified such things as appertain to the angels of heaven and to men of the church, from the Lord, and which witness concerning the Lord, or cause angels and men to witness concerning Him ; for angels and men cannot from themselves witness concerning the Lord, but the good and the truth which appertain to them from the Lord are what do this, that is, the Lord Himself, from His own good and truth appertaining to them, witnesses of Himself. In the Word, mention is frequently made of gardens and woods ; likewise of olive yards and vineyards, as also of trees of various kinds, as the olive, the vine, the fig, the cedar, the poplar, and the oak ; but no one has hitherto known, that each of them signifies somewhat spiritual appertaining to heaven and the church : it has indeed been known that a vineyard signifies the church, but this is not only the case with the vineyard, but also with the olive yard, likewise with the forest of cedar or Lebanon, yea, with the trees also, as the olive, the vine, the fig, the cedar, and it is by reason of their signifying the church, and the spiritual things appertaining thereto, that they are so often mentioned in the Word.   With respect to gardens and forests ; gardens or paradises specifically signify the intelligence and wisdom appertaining to the men of the church, and forests or groves, signify the intelligence of the natural man, which, viewed in itself, is science, subservient to the intelligence of the spiritual man; but the olive yard and vineyard signify the church, the olive yard, the celestial church, or the church which is in the good of love to the Lord, and the vineyard, the spiritual church, or the church which is in the good of charity towards the neighbor, and thence in the truths of faith: the olive and the vine have a similar signification, and this by reason that oil signifies the good of love to the Lord, and wine, the good of charity towards our neighbor, and the good of faith; whereas the fig tree signifies each church, as well the celestial as the spiritual, but external. The cause of these and such like significations is derived from representatives in the spiritual world, consequently from correspondence; for in the inmost heaven, where is the celestial kingdom of the Lord, and where love to the Lord reigns, their paradises and forests consist of olive yards and fig-trees; but in the second heaven they consist of vineyards, and various kinds of fruit trees; in like manner in the ultimate heaven, but with this difference, that in this heaven the trees are not so noble: the reason of the existence of such things in the heavens is, because they correspond to the wisdom, intelligence, love, charity, and faith, of the angels who are in those heavens.

From these considerations it may now appear, whence it is that the witnesses are called olive trees, viz. because by olive trees are understood all who constitute the celestial church of the Lord, that is, who are in the good of love to the Lord, and in the good of brotherly and social love. The signification of olive yards, olive trees, and olives, may also appear from the following passages; as in Zechariah: "Two olive trees were near the candlestick, one on the right [side] of the bowl, and the other near the left [side] thereof; and two berries of olives; these are the two sons of the olive tree standing near the Lord of the whole earth" (iv. 3, 11, 12, 14): the subject there treated of is concerning the foundation of the house or temple by Zerubbabel; and by the house or temple is signified the church, wherefore a candlestick was seen by the prophet, and near it two olive trees, almost similar to what was seen by John in the Apocalypse; and by the two olive trees and the olive berries are signified celestial goods, which are the goods of love to the Lord and of brotherly and social love; the former good is signified by the olive tree seen near the right hand of the bowl, and the latter by the olive tree at the left; the truths of this good are signified by the sons of the olive tree standing near the Lord of the whole earth, to stand near Him denoting to be and exist from Him. Inasmuch as olive trees signified those goods, therefore, "The cherubs in the midst of the house or temple were made of the wood of oil, likewise the doors to the secret place, and the posts" (1 Kings vi. 23–33); for the cherubs, as also the doors and posts to the secret place of the temple, signified guard, lest the Lord should be approached otherwise than by the good of love; the secret place signified where the Lord is, and the wood of oil, the good of love, because the olive yard,

olive tree, and olive, denote celestial things, which are of love. By
reason of the olive yard and olive tree signifying the church which
is principled in love to the Lord, "the oil of holiness, with which
all the holy things of the church were anointed, was made of the
oil of olive, and aromatics mixed therewith" (Exod. xxx. 23, 24);
for all things of the church, in proportion as they are derived from
love to the Lord, are in the same proportion holy and divine; hence
by that oil was induced a representative of the Lord, also of heaven
and the church, as may be seen where those things are explained in
the A. C. For the same reason, " Pure oil of olive was beaten for
the luminary in the tent of the assembly, which was lighted up every
evening" (Exod. xxvii. 20; Levit. xxiv. 2); by that luminary or
candlestick was there signified the spiritual church of the Lord, and
by the fire kindled in the lamps was signified spiritual love, which
is love towards our neighbor; in like manner by oil of olive pure
and beaten from which was the fire; but concerning this also see
what is said in the A. C. That the olive tree and olive signifies the
good of love, appears also from the following passages; thus in Hosea: "I will be as the dew to Israel, he shall blossom as the lily,
and he shall infix his roots as Lebanon; his branches shall spread,
and his honor shall be as of the olive, and his odor as of Lebanon"
(xiv. 6, 7): these things are said concerning the spiritual church,
which is signified by Israel: to be to him as the dew, signifies the
spiritual re-birth and existence thereof; the first state of the re-birth
or regeneration thereof is signified by, he shall blossom as the lily,
the lily denoting the blossom which precedes the fruit; the second
state of regeneration is signified by, he shall infix his roots, which
state is the existence thereof in the natural man, for there the roots
are fixed; the third state is signified by, his branches shall spread,
by which is signified the multiplication of scientific truth and knowledges; the fourth state which is the state of fructification, is signified by, his honor shall be as of the olive, the olive denoting the
good of love, of which honor is predicated, as may be seen above,
n. 288, 345; and the fifth state, which is the state of intelligence
and wisdom, is signified by his odor being to him as of Lebanon,
odor denoting perception, and Lebanon rationality, from which are
intelligence and wisdom. And in David: " I am as a green olive
tree in the house of God; I confide in the mercy of God to the age
and forever" (Psalm lvii. 10): it is said, as a green olive tree in the
house of God, because by the green olive is signified the good of
love, springing up by means of the truth of the Word; and by the
house of God is signified the church. Again: " Thy wife shall be
as a fruitful vine in the sides of thy house, thy sons as olive plants
round about thy tables; thus shall the man be blessed that feareth
Jehovah" (Psalm cxxxviii. 3, 4): by these words, in the natural
sense, which is the sense of the letter, are understood a wife and
sons, and the delights arising from marriage and prolification, but
in the internal sense, which is the sense of the spirit of the Word,
by wife is signified the affection of truth, and by sons, the truths
themselves thence springing up, for all truth, in which there is life, is

born from the affection of truth; and inasmuch as by wife is signified that affection, she is therefore compared to a fruitful vine, because by a vine is signified the church, and by a fruitful vine, the church as to the affection of truth; by the house is signified the spiritual mind, and by the sides thereof are signified all things which are in the natural man; by sons are signified the truths which are born from that spiritual affection, and these are compared to olive plants, because by truths are produced the goods of love and charity, which are olives; by round about the tables, are signified the delights arising from spiritual appropriation and nourishment. And in Moses: "It shall come to pass when Jehovah thy God hath introduced thee into the land, he shall give thee great and good cities which thou buildedst not, and houses full of every good which thou filledst not, and hewn cisterns which thou hewedst not, vineyards and olive yards which thou plantedst not" (Deut. vi. 10, 11): these words are to be understood altogether differently, in the spiritual sense, to what they are in the letter; for in the spiritual sense by the land of Canaan, into which they were to be introduced, is signified the church, wherefore by cities, houses, cisterns, vineyards, and olive yards, are signified such things as appertain to the church; by great and good cities are signified doctrinals, which teach the goods of love and charity; by houses full of every good are signified all things appertaining to wisdom; by cisterns hewn out are signified all things appertaining to intelligence in the natural man, which are knowledges and sciences; by olive yards and vineyards are signified all things appertaining to the church as to truths and goods. It is related concerning Noah, "That he sent out a dove from the ark, which returned to him about the time of evening, bearing the leaf of an olive plucked off in its mouth, and that hence he knew that the waters were diminished" (Gen. viii. 10, 11): by these things, in the spiritual sense, is described the regeneration of the man of the church, which is signified by Noah and his sons: in this case, by the dove which was last sent out, is signified the second successive state, which is when spiritual good begins to exist by truths, the falses being removed; for by the leaf is signified truth, and by the olive, good thence springing forth, and by the waters are signified falses; but these things may be seen more fully explained in the A. C. n. 870–892. And in Zechariah: "In that day His feet shall stand upon the mount of olives, which is before the face of Jerusalem from the east, and the mount of olives shall be cloven asunder, and part thereof [shall go] towards the rising and towards the sea with a valley exceeding great; and part of the mountain shall recede towards the north, and part thereof towards the south" (xiv. 4): what these things signify has been explained above, n. 405, where it was shown, that by the mount of olives is signified the divine love; for the mount of olives was on the east of Jerusalem, and Jerusalem signified the church as to doctrine; and all the church, and all the truth of doctrine, is illustrated and receives light from the Lord in the east; and the east in heaven is where the Lord appears as a sun; and inasmuch as the sun signifies the divine love, therefore the east and the mount of olives, which was on the east of Jerusalem, signify the same; forasmuch as that mountain signified, as was said, the divine love of the Lord, therefore the Lord ordinarily abode upon it; as it is written in the Evangelists, "That Jesus taught in the day time in the temple, and at night he went out and abode in the mount which is called the mount of olives" (Luke xxi. 37; chap. xxii. 39; John viii. 1); also, that "Upon that mountain He spake with His disciples concerning the last judgment" (Matt. xxiv. 3; Mark xiii. 3); and that "He went thence to Jerusalem and suffered;" besides various other circumstances which there took place, concerning which, see Matt. xxi. 1; chap. xxvi. 30; Mark xi. 1; chap. xiv. 16; Luke xix. 29, 37; chap. xxi. 37; chap. xxii. 39; John vii. 1: the reason why such circumstances there took place, was, because the mount of olives signified the divine love, and things significative, because they were representative of heaven and the church, were what at that time conjoined the Lord with heaven and the world: the angels of the inmost or third heaven also dwell in the east, upon mountains, where olive trees flourish above all others. And in Jeremiah: "Jehovah hath called thy name a green olive, fair and of goodly fruit; at the voice of a great tumult He hath kindled a fire upon it, and the shoots thereof are broken; for Jehovah Zeboath, who planted thee, hath spoken evil against thee, on account of the wickedness of the house of Israel and of the house of Judah" (xi. 16, 17): in this case, the house of Judah and Israel is called a green olive, fair and of goodly fruit, because by the olive and its fruit, is signified the good of love, and by green and fair in form, is signified the truth of that good, from which comes intelligence, for by the house of Judah is signified the church as to the good of love, and by the house of Israel the church as to truth of that good; by calling the name is signified, the quality thereof; the destruction and vastation of that church by the love of evil, is described by Jehovah kindling a fire upon it, and breaking the shoots thereof, by the fire is signified the love of evil, and by the shoots are signified truths, which are said to be broken when they perish by reason of that love; this is attributed to Jehovah from the appearance that all evil of punishment seems as if it was from God, because He is omnipotent, and does not avert it, mankind not being aware, that to avert the evil of punishment, would be contrary to order, for if it should be so averted, evil would increase until there would be no good remaining. And in Isaiah: "So shall it be in the midst of the land, in the midst of the people, as the shaking of the olive, as the gleaning when the vintage is consummated" (xxiv. 13): speaking also of the vastation of the church as to celestial good, and as to spiritual good; celestial good is the good of love to the Lord, and spiritual good is in its essence the truth from that good; celestial good is signified by the olive, and spiritual good, which is the truth from celestial good, is signified by the vintage; vastation is signified by the shakings and the gleanings after consummation. And in Moses: "Thou shalt plant vineyards and dress them, but the wine thou shalt not drink, because the worm shall devour it; thou shalt have olives in all thy border, but thou shalt not anoint thee with the oil, because thy olive shall be shaken off" (Deut. xxviii. 39, 40): by the vineyard is signified the spiritual church, and by the olive, the celestial church, whence by the vineyard is also signified the truth of the church, and by the olive, the good thereof; wherefore by planting a vineyard and ,dressing it, and not drinking the wine, is signified, that although the church is established and the truths of doctrine are taught, still the truth will neither affect nor perfect; wine denotes the truth of doctrine; because the worm shall devour it, signifies, that falses will destroy it; thou shalt have olives in all thy border, signifies, that the goods of love from the Lord by the Word, an'd by preaching from the Word, shall be in all the church; but thou shalt not anoint thee with the oil, signifies, that notwithstanding there shall be no fruition of any good, nor of any joy thence derived; for thy olive shall be shaken off, signifies, that that good will perish; these things are said concerning the curse which should come upon them if they should worship other gods, and should not keep the statutes and the judgments. And in Micah: " Thou shalt tread the olive, but shalt not anoint thee with the oil, and the must, but shalt not drink the wine" (vi. 15). And in Amos: " I have smote with blasting and mildew most of your gardens and your vineyards, and your fig trees and your olives the palmer-worm hath eaten; yet have ye not returned unto me" (iv. 9): by gardens are signified such things as appertain to spiritual intelligence; by blasting and mildew are signified evil and the false in extremes, or from the corporeal sensual pr n   e: by vineyards are signified the spiritual or interior truths of the church; by fig trees, goods and truths exterior, which are also called moral; but by the olives are signified the goods of the church; and by the palmer-worm is signified the false destroying the good. And in Habakkuk: " The fig tree shall not flourish, and there shall be no produce in the vines, the labor of the olive yards shall fail, and the field shall yield no meat" (iii. 17): by the fig tree here also are signified the external things of the church; by the vines, the internal things thereof; by the olive yard, the goods thereof; and by the field, the church itself with man. And in the first book of Samuel: "The king shall take your fields, and your vineyards, and your olive yards, and shall give them to his servants" (viii. 14): here also by fields, vineyards, and olive yards, similar things are signified, the subject treated of being concerning the right of a king, by which is there understood and described the dominion of the natural man over the spiritual, viz. that it shall destroy all the truths and goods of the church, and make them to serve the natural man, consequently to serve evils and falses. And in the book of Judges: " Jotham said unto the citizens of Shechem, who had made Abimelech king, the trees went to anoint over them a king, and they said to the olive, Reign thou over us: but the olive said to them, Shall I make my fatness to cease, which God and men honor in me, and go to move me over the trees ? And the trees said unto the fig tree,

Come, reign thou over us; but the fig tree said unto them, Shall
I make my sweetness to cease, and my good produce, and go to
move me over the trees? Likewise the trees said unto the vine,
Come, reign thou over us; but the vine said unto them, Shall I
cause my must to cease, that maketh glad God and men, and go to
move me over the trees? And all the trees said to the bramble,
Reign thou over us; and the bramble said unto the trees, If in truth
·ye anoint me for a king over you, come and confide in my shade,
but if not, let fire go out from the bramble and devour the cedars of
Lebanon" (ix. 7–16): by these words of Jotham is signified, that
the citizens of Shechem were not willing that celestial good, which
is the olive, neither the truth of that good, which is the vine, neither
moral good, which is celestial and spiritual external good, signified
by the fig tree, should reign over them, but the evil of the false appearing to them as good, which is the bramble; the fire from this is
the evil of concupiscence; the cedars of Lebanon are things rational
derived from truths.   From the passages above adduced, it may be
seen, that the olive tree and vineyard, in most places, are mentioned
together, which is on account of the marriage of good and truth in
every part of the Word; for by the olive and oil is signified the
good of the church, and by the vineyard and wine, the truth of that
good: that oil signifies the good of love and the delight of heaven
thence derived, may be seen above, n. 375; and that wine signifies
the good of charity and the truth of faith, may be seen n. 376.

639. " Which stand before the God of the earth"—That hereby
is signified which are divine things proceeding from the Lord, and
are of Him in heaven and in the church, appears from the signification of the God of the earth, as denoting the Lord, who is the God
of heaven and earth, and, specifically, the God of the church in heaven and in the world; for by earth in the Word is signified the
church, and the church is both in heaven and in the world; the
reason why heaven and the church also are there understood by
earth, is, because there are earths in the spiritual world equally as
in the natural world, and as to external appearance they are altogether similar in that world to what they are in this; hence it is,
that by the God of the earth, is understood the God of heaven and
earth, and specifically, the God of the church in heaven and in the
world: that the Lord is the God of heaven and earth, He teaches in
Matthew: " Jesus said, All power is given to Me in heaven and in
earth" (xxviii. 18): and from the signification of standing before
Him, as denoting, to be from Him, thus what is of Him in heaven
and in the church.   In the Word it is frequently said of angels and
of men of the church, that they stand before God, likewise, that
they walk before Him, and, in the spiritual sense, by standing before
God, is signified to be from Him, and by walking before God, is signified to live according to being from Him; for all the esse [or be-
ing] of heaven and the world, proceeds from the Lord, for the Divine
Proceeding is what created and formed all things in heaven and in
the world, and this is called the Word in John, chap. i. 1, 2, 3; and

the Word there mentioned is the Divine Proceeding, which is called divine truth, from which all things were made and created; inasmuch as this extends itself every way about the Lord, as a sun, therefore it is what is properly said to stand before Him, for this looks to or regards the Lord from every part and quarter of its common centre; this also is in its essence the Lord in heaven, because it is the Divine Proceeding, and that which proceeds is of Him from whom it proceeds, yea, it is Himself; just as the heat and light proceeding from the sun is of the sun; hence all the angels, who are recipients of this Divine Proceeding, which is called divine truth, turn themselves to the Lord, and hence are continually in His presence, for, as was said, the Divine Proceeding looks to the Lord as its centre from which it is derived and to which it returns; consequently also the angels, who are the recipients of divine truth, and as it were divine truths in form; from this circumstance it is, that the angels are said to stand before the Lord, to stand being properly predicated of divine truth, because it encompasses the Lord as a sun. To stand before God, signifies to be in the divine truth, consequently with the Lord, also in the following passages; thus in Luke : " The angel said, I am Gabriel, that standeth before God " (i. 19); and in the first book of Kings : "I saw Jehovah sitting upon His throne, and the universal host of the heavens standing near Him, at his right hand and at His left" (xxix. 19); and in Jeremiah : " There shall not be a man cut off to Jonadab to stand before me all the days" (xxxv. 19); and in David : " At thy right hand standeth the queen in best gold of Ophir" (Psalm lxv. 10); and in Luke : " Watch always, that ye may be accounted worthy to stand before the'Son of Man" (xxi. 36); and in the Apocalypse : " The great day of His anger cometh and who can stand " (vi. 17); " All the angels stood about the throne, and the elders and the four animals" (vii. 11); " I saw seven angels who stood before God" (viii. 2); and in Zechariah : " Two olive trees, and two berries of olives, which are the two sons of the olive tree, standing near the Lord of the whole earth" (iv. 12, 14); and in other places. It is also said concerning the Lord Himself, that He stood to judge, because it is said of the Divine Proceeding from the Lord, which is called divine truth, inasmuch as judgment is from it; thus in Isaiah : " Jehovah hath stood up to plead, and standeth to judge" (iii. 13); and in David : " God stood in the assembly of God, in the midst of the gods he will judge" (Psalm lxxxii. 1): by the assembly of God, and by the gods in the midst of whom Jehovah stood, are understood the angels, by whom, in the spiritual sense, are signified divine truths; and inasmuch as the Lord in heaven is divine truth, therefore to stand is predicated concerning Him. From these considerations it may now appear, that by standing before the God of the earth, is signified the Divine Proceeding from the Lord, which is of Him in heaven and in the church; that this is what is understood as likewise they who are therein principled, may appear also from this consideration, that to stand before the God of the earth is predicated of the two olive trees and the two candlesticks, by which is signified good and truth, consequently the Divine Proceeding; see also the preceding article, n 638.

640. Verses 5, 6. " And if any one shall be willing to hurt them fire shall go forth out of their mouth, and shall devour their ene mies; and if any one shall be willing to hurt them, he must thus be killed. These have power to shut heaven, that it rain no rain ii the days of their prophecy; and they have power over the waters to turn them into blood, and to smite the earth with every plague as often as they will."—"And if any one shall be willing to hut them," signifies the defence of them by the Lord, lest they should in any wise be injured; " the fire shall go forth out of their mouth and shall devour their enemies," signifies, that they who would bring hurt upon them, shall fall into evils and falses which are from hell and which will destroy them; " and if any one shall be willing to hurt them, thus he must be killed," signifies that according to their endeavor to bring evil upon them they perish; " these have power to shut heaven that it rain no rain in the days of their prophecy,' signifies, that they who reject the goods and goods and truths o heaven and the church, which proceed from the Lord, do not receive any influx from heaven; " and they have power over the waters to turn them into blood," signifies, that truths with them are turned into falses of evil; " and to smite the earth with every plague,' signifies that the church with such perishes by the concupiscences of evil; " as often as they will," signifies, as often as man assaults the goods of love and truths of doctrine which witness concerning the Lord, and from which man acknowledges and confesses the Lord, to bring evil upon them.

641. "And if any one shall be willing to hurt them"—Tha hereby is signified, the defence of them by the Lord, lest they should be in any wise injured, appears from what follows; that if any one shall be willing to hurt them, fire shall go forth out of their mouth. and shall devour their enemies; likewise, that if any one shall be willing to hurt them, he must thus be killed; from which words and those also which next follow, it is evident, that the defence of them by the Lord, lest they should in any wise be injured, is here signified. This is said concerning the two witnesses, by whom is signified the doctrine of the good of love to the Lord, and of the good of charity towards our neighbor, which is the doctrine of life. to which the doctrine of faith is subservient, which doctrines will be preached about the end of the church. What the following things contained in these two verses involve, has indeed been already said above, but inasmuch as they are amongst the things which are at present unknown, the same shall be repeated. When the end of the church is at hand, then the interior things of the Word, of the church, and of worship, are revealed and taught; the reason whereof is, in order that the good may be separated from the evil; for the interior things of the Word, of the church, and of worship, which are celestial and spiritual things, are received by the good, and rejected by the evil, whence separation is effected: moreover, the interior things of the Word, which are revealed in the end of the church, are

serviceable to the new church, which then begins to be established, for doctrine and for life; that this is the case, may appear from this consideration, that whilst the end of the Jewish church was at hand, the Lord Himself opened and taught the interior things of the Word, and especially revealed those things which were therein predicted concerning Himself, which being opened and revealed, the externals of the church were abrogated, which consisted principally of sacrifices, and of rituals and statutes which shadowed forth the Lord, and represented and thence signified the interior things of the church which were revealed by Him; that this would come to pass was also predicted in various passages in the prophets. The case is the same at this day, for it has now pleased the Lord to reveal various arcana of heaven, especially the internal or spiritual sense of the Word, which was hitherto entirely unknown, and therewith He hath taught the genuine truths of doctrine, which revelation is understood by the advent of the Lord in Matthew, chap. xxiv. 3, 30, 37: the reason of this revelation in the end of the church is, as was said above, viz. that separation may be effected of the good from the evil; likewise the establishment of a new church, and this not only in the natural world where men are, but also in the spiritual world where spirits and angels are; for the church is in both worlds, and revelation takes place in both, and thereby separation, as also the establishment of a new church. From these considerations it may appear, that by the above words concerning the two witnesses, is signified defence from the Lord lest they should be injured. If we take a view of the successive states of the church on our earth, it is evident that they have been similar to the successive states of man who is reformed and regenerated, in that, with a view to his becoming spiritual, he is first conceived, afterwards born, then grows up, and is afterwards led on further and further into intelligence and wisdom: the church from the most ancient times, even to the end of the Jewish church, increased as a man who is conceived, born, and grows up, and is then instructed and taught; but the successive states of the church after the end of the Jewish church, or from the time of the Lord even to the present day, have been as those of a man who grows in intelligence and wisdom, or is regenerated, for which end the interior things of the Word, of the church, and of worship, were revealed by the Lord when He was in the world, and now, lastly, things still more interior are made known; and in proportion as things interior are revealed, in the same proportion man may become wiser, for to become interior is to become wiser, and to become wiser is to become interior.

642. "Fire shall go forth out of their mouth, and shall devour their adversaries"—That hereby is signified that they who would offer injury to them shall fall into evils and falses which are from hell, and which destroy them, appears from the signification of fire, as denoting love in both senses, in this case, the love of self and of the world, and thence the love of evil and the false of every kind, concerning which see above, n. 68, 504, 539: hence it follows, that by fire going forth out of their mouth, is signified, that those who

are willing to hurt or would bring injury upon them, shall fall into
evils and falses of every kind, which are from hell: and from the
signification of devouring their adversaries, as denoting that they
shall perish by the falses of evil; for by adversaries in the Word
are signified falses of evil, and by enemies, evil, and the love of evil
and the false is what destroys. It is said, that fire shall go forth
out of their mouth; but this is said according to appearance, according to which it is also said, that fire and a flame goeth forth out
of the mouth of God, and that anger and wrath go forth from his
nostril, when notwithstanding nothing of wrath or anger can possibly proceed from Him, for He is Good Itself, Love Itself, and Mercy
Itself, from which nothing of fire, of anger, and wrath, can come
forth, but still it is said so, because it so appears: the reason that it
thus appears, is, because when an evil and infernal spirit assaults
anything divine, with the intention of doing hurt thereto, as when he
blasphemes the Lord or the Word, or any good and truth of doctrine, or any g d spirit or angel whom the Lord defends, he then
immediately deprives himself of the defence of the Lord; for every
spirit, as well evil as good, is in the defence or protection of the
Lord, on the deprivation of which he falls into evils and falses of
every kind, which are from hell, and then at the same time falls into
the hands of those who are thence, and are called punishers, who
then punish and torment him according 'to the evil which he did or
intended to do in the assault: from whence it may appear, that the
Lord does not do any evil to them, but that the evil spirit himself
does evil to himself, that is, the evil itself which appertains to him.
From these considerations it is evident, how it is to be understood,
that if any one shall be willing to hurt the two witnesses, fire shall
go forth out of their mouth and shall devour them, [the two witnesses
are the good of love and charity, and the truth of doctrine and faith,
and these are things divine, because they are from the Lord with
angel and with man,] namely, that it is not to be understood that
fire will go forth from them, but from the evil itself, which endeavors
to injure them, as has been now said; and that this is to be understood in the same manner, as when it is said, that fire, anger, and
wrath, proceed from Jehovah: but these things are more fully illustrated in the work concerning H. & H. n. 545–550, where the subject treated of is that the Lord casts no one into hell, but that the
evil spirit casts himself thither.

643. " And if any one shall be willing to hurt them, he must thus
be killed "—That hereby is signified, that according to the endeavor
of bringing in evil, they perish, appears from the signification of being
willing to hurt, as denoting the effort of bringing evil, for to will is
to make an effort; and from the signification of being killed, as denoting to perish, in the present case, as to spiritual life, which perishes solely from evils and the falses of evil, for thence comes spiritual death, as may be seen above, n. 315, 589. The reason why
it is here repeated, if any shall be willing to hurt them, is, because
thereby is understood that every one perishes according to the will, or
according to the effort of bringing in evil, for the will constitutes every

one's life : the reason that every one perishes according to the will of hurting the two witnesses, who are the two olives and the two candlesticks, that is the good of love and of charity, and the truth of doctrine and of faith, is, because they are in an opposite will, and the will that is opposed against the good of love and the truth of doctrine is hell, in proportion to the quantity of such opposition, and hence it is that it is said that he must thus be killed, that is, perish in proportion to the will to hurt them. Moreover, every man and spirit is in the protection of the Lord, the evil equally as the good; and to him who is in the protection of the Lord, no evil can happen, for it is not the will of the Lord that any one should perish or be punished : but every one is so far in the protection of the Lord, as he abstains from doing evil, but so far as he does not abstain from evil, so far he removeth himself from the protection of the Lord, and so far as he thus removes himself, so far he is hurt by evil spirits who are from hell: for infernal spirits are in a continual lust of doing evil to others, and so far as any are out of, or without, the divine protection of the Lord, that is, so far they do evil, they come into the power of those who do evil to them by punishing and depriving them of such things as appertain to spiritual life. In a word, so far as any one wills to do hurt to the goods of love and truths of doctrine, so far he is devoured by a fire and is killed, that is, he is so far possessed by evils and the falses of evil, and so far spiritually dies, and this is not affected from the Divine [principle] but from the evil itself which every one does.

644. " These have power to shut heaven, that it rain no rain in the days of their pr   he   "—That hereby is signified that they who reject the goods and truths of heaven and the church, which proceed from the Lord, do not receive any influx out of heaven, appears from the signification of shutting heaven, as denoting lest any influx out of heaven be received, concerning which we shall speak presently; and from the signification of rain, as denoting truth fertilizing, which is truth from which good is derived, and which flows down out of heaven, concerning which also we shall speak presently; and from the signification of their prophecy, as denoting prediction concerning the Lord, and concerning His advent, and concerning the good of love and truths of faith which are directed to Him, for this revelation, and preaching thence derived, in the end of the church, is what principally is understood by the days of the prophecy of the two witnesses: the reason that the Lord is especially preached in the end of the church, by the two witnesses, is because the two witnesses, which are the good of love to the Lord and the truth of faith, principally witness concerning Him, wherefore in what follows it is said, that " The testimony of Jesus is the spirit of prophecy " (Apoc. xix. 10). The reason why to shut heaven denotes to hinder the reception of any influx from heaven is, because it follows, that it rain no rain, by which is signified the influx of divine truth out of heaven : for it is a known thing that all the good of love and all the truth of faith flows in out of heaven, that is, from the Lord through heaven, with man, and this continually ;

whence it follows, that the good of love and the truth of faith are by no means of man, but of the Lord with him : both these flow-in, in proportion as evil and the false do not hinder, these being what shut heaven and prevent the influx thence : for evil and good, and the false and the true, are opposites, wherefore where the one is, the other cannot possibly be : for evil with man hinders the good from entering and the false hinders the truth; and good causes evil to be removed, and truth the false; for they are opposite to each other as heaven and hell are opposite ; wherefore the one acts against the other with a perpetual effort of destroying it, and that which prevails destroys the other.   There are also in every man two minds, the one interior, which is called the spiritual mind, the other exterior, which is called the natural mind ; the former being created for the reception of light from heaven, but the latter for the reception of light from the world; wherefore the spiritual mind, which is the interior mind of man, is heaven with him, and the natural mind, which is the exterior mind, is the world with him : the interior mind, which is heaven in man, is opened, in proportion as man acknowledges the Divine [principle] of the Lord, and man so far acknowledges as he is in the good of love and charity, and in the truths of doctrine and faith ; but this interior mind, which is heaven in man, is not opened in proportion 'as he does not acknowledge the Divine [principle] of the Lord, and does not live a life of love and faith : and that mind is so far shut as man is in evils and thence in falses, and when it is shut, then the natural mind becomes hell in man : for the evil and its false are in the natural mind, and therefore when the spiritual mind, which is heaven in man, is shut, then the natural mind, which is hell, has dominion : from these considerations it may appear, how it is to be understood, that heaven is shut, that it rain no rain.   It is not however to be understood that the two witnesses shut heaven, but evil and the false, which have rule in the men of the church at its end : this is said of the two witnesses in the same manner as it is said above that fire shall go forth out of their mouth, and devour their adversaries, when yet there is not any fire which goes forth from them and devours, as was explained in the two articles above. The reason why not to rain any rain, signifies no influx of divine truth out of heaven, is, because water, from which comes rain, signifies the truth of the Word, and the truth of doctrine and of faith thence derived, as may be seen above, n. 71, 483, 518, 537, 538 : and because rain water descends out of the clouds in heaven, therefore by raining rain is signified the influx of divine truth from the Lord in heaven ; and inasmuch as rain fertilizes the earth, therefore it signifies the divine truth, fertilizing and fructifying the church, whence by rain is also signified spiritual benediction. That by rain, in the Word, is not understood rain, but the influent Divine [principle], from which intelligence and wisdom, likewise the good of love and truth of faith in man, grow and fructify, and that by raining is signified influx, may appear from the following passages : Thus in Moses: " My doctrine shall flow down as the rain, My word shall drop as the dew, as droppings [stillæ] upon the

grass, and as the drops [guttæ] upon the herb" (Deut. xxxii. 2):
doctrine is here compared to rain, because by rain is signified the
divine truth proceeding, from which is the all of doctrine; for all
comparisons in the Word are also from correspondences: inasmuch
as the divine truth flowing down is signified by rain, it is therefore
said, my doctrine shall flow down as rain; by dew is signified good,
and whereas this is also signified by word, it is said, My word shall
drop as the dew; intelligence and wisdom thence derived are signified by droppings upon the grass, and drops upon the herb, for as
the grass and herbs of the field grow by virtue of the waters of the
rain and dew, so do intelligence and wisdom by virtue of the influx
of divine truth from the Lord; this was premised by Moses, because
in that chapter the twelve tribes of Israel are treated of, by whom,
in the spiritual sense, are signified all the truths and goods of the
church, consequently, doctrine in the whole complex. So again:
" The land which ye shall pass through to possess it, is a land of
mountains and valleys, and drinketh the waters of the rain of
heaven. And I will give the rain of your land in its season, the
early and the latter rain, that thou mayest gather thy corn, and thy
must, and thine oil. But if ye shall serve other gods, and not walk
in My statutes, the anger of Jehovah shall enkindle against you;
He will shut heaven that there be no rain, and the land shall not
yield her produce" (Deut. xi. 11, 14, 16, 17): by these words is
described the land of Canaan and its fruitfulness; but inasmuch, as
by that land, in the spiritual sense, is signified the church, it follows,
that all things contained in that description signify such things as
appertain to the church, as the mountains, valleys, corn, must, oil,
produce, and rain: a land of mountains and valleys signify the superior and inferior, or internal and external things of the church;
the internal things of the church are in the internal man, which is
called the spiritual man, and the external things of the church are
in the external man, which is called the natural man; that each of
these are of such a quality as to receive the influx of divine truth, is
signified by drinking the waters of the rain of heaven; that the divine
truth flows in with the man of the church, both when he is in a spiritual state and in a natural state, is signified by the rain being given
in its season, the early and the latter rain; for the man of the church
is alternately in a spiritual state and in a natural state, and the
influx and reception of divine truth in the spiritual state is understood by the early or morning rain, and in the natural state by the
latter or evening rain; spiritual and celestial good and truth, which
the man of the church thence possesses, are understood by the corn,
must, and oil, which they shall gather; that falses of doctrine and
of worship would hinder the influx and reception of divine truth,
whence there would be no growth of the spiritual life, is signified
by, if ye shall serve other gods, there shall be no rain, and the land
will not give her produce, other gods denoting falses of doctrine and
of worship. Again: " If ye walk in My statutes, and observe My
precepts, and do them, then will I give you rain in due season; and
the earth shall give its produce, and the tree of the field shall give

its fruit " (Levit. xxvi. 3, 4): here by the rain which shall be given in its season, and by the produce of the land, are signified similar things as above: and whereas the church at that time was merely an external church, representative of interior or spiritual things, therefore also it so came to pass, that when they walked in the statutes, and observed the precepts, and did them, they had rain in its season, and the earth yielded its produce, and the tree of the field its fruit, but still these things were representative and significative, rain representing and signifying the Divine [principle] flowing-in, produce, the truth of doctrine and the understanding of truth, and fruit of the tree, the good of love and the will of good: the same may also appear from what is recorded concerning those things in other passages: as that " The rain was withheld, and thence a famine took place in the land of Israel, for three years and a half, under Ahab, because they served other gods, and slew the prophets " (1 Kings xvii. and chap. xviii.; Luke iv. 25): this was representative, and thence significative, that no divine truth flowing-in out of heaven, could be received, on account of the falses of evil, which were signified by other gods and by Baal, whom they worshiped; by killing the prophets, was also signified, to destroy what was divine, for by a prophet, in the Word, is signified the doctrine of truth from the Word. So in Isaiah: " I will make My vineyard a desolation; it shall not be pruned nor weeded, the briar and the thorn shall come up; and I will command the clouds, that they rain no rain upon it " (v. 6): here likewise it is said of Jehovah, that He maketh the vineyard a desolation, and commandeth the clouds that they rain no rain upon it; when notwithstanding this is not done by Jehovah, that is by the Lord, for He always flows in as well with the evil as with the good, which is understood by his sending his rain upon the just and upon the unjust, Matt. iv. 45; but the cause hereof is in the man of the church, in that he does not receive any influx of divine truth, for when this is the case with man, he shuts up the interiors of his mind, which should receive, and these being shut, the divine influx is rejected: by the vineyard, which is laid into desolation, is signified the church; by not being pruned nor weeded, is signified that it cannot be cultivated and so prepared to receive; by the briar and thorn which shall come up, are signified the falses of evil; by commanding the clouds that they rain no rain, is signified the non-reception of any influx of divine truth out of heaven. So in Jeremiah: " The showers have been withheld, and there hath been no latter rain; but notwithstanding the forehead of a harlot remaineth to thee, thou hast refused to be ashamed " (iii. 3): again: " They said not in their heart, let us now fear Jehovah our God, that giveth the rain and the shower, the early and the latter, in its season: He reserveth unto us the weeks, the appointed times of harvest: your iniquities make these to decline " (v. 24, 25): and in Amos: " I have prohibited the rain from you, when as yet there were three months until harvest, so that I caused it indeed to rain upon one city, and upon another city I caused it not to rain; one field received the rain, but the field upon which it rained not, withered; whence two three cities wandered unto one city to drink waters, nor yet were they satiated : nevertheless ye have not returned unto Me" (iv. 7, 8): and in Ezekiel: " Son of Man, say, Thou art the land, which is not cleansed, which hath no rain in the day of anger, a conspiracy of her prophets in the midst thereof" (xxii. 24, 25): and in Zechariah : " Whosoever of the families of the land shall not go up to Jerusalem, to adore Jehovah Zebaoth, there shall be no rain upon them" (xiv. 17): in these passages also, rain signifies the reception of the influx of divine truth, from which comes spiritual intelligence ; and that no such intelligence exists by any influx on account of the evils and falses which refuse to receive and which reject it, is signified by there being no rain.   So in Jeremiah : " The great ones sent the little ones to seek waters; they came unto the pits and found no waters, because the earth was chapt, for there had been no rain in the earth ; the husbandmen were ashamed, they covered their heads" (xiv. 3, 4): by the great ones are understood those who teach and lead, and by the little ones, those who are taught and led; by waters are signified the truths of doctrine ; by pits in which there are no waters, are signified doctrinals in which there are no truths ; by there being no rain in the earth, is signified, that no influx of divine truth is received by reason of the falses of the church; by the husbandmen who were ashamed and covered their heads, are signified those who teach and their grief.   Again in Isaiah : " Then Jehovah shall give rain to thy seed, with which thou sowest the land, and bread of the produce of the earth, and it shall be fat and opulent; thy cattle shall feed in that day in a broad meadow" (xxx. 23): speaking of the advent of the Lord : the influx of divine truth proceeding from Him, is signified by the rain which the Lord shall then give to the seed, the rain is the divine influx, the seed is the truth of the Word; to sow the land, signifies, to plant and form the church: by the bread of the produce which Jehovah will give, is signified the good of love and charity, which is produced by the truths of the Word, vivified by influx divine ; by fat and opulent, is signified, full of the good of love and truths thence derived, for fat is predicated of good, and opulent, of truths; by the cattle shall feed in that day in a broad meadow, is signified the extension and multiplication thereof from the divine influx, and spiritual nourishment thence derived, cattle denoting the goods and truths with man, that day, the advent of the Lord, and the broad meadow, the Word, by which is the divine influx and spiritual nourishment,—breadth being predicated of the extension and multiplication of truth. Again in the same prophet: " As the rain and the snow descendeth out of heaven, and returneth not thither, but watereth the earth, and maketh it to bring forth and bud, that it may give seed to the sower, and bread to the eater; so shall My Word be that goeth forth out of My mouth; it shall not return unto Me in vain, but it shall accomplish that which I will, and it shall prosper to what I sent it" (lv. 10, 11): here the Word which goeth forth out of the mouth of God, is compared to the rain and snow from heaven, because by the Word is meant the divine truth proceeding from the Lord, which flows in with us by the Word; in like manner also, by "as the rain and snow descending out of heaven;" by the rain is signified truth spiritual, which is appropriated to man, and by snow, truth natural, which is as snow when it is only in the memory, but becomes spiritual by love as snow becomes rain water by heat; by watering the earth, that it may bring forth and bud, is signified to vivify the church, that it may produce the truth of doctrine and faith and the good of love and charity; the truth of doctrine and faith is signified by the seed which it giveth to the sower, and the good of love and charity by the bread which it giveth to the eater; it shall not return to Me in vain, but it shall accomplish that which I will, signifies that it shall be received, and that man shall be led from it to look to the Lord.   So in Ezekiel: " I will give them and the circuits of My hill, a blessing, and I will send down the rain in its season, there shall be rains of blessing; then the tree of the field shall give its fruit, and the earth shall give its produce" (xxxiv. 26, 27): by the circuits of the hill of Jehovah, are understood all who are in truths of doctrine and thence in the good of charity; by sending down the rain in its season is signified the influx of divine truth, agreeably to the affection and will of receiving; and inasmuch as thence is the fructification of good, and multiplication of truth, they are called rains of blessing, and it is said that the tree of the field shall give its fruit, and the earth shall give its produce; and by the tree of the field, and the earth, is signified the church and the man of the church, by the fruit of the tree of the field, the fructification of good, and by the produce of the earth, the multiplication of the truth thereof.   And in Joel : " Sons of Zion, rejoice and be glad in Jehovah your God, for He shall give you the former rain in justice, yea, he shall cause the rain to come down for you, the former and the latter in the first, that the corn floors may be full of pure corn, and the presses overflow with must and oil" (ii. 23, 24): by the sons of Zion are signified those who are in genuine truths, whereby they have the good of love, for by Zion is signified the celestial church, which is in the good of love to the Lord by genuine truths; that the Lord flows in with them with the good of love, and from that good into truths, is signified by, He shall give them the former rain in justice, justice in the Word being predicated of the good of love, and the just denoting those who are in that good, as may be seen above, n. 304; that the Lord flows in with the good of love into truths continually, is signified by, he shall cause the rain to descend, the former and the latter in the first; the good of brotherly and social love thence derived, is signified by the corn-floors being full of pure corn; and that thence they shall have the truth and good of love to the Lord, is signified by the presses overflowing with must and oil : with those who are of the celestial church of the Lord there is the good of brotherly and social love, which love, with those who are of the spiritual church, is called neighborly love or charity. And in Zechariah : " Ask of Jehovah the rain in its season; Jehovah shall make the clouds, and shall give to them the rain of the

shower, to man, the herb in the field " (x. 1) : by the rain here also
is signified the influx of divine truth from the Lord, from which man
has spiritual intelligence; the rain of the shower signifies divine
truth flowing-in in abundance, and by giving the herb in the field,
is signified knowledge of truth and good from the Word, and intelligence thence derived. And in David: " Thou visitest the earth,
and art delighted with it, thou enrichest it greatly; the river of God
is full of waters, thou preparest their corn, and so thou establishest
it; water the furrows thereof; lay down the ridges thereof; make
it liquid with drops; bless the budding thereof" (Psalm lxv. 10, 11):
by the earth is there signified the church; by the river full of waters is signified doctrine full of truths; by watering the furrows,
laying down the ridges, and making it liquid with drops, is signified, to fill with the knowledges of good and truth; by preparing the
corn, is signified all that nourishes the soul, wherefore it is added,
so thou establishest the earth, that is, the church; by blessing the
budding thereof, is signified, to produce continually anew, and to
cause truths to spring forth. Again: "Thou, O God causest the
rain of benevolences to drop" (Psalm lxviii. 9); and again: " He
shall descend as the rain, upon the herb of the meadow, as the drops
in the cleft of the earth, in His days the just shall flourish" (Psalm
lxii. 6, 7): in these passages also rain does not signify rain, but the
influx of divine truth with man, from which he has spiritual life.
And in Job: " My word they shall not repeat, and my discourse
shall drop upon them, and they shall wait for me as for the rain,
and they shall open their mouths for the latter rain" (xxix. 22, 23):
that by the rain is there understood truth which is spoken by any one,
and flows in with another, is evident, for word, discourse, and opening of the mouth, signifies truth proceeding from any one by speech,
whence it is called rain, and the latter rain, and also is said to drop,
by which is signified to speak. Again in Jeremiah: " The maker
of the earth by His power prepareth the globe, by His wisdom and
by His intelligence He stretcheth out the Heavens; at the voice
which He giveth, a multitude of waters in the Heavens; and He
maketh the vapors to ascend from the end of the earth; He maketh
lightnings for the rain, and bringeth the wind out of His treasures"
(x. 12, 13; ch. li. 16; Ps. cxxxv. 7): by the globe, which the maker
of the earth prepareth by His power is signified the church in the
universal terrestrial globe; power signifies the potency of divine truth;
by the heavens which He stretcheth out by wisdom and intelligence,
is signified the church in the heavens, corresponding to the church
on earth; wisdom and intelligence signify the Divine Proceeding,
from which angels and men have the wisdom of good and the understanding of truth, and to stretch out signifies the formation and extension of the heavens in general, and the extension of intelligence
and wisdom with every one who receives; at the voice which He
giveth a multitude of waters in the heavens, signifies, that from the
Divine Proceeding are derived spiritual truths in immense abundance, voice denotes the Divine Proceeding, waters denote truths,
and multitude, abundance; He maketh the vapors to ascend from

the end of the earth, signifies truths in the ultimate, such as are the truths of the Word in the literal sense, in which are contained spiritual truths, the end of the earth denoting the ultimates of the church, vapors denoting truths for those who are in ultimates, and to make them to ascend denoting to give spiritual truths from them, viz. from ultimate truths, because contained in them, which especially fructify the church; He maketh lightnings for the rain, signifies illustration from the influx of divine truth with them; and He bringeth the wind out of His treasures, signifies spiritual things in the Word out of heaven. So in Luke: "When ye see a cloud rising in the west, immediately it is said, A shower cometh, and so it is; and when the south wind bloweth, it is said, There will be heat, and it cometh to pass; ye hypocrites, ye know how to prove the face of the earth and of heaven, how is it that ye do not prove this time" (xii. 54, 55, 56): by this comparison the Lord teaches, that they see earthly things but not heavenly things; and the comparison itself, as is the case with all comparisons in the Word, is taken from correspondences: for by the cloud rising in the west is signified the advent of the Lord at the end of the church predicted in the Word, the cloud denoting the Word in the letter, the rising, the advent of the Lord, and the west, the end of the church; immediately it is said, that a shower cometh, signifies that then is the influx of divine truth; and when ye see the south wind blow, signifies preaching concerning His advent; it is said, there will be heat, signifies, that then is the influx of divine good: the same words also signify contentions and combats of truth from good with falses from evil, shower and heat also signifying those contentions and combats; for the comparison follows immediately after the Lord's saying "that He came not to send peace on the earth but dissension; and that the father shall be divided against the son, and the son against the father, the mother against the daughter, and the daughter against the mother" (erses 51, 52, 53), by which words is signified that contention andvcombat; that the same is also signified by a shower will be seen below: inasmuch as that comparison, viewed in its spiritual sense, involves the advent of the Lord, and that from blindness induced by falses they would not acknowledge Him, although He might have been known to them from the Word, it therefore follows, ye hypocrites ye know how to prove the face of the earth and of heaven, but ye do not prove this time, viz. the time of his advent, and the conflict which then took place of the false of evil with the truth of good. And in Hosea: "Then shall we know, and follow on to know Jehovah; His going forth is prepared as the cloud, and He shall come to us as the rain, as the latter rain that watereth the earth" (vi. 3): these words are said concerning the Lord and His advent; and inasmuch as from Him proceeds all divine truth, from which comes life and salvation to angels and men, therefore it is said, He shall come to us as the rain, as the latter rain watereth the earth; to water the earth denoting to make fruitful the church, which is said to be made fruitful, when truths are multiplied and intelligence thence increases, and when goods are fructified, and celestial love thence increases. So in 2 Samuel: "The Rock of Israel spake to me, as the light of morning, the sun ariseth, a morning without clouds; from the clear shining after rain, [there shall be] grass out of the earth" (xxiii. 3, 4); speaking also concerning the Lord, who, from divine truth which proceeds from Him, is called the Rock of Israel: that divine truth proceeds from His divine good, is understood by, as the light of the morning, the sun ariseth; comparison is made with light, because light signifies the divine truth proceeding, and with the morning, because the morning signifies the divine good, and with the rising sun, because the east or rising, and the sun, signify the divine love; that these are without obscurity is signified by the light of a morning without clouds; the illustration of the man of the church by and after the reception of divine truth from the divine good of the Lord, is signified by the clear-shining after rain, clear-shining or splendor denoting illustration, and rain denoting influx and consequent reception; that hence they who are of the church have science, intelligence, and wisdom, is signified by grass out of the earth, grass denoting spiritual nourishment, the same as pasture, and thence, science, intelligence, and wisdom, which are spiritual meats; and the earth denoting the church, and the man of the church. Again in Matthew: "Love ye your enemies, bless them that curse you, do good to them that hate you, and pray for them that hurt and persecute you, that ye may be the sons of your Father who is in the heavens; who maketh His sun to rise upon the evil and the good, and sendeth rain upon the just and the unjust" (v. 44, 45): neighborly love or charity is first described, which is to will good, and to do good, even to our enemies, by loving them, blessing them, and praying for them, for genuine charity regards only the good of another; to love there signifes charity, to bless, instruction, and to pray, intercession; the reason is, because inwardly in charity there is the end of doing good; that this is the Divine [principle] itself with man, as it is with regenerate man, is signified by, that ye may be the sons of your Father in the Heavens, the Father in the Heavens, is the Divine Proceeding, for all who receive this are called the sons of the Father, that is, of the Lord; by the sun which He maketh to rise upon the evil and the good, is signified, the divine good flowing-in; and by the rain which He sendeth upon the just and unjust is signified the divine truth flowing-in; for the Divine Proceeding, which is the Father in the Heavens, equally flows-in with the evil and the good, but the reception thereof depends upon man, although it is not of man himself to receive, but as of himself, for the faculty of receiving is continually given to him, and also flows-in, in proportion as man removes the evils which hinder or obstruct, by virtue of his faculty so to do, which also is continually given, the faculty itself appearing as of man, although it is of the Lord. From these considerations it may now appear, that by rain, in the Word, is signified the influx of divine truth from the Lord, whence man has spiritual life, and this because waters, of which rain consists, signify the truth of doctrine and the truth of faith: but whereas by waters, in the opposite sense, are signified falses of doctrine and of faith, therefore also by showers of rain, equally as by inundations of waters and by a flood, are signified not only falses destroying truths, but also temptations, in which man either falls or conquers : thus in Matthew : " Every one who heareth My words, and doeth them, I will compare with a prudent man, who built his house upon a rock ; and the shower descended, and the floods came, and the winds blew, and fell upon that house, yet it fell not. But he who heareth My words, and doeth them not, shall be compared to a foolish man, who built his house upon the sand; and the shower descended, and the floods came, and the winds blew, and beat upon that house, and it fell, and great was the fall of it " (vii. 24, 25, 26, 27): by the shower and by the floods are here understood temptations, in which man either conquers or falls ; by waters, the falses which usually flow-in in temptations, and by the floods, which there are inundations of waters from a shower, are signified temptations; by the winds which also blow and rush in, are signified the thoughts thence emerging, for temptations exist by irruptions of falses injected by evil spirits into the thoughts; by the house, into which they rush or break in, is signified the man, properly his mind, which consists of understanding or thought, and of will or affection ; he who receives only the Word of the Lord, that is divine truth, in one part of his mind, which is of the thought or understanding, and not· at the same time in the other part, which is of the affection or will, such a man yields in temptations, and falls into grievous falses, which are the falses of evil, wherefore it is said of that house, great was the fall of it; but he who receives divine truths in both parts, as well in the will as in the understanding, conquers in temptations; by the rock upon which that house is founded, is signified the Lord as to divine truth, or divine truth received in the soul and heart, that is in faith and love, which is in the understanding and will; but by the sand is signified divine truth received only in the memory, and thence some little in the thought, whence it is scattered and unconnected, because intermixed with falses, and falsified by the ideas entertained concerning it : hence then, it is evident, what is understood by hearing the Lord's words and not doing them : that such is the sense of the above words may also more clearly appear from those which precede. By an inundating rain or shower is signified an inundation of falses also in Ezekiel : " Say unto them that incrust with what is unfit, that it shall fall, because an inundating rain, because ye, O hail stones, shall fall, and a wind of storms shall break through : thus saith the Lord Jehovih, I will cause a wind of storms to break through in My wrath, and an inundating rain in Mine anger, and stones of hail in fervor for consummation, and I will destroy the wall which ye incrust with what is unfit " (xiii. 11, 13, 14): by the incrustation of what is unfit, is signified confirmation of what is false by fallacies, whereby the false appears as truth ; by the stones of hail are signified truths without good, thus without any spiritual life, which inwardly are all falses, for the ideas concerning them, which are dead, cause them to be merely crusts, and as pictures in which there is nothing alive ; such are the scientific truths appertaining to the natural man into which there does not flow-in anything from the spiritual; by the inundating rain and wind of storms, are signified falses and things imaginary rushing-in in abundance, also contentions concerning truths, which cause that nothing of truth can be seen, and so destroy man. Again in the same Prophet: " I will contend with Gog, with pestilence and blood, and I will cause it to rain an inundating rain, and stones of hail, fire and sulphur, upon him, and upon his wings, and upon the many people who are with him" (xxxviii. 23): by Gog are understood those that are in external worship without any internal; and inasmuch as that worship in like manner consists of crusts or shells, in which the kernels are either putrified or corroded by worms, therefore they are called an´ inundating rain and stones of hail, by which are signified falses and things imaginary rushing-in in abundance, which destroy man; evils of the false, and falses of evil, are signified by fire and sulphur. By " the deluge of waters, concerning which it is said that it inundated the whole earth, and destroyed all except Noah and his sons " (Gen. chap. vii. viii.), is also signified an inundation of falses, by which the most ancient church was at length destroyed; by Noah and his sons is signified the´new church which is called the ancient church, and the establishment thereof after the devastation of the most ancient church : but the particulars by which that deluge, and the salvation of the family of Noah, are there described, may be seen explained in the A. C. That waters signify truths, and, in the opposite sense, falses, may be seen above, n. 71, 483, 518, 537, 538; and that inundations of waters signify inundations of falses, and temptations, may also be seen above, n. 518.

645. " And they have power over the waters to turn them into blood "—That hereby is signified that truths, with them, are turned into falses from evil, appears from the signification of having power, when predicated of the two olive trees and two candlesticks, by which are signified the goods of love and truths of doctrine; not that they themselves have such power, viz. to turn truths into falses, because this is contrary to their nature, which is to turn falses into truths; for good cannot do evil; but still it appears as if they had this power, and also as if this was done by them, because it so comes to pass when they are injured; but it is the evil which is from hell; or hell from whence all evil comes, that turns the waters into blood, that is, truths into falses from evil: and from the signification of waters, as denoting truths, concerning which see above, n. 71, 483, 518, 537, 538; and from the signification of blood, as denoting the truth of the Word, and thence of doctrine derived from the Word, and, in the opposite sense, the false, specifically the truth of the Word falsified, for to shed blood signifies to offer violence to charity, and also to divine truth which is in the Word; but concerning the signification of blood in both senses, see above, n. 329.

646. " And to smite the earth with all plagues "—That hereby is signified that the church, with them, perishes by the concupiscences of evil, appears from the signification of the earth, as denoting the church, concerning which we have frequently spoken above; and

from the signification of plagues, as denoting such things as destroy
spiritual life, consequently such as destroy the church, which summarily have reference to the cupidities originating in the love of self
and of the world, thus to the concupiscences of evil, concerning
which see also above, n. 584; hence by turning the waters into
blood, is signified, that with those who will to hurt, and to bring
injury upon, the two witnesses, or upon the goods and truths of
heaven and the church, which acknowledge and confess the Lord,
goods are turned into evils and thence truths into falses.   That this
is the case, any one may see and conclude from this consideration,
that all the good of love and truth of faith is from the Lord, and
that they who do not acknowledge and confess the Lord, cannot
receive any good of love and truth of faith; for by non-acknow-
ledgement and by negation they shut up heaven against themselves,
that is reject all influx of good and truth from heaven, or by heaven
from the Lord; hence they remain in their proprium, which, viewed
in itself, is nothing but evil and the false thence derived; wherefore inasmuch as they think and will from their proprium or from
themselves, they cannot either think or will any other, than what
flows from the love of self and from the love of the world, and from
the concupiscence of those loves, and nothing at all which flows
from love to the Lord, and from love towards their neighbor: hence
it follows, that they who will and think from the loves of self and of
the world, and their concupiscences alone, cannot do otherwise than
will evils and think falses: that this is the case may be seen and
concluded by every one, who knows that all good and truth is from
the Lord, and all evil and the false from the proprium of man.   It
is to be observed, that so far as man acknowledges the Lord, and lives
according to His precepts, so far he is elevated above his proprium,
which elevation is out of the light of the world into the light of
heaven: man does not know that he is thus elevated above his proprium whilst he lives in the world, because it is not sensibly perceived by him, but still there is such elevation, or as it were attraction, of the interior understanding and interior will of man unto the
Lord, and thence a conversion of the face of man as to his spirit
unto Him: this, however, is manifested to the good man after death,
for then the conversion of the face is perpetual to the Lord, and
there is as it were an attraction unto Him as to a common centre,
concerning which conversion see what is said in the work concerning H. & H. n. 17, 123, 142, 143, 144, 145, 251, 272, 552, 561:
but inasmuch as it is according to divine order, that where attraction is, there ought to be impulsion, for attraction without impulsion
is not given, therefore it is according to divine order that there be
impulsion also with man, which, although it is there from the Lord,
yet it appears as if it was from man, and the appearance causes it
to be *as of* man: this impulsion as it were from man, corresponding
to the attraction from the Lord, is acknowledgment, thus reception
grounded in the acknowledgment and confession of the Lord, and
in a life according to His precepts, which must be on the part of
man, and from the liberty of his life, whilst man nevertheless ac-

knowledges, that this is also from the Lord, although, from the obscurity of perception in which he at present is, he does not feel it otherwise than as of himself.   These things are said in order that it may be known, that the man who denies the Lord cannot be otherwise than in evils and falses, because he cannot be drawn away from his proprium, that is, be elevated above it; hence neither can he be in any attraction, and consequent conversion of the interiors of his mind, unto the Lord.

647. " As often as they will"—That hereby is signified, as often as man assaults the goods of love and truths of doctrine which witness concerning the Lord, and from which man acknowledges and confesses the Lord, to bring evil upon them, appears from the signification of as often as they will, when predicated of the two witnesses, by whom are understood those who acknowledge and confess the Lord, not that they themselves will and do the evils which are hitherto related, but that the evil bring them upon themselves, when they assault the goods and truths which proceed from the Lord to bring evil upon them : for in the literal sense of the Word it is ascribed to Jehovah God, that is to the Lord, that He is angry, wrathful, that He is furious against the wicked, and that He does evil to them, yea, that He wills evil, when notwithstanding the Lord is never angry or wrathful, nor wills or does evil to any one ; for the Lord flows-in from good with good, and from truth with truths derived from good, with every man, for He wills to bring all to Himself and to save them : from these considerations it may appear, that this expression, as often as the witnesses will, is not to be understood as really applied to the two witnesses, but to the evil, denoting as often as they will, that is, do evil from will, that is, assault the goods and truths of heaven and the church with intent to bring hurt upon them. That it is not the Lord, nor, consequently, the good of love and truth of faith which are of the Lord with man and angel, that will evil to any one, may appear from this consideration, that the Lord God is not the cause of evil with any one, and He who is not the cause of evil, can neither be the cause of punishment, but the evil itself, which is in man, is the cause thereof : in the spiritual world where heaven and hell are, all things are so arranged, that the Lord never casts any one into hell, but the evil spirit casts himself there, as may be seen in the work concerning H. & H. n. 545–550 ; and this because the Lord is not the cause of the evil, and he who is not the cause of evil, cannot be the cause of any effect which exists from it : from these, considerations then it is evident, that the things contained in this verse, viz. " That the two witnesses have power to shut heaven, that it rain no rain, and that they have power over the waters to turn them into blood, and to smite the earth with every plague as often as they will," are not to be understood according to the literal sense, but according to the spiritual sense, which is, that they who do evil to the two witnesses, bring such things upon themselves : for so far as any one does evil to them, so far he shuts heaven against himself, and turns truths

with himself into falses, and so far destroys himself by concupiscences of evil.

648. Verses 7, 8. " And when they have finished their testimony,
the beast ascending out of the abyss shall make war with them, and
shall conquer them, and kill them   And their bodies [shall lie]
upon the street of the great city, which is spiritually called Sodom
and Egypt, where also our Lord was crucified."—"And when they
shall have finished their testimony," signifies in the end of the church,
when the Divine [principle] of the Lord is no longer acknowledged,
and thence there is no longer any good of love and truth of doctrine : " the beast ascending out of the abyss shall make war with
them," signifies assault from infernal loves : " and shall conquer them
and kill them," signifies the consequent destruction of all the good
and truth of the church : " and their bodies [shall lie] upon the street
of the great city," signifies the extinction thereof from the evils and
falses of doctrine : " which is spiritually called Sodom and Egypt,"
signifies, by the evils of the love of self, and by falses thence derived : " where also our Lord was crucified," signifies, by which,
namely, evils and falses thence derived originating in infernal love,
the Lord was rejected and condemned.

649. " And when they shall have finished their testimony "—
That hereby is signified in the end of the church, when the Divine
[principle] of the Lord is no longer acknowledged, and thence there
is no longer any good of love and truth of doctrine, appears from
the signification of testimony, as denoting the acknowledgment of
the Divine [principle] in the Lord, and thence the good of love and
truth of doctrine, concerning which we shall speak presently : and
from the signification of finishing, as denoting to end ; and whereas
this is ended in the end of the church, therefore the end of the church
is here signified by finishing : and inasmuch as there is then no
longer any acknowledgment of the Divine [principle] in the Lord,
therefore there is not any good of love and truth of Doctrine.   That
this is signified by testimony, may appear from what has been
hitherto said concerning the two witnesses, viz. that by them is understood the good of love and charity and the truth of doctrine and
faith, because these are what principally witness concerning the
Lord, for they are from the Lord, and are of Him with man, whence
by their testimony is signified, preaching concerning them : that the
acknowledgment of the Divine [principle] in the Lord is what is
here signified by testimony, appears from these words in the Apocalypse : " That the testimony of Jesus is the spirit of prophecy "
(chap. xix. 10) : for unless man acknowledge this from the heart,
and believe it from spiritual faith, he cannot be in any faculty of receiving the good of love and the truth of doctrine.   At the end of
the church the Lord is indeed preached, and also from doctrine
Divinity is attributed to Him like to the Divinity of the Father ; but
notwithstanding scarce any one thinks of his Divinity, by reason of
their placing it above or without His Humanity, wherefore when
they look to His Divinity they do not look to the Lord, but to the

Father as to another; when notwithstanding the Divinity, which is called the Father, is in the Lord, as He Himself teaches in John, (chap. x. 30, 38; chap. xiv. 7): hence it is that man does not think of the Lord otherwise than as of a common man, and from that thought flows his faith, howsoever he may say with his lips that he believes His Divinity: let any one explore, if he can, the idea of his thought concerning the Lord, whether it be not such as is here described, and when it is such, he cannot be conjoined to Him in faith and love, nor by conjunction receive any good of love and truth of faith: hence then it is, that in the end of the church, there is not any acknowledgment of the Lord, that is, of the Divine [principle] in the Lord and from the Lord: it appears indeed as if the Divine [principle] of the Lord was acknowledged, because it is affirmed in the doctrine of the church; but whilst the Divine [principle] is separated from His Human, His Divine [principle] is not yet acknowledged inwardly, but only outwardly, and to acknowledge it outwardly is to acknowledge it only with the mouth, and not in the heart, or with speech only and not in faith. That this is the case, may appear from Christians in the other life, where the thoughts of the heart are manifested: when it is granted them to speak from doctrine, and from what they have heard from preaching, then they attribute Divinity to the Lord, and call it their faith; but when their interior thought and faith is explored, it is found that they have a different idea concerning the Lord, which is as of a common man, to whom nothing divine can be attributed: the interior thought of man is the real ground of his faith, wherefore such being the thought and thence the faith of his spirit, it is evident, that there is not any acknowledgement of the Divine [principle] in the Lord and from the Lord, in the Christian world, at the end of the church. In a word, there is indeed an external acknowledgment of the Divine [principle] of the Lord, but no internal, and external acknowledgment is of the natural man alone, but internal acknowledgment is of his spirit itself; and the external is laid asleep after death, but the internal, being of his spirit, remains. From these considerations it may in a small degree appear, what is to be understood by the beast out of the abyss overcoming and killing the two witnesses, and by their bodies being seen in the street of the city which is called Sodom and Egypt and by the spirit of life afterwards entering into them.

650. "The beast ascending out of the abyss shall make war with them"—That hereby is signified assault from infernal love, appears from the signification of beast, as denoting the affection of the natural man in both senses, concerning which we shall speak presently: and from the signification of the abyss, as denoting hell, concerning which see above, n. 538; and from the signification of making war, as denoting to assault, for by wars, in the Word, are not signified wars, such as are in our world, but such as are in the spiritual world, all which are combats by falses from evil against truths from good; that such things are signified by wars in the Word will ap-

pear in the following pages, where wars are again mentioned : hence it may appear, that by the beast ascending out of the abyss and making war with the witnesses, is signified, infernal love orignating in the falses of evil about to assault the truths of good. Before it is shown that by beast is signified the love or affection of the natural man, something shall be said concerning assault: infernal love is principally the love of self, for the love of self is the love of the proprium of man, and the proprium of man is nothing but evil; wherefore so far as man is in that love, so far he is against the Lord, and consequently against the good of love and charity, and against the truth of doctrine and faith, thus against those two witnesses; hence it is, that the hells, where the love of self reigns, are the most dire and malignant, and diametrically opposite to the Lord, whence they continually assault the goods of love and of faith because these are from the Lord alone, and are the Lord with man and angel ; that those hells are more dire than the rest, may appear from this consideration, that they continually breathe the murder of those who confess the Divine [principle] of the Lord, consequently the murder of those who are in the good of love and in the good of faith to the Lord derived from the Lord: the reason why those hells are more malignant than the rest, is, because so far as man is in the love of self, and at the same time in the love of self-derived intelligence, so far his natural lumen is as it were in a sort of splendor, for the love of self is as fire which kindles that lumen, whence it is that such can think and reason ingeniously against the Divine [principle] and against all things of heaven and the church : sometimes I have been amazed when I have heard people of such a character, because I conceived that they might also be brought to receive faith even more than others, but I observed, that this was impossible, because in proportion as they were in light as to things corporeal, worldly, and natural, in the same proportion they were in darkness as to things celestial and spiritual, which darkness being seen by me, appeared altogether dusky, mixed with a fiery principle ; this I could confirm by much experience, if this were the place for expatiating on experiences : the love of self is what is here specifically understood by the beast ascending out of the abyss, which made war with the two witnesses, and killed them. That beasts signify the loves and affections of the natural man in both senses, may appear from many passages in the Word ; and whereas this has been hitherto unknown, and it appears strange to many that beasts signify the love or affection of the natural man, it may be necessary to confirm it from the Word, which we shall do presently. The reason why natural affections are signified by beasts, is, because those affections are altogether similar to the affections of beasts, and hence the man who does not imbibe spiritual affections by the goods and truths of heaven, differs but little from the beasts ; for man is distinguished above the beasts by the superaddition of the faculty of thinking and thence of willing spiritually, by virtue whereof he can eminently see and perceive abstract things ; but if this spiritual faculty is not vivified by the knowledges of truth and good, and afterwards by faith and the life of faith, he is no better than the beasts, except only that by virtue of that superior faculty, he is able to think and speak. Inasmuch as the affections of the natural man are signified by beasts, therefore those affections, when they are presented visible in the spiritual world in the correspondent forms of animals, appear altogether as forms of various beasts; thus as lambs, sheep, she-goats, kids, he-goats, heifers, oxen, cows; also as camels, mules, horses, asses; and also as bears, tigers, leopards, lions; likewise as dogs and serpents of various kinds; but such things are only appearances of the affections of the spirits who are present, and when they appear, it is also known there not only that they thence exist, but also from whom they are derived; but as soon as the affections cease, the appearances cease also. From these considerations also it may be manifest, whence it is that beasts are so often mentioned in the Word. But we proceed to confirmations from that source; thus in David: " Thou madest him to have dominion over the works of Thy hands, Thou hast put all things under his feet, the flock and the herd, and also the beasts of the field, the bird of heaven, and the fishes of the sea" (Psalm viii. 7, 8, 9): the subject treated of in the whole of that Psalm, is concerning the Lord, and His dominion over all things of heaven and the church; the things of heaven and the church, are understood here and in other passages of the Word by the works of the hands of Jehovah; and inasmuch as His dominion is over those things, and spiritual things, in the Word, are expressed by natural things, for the Word, in its bosom, is spiritual, hence by flock, herd, beasts of the fields, birds of heaven, and fishes of the sea, are not understood those things, but spiritual things appertaining to heaven and the church; by flock and herd are signified things spiritual, and things natural which are from a spiritual origin, by flock, viz. by lambs, kids, she-goats, sheep, and rams, things spiritual, and by herds, which are heifers, oxen, cows, and camels, things natural from a spiritual origin; by beasts of the field are signified the affections of the natural man, by the birds of the heavens, the thoughts thence derived, and by the fishes of the sea, the scientifies of the sensual natural man; if such was not the signification of these things, to what purpose could it be to describe the Lord's dominion over them? Again: "Thou, O God, causest the rain of benevolences to drop; thou didst confirm thy laboring heritage, thy wild beast, thy congregation, shall dwell therein" (Psalm lxviii. 10, 11): here beast is manifestly put for the people which receives the influx of divine truth from the Lord, for the heritage of God, whereby is signified the church, is called thy beast, thy congregation shall dwell therein; by rain of benevolences is signified the influx of divine truth from the divine clemency. So again: "Jehovah who sendeth out the fountains into the rivers; they go amongst the mountains, they afford drink to every beast; the wild asses break their thirst, near them the bird of the heavens dwelleth, from amongst the boughs they utter their voice: who maketh the grass to bud forth for the beast, and the herb for the service of man, to bring forth bread out of the earth. Thou disposest the darkness, that there may be night, in which every wild beast of the forest cometh forth ; the great sea and broad in spaces, there is the reptile without number, wild beasts small and great" (Psalm civ. 10, 11, 14, 20, 25) ; treating also of the Lord ; and by these words is described the establishment of the church with the gentiles ; wherefore by wild beasts, beasts, and birds, are signified such things as appertain to the man of the church. It is well to be noted, that in many passages, mention is made sometimes of wild beast and sometimes of beast, and that by wild beast is not understood wild beast according to the common idea concerning wild beasts; for wild beast, in the Hebrew tongue, is derived from an expression which signifies life, and hence for wild beast in certain passages it should be rather said animal ; this may appear also from this consideration, that the four animals, in which the cherubs were seen, whereby is signified the divine providence and defence, in Ezek. ch. j. to x. are called wild beasts, and in like manner by John in the Apocalypse, where the four animals about the throne are treated of, by which cherubs are also understood ; but still a distinction is carefully made in the Word between beasts and wild beasts, and by the former are signified the affections of the natural man, which appertain to the will, and by the latter, the affections of the natural man that appertain to the understanding : inasmuch as wild beast, in the Hebrew tongue, is derived from an expression which signifies life, therefore Eve, the wife of Adam, was named from that expression : this is premised in order that it may be known what is signified in the proper sense, by wild beast and what by beast. What is signified by Jehovah sending out fountains into the rivers, by their going among the mountains, and affording drink to every wild beast of the fields, by the wild asses breaking their thirst, and the birds of the heavens dwelling near them, was explained above, n. 483 ; by Jehovah causing the grass to bud forth for the beast, and herb for the service of man, to bring forth bread out of the earth, is signified the instruction and nourishment of the natural and spiritual man by truths from the Word, that he thence may have the good of love and charity; by grass is signified the truth of the natural man, which is scientific truth, as may be seen above, n. 507 : by beast is signified the affection thereof, which desires to be instructed and spiritually nourished ; by herb is signified the truth of the spiritual man ; by man, intelligence thence derived ; and by bread is signified the good of love and charity, which is nourished by truths; inasmuch as by darkness and by night is signified the lumen of the natural man, which, respectively to the light of the spiritual man, is as night, by the wild beast of the forest, the affection of scientifics, by the great sea and broad spaces, the natural principle itself, by the reptile which is without number, the scientifics therein, and by wild beasts great and small, the various affections, it is evident what is signified by, thou disposest darkness that it may be night, in which every wild beast of the forest cometh forth ; the great sea and broad in spaces, there is the reptile without number, wild beasts small and great. Again: " They shall sow fields and plant vineyards, and they shall yield the fruit of the produce, and he shall bless them so that they shall multiply exceedingly; and he shall not diminish their beast; and they are diminished and bowed down, through the vehemence of wickedness and sorrow" (Psalm cvii. 37, 38, 39) : the whole of that Psalm treats concerning the advent of the Lord and concerning redemption from Him; that they shall then possess truths, whereby the church shall be implanted with them, is signified by, they shall sow fields and plant vineyards; and that thence they shall possess the goods of the church, whence truths shall grow and increase, is signified by, they shall yield the fruit of the produce, and by Jehovah blessing them, that they multiply exceedingly; that in this case every good affection of the natural man shall remain with them, is signified by, he shall not diminish their beast; that those affections would otherwise have perished by evils, is signified by, they are diminished and bowed down through the vehemence of wickedness and sorrow. So again : "Praise Jehovah ye whales and all abysses, wild beast and every beast, reptile and every bird of wing" (Psalm cxlviii. 7, 10: in that Psalm, the things which shall praise Jehovah are enumerated by various things which are without life in the world, as fire, hail, snow, vapors, wind of storm, mountains, hills, trees, fruits, cedars, likewise, as in this case, by wild beasts, beasts, reptiles, and birds, which things themselves cannot praise Jehovah; who cannot see therefore, that to recount such things in the divine Word would be vain and superfluous, unless they were significative of such things in man as can praise, that is worship, Jehovah : from the science of correspondences it is known, that whales signify the scientifics of the natural man in general; abysses and seas, the natural principle itself, where scientifics are; wild beasts and beasts, the affections of the natural man, both of his understanding and of his will; reptiles, the sensual principle, which is the ultimate of the natural man; and birds of wing, the cogitative principle thence derived. Again : "Jehovah who prepareth rain for the earth, who causeth grass to grow upon the mountains, who giveth to the beast his food, to the sons of the raven which call upon Him " (Psalm cxlvii. 8, 9): the things here mentioned also signify spiritual things appertaining to heaven and the church : to what purpose would it be for the Word, which is given for the sole purpose of leading man in the way to heaven, by teaching him the truths of faith and goods of love, to say that Jehovah prepareth rain for the earth, causeth grass to grow upon the mountains, giveth to the beast his food, and to the sons of the raven which invoke Him? These things however are worthy of the divine Word, when by rain is understood the influx of divine truth, by mountains, the good of love, by causing grass to germinate, the instruction of the natural man by knowledges from the Word, by beasts, the affections of the natural man, which desire to be thence nourished, which nourishment is signified by giving them food, and when by the sons of the raven also are signified natural men who are in a dark lumen arising from fallacies concerning truth divine, as were men of the gentiles or nations, wherefore it is said, that He giveth food to the sons of the raven which call upon Him, for these can call upon Jehovah, but not the sons of the raven. Again: "Every wild beast of the forest is mine, the beasts in the mountains of thousands; I know every bird of the mountains, and the wild beasts of My fields are with Me" (Psalm l. 10, 11): these things are indeed said concerning sacrifices, and that the Lord doth not delight in them, but in confession of the heart and invocation, but still by the wild beast of the forest, the beast in the mountains, and by the bird of the mountains and wild beast of the fields, are signified similar things as above, viz. such as appertain to the man of the church. Again: "Thy justice is as the mountains of God, thy judgments are a great abyss; O Jehovah, thou preservest man and beast" (Psalm xxxvi. 7): by man and beast is signified the interior affection, which is spiritual, whence intelligence is derived, and the exterior affection, which is natural, whence comes science, corresponding to intelligence. Similar things are also signified by man and beast in the following passages: as in Jeremiah: "The God of Israel said, I have made the earth, man and beast, which are upon the faces of the earth, by my great power" (xxvii. 5; chap. xxxviii. 14): again in the same prophet: "Behold the days come, in which I will sow the house of Judah with the seed of man and with the seed of beast" (xxxi. 27): again: "As yet there shall be heard in this place, concerning which ye say, it is devastated, and there is no man nor beast, and in the cities of Judah, and in the streets of Jerusalem, that are devastated, so that there is no man, no inhabitant and no beast, the voice of joy and the voice of gladness" (xxxiii. 10, 11, 22): again: "The whole land shall be desolation that there shall not be man or beast" (xxxii. 43): "I will smite the inhabitants of this city, both man and beast; they shall die with a great pestilence" (xxi. 6): again: "A nation from the north shall come up against Babel, and shall bring her land into desolation, so that there shall be no inhabitant therein; from man even unto beast, they have moved themselves off, they have gone away" (l. 3): and again: "My anger and my wrath is poured out upon this place, upon man and upon beast" (vii. 20): and in Ezekiel: "When the land shall sin against Me, I will break its staff of bread, and I will send into it famine, and I will cut off from it man and beast" (xiv. 13, 17, 19): again: "I will stretch out my hand over Edom, and will cut off from it man and beast" (xxv. 13): so again: "I will destroy every beast of Egypt from over many waters, and the foot of man shall no more disturb them, neither shall the hoof of beast disturb them" (xxxii. 13): and again: "I will multiply upon you man and beast, that they shall grow and fructify" (xxxvi. 11): and in Zephaniah: "In consuming I will consume all things from upon the faces of the earth; I will consume man and beast, I will consume the bird of the heavens, and the fishes of the sea, and the stumbling blocks with the impious, and I will cut off man from the faces of the earth" (i. 2, 3): and in Zechariah: "The angel who came to measure Jerusalem said, Run, speak, saying, Jerusalem shall inhabit the suburbs, by reason of the multitude of man and of beasts in the midst thereof"

(ii. 7, 8) : again in the same prophet : "Let your hands strengthen themselves, for the temple shall be built; for before these days there was no price of man nor price of beast; for to him that went out and to him that entered, there was no peace from the enemy " (viii. 9, 10) : in these passages by man and beast is signified the interior or spiritual principle, and the exterior or natural principle ; consequently, by man, the spiritual affection of truth, from which is all intelligence, and by beast, the natural affection corresponding to the spiritual : the reason that the exterior or natural principle is signified by beast, is, because man, as to his external or natural man, is nothing but a beast; for he enjoys similar cupidities, and also pleasures, appetites, and senses, so that man as to such things is altogether like a beast, wherefore the natural man may be called the animal man ; but the reason that the internal or spiritual principle is signified by man, is, because man is man as to his internal or spiritual principle, enjoying the affections of good and truth such as appertain to the angels of heaven, and because man, by that principle in himself, rules his animal or natural man, which is a beast.   Forasmuch as the spiritual man and natural man is signified by man and beast, therefore in the history of creation, Gen. chap. i. it is related that in the same day, that is, the sixth, the beasts were created, and also man ; and afterwards, that to man was given dominion over the beasts : concerning the creation of beasts and of man in the same day, and concerning the dominion of man over the beasts, it is thus written : " God said, Let the earth produce the living soul, according to its species, and what moveth itself, and the wild beast of the earth according to its species, and it was so.   And God made the wild beast of the earth according to its species, and the beast according to its species, and everything that creepeth upon the ground according to its species.   And God said, Let us make man into our image, according to our likeness, and they shall rule over the fishes of the sea, and over the bird of the heavens and over the beast, and over all the earth, and over every creeping thing that creepeth upon the earth ; and the evening was and the morning was, the sixth day " (i. 24–31): by the creation of heaven and earth, in the spiritual sense of that chapter, is described the new creation or regeneration of the man of the most ancient church, whence by beast is there signified the external or natural man, and by man, the internal spiritual, and by his dominion over the beasts is understood the dominion of the spiritual man over the natural.   That it was granted to the man of that church to know all the affections of the natural man, in order that he might have dominion over them, is signified .by the words in Genesis: " Jehovah formed out of the ground every beast of the field, and every bird of the heavens, and brought unto the man, to see what he would call it; and whatsoever man called it, the living soul, that was its name; and man gave names to every beast, and to the bird of the heavens, and to every wild beast of the field " (ii. 19)ꞏ by calling the name is signified, in the spiritual sense, to know the quality of a thing, or of what quality it is, thus, in the present case, to know the qualities of all the affections, cupidities, pleasures, appetites, likewise thoughts and inclinations, of the natural man, and how they should agree and correspond with the affections and perceptions of the spiritual man: for from creation it was given to the spiritual man to see all things of the natural man, and at the same time to perceive the agreement or disagreement thereof with the spiritual, in order that the former might rule the latter, and admit such things as agree, and reject those which disagree, and thus become spiritual also as to effects, which are wrought by means of the natural man: but these things may be seen more fully explained in the A. C. n. 142–146. Inasmuch as by man, in the Word, is properly signified the internal or spiritual man, and by beast, the external or natural man, therefore it was commanded by God, that all the beasts and birds should be introduced with Noah in the ark: concerning which it is thus written in Genesis: "Jehovah said to Noah, Of every clean beast thou shalt take to thee sevens, sevens, male and female; and of the beast which is not clean, twos, male and female: and he took of the beast that was clean, and of the beast not clean, and of the bird, and of everything that creepeth upon the earth, twos, twos, entered unto Noah into the ark, male and female" (vii. 1–9): by Noah's flood, in the spiritual sense, is described the destruction of the most ancient church, and also the last judgment upon the men of that church; and by Noah and his sons, in the same sense, is understood and described the succeeding church, which is to be called the ancient church; hence it follows, that by the beasts introduced into the ark with Noah, are understood the affections of the natural man, corresponding to those of the spiritual, which appertained to the men of that church; but these things also may be seen explained in the A. C. Inasmuch as by man is signified the internal spiritual man, and by beast the external or natural, and by Egypt the natural man separate from the spiritual, which is then altogether destroyed, and is no longer man but beast, therefore where the destruction of Egypt is treated of, it is related, that "Jehovah caused it to rain hail, mingled with fire, and smote everything which was in the fields, from man even to beast" (Exod. ix. 22–25): concerning which also see the A. C.; by reason of the representation and consequent signification of the same thing, it is also written, that "Jehovah smote all the first born in the land of Egypt, from man even to beast" (Exod. xii. 12, 29). But on the other hand with the sons of Israel, by whom the church was represented, it was commanded, that "all the first born of man and of beast should be sacrificed to Jehovah" (Numb. xviii. 15). Because such things were represented and thence signified by man and beast, therefore, from a holy rite received in the ancient church, "The king of Ninevah proclaimed a fast, and commanded that neither man nor beast should taste or drink anything, and that man and beast should be covered with sackcloth" (Jonah iii. 7, 8). Inasmuch as by beasts are signified the affections in both senses, therefore it was prohibited to make the figure of any beast; concerning which it is thus written in Moses: "Ye shall not make to you the figure of any beast which is in the earth, the figure of any bird of wing which flieth under heaven, the figure of any reptile in the earth, the figure of any fish, which is in the waters under the earth" (Deut. iv. 17, 18): the reason was, because the posterity of Jacob, who, on account of the representation of the church being with them, were called the sons of Israel, were in externals without an internal principle, that is, were for the most part merely natural, wherefore if they had made to themselves the figure of any beast or bird, which signified affections and the like, they would have made to themselves idols, and have worshiped them: this also was the reason why the Egyptians, who were better acquainted with representatives than any other people, made to themselves figures of beasts, as of calves, serpents, and various other kinds, and this on account of their signification, for they were not intended for worship at the first; but their posterity, who from internal became external, consequently merely natural, looked upon those things not as representatives and significatives, but as things holy, appertaining to the church, and thence ascribed to them idolatrous worship; hence it was, that the posterity of Jacob, being altogether external men, were prohibited to make to themselves any figure of such things, for they were in heart idolatrous. Thus for example; the reason why they worshiped calves in Egypt, and afterwards in the wilderness, was, because a calf signifies the first affection of the natural man, together with its good of innocence : the gentiles also every where worshiped serpents, because the serpent signified the sensual principle which is the ultimate of the natural man, and the prudence thereof; and so in other cases. Whereas beasts signified the various things appertaining to the natural man, therefore it was also sometimes commanded, when certain cities, or regions, were given to the curse, that the beasts also should be slaughtered; which was by reason of their representing the evils and profane things which had place with the men who were given to the curse. It was also on account of the signification of beasts, as specifically denoting the various things existing with men of the church, that laws were prescribed concerning them, what kinds should be eaten and what should not be eaten (Levit. xi.): those which were to be eaten signifying goods, and those which were not to be eaten signifying evils; for the church of that time was a representative church, and therefore everything therein prescribed was representative and significative, especially beasts, concerning which it is thus written in Moses: " Ye shall distinguish between the clean beast and the unclean, and between the unclean bird and the clean, that ye may not make your souls abominable by beast and bird; and ye shall be holy to Me" (Levit. xx. 25, 26). From these considerations, it may now be seen whence it was that sacrifices of beasts of various kinds were permitted, as of lambs, sheep, kids, goats, heifers, oxen, also of turtle doves and pigeons, viz. because they signified things spiritual, and things natural from a spiritual origin; as lambs, innocence, sheep, charity, heifers and oxen, the affections of the natural man corresponding to those of the spiritual man ; hence it was that the beasts for the sacrifices were varied according to the causes for which they were offered, which would not have been done unless they had signified such things as appertain to the church. Whereas the man of the church at this day can scarcely be induced to believe that by beasts and wild beasts, in the Word, are signified the affections of good and truth which appertain to the man of the church, and this by reason of its appearing strange that anything appertaining to beasts should signify anything appertaining to man, therefore some more passages shall be adduced from the Word, by way of confirmation; thus in Ezekiel: "Say unto the king of Egypt, and unto his multitude, To whom art thou like in thy height? Behold Ashur is a cedar in Lebanon, fair in branch and shadowy forest; his height was exalted above all the trees of the field, and his branches were multiplied by many waters; all the birds of the heavens made their nests in his branches; and under his branches every wild beast of the field brought forth, and in his shade dwelt all great nations; he was fair in his greatness. But because thou art elated in the height, he shall be cut down; upon his ruin shall dwell every bird of the heavens, and upon his branches shall be every wild beast of the field" (xxxi. 2, 3, 5, 6, 10, 13): by the king of Egypt, and by his multitude, is signified the natural man with the scientifics therein; by Ashur, the cedar in Lebanon, is signified the rational principle, which is formed from scientifics on one part, and from the influx of spiritual truth on the other; by fair in branch and a shadowy forest, is signified intelligence by rational truths by means of scientifics; by the height above all the trees of the field, is signified elevation even to the interior rational, which is derived from the spiritual; by the branches being multiplied by many waters, is signified the abundance thereof by spiritual truths, which are derived from the knowledges of truth from the Word; by the birds of the heavens, which built their nests in his branches, are signified spiritual thoughts in things rational, for the rational principle is the medium between the internal spiritual man and the external natural; by the wild beast of the field which brought forth under his branches, are signified the affections of scientifics rationally perceived; by the great nations which dwelt in his shade, are signified the goods of the affections in the natural man; by being fair in his greatness, is signified intelligence; but by the bird of the heavens, and the wild beast of the field, of which it is afterwards said that they shall dwell upon his ruins, and in his branches, are signified falses of the thoughts, and evils of cupidities, arising from being elated in height, or proud in the love of self-derived intelligence: that thoughts of truth and the affections thereof are signified by the birds of heaven and the beasts of the field, is evident, for it is also said that great nations dwelt under the shade of the cedar. So in Daniel: "Behold a tree in the midst of the earth, and the height thereof was great; it reached even unto heaven, and its prospect was unto the end of the earth; the leaf thereof was fair, and the fruit thereof much, and in it was food for all; the beast of the field had a shade under it, and in its branches dwelt the birds of heaven; and all flesh was nourished from it. A watcher and holy one descended from heaven, crying aloud, hew down the tree and ut off its branches; shake off the leaf; disperse the flower thereof; et the beast get away from under it, and the birds from its branches; ut leave the stumps of the roots in the earth, and in a band of iron nd brass; in the herb of the field, and in the dew of the heavens, t it be dipped, and let his portion be with the beast in the grass of ie earth; they shall change his heart from man, and the heart of a east shall be given to him" (iv. 7-13). This was the dream of Ne-uchadnezzar, King of Babel, and thereby is described the establish-fent of the celestial church, and its increase to its full state, and fterwards the destruction thereof on account of domination over the oly things of the church, and on account of claiming to itself a right ver heaven: by the tree in the midst of the earth is signified that hurch; by the height thereof is signified the extension of percep-on and thence of wisdom; and by its prospect to the end of the arth, is signified the extension thereof even to the ultimates of the hurch; by the leaf thereof was fair, and the flower thereof much, re signified the knowledges and affections of truth and good, and itelligence thence derived; by food in it for all, is signified celes-al nourishment, which is from good and thence from truths; by the east of the field which had a shade under it, and the birds of the eavens which dwelt in its branches, are signified the affections of ood and thence the thoughts and perceptions of truth, which, inas-ouch as they are spiritual food, it is said that all flesh was nour-shed from it; but on account of domination originating in the love f self over the holy things of heaven and the church, over which he Babylonians at length claimed a right, the destruction thereof s afterwards described by these words: "a watcher and holy one lescended from heaven, crying aloud, Hew down the tree, and cut ff its branches; shake off the leaf; disperse the flower; let the beast ly from under it and the birds from its branches:" for with them the love of self, and elation of mind thence derived, increases even to the claiming a right over the holy things of the church, yea over heaven itself, and when this is the case, then everything belonging to the church perishes, as well as all perception and knowledge of truth and good; for the internal of the mind, where the spiritual principle resides, is shut, and the external, where the natural resides, has dominion, and thus man becomes sensual, until he differs but little from beasts; by the stump of the roots which should be left in the earth, is signified the Word, which is understood as to the letter only, and the knowledge thereof is as somewhat residing merely in the memory, and proceeding thence into the speech; by the bands of iron and brass is signified, that the interior truths and goods are kept close up and bound in ultimates, iron denoting truth in the ulti-mates, and brass denoting good in the ultimates, and these, sepa-rated from interior truths and goods, become falses and evils; and whereas the man of the church is then almost as a beast as to un-derstanding and as to will, in consequence of evils of the affections and falses of the thoughts having rule, it is said that his portion shall be with the beast in the grass of the earth, and his heart sh changed from man, and the heart of a beast shall be give

that this change and inversion took place on account of claiming a
right over the holy things of the church, and at length over heaven,
appears from verses 27, 28, 29, of that chapter, where are these
words : " The king said, Is not this great Babel, which I have built
for the house of the kingdom, by the strength of my fortitude and
for the glory of mine honor? Whilst the word was in the king's
mouth, there fell a voice from the heavens, saying, the kingdom
shall pass away from thee, and they shall expel thee from man, and
thy dwelling shall be with the beast of the field, they shall make
thee to taste the herb as oxen, until thou shalt know that the most
High ruleth in the kingdom of man, and giveth it to whomsoever
He will." That by Nebuchadnezzar, as king of Babel, in the beginning is signified the celestial church, and its advancement to a
full state of wisdom, appears also from Daniel, where, treating of
the statue seen by him in a dream, it is said, " The God of the heaven
hath given into thine hand the sons of man, the beast of the field,
and the bird of the heavens, and hath made thee ruler over all ;
thou art the head of the statue which is gold " (ii. 37, 38). By the
head of the statue which was of gold, is signified the celestial church,
which is the primary of all ; the reason why that church is signified
by the king of Babel in the beginning, is, because the church which,
afterwards became Babel or Babylon, commenced from the worship
of the Lord, and from love towards Him, and then there reigned
with them a zeal of extending and perfecting the church by the holy
goods and truths of heaven, but this from a cause as yet latent, viz.
the love of ruling, which however only broke out successively ; but
this subject will be further explained, when we come to treat of
Babylon. Again in Hosea : " I will establish for them a covenant
in that day with the wild beast of the field, and with the bird of the
heavens, and the reptile of the earth ; and the bow, and the sword,
and the war, will I break from the earth ; and I will make them to
lie down securely, and I will betroth thee to me for ever" (ii. 18, 19).
These things are said concerning the establishment of the new
church by the Lord, which is the subject there treated of ; that Jehovah, that is, the Lord, will not then establish a covenant with the
wild beast of the field, the bird of the heavens, and the reptile of the
earth, but with men in whom the church will be renewed, is evident ;
wherefore by those things are signified such things as are in man ,
viz. by the wild beast of the field, the affection of the knowledge
of truth, by the bird of the heavens, rational thought from a spiritual
ground, by the reptile of the earth, the scientific of the natural man,
specifically the sensual scientific ; by breaking the bow and the
sword from the earth, is signified the destruction of the falses that
fight against the truths of doctrine ; and that there shall be no longer
any dissension arising from combats between goods and evils, and
between truths and falses, is signified by, I will cause them to lie
down securely, and I will betroth thee to Me for ever. Again in
Isaiah : " The wild beast of the field shall honor Me, the dragons
and the daughters of the owl ; because I will give waters in the
wilderness, rivers in the desert, to give drink unto my people, mine

lect" (xliii. 20). That the wild beast of the field, dragons and laughters of the owl, are not here understood, is evident, for these cannot honor Jehovah; but that the men of the church are understood is manifest from its being said in what follows, to give drink to my people, mine elect: wherefore by the wild beast of the field are signified the affections of the knowledges of truth, by dragons, natural ideas, and by the daughters of the owl, sensual affections, or the sensual principle is affected with truths, and sees them in darkness, as owls see objects in the night; hence it is also evident, that the gentiles are hereby understood, with whom the new church was to be established, for before reformation they were in such obscure affection and natural thought; by giving waters in the wilderness, and rivers in the desert, is signified to imbue with truths, and hence with intelligence, those who were before in ignorance, waters denoting truths, rivers, intelligence, and wilderness and desert denoting ignorance; to give drink to the people of Jehovah and to His elect, signifies to instruct those who are in the truths of faith and in the good of charity; they are called people who are principled in the truths of faith, and they elect who are in the good of charity. So in Joel: "Is not the food cut off before our eyes from the house of our God, the gladness and the joy; the beast sigheth, the herds of the ox are perplexed, because there is no pasture for them; the flocks of cattle likewise are desolated; the beast of the field crieth unto thee, because the rivers of waters are dried up, and the fire hath devoured the dwellings of the wilderness" (i. 16, 18, 20). These things are said concerning the state of the church, when there are no longer any truths of doctrine or good of life therein: by the meat which is cut off from the house of God, is signified spiritual nourishment, which is from truths derived from good, the house of God denoting the church; the beast sigheth, the herds of the ox are perplexed, signifies a defect of the affections of truth and thence of knowledges in the natural man, and grief on that account, the herds of the ox denoting the things appertaining to the natural man in the whole complex; by there being no pasture for them, is signified, no instruction; the flocks of cattle are desolated, signifies the defect of spiritual truth and good which are of faith and charity; the beast of the field crieth unto thee, signifies the grief of those who are in natural affection, and thence in desire of the knowledges of truth and good; the rivers of waters are dried up, signifies the truths of doctrine dissipated by natural love; the fire hath devoured the dwellings of the wilderness, signifies that love, and the destruction thence of the knowledges of truth; the dwellings of the wilderness denote the things appertaining to the understanding and will of such persons, which otherwise would receive the truths and goods of the church. Again in the same prophet: "Fear, O earth, rejoice and be glad, that Jehovah doeth great things for thee; be not afraid, ye beasts of my fields, for the dwelling places of the wilderness are become herbous, for the tree shall bear its fruit, the fig tree and the vine shall yield their strength; sons of Zion, rejoice and be glad in Jehovah" (ii. 21, 22, 23). These things are said concerning the establishment of the church by the Lord; and by the earth which shall fear, rejoice, and be glad, is signified the church and its delight; the establishment thereof by the Lord, is signified by Jehovah's doing great things; hence by the beasts of His fields are signified those who are in the affections of good and desire instruction from the Word, beasts denoting those who are in the affections of good appertaining to the natural man, and fields denoting doctrinals from the Word; by the dwelling places of the wilderness becoming herbous, is signified that the knowledges of truth and good shall be with those with whom they were not before; the tree shall yield its fruit, signifies the production of the good of life by those knowledges, for a tree signifies a man of the church, specifically, the mind imbued with knowledges, and fruit, the good of life; the fig tree and the vine shall yield their strength, signifies the production of the effect from natural good and spiritual good together; inasmuch as by the beasts of the fields, the tree, the fig, and the vine, are signified such things as appertain to the man of the church, therefore it is said, sons of Zion rejoice and be glad in Jehovah; by the sons of Zion are understood those who are of the celestial church; to rejoice is predicated of the delight of good; and to be glad of the pleasantness of truth. So in Ezekiel: "In that day Gog shall come upon the land of Israel; and then shall be a great earthquake upon the land of Israel; and before me shall tremble the fishes of the sea, and the bird of the heavens, and the wild beast of the field, and every reptile creeping upon the earth, and every man upon the faces o the earth" (xxxviii. 18, 19, 20): by Gog is signified external sanctity without internal sanctity, thus those who are in such external sanctity; by the earthquake is signified a change of the state of the church; by the fishes of the sea trembling, and the bird of the heavens, the wild beast of the field, the reptile of the earth, and every man, is signified that all things of man, as to what appertains to the church with him, shall be changed; the fishes of the sea denote scientifics, the birds of the heavens denote thoughts thence derived, the wild beasts of the fields, the affections thence derived, the reptile of the earth, the thoughts and affections in the corporeal sensual principle, and man, all of them in the complex from first to last; if there was not such a signification, to what purpose would it be to say, that those things shall tremble before Jehovah? Again in Zechariah: "There shall be in that day a great tumult, Judah shall fight against Jerusalem, and so there shall be a plague of the horse, of the mule, of the camel, and of the ass, and of every beast which shall be in their camps: afterwards every one that remaineth shall go up to Jerusalem" (xiv. 13, 14, 15). Thus is described the last state of the old church, and the beginning of the new: the last state of the old church is described by the great tumult, when Judah shall fight against Jerusalem, by which is understood, the change which then takes place, and the fighting of the love of evil against the truths of the doctrine of the church; by the plague of the horse, of the mule, of the camel, of the ass, and of every beast, are signified such things as hurt and destroy the church, and the spiritual life of the men of the church; and by the horses, the mules, the camels, and the asses, are signified the things which appertain to their understanding and their will, consequently, which appertain to their knowledges and affections; the beast in particular signifies the affection of the natural man, and the plague of the beast, the hurting and destruction of that affection: what the rest signify hath been shown elsewhere, wherefore there is no occasion to repeat it in this place. Again in Jeremiah: "How long shall the earth mourn, and the herb of every field wither, on account of the wickedness of them that dwell therein? the beast and the bird are consumed" (xii. 4). By the earth is understood the church; by the herb of the field is signified the truth of the church sprung up and springing; by mourning and withering is signified to perish and be dissipated by concupiscences; by the beasts and birds which are consumed, are signified the affections of good and the thoughts of truth thence derived, which perish by reason of the evils in the church, wherefore it is said, on account of the wickedness of them that dwell in the earth. Again in Isaiah: "They shall be left together, the bird of the mountains, and the beast of the earth; but the bird shall abominate it, and every beast of the earth shall despise it" (xviii. 6). Speaking of the land shadowed with wings by which is understood the church, which, from the obscurity in which it is, catches at imaginary things for spiritual truths, and thence by reason of ignorance comes into the negation thereof: by birds and beasts are also there signified thoughts of truth and affections of good, as well rational as natural, which are said to abominate and despise it; that such abominating and contemning cannot be predicated of birds and beasts, is manifest, but of the affections of good and thoughts of truth, that is, of those that are in them. Again in Hosea: "They are all robbers, bloods touch bloods, and every one that dwelleth therein pineth away, to the wild beast of the field, and to the bird of the heavens, and even the fishes of the sea are collected together" (iv. 2, 3): here also by the wild beast of the field, and the bird of the heavens, and by the fishes of the sea, are signified similar things as above. Again in Ezekiel: "Thou son of man, say to every bird of every wing, and to every wild beast of the field, gather together and come, gather yourselves from around, upon my sacrifice which I sacrifice for you, a great sacrifice upon the mountains of Israel, that ye may eat flesh and drink blood: ye shall eat the flesh of the strong, and drink the blood of the princes of the earths; rams, lambs, and kids, and heifers, all fatlings of Bashan; ye shall eat fat unto satiety, and ye shall drink blood even unto drunkenness, of my sacrifice which I sacrifice for you; and ye shall be satiated upon my table with horse, and chariot, with the strong, and every man of war; so will I give my glory among the nations" (xxxix. 17, 18, 19, 20, 21): these things are said concerning the calling or convocation of the gentiles or nations to the church, and concerning the reception by them of the truth of doctrine in the good of love, which is the good of life, and of their intelligence thence in spiritual things; wherefore by the bird of every wing, and by every wild beast of the field, which shall be

gathered together from around to the great sacrifice upon the mountains of Israel, are understood all in whatever state they may be as
to the perception of truth and as to the affection of good : by the
bird of every wing, are understood all of whatsoever quality who
are in the perception of truth, and by every wild beast of the field,
all of whatsoever quality who are in the affection of good ; by gathering together from around, is signified from all sides without the
church ; by the great sacrifice is signified the worship of the Lord
from faith and love, for this was represented by the sacrifices in
general; and by the mountains of Israel are signified the goods of
spiritual love; by eating flesh and drinking blood, is signified, to
appropriate to themselves the good of love, and the truth of that
good; by eating the flesh of the strong and drinking the blood of
the princes of the earth, is signified that appropriation, the strong or
oxen denoting the affections of the natural man, and the princes of
the earth denoting the principal truths of the church; by rams,
lambs, kids, heifers, fatlings of Bashan, are signified all things appertaining to innocence, love, charity, and good, fatlings of Bashan
denoting the goods of the natural man from a spiritual origin ; hence
it is evident what is signified by eating flesh to satiety, and by drinking blood to drunkenness, viz. that they shall be filled with every
good of love and truth of faith; by being satiated upon the table
of the Lord with horse, and with chariot, with the strong, and
every man of war, is signified, to be instructed to the full from
the Word, by the horse being signified the understanding of truth,
by chariot, the doctrine of truth, by the strong and the man of
war, the truth of good combating against the falses of evil, and destroying it; inasmuch as these things are said concerning the calling
together of the nations or gentiles to the church of the Lord, it is
therefore added, so will I give my glory among the nations, glory
signifying divine truth in the light.   That such things are signified
by the bird of every wing and by the beast of the field, may further
appear from these words in Isaiah: " The saying of the Lord Jehovah, who gathereth together the outcasts of Israel: as yet I will
gather them to those that are gathered of Him : every wild beast of
My fields, come ye to eat, every wild beast in the forest " (lvi. 8, 9) :
by the outcasts of Israel, whom the Lord shall gather together, are
signified all in the church who are in truths from good and separated
from those therein who are in falses from evil ; the same are also understood by the wild beasts of the fields of the Lord Jehovah, for
fields signify the church as to the implantation of the truth of doctrine ; but the gentiles who are without the church are signified by
the wild beast in the forest, the forest denoting the natural and sensual man, and the wild beast his science, and obscure intelligence
thence derived : that such things are signified by the wild beast of
the field and the wild beast in the forest, is evident, for it is said,
come ye every wild beast of my fields, and every wild beast in the
forest, to eat, to eat denoting instruction and appropriation.   Inasmuch as most things in the Word have also an opposite sense, so
likewise have beasts and wild beasts, in which sense the former

signify evil affections, which are cupidities of adulterating and destroying the goods of the church, and the latter signify the cupidities of falsifying and thus of destroying the truths of the church : in this sense they are mentioned in the following passages; as in Ezekiel: " I will raise up over them one shepherd, who shall feed them, My servant David, he shall be to them for a shepherd: then I will make with them a covenant of peace, and I will cause the evil wild beast to cease out of the land, and they shall dwell confidently in the wilderness, and sleep in the forests : they shall be no more a prey to the nations, and the wild beast of the earth shall not devour them, but they shall dwell confidently, none making them afraid " (xxxiv. 23, 25, 28): these things are said concerning the advent of the Lord, and concerning the blessed state of heaven, and of those of the church who will come into the new heaven ; by the servant David, the shepherd whom Jehovah will raise up, is understood the Lord, who is called servant from serving and ministering, that is, accomplishing uses, as may be seen above, n. 409; by making with them a covenant of peace, is signified, conjunction with the Lord by divine things proceeding from Him, which are the goods of love and the truths of doctrine from the Word, thus by the Word ; by causing the evil wild beast to cease out of the land, is signified that evil cupidities and concupiscences shall no more invade and destroy them ; by dwelling confidently in the wilderness, and sleeping in the forests, is signified, that they shall be safe from the infestation of those things, although in them and amongst them, the wilderness and forests denoting where such things and such persons are : thus by these words the same things are signified as in Isaiah, chap. xi. 7, 8, 9 : inasmuch as the cupidities of evil and the false are what destroy the man of the church, therefore it is said, they shall no more be a prey to the nations, and the evil wild beast shall not devour them ; for by the nations are signified the cupidities of evil, and by the wild beasts of the earth, the cupidities of the false. So in Jeremiah : " Mine heritage is become as a lion in the forest, she uttered her voice against me, therefore I have hated her; as the bird Zabuah is mine heritage, about which are the birds; gather together every wild beast of the field, come ye to devour, many shepherds have destroyed my vineyard " (xii. 8, 9, 10): these things are said concerning the vastation of the church by the falses of evil : by heritage is signified the church; by the lion out of the forest, which uttereth his voice against God, is signified the false of evil in the whole complex; the bird Zabuah signifies reasonings from falses ; the wild beasts of the field, which shall be gathered together to devour, signify the cupidities of destroying the truth of the church by falses ; and because the church is understood which is so destroyed, therefore it is said, many shepherds have destroyed my vineyard, a vineyard denoting the spiritual church, or the church as to the affection of truth ; and whereas the vineyard signifies the church, it follows, that by the wild beast of the field is signified the cupidity of falsifying and thereby of destroying the truths of the church. Again in Isaiah : " There shall be no lion there, nor shall any

ravenous wild beast go up thereon, it shall not be found there"
(xxxv. 9): treating concerning the advent of the Lord, and His
kingdom in the heavens and in the earths; and by the lion and ravenous wild beast are signified the same things as above; that a
wild beast is not here understood must be evident to every one.
Again in Hosea : "I will meet them as a bear that is bereaved, and
I will rend the caul of their heart, and I will consume them as a
savage lion; the wild beast of the field shall tear them" (xiii. 8);
where also by the lion and the wild beast similar things are signified as above. Thus also in Zephaniah : "Jehovah shall stretch
out His hand over the north, and shall destroy Ashur, and shall
make Nineveh a waste, a dry place, as a wilderness; and the flocks
shall rest in the midst thereof, every wild beast of the nation; the
cormorant and the bittern shall lodge in the upper lintels thereof;
a voice shall sing in the window, a drought shall be in the threshold,
because the cedar thereof ·shall be stripped bare : such is the rejoicing city that dwelleth securely, saying in her heart, I and none
besides me : how is she become a waste, a place for the wild beasts
to lie down in, every one that passeth over her hisseth, and moveth
his hand" (ii. 13, 14) : thus is described the vastation of the church
by falses of doctrine originating in self derived intelligence : by the
north over which Jehovah will stretch out his hand, is signified the
church which is in falses; by Ashur which Jehovah shall destroy,
are signified reasonings from falses; by Ninevah which he shall
make a waste, a dry place as a wilderness, are signified falses of
doctrine : by flocks, the wild beast of the nation, the cormorant, and
the bittern, are signified affections of what is false, and falses themselves interior and exterior; by the upper lintels in which they shall
rest, are signified the knowledges of truth from the word falsified;
by the voice in the window is signified the preaching of what is false;
by a drought in the threshold, is signified the total desolation of
truth; by the cedar which is stripped bare, is signified the rational
principle destroyed; by the rejoicing city that dwelleth securely, is
signified the doctrine of what is false, with which they are delighted,
and in which they rest; saying in her heart, I and none besides me,
signifies the false of self-derived intelligence; by a place for the
wild beast to lie down in, is signified the state of the church vastated
as to truths; by every one that passeth over it shall hiss and move
his hand, is signified the contempt and rejection thereof by those
who are in the truths and goods of doctrine. Again in Moses : "I
will give peace in the earth, so that ye shall lie down securely, and
none shall make you afraid, and I will cause the evil wild beast to
cease out of the land, and the sword shall not pass through your
land" (Levit. xxvi. 6): by peace in the earth so that they shall lie
down securely and none make them afraid, is signified defence from
the irruption of the false in the church by virtue of confidence in the
Lord; by causing the evil wild beast to cease out of the land, is
signified immunity from the affection and cupidity of the false; and
by the sword which shall not pass through the land, is signified that
the false shall no more destroy the truth.   Again : "I will send the

hornet before thee, and it shall drive out the Hivite, the Canaanite, the Hittite before thee; I will not expel him from before thee in one year, lest the land be a desert, and the wild beast of the field multiply upon thee; by little and little will I expel him from before thee, until thou be fruitful, and inherit the earth " (Exod. xxiii. 28, 29, 30) : I will send the hornet before thee, signifies the dread of those who are in falses from evil; and it shall drive out the Hivite, the Canaanite, and the Hittite, signifies the flight of the falses which are from evils; I will not expel him from before thee in one year, signifies the flight or removal thereof not hasty; lest the land be desolate, signifies deficiency in such case and little of spiritual life; and the wild beast of the field be multiplied upon thee, signifies the afflux of falses from the delights of the love of self and of the world; by little and little I will expel him from before thee, signifies removal by degrees, according to order; until thou fructify, signifies according to the increase of good; and inherit the earth, signifies, and thus to be principled in good and regenerate; but these words may be seen further explained in the A. C. n. 9331-9338. Similar things are signified by these words in Moses : " Jehovah God shall expel the nations before thee by little and little, thou canst not expel them immediately, lest the wild beast of the field be multiplied against thee " (Deut. vii. 27) : by the nations expelled and to be expelled out of the land of Canaan by the sons of Israel, are signified evils and falses of every kind, by the land of Canaan, the church, and by the sons of Israel, the men of the church; wherefore by the wild beast of the field, which would be multiplied against them, are signified cupidities of the false from evil; for the man who is reformed and regenerated until the church appertain to him is reformed and regenerated by little and little; for he is conceived anew, born and educated; and this process is accomplished in proportion as the evils and falses thence derived, which are in him hereditarily and from birth, are removed, which is not effected in a moment, but through a great part of his life; hence it is evident what is signified in the spiritual sense by the nations not being expelled in one year, but by little and little, lest the wild beast of the field be multiplied against thee; for if evils and the falses thence derived were removed all at once, man would then have scarce any life, inasmuch as his life, into which he is born, is a life of evil, and thence of the false originating in cupidities, which are removed in proportion as goods and truths enter, for the former are removed by the latter. Whereas by wild beasts, in the opposite spiritual sense, are signified cupidities of the false from evil, and by birds the thoughts and reasonings from thence, and whereas the man of the church thereby spiritually perishes, therefore every where in the Word, where the vastation of the church is treated of, it is said, that they shall be given to the wild beasts and the birds to be devoured, as in the following passages : thus in David : "The boar in the wood trampleth upon it, and the wild beast of the fields eateth it down " (Psalm lxxx. 14): and in Hosea : " I will devastate her vine and her fig-tree, I will make them into a forest, and the wild beast of the field shall devour them"

(ii. 12): and in Ezekiel: " I will send upon you famine, and the
evil wild beast, and they shall bereave thee " (v. 17): speaking of
Jerusalem whereby is meant the church : again in the same prophet:
" I will give him to the wild beast to be devoured " (xxxiii. 27):
again : " The sheep are dispersed without a shepherd, and are for
food to every wild beast of the field " (xxxiv. 5, 8): again : " To
the wild beast of the earth, and to the bird of the heavens, have I
given thee for food " (xxix. 5): and again : " I will throw thee upon
the faces of the field, and I will make every bird of the heavens to
dwell upon thee, and I will satiate the wild beast of all the earth
from thee " (xxxii. 4): so in Jeremiah: " Their carcase shall be for
food to the bird of the heavens, and to the beast of the earth" (xvi. 4;
ch. xix. 7; ch. xxxiv. 5, 8): so in Ezekiel: " To the flying bird of
every wing, and to the wild beast of the field, have I given thee for
food " (xxxix. 4): and in David : " They have given the dead body
of thy servant to the bird of the heavens, the flesh of thy saints to
to the wild beast of the earth " (Psalm lxxix. 2): and in Jeremiah:
" I will visit upon them in four kinds; with the sword to kill, and
with dogs to tear, and with the birds of the heavens and the wild
beast of the earth to devour and to destroy " (xv. 3) : in these passages by wild beasts and birds are signified falses arising from the
cupidity of evil, and from reasoning ; and whereas by the nations in
the land of Canaan are signified the evils and falses of religion and
of worship, therefore the sons of Jacob did not bury the dead bodies
of the nations which they slew in war, but left them to be devoured
by the birds and wild beasts, which was not from the divine command, but from the innate cruelty of that people, thus from permis-
sion, in order that such things might be represented. Again in
David: " The enemy hath reproached Jehovah, and the foolish
people hath despised thy name ; give not the soul of thy turtle dove
to the beast: forget not the life of thy miserable ones forever "
(Psalm lxxiv. 18, 19): by the enemy which reproacheth Jehovah,
is signified hell and evil thence derived ; by the foolish people
which despiseth His Name, are signified falses, which are opposed
to the truths of doctrine, people denoting those who are in truths,
and, in the opposite sense, those who are in falses, who are the
foolish people, and the name of Jehovah signifying all truths of doctrine and of the church; give not the soul of thy turtle dove to the
beast, signifies, not to give spiritual good to those who are in the
cupidities of evil; by the life of thy miserable ones is signified the
spiritual life oppressed by evils and falses. So in Habakkuk: "The
violence of Lebanon hath covered thee, and the devastation of the
beasts hath dismayed them, by reason of the bloods of men, and the
violence of the earth, of the city, and of all that dwell therein " (ii.
17): by the violence of Lebanon is signified opposition made to the
truths perceived by the rational man from the Word, for Lebanon
signifes the church as to the perception of truth, from the rational
man; by the devastation of the beasts which dismayed them, is signified the destruction of verities by the cupidities of evil; by bloods
is signified the violence offered to the truths of the Word by evils;

and by the violence of the earth, of the city, and of all that dwell therein, is signified opposition made to the truths and goods of the Church and of its doctrine from the Word by falses. Again in Moses: " I will send amongst them the tooth of the beasts, with the poison of the reptiles of the earth " (Deut. xxii. 24): by the tooth of beasts is signified the sensual principle as to the cupidities of evil, for tooth corresponds to the ultimate of the life of man, which is the sensual principle; by the poison of the reptiles of the earth, are signified the falsities thence derived, which subtlely perverts truths by the fallacies of the sensual man. Again in Ezekiel : " When I entered and saw, behold every effigy of reptile and beast, abomination, and all the idols of the house of Israel, painted upon the wall round about " (viii. 10): by these and divers other things that were shown to the prophet, are signified the direful cupidities and falsities in which the Israelites were, by reason of their being altogether in externals without any internal principle, and they who were such turned all representatives into idolatry, whence arose the idolatries which existed both with them and the gentiles : and on this occasion by beasts and reptiles, of which images were made on account of their signifying affections of good and prudence, were represented the direful cupidities of evil and the false ; for so it comes to pass when the natural man separate from the spiritual, views holy things, and hence it is that they are called the idols of the house of Israel ; by the wall round about upon which they were seen painted, are signified the interiors every where in the natural man, for by the roof is signified the inmost principle, by the floor or pavement the ultimate, by the walls the interiors, and by the house the man himself, as to the things appertaining to his mind; the natural man is also interior and exterior, and the interior natural is where the filthy things of man reside, which the exterior doth not divulge, but counterfeits what is good, just and sincere. Inasmuch as wild beasts and beasts signified the goods of the understanding and the goods of the will, which are of the affections, and the ancients who were skilled in correspondences made representative and significative figures of them, which were not worshiped at first, but afterwards by their posterity, who from internal became merely external, hence wild beasts and beasts were made idols, and are so spoken of in the Word: as in Isaiah : " Bel bowed down, Nebo stooped, their idols are wild beasts and beasts " (xlvi. 1). In the prophecy of Isaiah, we read concerning " The beasts of the south " (ch. xxx. 6, and following verses), by which are signified the adulterations of good, and falsifications of truth, whence arise evils and falses of every kind with those of the church who are only in externals ; they are called the beasts of the south, because they are with those who have the Word, by virtue whereof they may be in the light of truth, which is the south. Again in Daniel: " I saw in vision when it was night, four beasts ascending out of the sea ; the first was as a lion, but had the wings of an eagle ; the second was like to a bear ; the third was a leopard, which had four wings, and the fourth was terrible and formidable " (vii. 3, 4, 5): by the beast out of the sea, is

there signified the love of dominion, to which the holy things of th
Word and the church are made subservient means; and by all fou
is signified the successive increase thereof, wherefore the last bea
is called formidable and terrible; but these things may be seen ex
plained in part, n. 316, 556. Things nearly similar are signified in
the Apocalypse by "the beast ascending out of the sea" (xiii. 1–
10): by "the beast ascending out of the earth" (xiii. 11–18): by
"the beast of the abyss" (xviii. 8): by "the scarlet beast" (xvii.
3): concerning which beasts a further account is given, ch. xix. 19,
20; ch. xx. 10; but what cupidities of evil and the false are signi
fied by each in particular, will be seen below, when we come to
treat of those beasts. From these considerations it may now ap
pear what is understood by these words in Mark: "The spirit im
pel ng Jesus caused Him to go into the wilderness forty days, and
He was with the beasts, and angels ministered unto Him" (i. 12,
13): by the Lord's being in the wilderness forty days, was represented the duration of all temptations, which the Lord underwent
and sustained above all in the universal globe of earths, and those
of the most cruel kind; for by forty days is signified an entire period
and duration of temptations, thus not that he was tempted then only,
but from childhood even to the last moment of his life in the world,
the last temptation being that in Gethsemane: for by temptations
the Lord subjugated all the hells, and also glorified His Humanity,
concerning which temptations see the D. of the N. J. n. 302; an
whereas temptations exist by evil spirits and genii who are fro
hell, thus by the hells, whence evils and falses and their cupiditie
and concupiscences arise, therefore by the beasts with which the
Lord was, are not understood beasts, but the hells and the evils
thence arising; and by the angels who ministered unto him, are not
understood angels, but divine truths, by which, from His own proper
power, He conquered and subjugated the hells; that by angels, in
the Word, are signified divine truths, may be seen above, n. 130,
200, 302, 593.

651. " And shall conquer them, and kill them "—That hereby is
signified the destruction thence of all the good and truth of the church,
appears from the signification of conquering and killing the two
witnesses, as denoting to destroy those things which are signified by
them, which are the good of love and charity, and the truth of doctrine and faith: that the affections of the natural man separate from
the affections of the spiritual man, which are evil cupidities of every
kind, arising from infernal loves, will destroy those things, is signified by the beast ascending out of the abyss: that it was predicted
that this would come to pass at the end of the church, when the last
judgment takes place, was said above: that to kill, in the Word,
signifies spiritually to kill, which is here to destroy the good of love
and truth of doctrine, may be seen above, n. 315.

652. " And their bodies [shall lie] upon the street of the great
city "—That hereby is signified the extinction of them from evils
and falses of doctrine, appears from the signification of bodies, as
denoting that the good of love and truth of doctrine, which are sig-

ied by the two witnesses, were extinguished; for to be killed sig-
ies to be extinguished, in this case spiritually, because with those
.o have altogether destroyed those things with themselves; it is in
e manner said concerning the Lord that He is slain and dead,
ereby is signified, that the Divine [principle] proceeding from
m, which is the divine good and divine truth, is rejected, for with
ıse who reject this Divine [principle] which proceeds from the Lord,
ı Lord is slain and dead, as may be seen above, n. 83: and from
ı signification of the street of the great city, as denoting the truth
ı good of doctrine, and, in the opposite sense, the false and evil of
ctrine; for by street is signified, in a good sense, truth leading,
ı, in the opposite sense, the false leading, concerning which we
ıll speak presently, and by city is signified doctrine, concerning
ıich see above, n. 223; it is said the great city, because great is
ıdicated of good, and in the opposite sense, of evil, as many or
ıch is predicated of truth, and, in the opposite sense, of the false,
ı above, n. 223: from these considerations it is now evident, that
the bodies of the two witnesses lying upon the street of the great
y, is signified the extinction of the good of love and of charity,
d of the truth of doctrine and of faith, by falses and -evils of doc-
ne; inasmuch as evils and falses of doctrine are signified, it is
erwards said of the great city, that it is spiritually called Sodom
d Egypt, and by Sodom are signified evils of the love, and by
ıypt, the falses thence derived, each appertaining to doctrine,
ıich destroy the church at its end, concerning which we shall
eak further in the following articles. The reason why street sig-
ıes the truth of doctrine, and, in the opposite sense, the false
ereof, is, because by way, in the spiritual sense of the Word, is
ınified truth leading to good, and, in the opposite sense, the false
ıding to evil, as may be seen, n. 97; and streets are ways in a
ıy: and inasmuch as city signifies doctrine, therefore by street is
ınified the truth and false of doctrine. In the spiritual world also
ere are cities, and streets in them as in the cities of the world, and
e quality of every one, as to the affection of truth and intelligence
ence derived, is there known from the places only where they
ıell, and also from the streets in which they walk: they who are
a clear perception of truth, dwell in the southern quarter of the
ıy, and also walk there; they who are in a clear affection of the
ıod of love, dwell in the eastern quarter, and also walk there;
ey who are in an obscure affection of the good of love, dwell in
e western quarter, and also walk there; and they who are in an
ıscure perception of truth, dwell in the northern quarter, and also
alk there: but it is contrariwise in the cities where they have
eir abode who are in the persuasion of the false from evil: from
ese considerations it may appear whence it is that street denotes
e truth or the false leading. That such things are signified by
reets may appear from the following passages: thus in Jeremiah:
Run ye through the streets of Jerusalem, and see, I pray, and know,
ıd seek in the broad places thereof, if ye can find a man that doeth
dgment, that seeketh verity; then will I pardon it" (v. 1). Inas-

much as by the streets in Jerusalem, and by the broad places thereof, are signified truths of doctrine, according to the states of affection and perception of those who are of the church, and by Jerusalem is signified the church as to doctrine, therefore it is said, run ye through the streets of Jerusalem, and see, and know, and seek in the broad places thereof; and inasmuch as judgment is predicated of truths, because all judgment is effected from laws and precepts, which are truths, and whereas by verity is signified the truth of doctrine and of faith, therefore it is said, if ye can find a man that doeth judgment and that seeketh verity: by the broad places are specifically signified the corners of the city, thus the quarters where they dwell, and whereas the habitations of all in the cities in the spiritual world are according to the clear and obscure affection of good and perception of truth, therefore by broad places are signified truths and goods according to every one's affection and perception. So in Isaiah: "Judgment is rejected backward, and justice standeth afar off; for verity stumbleth in the street, and rectitude cannot come" (ix. 14). By judgment and justice, in the Word, are signified truth and good; that these no longer exist, is signified by judgment being rejected backward and justice standing afar off; the wandering from the truths of doctrine, and there being thence no truth in the life, which is good of life, is signified by, verity stumbleth in the street, and rectitude cannot come, for all the good of life is procured by truths of doctrine, as man thereby learns how he ought to live; whereas street signifies where truth leads, therefore it is said, verity stumbleth in the street. And in Nahum: "The chariots raged in the streets, they ran to and fro in the broad places" (ii. 5). Inasmuch as by chariots are signified doctrinals of truth, and by streets and broad places, according to every one's affection and perception, as above, therefore it is said, the chariots raved in the streets, they ran to and fro in the broad places; to rave denotes to speak falses for truths, and by running to and fró is signified the wanderings of error. And in Judges: "In the days of Jael, the ways ceased, they that go in the paths, went crooked ways, they ceased, the broad ways in Israel ceased" (v. 6, 7). These words are in the song of Deborah and Barak, in which the desolation of truth in the church is treated of, and afterwards the restitution thereof; the desolation is described by the ways ceased, they that go in the paths went crooked ways, they ceased, the broad ways in Israel ceased; by ways and paths are signified the same as by streets and broad ways, viz. the truths of doctrine leading, and by going crooked ways, is signified wandering from truths. Again in Isaiah: "The city of emptiness shall be broke, every house shall be shut that no one may enter; there shall be a cry for wine in the streets, all joy shall be mingled together, the gladness of the earth shall be banished" (xxiv. 10, 11). By the city of emptiness, is signified the doctrine in which there is no truth, but the false; by house is signified good of the will, and thence of the life; hence it is evident what is signified by the city of emptiness shall be broken, every house shall be shut that no one may enter; by a cry for wine in the streets, is signified lamentation on account of the defect and commixtion of truth with the false, wine signifying the truth of the church from the Word, therefore it is said, in the streets, because street, also signifies truth, and whence it is sought: joy and gladness, are mentioned, because joy is predicated of the delight originating in the affection of good, and gladness of the delight originating in the affection of truth; the cessation of those delights is signified by, all joy shall be mingled together, gladness shall be banished from the earth, the earth denoting the church.   Again in Jeremiah: "How is the city of glory left, the city of my joy; wherefore the young men shall fall in the streets, and all the men of war shall be cut off" (xlix. 25, 26; chap. l. 30). by the city of glory is signified the doctrine of divine truth, and by the city of joy is signified the delight derived from the affection of good and truth therein; by the young men are signified those that are made intelligent by truths, and that the intelligence of truth would perish, is signified by, the young men shall fall in the streets; by the men of war are signified truths combating against falses, and that the defence of truth against falses would become none, is signified by, all the men of war shall be cut off.   Again in Ezekiel: "Ye have multiplied your slain in this city, so that you have filled the streets thereof with the slain" (xi. 6).   By the slain, in the Word, are understood those who perish by falses, for the sword with which they are slain, signifies the false destroying truth; by the city is signified here, as above, the doctrine of truth, whence it may be evident, what is signified by the slain in the city; by filling the streets with the slain, is signified the devastation of truth by falses. So in Lamentations: "They that did eat delicacies are devastated in the streets; and they that were educated upon purple have embraced dunghills.   The form of the Nazarites is obscured by blackness, they are not known in the streets.   They have wandered blind in the streets, they are polluted with blood.   They have hunted our steps so that we cannot go in the streets" (iv. 5, 8, 14, 18).   By streets here also are signified truths of doctrine leading to the good of life, or truths whereby the life is to be formed: the subject there treated of is concerning the church where the Word is, and the devastation thereof as to truths; wherefore by, they who did eat delicacies are devastated in the streets, is signified, that they who imbibed genuine truths from the Word have no longer any truths, delicacies denoting genuine truths from the Word; by, they who were educated upon purple have embraced dunghills, is signified, that they who imbibed genuine goods from the Word have nothing but falses of evil, purple denoting the genuine good of the Word, specifically, the celestial love of truth, and dunghills denoting the falses of evil; by, the form of the Nazarites is obscured by blackness, they are not known in the streets, is signified, that divine truth is in such obscurity that it does not appear to any one; for by the Nazarites was represented the Lord as to divine truth, whence they also signify divine truth from the Lord; by, they wandered blind in the streets, they are polluted with blood, is signified, that the

truths of the Word are no more seen, because they are falsified, the
blind denoting those who do not see truths; by, they have hunted
our steps, so that we cannot go in the streets, is signified seduction,
so that it is not known how to live, to hunt the steps denoting to
seduce by falses, and to go, denoting to live, whence to go in the
streets, denotes to live according to truths. So in Zephaniah : " I
will cut off the nations; their corners shall be devastated ; I will
desolate their streets, that none shall pass through ; their cities shall
be devastated, that there shall be no man, and no inhabitant" (iii. 6).
By the nations which shall be cut off are signified the goods of the
church ; by the corners which shall be devastated, are signified the
truths and goods thereof in the whole complex ; that such things are
signified by corners, may be seen above, n. 417; by the streets
which shall be desolated, that no one shall pass through, are signified the truths of doctrine ; for by the cities which shall be devastated, that there shall be no man and no inhabitant, are signified doctrinals, and by man and inhabitants, in the spiritual sense of the
Word, are understood all who are in truths and goods, thus, abstractedly, truths and goods themselves. Again in Zechariah : " I
will return to Zion, and I will dwell in the midst of Jerusalem,
whence Jerusalem shall be called the city of verity ; as yet males
and old women shall dwell in the steets of Jerusalem, and the streets
shall be filled with boys and girls, playing in the streets thereof"
(viii. 3, 4, 5). These things are said concerning the advent of the
Lord, and concerning the New Church to be established by Him ;
by Zion is understood the church as to the good of love, and by Jerusalem the church as to the truths of doctrine, wherefore Jerusalem
is called the city of verity ; by the males and old women, who shall
dwell in the streets of Jerusalem, are understood those that are
intelligent and wise by truths of doctrine ; by the boys and girls
playing in the streets, with whom the streets of the city shall be
filled, are signified the affections of truth and good and their delights, with which they shall abound who live in truths of doctrine.
Again in Jeremiah : " According to the number of thy cities have
been thy gods, O Judah ; and according to the number of the streets
of Jerusalem thou hast set altars for a shame, altars to burn incense
to Baal " (xi. 13). According to the number of thy cities were thy
gods, O Judah, signifies, that there were as many falses as doctrinals, cities denoting doctrinals, and gods the falses of religion; according to the number of the streets of Jerusalem thou hast set altars
for a shame, signifies as many kinds of worship as falses of doctrine,
streets denoting falses of doctrine, and altars denoting worship ; the
reason why worship from falses is here understood, is, because by
altars are understood the altars of incense, for it is said, altars to
burn incense to Baal, and incense signifies spiritual good, which, in
its essence, is truth from good, and in the opposite sense it signifies
the false from evil ; concerning this signification of incense, and the
altars of incense, see above, n. 324, 491, 492, 567. Again in the
same prophet : " Seest thou not what they do in the cities of Judah
and in the streets of Jerusalem? the sons gather wood, and the

Fathers kindle the fire; the women knead the dough to make cakes to Melecheth of the heavens, and to pour out drink offerings to other gods; I will cause to cease in the cities of Judah and in the streets of Jerusalem the voice of joy and the voice of gladness" (vii. 17, 18, 34). What these words signify in the spiritual sense may be seen fully explained above, n. 555; and that the cities of Judah denote the doctrinals of the church, and the streets of Jerusalem the truths of doctrine. Again: "Ye have not forgotten the evils which they did in the land of Judah and in the streets of Jerusalem"(xliv. 9). By the land of Judah is signified the church as to good, but in this case, as to evil; and by the streets of Jerusalem are signified the truths of doctrine, but in this case, the falses of doctrine. Again in Ezekiel: "By the hoofs of his horses shall Nebuchadnezzar king of Babel tread down all thy streets; he shall slay thy people with the sword, and he shall bring down the statues of strength to the earth; they shall make spoil of thy wealth" (xxvi. 11, 12). By Nebuchadnezzar king of Babel is signified the profanation of truth and consequent destruction thereof; by treading down all the streets with the hoofs of his horses, is signified the destruction of all the truths of the church by the fallacies of the sensual man; by slaying the people with the sword, is signified to destroy truths by falses; that thus all worship derived from truths would also be destroyed, is signified by bringing down to the earth the statues of strength, for statues signify holy worship from truths, and because all power appertains to truth from good, they are called statues of strength; that the knowledges of truth also would be destroyed, is signified by, they shall make spoil of thy wealth; that wealth and riches denote knowledges of truth, may be seen above, n. 236. Again in the same Prophet: "Thou hast built thee a lofty place, and thou hast made thee a high place in every street; upon every head of the way thou hast made thee a lofty place, and thou hast made thy beauty abominable" (xvi. 24, 25, 31). By high and lofty places with the ancients, was signified heaven, whence came the rite of sacrificing upon high mountains, and instead thereof upon places built up high, wherefore worship from evils and falses of doctrine is signified by making a lofty and high place in every street, and upon every head of the way; and whereas that worship was made idolatrous, therefore it is said that they made their beauty abominable; by beauty is understood truth and intelligence thence derived, for every one in the spiritual world is beautiful according to truths from good, and intelligence thence derived. So in Amos: "In all the streets shall be wailing, and in all the broad ways they shall say, Alas, alas; and they shall call the husbandman to the mourning" (v. 16). In all the streets mourning, and in all the broad ways they shall say, alas, alas, signifies grief on account of truth and good being every where devastated; and they shall call the husbandman to the mourning, signifies the grief of the men of the church on account thereof; the husbandman signifies the man of the church, because field signifies the church as to the implantation of truth. Again in David: "Our garners are full affording from

meat to meat, our flocks are thousands and ten thousands in our
streets; our oxen are burdened, no breach, nor flying away, nor
clamor in our streets" (Psalm cxliv. 13, 14).   By the garners full
of food, are signified doctrinals from the Word, thus the Word itself,
wherein are all the truths of doctrine from which is instruction and
spiritual nourishment; by the flocks being thousands and ten thousands in the streets, are signified goods and truths spiritual, by thousands of flocks, goods, and by ten thousands, truths; by oxen burdened, are signified natural goods and their affections; by no breach,
is signified their coherence; by none flying away, is signified no
loss of any; by no clamor in the streets, is signified no lamentation
any where over the want of them.   So in Job: "God who giveth
the rain upon the faces of the earth, and who sendeth the waters
upon the faces of the streets" (v. 10).   To give rain upon the faces
of the earth, signifies the influx of divine truth into all things with
those who are of the church; and to send waters upon the faces of
the streets, signifies the divine influx into truths of doctrine, to render man thereby spiritual.   Again in Isaiah: "In her streets they
have girded on sackcloth, upon the house-tops and in the streets
every one shall howl, coming down to weeping" (xv. 3).   Speaking of the city Ar in the land of Moab, whereby is signified the doctrine of those who are in truths from the natural man; grief over the
falses of their doctrine, from the first to the last, is signified by girding on sackcloth, and by howling in the streets and upon the house-
tops, house-tops denoting things interior, and street, things exterior
with them.   So again in Jeremiah: "Upon all the house tops of
Moab, and in the streets thereof, a whole mourning" (xlviii. 38).
Similar things are here signified as above.   Thus also in Daniel:
"Know thou and perceive from the going forth of the Word, unto
the restoring and building Jerusalem, unto Messiah the Prince; after
sixty and two weeks, the street and ditch shall be restored and built,
but in straitness of times" (ix. 25).   He who does not know the
spiritual sense of the Word, may suppose that by Jerusalem is here
signified Jerusalem, and that this is to be restored and built; also
that by the street and ditch, of which it is likewise said that it shall
be restored and built, is understood the street and ditch of that city;
but by Jerusalem is understood the church which will be established
by the Lord, and by the street and ditch is understood the truth of
doctrine, by street, truth, and by ditch, doctrine; what is signified
by the number of weeks, is not to be explained in this place.   From
these considerations it is now evident that the like is signified by
the street of the New Jerusalem in the following passages in the
Apocalypse: "The twelve gates were twelve pearls, and the street
of the city pure gold, as it were pelucid glass" (Apoc. xxi. 21;
and afterwards).   "He showed me a pure river of water of life,
bright as chrystal, going forth from the throne of God and the Lamb;
in the midst of the street thereof and of the river, on either side, was
the tree of life, making twelve fruits" (xxii. 1, 2): but these passages will be explained hereafter.   Again in Isaiah: "Thy sons have
fainted, they have lain in the head of all the streets, as a wild bull

in a net " (li. 20).   Speaking also of Jerusalem, that is, of the church vastated as to doctrine : by sons are meant those who are in truths of doctrine ; to faint and to lie in the head of all the streets, signifies to be deprived of all truth, the head or beginning of the streets denoting the entrance to truth, consequently all truth. Again in Lamentations : " The infant and suckling fainteth in the streets of the city; lift up to the Lord thy hands over the souls of thine infants, who have fainted through hunger in the head of all the streets " (ii. 11, 19). By the infant and the suckling is signified innocence, and also the goods and truths which are first born and vivified by knowledges from the Word with the men who are regenerating, and which, being the first, are also guiltless and harmless; the plenary defect of them is signified by fainting in the streets of the city, and in the head of all the streets; it is said through hunger or famine, because hunger or famine signifies deprivation, defect, ignorance, and at the same time the desire of knowledges; see above, n. 386. So in Nahum : " Her infants are dashed at the head of all streets, and over her honored men they cast lots, and all her great men are bound in chains " (iii. 10). By infants here also are understood the truths which are first born and vivified ; and by being dashed at the head of all streets, is signified to be dispersed and perish ; by the honored are signified the goods of love; by casting lots over them is signified the dissipation thereof; by the great men or nobles are signified the truths of good; and by being bound in chains is signified to be tied by falses, so that truth cannot come forth ; these things are said concerning the city of bloods, by which is signified doctrine in which the truths of the Word are falsified. Again in Jeremiah : " Death cometh up through our windows, it is come into our palaces, to cut off the infant from the street, the young men from the broad ways " (ix. 21): by death is here understood spiritual death which takes place when the false is believed to be the truth, and the truth the false, and the life is according to such belief; by windows are signified thoughts from the understanding ; by palaces, the more interior and thence more sublime things of the human mind; hence it is evident, what is signified by death ascending through the windows and coming into the palaces; by infants are signified here, as above, the truths which are first born by knowledges from the Word; by the young men are signified truths that are acquired, whence comes intelligence ; and by streets and broad ways are signified the truths of doctrine and truths of life, which lead to intelligence and wisdom; hence it is evident, what is signified by cutting off the infant from the street, the young men from the broad ways. Again in the same prophet; " I am full of the anger of Jehovah, I am wearied with holding in; pour out upon the infant in the street, and upon the assembly of young men; for also the man with the woman shall be taken, the old man with the full of days " (vi. 11). Where by the infant in the street and the young men are signified similar things as above ; by man and woman is signified truth conjoined to good and intelligence thence derived; and by the old man and full of days is signified wisdom. Inasmuch as street signifies the truth of doctrine leading, and, in the opposite sense, the false, therefore by the mud of the streets, the mire, and the dung, is signified the false originating in the love of evil; as in the following passages: thus in Isaiah: "Their carcase is become the dung of the streets" (v. 25). Again: "He shall make him a treading down as the mud of the streets" (x. 6). And in Micah: "He shall be for a treading down as the mire of the streets" (vii. 10). And in David: "I will bruise them small as the dust before the faces of the wind, as the mire of the streets I will beat them small" (Psalm xviii. 43). These things are also said from appearances in the spiritual world, for in the cities in that world where falses from evil reign, the streets appear full of dung, mire, and mud. Hence it may also appear what is signified by, "The Lord commanding the seventy, whom He sent to preach the Gospel, into whatever city ye enter, and they receive you not, go out in the streets thereof, and say, Even the dust of your city, that cleaveth unto us, do we shake off from us" (Luke x. 8, 9, 10). Because the streets of a city signify the truth of doctrine, according to which man should live, therefore it was customary to teach and to pray in the streets; as in the 2d book of Samuel: "Announce it not in Gath, evangelize it not in the streets of Askalon, lest peradventure the daughters of the Philistines rejoice" (i. 20). Hence also the Lord saith in Matthew: "When thou doest thine alms, do not sound a trumpet before thee, as the hypocrites do, in the synagogues and in the streets, that they may have glory of men: and if thou pray thou shalt not be as the hypocrites, for they love to pray standing in the synagogues, and in the corner of the streets, where they may be seen of men" (vi. 3, 5). And in Luke: "Then shall ye begin to say we have eaten and drunk in thy presence, and thou hast taught in our streets, but I shall say unto you, I know you not whence ye are" (xiii. 26, 27). From the signification of street, as denoting the truth of doctrine, it is also evident why the Lord said in the parable that "The householder commanded his servents, that they should go quickly into the streets and broad ways of the city, and bring in the poor, the maimed, the lame, and the blind" (Luke xiv. 21). Where by the poor, the maimed, the lame, and the blind, are not understood such in a natural sense, but in a spiritual sense, namely, such as had not the Word, and were therefore in ignorance of truth, and in want of good, but still desired truths in order to the attainment of good; such were the gentiles with whom the church of the Lord was afterwards established. Inasmuch as the street of a city signified either the truth or the false teaching and leading, therefore "the angels who came to Sodom, said that they would tarry all night in the street" (Gen. xix. 2). Hence also it was commanded, that "if the sons of Israel observed in any city that they served other gods, they should smite the inhabitants thereof with the sword, utterly destroying the city, and that they should bring all the spoil thereof into the midst of the street, and burn the city and all the spoil thereof with fire" (Deut. xiii. 14, 16, 17). By other gods are signified the falses of worship; by the sword, the destruction of the false by truths; by the spoil, the falsification of truth; and by fire, the punishment of the love of evil and its destruction. From the passages that have been adduced from the Word, it may now appear what is signified by the bodies of the two witnesses being cast upon the street of the great city, which is spiritually called Sodom and Egypt, and afterwards by their not being permitted to be laid in the tombs; for it was a custom with the Jewish and Israelitish nation to cast out the slain that were enemies into the ways and streets, and not to bury them, as a sign of their hatred; but still thereby was represented, that they were infernal evils and falses, which could not be raised again to life, that is, they who were in such evils and falses: this is also evident in Jeremiah: "The prophets prophesy, saying, There shall not be sword or famine in this land; by the sword and famine shall these prophets be consumed, and the people to whom they prophesy shall be cast out into the streets of Jerusalem, and there shall be none to bury them" (xiv. 15, 16). By a prophet is understood the doctrine of truth, but here the doctrine of the false, because they prophesied falses; and whereas streets signify where falses are, therefore it is said that they shall be cast into the streets of Jerusalem.

653. "Which is spiritually called Sodom and Egypt"—That hereby is signified by the evils of the love of self, and by falses thence derived, appears from the signification of Sodom, as denoting the love of self and thence evils of every kind, of which we shall speak presently; and from the signification of Egypt, as denoting the natural man separate from the spiritual, and thence the false of evil of every kind, concerning which also we shall speak presently; that by Sodom and Egypt is understood Jerusalem, consequently the church in which the goods of love are adulterated and the truths of doctrine falsified, is evident, for it is presently said, where also our Lord was crucified; for the evils of the love of self, and falses of doctrine, are what crucify the Lord, wherefore He was crucified by the Jews, because they were in those evils and falses; but of this also more hereafter. Here it shall first be shown that by Sodom, in the Word, is signified the love of self, and thence all evil, inasmuch as evils of every kind flow from the love of self; for he who loves himself only, loves his own proprium, and thence immerses all things of his will and understanding in his proprium, so that he cannot be elevated from it to heaven and to the Lord; hence it is, that he sees nothing from the light of heaven, but solely from the light of the world, which light, separate from the light of heaven, is mere darkness with respect to spiritual things appertaining to heaven and the church; "wherefore also the more man loves himself, the more he despises things spiritual, yea, denies them: hence also the internal spiritual mind, by which man is in the light of heaven, is shut, whence he becomes merely natural, and the mere natural man favors evils of every kind: for the evils into which man is born reside in the natural man, and are only removed from him in proportion as his interior mind, which receives the light of heaven, is opened; man's proprium also resides in the natural man, and this

is nothing but evil. That Sodom therefore signifies the love of self,
and thence evils of every kind, may appear from the passages in the
Word where Sodom is mentioned; thus in Ezekiel: "Thy elder
sister is Samaria, she and her daughters, dwelling at thy left hand;
but thy younger sister, dwelling at thy right hand, is Sodom and
her daughters; thou hast corrupted thyself more than they, in all
thy ways: Sodom thy sister hath not done, she and her daughters,
as thou hast done and thy daughters: behold this was the iniquity
of Sodom, pride, fulness of bread, and tranquility of rest, was to her
and her daughters, and she strengthened not the hand of the miserable and needy; whence they became elated, and committed abomination before me" (xvi. 46–50). The subject there treated of is
concerning the abominations of Jerusalem, which were principally
their adulterating the goods and truths of the Word and of the
church; by Samaria, where the Israelites were, is signified the spiritual church, in which spiritual good, which is the good of neighborly love or charity, is the essential; but by Jerusalem, where the
Jews were, is signified the celestial church, in which celestial good,
which is the good of love to the Lord, is the essential; for there are
two kingdoms, into which heaven and thence the church is distinguished, the spiritual kingdom and the celestial kingdom; concerning which see the work concerning H. & H. n. 20–28: these kingdoms were represented by the Israelites, whose metropolis was Samaria, and by the Jews, whose metropolis was Jerusulem: to spiritual good, which is the good of charity, is opposed infernal evil,
which is the evil of the love of the world, and to celestial good is
opposed diabolical evil, which is the evil of the love of self; from
the love of self flow evils of all kinds, and much worse than from
the love of the world, as may be seen in the N. J. n. 65–83; hence
it is, that more direful and abominable things are related of Jerusalem than of Samaria, and hence Jerusalem is not only called Sodom,
but it is also said that she did worse things than Sodom; as in these
words, Sodom hath not done as thou hast done, and thy daughters;
that the evil of the love of self was the evil of Sodom, is thus described: "this was the iniquity of Sodom, pride, fulness of bread,
tranquility of rest, and she strengthened not the hand of the miserable and needy:" by pride is understood the love of self; by fulness or satiety of bread is understood contempt of all good and truth
appertaining to heaven and the church, so as even to nauseate them;
by tranquility of rest is understood security and no anxiety on account of evil; and by not strengthening the hands of the miserable
and needy, is signified unmercifulness; whereas the love of self was
the love of Sodom, it is therefore said, that her daughters became
elated, and committed abomination before Jehovah; and by the
daughters that became elated, are signified the cupidities of that
love, and by the abomination before Jehovah, is signified every evil
against the Divine [principle] itself. Forasmuch as by the Chaldeans is signified the profanation and adulteration of the truth of
doctrine derived from the Word, and by the inhabitants of Babel the
profanation and adulteration of the good of love, therefore their over-

throw is also compared to the overthrow of Sodom and Gomorrah ; as in Jeremiah : " A sword against the Chaldeans, and against the inhabitants of Babel, according to the overthrow of God, Sodom and Gomorrah, and the vicinities thereof; not a man shall dwell there, nor shall the son of man tarry therein" (l. 37, 40); and in Isaiah : " So shall Babel be, the ornament of the kingdoms, the glory of the magnificence of the Chaldeans, as the overthrow of God, Sodom and Gomorrah" (xiii. 19). By Sodom is signified the evil of the love of self, and by Gomorrah the false of that love ; and whereas the love of self does not acknowledge any truth of the church, it is said, not a man shall dwell there, nor shall the son of man tarry therein, by man [vir] is signified intelligence, and, by son of man [filius hominis], the truth of the church. Inasmuch as by Edom is signified the natural man who is in falses from the love of self, and thence adulterates the goods of the church, therefore also the vastation thereof is compared to the overthrow of Sodom and Gomorrah; thus in Jeremiah : " Edom shall be a desolation as the overthrow of Sodom and Gomorrah, not a man shall dwell there, neither shall the son of man abide there" (xlix. 17); and in Zephaniah : " Moab shall be as Sodom, and the sons of Ammon as Gomorrah, a place abandoned to nettles, and a pit of salt, a waste for ever" (ii. 9). By Moab, as was said, is understood the natural man, who from the love of self adulterates the goods of the church, and by the sons of Ammon are signified those who falsify the truths thereof; and inasmuch as thence comes the devastation of all good and truth, therefore it is said, that it shall be a place abandoned to nettles, a pit of salt, a waste for ever ; the devastation of all good is signified by a place of nettles, and the devastation of all truth by a pit of salt; similar things are signified by Sodom and Gomorrah. Inasmuch as by Judah is signified celestial love, which is love to the Lord, from which comes all good, and, in the opposite sense, diabolical love, which is the love of self, from which comes all evil, therefore the devastation of the church which is signified by Judah and Jerusalem, is also compared to the overthrow of Sodom and Gomorrah ; as in Isaiah :- " Jerusalem hath stumbled, and Judah hath fallen ; the obduracy of their faces, witnesses against them, and their sin is as Sodom" (iii. 8, 9); again : " Hear the Word of Jehovah, ye princes of Sodom, hearken to the law of our God, ye people of Gomorrah" (i. 10). By the Word of Jehovah is understood the divine good, and by the law of God is understood the divine truth, for where good is treated of, the name Jehovah is used, but where truth is treated of, the name God is used ; and whereas the divine good to those who are in the love of self, is evil, it is said, their sin is as of Sodom, likewise hear the Word of Jehovah, ye princes of Sodom ; and whereas, the divine truth, to those who are in the false of the love of self, is false, it is said, hearken to the law of our God, ye people of Gomorrah. Again, in Moses : " Their vine is of the vine of Sodom, and the grapes thereof are of the fields of Gomorrah, grapes of gall, clusters of bitternesses" (Deut. xxxii. 32); treating of the dire falses with the posterity of Jacob, flowing from the evils of the love of self; but these words are particularly explained above, n. 519. So in Lamentations: "They that did eat delicacies are devastated in the streets, they that were educated upon purple have embraced dunghills; the iniquity of my people is become greater than the sin of Sodom, which is overturned as it were in a moment" (iv. 6). These things are said concerning those who are of the celestial kingdom and church of the Lord when changed into the contrary, for celestial love is what is turned into the love of self, which is diabolical love; what is signified by eating dainties, being educated upon purple, devastated in the streets, and embracing dunghills, was explained in the article above, n. 652; the reason why it is said of their iniquity, that it was greater than the sin of Sodom, was, because they had the Word, from which they could know the goods and truths of heaven and the church, or of doctrine and life, and had adulterated them, which the inhabitants of Sodom could not do; for he who knows the will of the Lord, and does it not, sins more than he who does not know it; all those also, with whom the love of self has rule, despise the holy things of heaven and the church, and deny the divine [principle] of the Lord; and to confirm the evils flowing from that love, they either adulterate the Word, or reject it as a writing not holy from any other reason than as being so received; hence it is, that they who do these things from the love of self are compared to Sodom and Gomorrah. That they who are instructed by the Lord concerning the truths and goods of the church, and yet reject and deny them, do worse than those of Sodom, appears from the words of the Lord concerning Capernaum, in Matthew: "Thou Capernaum, which art exalted even to heaven, shalt yet be pressed down to hell, for if the virtues had been done in Sodom which are done in thee, they would have remained even to this day; I say unto thee, that it shall be more tolerable for the land of Sodom, in the day of judgment, than for thee" (xi. 23, 24); for the Lord after He left Nazareth dwelt in Capernaum, see Matthew iv. 13, and there performed miracles, Matthew viii. 5–14; John iv. 46 to end. The Lord said like things concerning the cities in which the disciples preached His advent or Gospel, and were not received; as in these words: "Whatsoever house or city receiveth you not, neither heareth your words, when ye go out of that house or city, shake off the dust of your feet; verily I say unto you, it shall be more tolerable for the land of Sodom and Gomorrah, in the day of judgment, than for that city" (x. 14, 15; Mark vi. 11; Luke x. 10, 11, 13); for no one rejects the holy things of the church, and denies the divine [principle] of the Lord inwardly, but those who are in the love of self; they who are in the love of the world, and in the evils thence derived, may also reject the holy things of the church, but still not interiorly, that is from confirmation of the heart. The like is said concerning the prophets and the people who adulterate the truths and goods of the Word to confirm evils and falses; as in Jeremiah: "In the prophets of Jerusalem I have seen a horrible obstinacy, adulterating and walking in a lie; whilst they have strengthened the hands of evil doers, that not a man returneth from his wickedness, they are become to me as Sodom and the inhabitants thereof as Gomorrah" (xxiii. 14). By prophets are there understood those that teach the truths and goods of doctrine, and, in the abstract sense, which is the genuine spiritual sense, is understood doctrine from the Word, thus also the Word as to doctrine, wherefore by horrible obduracy is signified confirmation of heart against the truths and goods of the Word; by adulterating, and walking in a lie, is signified to pervert the goods and truths of the Word; by adulterating to pervert the goods of the Word by evils and falses; a lie denotes the false, and to go in a lie is to live in falses; the confirmation of evils and consequent power thereof over goods, is signified by strengthening the hands of evil doers; and the persisting in evils and falses of doctrine is signified by, not a man returneth from his wickedness; hence it is said, they are become as Sodom, and the inhabitants thereof as Gomorrah; as Sodom, signifies in evils flowing from the love of self, and the inhabitants thereof as Gomorrah, signifies an evil life from falses of doctrine. The evil which destroyed Sodom and Gomorrah, is described by these words in Moses: "That they desired to offer violence to the angels, and that therefore they were smitten with blindness, so that they could not find the gate where the angels were; and that therefore Jehovah caused it to rain upon Sodom and Gomorrah sulphur and fire, and overthrew those cities, and all the plain, and all the inhabitants of the cities, and the bud of the earth" (Gen. xix.). Their desiring to offer violence to the angels signified the desire of violating divine good and divine truth, for these are signified by angels; by the blindness with which they were smitten, that they could not find the gate, was signified a plenary rejection and negation of the divine [principle], and of the holy things of heaven and the church, so as not to be able to see or acknowledge anything appertaining thereto, which is signified by their not finding the gate where the angels were; by sulphur is signified the concupiscence of destroying the goods and truths of the church by falses; and by fire is signified the love of self and every evil which destroys, in this case their destruction. That by Sodom and Gomorrah are signified all evils and falses flowing from the love of self, has been told me from heaven; for when they who are in evils from that love perish, as was the case in the day of the last judgment, there appeared as it were sulphur and fire raining out of heaven, which was also seen by me; that such a thing was to take place on the day of the last judgment, was also predicated by the Lord in Luke: "In like manner as it came to pass in the days of Lot, in the day when Lot departed out of Sodom, it rained fire and sulphur out of heaven, and destroyed them all; according to this shall it come to pass, in the day in which the Son of Man shall be revealed" (xvii. 28, 29, 30). Whereas they who from the love of self confirm themselves in evils by falses against the goods and truths of heaven and the church, entirely eradicate with themselves every truth of doctrine and of the Word, also the good of spiritual and celestial love, therefore a total vastation takes place with them, which is thus described in Moses: "It shall be sulphur and salt, the whole land a burning, it shall not be sown, neither shall it bud forth, nor shall any herb come up thereon, according to the overthrow of Sodom and Gomorrah, of Admah and Zeboim" (Deut. xxix. 22). By sulphur is signified the vastation of all good by concupiscences originating in evils; by salt is signified the vastation of all truth by falses originating in those concupiscences; by the burning of the whole earth is signified the devastation of the church by the love of self; by, it shall not be sown, neither bud forth, nor any herb come up thereon, is signified no receptibility at all of the truth of the church, the herb denoting the truth of the church which is first produced; and because such is the devastation of good and truth from the love of self, therefore it is said, according to the overthrow of Sodom and Gomorrah, Admah and Zeboim, Admah and Zeboim signifying the knowledges of evil and the false; that such things would take place at the day of the last judgment, is evident from the signification of the words of the Lord above mentioned, which are spoken of the day in which the Son of Man shall be revealed.

654. That Egypt here signifies the natural man separate from the spiritual, and thence the falses flowing from the evils of the love of self, consequently from the conceit of self-derived intelligence, shall now be explained; for when the natural principle of man is separated from the spiritual, which takes place chiefly from the love of self, then from the evils of that love falses flow forth, all the false being derived from evil; for the false is the patron of evil, and the evil of the will is formed in the understanding by the ideas of the thought, which ideas are called falses, and whereas the falses flowing forth from the evils of the love of self, are attended with self-conceit, for man then thinks from his proprium, therefore also by Egypt is here signified the conceit of self-derived intelligence. But inasmuch as by Egypt is signified the natural man in both senses, namely, as well conjoined with the spiritual man as when separated from it, thus in a good sense and in a bad sense, therefore the various things which appertain to the natural man are also signified by Egypt, which in general have reference to knowledges and scientifics, for the truths and falses of the natural man are called knowledges and scientifics; but the truths themselves, when they have obtained life, which is effected by the life of faith, which is charity, appertain to the spiritual man, or spiritual mind of man, and these with their affections and pleasantnesses do not appear to the manifest sense and sight of the man, as is the case with the knowledges and scientifics of the natural man: the reason of this is, because man, so long as he lives in the world, thinks naturally and speaks naturally, and what is thought and spoken naturally is sensibly felt and perceived by him in a certain sight which appertains to his understanding, whereas his spiritual thought, which is conjoined with the affection of truth or of the false, does not appear before man has put off the natural body, and put on the spiritual body, which takes place after his decease, or departure from this world, and his entrance into the spiritual world when he thinks spiritually and speaks

spiritually, and no longer naturally as before. This comes to pass with every man, whether he be merely natural or at the same time spiritual; and thought with the mere natural man after death is still spiritual, but gross, without intelligence of truth or affection of good, for it consists of correspondent ideas, which indeed appear as material, but still are not so; but concerning the spiritual thought and the speech also thence derived of merely natural men in the spiritual world, the Lord willing, more will be said elsewhere. The reason why by Egypt, in the Word, is signified the natural man in both senses, good and bad, consequently all that which properly belongs to the natural man, is, because in Egypt the sciences were cultivated, especially the science of correspondences and representations, at the time when churches were representative; but whereas they made to themselves resemblances according to correspondences, which, when from internal they became altogether external, they began to worship with holy rites, and thus perverted the representatives of things spiritual and celestial to idolatrous purposes, and also to magic, hence it is, that by Egypt, in a bad sense, which is opposite to the former, is signified the false scientific of the natural man, and also what is idolatrous and magical. That such things are signified by Egypt may be abundantly confirmed from the Word; but before we proceed to such confirmation it is proper to be known, that with every man there is an internal, which sees from the light of heaven, which is called the internal spiritual man, or the internal spiritual mind, and an external, which sees from the light of the world, which is called the external natural man, or the external natural mind: with every man of the church the internal must be conjoined with the external, or the internal spiritual man with the external natural man: when they are thus conjoined, then the spiritual man, inasmuch as it is in the light of heaven, has dominion over the natural man, which is in the light of the world, and rules it as a master of a family rules his servant, and teaches it as a master teaches his disciple; from this conjunction man is a man of the church, and an angel; but when the natural man is not conjoined with the spiritual nor subordinate thereto, as is especially the case when the spiritual man is shut, as it is with those who deny the divine things of the Word and the church, who thence see nothing from the light of heaven, then the natural man is in blindness as to things spiritual, and by his rational principle perverts all the truths of the church, and by the ideas he has of them turns them into falses: this subject, viz. the conjunction of the spiritual man with the natural man, and the separation of the natural man from the spiritual, is much treated of in the Word, especially where treating concerning Egypt, inasmuch as by Egypt is signified the natural man as well conjoined with the spiritual man as separate therefrom; and where the natural man is treated of separate from the spiritual, Egypt is rebuked and rejected. Whereas Egypt, in an extensive sense, signifies the natural man, therefore the true scientific and the false scientific is also thereby signified, for truths and falses in the natural man are called scientifics; and whereas scientifics true and false are signified by Egypt, faith is also thereby signified, inasmuch as faith is of truth, and truth is of faith, whence faith conjoined to charity is also signified by Egypt in a good sense, and faith separate from charity in the opposite sense; for faith is conjoined to charity when the spiritual man is conjoined with the natural, and then by Egypt is signified the true scientific, but faith is separate from charity when the natural man is separate from the spiritual, and then by Egypt is signified the false scientific; for when the natural man is separate from the spiritual, man has then no truths, and if he imbibes truths from the Word or from the doctrine of the church, he still falsifies them by the ideas of his thought, whence all truth with him becomes false. So far concerning the significations of Egypt in the Word; it shall now therefore be first demonstrated from the Word itself, that by Egypt is signified the natural man conjoined to the spiritual, or the scientific vivified by the influx of spiritual light, or, what is the same, faith conjoined to charity, which in itself is faith; and afterwards it shall be demonstrated that by Egypt, in the opposite sense, is signified the natural man separate from the spiritual, or the scientific not vivified by any influx of spiritual life, or what is the same, faith separate from charity, which in itself is not faith. That by Egypt is signified the natural man conjoined to the spiritual, likewise the scientific vivified by the influx of spiritual light, which in itself is the true scientific or the truth of the natural man, and what is the same, faith conjoined to charity, which in itself is faith, appears from the following passages; as in Isaiah : " In that day there shall be five cities in the land of Egypt, speaking with the lip f Canaan, and swearing to Jehovah Zebaoth every one shall be called the city Cherez. In that day there shall be an altar to Jehovah in the midst of the land of Egypt, and a statue at the border thereof to Jehovah. They shall cry unto Jehovah on account of oppressions, who shall send unto them a Savior and Prince : then shall Jehovah become known to Egypt, and the Egyptians shall know Jehovah in that day, and shall make the sacrifice and meat offering. So Jehohovah shall smite Egypt in smiting and healing, whence they shall convert themselves unto Jehovah, who shall be intreated of them, and shall heal them. In that day there shall be a highway from Egypt into Ashur, and Ashur shall come into Egypt, and Egypt into Ashur, and the Egyptians shall serve with Ashur; in that day Israel shall be a third to Egypt and to Ashur, a blessing in the midst of the land, which Jehovah Zebaoth shall bless, saying, Blessed is my people Egypt, and Ashur the work of my hands, and Israel mine inheritance" (xix. 18–25). Here Egypt is put for the natural man conjoined to the spiritual, thus for the nations and people who were without the church, and who, not being in truths, were natural men, but who when they heard the gospel, acknowledged the Lord, and, being thence instructed in the truths of doctrine, received faith ; the advent of the Lord is understood by "in that day," which is there five times mentioned ; in that day there shall be five cities in the land of Egypt, speaking with the lip of Canaan, signifies that there shall be with them several doctrinals, according to the truths of the doctrine of the church itself, five denoting several; cities, doctrinals; the land of Egypt, the church of such nations; and the lip of Canaan, the truths of the doctrine of the church; every one shall be called the city Cherez, signifies the doctrine of the good of charity in every one, city denoting doctrine, and Cherez, which in the Hebrew tongue signifies the sun and the beaming of its splendor, denotes the good of charity and faith thence derived; in that day there shall be an altar to Jehovah in the midst of the land of Egypt, and a statue at the border thereof to Jehovah, signifies the worship of the Lord from the goods of charity, and thence from the truths of faith in all things appertaining to the natural man; by the altar to Jehovah is signified worship from the good of charity, and by the statue, worship from the truths of faith: by, in the midst of the land of Egypt, is signified every where and in all things of the natural man, and by the border or boundary, scientific truth; they shall cry unto Jehovah on account of oppressions, who shall send to them a Savior and Prince, signifies their grief on account of the defect or want of truth, and thence of spiritual good, and the advent of the Lord from whom they will receive them; to cry denotes grief, oppressions signify the want of truth and thence of spiritual good, and Savior and Prince signify the Lord, who is called Savior from the good of love, and Prince from the truth of faith; then Jehovah shall become known to Egypt, and the Egyptians shall know Jehovah in that day, signifies the acknowledgment of the Lord, and of His Divine [principle]; and they shall make the sacrifice and meat offering, signifies the worship of the Lord according to His precepts from the Word, thus from truths of doctrine and from the good of love; so shall Jehovah smite Egypt, in smiting and healing, whence they shall convert themselves unto Jehovah, and He shall be entreated of them and shall heal them, signifies temptations and thus conversion, and healing from falses by truths; in that day there shall be a highway from Egypt into Ashur, and Ashur shall come into Egypt and Egypt into Ashur, signifies that then the rational principle shall be opened to them by scientific truths and man shall view the scientifics appertaining to the natural man rationally, and thus intelligently; Egypt denotes the scientific principle which appertains to the natural man, and Ashur denotes the rational; in that day Israel shall be a third to Egypt and Ashur, a blessing in the midst of the land, signifies influx into each from spiritual light, Israel is the spiritual man, which has light from heaven, Egypt is the natural man, which has light from the world, and Ashur is the rational man, which is middle or mediate, and which receives light from the spiritual, and transmits it into the natural, which it thereby illustrates: which Jehovah shall bless, signifies influx from the Lord; saying, blessed is Egypt my people, signifies the natural man illustrated; and Ashur the work of my hands, signifies the rational man not from self but from the Lord; and Israel mine inheritance, signifies the spiritual man, which is called inheritance because all the spiritual principle is of the Lord, for it is His Divine Proceeding, from which is heaven and the church;

without such spiritual sense how could these prophecies be understood?   Again in Micah : " This is the day in which they
shall even come unto thee from Ashur and the cities of Egypt, and
thence from Egypt unto the river, and from sea to sea, and from
mountain to mountain " (vii. 12).   These things are also said concerning the establishment of the church by the Lord with the gentiles or nations, and describe the extension of that church from one
end to the other: one end of the land of Canaan was the river Euphrates, and the other was the river of Egypt; the extension of
truth from one end to the other is signified by " from sea to sea "
and the extension of good from one end to the other, by " from
mountain to mountain." That the extension of the land of Canaan,
by which is signified the church, was from the river of Egypt to the
river Euphrates of Assyria, appears in Moses : " In this day, Jehovah covenanted a covenant with Abraham, saying, To thy seed will
I give this land, from the river of Egypt even to the great river, the
river Euphrates " (Gen. xv. 18).   And in 1 Kings : " Solomon was
ruler over all the kingdoms from the river Euphrates to the land
of the Philistines, and even to the lands of Egypt " (v. 1).   For the
church, which in itself is spiritual, terminates in the natural man,
viz. in its rational and scientific [principles], for the rational principle is in the interior natural man, for it is the understanding thereof;
the scientific principle is there also, and the rational is born by means
of scientifics, for in these it sees its conclusions as in a mirror, and
confirms itself by them, but yet from a spiritual principle, without
which man can neither have the rational principle nor the true scientific, but ratiocination instead of the former, and a false scientific
instead of the latter ; these two principles therefore constitute the
boundaries of the spiritual church, which is signified by the land of
Canaan.   Again in Ezekiel : " Son of man, say unto Pharoah king
of Egypt, and unto his multitude ; to whom art thou made like in
thy greatness?   Behold Ashur is a cedar in Lebanon, fair in his
branches, and a shady forest, and high in height, and his shoot was
amongst the entwistings ; the waters caused it to grow, the abyss
made it high so that with its rivers they went about the plant, and
he sent out aqueducts to all the trees of the field, whence its height
was made high, and its branches were made long, through the many
waters he sent out : all the birds of the heavens made their nests in
its branches, and under its branches every beast of the field brought
forth, and in its shade dwelt all great nations; it was beautiful in
its greatness, in the length of its branches, for its root was with
many waters.   The cedars in the garden of God could not hide it;
the fir trees were not equal to its branches ; no tree in the garden of
God was equal to it in beauty ; they made it beautiful by the multitude of its branches, and all the trees of Eden, which are in the
garden of God emulated it " (xxxi. 1–8).   Inasmuch as by Pharaoh
king of Egypt is signified the intellectual principle of the natural
man, which is born and formed from scientific truths rationally seen,
hence it is that he is here called Ashur, by whom is signified the
rational principle, and is described by a cedar and its height, and

the length and multitude of its branches, and this because cedar also, in the Word, signifies the rational principle: but the greater part of this passage may be seen explained above, n. 650: whereas the rational principle is of such a nature and quality as to intellectual truths, and thence the natural is such as to scientific truths, therefore it is said that the cedars in the garden of God could not hide it, that the fir trees were not equal to its branches, and that no tree in the garden of God was equal to it in beauty: by the garden of God is signified the intelligence which appertains to the man of the church, who is in genuine truths; by the cedar is signified his rational principle which is from a spiritual origin; by the fir tree is signified the perceptive principle of the natural man; and by beauty is signified the affection of truth and thence intelligence; by their making it fair by the multitude of branches, is signified abundance of scientific truths rationally perceived; all the trees of Eden in the garden of God emulated it, signifies the perceptions of truth from celestial good, whence comes wisdom, trees signifying perceptions, where the celestial man is treated of, and knowledges where the spiritual man is treated of, and Eden in the garden of God signifying the wisdom which is from the good of love; that it is Pharaoh and Egypt which is here understood and described by Ashur and the cedar, appears also from the last verse of the same chapter, where it is said, this is Pharaoh and all his multitude. Inasmuch as all the spiritual intelligence and wisdom of man terminates in the natural, and there renders itself conspicuous, therefore in the passage above adduced, Pharaoh king of Egypt, by whom is signified the intellectual principle which is in the natural man born and formed from scientific truths, is compared to a cedar in the garden of God, consequently the land of Egypt is what is understood by the garden of God, in like manner as in Moses: "Lot lifted up his eyes, and saw all the plain of Jordon, that the whole abounded in waters, as the garden of Jehovah, as the land of Egypt, in coming to Zoar" (Gen. xiii. 10). The natural man as to his intellectual principle, as described above in Ezekiel, is also described by Senacherib the chief captain of the king of Assyria, but by blasphemies, in these words: "By the hand of thy embassadors thou hast reproached the Lord, and hast said, by the multitude of my chariots, I have ascended the heights of the mountains, the sides of Lebanon, where I will cut off the height of the cedars thereof, the choice of the firs thereof, and I will come on to the lodgings of his border, the forest of his grounds: I have digged and drunk strange waters, and I will dry up with the sole of my steps all the rivers of Egypt" (2 Kings xix. 23, 24). Similar things are here signified as in the passage adduced above, viz. things rational appertaining to the men of the church formed from scientific truths, and illustrated from the divine spiritual principle, which yet the king of Assyria, by whom is here signified the perverted rational, was desirous to destroy, for he made war upon Hezekiah, king of Judah; but because he blasphemed those things, and threatened to destroy all things from first to last appertaining to the church, which is formed with man, from the spiritual, in his ra-

tional and natural principles, therefore in that night a hundred and
eighty-five thousand were smitten in his camp by the angel of Jehovah, (verse 35): by the multitude of chariots of the king of Assyria
are there signified falses of doctrine; by the height of the mountains,
and the sides of Lebanon which he was desirous to ascend, are signified all the goods and truths of the church, which he was desirous
to destroy; by the height of the cedars and the choice of the firs,
which he desired to cut off, are signified rational and natural truths
as to perception; by the forest of the ground are signified scientifics;
by the rivers of Egypt which he would dry up with the sole of his
steps, is signified the science of the natural man from a spiritual origin, which he would blot out and annihilate by his sensual [princi-
ple], the sole of the steps of the king of Assyria denoting the sensual principle and ratiocination thence derived, which is from fallacies alone, and the rivers of Egypt denoting the intelligence of the
natural man, derived from scientifics, which are from a spiritual
origin when they are applied to confirm the truths of the church
which are spiritual.   Whereas every man with whom the church is
to be implanted must first be instructed in scientifics, for without the
instruction of the natural man by scientifics, which also consist of
various experiences from things of the world, and associations
therein, man cannot become rational, and if he does not become
rational he cannot become spiritual, for the rational principle of
man conjoins itself on one part with the spiritual, that is with heaven, and on the other part with the natural, that is with the world;
and whereas also the church was to be instituted with the sons of
Israel, therefore the natural man with them was first to be instructed,
that is, in truths naturally and also scientifically understood: in
order that this might be represented and signified, it came to pass
that Abraham, whose posterity were to represent the church, and
himself the head thereof, "sojourned in Egypt with his wife, and
there abode some time" (Gen. xii. 10, and following verses): and
afterwards "Jacob with his sons, who were then called the sons of
Israel, went by command into Egypt, and dwelt in Goshen, which
was the best of the lands of Egypt, and there remained a long time"
(Gen. xlvi. and following chapters); and this to the intent that they
might first be instructed in truths scientifically and naturally, and
not spiritually till afterwards; for by truths scientifically and naturally understood, every one procures to himself a rational principle
into which the spiritual can flow, and become operative; for man
imbibes the light of heaven, which is spiritual light, by the rational
principle, which appertains to his understanding, and by the rational
illustrated from the spiritual inspects knowledges and scientifics,
and chooses thence such as agree with the genuine truths and goods
of heaven and the church, which are spiritual, and rejects those
which disagree; thus man founds the church in himself: it is therefore said concerning Abraham and Jacob, that on account of the
famine in the land of Canaan they went to Egypt to sojourn there:
the reason why this was on account of the famine, is, because famine
signifies a defect or want of the knowledges of good and truth, and

so a desire for them, and to sojourn, in the Word, signifies to be
structed. From these considerations it is evident, what is under-
ood by these words in David : " Thou hast made a vine to journey
it of Egypt, thou hast driven out the nations, thou hast planted it,
ou hast purged before it, and caused its roots to take root, that it
led the land ; thou hast sent out its shoots unto the sea, and its
tle branches to the river" (Psalm lxxx. 9, 10). By the vine out
Egypt is signified the church, which the sons of Israel represented ;
' driving out the nations, is signified, to expel the evils of the na-
ral man, which are expelled by truths ; by planting it, purging
fore it, and causing its roots to take root, is signified instruction
cording to order, namely, the imbibing scientifics and knowledges,
en the being as in a wilderness, and tempted, and afterwards intro-
iced into the land of Canaan, that is into the church : these things
e signified in their order, by thou hast planted it, thou hast purged
thou hast caused its roots to take root, and it filled the earth ; by
nding out the shoots thereof unto the sea, is signified the increase
intelligence and the extension thereof to the ultimates of good
d truth appertaining to the church ; and by sending out the little
anches unto the river, is signified unto the rational principle ; that
' the river, namely, Euphrates, is signified the rational principle,
ay be seen above, n. 569. It is also written in Hosea, " When
rael was a boy, then I loved him, and out of Egypt have I called
y son " (xi. 1). By Israel, in the spiritual sense, is signified the
urch, and, in the supreme sense, the Lord, who, as He is the all
Heaven, is also the all of the church : and whereas the sons of
rael, were to represent the church, and it was according to divine
der that they should first be instructed in such things as might
rve the rational principle and thereby the spiritual, therefore they
st sojourned in Egypt, and afterwards were led in the wilderness,
at they might undergo temptations, and that the natural man
ight be thereby subdued ; for man cannot become rational, unless
apty and false scientifics be removed, and so the natural man be
rged from them, which is principally effected by temptations. In-
much as by Israel, in the supreme sense, is understood the Lord,
erefore the Lord Himself, when He was an infant, was carried
wn into Egypt, according to these words in Matthew : " The
gel of the Lord appeared to Joseph in a dream, saying, arise, take
e boy, and flee into Egypt, and remain there until I tell thee : and
arose and took the boy and his mother by night, and departed
to Egypt, and was there until the death of Herod ; that it might
fulfilled, which was spoken by the prophet, out of Egypt have
called my son" (ii. 13, 14, 15). Hereby also was signified the first
struction of the Lord, for the Lord was instructed as another man,
it by virtue of his divine [principle] he imbibed all things more
telligently and wisely than all others do ; but this departure into
gypt only represented instruction ; for as all the representatives
the Jewish and Israelitish church had respect unto Him, there-
re He also represented them in Himself and accomplished them,
r thus He fulfilled all things of the law ; since representatives were

the ultimates of heaven and the church, and all prior things, which
are things rational, spiritual, and celestial, enter into ultimates and
are in them, therefore the Lord was in ultimates by them, namely
by representatives : and whereas all strength is in ultimates, therefore from first principles by ultimates He subjugated all the hells,
and reduced to order all things in the heavens : hence it was that
the whole life of the Lord in the world was representative, even as
to all things related by the Evangelists concerning His passion,
which represented the quality of the church at that time as being
against the divine [being or principle], and against all the goods
and truths of heaven and the church.   From these considerations it
may appear what is understood by Egypt, where the church to be
established by the Lord is treated of, as in the following passages ;
thus in Isaiah: "Thus saith Jehovah: the labor of Egypt and the merchandize of Cush and of the Sabeans, men of length, shall come over
unto thee, and they shall be thine; they shall come after thee, in bonds
shall they come over unto thee, so that they shall bow themselves down
towards thee, they shall pray towards thee, surely God is only in thee,
and there is no God beside" (xlv. 14). These things are said concerning the Lord, who is treated of in the whole of that chapter ; by the
labor of Egypt, and by the merchandize of Cush and of the Sabeans,
is signified the delight of natural love arising from the acquisition of
the knowledges of truth and good ; those knowledges themselves
are signified by the Sabeans, who are called men of length from
good, for length signifies good and the quality thereof, and breadth
signifies truth and its quality; that they would accede to the church,
and acknowledge and adore the Lord, is signified by, they shall come
over unto Thee, they shall be Thine, they shall bow down them-
towards Thee: that the natural man with them should serve the
spiritual and thereby the Lord, is signified by, they shall come over
in bonds, for they are said to come in bonds, with whom the cupidities appertaining to the natural man are restrained; that they shall
ackowledge the Lord alone to be God, is understood by, they shall
pray towards Him, surely God is only in Him, and there is no God
beside.   Again in David : " Fat ones shall come out of Egypt, Cush
shall accelerate her hands to God; sing to God O ye kingdoms of
the earth, sing praises to the Lord " (Psalm lxviii. 32, 33); by the
fat ones out of Egypt, are signified the gentiles or nations, who are
in the affection of knowing truths, and by Cush are signified those
who imbibe them from the delight of the natural man ; the signification of Cush may appear from other passages in the Word where
Cush is mentioned, as in Gen. ii. 13; Zeph. iii. 5, 9, 10; Dan. xi.
43 ; the reception by the nations of the goods and truths of heaven
and the church from the Lord, is signified by, sing to God ye kingdoms of the earth, sing praises to the Lord.   Again in Hosea :
" With honor shall they come as the bird out of Egypt, and as the
dove from the land of Assyria, and I will cause them to dwell upon
their houses" (xi. 11); speaking also of the Lord, about to establish
a church with the gentiles: it is said, as the bird out of Egypt, because a bird signifies thoughts from scientific truths ; and it is said,
as a dove from the land of Assyria, because a dove signifies rational

good derived from spiritual good, and Assyria, the rational principle itself; by causing them to dwell upon their houses are signified the interiors of the mind formed by truths from good, and thus safe from the infestation of the falses of evil. Again in Isaiah: "It shall come to pass in that day, Jehovah shall shake from the spike of the river unto the river of Egypt; and ye shall be gathered one to another O sons of Israel: moreover it shall come to pass in that day that the great trumpet shall be sounded, and they shall come that were ready to perish in the land of Ashur, and that were expelled from the land of Egypt, and they shall bow down themselves to Jehovah in the mountain of holiness, in Jerusalem" (xxvii. 12, 13). In that day signifies the advent of the Lord; from the spike of the river unto the river of Egypt which Jehovah shall shake, signifies all rational and scientific truth subservient to spiritual; it is said, from the spike, because the spike or ear is what contains corn, by which is signified the truth and good which serves the spiritual man for nourishment; convocation unto the church by the Lord is signified by, in that day the great trumpet shall be sounded; that they shall accede to the church who otherwise would have perished by reasonings from scientifics, applied to confirm falses, is signified by, they shall come that were ready to perish in the land of Ashur, and they that were expelled out of the land of Egypt; that they shall adore the Lord, and that a church shall be formed from them, is signified by, they shall bow down themselves to Jehovah in the mountain of holiness, in Jerusalem, the mountain of holiness denoting the church as to the good of life, and Jerusalem the church as to truth of doctrine: these things indeed are said concerning the sons of Israel who were made captive in Assyria and in Egypt, but by the sons of Israel there and elsewhere are understood the nations who were to constitute the church of the Lord, and by their captivity in Assyria and in Egypt is signified the spiritual captivity in which man is from falses of religion. Again in Zechariah: "I will bring them again from the land of Egypt, and I will gather them together from Assyria, and I will bring them to the land of Gilead and Lebanon: he shall pass through the sea of straitness, but he shall smite the waves in the sea, and the pride of Ashur shall be cast down, and the staff of Egypt shall recede" (x. 10, 11); treating also concerning the restoration of the church by the Lord: by bringing again out of the land of Egypt, and gathering them together from Assyria, are signified similar things as in the above passage in Isaiah, which have been explained; by the land of Gilead and by Lebanon are signified the goods and truths of the church in the natural man; by he shall pass through the sea of straitness, but shall smite the waves in the sea, and the pride of Ashur shall be cast down, and the staff of Egypt shall recede, is signified, that the evils and falses of the natural man shall be dispersed, and the reasonings derived from scientifics which confirm them; to pass through the sea of straitness signifies temptations; the waves signify falses and evils; the pride of Ashur signifies reasonings from the conceit of self-derived intelligence; and the staff of Egypt signifies the scientific

principle which confirms.   Again in Ezekiel : " At the end of fort
years I will gather together Egypt from the people whither the
were dispersed, and I will bring them again into the land of Pathros
upon the land of their trading, that they may be there a humbl
kingdom, that thou mayest not exalt thyself any more over the nations ; and I will diminish them, that they shall not rule over the nations" (xxix. 13–16).   By Egypt is here signified the church with
those who are in a moral life, grounded in natural lumen ; the temptations which they will undergo, that the natural man may not rule
over the spiritual, is signified by forty years ; the scientifics by which
they confirmed falses, are signified by Egypt which Jehovah shall
gather from the people whither they were dispersed ; their illustration by the knowledges of truth, is signified by, I will bring them
again upon the land of Pathros, which is called the land of their
trading by reason of the knowledges which they procured for themselves, for to trade signifies to procure and communicate knowledges;
that the scientifics of the natural man shall not elate themselves,
and in their elation do evil to the truths and goods of the church,
and rule over them, is signified by, they shall be a humble kingdom,
that thou mayest not exalt thyself any more over the nations, and
I will diminish them, that they shall not rule over the nations; by
the nations first mentioned are signified the truths of the church,
and by the nations last mentioned are signified the goods of the
church.   Again in Zechariah : " All the residue of all the nations
that come against Jerusalem shall go up from year to year to adore
the king Jehovah Zebaoth, and to keep the feast of tabernacles ;
whoso goeth not up, there shall be no rain upon them ; and if a
family of Egypt go not up, nor come even with these, there shall be
a plague with which Jehovah shall smite the nations" (xiv. 16, 17,
18).   These words also are said concerning the advent of the Lord,
and the establishment of the church by Him ; by the king Jehovah
Zebaoth, whom they shall adore, is meant the Lord, by the feast of
tabernacles is signified the implantation of good by truths ; that there
is no influx of truth and good from the Lord with those who do not
accede to His church, is signified by, whoso 'cometh not up, there
shall be no rain upon them ; that they who are in natural light from
scientifics only, and with whom good cannot be implanted by truths,
will be in evils and falses of every kind, is signified by, if a family
of Egypt go not up, there shall be a plague with which Jehovah
shall smite the nations.   Again in Isaiah : " I am Jehovah thy God,
the Holy One of Israel, thy Savior ; I have given Egypt an expiation for thee, Cush and Sheba instead of thee; I will give man instead of thee, and a people for thy soul " (xliii. 3, 4).   These things also
are said concerning the Lord and concerning the redemption of those
who acknowledge Him, and from affection receive truths from Him ;
redemption is signified by expiation, and by, " instead of thee," and
" for thy soul ;" the natural affection of knowing truths derived from
spiritual affection, is signified by Egypt, Cush and Sheba ; their intelligence thence derived is signified by man ; and the church from
them, by people.   Inasmuch as by Egypt is signified the natural
man, and all the intelligence of the spiritual man is terminated and

has its foundation in the natural man, and in his knowledges and scientifics, therefore man without them is not intelligent or wise, nor indeed rational, for the spiritual man must act as one with the natural man as cause with effect, and he so acts as one by correspondences; hence it is, that in ancient times, when the representative church was also in Egypt, " the king of Egypt, or Pharaoh was called the son of the wise, and the son of the kings of antiquity" (Isaiah xix. 11); also " Egypt the corner stone of the tribes" (verse 13); for by the tribes are signified all the truths and goods of the church in a complex, and by the corner stone is signified the foundation thereof.   Hence also it is said of Solomon, by whom the Lord was represented as to his celestial and spiritual kingdoms, " That his wisdom was above the sons of the East, and above all the wisdom of the Egyptians" (1 Kings v. 10).   By the sons of the east are understood all who at that time were in the knowledges of truth and good, and thereby were made wise ; and by the Egyptians are understood all who were skilled in sciences, especially in the science of correspondences, and in intelligence thence derived, wherefore also the sciences of the Egyptians are called the hidden things of gold and silver, and desirable things, in Daniel : " The king of the north shall stretch out his hands over the lands, and the land of Egypt shall not escape, for he shall have dominion over the hidden things of gold and silver and over all the desirable things of Egypt" (xi. 42, 43).   On this account also it was commanded the sons of Israel, when they went out of Egypt, " that they should borrow from the Egyptians vessels of gold and vessels of silver, and raiment, which they carried away out of Egypt" (Exod. xii. 35, 36).   By vessels of gold and silver, and by raiment, are signified the sciences and knowledges of truth and good, which were taken away from Egypt, because they applied them to confirm evils and falses, and perverted them to idolatrous and magical purposes; wherefore when the Egyptians were deprived of them, and thus became merely natural, they were shortly afterwards drowned in the sea Suph, whereby was represented the lot of those who abuse the sciences to confirm evils and falses ; for after death they are deprived of all knowledge of truth and good, and when this deprivation is accomplished, they are cast down into hell, which was also represented by the drowning of the Egyptians in the sea Suph.   Whereas by Egypt is signified science, from which man hath intelligence, therefore where Tyre is treated of it is said " Fine linen of needle work from Egypt was thy spreading forth, which was to thee for a sign" (Ezek. xxvii. 7). By Tyre are signified the knowledges of truth, and by fine linen of needle work from Egypt is signified the scientific principle grounded in spiritual truth, needle work denoting scientifics, and fine linen spiritual truth ; spreading forth and sign, signify manifestation, for spiritual truths are manifested by sciences, for they thereby appear to the sight and perception of the natural man.   Inasmuch as all scientifics which serve the spiritual man for the confirmation of truths are from the Lord, namely, all the application of them to confirm the truths and goods of heaven and the church, therefore " Joseph was carried down into Egypt, and was there made ruler of the whole

land " (Gen. xli. 1); for by Joseph, in the supreme sense, is understood the Lord as to the divine spiritual [principle], and thence also
the truth of doctrine, which hath its foundation upon the scientifics
of the natural man, as was said above, n. 448; and whereas the
natural man, or natural principle of man, must be subordinate to the
spiritual, that it may serve for the confirming and executing the arbitrations of the spiritual man, therefore Joseph, on account of the
representation of that dominion, was made ruler over Egypt, and
under his auspices Egypt had provision or corn in abundance, so
that the neighboring countries were supplied therefrom, and even
the land of Canaan itself. Inasmuch as Solomon represented the
Lord as to each kingdom, as well the celestial as the spiritual, and
all of both kingdoms are in intelligence and wisdom by knowledges
of truth and good and by scientifics which confirm them, therefore
"Solomon took the daughter of Pharaoh to wife, and brought her
into the city of David " (1 Kings iii. 1); and also afterwards " built
for the daughter of Pharaoh a house near the porch" (1 Kings vii.
8); by which also was represented, that science, upon which all
intelligence and wisdom is founded, is signified by Egypt in a good
sense ; and whereas every man of the church hath a spiritual, a rational, and a natural principle, therefore Solomon built three houses,
the house of God, or the temple, for the spiritual principle, the house
of the forest of Lebanon for the rational, (for the cedar and thence
Lebanon signifies the rational principle,) and the house for the daughter of Pharaoh for the natural ; these arcana do not appear in the
historic sense of the Word, but nevertheless they lie concealed in
the spiritual sense thereof.   Hitherto we have treated concerning
the signification of Egypt in a good sense, it now follows that we
treat also of its signification in a bad or opposite sense, in which
Egypt signifies the natural man separate from the spiritual, or scientific truth separate from spiritual good, which in itself is false; or,
what is the same thing, faith separate from charity, which in itself
is not faith; for man is born natural, and at first imbibes scientifics
from his master or parent, likewise from the reading of books, and
at the same time from his life in the world, and unless he become
spiritual, that is, be born anew, he applies the scientifics which he
hath imbibed to confirm the appetites and pleasures of the natural
man, in a word, to confirm his loves, which are all contrary to divine order; and this natural man is what is signified by Egypt in
the opposite sense, as may appear from the following passages ; thus
in Ezekiel : " Because Pharaoh is lifted up in height, and hath shot
up his top amongst the entwistings, and his heart is lifted up in his
height, I will give him into the hand of the strong one of the nations ; according to his impiety I have rejected him, wherefore
strangers shall cut him off, the violent of the nations and shall cast
him down; upon the mountains and the valleys, are his branches
fallen ; whence all the people of the earth are gone down from his
shade and have forsaken him ; upon his ruin shall dwell every bird
of the heavens, and every wild beast of the field shall be upon his
branches ; all shall be delivered up to death, unto the lower earth,

in the midst of the sons of man, unto them that go down into the pit. In the day when he shall go down into hell I will cover over him the abyss, and I will restrain the floods thereof, that the great waters may be shut up, and I will darken Lebanon over him, and all the trees of the field shall languish over him. To whom art thou thus become like in glory and in greatness, among the trees of Eden, when thou shalt be brought down with the trees of Eden into the lower earth, when thou shalt lie in the midst of the uncircumcised, with them that are slain by the sword; this is Pharaoh, and all his multitude" (xxxi. 10–18). By Pharaoh is here signified the same as by Egypt, viz., the natural man as to science and intelligence thence derived; the conceit of self-derived intelligence from science, is understood by being lifted up or elated in height, and shooting up his top amongst the entwistings, and by his heart being elated in his height; the entwistings signify the scientifics of the natural man: that scientifics were applied to the confirmation of the cupidities of evil and the false, is signified by, I will give him into the hand of the strong one of the nations, the strong one of the nations denoting the false of evil; that the falses of evil will destroy him, is signified by, the strangers shall cut him off, the violent of the nations shall cast him down; that all scientific and rational truths were dispersed by evils and falses, is signified by upon the mountains and the valleys are his branches fallen; that all the truths of the church were driven away, is signified by, all the people of the earth are gone down from his shade, and have forsaken him; that thoughts and affections of the false succeed in the place thereof, is signified by upon his ruin shall dwell every bird of the heavens, and every wild beast of the field shall be upon his branches; that all things are damned and infernal, is signified by, all shall be delivered up to death, unto the lower earth, in the midst of the sons of man, unto them that go down into the pit; the sons of man denote those who are in self-derived intelligence, and the pit denotes where they are who are in falses of doctrine; restraint to prevent any scientific and rational truths entering, is signified by I will cover over him the abyss, and I will restrain the streams thereof; that neither spiritual truths may enter, is signified by, the great waters shall be shut up; that there will be no rational principle, is signified by, I will darken over him Lebanon; that neither shall there be any knowledges of truth appertaining to the church, is signified by, all the trees of the field shall languish upon him; that there shall be no longer any understanding of truth, nor any perception of the knowledges of good, on account of the conceit of self-derived intelligence, is signified by, to whom art thou thus like in glory and in greatness amongst the trees of Eden; because the knowledges of good were altogether perverted by applications to evil, is signified by, when thou shalt be brought down with the trees of Eden into the lower earth, the trees of Eden denoting the knowledges of good from the Word, which the natural man perverted and falsified; that they shall be amongst those in hell, who, by a faith separate from the life of charity have extinguished in themselves all truth, is signified by,

when thou shalt lie in the midst of the uncircumcised with them that
are slain by the sword, the slain with the sword denoting those who
extinguish truths in themselves by falses; that all these things are
said of the natural man deprived of the light which is from the spiritual man, is signified by, this is Pharaoh and all his multitude,
Pharaoh denoting the natural man, and his multitude denoting every
scientific therein. Again in the same prophet: " Son of man, prophecy and say, howl ye, alas the day, a day of cloud, it shall be the
time of the nations, in which a sword shall come into Egypt, and
they shall take its multitude, and shall overturn her foundations;
and they that uphold Egypt shall fall, and the pride of her strength
shall come down, from the tower of Sevene they shall fall in it by
the sword; then shall they be devastated in the midst of the lands
that are devastated, and the cities thereof shall be in the midst
of the cities that are desolate; that they may know that I am
Jehovah, when I shall set a fire in Egypt, and all her helpers shall
be broken: and I will cause the multitude of Egypt to cease by the
hand of Nebuchadnezzar king of Babel, he and his people with him,
the violent of the nations, who shall be brought to destroy the land;
and they shall draw the sword against Egypt, and shall fill the land
with the slain; then will I make the rivers dry, and I will sell the
land into the hand of the wicked, and I will lay waste the land and
the fullness thereof by the hand of strangers, there shall no more be
a prince out of the land of Egypt: I will set a fire in Egypt, and I
will disperse Egypt amongst the nations, and I will scatter them
through the lands " (xxx. 1 to end). These things are summarily
taken from that chapter: it is a lamentation over the church vastated by falses which favor the evils of the natural man: for from the
natural man separate from the spiritual flow all evils, and thence
all falses, which pervert and destroy the truths and goods of the
church: lamentation over that vastation is signified by, howl ye,
alas the day, a day of cloud, it shall be the time of the nations; a
day of cloud denotes the state of the church, when truths are
not understood, consequently when in falses, and the time of the
nations denotes the state of the church arising from evils; that the
false will destroy the whole natural man, and all things that are
therein, by application to evils, is signified by, a sword shall come
into Egypt, and they shall take the multitude thereof, and the foundations thereof shall be overturned; that there will be no confirmations nor corroborations of truth by the scientifics of the natural
man, is signified by, they that uphold Egypt shall fall, and the pride
of her strength shall come down; that falses will destroy the understanding of truth, is signified by, from the tower of Sevene they
shall fall in it by the sword; that all things appertaining to the
church and to the doctrine of the church will perish, is signified by
then shall they be devastated in the midst of the lands that are devastated, and the cities thereof shall be in the midst of the cities that
are desolated; the evil lusts arising from the natural man are signified by the fire which Jehovah will set in Egypt; that there will be

no longer any confirmations of truth from the natural man, is signified by, all her helpers shall be broken; that the cupidities of the love of self and falsities thence derived will devastate, is signified by, the hand of Nebuchadnezzar, king of Babel, he and his people: that thus the church will be devastated by the falses of evil offering violence to the goods of charity and truths of faith, is signified by the violent of the nations being brought to destroy the land, and drawing their sword against Egypt, and filling the land with the slain; that thus truth is not understood, is signified by, I will make the rivers dry; because instead of good in the church there is evil, and instead of truth the false, is signified by, I will will sell the land into the hand of the wicked, and I will vastate the land and the fulness thereof by the hand of strangers; that there will not be any truth as head or primary, and hence not any truth of life from the Lord, is signified by, there shall be no more a prince out of the land of Egypt; that nothing but evils from the love of self will occupy the natural man, is signified by, I will set fire to Egypt, and I will disperse Egypt amongst the nations; that hence all things of the church will be dissipated, is signified by, I will scatter them through the lands. Again in Isaiah: "The prophecy of the beasts of the south: in a land of straitness and anguish, the young lion and the old lion are before them, the viper and the fiery flying serpent; they carry their wealth upon the shoulders of asses, and their treasures upon the back of camels, unto a people they have not profited, and Egypt, vanity and emptiness, they shall help" (xxx. 6, 7). By the beasts of the south, are signified the cupidities, which are from the natural man, extinguishing the light which the man of the church ought to possess from the Word; by the land of straitness and anguish, is signified the church where there will be no good of charity nor truth of faith; by the young lion and the old lion who were before them, is signified the power of the false destroying the truth and good of the church; by the viper and fiery flying serpent, is signified the crafty and subtle reasoning of the sensual principle; by, they carry their wealth upon the shoulders of asses, and their treasures upon the back of camels, are signified the scientifics of the sensual and natural man, from which they draw all their conclusions; wealth and treasures denote the knowledges of truth and good from the Word, but in this case, false scientifics, because from self derived intelligence, asses denoting such things as appertain to the sensual man, and camels such as appertain to the natural; by Egypt, which is vanity and emptiness, is signified both, as well the sensual as the natural principle, which, viewed in themselves, are void of either good or truths. Again in the same prophet: "Wo to them that go down into Egypt for aid, and lean upon horses, and confide upon chariots because they are many, and upon horsemen because they are exceedingly strong; but they look not unto the Holy One of Israel, and seek not Jehovah; for Egypt is man and not God, and his horses are flesh and not spirit" (xxxi. 1, 3). By these words is described the state of those who desire to be wise from themselves, consequently from self-derived intelligence, and

not from the Lord, in those things which appertain to heaven and
the church; and whereas such are merely natural, and take up everything from the fallacies of the senses, and from scientifics perversely
applied, whereby they pervert and falsify the truths and goods of
the church, therefore it is said of them, Wo to them that go down
into Egypt for aid, and look not unto the Holy One of Israel, nor seek
Jehovah; the imaginations which are derived from the fallacies of
the senses, are signified by the horses of Egypt on which they lean;
falses of doctrine confirmed by scientifics in great abundance, are
signified by the chariots on which they confide, because they are
many; and the reasonings thence derived whereby they assault
truths, are signified by the horsemen who are exceedingly strong;
that the natural man has no understanding of divine things from
himself, is signified by, Egypt is man and not God; that his intelligence is from the proprium, in which there is no life, is signified by,
his horses are flesh and not spirit, the horses of Egypt denoting
things of the imagination, which in themselves are dead, because
they are fallacies, flesh denoting the proprium of man, and spirit denoting life from the Lord.   Again in Jeremiah: " Against Egypt,
against the army of Pharaoh king of Egypt, which was at the river
Euphrates, which Nebuchadnezzar king of Babel smote: who is this
that cometh up as a stream, whose waters are moved as streams:
Egypt cometh up as a stream, and as streams the waters are moved;
for He saith, I will come up, I will cover the earth, I will destoy the
city and them that dwell therein; go ye up ye horses, and rave ye
chariots, and come forth ye mighty men; the sword shall devour
and be saturated, and shall be made drunk with their blood: go up
to Gilead, and take balsam, O virgin daughter of Egypt, in vain
hast thou multiplied medicines, healing is not for thee" (xlvi. 2,
7–11, and also 14–26).   That by Egypt here also is signified the
natural man with the scientifics thereof, separate from the spiritual,
which comes to pass through the conceit of self-derived intelligence,
which destroys the truths and goods of the church by reasonings
from scientifics, is evident from all the particulars when viewed in
the spiritual sense: for by the army of the king of Egypt, which
was at the river Euphrates, are signified scientifics falsely applied
and reasonings from them; which Nebuchadnezzar king of Babel
smote, signifies the destruction thereof by the conceit of self-derived
intelligence; who is this that cometh up as a stream, whose waters
are moved as streams, signifies self-derived intelligence and the
falses thereof endeavoring to destroy the truths of the church; Egypt
cometh up as a stream, and as streams the waters are moved, signifies
the natural man reasoning from himself, or from the proprium,
against the truths of the church; for he hath said, I will go up, I
will cover the earth, I will destroy the city and them that dwell
therein, signifies the effort and desire of destroying the church, and
the truths and goods of the doctrine thereof; come up ye horses,
and rave ye chariots, and go forth ye mighty men, signifies by things
imaginary derived from fallacies, and by falses of doctrine confirmed
from scientifics, from which they appear to themselves strong; the

sword shall devour and shall be saturated, and shall be made drunk with their blood, signifies the total destruction of the natural man by falses and by falsifications of truth; go up to Gilead and take balsam, O virgin, daughter of Egypt, signifies the truths of the literal sense of the Word, also reason and patronizing or support thence derived; for by Gilead is signified reasoning from the literal sense of the Word whereby falses are confirmed; for Gilead was not far from Euphrates, and thence was carried wax, balsam and myrrh, and it was made the inheritance of the sons of Manassah and the half tribe of Gad (Gen. xxxi. 21; chap. xxxvii. 25; Numb. xxxii. 29; Joshua xiii. 25). Hence Gilead, besides other things, signifies reasonings from the literal sense of the Word; by balsam is signified application and thence confirmation of the false, and by the daughter of Egypt, the affection of the false which belongs to such a church; in vain hast thou multiplied medicines, healing is not for thee, signifies that such things, however great the abundance thereof, afford no help, inasmuch as thereby truths themselves are falsified. Again in Moses: "The Egyptians pursued the sons of Israel, and came behind them, all the horses of Pharaoh, his chariots and his horsemen, into the midst of the sea: but Jehovah looking unto the camp of the Egyptians, disturbed them, and removed their chariot wheels, and the waters returned, and covered the chariots and horsemen with the whole army of Pharoah" (Exod. xiv. 25–28; chap. xv. 19, 21). By the horses of Pharaoh are signified things imaginary, as being fallacies, which are scientifics originating in the intellectual principle perverted, and applied to confirm falses; by his chariots are signified doctrinals of the false, and by horsemen, reasonings thence derived; by the chariot wheels is signified the faculty of reasoning; but these things may be seen more particularly explained in the A. C. n. 8208–8219, 8332–8335, 8343. On account of such signification of the horses of Egypt, it was prescribed by Moses, "If the people desire a king, a king shall be set over them, whom Jehovah God shall choose from the midst of the sons of Israel: a man that is a stranger who is not thy brother, shall not be set over them: only he shall not multiply to himself horses, nor bring back the people into Egypt, that he may multiply horses; for Jehovah hath said to you, ye shall not add to return in this way any more: neither shall he multiply to himself wives that his heart may not turn back, neither shall he multiply to himself too much gold and silver" (Deut. xvii. 15, 16, 17). What are signified by the things here prescribed to a king, cannot possibly be seen, except it be known what is signified in the spiritual sense by a king, by the sons of Israel, by Egypt and the horses thereof, likewise by wives, and by silver and gold; by a king is signified truth from good; by Egypt, the natural man; by his horses, scientifics; by wives, the affections of truth and good; and by silver and gold, the truths and goods of the church, and, in the opposite sense, the falses and evils thereof; and whereas by a king is signified truth from good, and by the sons of Israel, the church consisting of those who are in truths from good, therefore it is said that if the people desire it, a king shall be set over them, whom Jehovah God shall choose out of the midst of the sons of Israel, and that a strange man who is not a brother shall not be set over them, a strange man not a brother denoting a religious principle not agreeing with good, or a false principle in which there is no good; and whereas by Egypt is signified the natural man, and by horses, false scientifics which are things imaginary, therefore it is said, only he shall not multiply to himself horses, nor bring back the people into Egypt that he may multiply horses; whereas by wives are signified the affections of truth and good, which become affections of evil and of the false when one man has several wives, therefore it is said, neither shall he multiply to himself wives that his heart may not turn back; and whereas by gold and silver are signified the goods and truths of the church, but in this case evils and falses, when they are viewed only by the natural man, therefore it is also said, neither shall he multiply to himself too much gold and silver; but to come nearer to the point, by these words is prescribed, that truth shall not have rule over good, as is the case when the natural man rules over the spiritual; this is signified by its being said, that he shall not bring back the people into Egypt to multiply horses, nor take several wives, for by wife and husband is signified the affection of good corresponding to the affection of truth, which correspondence is given in the marriage of a man with one wife, but not with several; more things of a similar nature are prescribed in the law of a king in 1 Sam. viii. 10–18; inasmuch as Solomon not only procured to himself horses from Egypt, but also multiplied wives, and heaped together gold and silver, therefore he became idolatrous, and after his death the kingdom was divided. Again it is written in Isaiah: " The prophecy concerning Egypt: Jehovah rideth upon a light cloud, and cometh into Egypt, whence the idols of Egypt shall be moved before Him, and the heart of the Egyptian shall melt in the midst of him. I will shut up Egypt into the hand of a hard lord, and a vehement king shall rule over them. Then the waters shall fail in the sea, and the river shall be wasted and dried up, and the streams shall recede, and the rivers of Egypt shall be dried up, the reed and the flag shall wither; therefore the fishers shall mourn, and all that cast the hook into the stream shall be sad, and they that spread the net upon the faces of the waters shall languish; they also that make thread of silk, and the weavers of curtains, shall blush. How say ye unto Pharaoh, I am the son of the wise, the son of the kings of antiquity? Where now are thy wise men, that they may declare? Come to thyself, and let them know what Jehovah hath consulted upon Egypt: the princes of Zoan are become fools, the princes of Noph are carried away, and they have seduced Egypt the corner stone of his tribes; there shall be no work for Egypt which the head or the tail, the branch or the rush, may do" (xix. 1–17). That by Egypt is signified the natural principle of man separate from his spiritual principle, may appear also from these words viewed in their internal sense; and man becomes merely natural, when in his life he does not look to the Lord, but only to himself, and to the world, whence he comes into the conceit of self-derived intelligence, which is common with the learned, who thereby pervert their rational principle, and shut the spiritual mind : in order that it may be known that the natural man is signified by Egypt, self-derived intelligence by the river thereof, and falses by the waters of the river of Egypt, we will explain in a series the things which are here summarily adduced from that chapter: Jehovah rideth upon a light cloud, and cometh into Egypt, signifies the visitation of the natural man from divine truth spiritual natural, for visitation is inquisition into the quality of man, and inquisition is effected by divine truth ; a light cloud denotes the divine truth spiritual natural, from which it appears what is the quality of man as to his natural principle ; whence the idols of Egypt shall be moved before Him, and the heart of the Egyptian shall melt in the midst of Him, signifies a heap and crowd of falses in the natural man, whence worship is derived, and his terror on account of visitation ; I will shut up Egypt into the hand of a hard lord, and a vehement king shall rule over them, signifies, that the evil of the false, and the false of evil, shall reign therein, a hard lord denoting the evil of the false, and a vehement king, the false of evil : then the waters shall fail in the sea, and the river shall be wasted and dried up, signifies, that there shall not be any truths in the natural man, nor any intelligence thence derived ; and the streams shall recede and the rivers of Egypt shall be dried up, signifies, that it shall turn itself from truths to falses, whence intelligence, being without truths from the light of the spiritual man, will become dead ; the reed and the flag shall wither, signifies, that all perception of truth and good from the sense of the letter of the Word, otherwise appertaining to the sensual man, will vanish : therefore the fishers shall mourn, and all that cast the hook in the stream shall be sad, and they that spread the net upon the faces of the waters shall languish, signifies, that they who teach and instruct will labor in vain by truths from the Word to reform the natural man, fishermen and they who spread the net upon the faces of the waters denoting those that teach and instruct natural men from the Word, specifically, from the literal sense thereof; fish signify knowledges thence derived, and to be sad and to languish denote laboring ; they that make thread of silk, and the weavers of curtains, shall blush, signifies those who teach spiritual truths in a natural manner, thread of silk denoting spiritual truths, curtains denoting natural truths from a spiritual origin, and to work and weave them denoting to teach ; how say ye unto Pharaoh, I am the son of the wise, a son of the kings of antiquity, where now are thy wise men, signifies, that the wisdom and intelligence of the natural man from the spiritual is perished, for the natural man is formed to receive intelligence and wisdom from the spiritual man, which takes place when both act as one, like cause and effect ; the princes of Zoan are become foolish, the princes of Noph are carried away, signifies, that the truths of wisdom and intelligence derived from spiritual light in the natural man are turned into the falses of insanity ; Zoan and Noph were in the land of Egypt, and signified the illustration of the natural man from spiritual light ; and they have seduced Egypt the corner stone of the tribes, signifies that the natural man was perverted, in which, notwithstanding, all the goods and the truths of the church have their foundation ; there shall be no work for Egypt which the head or the tail, the branch or the rush, may do, signifies, that they have no longer any intelligence, nor science of truth, consequently no truth either spiritual or natural. Again in Ezekiel: " Son of man, set thy faces against Pharaoh king of Egypt, and prophesy against him, and against all Egypt ; speak and say, Thus saith the Lord Jehovah, behold I am against thee, Pharaoh king of Egypt, the great whale, that lieth in the midst of his rivers, which hath said, the river is mine, and I have made myself : wherefore I will put hooks into thy jaws, and I will cause the fish of thy rivers to stick to thy scales, and I will leave thee in the wilderness, thee and all the fish of thy rivers ; thou shalt fall upon the faces of the field, thou shalt not be collected, neither gathered together ; to the wild beast of the earth, and to the bird of heaven have I given thee for meat, that all the inhabitants of Egypt may know that I am Jehovah, because they have been a staff of reed to the house of Israel ; when they held thee by the hand, thou didst break, and thrust through all their shoulder, and when they leaned upon thee, thou brakest, and didst make all their loins to stand. Behold I bring against thee the sword, and I will cut off from thee man and beast, that the land of Egypt may become a solitude and a waste, because he hath said, my river is mine, and I have made it ; therefore I am against thee, and against thy rivers, and I will make the land of Egypt utterly waste from the tower of Sevene unto the border of Cush, and her cities shall be a solitude forty years " (xxix. 1–12). By these words also is described the natural man deprived of all truth and good by conceit originating in science and self intelligence thence derived ; and whereas Pharaoh king of Egypt signifies the science of the natural man, and thence self-derived intelligence, therefore it is said behold I am against thee, Pharaoh King of Egypt, the great whale that lieth in the midst of his rivers ; by the great whale is signified the scientific principle of the natural man in general, in this case, the false scientific, and by the river is signified self-derived intelligence : who hath said, the river is mine, and I have made myself, signifies intelligence from self and not from the Lord, whence these words involve the conceit of self-derived intelligence ; wherefore I will put a hook into thy jaws, signifies false speaking and chastisement on account thereof ; and I will cause the fish of thy rivers to stick to thy scales, signifies the false scientifics of the lowest sort originating in the fallacies of the senses, fishes denoting scientifics, and scales denoting the fallacies of the senses, which are scientifics of the lowest sort ; and I will leave thee in the wilderness, thee and all the fish of thy rivers, signifies the being divested of truths together with all scientifics from which comes intelligence ; upon the faces of the field shalt thou fall, thou shalt not be collected, neither gathered together, signifies their religious principle without any coherence or restitution ; to the wild beast of the earth and to the bird of heaven have I given thee for meat, signifies the being consumed by affections and thoughts of the false; that all the inhabitants of Egypt may know that I am Jehovah, signifies, that they may know and believe that all truth and good, even in the natural man, are from the Lord; because they were a staff of a reed to the house of Israel, signifies confidence with the men of the church in the scientifics of the sensual man, which are fallacies, concerning which see above, n. 627; when they held thee by the hand thou didst break and thrust through all their shoulders, signifies, that by such faith all the power of truth perishes; and when they leaned upon thee thou brakest, and didst make all their loins to stand, signifies, that by such confidence the faculty of receiving the good of love perishes; behold I will bring against thee the sword, and I will cut off from thee man and beast, signifies, that the false will destroy all intelligence of truth and affection of good in the natural man; that the land of Egypt may become a solitude and a waste, signifies, that the natural man will thence be destitute of all truth and good; because he said, my river is mine, and I have made it, signifies on account of the conceit of self-derived intelligence; and I will make the land of Egypt utterly waste from the tower of Sevene unto the border of Cush, signifies the destruction of the church from first principles to ultimates, in the natural man; her cities shall be a solitude forty years, signifies doctrinals derived from mere falses until there is not any truth remaining, forty years signifying an entire period of vastation of the church, and also an entire duration of temptations. Thus also in 2 Kings: "If thou hast trusted upon the staff of a broken reed, upon Egypt, upon which if a man lean it entereth into his hand, and pierceth it; so is Pharaoh King of Egypt to all that trust in him" (xviii. 21). By the staff of a reed and by leaning upon it, are signified similar things as above. Hence also Egypt is called in David, "The wild beast of the reed, the congregation of the strong which disperseth the people" (Psalm lxviii. 31). By the wild beast of the reed is signified the affection or cupidity of the false originating in the scientifics of the sensual man, which are fallacies; these are called the congregation of the strong, because they strongly persuade; and whereas they disperse the truths of the church, it is said, which disperseth the people. Again in Hosea: "Ephraim shall be as a silly dove, without heart; they called to Egypt, they have departed to Assyria; woe unto them, because they have wandered from Me, devastation to them, because they have trespassed against Me; their princes shall fall by the sword, for the indignation of their tongue; this is their derision in the land of Egypt" (vii. 11, 13, 16). The subject there treated of is concerning the pride of Israel, whereby is signified the conceit of self-derived intelligence in such things as appertain to the church: that by Egypt is signified the natural man, and the science thereof, is evident, from the mention made of Ephraim, who is much treated of in this prophet, and signifies the intellectual principle of the church and the truth of the doctrine thereof in the natural man, concerning which signification, see above, n. 440; wherefore by, Ephraim shall be as a silly dove without heart, is signified, that now there will be no intellectual principle, because there is no truth, nor affection of truth and good; by their calling to Egypt and departing to Assyria, is signified their confiding in the scientifics of the natural man and in reasonings thence derived, which deceive; woe unto them, because they have wandered from Me, signifies aversion from truths which are from the Word; devastation to them because they have trespassed against Me, signifies deprivation of all truth on account of their receding; their princes shall fall by the sword, signifies that primary truths will be destroyed by falses; for the indignation of their tongue, this is their derision in the land of Egypt, signifies the rebuking of doctrine from the natural man, and the contempt thereof. Again in the same prophet: " Israel, thou hast committed whoredom under thy God; they shall not dwell in the land of Jehovah, and Ephraim shall return to Egypt, and they shall eat the unclean thing in Assyria: lo, they are gone away because of devastation; Egypt shall gather them, Moph shall bury them; the desirable [places] for their silver, the thistle shall possess them; thorns shall be in their tents " (ix. 1, 3, 6). The subject treated of in the whole of that chapter is concerning the understanding of the Word destroyed, which is here signified by Ephraim: by the whoredom of Israel under his God, is signified the falsification of the truth of the Word; they shall not dwell in the land of Jehovah, signifies, that they shall not have the life of good, such as in the life of heaven; and Ephraim shall return into Egypt, signifies the understanding of truth destroyed, whence they become natural; and they shall eat the unclean thing in Assyria, signifies the rational principle abounding in falses of evil; lo, they are gone away because of devastation, signifies aversion or the turning away from the Lord by the falsification of truth; Egypt shall gather them, signifies that they have become merely natural; Moph shall bury them, signifies spiritual death by application of the truths of the literal sense of the Word to the falses of evil; the desirable [places] for their silver, signifies the knowledges of truth; the thistle shall possess them, signifies, that evil shall pervert them; thorns shall be in their tents, signifies the false of evil in worship. Again: " Israel shall not return into Egypt, the Assyrian here is their king " (xi. 5). Israel shall not return to Egypt, signifies, that the man of the church made spiritual, shall not become natural; the Assyrian here is their king, signifies that in such case reasonings derived from falses would have rule: the man of the church from spiritual becomes natural, when he separates faith from charity, that is believes the Word, and does not live according to the precepts thereof; likewise, when he arrogates to himself intelligence, and does not attribute it to the Lord, whence arises conceit, from which man becomes natural; for man is first natural, afterwards he becomes rational, and lastly spiritual: when man is natural he is then in Egypt, when he becomes rational, he is then in Assyria, and when he becomes spiritual, he is then in the land of Canaan, thus in the church. So again: " Ephraim feedeth upon wind, and followeth after the east wind; every day he multiplieth a lie and vastation, and they make a covenant with Assyria, and oil is carried down into Egypt" (xii. 2). By Ephraim is signified the church, in which the understanding of truth is destroyed ; by feeding upon wind, is signified to imbibe the false ; by the east wind is signified the drying up and dissipation of truth ; by oil being carried down into Egypt, is signified the perversion of the good of love by the scientifics of the natural man ; but these words may be seen particularly explained above, n. 419. Again in Isaiah : " Woe to the refractory sons, that take counsel but not of Me, and found a molten image but not by My spirit, that they may add sin upon sin ; who depart to go down to Egypt, but ask not of My mouth, and to confide in the shade of Egypt ; therefore the strength of Pharaoh shall become a shame, and trust in the shade of Egypt a reproach" (xxx. 1, 2, 3). Woe to the refractory sons, signifies lamentation concerning the damnation of those who avert themselves ; taking counsel but not of Me, signifies thoughts and conclusions concerning the things of heaven from self and not from the Lord ; and founding a molten image but not by My spirit, signifies worship from the infernal false and not from divine truth ; who depart to go down into Egypt, but have not asked at My mouth, signifies, from the proprium of the natural man, and not from the Word ; and to confide in the shade of Egypt, signifies, and to have faith and confidence in such things as are suggested by the natural man, who is no light of heaven ; therefore shall the strength of Pharaoh become a shame, and trust in the shade of Egypt a reproach, signifies, that there will be no faculty of resisting evils from self-derived intelligence, nor from science in the natural man, shame and reproach signifying the state of such, when, on account of evils, they are esteemed as evil. Again in Jeremiah : " Thou hast forsaken Jehovah thy God, in the time when He led thee into the way ; what hast thou to do with the way of Egypt to drink the waters of Sihor ? and what hast thou to do with the way of Assyria to drink the waters of the river ? why goest thou about so strenuously to change thy way ? thou shalt be ashamed also of Egypt, as thou wast ashamed of Assyria " (ii. 17, 18, 36). These words also treat of the man of the church who by falses of doctrine and evils of life becomes external and merely natural : thou hast forsaken Jehovah at the time when he led thee into the way, signifies aversion to be reformed of the Lord by truths that lead to him ; what hast thou to do with the way of Egypt to drink the waters of Sihor, signifies instruction solely from the natural man, whence come mere falses ; what hast thou to do with the way of Assyria to drink the waters of the river, signifies reasonings thence derived, whence come falses of faith ; why goest thou about so strenuously to change thy way, signifies strong resistance to the being reformed, and made spiritual ; thou shalt be ashamed also of Egypt as thou wast ashamed of Assyria, signifies that it is a perverse and vile state to be led by the natural man, and by reasonings thence derived, because by falses and evils originating in the proprium. Again in Lamentations : " Our inheritance is turned away to strangers, our houses unto aliens ; we drink our waters for silver ; our wood is sold for a price ;

we have given the hand to Egypt, to Assyria, that we may be satisfied with bread; servants rule over us, none delivereth us out of
their hands" (v. 2, 4, 6, 8). Our inheritance is turned away to
strangers, signifies the truths of the church converted into falses; our
houses unto aliens, signifies the goods of the church turned into
evils; we drink our waters for silver, signifies instruction from
ourselves, whence come mere falses; our wood is sold for a
price, signifies instruction also from ourselves, whence come
mere evils; whereas man is instructed and reformed gratis, or
without silver and price by the Lord (Isaiah lv. 1), therefore
by drinking for silver and procuring wood for a price, and thence
growing warm, is signified from ourselves; and whereas to
be instructed from man's self is to be instructed from the natural
man and the scientifics thereof, and conclusions thence derived,
therefore it is said, we have given the hand to Egypt, to Assyria,
that we may be satisfied with bread, by Egypt being signified the
natural man, whence come falses, and by Assyria, the natural man
reasoning from falses, whence come evils; and whereas the things
appertaining to the natural man, are respectively things of service,
for the natural man was made to serve the spiritual, therefore when
the natural rules over the spiritual, then the servants have dominion,
and this is understood by, servants rule over us, none delivereth us
out of their hands. Again in Jeremiah: "If ye say, we will not
dwell in this land, saying no, but we will go to the land of Egypt,
where we shall not see war, nor hear the voice of the trumpet, nor have
hunger of bread, and there will we dwell: but if ye set your faces
to go to Egypt, and go to sojourn there, it shall come to pass that
the sword of which ye were afraid, shall overtake you in the land
of Egypt, and the famine about which you were solicitous shall
there adhere to you in Egypt, and there shall ye die; and all the
men who set their faces to go to Egypt to sojourn there, shall die
by the sword, by famine, and by pestilence, none of them shall remain or escape, and ye shall be for a curse, for astonishment, for
execration and for a reproach, neither shall ye see this land any
more'" (xlii. 13–18, and following verses). We frequently read
both in the historical and prophetical parts of the Word, that the
people of Israel were inflamed with a desire of returning to Egypt,
and that this was forbidden them, and plagues and punishments
thereupon denounced against them; but no one has heretofore
known the reason: the reason was, because the sons of Israel were
to represent the church from its first rise to its end, and the church
with man is first formed by sciences and knowledges in the natural
man, which man is first cultivated by them, for every man is born
natural, wherefore the natural man is first to be cultivated in order
that he may serve ultimately for a basis to the man's intelligence and
wisdom: afterwards by means of the sciences and knowledges which
are implanted, in the natural man, the intellectual principle is formed,
in order to man's becoming rational: but to the intent that from
rational he may become spiritual, he must of necessity undergo
temptations, for thereby the rational principle is subdued, which
would otherwise call forth from the natural principle such things as

vor concupiscences, and would consequently destroy it: lastly when man by that way has been made rational, he then becomes spiritual, for the rational is the medium between the spiritual and the natural, wherefore the spiritual flows into the rational, and thereby into the natural: in a word, man must first enrich the memory with sciences, afterwards his understanding must be thereby cultivated, and lastly the will: memory is of the natural man, understanding is of the rational, and will is of the spiritual: this is the way of the reformation and regeneration of man; it was for this reason that the sons of Israel were first led into Egypt, afterwards into the wilderness to undergo temptations, and lastly into the land of Canaan, for, as was said, they were to represent the church from its first rise to its ultimate end: by their abiding and sojourning in Egypt was represented the instruction of the natural man; by the wanderings forty years in the wilderness were represented temptations, by which the rational man is formed; and by the land of Canaan, into which they were lastly introduced, was represented the church, which, considered in itself, is spiritual. But they who are not willing to be reformed and regenerated, stop in the first way, and remain natural; wherefore the sons of Israel, inasmuch as they were not willing, so often lusted to return into Egypt, concerning which so much is said in the book of Exodus; for they were merely natural, and could not, without great difficulty, become at all spiritual: but still they could represent those things which belong to the spiritual church, and hence it was, that they were led into Egypt, and afterwards into the wilderness, and lastly into the land of Canaan, by which was represented the rise, and progress, and final establishment of the church in man. From these considerations it may now appear whence it is, that it was so severely prohibited the sons of Israel to return into Egypt; for thereby they would have represented the men of the church from spiritual becoming natural, and when the spiritual man becomes natural he no longer sees any truths nor has any perception of good, but falls into falses and evils of every kind. But we will now explain the signification of the passage above cited: if ye say we will not dwell in this land, saying no, but we will go into the land of Egypt, signifies aversion to the spiritual state, in which they are who are of the church, and a desire to the natural state, and to those things which are of the natural man; where we shall not see war, nor hear the voice of the trumpet, nor have hunger of bread, signifies, that they will then suffer no infestation from falses and evils, because there will then be no temptations; for war signifies infestation and combat from evils and falses, and not to hunger for bread signifies not to desire good, which is the case with those who are in falses and evils, consequently with those who are merely natural, and such experience no infestation from evils and falses, because they are in them, and do not know anything concerning truths and goods; and there will we dwell, signifies natural life; but if ye set your faces to go to Egypt, and shall go to sojourn there, signifies, if from love they desire natural life; it shall come to pass that the sword of which ye were afraid shall there overtake you in the land of Egypt, signifie

falses destroying truths; and the famine of which ye were solici—
tous, shall there adhere to you in Egypt, signifies the defect or wan——
of the knowledges of truth and good; and there shall ye die, signi—
fies the consequent desolation of the church and condemnation; and——
all the men who set their faces to go into Egypt to sojourn there,——
shall die by the sword, by the famine, and by pestilence, signifies——
similar things as before, pestilence denoting the vastation of all good——
and truth; none of them shall remain or escape, signifies, that nothing at all of truth and good shall remain; and ye shall be for a——
curse, for astonishment, for execration, and for a reproach, signifies——
all things appertaining to condemnation; neither shall ye see this
place any more, signifies, that there shall be nothing of the church
with them any more. Again in Ezekiel: " There were two women,
the daughters of one mother, who committed whoredom in Egypt;
their names were Ohola, the elder born, which is Samaria, and
Oholibah, which is Jerusalem: Ohola committed whoredom under
me, and loved the Assyrians her neighbors, and gave her whoredoms upon the choice of all the sons of Ashur; nevertheless she
forsook not her whoredoms from Egypt, for they lay with her in her
youth; therefore I delivered her into the hands of her lovers, the
sons of Ashur, they discovered her nakedness, they took her sons
and her daughters, and at length slew her herself with the sword.
Her sister Oholibah saw and corrupted her love more than she, and
her whoredoms above the whoredoms of her sister; she doted on
the sons of Ashur; for she added to her whoredoms; for when she
saw men painted upon the wall, the images of the Chaldeans painted
with vermilion, all having the appearance of dukes, the likeness of
the sons of Babel, of the Chaldeans; and the sons of Babel came
to her to the congress of loves, and they polluted her by their
whoredom; she multiplied her whoredoms whilst she remembered
the days of her youth, in which she committed whoredom in the
land of Egypt, she doted above their concubines, because their flesh
was the flesh of asses, and their issue the issue of horses: thus thou
commendest the lewdness of thy youth, when thou adornedst thy
paps from Egypt; wherefore, Oholibah, I will stir up thy lovers
against thee, the sons of Babel, and all the Chaldeans and all the
Assyrians with them; they shall take thy sons and thy daughters,
and thy posterity shall be consumed by fire; they shall strip thee
of thy garments, and shall take the vessels of thine adorning; thus
will I cause thy wickedness to cease from thee, and thy whoredom
from the land of Egypt, that thou mayest not lift up thine eyes unto
them, nor remember Egypt any more: thou shalt be filled with
drunkenness and sadness, with the cup of devastation and desolation " (xxiii. 2–33, and further to the end). In order to confirm the
signification of Egypt as denoting the natural man, in this case the
natural separate from the spiritual, and Ashur the rational, but here
ratiocination from those things which are of the natural man;. the
above words shall be summarily explained: there were two women
the daughters of one mother, who committed whoredom in Egypt,
signifies the falsifications of truth and good, and that as the sons of
Jacob were merely natural men, they imbibed the idolatries of the

Egyptians, whereby was signified that they falsified all the truths of the church; their names were Ohola the elder born, which is Samaria, and Oholibah, which is Jerusalem, signifies both the spiritual and the celestial church, which the posterity of Jacob represented, the Israelites, who were in Samaria, representing the spiritual church, and the Jews who were in Jerusalem, the celestial church, both from the same mother, which is divine truth; Ohola committed whoredom under me, signifies the falsification of divine truth which is in the Word; and she loved the Assyrians her neighbors, and gave her whoredoms upon the choice of all the sons of Ashur, signifies confirmations by many reasonings; but yet she forsook not her whoredoms from Egypt, for they lay with her in her youth, signifies that they still prosecuted their idolatries; therefore I delivered her up into the hand of her lovers the sons of Ashur, signifies reasonings confirming idolatries; they discovered her nakedness, they took her sons and her daughter, and at length slew her herself with the sword, signifies deprivation of all truth and good, and consequent extinction of the church with them, nakedness denoting deprivation, sons and daughters denoting truths and goods, and Ohola, the church; her sister Oholibah saw, and corrupted her love more than she, and her whoredoms above the whoredoms of her sister, signifies the devastation of the celestial church represented by the Jewish nation in Jerusalem, which is said to have corrupted her love more than her sister, when she perverted and adulterated the goods of the Word, and of doctrine thence derived, because the sin is greater with those who corrupt or pervert the goods of the church than with those who pervert the truths thereof; she doated on the sons of Ashur, signifies, by ratiocinations against truths and goods; she added upon her whoredoms, when she saw men painted upon the wall, the images of the Chaldeans painted in vermilion, signifies phantasies from the fallacies of the senses, which are of the sensual man, and from thence argumentations, whence come falsifications; all of them having the appearance of dukes, the likeness of the sons of Babel, the Chaldeans, signifies their appearance as chief truths, preferable to all others; and they came to her, the sons of Babel, and polluted her by their whoredom, signifies conjunction with the falses of evil originating in the love of self; she multiplied her whoredoms, whilst she remembered the days of her youth, when she committed whoredom in the land of Egypt, signifies confirmation of idolatries, and the falses of evil imbibed from the natural man, and thus increase of falsifications; she doated above their concubines, because their flesh was the flesh of asses, and their issue the issue of horses, signifies the cupidities of love towards those things, because from their voluntary proprium, and thence from their intellectual proprium, the flesh of asses denoting the voluntary proprium, and the issue of horses the intellectual proprium thence derived, which pervert all things; thus thou commendest the lewdness of thy youth, when thou adornedst thy paps from Egypt, signifies the love of the false implanted at an early age, and delectation thence derived; wherefore, Oholibah, I will stir up thy lovers against thee,

the sons of Babel, and all the Chaldeans, and the Assyrians with
them, signifies the destruction of the church by the evils originating
in the love of self, and by falses originating in the conceit of self
derived intelligence, in which there is a deadly hatred against th
goods and truths of doctrine; they shall take thy sons and th
daughters, signifies the goods and truths of the church, which th
will destroy; and thy posterity shall be consumed by fire, signifi
that all other things appertaining to the church shall thence
by earthly loves; they shall strip thee of thy garments, a
the vessels of thine adorning, signifies the deprivation of all intelli
gence and science, which are the adorning of the church; thus will
I cause thy wickedness to cease from thee, and thy whoredom from
the land of Egypt, signifies, that so truths can no longer be falsified;
that thou mayest not lift up thine eyes upon them, nor remember
Egypt any more, signifies, when there is no more any understand
ing of truth, nor science of truth; thou shalt be filled with drunken
ness and sadness, signifies insanity in things spiritual, and aversion
or turning away from them; with the cup of devastation and deso
lation, signifies the falses of evil which entirely devastate and deso
late all the goods and truths of the church. So again in the same
prophet: "Thou hast committed whoredom with the sons of Egypt
thy neighbors, great in flesh, and thou hast multiplied thy whoredom,
and thou committedst whoredom with the sons of Ashur, and couldst
not be satiated; and thou hast multiplied thy whoredom even to Chaldea the land of thy trading, but neither then wast thou satiated" (xvi.
26, 28, 29); speaking of the abominations of Jerusalem, whereby is
signified the church as to doctrine, and by whoredoms are signified
the falsifications of the truth of doctrine and of the Word; thou
committedst whoredom with the sons of Egypt thy neighbors, great
in flesh, signifies falsification by the natural man, in which are all
evils and falses, flesh denoting the proprium of man, which resides
in the natural man, and in itself is nothing but evil and the false
thence derived; and thou hast committed whoredom with the sons
of Ashur, signifies falsifications by reasonings; and thou couldst
not be satisfied, signifies the cupidity of falsifying truths without end;
and thou hast multiplied thy whoredom even unto Chaldea, the
land of thy trading, signifies falsifications from the sensual man,
where are mere fallacies, from which man altogether rejects and denies, and also blasphemes, truths, the land of trading signifying
whence all falses are procured, and the sensual principle is the
source of all evils and falses thence derived; man also is born first
sensual, afterwards he becomes natural, then rational, and at length
spiritual, and they who falsify the truths of the church become again
natural, and at length sensual; but neither then wast thou satiated,
signifies the immense cupidity of destroying the truths of the church.
Again in Joel: "Egypt shall be a desolation, and Edom a wilderness of desolation, because of the violence of the sons of Judah,
whose innocent blood they shed in their land" (iv. 19). Egypt
shall be a desolation, signifies, that the natural man will be without
truths, and thence in mere falses; and Edom a wilderness of deso-

tion, signifies, that the natural man will be without goods, and
hence in mere evils; because of the violence of the sons of Judah,
whose innocent blood they shed in their land, signifies, because they
offered violence to the truths and goods of the Word, which they
perverted.   Similar things are involved in the wars between the
sons of Israel and the Egyptians; likewise between the sons of Israel and the Assyrians; as also between the Assyrians and Egyptians, see 2 Kings xxiii. 29 to end; chap. xxiv. Isaiah x. 3, 4, 5;
and in 1 Kings: " That under king Rehoboam, the king of Egypt
came up against Jerusalem, and took the treasures of the house of
Jehovah and the treasures of the house of the king; and that he took
the shields which Solomon had made, and various other things"
(xiv. 25, 26); for in all the historical parts of the Word, as well as
in the prophetical parts, there is a spiritual sense, inasmuch as they
are representative of spiritual and celestial things appertaining to
heaven and the church, and the words thereof are significative; thus
by the king of Egypt taking the treasures of the house of Jehovah,
and of the house of the king, and several other things, was represented the devastation of the church as to the knowledges of good
and truth by scientifics falsely applied, which are in the natural man.
The quality of the natural man, when subordinate to the spiritual,
and when separate therefrom, is fully described in Exodus in the internal sense: the quality of the natural man when subordinate, and
thus conjoined to the spiritual, is described where Joseph is treated
of, and the sons of Israel being called by him thither, and dwelling
in the land of Goshen, which was the best of the lands of Egypt:
where Joseph is treated of, the dominion of the Lord over the natural man is described, for by Joseph in the spiritual sense, is understood the Lord, and by Egypt, the natural man, and by the sons of
Israel, the spiritual man.   But afterwards the quality of the natural
man is described, when separate from the spiritual, by Pharaoh's
making the sons of Israel to serve grievously; and the vastation
thereof afterwards as to all the truths and goods of the church is described by the miracles there performed, which were so many plagues;
and, lastly, the destruction thereof, by the drowning of Pharaoh and
all his host in the sea Suph: the miracles, by which, in the spiritual
sense, is described the vastation of the natural man separate from
the spiritual, were these: " That the rod of Aaron was turned into
a serpent; that the waters of the river were turned into blood, so
that the fish died, and the river stunk" (Exod. vii.); " That from
the rivers and ponds were produced frogs upon the land of Egypt;
that the dust of the earth was turned into lice; that swarms of noxious flying insects were sent into the house of Pharaoh, of his servants, and into all the land of Egypt" (Exod. viii.); " That there was
a boil breaking forth with blains upon man and upon beast; that a
rain of grievous hail mingled with fire rained upon the land of Egypt"
(Exod. ix.); " That locusts were sent upon the land, which devoured
the herb, and all the fruit of the tree; that a thick darkness came
over all the land of Egypt" (Exod. x.); " That all the first-born in
the land of Egypt died" (Exod. xi.); lastly, " That after the sons of Is-

rael borrowed of them, and thus took away surreptitiously their vesself of gold and silver, and raiment," by which were signified the knowledges of good and truth, the Egyptians were drowned in the sea Suph, by which is signified hell ; by all those things is described how the natural man is vastated, which takes place when he rejects from himself all the truths and goods of the church, and imbibes falses and evils, until there is no longer any truth or good of the church remaining ; but all those things may be seen explained at large in the A. C. where the book of Exodus is unfolded. Hence it may appear what is signified "by the plagues and diseases of Egypt" in Deut. xii. 15; chap. xxviii. 60; also what "by being drowned in the river of Egypt," Amos viii. 8; chap. ix. 15 ; and whence it is that "Egypt is called a land of bondage or servitude," Micah vi. 4; likewise "the land of Ham," Psalm cxxvi. 23 ; and "a furnace of iron," Deut. iv. 20; 1 Kings viii. 5. From all that has been adduced it may now fully appear, that Egypt signifies the natural man in both senses.

655. " Where also our Lord was crucified "—That hereby is signified by which, viz., evils and falses thence derived originating in infernal love, He was rejected, and condemned, appears from this consideration, that evils themselves and their attendant falses arising from infernal love are what reject and condemn the Lord, and these are signified by Sodom and Egypt, wherefore it is said concerning the city of Jerusalem, that it is so called spiritually, for to be spiritually called Sodom and Egypt, signifies evil itself and the false thence derived. The hells are distinguished into two kingdoms, opposed to the two kingdoms in the heavens, the kingdom opposed to the celestial kingdom is backward, and they who are there are called genii, and this kingdom is what is understood in the Word by the devil; but the kingdom opposed to the spiritual kingdom is forward, and they who are there are called evil spirits; this kingdom is what is understood in the Word by Satan : these hells, or these two kingdoms into which the hells are distinguished, are understood by Sodom and Egypt ; whether we say evils and the falses thence derived, or those hells, it is the same thing, inasmuch as all evils and thence all falses ascend from them. By the Jews who lived at Jerusalem crucifying the Lord, was signified that the evils and consequent falses which they loved, crucified Him ; for all things recorded in the Word concerning the Lord's passion represented the perverted state of the church with that nation; for although they accounted the Word holy, yet by their traditions they perverted all things therein contained, until there was no longer any divine good and truth remaining with them, and when this is the case, then evils and falses from infernal love succeed in their place, and these are what crucify the Lord ; that such things are signified by the Lord's passion may be seen above, n. 83, 195, 627. That the Lord's being said to be slain signifies His being rejected and denied, may also be seen above, n. 328 ; and concerning the nature and quality of the Jews, see above, n. 122, 433, 619 ; and in the D. of the N. J. n. 248. Forasmuch as it is here said, where our Lord was crucified, it shall be explained what crucifixion, or suspension upon

wood, signified with the Jews. There were two punishments of death with them, crucifixion and stoning; and by crucifixion was signified condemnation and the curse on account of the destruction of good in the church, and by stoning was signified the same on account of the destruction of truth in the church; and the reason why crucifixion signified condemnation and the curse on account of the destruction of good in the church, was, because wood, upon which they were suspended, signified good, and, in the opposite sense, evil, both appertaing to the will; and the reason why stoning signified condemnation and the curse on account of the destruction of truth in the church, was, because a stone, with which stoning was effected, signified truth, and, in the opposite sense, the false, both appertaining to the understanding; for all things which were instituted with the Israelitish and Jewish nation were representative and thence significative; that wood signifies good, and, in the opposite sense, evil, and that a stone signifies truth, and, in the opposite sense, the false, may be seen in the A. C. n. 643, 3720, 8354. But whereas it has been hitherto unknown whence the punishments of the cross and of stoning were derived with the Jews and Israelites, and it is here of importance that it may be known, we will adduce some passages from the Word from which it may appear that those punishments were representative. That suspension upon wood, or crucifixion, was denounced on account of the destruction of good in the church, and that thus was represented the evil originating in infernal love, whence comes condemnation and the curse, may appear from the following passages in Moses: "If a son shall be stubborn and rebellious, obeying not his father and mother, all the men of the city shall stone him with stones that he die. And if there shall be in a man the crime and judgment of death and murder, thou shalt suspend him upon wood; his carcase shall not remain all night upon the wood, but burying thou shalt bury him in the same day; for he that is suspended is the curse of God, and thou shall not pollute thy land" (Deut. xxi. 20–23). By not obeying the voice of father and mother is signified, in the spiritual sense, to live contrary to the precepts and truths of the church, wherefore the punishment of stoning was denounced for it; the men of the city who were to stone him signify those who are in the doctrine of the church, a city denoting doctrine; by the crime and judgment of death, for which a man should be suspended upon wood, was signified the doing evil against the good of the Word and of the church; this being a crime of death he was to be hung upon wood, for wood, in the Word, signifies good, and, in the opposite sense, evil; by its being said that the body shall not remain all night upon the wood, but be buried in the same day, was signified, that there may not be a representative of eternal damnation; lest they should pollute the land, signifies, that it would be a scandal to the church. And in Lamentations: "Our skins are become black as an oven, because of the storms of famine: they ravished the women in Zion, the virgins in the cities of Judah: their princes are hanged up by the hand, the faces of the elders are not honored, the young men they have led away to grind, and the boys

fall together in wood " (v. 10–13). By Zion is understood the ce—
lestial church, which is in the good of love to the Lord, and was
represented by the Jewish nation; by the virgins in the cities of
Judah are signified the affections of truth originating in the good of
love; the perishing of truths from good by falses from evil, is sig—
nified by, their princes are hanged up by the hand; by the faces of
the elders which are not honored, are signified the goods of wisdom;
by the young men who are led away to grind, are signified truths
derived from good, and by grinding is signified to procure falses and
confirm them from the Word; by the boys who fall together in
wood, are signified goods just springing up and perishing by evils.
Inasmuch as the good of love is signified by a baker, in like manner
as by bread, and the truth of doctrine by a butler, in like manner as
by wine, therefore " The baker was hung up on account of his crime
against king Pharaoh" (Gen. xl. 19–22; chap. xli. 13); which may
be seen explained in the A. C. n. 5139–5169. Whereas by Moab
are understood those who adulterate the goods of the church, and
by Baalpeor is signified the adulteration of good, hence it came to
pass, "That all the heads of the people were hung up before the
sun, because the people committed whoredom with the daughters of
Moab, and bowed down themselves to their gods, and adjoined themselves to Baalpeor" (Numb. xxv. 1–4); by committing whoredom
with the daughters of Moab, is signified to adulterate the goods of
the church, and by being hung up before the sun, is signified condemnation and the curse on account of the destruction of the good of
the church. Inasmuch as by Ai were signified the knowledges of
good, and, in the opposite sense, the confirmations of evil, therefore
" The king of Ai was hung up upon wood, and afterwards cast to
the door of the gate of the city, and the city itself was burned"
(Josh. viii. 26–29). And whereas by the five kings of the Amorites
were signified evils and falses thence derived, destroying the goods
and truths of the church, therefore " Those kings were hung up by
Joshua, and afterwards cast into the cave of Makkedah" (Joshua x.
26, 27); by the cave of Makkedah is signified the dire false originating in evil. By hanging upon wood, or crucifying, is also signified
the punishment of evil destroying the good of the church, in Matthew: " Jesus said, I send unto you prophets, wise men and scribes;
and some of them ye shall kill, crucify, and scourge in your synagogues, and persecute them from city to city" (xxiii. 34): all things
which the Lord spake He spake from the divine [principle], but the
divine things from which He spake fell into the ideas of natural
thought and expressions thence derived according to correspondences, such as occur in this and other passages in the Evangelists;
and whereas all the words have a spiritual sense, therefore by prophets, wise men, and scribes, according to that sense, are not meant
prophets, wise men, and scribes, but instead thereof the truth and
good of doctrine and of the Word; for spiritual thought and speech,
such as is that of the angels, is without any idea of person; and hence
by a prophet is signified the truth of doctrine, by wise men, the good
of doctrine, and by scribes, the Word from which doctrine is derived;

whence it follows that to kill has reference to the truth of the doctrine of the church, which is signified by prophets, to crucify has reference to the good of doctrine, which is signified by wise men, and to scourge has reference to the Word, which is signified by scribes; and that thus to kill signifies to extinguish; to crucify, to destroy; and to scourge, to pervert; that they will wander from one false of doctrine into another, is signified by persecuting them from city to city, a city denoting doctrine; this is the spiritual sense of the above words. Again: " Jesus said unto the disciples, that He should suffer at Jerusalem, and that the Son of Man should be delivered to the chief priests and scribes, and that they should condemn Him, and deliver Him up to the gentiles, to be mocked, to be scourged, and to be crucified, and that on the third day he should rise again" (xx. 18, 19; Mark x. 32, 33, 34).   The spiritual sense of these words is, that divine truth, in the church where mere falses of doctrine and evils of life reign, shall be blasphemed, the truth thereof perverted, and the good thereof destroyed; the Son of Man signifies divine truth which is the Word, and Jerusalem signifies the church where mere falses and evils reign; by the chief priests and scribes are signified the adulterations of good and falsifications of truth, both from infernal love; by condemning Him and delivering Him to the gentiles, is signified, to adjudge divine truth and divine good to hell, and to deliver them to the evils and falses which are thence, the gentiles or nations signifying the evils which are from hell and destroy the goods of the church; to be mocked, to be scourged, and to be crucified, signifies blasphemation, falsification, and perversion of truth, and the adulteration and destruction of the good of the church and of the Word, as above; and the third day He shall rise again, signifies the plenary glorification of the human [principle] of the Lord. From these considerations it may appear, what is signified, in the spiritual sense, by the crucifixion of the Lord; likewise, by the various mockings which then took place; as that they set a crown of thorns upon His head; that they smote him with a reed; and that they spit in His face, besides other things related in the Evangelists, viz., that the Jewish nation so nefariously treated the divine truth and good itself, which the Lord was; for the Lord suffered the wicked state of that church to be represented in Himself, and this was signified by " His bearing their iniquities" (Isaiah liii. 11); for it was common for the prophets to take upon themselves the representation of the wicked state of the church; thus the prophet Isaiah was commanded to go naked and barefoot three years, in order to represent the church being destitute of good and truth (Isaiah xx. 3, 4): the prophet Ezekiel bound in cords laid siege to a tile, on which was portrayed Jerusalem, and did eat cake made of barley with the excrement of the ox, to represent that the truth and good of the church was thus obsessed by falses and defiled by evils (Ezek. iv. 1–13): the prophet Hosea was commanded to take a harlot to himself for a woman, and children of whoredoms, in order to represent what was then the quality of the church (Hosea i. 1–11); besides other circumstances of a like nature: that this was to bear the iniquities of the house of Israel or the church, is openly declared in Ezek. chap. iv. 5, 6. From these considerations it may appear, that all things which are recorded concerning the passion of the Lord, were representative of the state of the church at that time with the Jewish nation. So far concerning the signification of the punishment of suspension upon wood, or crucifixion : that the other punishment of death, with the sons of Israel, which was stoning, was significative of condemnation and the curse on account of the destruction of the truth of the church, it does not belong to this place to confirm from the Word, but it may appear from the passages where stoning is mentioned ; as in Exod. xxi. 28–33 ; Levit. xxiv. 10–17, 23 ; Numb. xv. 32–37 ; Deut. xiii. 11 ; chap. xvii. 5, 6, 7 ; chap. xxii. 20, 21, 24 ; Ezek. xvi. 39, 40, 41 ; chap. xxiii. 45, 46, 47 ; Matt. xxiii. 37 ; Luke xiii. 34 ; chap. xx. 6 ; John viii. 7 ; chap. x. 31, 32 ; and elsewhere.

656. "And they of the people, and tribes, and tongues, and nations shall see their bodies three days and a half, and they shall not permit them to be put in monuments. And they that dwell upon the earth shall rejoice over them and shall be glad, and they shall send gifts one to another, because those two prophets tormented them that dwell upon the earth."—"And they of the people, and tribes, and tongues, and nations shall see," signifies, with all who are in falses and evils of religion, of doctrine, and of life ; "their bodies three days and a half," signifies the plenary extinction of divine truth and divine good ; "and they shall not permit their bodies to be put in monuments," signifies their rejection and damnation ; "and they that dwelt upon the earth shall rejoice over them and shall be glad," signifies the delights of infernal love with those who are against the goods and truths of the church ; "and they shall send gifts one to another" signifies their concovation : "because those two prophets tormented them that dwell upon the earth," signifies anxiety of heart from them in the devastated church.

657. "And they of the people, and tribes, and tongues, and nations shall see"—That hereby is signified, with all who are in falses and evils of religion, of doctrine, and of life, appears from the signification of seeing, as denoting to know, to perceive and to understand ; and from the signification of people and tribes, as denoting those who are in falses of doctrine and of religion ; for by people, in the Word, are understood all who are in truths or in falses, whether they are of the church or of some religion out of the church, as may be seen, n. 175, 331, 625 ; and by tribes, in the Word, are understood all who are in truths or in falses of doctrine, for tribes denote all truths and falses of doctrine, see above, n. 330, 430, 431, 454 ; hence it may appear that people and tribes signify all who are in truths or falses of religion and of doctrine, in this case who are in falses, because it is said that they shall see the bodies of the witnesses three days and a half, and not permit them to be put in monuments ; and from the signification of tongues and nations, as denoting those who are in evils of doctrine and of life, for by tongues are signified goods or evils of doctrine and thence of religion, as may be seen above, n. 330, 445, 625 ; and by nations are signified goods or

evils of life, see also above, n. 175, 331, 625; from which it may appear, that tongue and nations, signify all who are in goods or evils of doctrine and of life, in this case who are in evils, because it is said concerning them, that they shall see the bodies of the witnesses upon the street of the great city, and not permit them to be put in monuments.

658. " Their bodies three days and a half"—That hereby is signified the plenary extinction of divine truth and divine good, appears from the signification of the bodies, namely, of the witnesses, as denoting those who have extinguished with themselves all divine truth and divine good; for by the two witnesses, whom they slew, are signified the goods of love and charity and the truths of doctrine and faith, as may be seen above, n. 228, 635; hence by their bodies, when slain, is signified that those principles were extinguished; but whereas the good of love and charity and the truth of doctrine and faith cannot be extinguished, except only with those who are in falses of doctrine and in evils of life, therefore they are understood, inasmuch as others do not see the goods of love and truths of doctrine extinguished; for every one sees the things which are of the Lord, and thence the things which are of heaven and the church, according to the quality of his state, this being the ground whence his sight proceeds, wherefore he cannot see otherwise than agreeable to that quality; thus he who denies the Lord and his divine [principle] in heaven and in the church does not see them, because he sees from a negative principle, wherefore such a one does not see the witnesses alive, but their bodies as carcases, that is, the goods of love and truths of doctrine as none, consequently extinguished; and from the signification of three days and a half, as denoting what is plenary or full, in this case, a plenary extinction. The reason why three and a half denote what is plenary, is, because the number three signifies an entire period or duration from beginning to end, consequently, where the church is treated of, as in the present case, three and a half signifies even unto its end, and at the same time to a new beginning, wherefore it follows that after three days and a half the spirit of life from God entered into them and that they stood upon their feet, by which is signified the beginning of a new church after the end of the old; for all the good of love and truth of doctrine is extinguished in the end of the church, and then also it is raised up again, which is effected with those in whom a new church is established by the Lord, which is also signified by the spirit of life which entered into them. A plenary or full state is signified by three days and a half also for this reason, that the same is signified by this number as by the number seven, for it is the half thereof, and by a number halved, as also by a number doubled, is signified the same as by number itself which is halved or doubled; and by the number seven is signified all, likewise, what is full and plenary, and it is predicated of what is holy appertaining to heaven and the church, concerning which see above, n. 20, 24, 257, 299; that the greater numbers and congregates of lesser, signify the same as the simple numbers from which they arise by multiplication, may be also seen above, n. 430; and that three signify an entire period greater or less from beginning to end, may be seen above, n. 532.

659. "And will not permit them to be put in monuments"—That hereby is signified their rejection and damnation, appears from the signification of not being put in monuments, or not being buried, as denoting eternal damnation; for by burial, in the Word, is signified resuscitation into life and resurrection, inasmuch as when man dies and is buried, he is then raised up or rises again into life eternal; for man lives after death equally as in the world, but he lays down the terrestrial or material body, which served him for use in the natural world, and continues life in a spiritual body, wherefore burial is only a rejection as it were of the husk which he carried about in the natural world.   The reason why burial signifies resuscitation into life eternal, or resurrection, is, because the angels do not know what the death of man is, nor consequently what his burial is, inasmuch as there is no death nor burial with them; and still they perceive all things in the Word spiritually; wherefore where the death of man is mentioned, instead of death they perceive his transmigration from one world into another; and where burial is mentioned, they perceive his resurrection into life; from hence it follows that not to be buried signifies not to be raised again into life, but into damnation, by which is understood spiritual death; every man, indeed, after his departure out of the world, is raised up and rises again, but some to life and some to damnation, and whereas to be buried signifies resurrection to life, hence not to be buried signifies damnation, but, in this case, by those who reject the goods of love and truths of doctrine, which are signified by the two witnesses; therefore by not being put in monuments, or not buried, is not understood damnation except in the idea of those only who condemn such things.   What is signified therefore by sepulchres, in the Word, likewise by being buried and not buried, may appear from adducing some passages where they are mentioned.   That sepulchres signify things unclean, consequently also things infernal, by reason of the carcases and bones which are therein, appears from various passages in the Word; as in Isaiah: "A people who provoke me to anger before my faces continually, who burn incense upon bricks, who sit in the sepulchres, and pass the night in waste places, who eat the flesh of swine" (lxv. 3, 4).   To provoke Jehovah to anger before His faces, signifies to sin against truths and goods of the Word, and to recede from the worship there commanded, the faces of Jehovah are the things revealed in the Word; to burn incense upon bricks, signifies worship from falses of doctrine, bricks denoting falses of doctrine, and to burn incense denoting worship from them; to sit in the sepulchres, signifies to be in filthy loves; to pass the night in waste places, signifies to remain and live in falses, waste places denoting where there are no truths; to eat the flesh of swine, signifies to appropriate to themselves infernal evils.   So in Moses: "Whosoever shall touch upon the surface of the field one slain with the sword or dead, or the bone of a man, or a sepulchre, he shall be unclean seven days, and afterwards he shall be purified" (Numb. xix. 16, 18).   By touching, in the Word, is signified to communicate; wherefore lest falses and evils should be communicated,

and thus appropriated, it was prohibited to touch things unclean, as in this case the slain by the sword, the dead, the bone of a man, and a sepulchre; because by the slain with the sword are signified those who perish by falses, and are thence condemned to hell; and by the dead are signified those who perish by evils; by the bone of a man is signified infernal falses, and by sepulchre, infernal evil. Again in Ezekiel: "Wail over the multitude of Egypt and make her go down with them that go down into the pit: they shall fall by the sword in the midst of the slain; there is Ashur and his whole congregation, his sepulchres are about him, all the slain who fell by the sword to whom sepulchres were given in the sides of the pit, and his congregation is about his sepulchre; Elam and all his multitude is about his sepulchre, all the uncircumcised, slain with the sword" (xxxii. 18, 20–24). By the multitude of Egypt are signified scientifics of the natural man, which are dead, because they descend not and are not formed as effects, conclusions, and confirmations, from the truths of the spiritual man; by Ashur are signified ratiocinations from such scientifics; wherefore by, wail over the multitude of Egypt, and make her go down with them that go down into the pit, is signified grief on account of the damnation of those who are therein principled, the pit denoting the hell where such dead scientifics prevail, that is, scientifics separate from truths, because applied to confirm falses of doctrine and evils of life; by the slain with the sword, here as above, are signified those who are condemned to hell by falses; there is Ashur and his whole congregation, signifies ratiocinations from those falses; by the sepulchres which are about Ashur and in the sides of the pit, where Elam is, and all the uncircumcised slain with the sword, are signified the hells where those falses are, i. e. those who are in such falses. It is to be observed, that falses and evils of every kind correspond to whatever is unclean and hideous in the natural world, and the more dire falses and evils, to stinking cadaverous, and also to excrementitious substances, and those of a milder kind to marshy places; hence it is that the dwellings of those in the hells who are in such falses and evils, appear like pits and sepulchres; and if ye are disposed to believe it, such evil genii and spirits also dwell in the sepulchres, privies, and marshes which are in our world, although they are ignorant of it; the reason is, because they correspond, and things which correspond conjoin: the same may be concluded also from this consideration, that nothing is more delightful than cadaverous stenches to those who have been assassins and poisoners, likewise to those who perceived delight in violating women; and there is nothing more delightful than excrementitious stenches, to those who have been eaten up with the love of ruling imperiously, likewise to those who took delight in adulteries and none in marriages; and there is nothing more delightful than a marshy, and likewise a urinous stench, to those who have confirmed themselves in falses, and extinguished in themselves the affection of truth; hence it is that the hells in which they are, appear according to the correspondent delights, some as pits and some as sepulchres.

From these considerations it may also appear whence it was "The they who were obsessed by demons were in the sepulchres and came out thence" (Matt. viii. 28, and following verses; Mark v. 2, 3, 5 Luke viii. 27): viz. because they who obsessed, whilst they lived in the world were in falses from evil, or in knowledges from the Word, which they made dead by applying them to confirm evils, and likewise to destroy the genuine truth of the church, especially the truths concerning the Lord, concerning the Word, and concerning life after death, which dead knowledges in the Word are called traditions; hence it was that those who were obsessed by such, after they had become demons, were in the sepulchres, and the demons themselves were afterwards cast out into the swine, who precipitated themselves into the sea, the reason whereof was, because they had lived in the world in sordid avarice, which swine correspond to and thence signify; the reason why they precipitated themselves into the sea, was, because the sea there signified hell. Again in David: "I am reputed with them that go down into the pit. I am become as a man that hath no strength: I am amongst the dead, neglected, as the slain that lie in the sepulchre, whom thou rememberest no more, and who are cut off from thy hand; thou hast laid me in the pit of the lower parts, in darkness, in the deeps: shall Thy mercy be declared in the sepulchre, Thy truth in perdition," (Psalm lxxxviii. 5, 6, 7, 12). The subject there treated of is concerning temptations, in the supreme sense concerning the temptations of the Lord, the quality of which is here described, which was such, that He seemed to Himself to be as it were in hell, amongst the damned, so exceedingly direful and enormous were the temptations which the Lord sustained; wherefore I am reputed with those that go down into the pit, signifies, that He seemed to Himself as it were in hell, the pit denoting hell; I am become as a man that hath no strength, signifies that He then seemed to Himself to be as without power, for temptations immerse man into evils and falses, in which there is no power; amongst the dead, neglected, signifies amongst those in whom there is nothing of truth and good, and who are therefore rejected; as the slain that lie in the sepulchre, signifies as those who are in falses from evil, the slain denoting those who perish by falses, and the sepulchre denoting hell, by reason that they who are in hell are spiritually dead; whom thou rememberest no more, and who are cut off from thy hand, signifies who are deprived of all truth and good; thou hast laid me in the pit of the lower parts, signifies, in the places of hell where such are; in darkness, signifies as it were in falses; in the depths, signifies as it were in evils; prayer arising from grief then follows, that He may be delivered from the temptations; and amongst the reasons why He should be delivered from them, is this also, shall thy mercy be declared in the sepulchre, and thy truth in perdition, whereby is signified, that in hell where and whence evils and falses are, divine good and divine truth cannot be proclaimed; mercy denotes the divine good of the divine love, and truth is the divine truth of the divine wisdom; the sepulchre denotes hell where and whence evils are, and perdition denotes the hell where and whence falses are : from these considerations it is also evident, that by sepulchre is understood hell, and especially from this consideration, that they who are in hell are spiritually dead. So in Isaiah : " That He might give the impious to their sepulchre, and the rich in their deaths " (liii. 9). The whole of that chapter treats concerning the Lord, and here concerning His victories over the hells : by the impious whom He should give to the sepulchre, are understood the evil who shall be cast down into hell, which is manifestly called a sepulchre by reason of those who are there being spiritually dead ; by the rich whom he should give in their deaths, are understood those of the church who are in falses from evil, who are called rich by reason of the knowledges of truth and good which they have from the Word ; falses from evil are signified by deaths, inasmuch as they who are in them are spiritually dead. They who think evil concerning God and their neighbor, and yet speak well, and they who think insanely concerning the truths of faith and the goods of love whilst they speak sanely, are inwardly sepulchres and outwardly whitened, according to these words of the Lord : " Woe unto you, scribes and pharisees, hypocrites, for ye make yourselves like to whitened sepulchres, which appear indeed beautiful without, but within are full of bones of the dead and all uncleanness " (Matt. xxiii. 27, 29 ; Luke xi. 47, 48).   And in David : " There is no rectitude in their mouth, their midst is perditions ; their throat is an open sepulchre, they flatter with their tongue" (Psalm v. 10).   The mouth signifies outwardly or without, and the midst inwardly or within ; that within is hell, is signified by, their throat is an open sepulchre ; and that without is what is hypocritical and as it were sane, is signified by, they flatter with their tongue.   From these and other passages in the Word it may now manifestly appear what is signified by sepulchre. When therefore the subject treated of is concerning those who are in falses from evil, then by their sepulchre is understood the hell from which and in which that false is ; but where the subject treated of is concerning those who are in truths from good, then by sepulchre is understood the removal and rejection of the false from evil, and by burial is understood resuscitation and resurrection into life, likewise also regeneration : for with man who is in truths from good the false from evil is removed and rejected into hell, and the man himself, as to his interiors, which are of his spirit, rises again, and enters into the life of truth from good, which is spiritual life : in this sense burial is understood in the following passages : as in John : " Marvel not, for the hour cometh, in which all who are in the monuments shall hear the voice of the Son of Man, and shall come forth ; they who have done goods unto the resurrection of life, but they who have done evils unto the resurrection of judgment" (v. 28, 29).   By these words is not understood that they who are in the sepulchres or monuments shall hear the voice of the Lord and come forth, inasmuch as all men live after death equally as in the world, but with this sole difference, that after death they live in a spiritual body, and not in a material body ; wherefore by going forth out of the sepulchre is signified, out of the material body, which first takes place with every one immediately after death, and afterwards when the last judgment takes place, for then the exteriors are removed and the interiors are opened in all wíth whom this was not accomplished before, when they whose interiors are heavenly, rise into life, but they whose interiors are infernal, rise into death, which is signified by, they who have done goods shall go unto the resurrection of life, but they who have done evils unto the resurrection of judgment. That this is meant by going forth out of the sepulchres or monuments is still more evident in these words of the prophet Ezekiel : "Behold I am about to open your sepulchres, and I will cause you to ascend out of your sepulchres, O my people, and I will bring you upon the land of Israel, that ye may know that I am Jehovah, when I shall have opened your sepulchres, and shall have caused you to ascend out of your sepulchres, O my people, and I shall have given My spirit in you that ye may live, and I shall have placed you upon your land" (xxxvii. 13, 14). The subject here treated of is concerning the dry bones seen by the prophet upon the faces of the valley, upon which nerves appeared adduced and flesh came upon them, and they were covered with skin, and which, after the spirit of God came into them, revived, and stood upon their feet : that by those bones is understood the whole house of Israel, is openly declared in these words, " Son of man these bones are the whole house of Israel, behold they say, Our bones are dried up, our hope hath perished, we are cut off for our parts" (verse 11). The reason of the house of Israel being likened to dry bones, was, because they were in falses and evils, which have not any life, because no correspondence with heaven as to nerves, flesh, and skin, for by bones are signified truths in the ultimate of order, upon which spiritual truths have their foundation, but dry bones signify falses derived from evil ; hence it may appear that by opening the sepulchres, and causing the people to ascend out of the sepulchres, is signified to raise up out of falses from evil, thus from the dead, and to endow with truths from good, thus with life, which life is the spirit of God, from which they revived ; this therefore is what is meant by causing to ascend out of the sepulchres ; the church to be formed of them, is signified by the land of Israel, upon which they shall be brought, and upon which they shall be placed together. It is recorded in Matthew, "That after the passion of the Lord the monuments were opened, and many bodies of those that slept went out of the monuments into the holy city and appeared to many" (xxvii. 52, 53). By the monuments being opened, and many bodies of them that slept appearing, is signified the like as above in Ezekiel, where it is said Jehovah would open the sepulchres, and cause them to ascend out of the sepulchres, namely, the regeneration and resurrection of the faithful unto life, not that the bodies themselves, which lay in the monuments, rose again, but that they appeared, to the intent that both regeneration and resurrection to life from the Lord might be signified : moreover, by the same words are understood those who are said in the Word to be bound in the pit, whom the Lord liberated, after He had finished the whole work of redemption : for many of the

.ithful could not be saved, before the Lord came into the world and '
abjugated the hells, and in the mean time they were detained in
te places which are called pits, even to the coming of the Lord,
at were liberated by the Lord immediately after his advent: these
its were also represented by the sepulchres which were opened,
ad they who were therein by those that slept, who after the Lord's
surrection, as it is said, appeared to many in the holy city; the
oly city was Zion and Jerusalem, but thereby is understood
eaven, whither they were raised up by the Lord, for both Zion and
Jerusalem were rather profane than holy: from these considerations
may appear what that miracle and that appearance represented
id signified. Inasmuch as by the land of Canaan is not only sig-
fied the church, but also heaven, and by burial is signified resur-
ction into life, therefore "Abraham bought of Ephron a field in
hich was the cave of Machpelah which is before Mamre" (Gen.
ciii.): and "there Abraham, Isaac, and Jacob, with their wives,
ere buried" (Gen. xxiii.; chap. xxv. 9, 10; chap. xxxv. 29; chap.
ix.; chap. l). The particular things related concerning that cave,
mely, that it was in the field of Ephron, which is before Mamre,
id so on, were significative of resurrection unto life, which may be
en explained in the A. C. On this account also Joseph com-
anded "that his bones should be brought up into the land of
anaan" (Gen. l. 24, 25, 26): "which was also done" (Exod.
ii. 19; Joshua xxiv. 32). And this because the land of Canaan,
was said, signified the heavenly Canaan, which is heaven. On
xount of the representation of resurrection into heaven by burial,
so, "David and the kings after him were buried in Zion" (1 Kings
10; chap. xi. 43; chap. xiv. 17, 18; chap. xv. 8, 24; chap.
cii. 51; 2 Kings viii. 24; chap. xii. 22; chap. xiv. 20; chap.
r. 7, 38; chap. xvi. 20). The reason of which was, because
ion signified the celestial church and heaven, where the Lord
. That burial signifies resurrection may also appear from this
nsideration, that it is frequently said concerning the dead, that
ey were gathered to their fathers and to their pepole; to their
thers, in Genesis: "Jehovah said unto Abraham, Thou shalt
me unto thy fathers in peace, and shalt be buried in a good
d age" (xiv. 15): and in 2 Kings: "Jehovah said of Josiah
ing of Judah, Behold I gather thee unto thy fathers, and thou
alt be gathered into thy sepulchre in peace" (xxii. 20): and
their people, in Genesis: "Abraham expired and died in a good
d age, an old man and full of days, and was gathered unto his
eople" (xxv. 8): and in another place: "Isaac expired and died,
id was gathered unto his people, an old man and full of days"
:xxv. 29): and again: "Jacob expired, and was gathered unto
is people" (xlix. 33). In all which passages to their fathers and
their people denote to their own, that is, to their like in the other
fe, for every one after death comes to his like, with whom he is to
ve for ever: it cannot be meant to be gathered to their fathers, and
their people in the sepulchre, for it is also said concerning Abra-
am, that he should be gathered to his fathers, and that he was
athered to his people when dead, whereas he was buried in a new

sepulchre, where none of his fathers or of his people were before him, except Sarah his wife. So in Job: " Thou shalt know that thy tabernacle shall be peace, and thy children as the herb of the land, thou shalt come in old age unto the sepulchre, as a shock of corn cometh up in its season" (v. 24, 25). By tabernacle, in the Word, is signified the holy principle of worship, and the good of love, be- cause divine worship, in the most ancient times, was performed in tabernacles, and because their worship was from the good of celes- tial love, therefore by a tabernacle is also signified that good, and inasmuch as genuine peace appertains to celestial good, therefore it is said, thou shalt know that thy tabernacle shall be peace; the truths from that good and their increasings are signified by the chil- dren which shall be as the herb of the land, for truths from good are signified by sons and children and likewise by the herb of the land; that after being endued with wisdom he should come into heaven, is signified by, thou shalt come in old age into the sepulchre, old age denoting wisdom, and to come to the sepulchre, or to be buried, de- noting resurrection : hence it is also added, as a shock of corn cometh up in its season. From these few instances it may appear, that sepulchres, by reason of the inanimate carcases and bones therein, signify things infernal, and that burial signifies the rejection thereof, consequently also resurrection : for when man rejects or puts off his material body, he then puts on the spiritual body, with which he rises again : hence also it is, that the death itself of man, in the spiritual sense, signifies the continuation of his life, although in a bad sense it signifies damnation, which is spiritual death : whereas burial, with respect to man, signifies resurrection, and also regeneration, therefore with respect to the Lord it signified the glo- rification of His Humanity ; for the Lord glorified His whole Hu- manity, that is, made it divine, wherefore He rose again the third day with the Humanity glorified or made divine : unless this had been accomplished, no man could have risen again to life; for the resurrection of man unto life is solely from the Lord, and indeed from the union of His divine [principle] with His human, which is properly understood by glorification, and by virtue whereof man has salvation : this also is involved in what the Lord said concerning the woman " who poured balsamic ointment upon His head, that she did it unto His burial " (Matt. xxvi. 7, 12; Mark xiv. 8; John xii. 7). For by unition is signified that glorification ; and whereas by virtue thereof man has salvation, therefore He said concerning the woman, " Verily I say unto you, wheresoever this gospel shall be preached in the whole world, there also shall be reported what this woman hath done for a memorial of her " (Matt. xxvi. 13). This was also represented " by the man who was cast into the sepulchre of Elisha reviving when he touched his bones " (2 Kings xiii. 20, 21). For by Elisha was represented the Lord as to divine truth, which constitutes the life of heaven, into which man is raised up or resuscitated. Inasmuch as to be buried and burial signifies both re- suscitation into life and regeneration ; therefore by not being buried, and by being dragged out of the monuments, is signified no resurrec- tion to heaven, nor regeneration, but resurrection to hell, and consequently damnation : as in the following passages; thus in Isaiah : "Thou art cast out of thy sepulchre as an abominable shoot, the raiment of the slain thrust through with the sword, who go down to the stones of the pit, as a carcase trodden under foot; thou shalt not be joined with them in the sepulchre, for thou hast destroyed thy land, thou hast slain thy people, the seed of evil doers shall not be named for ever" (xiv. 19, 20). Those things are said concerning the king of Babel, by whom is signified the profanation of divine truth; wherefore by, thou art cast out of thy sepulchre, is signified condemnation to hell; as an abominable shoot, the raiment of the slain, thrust through with the sword, signifies the falsification of truth and profanation thereof, an abominable shoot denoting truth falsified, and the raiment of the slain, thrust through with the sword, denoting truth adulterated and altogether destroyed by dire falses; who go down to the stones of the pit, as a carcase trodden under foot signifies to the hell where are the falses of evil, a carcase trodden under foot denoting the infernal spirit, with whom everything is spiritually dead, by reason of good being altogether destroyed; thou shalt not be joined with them in the sepulchre, signifies no consociation with those who rise again to life, for to be laid in the sepulchre, or to be buried, signifies that resurrection, and on the other hand, to be cast out of the sepulchre signifies damnation; thou hast destroyed thy land, thou hast slain thy people, signifies the destruction of the church, and of those therein who were in truths from good, by the falses of evil; the seed of evil doers shall not be named for ever, signifies eternal dissociation and separation. Again in Jeremiah : "Jehovah hath said concerning the sons and concerning the daughters who are born in this place, and concerning their mothers who bare them and concerning their fathers who begat them in this land; they shall die sickly deaths, so that they shall not be lamented, neither buried; they shall be for dung upon the faces of the earth; they shall be consumed by the sword, and by famine, and their carcase shall be for meat to the birds of the heavens, and to the beast of the earth" (xvi. 3, 4). Treating of the church vastated as to all good and truth; by sons and daughters, and by mothers and fathers, in the spiritual sense, are not understood sons and daughters, mothers and fathers, but the truths and goods of the church, both exterior and interior, sons and daughters denoting truths and goods exterior, mothers and fathers denoting truths and goods interior, which are called mothers and fathers because they beget and produce the exterior; they shall die sickly deaths, so that they shall not be lamented neither buried, signifies condemnation to hell on account of dire falses; they shall be for dung upon the faces of the earth, signifies the filthy infernal principle which is the evil that defiles the good and truth of the church; to be consumed by sword and famine, signifies to be destroyed by falses and evils; and their carcase shall be for meat to the birds of the heavens and to the beast of the earth, signifies, to be consumed then, and also further, by the cupidities of the love of evil and the false. Again in the same prophet : "A tumult cometh even to the end of the earth, for Jehovah hath a controversy against the nations; He shall enter into judgment with all flesh, He shall give up the impious to the sword; the slain of Jehovah shall be in that day from the end of the earth unto the end of the earth, they shall not be lamented, nor gathered, neither buried, they shall be for dung upon the faces of the earth" (xxv. 32, 33).   By these words is described the devastation of the church at its end when the last judgment takes place : the tumult even to the end of the earth because of the controversy of Jehovah against the nations, signifies the consternation of all who are of the church whilst their evils are visited and detected, the earth denoting the church, the nations, those who are in evils, and abstractedly, evils, and the controversy of Jehovah against them, visitation and detection; He shall enter into judgment with all flesh, signifies the universal judgment which takes place in the end of the church; He shall give up the impious to the sword, signifies that the unfaithful shall perish by their own falses; the slain of Jehovah in that day shall be from the end of the earth unto the end of the earth, signifies those who perish by falses of every kind, the slain of Jehovah denoting those who perish by falses, and from the end of the earth even to the end of the earth, denoting from first principles to the ultimates of the church, consequently falses of every kind; they shall not be lamented, neither gathered nor buried, signifies that there will be no more any restoration or salvation, but condemnation, lamentation signifying grief on account of such a state of man, and no lamentation signifying no grief, on account of man's being such as to admit of no restoration; they shall be for dung upon the faces of the earth, signifies merely falses and evil, without reception of life from heaven; for if man does not receive life by the truths of faith and goods of charity, he is merely dead, being in mere falses of evil and evils of the false, which are carcase and dung upon the faces of the earth.   Again in the same prophet : " Against the prophets who prophesy a lie in the name of Jehovah : the people to whom they prophesy shall be cast away in the streets of Jerusalem ; on account of famine and the sword, there shall be none to bury them, themselves, their wives, and their sons, and their daughters" (xiv. 16).   Where not to be buried denotes not to rise again to life but to damnation; the rest may be seen explained above, n. 652.   Again : " In that time they shall bring out the bones of the kings of Judah and the bones of the princes thereof, and the bones of the priests, and the bones of the prophets, and the bones of the inhabitants of Jerusalem, out of their sepulchres, and shall spread them out to the sun, and to the moon, and to all the host of the heavens, which they have loved, and which they have served, and which they have gone after, and which they have sought, and to which they have bowed down themselves ; they shall not be gathered neither buried, they shall be for dung upon the faces of the earth " (viii. 1, 2).   By bringing out the bones from the sepulchres, is signified to dissociate from their people, that is, to cast out from communion with those who are in heaven, abroad amongst the damned, as is the case when the evil enter the societies of the good, and being afterwards detected, are cast out:

for concerning them that are buried it is said that they are gathered to their people, as above concerning Abraham, Isaac, and Jacob, whence it follows, that to be drawn out of the sepulchre, denotes to be cast out from them; all who are of the church, likewise all things appertaining to the church, are signified by the kings, princes, priests, prophets, and inhabitants of Jerusalem; by kings the truths themselves of the church in the whole complex; by princes, principal truths; by priests, the goods of doctrine; by prophets, the truths of doctrine, and by the inhabitants of Jerusalem, all things of the church thence depending; in this case by their bones, which are to be drawn out, are signified falses and evils, which have nothing in common with truths and goods; by spreading them out to the sun, to the moon, and to all the host of the heavens, is signified to be given up to diabolic loves, and thence to evils and falses which are from hell; for the sun signifies love in both senses, the moon, faith in both senses derived from that love, and the host of the heavens, falses and evils of every kind; to spread out the bones therefore in this case, is altogether to deliver them up to such things, so as to be nothing but loves and cupidities of evil and the false; which they have loved, which they have served, after which they have gone, which they have sought, and to which they have bowed down themselves, signifies affection and propensity to those things exterior and interior, and worship thence derived; they shall not be gathered, neither buried, signifies that they shall never return to the societies which belong to heaven, but remain with those who are in hell; they shall be for dung upon the faces of the earth, signifies such a dead and unclean principle, as is cast out and trodden under foot.   Hence it may also appear what is signified "by the bones of Josiah the king being taken out of the sepulchre and burnt upon the altar" (2 Kings xxiii. 16): "by Jezebel being eaten by the dogs in the field, and none to bury her" (2 Kings ix. 10): and "by Jehoiakim, the son of Josiah, King of Judah, being buried with the burial of an ass, drawn out, and cast afar off beyond the gates of Jerusalem" (Jeremiah xxii. 19).   The like is also signified by being buried in Tophet, and in the valley of Hinnom, in Jeremiah: "Behold the days come in which it shall no more be called Tophet, or the valley of the son of Hinnom, but the valley of slaughter; and they shall bury in Tophet till there is no room, and the carcase of this people shall be for meat to the bird of the heavens, and to the beast of the earth, and none shall fray them away" (vii. 32, 33).   And again: " I will break this people and this city as the vessel of a potter is broken, which cannot be repaired any more, and they shall bury in Tophet, because there is no place to bury, and I will make this city as Tophet" (xix. 11, 12).   Tophet and the valley of Hinnom signified the hells, Tophet, the hell from behind, which is called the devil, and the valley of Hinnom, the hell from before, which is called Satan; for in the city Jerusalem, and about it, all places correspond to places in the spiritual world, and in that world the habitations are according to divine order; in the midst are those who are in the greatest light or wisdom: in the borders, those who are in the least;

to the east and west, those who are principled in love; to the south
and north, those who are principled in intelligence: such is the
ordination of the universal heaven: the like also prevails in every
society, in every city, and in every house, and this on that account,
because the lesser forms in the heavens are also according to the
likeness of the greatest form: and whereas Jerusalem signified
heaven and the church as to doctrine, hence also the places there
were representative according to their quarters and distances from
the temple and from Zion.   Hence Tophet and the valley of Hinnom, being the most unclean places, and impiously idolatrous, represented and thence signified the hells: from these considerations
it is evident what is signified by burying in Tophet, and in the
valley of Hinnom.

660. "And they that dwell upon the earth shall rejoice over them
and shall be glad"—That hereby are signified the delights originating in infernal loves with those who are against the goods and
truths of the church, appears from the signification of them that
dwell upon the earth, as denoting those who are in the church, and
in the present case, those therein who are in evils and thence in
falses, consequently who are against the goods and truths thereof;
and from the signification of rejoicing and being glad, as here denoting the delight of infernal love; for all joy and all gladness is of
love; for every one rejoices and is glad when his love is favored,
and when he arrives at and obtains the object of his love; in a word,
all the joy of man proceeds from his love, and all sadness and grief
of mind from opposition thereto.   The reason why to rejoice and to
be glad are both mentioned, is, on account of the marriage of good
and truth in every part of the Word; for joy is predicated of good,
because it is of the love, being properly of the heart and will, and
gladness is predicated of truth, because it is of its love, being properly of the mind and its thought, wherefore we say joy of heart and
gladness of mind: for every where in the Word there are two expressions, one of which has reference to good and the other to truth,
and this because the conjunction of good and truth constitutes both
heaven and the church; hence both heaven and the church are compared to a marriage from this circumstance, that the Lord is called
bridegroom and husband, and heaven and the church, bride and
wife; wherefore every one who is not in that marriage, is not an
angel of heaven, nor a man of the church; the reason whereof also is,
because good is not given with any one unless it is formed by truths,
nor is truth given unless it lives from good; for all truth is the form
of good, and all good is the esse of truth, and inasmuch as one without the other is not given, it follows that the marriage of good and
truth is necessary to constitute the man of the church as well as the
angel of heaven: all intelligence and wisdom is also derived from
that marriage, for from it goods and truths are continually born, by
which the understanding and will is formed.   These things are said
in order that it may be known, why to rejoice and be glad are mentioned together, namely, because to rejoice is predicated of good and
its love or affection, and to be glad is predicated of truth, and of its

love or affection : thus also in the following passages: "The heavens shall be glad, and the earth shall rejoice" (Psalm xcvi. 11). "Let all that seek Thee rejoice and be glad in Thee" (Psalm xl. 17; Psalm lxx. 5). "The just shall be glad, and exult before God, and shall rejoice in gladness" (Psalm lxviii. 4). "That we may rejoice all our days, make us glad according to the days in which thou hast afflicted us" (Psalm xc. 14, 15). "Be glad in Jerusalem, and exult in her, all ye that love her, rejoice a joy with her, all ye that mourn over her" (Isaiah lxvi. 10). "Rejoice and be glad, O Daughter of Edom" (Lam.-iv. 21). "Behold joy and gladness to kill the ox" (Isaiah xxii. 13). "They shall obtain joy and gladness, sorrow and sighing shall flee away" (Isaiah xxxv. 10; chap. li. 11). "Joy and gladness shall be found in her, confession and the voice of singing" (Isaiah li. 3). "Make me to hear joy and gladness" (Psalm li. 10). "Joy and gladness is cut off from the house of our God" (Joel i. 16). "The fast of the tenth shall be to the house of Judah for joy and for gladness" (Zech. viii. 19). "The voice of joy and the voice of gladness, and the voice of the bridegroom and the voice of the bride" (Jer. vii. 34; chap. xxv. 10; chap. xxxiii. 11). In the place of joy, exultation is also mentioned, because exultation, in like manner as joy, is predicated of good, being of the love of the heart and the will; as in the following passages: "Jacob shall exult, Israel shall be glad" (Psalm xiv. 7; Psalm liii. 7); "I exult and am glad in thy benignity" (Psalm xxxi. 7). "Be glad in Jehovah and exult, O ye just" (Psalm xxxii. 11). "The mount of Zion shall be glad, and the daughters of Judah shall exult" (Psalm xlviii. 12); "Let all that confide in Thee be glad, and let them that love Thy name exult in Thee" (Psalm v. 12). "This is the day which Jehovah hath made, we will exult and be glad in it" (Psalm cxviii. 24.) "We will exult and be glad in His salvation" (Isaiah xxv. 9). "Be glad and exult for ever in the things which I create" (Isaiah lxv. 18). "Exult and be glad that Jehovah hath magnified His doing" (Joel ii. 21). "Sons of Zion exult and be glad in Jehovah your God" (Joel ii. 23; Habakkuk i. 15). "Be glad and exult from all thy heart, O daughter of Jerusalem" (Zephan. iii. 14). "Gladness and exultation is taken away from Carmel" (Isaiah xvi. 10; Jeremiah xlviii. 33). "The angel said unto Zechariah, thou shalt have gladness and exultation, and many shall rejoice upon His nativity" (Luke i. 14). In all these passages, exultation signifies the delight originating in the love and affection of good, and gladness signifies the pleasantness originating in the love and affection of truth.

661. "And they shall send gifts one to another"—That hereby is signified their consociation, appears from the signification of sending gifts, as denoting to be consociated by benevolence from love and friendship; for gifts proceeding from that mind, and that affection, consociate both the well-disposed and the ill-disposed, in this case, those who are against the goods of love and truths of doctrine, which are signified by the two witnesses who were slain and cast into the street of the great city, which is spiritually called Sodom

and Egypt. It is to be observed, that to the ill-disposed and impious, nothing is more delightful than to destroy the goods of love and truths of doctrine, wherever they are, and to do evil to those who are principled in them; for they burn with hatred against such things, and hence it is that from the hell, where such persons are, there continually expires a deadly hatred against celestial love and spiritual faith, consequently against heaven, and especially against the Lord Himself; and as often as they are permitted to do evil, they are in the delight of their heart; such is the beastly nature of those who are in hell; this therefore is what is understood by, they shall rejoice and be glad over them. The ill disposed also enter into friendships and consociate with the simple good, to bring hurt upon them; the delight of hatred, which is the delight of their love, is what consociates, and then they appear as if they were friends in heart, when notwithstanding they are enemies; this therefore, is what is signified by sending gifts one to another. Inasmuch as gifts captivate the mind and consociate, therefore in ancient times, it was customary to give gifts to the priest, and to the prophet, likewise to a prince and king, when they approached them, 1 Sam. ix. 7, 8; and it was also appointed, "That they should not appear empty, that is, without gifts, before Jehovah, but in their feasts every one should bring a gift according to his blessing," (Exod. xxiii. 15; chap. xxxiv. 20; Deut. xvi. 16, 17); and hence also "the wise men from the east brought to the Lord, as soon as He was born, gifts, gold, frankincense, and myrrh" (Matt. ii. 11); according to the prediction in David, Psalm lxxii. 10; and for the same reason,. the oblations upon the altar, which were sacrifices, and also the meat-offerings and drink-offerings, were called gifts, Isaiah xviii. 10; chap. lvii. 6; chap. lxvi. 20; Zephan. iii. 10; Matt. v. 23, 24, and elsewhere; and this because external gifts signified internal or spiritual gifts, viz. such as proceed from the heart, and of consequence are of the affection and faith; and whereas by these conjunction is effected, therefore by gifts in the spiritual sense, is signified conjunction, when predicated of God, and consociation, when predicated of men.

662. "Because those two prophets tormented them that dwell upon the earth"—That hereby is signified anxiety of heart occasioned by them in the devastated church, appears from the signification of the two witnesses, who are here called two prophets, as denoting the goods and truths of doctrine; and from the signification of tormenting, as denoting anxiety of heart: and from the signification of them that dwell upon the earth, as denoting those who live in the church, in this case, in the devastated church; hence by those words is signified anxiety of heart arising from the goods of love and truths of doctrine to those who are of the devastated church; for the subject here treated of is concerning the end of the church, when the loves of self and of the world, and their concupiscences, and the evils and falses of those concupiscences, have rule, in which case the goods of love and truths of doctrine torment men, for inwardly

or in their hearts they entertain hatred towards them, howsoever they may confess them with their lips, and when anything enters which a man hates, it inwardly torments him : howbeit the man of the church, who is of such a quality and nature during his abode in the world, does not know that he is in such hatred against those two witnesses, and that he is inwardly tormented by them, by reason that he does not know the state of his interior thought and affection, but only of his exterior thought and affection, which immediately falls into the speech ; but when he comes into the spiritual world, his exterior thought and affection is laid asleep, and the interior is opened, and then he feels a repugnance arising from hatred against the goods of love and truths of doctrine, insomuch that he cannot bear to hear them ; wherefore when such a man enters any angelic society, where spiritual love and faith prevail, he is vehemently tormented, which is a sign of interior repugnance, arising from hatred against them.   From these considerations it may appear what is signified by the two prophets tormenting them that dwell on the earth. By them that dwell on the earth are understood, in a good sense, those in the church who are in good as to life, but here, those who are in evil, for such are inwardly tormented by the goods of love and truths of doctrine.   That to dwell signifies to live, consequently life, may appear from the passages in the Word, where dwelling is mentioned ; as in Isaiah xi. 6 ; chap. xiii. 20 ; chap. xxxvii. 16 ; Jerem. ii. 6, 15 ; chap. li. 13 ; Dan. ii. 22 ; chap. iv. 9 ; Ezek. xxxi. 6 ; Hosea ix. 2, 3 ; Psalm xxiii. 6 ; Psalm xxvii. 4 ; Psalm lxxx. 2 ; Psalm ci. 7 ; Zephan. iii. 6 ; and elsewhere.

663.   Verses 11, 12.   " And after three days and a half the spirit of life from God entered into them, and they stood upon their feet, and great fear fell upon them that saw them.   And they heard a great voice out of heaven, saying to them, ascend hither.   And they ascended into heaven in a cloud and their enemies saw them."— " And after three days and a half," signifies when the state was complete, thus the end of the old church, and the beginning of the new church : " the spirit of life from God entered into them," signifies illustration and reception of the influx of divine truth from the Lord with some for the beginning of a new church : " and they stood upon their feet," signifies a new life such as appertains to the man of the church when regenerate ; " and great fear fell upon them that saw them," signifies a state of anxiety with those who have not received and acknowledged : " and they heard a great voice out of heaven, saying to them," signifies the divine providence of the Lord : " ascend hither," signifies separation and thence protection : " and they ascended into heaven in a cloud," signifies separation as to things internal, and the protection thereof : " and their enemies saw them," signifies knowledge and acknowledgment with those who are inwardly against the goods and truths of the Word and of the church.

664.   " And after three days and a half"—That hereby is signi-

fied when the state is complete, thus the end of the old church, and the beginning of a new church, may appear from the signification of three days and a half, as denoting what is full or complete unto the end of the old church, when a new church commences, concerning which see above, n. 658. The reason why it is said, after three days and a half, is, because days, in the Word, signify states, here, the last state of the church; for all times, in the Word, as hours, days, months, years, ages, are significative of states, as in this case, the last state of the church, in which there is no longer any good of love or truth of faith remaining. Inasmuch as by days are signified states, and the establishment of the most ancient church is treated of in the first chapter of Genesis, and this was successively accomplished from one state to another, therefore it is there said that the evening and the morning was the first, the second, the third, the fourth, the fifth, and sixth days, unto the seventh, when it was complete, Gen. i. 5, 8, 13, 19, 23, 31; and by the days there mentioned are not understood days, but the successive states of the regeneration of men at that time, and the establishment of the church with them; the like is signified by days in other parts of the Word.

665. " The spirit of life from God entered into them"—That hereby is signified illustration and reception of divine truth from the Lord with some, to commence a new church, appears from the signification of the spirit of life from God, as denoting the divine truth proceeding from the Lord, concerning which we shall speak presently; and from the signification of entering into them, viz. into the witnesses that were slain and cast into the streets, as denoting illustration and the reception of influx, namely, of divine truth, which is signified by the spirit of life; that this takes place with some for the commencement of a new church, is evident from the following verse, where it is said, that they ascended into heaven in a cloud, thus with some, for by the two witnesses are signified the goods of love and truths of doctrine, consequently those who receive them, or with whom they are, for all such are witnesses. When the end of the church is at hand, it is then provided by the Lord that a new church should succeed, because without a church in which the Word is, and in which the Lord is known, the world cannot possibly subsist; for without the Word and thence the knowledge and acknowledgment of the Lord, heaven cannot be conjoined to the human race, nor, consequently, can the divine truth proceeding from the Lord flow in with new life; and without conjunction with heaven and thereby with the Lord, man would not be man but a beast; hence it is that a new church is always provided by the Lord, when the old church comes to its end: the reason why the commencement or beginning only of a new church is understood, and not yet its establishment, will be shown in the explication of the following verse. That by the spirit of life from God, or by the spirit of God, and by the holy spirit, is understood the divine proceeding from the Lord, which is called the divine truth, from which comes all wisdom and intelligence, may be seen above, n. 24, 183, 318: this divine proceeding is what illustrates man, and flows in

with him, when he is reforming and regenerating, thus when the church commences and is establishing with him, as may manifestly appear from the passages adduced above from the Word, n. 183; the same may also appear from these words in Ezekiel : " Jehovah said unto me, Prophesy upon the spirit, and prophesy, Son of Man, and say unto the wind, thus saith the Lord Jehovih, Come, O spirit, from the four winds, and breathe into these slain that they may live; and when I prophesied the spirit entered into them, and they revived, and stood upon their feet, an exceeding great army" (xxxvii. 9, 10); treating of the dry bones seen by the prophet upon the faces of the valley, by which is signified the house of Israel, as is manifestly declared, verse 11, of the same chapter; and by the house of Israel is signified the church, which is there compared to dry bones because there was no good of love nor truth of doctrine therein ; the establishment of a new church by the inspiration of new life, or by regeneration, is described by nerves, flesh, and skin, with which the bones were clothed and encompassed, and especially by the spirit which entered into them, and from which they revived; by the spirit in them is there also signified the reception of the influx of divine truth, and spiritual life thence derived : the reason why the prophet said unto the wind, come, O spirit, from the four winds, is, because by the four winds are signified the four quarters in the spiritual world, and by the four quarters there, are signified the goods of love and truths of doctrine in every complex, concerning which see above, n. 417, 418, 419, 422, and in the work concerning H. & H. n. 141–151.

666. "And they stood upon their feet"—That hereby is signified new life, such as is that of the man of the church, when regenerate, appears from the signification of standing, as denoting to be and to live, and also to sustain, concerning which see above, n. 414; and from the signification of feet, as denoting the natural principle, which is the ultimate of divine order, and the basis upon which things prior or superior rest and subsist, concerning which also, see above, n. 69, 600, 606; hence by standing upon the feet is signified life in fulness, because in the ultimate ; the reason why new life is signified, is, because the witnesses, who are here treated of, were slain and revived : the reason why such life is here understood by standing upon the feet as appertains to the regenerate man of the church, is, because these things are said of the two witnesses, by whom are understood all who are in the goods of love by truths of doctrine, who are those that are regenerated ; likewise because when the natural principle, which is signified by the feet, is regenerated, the whole man has life, such as appertains to the regenerate, according to the words of the Lord in John : "Jesus said unto Peter, He who is washed, needeth only to be washed as to the feet, and he is wholly clean" (xiii. 10). By being washed is signified to be purified from evils and falses, which is to be regenerated, wherefore he who is washed signifies he who is purified, that is, regenerated, as to the spiritual principle, which is the good of love and truth of doctrine, which are first to be received in the memory and understanding, that is, to be known

and acknowledged; has need only to be washed as to the feet, signifies, that the natural or external man is then to be purified or regenerated, which is done by a life according to the precepts of love
and faith, that is, according to the goods and truths of doctrine from
the Word; when this takes place, the man himself is purified or regenerated; for to live according to the goods and truths of doctrine
from the Word, is to will them, and thence to do them, which is the
same thing as to be affected with them, and to love them; for what
becomes of the will, becomes also of the affection and of the love,
consequently, of the man himself, for the will is the man himself,
inasmuch as man is his own love and his own affection; hence it is
said, that then the whole man is clean.   From these considerations
it is evident whence it is, that to stand upon the feet denotes life
such as appertains to a regenerate man; hence also it is said concerning the dry bones seen by the prophet on the face of the valley,
after they were covered with nerves, flesh, and skin, "When I prophesied concerning the spirit, the spirit entered into them, and they
revived and stood upon their feet" (Ezek. xxxvii. 10); where also
by standing upon the feet is signified new life, such as appertains
to a regenerate man; for by the dry bones to which the house of
Israel is likened, is signified the state of the church destitute of the
goods of love and truths of doctrine; and by the clothing of nerves,
flesh, and skin, is signified regeneration; and by the spirit which
entered, new life by the influx and reception of divine truth; wherefore it is then said, that they revived and stood upon their feet. The
like is signified by standing upon their feet in other parts of the
Word; as again in the same prophet: "The voice spake with me
and said, Son of Man, stand upon thy feet, that I may speak unto
thee; then the spirit came into me, when he spake unto me, and
set me upon my feet, and I heard him speaking to me" (Ezek. ii.
1, 2); and again: "I fell upon my faces, but the spirit came into
me, and raised me upon my feet" (Ezek. iii. 23, 24): these things
were done, because life itself, when it is in its fulness, is signified
by standing upon the feet, and it is then in its fulness when the natural principle lives from the spiritual; for the ultimate of man's
life is in his natural principle, and this ultimate is as a basis to his
interior and superior principles, which therein terminate and subsist,
wherefore unless life be in the ultimate, it is not full, and consequently not perfect; moreover, all the interior or superior principles
co-exist in the ultimate, as in their simultaneous principles, whence
according to the quality of the ultimate, such are the interior or superior principles, for these accommodate themselves to the ultimate,
because it receives them.   The like is also signified by standing
upon the feet in David: "Thou makest my feet to stand in the
breadth" (Psalm xxxi. 9).   By breadth is signified the truth of doctrine from the Word, wherefore by causing his feet to stand in the
breadth is signified, to cause him to live according to divine truths.
So again: "Thou hast made me to ascend out of the pit of devastation, out of the mire of clay, and hast set my feet upon a rock"
(Psalm xl. 3).   By the pit of devastation is signified the false of

doctrine, and by the mire of clay is signified evil of the life: and by setting his feet upon a rock is signified the same as above, by causing his feet to stand in the breadth, for by a rock is also signified the truth of doctrine from the Word, and, in the supreme sense, the Lord as to divine truth.   Hence also it is evident, what in the spiritual sense is signified in these words in another place : "Jehovah will not suffer my feet to stagger" (Psalm cxxi. 3) : namely, that he will not suffer the natural principle to wander away from truths; or in proportion as the natural principle wanders, the interiors which are of the understanding and will, wander also.

667. "And great fear fell upon those that saw them"—That hereby is signified a state of anxiety with those who did not receive and acknowledge, appears from the signification of great fear, as denoting a state of anxiety, for by fear, in the Word, are signified various changes of the state of the interiors of man, in the present case therefore, a state of anxiety ; and from the signification of upon those that saw them, as denoting, with those that could not sustain the presence of the witnesses, and who therefore slew and cast them out, to whom therefore to see them alive, caused grief and anxiety of heart, consequently denoting with those who did not receive and acknowledge the good of love, and the truth of doctrine.   In these words are described the state of those who are against the goods of love and truths of doctrine, at the end of the old church and beginning of the new, who then come into anxiety from the presence of those who receive love and faith to the Lord, of whom the new church is formed : this however takes place in the spiritual world, but not in the natural world: for in the spiritual world there is a communication of affections, and spiritual affection, which is of love and faith to the Lord, and which now commences with some, strikes such anxiety into the evil.   This therefore is what is understood by great fear falling upon those that saw them.

668. "And they heard a great voice out of heaven, saying to them"—That hereby is signified the divine providence of the Lord, appears from the signification of a great voice out of heaven, as denoting the divine providence of the Lord : by a voice out of heaven is signified all that proceeds from the Lord, which, in general, is called divine truth, and, with us in the world, the Word, thus specifically it signifies every precept and command which is in the Word, and which is called a voice out of heaven, because it descended from the Lord through or by heaven, and continually descends with those who read the Word from a spiritual affection of truth : but the reason why it is the divine providence of the Lord which is signified in this place by the voice out of heaven, is, because the subject treated of is concerning the state of heaven and of the church at the end thereof, when it is provided by the Lord that a hasty change may not bring evil upon those who are to be separated, of whom many are to come into heaven, and many are to be cast into hell : this is the reason why it now follows, that the two witnesses, by command, ascended into heaven in a cloud, and their enemies saw them, and this in order that they might be separated, lest the

successive progression of things according to order should be disturbed by their presence and consequent communication with the
evil, concerning which see above.   But this arcanum cannot be described in a few words, but in what now follows, it will be elucidated as far as possible.

669. "Ascend hither"—That hereby is signified separation and
thence protection, appears from the signification of ascending into
heaven, when predicated of the witnesses, by whom are signified
the goods of love and truths of doctrine, as denoting to be separated
from those with whom the goods of love and truths of doctrine are
not, thus to be separated from the evil; and whereas the cause of
separation is, that those things, namely, the good of love and truth
of doctrine, may not be hurt by the evil, hence by "ascend hither"
is also signified protection: for if those things were communicated
to the evil, they would be received by them exteriorly, but interiorly
they would hurt them, by denying and laughing them to scorn;
hence also it would come to pass that the evil would be conjoined
with the simple good, who cannot perceive their interiors, nor, consequently, that they are evil; and the simple good are those who
constitute the ultimate or lowest heaven, wherefore unless they were
separated, hurt might be brought upon those who are in that heaven
by a conjunction with their externals; but concerning this circumstance more may be seen in the work concerning the L. J. n. 70.
This is what is involved in its being commanded the two witnesses
to ascend into heaven, whereby is also signified their protection.

670. "And they ascended into heaven in a cloud"—That hereby
is signified separation as to internals, and their protection, appears
from the signification of ascending into heaven, when predicated of
the two witnesses, as denoting separation from the evil, namely,
from those who are in evils of the life, and also their protection,
concerning which see the preceding article, n. 669; and from the
signification of a cloud, as denoting the ultimate of divine truth, or
the external of the Word, which is called the literal sense thereof,
concerning which see above, n. 36, 594: this is the external in
which many of the evil also are; for all who lead an evil life,
although they are in externals, still think in themselves against the
goods and truths of the Word, of doctrine, and of the church; the
reason is, because from the life they are in the love of evil, and the
love draws the interiors of the mind, thus the thoughts of the spirit,
to its side, wherefore such persons, when they are left to think alone,
altogether deny those things which they confess with their lips before
the world: this external, which also has place with the impious and
the evil, is what is here understood by a cloud; wherefore by their
ascending into heaven in a cloud, is signified separation as to internals, but not as to externals: the reason why separation as to internals, and not as to externals, is understood, is, because the internals
of the two witnesses were spiritual and celestial, but the internals
of the evil were infernal and diabolical; and the internals which are
celestial and spiritual, are actually in heaven; wherefore it is said
that they ascended thither, in order that as to internals they might

be separated from the evil, and thereby be preserved from hurt. It may be expedient here to say a few words more on this subject, in order that it may be known what is especially involved in the ascent into heaven of the two witnesses that were slain and revived. In the end of the church, when there is no faith in consequence of there being no charity, the interior things of the Word are manifested, which are to serve the new church for doctrine and life: this was done by the Lord Himself, when the end of the Jewish church was at hand, for then the Lord Himself came into the world, and opened the interiors of the Word, especially those concerning Himself, concerning love to Him, and love towards our neighbor, and concerning faith in Him, which before lay stored up in the interiors of the Word, being in the representatives thereof, and thence in singular the things appertaining to the church and worship: those truths therefore which the Lord disclosed, were interior truths, and in themselves spiritual, which afterwards served the new church for doctrine and life, according to what was just said above: but still those truths were not immediately received, nor till after a certain period of time, as is well known from ecclesiastical history; the reason was, because they could not be received before all things in the spiritual world were reduced to order; for the spiritual world is conjoined to the natural world with men, wherefore unless that world had been first reduced to order, the goods of love and truths of doctrine could not be understood nor perceived by men in the natural world: this was the reason why so long a time intervened before the Christian church was universally established in the European orb; for all effects which exist in the natural world, derive their origins from causes in the spiritual world, especially those which concern the things of the church. These things are mentioned in order that it may be known, what is specifically signified by the two witnesses being commanded to ascend into heaven, namely, that the goods of love and truths of doctrine, manifested in the last time of the church, may not be hurt by the evil. The case was similar when the most ancient church, which was before the deluge, arrived at its end, for then the representatives of celestial things, which were with the most ancient people, were collected together into one, by those who were called Enoch, and reserved for the use of the new church after the deluge, which was called a representative church, because the laws and statutes thereof, and the worship in general, consisted of representatives, or of such things in the natural world as corresponded with spiritual things in the spiritual world: the same things took place with respect to these, namely, that they were separated from the evil by being taken into heaven, and thus protected, and this until the old church arrived to its ultimate or last, when the new church was to be established: this is described by these words in Genesis: "And Enoch walked with God, and was no more, for God took him" (v. 24). That such things are signified by Enoch, by his walking before God, and being taken by God, may be seen in the A. C. n. 518–523. The case is the same at this day: the present church, which is called the Christian church, is at this day

arrived at its end, wherefore arcana of heaven and the church are
now revealed by the Lord, to serve the new church, which is understood by the New Jerusalem in the Apocalypse, for doctrine of life
and faith; and this doctrine is also taken up into heaven, lest before
the establishment of the new church it should be hurt by the evil:
this therefore is what is signified by its being said of the two witnesses, that they ascended into heaven; and also by the words of
the following chapter, where treating of the woman about to bring
forth the boy, before whom stood the dragon, it is said, "that the
boy was caught up to God, and to His throne" (Apoc. xii. 5).
What is particularly understood by the woman and by the boy there
mentioned, will be seen in the explication of the following chapter.
From these considerations it may now appear, what arcanum is involved in the two witnesses ascending by command into heaven in
a cloud.

671. "And their enemies saw them"—That hereby is signified
knowledge and acknowledgment with those who are inwardly against
the goods and truths of the Word and of the church, appears from
the signification of seeing, as denoting to understand, consequently
to know and to acknowledge, concerning which see above, n. 11,
37, 260, 354, 529; and from the signification of enemies, as denoting those who are against the goods of love and truths of doctrine, consequently those who are in evils and falses, for these are
understood by enemies and foes in the Word, in its spiritual sense:
hence it is evident, that by their enemies seeing them, is signified
knowledge and acknowledgment with those who are against the
two witnesses, which are the goods of love and truths of doctrine.
The arcanum here involved, is this; by enemies are here understood those who are inwardly against the goods of love and truths
of doctrine, but still not outwardly; for with the mouth they act as
friends, but in heart they are enemies; wherefore they profess those
things before the world, but in their spirit, in which they are when
they meditate alone with themselves, they deny them: these, therefore, are the enemies who see, for when they are in their corporeal
natural thought, in which they are as often as they are in society
with others, then they see, that is, know and acknowledge them;
but when they are in their spiritual natural thought, in which they
are as often as they are alone, and think concerning the things of
faith, then they do not acknowledge: hence it is that it is said, that
those two witnesses ascended into heaven in a cloud; for by the
cloud is signified the external of the Word, of the church, and of
worship, which, and from which, they see; that the cloud there signifies such external, may be seen in the article just above. In various passages of the Word, mention is made of foes and enemies
[hostes et inimici] and thereby are understood evils and falses, by
foes evils, and by enemies falses; for the Word in its bosom is spiritual, wherefore no other than spiritual foes and enemies can be
there understood: that this is the case may appear from the following passages; as in David: "Jehovah, how are my foes multiplied,
many are they that rise up against me, that say of my soul, there is

o help for him in God" (Psalm iii. 1): again: "Make wonderful Thy mercy, O Thou Saviour of them that trust in Thee: from them hat rise up against me, keep me by Thy right hand, from the imnious who are against my soul, who compass me about" (Psalm :vii. 7, 8): again: "Deliver me not up to the desire of my foes, or witnesses of a lie have risen up against me, who breath out viosence, lest I should believe to see good in the land of life" (Psalm :xvii. 12, 13): again: "Liberate me from my foes, O my God, rom them that rise against me, lift me up: liberate me from the rorkers of iniquity, behold they lay snares for my soul" (Psalm lix. , 3): and in Isaiah: "The impious acteth perversely in the land f uprightness, but Jehovah, Thou hast lifted up thine hand, fire hall devour thine enemies" (xxvi. 10, 11). besides a variety of assages in the prophetic Word, where foes and enemies are menoned, and also in the historic Word, treating of foes, wars, and attles: for as war signifies spiritual war, which is between truth nd falses, and consequently the arms of war, as spears, bows, arows, and swords, signify such things as appertain to spiritual war, o likewise do foes and enemies. That wars, in the Word, are significative, and also the arms of war, as bows, arrows, and swords, as been frequently shown in the preceding pages.

672. Verse 13. "And in that hour there was a great earthquake, nd the tenth part of the city fell, and there were slain in the earthuake, the names of men seven thousand; and the rest were affrighted, and gave glory to the God of heaven."—"And in that our," signifies during that state: "there was a great earthquake" gnifies a remarkable change of the state of the interiors with those ho are of the church: "and the tenth part of the city fell" signies, that no truths of doctrine any more existed with those who reained: "and there were slain in the earthquake the names of men even thousand," signifies, that in that change of state all the truths f good, and consequently all things of heaven and the church, also erished with them: "and the rest were affrighted," signifies the commotion of mind and conversion of those who were in some deree spiritual: "and they gave glory to the God of heaven," signies that they acknowedged and worshiped the Lord.

673. "And in that hour"—That hereby is signified during that tate, appears from the signification of hour, as denoting state, in his case, therefore, that state when the two witnesses ascended into eaven, and their enemies saw them. The reason why hour signiies state, is, because times, in the Word, and all expressions appertaining to time, as hours, days, weeks, months, years, ages, and moreover morning, noon, evening, night, likewise spring, summer, autumn and winter, signify states of the life; that such things are ignified by times, is shown and illustrated in the work concerning L. & H. under the article concerning time in heaven, n. 162–169; s also above in this work, n. 571, 610, 664; and that hour signifies ny duration of state, greater or less, may be seen above, n. 194; nd that the annexed number determines the state as to the quality hereof, n. 488.

674. " There was a great earthquake"—That hereby is sig
remarkable change of the state of the interiors with those v
of the church, appears from the signification of a great eartl
as denoting a remarkable change of the state of the church ;
the earth is signified the church, by motion or quaking, ch
state, and by great, what is remarkable : that an earthquake
Word, signifies a change of the state of the church, may 1
above, n. 400, 499. That a change of state as to the tru
goods of the church, existed from causes contained in the pr
verse, viz. from the two witnesses that were slain and res
life, ascending by command into heaven in a cloud, and th
mies seeing them, is evident ; whence it may appear also,
cause was the separation of the good from the evil, as was al
the articles above, where the ascent of the two witnesses
plained ; but these things cannot be shown to the undersl
unless it be previously known how this matter is circumsta
the spiritual world ; for the things mentioned in this verse, i
that there was a great earthquake, that the tenth part of
fell, and that the names of men seven thousand were kille
earthquake, likewise, that the rest were affrighted and gave
the God of heaven, come to pass, and also did come to pas
the last judgment took place, but in the spiritual world an
the natural world ; for when the good there are to be separat
the evil, and the good to be protected lest they should be
the evil, then the good are taken away from the societies,
evil left, according to the words of the Lord in Matthew :
shall be in the field, one shall be taken, the other shall be l
shall be grinding at a mill, one shall be taken, the other shall
(xxiv. 40, 41) ; which may be seen explained in the A. C.
4335 : and when the good are taken away, then in the soc
which the good and evil were together, a remarkable chan
place as to those things which are of the church. But the
that change shall be further disclosed : in the spiritual wol
is a communication of all affections, and sometimes of thoug
within every society there is a common or general commu
extending itself from the midst thereof every way, even to tl
daries, nearly as light is extended from the centre to the ci
ences : the variations and changes of affections arising from
nication and its extension, exist by virtue of the influx
tions from other societies, which are either above or at th
likewise from the new comers who enter the society ; and i
this circumstance, that few or many are taken away from the
the societies upon which the last judgment took place, con
both good and evil, but of such evil as were inwardly ag
goods of love and truths of doctrine, but not outwardly ;
wardly they could act according to rectitude and justice, as
what was pious and true, not for the sake of rectitude, justic
and truth themselves, but from habit acquired in the world
sake of fame, glory, honor, gain, and various delights of the
loves ; likewise on account of the laws and their penalties ;

sons, although inwardly evil, could still be together with
o were not only outwardly but also inwardly good : when
: the good are separated from those who appeared good in
rnal form only, then the external good of the latter vanished,
internal evil opened or discovered itself ; for they were kept
external good only by communication with those within the
:iety, who, as was said, were inwardly as well as outwardly
rherefore when by the removal of these the external good
:n away from the evil their interiors were opened, which
d with mere evils and falses, and hence their real quality
le manifest. These things, therefore, are what are specifi-
derstood by the two witnesses ascending by command into
ia a cloud, and their enemies seeing them ; and by what is
ited as a consequence thereof, that in that hour there was a
rthquake, that is, that when that state took place, a remark-
inge was wrought as to those things which appertain to the

"And the tenth part of the city fell"—That hereby is sig-
at there no longer existed any truths of doctrine with those
rained, appears from the signification of the number ten, as
; all and all things, likewise many and many things ; and of
1 part, as denoting all and much, concerning which we shall
esently ; and from the signification of city, as denoting doc-
d also the truth of doctrine, for doctrine, that it may be the
of the church, consists of truths from the Word ; that a city
doctrine may be seen above, n. 223 ; and from the signifi-
f falling, as denoting to be parted or severed, consequently
rist, to be parted or severed and not to exist being predi-
truths of doctrine, when falling is predicated of a city. For
particular thing is allotted its own proper and analogous
on, according to the correspondence of the subject in the
sense and of the subject in the spiritual sense, and the
ia the natural sense is here a city, and the subject in the
sense is the truth of doctrine ; that no truths any longer
with those that remained, follows as a consequence from
is shown in the preceding article concerning the good being
ray from the societies in which the good and evil were to-
ind being taken up into heaven ; whence, the evil being de-
f their communication with the good, no truths could any
emain with them, inasmuch as it was only by virtue of that
ication that they could be as it were in truths as to the ex-
nd thence also speak concerning them from doctrine ; for in
tual world there is a communication of affections and thence
hts, and by virtue of such communication, one is held by
r, thus all in the same society mutually, and also the evil
rood, in a similar affection, consequently in a similar good ;
:vil in those societies were such as in an external form could
in appearance of sanctity, of piety, of intelligence, of zeal
hurch and its doctrine, and likewise in the life an appear-
if they were just and sincere from the heart, although in-

wardly in themselves they possessed nothing of such things; these are the evil, with whom there no longer existed any truths of doctrine, after the good were taken away, who are understood by the two witnesses, who ascended by command into heaven. It is to be observed that there were many societies so composed in the spiritual world, and these societies, taken together, are understood by the former heaven which passed away (Apoc. chap. xxi. 1); concerning which societies or which heaven, see what is related in the small work concerning the L. J.; in these societies were such of the evil as are above described, and, together with them, the good; and so long as they were conjoined in one society, the evil as to externals appeared as good, but when they were separated, then the external good, which was only simulated and hypocritical, was parted or severed with them, and their interiors were manifested, which were infernal, abounding with mere evils and falses thence derived. Such a separation, and such state in consequence thereof, took place in the spiritual world a little before the last judgment, and this is the state, therefore, which is here described; for the subject here treated of is concerning the last time of the church, when the universal judgment is at hand. That the number ten signifies all and all things, likewise many and many things, may appear from the passages in the Word where that number occurs; as in Moses: "Jehovah hath commanded you His covenant, which He covenanted with you to do, the ten words, which He wrote upon the two tables of stone," (Deut. iv. 13); and again: "Jehovah wrote upon the tables, according to the former writing, the ten words which He spake unto you in the mount of fire," (Deut. x. 4); the reason why the decalogue consisted of ten words or ten precepts, was, because by ten are signified all, and hence by ten words is understood the law in the whole complex. Inasmuch as ten signify all, therefore the Lord "compared the kingdom of heaven to ten virgins, having lamps, and going to meet the bridegroom, of whom five were prudent and five foolish" (Matt. xxv. 1, 2, and following verses); by the ten virgins to whom the kingdom of the heavens is likened, are signified all who are of the church; for ten signify all, and virgins the church; but by five are signified some or some part, thus that some were prudent and some foolish; by lamps are signified the knowledges of truth and good, in this case, from the Word, likewise the truths of doctrine and of faith; by oil is signified the good of love and charity; by the bridegroom is understood the Lord, and by nuptials is understood heaven and the church, which are called nuptials from the marriage of good and truth; and inasmuch as where that marriage is not, there neither exists heaven nor the church, therefore they are called foolish who know the truths of faith and have not the good of love, and they who have the good of love, are called prudent; for, as was said, lamps there denote the truths of faith, and oil, the good of love; the reason why virgins signify the church, is, because virgin and daughter, in the Word, signify the affection of good and truth, and it is by virtue of that affection that a church is a church; hence it is that so frequent mention is made of the virgin and the daughter of Zion, the virgin or daughter of Jerusalem, the virgin and daughter of Israel and of Judah, by which expressions is everywhere understood the church. Whereas ten signify all and many, therefore also the Lord " said concerning the nobleman who went into a far country, that he called his ten servants, and gave them ten pounds to trade ; and after they had traded, one said that his pound gained ten pounds, to whom he said, thou shalt have power over ten cities ; and the second said, thy pound hath made five pounds, to whom he said, be thou over five cities ; and concerning the third, who laid his pound in a napkin, and did not trade with it, he said, take from him the pound and give it to him who hath ten pounds" (Luke xix. 12, 13, 14, 15, 16, 17, 18, 19, 20, 24) : the numbers ten and five are also here used, because ten signify all and all things, and five signify some and somewhat ; by the ten servants, whom the nobleman, when he went into a far country, called to himself, are understood all who are in the world, and specifically, all who are of the church, for by the nobleman is understood the Lord, and by his departure into a far country is understood His departure out of the world, and then as it were absence ; by the ten pounds which he gave to the ten servants to trade with, are signified all the knowledges of truth and good from the Word, with the faculty of perceiving them ; for a pound, which was silver and money, signifies the knowledges of truth and the faculty of perceiving them, and to trade, signifies to procure thereby intelligence and wisdom ; they who procure for themselves much, are understood by the servant, who from the pound gained ten pounds ; and they who procure for themselves some, are understoood by him who gained five pounds ; by the cities which are there said to be given them, are signified the truths of doctrine, and by possessing them is signified intelligence and wisdom, and life and felicity thence derived ; hence it is evident, what is signified by ten cities and by five cities ; whereas they who procure for themselves nothing of intelligence, are as the foolish virgins spoken of above, who only possess truths in the memory, and not in the life, therefore they are deprived of them after their departure out of this world ; but they who possess truths as well in the life as in the memory, increase in the riches of intelligence to eternity, therefore it is said, that they should take the pound from him who gained nothing with it, and should give it to him who had ten pounds. The case is similar with those " to whom talents were given, to one five, to another two, and to a third one ; of whom the first from his five talents gained other five ; and the second from two talents gained other two ; and the third deposited his talent in the earth ; concerning whom the Lord said, take from him that hath not traded and gained, and give to him that hath ten talents, for to every one that hath shall be given, that he may abound, and from him who hath not shall be taken away, even that which he hath" (Matt. xxv. 14–30). By five and by ten here also are signified something and much, and thus, that the first from some knowledges of truth and good procured for himself much wisdom ; the reason why from him who has procured for himself nothing of intelligence, is taken away that which he hath, and given to him who has much, is, because after death, when man becomes a spirit, he carries with him all and everything which he has imbibed from the Word, and from the doctrine of the church; but they who have thereby procured for themselves nothing of intelligence, are inwardly evil, and therefore abuse the truths and goods of heaven and the church, which they possessed in the memory only, to the purposes of ruling over, and doing evil to, the simple good who belong to the ultimate heaven; this is the reason why those truths and goods are taken away from them, and given to those who have much, inasmuch as these latter do not abuse but perform uses with them. That they do not procure for themselves spiritual intelligence in the world by the knowledges of truth and good from the Word, are inwardly evil, may appear from this consideration, that all are born into evils of every kind, and these cannot be removed, except by divine truths from the Word, namely, by the application thereof to uses, and thereby reception in the life; wherefore to those who have gained it is said, " Well done, good and faithful servants, ye have been faithful over a few things, I will make you rulers over many things, enter ye into the joy of your Lord" (verses 21, 23); and to him who gained nothing, " Cast out the unprofitable servant into outer darkness, there shall be wailing and gnashing of teeth" (verse 30). By reason of the number ten signifying all and much, it is therefore used by the Lord in other passages, where all and much is to be understood; as again in Luke : " What woman having ten pieces of silver, if she lose one piece, doth not light a candle and sweep the house, and seek diligently till she find it" (Luke xv. 8). By ten is here signified much; the reason why mention is made of woman, and of her lighting a candle, and sweeping the house, is, on account of the spiritual sense in singular the things of the Word : in this sense, by woman is signified the church as to the affection of truth, consequently also, the affection of truth itself appertaining to the church·; by a piece of silver is signified truth, and by losing the piece of silver, to lose one of the truths or of the knowledges of truths; by lighting a candle is signified inquisition in herself from affection; by sweeping the house, is signified to run over the whole mind, and to take a view of everything therein, in order to discover where the truth has hid itself; such is the spiritual sense of these words. The same as is signified by ten is also signified by a hundred, namely, much; therefore a similar parable speaks of " a hundred sheep and losing one" (Matt. xviii. 12, 13; Luke xv. 3-8). By ten is signified all and much, also, in the following passages; as in Isaiah : " Many houses shall be a devastation, great and fair, without inhabitant; for ten acres of vineyard shall yield one bath" (v. 9, 10); treating of the desolation of truth with those who are of the church; by many houses which shall be a devastation, are signified the men of the church, specifically as to truths from good; by grea and fair, namely houses, is signified the affection of good and intelligence of truth, for great is predicated of good and the affection thereof, and fair is predicated of truth and the intelligence thereof; by ten acres of vineyard shall yield one bath, is signified, that in all things appertaining to the church with man, there is scarce any truth from good, for by the bath is signified the same as by wine, namely, truth derived from good, wherefore by ten acres of vineyard are signified all things of the church with man. And in Moses: " If ye will go contrary to me, I will break the staff of bread, that ten women shall bake your bread in one oven, and I will bring your bread again in weight" (Levit. xxvi. 26); by breaking the staff of bread, is signified deprivation of spiritual food, and thence of spiritual nourishment, for by bread is signified everything that nourishes the soul, and specifically, the good of love ; wherefore by ten women shall bake your bread in one oven, is signified, that in all things of the church with man there is so little either of good or truth, as scarce to amount to anything ; by ten women, are signified all things of the church ; by bread is signified good and truth which nourish the soul ; and by the oven is signified where spiritual food is prepared, thus the man with whom it is; by bringing the bread again in weight, is signified the defect or want and penury of such things as spiritually nourish. And in Zechariah : " Many people and numerous nations shall come to seek Jehovah Zebaoth in Jerusalem, and to deprecate the faces of Jehovah ; in those days ten men out of all the tongues of the nations, shall take hold of the wing of a man that is a Jew, saying we will go with you, for we have heard that God is with you" (viii. 22, 23); these things are said concerning the convocation and accession of the gentiles to the church by the Lord ; and by ten men out of all tongues, are signified all of whatsoever religion who come to seek Jehovah Zebaoth in Jerusalem, that is, who are willing to accede to the church, and to confess the Lord, wherefore ten men denote all such, and the tongues of the nations, the religious principles ; but this may be seen further explained with the rest of the passage, n. 433, where it is shown, that by Jerusalem is not understood Jerusalem, nor by the Jew, any Jew. And in Amos: " Jehovah saith, I hate the pride of Jacob, and his palaces, whence I will shut up the city, and the fulness thereof ; if there be left ten men in one house they shall die" (vi. 8, 9). By the pride of Jacob and by his palaces which Jehovah hates, are signified the love and faith of what is false with those who are of the church, by pride, the love of the false, and by palaces, the falses themselves, which are called palaces because such are proud, and because their falses are adorned and trimmed out in the external form, so as to appear magnificent, although they are most vile, as cottages full of rubbish and uncleannesses ; by shutting up the city and the fulness thereof, is signified, to condemn the doctrine, because obsessed and full of falses originating in evil, city denoting doctrine, and its fullness the falses of evil contained in it ; wherefore if there shall be left ten men in one house they shall die, signifies that all truths of good with every one shall perish, ten men [viri] denoting all truths, house denoting man as to good, and to die denoting to perish. And in Zechariah : " The prophet saw a scroll flying, the length thereof twenty cubits, and the breadth thereof ten cubits: this is the curse going over the faces of the whole earth" (v. 2, 3). The reason why the flying scroll, by which was signified the curse going forth over the faces of the whole earth, was in length twenty cubits, and in breadth ten, was, because by twenty and by ten is signified all, and in this place, all good changed into evil, and all truth into falses, twenty being predicated of good and of the all thereof, and ten of truth and of the all thereof; length also is significative of good and breadth of truth, concerning which see above, n. 197. Inasmuch as ten signify all and many, therefore by ten times is signified oft times and always, in the following passages ; as in Daniel : "There was not found of all them any like to Daniel, Hannani.h, Misael, and Azariah ; in all matters of wisdom and intelligence, which the king sought of them, he found them ten times above all the astrologers and diviners who were in all his kingdom" (i. 19, 20) : and in Moses : "All the men, who saw My glory and My signs, which I did in Egypt and in the wilderness, and who tempted Me these ten times, shall not see the land" (Numb. xiv. 21, 22, 23); and in Job : "Ten times have ye reproached me, ye blushed not, ye hardened yourselves against Me" (xix. 3). By ten times, in these passages, is signified at all times or always, and oft times. In Daniel and the Apocalypse horns are attributed to the beasts, to some ten, to some seven, and to some three, and by the horns is signified the power of the false against the truth, and of evil against good, and by the ten horns, the highest power: thus in Daniel : "The fourth beast ascending out of these, had ten horns ; and to the ten horns from the same kingdom ten kings shall arise" (viii. 7, 20, 24). By the ten horns of the beast is there signified the highest power of the false against truth ; by ten kings are signified falses in every complex, and by kingdom is signified the church perverted. And in the Apocalypse: "The dragon had seven heads and ten horns, and upon the heads seven diadems" (xii. 3); again : "The beast ascending out of the sea had seven heads and ten horns, and upon his horns ten diadems" (xiii. 1); and again : "The woman sitting upon the scarlet beast full of names of blasphemy, had seven heads and ten horns ; the ten horns, which thou sawest, are ten kings, which have not yet received the kingdom ; yet they receive power as kings one hour with the beast," (xvii. 3, 7, 12). What is signified in these passages as to each particular, will be seen when we come to the explication of them. Inasmuch as ten signify all persons and all things, it follows that the tenth part signifies the all ; from hence tenths and tithings derived their origin, and signified that everything was holy and blessed, when the tenth part of the corn-floor and of the wine-press, or of the corn and the wine, was given to the Levites ; and in like manner for the Levites, when the tenth part was again tithed and given to Aaron ; concerning these it is thus written in the Word : "Tithing thou shalt tithe all the produce of thy seed, which shall be brought into the field year by year" (Deut. xiv. 22); and again : "Say unto the Levites, that the tenths shall be given to them for an inheritance, and that they shall take therefrom a heave-offering to Jehovah, tenths of the tenths, and this from the corn of the corn floor, and from the fulness of the wine-press; and the tenth of the tenth shall they give to Aaron the priest" (Numb. xviii. 24–28). That the tenth signified benediction in all things, thus that everything was holy and blessed, appears in Malachi : " Bring all the tenths to the house of treasure, that there may be food in my house; then prove ye me in this, if I will not open to you the windows of heaven, and pour out upon you a blessing, until there is no more any room" (iii. 10). By opening the windows and pouring out a blessing, is signified the divine [principle] flowing in, whence comes intelligence and eternal life, the same as is signified by rain treated of above, n. 644, which is also properly understood by the blessing which should be given if the tenths were brought, wherefore it is here signified, that by them everything would be blest. In order that all things might be blessed which Abraham took from his enemies, it is said, " that he gave to Melchisedeck, who was king in Salem, and at the same time priest to God most high, tenths of all " (Gen. xiv. 18, 19); so likewise Jacob vowed a vow, " that if he should return in peace unto the house of his father, everything that Jehovah gave him tithing should be tithed " (Gen. xxviii. 21, 22). From these passages, besides many others, it may appear what is signified, in the Word, by ten and the tenth part. The cause of this signification of the number ten, as denoting all things, is derived from heaven itself; for heaven in the whole and every part has reference to man, whence it is called the grand man ; all the powers of the life of that grand man or heaven, terminate in the two hands and two feet, and the hands, as also the feet, terminate in ten fingers or toes, wherefore as all things appertaining to man, as to power and as to support, are ultimately collated into ten fingers, therefore ten signify all things appertaining to him ; and moreover ultimates, in the Word, also signify all things.

676. " And there were slain in the earthquake the names of men seven thousand"—That hereby is signified that in that change of state all truths of good perished with them, and thereby all things of heaven and the church, appears from the signification of being slain, as denoting to be spiritually slain, which is to perish by evils and falses, concerning which see above, n. 315, 547, 572, 589 ; and from the signification of earthquake, as denoting change of the state of the interiors with those who are of the church, concerning which see above, n. 674; and from the signification of names of men, as denoting the truths of good, and thence the understanding of truth, concerning which we shall speak presently ; and from the signification of seven thousand, as denoting all things of heaven and the church, for the number seven signifies all, and is predicated of the holy things of heaven and the church, as may be seen above, n. 257, and the signification is retained when it is multiplied by 10, or 100, or 1000, for these numbers signify all : hence it may appear that by the names of men, seven thousand, being slain in the earthquake, is signified, that in that change of state all the truths of good perished, and thereby all things of heaven and the church. That

by names of men are signified truths originating in good, and thence the understanding of truth, may appear from the signification of name, as denoting the quality of a thing and state with man ; and from the signification of man, as denoting intelligence, thus also the understanding of truth. The reason why name signifies the quality of a thing and state with man, is, because names of persons are not given in the spiritual world as in the natural world, but in the spiritual world all are named according to the quality of their life, thus with a difference within the societies and without them : within the societies the quality of the state of every one's life is constant, for every one there dwells in a certain quarter, and at a certain distance from the midst, according to the quality of his affection and of his intelligence, wherefore according to this quality is his name ; hence it is, that when the name of any one in a society is heard, his quality is also recognized ; it is from this circumstance, that by name, in the spiritual sense is signified the quality of a thing and the state of life ; but without or out of the societies, the denomination according to the quality of the state of life of any one is not constant ; for before the man-spirit comes into any society, he passes through several states, in order that he may put off the things that disagree with his ruling love, and put on such as agree therewith ; but still every one is named according to the state in which he is, and also according to the idea and perception of the quality thereof ; that names, in the spiritual world, are pronounced spiritually, may be seen above, n. 102 ; that hence name, in the Word, signifies the quality of the state of the life, n. 148 ; and that hence the name of Jehovah, and the name of the Lord, signifies all things whereby He is worshiped, thus all things of love and faith, n. 102, 135 ; and that man, in the Word signifies the spiritual affection of truth, and thence the understanding of truth, n. 280, 546 ; from which it may appear what is signified by the names of men. The reason of the truths of good perishing, and consequently the understanding of truths thence derived, by the remarkable change of state which is signified by a a great earthquake, was shown in the article above, namely, that in the end of the church, when the last judgment takes place, they who are spiritually good are taken away from those who are only naturally so, and when this is the case, then from the latter are also taken away all truths of good, consequently also all understanding of truth ; for with the natural in whom there is nothing spiritual, truths and goods reside in their externals, and falses and evils in their internals, hence when the good with whom they had communication as to externals are taken away, the externals are also taken away, and the internals are made manifest, which, as was said, abound with mere falses of evil : hence then it is, that by these words are signified, that with those who remained all truths of good and all understanding of truth perished.

677. " And the rest were affrighted"—That hereby is signified the commotion of mind and conversion of those who were somewhat spiritual, appears from the signification of the rest, as denoting those who were not merely external and natural, but also somewhat in-

ternal and spiritual, concerning which we shall speak presently; and from the signification of being affrighted, as denoting to be moved in the mind, and turned away from those who were merely natural, and thence in mere falses and evils. That to be affrighted signifies such commotion and conversion will be seen below; but first something shall be said concerning those who are understood by the rest that were affrighted and gave glory to the God of heaven, as being not merely natural but also somewhat spiritual; for they who are merely natural, when the truths of good which were with them in the externals are taken away, experience no commotion from the influx of falses and evils from hell, still less do they convert themselves; for their own proper thought and will, which interiorly lay hid with them, consists merely of falses and evils thence derived, and of evils and falses thence derived, wherefore, when they are in these, they become enraged against truths and goods, and thence ardently lust to extinguish them: hence it is, that the evil, when they are no longer in externals, have no terror for evils and falses, nor even for hell, for these things are of their love, consequently the delights of their life; but the case is otherwise with such as are also somewhat spiritual; these experience commotion of mind and terror, when they are infested from evils and falses, which takes place when they are amongst the evil, for they fear the loss of their spiritual life, on account of which their minds are agitated and afraid, whence they supplicate the Lord for aid, and turn themselves away from the evil. When societies are purified in the spiritual world, which takes place as often as the evil, especially hypocrites, have insinuated themselves into them, and commixed themselves with the good there (the signs of whose presence are obscuration of the understanding, deprivation of the perception of good, a dulness of the affection of truth, and similar other things), then influx is let in from hell, at which the evil rejoice, whilst the good experience commotion of mind, and by conversion are separated, wherefore they who being affrighted convert themselves are preserved, and the rest are cast out. From these considerations it may appear whence it is that it is said, that some were affrighted, and that this signifies the commotion of mind and conversion of those who are somewhat spiritual. Mention is frequently made in the Word of being affrighted, dismayed, and the like, both concerning the good and the evil, and by terror and consternation is signified a state of commotion and change of mind arising from imminent or visible danger of life, but differently with the good and with the evil; with the good it is a commotion of mind, and change of state, arising from the imminent and visible danger of the soul, but with the evil it arises from the imminent and visible danger of the bodily life; the reason of this is, because the good regard the life of the soul as principal and final, and not so the life of the body, whereas the evil regard the life of the body as principal and final, and not so the life of the soul, which, indeed, they do not believe in, in their heart, and they who do believe, still love only the things which are of the body, such as appetites and pleasures of various kinds; but the case is reversed with the good. In order that it may be known, that to be affrighted, dismayed, to dread, and the like, signify commotion of the mind arising from the change of the state of the interiors, some passages shall be adduced from the Word by way of confirmation; thus in David: "My heart trembleth in the midst of me, and the terrors of death are fallen upon me, fear and trembling came upon me and horror hath covered me" (Psalm lv. 5, 6). These things are said concerning temptations, in which evils and falses break in from hell, and strike with terrors for fear of damnation; for, as was said above, the good are terrified and tremble from imminent dangers of the soul, thus from the irruption of evils into the thoughts and intentions of the will; there are, therefore various commotions of the mind, which are specifically signified by trepidation of the heart, terrors of death, fear, trembling, and horror, which are there mentioned according to the order in which they succeed. And in Isaiah: "The isles came and were afraid, the ends of the earth trembled, they drew near and came" (xli. 5); speaking of the advent of the Lord; and by the isles and ends of the earth are understood the nations which are remote from the truths of the church, and by their fear and trembling are signified commotions of mind arising from the dread of perishing. And in Ezekiel: "All hands are let down, and all knees go into waters, whence they shall gird themselves with sacks, terror shall cover them, and upon all faces shall be shame, they shall cast their silver into the streets, and their gold shall be an abomination" (vii. 17, 18, 19); where the advent of the Lord is also treated of: the various commotions of the mind arising from grief on account of evils, and from joy on account of goods, are described by various kinds of fear and grief, as by the hands being let down, the knees going into waters, terror covering them, and shame upon all faces by which are signified, not only various commotions of the mind, and changes of the states of the life, but also conversions from falses and evils; for the falses which they shall reject are signified by the silver which they shall cast into the streets, and the evils by the gold, which shall be an abomination; by all knees, going into waters, is signified grief on account of the good of love being destroyed, and joy that it is now recovered, the knees signifying the love of good and to go into waters signifies to weep. That the holy tremor which occupies, vibrates, and penetrates through all the interiors of the head, when the Divine [principle] flows in and fills, is also called fear, terror, dread, may appear from the following passages: thus in Luke, "When Zacharias saw the angel, he was troubled, and fear fell upon him, and the angel said, Fear not, Zacharias" (i. 12, 13): in like manner, "When the virgin Mary saw the angel, he said unto her, Fear not" (i. 30): again: "When the angel of the Lord stood before the shepherds, and the glory of the Lord shone round about them, they feared a great fear, but the angel said to them, Fear not, behold, I bring to you good tidings of great joy, which shall be for all people" (Luke ii. 9). "When Jesus was transformed and seen in glory, it is said that Peter, James, and John, were afraid when they entered into the cloud" (Luke viii. 21): and

" when they they heard the voice out of the cloud, saying, This is my beloved Son, that they fell upon their faces and feared exceedingly ; but Jesus drew near and touched them, saying, Arise, fear not" (Matthew xvii. 6, 7 ; Mark ix. 6) : also " when the Lord healed the paralytic, it is said, that fear came upon them all, and they glorified God, and were filled with fear, saying, This day we have seen prodigies " (Luke v. 26) : and " when the Lord raised to life the young man that was carried out of Nain, it is said, that fear seized them all, and they praised God" (Luke vii. 16) ; in like manner as here in the Apocalypse, " That they were affrighted and gave glory to the God of heaven :" moreover " when the women entered into the monument, they saw an angel sitting at the right side, clothed in a white robe ; and they were afraid" (Luke xxiv. 5, 6) : and " when the women departed out of the monument, they were seized with fear, trembling, and amazement, and at the same time with great joy, and they told no one, because they were afraid, wherefore Jesus said to them, Fear not, declare to the brethren" (Matthew xxviii. 8, 10 ; Luke xxiv. 6, 7) : also " the two disciples going to Emmaus, said unto Jesus, Certain women terrified us" (Luke xxiv. 22). From these passages it may be concluded, that by terror and dread, in the Word, are understood various commotions of mind arising from the influx of such things as cause amazement, and also conjoined with joy. Moreover by terror, in the spiritual sense, is signified terror on account of evils and falses which are from hell, for these terrify the spiritual man, inasmuch as they are opposed to goods and truths, which the spiritual man loves, and for the loss of which he is afraid ; in this sense terror is mentioned in many passages of the Word ; as in Isaiah : " About the time of evening, behold terror, before the morning it is not" (xvii. 14). Evening signifies the last time of the church, when there is nothing but evils and falses, which are called terror, because they are hell ; but the morning signifies the first time of the church, when evils and falses are not, wherefore it is said, before the morning the terror is not. Again in Jeremiah : " Fear thou not, my servant Jacob, and be not afraid, O Israel, for behold, I keep thee from afar ; Jacob shall be tranquil, and quiet, none shall affright him" (xxx. 9, 10) : and in Zephaniah : " The remains of Israel shall feed and rest, none making them afraid" (iii. 13). By Jacob and Israel are understood those who are in goods and truths within the church ; and by none affrighting or making them afraid, is signified, that nothing of evil or of the false from hell shall infest : the like is also signified in many other passages. But what is signified by fearing God, in the spiritual sense of the Word, will be shown in the explication at the 18th verse of this chapter.

678. " And they gave glory to the God of heaven"—That hereby is signified that they acknowledged and worshiped the Lord, appears from the signification of giving glory or of glorifying, as denoting to acknowledge and worship, concerning which we shall speak presently ; and from the signification of the God of heaven, as denoting the Lord. That the Lord is the God of heaven, He himself made manifest whilst He was in the world, and when He departed

out of the world: whilst He was in the world, He said, "The Father hath given all things into the hand of the Son" (John iii. 35): again: "The Father hath given to the Son power over all flesh" (xvii. 2): and in Matthew: "All things are delivered unto me by the Father" (xi. 27): and when He departed out of the world, He said to His disciples, "All power is given to me in heaven and in earth" (Matthew xxviii. 16): from which it is evident that the Lord is the God of heaven. The reason why to give glory denotes to acknowledge and worship Him, is, because to give glory signifies that glory belongs to Him alone, because He is the God of heaven and earth, and at the same time to acknowledge that all things of the church are from Him, thus all salvation and eternal life: from these considerations it follows, that to give glory and to glorify, when predicated concerning God, is to worship and adore Him. Glory, in the Word, when predicated of the Lord, properly signifies the divine truth proceeding from Him, by reason that that divine truth is the light of heaven, and from that light angels and men derive not only all their intelligence and wisdom, but also all their felicity; and moreover all magnificence in the heavens, which is ineffable, is thence derived: these things, therefore, are what are properly signified by the glory of God: hence it also follows, that the glory of the Lord is to illustrate angels and men, and to gift with intelligence and wisdom, and to bless with all things happy and delightful, and also to give magnificence to all things in the heavens, and that this glory is not from the love of glory, but from love towards the human race; wherefore the Lord says in John: "In this is My Father glorified, that ye bear much fruit, so shall ye be My disciples" (xv. 8): and elsewhere, "The words which Thou hast given to Me, I have given them; and I am glorified in them" (xvii. 8, 10). That this is the glory of the Lord, may appear from this consideration, that the light of heaven, from which is all the wisdom, beauty, and magnificence in the heavens, proceeds from the Lord as a sun, and the divine love of the Lord is what appears to the angels as a sun; hence it is manifest, that the light of heaven, which in its essence is divine truth and divine wisdom, is the divine love proceeding, and love wills no other than to give that which is its own to another, thus to fill others with beatitude; and if this be the will of all love, what must it be of the divine love? The Lord, however, cannot give His glory to another, and fill him with wisdom and beatitude, unless He be acknowledged and worshiped, for hereby man conjoins himself to Him from love and faith; for acknowledgment and worship, in order to be true acknowledgment and worship, must be from love and faith, and without conjunction thereby it is not possible for any good to flow in from the Lord, because it is not received: from these considerations it is now evident, that to give glory to the God of heaven, is to acknowledge and worship the Lord. That glory signifies the divine truth proceeding from the Lord, and that the glory of the Lord with man is the reception of divine truth, may be seen above, n. 34, 345. That the glorification of the Lord is from the Lord Himself, and that with men and angels it is reception and acknowledgment that all good and truth, and the all of salvation and life, is from the Lord, may also be seen above, n. 228.

679. Verses 14, 15. "The second woe is passed, behold, the third woe cometh quickly. And the seventh angel sounded, and there were great voices in heaven, saying, The kingdoms of the world are become our Lord's and His Christ's, and He shall reign to ages of ages."—"The second woe is passed, behold, the third woe cometh quickly," signifies lamentation upon the last vastation of the church now certainly at hand: "and the seventh angel sounded," signifies the influx of divine truth through the heavens from the Lord, and thence the last changes: "and there were great voices in heaven," signifies illustration and joy in the superior heavens: "saying, The kingdoms of the world are become the kingdoms of our Lord and of His Christ," signifies all things in the heavens and in the earths subject to the Lord, when the evil are separated from the good, and the divine good and divine truth proceeding from the Lord is clearly received: "and He shall reign to ages of ages," signifies His dominion by divine truth to eternity.

680. "The second woe is passed, behold the third woe cometh quickly"—That hereby is signified lamentation over the last vastation of the church, now certainly at hand, appears from the signification of woe, as denoting lamentation on various accounts, especially for such things as devastate the church, concerning which see above, n. 532; and whereas the number three signifies what is complete, therefore the third woe signifies the last lamentation, when the devastation is full; that three signify what is complete and thus the end, may be seen above, n. 435, 506, 532; and from the signification of coming quickly, as denoting certainly at hand and coming to pass; that quickly signifies certain, may be seen also above, n. 7, 216. What this third woe, which is to come quickly, involves, may appear from the things which follow, viz., that it involves the last state of the church, when there is no more any truth or good, and in such case the state of separation, which then takes place, of the evil from the good, and of the good from the evil, and at length the last judgment, which is effected by a plenary separation, and then the casting down of the evil into hell, and elevation of the good into heaven.

681. "And the seventh angel sounded"—That hereby is signified the influx of divine truth through the heavens from the Lord, and the last changes consequent thereupon, appears from the signification of sounding, when predicated of the angel, as denoting the influx of divine truth from the Lord, and consequent change in the inferior parts, where the evil are, concerning which see above, n. 489, 502. The reason of this signification of the angel's sounding, is, because a trumpet signified divine truth to be revealed, and also already revealed, as may be seen above, n. 55, 262: the reason why it is the last change from the influx of divine truth from the Lord, which is understood by the sounding of the seventh angel, is, because the number seven signifies what is full and ultimate, or last, concerning which see above, n. 20, 24, 257, 299, 486: the changes in the lower

parts, where the evil are, occasioned by a more intense or gentle influx of divine truth through the heavens from the Lord, and thus by various influxes, have been amply treated of above, n. 413, 418, 419, 426, 489, 493, wherefore it is unnecessary to say any more concerning them in this place; that by those influxes were effected separation of the evil from the good, and casting down of the evil into hell, and various other changes, may be seen in the places cited. From these considerations it is now evident what is signified by the seven angels sounding.

682. "And there were great voices in the heavens"—That hereby is signified illustration and joy in the superior heavens, appears from the signification of great voices in the heavens, as denoting illustration, wisdom, and joy, in the superior heavens; for by voices, in the Word, are signified various things; as the divine truth, revelation, the Word itself which is with us, likewise every precept and command of the Word; these however are signified by voices out of heaven, but by voices in heaven is signified illustration, from which the angels have wisdom and thence joy; for when the angels are in illustration, they are also in wisdom, and then they have great voices, whereby they express the arcana of wisdom: the reason why joy thence is also mentioned, is, because the angels have joy from wisdom, whence also it is that the voices are called great, for great is predicated of the affection of good and truth, from which comes joy in the heavens. The reason why the superior heavens are understood, is because by them and from them influxes descend into the lower parts, whereby the evil are separated, who as to externals were conjoined to those who were in the lower or inferior heavens, and so long as this conjunction had place the latter could not be in illustration and joy, but only in proportion as they were separated; hence it is that the superior heavens are understood: for there is such a connexion between superior things and inferior things, in the spiritual world, that in proportion as the latter are in order, so also are the former: for inferior things there are as the lower parts of a house, and as the foundations thereof, so far therefore as these are entire, so far the parts above are in a firm, secure, and perfect state, being thereby preserved from nodding, tottering, and from clefts or breaches; or they are as the exterior things in man, as the organs of sight, taste, hearing, and touch, for in proportion as these are free from hurt, in the same proportion his interiors see, taste, and hear well, and have sensation by touch, for interior things are what perceive or feel in exterior things, the latter having nothing thereof of themselves: the case is similar with respect to the heavens, the superior terminating in and standing upon the inferior, between which therefore there is such a connexion, the one being contained in the other, as subsists between things prior and posterior, or as between causes and effects; if the effect does not altogether correspond to its cause, that is, if it has not everything formed in itself, which is in the efficient cause, which has reference to powers and endeavors of acting, then the cause falls to decay, and acts imperfectly; for all things of the cause are inscribed on the

effect, wherefore the cause is what alone acts, and not the effect, in any case whatever, separate from the cause. Similar is the case with the heavens superior and inferior : in the superior heavens are causes, and effects corresponding to the causes present themselves in the inferior heavens. These things are said, in order that it may be known, whence it is, that by great voices in heaven, are signified illustration, from which comes wisdom and joy in the superior heavens, when the inferior heavens are purified, that is when the evil are separated and removed from the good.

683. " Saying, The kingdoms of the world, are become our Lord's and His Christ's"--That hereby are signified all things in the heavens and in the earths subject to the Lord, when the evil are separated from the good, and that then the divine good and divine truth proceeding from the Lord is clearly received, appears from the signification of the kingdoms of the world when become the Lord's, as denoting the reception of the Divine Proceeding from the Lord in love and faith, concerning which we shall speak presently ; and from the signification of the Lord and his Christ, as denoting the Lord as to the divine good of divine love, and as to the divine truth proceeding from that love ; that the Lord is called Lord from divine good, and Christ from divine truth, will be seen below. That the kingdom of the Lord is the reception of divine good and divine truth, thus with those who receive may appear from this consideration, that the Lord reigns with angels of heaven, and with men of the church by that which proceeds from Him, which is commonly called divine good and divine truth, likewise justice and judgment, and also love and faith : these are the things by which the Lord reigns, consequently, they are properly the kingdom of the Lord, with those who receive them ; for when they reign in angels and men then the Lord Himself reigns, inasmuch as the things which proceed from the Lord are Him, and the Lord in heaven is no other than the Divine Proceeding. The Lord indeed not only rules those who receive divine celestial and spiritual things from Him, but also those who do not receive, as all who are in hell, but still it cannot be said, that the kingdom of the Lord is there, inasmuch as they are altogether unwilling to be governed by the Divine which proceeds, and according to the laws of its order, yea, they deny the Lord, and avert themselves from Him ; but still the Lord rules them, not as the subjects and citizens of His kingdom, but as refractory and rebellious, keeping them in bonds that they may not do evil to each other, and especially to those who are of His kingdom. That the kingdom of the Lord is what proceeds from Him and is received, may appear from the passages in the Word where the kingdom of God is mentioned : as in the Lord's prayer : " Thy kingdom come, Thy will be done, as in heaven, so also in the earth" (Matt. vi. 10). That by kingdom is there understood the reception of divine good and divine truth which proceed from the Lord, and in which the Lord is with the angels of heaven and with men of the church, is evident, for it follows, Thy will be done, as in heaven so also in the earth, and the will of God is done when those things are received

in the heart and soul, that is, in love and faith. So in another place: "Seek ye first the kingdom of the heavens and the justice thereof, and all things shall be added to you" (Matt. vi. 33). By the kingdom of the heavens, in the spiritual sense, is understood the divine truth, and by justice, the divine good, wherefore it is said, seek first the kingdom of the heavens and the justice thereof; and, in the supreme sense, by the kingdom of the heavens is understood the Lord, inasmuch as He is the all of His kingdom, and by justice, in the same sense, is signified the merit of the Lord; and whereas man, who is ruled by the Lord, wills and loves only such things as are of the Lord, he is led unknown to himself to the felicities of eternity, therefore it is said, that all things shall be added to him, whereby is understood, that all things shall happen for salvation according to his wishes. Inasmuch as heaven is heaven from the reception of divine truth from the Lord, and in like manner the church, therefore heaven and the church are understood in the general sense by the kingdom of God, and by the kingdom of the heavens: hence they who receive divine truth, are called by the Lord the sons of the kingdom, in Matthew: " The field is the world, the seed are the sons of the kingdom, the tares are the sons of the evil one" (xiii. 38). That they who receive divine truth are understood by the sons of the kingdom, is evident, for it is said, the seed are the sons of the kingdom, and the tares are the sons of the evil one, and by seed is meant divine truth, and by tares the infernal false, and they are called sons, because sons, in the spiritual sense of the Word, signify truths, and, in the opposite sense, falses, as may be seen above, n. 166. Moreover, that the kingdom of God signifies the church as to truths from good, and also heaven, may be seen above, n. 48; and that the kingdom of God with man, signifies to be in truths from good from the Lord, consequently to be in wisdom, and thence in the power of resisting falses and evils, and thus that to reign is of the Lord alone, may be seen also above, n. 333.

684. It is said that the kingdoms of the world are become our Lord's and His Christ's, and thereby is signified, that divine good and divine truth is then received, when the evil are separated from the good and cast into hell; for then both the superior and inferior heavens can be in illustration, and thence in the perception of good and truth, which could not be the case so long as the evil were conjoined with the good; the reason is, because so long as that conjunction had place, the interiors of the angels, who are in the inferior heavens, could not be opened, but only the exteriors, and the Lord does not reign in externals with spirits and men separate from internals, but in internals and from them in externals; wherefore before the interiors of the angels of the ultimate heaven were opened, which are spiritual and celestial, that heaven could not become the kingdom of the Lord as it could after the separation of the evil from them. The reason why it is said, our Lord's and His Christ's, is, because by Lord is here understood the same as by Jehovah in the Old Testament, and by Father in the New, namely, the Lord as to the Essential Divine [principle] and also as to divine good, and by

Christ is understood the same as by God in the Old Testament, and by Son of God in the New, namely, the Lord as to the Divine Human [principle] and also as to divine truth : for by Christ is signified the same as by Anointed, Messiah, and King, and by Anointed, Messiah, and King, is understood the Lord as to divine truth, and also as to the Divine Human [principle], when He was in the world, for then the Lord, as to His Human [principle], was divine truth : the like is therefore signified by the Anointed of Jehovah, for the Essential Divine [principle], which is called Jehovah and Father, and in its essence was the divine good of divine love, anointed the Divine Human [principle], which is called the Son of God, and which in its essence, during the Lord's abode in the world, was divine truth, for anointing signified that the Divine Human [principle] of the Lord proceeded from His Essential Divine [principle], consequently divine truth from His divine good. Hence it is evident, that the Lord alone, as to the Divine Human [principle], was essentially the Anointed of Jehovah, but that kings and priests were called the anointed of Jehovah representatively, for the oil, with which the anointing was performed, signified the divine good of the divine love: now inasmuch as the divine truth with the Lord was what was anointed of the divine good, hence it is that by Christ, and likewise by Messiah and Anointed, and also by King, is signified the divine truth proceeding from the divine good of the divine love of the Lord : that this is the case, may appear from the passages in the Word where Christ, Messiah, and Anointed are mentioned : that Christ is the Messiah or Anointed appears in John : " Andrew found his brother Simon, and said to him, We have found the Messiah, which is, when interpreted, the Christ" (i. 42) : and again : " The woman of Samaria said, I know that Messiah cometh, which is called Christ" (iv. 25) ; from which passages it is evident, that the Lord is called Christ from His being the Messiah, whose advent was predicted in the Word of the Old Testament ; for Anointed is called Christ in the Greek tongue, and Messiah in the Hebrew, and Anointed is King : hence it is that the Lord was called King of Israel, and King of the Jews, which He also confessed before Pilate, whence it was written upon the cross, " The King of the Jews" (Matt. xxvii. 11, 29, 37, 41 ; Luke xxiii. 1–4, 35–40) : and in John : " Nathaniel said, Thou art the Son of God, the King of Israel" (i. 46–50). And whereas Messiah, Christ, Anointed, and King, are synonimous terms, so also is Son of God, and each of those names, in the spiritual sense, signifies divine truth ; that this is the signification of king may be seen above, n. 31, 553, 625 ; the reason why He is also called Son of God, is, because sons, in the Word signify truths, whence Son of God signifies divine truth : that sons denote truths, may be seen above, n. 166. The like is also signified by Christ and by Messiah : that by Christ is signified divine truth, appears in Matthew : " Be not ye called Rabbi, one i your teacher, Christ" (xxiii. 8). By Rabbi and teacher is sign᾽ one that teaches truth, thus, abstractedly, the doctrine of trut᷄ in the supreme sense, divine truth, which is Christ ; that

alone is divine truth, is therefore understood by, be not ye called
Rabbi, one is your teacher, Christ: so again: " See that no one
seduce you; for many shall come under My name, saying, I am
Christ, and shall seduce many.   If any one say to you, Lo, here is
Christ, or there, believe not, for there shall arise false Christs and
false prophets" (xxiv. 5, 23, 24; Mark xiii. 21, 22, 23): where it
is not to be understood, that any will arise who will call themselves
Christ or Christs, but that they will falsify the Word, or say that
this or that is divine truth, when it is not; they who confirm falses
from the Word, are understood by false Christs, and they who
hatch or propagate falses of doctrine, are understood by false prophets; for the subject treated of in these two chapters is concerning the successive vastation of the church, thus concerning the falsification of the Word, and at length concerning the profanation of
truth thence derived; but these things may be seen further explained
in the A. C. n. 3353–3356, and n. 3897–3901.   And whereas the
Son of God also signifies divine truth, as was just said, therefore He
is sometimes called Christ the Son of God, as in Matt. xxvi. 63;
Mark xiv. 60; Luke iv. 41; chap. xxii. 66 to the end; John vi.
69; chap. xi. 26, 27; chap. xx. 31.   In a word, the reason why
the Lord, when He was in the world, was called Christ, Messiah,
Anointed, and King, was, because in Him alone was the divine
good of the divine love, from which proceeds divine truth, and this
was represented by anointing; for the oil with which anointing was
performed, signified the divine good of divine love, and the king
who was anointed signified divine truth, wherefore kings, when they
were anointed, represented the Lord, and were called the anointed
of Jehovah; but still the Lord alone as to His Divine Human [prin-
ciple], was the Anointed of Jehovah, inasmuch as the divine good
of the divine love was in Him, and this was the Jehovah and
Father from which the Lord had the esse of life; for that He was
conceived of Jehovah, is well known, consequently from the divine
good of the divine love, which was in Him from conception, the
Lord was divine truth as to His Human [principle] so long as He
was in the world: from which it may appear, that the Lord alone
was essentially the Anointed of Jehovah, and that kings were so
called only representatively: hence then it is, that the Lord, as to
His Divine Human [principle], was called Messiah and Christ, that
is, Anointed.   This may also appear from the following passages:
as in Isaiah: " The spirit of the Lord Jehovih is upon Me, therefore Jehovah hath anointed Me to publish good tidings to the poor,
He hath sent me to bind up the broken in heart, to preach liberty to
the captives, the opening of the prison to the bound, to proclaim the
year of the good pleasure of Jehovah, and the day of vengeance to
our God, to console all that mourn" (lxi. 1).   These things are
manifestly said concerning the Lord: His Divine Human [princi-
ple] is understood as being what the Lord Jehovih anointed to publish good tidings to the poor, and sent to bind up the broken hearted,
and so on, for the Lord performed those things from His Humanity;
but the particulars of this passage may be seen explained above, n.
183, 375, 612.   So in David: " The nations were tumultuous, and

the people meditated vanity; the kings of the earth stood up and the rulers consulted together against Jehovah and against His Anointed. I have anointed My king upon Zion, the mountain of My holiness. I will announce concerning the statute, Jehovah hath said unto Me, Thou art My Son, to-day have I begotten Thee; ask of Me, and I will give the nations for Thine inheritance, and the uttermost parts of the earth for Thy possession. Kiss the Son, lest He be angry, and ye perish in the way, for His anger will kindle shortly, blessed are all they that confide in Him" (Psalm ii. 1, 2, 6, 7, 12). That by the Anointed of Jehovah is here understood the Lord as to the Divine Human [principle] is evident, for it is said, Jehovah hath said unto Me, Thou art my Son, to-day have I begotten Thee, kiss the Son lest ye perish, blessed are all they that trust in Him: these things indeed, in the sense of the letter, are said concerning David, but by David, in the Word, is understood the Lord as to divine truth, or as King, as may be seen above, n. 205; it is also evident that the subject here treated of is concerning the advent of the Lord, and at length concerning the last judgment accomplished by Him, and afterwards concerning His kingdom over all things of the world; the spiritual things which lie concealed, and are signified in the particulars of this passage are these; the nations made a tumult, and the people meditated vanity, signify the state of the church and of the former heavens, that it was to pass away, nations denoting those who are in evils, and people those who are in falses, concerning which see above, n. 175, 331, 625: the kings of the earth stood up, and the rulers consulted together against Jehovah, and against His Anointed, signifies the falses of the church and the evils thereof, as being altogether against the divine good and against the divine truth, thus against the Lord, the kings of the earth denoting the falses of the church, and the rulers the evils thereof, and Jehovah denoting the Lord as to the essential divine [principle] thus as to divine good, and Anointed denoting the Lord as to the divine human [principle] thus as to divine truth; I have anointed My king upon Zion, the mountain of My holiness, signifies the human [principle] of the Lord as to divine truth proceeding from the divine good of His divine love, and thence His kingdom over all things of Heaven and the church, Zion and the mountain of holiness denoting heaven and the church, consequently all things thereto appertaining; I will announce concerning the statute, signifies an arcanum of the divine will and providence; Jehovah hath said unto Me, Thou art my Son, to-day have I begotten Thee, signifies the Lord as the Anointed, Messiah, Christ and King, thus as to His human [principle] conceived and afterwards born of His essential divine [principle] or Jehovah; to-day signifies a statute from eternity, and thence has respect to the conjunction and union accomplished in time; ask of Me, and I will give the nations for thine inheritance, and the ends of the earth for Thy possession, signifies His kingdom and dominion over all things of heaven and the church, which shall be His; kiss the Son, signifies conjunction with the Lord by love, to kiss denoting conjunction from love; lest He be angry, and ye perish in the way, signifies lest evils invade you and ye be condemned, for to be angry, where it is predicated of the Lord, signifies the aversion or turning away of men from Him, consequently their anger and not the Lord's, and evils are the things which avert themselves, and afterwards are angry; because His anger will kindle shortly, signifies the last judgment, and dejection of the evil into hell; blessed are all they that confide in Him, signifies salvation by love and faith in the Lord. Again: " Thou art fair far above the sons of men, grace is poured upon Thy lips: gird Thy sword upon Thy thigh, O Powerful in Thy glory and Thine honor; and mount up in Thine honor, ride upon the word of verity, and of the meekness of justice, and Thy right hand shall teach Thee wonderful things; Thine arrows are sharp, the people shall fall under Thee, the enemies of the king from the heart. Thy throne, O God, is to the age and eternity; a sceptre of rectitude is the sceptre of Thy kingdom: Thou hast loved justice and hated evil, therefore God hath anointed thee, Thy God, with the oil of joy above Thy fellows; all Thy garments with myrrh, aloes, and cassia; the daughters of kings are amongst thy precious ones; at thy right hand standeth the queen in best gold of Ophir" (Psalm xlv. 3–10). That these things also are said concerning the Lord, is evident from all the particulars of that Psalm, and consequently that it is Himself of whom it is said, God hath anointed Thee, Thy God, with the oil of joy, and all Thy garments with myrrh, aloes, and cassia : the signification thereof may appear from the series, namely, that He has divine wisdom, and that from Him is the doctrine of divine truth, is signified by, Thou art fair, far above the sons of men, grace is poured upon Thy lips, to be fair signifies to be wise, the sons of men signifying those that are intelligent in divine truths, and lips signifying doctrinals: His omnipotence by virtue of divine truth proceeding from divine good, and thence the destruction of falses and evils, and subjugation of the hells, is signified by, gird Thy sword upon Thy thigh, O powerful in Thy glory and Thine honor, and in Thine honor mount up, ride upon the word of verity, Thy right hand shall teach Thee wonderful things, Thine arrows are sharp, the people shall fall under Thee, the enemies of the king from the heart; by sword is signified truth combating against the false, and destroying it ; by the word of verity, the same as by chariots, viz. the doctrine of truth; by riding upon it, to instruct and combat; by the right hand, omnipotence; by arrows, truths combating ; by people, those who are in falses of evil; and by the enemies of the king, those who are against truths, thus the hells : that hence the kingdom and dominion would be His for ever, is signified by, Thy throne, O God, is to the age and eternity, a sceptre of rectitude is the sceptre of Thy kingdom, the sceptre of rectitude denoting the divine truth which has power and the kingdom: whereas he vindicated the good from damnation by destroying the evil, and that on that account the essential divine [principle] united itself to His human, is signified by, Thou hast loved justice and hated evil, therefore God has anointed Thee, Thy God, with the oil of joy above Thy fellows; to love justice and to hate evil, signifies to vindicate the good from damnation by destroying the evil; to anoint with the oil of joy, signifies to unite himself by victories in temptations; God, Thy God, signifies the reciprocal unition of the human [principle] with the divine, and of the divine with the human; divine truths united to divine goods are signified by, He hath anointed all thy garments with myrrh, and aloes, and cassia; myrrh signifies the good of the ultimate degree, aloes the good of the second, and cassia the good of the third, in like manner as those three spices or perfumes mixed with the oil of olive, whence was made the oil of holiness for anointing (Exod. xxx. 23, 24); which oil signified the divine good of the divine love, and the garments which were anointed signified divine truth; that spiritual affections of truth belong to those who are of His kingdom, is signified by, the daughters of kings are amongst thy precious ones, the daughters of kings denoting the spiritual affections of truth, which are called precious when the truths are genuine: and that heaven and the church are in his protection and conjoined to Him, because principled in love to Him from Him, is signified by at thy right hand stands the queen in best gold of Ophir; the queen signifies heaven and the church; at thy right hand signifies in His protection by virtue of conjunction with Him; and best gold of Ophir signifies the good of love to the Lord. Again in David: "I have made a covenant with Mine elect, I have sworn to David My servant, thy seed will I establish for ever, and I will build up Thy throne to generation and generation. Thou hast spoken in vision to thine Holy One, and hast said, I have laid help upon one that is Mighty, I have exalted one chosen out of the people; I have found David my servant, with the oil of My holiness have I anointed Him, with whom my hand shall be established; Mine arm also shall strengthen Him. I will beat down His enemies before Him, and will smite them that hate Him; I will set His hand in the sea, and his right hand in the rivers; He shall call me, Thou my Father, my God, and the rock of my salvation; also I will give him [to be] My first born, higher than the kings of the earth; and My covenant shall be established with Him, and I will make His seed [to endure] for ever, and His throne as the days of the heavens. Once have I sworn by My holiness I will not lie unto David, His seed shall be for ever, and His throne as the sun before Me, as the moon established for ever a faithful witness in the clouds" (Psalm lxxxix. 4, 5, 21, 22, 24, 26, 27, 28, 29, 30, 36, 37, 38). That by David in this Psalm is not understood David, but the Lord as to His royalty, which is the divine spiritual [principle] and is called divine truth, is evident from all that is here said concerning Him, viz. that His seed and throne shall be as the days of the heavens, and as the sun and the moon for ever, that He shall set His hand in the sea, and his right hand in the rivers, and that He shall call Jehovah His father, and shall be His first-born, higher than the kings of the earth, with other things of a like nature, which cannot be said concerning David, his sons, or his throne; that by David in the Word is understood the Lord, may be seen above, n. 205; but to proceed to the explication of singular the expressions; I have made a covenant with Mine elect, I have sworn to David My servant, signifies the unition of the Lord's divine [principle] with His human, to make a covenant denoting unition, to swear denoting confirmation thereof, elect being predicated of good, and servant of truth; I will establish thy seed for ever, and I will build up thy throne to generation and generation, signifies divine truth, and heaven and the church, from Him, seed denoting divine truth and those who receive it, and throne denoting heaven and the church : thou hast spoken in vision to thine Holy One, signifies a prophetic arcanum concerning the Lord; I have laid help upon one that is mighty, I have exalted one chosen out of the people, signifies the divine truth whereby divine good operates all things, which is called a help upon one that is mighty, and, in other passages, the right hand of Jehovah; divine majesty and power thence derived, is signified by, the exaltation of one chosen out of the people; I have found David My servant, with the oil of holiness have I anointed Him, signifies the Lord as to the Divine human [principle] and union with the essential divine, which union, in the Word of the New Testament, is called glorification, and is understood by the anointing with the oil of holiness, for the oil of holiness signifies the divine good of divine love, and to be anointed signifies to be united to divine truth, which appertained to the Lord's human [principle] in the world : with whom My hand shall be established, Mine arm also shall strengthen Him, signifies omnipotence thence derived, the hand denoting the omnipotence of truth from good, and the arm the omnipotence of good by truth; I will beat down His enemies before Him, and I will smite them that hate Him, signifies combat attended with victory against evils and falses, thus against the hells; I will set His hand in the sea, and His right hand in the rivers, signifies the extension of His dominion and kingdom over all things of heaven and the church, for seas and rivers are the ultimates of heaven, and the ultimates signify all; He shall call Me, Thou My Father, My God, and the rock of My salvation, signifies the divine human [principle] which is the Son of God, conceived of the Essential Divine, and afterwards born, and whereas divine truth and divine power was thence derived to the Lord's human [principle] He is also called God and the Rock of Salvation; also I will give Him to be My first-born, higher than the kings of the earth, signifies, that He is above all the good and truth of heaven and the church, because the goods and truths of heaven and the church are from Him; and My covenant shall stand fast with Him, signifies eternal union; I will make His seed to endure for ever, and His throne as the days of the heavens, signify here as above, the days of the heavens denoting the states of the whole heaven, which are from His Divine [principle]; once have I sworn by my holiness, I will not lie unto David, signifies eternal confirmation, because from the Divine [principle], concerning the Lord, and concerning the union of His Human [principle] with the Essential Divine; His seed shall endure

for ever, and His throne as the sun before Me, as the moon it shall
be established for ever, signify similar things as above, where treating of His seed and of his throne; it is said as the sun and as the
moon because of the sun is predicated eternity as to divine good,
and of the moon as to divine truth, for these are signified by the
sun and the moon; a faithful witness in the clouds, signifies acknowledgment and confession from the Word concerning the Divine
in the Human [principle] of the Lord, which, that it is a witness in
the clouds, may be seen above, n. 10, 27, 228, 392, 649. Again:
" Jehovah remember David in all his labor; how he sware unto
Jehovah, and vowed to the Mighty One of Jacob, surely I will not
enter within the tent of my house, nor go up into my bed, until I
find out a place for Jehovah, habitations for the Mighty One of
Jacob. Lo, we have heard of Him in Ephratah, we found him in
the fields of the forest; we will enter into His habitations, we will
bow down ourselves at his footstool. Arise, Jehovah, to Thy rest,
Thou and the ark of Thy strength : let Thy priests be clothed with
justice, and let Thy saints jubilate; for Thy servant David's sake,
turn not away the face of thine anointed. In Zion will I make the
horn of David to bud, I will set a lamp for Mine anointed, His enemies will I clothe with shame, but upon Himself shall His crown
flourish " (Psalm cxxxii. 2, 3, 5–10, 17, 18); where also by David
and by anointed or Christ is not understood David, but the Lord as
to the Divine Human [principle], for it is said, that His habitations,
viz. the habitations of that Mighty One of Jacob, are found in Ephratah, which is Bethlehem, and that they bowed themselves down at
His footstool; but this will better appear from the explication of the
particulars in their order; by swearing to Jehovah, and vowing to
the Mighty One of Jacob, is signified irrevocable asseveration before
the Lord, who is called Jehovah from the Divine in first principles,
and the Mighty One of Jacob from the Divine in ultimates, in which
the divine power is in its fulness; I will not enter within the tent
of my house, nor go up into my bed, signifies not to enter into and
know the things which appertain to the church, and to the doctrine
thereof, the tent of the house denoting the holy things of the church,
and the bed, the doctrine thereof; until I find out a place for Jehovah, habitations for the Mighty One of Jacob, signifies, before I
shall know the advent of the Lord, and the arcana of the union of
His Human [principle] with the Divine, for these things, in the supreme sense, are the place of Jehovah, and the habitations of
the Divine Human [principle] of the Lord; lo, we have heard of
Him at Ephratah, we found Him in the fields of the forests, signifies,
in the spiritual sense of the Word, and also in the natural, for
Ephratah and Bethlehem signify the spiritual natural [principle],
and the fields of the forest the natural, both appertaining to the
Word, for there the Lord is found; we will enter into His dwelling
places, we will bow down ourselves at His footstool, signifies that
He is there found, forasmuch as He is the Word, and His dwelling
places or habitations denote those things which appertain to the spiritual sense, consequently the heavens, which are in that sense, and

His footstool denotes those things which appertain to the natural sense, consequently also the church, inasmuch as in the church are divine truths in their ultimates, which serve the spiritual things of the Word and the heavens, thus the Lord Himself who dwells therein, for a footstool ; rise, Jehovah, into Thy rest, Thou and the ark of Thy strength, signifies the unition of the Essential Divine [principle] with the Human in the Lord, and thence peace to all in heaven and the church, the rest of Jehovah denoting that unition, and the ark of His strength denoting heaven and the church ; let Thy priests be clothed with justice, and Thy saints jubilate, signifies thence worship originating in love with those who are in celestial good, and worship originating in charity with those who are in spiritual good, for priests denote those who are in the celestial kingdom of the Lord, and they are called saints who are in the spiritual kingdom : for the sake of David Thy servant turn not away the face of Thine Anointed, signifies, that they may be enkindled with love and illustrated with the light of truth, since divine truth is united with divine good in the Lord, thus the Essential Divine [principle] with the Human, and the Human with the Divine, for David as a servant signifies the Human [principle] of the Lord as to divine truth, and Anointed signifies the same united with divine good, and His face signifies divine love and illustration thence derived ; in Zion will I make the horn of David to bud, signifies the power of divine truth from Him in heaven and in the church ; I will place a lamp for Mine Anointed, signifies the illustration of divine truth from the unition of the Divine and Human [principles] in the Lord, the lamp denoting divine truth as to illustration ; His enemies will I clothe with shame, signifies the subjugation of the hells, and consequent dissipation of evils ; but upon Himself shall His crown flourish, signifies perpetual and eternal victory over them.   From the passages that have been now adduced from the Word, it may appear, that the Lord is called Anointed, which is Messiah, or Christ, from the unition of divine good with divine truth in His Human [principle], for the Human [principle] of the Lord from that union is understood by the Anointed of Jehovah.   In like manner in 1 Samuel : " Jehovah will judge the ends of the earth, and will give strength to His King, and exalt the horn of His Anointed" (ii. 10).   These words are in the prophetic [song] of Hannah the mother of Samuel, which was spoken before there was any king or anointed over Israel, wherefore by King and Anointed is there understood the Lord, to whom is given strength, and the horn is exalted, when the Divine [principle] was united with the Human ; for by strength is signified the power of good over evil, and by horn the power of truth over the false, and truth is said to be exalted, when it becomes interior, and in the same degree also it becomes more powerful.   So likewise in Lamentations : " The spirit of our nostrils, the anointed of Jehovah, was taken in their pits, concerning whom we said, in his shade shall we live amongst the nations" (iv. 20).   By the anointed of Jehovah, in the sense of the letter, is here understood the king who was made captive, but in the spiritual sense is understood the Lord, wherefore it is said, the spirit of our nostrils, that is, the life of the perception of good and truth; taken in the pits, signifies rejected by those who are in falses of evil, pits denoting falses of doctrine; to live in His shade signifies to be in His protection against falses of evil, which are signified by nations. Whereas by Anointed, Messiah, or Christ, is signified the Lord as to the Divine Human [principle], thus as to the divine good united with divine truth, therefore by anointing is signified that unition; concerning which the Lord thus saith: " I am in the Father and the Father in Me, believe Me that I am in the Father and the Father in Me" (John xiv. 7–11; and elsewhere). " The Father and I are one; know ye and believe, that I am in the Father and the Father in Me" (John x. 30, 38): and whereas this was represented by the anointing of Aaron and his sons, "therefore the things that were holy to Jehovah with the sons of Israel, were given to Aaron and His sons for the anointing" (Numb. xviii. 8). Those things are enumerated from verse 9–19 of that chapter; but concerning anointings, as that the Lord alone, as to the Divine Human [principle], was the Anointed of Jehovah, because in Him was the divine good of divine love, which was signified by oil, and that all other anointings with oil were only representative of Him, see what has been said above, n. 375. These things are said concerning the Anointed of Jehovah, because the Anointed of Jehovah is Christ, in order that it may be known that by the Lord and His Christ, in this passage in the Apocalypse, are not understood two, but one, or that they are one, as the Anointed of Jehovah and the Christ of the Lord, Luke ii. 26. Inasmuch as the subject here treated of is concerning the Lord, in order to elucidate also whence it is that He was called Christ, that is, Messiah, or Anointed, it is of moment that the following passage concerning Him in Daniel be explained: " Seventy weeks are decided upon thy people, and upon thy city of holiness, to consummate prevarication, and to seal up sins, and to expiate iniquity, and to bring in the justice of ages, and to seal up the vision and the prophet, and to anoint the Holy of Holies. Know therefore and perceive, from the going forth of the Word even to restore and to build Jerusalem, even to Messiah the prince, shall be seven weeks; afterwards in sixty and two weeks, the street and the ditch shall be restored and built, but in straitness of times. But after sixty and two weeks Messiah shall be cut off, but not for Himself: afterwards the people of the prince that shall come, will destroy the city and the sanctuary, so that the end thereof shall be with an inundation, and even to the end of the war desolations are decided. Yet He shall confirm the covenant with many for one week, but in the midst of the week He shall cause the sacrifice and meat-offering to cease: at length upon the bird of abominations shall be desolation, and even to the consummation and decision it shall drop upon the devastation" (Dan. ix. 24, 25, 26, 27). The sense of these words has been investigated and explained by many of the learned, but only as to the literal sense, but not yet as to the spiritual sense, for this sense has been hitherto unknown in the christian world; in this sense the following things are signified by those words: seventy weeks are decided upon thy people, signifies the time and state of the church which then existed with the Jews, even to the end thereof, seventy weeks denoting a full state from beginning to end, and people those who then belonged to the church; and upon thy city of holiness, signifies the time and state of the end of the church as to the doctrine of truth from the Word, city denoting the doctrine of truth, and the city of holiness divine truth, which is the Word; to consummate prevarication, and to seal up sins, and to expiate iniquity, signifies, when there are nothing but falses and evils in the church, thus when iniquity is fulfilled and consummated; for before this is the case, the end does not come, the reason whereof may be seen in the work concerning the L. J. where it is shown, that if the end should come before, the simple good would perish, who, as to externals, are conjoined with those who make a pretence of truths and goods, and make a counterfeit and hypocritical show thereof in externals; wherefore it is added, to bring in the justice of ages, whereby is signified, to save those who are in the good of faith and charity; and to seal up the vision and the prophet, signifies, to fulfil all things which are contained in the Word; to anoint the Holy of Holies, signifies, to unite the Essential Divine [principle] with the Human in the Lord, for this is the Holy of Holies: know therefore and perceive, from the going forth of the Word, signifies, from the end of the Word of the Old Testament, this being to be fulfilled in the Lord, for all things of the Word in the Old Testament, in the supreme sense, treat concerning the Lord, and concerning the glorification of His Humanity, and thence concerning His dominion over all things of heaven and the world; even to restore and build Jerusalem, signifies when the new church was to be established, Jerusalem denoting that church, and to build denoting to establish anew; even to Messiah the Prince, signifies even to the Lord, and the divine truth in Him and from him, for the Lord is called Messiah from the Divine Human [principle] and Prince from divine truth; seven weeks signify a full time and state; afterwards in sixty and two weeks the street and the ditch shall be restored and built, signifies the full time and state after His advent until the establishment of the church with its truths and doctrine, sixty denoting a full time and state as to the implantation of truth, in like manner as the number three or six, and two denoting those things as to good, thus sixty and two together signify the marriage of truth with some little good; the street signifies the truth of doctrine, and the ditch, doctrine; concerning the signification of street, see above, n. 652, and of a ditch or well, n. 537; but in straitness of times, signifies scarcely and with difficulty, because with the nations or gentiles with whom there is but little spiritual perception of truth; but after sixty and two weeks, signifies after a full state and time of the church now established as to truth and as to good; Messiah shall be cut off, signifies, that they shall recede from the Lord, which took place principally with those of Babylon, by the transferring of the divine power of the Lord to the popes, and thus by the non-acknowledgment of the Divine [principle] in His. Human : but not for Himself, signifies, that still the power and the Divine [principle] is His ; afterwards the people of the prince that shall come shall destroy the city and the sanctuary, signifies, that thus doctrine and the church will perish by falses, city denoting doctrine, sanctuary, the church, and the prince that shall come, the reigning false ; so that the end shall be with an inundation, and even to the end of the war desolations are decided, signifies the falsification of truth, until there is no longer any combat between the truth and the false, inundation signifies falsification of truth, war, the combat between what is true and what is false, and desolation, the last state of the church, when there is no longer any truth but merely what is false ; yet He shall confirm the covenant with many for one week, signifies a time of reformation, when the Word is again read, and the Lord acknowledged, that is, the Divine [principle] in His Human, which acknowledgment and thence conjunction of the Lord by the Word is signified by covenant, and the time of reformation by one week ; but in the midst of the week he shall cause the sacrifice and the meat-offering to cease, signifies that still interiorly with those who are the reformed, there will be no truth and good in their worship, sacrifice denoting worship from truths, and the meat-offering worship from goods, by the midst of the week is not signified the midst of that time, but the inmost of the state with the reformed, for midst signifies inmost, and week, the state of the church ; the reason that there was no truth and good inwardly in worship after the reformation, is, because they assumed faith for the essential of the church, and separated it from charity, and when faith is separated from charity, then in the inmost of worship there is neither truth nor good, for the inmost of worship is the good of charity, and the truth of faith proceeds from it; at length upon the bird of abominations shall be desolation, signifies the extinction of all truth by the separation of faith from charity, the bird of abominations denoting faith alone, thus faith separated from charity, for a bird signifies thought concerning the truths of the Word and the understanding of them, which becomes a bird of abominations when there is not any spiritual affection of truth, which alone illustrates and teaches truth, but only a natural affection, which is for the sake of fame, glory, honor, and gain, and which, being infernal, is abominable, inasmuch as mere falses flow from it ; and even to the consummation and decision it shall drop upon the devastation, signifies the extreme state thereof, when there is nothing of truth of faith remaining, and when the last judgment takes place : that these last words were predicted in Daniel concerning the end of the Christian church, is evident from the Lord's words in Matthew : " When ye shall see the abomination of desolation predicted by Daniel the prophet standing in the holy place, let him who readeth understand" (xxiv. 15). For the subject treated of in that chapter is concerning the consummation of the age, thus concerning the successive vastation of the Christian church, wherefore the devastation of this church is understood by those words in Daniel ; but what they signify in the spiritual sense, may be seen explained in the A. C. n. 3652. From these consider-

ations it may now appear, what is signified by the kingdoms of the
world becoming the Lord's and His Christ's : and also what is signified by the Lord's Christ, or the Christ of the Lord, in Luke : "It
was answered to Simeon by the Holy Spirit, that he should not see
death, before he had seen the Christ of the Lord" (ii. 26).

685. "And He shall reign for ages of ages"—That hereby is signified His dominion by divine truth to eternity, appears from the
signification of reigning, when attributed to the Lord, as denoting to
rule by divine truth, concerning which we shall speak presently;
and from the signification of for ages of ages as denoting to eternity :
the reason why for ages of ages denotes to eternity, is, because the
literal sense of the Word is natural, to which the spiritual sense corresponds, and the natural sense of the Word consists of such things
as are in nature, which in general have reference to times and
spaces, also to places and persons, and ages of ages have relation
to times, to which eternity corresponds in the spiritual sense : the
case is similar with generations of generations, where the subject
treated of is concerning the propagation of faith and charity in the
church. The reason why to reign, when predicated of the Lord,
signifies to rule by divine truth, is, because rule or dominion is predicated of good, and to reign of truth, for the Lord, is called Lord
from divine good, and king from divine truth; hence it is that
every where in the Word both are mentioned, namely, dominion and
kingdom, or to rule and to reign, as in the following passages : thus
in Micah : "Thou, O little hill of the daughter of Zion, unto thee
shall come and return the former dominion, the kingdom of the
daughter of Jerusalem" (iv. 8). Inasmuch as by the daughter of
Zion is signified the celestial church, the essential principle of which
is the good of love, therefore dominion is predicated thereof, and
kingdom is predicated of the daughter of Jerusalem, because the
spiritual church is thereby signified, the essential principle whereof
is the truth of doctrine. And in David : "Thy kingdom is the kingdom of all ages, and thy dominion to every generation and generation" (Psalm cxlv. 13) : and in Daniel : "To the Son of Man was
given dominion, glory, and a kingdom : His dominion is the dominion of an age, and His kingdom that which shall not perish" (vii.
14) : again : "The kingdom and dominion, and majesty of the
kingdoms, shall be given to the people of the saints of the Most
High" (vii. 27). In these passages, dominion is predicated of good,
because from good the Lord is called Lord, and kingdom is predicated of truth, because from this the Lord is called king; as in the
Apocalypse : "He who sat upon the white horse, had upon His
vestment and upon His thigh, a name written, King of kings and
Lord of Lords" (xix. 16). King of kings is predicated of the name
upon the vestment, and Lord of lords of the name upon the thigh,
for by vestment is signified truth, and here divine truth, because concerning the Lord, and by the thigh is signified good, and here the
divine good of divine love. So likewise, as applied to men, in
David : "The kings of the earth stood up, and the rulers consulted
together" (Psalm ii. 2). From these considerations it may appear,

what is specifically signified by reigning for ages of ages. That kingdom signifies heaven and the church as to the truth of doctrine, may be seen above, n. 48 : and hence that to reign belongs to the Lord alone, and, when predicated of men, that it is to be in truths by virtue of good from the Lord, and thence in the power of resist-.ng falses from evils, may be seen above, n. 333.

686. Verses 16, 17. "And the four and twenty elders, who sat)efore God upon their thrones, fell upon their faces and adored God saying, We give Thee thanks, Lord God Almighty, Who art, Who wast, and Who art to come, that Thou hast gained Thy great power, and entered upon the kingdom."—" And the four and twenty elders who sat before God upon their thrones," signifies the superior hea-vens in light and power from the Lord, to separate the evil from the good before the day of the last judgment, which is about to come shortly : "fell upon their faces and adored God," signifies their adoration of the Lord from a most humble heart, " saying, We give Thee thanks, Lord God Almighty," signifies acknowledgment that the all of being, life, and power, is from the Lord : " Who art, Who wast, and Who art to come," signifies from Himself who is all in all things of heaven and the church from eternity to eternity : " that thou hast gained Thy great power, and entered upon the kingdom," signifies the establishment of the new heaven and new church, at the destruction of the former heaven and former church.

687. " And the four and twenty elders, who sat before God upon their thrones "—That hereby are signified the superior heavens in light and power from the Lord, to separate the evil from the good before the day of the last judgment shortly to come, appears from the signification of the four and twenty elders, as denoting the supe-rior heavens, concerning which see above, n. 122, 362, 462 ; and from the signification of sitting upon thrones, as denoting to be in operation to judge, for by thrones are signified the heavens, and by sitting upon thrones is signified to judge; and whereas the angels do not judge, but the Lord alone, and the Lord disposes those hea-vens by his influx and presence, in order thence to perform judg-ment upon those who were gathered together below the heavens, therefore by these words is signified the superior heavens being in light and power from the Lord, to separate the evil from the good before the day of the last judgment. That this is the internal sense of these words, is manifest from the things which follow in this chapter, also from what was said above on this subject. From the things which follow in this chapter, it is evident, that the superior heavens are in light and power from the Lord, on which account it is said that they fell upon their faces and adored God, and gave thanks that He had gained His great power and entered upon the kingdom, and afterwards, that the temple was opened in heaven, and the ark of the covenant seen in the temple, these latter things signifying the light there, and the former signifying the power, both from the Lord alone : that it is to separate the evil from the good before the day of the last judgment is also evident, for it is said that the nations were angry, and that his anger is come, and the time of

judging the dead; and afterwards, that there were lightnings and
voices, and thunders, and an earthquake, and great hail, by which
is signified the separation of the evil from the good, and the sign of
the presence of the last judgment: whereas these are the things
treated of, and by the twenty-four elders sitting before God upon
the thrones, are understood the superior heavens disposed for the
last judgment to be thence executed, it follows that such things are
involved in the words now under consideration.   The same also appears from what had been said above upon this subject, where it
was shown, that the superior heavens, before the last judgment,
were put into a state of light and power, in order that the influx might
descend from them into the lower parts, by which the evil might be
separated from the good, and afterwards the evil cast down into
hell, see n. 411, 413, 418, 419, 426, 493, 497, 674, 675, 676.   That a
throne signifies heaven in general, specifically the heavens which
constitute the spiritual kingdom of the Lord, and, abstractedly, the
divine truth proceeding from the Lord, and that it is predicated of
judgment, may also be seen above, n. 253, 297, 342, 460, 482;
where it is also shown, that although it is said of the twenty-four
elders that they sat upon thrones, likewise of the apostles that they
should sit upon twelve thrones judging the twelve tribes of Israel,
and also of the angels, that they will come with the Lord to judgment, still it is the Lord alone who will judge; for by the twenty-
four elders, the twelve apostles, and the angels, are understood all
the truths of the church, and, summarily, the divine truth, from
which comes judgment; and whereas divine truth is understood
by them, and all divine truth proceeds from the Lord, therefore
judgment belongs to the Lord alone: who cannot see, that to judge
myriads of myriads, every one according to the state of his love and
faith, as well in his internal man as in the external, cannot be possible to any angels, but to the Lord alone, by virtue of the Divine
[principle] which is in Him, and which proceeds from Him; likewise,
that to judge all in the heavens, and all in the earths, belong to infinite
wisdom, and infinite power, not the least part whereof can fall into
finite beings such as the angels are, and such as were the elders of
Israel, and the apostles of the Lord, all of whom taken together
cannot p ss   judge so much as one man or one spirit; for he who
is to judge, must see every state of the man who is to be judged,
from infancy to the last period of his life in the world, and
what the state of his life will be afterwards to eternity: for there
must be what is eternal and what is infinite in every view, and
consequently in all and singular the things appertaining to judgment, which is in the Divine [principle] alone, and from It alone,
inasmuch as It is the Infinite and Eternal.   In the Word, mention
is frequently made of walking before God, of standing before God,
and, as in the present case, of sitting before God; what is signified
by standing before God may be seen above, n. 414; what by walking before God, n. 97; but what is signified by sitting before God,
as is here said of the twenty-four elders, may appear from the passages in the Word, where sitting is mentioned: for in the spiritual

world, all things appertaining to man's motion or rest, signify things appertaining to his life, inasmuch as they thence proceed; walkings and journeyings relate to the movements of man, and thence signify progression of life, or progression of the thought from the intention of the will; but standings and sittings appertain to the rest of man, and thence signify the esse of life, from which is the existere thereof, thus to cause to live; wherefore to sit upon thrones, when predicated of judgment, signifies to be in operation to judge, consequently also to judge, whence comes the expression of sitting in judgment, which denotes to do judgment: to sit upon a throne likewise, when treating of a kingdom, signifies to be king or to reign. What is signified moreover by sitting, in the spiritual sense, may appear from the following passages : thus in David : "Blessed is the man who walketh not in the counsel of the impious, and standeth not in the way of sinners, and sitteth not in the seat of the scornful" (Psalm i. 1). To walk, to stand, and to sit, are here mentioned, because one follows another, for to walk is expressive of the life of the thought from intention, to stand is expressive of the life of the intention from the will, and to sit of the life of the will, thus of the esse of the life: counsel, also, of which walking is predicated, has respect to the thought, way, of which standing is predicated, has respect to intention, and to sit in a seat has respect to the will, which is the esse of a man's life. Inasmuch as Jehovah, that is, the Lord, is the very esse of the life of all, therefore to sit is predicated of Him, in various parts of the Word: as in David, "Jehovah shall sit to eternity" (Psalm ix. 8); again, "Jehovah shall sit upon the flood, and He shall sit a King to eternity" (Psalm xxix. 10): and again, "God reigneth over the nations; God sitteth upon the throne of His holiness" (Psalm xlvii. 9): and in Matthew: "When the Son of man shall come in His glory, and all His holy angels with him, then shall He sit upon the throne of His glory" (xxv. 31). To sit upon the throne of His glory, signifies to be in His divine truth, from which is judgment: again: "When the Son of Man shall sit upon the throne of His glory, ye also shall sit upon twelve thrones, judging the twelve tribes of Israel" (xix. 20; Luke xxii. 30). Inasmuch as by the angels, likewise by the twelve apostles, and also by the twelve tribes of Israel, are signified all the truths of the church, and, in the supreme sense, the divine truth, therefore by sitting upon thrones is not understood that they themselves will so sit, but the Lord as to divine truth, from which is judgment ; and by judging the twelve tribes of Israel, is signified to judge all according to the truths of their church; hence it is evident, that by sitting upon a throne, when predicated of the Lord, is signified to be judging, consequently to judge ; it is said, the throne of glory, because glory signifies the divine truth, as may be seen above, n. 34, 288, 345, 678. Again in the evangelists : "David saith in the book of Psalms, the Lord said to my Lord, sit thou at My right hand, until I make thine enemies thy footstool" (Mark xiii. 36; Luke xx. 42, 43; Psalm cx. 1). The Lord said to my Lord, signifies the Essential Divine [principle], which is called the Father, to the Divine Human [principle], which is the Son ; sit Thou at My right hand, signifies divine power, or omnipotence by divine truth; until I make thine enemies thy footstool, signifies until the hells are conquered and subjugated, and the evil cast thither, enemies denoting the hells, consequently the evil, and footstool the lowest region under the heavens, under which are the hells; for the Lord whilst He was in the world, was divine truth, to which belongs omnipotence, and by which He conquered and subdued the hells.   Again: "Jesus said, hereafter shall ye see the Son Man sitting at the right hand of power, and coming upon the clouds of heaven" (Matt. xxvi. 63, 64; Mark xiv. 61, 62; Luke xxii. 69).   Where to sit at the right hand of power signifies the divine omnipotence of the Lord over the heavens and over the earths, after he had subjugated the hells and glorified his humanity; to come upon the clouds of heaven signifies by divine truth in the heavens, for since the Lord united his Human to the Essential Divine [principle], the divine truth proceeds from Him, and He Himself is therein with angels and with men because in the Word, which is divine truth, in which and from which is the divine omnipotence.   So again it is written: "The Lord, after he had spoken with them, was taken up into heaven, and sat down at the right hand of God" (Mark xvi. 19); where to sit down at the right hand of God signifies the same thing, namely, His divine omnipotence by divine truth: from which it is evident, that to sit denotes esse or to be, and to sit at the right hand denotes to be omnipotent.   Whereas to sit signifies esse or to be, hence to sit upon a throne signifies to be king and to reign, as in Exodus xi. 5; Deut. xvii. 18; 1 Kings i. 13, 17, 20; Jeremiah xvii. 25; chap. xxii. 2, 30, and elsewhere; in like manner, "to sit on the right hand and on the left" (Matthew xv. 21, 23; Mark x. 37, 40).   Thus also in Isaiah: "Descend and sit upon the dust, O virgin daughter of Babel, sit upon the earth, there is no throne, O daughter of the Chaldeans; sit in silence and enter into darkness, O daughter of the Chaldeans; for they shall no more call thee, the lady of the kingdoms; hear this thou delicate, that sitteth securely, saying, I shall not sit a widow, neither shall I know bereaving" (xlvii. 1, 5, 8). The subject here treated of is concerning the profanation of good and truth; for by the daughter of Babel is signified the profanation of good, and by the daughter of the Chaldeans the profanation of truth; and the reason why such things are signified by them, is, because they use the divine goods and truths which are in the Word and from the Word, as means of bearing rule, whence the Babylonians and Chaldeans regard themselves, or their own empire, as ends, and the holy things of the church from the Word as means, thus they do not regard the Lord and His dominion as an end, nor their neighbor and love towards him: to descend and sit upon the dust and in the earth, signifies to be in evils and thence in damnation; to sit in silence and enter into darkness, signifies to be in falses and thence in damnation; to sit securely signifies to be in confidence that their rule or empire will remain, and that they shall not perish; not to sit a widow, and not to know bereaving, signifies not to be in want of attendants, clients, and worshipers; there is no throne for thee, O daughter of the Chaldeans, they shall no more call thee a lady of kingdoms, signifies, that they shall bear rule no longer because of their subversion and damnation in the day of the last judgment, which is treated of in the same chapter. Again in the same prophet : "Thou hast said in thine heart, I will ascend the heavens, over the stars of God will I exalt my throne, and I will sit in the mount of the assembly, in the sides of the north" (xiv. 13); where also to sit signifies esse or to be, and has respect to empire or rule ; the subject treated of is also concerning Babel, which is called there Lucifer, and concerning the concupiscence of the profane love of ruling over all things of heaven; but what is signified in particular by exalting the throne above the stars of God, by sitting in the mount of the assembly, and in the sides of the north, will be explained in the following pages when we come to treat of Babylon. Again in Ezekiel : "All the princes of the sea shall descend from their thrones, they shall sit upon the earth" (xxvi. 16). Treating of Tyre, whereby is signified the church as to the knowledges of truth, but in the present case, of Tyre vastated, in which those knowledges are falsified ; wherefore by all the princes of the sea descending from their thrones, is signified that the knowledges of truth shall reign no more with the men of that church, for all reigning is of divine truth; to descend from the thrones, signifies from governing, consequently not to reign, and the princes of the sea denote the knowledges of truth, and those who are in them; they shall sit upon the earth, signifies that they will be in truths falsified, that is, in falses, for to be upon thrones, signifies to be in the truths of heaven, and to sit upon the earth, signifies to be in falses, inasmuch as under the earths in the spiritual world are the hells, from which evils and falses are continually exhaling. The like is signified by sitting, in the following passages, thus in Luke : "Who sit in darkness and in the shadow of death" (i. 79); and in Isaiah : "To open the blind eyes, to bring the bound out of the prison, and them that sit in darkness out of the prison house" (xlii. 7); and in Jeremiah : "I have not sat in the counsel of mockers, nor was I glad; I sat solitary because of thy hand, for thou hast filled me with indignation" (xv. 17); and in David : "I have not sat with men of vanity, nor have I entered with the hidden" (Psalm. xxvi. 4); and in Luke : "That day shall come as a snare upon all who sit upon the faces of the whole earth" (xxi. 35). Inasmuch as to sit signifies to be, and to abide in that state, and appertains to the will, therefore it is also said in David, "Jehovah, thou hast searched me and known me; thou knowest my sitting and my rising; thou understandest my thought afar off" (Psalm cxxxix. 12); where to know his sitting has respect to the esse of life which is the will, and to know his rising has respect to his intention thence derived; and whereas the thought follows the intention of the will, it is added, thou understandest my thought afar off. And in Micah : "Then shall he stand and feed in the name of Jehovah, and they shall sit, for now shall he increase unto the ends of the earth" (v. 3); treating of the Lord and of the doctrine of divine truth from Him, which is understood by, then shall he stand and feed, or rule, in the name of Jehovah; and that the men of the church shall be in that doctrine, is signified by, they shall sit; and that the doctrine of divine truth shall abide to eternity, is signified by, he shall increase unto the ends of the earth. So likewise in Isaiah : " Shake thyself from the dust, arise, sit, O Jerusalem, open the bands of thy neck, O captive daughter of Zion" (lii. 2); treating of the establishment of the new church by the Lord, which, together with its doctrine, is here signified by Jerusalem, and by the daughter of Zion; to reject falses and evils, and to be in truths and goods, is signified by shaking herself from the dust, rising, and sitting, likewise by opening the bands of the neck, the bands of the neck denoting falses, which hinder truths from entering. That to sit is an expression significative of essence and endurance in the state of a thing and of the life, may appear from those passages in the Word where mention is made of sitting before Jehovah, of standing before Him, and of walking before Him; that to sit before Jehovah denotes esse, or to be with Him, thus also to will and to act from Him; and that to stand before Him denotes to look to, or regard and understand, what He wills; and that to walk before Him denotes to live according to His precepts, thus from Him. Whereas to sit involves such things, therefore the same expression, in the Hebrew tongue, signifies to abide and to dwell. It was on account of such things being signified by sitting, that " An angel of the Lord was seen sitting upon the stone, which he had rolled away from the door of the sepulchre" (Matt. xxviii. 2); and therefore also " Angels were seen in the sepulchre, one sitting at the head, and the other at the feet" (John xx. 12; Mark xvi. 5); which things were representative of the glorification of the Lord and introduction into heaven by Him; for by the stone which was placed before the sepulchre, and was rolled away by the angel, is signified divine truth, consequently the Word, which was shut by the Jews, but opened by the Lord; that stone signifies truth, and, in the supreme sense, divine truth, may be seen in the work concerning H. & H. n. 417, 534; and whereas by a sepulchre, in the spiritual sense, is signified resurrection and also regeneration, and eminently so by the sepulchre where the Lord was, and by angels in the Word is signified divine truth, therefore angels were seen, one sitting at the head and the other at the feet, and by the angel at the head was signified divine truth in first principles, and by the angel at the feet divine truth in ultimates, both proceeding from the Lord, by which, when it is received, regeneration and resurrection are effected. That to be buried, burial, and sepulchre, signify regeneration and resurrection, may be seen above, n. 659; and that angels, in the supreme sense, signify the Lord as to divine truth, and, in the respective sense, the recipients of divine truth, and thus, abstractedly, divine truths from the Lord, may be seen above, n. 130, 200, 302. Moreover mention is sometimes made in the Word of sitting before Jehovah when in great joy, likewise sitting when in great mourning, the reason whereof is, because sitting has respect to the esse of man, which appertains to his will and love;

concerning weeping and sitting before Jehovah, see Judges xx. 26; chap. xxi. 2.

688. "Fell upon their faces and adored God"—That hereby is signified the adoration of the Lord with them from a most humble heart, appears from the signification of falling upon their faces, as denoting the greatest humiliation of heart, for it is a gesture of the body corresponding to humiliation of the heart, thus a gesture representative of the humiliation of the whole man; the adoration of God in such case is what flows forth from that heart, which is various according to the object upon which the mind is engaged. The reason why to fall upon the faces before God is the representative gesture of deepest humiliation, is, because the face is the form of man's affections, consequently of the interiors appertaining to his mind (mens) and mind (animus), for the affections shine forth in the face, as in their type, whence it is that the face is called the index and image of the mind; wherefore, when man acknowledges that all things with himself are averted from God, and therefore cursed, and that hence he neither can nor dares to look unto God, who is essential holiness, and if he should from himself in such a condition look up, that he would spiritually die, then the man from such thought and acknowledgment, falls upon the face to the earth; and whereas his proprium is hereby removed, he is then filled by the Lord, and elevated so as to be able to look up unto Him. It is said, that they adored God, by reason that by God, in the Word, is understood the divine proceeding which is called divine truth; and inasmuch as this divine [proceeding] is truth with the angels, for they are the recipients thereof, and constitutes their wisdom, therefore the angels in the Word, are called gods, and signify divine truths; in the Hebrew tongue also, God is called Elohim, in the plural, wherefore by God, in the Word, is understood the divine [principle] which is with the angels of heaven and with men of the church, which is the divine proceeding; and inasmuch as the superior heavens were now in illustration and in power, on account of the separation of the evil from the good in the lower parts, and on account of the last judgment shortly to take place, therefore it is said that they adored God, by which it is evident, that the Lord was then with them, for their illustration and power was from the more intense and powerful influx of the divine truth, which proceeds from the Lord.

689. "Saying, we give Thee thanks, Lord God Almighty"— That hereby is signified that all esse or being, life, and ability, is from the Lord, appears from the signification of saying and giving thanks, as denoting to acknowledge, inasmuch as by falling upon the face, and adoring, and then giving thanks, nothing else can be signified than acknowledgment, in this case, of the omnipotence of the Lord; and from the signification of the Lord God, as denoting the Lord as to divine good and as to divine truth, for where divine good is understood in the Word, there Lord and Jehovah are mentioned, and where divine truth is understood, God is mentioned, whence by the Lord God and by Jehovah God is understood the Lord as to divine good and as to divine truth; moreover Jehovah, in

the Old Testament, is called Lord in the New; and from the signification of Almighty, as denoting to be, to have life and ability, of Himself, and also that the esse or being, life, and ability of angels and men, is from Him; that these things are understood by Omnipotence, may be seen above, n. 43; likewise, that by the divine omnipotence is understood what is infinite, n. 286.   As to what concerns the divine omnipotence, it does not involve any power of acting contrary to order, but it involves all power of acting according to order, for all order is from the Lord; hence it follows, that no one has any power of acting according to order, except from him who is the source of order; hence also it may appear that it is of the divine omnipotence to lead man according to order, and this every moment from the beginning of his life even to eternity, and this according to the laws of order, which are innumerable and ineffable in number; it is to be observed, however, that this can only take place in proportion as man suffers himself to be led, that is, in proportion as he does not will to be led of himself, for in proportion as he wills this, he is carried away contrary to order; and whereas it is of the divine omnipotence to lead man who wills to be led, according to order, consequently not any one contrary to order, therefore, it is not of the divine omnipotence to lead any one to heaven who wills to lead himself, because it is a law of order, that what man acts, he should act from rationality and from liberty, inasmuch as that which is received in rationality, and acted from liberty, remains with man, and is appropriated to him as his own, but not that which is not received in rationality and acted from liberty; hence it may appear that it is not of the divine omnipotence to save those who do not will to be led according to order, for to be led according to order is to be led according to the laws of order, and the laws of order are the precepts of doctrine and of life from the Word, wherefore to lead man according to these, who wills to be led, every moment and continually to eternity, is of the divine omnipotence; for in every moment there are infinite things to be seen, infinite things to be removed, and infinite things to be insinuated, in order that man may be withheld from evils, and held in goods, and this continually in a wonderful connection, according to order.   It is also of the divine omnipotence to protect men from the hells, so far as it can be done without hurting their liberty and rationality; for all the hells are as nothing against the divine power of the Lord, and without this power of the Lord no man could possibly be saved; but more particulars concerning the divine omnipotence, may be seen above, n. 43.

690. " Who art and who wast and who art to come"—That hereby is signified from Him who is the all in all of heaven and the church from eternity to eternity, appears from the explication of the same words above, n. 23, 41, 42.

691. " That thou hast gained thy great power, and entered upon the kingdom"—That hereby is signified the establishment of the new heaven and the new church, at the destruction of the former heaven and church, appears from the signification of gained His great power, and entering upon the kingdom, as denoting that after

the former heaven and former church are destroyed, a new heaven and new church are established; that this is what is here understood is evident from this consideration, that the Lord has then omnipotence and the kingdom; for then His will is done, inasmuch as the angels of heaven and men of the church then suffer themselves to be led by Him; for hereby He rules all, according to order, from Himself, keeping them in divine goods and truths, which proceed from Him, and withholding them from evils and falses which are from hell; which could not be accomplished, before the evil were separated from the good, and the former cast down into hell, and a new heaven formed of the latter; these things were actually accomplished by the last judgment, which is treated of in what follows. That then the Lord has power and the kingdom, may be illustrated by a comparison with the sun of this world; so long as the winter continues the sun has not any power or any kingdom in the earth, because the heat thereof is not received, for the cold of the air and of the earth extinguish it; but when spring returns, then comes the power and kingdom of the sun, for then the heat thereof is received, and also the light, because conjoined to the heat, by virtue whereof the whole earth begins to flourish; similar is the case with the power and the kingdom of the Lord, which come when the evil are separated from the good and cast down into hell, for these are as the colds of winter, which extinguish the spiritual heat of the sun, which is love, and prevent the power and kingdom of the Lord from taking place, although with respect to, or viewed in, Himself, He is perpetually in a like omnipotence, but not so in the subjects thereof, before the new heaven and new church are formed.

. 692. Verse 18. " And the nations were angry, and thy anger is come, and the time of the dead, that they should be judged, and to give reward to his servants the prophets and saints, and to them that fear thy name, small and great, and to destroy them that destroy the earth."—" And the nations were angry," signifies the contempt, enmity, and hatred, of the evil against the Lord, and against the divine things which are from Him, which are the holy things of heaven and the church; " and thy anger is come, and the time of the dead that they should be judged," signifies the last judgment upon those who inwardly possess nothing of good and truth; " and to give reward to his servants the prophets and saints," signifies heaven to those who are in truths of doctrine, and in a life according to them; " and to them that fear thy name, small and great," signifies, and to all who worship the Lord of whatsoever religion they are; and to destroy them that destroy the earth," signifies hell to those who destroy the church.

· 693. " And the nations were angry"—That hereby is signified the contempt, enmity and hatred of the evil against the Lord and against the divine things which are from Him, which are the holy things of heaven and the church, appears from the signification of nations, as denoting those who are in the goods of the church, and, in the opposite sense, who are in evils, in this case, those who are in evils, inasmuch as it is said, that they were angry; that nations signify those who are in goods and who are in evils, and, abstractedly, the goods and evils of the church, and that people signify those who are in truths and who are in falses, and, abstractedly, the truths and falses of the church, may be seen above, n. 175, 331, 625; and from the signification of being angry, when predicated of the evil, who are signified by nations, as denoting to be in contempt, in enmity, and in hatred, against the Lord and against the divine things which are from Him, which are the holy things of heaven and the church. The reason why these and other things of a like nature, are signified by being angry, is because every one is inflamed with wrath and anger, when his love is assaulted, and the delight of his love, for hence comes all wrath and anger, the reason whereof is, because the love of every one is his life, wherefore to hurt the love is to hurt the life, and when this is hurt a commotion of the mind take place, which produces wrath and anger : the case is similar with the good, when their love is assaulted, but with this difference, that with them there is no anger nor wrath, but zeal ; this zeal is indeed called anger in the Word, although it is not so in reality, but is so called because it appears similar thereto in the external form, whilst notwithstanding, it is inwardly nothing but charity, goodness, and clemency; wherefore the zeal which appears as anger does not continue any longer than till the person, against whom it was enkindled, repents and turns himself away from the evil; anger with the evil is of a different nature, for this inwardly conceals in itself hatred and revenge, which they love, wherefore it continues and is rarely extinguished. Hence it follows that anger belongs to those who are in the loves of self and of the world, for such are also in evils of every kind, but zeal belongs to those who are in love to the Lord, and in love towards their neighbor, wherefore zeal regards the salvation of man, but anger his damnation : the evil man, who is angry, also intends the latter, but the good man, who is zealous, intends the former. The reason why the nations being angry here signifies the contempt, enmity, and hatred, of the evil against the Lord, and against the divine things which are from Him, thus against the holy things of heaven and the church, is, because at the end of the church, a little before the last judgment, which is the subject here treated of, a change takes place in the state of those who were in the former heaven and former earth, which is effected by the separation of the good from the evil ; for, in consequence of this separation, the externals of the evil, by which and from which they made a pretence of, and hypocritically spoke and did what was good and true, are shut, and the internals, which with them were infernal, are opened, and these being opened, their contempt, hostility, and hatred, manifestly break out, with scorn against the Lord and against the holy things of heaven and the church, for with such persons those things lie inwardly concealed, but covered over by the loves of self and of the world, from which they can do good and speak truths for the sake of self and of the world, because the holy things of heaven and the church serve them as means to obtain their ends, which are fame, glory, honor, and gain, in a word, themselves and the world, and the means are loved for the sake of the ends; but whereas the end which is of the love, and thence of the intention and will, is thus corporeal and worldly, consequently infernal, therefore the goods and truths, which appertain to heaven and the church, with them stick only in their externals, but not at all in their internals, which are occupied by evils and falses; for the goods and truths of heaven penetrate into the internals with those only who make the holy things of heaven and the church their ends, that is, who make them to be of their love, and thence of their intention and will, in which case the spiritual mind is opened, and thereby man is led of the Lord; but the contrary is the case when the goods and truths of heaven and the church are not considered as ends, but as means only, for as was said above, ends are what appertain to man's ruling love, and when this is the love of self, it is also the love of his proprium, which, viewed in itself is nothing but evil, and so far as man acts from it he acts from hell, consequently also against the Divine [being or principle]. It is moreover to be observed, that in all evil there is anger against the Lord, and against the holy things of the church: that this is the case, has manifestly appeared to me from the hells, where all are in evils and from which all evils are derived; for when those who are there do but hear the Lord named, they become inflamed with vehement anger, not only against Him, but also against all who confess Him; hence hell is diametrically opposite to heaven, and in the continual effort of destroying it, and of extinguishing the divine things thereto belonging, which are the goods of love and truths of faith; from these considerations it is evident, that evils are angry with goods, and the falses of evil with truths; and hence it is, that by anger, in the Word, is signified evil in all its complex. In like manner in the following passages; as in Luke: "Jesus said, woe to them that are with child and to them that give suck in those days, for there shall be great straitness upon the earth, and anger in the people" (xxi. 23); these words relate to the consummation of the age, which is the last time of the church; that then good and truth cannot be received, is signified by, woe to them that are with child and to them that give suck; the rejection of good on account of the evil which then rules in the church, and the rejection of truth on account of the false, is signified by, there shall be great straitness upon the earth, and anger in the people, straitness here denoting the ruling evil, and anger the ruling false from evil, for in the end of the church the evil are tortured at the presence of good, and angry at the presence of truth. So in Isaiah: "Surely in Jehovah is justice and strength, unto Him shall they come, and all who were incensed against Him shall be ashamed" (xlv. 24). By all who were incensed against Jehovah shall be ashamed, is signified, that all who are in evils and falses shall recede from them, to be angry against Jehovah signifies to be in falses from evil. Again in Moses: "Simeon and Levi are brethren, in their anger they slew a man, and in their good pleasure they unstrung an ox; cursed be their anger, because it is vehement, and their wrath, because it is hard; I will divide them in Jacob, and disperse them in Israel" (Gen. xlix. 5, 6, 7).

By Reuben, Simeon and Levi are signified faith, charity, and works
of charity, but there by Reuben is signified faith separated from charity, whence there is neither charity nor any work of charity, inasmuch as these three cohere together; for according to the quality of
the faith, such is the charity, and according to the quality of the
charity, such is the work of charity, wherefore they are inseparable,
one being of the other, and thus as the other; and whereas Reuben,
on account of his adultery with the handmaid, his father's concu-
bine, was accursed, therefore Simeon and Levi were also rejected,
and their rejection is signified by being divided in Jacob and dispersed in Israel: now whereas faith, which was represented by
Reuben, was not to be accepted as the first principle of the church,
but spiritual good, which is truth in the understanding and will,
therefore Joseph was received for the first begotten of the church in
the place of Reuben, for by Joseph was represented spiritual good,
which in its essence is truth in the understanding and will; hence
it may appear what is signified by the anger of Simeon and Levi
which is vehement, and by their wrath which is hard, namely, aversion from good and truth, thus the evil and false in every complex;
for when charity recedes from faith, then there is no more any good,
nor any truth; but these things may be seen explained more at
large in the A. C. n. 6351–6361. Again in Matthew: "Jesus
said, it hath been said to them of old time, whosoever shall kill,
shall be obnoxious to the judgment, but I say unto you, whosoever
shall be angry with his brother rashly, shall be obnoxious to the
judgment" (v. 21, 22). By being angry with his brother rashly, is
here also signified enmity and hatred against good and truth: they
also who are in such enmity and hatred, continually kill in mind,
intention, and will, for only make it allowable, that is, remove the
obstacles, which arise from the laws and the consequent fear of punishment and of life, or of the loss of fame, honor, or gain, and they
would actually kill, since what a man bears or cherishes in his
mind, this he does where there is opportunity; the reason why he
who is rashly angry with his brother is obnoxious to the judgment,
as he who kills, is because by being angry is signified to think, intend, and will, evil to another, and all evil of the will is in the life
of man's spirit, and returns after death, and hence it is, that he is
then obnoxious to the judgment; for what is of the intention and
will, is judged as if it were done. But there is no need to adduce
more passages to show the signification of anger and wrath with
those who are in evil, because it is self evident that all evil conceals
in itself anger against good, for it wills to extinguish it, and also to
kill those in whom good is, if not as to the body yet as to the soul,
which is done entirely from anger and with anger.

694. "And thy anger is come, and the time of the dead that they
should be judged"—That hereby is signified the last judgment upon
those who inwardly possess nothing of good and truth, appears from
the signification of anger, when predicated of the Lord, as denoting
the last judgment, concerning which see above, n. 413; that this is
signified by the anger here mentioned is evident, for it follows, and

the time of the dead, that they should be judged; and from the signification of the dead, as denoting those who inwardly in themselves
possess nothing of good and truth; the reason why such are called
dead, is, because the essential life of man is his spiritual life, for by
this he is a man, and is distinguished from the beasts, which have
only a natural life; with man the natural life without the spiritual life is dead, inasmuch as it has not in itself heaven, which is
called life and also eternal life, but hell, which is spiritually called
death: that they are understood by the dead mentioned in the Word,
who live a natural life alone, and not at the same time a spiritual
life, may be seen above, n. 78; also, that by death, when predicated of man, is understood the defect or want of the faculty of understanding truth and perceiving good, may also be seen above, n. 550:
and this defect is, where the internal spiritual man is not formed,
for this is formed by truths from good: in this internal man resides
the faculty of understanding truth and of perceiving good, for this
man is in heaven and in the light thereof, and he who is in the light
of heaven is alive or living, but when the natural man only is formed,
and not at the same time the spiritual, then there is not any faculty
of understanding and perceiving the truths and goods of heaven, and
the church, because such a man has not any light from heaven, and
hence it is that he is called dead. That they who do not inwardly
possess any thing of good and truth, are here understood by the
dead who are to be judged, may appear also from what goes before,
where the separation of the evil from the good before the last judgment is treated of, and that the evil, when they are separated, come
into their interiors, which abound with mere evils and falses: from
which it is evident, that inwardly they were dead, although in the
external form they appeared as alive.

695. "And to give reward to his servants the prophets and
saints"—That hereby is signified heaven to those who are in truths
of doctrine and in a life according to them, appears from the signification of giving reward, as denoting salvation, consequently heaven; and from the signification of his servants the prophets, as denoting those who are in the truths of doctrine, for they are called
servants of the Lord who are principled in truths, because truths
serve for the producing, confirming, and preserving of good, and
whatever serveth good, serveth also the Lord, for all good is from
the Lord, and they are called prophets, who teach doctrine, whence,
in an abstract sense, doctrine is signified by them; that they are
called servants of God who are principled in truths, may be seen
above, n. 6, 409, and prophets who teach doctrine, and abstractedly
doctrines, n. 624; and from the signification of saints, as denoting
those who are in the truths of doctrine from the Word, and in a life
according thereto, concerning which see above, n. 204: hence it is
evident, that by giving reward to his servants the prophets, and
saints, is signified heaven to those who are in the truths of doctrine
from the Word, and in a life according thereto. That by reward
is signified salvation, consequently heaven, may appear without
explication; but inasmuch as few know what is properly under-

stood by reward, it shall be explained: by reward is properly
understood that delight, satisfaction, and blessedness, which is
contained in the love or affection of good and truth, for that love
or that affection has in itself all the joy of heart, which is called
heavenly joy, and also heaven; the reason is, because the Lord is
in that love or in that affection, and with the Lord is also heaven;
this joy, therefore, or this delight, satisfaction, and blessedness, is
what is properly understood by the reward which they shall receive
who do good and speak truth from the love and affection of good
and truth, thus from the Lord, and by no means from themselves;
and whereas they act and speak from the Lord, and not from themselves, therefore the reward is not of merit but of grace; from
these considerations it may appear, that he who knows what heavenly
joy is, may know also what reward is; what heavenly joy is in its
essence may be seen in the work concerning H. & H. n. 395—414:
this therefore is signified by the reward which is given to those who
are in truths from good: but the reward of those who are in falses
from evil, is joy or delight, satisfaction and blessedness, in the world,
but hell after their departure out of the world.   Hence it may appear what is signified by reward in the following passages: thus in
Isaiah : "Behold the Lord Jehovih cometh in might; behold His
reward is with Him, and the price of His work is with Him" (xl.
10): and in the Apocalypse: "Behold I come quickly, and My
reward with Me, to give every one as his work shall be" (xxii. 12):
and again in Isaiah : "Say to the daughter of Zion, Behold thy salvation cometh, and the price of work with Him" (lxii. 11). Behold
the Lord Johovih cometh in might, behold thy salvation cometh, and
behold He comes quickly, signify the first and second advent of the
Lord : His reward is with Him, signifies heaven, and all things
thereto appertaining, as above, inasmuch as where the Lord is,
there is heaven, for heaven is not heaven from the angels there, but
from the Lord with the angels; that they shall receive heaven according to the love and affection of good and truth from the Lord, is
understood by, the price of His work before Him, and by giving to
every one according as His work shall be: by the work for which
heaven shall be given as a reward, nothing else is meant than what
proceeds from the love or affection of good and truth, inasmuch as
nothing else can produce heaven in man; for every work derives
all that it has from the love or affection whence it proceeds, as the
effect derives all that it has from the efficient cause, wherefore according to the quality of love or affection, such is the work; and
hence it may appear what is understood by the work according to
which it shall be given to every one, and and what by the price of
his work.   In like manner in Isaiah : "I Jehovah, who love judgment, will give the reward of their work in truth, and will make
with them a covenant of eternity" (lxi. 8).   By the judgment which
Jehovah loves is signified truth in faith, in affection, and in act, for
man has judgment from truth, as well when he thinks and wills it,
as when he speaks and acts according to it: and whereas this is
signified by judgment, therefore it is said, I will give the reward of

their work in truth, that is, heaven according to the faith and affection of truth in act: and whereas thence is conjunction with the Lord, from whom reward comes, therefore it is also said, I will make with them a covenant of eternity; for by covenant, in the Word, is signified conjunction by love, and by a covenant of eternity, conjunction by the love of good and truth, for this love conjoins, inasmuch as it is of the Lord Himself, for it proceeds from Him. That to love good and truth for the sake of good and truth is itself reward, is evident, inasmuch as the Lord and heaven are in that love, as may also appear from the following passages: thus in Matthew: "Do not ye your alms before men, to be seen of them, otherwise ye will have no reward with your Father, who is in the heavens: when thou doest alms do not sound a trumpet before thee, as the hypocrites do, in the synagogues and in the streets, that they may have glory from men; verily I say unto you, they have their reward; but thou when thou doest alms, let not thy left hand know what thy right hand doeth, that thine alms may be in secret; then thy Father who seeth in secret, shall reward thee in what is manifest. And if thou prayest, thou shalt not be as the hypocrites, for they love to pray standing in the synagogues, and in the corners of the streets, that they may be seen of men; verily I say unto you, that they have their reward; but thou, when thou prayest, enter into thy chamber, and shut thy door, and pray to th Father who is in secret; then thy Father who seeth in secret, shall reward thee in what is manifest" (vi. 2, 3, 4, 5, 6). By alms, in a universal sense, is signified all the good which a man wills and does, and by praying, in the same sense, is signified all the truth which a man thinks and speaks: they who do these things that they may be seen, that is, that they may appear, do them for the sake of themselves and the world, because for the sake of glory, which is the delight of their love, and which they receive from the world: inasmuch as the reward of such persons is the delight of glory, it is said that they have their reward; howbeit the delight of glory, which in the world appears to them as heaven, after their departure out of the world is changed into hell: but they who do good and speak truth, not for the sake of themselves and the world, but for the sake of good itself and truth itself, are understood by those who do their alms in secret, and who pray in secret, for such act and pray from love or affection, thus from the Lord, and this is to love good and truth for the sake of good and truth; concerning these therefore it is said, that their Father in the heavens will reward them in what is manifest; wherefore to be in goods and truths from love and affection, which is the same thing as to be in them from the Lord, is reward, inasmuch as heaven is therein, and all the blessings and satisfaction of heaven. So in Luke: "When thou makest a dinner or a supper, call not the rich, lest they also call thee again, and a recompense be made thee; but call the poor, then shalt thou be blessed, for they cannot recompense thee; for thou shalt be recompensed at the resurrection of the dead" (xiv. 12, 13, 14). By making a dinner and a supper, and bidding or calling thereto, is signified the same as by giving to eat and drink, or by giving bread and wine, viz. to do good to our neighbor, and teach truth, and thereby to be consociated as to love; they therefore who do this with a view to be recompensed, do it not for the sake of good and truth, thus not from the Lord, but for the sake of themselves and the world, and thus from hell; but they who do those things, not for the end of recompense, do them for their own sake, viz. for the sake of good and truth, and thus from good and truth, consequently from the Lord, from whom they are with man; the heavenly blessedness which is in those deeds, and thence from them, is reward, and is understood by the recompense in the resurrection of the dead. Again: "Rather love ye your enemies, and do good, and lend, hoping for nothing again; then shall your reward be much, and ye shall be the sons of the Highest" (vi. 35). Similar things are signified by these words as by those above, viz. that good should not be done for the sake of recompense, that is, for the sake of self and the world, thus not for the sake of fame, glory, honor, and gain, but for the sake of the Lord, which is for the sake of good and truth itself which are with them from the Lord, consequently in which the Lord is: by loving their enemies and doing good to them, is there understood, in the proximate sense, to love and to do good to the Gentiles, which is done by teaching them truth and by leading them to good, for the Jewish nation called their own people brethren and friends, but the Gentiles they called foes and enemies; by lending is signified to communicate the goods and truths of doctrine from the Word; hoping for nothing again, signifies, not for the sake of any thing of self and of the world, but for the sake of good and truth; then shall your reward be much, signifies, that then heaven shall be theirs with its blessings and delights; and ye shall be the sons of the Highest, signifies, because they do these things not from themselves but from the Lord; for he who does good and teaches truth from the Lord, is the Lord's son, but not he who does good from himself, as is the case with every one who regards honor and gain in what he does. Again in Matthew: "Whoso receiveth a prophet in the name of a prophet, shall receive a prophet's reward; whoso receiveth a just man in the name of a just man, shall receive a just man's reward; whoso shall give to drink to one of these little ones, a cup of cold [water] only, in the name of a disciple, he shall not lose his reward" (x. 41, 42). How these words of the Lord are to be understood, no one can see except from their internal or spiritual sense; for who can know what is meant by receiving a prophet's reward, and a just man's reward, and what by receiving a prophet and a just man in the name of a prophet and a just man? likewise what is meant by the reward which he shall receive, who gives to drink to one of the little ones, a cup of cold [water] only in the name of a disciple? who without the internal spiritual sense, can see that by these words is understood, that every one shall receive heaven and the joy thereof according to his affection of truth and good and according to obedience; that this is the sense will evidently appear, when by the prophet is understood the truth of doctrine, by the just, the good of love, and by a disciple, the truth and good of the Word and of the church, and when by receiving them in their name is understood for their own sake, and according to their quality with those who do and teach them; likewise, when by reward is understood heaven, as it was said above, viz. that heaven is with every one according to the affection of truth and good, and according to the quantity and quality thereof: for all things of heaven are inscribed on those affections, inasmuch as no one can have those affections but from the Lord, for it is the Divine Proceeding from the Lord, in which and from which is heaven : by giving to drink a cup of cold [water] only, to one of the little ones in the name of a disciple, is meant to do good and teach truth from a principle of obedience, for by water is signified truth in affection, and by cold water, truth in obedience, for obedience alone is a natural affection and not spiritual, wherefore it is respectively cold ; and by the disciple in whose name or for whose sake it is done, is signified the truth and good of the Word and of the church : that by a prophet is signified the truth of doctrine, may be seen above, n. 624; that by a just man is signified the good of love, n. 204; that by a disciple is signified the truth and good of the Word and of the church, n. 100, 122; and that by name is signified, the quality of a thing and state, n. 102, 135, 148, 676. Again in Mark : " Whosoever shall give you a cup of water to drink in My name, because ye belong to Christ, verily I say unto you, he shall not lose his reward" (ix. 41). By these words also is signified, that they shall receive the delight of heaven, who from affection hear, receive, and teach, the truth, by reason of truth and the affection thereof being from the Lord, thus for the sake of the Lord, and consequently also for the sake of truth, for by doing this because they belong to Christ, is signified, for the sake of divine truth proceeding from the Lord : that Christ is the Lord as to divine truth, and thence divine truth proceeding from the Lord, may be seen above, n. 584, 585. Again in Zechariah : " The foundation of the house of Jehovah Zebaoth is laid, that the temple might be built ; for before these days there was no reward of man, neither reward of beast, and to him that went in and him that came out, no peace from the enemy : now shall there be seed of peace, the vine shall give its fruit, and the earth shall give its produce, and the heavens shall give their dew" (viii. 9, 10, 12). These things are said concerning the new church to be established by the Lord at the devastation of the old; the new church which shall be established, is signified by the house of Jehovah Zebaoth whose foundations are laid, and by the temple which shall be built ; the house of Jehovah signifies the church as to good, and the temple the church as to truth, concerning which see above, n. 220 ; that before this there was not any spiritual affection of truth and good, nor natural affection of truth and good, is signified by, before these days there was no reward of man, neither reward of beast, for by man is signified the spiritual affection of truth, and by beast, the natural affection of good, and by reward, heaven, which is given to those who are in the affections of truth and good ; that man signifies

the spiritual affection of truth, and thence intelligence, may be seen
above, n. 280, 456, 547 ; and that beast signifies natural affection,
n. 650 ; to him that came out and him that went in, no peace from
the enemy, signifies, that before this they were infested from hell in
every state of life, the state of life from beginning to end being signified by going out and coming in, infestation from evils and falses
thence derived by no peace, and hell, whence evils and falses arise,
by the enemy ; the seed of peace signifies the truth of heaven and
the church, which is from the Lord, and which is called the seed of
peace, because it defends from the hells, and gives security ; the
vine shall give its fruit, and the earth its produce, signifies, that the
spiritual affection of truth shall produce the good of charity, and the
natural affection of good and truth shall produce the works of
charity, the vine denoting the church as to the spiritual affection of
truth, the earth the church as to the natural affection of truth, fruit,
the good of charity, and produce, the works of that good ; the
heavens shall give their dew, signifies, that these things shall be
from influx through heaven from the Lord.   Again in John : " Lift
up your eyes, and look upon the fields that they are white already
to harvest, and he who reapeth receiveth reward and gathereth fruit
unto life eternal, that he who soweth and he who reapeth may rejoice together" (iv. 35, 36.)   These words relate to the new church
to be established by the Lord ; its being at hand, is signified by the
fields being white already to the harvest ; those of the church who
are in the spiritual affection of truth, and thence in heaven, are understood by, he who reapeth receiveth reward, and gathereth fruit
unto life eternal ; and the Lord Himself, from whom the affection of
truth and heaven are derived, is understood by Him that soweth ;
hence it may appear what is meant by their rejoicing together.
Again in Jeremiah : " Rachel weeping for her sons, refuseth to be
comforted for her sons because there was not any ; but refrain thy
voice from weeping and thine eyes from tears, for thy labor shall be
rewarded ; for they shall return from the land of the enemy, and
there is hope in thine extremity, for thy sons shall return in their
own border" (xxxi. 15, 16, 17 ; Matt. ii. 18).   That these words
relate to the infant children who were slain in Bethlehem by command of Herod, is evident from the passage cited in Matthew, but
what was thereby signified, is not yet known : the signification is,
that when the Lord came into the world, there was not any spiritual
truth remaining ; by Rachel was represented the internal spiritual
church, and by Leah, the external natural church ; by Bethlehem,
the spiritual [principle], and by the boys who were slain, truth from
a spiritual origin ; that there was not any spiritual truth remaining
any longer, is signified by Rachel weeping for her sons, and refusing
to be comforted for her sons, because there was not any ; that grief
on that account should afterwards cease, by reason of the Lord's
being born, from whom there should be a new church, which should
be in truths from a spiritual affection, is signified by, refrain thy
voice from weeping and thine eyes from tears, for thy labor shall be
rewarded, by labor, is signified the Lord's combat against the hells,

and subjugation of them, that a new church might be established, and by His reward is signified heaven to those who will be of that church, from a spiritual affection of truth; the establishment of a new church in the place of the former, which perished, is signified by, they shall return from the land of the enemy, and there is hope in thine extremity; also by thy sons shall return into their own border; to return from the land of the enemy, signifies to be led out of hell, hope in extremity signifies the end of the former church and beginning of the new, and the sons returning into their own border, signifies that spiritual truths will exist with those who will be of that new church. Again in Isaiah: "I said, I have labored in vain, I have spent my strength to emptiness and vanity: yet surely my judgment is with Jehovah and the reward of my work with my God" (xlix. 4). Speaking also concerning the establishment of the new church from the Lord: that it could not be established with the Jewish nation, because truths could not be received by that nation from any spiritual affection, is understood by, I said I have labored in vain, I spent my strength to emptiness and vanity: that still a spiritual church is provided by the Lord, viz. with the gentiles, is signified by, my judgment is with Jehovah, and the reward of my work is with my God; by reward is here signified the church which is in the spiritual affection of truth; by labor and by work is signified the combat of the Lord against the hells, and the subjugation of them, whereby the Lord restored the equilibrium between heaven and hell, in which man can receive truth, and become spiritual; concerning which equilibrium see in the work concerning H. & H. n. 589–603, and in the small work concerning the L. J. n. 33, 34, 73, 74. Again in David: "Lo·sons are the heritage of Jehovah, the fruit of the belly a reward; as arrows in the hand of the mighty, so are the sons of youth; blessed is the man who hath filled his quiver from them; they shall not be ashamed, when they speak with their enemies in the gate" (Psalm cxxvii. 3, 4). What things are here signified by sons, the fruits of the belly, arrows, the quiver, and by the enemies in the gate, may be seen above, n. 357; where it is also shown that by reward is signified the felicity of those who are in heaven. Thus also in the Evangelists: "Blessed are ye when men revile you, and persecute you, and say all manner of evil against you falsely for the sake of Christ: rejoice ye and be exceeding glad, for your reward is much in the heavens; for so persecuted they the prophets who were before you" (Matt. v. 11, 12; Luke v. 22, 23). These things are said concerning those who fight and conquer in temptations induced by evils, and thus from hell; temptations are signified by revilings, persecutions, and saying evil falsely for the sake of Christ, for temptations are assaults and infestations of truth and good by falses and evils; by Christ is understood divine truth from the Lord, which is assaulted, and on account of which they are infested; rejoice and be exceeding glad, because great is your reward in the heavens, signifies heaven, with the joy thereof, to those who are in the spiritual affection of truth, for such alone fight and conquer, by reason that the Lord is in that affection,

who resists and conquers for man in the combats of temptations; for
so persecuted they the prophets who were before you, signifies, that
formerly likewise they assaulted the truths of doctrine which were
with those who were in the spiritual affection of truth, for by prophets, abstractedly from persons, are signified the truths of doctrine
from the Word or from the Lord. From the passages which have
been now adduced from the Word, it may appear, that by reward
is signified heaven, as to its blessedness, satisfaction, and delight,
which is given to those who are in the spiritual affection of truth
and good : also, that reward is that affection itself; for whether we
speak of that affection or heaven it is the same thing, inasmuch as
in that affection and from it is heaven. But they who speak truth
and do good, not from a spiritual, but from a natural affection only,
and think continually of heaven as a reward, were represented in
the Israelitish church, by mercenaries or hirelings concerning whom
in that church, various statutes were given, as : "That the hirelings
should not eat of the passover" (Exod. xii. 43, 45); "That they
should not eat of the holy things" (Levit. xxii. 10); "That the wages
of the hireling should not abide with any one all night until the
morning" (Levit. xix. 13); and in Deuteronomy : "Thou shalt not
oppress the hireling that is poor and needy, of thy brethren, or of
the stranger who is in thy land, and in thy gates; in his day thou
shalt give him his hire, so that the sun may not go down upon it,
lest he cry against thee unto Jehovah and it be in thee a sin" (xxiv.
14, 15) : and in Malachi: " I will be against the oppressors of a hireling in his wages, of the widow and of the fatherless, and them that
turn aside the stranger and fear not me" (iii. 5); besides other passages. The reason why the hirelings were not to eat of the passover,
nor of things sanctified, was because by them were represented those
that are natural and not spiritual, and the spiritual are of the church
but not so the natural : for to look to heaven as a reward, on account of the good which they do, is natural, for the natural [princi-
ple] regards good as being from itself, and consequently heaven as
the reward thereof, whence the good becomes meritorious : but it is
otherwise with the spiritual [principle], this acknowledges good not
as being from itself, but from the Lord, whence it also acknowledges
heaven to be from mercy, and not from any merit : but inasmuch as
the natural still do good, although not from a spiritual but from
a natural affection, which is obedience, and then think concerning
heaven as a reward, therefore they are mentioned amongst the needy,
the poor, the strangers, the fatherless, and the widows, by reason of
their being in a state of spiritual poverty ; for genuine truths are to
them in obscurity, because light from heaven does not flow in by or
through the spiritual man into their natural, hence it is that they are
classed amongst such as are mentioned above, and that it is commanded that their hire or reward should be given them before the
going down of the sun : such persons are also in the lowest parts of
the heavens, where they are in a state of servitude, and are rewarded
according to their works : see what is further said concerning them,
in the D. of the N. J. n. 150–158. But the mercenaries or hirelings

who do not think of reward in heaven, but of reward in the world, thus who do good for the sake of gain, whether it be honor or wealth, consequently from the love of honor or wealth, which is for the sake of self and the world, are infernal natural; these hirelings are understood by these words in John: "I am the good shepherd; the good shepherd giveth his soul for the sheep, but the hireling seeth the wolf and forsaketh the sheep, and fleeth, because he is a hireling" (x. 11, 12, 13); and in Jeremiah: " Egypt is a very beautiful heifer, but destruction cometh from the north, her hirelings are as fatted calves, for they also turned themselves back, they flee together, they stood not, because the day of their destruction came upon them" (xlvi. 20, 21 ; and also elsewhere, as in Isaiah xvi. 14; chap. xxi. 16). Inasmuch as by reward, in the Word, is signified heaven, which they have who are in the spiritual love of truth and good, so, in the opposite sense, by reward is signified hell, which they have who are in the love of the false and evil: the latter is signified in these words in David: "He putteth on cursing as his garment, and it entered into the midst of him as waters, and as oil between his bones: this is the reward of mine adversaries from with Jehovah, and of them that speak evil against my soul" (Psalm cix. 18, 20). These words, in the spiritual sense, are to be understood concerning the Lord, for where David speaks concerning himself in the Psalms, it is understood in that sense concerning the Lord, for David as a king, represented the Lord, and thence signifies Him as to the Divine Spiritual [principle], which is the royalty of the Lord: the reward of them that are adversaries to the Lord, and that speak evil against His soul, is described as hell originating in the love of the false and evil, viz. by putting on cursing as his garment, and by its entering into the midst of him as waters, and as oil between his bones; hell is thus described as received in the externals and in the internals; as received in the externals by the cursing being put on as a garment, and as received in the internals by its entering in the midst of him as waters, and as oil between his bones; it is said as waters and as oil, because waters signify the falses of faith, and oil, evils of the love, whence by both is understood the love or affection of the false and evil, which is hell: this may appear also from this consideration, that love imbibes all things which agree with it, altogether as a spunge does waters and oil; for the love of evil nourishes itself from falses, and the love of the false nourishes itself from evils ; and whereas love is of such a nature, it is therefore said that cursing entered into the midst of him as waters, and as oil between the bones. Whereas by reward, in the opposite sense, is signified hell as to the affection of the false from evil, therefore the falsification of truth in the Word is every where called the reward of whoredom; as in Hosea: "Rejoice not O Israel, to exultation as the nations, because thou hast committed whoredom under thy God ; thou hast loved the reward of whoredom upon all corn-floors ; the floor and the press shall not feed them, and the must shall lie to her" (ix. 1, 2); to commit whoredom under God, signifies to falsify the truths of the Word, and to apply the holy things of the church to idolatrous purposes; to love the reward of whoredom, signifies the delight of falsifying and of the false, likewise of idolatry, from infernal love; upon all corn-floors, signifies all things of the Word and of doctrine from the Word, for corn, of which bread is made, signifies everything that spiritually nourishes, and the floor signifies where it is collected together, consequently the Word; the floor and the press shall not feed them, signifies, that they will not imbibe from the Word the good things of charity and love, thus not anything which nourishes the soul, for the floor there denotes the Word as to the goods of charity, and the press, as to the goods of love, and by the press is here understood oil, for which there were presses as well as for wine; and the must shall lie to her, signifies, that neither shall there be any truth of good, for must signifies the same as wine, viz. truth derived from the good of charity and love. Again in Micah: " All the sculptured things of Samaria shall be beaten to pieces, and all the rewards of her whoredom shall be burned in the fire, and I will lay waste all their idols, for she gathered them from the reward of whoredom, therefore, to the reward of whoredom shall they return; upon this will I wail and howl, I will go spoiled and naked" (i. 7, 8). By Samaria is understood the spiritual church as to truths of doctrine, in this case, as to falses of doctrine; for by their sculptured things are signified things falsified, which are from self-derived intelligence; by the rewards of her whoredom which shall be burned in the fire, are signified falsifications of truth from the love of the false by evil and infernal delight thence derived; and whereas that love is from hell, it is said, that they shall be burned in the fire, fire denoting love in both senses; and I will lay waste all their idols, signifies, that falses shall be destroyed; for from the reward of whoredom she gathered them, signifies, from the love of the false which is from evil, and thence from infernal delight; therefore to the reward of whoredom shall they return, signifies, that all things of that church shall be truths falsified, being derived from that source: upon this will I wail and howl, signifies the grief of the angels of heaven and the men of the church in whom the church is, and thus with whom the Lord is; I will go spoiled and naked, signifies mourning on account of the vastation of all truth and good; that sculptured things and idols signify doctrinals from self-derived intelligence favoring the loves of self and of the world, and the false principles thence conceived, consequently the falses of doctrine, of religion, and of worship, may be seen above, n. 587, 654. Again in Ezekiel: "Thou hast built thy little hill at the head of every way, and thy high place in every street; neither wast thou as a harlot to glory in reward; the adulterous woman took strangers under her man; they give reward to all whores, but thou hast given thy rewards to all thy lovers, and hast rewarded them, that they might come unto thee from all sides in thy whoredoms; so the contrary was done in thee from other women in thy whoredoms, that none went after thee to commit whoredom in giving reward, and no reward is given to thee, thou hast been therefore contrary" (xvi. 31,

32). The subject treated of in that chapter is concerning the abominations of Jerusalem, or of the Jewish church, in that they not only perverted and adulterated the goods of the Word, but also received falses of religion and of worship from the idolatrous nations, and thereby adulterated the truths and goods of the Word, and confirmed their adulterations; what is signified by building a little hill in the head of every way, and making a high place in every street, may be seen above, n. 652; that by adulteries and whoredoms, in the Word, are signified the adulterations and falsifications of the truth and good of the church, may be seen above, n. 141, 511; by not being as a whore to glory in reward, is signified, that they did not so falsify the truths of the Word from any delight of affection; by an adulterous woman taking strangers under her man, is signified the perversion of the truths and goods of the Word by the falses of other nations; by, they give reward to all whores, but thou gavest thy rewards to all thy lovers, and rewardedst them, is signified, that they loved the falses of religion and of worship belonging to other nations; a reward or gift of whoredom denotes the love of falsifying by the falses of others; that they might come to thee from all sides in thy whoredoms, signifies, that falses were everywhere searched for, whereby they falsified truth; thus it was contrary in thee from other women in whoredoms, that none went after thee to commit whoredom in giving reward, and no reward was given thee, thou wast therefore contrary, signifies the delight of the love and affection of falsifying the truths of their church by the falses of other religions, and of confirming the falsifications; the delight of the love and affection towards the falses of other religions, is here understood by reward or the gift of whoredom. From all that has been now adduced, it may appear what is spiritually understood by reward in both senses; for that is spiritual reward which affects with delight and joy; as for example, the riches, possessions, honors, and gifts, with which a man is recompensed for well doing; these things are not reward spiritually understood, but the delights and joys which proceed from them; much more is this the case with heavenly reward, which is given to the man of the church who lives well, and which is the spiritual affection of truth, and thence intelligence and wisdom, and whence comes all beatitude and felicity; moreover in heaven there is opulence and magnificence which proceed from heavenly love, as the consequent correspondence thereof, but still opulence and magnificence in heaven are not regarded as reward, but the spiritual principle in which they originate, and from which they are derived. This also is what is understood by the price of the work, and by the reward, which is in the Lord and from the Lord (Isaiah xl. 10; chap. lxi. 8; chap. lxii. 11; Luke vi. 35; chap. xiv. 12, 13, 14; and elsewhere).

696. "And to them that fear thy name small and great"—That hereby is signified, and to all who worship the Lord from whatever religion, appears from the signification of fearing the name of the Lord God, as denoting to worship the Lord, concerning which we shall speak presently; and from the signification of small and great,

as denoting from whatever religion ; for by the small are understood those who know but little of the truths and goods of the church, and by the great, those who know much, thus those who worship the Lord little and much ; for in proportion as man knows the truths of faith, and lives according to them, in the same proportion he worships the Lord, for worship is not from man, but from the truths originating in good which are with man, inasmuch as these are from the Lord, and the Lord is in them; the reason why by them that fear Thy name small and great, are understood all who worship the Lord from whatever religion, is, because just before, mention is made of the servants, the prophets, and of the saints, by whom are understood all within the church who are in the truths of doctrine, and in a life according to them, wherefore by them that fear Thy name small and great, are understood all without the church who worship the Lord according to their religion, for these also fear the name of God, who worship the Lord, and live in any faith and charity, according to the principles of their religion ; moreover, the subject treated of in this verse, is concerning the last judgment upon all, as well the evil as the good, and the last judgment takes place upon all, as well those who are within the pale of the church, as those who are without, and then all are saved who fear God, and live in mutual love, in uprightness of heart and sincerity from a principle of religion, for all such, as to the soul, are, by intuition of faith, in God, and, by a life of charity, consociated with the angels of heaven, and thus conjoined with the Lord and saved ; for every one after death comes to his own in the spiritual world, with whom he was consociated as to his spirit during his life in the natural world. The reason why small and great signify less and more, viz. who worship the Lord, thus who are less and more in truths from good, is, because the spiritual sense of the Word is abstracted from all respect to persons ; for it simply regards the thing, and in the expression, small and great, there is respect to person, for thereby are understood the men who worship God ; hence it is, that instead of small and great, is understood in the spiritual sense, less and more, thus those who worship more and less from genuine truths and goods ; the case is the same also with respect to the servants, the prophets, and saints, treated of just above, by whom, in the spiritual sense, are not understood prophets and saints, but, abstractedly from persons, the truths of doctrine and a life according to them ; whilst these are understood, all who are in the truths of doctrine and in a life according to them, are also inclusively comprehended, for these things are in subjects which are angels and men ; but to think in such case of angels and men only, is natural, but to think of the truths of doctrine and the life which constitutes angels and men, this is spiritual : hence it may appear, how the spiritual sense, in which the angels are, distinguishes itself from the natural sense, in which men are, viz. that in everything which men think, there inheres somewhat derived from person, space, time and matter, but that the angels think, abstractedly from these, of things only ; hence it is that the speech of angels is incomprehensible to man, inasmuch as it flows from intuition of the thing, and consequently from a wisdom abstracted from such things as are proper to the natural world, and thus respectively indeterminate to such things. The reason why to fear Thy name, signifies to worship the Lord, is, because to fear signifies to worship, and Thy name signifies the Lord; for in the preceding verse, it is said, that the twenty-four elders gave thanks to the Lord God, Who is, and Who was, and Who is to come, wherefore by fearing Thy name is here understood the worship of the Lord: in the Word, both of the Old and New Testament, mention is made of the name of Jehovah, the name of the Lord, the name of God, and of the name of Jesus Christ, and in such places by name are understood all things whereby He is worshiped, thus all things of love and faith, and, in the supreme sense, the Lord Himself is understood, because where he is there also are all things of love and faith; that such things are signified by the name of Jehovah, of the Lord God, and of Jesus Christ, may be seen above, n. 102, 135, 224; and is also evident from these words of the Lord: " If two of you shall agree in My name upon earth, concerning everything whatsoever they shall ask, it shall be done for them of My Father, who is in the heavens; for where two or three are gathered together in My name, there am I in the midst of them" (Matt. xviii. 19, 20); where by agreeing together in the name of the Lord, and being gathered together in His name, is not understood in the name alone, but in those things which are of the Lord, which are the truths of faith and goods of love, by which He is worshiped. The reason why fear, when predicated concerning the Lord, signifies worship and to revere, is, because in worship and in all things appertaining thereto, there is a holy and reverential fear, which is grounded in the consideration, that the object of worship is to be honored, and not by any means to be injured : the case herein is as with infants towards their parents, with parents towards their children, with wives towards their husbands, and husbands towards their wives, likewise as with friends towards friends, with whom there is a fear lest they should be hurt, and at the same time a respect; this fear attended with respect, is in all love and in all friendship, insomuch that love and friendship, without such fear and respect, is as food not salted, which is unsavory; hence then it is, that to fear the Lord denotes to worship Him from such love. It is said that by fearing Thy name is signified to worship the Lord, and yet that by them that fear Him, are understood those who are without the pale of the church, to whom the Lord must however be unknown, by reason of their not having the Word; it is therefore to be observed, that notwithstanding their ignorance of the Lord, all such are accepted by Him as have an idea of Humanity concerning God, for God under a human form is the Lord; but all those who do not think of God as a man, whether they be within or without the pale of the church, on their coming into the spiritual life, which takes place after their departure out of this world, are not accepted of the Lord, because they have not any determinate idea concerning God, but only an indeterminate idea, which is no idea at all, or if it be any, is still dissipated; this is the reason why all, who come from

the earths into the spiritual world, are first explored as to the quality of their idea concerning God, and if it be not as of a man, they
are sent to places of instruction, where they are taught that the Lord
is the God of heaven and earth, and that, when they think of God,
it is necessary that they think of the Lord, and that otherwise they
cannot have any conjunction with God, nor consequently any consociation with the angels : all who have lived a life of charity, then
receive instruction, and worship the Lord ; but all those who declare themselves to have been in the faith, but were not in the life
of faith, which is charity, do not receive instruction, wherefore they
are separated, and are sent away into places below the heavens,
some into the hells, and some into the earth which is called in the
Word the lower earth, where they suffer severely ; still, however,
the gentiles to whom the laws of religion were laws of life, receive
doctrine concerning the Lord more readily than the Christians, and
this more especially by reason of their having no other idea concerning God than as of a Divine Man.   These things are said in order
that it may be known whence it is that by fearing Thy name is understood to worship the Lord.   Inasmuch as mention is frequently
made in the Word of fearing Jehovah God, and thereby is understood
to worship Him, therefore it shall be explained in a few words what
worship in particular is thereby understood; all worship of Jehovah
God must be from the good of love by truths ; the worship which is
from the good of love alone, is not worship, neither is that worship
which is from truths alone without the good of love, but both are
necessary ; for the essential of worship is the good of love, but good
exists and is formed by truths, and hence all worship must be by
truths from good : this being the case, therefore in most passages in
the Word, where mention is made of fearing Jehovah God, mention
is also made of keeping and doing His words and precepts, wherefore
by the former expression is signified worship by truths, and by the
latter is signified worship from the good of love, for to do is of the
will, thus of the love and of good, and to fear is of the understanding, thus of faith and of truth, for all truth which is of faith is properly of the understanding, and all good which is of love is properly
of the will : hence it may be seen, that the fear of Jehovah God is
predicated of worship by truths of doctrine, which are called also the
truths of faith ; the ground and reason why this worship is understood
by the fear of Jehovah God, is, because divine truth causes fear, for
it condemns the evil to hell, but not so divine good, for this takes
away condemnation in proportion as it is received in truths by man
and angel ; hence it may appear, that in proportion as there is fear
for God, in the same proportion man is in the good of love, and in
proportion as dread and terror are evanescent or disappear, and become a holy fear attended with reverence, in the same proportion man
is in the good of love and thence in truths, that is, there is so much of
good in his truths; hence it follows, that fear in worship is various with
every one, according to the state of his life, and also that sanctity
attended with reverence, which is inwardly in fear with those that
are in good, is likewise various according to the reception of good
thine will, and according to the reception of truth in the understand-

ing, that is, according to the reception of good in the heart and the reception of truth in the soul. But these observations will appear more evidently from the following passages in the Word; thus in Moses: "What does Jehovah God ask of thee, but that thou mayest fear Jehovah thy God, to go in all His ways, and to love Him, and to serve Jehovah thy God from thy whole heart, and from thy whole soul" (Deut. x. 12, 20); mention is here made of fearing Jehovah God, of going in His ways, of loving Him, and of serving Him, by all which expressions is described worship by truths from good; worship by truths is understood by fearing Jehovah God and serving Him, and worship from good by going in His ways and loving Him; wherefore it is also said, from the whole heart, and from the whole soul, heart denoting the good of love and charity which is of the will, and soul the truth of doctrine and faith which is of the understanding; for heart corresponds to the good of love, and in man to his will, and soul corresponds to the truth of faith, and in man to his understanding, for by soul is understood the animation or respiration of man, which is also called his spirit: that soul in the Word signifies the life of faith, and heart the life of love, may be seen in the A. C. n. 2930, 9250, 9281. Again: "Ye shall go after Jehovah your God, and shall fear Him, that ye may keep His precepts, and hear His voice and serve Him and adhere to him" (Deut. xiii. 5). To go after Jehovah God to keep His precepts, and to adhere to Him, signify the good of life, thus the good of love, from which worship is derived; and to fear Jehovah God, to hear His voice, to serve Him, signify the truths of doctrine, thus the truths of faith by which worship is performed. Inasmuch as all worship of the Lord must be by truths from good, and not by truths without good, nor by good without truths, therefore in every part of the Word there is a marriage of good and truth, as in the passages already adduced, and also in the following: concerning this marriage of good and truth, as contained in every part of the Word, see what is said above, n. 238 at the end, n. 288, 660. Again in Moses: "Thou shalt fear Jehovah thy God, thou shalt serve Him, and shalt adhere to Him, and thou shalt swear in His name" (Deut. x. 12). Where also to fear Jehovah God, and to serve Him, involve the truths of worship, and to adhere to Jehovah God, and to swear in His name, involve the good of worship; for to adhere is an expression which has relation to the good of love, inasmuch as he who loves also adheres, and in like manner to swear in the name of Jehovah, for thereby is confirmed what is about to be done: the reason why to serve involves the truths of worship, is, because by servants, in the Word, are understood those who are in truths, and this by reason that truths serve good, as may be seen above, n. 6, 409. Again: "That thou mayest fear Jehovah thy God, to keep all His statutes and His precepts: thou shalt fear Jehovah thy God, and shalt serve Him, and shalt swear in His name; ye shall not go after other gods: Jehovah hath commanded us to do all these statutes, to fear Jehovah our God" (Deut. vi. 2, 13, 14, 24). Worship by truths from good or by faith from love, is likewise here described;

by fearing Jehovah God and by serving Him is understood worship by the truths of faith, and by keeping and doing His precepts and statutes, and by swearing in the name of Jehovah, is understood worship from the good of love, for to keep and to do the statutes and precepts, appertains to the good of life, which is the same as the good of love, inasmuch as he who loves lives; so likewise with respect to swearing in the name of Jehovah, for to swear denotes confirmation in life : that to fear Jehovah and to serve Him, denotes worship according to truths of doctrine, was shown above : for there are two things, which constitute worship, viz. doctrine and life, doctrine without life does not constitute it, neither life without doctrine.   Thus also in the following passages : " Gather together the people that they may hear, and that they may learn and fear Jehovah your God, and may keep all the words of the law to do them" (Deut. xxxi. 12) : again : " If thou keepest not all the precepts of this law to do them, to fear this magnificent and venerable name, Jehovah thy God" (Deut. xxviii. 58) : so again : " The king shall write for himself a copy of the law, and he shall read in it all the days of his life, wherein he may learn to fear Jehovah his God, to keep all the words of the law, and the statutes, to do them" (Deut. xvii. 29).   Again : "Thou shalt keep the precepts of Jehovah thy God, going in His ways and fearing Him" (Deut. viii. 6) : and again : " Who will give that they may have a heart to fear Me, and to keep My precepts all his days" (v. 26).   In all these passages the fear of Jehovah God is adjoined to the keeping and doing the precepts of His law, likewise to the going in His ways, by reason, as was said, that all worship of God, which is internal spiritual, consisting in the good of life, must be performed according to truths of doctrine, inasmuch as these must teach : worship according to truths of doctrine is signified by fearing Jehovah, and worship from the good of life by keeping the precepts and going in His ways, to go in the ways of Jehovah denoting to live according to the truths of doctrine ; and whereas worship according to the truths of doctrine is understood by fearing Jehovah, therefore it is said that the fear of Jehovah shall be learned from the law : it is however to be observed, that the fear of Jehovah denotes internal spiritual worship, which must be in external natural worship, for internal spiritual worship is to think and understand truths, thus to think reverently and holily concerning God, which is to fear him, and external natural worship is to do those truths, which is to keep the precepts and words of the law. So in David : " Teach me, Jehovah, Thy way, teach it me in truth, unite my heart to the fear of Thy name" (Psalm lxxxvi. 11). Where by teaching the way is signified to teach truth according to which the life ought to be formed, wherefore it is said, teach it in truth ; that the good of love must be conjoined with the truths of faith, is signified by, unite my heart to the fear of Thy name, the heart signifying the love, and fear the holy principle of faith, which must be united, or be together in worship.   Again : " Blessed is every one that feareth Jehovah, that walketh in his ways" (Psalm cxxviii. 1). To fear Jehovah here also denotes to think reverently and with sanctity concerning God, and to walk in His ways denotes to live according to divine truths, worship is performed by both, but in external worship, which is to live according to divine truths, there must be internal worship, which is to fear Jehovah, wherefore it is said that he is blessed who feareth Jehovah, who walketh in His ways. So again : " Blessed is the man who feareth Jehovah, who delighteth greatly in His precepts"(Psalm cxii. 1): where the same things are signified; for to delight greatly in the precepts of Jehovah is to love them, consequently to will and do them. So in Jeremiah : " They feared not, neither went they in My law, nor in My statutes" (xliv. 9): where not to fear denotes not to think concerning God from the truths of the Word, thus not to think holy and reverently ; not to go in the law of God, nor in his statutes, denotes neither to live according to them, precepts denoting the laws of internal worship, and statutes the laws of external worship. So in Malachi : " If I am a Father, where is My honor? if I am Lord, where is the fear of me ?" (i. 6.) Honor and fear are here mentioned, because honor is predicated of worship from good, and fear of worship by truths; that honor is predicated of good, may be seen above, n. 288, 345; wherefore also honor is predicated of Father, and fear of Lord, for Jehovah is here called Father from divine good, and Lord from divine truth. Again in the same prophet: "My covenant was with Levi, of life and of peace, which I gave him with fear; and he feared Me" (ii. 5). By Levi is here understood the Lord as to the Divine Human [principle], and by the covenant of life and of peace is signified the union of His Divine [principle] therewith, and by fear and by fearing, is signified holy truth, with which there is union. So in Isaiah : " The spirit of Jehovah rested upon Him, the spirit of wisdom and intelligence, the spirit of counsel and might, the spirit of science and of the fear of Jehovah, whence His incense was in the fear of Jehovah" (xi. 2, 3). These words also relate to the Lord, and thereby is described the divine truth, in which and from which is all wisdom and intelligence : the divine truth which was in the Lord, when He was in the world, and which after the glorification of His Human [principle] proceeds from Him, is understood by the spirit of Jehovah, which rested upon Him ; that thence He had divine wisdom and divine power, is understood by the spirit of wisdom and intelligence, and by the spirit of counsel and might ; that thence He had omniscience and essential sanctity in worship, is understood by the spirit of science and of the fear of Jehovah ; and whereas fear signifies the holy principle of worship from divine truth, it is therefore added, whence His incense was in the fear of Jehovah, for to offer incense signifies worship from the Divine spiritual [principle] which is divine truth, concerning which see above, n. 324, 491, 492, 494, 567 ; it is said, the spirit of wisdom and intelligence, of science and of fear, and by spirit is understood the Divine Proceeding, by the spirit of wisdom, the Divine Celestial, which is the Divine Proceeding received by the angels of the inmost or third heaven, by the spirit of intelligence is meant the Divine Spiritual [principle], which is the Divine Proceeding received by the angels of the middle or second heaven, by the spirit of science is meant the

Divine Natural [principle], which is the Divine Proceeding received by the angels of the ultimate or first heaven, and by the spirit of the fear of Jehovah is understood all the holy principle of worship from those divine principles.   So in Jeremiah: "I will give unto them one heart and one way, to fear Me all their days for good unto them; and I will make with them the covenant of an age; and My fear will I give into their heart, that they may not recede from with Me" (xxxii. 39, 40).   I will give them one heart and one way to fear Me, signifies one will and one understanding to worship the Lord, the heart denoting the good of the will, way the truth of the understanding, which leads, and fear the holy worship thence derived; I will make with them the covenant of an age, and My fear will I give into their heart, signifies conjunction by the good of love, and by the truth of that good in worship, covenant denoting conjunction, and fear in the heart, the holy principle of worship from truth in the good of love; that they may not recede from with Me, signifies for the sake of conjunction; inasmuch as conjunction with the Lord is effected by truths from good, and not by truth without good, nor by good without truths, therefore both are here mentioned.   Again in David: "O house of Aaron, confide in Jehovah, ye that fear Jehovah, confide in Jehovah" (Psalm cxv. 10, 11).   By the house of Aaron are signified all who are in the good of love, and by them that fear Jehovah are signified all who are in truth from that good. And in the Apocalypse: "The angel who had the everlasting gospel, said, Fear God, and give glory and adore Him" (xiv. 7).   By fearing God and giving glory to Him, is signified to worship the Lord from holy truths; and to adore Him signifies from the good of love. Again in David: "Let all the earth fear Jehovah; let all the inhabitants of the globe be afraid of him; behold, the eye of Jehovah is upon them that fear Him, that hope in His mercy" (Psalm xxxiii. 8, 10): and again: "The good pleasure of Jehovah is in them that fear Him, upon them that hope in His mercy" (Psalm cxlvii. 11). Inasmuch as the fear of Jehovah signifies the reception of divine truth, and mercy the reception of divine good, therefore it is said that the eye and the good pleasure of Jehovah are upon them that fear Him, upon them that hope in His mercy.   Again in Isaiah: "The powerful people shall honor Thee, the city of the strong nations shall fear Thee" (xxv. 3).   Here also worship from good is signified by honoring, for honor is predicated of the good of love, and worship from truths is signified by fearing the Lord, as was said above; powerful people signifies the men of the church who are in truths from good, for from them comes all power; the city of the strong nations signifies those who are in the truths of doctrine, and thereby in the good of love; and inasmuch as all spiritual power is thence derived, therefore they are called the strong nations; from these words also it manifestly appears, that there is a marriage of good and truth in every part of the Word; for to honor is predicated of good, to fear of truth, both of them in worship; people also is predicated of those who are in truths and thereby in good, and nations of those who are in goods and thence in truths; and whereas all power in the spiritual world

·is from the conjunction of good and truth, therefore people are called powerful, and nations are called strong. The fear of Jehovah signifies worship in which there is sanctity by truths, also in the following passages; as in Isaiah : " The heart of this people hath receded far from Me, and their fear toward Me is become a precept taught of men" (xix. 13); again : " Who is there amongst you that feareth Jehovah, that heareth the voice of His servant, that walketh in darkness, and hath no brightness ; that confideth in the name of Jehovah, and leaneth upon his God " (l. 10); and in Jeremiah : " They shall hear all the good which I do unto them, that they may fear and be moved for all the good, and for all the peace which I am about to do to it" (xxxiii. 9); and in David : " The angel of Jehovah encampeth about them that fear Him, to deliver them. Fear Jehovah, ye His saints, for there is no want to them that fear Him" (Psalm xxxiv. 8, 10); again : " Who have no changes, neither fear they God " (Psalm lv. 20); and again : " The fear of Jehovah is the beginning of wisdom, a good understanding have all they that do it" (Psalm cxi. 10); inasmuch as fear has respect to divine truth from which comes all sanctity in worship, and all wisdom and intelligence, therefore it is said, the fear of Jehovah is the beginning of wisdom; a good understanding, that is, intelligence, have all they that do it. Again : " They that fear Jehovah shall praise Him, all the seed of Jacob shall honor Him, and the seed of Israel shall be afraid of Him" (Psalm xxii. 24); and in Luke : " The mercy of God is to generation of generations to them that fear Him" (i. 50). That to fear Jehovah God involves and thence signifies to account Him holy, and to revere Him, consequently to worship Him with sanctity and reverence, may also appear from these passages ; as in Moses : " Ye shall observe My sabbath, and My sanctuary shall ye fear" [revere], (Levit. xix. 13 ; chap. xxvi. 2); and again : " The work of Jehovah how is it to be feared [revered], that which I will do" (Exodus xxxiv. 10); and again : " And Jacob feared and said, how is this place to be feared [revered], this is none other but the house of God, and the gate of heaven" (Gen. xxviii. 17). That to fear, when it is predicated of the Divine [principle], and of the holy [principle] of heaven and the church, signifies to revere and to have reverence, is evident from the above passages, and also from this consideration, that the same expression which signifies to fear, in the Hebrew tongue, signifies also to revere and to venerate. This is likewise evident from these words in Luke : " There was a judge in a certain city who feared not God, neither revered man, who said within himself, although I fear not God, nor revere man" (xviii. 2, 4); where it is said to fear God, and to revere man, because to fear signifies to revere in a superior degree. So in Matthew : " Jesus said, Fear not them who can kill the body, but who are not able to kill the soul ; rather fear Him who can destroy both soul and body in Gehenna" (x. 28; Luke xii. 4, 5, 7); but by fearing in this passage is signified the fear of spiritual death, consequently natural fear, which is fearfulness and dread ; but spiritual fear is holy fear, which is inwardly in all spiritual love, and is various according to the qua-

lity of the love and according to the quantity thereof: in this fear the
spiritual man is principled, who also knows that the Lord cannot do
evil to any one, much less destroy any one, as to body and soul in
Gehenna, but that He does good to all, and that He wills to raise up
every one as to body and soul into heaven to Himself; hence the
fear of the spiritual man is a holy fear, lest by evil of life and by
false of doctrine he should avert that divine love in himself, and so
hurt it; but natural fear, is a fearfulness, dread, and terror, of dangers, punishment, and thus of hell, which fear is inwardly in all corporeal love, and also is various according to the quality of the love,
and according to the quantity thereof; the natural man who is in such
fear, does not know otherwise than that the Lord does evil to the
evil, condemns them, casts into hell, and punishes, and hence it is
that such persons fear and dread the Lord: in this fear were most
of the Jewish and Israelitish nation, by reason that they were natural men; hence it is that mention is so frequently made in the
Word of being afraid and trembling before Jehovah, and that it is
said of the sons of Israel that they were sore afraid when the divine
law or divine truth was promulgated from mount Sinai (Exod. xx.
Deut. v). This fear is also what is partly understood by " the dread
of Isaac by whom Jacob swear to Laban" (Gen. xxxi. 42, 53); for
by Abraham, Isaac, and Jacob, in the Word, is understood the
Lord, by Abraham the Lord as to the divine celestial [principle], by
Isaac as to the divine spiritual, and by Jacob, as to the divine natural; the divine spiritual [principle], signified by Isaac, is the divine
truth, which terrifies natural men, and whereas Laban was a natural man, therefore it is said, Jacob sware to him by the dread or terror of Isaac. A fear nearly similar is understood in these words in
Isaiah: " Ye shall sanctify Jehovah Zebaoth, for He is your fear
and your dread" (viii. 13): where fear is mentioned for the spiritual
man, and dread for the natural man. That the spiritual man may
not be in such fear, as is that of the natural man, it is sometimes
said, fear not, as in Isaiah: " Fear not, O Jacob and Israel, for I
have redeemed thee, calling thee by name, thou art Mine" (xliii. 1);
and in Luke: " Fear not, little flock, for it hath pleased your Father to give to you the kingdom" (xii. 32); and in Jeremiah: " Fear
not, Jacob My servant, and be not afraid, O Israel, for I will keep
thee from afar; Jacob shall be tranquil and quiet, none making him
afraid" (xxx. 9, 10); besides various other passages. Moreover,
that fear, terror, consternation and the like, signify various commotions of the mind [animus], and changes of the state of the mind
[mens], may be seen above, n. 667, 677.

697. " And to destroy them that destroy the earth"—That hereby
is signified hell to those who destroy the church, appears from the
signification of destroying, when predicated of those who destroy
the church, as denoting damnation and hell; for when to give reward to His servants the prophets and saints, signifies salvation and
heaven to those who are in truths from good, thus who constitute
the church, of consequence to destroy it signifies damnation and
hell; and from the signification of earth, as denoting the church,

concerning which see above, n. 29, 304, 413, 417; hence to destroy the earth, signifies to destroy the church. That by earth, in the Word, is understood the church, has been shown in many passages above, likewise also in the A. C.; there are several reasons for this signification of earth, and this amongst the rest, that by the earth, when no particular earth or land is mentioned, as the earth or land of Egypt, of Edom, of Moab, of Assyria, of Chaldea, of Babel, and others, the land of Canaan is understood, and when that land is understood, they who are in a spiritual idea cannot think of any land or earth, inasmuch as such thought is merely terrestrial and not heavenly, but they think of the quality of the nation there as to the church; in like manner as when any land is mentioned, whilst a person is in the idea of the church, of religion, or of worship, the land is not then thought of, but the people or nation inhabiting it, as to their quality with respect to the church, religion, or worship; hence it is, that the angels, who are spiritual, when man reads in the Word concerning earth or land, think of the church, and what the angels think, this is the spiritual sense of the Word; for the spiritual sense of the Word is for angels, and also for men who are spiritual; for the Word in the letter is natural, but still inwardly, or in its bosom, it is spiritual, and when what is natural is removed, the spiritual principle which is within or in its bosom becomes manifest. Moreover there are earths or lands in the spiritual world, or in the world where spirits and angels are, equally as in the natural world where men are, and those earths or lands as to external appearance are altogether similar; for there are in that world, plains, valleys, mountains, hills, rivers, and seas, and also fields, meadows, forests, gardens, and paradises; the earths or lands, also, there, are beautiful in appearance, altogether according to the state of the church with those who dwell upon them, and undergo changes according to the changes of the church with the inhabitants; in a word, there is a full correspondence of the earths or lands there, with the reception of the good of love and truth of faith with the inhabitants thereof; and hence also it is, that by earth or land in the Word, is signified the church, for the quality of the earth or land is according to the quality of the church there, which is caused by correspondence; for in that world, the earth itself makes one with the church, as the correspondent with its subject to which it corresponds, altogether as the effect with its efficient cause, as the eye with its sight, as the speech with its understanding, as the action with the will, as the countenance or features of the face with the affection of the thought, in a word, as the instrumental with its principal, of which it is said that they make one thing; so it is in the spiritual world, as to the quality of the earth or land with the quality of the church; from these considerations it may appear, whence it is that by earth or land, in the Word, is signified the church, and that to destroy the earth here signifies to destroy the church. The same is understood also in the following passages; as in Isaiah: "Is this the man that moveth the earth, that maketh the kingdoms to tremble, that hath made the globe a wilderness, and destroyed the cities thereof? Thou hast de-

stroyed thy earth, thou hast slain thy people" (xiv. 16, 17, 20);
speaking of Lucifer, by whom is there understood Babel, as is evident from what precedes and from what follows; and by the earth
which he moved and destroyed, is signified the church, by the kingdoms
which he makes to tremble, are signified the churches into which the
general church is distinguished; by the globe which he made a wilderness, is signified the church in general; by the cities which he
destroyed, are signified the truths of the doctrine thereof; and by
the people which he slew, are signified the men of the church, whose
spiritual life he destroyed.   So in Jeremiah: "Behold, I am against
thee, O destroying mountain, destroying the universal earth" (li. 25);
treating also of Babel, which is called a destroying mountain, because a mountain there signifies the love of ruling over heaven and
earth, to which the goods and truths of the church are made to serve
as means, wherefore to destroy the universal earth, signifies, to destroy the whole church.   So in Daniel: "The fourth beast ascending out of the sea shall devour the whole earth, and shall tread it
down, and break it in pieces" (vii. 23).   By this beast is also signified the love of ruling over the universal heaven and the universal
earth, which love prevails with those who are of Babel, as may be
seen above, n. 316, 556; wherefore by devouring, treading down,
and breaking in pieces the earth, is signified altogether to destroy
the church; any one may see, that it is not any beast which is here
meant, that will ascend out of the sea, devour, tread down, and
break in pieces all the earth, but some evil and diabolic love, which
will do those things to the church.   It is written in Moses: "There
shall not be any more a deluge to destroy the earth" (Gen. ix. 11);
where by the earth is also signified the church, which was destroyed
by the antediluvians, but should no more be destroyed.   Again in
Isaiah: "Jehovah emptieth the earth, and maketh it void, and He
overturneth the faces thereof.   In emptying, the earth shall be emptied, and in spoiling it shall be spoiled; the habitable earth shall
mourn, shall be confounded, the globe shall languish, shall be confounded, the earth itself shall be profaned, by reason that they have
trangressed the laws, transcended the statute, rendered vain the
covenant of eternity, wherefore the curse shall devour the earth.
The cataracts from on high are opened, and the foundations of the
earth are removed; in breaking the earth is broken, in moving the
earth is moved, tottering the earth tottereth as a drunkard, and it is
moved to and fro as a cottage" (xxiv. 1, 3, 4, 5, 6, 18, 19, 20).
That by the earth here mentioned is not understood the earth, but
the church, must be evident to every one; the reason why the church
is thus described, is, because the earths or lands in the spiritual
world, upon which angels and spirits dwell, undergo such changes
according to the changes of the state of the church with the inhabitants thereof, even as to be moved; the reason why it is said that
Jehovah empties the earth and makes it void, likewise that in emptying it shall be emptied, and in spoiling it shall be spoiled, is, because the earths or lands there, when the church is devastated with
those who dwell upon them, altogether change their appearance;
the paradises with their flowrets, verdures, and the like, with which

they before flourished, disappear, and instead thereof appearances most unpleasant take place, as sands and rocky places, also heaths full of thickets and briars, with other things of a like nature, corresponding to the falses and evils which devastated the church ; the devastation thereof as to the good of love and charity, is signified by emptying the earth, and the desolation thereof as to the truth of doctrine and faith, is signified by making it void and spoiling it; and the change itself by overturning the faces thereof ; the habitable earth shall mourn, shall be confounded, the globe shall languish, shall be confounded, the curse shall devour the earth, signifies that there shall not anything grow there or flourish, but that it shall be barren, and filled with things useless, by reason whereof the earth is said to mourn, to languish, and to be devoured with a curse ; whereas these things take place when they that dwell there have no longer any concern for the holy things of the church, therefore it is said, by reason that they have trangressed the law, transcended the statute, rendered vain the covenant of eternity ; inasmuch as the earths there are sometimes inundated, sometimes violently shaken, and also here and there cleave asunder and open towards hell, which is beneath, and lifts itself up, and this takes place according to the quantity and quality of the falses and evils which are loved, and consequent falsification and denial of the goods and truths of the church, therefore it is said, that the cataracts from on high are opened, the foundations of the earth are moved, the earth is broken and totters as a drunkard : these things also actually take place in the spiritual world, when the state of the church is there changed into the contrary. From these considerations it may appear whence it is, that by the earth, here and elsewhere in the Word, is understood the church.

698. Verse 19. "And the temple of God was opened in heaven, and the ark of His covenant was seen in His temple ; and there were lightnings, and voices, and thunderings, and an earthquake, and great hail."—" And the temple of God was opened in heaven," signifies the appearing of the new heaven and new church, where the Lord is worshiped : " and the ark of His covenant was seen in His temple," signifies the divine truth, whereby there is conjunction with the Lord ; " and there were lightnings, voices, and thunderings," signifies, conflicts and confused crowds of thoughts, also ratiocinations from evil and the false concerning good and truth, which then take place in the lower parts, where the evil are ; " and an earthquake," signifies a change of state as to those things which appertain to heaven and the church with them ; and " great hail," signifies the infernal false destroying the truths and goods of the church.

699. " And the temple of God was opened in heaven"—That hereby is signified the appearing of the new heaven and new church, where is the worship of the Lord, appears from the signification of the temple, as denoting heaven and the church, in this case, the new heaven and new church, the appearing of which is signified by the temple being opened ; that temple, in the supreme sense, signifies

the Lord as to His divine human [principle], and the divine truth proceeding from Him, and, in the respective sense, heaven and the church, may be seen above, n. 220, 391, 630. The reason why temple here signifies the new heaven and new church, where is the worship of the Lord, is, because the subject treated of in this chapter is concerning the changes of state which precede the last judgment, viz. concerning the separation of the evil from the good, and concerning their removal from the places where they were before: when this is accomplished, then the new heaven and new church appear to those who are in the superior heavens: these could not appear to them so long as they were conjoined with the evil, because their interiors were closed, lest they should be hurt by the evil, with whom there was a communication as to externals; but when they were separated and removed, then the interiors with the good, which in themselves were heavenly, were opened, and these being opened, heaven and the church became manifest, for in proportion as the interiors, which are celestial and spiritual, are opened, in the same proportion heaven becomes manifest, that is, the quality thereof as to the church with those in whom heaven and the church is. That this is the case, no one could possibly know from his own intelligence, inasmuch as the things here related are arcana of heaven, which are to be learnt only from revelation: for who could possibly know in what manner the last judgment was performed, likewise the nature and quality of the changes which preceded in the spiritual world, and those which followed? In order, however, that these things might be known, they were manifested to me, wherefore it is allowed here to describe them from revelation. The reason why it is here said, the new heaven and new church, where is the worship of the Lord, is, because in the new heaven and new church the Lord alone is worshiped; for the Divine [principle] is not there distinguished into three persons, but into a trine in one person, concerning which Trinity see what is written in the D. of the N. J. from n. 280–310: this also is what is signified in the Apocalypse, where, treating of the New Jerusalem, it is said, "And I saw no temple therein, because the Lord God Almighty, and the Lamb, is the temple thereof" (chap. xxi. 22). By the Lord God Almighty and the Lamb, is understood the Lord as to the Essential Divine [principle] and the Divine Human: the reason why no temple was seen there, is, because by temple, in the supreme sense, is signified the Lord as to divine truth and as to worship, as was shown above, n. 220, 391, 630; and because by the New Jerusalem is understood the church as to doctrine, or the doctrine of the New Jerusalem. But still there are temples in heaven, in which the Lord is preached, and divine truth is taught.

700. "And the ark of His covenant was seen in His temple"— That hereby is signified the divine truth, whereby there is conjunction with the Lord, appears from the signification of the ark of the covenant, as denoting the divine truth proceeding from the Lord, concerning which more will be said presently. The reason why the ark of the covenant was seen, was, because the temple appeared, and in the midst of the temple of Jerusalem was the ark, in which

were deposited the two tables of the law, by which, in the universal sense, was signified the divine truth proceeding from the Lord, thus the Lord Himself, who is the divine truth in the heavens, whence He is also called the Word, in John, ch. i. 1, 2, 14 : the reason of this signification of the ark was, because the tent of the assembly represented the three heavens; the court thereof represented the ultimate or first heaven, the tent itself even to the veil, where were the tables for the breads, the altar of incense, and the candlestick, represented the middle or second heaven, and the·ark which was within the veil, upon which was the propitiatory with the cherubs, represented the inmost or third heaven, and the law itself, which was in the ark, represented the Lord as to divine truth or the Word; and whereas conjunction with the Lord is by the Word, therefore that ark was called the ark of the covenant, for covenant signifies conjunction. That the tent or tabernacle represented the form of heaven, and that together with the court is represented the three heavens, and that the Holy of Holies, which was the inmost, where the ark was, in which were the tables of the law, represented the third or inmost heaven, and that the law or testimony represented the Lord Himself, may be seen in the A. C. n. 3478, 9457, 9481, 9485 : and that the tabernacle, equally as the temple, in the supreme sense signifies the Lord, in the respective sense, heaven and the church, and thence the holy principle of worship, n. 9457, 9481, 10,242, 10,245, 10,505, 10,545 : also that covenant, in the Word, signifies conjunction, and that all things appertaining to the church, as well internal as external, are signs of the covenant, and that they are called covenant, because conjunction is effected by them, n. 665, 666, 1023, 1038, 1864, 1996, 2003, 2021, 2037, 6804, 8767, 8778, 9396, 9416, 10,632 : and that the law promulgated on mount Sinai was thence called the covenant, and the ark in which the law was, the ark of the covenant, n. 6804, 9416. That the ark, with the covenant, or with the testimony included, signifies the Lord as to the Divine Celestial [principle] which is the divine truth in the inmost or third heaven, may appear from what is said concerning the ark in the Word: as in Moses: " Let them make for Me a sanctuary, that I may dwell in the midst of them, according to all that I have shown thee, the form of the dwelling place: especially let them make the ark of shittim wood : and thou shalt overlay it with pure gold, within and without shalt thou overlay it ; and thou shalt make for it a border of gold round about, four rings of gold for the staves; and thou shalt give into the ark the testimony, which I shall give thee ; and thou shalt make the propitiatory of pure gold ; and shalt make two cherubs of gold, solid shalt thou make them from the propitiatory, so that the cherubs shall stretch out their wings, and shall cover with their wings the propitiatory, and their faces towards the propitiatory : and thou shalt give the testimony into the ark; and I will meet thee there, and I will speak with thee from above the propitiatory, from between the two cherubs which are over the ark of the testimony, all that I shall command thee for the sons of Israel" (Exod. xxv. 8–22). " Thou shalt make a veil of blue, and purple (hyacinthinum), and scarlet double dyed, and fine twined linen, with cherubs : thou shalt give it upon four pillars of shittim overlaid with gold; and thou shalt give the veil under the handles: and thou shalt bring in thither within the veil, the ark of the testimony, so that the veil shall divide unto you between the holy and the Holy of Holies; and thou shalt give the veil before the ark in the Holy of Holies" (Exod. xxvi. 31–34). It was said above, that the tent where were the ark, the candlestick, the table for the breads, and the altar for the incense, together with the court, represented the three heavens, and that the place within the veil, where the ark was, which contained the law or testimony, represented the third heaven : the reason why this place represented this heaven was, because there was the law, by which is understood the Lord as to divine truth or as to the Word (for such is the signification of that law in an extensive sense), and the divine truth proceeding from the Lord is what forms the heavens : this is received in the greatest purity by the angels of the third heaven, because they are in conjunction with the Lord by virtue of love to Him; for all the angels in that heaven are principled in love to the Lord, wherefore they see divine truth as it were implanted in themselves, although it continually flows-in from the Lord, and hence it is, that that heaven, above the rest, is said to be in the Lord, because in the Divine [principle] which proceeds from Him : this heaven was represented by the ark in which was the law, that is, the Lord : this was the reason that the ark was overlaid with gold, within and without, and, that the propitiatory was over the ark, and over the propitiatory, and from it, two cherubs, which were of pure gold; for gold, from correspondence, signifies the good of love, in which the angels of the third heaven are principled ; by the propitiatory was signified the hearing and reception of all things appertaining to worship, which originates in the good of love from the Lord ; and by the cherubs was signified the Lord's providence and guard, that He may not be approached except by the good of love, and that heaven, with the angels thereof, is protection lest any thing should be elevated to the Lord Himself except what proceeds from the good of love to Him derived from Him; for all worship of God passes through the heavens even unto the Lord, and is purified in the way, even till it is elevated to the third heaven, and is there heard and received by the Lord, all impurities being wiped off in the way; hence it is that cherubs of gold were placed over the propitiatory, which was over the ark, and hence that place was called the sanctuary, and also the Holy of Holies, and was distinguished from the exterior part of the tabernacle by the veil. That the tent, together with the court, represented the three heavens, may also appear from this consideration, that all things which were instituted with the sons of Israel, were representative of heavenly things; for the church itself was a representative church, so that the tabernacle, together with the altar, was in an especial manner the most holy representative of worship: for worship was performed upon the altar by burnt offerings and sacrifices, and in the tabernacle by burning of incense, also by the lamps which were daily lighted up, and by the breads which were daily disposed in order upon the table: all these things represented all worship in heaven, and in the church, and the tent itself with the ark, the heavens themselves: hence it was, that the tabernacle was called the dwelling place of Jehovah God, as heaven itself is called: that the heavens were represented by the tabernacle may also appear from this consideration, that the form thereof was shown to Moses by the Lord upon mount Sinai, and what was shewn in form by the Lord must necessarily represent either heaven or the things appertaining to heaven: that the form of the tabernacle was shown to Moses upon mount Sinai, appears from these words which were spoken to Moses: "Let them make for Me a sanctuary, that I may dwell in the midst of them, according to all that I have shown thee, the form of the dwelling place:" and afterwards: "See and make them in their form, which thou wast made to see in the mount" (Exod. xxv. 8, 9, 40). Hence it is, that it is called the sanctuary, and it is said, that I may dwell in the midst of them. With respect to the signification of the ark in particular, likewise of the propitiatory over it, as also of the cherubs over the propitiatory, of the border of gold round about the ark, of the four rings for the staves, of the veil, of the handles, and the rest, see what is said and shown in the A. C. n. 9546–9577, where they are explained. The sanctity itself of the whole tabernacle was from the testimony, that is, from the two tables of stone on which the law was inscribed, by reason that the law signified the Lord as to divine truth, and thence as to the Word, for this is divine truth: that the Lord is the Word, is evident from John, where it is said, "The Word was with God, and God was the Word, and the Word was made flesh, and dwelt amongst us" (chap. i. 1, 2, 14). That the law which was called both the testimony and the covenant, was placed in the ark, and likewise the book written by Moses, appears from these words: "Thou shalt give the testimony which I shall give thee, into the ark" (Exod. xxv. 16; chap. xl. 20): "I put the tables of the law in the ark which I made, that they might be there, even as Jehovah commanded me" (Deut. x. 5): and concerning the book of the law written by Moses: "When Moses had finished writing the words of this law upon the book even to the making and end thereof, Moses commanded the Levites that bare the ark, to take the book of the law, and put it by the side, of the ark of the covenant, that it may be there for a witness" (Deut. xxxi. 25, 26): from which it is evident, that within the ark there was nothing but the two tables of stone, on which the law was written, and that the book of Moses was by the side of it. That there was nothing in the ark but the two tables of the covenant appears from 1 Kings: "There was nothing in the ark but the two tables of stone, which Moses put there in Horeb, the covenant which Jehovah covenanted with the sons of Israel" (viii. 9). That the book of Moses, which was laid by the side of the ark, was afterwards taken out, and preserved in the temple, appears from what is written in 2 Kings, that "Hilkiah the high priest found the book of the law in the house of Jehovah and gave it to Shaphan, who told it unto the king, and read it before the king" (2 Kings xxii. 8–11. That by the ark was represented the Lord as to divine truth, and that it consequently signified the divine truth which is from the Lord, and thus the Word, may appear also from this consideration, that the Lord spake thence with Moses, for it is said, " Thou shalt give the testimony into the ark, and I will meet thee there, and I will speak with thee from between the two cherubs, which are over the ark of the testimony, all that I shall command thee for the sons of Israel" (Exod. xxv. 21, 22): and elsewhere, " When Moses entered in the tent of the assembly to speak with Him, he heard the voice of one speaking unto him from over the propitiatory, which was over the ark of the testimony, from between the two cherubs ; thus He spake unto him" (Numb. vii. 89). The reason why the Lord thence spake unto Moses, was, because the law was there, and by that law, in an extensive sense, is signified the Lord as to the Word, and the Lord speaks with man from the Word : the reason why it was from over the propitiatory between the two cherubs, was, because by the propitiatory is signified the removal of falsities originating in evil loves, and thence reception and hearing, and by the cherubs, defence, lest He should be approached except by the good of love. Inasmuch as the Lord in heaven and in the church is the divine truth or the Word, and this is understood by the law included in the ark, and whereas the presence of the Lord is in the law or the Word, therefore, where the ark was, there was Jehovah or the Lord, as may appear from these words in Moses : "Moses said unto Hobab, leave us not I pray, forasmuch as Thou knowest how we are to be encamped in the wilderness, whence Thou wilt be to us instead of eyes ; and it shall be when Thou shalt go with us, yea it shall be that the good which Jehovah shalt do to us, we will also do to thee. And they went forward from the mount of Jehovah a journey of three days, and the ark of the covenant of Jehovah going before them the journey of three days to search out for them a rest ; and the cloud of Jehovah was upon them by day, when they went forward out of the camp. When the ark went forward, Moses said, arise Jehovah, that Thine enemies may be dispersed, and Thy haters may flee from before Thy faces ; and when it rested, he said, return Jehovah, the myriads of the thousands of Israel" (Numb. x. 31–36). From all the particulars of this passage it is evident, that Jehovah or the Lord is there understood by the ark, by reason of His presence in the law, which was in the ark, thus by reason of His presence in the Word : inasmuch as the Lord is there understood by the law, and thence by the ark, therefore when it went forward, Moses said, arise Jehovah, that thine enemies may be dispersed, and Thy haters may flee from before thy faces : and when it rested, he said, return Jehovah, the myriads of the thousands of Israel : but the same words involve things still more interior, viz. that the Lord, by His divine truths, leads men and defends them against falses and evils, which are from hell, especially in states of temptation, which are specifically signified by the journeyings of the sons of Israel in the wilderness forty years ;

that He leads them continually by His divine truth is signified by the ark of the covenant of Jehovah going forward before them, a journey of three days, to search out a rest for them; by the ark of Jehovah is understood the Lord as to divine truth; by its going forward a journey of three days is understood His auspices and leading from beginning to end, and by searching out a rest is signified salvation, which is the end; but protection from falses and evils, which are from hell; is signified by the cloud of Jehovah upon them by day, likewise by the words of Moses when the ark went forward, arise Jehovah, that thine enemies may be dispersed, and that thy haters may flee from before Thy faces: by the cloud of Jehovah by day, is also signified defence by divine truth in ultimates, such as is the Word in the sense of the letter, for the Lord by this may be approached also by the evil, and by this He defends the interior things of the Word which are celestial and spiritual; that this sense of the Word is signified by a cloud, may be seen above, n. 594; by enemies and haters are signified falses and evils, which are from hell, by enemies falses, and by haters evils, consequently also the hells themselves as to those falses and evils; truths from good which are implanted in man after temptations, are signified by Moses saying, when the ark rested, return Jehovah, the myriads of the thousands of Israel; by the resting of the ark is signified the state after temptations, when evils and falses are removed, by returning is signified the presence of the Lord, which is then manifest, for in temptations the Lord appears as absent, and by the myriads of the thousands of Israel is signified the truths derived from good, which are then implanted, and from which the church exists; that myriads are predicated of truths, and thousands of goods, may be seen above, n. 336. Similar things are signified by these words in David: "Lo, we heard of Him in Ephratah, we found him in the fields of the forest; we will enter into His dwelling places, we will bow down ourselves at His footstool. Arise Jehovah to thy rest, Thou and the ark of Thy might; let Thy priests be clothed with justice, and let Thy saints jubilate" (Psalm cxxxii. 6–9). The subject treated of in that psalm is manifestly concerning the Lord, who is also there understood by David, as may appear from its being said, we have found Him in Ephratah and in the fields of the forest, likewise from its being said, we will bow down ourselves at His footstool; Ephratah is Bethlehem, where the Lord was born, and by Ephratah is signified the Word as to its natural sense, and by Bethlehem the Word as to the spiritual sense; and inasmuch as the Lord is the Word, it was therefore his will to be born there; by the fields of the forest are signified those things which appertain to the natural sense of the Word, thus which appertain to the sense of the letter; the spiritual sense of the Word is also signified by His dwelling places, and thence also heaven, inasmuch as heaven is in that sense; and by the footstool to which they shall bow down themselves is signified the natural sense of the Word, and thence also the church on earth, inasmuch as the church is in that sense; that the footstool of the Lord is the church in the earths, may be seen above, n. 606; by the rest to which Jehovah should arise is signified the unition of the Divine and Human [principles] in the Lord, and his conjunction with heaven and the church; and whereas the Lord had rest and peace, and also they who were in heaven and in the church, when he subjugated the hells and disposed all things there and in the heavens into order, it is said, arise, Thou and the ark of Thy might, by Thou being understood the Lord Himself, and by the ark of Thy might, the divine truth proceeding from Him, for by this the Lord has divine power; by the priests who shall be clothed with justice, and by the saints who shall jubilate, are signified the same as by thousands and myriads of Israel mentioned above, viz. by priests those who are in good, and by saints, those who are in truths, thus, abstractedly, the goods and truths of heaven and the church; that by priests in the abstract sense, are signified the goods of the church, may be seen above, n. 31, to the end, and that by saints, in that sense, are signified the truths of the church, n. 204, 328; more particulars of that psalm may also be seen explained above, n. 684. Inasmuch as the ark, by virtue of the law which was in it, signified the Lord as to divine truth, and the Lord has omnipotence from divine good by divine truth, hence it is that so many miracles were performed by the ark: as when the waters of Jordon were divided by it, so that the sons of Israel passed over on dry ground; when the wall of the city of Jericho fell down; when Dagon, the god of the Ashdodites, fell down before it; when the Ashdodites, the Gittites, the Ekronites, and Bethshemites, were smitten with plagues on account of it; when Uzzah died, because he touched it; and when Obed-edom, into whose house it was introduced, was therefore blessed: and inasmuch as those historical circumstances involve arcana, which can only be manifested by the spiritual sense, therefore I am willing to explain them here, in order that it may be known what the ark signifies in a strict and in an extensive sense. First, concerning the waters of Jordon being divided so that the sons of Israel passed through on dry ground, as it is written in Joshua: "Joshua and all the sons of Israel came unto Jordon; and at the end of three days Joshua commanded, saying, when ye shall see the ark of the covenant of Jehovah, and the priests the Levites bearing it, ye shall also journey from your place and shall go after it, but there shall be a space between you and it, about two thousand cubits, ye shall not approach unto it. And the priests took up the ark of the covenant and went before the people; and Joshua said, when ye shall come to the brink of the waters of Jordan, ye shall stand still in Jordan. And he said unto the people, behold the ark of the covenant of the Lord of the whole earth passing over before you into Jordan; and take ye twelve men of the tribes of Israel; and when the soles of the feet of the priests that bear the ark of the Lord of the whole earth shall rest in the waters of Jordan, the waters of Jordan shall be cut off, and the waters that come down from above shall stand in one heap. And it came to pass when the priests came unto Jordan, and the feet of the priests that bare the ark were dipped in the brink of the waters, and Jordan was full, as it was wont to be all the days of harvest, the waters that came down from above stood in a heap, lengthening themselves out very far from the city Adam, and those that came down upon the sea of the plain, the sea of salt, were consumed and cut off, so that the people could pass through towards Jericho. And the priests stood on the dry ground in the midst of Jordan; and all the people passed through on dry ground. Afterwards Jehovah said unto Joshua, take to you twelve men, one of a tribe, and take up from the midst of Jordan, from where the feet of the priests stood, twelve stones, which ye shall bring over with you, and leave in the place where ye pass the night. And the sons of Israel did so; and they took up twelve stones out of the midst of Jordan, according to the numbers of the tribes of Israel, and they carried them into the place where they passed the night. Then after that all the people had finished to pass over, the ark of Jehovah passed over, and the priests: and it came to pass, when the priests were come up, and the soles of their feet were lifted up out of Jordan, the waters of Jordan returned into their place. And the twelve stones which they took out of Jordan, Joshua set up in Gilgal" (Josh. iii. 1–17; chap. iv. 1–20). All the historical parts of the Word, as well as the prophetical parts thereof, contain a spiritual sense, which does not treat concerning the sons of Israel or concerning nations and people, but concerning the church and its establishment and progression, for herein consists the spirituality of the Word, which the natural historic sense serves to contain: hence also all the miracles which are described in the Word, as the miracles performed in Egypt and afterwards in the Land of Canaan, involve such things as appertain to heaven and the church, whereby also those miracles are divine. By the miracle above cited is signified the introduction of the faithful into the church, and by the church into heaven: by the sons of Israel, in the spiritual sense, are there understood the faithful, who, after suffering temptations, which are signified by their wanderings in the wilderness, are introduced into the church; for by the land of Canaan, into which the sons of Israel were introduced, is signified the church, and by Jordan is signified the first entrance into it; by the waters of Jordan are signified introductory truths, such as are those of the literal sense of the Word, for those truths also first introduce, but here by Jordan and the waters thereof, as taken in the opposite sense, are signified the falses of evil which were from hell, by reason that the land of Canaan was then full of idolatrous nations, by which are signified all kinds of evils and falses which constitute hell, for which reason they were also to be expelled, that room might be made for the church which was to be there established; and whereas the waters of Jordan then signified the falses of evil, therefore they were divided and removed, that a passage might be given to the sons of Israel, by whom the church might be represented. Now inasmuch as the Lord alone removes and dissipates the falses of evil which are from hell, and by His divine truths introduces the faithful into the church and into heaven, and whereas by the ark, and the law inclosed in it, was represented the Lord as to divine truth, therefore it was commanded that the ark should go before the people and so should lead them; wherefore it came to pass, that as soon as the priests bearing the ark dipped their feet in the waters of Jordan, those waters were divided and went down, and the people passed over on dry land, and that after this was accomplished, the waters returned: but those same waters now signified introductory truths; for Jordon was the first boundary of the land of Canaan, by which land, after the sons of Israel had entered into it, was represented the church, and by that river introduction into it. Inasmuch as the waters of Jordan thus signified introductory truths, therefore it was also commanded that they should take up out of the midst thereof twelve stones, and should carry them over into the first place where they should pass the night, and this because stones signify truths, and twelve stones, according to the number of the tribes of Israel, signified the truths of the church. The reason why Joshua set up those stones in Gilgal from the east of Jericho, was, because Gilgal signified the doctrine of natural truth, which is serviceable for introduction into the church. From these few observations it may appear, what things appertaining to heaven and the church were represented by that miracle, and that the ark, by virtue of the law in it, signified the Lord as to divine truth, on which account it is also called the ark of the covenant of the Lord of the whole earth, by reason of the conjunction with the Lord by divine truth, for by it conjunction is effected, which is signified by covenant, and this is what constitutes heaven and the church, which are specifically signified by the whole earth, yea, by which all things were created and made, according to the Lord's words in John, chap. i. 1, 2, 3, 10; and in David, Psalm xxxiii. 6; by the Word is there understood divine truth. The second miracle which was performed by the ark, was the falling down of the wall of Jericho, which is thus described in Joshua: "The city of Jericho was shut: and Jehovah said unto Joshua, I have given into thy hand Jericho, and the king thereof, and the mighty in strength: ye shall go round the city, all the men of war, once a day for six days, and seven priests shall carry seven trumpets of them that jubilate before the ark; but in the seventh day ye shall go round the city seven times, and the priests shall sound with the trumpets, and then the people shall shout with a great shouting, and the wall of the city shall fall underneath itself, and the people shall go up. Then Joshua made them go round the city once in the first day, as it was said; after which they returned into the camp, and passed the night in the camp: in like manner the day after; and the seven priests carried the seven trumpets of them that jubilate before the ark of Jehovah, marching as they went, and sounded the trumpets, before whom went the men of war, and also the rear company marching after the ark, in going and sounding the trumpets: and so they did six days: and in the seventh day they went about the city seven times, and the seventh time the people shouted: and when the people heard this, then the wall of the city fell flat under itself, and the people went up into the city, and gave to the curse all things which were in the city, from male even to female, and from the boy to the old man; and they burned the city with fire, and all things that were in it; only the silver and gold, and the vessels of brass and iron, they gave into the treasury of the house of Jehovah. And Joshua adjured them, saying, cursed be the man against Jehovah, who shall rise up and build this city; with his first born he shall lay the foundation of it, and with the youngest he shall set up its gates" (Joshua vi. 1–26). No one can know what there is divine in this miracle, unless he knows what the city of Jericho, which was burned in the land of Canaan, signified, what the wall thereof which fell flat, what the inhabitants who were devoted to the curse, likewise what was signified by the gold and silver, and vessels of brass and iron, which were given into the treasury of the house of Jehovah; moreover what by sounding the trumpets and shouting, as also by going about it six days, and seven times on the seventh day: by the city Jericho is signified instruction in the knowledges of good and truth, whereby man is introduced into the church; for Jericho was a city not far from the river Jordan, by which river is signified introduction into the church, as was shown above; for all the places in the land of Canaan were significative of things celestial and spiritual appertaining to the church, and this from the most ancient times; and whereas the sons of Israel were to represent the church, and the Word was to be written amongst them, in which those places were to be mentioned according to their spiritual signification, therefore they were introduced thither: Jordan signified that introduction, and Jericho instruction; and whereas Jericho signified instruction, it also signified the good of life, because no one can be instructed in truths of doctrine but he who is in the good of life: but when the land of Canaan was possessed by idolatrous nations, the signification of places and cities in that land was changed into the contrary, and hence Jericho then signified the profanation of truth and good: from these observations it follows, that the city itself signified the doctrine of the false and evil, which perverted the truths and goods of the church and profaned them; that the wall thereof signified the falses of evil defending that doctrine, and that the inhabitants signified the profane; and whereas all profanation arises from infernal love after the acknowledgment of truth and good, therefore the city was burned with fire, the inhabitants given to the curse, and the wall thereof fell flat, for fire signifies infernal love, curse, a total blotting out and the falling down of the wall, a stripping or making bare to everything evil and false: by the priests sounding the trumpets was signified the preaching of divine truth from divine good; by the shouting and acclamation of the people was signified consent and confirmation; by going round the city was signified the taking a view on all sides of the false and evil, and the dissipation thereof by the influx of divine truth from the Lord, which influx was signified by the carrying round the ark; by the priests being seven in number, and by their going round the city seven days, and seven times on the seventh day, was signified what was holy, and the holy preaching of divine truth, for seven signifies what is holy, and, in the opposite sense, what is profane, wherefore as there was holiness on the one part, and what was profane on the other, there were seven priests with seven trumpets, and they went about the city seven times. The reason why the gold, the silver, and vessels of brass and iron, were given into the treasury of the house of Jehovah, was, because they signified the knowledges of spiritual and natural truth and good, gold and silver the knowledges of spiritual truth and good, and vessels of brass and iron the knowledges of natural truth and good, which, with those who profane, are changed into dire falses and evils, but inasmuch as they are still knowledges although applied to evils, they serve for use with the good, by application to good, and therefore these things were given into the treasury of the house of Jehovah; this also is what is understood by the pounds which were taken away from the evil, and given to the good; likewise by the unjust mammon; as also by the gold, silver, and raiment, which the sons of Israel took away from the Egyptians, and afterwards bestowed on the tabernacle; and also by the gold and silver which David amassed from the spoils of the enemy, and left to Solomon to build the temple. That he should be cursed who rebuilt Jericho, and that he should lay the foundation thereof with his first born, and set up the gate with his youngest, signified the profanation of divine truth from first to last, if instruction therein should be represented elsewhere than in Jerusalem, by which the church was to be signified as to the doctrine of truth and good, and as to instruction from the Word; that this profanation took place under king Ahab by Hiel the Bethelite, is recorded in 1 Kings, chap. xvi. 34; and it is said concerning Ahab, that he did evil in the eyes of Jehovah above all the kings of Israel, verse 30, 33. From this miracle performed by the ark, it may also appear that the ark, by virtue of the law in it, represented the Lord as to divine truth, and thence signified divine truth proceeding from the Lord. The THIRD miracle performed by the ark, which was when Dagon, the god of the Ashdodites, fell before the ark, and the Ashdodites, Gittites, Ekronites, and Bethshemites, were smitten with plagues on account thereof, is thus described in the 1st book of Samuel: "Israel went out against the Philistines to war: and Israel was smitten before the Philistines to four thousand men: wherefore the elders said, let us receive unto us out of Shiloh the ark of the covenant of Jehovah, and let it come into the midst of us, and deliver us out of the hand of the enemy: and they carried down the ark of the covenant of Jehovah Zebaoth that sitteth upon the cherubs, and with the ark the two sons of Eli. And it came to pass when the ark came to the camp, all Israel shouted with a great shouting: the Philistines heard and knew that the ark of Jehovah was come to the camp, and they feared for themselves, saying, God is come to the camp; wo unto us! who shall deliver us out of the hands of these magnificent gods, these gods who smote the Egyptians with every plague? but be strong and quit yourselves like men, O ye Philistines, that ye may not serve the Hebrews. And the Philistines fought, and Israel was smitten with a great slaughter, to thirty thousand footmen; and the ark of God was taken, and both the sons of Eli slain. And the Philistines took the ark, and brought it down to Ashdod, into the house of Dagon, and they set it near Dagon. When the Ashdodites arose in the morning, behold Dagon lay upon his faces on the earth before the ark of Jehovah; and they set him up again in his place; but when they arose the next morning, Dagon lay upon his faces on the earth before the ark, and at the same time the head of Dagon and the two palms of his hands were cut off upon the threshold. And the hand of Jehovah was heavy upon the Ashdodites, and He smote them with hemorrhoids, Ashdod, and the borders thereof; then the Ashdodites, said, the ark of Israel shall not remain with us: wherefore the Lords of the Philistines let the ark of the God of Israel be carried over unto Gath; and they carried it over unto Gath; but the hand of Jehovah came against the city, and smote the men of the city from the least to the greatest, whilst the hemorrhoids were stopped up with them: wherefore they sent the ark of God to Ekron: but the Ekronites cried out that they should be slain; and the men that died not were smitten with hemorrhoids: therefore the lords said, that they would send back the ark into its place. When the ark had remained in the field of the Philistines seven months, the Philistines called the priests and diviners, saying, what shall we do with the ark of Jehovah, how shall we send it back to its place? And they said, send it not again empty, but send with it a trespass-offering, then shall ye be healed, namely, according to the number of the lords of the Philistines, five hemorrhoids of gold, and five mice of gold, because one plague is upon you all, and upon your lords; ye shall make images of your hemorrhoids, and images of your mice, which vastated the land; and make a new cart, and take two milch kine upon which no yoke has yet come, and tie the kine to the cart, and bring their sons home from them, and put the ark of Jehovah upon the cart, and the vessels of gold put into a coffer at the side thereof; and see if it go up the way of the coast to Bethshemesh: and they did so. Then the cows went in a straight way upon the way to Bethshemesh in one path, and they lowed; and the lords of the Philistines went after them. And the cart came into the field of Joshua the Bethshemite, and stood there: and there was a great stone in the place; then they clave the wood of the cart, and offered the kine for a burnt offering to Jehovah. And the Levites set down the ark of Jehovah, and the coffer in which were the vessels of gold, upon that great stone, and the men of Bethshemesh offered burnt offerings, and sacrificed sacrifices to Jehovah: but the Bethshemites were smitten because they saw the ark of Jehovah, to the number of fifty thousand and seventy men. But the men of Kirjathjearim caused the ark of Jehovah to come up, and brought it into the house of Abinadab in Gibeah, and it remained there twenty years. Then Samuel said, if with the whole heart ye will return to Jehovah, remove ye the gods of the stranger and Ashtaroth, and prepare your heart towards Jehovah, and serve him alone, then shall he deliver you out of the hand of the Philistines" (chap. iv. 1–11; chap. v. 1, 2; chap. vi. 1–21; chap. vii. 1, 2, 3). What is signified by the ark being taken by the Philistines, and by the Philistines being smitten with hemorrhoids on account of the ark in Ashdod, Gath, and Ekron, likewise by the mice devastating their land, and by so many dying there and in Bethshemesh, cannot possibly be known, unless it be known what the Philistines, and specifically the Ashdodites, Gittites, Ekronites, and Bethshemites represented, and thence signified; likewise what was signified by the hemorrhoids and by the mice; as also by the images thereof made of gold; and moreover by the new cart, and the milch kine: that they were all representative of such things as appertain to the church, must be evident to every one, for otherwise to what purpose could it be that the Philistines should be smitten with such plagues, and that the ark should be so brought back? The Philistines represented, and thence signified, those who make no account of the good of love and charity, nor consequently of the good of life, placing the all of religion in science and knowledge; hence they were like those at this day who make faith alone, that is, faith separate from charity, the essential of the church and the essential of salvation; and on this account they were called the uncircumcised, for to be uncircumcised signifies to be void of spiritual love, consequently of good; and whereas they had reference to those within the church, therefore they were not spiritual, but merely natural; for they who make no account of the good of charity and of life, become merely natural, yea sensual, loving only worldly things, neither can they understand any truths spiritually, and those which they apprehend naturally, they either falsify or defile; such are they who are understood in the Word by the Philistines: hence it may appear, whence it was that the Philistines so often fought with the sons of Israel, and that sometimes the Philistines conquered, and sometimes the sons of Israel: the Philistines conquered when the sons of Israel departed from the statutes and precepts by not doing them, and the sons of Israel conquered when they lived according to them; to live according to the precepts and statutes was their good of love and good of life. The reason why the sons of Israel were now conquered by the Philistines, was, because they departed from the worship of Jehovah to the worship of other gods, and especially to the worship of Ashtaroth, as may appear from the words of Samuel to them, 1 Sam. vii. 3; this was the cause also of the ark being taken by the Philistines. When it is thus known that by the Philistines were represented, and thence signified, those who make no account of the good of love, of charity, and of life, it may be known why they were smitten by hemorrhoids ón account of the ark, and died in consequence thereof; likewise, why the mice devastated the land; for hemorrhoids signify truth defiled by evil of the life, as is the case with those who are destitute of good, for blood signifies truth, and the corrupt matter of the hemorrhoids, truth defiled, and the posterior part, where the hemorrhoid was, signifies natural love with those who are not spiritual, which is the love of the world; and mice signify the falses of the sensual man, which, as it were, eat up and consume all things of the church, as mice do the corn with other produce of the fields, and also the roots in the earth : these therefore were their plagues, by reason of their being of such a nature and quality, for they who are without good, defile truths, and also devastate all things of the church. The reason why these things took place on account of the ark, was, because the ark signified divine truth which proceeds from the Lord, and this is not given genuine except with those who are in the good of love and thence in the good of life; and when the divine truth flows in with those who are not in good, it produces effects which correspond to the falses of their doctrine and the evils of their life, similar to what takes place in the spiritual world, where, when divine truth flows in with such persons, the defilement of truth and devastation of good appears in the likeness of hemorrhoids and mice. The reason why Dagon the god of the Ashdodites, by reason of the nearness and presence of the ark, was cast down to the earth, and afterwards his head and the palms of his hands were cast upon the threshold of his house, was, because Dagon signified their religious principle, which being destitute of spiritual good, was also destitute of all intelligence and power; for the head signifies intelligence, and the palms of the hands signify power: the like also takes place in the spiritual world, when divine truth flows in out of heaven with such persons, for they then appear as if they had no head, and without the palms of their hands, because they have no intelligence nor power. The reason why, by the advice of their priests and diviners, they made golden images of the hemorrhoids and of the mice, and set them at the side of the ark upon a new cart, to which they tied two milch kine upon which no yoke had ascended, was because gold signifies the good of love, which heals and purifies from falses and evils, which are signified by hemorrhoids and mice, and because a cart signifies the doctrine of natural truth, and a new cart, that doctrine untouched and not defiled by the falses of their evil; and the milch kine, upon which there had been no yoke, signified natural good not yet defiled by falses, for to carry a yoke signifies to serve, and in this case to serve falses which defile good; and whereas those things were in agreement with divine truth, which was signified by the ark, therefore they were made use of and applied as representatives, and afterwards the Levites offered them for a burnt offering, which they burned with the wood of the cart. The reason why the ark with the gifts was deposited upon a great stone, near which the kine stood still, was, because stone signifies divine truth in the ultimate of order. The reason why all this was done by the advice of the priests and diviners of the Philistines, was, because the science of correspondences and representations was a common science at that time, for it was their theology, known to the priests and diviners, who were their wise men ; but whereas at that time they were for the most part become merely natural, they regarded those things idolatrously, worshiping the externals, and not thinking of the internal things which they represented. From these observations it may appear, what all the particulars which are ad-

duced above from the book of Samuel, signify in their series, and
that the ark, by virtue of the law in it, signifies divine truth
proceeding from the Lord.   FOURTHLY, concerning the two miracles
performed by the ark, which relate to the death of Uzzah and the
blessing of Obededom, it is thus written in 2 Samuel: " David arose
and departed, and all the people that were with him, from Baal of
Judah, to bring up thence the ark of God, whose name is invoked,
the name of of Jehovah Zebaoth that sitteth between the cherubs
over it : and they caused the ark of God to be carried upon a new
chariot, and they brought it from the house of Abinadab, which is in
Gibeah, and Uzzah, and Abio, the sons of Abinadab, were leading
the chariot.   And David and all the house of Israel were playing
before Jehovah, upon all kinds of instruments made of fir wood, and
upon harps, and with psalteries, and with timbrels, and with dulci-
mers, and with cymbals.   And when they came to the corn floor of
Nachon, Uzzah put forth [his hand] to the ark, and took hold of it,
because the oxen had turned aside: and the anger of Jehovah was
kindled against Uzzah, and God smote him for his error, so that he
died there at the ark of God : and David was grieved at it, and
David feared Jehovah in that day, saying, how shall the ark of Jehovah come unto me ? and David would not himself set the ark of
Jehovah with himself in the city of David, but he carried it aside
into the house of Obed-edom the Gittite.   When the ark of Jehovah
had remained in his house three months, Jehovah also blessed
Obed-edom and all his house : and this was told to king David,
and David went, and brought up the ark of God from the house of
Obed-edom into the city of David with joy ; and when they that
bare the ark of Jehovah had gone forward six paces, he sacrificed an
ox and a fatling ; and David danced with all his might before Jehovah, girt with a linen ephod : and David and all the house of Israel
brought up the ark of Jehovah with a shout and with the sound of a
trumpet, and brought the ark of Jehovah into the city of David,
which is Zion, and set it up in its place within the tent which David
had spread for it" (vi. 1–17).   These historical particulars, in the
internal or spiritual sense, involve many things which cannot appear to view in the sense of the letter, which is the historical sense;
thus something is involved in the ark being brought from the house
of Abinadab into the house of Obed-edom, and at last into the city
of David, which is Zion; something again, when it was being brought
in, their playing, and sounding all kinds of instruments of music, and
in David himself dancing ; likewise in the ark being brought upon
a new chariot, to which oxen were tied; as also in Uzzah, the son
of Abinadab dying, and in Obed-edom with his house being blessed:
all these things, notwithstanding their being historical events, contain in their bosom such things as appertain to heaven and the
church, in like manner as the ark itself, which, on account of the
law in it, represented the Lord as to divine truth, wherefore it is
called the ark of God whose name is invoked, the name of Jehovah
Zebaoth sitting between the cherubs : with respect to the ark being
brought out of the house of Abinadab, first into the house of Obed-

edom, and at last into the city of David, which is Zion, no one can know what arcana are herein involved, but he who knows what was signified by Gibeah, and by Baal of Judah there, where Abinadab was, and what by Gath, where Obed-edom was, and lastly what by Zion, where David was: all the tracts or countries, with the cities in them, in the land of Canaan, were representative, as in the spiritual world, with respect to the regions there, and the cities of those regions: in every region, and also in every city whatever, in the spiritual world, they who are in the good of love dwell to the east and west, they who are in a clear good of love to the east, and they who are in an obscure good of love to the west; and they who are in the light of truth dwell to the south and the north, they who are in a clear light of truth to the south, and they who are in an obscure light of truth to the north: the case was similar in the land of Canaan in the tracts thereof, and in the cities of those tracts: these, with respect to their quarters, corresponded to the regions in the spiritual world, and to the cities of those regions, but with this difference, that men on earth cannot be thus arranged in their quarters as to the good of love, and as to the light of truth, as spirits and angels are in the spiritual world, wherefore in the land of Canaan and in the cities thereof the places themselves represented, and not persons; that this was the case, may appear from the partition of the land of Canaan into inheritances, which fell by lots to the tribes according to their representation of the church; likewise from Jerusalem and Zion representing the church itself, Jerusalem the church as to the truth of doctrine, and Zion the church as to the good of love: if therefore it be known what is particularly signified, as appertaining to heaven and the church, by Gibeah, and by Baal of Judah there, where Abinadab was, and what by Gath where Obed-edom was, it may be known what is signified by the ark being brought from Abinadab to Obed-edom, and at last into Zion: from the signification of those cities, it may appear, that by the translation of the ark was represented the progression of the church in man, from its ultimate to its inmost, as from one heaven into another even to the supreme, which is the third heaven: Baal of Judah, where Abinadab was, signified the ultimate of the church, which is called its natural principle, for this was represented by Gibeah, where Baal of Judah was; but Gath, where Obed-edom was, who was thence called a Gittite, signified the spiritual [principle] of the church, which signification it put on after the sons of Israel had taken the cities from Ekron even to Gath from the Philistines (1 Sam. vii. 13, 14, 15): but Zion, where David dwelt, signified the inmost [principle] of the church, which is called its celestial principle. From these considerations it is evident, that the translation of the ark signified the progression of the church with man from its ultimate to its inmost, and this because those progressions are effected by divine truth, which was signified by the ark: for the man of the church advances from the natural principle to the spiritual, and through this to the celestial, and this continually from the Lord by His divine truth; the natural [principle] is the good of life, the spiritual is the good of charity towards our neighbor, and the celestial is the good of love to the Lord; in a similar progression are the goods of the three heavens, wherefore the ascent through them in their order was also represented. By their playing and sounding all kinds of instruments of music, when the ark was being brought, and by David's dancing, was represented the gladness and joy which result from the affection of truth and good from the Lord by the influx of divine truth, which was signified by the ark; the instruments mentioned, on which they played in the first journey from the house of Abinadab to the house of Obed-edom, represented the gladness of mind resulting from the natural and spiritual affection of truth; and the dancing of David, likewise the shouting and sound of the trumpet, represented the joy of heart resulting from the affection of spiritual and celestial good; that harmonies of musical sounds are from the spiritual world, and signify affections with their gladnesses and joys, may be seen above, n. 323, 326; and that Zion signifies the third heaven, and thence the inmost [principle] of the church, may also be seen above, n. 405. The ark being brought upon a new chariot, and oxen being tied to the chariot, represented and thence signified the doctrine of truth derived from the good of love, the chariot signifying the doctrine of truth, and the oxen the good of love, each in the natural man, for divine truth which is signified by the ark, subsists and has its foundation upon the doctrine of natural truth which is derived from good; hence it was that the ark was set upon a chariot, and oxen before the chariot: that a chariot signifies the doctrine of truth, may be seen above, n. 355; and that an ox signifies natural good, may be seen in the A. C. n. 2180, 2566. The reason why Uzzah, the son of Abinadab, died because he laid hold of the ark with his hand, was, because to touch with the hand signifies communication, which is effected with the Lord by the good of love, and yet Uzzah was not anointed, as were the priests and Levites, to whom the representation of the good of love acceded by anointing, and yet the cherubs, which were over the propitiatory which was over the ark, signified guard that the Lord should not be approached except by the good of love; that the representation of the good of love was put on by anointing, may be seen above, n. 375. That this circumstance also took place, in order that David might not bring the ark to Zion before the progression, which was also represented, was finished, according to what was said above, may appear from this consideration, that David grieved at the death of Uzzah, and feared to bring the ark into his own city, which was Zion, verses 8, 9, 10. The reason why Obed-edom was blessed, and his house, on account of the ark, was, because blessing from the good things of the world, signifies blessing from the good things of heaven, which proceed solely from the Lord by the reception of divine truth represented by the ark, which good things are given to those who are in spiritual good, which Obed-edom in Gath represented, as was said above. Lastly, the introduction of the ark into Zion, and into the tent which was spread out for it by David, signified ascent into the third heaven, and conjunction of divine truth with the good of love, for Zion represented the inmost principle of the church, and thence the inmost of the heavens, which is the supreme or third heaven, where the angels are in the good of love to the Lord, and where is guard or defence lest the Lord should be approached except by the good of love, which is represented by the cherubs over the ark. The like was also signified by the ark being introduced into the inmost part of the temple built by Solomon, concerning which it is thus written in 1 Kings: "Solomon prepared the oracle in the midst of the house, that he might set in it the ark of the covenant of Jehovah ; and he made in the oracle two cherubs of the wood of oil, and set them in the midst of the inner house, and they stretched out the wings to the wall on each side, and their wings touched each other in the midst of the house; and he overlaid the cherubs with gold. And Solomon brought up the ark of the covenant of Jehovah from the city of David, which is Zion. And all the elders of Israel came, and the priests carried the ark, and brought up the ark of Jehovah, and the tent of assembly, and all the vessels of holiness which were in the tent; and Solomon and all the congregation with him were before the ark ; and the priests brought the ark of the covenant of Jehovah into its place, into the oracle of the house, into the holy of holies, even under the wings of the cherubs; for the cherubs spread out their wings over the place of the ark, so that the cherubs covered the ark and the staves thereof from above, and the heads of the staves were seen from the holy [place], towards the faces of the oracle, but they were not seen without. And Solomon said, I have appointed there the place of the ark, wherein is the covenant of Jehovah, which He covenanted with our fathers, when He brought them forth out of the land of Egypt" (vi. 19, 23, 27 ; chap. viii. 1–8, 21). Inasmuch as the ark in the tent of assembly represented the third heaven where the Lord is, and the tent itself, without the vail, the second heaven, and the court the first heaven, so likewise did the temple ; for the temple with its courts represented also the three heavens, wherefore there was nothing in the temple, nor out of the temple within the courts, which did not represent somewhat of heaven, and this by reason that the Lord at that time was present in representatives; for the churches which were before the advent of the Lord, were representative churches, and at last also of such a quality as was the church which was instituted with the sons of Israel ; but when the Lord came into the world, then the externals which represented were abolished, because it was the Lord Himself whom the representatives of the church shadowed forth and signified, and whereas they were external things, and as it were veilings or coverings, within which was the Lord, therefore when He came, these coverings were taken away, and He Himself appeared manifest with heaven and with the church, in which He is the all in all. The chief representatives of the Lord, and thence of heaven and the church, were the tent of assembly, with the table, the candlestick, the altar of incense, and the ark, therein contained;

likewise the altar with the burnt offerings and sacrifices, and after——
wards the temple; and the same was represented by the temple,
as by the tent of assembly, with this difference, that the tent of assembly was a more holy representative of the Lord, of heaven, and
of the church, than the temple. From these considerations it may
appear that the oracle or secret place [adytum] of the temple, where
the ark was, in like manner as in the tent of assembly, represented
the Lord as to divine truth, and thence also the third heaven, where
the angels are conjoined to the Lord by love to Him, and thence
have divine truth inscribed on their hearts. But what was signified
by the cherubs in the temple, and by their wings, likewise by the
staves, which are also mentioned, shall be explained in a few
words: by the cherubs was signified defence lest the Lord should
be approached otherwise than by the good of love, wherefore also
they were made of the wood of oil, by which wood is signified the
good of love, as may be seen above, n. 375: by the wings of the
cherubs is signified the divine spiritual [principle], which descends
from the divine celestial, in which the third heaven is, into the
second, and is there received, wherefore the wings touched each
other in the midst of the house, and thence were stretched forth to
the wall on each side : but by the staves, with which the ark was
carried, was signified divine power, thus the same as by arms. From
these and the preceding observations may appear what is signified in
the Word by the ark of the covenant. Moreover by the ark is signified the representative of the church in general, in like manner as
by the daily or continual [sacrifice] in Daniel, which was to cease
at the Lord's coming into the world: in this sense it is mentioned in
Jeremiah : "I will give you pastors according to my heart, and
they shall feed you with knowledge and intelligence : and it shall
come to pass when ye shall be multiplied, and bear fruit in the land,
in those days they shall no more say, the ark of the covenant of Jehovah, neither shall it come up upon the heart, nor shall they make
mention thereof, neither shall they desire it, neither shall it be repaired any more" (iii. 15, 16). These things are said concerning
the advent of the Lord, and concerning the abolition of the representative rites of the Jewish church which should then take place :
that the interior things of the church should be manifested, which
were veiled over by the representative external rites, and that they
should then become interior or spiritual men, is signified by pastors
being given according to the heart of the Lord, who shall feed them
with knowledge and intelligence ; by pastors are understood those
who teach good and lead thereto by truths; the multiplication of
truth and fructification of good, is signified by, then it shall come to
pass, when ye shall be multiplied and bear fruit in the land in those
days; that then conjunction with the Lord will be by the interior
things of the Word and not by things exterior, which only signified
and represented things interior, is signified by, they shall no more
say, the ark of the covenant of Jehovah, the ark of the covenant of
Jehovah there denoting the externals of worship, which were then
to be abolished, the same as by the daily or continual [sacrifice]

which was to cease, as mentioned in Daniel, chap. viii. 13; chap. xi. 31; chap. xii. 11; that there was to be no longer external worship, but internal, is signified by, it shall not come into the heart, neither shall they make mention thereof, neither shall they desire it, neither shall it be repaired any more. Hence also it may appear, that the ark of the covenant seen by John in the temple of God, which is the vision now treated of, was an appearing of the divine truth, whereby is effected the conjunction of the new heaven and new church with the Lord, and that this was so seen in order that the Word in the letter might be every where like to itself, consisting of such things as were externals of worship and representing things internal; in like manner as above, chap. viii. 3, 4, where he saw the altar and incense before the throne; for the Word in the letter consists of mere correspondences, such as were in the representative churches, and which were thence made use of in writing the Word, inasmuch as interior things of heaven and the church, which are spiritual and celestial, are therein contained.

701. Forasmuch as the ark is called the ark of the covenant, it remains also to be confirmed from the Word that it was so called because the law was in it, and by the law, whereby, in an extensive sense, is meant the Word, is signified the Lord as to divine truth, which is the Word, thus the divine truth or Word which is from the Lord, and in which the Lord is, inasmuch as all divine truth proceeds from Him; when this is received by man, conjunction with the Lord is effected, and this conjunction is what is signified by covenant. How conjunction of the Lord with man is effected, and of man with the Lord, shall also be explained in a few words: the Lord continually flows in with all men with light which enlightens, and with the affection of knowing and understanding truths, also of willing and doing them; and whereas that light and that affection continually flows in from the Lord, it follows, that in proportion as man receives of that light, in the same proportion he becomes rational, and in proportion as he receives of that affection, in the same proportion he becomes wise, and is led by the Lord; that affection with its light draws or attracts to itself the truths which man from infancy has learnt from the Word, from doctrine derived from the Word, and from preaching, and conjoins to itself; for all affection desires to be nourished by the knowledges which agree with it; from this conjunction is formed man's spiritual love or affection, by which he is conjoined to the Lord, that is, by which the Lord conjoins man to himself. But in order to the reception of that light and that affection, there is also given to man a freedom of choice, which, inasmuch as it is from the Lord, is also the gift of the Lord with man, and is never taken away from him, for that freedom appertains to man's affection or love, consequently also to his life; man, by virtue of freedom, can think and will what is evil, and also think and will what is good; in proportion therefore as from that freedom, which appertains to his love, and thence to his life, he thinks falses and wills evils, which are contrary to the truths and goods of the Word, in the same proportion he is not conjoined to

the Lord; but in proportion as he thinks truths, and wills goods, which are from the Word, in the same proportion he is conjoined to the Lord, and the Lord causes those truths and goods to be of his love and thence of his life; from these considerations it may appear that that conjunction is reciprocal, viz. of the Lord with man, and of man with the Lord; such is the conjunction which is understood by covenant in the Word. It is a great fallacy to believe that man can contribute nothing to his salvation, because the light of seeing truths and the affection of doing them, likewise also the freedom of thinking and willing them, are from the Lord, and nothing thereof from man; but inasmuch as those things appear to man as if they were in him, and, when they are thought and willed, as if they were from him, therefore, on account of that appearance, man ought to think and will them as from himself, but still to acknowledge that they are from the Lord, otherwise nothing of truth and good, or of faith and love, can be appropriated to him; he who hangs down his hands, and waits for influx, cannot receive anything, neither can he have any reciprocal conjunction with the Lord, nor consequently be in the covenant. That this is the case, may clearly appear from this consideration, that the Lord has said in a thousand passages in the Word, that man should do good, and that he should not do evil, which the Lord would by no means have said, unless somewhat was given to man, by virtue whereof he has the ability to do, and that which is given to man, appears to him as his own, although it is not his; and as this is the case, therefore the Lord thus speaks in John: "I stand at the door and knock; if any man hear My voice, and open the door, I will come in unto him, and will sup with him, and he with Me" (Apoc. iii. 20). That covenant signifies conjunction with the Lord by reception of divine truth in the understanding and will, or in the heart and soul, that is in the love and faith, and that conjunction is effected reciprocally, may appear from the various passages in the Word where covenant is mentioned: for from the Word it is evident, 1. That the Lord Himself is called the covenant, because conjunction is effected by Him with Him by means of the divine [principle] which proceeds from Him: 2. That the divine proceeding, which is divine truth, thus the Word, is a covenant, because this conjoins: 3. That the precepts, judgments, and statutes, commanded to the sons of Israel, were to them a covenant, because by them conjunction with the Lord was then accomplished: 4. That moreover whatever conjoins is called covenant. As to what concerns the first, viz. That the Lord Himself is called covenant, because conjunction is effected by Him with Him by means of the divine [principle] which proceeds from Him, appears from the following passages: thus in Isaiah: "I Jehovah have called Thee in justice, and I will hold thine hand, and I will guard thee, and I will give Thee for a covenant of the people, and for a light of the nations" (xlii. 6). These words are spoken concerning the Lord, who is called a covenant of the people, and a light of the nations, by reason that covenant signifies conjunction, and light divine truth; by people are understood those who are in truths and by nations those who are in goods, as may be seen above, n. 175, 331, 625; to call Him in justice, signifies, that He may accomplish justice by separating the evil from the good, and by saving the lat-. ter but condemning the former; to take hold of the hand and to guard, signifies, by virtue of the divine omnipotence, which the hells cannot resist; by Jehovah doing this, is signified, that it is done by the divine [principle] in the Lord. Again, in the same prophet: "I have given Thee for a covenant of the people, to restore the earth, and to inherit the devastated inheritances" (xlix. 9); treating also of the Lord; and to give for a covenant of the people, signifies, that conjunction may be with Him and by Him; to restore the earth, signifies the church; and to inherit the devastated inheritances, signifies to restore the goods and truths of the church which were destroyed. So in David: "I have covenanted a covenant with Mine elect, and I have sworn to David my servant, even for ever will I establish thy seed, for ever will I keep to Him My mercy, and My covenant shall be stable" (Psalm lxxxix. 4, 5, 29). By David is here understood the Lord as to His royalty or kingly office, as may be seen above, n. 205, who is called elect from good, and servant from truth; to make a covenant and swear to Him, signifies the union of His divine [principle] with His human, to make a covenant denoting to be united, and to swear denoting to confirm it; even for ever will I establish thy seed signifies the eternity of divine truth from Him; for ever will I keep to Him My mercy, signifies the eternity of divine good from Him; My covenant shall be stable, signifies the union of the divine [principle] and Human in Him: this is the sense of those words, whilst instead of David is understood the Lord as to the divine human [pr n   e], and the royalty thereof, concerning which it is thus said in the sense of the letter, because in that sense David is treated of, with whom there was no such eternal covenant. Thus also in 2 Samuel: "The God of Israel said, the rock of Israel spake to me, and He [shall be] as the light of the morning [when] the sun ariseth, of a morning without clouds, the grass in the earth from the clear shining after rain: is not my house firm with God, because He hath set for me a covenant of eternity, to set over all and to keep" (xxiii. 3, 4, 5). These words were spoken by David; and by the God of Israel, and the rock of Israel, is understood the Lord as to divine truth; what is signified by He [shall be] as the light of the morning [when] the sun arises, of a morning without clouds, the grass out of the earth, by the clear shining after rain, may be seen above, n. 644: hereby is described the divine truth proceeding from the Lord, from which comes all germination of truth and fructification of good; is not my house firm with God, signifies the church conjoined with the Lord by divine truth, the house of David denoting the church; because he has set for me a covenant of eternity, signifies, that from the union of His human [principle] with the divine He has conjunction with the men of the church; to set over all and to keep, signifies by virtue whereof He rules all things and all, and saves those who receive. So in Malachi: "Ye shall know that I have sent unto you this precept,

that My covenant may be with Levi : My covenant was with him
of life and of peace, which I gave to him with fear, that he might
fear Me : the law of verity was in his mouth, and perversity was not
found in his lips.   But ye have receded from the way, ye have
caused many to stumble in the law, ye have corrupted the covenant
of Levi" (ii. 4, 5, 6, 8).   By the covenant of Jehovah with Levi, in
the supreme sense, is signified the union of the divine [principle]
with the human in the Lord, and in the respective sense, the conjunction of the Lord with the church ; for the Lord is understood
by Levi as well as by David, but by Levi as to divine good, which
is the sacerdotal or priesthood of the Lord, and by David as to the
divine truth, which is the royalty of the Lord ; that the Lord is understood by Levi is evident, from its being said, the law of verity
was in his mouth, and perversity was not found in His lips, by the
law of verity being signified divine truth from divine good, and by
lips being signified the doctrine of truth and instruction ; and from
its being afterwards said, " the lips of the priest shall keep science"
and " they shall seek the law from His mouth, because He is the
angel of Jehovah Zebaoth" (verse 7) : by the covenant of life and of
peace, is signified that union and that conjunction which were
spoken of just above, by virtue whereof the Lord Himself was made
life and peace, from which man has eternal life, and peace from the
infestation of evils and falses, thus from hell; what is signified by
His fear may be seen above, n. 696 : they who live contrary to divine truth, are understood by those that have receded from the way,
caused many to stumble in the law, and corrupted the covenant of
Levi; by receding from the way and stumbling in the law, is signified to live contrary to divine truth, and by corrupting the covenant
of Levi, is signified corrupting conjunction with the Lord.   Again, in
the same prophet : " Behold, I send mine angel, who shall prepare
the way before Me ; and suddenly the Lord shall come to His temple, and the angel of the covenant whom ye desire" (iii. 1).   That
the advent of the Lord is there proclaimed, is manifest ; that the
Lord is there called Lord from divine good, and the angel of the covenant from divine truth, may be seen above, n. 242, 433, 444, where
the rest of the passage is also explained.   From the above observations it may appear, that by covenant, when predicated of the Lord,
is understood either Himself, or the union of His divine [principle]
with the human in Him, and that, in respect to those who are in
heaven and in the church, is meant conjunction with Him, by the
divine [principle] which proceeds from Him. 2dly, That the divine
proceeding, which is divine truth, consequently the Word, is a covenant because it conjoins, may appear from the following passages;
thus in Moses : " Moses coming down from Mount Sinai related to
the people all the words of Jehovah, and all the judgments ; and all
the people answered with one voice, and said, all the words which
Jehovah hath spoken will we do ; and Moses wrote all the words
of Jehovah in a book ; and he took the book of the covenant, and
read it in the ears of the people, and they said, all that Jehovah
hath spoken, we will do and will hearken.   And Moses took half

of the blood of the burnt-offerings, and sprinkled upon the people, and said, behold the blood of the covenant, which Jehovah hath covenanted with you respecting all these words ; and they saw the God of Israel, under whose feet was as it were the work of sapphire stone" (Exodus xxiv. 3, 4, 7, 8, 10). That divine truth, which with us is the Word, is a covenant, may appear from all the particulars here related, viewed in the internal or spiritual sense; for Moses, who read those things to the people, represented the law, that is, the Word, as may appear from various places where it is said, Moses and the prophets, and in others, the law and the prophets, consequently Moses denotes the law, and the law, in an extensive sense, signifies the Word, which is divine truth ; the same may also appear from this consideration, that Mount Sinai signifies heaven, whence divine truth comes; and from this, that the book of the covenant, which was read before the people, signifies the Word; and that the blood, of which half was sprinkled upon the people, also signifies divine truth, which is the Word, and whereas it conjoins, it is called the blood of the covenant ; and inasmuch as all conjunction by divine truth is with the Lord, therefore the God of Israel, who is the Lord, was seen by Moses, Aaron and his sons, and the seventy elders : the reason, why it is said, that there was seen under His feet as the work of sapphire stone, is, because when by the Lord is understood the Word, by His feet is understood the Word in its ultimates, that is, in the literal sense thereof, for the sons of Israel did not see it interiorly ; as the work of sapphire, signifies pellucid from internal truths, which are the spiritual sense of the Word; but these things may be seen particularly expounded in the A. C. n. 9371-9412.   The nature and quality of the conjunction, which is signified by covenant, may also appear from what is here adduced, viz. that it is as covenants are wont to be made in the world, which are on the part of one and on the part of the other; in like manner, the covenants which the Lord makes with men, must be on the part of the Lord, and on the part of man ; that they must be on the part of each, is for the sake of conjunction; the things which were on the part of the Lord, are related in the preceding chapter, viz. that He will bless their bread and their waters, that He will take away their diseases, and that they shall possess the land of Canaan from the sea Suph even to the river Euphrates (Exod. chap. xxiii. 25-31); and there by blessing their bread and their waters, in the internal spiritual sense, is signified the fructification of good and multiplication of truth, bread signifying all the good of heaven and the church, and waters all the truths of that good ; by taking away diseases, is signified to remove evils and falses which are from hell, for these are diseases in the spiritual sense ; and by possessing the land from the sea Suph to the river Euphrates, is signified the church with all the extension thereof, which is from the Lord with those who are conjoined to Him by divine truth ; but the things which must be on the part of man, are related in the three chapters which precede, and are summarily understood, in the passage adduced above, by the words of Jehovah and the judgments, which Moses, descending from Mount

Sinai, related to the people, to which the people said with one voice, all the words which Jehovah has spoken, we will do, and will hearken: hence it was that Moses divided the blood of the burnt-offerings, and the half thereof, which was for the Lord, he left in the bowls, and the other half he sprinkled upon the people. That conjunction of the Lord with men is effected by divine truth, is also understood by blood in the Evangelists: "Jesus took the cup, saying, drink ye all of it, this is My blood, the blood of the new covenant" (Matt. xxvi. 27; Mark xiv. 22; Luke xxii. 20). Here blood is called the blood of the new covenant, because blood signifies the divine truth proceeding from the Lord, and covenant signifies conjunction: that blood signifies the divine truth proceeding from the Lord, and received by man, may be seen above, n. 329, 476; and that to drink signifies to receive, to appropriate, and thus to be conjoined, may also be seen above, n. 617. So likewise in Zechariah: "By the blood of thy covenant, I will send forth thy bound out of the pit in which there is no water" (ix. 11); speaking concerning the Lord who is manifestly treated of in that chapter; and by the blood of the covenant is understood, as above, the divine truth, by which conjunction is effected with the Lord; who they are that are understood by the bound in the pit, in which there is no water, may be seen above, n. 537. Forasmuch as the Lord called His blood, by which is understood the divine truth proceeding from Him, the blood of the new covenant, it shall be explained in a few words what is understood by the old covenant and what by the new covenant: by the old covenant is understood conjunction by divine truth such as was given to the sons of Israel, which was external, and thence representative of divine truth internal: no other divine truth was given to them, because they could not receive any other, for they were external and natural men, and not infernal or spiritual, as may appear from this consideration, that those who knew something concerning the advent of the Lord, thought no otherwise concerning Him, than that He was to be a king, who should raise them above all the people in the universe, and who would thus establish a kingdom with them on earth, and not in the heavens and thence in the earths with all who believe in Him; wherefore the old covenant was a conjunction by such divine truth as is contained in the books of Moses, and was called the precepts, judgments, and statutes, in which however lay concealed the divine truth such as is in heaven, which is internal and spiritual; this divine truth was opened by the Lord when He was in the world; and as by this alone is effected conjunction of the Lord with men, therefore it is understood by the new covenant, and also by his blood, which is thence called the blood of the new covenant: the same is also understood by wine. Concerning this new covenant, which was to be entered into with the Lord when He should come into the world, frequent mention is made in the Word of the old covenant; as in Jeremiah: "Behold the days come, in which I will make a new covenant with the house of Israel and with the house of Judah, not as the covenant which

I made with your fathers, because they rendered My covenant vain; but this is the covenant, which I will make with the house of Israel after these days: I will give my law in the midst of them, and upon their heart will I write it, and I will be to them for a God, and they shall be to Me for a people; neither shall they teach any more a man his companion, or a man his brother, saying, know ye Jehovah, for they shall all know Me, from the least of them even to the greatest of them" (xxxi. 31–34). By the house of Israel and the house of Judah, with whom it is here said that the Lord will make a new covenant, are not understood the sons of Israel or Judah, but all who are in truths of doctrine and in the good of love to the Lord derived from the Lord; that these are understood by the sons of Israel and by Judah, in the Word, may be seen above, n. 433; that by the days that come is meant the advent of the Lord, is evident: that conjunction with the Lord should then take place by divine truth internal and spiritual, is understood by these words, this is the covenant which I will make with the house of Israel after those days, I will give My law in the midst of them, and upon their heart will I write it; whereby is signified, that they shall then receive divine truth inwardly in themselves; for divine truth spiritual is received by man inwardly, thus otherwise than with the sons of Israel and the Jews, who received it from without only; for when man receives divine truth within himself, that is, makes it of his love and thence of his life, then truth is known by virtue of truth itself, inasmuch as the Lord flows in into His own truth with man, and teaches him; this is understood by these words, they shall no more teach a man his companion, or a man his brother, saying, know ye Jehovah, for they shall all know Me, from the least even to the greatest; the conjunction itself thereby effected, which is understood by the new covenant, is understood by, I will be to them for a God, and they shall be to Me for a people. Again, in the same prophet: " They shall be to Me for a people, and I will be to them for a God, and I will give to them one heart and one way, to fear Me all their days, and I will make with them an eternal covenant, that I will not turn Me away from after them, that I may do them good; and I will give My fear into their heart, that they may not recede from with Me" (xxxii. 38, 39, 40); treating also concerning the Lord, and concerning a new covenant with Him: conjunction hereby is understood by, I will be to them for a God, and they shall be to Me for a people, and is further described by gving to them one heart and one way, to fear Him all their days, and by not turning away from them, and giving His fear into their heart, that they may not recede from with Him: by one heart and one way, to fear Me, is signified, one will of good and one understanding of truth to worship the Lord; and inasmuch as the conjunction is reciprocal, viz. of the Lord with them, and of them with the Lord, therefore it is said, that He will not turn away from after them, to do them good, and that they shall not recede from with Him; hence it is evident, what is signified by the eternal covenant, which He will enter into with them, viz. conjunction by divine truth spiritual, which, being received, constitutes the life of man,

whence comes eternal conjunction. Again in Ezekiel: " I will
raise up over them one shepherd, who shall feed them, My servant
David : I Jehovah will be to them for a God, and My servant David
a prince in the midst of them; then will I make with them a covenant of peace, I will cause the evil beast to cease, that they may
dwell confidently in the wilderness, and sleep in the forests" (xxxiv.
23, 24, 25) : these things also are said concerning the Lord : and by
David who shall feed them, and who shall be a prince in the midst
of them, is understood the Lord as to divine truth, who is called a
servant from serving ; conjunction with the Lord by divine truth is
understood by the covenant which He will make with them ; it is
called a covenant of peace by reason that man by conjunction with
the Lord has peace from the infestation of evil and the false from
hell ; therefore it is also said, I will cause the evil beast to cease
that they may dwell confidently in the wilderness, and sleep in the
forests ; by the evil beast is understood the false and evil from hell,
and by dwelling confidently in the wilderness, and sleeping in the
forests, is signified, that they shall be safe from all infestation thereof
everywhere.   Again, in the same prophet : " My servant David shall
be a king over them, that there may be one shepherd to them all ;
and I will make with them a covenant of peace, a covenant of eternity shall it be with them ; and I will give them, and multiply them ;•
and I will set My sanctuary in the midst of them for ever, and My
dwelling place with them ; and I will be to them for a God, and they
shall be to Me for a people" (xxxvii. 24, 26, 27) : here also by David
is understood the Lord ; for that David was not to come again to be
their king and shepherd, is evident, but the Lord is called king from
divine truth, for this is the royalty of the Lord, and divine good is
His priesthood ; He is also called shepherd, because He will feed
them with divine truth, and thereby lead to the good of love and
thus unto Himself ; and whereas conjunction is thence, it is said, I
will make with them a covenant of peace, a covenant of eternity;
what the covenant of peace signifies, was said above, likewise that
conjunction is understood by, I will be to them for a God, and they
shall be to Me for a people : by the sanctuary which He shall set in
the midst of them, and by the dwelling place which shall be with
them, are signified heaven and the church, which are called a sanctuary from the good of love, and a dwelling place from the truths of
that good, for the Lord dwells in truths which are derived from good.
So in Hosea : "I will make for them a covenant in that day, with
the wild beast of the field, with the bird of the heavens, and with
the reptile of the earth ; and the bow, and the sword, and the war,
will I break from off the earth ; and I will cause them to lie down
securely : and I will betroth thee to Me for ever" (ii. 18, 19); treating concerning the establishment of the new church by the Lord :
that the Lord would not then make a covenant with the wild beast
of the field, with the bird of the heavens, and with the reptile of the
earth, is evident, wherefore by those things are signified such things
as appertain to man ; by the wild beast of the field, the affection of
truth and good, by the bird of the heavens, spiritual thought, and by

the reptile of the earth, what is scientific appertaining to the natural man; what the rest of this passage signifies, may be seen above, n. 650; hence it is evident, that the covenant which the Lord will make, is a spiritual covenant, or a covenant by spiritual truth, and not a covenant by natural truth, the latter being the old covenant made with the sons of Israel, and the former the new covenant. Inasmuch as by the law, which was promulgated by the Lord from Mount Sinai, in an extensive sense is signified the Word, therefore also the tables, on which that law was inscribed, are called the tables of the covenant; as in Moses: "I went up into the mountain to receive the tables of stone, the tables of the covenant which Jehovah made with you; at the end of forty days and forty nights, Jehovah gave to me two tables of stone, the tables of the covenant" (Deut. ix. 9, 11): by those tables, that is, by the law written upon them, is understood the divine truth, by which there is conjunction with the Lord, by virtue of which conjunction they are called the tables of the covenant; and inasmuch as all conjunction, like a covenant, is effected on the part of one and on the part of the other, thus reciprocally on both sides, therefore there were two tables, and they were of stone; the reason of their being of stone, was, because by stone is also signified divine truth in ultimates, concerning which see the A. C. n. 643, 3720, 6426, 8609, 10,376. Hence it is that the ark, in which those tables were deposited, was called the ark of the covenant, and with the sons of Israel, it was the most holy of worship, as was shown in the preceding article. 3dly. That the precepts, judgments, and statutes, commanded to the sons of Israel, were to them a covenant, because by them conjunction with the Lord was then effected, may appear from the following passages: thus in Moses: "If ye walk in My statutes, and observe My precepts, and do them, I will have respect unto you, and will make you fruitful and multiply you, and I will confirm My covenant with you.' But if ye reprobate My statutes, so that ye do not all My precepts, whilst ye make My covenant vain, I will do contrary to you" (Levit. xxvi. 3, 9, 15, and following verses): in the preceding chapter were set forth the statutes and precepts which were to be observed and done, and in this chapter the goods which they should enjoy if they kept those precepts and statutes, and afterwards the evils which should come upon them if they did not keep them; but the goods which they should enjoy were terrestrial and worldly goods, and so likewise were the evils, by reason that they were terrestrial and natural men and not celestial and spiritual; hence neither did they know anything of the goods which inwardly affect man, nor of the evils which inwardly afflict him; but still the externals which they were bound to observe, were such as inwardly contained in themselves things celestial and spiritual, by which conjunction is effected with the Lord; and inasmuch as those were perceived in heaven, therefore the externals which the sons of Israel were to observe, were called a covenant; but the nature and quality of the conjunction of the Lord with the sons of Israel by those things may be seen in the Doctrine of the New Jerusalem, n. 248.

Similar things are understood by covenant in the following passages: thus in Moses: "Jehovah said unto Moses, write thou these words, because upon the mouth of these words have I made a covenant with thee and with Israel" (Exod. xxxiv. 27): again: "Keep ye the words of this covenant, and do them, ye that stand here this day, your heads, your tribes, your moderators, and every man of Israel, to pass over into the covenant of Jehovah, and into His oath, which Jehovah God maketh with thee this day, that He may appoint thee this day for a people, and that He may be to thee for a God; not with you only do I make this covenant, and this oath, but also with every one who is not here with you this day" (Deut. xxix. 8, 9, 11 –14): and in 2 Kings: "King Josiah sent, and gathered unto him all the elders of Judah and Jerusalem; and the king went up to the house of Jehovah, and every man of Judah, and all the inhabitants of Jerusalem with him, likewise the priests and the prophets, and the whole people from small even to great; and he read in their ears all the words of the book of the covenant found in the house of Jehovah; and the king stood at a pillar, and made a covenant before Jehovah, to go after Jehovah, and to keep His precepts, and His testimonies, and His statutes, with all the heart and with all the soul, to establish all the words of this covenant written upon this book; and all the people stood in the covenant" (xxiii. 1, 2, 3); besides other places, as Jeremiah xxii. 8, 9; chap. xxxiii. 20, 21, 22; chap. l. 5; Ezek. xvi. 8; Malachi ii. 14; Psalm lxxviii. 37; Psalm l. 5, 16; Psalm ciii. 17, 18; Psalm cv. 8, 9; Psalm cvi. 45; Psalm cxi. 5, 9; Deut. xvii. 2; 1 Kings xix. 14; in all which passages the covenant is mentioned, and thereby are signified the external rites which the sons of Israel were to observe. But with respect to the covenant which the Lord made with Abraham, Isaac and Jacob, this was not the same as that made with the posterity of Jacob, but it was a covenant on the part of the Lord that their seed should be multiplied, and that to it should be given the land of Canaan; and on the part of Abraham, Isaac, and Jacob, that every male should be circumcised; that it was another covenant which was made with the posterity of Jacob, appears in Moses: "Jehovah God made with us a covenant in Horeb, not with our fathers did Jehovah God make this covenant, but with us" (Deuteronomy v. 2, 3). Concerning the former covenant, it is thus written in Moses: "Jehovah brought Abraham forth abroad, and said, look towards heaven, and number the stars; and He said to him, thus shall thy seed be; and he said to him, take to thee a heifer of three years old, and a she-goat of three years old, and a ram of three years old, and a turtle dove, and a young pigeon; and he divided them in the midst, and he gave each part opposite to its other; and the birds he did not divide. And the sun went down, and there was a thick darkness; and Lo! a furnace of smoke and a torch of fire passed between the pieces. In that day Jehovah made a covenant with Abraham, saying, to thy seed will I give this land, from the river of Egypt even to the great river Euphrates" (Gen. xv. 5–18); and afterwards: "I will give My covenant between Me and thee, and I will multiply thee exceedingly; I, behold My covenant is with thee, and thou shalt be for a father of a multitude of nations, and I will make thee exceeding fruitful; and I will give to thee, and to thy seed after thee, all the land of thy sojournings, all the land of Canaan, for an eternal possession. This is My covenant which ye shall keep between Me and you, and between thy seed after thee; every male shall be circumcised to you; he who is not circumcised in the flesh of his foreskin, that soul shall be cut off from his people, he hath made my covenant vain; and my covenant will I set up with Isaac, whom Sarah shall bear to thee" (Gen. xvii. 1–21). From these things it may appear what was the nature of the covenant entered into with Abraham, viz. that his seed should be multiplied exceedingly, and that the land of Canaan should be given to him for a possession; the precepts, judgments, and statutes themselves, by which the covenant was to exist, are not mentioned, but still they are signified by the heifer, she-goat, and ram of three years old, and by the turtle dove and young pigeon, for by those animals are signified such things as appertain to the church, and by the land of Canaan itself is signified the church; and whereas the Lord foresaw that the posterity of Abraham from Jacob would not keep the covenant, hence there appeared to Abraham a furnace of smoke and a torch of fire passing between the pieces, and by the furnace of smoke is signified the dense false, and by the torch of fire the dire evil, which would take place with the posterity of Jacob; the same is also confirmed in Jeremiah, chap. xxxiii. verses 18, 19, 20: that Abraham divided the heifer, the she-goat, and the ram, and gave each part opposite to its other, was agreeable to the ritual of covenants, which are between two parties; but these things may be seen fully explained in the A. C. from n. 1783 to 1860. The reason why the covenant was made by circumcision, was, because circumcision represented purification from the loves of self and of the world which are corporeal and terrestrial loves, and their removal, wherefore also circumcision was performed by a little knife of stone, which signified the truths of doctrine, whereby all purification from evils and falses, and the removal thereof, is effected; but the particulars relating to that covenant may also be seen explained in the A. C. n. 1987–2095; and concerning circumcision, n. 2039, 2046, 2632, 2799, 4462, 7044, 8093. But whereas by Abraham, Isaac, and Jacob, in the internal sense, is understood the Lord, hence by their seed are signified all who are of the church of the Lord, which church is also understood by the land of Canaan, which their seed was to inherit. There was also a covenant entered with Noah, "that men should no more perish by the waters of a deluge, and that the bow should be in the cloud for a sign of that covenant" (Gen. vi. 17, 18; chap. ix. 9–17). That that covenant also involves the conjunction of the Lord by divine truth, may appear from the explication of the above words in the A. C. n. 659–675, and 1022–1059; that the bow in the cloud, or the rainbow, signifies regeneration, which is effected by divine truth and by a life according thereto, and that hence that bow was taken for a sign of the covenant, may also be seen in the same work, n. 1042. Fourthly, that, moreover, whatever conjoins is called covenant; as the sabbath, in Moses: "The sons of Israel shall keep the sabbath in their generations, the covenant of an age" (Exod. xxxi. 16). The reason why the sabbath was called the covenant of an age, was, because the sabbath, in the supreme sense, signified the union of the divine [principle] with the human in the Lord, and, in the respective sense, the conjunction of the Lord with heaven and the church, and, in the universal sense, the conjunction of good and truth, which conjunction is called the heavenly marriage; hence the rest on the day of sabbath signified the state of that union, and of that conjunction, inasmuch as thereby the Lord has peace and rest, and thereby also is peace and salvation in the heavens and in the earths : that such things are signified by sabbath, and by rest on the occasion, may be seen in the A. C. n. 8494, 8495, 8510, 10,356, 10,360, 10,367, 10,668, 10,730. The salt in the sacrifices was also called the salt of the covenant, as appears in Moses: "Thou shalt not cause the salt of the covenant of thy God to cease upon thine offering; upon all thine offering thou shalt offer salt" (Levit. ii. 13). The reason of the salt upon the offering being called the salt of the covenant, was, because by salt is signified the desire of truth to good whence comes the conjunction of each with the other; concerning this signification of salt, see the A. C. n. 9207. A wife is also called a wife of the covenant, as in Malachi : "Jehovah hath been a witness between thee and the wife of thy youth, against whom thou hast dealt perfidiously, when she was thy companion, and a wife of thy covenant" (ii. 14.) A wife is there called the wife of a covenant, by virtue of conjunction with her man, but by the wife there mentioned is signified the church, and by a wife of youth the ancient church, against which the Jewish church is said to have dealt perfidiously; and whereas each was representative, and in this respect alike, and so were conjoined, therefore it is said, when she was thy companion and a wife of thy covenant. In the book of Job mention is made of a covenant with the stones of the field, in these words: "Thou shalt not be afraid of the wild beast of the field, for with the stones of the field is thy covenant, and the wild beast of the field shall be at peace with thee" (v. 22, 23). By the covenant with the stones of the field is signified conjunction with the truths of the church, for stones signify truths, field, the church, and covenant, conjunction; by the wild beast of the field is signified the love of the false, of which the man of the church is not afraid, and which is pacific, when there is conjunction with the church by truths. Mention is also made of a covenant with wild beasts and birds, in Hosea: "I will make for them a covenant in that day with the wild beast of the field, with the bird of the heavens, and with the reptile of the earth" (ii. 18); and in Moses: "God said to Noah, behold I set up my covenant with you, and with every living soul which is with you, to the bird, to the beast, and to every wild beast of the earth with you, of all that go out of the ark, as to every wild beast of the earth" (Gen. ix. 9, 10). By the covenant with beast, wild beast, bird, and reptile of the earth, is signified conjunction with such things in man as are signified by them ; for by beast is signified the affection of good, by wild beast, the affection of truth, by bird, what appertains to the thought, and by the reptile of the earth, what is scientific, living from those affections. Mention is also made of a covenant with death, in the prophet Isaiah : "Ye have said, we have made a covenant with death, and with hell we have made a vision ; your covenant with death shall be abolished, and your vision with hell shall not stand" (xxviii. 15, 18). To make a covenant with death signifies conjunction by the false from hell, whence man dies spiritually ; to make a vision with hell, signifies divination as it were prophetic from hell. From the passages that have been now adduced in their series, it may appear, that by covenant, where the subject treated of is concerning the Lord, is signified conjunction by divine truth : conjunction with Him is effected indeed by the good of love, but whereas the Lord flows in with man by good into truths, whence man has the affection of truth, and man receives the good of the Lord in truth, by virtue whereof he acknowledges, confesses, and adores the Lord, hence the good of love conjoins by truth, comparatively as the heat of the sun, in the time of spring and summer, conjoins itself with the fructifications of the earth.

702. "And there were lightnings, voices, and thunderings"—That hereby is signified, that then in the lower parts, where the evil are, were conflicts and tumults of thoughts, and ratiocinations from evils and falses concerning goods and truths, appears from the signification of lightnings, voices, and thunderings, as denoting illustrations, thoughts, and perceptions, concerning which see above, n. 273 ; and, in the opposite sense, as here, conflicts and tumults of thoughts, and ratiocinations from evils and falses, concerning the goods and truths of the church, concerning which also see above, n. 498 : in the strict sense by lightnings are signified darkenings of the understanding, by voices, ratiocinations, and by thunderings, conclusions of the false from evil, and whereas from these, according to the state of the interiors of those with whom they are, there arise conflicts and tumults of affections and thoughts, and thence ratiocinations from evils and falses concerning the goods and truths of the church, therefore from the series consequent upon what goes before, these are the things signified by those words. Forasmuch as in the superior heavens was seen the temple and the ark of the covenant in the temple, by which is signified the appearing of the new heaven where is the worship of the Lord, and the representation of divine truth, by which is conjunction, as may appear from the explication above, hence it follows of consequence, that lightnings, voices, and thunderings, likewise also an earthquake and hail, took place in the parts below. That such things take place in the parts below by influx out of the superior heavens, has been already elucidated ; but whereas they are such as do not fall into any one's understanding except by living revelation, and knowledge thence derived concerning the influx of superior things into inferior things in the spiritual

world, inasmuch as these things have been revealed to me, and thence are known, the arcanum shall here be briefly expounded. In the spiritual world, by which are understood both the heavens and the hells, such is the arrangement, that the heavens are as expanses one above the other, and under the heavens is the world of spirits, and under this are the hells, one below another: according to this successive arrangement descends the influx from the Lord, thus through the inmost heaven into the middle, and through this into the ultimate, and from these in their order into the subjacent hells. The world of spirits is in the midst, and receives influx as well from the heavens as from the hells, every one there according to the state of his life. But this arrangement of the heavens and the hells underwent changes from one judgment to another, which were occasioned by this circumstance, that the men who flocked into the spiritual world from the earths, from which the heavens and the hells receive their inhabitants, were of divers affections, some being more or less spiritual or internal, and some more or less natural or external; and inasmuch as the Lord does evil to no one, but good to all, therefore He permitted them who lived in a moral and as it were spiritual life in externals, from a conformity to mode and custom in the world, however interiorly they were conjoined with hell, to form to themselves, in the world of spirits, a resemblance of heaven in various places, and then the arrangements of the heavens above them, and of the hells below them, were so disposed, that their interiors, by which they were conjoined with hell, might as far as possible be kept closed, and their exteriors, by which they were conjoined with the ultimate heaven, be kept open; and then also it was provided, that the superior heavens should not flow in immediately, because by such immediate influx their interiors would be opened, which were infernal, and their exteriors would be closed, which appeared as spiritual; for the influx of the superior heavens is into the interiors, which are what properly belong to spirits, and not into the exteriors, which do not properly belong to them. But when such imaginary heavens were so far multiplied that the influx thence from the hells began to prevail over the influx from the heavens, and thereby the ultimate heaven, which was conjoined with them, began to totter, then the last judgment impended, and a separation was made by turns of the evil from the good in those new imaginary heavens, and this by immediate influx from the superior heavens, and by that influx their interiors were opened, which were infernal, and their exteriors were closed, which were as it were spiritual, as was said above. From these considerations it is now evident, whence it was that the temple appeared and the ark in the temple, by which is signified the divine truth, with which the superior heavens were illustrated, from which influx might be effected into the parts below, where the evil had their abode: from this influx it came to pass, that in the parts below where the evil were, there were seen lightnings, and that there were heard voices and thunderings, likewise that there was a great earthquake, and hail: the influx out of the heavens, that is, through the heavens from the Lord, is nothing else but an influx of the love of good and of the affection of truth, but it is turned with the evil into such things as correspond with their evils, and with the falses thence derived, thus which correspond with their love of evil and affection of what is false; and whereas the conflicts and tumults of thoughts and ratiocinations from evils and falses concerning the goods and truths of the church, in which they were, correspond to lightnings, voices, and thunderings, therefore they are here signified by them; for the subject here treated of is concerning the state of heaven proximately before the last judgment.　The existence of conflicts and tumults of thoughts and of ratiocinations from evils and falses concerning the goods and truths of the church with those who are inwardly evil, and appear outwardly good, after their interiors were opened, and their exteriors closed, arises from the conflict of their interiors with their exteriors in the first state of separation, but as soon as the exteriors are altogether closed, and they are left to their own interiors, then the conflict ceases, for then they are fully in the love of their own evil, and in the affection of their own false, and thence in the delight of their own life, wherefore they then cast themselves down into hell to their like, which takes place at the day of the last judgment.

703. " And an earthquake"—That hereby are signified changes of state as to those things which are of heaven and the church with them, appears from the signification of an earthquake, as denoting a change of the state of the church, concerning which see above, n. 400.　That in the spiritual world there are earths, hills, mountains, and so forth, and that they are shaken when the state of the church with them is changed into evil and the false, and that such concussions or earthquakes are understood by the earthquakes mentioned in the Word, may also be seen above, n. 400, 409.

704. " And a great hail"—That hereby is signified the infernal false destroying the truths and goods of the church, appears from the signification of hail, as denoting the infernal false destroying the truth of the church, concerning which see above, n. 503; and whereas it is called a great hail, and great is predicated of good, and much of truth, concerning which see above, n. 696, therefore also a great hail signifies the infernal false which destroys the goods of the church.　The reason why, besides lightnings, thunderings, and an earthquake, a great hail also was seen, is, because in the spiritual world appear all things which are in the natural world, as mists, clouds, rains, snow, and hail, which are indeed appearances, but real, arising from correspondences; for the divine celestial and spiritual things, which are proper to the affections and the thoughts thence derived, thus to the good of love and the truth of that good, with the angels, when they descend into the sphere next below, put on forms like natural things, and thus present themselves before the eyes to be seen; thus are formed correspondences; this is the case with respect to lightnings and thunders, and also to hail; this latter, viz. hail, is formed by the flowing down of divine truth where the evil are, who by reasoning conclude falses, and thereby fight against truths and destroy them; for when the divine truth flows out of the

heavens into the sphere which is about the evil, and which appears as a mist, formed from their evil affections and falses thence derived, then that influx is turned into various things, and into hail, with those who think from evils and falses against the goods and truths of heaven and the church, and vehemently resist them; the reason is, because their affections and thoughts thence derived, which are of the false against truths, are void of all celestial heat, and hence the rain which also thereupon falls from the heavens into the parts below, congeals into snow or into hail, and that hail destroys all things which are green and grow with them, and also their habitations altogether similar to what is written concerning the hail in Egypt: the reason why it destroys is, because the things which are green and grow, signify the truths of the church, and their habitations its goods, which they destroy in themselves; this comes to pass, as was said, from correspondence.   The hail also appears congealed into parts greater or less according to the more strong or light resistance of the truths by falses, the greater parts are called, in the Word, stones of hail, because by stones also are signified falses. From these considerations it may now appear whence it is, that by a great hail is signified the infernal false destroying the truths and goods of the church.

CHAPTER XII.

1. And a great sign was seen in heaven: a woman encompassed with the sun, and the moon under her feet, and upon her head a crown of twelve stars.

2. And she bearing in the womb, cried, travailing [in birth], and being pained to bring forth.

3. And there was seen another sign in heaven; and behold, a great red dragon, having seven heads, and ten horns, and upon his heads seven diadems.

4. And his tail drew a third part of the stars of heaven, and cast them to the earth: and the dragon stood before the woman about to bring forth, that when she had brought forth he might devour her child.

5. And she brought forth a male son, who was to rule all nations with an iron rod; and her child was caught up to God and His throne.

6. And the woman fled into the wilderness, where she hath a place prepared of God, that they may nourish her there a thousand two hundred and sixty days.

7. And there was war in heaven: Michael and his angels fought with the dragon, and the dragon fought and his angels,

8. And prevailed not, and their place was not found any more in heaven.

9. And that great dragon was cast down, the old serpent, called the devil and satan, which seduceth the whole world: he was cast down into the earth, and his angels were cast down with him.

10. And I heard a great voice saying in heaven; Now is come the salvation, and the power, and the kingdom of our God, and the authority of His Christ, for the accuser of our brethren is cast down, that accuseth them before our God days and nights.

11. And they conquered him through the blood of the Lamb, and through the word of their testimony: and they loved not their soul unto death.

12. Therefore rejoice, ye heavens, and ye that dwell in them: Woe to the inhabitants of the earth and of the sea, for the devil is come down unto you, having great anger, knowing he hath but a little time.

13. And when the dragon saw that he was cast into the earth, he persecuted the woman who brought forth the male [child].

14. And there were given to the woman two wings of a great eagle, that she might fly into the wilderness into her place, where she should be nourished a time, and times, and half a time, from the face of the serpent.

15. And the serpent cast out of his mouth water as a flood after the woman, that he might make her be carried away by the flood.

16. And the earth helped the woman; and the earth opened her mouth, and swallowed up the flood, which the dragon cast out of his mouth.

17. And the dragon was angry against the woman, and went to make war with the rest of her seed, who keep the commandments of God, and have the testimony of Jesus Christ.

18. And I stood upon the sand of the sea.

EXPLICATION.

705. Verses 1, 2. "And a great sign was seen in heaven: a woman encompassed with the sun, and the moon under her feet, and upon her head, a crown of twelve stars. And she bearing in the womb, cried, travailing [in birth], and being pained to bring forth."—" And a great sign was seen in heaven" signifies divine testification concerning the future church, and concerning the reception of its doctrine, and by whom it will be assaulted: "a woman encompassed with the sun" signifies the church with those who are in love to the Lord, and thence in love towards their neighbor: "and the moon under her feet" signifies faith with those who are in charity: "and she, bearing in the womb" signifies doctrine in its birth from the good of celestial love: "cried, travailing [in birth] and being pained to be delivered" signifies non-reception by those who are in the church; and the resistance of those who are in faith separate from charity.

706. "And a great sign was seen in heaven"—That hereby is signified divine testification concerning the future church, and concerning the reception of its doctrine, and by whom it will be assaulted, appears from the signification of a great sign in heaven, as denoting divine manifestation and testification : that it is concerning the church, and concerning the reception of its doctrine, likewise concerning the assaulting thereof, appears from the things following, for by the woman is understood the church, by her male son, doctrine, and by the dragon and his angels, and afterwards by the beasts, are understood those who are about to assault the church and its doctrine.   The reason why this vision is called a great sign, is, because by a sign is understood divine manifestation concerning things future, also testification, in the present case concerning the future church and its doctrine, and also concerning the assaulting thereof by those who are understood by the dragon and by the beasts ; this is called a sign, because it manifests and testifies. Signs and miracles are frequently mentioned in the Word ; and by a sign is understood, that which indicates, witnesses, and persuades, concerning the subject of inquiry, but by miracle is understood that which excites, strikes, and induces astonishment ; thus a sign moves the understanding and faith, and a miracle the will and its affection, for the will and its affection is what is excited, struck, and amazed, and the understanding and its faith is what is persuaded, indicated to, and for which testification is made.   That there is such a difference betwixt a sign and a miracle, may appear from this consideration, that the Jews, although they saw so many miracles performed by the Lord, still asked of him signs ; and also from this, that the prodigies performed in Egypt and in the wilderness are sometimes called signs and sometimes miracles, and also sometimes both : and moreover it is manifest from this consideration, that in every part of the Word there is a marriage of truth and good, consequently also of the understanding and will, for truth appertains to the understanding and good to the will, and hence also signs have reference to the things which are of truth, thus which are of faith and the understanding, and miracles to the things which are of good, thus which are of affection and the will: hence then it is evident, what is specifically understood by signs, and what by miracles, where they are both mentioned in the Word ; as in the following passages. Thus in Moses : " I will harden the heart of Pharaoh, that I may multiply My signs and My miracles in the land of Egypt" (Exod. vii. 3): again : " Jehovah gave signs and miracles great and evil in Egypt, in Pharaoh, and in every man of his" (Deut. vi. 22): again : " Hath Jehovah assayed to come to take to himself a nation out of the midst of a nation, by miracles, by signs, and by wonders" (Deut. iv. 34): and in David : " They remembered not the day in which Jehovah set signs in Egypt, and prodigies in the field of Zoan" (Psalm lxxviii. 42, 43): again : " They set amongst them the words of his signs and miracles in the land of Ham" (Psalm cv. 27): again : " He sent signs and miracles into the midst of thee, O Egypt, into Pharaoh and all his servants" (Psalm cxxv.

9): and in Jeremiah: "Who hast set signs and miracles in the land of Egypt, and even to this day, also in Israel, and in men, and hast led thy people Israel out of the land of Egypt, by signs and by miracles" (xxxii. 20, 21): from these passages it is evident, that the prodigies performed in Egypt, and afterwards with the sons of Israel, are called signs and miracles, signs because they testified and persuaded, and miracles because they excited and induced astonishment; they agree, however, in this, that the things which excite and induce astonishment also testify and persuade, as those things which excite the will, also persuade the understanding, or as those things which move the affection also move the thought by persuasion. In like manner it is written in the Evangelists, "In the consummation of the age there shall arise false Christs, and false prophets, they shall give great signs and miracles, and shall lead into error, if it is possible, even the elect" (Matthew xxiv. 24; Mark xiii. 22): here also by great signs and miracles similar things are signified, viz. that they will testify and persuade, also that they will strike and induce astonishment, whence arises strong persuasion: who are meant by false Christs and false prophets, likewise by the elect, may be seen above, n. 624, 684. Again in Moses: "If there shall arise in the midst of thee a prophet, or a dreamer of dreams, who shall give thee a sign or a miracle, and the sign or miracle come to pass which he spake unto thee, saying let us go unto other gods, thou shalt not obey" (Deut. xiii. 2, 3, 4): mention is here made of a prophet and a dreamer of dreams, also of a sign and miracle, because a sign has reference to a prophet, and a miracle to a dreamer of dreams, by reason that by a prophet is meant one who teaches truths, and, in the abstract sense, the doctrine of truth, and by a dreamer of dreams is meant one who excites to do a thing, and in the abstract sense, excitation, by virtue of which a thing is done; this latter also appertains to a miracle as the former does to a sign: for prophets were instructed by a living voice from the Lord, and dreamers by representatives exciting to action; these, [viz. representatives,] flowed into the affection of the person dreaming, and thence into the sight of the thought, for when man dreams, his natural understanding is laid asleep, and his spiritual sight is opened, which derives its all from the affection; but in this passage is meant the sight which derives its all from an evil affection, for it is said concerning the prophets who teach falses, and who dream vain things, for by other gods are understood the falses and vain things which they heard and saw. That signs signify testifications, which indicate and persuade to believe, appears from the following passages: as in Moses: "If they will not believe thee, nor hear the voice of the first sign, yet they will believe the voice of the latter sign: and if they will not believe these two signs, nor hear thy voice, thou shalt take of the waters of the river, and they shall become blood" (Exod. iv. 8, 9); speaking of the miracles performed by Moses, when the Lord appeared to him in the bush, which are called signs, because they were to testify and persuade them to believe that Moses was sent to lead them out of Egypt, wherefore it is three times said that

they may believe, and also that they may hear his voice.   Again:
" Jehovah said unto Moses, how long will this people not believe
in Me, for all the signs which I have done in the midst of them : all
the men who have seen My glory, and the signs which I did in
Egypt and in the wilderness, shall not see the land" (Numb. xiv.
11, 22); here likewise miracles are called signs, because mention is
made of believing ; for, as has been already said, miracles are called
signs, by reason of their tendency to persuade and induce faith;
and whereas signs, with those who, by reason of fear, were not willing to enter into the land of Canaan, did not induce faith, therefore
it is said concerning them, that they should not see the land.   Similar things are signified by signs in Exod. xiv. 17; and chap. x. 1, 2.
Again in the evangelists: "The scribes and Pharisees said, Master,
we desire to see from thee a sign : and He answering said, a wicked
and adulterous generation seeketh a sign, but no sign shall be given
to it except the sign of Jonas the prophet; even as Jonas was in the
whale's belly three days and three nights, so shall the Son of Man
be in the belly of the earth three days and three nights" (Matthew
xii. 38, 39, 40; Luke xi. 16, 29, 30).   That by a sign is here understood testification that they might be persuaded and might believe that the Lord was the Messiah and the Son of God who was
to come, is evident, for the miracles which the Lord performed in
great abundance, and which they saw, were no signs to them, by
reason that miracles, as was said above, are signs only with the
good : the reason why Jonas was in the belly of the whale three
days and three nights, and that this was taken for a sign, was, because it signified the burial and resurrection of the Lord, thus the plenary glorification of His human [principle] ; three days and three
nights also signify to the full. Again in Matthew: "The Pharisees and
the Sadducees, tempting, asked Jesus to show them a sign from heaven: He answering said when it is evening, ye say, it will be serene, for
the heaven is red: and in the morning, it will be tempestuous to-day, for
the heaven is red and lowering; ye hypocrites, ye know how to discern
the face of the heaven, but the signs of the times ye cannot; a wicked
and adulterous nation requireth a sign, but no sign shall be given to it,
except the sign of the prophet Jonas" (xvi. 1-4).   By the sign which
they asked from heaven, is here also understood testification, that
they might be persuaded and believe that the Lord was the Son of
God, although miracles were performed, which they did not call
signs : the reason why the Lord then spake of evening and of morning is, because by evening and morning is signified the advent of the
· Lord, and, in the present case, when the church with the Jews was
devastated, who were then in a state of serenity, because they knew
not the Lord, and lived securely in falses from evil; this is the evening ; but when they knew Him, and by reason of falses from evils
in which they were, denied Him, and assaulted, this state is signified by the morning when it is tempestuous; hence it is, that the
Lord said, ye hypocrites, ye know how to discern the face of the
heaven, but the signs of the times, viz. His advent, ye cannot: and
because they were a depraved and adulterous nation, viz. that adul-

terated the Word, therefore He said, that a sign should not be given them. Thus also in Mark: " The Pharisees began to dispute with Jesus, seeking of him a sign from heaven; and He, sighing in His spirit, said, why doth this generation seek after a sign? verily I say unto you, a sign shall not be given unto this generation" (viii. 11, 12). That a sign here signifies testification, from which they might manifestly know, acknowledge, and believe, that the Lord was the Messiah and Son of God whom they expected from the predictions in the prophets, may appear from Jesus sighing in spirit, and saying, why doth this generation seek after a sign, verily I say unto you, a sign shall not be given to this generation; the reason whereof was, because if this had been manifestly revealed or told them from heaven, and they had thereby been persuaded, so as to acknowledge and believe, still they would have afterwards rejected, and to reject after acknowledgment and faith is to profane, and the lot of profaners in hell is the worst of all; that on this account manifest testification was not given them from heaven, appears from these words in John: " He hath blinded their eyes and hardened their hearts, that they may not see with their eyes and understand with their heart, and convert themselves, and I might heal them" (xii. 40); where to convert themselves and be healed implies to profane, as is the case when truths and goods are acknowledged, especially when the Lord is acknowledged, and afterwards denied; this would have been the case, if the Jews had converted themselves by a sign and been healed; to see with the eyes and understand with the heart, signifies, to receive in the understanding and will, or in the faith and love: from these considerations it is evident, that a sign signifies manifest testification; concerning the lot of profaners see the D. of the N. J. n. 172. Again in John: " The disciples said unto Jesus, what sign showest Thou, what dost Thou work, that we may see and believe Thee? our fathers did eat manna in the wilderness, as it is written, He gave them bread out of heaven to eat. Jesus said unto them, verily, verily, I say unto you, Moses gave you not bread from heaven, but my father giveth you the true bread from heaven; for the bread of God is He who descendeth from heaven and giveth life to the world" (vi. 30–33). Here also the disciples desired a sign; and that thereby is signified testification that they might be-'eve, appears from their saying, what dost Thou work that we may ee and believe? the reason why they then spake concerning manna, ınd the Lord answered concerning bread from heaven, was, because ɒy bread is signified all good and truth which nourishes the soul, and in the supreme sense the Lord Himself, from whom is the all of doctrine and the all of spiritual nourishment, by which He testified that they may see and believe; that nevertheless testification, which is a sign from heaven, was given to the three disciples, Peter, James, and John, appears from the transformation of the Lord, for then they saw His glory, and also heard a voice out of heaven, saying, " This is my beloved Son, hear ye Him" (Matt. xv. 5; Mark ix. 7; Luke ix. 35). Again in John: " When Jesus cast out of the temple them that sold therein, the Jews said, what sign showest Thou that Thou doest these things? Jesus answered and said to them, dissolve this temple, yet in three days I will raise it up" (ii. 16, 18, 19). That by showing a sign is here signified to testify by somewhat stupendous, or by a voice from heaven, is evident; but whereas such testification would rather have condemned than saved them, as has been said just above, therefore He answered them concerning the temple, by which He understood His body, that this should be dissolved, that is, should die, and rise again glorified the third day; this also is what the Lord understood by the sign of Jonah in the belly of the whale three days and three nights; that by temple, in the supreme sense, is signified the Lord's body, may be seen in John ii. 21. Again, in Luke: "The angel said to the shepherds, To-day is born to you a Savior, who is Christ the Lord, in the city of David; and this shall be a sign to you, ye shall find the infant wrapped in swaddling clothes lying in a manger" (ii. 11, 12, 16). Inasmuch as by a sign is understood testification that they might believe that the Savior of the world was born, therefore it is said, that they should find him lying in a manger wrapped in swaddling clothes; but that this was a testification cannot be known to any, unless it be known what is understood by a manger, and what by swaddling clothes; by a manger is understood the doctrine of truth from the Word, by reason that horses signify the understanding of the Word, as may appear from the things shown above, n. 355, 364, and in the small work concerning the W. H. n. 2, 3, 4; hence by a manger where horses are fed, is signified the doctrine of truth from the Word: it is said also in verse 7 of that chapter, that this was done, because there was no place in the inn, for by an inn is signified a place of instruction, as also in Luke x. 34; chap. xxii. 11; Mark xiv. 14, and elsewhere; and this was the case with the Jews, who were then in mere falses, by the adulteration of the Word: this therefore is what is signified by there being no place in the inn; for if it had pleased the Lord, he could have been born in the most splendid palace, and reposed in a bed adorned with precious stones, but this would have been among those who were not in any doctrine of truth, nor in any heavenly representation; it is also said that He was wrapped in swaddling clothes, because swaddling clothes signify the first truths, which are truths of innocence, which also are truths of divine love; for nakedness, when predicated of an infant, signifies the deprivation of truth: from these considerations it may appear whence it was, that it was said by the angels, this shall be a sign unto you, ye shall find the infant wrapped in swaddling clothes lying in a manger. Again, it is written in the Evangelists: "The disciples said unto Jesus, what shall be the sign of Thy coming and of the consummation of the age?" (Matt. xxiv. 3; Mark xiii. 4; Luke xxi. 7.) By the coming of the Lord and the consummation of the age, is signified the beginning of the new church and the end of the former church, by the coming of the Lord, the beginning of a new church, and by the consummation of the age, the end of the old church, wherefore in those chapters the Lord instructs His disciples concerning the successive vastation of the former church, and concerning the establishment of the new church at the end thereof; but He instructs and teaches them by mere correspondences, which cannot be unfolded and known except by the spiritual sense, and inasmuch as the expressions by which the Lord spake were correspondences, therefore they were all signs, consequently testifications : they are also called signs by the Lord in Luke : " There shall also be terrible and great signs from heaven : there shall be signs in the sun, the moon, and the stars, and upon the earth straitness of nations in desperation, the sea and the billows resounding" (xxi. 11, 25) ; and in Matthew : " And then shall appear the sign of the Son of Man ; and then shall all the tribes of the earth wail, and they shall see the Son of Man coming in the clouds of heaven with power and great glory" (xxiv. 30). What is signified by these and the other things contained in the same chapter in the spiritual sense, may be seen in the A. C.; and what is signified by the appearance of the Son of Man in the clouds of heaven, in the work concerning H. & H. n. 1; wherefore it is unnecessary to explain them further in this place. Again, in Mark : " Jesus said unto the disciples, these signs shall follow them that believe ; in my name they shall cast out demons ; they shall speak with new tongues ; they shall take up serpents ; if they drink any deadly thing, it shall not hurt them ; they shall lay hands on the infirm, and they shall recover. And they went out and preached every where, the Lord working with them by signs following" (xvi. 17, 18, 20). Although these were miracles, yet they were called signs, because they testified of the divine power of the Lord who operated them, wherefore it is said, the Lord working with them by those signs ; they would have been called miracles, if applied to the evil, for with them such things only induce a stupor and strike the mind, and yet do not persuade to believe ; but the case is otherwise with the good, for with these the same things are testifications which persuade to believe, wherefore also they are called signs, and it is said, these signs shall follow them that believe. But how those signs would persuade to believe, shall also be briefly explained ; those miraculous signs, as that they should cast out demons, speak with new tongues, take up serpents, that if they drank any deadly thing it should not hurt them, and that they should restore the sick by the laying on of hands, were in their essence and in their origin spiritual, from which those things flowed and came forth as effects : for they were correspondences, which derive their all from the spiritual world by influx from the Lord ; as that they should cast out demons in the name of the Lord, derived all its effects from this circumstance, that the name of the Lord spiritually understood is the all of doctrine out of the Word from the Lord, and that demons are falses of every kind, which are so cast out, that is, removed, by doctrine out of the Word from the Lord ; that they should speak with new tongues, derives its effect from this, that new tongues denote doctrinals for the new church; that they should take up serpents was, because serpents signify the hells as to malice, and so that they should be safe from the infestation thereof; that they should not be hurt if they drank the deadly thing, denoted that the malice of the hells should not infect them ;

and their restoring the infirm by laying on of hands, signified, that by communication and conjunction with heaven, thus with the Lord, they should restore to health from spiritual diseases, which are called iniquities and sins, the laying on of the hands of the disciples corresponding to communication and conjunction with the Lord, and so as to the removal of iniquities by His divine power.   Thus also in Isaiah : " Jehovah said unto Ahaz, ask thee a sign of Jehovah ; direct into the deep, or lift up above; the Lord giveth you a sign ; behold a virgin shall conceive and bring forth a son, and shall call His name God with us" (vii. 11, 14).   The reason why these things were said to Ahaz, king of Judah is, because the king of Syria and the king of Israel made war against him, even unto Jerusalem, on whose side also was the tribe of Ephraim, but still they did not prevail, by reason that the king of Syria there represented the external or natural [principle] of the church, the king of Israel the internal or spiritual [principle] thereof, and Ephraim the intellectual [principle], but in this case, those three principles, namely, the natural, spiritual, and intellectual, perverted, which were desirous to assault the doctrine of truth, signified by the king of Judah and Jerusalem, wherefore they did not succeed; but in order that Ahaz might be assured of their attempt being in vain, it is said to him, that he might ask a sign, that is, a testification that he might be assured, and option was given him, whether it should be from heaven or from hell, which was signified by direct into the deep, or lift up above; for the king was evil, but whereas Jerusalem, by which is signified the doctrine of truth from the Word, was not to be destroyed by such before the advent of the Lord, therefore a miraculous sign was given to him testifying concerning that subject, viz. that a virgin shall conceive and bring forth a son, whose name shall be God with us : that that church should afterwards be destroyed, follows in that chapter. Again, in the same prophet : " This shall be a sign to thee from with Jehovah, behold I will bring back the shadow of the degrees which is gone down in the sun-dial of Ahaz, ten degrees backward, that the sign may return ten degrees in the degrees which it hath gone down" (xxxviii. 7, 8).   This sign was given to king Hezekiah for a testification that the Lord would defend him and Jerusalem from the king of Assyria, as is said verse 6 of that chapter, by which king was signified the rational principle perverted, destroying all things of the church, wherefore by this sign in like manner was represented the new church, which was to be established by the Lord, but in this case that the time which was told to Ahaz just above, should be further protracted ; by the retraction of the shadow which was gone down in the sun-dial of Ahaz, is signified the retraction of the time before it should take place, the degrees of the sun-dial of Ahaz signifying the time until the advent of the Lord, and the shadow the progression of time from the rising to the setting ; by its being drawn backwards ten degrees, is signified the prolongation of the time as yet by several years, for ten signify several or more, and by the sun which should go back, is signified the advent of the Lord; but this is to be further illustrated ; the advent of the Lord took place when the Jewish church was at an end, that is, when there was not any good and truth therein remaining ; this is understood by, when iniquity was consummated, and also by the fulness of times, in which the Lord was to come ; the entire time of the duration of the Jewish church was represented by the degrees of the sun-dial of Ahaz, the beginning thereof by the first degree, which is when the sun is in its rising, and the end thereof by the last degree in the setting ; hence it is evident, that by the retraction of the shade from the setting towards the rising is understood the prolongation of that time ; the reason why this came to pass in the degrees of the sun dial of Ahaz, was, because Ahaz was a wicked king, and profaned the holy things of the church, wherefore if his successors had done in like manner, the end of the church would have been brought on shortly ; but as Hezekiah was an upright king, the time was prolonged, for thereby the iniquity of that nation did not so soon arrive at its consummation, that is, at its end. Again, in the same prophet : " Say ye unto the king Hezekiah, this shall be a sign to thee, in this year ye shall eat that which springeth up spontaneously, and in the second year that which further groweth from the same ; but in the third year, sow ye, reap, and plant vineyards, and earth the fruit thereof" (xxxvii. 30). This was said to Hezekiah the king, when Senacherib, king of Assyria, made war against him, and spake proudly of himself, and contumeliously of God and of Israel, wherefore also one hundred and eighty thousand were smitten in his camp, and himself was slain by his sons ; the reason why this was done was, because by Assyria is signified the rational [principle], and the same by the king of Assyria, and by Judea, the celestial [principle] of the church, and the spiritual [principle] by the king thereof ; but in this case by the king of Assyria is signified the rational [principle] perverted, which by false reasonings destroys all the celestial and spiritual things of the church, which are the goods and truths thereof ; and inasmuch as by Judea and by the king thereof is signified the celestial and spiritual principle of the church, which should be from the Lord when He came into the world, therefore such things are said, by which is described the regeneration of those who should be of that church ; wherefore by the sign, that they should eat in the first year that which springs up spontaneously, is signified celestial good which shall be implanted in them from the Lord ; by that which grows further in the second year, is signified the truth of that good which shall thence be derived ; by sowing, reaping, planting vineyards, and eating the fruit thereof, are signified all the goods and truths which thence flow forth ; by sowing and reaping is signified the implantation of good and reception thereof ; by planting vineyards the implantation of truth and reception thereof ; and by eating the fruits of them, the fruition of goods, and satisfaction thence derived, appertaining to the regenerate man ; these things are called a sign, because they are testifications concerning the celestial church with those who are understood in the spiritual sense by Judah, whose regeneration is effected from the Lord by the implantation of celestial good, afterwards by the implantation of spiritual good which in its essence is the truth of celestial good, and lastly, by multiplication and fructification in the natural man. Again: "Thus saith Jehovah, the Holy One of Israel, and his Former: They asked of Me signs concerning My sons, and concerning the work of M hands they command Me; I have raised him up in justice and I will rectify all his ways. He shall build My city and let go my captivity, not for price, neither reward" (xlv. 11, 13). The subject treated of there also is concerning the advent of the Lord, and the establishment of the church from him: the Lord is understood by Jehovah, the Holy one of Israel, and his Former, who is called the Holy One of Israel from divine truth, and his Former from the establishment of the church thereby; and Israel denotes the church; therefore by His sons concerning whom they asked signs, are understood those who are in truths from the Lord, and by the work of His hands, is understood their formation, and the establishment of the church with them; I have raised Him up in justice, and all His ways will I rectify, signifies that to Him appertain divine good and divine truth, for justice, in the Word, is predicated of good, and ways signify truths leading, in this case, divine truths, because predicated of the Lord; He shall build my city, and my captivity He shall let go, signifies that He shall restore the doctrine of truth, and, that He shall liberate those who are in falses from ignorance, for a city signifies the doctrine of truth, and captivity the falses of ignorance, in which the gentiles were, and thereby in spiritual captivity; not for price neither reward, signifies gratis from love divine. Again: "Let them relate to you the things which shall happen, declare ye those former things, and we will set our heart, and know the latter end of them; or cause us to hear things to come, declare to us a sign for the future, that we may know that ye are gods" (xli. 22, 23). That to tell things past and to come belongs to the Lord alone, and not to any man or any spirit, is expressed by declaring a sign for the future, that we may know that ye are gods; this concludes the things which precede, wherefore to declare a sign is to testify by persuading to believe. Thus also in Ezekiel: "Take to thee a pan of iron, and set it for a wall of iron betwixt thee and the city, and thou shalt set thy faces against it, that it may be for a siege, and thou shalt straiten it: this [shall be] a sign to the house of Israel" (iv. 3). These and the rest of the things in that chapter are representative of the state of the church with the Jewish nation, signifying that there was not with them any truth but what was falsified and adulterated, which in itself is false; such truth is signified by the pan of iron which he should set for a wall between him and the city; and whereas this, like iron, is hard, secluding and admitting not any genuine truth, it is said, that it may be for a siege, and thou shalt straiten it; that this sign should witness concerning the church as being such, is signified by this shall be a sign to the house of Israel, a sign denoting testification, and the house of Israel the church. So in David: "The enemy hath destroyed all things in the sanctuary; the enemies roared in the midst of thy feast: they have set their signs [for] signs. We see not our signs, there is no more a prophet" (Psalm lxxiv. 3, 4, 9). The enemy has destroyed all things in the sanctuary, signifies, that evil has destroyed the holy things of the church: the enemies have roared in the midst of thy feast, signifies, that falses have destroyed all things of worship: they have set their signs for signs, signifies, that they have testified and persuaded by every means; we see not our signs, signifies, that no testifications of truth were received in the church; there is no more a prophet, signifies no doctrine of truth. Again: "Jehovah make me a sign for good, that my haters may see and be ashamed, that Thou Jehovah hast helped me, and consoled me" (Psalm lxxxvi. 17). To make a sign for good, signifies testification, that Jehovah will help and console him, as it follows, for this is the good for which Jehovah makes a sign; and because a sign is thus for a testification thereof, therefore it is said, that my haters may see and be ashamed. Again: "God who strengtheneth the mountains by His might, is girded with power; who maketh the tumult of the seas to cease, the tumult of the waves thereof and the noise of the people, that the inhabitants of the ends may fear from thy signs" (Psalm lxv. 7, 8). Thus is described the divine power of the Lord, by things testifying that they may believe; but the things testifying, which are signs, are not that He strengtheneth the mountains, maketh the tumult of the seas and of the waves thereof to cease, and the noise of the people, for these are not such signs as can persuade those who ascribe all things to nature, but those things are the signs, testifying the divine power of the Lord, which are understood in the spiritual sense, in which heaven and the church are the subjects treated of; for in that sense, by the mountains which God strengtheneth by His might, are understood the superior heavens, because the angels of those heavens dwell upon mountains, and in the abstract sense is understood love to the Lord and neighborly love; these are what the Lord, being girded with power, strengtheneth by His might, that is, makes them to subsist for ever; that mountains have such a signification, may be seen above, n. 405; by the tumult of the seas and the tumult of the waves, are understood the disputations and ratiocinations of those who are beneath the heavens, and are natural and sensual; that seas signify those things which appertain to the natural man, thus those who are natural, and that hence the tumults and waves thereof signify their disputations and ratiocinations, may be seen also above, n. 342; by the noise of the people are understood contradictions from falses, for by people are signified those who are in truths, and, in the opposite sense, who are in falses, as may be seen above, n. 175, 331, 625; that the inhabitants of the ends may fear from thy signs, signifies holy worship from faith concerning the divine power with those who are in the ultimates of heaven and the church; that to fear denotes to worship the Lord from charity and faith, may be seen above, n. 696; and that the inhabitants of the ends denote those who are in the ultimates of heaven and the church, and there in the faith of charity, appears from this consideration, that the ends are the ultimates of heaven and the church: from these considerations it may appear, that signs here signify testifications concerning the divine power of the Lord. Again, in Jeremiah : "This shall be a sign to you, that I will visit upon you in this place, that ye may know that My words stand upon you for evil ; behold I give the king of Egypt into the hand of his enemies, and into the hand of them that seek his soul" (xliv. 29, 30). The subject there treated of is concerning those of the church who were become natural, who are understood by them that sojourned into Egypt, and thence returned : that they were to be destroyed by evils and falses, is understood by the king of Egypt being to be given into the hand of his enemies, and into the hand of them that seek his soul, enemies there denoting those who are in evils, and them that seek the soul, those who are in falses, thus, abstractedly, evils and falses ; that Egypt is the natural man, may be seen above, n. 654 ; this is called a sign, because it is a testification that the things should come to pass, wherefore it is said, that ye may know that My words shall stand upon you for evil. That a sign denotes testification concerning the certainty of a thing, appears also from the following passages : thus in Isaiah : "Hezekiah said, what is the sign that I am to go up into the house of Jehovah" (xxxviii. 12) : and in the book of Judges : "Gideon said unto the angel of Jehovah, show me a sign that thou art he who speaketh to me : which sign was, that when he touched with the staff the flesh and leavened cakes, which Gideon offered, a fire would come up out of the rock, and consume them" (vi. 17, 21) : and in Samuel : "This shall be a sign to thee, which shall come upon thy two sons ; in one day they shall both die" (ii. 34) : and in the same book : "If the Philistines say, come up unto us, then will we come up, because Jehovah hath given them into our hands : this shall be a sign to us" (xiv. 10). Almost similar things are signified by the "Signs of the covenant" (Gen. ix. 13 ; chap. xvii. 11 ; Ezek. xx. 12, 20 ; and elsewhere), viz. testifications concerning conjunction. Testifications are also signified by the signs, which appeared as miracles, performed by them that were evil, in the following passages : thus in Isaiah : "Jehovah rendereth vain the signs of the liars, he rendereth the diviners insane, rejecting the wise man backward, and maketh their science foolish" (xliv. 25) : and in Jeremiah : "Jehovah saith, learn not the way of the nations, and be not dismayed at the signs of the heavens, for the nations are dismayed at them, the statutes of the nations are vanity" (x. 2, 3) : and in the Apocalypse : "The beast that ascendeth out of the earth made great signs, so that he even maketh fire to come down from heaven to the earth before men, and seduceth them that worship upon the earth, on account of the signs which were given him to make" (xiii. 13, 14) : again : "They are the spirits of demons, making signs to go forth unto the kings of the earth, to gather them together to the war of that great day" (xvi. 14) : and again : "The beast was taken, and with him the false prophet, who made signs before them, by which he seduced those who received the mark of the beast" (xix. 20). But what is understood by signs upon the hand and in the forehead, may be seen above, n. 427.   But the signs which were set upon the mountains to gather the people together to war, to battle, and so on, signified indications to the performance of things commanded: as in Isaiah : " In that day there shall be a root of Jesse, which shall stand for a sign of the people : [to it] shall the nations seek, and his rest shall be glory.   When he shall lift up a sign to the nations, and shall gather together the outcasts of Israel and the dispersed of Judah from the four winds of the earth" (xi. 10, 11, 12) : and in Jeremiah : " Set thee up signs, make thee pillars, set thy heart to the highway, the way thou goest" (xxxi. 21) : again : " Announce amongst the nations, and cause [it] to be heard, and lift up a sign, Babel is taken" (1, 2) : and again : " Against the walls of Babel lift up a sign, keep custody, appoint guards : lift up a sign in the land, sound the trumpet amongst the nations" (li. 12, 17) : besides other passages, especially in the historical parts of the Word.   From all that has been adduced from the Word, it may appear, that by a great sign seen in heaven is signified divine manifestation and testification ; as also in verse 3 of this chapter, and afterwards in chap. xv. 1.

707. " A woman encompassed with the sun"—That hereby is signified the church with those who are in love to the Lord, and thence in love towards their neighbor, appears from the signification of woman, as denoting the spiritual affection of-truth, by virtue of which the church is a church, consequently also the church as to that affection, concerning which see above, n. 555 ; that it is the new church to be established by the Lord after the end of the present church in the christian world, follows of consequence ; and from the signification of the sun, as denoting the Lord as to divine love, thus also love to the Lord from the Lord, concerning which also see above, n. 401, 412 ; and from the signification of being encompassed, as denoting to live from it, for the life of the love of every one, as well of man as of a spirit and angel, forms a sphere about them, from which they are perceived, even afar off, as to their quality ; by that sphere also consociations and conjunctions are effected in the heavens, and also in the hells ; and whereas the subject here treated of is concerning the church which is in love to the Lord from the Lord, and that church is understood by the woman, and that love by the sun, hence by the woman encompassed with the sun is signified the church with those who are in love to the Lord from the Lord : the reason why it is also said, and thence in love towards their neighbor, is, because neighborly love is derived from love to the Lord, as a posterior [principle] from its prior, or as what is exterior from its interior, in a word, as an effect from its efficient cause ; for love to the Lord is to love and to will those things which are of the Lord, consequently those things which the Lord has commanded in the Word, and love towards the neighbor is from that will to do, thus consisting in the performance of uses, which are effects.   That by this woman is signified the new church, which is to be established by the Lord, after the end of this which is in the christian world, may appear from the things which follow in this

chapter; namely, that she brought forth a male son, which the dragon desired to devour, and which was caught up to God, and that
the woman fled into a wilderness, where also the dragon was desirous to destroy her; for from what follows it will appear, that by
the male son is understood the truth of the doctrine of that church,
and by the dragon are understood those who are against the truths
of that doctrine; that the church which is here understood by the
woman is the same church with the New Jerusalem, which is described chap. xxi. and is called the bride, the lamb's wife, verse 9,
will be seen in the explication of that chapter.

708. "And the moon under her feet"—That hereby is signified
faith with those who are natural and in charity, appears from the
signification of the moon, as denoting faith in which is charity, concerning which we shall speak presently; and from the signification
of feet, as denoting things natural, concerning which see above, n.
69, 600, 632; in this case, therefore, those who are natural, because
it is said concerning the woman, by whom is signified the church,
and by the sun with which she was encompassed, love to the Lord
from the Lord and neighborly love, as was shown in the preceding
article: hence by the woman encompassed with the sun, is signified
the church with those who are celestial and thence spiritual, and by
the moon under her feet is signified the church with those who are
natural and sensual, and at the same time in the faith of charity:
for the goods and thence the truths of heaven and the church succeed in order, as the head, the body, and the feet with man: in the
head of the grand man, which is heaven, are those who are in love
to the Lord from the Lord, and these are called celestial; but in the
body, from the breast even to the loins of that grand man, which is
heaven, are those who are in love towards their neighbor and
these are called spiritual; but in the feet of the grand man, which is
heaven, are those who are obscurely in the faith of charity, and
these are called natural. But in order that this may be clearly understood, it is to be observed, that there are two kingdoms into
which the heavens are distinguished, one which is called the celestial, and the other the spiritual; and that there are three heavens,
a supreme which is called celestial, a middle which is called spiritual, and an ultimate or last which is celestial and spiritual natural.
But besides these distinctions of the heavens, there is also a further
distinction, there being some who receive light, that is intelligence,
from the Lord as a sun, and some who receive light and intelligence
from the Lord as a moon: they who receive the light of intelligence
from the Lord as a sun, are those with whom the intellectual principle, and the rational thereof, have been open, and who from a spiritual affection of truth thence derived, thought rationally concerning
things to be believed; but they who receive light from the Lord as
a moon, are those with whom the intellectual and rational principle
was not interiorly opened, but only the natural, and who thence,
from the memory, thought concerning things to be believed, and to
think of such things from the memory, is to think only from such

things as they have heard from masters or preachers, which they say and also believe to be truths, although they might be falses, for they do not see them from any further ground: these also, if they were in the faith of charity during their abode in the world, are in the heavens under the Lord as a moon, for the lumen, from which their intelligence is derived, is as the lumen of the moon in the night time, whereas the light from which their intelligence is derived who are in the heavens under the Lord as a sun, is as the light of day: what the difference is, may appear from the difference of the light of the sun in the day and of the moon in the night: the difference herein also is such, that they who are under the Lord as a moon, cannot see any thing in the light of those who are under the Lord as a sun, by reason that with them there is not genuine light, but a reflected light, which can receive falses, if good only appear in them, equally as truths.   Inasmuch as they who are in the heavens under the Lord as a moon are all natural and sensual, and have nothing in common with those who are in the heavens under the Lord as a sun, and also are in falses, in which however there is good, hence the moon was seen under the feet of the woman, and thereby is understood the faith which is with those who are natural.   So far concerning the faith with those who are in the heaven under the Lord as a moon; something shall also be briefly said concerning their affection, from which faith derives its life : their affection of knowing truth and doing good, is, like themselves, natural, deriving its quality more or less from the glory of erudition, and from fame, which has respect to honors and gain as rewards, herein differing from the spiritual affection of knowing truth and doing good which has place with those who are in heaven under the Lord as a sun, for with these, this affection is separated from natural affection, so that the latter is under the feet; hence also it is, that the moon, by which not only faith, but also the affection thereof, is signified, was here seen under the feet.   But a fuller idea upon this subject, may be obtained from what is said and shown in the work concerning H. & H.; as that heaven is distinguished into two kingdoms, n. 20–28: concerning the sun and moon in heaven, and concerning the light and heat in the heavens, n. 116–140; concerning the correspondence of heaven with all things of man, n. 103–115: and in the D. of the N. J. concerning those who are in falses from good, n. 21.   That the sun signifies the Lord as to divine love, and thence love to the Lord from the Lord, and that the moon signifies the truth of faith, may be seen above, n. 401.   And moreover concerning the heavens which are under the Lord as a sun, and as a moon, see n. 411, 422, 527, also above.   To which it may be added, that those heavens which are under the Lord as a moon, are also three, superior, middle, and inferior, or what is the same, interior, middle, and exterior, but still all in these heavens are natural : the reason why they are interior, middle, and exterior, is, because the natural [principle] is distinguished into three degrees in like manner as the spiritual ; the exterior natural communicates with the world, the interior with heaven, and the middle conjoins; but still they who are in the heavens under the Lord as a moon, cannot enter into the heavens which are under the Lord as a sun, because their interior sight or understanding is formed to receive the lunar light there, and not to receive the solar light: they are comparatively not unlike those birds who see in the night and not in the day time, wherefore when they come into the solar light which they enjoy who are under the Lord as a sun, their sight is darkened. But they who are in those heavens, are such as were in charity according to their religious principle, or according to their faith; whereas they who were merely natural, and not in a faith grounded in charity, are in the hells under those heavens. From these considerations it may appear, that by the moon is here understood faith with those who are natural and in charity; and that the moon was seen under the feet, because they who are in the heavens under the Lord as a moon have nothing common with those who are in the heavens under the Lord as a sun, insomuch that they cannot rise up unto them.

709. "And upon her head a crown of twelve stars"—That hereby is signified the wisdom and intelligence of those who are of that church, by the doctrinals and knowledges of all things appertaining to truth and good from the Word, appears from the signification of the head, as denoting wisdom and intelligence, concerning which see above, n. 553, 578, in the present case, the wisdom and intelligence of those who are of that church which is signified by the woman encompassed with the sun, and the moon under her feet; and from the signification of a crown, as also denoting wisdom and intelligence, concerning which also see above, n. 126, 218, 272; and from the signification of stars, as denoting doctrinals and knowledges of truth and good from the Word, concerning which see, n. 72, 402, 535: and from the signification of twelve, as denoting all, and as being predicated of truths and goods, see n. 430; hence it may appear that by the crown of twelve stars upon the head of the woman, is signified the wisdom and intelligence of those who are of that church, by the doctrinals and knowledges of all things appertaining to truth and good from the Word. The reason why this is said concerning the woman encompassed with the sun and the moon under her feet, and follows immediately after this description of her, is, because the sun signifies celestial and spiritual love, and the moon, faith originating in charity, and from these flow forth all wisdom and intelligence; for from the Lord as a sun proceeds heat and light, and heat is the good of love and light is the truth from that good, and these two constitute wisdom and intelligence with angels and men, for the good of love enters their will, and the truth from that good enters their understanding, and in the will and understanding together resides wisdom.

710. "And she bearing in the womb"—That hereby is signified doctrine nascent from the good of celestial love, appears from the signification of bearing in the womb, when predicated of the church, which is signified by the woman, as denoting the doctrine of truth nascent from the good of celestial love; for by the womb is signified inmost conjugial love, and thence celestial love in every com-

plex, and by the embryo in the womb, the truth of doctrine from the good of celestial love, the same as by the male son which the woman brought forth, which is treated of in the following verse, by whom is signified the doctrine of truth from the good of love, with the difference, that the embryo, being as yet in the womb, derives more from the good of innocence than after it is born, hence by embryo is signified the doctrine of truth equally as by son, but by the latter is signified the doctrine itself, whereas by the former is signified nascent doctrine. From these considerations then it is evident, that by bearing in the womb is signified the doctrine of truth nascent from the good of celestial love. The reason why the womb signifies the inmost good of love, is, because all the members allotted to generation, as well with males as females, signify conjugial love, and the womb, the inmost [principle] thereof, because there the fœtus is conceived, and takes its growth, until it is born ; it is also the inmost of the genital members, and from it is also derived the maternal love, which is called storge. Inasmuch as man who is regenerating is also conceived, and as it were carried in the womb and born, and inasmuch as regeneration is effected by truths from the good of love, hence by carrying in the womb, in the spiritual sense, is signified the doctrine of truth from the good of love ; there is also a correspondence of the womb with the inmost good of love ; for the universal heaven corresponds to all things with man, concerning which correspondence see the work concerning H. & H. n. 87–102 ; this is also the case with the members allotted to generation, and these correspond there to celestial love : this love also flows in out of heaven with mothers during the time of gestation, and also with the embryos ; hence exists the love of the infant with mothers, and innocence with infants. From these considerations it may appear whence it is, that the womb signifies the inmost good of love, and that gestation signifies the doctrine of truth nascent from the good of love. That such things are signified by the womb, and by carrying in the womb may appear from the following passages in the Word ; as in Isaiah : "Attend unto me, O house of Jacob, and all the remains of the house of Israel carried from the womb, borne from the matrix, even unto old age ; I am the same, and even to hoariness I will carry ; I have made, I will carry, and I will bear and rescue" (xlvi. 3, 4) ; treating of the reformation of the church, and of the regeneration of the men of the church by the Lord ; the church is signified by the house of Jacob and by the house of Israel, the external church by the house of Jacob, and the internal by the house of Israel ; by them that are carried from the womb are signified those who are regenerating by the Lord, and by them that are borne from the matrix are signified the regenerate ; inasmuch as the man who is regenerating is first conceived by the Lord, and afterwards born, and lastly educated and perfected, and inasmuch as regeneration is in this respect like to the natural generation of man, therefore by being carried from the womb is signified the state of the man to be regenerated from conception to nativity ; the nativity itself, and afterwards education and perfection, being signified by being

borne from the matrix, even unto old age, I am the same, and even
to hoariness I will carry : like things are signified by, I have made,
I will carry, and I will bear and rescue ; but by the former expressions is understood regeneration by the goods of love and charity,
and by the latter is understood regeneration by truths from those
goods ; by rescuing is understood to take away and remove evils
and falses which are from hell.   So in Hosea : " Ephraim, his glory
shall fly away as a bird, from the birth, and from the belly, and from
conception : yea, though they have brought up their sons, yet will
I make them bereaved of man [homo].   Give to them, O Jehovah,
an abortive matrix and dry paps.   Ephraim is smitten, their root is
dried up, they shall not bear fruit, even when they have generated
I will slay the desires of their belly" (ix. 11, 12, 14, 16).   By Ephraim
is understood the church as to the understanding of truth and good :
that there would be no more any understanding of divine truth in
the church, is signified by, Ephraim, his glory shall fly away as a
bird, glory signifying divine truth, and to fly away signifying to be
dissipated ; it is said to fly away, because mention is made of a bird,
and mention is made of a bird, because by birds are signified things
appertaining to the understanding and the thought thence derived ;
from the birth, and from the belly, and from conception, signifies,
the dissipation of all truth from the ultimates thereof to first [princi-
ples], the birth signifying the ultimates thereof, because that which
is born from the belly and from conception signifies what is before
nativity, thus all things from ultimates to first principles, for when
the ultimates perish, things prior also successively fall away ; though
they have brought up sons, I will make them bereaved of man, signifies, although they have procured for themselves truths, yet still
they will be without intelligence, sons denoting the truths of the
church, and man denoting intelligence, whence by making them bereaved of man, is signified that still they have not intelligence ; give
them, O Jehovah, an abortive matrix and dry paps, signifies that
they have no more truths from any good, but falses from evil, an
abortive matrix signifying falses from evil in the place of truth from
good, and in like manner dry paps, but matrix signifies truths from
the good of love, and paps truths from the good of charity ; in the
present case, the falses from evil contrary to them ; Ephraim is
smitten, their root is dried up, signifies, that there was no more any
understanding of truth even from first [principles], Ephraim here, as
above, denoting the understanding of the truth of the church, and
root the first principle thereof ; they shall not yield fruit, signifies,
not any good, for where there are not truths there is not good ; even
when they have generated I will slay the desires of their belly, signifies, though they have procured for themselves truths that still they
will perish, the desires of the belly signifying truths procured ; the
belly is mentioned instead of the womb, from the appearance of the
swelling of the belly with those who are with child, but still the
term belly is used where truths are treated of, and the womb where
good is treated of.   And in David : " For thou art my bringer forth
from the womb, making for me confidence from my mother's paps ;

upon Thee have I been cast from the belly of my mother, O Thou my God" (Psalm xxii. 10, 11). Here also is described the spiritual regeneration of man by such things as belong to natural generation from the mother; hence by, Thou art my bringer forth from the womb, is signified to be regenerated from the Lord, and made a man of the church; by, thou makest for me confidence from my mother's paps, is signified the being led afterwards, and spiritually educated, the mother's paps signifying spiritual nourishment in such things as appertain to the church, and mother denoting the church; by, I have been cast upon thee from the womb, is signified, that the Lord operated all things from the good of love; and by, from the belly of my mother, Thou my God, is signified, that he operated all things by truths, for, as was said above, where the subject treated of is concerning the good of love, the term womb is used, and where it 'is concerning truths from that good, the term belly is used; hence also it is said, Thou my God, for where the good of love is treated of, the Lord is called Jehovah, and where truths are treated of, He is called God. And in the Evangelists: "Woe to them that are with child, and to them that give suck in those days" (Matt. xxiv. 19; Mark xiii. 17; Luke xxi. 23). The subject treated of in those chapters is concerning the consummation of the age, whereby is understood the end of the church when the last judgment takes place, hence by those that are with child and those that give suck in those days, over whom lamentation is made, are understood, those who then receive the goods of love and the truths of that good; they that are with child denote those who receive the good of love, and they that give suck denote those who receive the truths of that good, for the milk which is given to suckle signifies truth from the good of love; the reason why it is said, woe unto them, is, because they are not able to keep the goods and truths which they receive, for then hell prevails, and takes them away, whence arises profanation; the reason why hell then prevails is, because in the end of the church the falses of evil reign, and take away the truths of good; for man is held in the midst between heaven and hell, and before the last judgment the influx which arises out of hell prevails over that which descends from heaven; see more particularly upon this subject the work concerning H. & H. n. 538, 540, 541, 546, 589–596; and the small work concerning the L. J. n. 73, 74. Again, in Luke.: "Behold the day shall come, in which they shall say, blessed are the barren and the bellies which have not born and the paps which have not suckled" (xxiii. 29). These words have a similar signification, inasmuch as they are also spoken of the last time of the church, and by the barren, and the bellies that have not born, are signified those who have not received genuine truths, that is, truths from the good of love, and by the paps which have not suckled, are signified those who have not received genuine truths from the good of charity; for all truths are from good, and goods are of two-fold kind, celestial good, which is the good of love to the Lord, and spiritual which is the good of charity towards the neighbor; the nified by paps as by milk, viz. truth from good. Aga'　　e same evangelist: " A woman lifting up her voice from the people said concerning Jesus, blessed is the belly which bare Thee, and the paps which Thou hast sucked; but Jesus said, yea, rather blessed are they who hear the Word of God and keep it" (xi. 27, 28). Inasmuch as to bear in the belly and to give suck with the breasts signifies the regeneration of man, as was said above, therefore the Lord answered, blessed are they who hear the Word of God and keep it, by which is described the regeneration which is effected by truths from the Word, and by a life according to them; by hearing the Word of God is signified to learn truths from the Word, and by keeping it is signified to live according to them. So in John: " Nicodemus said, how can a man be generated when he is old? he cannot enter into the womb of his mother a second time? Jesus answered, verily, I say unto you, unless a man be born of water and the spirit, he cannot enter into the kingdom of the heavens: that which is born of the flesh is flesh, but that which is generated of the spirit is spirit" (iii. 4, 5, 6). That Nicodemus understood natural generation instead of spiritual, concerning which the Lord spake, is evident, wherefore the Lord teaches him concerning regeneration that is effected by truths from the Word, and by a life according thereto, which is signified by being generated of water and the spirit, for water, in the spiritual sense, is truth from the Word, and the spirit is the life according thereto; that man is born natural, and becomes spiritual by a life according to truths from the Word, is signified by, what is born of the flesh is flesh, and what is born of the spirit is spirit; that the natural man, unless he becomes spiritual, cannot be saved, is understood by, unless a man be generated of water and the spirit, he cannot enter into the kingdom of the heavens. Inasmuch as the Lord alone reforms and regenerates men, therefore in the Word He is called the Former from the womb, as in Isaiah: " Jehovah, thy Maker and Former from the womb helpeth thee" (xliv. 2. 24); again: " Jehovah hath called me from the womb, from the bowels of my mother He hath remembered my name. Thus saith Jehovah, my Former from the womb, for His servant, to bring back Jacob unto Himself, and Israel shall be gathered to Him" (xlix. 1, 5). The Lord, in many parts of the Word, is called Creator, Maker, and Former from the womb, and also Redeemer, by reason that He creates man anew, reforms, regenerates, and redeems; it may be supposed that the Lord is so called because He created man and forms him in the womb, but still it is a spiritual creation and formation which is there understood; for the Word is not only natural, but also spiritual, natural for men who are natural, and spiritual for the angels who are spiritual, as may also appear from this consideration, that the things here said, are said concerning Israel, and, in the supreme sense, concerning the Lord; by Israel is understood the church, thus every man of the church; and inasmuch as the Lord knows the quality of every one as to the good of love and truth of faith, therefore it is said, Jehovah hath called me from the womb, from the bowels of my mother he hath remembered my name; ·by calling and knowing the name of any one, is signified to know his quality; from the womb, denotes as to the good of love, and from the bowels of my mother, as to truths from that good; by Jacob who shall be brought back unto Him, and by Israel who shall be gathered to Him, is signified the church, by Jacob the external church, and by Israel the internal church, the latter being in the spiritual man, the former in the natural. And in Jeremiah: " Before I formed thee in the womb I knew thee, and before thou camest forth from the womb I sanctified thee, I will give thee a prophet to the nations" (i. 5). These things are indeed said concerning the prophet Jeremiah, but still by prophet in the spiritual sense is understood one that teaches truth, and in the abstract sense, the doctrine of truth; hence by forming him in the womb and knowing him before he came forth from the womb, is signified foresight that he could be in truth from good by regeneration, thus that he could receive and teach the Word; this is also to sanctify and to give a ·prophet to the nations, the nations denoting those who are in good, and from good receive truths. So in David: "I have been laid upon Thee from the womb, Thou art He that brought me forth from the bowels of my mother" (Psalm lxxi. 6); by which similar things are signified. Again: "Lo sons [are] the heritage of Jehovah, the fruit of the belly a reward" (Psalm cxxvii. 3); where by sons are understood those who are in truths from good, as also in other passages in the Word; and by the fruit of the belly are understood those who are in good by truths, who have heaven, which is the heritage and also reward. Again, in Isaiah: "Can a woman forget her infant, and not have compassion on the son of her belly? yea, though they may forget, yet will I not forget thee" (xlix. 15). This is said, because in the spiritual sense regeneration is understood, wherefore comparison is made with a woman, and her love towards her infant; the case is the same with those who are regenerated by the Lord. Again: "Jehovah sware to David in verity, of the fruit of thy belly will I set upon thy throne" (Psalm cxxxii. 11). By David here, as in other places, is understood the Lord as to the spiritual kingdom, which is His royalty, wherefore by setting the fruit of His belly upon His throne, is understood one who is regenerating by Him, the regenerate being called the fruit of His belly, because they are in truths and in a life according to them; by the throne is understood heaven; those things are what are signified by the above words in their spiritual sense, but in the supreme sense the Lord is understood, and His glorification. Again: Thou possessest my reins, Thou hast covered me in my mother's belly" (Psalm cxxxix. 13). By possessing the reins is signified to purify truths from falses, see above, n. 167; and by covering in the mother's belly, is signified, to defend from the falses of evil which are from hell, and this from the beginning of regeneration and afterwards continually. Again: " The impious are estranged from the womb, they go astray from the belly, speaking a lie" (Psalm lviii. 4); where it is not understood that the impious are estranged from the womb, and that they go astray from the belly, that is, from the first nativity, for no one from this nativity is estranged from God and goes astray, but to be es-

tranged from the womb signifies to recede from good to evil from the
first day when they could be reformed, and to go astray from the
belly signifies to recede in like manner from truths to falses; to
speak a lie also signifies to believe falses; the reason why it is said
that they receded from the first day when they could be reformed, is,
because the Lord is in the endeavor to reform all, whomsoever they
may be, beginning from childhood and continuing through adolescence to youth, but they who do not suffer themselves to be reformed
are said immediately to recede.   And in Hosea: " The iniquity of
Ephraim is bound up, his sin is hid, the griefs of a travailing woman
shall come upon him; he is a son not wise, because time doth not
stand in the womb of sons" (xiii. 12, 13).   By Ephraim is signified
the understanding of truth, in this case the understanding perverted,
which is of the false instead of truth; the false thereof is signified
by iniquity and the evil of the false by his sin; hence he is called
a son not wise; the not receiving reformation is signified by, the
griefs of a travailing woman shall come upon him; and the not continuing in a state of reformation is signified by, time doth not stand
in the womb of sons.   And in Isaiah: " I knew thou wouldest act
perfidiously in acting perfidiously, and thou wast called by the name
of a trespasser from the womb" (xlviii. 8).   These things are said
concerning the house of Jacob, by which is signified the church perverted: to act perfidiously, signifies against the revealed truths; and
to be called by the name of a trespasser from the womb, signifies
recession from truths from the first time in which reformation could
be effected; by being called by a name is signified quality as to
such things.   Again, in Hosea: " Jacob supplanted his brother in
the womb, and in his strength he fought powerfully with God " (xii.
4).   In order to know what is understood by these words in the internal sense, it is necessary to be observed, that Jacob and his posterity, even from their fathers, were merely natural, consequently
against the good of heaven and the church; for he who is natural
and not at the same time spiritual, is against that good, for this is
procured solely by the conjunction of truth and good, first in the
spiritual man, and afterwards in the natural; but by Esau is signified natural good in spiritual: now whereas Jacob and his posterity
were of such a nature, and whereas they rejected all such good,
and this from the first time, therefore it is said of Jacob, that in the
womb he supplanted his brother; moreover by the combat of Jacob
with the angel, which is treated of in Genesis xxxii. 25–32, is described their contumacy, with which they insisted upon possessing
the land of Canaan, by which is understood, that the church might
be instituted amongst them; this contumacy is described by that
combat, and also by what is said in the verse following in Hosea:
" And he fought powerfully with the angel, he wept and entreated
him," but that still they would be destitute of any good of celestial
and spiritual love is understood by the angel touching the hollow of
Jacob's thigh, and by its being put out of joint in wrestling with the
angel (Gen. xxxii. 25, 32); for by the thigh is signified the conjunction of good and truth, and by its being put out of joint is signi-

fied that there was no conjunction of truth with good, with Jacob and his posterity; but more may be seen about this subject in the A. C. n. 4281. That the Israelitish and Jewish nation was not elected, but received in order to represent a church, by reason of the contumacy of their fathers, and of Moses, may be seen in the same work, n. 4290, 4293, 7051, 7439, 10,430, 10,535, 10,632. So again, in Moses: "The sons strove with each other in the belly of Rebecca; and Jehovah said, two nations are in thy womb, and two people shall be separated from thy bowels, and people shall prevail over people, and the greater shall serve the lesser. And the days were fulfilled to bring forth, and lo, twins were in her womb; and the first came forth wholly red, as a hairy garment, and they called his name Esau; and afterwards his brother came forth, and his hand took hold of the heel of Esau, and he called his name Jacob" (Gen. xxv. 20, 26). These historical particulars involve the things said above concerning Jacob and his posterity, viz. that they were merely natural, and thence not in any natural good from spiritual, which is signified by Esau; that the posterity of Jacob were without that good, is signified by Jacob, as he came forth out of the womb of his mother, taking hold of the heel of Esau, the heel denoting the ultimate natural [principle]; but these things also may be seen explained in the A. C. Again: "From the God of thy father and He will help thee, and from Schaddai, and He will bless thee, with the benedictions of heaven from above, with the benedictions of the abyss lying beneath, the benedictions of the paps, and of the womb" (Gen. xlix. 25). This is the benediction of Joseph by his father Israel, concerning which also see the A. C. n. 6428–6434, where it is shown that the benedictions of the paps signify the affections of good and truth, and the benedictions of the womb the conjunction of good and truth, thus regeneration. Again: "That Jehovah may love thee, and bless thee, and multiply thee, that He may bless the fruit of thy belly, and the fruit of thy land, thy corn and thy new wine, thy oil, the young of thy oxen, and the rams of thy flock" (Deut. vii. 13; and elsewhere); "Blessed be the fruit of thy belly, and the fruit of thy land, the young of thy oxen, and of the cattle of thy flock" (Deut. xxviii. 4). These words were spoken to the sons of Jacob, who understood them only in a natural manner, that is, according to the sense of the letter, because they were merely natural, and not in the least spiritual; but by those benedictions are signified spiritual benedictions, which appertain to heaven and thence to eternal life; for by the fruit of the belly is signified the good of love and the truth of that good; by the fruit of the earth is signified everything appertaining to the church; by the corn and new wine is signified all good and truth in the natural man; by the young of the oxen, and of the cattle of the flock, are signified their affections exterior and interior; in general by all those things are signified the fructification and multiplication of truth and good. Again, in Isaiah: "Behold I stir up against them the Mede, who shall not esteem silver, and in gold they shall not take delight; whose bows shall dash in pieces the young men, and they shall have no pity on the fruit of the belly; their eye shall not spare the sons" (xiii. 17, 18). By the Mede are understood those who make no account of the truth and good of the church, and destroy those things which are thence of the understanding and love; by the silver which they shall not esteem, and by the gold with which they shall not be delighted, is signified the truth and good of heaven and of the church, by silver their truth, and by gold their good; their bows shall dash in pieces the young men, and they shall have no pity on the fruit of the belly, signifies, that falses of doctrine will destroy all the understanding of truth, and all the good of love, bow denoting the false of doctrine, young men the intelligence of truth, and the fruit of the belly, the good of love; their eye shall not spare the sons, signifies that their perverted understanding and insanity will devastate all the truth of the church, sons denoting truths, and the eye, the understanding perver,ed, which is insanity; it is to be observed, that by the Mede is not understood the Mede, but such persons and things in the church as devastate it. And in Matthew: "The Pharisees said, is it lawful for a man to put away his wife for every cause? Jesus answering said, have ye not read that He who made them from the beginning, made them male and female, and said, for this cause a man shall leave father and mother, and shall adhere to his wife, and they two shall be one flesh; wherefore they are no more two but one flesh; what therefore God hath joined together let no man put asunder. Moses for the hardness of your heart permitted you to put away your wives, but from the beginning it was not so; I say unto you, that whosoever shall put away his wife, except for fornication and take another, committeth adultery, and whosoever taketh her that is put away, committeth adultery. The disciples said, if the case of a man be so with his wife, it is not good to marry: but Jesus said, all cannot receive this word, but they to whom it is given; for there are eunuchs who were so born from their mother's womb, and there are eunuchs who were made eunuchs of men, and there are eunuchs who have made themselves eunuchs for the sake of the kingdom of God: he who is able to receive it, let him receive it" (xix. 3–12). That there are interior arcana contained in these words, may appear from the Lord's saying, that all cannot receive them, but they to whom it is given; the interior arcanum contained in the above words spoken by the Lord can be but little apprehended by men, but it is apprehened by all the angels in heaven, because they perceive the words of the Lord spiritually, and the arcana therein contained are spiritual, viz. these: that there are marriages in the heavens equally as on earth, but in the heavens, marriages are of like with their like: for man is born to act from understanding, but woman from affection, and the understanding with men is the understanding of truth and good, and the affection with woman is the affection of truth and good; and whereas all understanding derives life from affection, therefore they are conjoined, as the affection which is of the will is conjoined with a correspondent thought which is of the understanding: for the understanding with every one is various, as the truths from which the understanding is formed are various; in general there are truths celestial, truths spiritual, truths moral, truths civil, yea, there are truths natural, and of every order of truth there are species and varieties innumerable; and whereas in consequence thereof, the understanding of one is never like the understanding of another, nor the affection of one like that of another, and still understanding and affection act as one, therefore they are so conjoined in heaven, that the correspondent affection which is of the woman is conjoined to the correspondent understanding which is of the man : hence it is that the life of each is by virtue of correspondence full of love : now inasmuch as two various affections cannot correspond to one intellect, hence in heaven there is never given, neither can be given, several wives to one man. From these considerations it may also be seen and concluded, what is spiritually understood by the above words of the Lord : by a man shall leave father and mother, and shall adhere to his wife, and they shall be one flesh, is signified, that the man shall leave that evil and false which he has from his religion, and which defiles his understanding, thus which he has from father and mother, and that his understanding, being separated from them, shall be conjoined with the correspondent affection which is of the wife, whence the two become one affection of truth and good : this is understood by the one flesh, in which the two are to be, for flesh, in the spiritual sense, signifies the good which is of the love or affection : wherefore they are no more two but one flesh, signifies, that so the understanding of truth and good, and the affection of good and truth, are not two, but one, in like manner as the understanding and the will are indeed two, but still one, also as truth and good, likewise faith and charity, which indeed are two, but still one, namely, when truth is of good, and good is of truth, likewise when faith is of charity, and charity is of faith ; hence also is love conjugial : the reason why Moses for the hardness of their heart permitted them to put away a wife for every cause, was, because the Israelites and Jews were natural and not spiritual, and they who are merely natural, are also hard in heart, inasmuch as they are not in any conjugial love, but in lascivious love, such as is that of adultery; the reason why it is said that whosoever putteth away a wife except for fornication, and taketh another, committeth adultery, is, because fornication signifies the false, and with a woman the affection of what is evil and false, thus an affection which by no means agrees with the understanding of truth and good, and because, by reason of that discordance, conjugial love, which is of truth and good, and thence is heaven and the church with man, entirely perishes, for when the interior conjunction, which is of minds [mens] and minds [animus], perishes or is no more, the marriage is dissolved : the reason why he who who takes her that is put away also commits adultery, is, because by her that is put away on account of fornication, is understood the affection of evil and the false, as was said above, which is not to be conjoined with any understanding of truth and good, for in this case the understanding is perverted, and becomes also of the false and evil, and the conjunction of the false and evil is spiritual adultery, as the con-

junction of truth and good is spiritual marriage. The reason why
the Lord afterwards spake concerning eunuchs, was, because the
disciples said, if the case of a man with his wife be so, it is not good
to marry, and because marriages with the Jewish nation, which was
a nation hard in heart, by reason of their being in falses from evil,
were not marriages but adulteries, understood in a spiritual sense,
wherefore also that nation was called by the Lord an adulterous
generation : hence it was that the Lord spake concerning eunuchs,
by whom are understood those who do not desire to enter into marriage, that is, to be conjoined, with the affection of evil, because
thereby the understanding of truth and good would be perverted and
dissipated ; thus by eunuchs are understood as well the married as
the unmarried, with whom the understanding of truth and good is
conjoined with the affection of truth and good ; the reason why they
are called eunuchs is, because they have not a lacivious principle,
like those who from hardness of heart, in which the Jews were
principled, take several wives, and divorce them for every cause.
In order to understand more fully these words of the Lord concerning eunuchs, it is first to be observed, that the marriage of the understanding of truth and good with the affection of truth and good,
is in general from a three-fold origin, and thence in a three-fold degree : in the supreme degree is the marriage of those who are called
celestial, in an inferior degree between those who are spiritual, and
in the lowest degree between those who are natural; for there are
so many degrees of the interiors of man, whence there are three
heavens, and they who are in the supreme heaven are called celestial, they who are in the inferior, spiritual, and they who are in the
lowest, natural ; the marriage of the understanding of truth and good
with the affection of truth and good with the celestial, is understood
by the eunuchs who are born eunuchs in the mother's womb, by
reason that these, when they are regenerated, receive truths immediately in the life, through the love thereof, whence they know
truths by virtue of the truths themselves, and their regeneration from
the Lord by love to Himself, is signified by being made eunuchs in
the womb, thus without any lascivious principle of adultery; but
the marriage of the understanding of truth and good with the affection of truth and good with the spiritual, is understood by eunuchs
who are made eunuchs of men, for these are not regenerated in the
womb, that is, by love, but by truths first received in the memory,
and afterwards intellectually in the thought, and so at last in the
life by a certain spiritual affection ; these are said to be made eunuchs of men, because they are reformed by the intellect from the
memory, and man signifies that intellect, as where man and wife
are mentioned above ; but the marriage of truth and good with the
affection of truth and good with the natural, is understood by the
eunuchs who make themselves eunuchs ; for the natural, by sciences
and knowledges, procure to themselves a natural lumen, and by the
good of life according to them they procure affection, and thence
conscience ; and inasmuch as these know no other, than that they
do this themselves, for the natural man does not enjoy the intelli-

gence of the spiritual man, nor the perception of the celestial man, hence it is that they are understood by those who make themselves, but it is so said from appearance only, and by reason of their obscure faith.   These are the things therefore which are understood by becoming eunuchs for the sake of the kingdom of God : and whereas but few apprehend these things, therefore the Lord says, he who can receive it, let him receive it.   But for farther illustration on this subject, see what is said in the work concerning H. & H. concerning the two kingdoms into which the heavens are distinguished, and concerning the three heavens, according to the three degrees of the interiors of man, n. 20–40 ; and concerning marriages in heaven, n. 366–386.   It is said concerning John the Baptist, "That he was filled with the Holy Spirit in his mother's womb ; and that the embryo exulted in the womb at the salutation of Mary" (Luke i. 15, 41, 44) ; but by this was signified that he was about to represent the Lord as to the Word, as did Elias ; for in the Word, which is divine truth, there is every where the marriage of divine good and divine truth, and divine good united with divine truth is the divine proceeding from the Lord, which is called the Holy Spirit : the exultation in the womb at the salutation of Mary, represented the joy arising from the love of the conjunction of good and truth, thus the joy of celestial conjugial love, which is in every part of the Word ; that John the Baptist, in like manner as Elias, represented the Lord as to the Word, may be seen in the A. C. n. 7643–9372.   What is signified by the male which first opens the womb, as mentioned in Moses, shall also be explained ; the words are these : " When Jehovah hath brought thee into the land of Canaan, thou shalt make to pass to Jehovah every opening of the womb, and every opening of the fœtus of beast, as many as are males shall be Jehovah's ; but every first born amongst thy sons thou shalt redeem.   And it shall come to pass that if thy son shall ask thee in time to come, why is this, thou shalt say unto him, by might of hand Jehovah brought us out of Egypt, out of the house of servants, when he slew all the first born in the land, from the first born of men even to the first born of beast ; wherefore I sacrifice to Jehovah every opening of the womb, males, and all the first born of my sons I redeem" (Exod. xiii. 11, 15 ; chap. xxxiv. 19, 20).   That the Levites were accepted in the place of them, may appear from these words : " Behold I have accepted the Levites, from the midst of the sons of Israel, instead of all the first born, the openings of the womb of the sons of Israel, that the Levites may be Mine ; because every first born is Mine : in the day when I smote all the first born in the land of Egypt, I sanctified to Me all the first born in Israel from man even to beast ; they shall be Mine" (Numb. xiii. 12, 13 ; chap. viii. 16, 17).   The spiritual meaning which lies concealed in this statute, cannot appear, unless it be known that natural generations and nativities signify spiritual generations and nativities ; likewise also, that all the members of generation correspond to celestial love, and the things thence produced, which are uses, and are called the truths of that love : inasmuch as this is the case, and marriage, in the spiritual sense, signi-

fies the marriage of good and truth, as was said above, hence
it may appear what is signified in the same sense by the opening
of the womb, or the first born male : by the opening of the womb,
or the first born male, is signified that which is first born from
celestial love, and the perception of good and truth; that this is
truth from good, which is in the place of a principle to the rest, is
evident, and this in its essence is spiritual good, for this good, in its
form, is truth from good, or what is the same, truth from good, in its
essence, is spiritual good; this is signified by the opening of the
womb, the first born male, by reason that the womb corresponds to
inmost conjugial love, which, in its essence, is celestial love, and
from this love is produced spiritual good, which, in its form, is truth
from good, and, specifically, that truth from good which is in place
of a principle to the rest : that which is in the place of a principle,
is the all in the things which succeed as to their essential, because
it is the reigning principle in them; inasmuch as this is signified by
the opening of the womb, or the first born male, therefore it was
sanctified to Jehovah, and thereby all the subsequent births were
also sanctified.   It is to be observed, that the goods of heaven and
the church are of three degrees, the good of the inmost degree,
which is also that of the inmost heaven, is called the good of celestial love, the good of the inferior degree, which is also the good of
the middle heaven, is called the good of spiritual love, and the good
of the lowest degree, which is the good of the ultimate heaven, is
called natural good : these goods, as they follow in order, so also
they are born in order; the good of natural love is born from the
good of spiritual love, and the good of spiritual love is born from the
good of celestial love ; hence it is that by the opening of the womb,
the first born male, is signified the good of spiritual love, born from
the good of celestial love. Inasmuch as by beasts are signified affections, by beasts of the herd exterior affections, and by beasts of the
flock interior affections, therefore also the first born of these were
sanctified.   That this is the case, may also appear from this consideration, that the Levites were received in the place of all the first born;
for by Levi, and thence by the Levites, is signified spiritual good
from celestial good, and hence also the priesthood, by which is signified celestial good, was given to Aaron and his sons, and the ministry of this good, by which is signified truth from good, was given
to the Levites; concerning this signification of the tribe of Levi, see
above, n. 444.   The reason why the statute concerning the first born
was given to the sons of Israel on account of all the first born of
Egypt being slain, was, because by the first born are there signified
the falses from evil contrary or opposite to truths from good, thus
infernal evil contrary or opposite to spiritual good, and because
when those falses from evil with man are slain, that is, removed,
then first truths from good, or spiritual good, flows in from the Lord,
and is received by man.   From these considerations it may appear,
what was represented and signified by that statute in the spiritual
sense.   What was signified by "God shutting every womb of the
house of Abimelech on account of Sarah, Abraham's wife, and that

after Abraham prayed for them, God healed Abimelech, his wife, and their maid-servants, and they brought forth" (Gen. xx. 1 1, 18); may be seen explained in the A. C.

711. " Cried, travailing [in birth], and being pained to be delivered"—That hereby is signified non-reception by those in the church who are natural and sensual, and their resistance, appears from the signification ot crying, travailing in birth, and being pained to be delivered, when predicated of the doctrine of truth nascent from celestial love, which is understood by the male which the woman brought forth, as denoting non-reception thereof, and also resistance; the reason why this comes from those in the church who are natural and sensual, is, because such are understood by the dragon treated of in what follows. That to travail in birth and bring forth denotes to travail in birth and bring forth such things as appertain to the church, in the present case, which appertain to the doctrine of truth and good, may appear from what has been said and shown in the preceding article concerning the womb, the openings thereof, and concerning birth; and also from the following parts of this chapter, where the expression to bring forth is made use of. In the mean time it is sufficient here to observe only, that by the male, which the woman brought forth, is understood the doctrine of the New Jerusalem, which was given from the Lord out of heaven; that the dragons then stood around, and vehemently, and with all their might, withstood, and this even to the crying out and torment of those who were for that doctrine, I can testify; hence it may appear that they who are like them in the world will also withstand that doctrine to prevent its being received; the nature and quality of such will be explained in what follows, where the dragon and the beasts are treated of. But what is specifically signified by crying out, travailing in birth, and being pained to be delivered, in other parts of the Word, may be seen in the article below, n. 721, where the expressions are explained.

712. Verses 3, 4. " And there was seen another sign in heaven; and behold a great red dragon having seven heads, and ten horns, and upon his heads seven diadems. And his tail drew a third part of the stars of heaven, and cast them to the earth. And the dragon stood before the woman about to bring forth, that when she had brought forth he might devour her child."—" And there was seen another sign in heaven," signifies divine revelation concerning the assaulting of the doctrine which is for the new church, and by whom; " and behold a great red dragon," signifies all who are merely natural and sensual from the love of self and of the world, and still know some things, more or less, from the Word, from doctrine thence derived, and from preaching, and think to be saved by science alone without life; " having seven heads," signifies the science of the holy things of the Word, which they have adulterated; " and ten horns" signifies much power; " and upon their heads seven diadems," signifies divine truths in the ultimate of order, which are the truths of the literal sense of the Word, adulterated and profaned; " and his tail drew a third part of the stars of heaven," sig-

nifies the falsification and adulteration of all the truths of the Word;
" and cast them to the earth," signifies their extinction and destruction ; " and the dragon stood before the woman about to bring forth,"
signifies the hatred of those who are understood by the dragon,
against the church with those who will be in the doctrine and thence
in the life of love and charity from the Lord; " that after she had
brought forth he might devour her child," signifies that they might
destroy the doctrine of that church in its first rise.

713. " And there was seen another sign in heaven"—That hereby is signified divine revelation concerning the assaulting of the doctrine which is for the new church, and by whom, appears from the
signification of a great sign, as denoting divine revelation, manifestation, and testification, concerning which see above, n. 706; that it
is concerning the assaulting of the doctrine which is for the new
church, and by whom, appears from the following verse, in which
this sign is described. They who will assault the doctrine are understood by the great red dragon, the old serpent, and the assaulting
itself is described by the dragon standing before the woman about
to bring forth, that he might devour her child, and afterwards, by
the combat of the dragon with Michael, and lastly, by his pursuing
the woman into the wilderness, and there casting out water after her
as a flood; and moreover in the following verses. But the nature
and quality of those who are understood by the dragon, will be explained in the following article: here we shall only observe, that
they are those who have communication with the angels of heaven,
but only by things external, but not by things internal ; for it is
said that that dragon was seen in heaven, whereas they who have
no communication with heaven, cannot be seen there, for they are
in hell; such are they who deny God, especially the Lord, who
make no account of and blaspheme the Word, and who have no
faith concerning life eternal, in a word, all those who love themselves
and the world above all things, and live a life of enmity, hatred, revenge, and deceit, in which they perceive delight. These things
are said in order that it may be known, that such persons are not
understood by the dragon, but they who, during their abode in the
world, have an external communication with heaven, which communication is derived to them from the reading of the Word, from
preaching thence derived, and from external worship according to
the statutes of their church, but who still are not in any life according to the precepts of the Lord; hence it is that such have indeed
communication with heaven, but not internal ; whence it is that they
are called the devil and satan will also be explained in what follows.

714. " And behold a great red dragon"—That hereby are signified all who are merely natural and sensual from the love of self,
and still know some things, more or less, from the Word, from doctrine thence derived, or from preaching, and think to be saved by
science alone without life, appears from the signification of the dragon, as denoting the merely natural and sensual man, who is notwithstanding in the science of things in themselves spiritual, whe-

ther they be from the Word, or from preaching, or from religion, concerning which we shall speak presently; and from the signification of great and red, as denoting to be in the love of self, and in the evils thereof; for great, in the Word, is predicated of good, and, in the opposite sense, of evil, as much is predicated of truths, and, in the opposite sense, of falses, as may be seen above, n. 336, 337, 424; and red is predicated of love in each sense, namely, of celestial love, which is love to the Lord, and, in the opposite sense, or diabolic love, which is the love of self, concerning which also see above, n. 364 : hence it may appear, that by a great red dragon are understood all who are merely natural and sensual from the love of self, and still know some things, more or less, from the Word, either from doctrine thence derived, or from preaching, and think to be saved by science alone without the life of charity; the reason why they so think, is, because all those become merely natural and sensual, who live to the body and to the world, and not to God and heaven; for every one is interiorly formed according to his life, and to live to the body and to the world is to live natural and sensual, and to live to God and heaven is to live spiritual; every man is born sensual from his parents, and by a life in the world becomes natural more and more interiorly, that is rational, according to moral and civil life, and the lumen thence acquired, but afterwards he becomes a spiritual man by truths from the Word, or from doctrine derived from the Word, and by a life according to them : hence it may appear, that he who knows those things which the Word, of which doctrine or a preacher teaches, and does not live according to them, however learned and erudite he may appear, still is not spiritual, but natural, yea, sensual, for science and the faculty of reasoning do not make man spiritual, but life itself; the reason is because science with the faculty of reasoning thence derived, is only natural, wherefore it can also be given with the evil, yea, with the worst of men, but truths from the Word, together with a life according to them, make man spiritual; for life is to will truths and to do them from the love thereof, and this cannot be given from the natural man alone, but from the spiritual, and from the influx of this into the natural; for to love truths, and from love to will them, and from that will to do them, is from heaven, that is, through heaven from the Lord, and is in its nature heavenly and divine; this cannot flow in immediately into the natural mind, but mediately through the spiritual mind, which can be opened and formed to the reception of heavenly light and heat, that is, to the reception of divine truth and divine good : the reason why these cannot flow immediately into the natural mind, is, because in this mind reside man's hereditary evils, which are of the love of self and the world, whence the natural man, viewed in himself, loves only himself and the world, and from love wills, and from will does those hereditary evils, and these are the things which oppose the influx of anything out of heaven, and the possibility of its reception, wherefore it is provided of the Lord that these evils may be removed, and so a place may be given for the truths and goods of spiritual love, namely, by the opening and formation of the spiritual mind, which is above the natural mind, and by the influx thence of heaven from the Lord, thereby into the natural mind. These things are said, in order that it may be known, that to know the things which are of the Word, and of the doctrine of the church, does not make man spiritual, but a life according to those things which the Lord has commanded in the Word; consequently, that it is possible to know many things from the Word, and yet remain natural and sensual. These are therefore they who are signified, in the Word, by the dragon; and the reason why they are signified is, because the dragon is a genus of serpent, which not only creeps upon the ground, but also flies, and thence appears in heaven; and it is from this flight and this appearance that they who are in the science of truths from the Word, and not in a life according to them, are understood by the dragon; for by serpents in general are signified the sensual things of man, as may be seen above, n. 581, and hence also it is that the dragon, in the ninth verse of this chapter, and in the second verse of chapter xx. is called the old serpent. Forasmuch as in the following parts of this chapter, and also afterwards, the dragon is treated of, it shall be explained what sort of persons, generally and specifically, are thereby signified; in general are signified those who are more or less natural, and yet in the science of things spiritual from the Word, but those are specifically signified who have confirmed themselves in faith separate from charity in doctrine and life: these constitute the head of the dragon; but they who from self-derived intelligence hatch for themselves dogmas from the Word, constitute the body; and they who study the Word without doctrine, constitute the external parts: all these also falsify and adulterate the Word, inasmuch as they are in the love of self and thence in the pride of self-derived intelligence, from which they become merely natural, yea, sensual, and the sensual man cannot see the genuine truths of the Word, by reason of fallacies, of obscurity of perception, and of the evils of the body there residing, for the sensual principle adheres to the body, whence such things are derived. 1. It is to be explained that by the dragon in general are understood those who are natural, more or less, and yet in the science of things spiritual from the Word: the reason why these are so signified is, because by serpents in general are signified the sensual things of man, and thence sensual men, wherefore by the dragon, which is a flying serpent, is signified the sensual man, who yet flies towards heaven, in that he speaks and thinks from the Word, or from doctrine derived from the Word; for the Word itself is spiritual, because it is in itself divine, and thence in heaven; but inasmuch as the mere science of spiritual things from the Word does not make man spiritual, but a life according to those things which are commanded in the Word, hence all those who are in science from the Word, and not in a life according thereto are natural, yea, sensual. The sensual who are understood by the dragon, are those who see nothing from the light of heaven, but only from the light of the world, and who from this light alone can speak concerning divine things, and also reason with acuteness and alacrity excited by the

fire of the love of self and the conceit of self intelligence thence derived ; but still such persons cannot see whether the things they so
argue for be truths or not, calling that truth which they have imbibed from their childhood from a master or preacher, and afterwards from doctrine, and which they have since confirmed from some
passages of the Word not interiorly understood : inasmuch as these
see nothing from the light of heaven, they do dot see truths, but in
place thereof falses, which they call truths ; for truths themselves
cannot be seen except in the light of heaven, and not in the light of
the world, unless the latter light be illustrated by the former ; and
whereas such is their nature and quality, they love no other life than
what is corporeal and worldly ; and inasmuch as the pleasures and
concupiscences of this life reside in the natural man, hence their interiors are filthy and beset with evils of every kind, which close
every way for the influx of the light and heat of heaven ; whence
they are inwardly devils and satans, howsoever they may appear,
from their discourse and simulated gestures, as spiritual men and
Christians ; hence also it may appear that such persons are merely
sensual, for they can speak outwardly concerning the holy things of
the church, whilst inwardly they believe nothing, and they who suppose themselves to believe, have only a belief in what is historical,
and thence of a persuasive kind, derived from an instructor or from
self-intelligence, which in itself is false, but which they still believe
for the sake of fame, honor, and gain ; such are the dragons in general.   But there are several species of those who are signified by the
dragon, for there are those who have reference to the head, those
who have reference to the body, and to the external parts. 2. They
who specifically have reference to the head of the dragon, are those
who are in faith alone, which is a faith separate from charity, and
have confirmed themselves therein in doctrine and in life ; the reason why these have reference to the head of the dragon, is, because
they are, for the most part, men of erudition, and believed; to be
learned ; for they have confirmed themselves in the persuasion, that
by thinking only the things which the church teaches, and which
they call believing, they shall be saved : but the quality of their
doctrine and their life shall be unfolded : their doctrine is, that God
the Father sent His Son, born from eternity, into the world, that He
might become man, fulfil all things of the law, bear the iniquities of
all, and suffer the cross, and that thereby God the Father was reconciled and moved to compassion, and that those would be received
into heaven, who should be in a faith concerning those things,
grounded in confidence, and that the confidence of that faith, together
with the Lord, would intercede and save ; consequently, that that
faith is given to mankind, who were separated from God the Father,
as a medium of reception and salvation, because after Adam ate of
the tree of science, man was no more in a state to do good of himself, for with the image of God he thence lost his free will ; lastly,
that the things above mentioned are the merit of the Lord, by which
alone man can be saved : these are the primary things of the faith
which has place with those who are in faith alone, as to doctrine.

That it is not possible for any one to perceive and thereby believe anything of those dogmas from any spiritual sight, which is of the understanding, but only to know scientifically, and thence to speak such things from the memory, without any understanding, so that there is nothing of intelligence in that doctrine, shall, the Lord willing, be expounded and illustrated elsewhere. But what is the nature and quality of the same persons, as to the life, shall also be explained : they teach, that man is led of God by faith alone, even to the effort of doing good, and that the g d in act contributes nothing itself to salvation, but only faith ; and that then nothing of evil condemns him, because he is in grace, and justified : they also devise in their thought certain degrees, which they call progressions of faith alone unto the ultimate state of justification: the first degree or progression is information in such things as appertain to faith, especially in those above mentioned; the second is confirmation from the Word, or from preaching ; the third is mental inquisition, whether it be so or not; and whereas there then flows in a doubting and thence wavering, which is temptation, they hold it necessary to confirm themselves from the Word concerning the operation of faith, whence comes the confidence which they call victory: they add, that care is to be taken lest the understanding proceed any further than to confirmations from the Word concerning justification by faith alone, and if it go further, and be not kept under the obedience of faith, that then they fall; the fourth and last degree is the effort to do good, and they affirm that that is an influx from God, and nothing thereof from man ; also, that it is the fruit of faith ; for they say that when man is thus fully justified, nothing of evil can afterwards condemn him, nor does anything of good save him, but faith alone: from these observations it may appear, what is the quality of such persons as to life, viz. that they live to themselves and not to God, and to the world and not to heaven, for this follows of consequence from the faith which teaches that evils do not condemn and that goods do not save; neither do they know, that faith without the life of charity is not faith, and that man ought to shun evils and do good as of himself, yet believing that it is from the Lord, and that otherwise evils cannot be shaken off, nor goods appropriated : but more also will be elsewhere said on these subjects. Such is the doctrine and life with those who form the head of the dragon, who for the most part are learned dignitaries, but few among the vulgar; the reason is, because the former consider those things as the secrets of theology which cannot be apprehended by the vulgar, by reason of their secular employments: another reason why such are dragons as to the head, is, because they pervert and falsify all the things of the Word which teach love, charity, and life ; for the Word, viewed in itself, is only the doctrine of love to the Lord and of charity towards the neighbor, and in no case the doctrine of faith separate from charity : they falsify all things of the Word by this, that they call them either faith, or fruit of such a quality, which they do not eat, consequently do not nourish themselves by it, because they think nothing about doing : neither do they admit those principles any further than into the memory and thence into the thought proximate thereto, which is the sensual thought in which there is nothing spiritual, and which does not explore the truth of a thing; wherefore they take heed lest anything should enter the interior sight' which is of the understanding, being unwilling to know that all those things which are said concerning their faith are contrary to an enlightened understanding as they are contrary to the genuine sense of the Word. Hence also it is, that they who constitute the head of the dragon have not any genuine truth, for from a false principle, such as is that of faith alone, there cannot possibly flow anything but falses in a continual series, nor is faith alone possible to be given, for faith without charity is not faith, inasmuch as charity is the soul of faith, wherefore to speak of faith alone is to speak of what is without a soul, and thus without life, which in itself is dead. 3. That they who from self-derived intelligence have hatched for themselves dogmas from the Word, constitute the body of the dragon, may appear from this consideration, that all those who study the Word, and are in the love of self, are also in the conceit of self-derived intelligence, and all who are in this conceit, and at the same time excel in ingenuity from natural lumen, hatch for themselves dogmas thence; from this origin are all the heresies and all the falsities in the Christian world: it may be expedient here to explain what the intelligence from man's proprium is, and what that is which is not from his proprium: the intelligence from a man's proprium is that which is from himself, but the intelligence which is not from his proprium is from the Lord: all those derive intelligence from their proprium, who are in the love of self, for the love of self is the very proprium of man, and they are in the love of self who read the Word and thence collect dogmas for the sake of fame, honor, and glory; and inasmuch as they cannot see any truths but only falses, therefore they are in the body of the dragon; for they collect and hatch such things from the Word as favor their loves and the evils thence arising, and those things which are contrary to their dogmas, which are truths from good, they either do not see, or pervert; but all those have intelligence from the Lord, who are in the spiritual affection of truth, that is, who love truth because it is truth, and because it is serviceable to eternal life, and to the life of the souls of men: it is said that their intelligence is not from proprium but from the Lord, because these are elevated from their proprium whilst they read the Word, and this even into the light of heaven, and are thereby illustrated, for in this light truth appears from the truth itself, because the light of heaven is divine truth: but they who are in the love of self and thence in the conceit of self-derived intelligence, cannot be elevated from their proprium, for they continually regard themselves, and this in everything which they do; hence also it is that such place the all of salvation in the faith of their own dogmas, thus in knowing and thinking, and not at the same time in the life, thus not at the same time in willing and doing: these, therefore, constitute the body of the dragon: the heart of this body is the love of self, and the soul of the respiration or of his spirit, is the conceit of self-derived intelligence; from these two the dragon is called a great red dragon, and red, in the original Greek text, is derived from the principle of flame or what is flaming, thus from love and pride. 4. That they who study the Word without doctrine, and at the same time are in the love of self, constitute the externals of the draconic body. Externals are what proceed from the interiors, and involve, include, and contain them, as the skins, scales, and prominences on every part: the reason why such persons constitute these externals of the body of the dragon, is, because they are without any intelligence of the spiritual things of the Word: for they know the Word only as to the sense of the letter, which is of such a nature, that if doctrine does not shine through it, it may lead into errors and falses of every kind; consequently, they who study the Word without doctrine, can confirm as many heresies as they will, and also embrace and even patronize the loves of self and of the world, and the evils thence arising; for the literal sense of the Word is the ultimate sense of divine truth, thus for the natural and sensual man, accommodated to his apprehension, and oft times to favor him, wherefore unless it be read and viewed from doctrine, as from a lamp, the mind may be carried thereby into darkness concerning many things appertaining to heaven and the church; and yet such persons believe themselves to be wise above all others, when notwithstanding they know nothing of genuine wisdom. 5. That all those who constitute the dragon, adore God the Father, and view the Lord as a man like themselves, and not as God, and if they do regard Him as God, regard His divine [principle] as above the human, and not within it, will be illustrated when we come to treat concerning the combat of the dragon with Michael. 6. From these observations it may now appear, that by the tail of the dragon is understood the falsification and adulteration of the Word by those who constitute his head, his body, and the extreme parts; for the tail, as is the case with the tail of every animal, is a continuation of the spine, which is protended from the brains, and so is moved, bent, and vibrated, according to the appetites, concupiscences, and pleasures of the head and body, with which it is as it were soothed; and inasmuch as all those who constitute the dragon, being natural and sensual from the love of self, and thence in the conceit of self-derived intelligence, falsify and adulterate the Word, therefore it is said, that the dragon with his tail drew a third part of the stars of heaven and cast them to the earth; by the stars of heaven are signified the knowledges of truth and good from the Word, consequently truths from good thence derived, and by casting them to the earth is signified to pervert and adulterate, and so to destroy them. That the persons above described constitute the dragon, and that the adulteration and destruction of the truth of the Word are understood by his tail, it has been given me to see twice or thrice in the spiritual world, for in this world all things which appear are representative of things spiritual; when such persons are seen in the light of heaven, they are seen as dragons with a long tail; and when several such are seen, the tail appears extended, from the south, through the west, into the north, and that tail appears also as it were to draw down stars from heaven, and cast them to the earth. Inasmuch as such persons are understood by the dragon, and the falsification and adulteration of the Word by the tail of the dragon, hence by the habitation and den or bed of dragons, mentioned in the Word, is signified where there is nothing but what is merely false and evil; as in the following passages; thus in Isaiah: "The dry place shall become a lake, and the thirsty land springs of waters; in the habitation of dragons shall be the bed thereof, grass instead of reed and rush" (xxxv. 7); treating concerning the advent of the Lord and the establishment of a new church from Him with the gentiles; and by those words is understood that the truths and goods of the church shall be where they were not before, yea, where there were falses and evils: where falses and evils were before, is signified by the dry and thirsty place, and by the habitation of dragons, likewise by the reed and rush; but the truths and goods which they shall then have, are signified by the lake, by the springs of waters, by the bed where dragons were before, likewise by grass. And in Jeremiah: "I will lay Jerusalem in heaps, a habitation of dragons, and the cities of Judah will I reduce to wasteness that there be no inhabitant" (ix. 11); and again: "The voice of a noise, behold, a great tumult cometh from the land of the north, to reduce the cities of Judah to wasteness, to a habitation of dragons" (x. 22). By Jerusalem is understood the church as to doctrine; and by the cities of Judah are understood doctrinals, which are truths from the Word; the falsification of truth, and adulteration of good, from which arise mere falses and evils, are signified by laying Jerusalem in heaps, and by reducing the cities of Judah to wasteness, to a habitation of dragons, for truth falsified is merely false, and good adulterated is merely evil; the voice of a noise and a great tumult from the land of the north, signifies falses combating against truths, and evils against goods; the land of the north is where they are who are in the falses of evil. Again: "Hazor shall become a habitation of dragons, a desolation even for an age; a man shall not dwell there nor shall the son of man tarry there" (xlix. 33). By Hazor are signified spiritual treasures, which are the knowledges of truth and good from the Word; the vastation thereof even until they are no more, but in the place thereof falses and evils, is signified by, Hazor shall become a habitation of dragons, a desolation even for an age; that there will not be any truth of the church remaining, is signified by, a man shall not dwell there, nor shall the son of man tarry there; the son of man is the truth of the church. And in Isaiah: "The thorn shall come up in her palaces, the thistle and bramble in the fortresses thereof; it shall be a habitation of dragons, a court for the daughters of the owl" (xxxiv. 13); treating concerning Edom, and concerning the gentiles, by whom are understood those who are in falses and evils; the falses and evils in which they are, are signified by thorns, the thistle, and bramble; the dogmas defending them are signified by palaces and by fortresses; the devastation of all good and truth is signified by being a habitation of dragons, and a court for the daughters of the owl, owls denoting those who for truth see falses, and their daughters the concupiscences of falsifying truths. Again : " The Ijim shall answer in her palaces, and dragons in the temples" (xiii. 22); treating of Babel, whereby is signified the adulteration and profanation of good and truth : by her palaces in which are the Ijim, and by the temples in which are dragons, are signified the goods and truths of the Word and of the church, which are adulterated and profaned ; by the Ijim are signified adulterated and profaned truths, and by dragons adulterated and profaned goods. And in Micah : " Upon this will I wail and howl, I will go spoiled and naked, I will make a wailing as dragons, and a mourning as the daughters of the owl" (i. 5); treating of the vastation of Samaria, whereby is signified the spiritual church as to doctrine, in the present case vastated : devastation as to truth and good is signified by going spoiled and naked ; lamentation thereupon is signified by wailing and howling, lamentation upon devastated good by making a wailing as dragons, and lamentation upon devastated truth by making a mourning as the daughters of the owl ; the wailing and mourning being like dragons and daughters of the owl, is said representatively, as also his going spoiled and naked, spoiled signifying the same as the dragon, namely, to be destitute of goods, and naked the same as the daughters of the owl, namely, to be destitute of truths.   And in Jeremiah : " Nebuchadnezzar king of Babel hath constituted me an empty vessel, he hath swallowed me down as a whale, he hath filled his belly from my delicacies, he hath dispelled me : let Babel be a heap, a habitation of dragons, for a hissing and astonishment, and without inhabitant" (li. 34, 37).   Here also by Babel and by Nebuchadnezzar is signified the adulteration and profanation of good and truth : the dispersion of all truth and consequent destruction of all good, is signified by, he hath constituted me an empty vessel, he hath swallowed me down as a whale, he hath filled his belly from my delicacies, he hath dispelled me ; by a whale is signified the same as by a dragon ; they are also denoted by the same expression in the original tongue ; the devastation of all truth and good by reason of the adulteration and profanation of them, is signified by Babel being a heap, a habitation of dragons, for a hissing and astonishment, and having no inhabitant, no inhabitant denoting no good with any one.   And in Job : " I walked black without the sun, I stood in the congregation, I cried out, I am become a brother to the dragons, and a companion of the daughters of the owl" (xxx. 28, 29); speaking of his state in temptations, in which man thinks himself to be damned ; wherefore to walk black without the sun, signifies as a devil, without the good of love ; to stand in the congregation and cry out, signifies, amongst truths and yet in falses; to become a brother to the dragons, and a companion to the daughters of the owl, signifies, to be in conjunction and one with those who are in evils without good, and who are in falses without truths, dragons denoting those who adulterate goods and pervert them into evils ,and the daughters of the owl those who do the same to truths.

And in David : "Our heart hath not receded backward, nor hath our step declined from thy way, for thou hast broken us in the place of dragons, and covered us with the shade of death" (Psalm xliv. 19, 20) ; treating also concerning temptations; that he was then secluded from influx out of heaven, like the sensual man, so as not to perceive what was good and what was true, is signified by God breaking him in the place of dragons, and covering him with the shade of death, the place of dragons denoting where they who are dragons are in hell, namely, who have destroyed all good in themselves ; the false in which the same are, is called the shade of death. Again : "Thou shalt tread upon the lion and the asp, the lion and the dragon shall he trample under foot ; because he desireth me, I will deliver him, I will exalt him, because he hath known my name" (Psalm xci. 13, 14). To destroy falses interior and exterior which vastate the truths of the church, is signified by treading upon the lion and asp, and to destroy the falses interior or exterior which vastate the goods of the church, is signified by trampling under foot the lion and dragon : to withdraw from falses and to lead to interior truths and goods him who is in doctrine from the Word, is signified by, I will deliver him, I will exalt him, because he hath known My name ; to deliver is to withdraw from falses, to exalt is to lead to interior truths, and to know My name is to be in doctrine from the Word. And in Malachi : "Esau have I hated; and I have laid his mountains waste, and his heritage to the dragons of the wilderness" (i. 3). By Esau are understood those who are in good as to the natural man, in this case those who are in evil as to the same, wherefore it is said, Esau have I hated ; that the goods of love appertaining to the natural man were destroyed, is signified by, I have laid his mountains waste ; and that the truths of those goods were destroyed by the falses of the sensual man, is signified by, his heritage to the dragons of the wilderness. And in Ezekiel : "Behold I am against thee, Pharaoh king of Egypt, the great dragon [or whale] who lieth in the midst of his rivers, who saith, my river is mine, and I have made myself" (xxix. 3, 4 ; chap. xxxii. 2). The conceit of self-derived intelligence appertaining to the natural and sensual man is here described ; Pharaoh, king of Egypt, signifies the natural and sensual man ; the dragon or whale the same as to scientifics, which are made falses or falsified from self-derived intelligence ; but these words may be seen explained above, n. 513. And in Moses : Their vine is of the vine of Sodom and of the fields of Gomorrah ; the grapes thereof are grapes of gall, clusters of bitternesses to him ; their wine is the poison of dragons, and the cruel gall of asps" (Deut. xxxii. 32, 33). These words also may be seen explained above, n. 519, where it is shown, that their wine being called the poison of dragons, and the cruel gall of asps, signifies, that the truth of the church, with the posterity of Jacob, was external, in which inwardly were infernal evils and falses ; dragons and asps signify sensual things, which are the ultimates of the natural man, full of horrible evils and falses, confirming them ; the reason whereof is, because the natural principle in such case receives nothing

through the spiritual mind from the Lord, wherefore what it receives
is from hell.   That by the dragon are signified such things as are
above related, may more fully appear from what follows in this chapter; namely, from his enmity against the woman about to bring
forth, and flying into the wilderness; likewise, from his combat with
Michael; and moreover in chapter xvi. 13, 14, 15; chap. xx. 2, 7,
8, 10, 14; where it is said concerning him, that he was bound for a
thousand years, and afterwards being loosed went forth to seduce
the nations, and gather together Gog and Magog to war against the
saints, but that afterwards he was cast into a lake of fire and sulphur; from all which circumstances it may appear that by the dragon are understood those who do not possess any good of charity
and love, by reason of their not acknowledging it as any means serviceable to salvation, but only somewhat scientific, which from persuasion they call faith; and when the good of charity and love is
not implanted from the life of man, evil is in the place thereof, and
where evil is, there is the false.   Inasmuch as by serpents are signified sensual things, which are the ultimates of the natural man, and
these are not evil except with those who are evil, and inasmuch as
dragons are expressed by the same word in the original tongue as
serpents not poisonous, hence by dragons, when such serpents are
thereby understood, are signified in the Word sensual things not
evil, or as applied to persons, sensual men not evil.   That dragons
and such serpents are expressed in the Hebrew tongue by the same
word, may appear in Moses : " When it was commanded him, out of
the bush, to cast his rod to the ground, and when it became a serpent he took hold of it by the tail, and it became again a rod in his
hand" (Exod. iv. 3, 4); and afterwards : "That Moses took the
rod and cast it down before Pharaoh, when it became a serpent [dra-
gon], and that the magicians did the like with their rods; but the
rod of Moses, then a serpent [dragon], swallowed up the serpents
[dragons], of the magicians" (Exod. vii. 9–12).   In the original
tongue the serpent in the former passage is expressed by a different
word to what it is in the latter : in the former passage the common
word by which it is expressed in other parts of the Word is used,
but in the latter the same word is used as is used for dragon; so
that it may also be interpreted that the staff or rod of Moses cast before Pharaoh, was converted into a dragon; from this it follows,
that by the dragon, equally as by the serpent, in a good sense, is
signified the sensual [principle], which is the ultimate of the natural
man, not evil or not malignant.   In this milder sense also dragons
are mentioned in Isaiah : " The wild beast of the field shall honor
me, the dragons and the daughters of the owl, because I will give
waters in the wilderness, rivers in the desert, to give drink to my
chosen people" (xliii. 20); and in Jeremiah : "The hind brought
forth in the field, but left it because there was not grass; and the
wild asses stood upon the hills, they snuffed up the wind as dragons,
their eyes were consumed because there was no herb" (xiv. 6).   In
these passages the same word is used for dragons as for serpents in
general, and whales in the sea are also expressed by the same word,

by which also the same is signified, namely, the natural principle of man in common, which is the sensual principle; wherefore in the place last cited it may also be interpreted, they snuffed up the wind as whales; in like manner as in Isaiah, chap. li. 9.; in Jeremiah, chap. li. 34; in Ezekiel, chap. xxix. 3, 4; and in David, Psalm lxxiv. 33, 34. There are also men merely sensual who are good.

715. "Having seven heads"—That hereby is signified the science of the holy things of the Word, which they adulterated, and thence insanity, but still cunning, appears from the signification of head, as denoting intelligence and wisdom, and, in the opposite sense, insanity and foolishness, concerning which see above, n. 553, 578; that it also denotes cunning or craftiness, n. 578; and from the signification of seven, as denoting all and all things, and as being predicated of what is holy, concerning which see above, n. 257, in this case therefore of the holy things of the Word, which they adulterated: inasmuch as the number seven is predicated of things holy, it is also, in the opposite sense, predicated of those things adulterated and profaned, for every expression in the Word has also an opposite sense, and the opposite to what is holy is what is profane: from these considerations it is evident, that by the seven heads, which the dragon was seen to have, are not understood heads, nor seven, but the science of holy things from the Word, which they adulterated, and thence insanity, but still cunning. The reason why insanity is signified by the head of the dragon, is, because the intelligence appertaining to the man of the church is derived from genuine truths, which are from the Word; the understanding which is truly human is formed and perfected by truths natural, civil, moral, and spiritual, the interior understanding by truths spiritual, but the exterior by truths moral and civil; hence the quality of the understanding is according to the quality of the truths from which it is formed: all spiritual truths are from the Word, and make one with the good of love and charity; if therefore man places the all of the church and of heaven in faith, and separates from that faith the good of charity and love, as they do who constitute the head of the dragon, as was said in the preceding article, then the interior understanding cannot be formed, whence, instead of intelligence in things spiritual, they have insanity: for from a false principle flows falses in a continual series, and, by reason of the separation of the good of charity, no genuine truth can possibly be given them, inasmuch as all truth is of good, yea, is good in form: from hence it is evident that by the head of the dragon is signified insanity in things spiritual. The reason why by the head of the dragon, is also signified cunning, is, because all those who constitute his head, are merely natural and sensual, who, if they have at the same time studied the Word and the doctrine of the church, and have seized upon falses for truths, and also confirmed these scientifically, are cunning above all others: but this cunning does not so manifest itself in the world as afterwards when they become spirits: for in the world they cover over their cunning with an external piety and feigned morality, which conceal it from view, but whereas it resides in their spirits, it be-

comes very manifest when externals are removed, as is the case after death in the spiritual world : it is however to be observed, that
the cunning which is signified by the head of the dragon, is cunning
in perverting the truths and goods of the Word by reasonings
grounded in fallacies and in sophistry, also in persuasive principles,
by which the understanding is fascinated, thus inducing upon falses
the appearance of truths ; that this is the case, may also appear
from the serpent which seduced the first parents, concerning which
it is said, "that he was cunning above every wild beast of the field"
(Gen. iii. 1) : for by that serpent is signified the same as by the dragon here mentioned, wherefore the latter is also called the old serpent that seduceth the whole world, verse 9th of this chapter.

716. "And ten horns"—That hereby is signified much power, appears from the signification of horn, as denoting the power of truth
against the false and evil, and, in the opposite sense, the power of
the false against truth and good, concerning which see above, n.
316, 567 ; and from the signification of ten, as denoting all and all
things, likewise many and many things, concerning which also see
above, n. 675 ; hence it may appear that by the ten horns is signified much power. That the dragon had much power, appears from
the things which follow, viz. that on account thereof the male child
which the woman brought forth was caught up unto God ; that his
tail drew down from heaven the third part of the stars ; likewise,
that he fought with Michael and his angels ; and afterwards, that
he excited Gog and Magog, and a great number of the nations, to
war against the saints. The reason why such power is attributed
to the dragon, is, because by him are understood those who separate
faith from the goods of charity, which are works, and confirm themselves therein by the literal sense of the Word, which they thus bend
back from its genuine sense and as it were draw down from heaven ;
and, because, in the end of the church, which the Apocalypse treats
of, there is no charity remaining, whence the dragon then has power ;
for every one at the end of the church desires to live to himself, to
the world, and to his own natural temper, and few to the Lord, to
heaven, and to life eternal, and the principle concerning faith alone,
which is faith separate from charity, favors that life, and like the
current of a river carries away all so to believe and so to live : hence
it is that the dragon, by which such persons and such things are signified, appeared to have ten horns. It has been said before that
falses from evil have not the least power, but it is to be observed,
that they have no power against truth derived from good ; for truth
derived from good is from the Lord, and all power belongs to the
Lord by His divine truth ; but the reason why falses from evil are
said to have power, which is signified by the ten horns of the dragon, is, because they prevail against those who are principled in them,
for they act as one, and man is in evil and thence in falses hereditarily from his parents, and afterwards from actual life, especially
in the end of the church, and those falses from evil cannot be expelled from man in a moment but by degrees, for if they were to be
expelled in a moment, man would expire, inasmuch as they consti-

tute his life; and whereas the state of man is such at the end of the church, therefore the falses of evil prevail, although they have not the least power against truth from good; the Lord by His divine truth could immediately reject the falses of evil which are with man, but this would be to cast man immediately into hell, for they are first to be removed, and so far as they are removed, so far room is given for truths from good to be implanted, and man is reformed. The same persons who are here understood by the dragon are also understood by the goat who fought with the ram in Daniel, chap. viii. and also by the goats in Matthew, chap. xxv. for by the goats are there signified those who are in faith separate from charity, and by the ram and the sheep, those who are in charity.

717. "And upon his heads seven diadems"—That hereby are signified divine truths in the ultimate of order, which are the truths of the literal sense of the Word, in this case those truths adulterated and profaned, appears from the signification of the heads of the dragon, as denoting the scientific truths of the Word, which are adulterated and profaned; that they signify insanity in things spiritual, but still cunning in deceiving and seducing, may be seen above, n. 714; and from the signification of diadems or precious stones, as denoting divine truths in the ultimate of order, which are the truths of the literal sense of the Word, concerning which we shall speak presently; and from the signification of seven, as denoting all things, and being predicated of things holy, and, in the opposite sense, of things profane, concerning which see above, n. 715, in this case concerning things profane, because concerning the truths of the Word adulterated, and thereby profaned; hence it is evident, that the seven diadems upon the heads of the dragon, signify divine truths in the ultimate of order, in the present case, adulterated and profaned. The reason why precious stones, which are diadems, signify divine truths in the ultimate of order, which are the truths of the literal sense of the Word, is, because a stone signifies truth, whence precious stones signify divine truths: the reason why they denote divine truths in the ultimate of order, which are the truths of the literal sense of the Word, is, because those truths are translucent, for in them there is a spiritual sense, and in this sense is the light of heaven, from which all things of the literal sense of the Word are pellucid, and also, according to the series of things treated of in the internal sense, are variegated, whence arise modifications of heavenly light, which present colors such as appear in the heavens, and thence in precious stones of various kinds. The reason why diadems were seen upon the heads of the dragon, is, because the truths of the literal sense of the Word shine, wherever they are, as well with the evil as with the good, for the spiritual light which is in them, is not extinguished by their being with the evil, for heaven still flows into those truths; but whereas the evil adulterate them, and thence do not see anything of the light of heaven in them, yet still believe them to be holy, by reason of their applying them to confirm the falses of their religion, hence from the faith they have in their sanctity they still shine before them; and inasmuch as this is

the case, and by those truths they procure to-themselves communication with the heavens, therefore they are at length deprived of them, and left to their own falses in which there is not any light, which takes place when they are let down into hell. That the truths of the literal sense of the Word appear as diadems, may be manifest from the diadems in the spiritual world: in the palaces of the angels in heaven there are various things which are refulgent from precious stones; and precious stones are also sometimes sent down into the parts below, and are presented as a gift to those who have done any good, yea, they are also sold there as in the world, especially by the Jews, who also trade with them there; the reason why it is given and granted to the Jews in the spiritual world, as in the natural world, to trade with them, is, because they account the Word holy as to the literal sense; hence also it is that the noble women below the heavens also adorn themselves with diadems in like manner as in the world; and when it is inquired whence those diadems are in heaven, and thence in the parts below, it is said, that they are from the Lord, and from the spiritual light which is from Him, and that they are the ultimates of that light, which are called effects, also, that they are representative forms of the affections of truth from good, thus that they are divine truths in the ultimate of order, such as are the truths of the literal sense of the Word. Such being the origin of precious stones, it is therefore also permitted to some in the world of spirits to form diadems by ingrafting certain truths from the literal sense of the Word, but these diadems are not genuine and of a crystalline hardness, because made by art. From these considerations it may now appear what is signified by diadems, or by precious stones, in the following passages; as in Isaiah: "O thou afflicted, tossed with tempest and not comforted, behold I will lay thy stones with stibium, and thy foundations in sapphires, and I will make thy suns a carbuncle, and thy gates into fire-stones [pyropus], and all thy border into stones of desire, and all thy sons shall be taught of Jehovah" (liv. 11, 12, 13). These things are said of the barren who brought not forth, and who should have many sons; and by the barren are signified the gentiles, who had not divine truths, because they had not the Word, whence they are called the afflicted and tossed with tempest and not comforted, to be afflicted and tossed with tempest being predicated of falses, by which they were infested and carried every way; that the Lord, when He came, would reveal to them divine truths, and instruct them is signified by, I will lay thy stones with stibium, and thy foundations in sapphires, and I will make thy suns a carbuncle, and thy gates into fire-stones [pyropus], and all thy borders into stones of desire; that by the precious stones here mentioned are understood divine truths in the ultimate of order, such as are those of the literal sense of the Word, in which are contained internal truths, such as are those in the spiritual sense of the Word, is evident, for by the foundations, gates, and borders, which were to be laid with those stones, are signified ultimate principles, whence it follows that in the above passage by stones in general, and by sapphires, carbuncle,

and fire-stones, are signified such truths as are in the literal sense of
the Word, which are ultimate truths, because for the natural and
sensual man; inasmuch as the instruction of the gentiles in divine
truths is thereby understood, therefore it follows, and all thy sons
shall be taught of Jehovah; but what is specifically signified by the
sapphire, carbuncle, and fire-stone, it is not necessary to explain in
this place, only that precious stones in general signify ultimate
truths.   Inasmuch as the city of the New Jerusalem signifies the
doctrine of the New Church, and the foundation of its wall ultimate
divine truths, and the gates introductory divine truths, therefore the
foundations are described by twelve precious stones, and the gates
by pearls, in the Apocalypse: " The foundations of the walls of the
city of the New Jerusalem were adorned with every precious stone:
the first foundation jasper, the second sapphire, the third chalce-
dony, the fourth emerald, the fifth sardonyx, the sixth sardius, the
seventh chrysolite, the eighth beryl, the ninth topaz, the tenth chrysoprasus, the eleventh hyacinth, the twelfth amethyst.   The twelve
gates were twelve pearls, every gate was a pearl.   And the street
of the city was pure gold, as it were pellucid glass" (xxii. 18–21).
By these twelve precious stones, of which were the foundations,
and by the twelve pearls, of which were the gates, are signified ultimate divine truths, which are the truths of the literal sense of the
Word, upon which the doctrine of that church is founded, and by
which man is introduced as by gates; the reason why the foundations are said to be of precious stones, and the gates of pearls, is,
because the literal sense of the Word contains in itself the spiritual
sense, thus the light of heaven, from which the literal sense is pellucid, as those stones are from light and from fire; but more will be
said upon this subject, when we come to the explication of that
chapter.   Similar things are signified by the precious stones which
made the breast-plate of judgment, called urim and thummim, which
was upon the ephod of Aaron, and also by those which were set
upon the shoulder of the ephod; as in Moses: " They shall make
the ephod of gold, blue, purple scarlet double dyed, and fine twined
linen, the work of a contriver; thou shalt take two onyx stones,
and shalt engrave upon them the names of the sons of Israel, the
work of the engraver of stone, with the engravings of a seal thou
shalt engrave the two stones upon the names of the sons of Israel;
thou shalt make them to be set in ouches of gold; and thou shalt
put the two stones upon the shoulders of the ephod.   And thou shalt
make the breast-plate of judgment with the work of a contriver, as
the work of the ephod shalt thou make it, and thou shalt fill it with
filling of stones: there shall be four orders of stones; the first order
a ruby, a topaz, a carbuncle; the second order a chrysoprasus, a
sapphire, and a diamond; the third order a cyanus, an agate, and
an amethyst; and the fourth order a beryl, an onyx, and a jasper:
the stones shall be upon the names of the sons of Israel, twelve upon
their names, the engravings of a seal for every one upon his name,
they shall be for the twelve tribes: this is the breast plate of judgment, urim and thummim" (Exod. xxviii. 6–30).   What these things

involve, no one can know, unless it be known what Aaron represented, and what his garments thence signified, and the ephod in
particular, for it was on account of their being significative that they
were called the garments of holiness; likewise what was signified
by the breast plate upon the ephod, which was called the breast-
plate of judgment, urim and thummim; also what was signified by
the twelve tribes of Israel, and what by the twelve stones upon their
names : as to what respects Aaron himself, he represented the Lord
as to the priesthood, which is His celestial kingdom; but his garments in general represented the spiritual kingdom, for this in the
heavens invests the celestial kingdom; for there are two kingdoms
into which the heavens are distinguished, the celestial kingdom and
the spiritual kingdom; that is called the celestial kingdom where
the divine good proceeding from the Lord is received, and that the
spiritual kingdom where divine truth is received; wherefore divine
truth is signified by the garments of Aaron in general, and by the
ephod divine truth in ultimates, inasmuch as that was the ultimate
clothing; that garments in general signify truths, and that the garments of the Lord, which appeared bright as light, when He was
transfigured before the three disciples, signified the divine truth proceeding from Him, and in like manner the garments divided by the
soldiers, may be seen above, n. 64, 65, 195, 271, 395, 475, 476, 637;
hence it may appear, that by the twelve stones in the breast-plate
of the ephod were signified divine truths in ultimates, in like manner
as by the twelve sons of Israel, and by the twelve tribes; that both
these, in the Word, signify the truths of the church in every complex, may be seen above, n. 431, 657. The reason why that breast-
plate was composed of precious stones, under which were the names
of the twelve sons of Israel, was, that responses might be made
thereby from heaven, which were represented in the breast plate,
and from it, by variegations of the colors effulgent from those stones,
according to the representations of divine truths in the heavens;
for the divine truths which flow down from the Lord through the
heavens towards the parts below, are there exhibited or presented
to view by variegations of colors; from which it may appear, that
by precious stones are also signified divine truths in ultimates : but
these things may be seen more fully explained in the A. C. n. 9856–
9099; and concerning the two onyx stones which were upon the
shoulders of the ephod, n. 9831–9855; that the ephod signified the
external of the spiritual kingdom, which is divine truth in ultimates,
n. 9824; but what is specifically signified by the ruby, the topaz,
and the carbuncle, n. 9865 : what by the chrysoprasus, the sapphire,
and the diamond, n. 9868 : what by the cyanus, the agate, and the
amethyst, n. 9870; and what by the beryl, the onyx, and the jasper, n. 9872. Similar things are also signified by the precious
stones by which the sciences of the knowledges of truth and good,
and thence the intelligence of the king of Tyre, is described in Ezekiel : "King of Tyre, thou full of wisdom and perfect in beauty;
thou hast been in Eden, the garden of God; every precious stone

was thy covering, the ruby, the topaz, and the diamond, the beryl, the sardonyx, and the jasper, the sapphire, chrysoprasus, and the emerald, and gold. Thou art the cherub, the expansion of covering, and I have set thee; thou hast been in the mountain of the holiness of God, thou hast walked in the midst of the stones of fire" xxviii. 12, 13). Inasmuch as by the king of Tyre are signified the knowledges of the truth of the church from the Word, and indeed from the literal sense thereof, hence it is said that he was in Eden the garden of God, Eden the garden of God signifying intelligence by the Word from the Lord; for Eden, as the east, denotes the Lord, and the garden of God is intelligence from Him, and whereas true intelligence can only be procured, that is, be given, by the knowledges of truth and good from the Word understood according to their genuine sense, hence it is said, every precious stone was thy covering, every precious stone signifying the knowledges of truth and good, and covering signifying the external of the Word, which covers the internal thereof; the external of the Word is the literal sense covering the internal, which is the spiritual sense; inasmuch as man has thence wisdom and intelligence, therefore it is said, king of Tyre, thou full of wisdom and perfect in beauty, beauty signifying intelligence, because all beauty in the heavens is according thereto: the literal sense of the Word is also understood by the cherub, the expansion of covering, for cherubs signify defence that the Lord may not be approached except by the good of love, and the literal sense of the Word, inasmuch as it covers the interiors thereof, is what defends: the mountain of holiness signifies the church as to the doctrine of love and charity; and the stones of fire in the midst of which he walked, signify truths from the good of love, according to which is the life: that by precious stones are here signified truths pellucent from the light of heaven, which is divine truth, may manifestly appear from this consideration, that by Tyre, in the Word, are signified the knowledges of truth and good, which knowledges are ultimate truths, such as are of the literal sense of the Word; that Tyre signifies the knowledges of truth and good, may be seen above, n. 514. Again, in the same prophet: "Syria was thy trader by reason of the multitude of thy works, purple, and needle-work, and fine linen, and coral, and fire-stone [pyropus] with chrysoprasus, they gave in thy tradings; the traders of Sheba and Raamah, these were thy traders by the chief of all spices, and by every precious stone and gold" (xxvii. 16, 22); treating also of Tyre, whereby are signified the knowledges of truth and good appertaining to the church from the Word, as above: inasmuch as by Syria and by Sheba and Raamah are likewise signified the knowledges of truth and good, and by tradings the acquisitions thereof, therefore it is said that those nations gave precious stones in their tradings; the knowledges of truth and good are truths in ultimates, such as are those of the literal sense of the Word. And in Job: "A place the stones thereof are of sapphire, and its dust of gold; whence is wisdom found, and what is the place of intelligence? gold is not given in comparison with it, neither is silver weighed for the price of it; it cannot be valued with the gold of Ophir ; the precious onyx and the sapqpire, the gold and the diamond, cannot equal it, the coral and the gabish shall not be mentioned with it; and the choice of wisdom is above pearls, the topaz of Ethiopia shall not contend with it ; lo, the fear of the Lord is wisdom, and to depart from evil is intelligence" (xxviii. 6, 12, 13, 15–19, 28).   Inasmuch as all wisdom and intelligence is from ultimate divine truths spiritually understood, and those truths are understood by the precious stones there named, as the onyx, the sapphire, the diamond, the topaz, and pearls, and inasmuch as these stones, so far as they are of earthly materials, and accounted precious in the world, are of no account to intelligence and wisdom, therefore it is said, that they are not to be compared therewith, neither gold and silver ; comparisons are made with such things, because they are significative, and it is meant that otherwise they are respectively as nothing. . And in David : " Thou Jehovah shalt arise and have mercy upon Zion, because Thy servants desire the stones thereof" (Psalm cii. 14, 15).   By the stones of Zion which the servants of Jehovah desire, are understood divine truths, for by Zion, upon which Jehovah shall have mercy, is understood the church which is in celestial love.   And in Zechariah : " Behold the stone which I have given before the chief priest Joshua, upon one stone seven eyes: behold I engrave the engraving of it; in that day a man shall cry aloud to his companion, under the vine and under the fig-tree" (iii. 9, 10).   These things are said concerning the advent of the Lord ; and by the stone given before Joshua the priest, is signified divine truth, which is the Word ; seven eyes in one stone signify divine wisdom and intelligence, which are of divine truth, thus of the Word, seven being predicated of the holy things of heaven and the church, and eyes denoting intelligence and wisdom ; to engrave an engraving signifies the representative and significative thereof ; by the vine and the fig-tree under which they shall come, is signified the church and doctrine from internal and external truths, internal truths are what are called spiritual, and external truths are what are called natural, and the former are signified by the vine, and the latter by the fig-tree.   And in Moses : " They saw the God of Israel, and under His feet was the work of sapphire stone, as the substance of heaven as to cleanness" (Exod. xxiv. 10).   By the God of Israel is understood the Lord ; by the work of sapphire stone under His feet, is understood divine truth in ultimates, such as the Word is in the letter, for the sole of the feet signifies the ultimate, which alone could be seen by the Jewish nation, for they were in the external of the Word, of the church, and of worship, and not in internals : the sapphire stone signifies translucidity from internal truths : as the substance of heaven as to cleanness, signifies the translucence of the angelic heaven; but these things are explained more fully in the A. C. n. 9406, 9407, 9408. Inasmuch as a precious stone signifies divine truth in ultimates translucent from interior truths, therefore the luminary of the city New Jerusalem is described in the Apocalypse, as " like to a stone most precious, as jasper stone, like resplendent chrystal" (xxi. 11); and inasmuch as by the white horse, in the same book, is signified the understanding of the Word, and by Him that sat thereon the Lord as to the Word, therefore it is said, "that upon the head of Him who sat upon the white horse were many diadems, and that His name was called the Word of God" (Apoc. xix. 12, 13). So far concerning precious stones with those who are in divine truths; something shall now be said concerning the same with those who are in infernal falses, to whom precious stones are also given whilst they live in the world, because they also have the knowledges of truth and good from the natural sense of the Word, which is the sense of the letter, whence it is that precious stones or diadems are equally ascribed to them, as in the present case to the dragon, upon whose heads were seen seven diadems; the reason is, because the Word is still the Word, and the truths thereof are still truths in themselves, whether they be with the evil or with the good; the perversion and falsification of them by the evil does not change their essence. From hence it is that in the following parts of the Apocalypse, the like were seen upon the woman sitting on the scarlet beast, by whom Babylon is described; thus it is written: "The woman that sat upon the scarlet beast was full of names of blasphemy, and had seven heads and ten horns; she was clothed in purple and scarlet, and adorned with gold, and precious stones, and pearls, and upon her forehead a name written, Babylon the great" (Apoc. xvii. 3, 4, 5). But more of this in what follows; in like manner it is written in another passage in the Apocalypse: "The merchants of the earth shall weep and wail over Babylon the great, that her merchandize no one buyeth any more, the merchandize of gold and silver, and precious stone, and of pearl and fine linen, and of purple, and silk, and scarlet; and the merchants shall say alas! alas! the great city which was clothed in fine linen, and purple, and scarlet, adorned with gold, precious stone, and pearls" (xviii. 11, 12). Inasmuch as by precious stones, purple and fine linen, are signified the knowledges of truth and good from the Word, therefore it is said concerning "the rich man at whose gate lay Lazarus, that he was clothed with purple and fine linen" (Luke xvi. 19, 20). By the rich man is understood the Jewish nation, which, because it had the Word in which are divine truths, is said to be clothed in purple and fine linen; and by the poor Lazarus are understood the gentiles, who had not the Word, nor, consequently, truths; hence it is evident, that garments of purple and fine linen appertained to the rich man although he was evil, and afterwards cast into hell. It is also said concerning the king of the north, who made war against the king of the south, in Daniel, "that he shall honor God, fortifications upon his station, a God whom his fathers knew not shall he honor, with gold, silver, and precious stone, and desirable things; he shall make strong holds of fortifications with a strange god, whom he shall acknowledge and greatly honor" (xi. 38, 39). The subject treated of in this chapter is concerning the war of the king of the north with the king of the south; and by the king of the north are understood those who are in science from the Word, and yet not in the life

thereof, thus also those who are in faith alone so called, and yet not
in charity, the latter being rejected as not conducing to salvation;
but by the king of the south are understood those who are in intelligence from the Word, because in charity; these are the king of
south, or kings of the south, for the south signifies light, and
light signifies intelligence, and the light of intelligence is from the
Word, with those who are in charity, which is the life of faith; but
the reason why the former are understood by the king of the north,
is, because the north signifies night, and also a cold light, such as
is the light of winter, from which, inasmuch as there is no heat,
there is no fructification; for spiritual heat is charity, and all germination is from heat by light: by the war between those kings is
described the last time of the church, when the all of salvation is
placed in science from the Word, and nothing thereof in the life,
thus, with the Jewish nation, in traditions, by which they falsified
the Word, and the truths of the Word become traditions when there
is no life of charity; in like manner, the truths of the Word become
falses when faith is separated from charity: from these considerations it may appear, that by the king of the north, are also understood those who are in faith alone, that is, in faith without charity.
The same are also understood in Daniel by the he-goat which fought
with the ram; and also by the dragon in this chapter, with this difference, that by the dragon are properly understood the men of erudition who have confirmed themselves by doctrine and life in faith
separate from charity, for these have poison as dragons, which destroys charity; hence it is that the angel Michael is also mentioned
in Daniel, as well as in this chapter, see Daniel chap. xii. 1; that
they pervert and falsify the truths of the Word, who place the all of
the church in the science of knowledges thence derived, and nothing
in the life, is understood by the king of the north honoring a strange
god which their fathers knew not, and by honoring him with gold,
silver, precious stones, and pearls; his god denoting the truths of
the word falsified, inasmuch as where God is mentioned in the Word,
the Lord is understood as to divine truth, thus also the divine truth
proceeding from the Lord, and when Jehovah is mentioned, the
Lord is understood as to divine good, thus also the divine good proceeding from the Lord, therefore it is that by the strange god, whom
his fathers knew not, are understood the truths of the Word falsified,
which in themselves are falses, and not acknowledged by those who
were before of the church; those truths and goods of the Word
themselves, although falsified, are signified by precious stones and
by desirable things, likewise by gold and silver, for the truths of the
Word do not change their essence by being with those who are evil;
by the fortifications upon the station, and by the strong holds of fortifications, are signified such things as are of self-derived intelligence, confirmed by the literal sense of the Word, which is of such
a nature, that if it be not interiorly understood, it may be construed
to confirm any heresies whatever. From these considerations it may
now appear, what is signified by the seven diadems upon the heads
of the dragon.

718. " And his tail drew the third part of the stars of heaven"—
That hereby is signified the falsification and adulteration of all the
truths of the Word, appears from the signification 'of drawing with
the tail, when predicated of the dragon, as denoting falsification and
adulteration, concerning which we shall speak presently; and from
the signification of the third part, as denoting all and as predicated
of truths, concerning which see above, n. 384, 506; and from the
signification of the stars of heaven, as denoting the knowledges of
truth and good from the Word, concerning which also see above, n.
72, 402; thus also as denoting truths, for the knowledges of truth
and good are the truths of the natural man, from which is the intelligence of the rational and spiritual man: hence it may appear that
by drawing with the tail the third part of the stars of heaven, when
spoken of the dragon, is signified to falsify and adulterate the truths
of the Word. The reason of this signification is, because by the
dragon in general are understood all who acknowledge the Word,
and read it, and still do not live according to it, and this because
they separate life, which is charity, from faith, and believe it is
enough to think those things which are in the Word, and to persuade themselves that they are saved by thinking and speaking certain expressions thereof from trust and confidence, and that faith
alone justifies and saves, without any regard to the life or works;
that these are understood by the dragon, may be seen above, n. 714:
since in order to confirm their dogmas from the Word, such persons
adduce the passages wherein faith is mentioned, and where faith is
spoken of, but where love and charity are mentioned, and doing is
spoken of, they pervert them by application to faith alone, and so
falsify the Word, which from beginning to end is the doctrine of love
to the Lord and of charity towards the neighbor, therefore this falsification and adulteration of the truths of the Word is understood
by the dragon drawing down with his tail the third part of the stars
of heaven; for the tail is the continuation of the cerebrum through
the spine of the back, of which it is an appendix, and so is actuated
from the head and the body according to the appetites and desires
of the natural man, wherefore the motions of the tail are effects
flowing from the delights of the loves in which the sensual man is,
and the loves of the sensual man are what falsify and adulterate the
truths of the Word: that the tail signifies the sensual principle,
which is the ultimate of the natural man, may be seen above, n. 559;
whether we say that the loves of the sensual man falsify and adulterate the truths of the Word, or that the sensual principle does this,
it amounts to the same, for the sensual principle loves to live to the
body and the world, thus to its own inclination, and this life is perceived sensitively, but not the interior life, wherefore the latter it
denies.

719. It is said, that the sensual principle falsifies and adulterates
the truths of the Word, but it is also expedient to be known how
this can be effected, for they who do not know how the case herein
is, and the quality of the Word, may suppose that the truths of the

Word, inasmuch as they are truths, and are extant in the literal sense thereof, cannot be made falses : to illustrate this we will take an example from nature, which is thence perceptible to the natural man : it appears before the eyes, as if the sun was carried every day about the earth, and also once every year, and hence it is said in the Word that the sun rises and sets, and thereby causes the day, noon, evening, and night, also the seasons of spring, summer, autumn, and winter, and thus days and years, when notwithstanding the sun stands unmoved, and the earth revolves daily, and is carried about the sun yearly, consequently the progression of the sun is only an appearance and thence a fallacy : when therefore this truth is known and received, that the sun is not moved but the earth, then each becomes true ; namely, that the sun stands unmoved in the centre of its world, and also that he progresses ; that he stands unmoved is true for the rational man, and that he progresses for the sensual, thus in both cases it is truth, actually for the rational man, and apparently for the sensual : but if that phenomenon be not illustrated by the rational man, then what is false is believed, namely, that the sun actually progresses, and so the truth that the sun is not moved out of its place, but the earth, is falsified, but it is not falsified when the rational man illustrates the matter. The case is similar with singular the things of the Word in the sense of the letter; this sense, inasmuch as it is the ultimate, is natural, and adapted to the apprehension of the sensual man, thus of infants and of the simple, wherefore most things in that sense are appearances of truth, which, unless they are at the same time perceived from a spiritual, that is, from an enlightened understanding, become falses, for they are then believed as if they were actually and not only apparently true ; but the case is otherwise when they are at the same time perceived intellectually and spiritually, for then all things of the Word become true, in the genuine sense actually true, and in the literal sense apparently true, as was said above concerning the sun : from these considerations it may appear how innumerable things in the Word are falsified and adulterated ; as that God tempts, that he is angry, that he does evil, that he casts into hell ; likewise, that at the day of the last judgment the Lord will come in the clouds of heaven, that then the sun and the moon will withdraw their light, and that the stars will fall from heaven; also that the world with the earth will perish, and a new creation of all things take place ; besides other things of a like nature, which are truths of the literal sense of the Word, but which become falses if they are not at the same time perceived from an enlightened understanding : but in what follows, it will be explained, how faith alone, which is faith separate from charity, falsifies all things of the Word.

720. " And cast them to the earth"—That hereby is signified the extinction and destruction thereof, appears from the signification of casting to the earth, when predicated concerning the stars, by which are signified the knowledges of truth and good from the Word, consequently truths, as denoting to extinguish and destroy them, since truths are extinguished and destroyed when they are falsified and

adulterated; truths falsified and adulterated are greater falses than those from any other origin, for falses from any other origin do not so extinguish and destroy truths, but give some room for them, either in or near themselves; by falses from other origins, are meant especially those which arise from ignorance, from fallacies, and from religion with those who have not the Word. It is to be observed, that they who live in evil, and yet say that they are saved, because they have faith, have scarce any genuine truth, however many things they know and draw forth from the literal sense of the Word; for such is the nature of this sense, that if it be not interiorly comprehended, it may be explained in different manners, and if it be not viewed from genuine truths, is believed according to the letter only, and so is falsified, according to what was shown in the preceding article by comparison with the progression and station of the sun: that such persons have scarce any genuine truth, was discovered from some in the spiritual world, who had confirmed faith alone in doctrine and life, who being explored by the angels, it was found that they did not even know or acknowledge one genuine truth, at which the angels wondered: hence it was evident that they had extinguished and destroyed in themselves the truths of the Word: this therefore is signified by the dragon drawing down the third part of the stars of heaven with his tail, and casting them to the earth; as is also said of the he-goat in Daniel: "The horn of the he-goat of the she-goats, grew even to the army of the heavens, and cast down of the army to the earth, and of the stars, and trampled them under foot; and he cast truth to the earth" (viii. 10, 12). By the army of the heavens are understood all the truths and goods of heaven and the church. The like is signified by "the stars which shall fall from heaven" (Matthew xxiv. 29).

721. "And the dragon stood before the woman, that was about to bring forth"—That hereby is signified, the hatred of those who are understood by the dragon, against the church with those who will be in the doctrine and thence in the life of love and charity from the Lord, appears from the signification of the dragon, as denoting those who are in the science of the knowledges of truth from the literal sense of the Word, and not in a life according thereto, concerning which see above, n. 714; and from the signification of the woman, as denoting the church which is in the doctrine, and thence in the life, of love to the Lord and charity towards the neighbor, concerning which see above, n. 707; that it denotes the hatred of those who are signified by the dragon, against that church and its doctrine, is meant by standing before the woman about to bring forth, and by being willing to devour the birth; and from the signification of bringing forth, as denoting to produce such things as appertain to the church, which are doctrinals, in the present case concerning love to the Lord and concerning charity towards the neighbor, for by the male son which the woman brought forth, is signified the doctrine of that church. The reason why such things are signified by bringing forth, is, because by generations, births, and nativities, in the Word, are understood spiritual generations,

births, and nativities, which are effected by truths and by a life according thereto; hence it is that where spiritual generation, which is called regeneration, is treated of in the Word, it is described by natural generation and birth; as in John: "Jesus said to Nicodemus, unless a man be born again, he cannot see the kingdom of God. Nicodemus said, how can a man be born when he is old, can he enter a second time into his mother's womb, and be born? Jesus answered, verily, verily, I say unto thee, unless a man be born of water and the spirit, he cannot enter into the kingdom of God; that which is born of the flesh is flesh, but that which is born of the spirit is spirit" (iii. 3–6). Inasmuch as Nicodemus understood not the spiritual sense of the Lord's words, that a man must be born again, the Lord explained, that to be born again signified to be born of water and the spirit, thus to be regenerated, namely by truths from the Word, and by a life according thereto, for water signifies truths, and a spirit a life according to them. But in other passages in the Word, where to travail in labor, to bring forth, to beget, and to generate, are mentioned, spiritual travailing, birth, nativity and generation are understood, although they are not explained, inasmuch as the Word in the letter is natural, but in the bosom spiritual: the reason why to bring forth signifies to bring forth spiritually, is, because the man who is regenerating is also in like manner as it were conceived, carried in the womb, born, and educated, as a man is conceived from his father, carried in the womb of his mother, born, and afterwards educated. In order to confirm the spiritual signification of births and nativities, some passages shall be here adduced from the Word: thus in Isaiah: "Blush, O Zidon, the sea hath said, the fortification of the sea, saying, I have not travailed neither brought forth, I have not educated young men, nor brought up virgins; when Egypt hath fame, they shall be seized with grief as at the fame of Tyre" (xxiii. 4, 5). By Zidon and Tyre are signified the knowledges of good and truth from the Word; that the church has not thereby procured for itself any intelligence and wisdom, nor affected any uses, is signified by not travailing nor bringing forth, by not educating young men nor bringing up virgins, young men denoting the truths of the church, and virgins the goods thereof: but these things may be seen explained above, n. 275. Again: "Thy chastening is upon them, as a pregnant woman that draws near to her delivery, crying out in her pangs; so have we done before Thee, Jehovah: we have conceived, we have travailed in labor, we have as it were brought forth wind, we have not wrought salvation in the earth, neither have the inhabitants of the world fallen; thy dead shall live" (xxvi. 16–19). These things are said of the last times of the church, when falses and evils so far increase, that they cannot be reformed and regenerated; this state is understood by the chastening of Jehovah upon them; that then the perception, and acquisition of any degree of truth is effected with difficulty, is signified by a pregnant woman, who draws near to her delivery, crying in her pangs; that in the place of truths they imbibe vanities, in which there are no truths, is signified by, we have conceived, we have travailed, we have as it were brought forth wind, wind denoting such vanities; that no uses of life are from them, is signified by, we have not wrought salvations to the earth ; that still when the Lord should come they should be taught and regenerated by truths from Him, is signified by, thy dead shall live, and by the things which follow. Again : " Sing, O barren, thou that didst not bear, break forth into singing and cry aloud, thou that didst not travail with child, for more are the sons of the desolate than the sons of the married" (liv. 1) : treating of the advent of the Lord and of the new church to be established by Him with the Gentiles, who are understood by the barren, who did not bear, and by the desolate who shall have many sons; they are called barren because they knew not the Lord, neither had the Word where truths are, wherefore they could not be regenerated ; sons denote truths from the Lord by the Word ; the church which is in possession of the Word, from which the Lord is known, is understood by the married who hath no sons; the joy of those who are of the new church, and who before had not truths, is signified by her breaking forth into singing and crying aloud, who did not travail, to travail denotes to have in the womb. And in 1 Samuel : " They who were stricken are girt about with strength, they that were full have hired themselves out for bread, and the hungry have ceased, even till the barren have borne seven, and she that bare many hath failed" (ii. 5) : this is the prophetic song of Hannah the mother of Samuel : by the stricken who are girt about with strength, are understood the gentiles, with whom the church was to be established, who are said to be stricken by reason of the want of the knowledges of truth, and being thence rejected by those who were of the Jewish church ; to be girt about with strength, signifies that they are gifted with truths from good, and thence with power ; by the full who were hired for bread, and the hungry who ceased, are understood those who were of the Jewish church, who are said to be full because they had truths in abundance, and to be hired for bread because they could not be brought to learn and to do them, except as hirelings; that they neither desired to know them, is signified by, the hungry have ceased ; the same church is also understood by, she that bare many hath failed; but the gentiles or nations which would acknowledge the Lord, and receive the Word, and thence suffer themselves to be regenerated into the church, are understood by the barren who shall bear seven, seven denoting all and many, and being predicated of the holy things of the church. And in Jeremiah : " She that bear seven shall languish, she shall breathe out her soul, her sun shall set whilst it is yet day" (xv. 9). By these words is signified that the church which possesses all truth, because it possesses the Word, shall perish, until nothing of truth and good remains ; by bearing seven is signified to be gifted with all truths from the Word ; by languishing, and by her sun setting, is signified successively, and at length altogether to perish ; by breathing out the soul is signified to perish as to all truths, and by the sun setting is signified as to all the goods of love; when it is as yet day, signifies, whilst the Word

is still acknowledged.   Again in Isaiah : " Before she travailed she
brought forth, before grief came upon her she is delivered of a male;
who hath heard such a thing, who hath seen such a thing ? shall the
earth be made to travail in one day ? shall a nation be born at once ?
as soon as Zion travailed she brought forth her sons ; shall I break
and not generate, saith Jehovah, shall I cause to be generated, and
shut the womb ? rejoice with Jerusalem, exult in her, all ye that
love her, that ye may suck and be saturated from the pap of her
consolations" (lxvi. 7, 8, 9, 10) : treating also of the advent of the
Lord and of the establishment of the church with the gentiles : their
reformation and regeneration is described by travailing, bringing
forth, being delivered of a male, and by breaking the matrix and
generating ; for, as was said above, the man who is generated anew,
is in like manner as it were conceived, carried in the womb, born,
educated, and grows to adolescence, as from a father and mother;
by Zion and Jerusalem is understood the church and its doctrine,
and by sucking and being saturated from the breast of her consolations, is signified to be fully instructed in truths originating in good
from the delight of love according to desire ; by one day in which
those things shall take place is signified the advent of the Lord.
Again in David : "from before the Lord bring forth, O earth, from
before the God of Jacob" (Psalm cxiv. 7).   By bring forth, O earth,
is signified the establishment of the church, or the reformation of
those who will be of the church, to bring forth denoting to receive
truths and to be reformed, and the earth denoting the church ; it is
said, from before the Lord and from before the God of Jacob, because
reformation is understood as to good and as to truth, for the Lord is
called Lord from good, and God from truth.   Again, in Jeremiah :
" Behold I bring them from the land of the north, and I will gather
them together from the sides of the earth ; amongst them the blind
and the lame, the pregnant woman and her that is bringing forth
together, they shall return hither a great company" (xxxi. 8) : treating also of the restoration of the church with the gentiles by the
Lord : the gentiles or nations which are in falses, and which are in
appearances of truth, such as the truth of the Word in the literal
sense, are understood by the land of the north, and by the sides of
the earth, the north signifying falses, and the sides of the earth such
ultimate truths, hence it is also said, the blind and the lame, the
woman with child and her that brings forth together, the blind denoting those who are not in truths, and the lame those who are not
in goods, the woman with child those who receive truths, and her
who brings forth those who do them ; the establishment of the
church with them is signified by, behold I bring them, I will gather
them together, and they shall return hither a great company.
Again, in Isaiah : "Look unto the rock from which ye were hewn,
and to the digging of the pit from which ye were digged ; look unto
Abraham your father, and unto Sarah who bare you ; for I have
called him only, and I will bless him, and will multiply him ; for
Jehovah shall console Zion, He shall console all her wastenesses,
and shall make her wilderness as Eden, and her desert as the garden

of Jehovah" (li. 1, 2, 3).   These things also are said concerning the Lord, and concerning the new church from Him: the Lord as to divine truth, and as to the doctrine of truth, is understood by the rock from which they were hewn, and by the pit from which they were digged, see above, n. 411: but the Lord as to the Divine [principle], from which comes reformation, is understood by Abraham to whom they should look, and by Sarah who bare them: for by Abraham, Isaac, and Jacob, in the Word, are not understood those persons, but the Lord as to His Divine [principle] Itself, and the Divine Human, as may be seen in the A. C. n. 1893, 2833, 2836, 3245, 3252, 3305, 3439, 3703, 4615, 6089, 6185, 6276, 6804, 6847; but the heavenly marriage, which is of divine good and divine truth, from which comes all reformation and thence the church, is signified by Abraham, and Sarah, who bare them; inasmuch as the Lord is understood by Abraham, therefore it is said, I have called him only, and I will bless him, and will multiply him, and afterwards that Jehovah shall console Zion and all her wastenesses, Zion denoting the new church, wastenesses, truths destroyed, and consolation, the restoration of the church; that they who will be of that church will acknowledge the Lord, and receive love to Him, and thence wisdom, is signified by his making her wilderness as Eden, and her desert as the garden of Jehovah, Eden signifying love to the Lord, and the garden of Jehovah wisdom thence derived.   And in Micah: "O cliff of the daughter of Zion, unto thee shall come and shall return the kingdom, the kingdom of the daughter of Jerusalem: now wherefore dost thou shout in shouting? is not the king in thee, hath thy counsellor perished, that grief seizeth thee as a woman in travail? be in travail, and bring forth, O daughter of Zion, for thou shalt go out from the city, and shalt dwell in the field" (iv. 8, 9, 10).   The subject there treated of is concerning the spiritual captivity in which the faithful are, when they tarry in the church where there is no more truth and good; their lamentations that they are in that church is signified by, wherefore dost thou shout in shouting, likewise by, wherefore does grief seize thee as a woman in travail; when notwithstanding they have the truths of doctrine and also the understanding of them, is signified by, is not the king in thee, hath thy counsellor perished, king denoting truth of doctrine from the Word, and counsellor, the understanding thereof; that there shall be a church with those who are in the good of charity, and thence in truths of doctrine, is signified by the daughter of Zion to whom the kingdom shall come, and by the daughter of Jerusalem, kingdom also denoting the church; the establishment of the church and reformation of those who are of the church, is understood by, travail and bring forth, O daughter of Zion; for thou shalt go out from the city, and dwell in the field, signifies, that they shall recede from the doctrine in which there is no more any truth and good, and shall abide where they are in abundance; the city denotes the doctrine from which they shall recede, the field denotes where there are truths and goods in abundance, and to go out denotes to recede, namely, from that doctrine, and so to be liberated from spiritual captivity. Again, in David : "Jehovah raiseth the bruised out of the dust, He lifteth up the needy from the dunghill, to place him with princes, with the princes of his people, who make the barren house to dwell, the mother of sons glad" (Psalm cxiii. 17, 18, 19) : that they who are in falses from ignorance, and thence not in goods, are to be instructed from the Lord in truths, is signified by Jehovah raising the bruised from the dust, and lifting up the needy from the dunghill, the bruised and the needy denoting those who are in falses from ignorance and thence not in goods ; the primary truths of the church in which they are to be instructed, are signified by princes, the princes of the people, with whom they are to be placed ; that the life derived from the marriage of truth and good shall be with those with whom it was not before, is signified by making the barren house to dwell, the mother of sons glad, to dwell denoting to live, the barren house, where there was no marriage of truth and good, and the glad mother of sons, the church, wherein are truths born from good.   And in Hosea : "As to Ephraim, as a bird his glory shall fly away, from the birth and from the belly and from conception" (ix. 11).   That by these words is signified that all understanding of truth will perish from ultimates to first [principles], may be seen above, n. 710, where they are explained. And in Luke: "Woe to them that bear in the womb, and to them that give suck, in those days, for there shall be great straitness and anger in this people" (xxi. 23) ; again : " Behold the days shall come, in which they shall say, blessed are the barren, and the bellies which have not borne, and the paps which have not suckled" (xxiii. 29) ; also in Matthew (xxiv. 19 ; Mark xiii. 17).   That these things are said concerning those who are in the end of the church, when no genuine truths, but what are falsified, can be received, may also be seen above, n. 710. And in Jeremiah : "The partridge gathereth but doth not bring forth, making riches, but not with judgment : in the midst of his days he forsaketh them, and in his latter end becomes foolish" (xvii. 11). By the partridge are understood those who learn many things from the Word, and from the doctrines of the church, but not for the sake of the uses of life, to bring forth denoting to perform uses, thus to live, and so to be reformed ; by the riches not gotten with judgment, are signified spiritual riches, which are the knowledges of truth and good, to procure which to himself not for the sake of use, is to make riches not with judgment ; that those knowledges which are not made knowledges of the life, perish, is signified by his forsaking them in the midst of his days ; that at length they will have no knowledges of truth but what are falsified, is signified by, in his latter end he shall become foolish.   Forasmuch as a mother signifies the church, and sons and daughters the truths and goods thereof, and in the ancient churches, and afterwards in the Jewish churches, all things were representative, and thence significative, therefore it was a reproach and ignomy to women to be barren, and hence it is written, that "Rachel was angry with Jacob that she bare no children, and said, when she brought forth Joseph, God hath gathered my reproach" (Gen. **xxx.** 1. 23). For the same cause, Elizabeth after she had conceived, said, "Thus hath the Lord dealt with me in the days in which He looked upon me to take away my reproach among men" (Luke i. 24, 25). Hence also it is evident, that to travail with child, to bring forth, and to generate, signify the procreation of such things as appertain to the church. Thus again in Isaiah : "Woe to him that saith to the father, what begettest thou, or to the woman, what bringest thou forth" (xlv. 10); treating also of reformation, and that it is from the Lord and not from man. Again : "King Hezekiah said, when he heard the words of Rabshakeh, this day is a day of straitness, and of reproach, and contumely, and the sons are come to the mouth of the matrix, and there is not strength to bring forth" (xxxvii. 3). That truths from the Word may be heard and known, and yet reformation not be effected thereby, is signified by the sons coming to the matrix, and no strength to bring forth ; to bring forth signifies to make truths fruitful by doing them, whence comes reformation ; that this was a grief of heart and mind, and disgraceful to the church, is signified by a day of straitness, reproach and contumely. And in Ezekiel : "I will pour out my fury upon Sin, the strength of Egypt, and will cut off the multitute of No ; I will give fire in Egypt ; Sin shall travail in labor, and there shall not be [strength] to break through" (xxx. 15, 16). By Egypt, Sin, and No, are signified the scientifics and fallacies appertaining to the natural man, which hinder his being reformed by truths from the Word ; that these will be known, but still not received in the life, and thus no reformation effected, is signified by, Sin shall travail in labor, but there shall not be [strength] to break through, namely, the matrix. Inasmuch as by travailing in labor is signified to receive the truths of the Word by hearing or reading, and by bringing forth is signified to make fruitful and produce them in act, which is to live according to them, and so to be reformed, therefore when these things are effected with straitness and difficulty, on account of the falses and evils which rule in the church, and which hinder and pervert truths and goods, therefore it is then said, that they are seized with grief as a woman in labor ; and inasmuch as this is the case in the end of the church, therefore it is said in the Word concerning those who live at that time ; as in this chapter of the Apocalypse, "that the woman being with child, cried out, travailing in birth, and being pained to be delivered" (verse 2); whereby is signified, that spiritual truths and goods, which are from the Word, cannot be received, but with the greatest difficulty and with straitness, by reason of the hindrance arising from the evils and falses which are then in the church, and which occupy the minds of those who attend to religion. This is also signified by the griefs as of a woman in travail, in Jeremiah : "I heard a voice as of one sick, as of one in travail with her firstborn, the voice of the daughter of Zion : she sigheth, she stretcheth out her hands : woe to me now, for my soul is desolated by the slayers" (iv. 31). By the daughter of Zion is understood the church which is in truths of doctrine from the good of love ; this is said to

sigh and to stretch out the hands, being desolated by the slayers, the
slayers denoting those who destroy the spiritual life of man by falses
and evils; and whereas on this account spiritual truths and goods
cannot be received except with straitness and difficulty, therefore
there is said to be a lamenting as of a woman sick and bringing forth
the first-born: by the first-born is signified the first [principle] of
the church, from which all other things flow as from their beginning.
Again: "We have heard the fame of a people coming from the land
of the north; our hands are slackened, straitness hath seized us,
grief as of a woman in travail; go not out into the field, and go not
into the way, because of the sword of the enemy, terror on e ery
side" (vi. 24, 25). By the people coming from the land of the north
are understood those who are in the falses of evil, and, abstractedly,
the falses of evil which are in the church, then vastated; that then
the reception of truths in faith and in love will be attended with
difficulty, through the hindrances arising from the falses of evil, and
that hence there will be pain and grief of mind and heart, is signified by the hands being slackened, straitness seizing them, and
grief as of a woman in travail; that then the things which are of the
church and of the doctrine thereof are not to be consulted, is signified by go not out into the field, go not into the way, the field
denoting the church, and the way doctrine; the reason of this,
namely, because the false from hell invades, from which the truth is
falsified and extinguished, is signified by the sword of the enemy
and terror being on every side, sword denoting the false destroying
truth, enemy denoting hell, and terror, spiritual death.   From these
considerations it may appear what is understood by the words of the
Lord in Matthew: "Then let not him who is upon the house come
down to take anything out of the house, and let not him who is in
the field return back: woe to them that are with child, and to them
that give suck in those days; then shall be great affliction, such as
was not from the beginning of the world until now" (xxiv. 17, 18,
19, 21). These things are also said concerning the state of the
church about its end, when falses of evil and evils of the false have
rule, and the truths of the Word are not received except falsified and
adulterated: this is understood by, woe to them that are with child,
and to them that give suck in those days, and also by the great
affliction which shall then take place; but these and the other particulars of that chapter may be seen explained in their order in the
A. C. Again, in Jeremiah: "Ask and see; doth a man bring forth?
Wherefore do I see every man, his hands upon his loins, as a woman
in travail, and all faces are turned into paleness, because it is a great
day there is none like it" (xxx. 6, 7); treating also of the last state
of the church, when the last judgment takes place; the great day is
the advent of the Lord and judgment then from Him; by asking and
seeing whether a male bringeth forth, is signified, whether the truth
of the Word without the good of life can produce anything of a
church, inasmuch as the all of the church is produced by the marriage of good and truth, the male signifying the truth of the church,
and the wife the good of the church: wherefore do I see every man

his hands upon his loins as a woman in travail, signifies, why is it thought that truth without good produces such things as appertain to the church; the loins signify marriage, in the spiritual sense, the marriage of truth and good, but the loins of a man as of a woman in travail, signify, as if there was a marriage of truth alone without good; all faces are turned into paleness, signifies that there is nothing of good, because nothing of love and charity, the face denoting the affections which are of the love of good, whence paleness signifies those affections being extinguished.   And in Isaiah: " My loins are filled with great pain, pains take hold upon me, as the pains of a woman in travail" (xxi. 3); speaking also of the last state of the church, when the truths and goods thereof cannot be received, except with much painful effort, by reason of the evils and falses which then hinder: the loins, which are said to be filled with pain, signify the marriage of good and truth, from which is heaven and the church, which are said to be filled with pain, when truth cannot be conjoined with good; those hindrances therefore are signified by the pains as of a woman in travail which take hold upon her.   Grief or pain as of a woman in travail is also predicated of those, who, on account of falses conjoined with evils of life, cannot receive truths any more, which they nevertheless desire to receive when destruction hangs over them, especially in the spiritual world, when the last judgment is at hand: the efforts of such, which are then in vain, are signified by the griefs of a travailing woman in the following passages; as in Isaiah: "Howl ye, for the day of Jehovah is nigh: on account thereof all hands are slackened, and every heart of man melteth, and they are sore afraid: torments and pains seize them, they labor as a woman in travail, a man is amazed towards his companion, their faces are faces of flames" (xiii. 6, 7, 8).   The day of Jehovah which is near, signifies the last judgment performed by the Lord when He was in the world; their terror on account of the destruction then impending, is signified by, all hands are slackened, and every heart of man melteth, and they are sore afraid; that their attempts to receive the truths and goods of heaven and the church are then in vain, by reason of the falses of evil in which they were and still are, is signified by, torments and pains seize them, they labor as a woman in travail; that they are in the evils of hatred and anger, is signified by their faces being faces of flames.   And in Jeremiah: "O inhabitant of Lebanon, who makest thy nest in the cedars, what grace wilt thou find when pains shall come upon thee, pain as of a woman in travail? I will give thee into the hands of them that seek thy soul" (xxii. 23); treating of those who have the Word, and thence truths and the understanding thereof, who are said to dwell in Lebanon, and to have their nests in the cedars; their destruction at the last judgment, and their effort then to receive truths, but in vain, from the hindrances arising from the falses of evil, is signified by, what grace wilt thou find when pains come upon thee, pain as of a woman in travail; that the falses of evil which are from hell will then carry them away, is signified by, I will give thee into the hand of them that seek thy soul.   Again, in the same prophet:

" Damascus is made remiss, and hath turned herself to flee, and horror hath seized upon her, straitness and pains have taken hold of
her as a woman in travail" (xlix. 24); and again : " The king of
Babel heard the fame of the people coming from the north, whence
his hands were made remiss, straitness seized him, pain as of a woman in travail " (l. 43); and in Moses : " The people heard, the
pain of travailing women seized the inhabitants of Philistea" (Exod.
xv. 14).   By the pains of travailing women, in these passages, are
signified similar things as above.   And in Hosea : " The pains of
a travailing woman shall come upon Ephraim, he is a son not wise,
for the time doth not stand in the womb of sons" (xiii. 13); these
words are explained above, n. 710.   Again, in Moses: " Jehovah
God said unto the woman, in multiplying I will multiply thy pain,
and thy conception, in pain shalt thou bring forth sons; and thy
obedience shall be to thy man, and he shall rule over thee" (Gen.
iii. 16).   It is not understood by these words that women shall bring
forth sons in pain, but by the woman is understood the church,
which from celestial was become natural, this being signified by eating of the tree of science ; that the man of the church can scarcely,
or with difficulty, be regenerated by truths, and by a life according
to them, and that he will undergo temptations in order that truths
may be implanted, and conjoined to good, is signified by pain and
conception being multiplied, and by bringing forth sons in pain, conception signifying the reception of truth which is from good, and to
bring forth sons signifying to produce truths from the marriage of
truth and good; inasmuch as the natural man is full of concupiscences from the love of self and of the world, and these cannot be
removed except by truths, therefore it is said, thy obedience shall
be to the man, and he shall rule over thee, the man [vir] denoting,
in this as well as in other parts of the Word, the truths of the church ;
that man is reformed and regenerated by truths, and by a life according to them, has been frequently shown above.   From these considerations, it may now appear, that by conceptions, births, nativities, and generations in the Word, are understood spiritual conceptions, births, nativities, and generations.

722. ".That when she had brought forth, he might devour her
child "—That hereby is signified that they might destroy the doctrine of that church in its first rising, appears from the signification
of the child, which the woman was about to bring forth, as denoting
the doctrine of the church, for this is understood by the male son
whom she brought forth, will be seen in the following article ; and
from the signification of devouring, as denoting to destroy ; for pre-
dicates follow their subjects, and when the dragon is the subject,
then the predicate thereof is to devour, but when the doctrine of the
church is the subject, then the predicate thereof is to destroy, hence
it is that to destroy is here signified by devouring; the reason why
it is signified to destroy in its first rising, is, because it is said that
after the woman brought forth, he might devour her child.   That to
devour and to eat signifies to destroy in other passages also of the
Word, when predicated of wild beasts, by which are signified falses

and evils, appears in Ezekiel : " One of the whelps of the lion grew up, which became a young lion, which learned to seize the prey, and devoured man" (xix. 3, 6) ; where to devour man signifies to destroy the understanding of truth and intelligence.   And in Hosea : " I will meet them as a bear bereaved, and I will devour them as a fierce lion, a wild beast of the field shall tear them" (xiii. 8) ; and in Daniel : " Lo, a beast like to a bear, which had three ribs in the mouth between the teeth, to which it was said, rise, devour much much flesh" (vii. 5).   Moreover in the Hebrew tongue, to eat is in many passages put for consuming, ruining, and destroying ; as in Jeremiah : " They have eaten Jacob, they have eaten him and consumed him, and have laid waste his habitations" (x. 25) ; and elsewhere.

723. Verse 5. "And she brought forth a male son, who was to rule all nations with a rod of iron : and her child was caught up unto God and His throne."—" And she brought forth a male son," signifies the doctrine of truth for the church which is called the New Jerusalem : " who is to rule all nations with a rod of iron," signifies, which by the power of natural truth from spiritual shall argue with and convince those who are in falses and evils, and yet in the church, where the Word is : " and her child was caught up unto God and His throne," signifies protection of the doctrine by the Lord, because for the New Church.

724. " And she brought forth a male son"—That hereby is signified the doctrine of truth, which is for the New Church, which is called the New Jerusalem, appears from the signification of a son, as denoting truth, and of a male son, as denoting the genuine truth of the church, consequently also the doctrine thereof, for the truth of the church from the Word is doctrine, inasmuch as this contains the truths which are for the church : howbeit the genuine doctrine of the church is the doctrine of good, thus the doctrine of life, which is of love to the Lord and of charity towards the neighbor, but still it is a doctrine of truth, for doctrine teaches life, love, and charity, and so far as it teaches these it is truth ; for when man knows and understands what good is, what life is, what love is, and what charity is, he then knows and understands those things as truths, for he knows and understands the quality of good, how he is to live, also what is meant by love and charity, and the quality of the man who is in the life thereof; and so long as these things are things of science and of the understanding, they are nothing but truths, and thence doctrines; but as soon as they pass from science and from the understanding into the will, and thence into act, they are then no longer truths but goods, for man interiorly wills nothing but what he loves, and what he loves that is to him a good : from these considerations it may appear, that all the doctrine of the church is a doctrine of truth, and that the truth of doctrine becomes good, and the good of love and charity, when from doctrine it passes into life. This doctrine, which is here signified by a male son, is especially the doctrine of love to the Lord, and of charity towards the neighbor, thus the doctrine of the good of life, which nevertheless is still a doc-

trine of truth : that the doctrine of the good of love, and thence of
life is here signified by a male son, may appear from this consideration, that the woman, who brought forth the son, was seen encompassed with the sun, and upon her head a crown of twelve stars, and
by the sun is signified love to the Lord, and by the crown of twelve
stars are signified the knowledges of good and truth, and from a
woman and mother of such description, no other offspring could be
generated, but that of love and that of good, consequently doctrine
concerning them ; this therefore is the male son.   The reason why
that doctrine is for the New Church, which is called New Jerusalem, is, because the woman treated of in this chapter, is the same
who is called the bride the lamb's wife, which was the holy city Jerusalem descending from God out of heaven (ch. xxi. 9, 10); hence it
is that she was seen encompassed with the sun, for by the sun is understood the Lord as to divine love, as may be seen above, n. 401,
525, 527, 708 : another reason why a male son signifies the doctrine
of the church, is, because a son, in the Word, signifies truth, and
the doctrine of the church is truth in every complex.   That a son,
in the Word, signifies truth, may appear from what has been said
before concerning the woman, concerning the womb, and concerning
bringing forth, namely, that the woman signifies the church, the
womb the inmost [principle] of love and the reception of truth from
good, and to bring forth the production and fructification thereof;
concerning the woman, see above, n. 707 ; concerning the womb, n.
710 ; and concerning bringing forth, n. 721 : hence it follows, that
by sons and daughters, inasmuch as they are births, are signified the
truths and goods of the church, by sons truths, and by daughters
goods ; in a word, that by all names which appertain to marriage,
and thence to procreation, on earth, are signified such things as appertain to the marriage of good and truth, consequently by father,
mother, sons, daughters, sons in law, daughters in law, grandsons,
and several others are signified goods and truths procreating, and
goods and truths procreated, and moreover goods and truths thence
derived in their order : but it is to be observed, that goods and truths
procreating are in the spiritual man, and those which are procreated
are in the natural man, and that the former, which are in the spiritual man, are as father and mother, and that the latter, which are
in the natural man, being derived from the former, are as brothers
and sisters ; and that afterwards the truths and goods which are procreated anew as from sons married within affinity, and from daughters married also within the same, are in the natural man, after that
the former as parents have been elevated into the spiritual man, for
there all conception takes place, and all travail or gestation in the
womb, but the birth itself takes place in the natural man ; hence the
spiritual man is continually enriched by the elevation of truths and
goods out of the natural man, which as parents will procreate anew ;
there also all things are consociated as the societies of heaven, according to the affections of truth and good, and their propinquities
and affinities : hence it is evident, that those spiritual procreations, as
the natural procreations from a father and mother, are multiplied as

families and houses on earth, and as trees fructify from seeds, whence come gardens, which are called paradises in the spiritual man, but groves and orchards in the natural, and shady forests in the sensual. But whereas sons are frequently mentioned in the Word, and it has not yet been known that they signify the truths of the church and of doctrine, out of many passages the following only shall be adduced by way of confirmation: thus in the evangelists: "Jesus said, he who leaveth houses, brethren, sisters, father, mother, wife, children, lands, for My name's sake, shall receive a hundred fold, and shall attain an inheritance of life eternal" (Matthew xix. 29; Mark x. 29, 30). "Every one who cometh to Me, and hateth not his father, wife, children, brethren and sisters, yea, his own soul, is not My disciple" (Luke xiv. 26). Who cannot see that a father, a mother, a wife, children, brethren, and sisters, also houses and lands, are not here understood, but such things are of the man himself, and are called the things of his proprium? for these things man is to relinquish and hate, if he desires to worship the Lord, and to be His disciple, and to receive a hundred fold, and to attain an inheritance of life eternal; the things which are a man's own, or of his proprium, are those which are of his love and thence of his life into which he is born, consequently they are evils and falses of every kind; and whereas those things are of his love and life, therefore it is said, that he ought also to hate his own soul: these evils and falses are signified by father and mother, wife, children, brethren and sisters; for all things which are of the love and life of man, or which are of the affection and thence of the thought, or of the will and thence of the understanding, are formed and conjoined as generations, descending from one father and one mother, and are also distinguished as into families and houses; the love of self and the love of the world thence derived, are their father and mother, and the cupidities thence arising, and the evils and falses thereof, are the children, which are brethren and sisters: that these things are understood, may manifestly appear from this consideration, that it is not the will of the Lord that any one should hate his father and mother, neither wife and children, nor brethren and sisters, inasmuch as this would be contrary to the spiritual love implanted in every one from heaven, which is of parents towards children, and of children towards parents, likewise contrary to conjugial love, which is of the husband towards the wife, and of the wife towards the husband, as also contrary to mutual love, which is of brothers and sisters towards each other; yea, the Lord even teaches that enemies are not to be hated, but loved. From these considerations it is evident, that by the names of consanguinities, affinities, and kindreds, in the Word, are understood consanguinities, affinities, and kindreds in a spiritual sense. Again: "Jesus said to his disciples, the brother shall deliver the brother to death, the father the son, and children shall rise up against their parents, and shall give them to death" (Matthew x. 21; Mark xiii. 12). "The father shall be divided against the son, and the son against the father, the mother against the daughter, and the daughter against the mother, the mother in law against the daughter in law, and the daughter in law against the mother in law" (Luke xii. 53). That neither are these things to be understood according to the letter, appears from the words preceding, where Jesus says, that He came not to give peace upon the earth, but division, and that there shall be five in one house divided, three against two and two against three, by which is signified, that falses and evils will combat against truths and goods, and vice versa, as is the case when man comes into temptations and is reforming; this combat is signified by division and insurrection; that the father shall be divided against the son, and the son against the father, signifies, that evil will fight against truth, and truth against evil, the father there denoting the evil, which is the proprium of man, and the son denoting the truth which man has from the Lord; that the cupidity of the false will fight against the affection of truth, and the affection of truth against the cupidity of the false, is signified by the mother shall be divided against the daughter, and the daughter against the mother, the mother there denoting the cupidity of the false, and the daughter the affection of truth; and so on: that these words are to be so understood, is also evident from the words of the Lord elsewhere, where he says, that "in Him they shall have peace" and consequently not division: (John xiv. 27; xvi. 33). Again, in Luke: "The angel said to Zechariah concerning John, he shall go before the Lord in the spirit and power of Elias, to convert the hearts of the fathers to the sons" (i. 17): and in Malachi: "I will send to you Elias the prophet, before the great and terrible day of Jehovah cometh, that he may convert the heart of the fathers to the sons, and the heart of the sons to their fathers, lest I come and smite the earth with a curse" (iii. 23, 24). It was by baptism that John the Baptist was to prepare the people for the reception of the Lord, for baptism represented and signified purification from evils and falses, and also regeneration by the Word from the Lord; and unless this representation had preceded, it would not have been possible for the Lord to manifest Himself, to teach and to abide in Judea and in Jerusalem, inasmuch as the Lord was the God of heaven and God of earth under a human form, who could not possibly be together with a nation which was in mere falses as to doctrine, and in mere evils as to life, wherefore unless the representative of purification from falses and evils by baptism, had prepared that nation for the reception of the Lord, it would have perished with diseases of every kind at the presence of His Divine [principle]; this therefore is what is signified by, lest I come and smite the earth with a curse; that this would have been the case is well known in the spiritual world, for there they who are in falses and evils are direfully tormented and spiritually die at the presence of the Lord. The reason why such preparation could be effected by the baptism of John, was, because the Jewish church was a representative church, and all conjunction of heaven with them was by representatives, as may also appear from the washings there commanded; as that all who were made unclean should wash themselves and their garments, and were thence accounted clean; in like manner that the priests and Levites should wash themselves, before they entered the tent of assembly and then the temple, and before they ministered in holy offices ; in like manner that Naaman was cleansed from leprosy by washing in Jordan ; the washing and baptism itself did not indeed purify them from falses and evils, but only represented and thence signified purification from them, which notwithstanding was received in heaven, as if they themselves were purified : thus heaven was conjoined with the people of that church, by the baptism of John and when heaven was thus conjoined to them, the Lord, who was the God of heaven, could manifest Himself, teach, and abide amongst them: that "Jerusalem and all Judea went out to John, and all the confines of Jordon, and were baptized by Him in Jordan, confessing their sins" may appear in Matthew chap. iii. 5, 6; and that He said to them, " O generation of vipers, who hath warned you to flee from the anger to come" (Luke iii. 7). That the conjunction of heaven with the Jews and Israelites was by representatives, may be seen in the D. of the N. J. n. 248. This now was the reason why John was sent before to prepare the way of the Lord, and to prepare a people for Him. From these considerations it may be concluded, what is signified by converting the heart of the fathers to the sons, and the heart of the sons to the fathers, namely, that it is to induce a representation of the conjunction of spiritual goods with truths, and vice versa, thus of regeneration by the Word from the Lord ; for regeneration is the conjunction of goods with truths, and of truths with goods, and it is the Lord who regenerates, and the Word which teaches. The reason why it is said concerning John, that he should go before the Lord in the spirit and power of Elias, and that he was Elias, was, because John, in like manner as Elias, represented the Lord as to the Word, and thence signified the Word, which is from the Lord ; and whereas in the Word there is divine wisdom and divine power, this is what is understood by the spirit and power of Elias : concerning the Word, as being of such a nature, see the work concerning H. & H. n. 303–310 ; and in the small work concerning the W. H. That sons signify truths from the Word, may also appear from the following passages : thus in David : " Lo sons are the heritage of Jehovah, the fruit of the belly a reward ; as arrows in the hands of the mighty, so are the sons of youth ; blessed is the man who hath filled his quiver from them, they shall not be ashamed when they speak with their enemies in the gate" (Psalm cxxvii. 3, 4, 5). By the sons who are the heritage of Jehovah, and by the fruit of the belly which is a reward, are understood the truths and goods of the church, by sons truths, and by the fruit of the belly goods, for both these are rewards and the heritage of Jehovah, that is, heaven, which is from truths and goods, namely, from the reception of them ; by the sons of youth, who are as arrows in the hands of the mighty, are signified the truths of the ancient church, which were natural truths from a spiritual origin ; this church is understood by youth ; and whereas all power is in those truths against evils and falses, therefore it is said, as arrows in the hand of the mighty, arrows denoting truths destroying falses ; doctrine from truths is signified by the quiver the same as by the bow; and whereas they who are in doctrine from those truths fear nothing from falses, it is said, blessed is the man who hath filled his quiver from them, they shall not be ashamed when they speak with their enemies in the gate, not to be ashamed denoting not to be conquered, and enemies in the gate denoting the falses of evil which are from hell. Again: " Deliver me out of the hand of the son of the stranger, whose mouth speaketh vanity, and their right is the right hand of a lie ; for our sons are as great plants, made in their youth, and our daughters as corners cut out in the figure of a palace" (Psalm cxliv. 11, 12). That by the sons of the stranger are here understood falses, is evident, for it is said, whose mouth speaketh vanity, and their right hand is the right hand of a lie; and that by our sons are signified truths, is also evident, for it is said, that they are as plants made in youth, plants also denoting truths, and youth denoting here, as above, the ancient church, which was in genuine truths ; by our daughters are signified the affections of truth, which are therefore compared to corners cut out in the figure of a palace,.because a palace is a representative of the understanding in which truths are in a beautiful form, and they are in a beautiful form, when they are from the affection of truth. And in Micah: "Induce baldness and shave thyself, because of the sons of thy delight, dilate thy baldness as the eagle, because they have migrated from thee" (i. 16). Mourning on account of the truths of the church being destroyed, is described by inducing and dilating baldness, and by shaving themselves, for the hair signifies truths in ultimates, and they who are without truths in ultimates, are also without internal truths ; hence it is that, in the spiritual world, they who are in no truths from good appear bald ; the truths of the church being destroyed, is signified by, thy sons have migrated from thee ; and they are called sons of delights from the love of them and the delights thence arising. And in Zechariah : " I saw two olives near the right hand of the candlestick and near the left, and he said, these are the two sons of the olive standing near the Lord of the whole earth" (iv. 11, 14). By the two olives are signified the two churches, the celestial church, and the spiritual church, the former at the right hand of the candlestick, and the latter at the left ; by the sons of the olive are signified the truths of those churches, which are doctrinals. Again : " I will bend Judah for me, I will fill Ephraim with the bow, and I will stir up thy sons, O Zion, with thy sons, O Javan, and I will set thee as the sword of the mighty" (ix. 13). By the sons of Zion and by the sons of Javan, are signified the truths of the Word internal and external, by the sons of Zion truths internal, and by the sons of Javan truths external; what the rest signify may be seen above, n. 357, 433, where they are explained: inasmuch as by sons are signified truths, it is said, that they shall be placed as the sword of the mighty, the sword of the mighty signifying truth powerfully destroying the false. And in Isaiah : " I will raise up against them the Mede, whose bows shall dash in pieces the young men, and they shall have no compassion on the fruit of the belly, their eye shall not spare the sons" (xiii. 17, 18). Inasmuch as by the Mede, are understood those who make no account of the truths and goods of the church, therefore it is also said, their eye shall not spare the sons, for the sons are the truths of the Word and of the church; but these things may be seen explained above, n. 710. And in Jeremiah : " My tent is devastated and all my cords plucked away, my sons have departed from me, and they are not" (x. 20). By the tent which is devasted is signified the church as to the good of love and worship therein originating, for all worship in old time was performed in tents, and afterwards in the tent of assembly, in memory whoreof the feast of tents or tabernacles was instituted ; all my cords are plucked away, signifies, that there is no conjunction of truth with good, nor of truths with each other, which thereby fall asunder, and thence no conjunction of heaven with the church ; my sons have departed from me, and they are not, signifies that the truths of the church from the Word are dissipated, and that man has thereby removed himself from the Lord. Again, in the same prophet : " Behold I bring back the captivity of the tents of Jacob, and I will have mercy on his dwelling places, that the city may be built on its own heap, and the palace shall be inhabited after its own manner, and his sons shall be as aforetime, and his congregation shall be established before me" (xxx. 18, 20). By the tents of Jacob and his dwelling places are signified all things of the church and its doctrine, by tents the goods thereof, and by dwelling places the truths ; by their captivity is signified spiritual captivity, which is, when on account of falses, which have rule, the truths and goods of the Word cannot be perceived ; to shake off falses and teach truths, is signified by bringing back the captivity ; that the city may be built upon its own heap, signifies doctrine derived from truths, which was fallen away by means of falses : the city is doctrine ; and the palace shall be inhabited, according to its manner, signifies the spiritual understanding of truths, as with the ancients, palace denoting the understanding of spiritual truths, for, in the understanding are spiritual truths in their forms, which, when they are presented to be seen, appear as palaces ; his sons shall be as aforetime, and his congregation shall be established before Me, signifies, that the truths of the church shall be as with the ancients, and that their forms shall abide as they did with them in a repaired conjunction ; the sons there denote truths, and the congregation denotes the conjunction of them and disposition into forms, such as has place with the man of the church in the understanding, whence he has intelligence ; according to its manner and aforetime, denotes as with the ancients. And in Lamentations : " Mine eye runneth down with waters, because the counsellor who recreateth my soul is far from me : my sons are become devastated, in that the enemy hath prevailed" (i. 16). Mourning on account of the church being devastated, is understood by, mine eye runneth down with waters ; the devastation thereof as to truths, is signified by, my sons are become devastated ; that this is done by the falses of evil, is signified by, the enemy hath prevailed, the enemy denoting the false of evil, and the hell whence it rises. Again, in Isaiah : " Stir up, stir up, arise Jerusalem, who

hast drunk out of the hand of Jehovah the cup of his anger; thou
hast sucked out the dregs of the cup of trembling; there is none who
leadeth her of all the sons whom she hath brought forth, nor any
who taketh her by the hand of all the sons whom she hath educated;
thy sons have fainted, they have lain in the head of all the streets"
(li. 17, 18, 21). The restoration of the church, which was fallen
into mere falses of evil, is signified by, stir up, stir up, arise Jerusalem, who hast drunk out of the hand of Jehovah the cup of his
anger, thou hast sucked out the dregs of the cup of trembling; Jerusalem denotes the church, as to doctrine, to stir up and arise denotes
the restoration thereof, to drink the cup of anger denotes the false,
and the dregs of the cup mere falses, from which are evils, and to
attract them is signified by drinking and sucking them out; there is
none who leadeth her of all the sons whom she hath brought forth,
nor any who taketh her by the hand of all the sons whom she hath
educated, signifies, that no truths of the Word which she has learned
and imbibed withdraw her, sons there denoting truths; thy sons
have fainted, they have lain in the head of all the streets, signifies,
that truths are dissipated by falses of every kind; inasmuch as sons
denote truths, by fainting is signified to be dissipated, and by laying
in the head of all the streets, is signified by falses of every kind, for
the streets of a city signify doctrinal truths, but here doctrinal falses.
Again, in the same prophet: "Fear not, Jacob, from the east I will
bring thy seed, and from the west I will gather thee, I will say to
the north, give, and to the south, keep not back, bring my sons from
afar, my daughters from the extremity of the earth" (xliii. 5). These
things are not said concerning the posterity of Jacob, but concerning
the gentiles, of whom the church is to be formed: by Jacob and his
seed are understood those who will be of that church: that it is to
be formed of those who are in falses from ignorance, and thence in
obscurity as to truths, is signified by, from the west I will gather
thee, and I will say to the north, give; and that these are not to be
repelled by those who are in the good of love and in truths of doctrine from a clear [principle], but to be accepted, is signified by,
from the east will I bring thy seed, and I will say to the south, keep
not back, for the east signifies the good of love in clearness, the
south the truth of doctrine in clearness, the west the good of love in
obscurity, and the north the truth of doctrine in obscurity, such as
exists with those who, from ignorance of truth, are in falses, and
yet desire truths; the reason why those quarters have such significations, is, because, in the spiritual world, all dwell distinctly in
those quarters according to the light of truth and affection of good
in which they are principled; similar things are signified in Matthew, where it is said, "That the elect are to be gathered together
from the four winds, from the boundaries of heaven even to their
boundaries" (xxiv. 11). That all who are in falses from ignorance,
and yet in the desire of truth, are to be brought into that church, is
signified by, bring my sons from afar, and my daughters from the
extremity of the earth, sons denoting those who are in truths, and
daughters those who are in the affection thereof, and hence also ab-

stractedly from persons, they signify truths and their affections, and afar off and the extremity of the earth, signify removal from the light of truth, because in falses from ignorance, by reason of their not having the Word, or not understanding the sense thereof. Again, in the same prophet: " They shall hasten thy sons; thy destroyers and thy devastators shall go out from thee; behold I will lift up My hand towards the nations, and towards the peoples will I raise up My sign, that they may bring thy sons in the bosom, and carry thy daughters upon the shoulder" (xlix. 17, 22); also treating of the establishment of a new church by the Lord; and by the sons whom they shall hasten, and whom they shall bring in the bosom, and by the daughters whom they shall carry upon the shoulder, are understood all who are in truths and in the affection thereof, and, abstractedly from persons, truths themselves and their affections with those who will be of the new church; destroyers and devastators signify the falses of evil; that these will be removed is signified by, they shall go out from thee. Again: " The isles shall confide in me, and the ships of Tarshish in the beginning, to bring thy sons from afar, their silver and their gold with them" (lx. 9); also treating of the church of the gentiles; and by the sons who shall be brought, are signified those who will receive truths; the rest may be seen explained above, n. 50, 406, 514. And in Hosea: " I will not destroy Ephraim, they shall go after Jehovah, as a lion he shall roar, because he shall roar, and with honor shall sons accede from the sea, with honor they shall come, as a bird trom Egypt, and as a dove from the land of Assyria, and I will cause them to dwell in their own houses" (xi. 9, 10, 11). By the sons from the sea are signified scientific and rational truths; wherefore it is said, that they shall come as a bird from Egypt, and as a dove from the land of Assyria. By Egypt is signified the natural [principle], and by Assyria the rational, both as to truths; but these things also are explained above, n. 275, 601, 654. And in David: " Hear this, all ye people, perceive in the ear, all ye inhabitants of the age, as well the sons of a man [homo] as the sons of a man [vir], the rich and the needy together; my mouth shall speak wisdoms, and the meditation of my heart intelligences" (Psalm xlix. 2, 3, 4). By the sons of man [homo] are signified spiritual truths which are from the Lord by the Word, which are doctrinals, and by the sons of man [vir] are signified rational and natural truths, which are from the understanding, thus the understanding of the Word; by the rich and the needy, are signified those who attain much wisdom from them, and those who attain but little. Again, in David: " Jehovah return, look down from the heavens, and see and visit this vine, and the shoot which Thy right hand hath planted, and upon the son whom Thou hast made strong for Thyself; let Thy hand be for the man of Thy right hand, for the son of man whom Thou hast made strong for Thyself " (Psalm lxxx. 15, 16, 18). David spake these words concerning the church and concerning himself, which is the sense of the letter, for he understood himself by the shoot and by the son; but in the spiritual sense, by the vine and by the shoot which Jehovah planted is signified the spiritual church, represented by the sons of Israel; by the son whom he made strong for himself, is signified the truth of doctrine from the Word; by the man of the right hand, for whom is the hand, and by the son of man, whom he had strengthened for himself, is signified the truth of the Word in the natural sense, which is the sense of the letter, and the truth of the Word in the spiritual sense, which is the internal sense. And in Ezekiel: "Behold I am about to profane my sanctuary, the magnificence of my strength, the desire of your eyes, and the indulgence of your soul; and your sons, and your daughters, whom ye have left, shall fall by the sword" (xxiv. 21, 25). In these words are described the devastation of all truth appertaining to those who are of the church; by the sanctuary which he will profane, is signified the Word from which is the church, for this is the essential sanctuary, inasmuch as it is divine truth; from its power against falses and evils, which are from hell, it is called the magnificence of the strength of Jehovah; from the intelligence and heavenly life thence derived, it is called the desire of your eyes and the indulgence of your soul; that all truths with the affection of them will perish by falses, is signified by, your sons and your daughters shall fall by the sword, sons denoting truths, daughters, the affections of truth, and the sword, the false destroying the truth. And in Moses: "When the Most High gave to the nations an inheritance, when He separated the sons of man, He appointed the boundaries of the people, according to the number of the sons of Israel" (Deut. xxxii. 8). These things are said concerning the ancient churches, which were before the Israelitish, and concerning the establishment of them by the Lord; by the nations are understood those who were in the good of love, and by the sons of man those who were in the truths of doctrine from that good; that all truths and goods were granted them, is signified by, he appointed the boundaries of the people according to the number of the sons of Israel; that the twelve tribes, or the twelve sons of Israel, represented and thence signified the church, as to all truths and goods, may be seen above, n. 39, 430, 657. And in Jeremiah: "Shame hath devoured the labor of our fathers from our childhood, their flock and their herd, their sons and their daughters; we lie in our shame, and our ignominy covereth us" (iii. 24, 25). Again: "Behold I bring upon you a nation from afar, O house of Israel, which shall devour thy harvest and thy bread, they shall devour thy sons and thy daughters, they shall devour thy flock and thy herd, they shall devour thy vine and thy fig-tree, they shall devour thy fortifications in which thou confidest, with the sword" (v. 17). By these words, in the spiritual sense, is described the devastation of all things of the church with the Israelites; by the nation from afar is signified the false of evil, which is the false of the sensual man, destroying truths; by harvest, bread, sons, daughters, flock, herd, vine and fig-tree, which that nation shall devour, are signified all things of the church, by harvest and bread the truths and goods thereof as to nourishment, by sons and daughters the truths and goods thereof as to generation, by flock and herd, truths and goods spiritual and natural, by vine and fig-tree, the spiritual church internal and external thence derived. And in Ezekiel: "Though three men, Noah, Daniel, and Job, were in the midst thereof, as I live they shall not deliver their sons or their daughters, they only shall be delivered, and the earth shall become a desolation; I will bring a sword upon the earth, and I will cut off from it man and beast" (xiv. 16, 17, 18, 20). By these words also is described the devastation of the church as to all truths of good and goods of truth, except with those who, by truths from the Word, and by temptations, are reformed; these are signified by Noah, Daniel, and Job: that with the rest all the truths of good and goods of truth will perish, is signified by, they shall not deliver their sons or their daughters, but they only shall be delivered; the devastation of the church by falses, is signified by the earth shall become a desolation, and I will bring a sword upon the earth, the earth denoting the church, and the sword the false destroying the truth; that all truth, spiritual and natural, will be destroyed, and that all intelligence and science of truth will thence perish, is signified by, I will cut off from it man and beast. Again, in the same prophet: "The fathers shall eat the sons in the midst of thee, and the sons shall eat their fathers; I will execute judgments in thee, and I will disperse all thy remains into every wind" (v. 10); and in Moses it is said amongst the curses, "that they should eat the flesh of their sons and daughters" (Levit. xxvi. 29). By the fathers shall eat the sons, and the sons the fathers, is signified, that evils will destroy truths, and falses destroy goods, the fathers denoting evils and goods, and the sons falses and truths; and whereas everything appertaining to spiritual life with man thereby perishes, it is said that judgments shall be executed, and the remains dispersed into every wind, the remains denoting the truths and goods stored up in man from his infancy and childhood by the Lord. We read also, that they led away their sons to idols to be devoured, and for meat, also through the fire; as in the following passages; thus in Ezekiel: "Thou hast taken thy sons, whom thou hast brought forth to me, and hast sacrificed them to be devoured; is this of thy whoredoms a small thing? thou hast slaughtered my sons, and hast delivered them up, whilst thou madest them to pass through for them; thou art the daughter of thy mother, and the sister of thy sisters, who loathed their husbands and sons" (xvi. 20, 26, 45). These things are said concerning the abominations of Jerusalem; and by sacrificing their sons and daughters to idols to be devoured, is signified to destroy and consume all the truths and goods of the church; in like manner the truths from the Word, by slaughtering the sons, and making them to pass through to them; that they destroyed the truths and goods of the Word by falsifications and adulterations, is signified by whoredoms there and elsewhere in that chapter. Again: "I will pollute them with their gifts, in that they led away every opening of the womb, that I might devastate them; wherefore offer ye gifts, when ye lead away your sons through the fire? ye are polluted by all your idols" (xx. 26, 31). To destroy truths by the evils of the love of self, and by cupidities originating in the proprium, is signified by leading away the sons through the fire; and to destroy them by falses, is signified by being polluted with idols; that idols signify falses of doctrine, and the worship which is from self-derived intelligence, may be seen above, n. 587. Again, in the same prophet: "Oholah and Oholibah committed whoredom, and blood [was] in their hands, and with their idols they committed whoredom; their sons also whom they begat to Me, they led away to them for meat" (xxiii. 37). By Oholah and Oholibah are understood Samaria and Jerusalem, and by Samaria is understood the spiritual church, and by Jerusalem the celestial church, each as to doctrine; the falsifications and adulterations of the Word are signified by their committing whoredom, and by blood being in their hands; the falses which thence arise from self-derived intelligence, are signified by their idols with which they committed whoredom; hence it is evident what is signified by leading away their sons to the idols for meat, namely, that they destroyed the truths of the Word by falses. Inasmuch as sons signify truths, therefore the seeds which fell into the good land are called by the Lord, sons of the kingdom; and the tares which are falses, sons of the evil (Matt. xiii. 13). Likewise they who are in truths are called sons of light (John xii. 36). They who are in the marriage of truth and good, from the Lord, sons of the nuptials (Mark ii. 20); and they who are regenerated, sons of God (John i. 11, 12, 13). Inasmuch as by stones, in the Word, are signified truths, John the Baptist said, "God is able from these stones to raise up sons unto Abraham" (Luke iii. 8). That by stones are signified the truths upon which the interior truths of the Word are founded, may be seen in the A. C. n. 643, 1298, 3720, 6426, 8609, 10,376. As by sons are signified truths, so in the opposite sense they also signify falses; as in some of the passages adduced above, and in these words of Isaiah: "Prepare the slaughter for her sons, for the iniquity of their fathers, that they may not rise and possess the earth, and the faces of the earth he filled with cities. I will rise against them, and I will cut off from Babel the name and the residue, and the son and the grandson; and I will make her a heritage for the bittern, and lakes of waters, and I will sweep her with the besom of destruction" (xiv. 21, 22, 23). The subject there treated of is concerning the total vastation of truth with those who are understood by Babel, whereby is signified the adulteration of the Word and profanation; that truths were altogether destroyed with them by the adulteration of the Word, is signified by, prepare the slaughter for her sons, that they may not rise and possess the earth, and the faces of the earth be filled with cities; by the earth is understood the church in which are truths, and by cities are understood doctrinals from mere falses; that all truths would perish from first to last, is signified by cutting off from Babel the name and the residue, the son and the grand-son; that nothing of truth would remain, is signified by sweeping her with the besom of destruction. It is to be observed, that by sons, in the passages above adduced, are signified those who are in truths, or those who are in falses; but whereas the spiritual sense of the Word has not anything in common with persons, therefore in that sense by sons are signified truths or falses abstracted from the idea of person; the reason why the spiritual sense is of such a quality, is, because the idea of person confines the thought and the extension thereof into heaven in every direction; for all thought which proceeds from the affection of truth, makes its way through heaven on all sides, nor is it terminated except as light into shade, but when person is at the same time thought of, then the idea is terminated where the person is, and therewith also, intelligence; this is the reason why by sons, in the spiritual sense, are signified truths or falses abstractedly.

725. The reason why a male son signifies the doctrine of truth for the church which is called the New Jerusalem, is, because by son is signified truth, as has been just now shown above, and by a male son the truth of doctrine from the Word, consequently the doctrine of genuine truth which is for the church; the reason why it denotes doctrine for the church which is called the New Jerusalem, is, because by the woman who brought forth the male son, that church is understood, as was also shown above. The doctrine of truth which is for the church, is also signified by male in the following passages: thus in Moses: " God created man into His image, into the image of God created He him, male and female created He them " (Gen. i. 27). Again: " Male and female created He them, and blessed them, and called their name man, in the day in which they were created" (Gen. v. 2). What those things involve which are related in the first chapter of Genesis concerning the creation of heaven and earth, concerning paradise, and concerning the eating of the tree of science, no one can know unless from the spiritual sense, for those historical circumstances are factitious historical circumstances, but still holy, because singular the things thereof inwardly, and in their bosom, are spiritual. The subject there described is the establishment of the most ancient church, which was the most excellent of all the churches in this earth; its establishment is described by the creation of heaven and earth, the intelligence and wisdom thereof by the garden of Eden, and the declension and fall thereof by the eating of the tree of science: hence it is evident that by the man, who is called Adam and Eve, is understood that church, for it is said male and female created He them, and called their name man; and whereas that church is understood by both, it follows, that by male is understood the truth thereof, and by female the good, thus also by male the doctrine, and by female the life, inasmuch as the doctrine of truth is also the doctrine of love and charity, thus a doctrine of life, and the life of good is also the life of love and charity, thus a life of doctrine, that is, a life according to doctrine; these two are understood by male and female, and, taken together, and conjoined in marriage, are called man, and also make the church, which, as was said above, is understood by man; therefore also Adam was so called from ground, and ground, from the reception of seeds, signifies the church as to truths of doctrine, for seeds in the Word signify truths; and Eve was so called from life, as it is said, " Because she was to be the mother of all living" (Gen. iii. 20). The reason why these two, namely, doctrine

and life, taken together and as it were conjoined in marriage, are
called man, and also make the church, is, because man is man from
the understanding of truth and from the will of good, consequently
from the doctrine of life, because this is of understanding, and
from the life of doctrine, because this is of the will; the case is the
same with the church, for the church is in man, and is the man himself.   That those two, which are signified by male and female, shall
not be two but one, the Lord teaches in the evangelists : " Jesus
said, Have ye not read, that He who made them from the beginning
of the creation, made them male and female, and they two shall be
one flesh? wherefore they are no more two but one flesh" (Matt.
xix. 4, 5, 6; Mark x. 6).   These things also, as is the case with
every part of the Word, are to be understood, not only naturally,
but also spiritually, otherwise no one can know what is signified by
male and female, or husband and wife, being no more two but one
flesh, as it is also said in Gen. ii. 24: by male and female, in the
spiritual sense, is signified here, as above, truth and good, consequently also the doctrine of truth, which is a doctrine of life, and the
life of truth, which is the life of doctrine ; these must be not two but
one, inasmuch as truth does not become truth with man without the
good of life, nor does good become good with any one without the
truth of doctrine, for good does not become spiritual good except by
truths, and spiritual good is good, but not natural good without it;
when these are one, then truth is of good and good is of truth, and this
one is understood by one flesh : the case is the same with doctrine and
life ; these also make one man of the church, when the doctrine of life
and the life of doctrine are conjoined with him, for doctrine teaches how
he is to live and do, and the life lives and does it: from these considerations also it may appear, that by a male son is signified the doctrine
of love and charity, consequently, the doctrine of life.   Inasmuch
as the truth of doctrine, or the doctrine of truth, is signified by a
male, therefore a law was enacted, " That every male opening the
womb should be holy to Jehovah" (Exod. xiii. 12, 15 ; Deut. xv.
19; Luke ii. 23) : for from the marriage of truth and good, which is
understood in the spiritual sense by the marriage of a man and
woman, as was said above, are born truths and goods, which thence
are signified in that sense by sons and daughters, truths by sons,
and goods by daughters : and whereas every man is reformed and
regenerated by truths, for without truths man does not know what
is the nature and quality of good, nor, consequently, the way to
heaven, hence it is that the truth first born from the marriage of
truth and good was sanctified to Jehovah ; the truth first born is
also the doctrine of truth, for that which is first is the all in what
follows, thus it is all truth, and all truth is doctrine : it is, however,
to be well observed, that by the first-born is signified the truth
which originates in the good of charity, consequently the good of
charity in its form and in its quality, thus truth, for the form of good
and the quality of good is truth ; the reason why this is signified by
the first-born, is, because from the good of love, which is signified
by the womb and the infant there, nothing else can be born but the

good of charity, and this good does not become good until it is formed and qualified, thus until it is in the form in which it has its quality, and its form is called truth, but still is good in form. From all that has been said it may also appear, why it was commanded, " That every male should appear three times in the year before the face of the Lord Jehovah" (Exod. xxiii. 17; chap. xxxiv. 23; Deut. xvi. 16): viz. in the three feasts, by which was signified the all of regeneration, from first to last; and whereas the all of regeneration is effected by truths of doctrine made of the life by the Lord, therefore all the males, by whom were signified truths, were to present themselves before the Lord, that they might be cleansed and afterwards led of Him; by three times in the year, also, is signified continually, and by the face of· Jehovah the divine love, by which man is led: moreover, this was done because by Jerusalem was signified the church as to doctrine, and thence also the doctrine of the church.   Inasmuch as the burnt-offerings and sacrifices were significative of things celestial and spiritual, the burnt offerings of things celestial, and the sacrifices of things spiritual, therefore the law concerning them was, " That the burnt-offerings should be of males that were entire, either from the flock or from the herd; but the sacrifices either of males or females" (Levit. i. 2. 3; chap. iii. 1, 6).   The reasons were, because celestial things are those which are of love to the Lord thus of the marriage of good and truth, but spiritual things are those which are of charity towards the neighbor, thus not of the marriage but of the consanguinity of truth with good, and truths and goods in consanguinity are as sisters and brothers, but in marriage they are as husband and wife; hence it was that the burnt-offerings were of males that were entire, by which are signified genuine truths from the Word, or from doctrine derived from the Word, which were conjoined to the good of love to the Lord, which good was signified by the altar and its fire; but the reason why the sacrifices were either of males or females, was, because by males were signified truths, and by females goods, but not conjoined by marriage but consanguinity; and whereas both, as brothers and sisters, are from one parent, worship was accepted from truths equally as from goods, that is, from males equally as from females.   Inasmuch as all spiritual nourishment is from truths which are from good, therefore it is said in the law, " That a male should eat the holy things among the priests" (Levit. vi. 11, 22; ch. vii. 6). · The reason of this statute was, because by males are signified truths of doctrine, which are doctrinals, as above, and by priests the goods of love, which are goods of the life, and by their eating together of the holy things which belonged to Aaron and his sons, was signified spiritual nourishment.   Again, in Moses: " When they draw near unto a city and fight against it, thou shalt invite it to peace; if it accept not, thou shalt smite every male thereof with the edge of the sword, but the women, the infants, the beasts, and the booty, thou shalt take" (Deut. xx. 10–14). The reason why every male in a city which did not accept peace should be smitten with the edge of the sword, but not the women, infants, and beasts, was, because by a city is signified doctrine, and by a

city of the gentiles in the land of Canaan, the doctrine of the false;
in like manner by the males of that city; and by not accepting peace
is signified the not agreeing with the truths and goods of the church,
which were signified by the sons of Israel; by the edge of the sword,
with which the males should be smitten, is signified truth destroying
the false; and whereas falses only fight against truths and goods,
and destroy them, but not evils without falses, therefore the women,
infants, and beasts, which with the gentiles signified evils, were not
smitten, for by truths evils can be subdued, amended, and reformed.
And in Jeremiah : " Cursed be the man who hath declared to his
father, saying a male son is born to thee, in gladdening he hath
made him glad; let this man be as the cities which Jehovah overturneth" (xx. 15, 16).   Treating of those who are in the devastated
church, in which nothing but falses have rule and are accepted;
hence by cursed be the man who hath declared to his father, saying,
a male is born to thee, is signified, who acknowledges the false and
declares it for truth, thus the doctrine of the false for a doctrine of
truth ; by gladdening he made him glad, is signified, acceptation of
the false from affection ; let this man be as the cities which Jehovah
overturneth, signifies, as with the doctrines which are from mere
falses, which the Lord exterminated from the church, and destroyed
as the cities in the land of Canaan ; comparison is made with cities,
because cities also signify doctrines.   And in Ezekiel : " Thou hast
taken the vessels of thine adorning, of my gold and of my silver,
which I gave to thee, and hast made thee images of a male with
which thou hast committed whoredom" (xvi. 17).   Treating of the
abominations of Jerusalem, by which are signified the falsifications
and adulterations of the Word, which are made by applications to
the cupidities of corporeal and earthly loves : the vessels of adorning
from the gold and silver of the Lord, signify the knowledges of good
and truth, which are the goods and truths of the literal sense of the
Word ; these are called vessels, because they contain in themselves
spiritual truths and goods, and vessels of adorning, because they are
the appearances, and thus the forms, of things interior, those which
are of gold signifying those which are from good, and the silver
those which are from truth ; thou hast made to thee images of a
male, with which thou hast committed whoredom, signifies falses
appearing as truths of doctrine, which are falsified, the images of
a male denoting appearances of truth, which yet are falses, and to
commit whoredom denoting to falsify.   And in Malachi : " Cursed
be the defrauder in whose flock is a male, and he voweth and sacri-
ficeth what is corrupt to the Lord" (i. 14).   By a male in the flock
is signified genuine truth of doctrine from the Word ; by what is
corrupt is signified what is falsified ; and by vowing and sacrificing
is signified to worship, thus from things falsified ; when the truth is
known, that such a worship, inasmuch as it is fraudulent, is infernal,
is signified by, cursed be the defrauder.   From all that has been now
said and shown from the Word concerning the signification of male,
and concerning the signification of sons, it may appear that by the
male son, which the woman who was encompassed with the sun,

and upon whose head was a crown of twelve stars, brought forth, is signified the doctrine of truth, thus the doctrine of love and charity for the church which is called the New Jerusalem, which is treated of in the xxi. chap. of this book.

726. "Who was to rule all nations with a rod of iron"—That hereby is signified, which by the power of natural truth from spiritual shall argue with and convince those who are in falses and evils, and yet in the church where the Word is, appears from the signification of ruling or feeding [pascere] as denoting to teach, concerning which see above, n. 482, but in this case to argue with and convince, because it is said that he is to rule or feed them with a rod of iron; and from the signification of all nations, as denoting those who are in falses and evils, concerning which also see above, n. 175, 531, 625; and from the signification of a rod of iron, as denoting the power of natural truth from spiritual, for by a rod or staff is signified power, and it is predicated of divine truth spiritual, and by iron is signified truth in the natural man; the reason why it is the power of the truth of the natural man from the spiritual which is signified by the rod of iron, is, because all the power which appertains to truths in the natural man, is from the influx of truth and good from the spiritual man, that is, from the influx of divine truth from the Lord through the spiritual man into the natural; for power appertains to the Lord alone, and he exercises it by the divine truth which proceeds from Him. But in order that these things may be more clearly perceived, it is to be shown, I. That the Lord has infinite power. II. That the Lord has this power from Himself by His divine truth. III. That all power is together in ultimates, and that hence the Lord has infinite power from first [principles] by ultimates. IV. That angels and men, in proportion as they are receptions of divine truth from the Lord, in the same proportion are powers. V. That power resides in the truths of the natural man, in proportion as this receives influx from the Lord through the spiritual man. VI. That the truths of the natural man have nothing of power, without that influx. I. That the Lord has infinite power, may appear from these considerations; that He is the God of heaven and the God of earth; that He created the universe, full of so many innumerable stars, which are suns, consequently so many worlds therein, and earths in the worlds; that they exceed several hundred thousand in number; and that He alone continually preserves and sustains the same, inasmuch as He created them; likewise, that as he created the natural worlds, so also He created the spiritual worlds above them, and perpetually fills these with angels and spirits to the number of myriads of myriads; and that He has hid the hells under them, which are also as many in number as the heavens; moreover, that He alone gives life to all and singular the things which are in the worlds of nature and in the worlds above nature; and whereas He alone gives life, that no angel, spirit, or man, can move a hand or foot, except from Him: the quality of the infinite power of the Lord is especially evident from this consideration, that He alone receives all who come from

so many earths into the spiritual worlds, who are some myriads from our earth every week, and consequently so many myriads from so many thousand earths in the universe, and not only receives, but also leads by a thousand arcana of divine wisdom, every one to the place of his life, the faithful to their places in the heavens, and the unfaithful to their places in the hells, and that He every where rules the thoughts, intentions, and wills, of all, singularly as well as universally, and causes all and every one in the heavens to enjoy their felicity, and all and every one in the hells to be held in their bonds, insomuch that not one of them can lift up a hand, much less rise out, to the injury of any angel; also that all are thus held in order, and in bonds, howsoever the heavens and the hells may be multiplied, to eternity: these and several other things, which by reason of their abundance cannot be enumerated, would not be possible, unless the Lord had infinite power. That the Lord alone rules all things, He Himself teaches in Matthew: " All power is given to Me in heaven and in earth" (xxviii. 18). " And that He is the life" (John v. 26; chap. xi. 25, 26; chap. xiv. 6). II. That the Lord has infinite power from Himself by His divine truth; the reason is, because the divine truth is the Divine Proceeding, and from the Divine which proceeds from the Lord, all those things take place which have been said above concerning His infinite power: divine truth viewed in itself is the divine wisdom, which extends itself on all sides, as the light and heat in our world from the sun; for the Lord appears in the spiritual world, where angels and spirits are, as a sun, from divine love, and all which proceeds from that sun is called divine truth; and the proceeding is what produces, and also is Him, because from Him, wherefore the Lord in the heavens is divine truth. In order however that it may be known, that the Lord has infinite power by divine truth, somewhat shall be said concerning its essence and existence: this cannot be comprehended from the natural man and his lumen, unless by means of such things as proceed from the sun of the world, from which and by which it has all power in its world, and in the earths which are under its heat and light: from the sun of the world, as from their fountain, have issued auras and atmospheres, which are called ethers and airs, whence proximately about it is pure ether, and more remote from it ethers less pure, and at length airs, but both the former and latter surrounding the earths: those ethers and airs give heat when acted upon in the gross [volumatim actæ], and give light when modified singly [singillatim modificatæ]; and by these the sun exercises all its power, and produces all its effects out of itself, thus by ethers and by airs, through the mediation of heat and at the same time of light. From these considerations some idea may be formed concerning the infinite power of the Lord by divine truth: from Him as a sun have emaned in like manner auras and atmospheres, but spiritual, because from divine love, which makes that sun: that there are such atmospheres in the spiritual world, may appear from the respiration of angels and spirits: those spiritual auras and atmospheres which are proximate to the Lord as a sun, are the most pure, but according to the degree in which they are removed from Him, they are less and less pure: hence it is, that there are three heavens, the inmost heaven in a purer aura, the middle heaven in an aura less pure, and the ultimate heaven in an aura still less pure; those auras or atmospheres, which are spiritual, because they existed from the Lord as a sun, being generally acted upon, present heat, and being particularly modified, present light; and that heat, which in its essence is love, and that light, which in its essence is wisdom, specifically, are called divine truth, but taken together with the auras, which are also spiritual, they are called the Divine Proceeding: from these then the heavens were created, and also the worlds; for from the spiritual world all things which are in the natural world exist, being produced thence as affects from their efficient causes. From these considerations now, as in a natural mirror, may be viewed the creation of heaven and earth by the divine truth proceeding from the Lord as a sun, which is above the angelic heavens; and also it may in some degree be comprehended, that the Lord has infinite power by the Divine Proceeding, which in general is called divine truth: this is also understood by these words in John: "In the beginning was the Word, and the Word was with God, and God was the Word; all things were made by Him, and without Him was not anything made that was made: and the world was made by Him" (i. 1, 3, 10): and in David: "By the Word of Jehovah were the heavens made" (Psalm xxxiii. 6): the Word signifies divine truth. III. That all power is together in ultimates, and that hence the Lord has infinite power from first [principles] by ultimates. In order to understand this, it shall first be explained what is understood by ultimates: first principles are those which are in the Lord and which proximately proceed from Him; ultimates are the things which are most remote from Him, which are things in nature, and the ultimate things of nature; these are called ultimates, because spiritual things, which are prior, terminate in them, and subsist and rest upon them as upon their bases, wherefore they are unmoved; hence these are called the ultimates of divine order. The reason why all power is in ultimates, is, because prior things are together in them, for they co-exist therein in order, which is called simultaneous order: for there is a connexion of all things from the Lord Himself through the things which are of heaven and which are of the world even to those ultimates; and whereas prior things are in ultimates, as was said, which successively proceed, it follows that in ultimates from first principles resides essential power: howbeit the divine power is power by the Proceeding Divine [principle] which is called divine truth, as was shown in the preceding article. Hence it is that the human race, with respect to the heavens, is as the basis to a column, or the foundation to a palace; consequently, the heavens subsist in order upon those things of the church which are with men in the world, thus upon divine truths in ultimates, such as are the divine truths in the literal sense of the Word: the nature and quality of the power which is in these truths, cannot be described in a few words; they are the ultimates with man into which the Lord flows-in from Himself, thus from first principles, and rules, and contains in order and connection, all things which are in the spiritual world. Now inasmuch as the divine power itself resides in those ultimates, therefore the Lord Himself came into the world, and was made man, that He might be at the same time in ultimates as He is in first principles, to the end that by ultimates, from first principles, He might reduce all things into order which were become inordinate, viz. all things in the hells, and also in the heavens: this was the cause of the advent of the Lord: for at the time proximately before His advent, there was not any divine truth in ultimates with men in the world, nor any at all in the church, which was then with the Jewish nation, but what was falsified and perverted, in consequence of which there was not any basis to the heavens; wherefore unless the Lord had come into the world, and so assumed Himself what was ultimate, the heavens, which were from the inhabitants of this earth, would have been translated elsewhere, and all the human race in this earth would have perished in eternal death: but now the Lord is in His fulness, and so in His omnipotence, in the earths, as He is in the heavens, because He is in ultimates and in first principles together: thus the Lord can save all who are in divine truths from the Word, and in a life according to them, for with these He can be present and dwell in the ultimate truths from the Word, inasmuch as ultimate truths also are His, and are Him, because from Him: according to His words in John: "He who hath My precepts, and doeth them, he it is who loveth Me; and My Father loveth him, and we will come unto him, and make our abode with him" (xiv. 21, 23). IV. That angels and men, in proportion as they are receptions of divine truths from the Lord, in the same proportion are powers. This may appear from what has been said above, namely, that the Lord has infinite power, and that power appertains to Him alone by His divine truth; also from this consideration, that angels are nothing else but forms recipient of divine truth, and in like manner men; hence it is that by angels, in the Word, are signified divine truths, and that they are called gods; it therefore follows of consequence, that according to the measure and quality of their reception of divine truth from the Lord, in the same measure and quality they are powers. V. That power resides in the truths of the natural man, in proportion as this receives influx from the Lord through the spiritual man. This also follows of consequence from what has been before observed, concerning all power being in divine truths in ultimates from first principles, the natural man being the receptacle of ultimates. But it is to be observed, that to the natural mind of man there are two ways, one from heaven, the other from the world; the way from heaven leads through the spiritual mind into the rational, and through this into the natural, and the way from the world through the sensual mind, which is proximately extant to the world, and adheres to the body: hence it may appear, that the Lord does not flow in with Divine Truth into the natural man, unless through the spiritual; and in proportion as the natural man thence receives influx, in the same proportion power resides there. By the power there is understood power against the hells, which is the power of resisting evils and falses, and of removing them; and in proportion as they are resisted and removed, in the same proportion man comes into angelic power, and also into intelligence, and becomes a son of the kingdom: concerning the power of the angels, see the work concerning H. &. H. n. 228–233; and concerning their wisdom and intelligence, n. 265–275. VI. That the truths of the natural man have nothing of power without that influx. This also follows as a consequence from what has been just now said; for the truths of the natural man, without influx through the spiritual man, have in themselves nothing of the Lord, consequently also nothing of life, and truths without life are not truths, yea, interiorly viewed, they are falses, and falses have not the least of power, inasmuch as they are opposite to truths, to which all power appertains. These things have been now adduced, in order that it may be known what is understood by the power of natural truth from spiritual, which is signified by the rod of iron, with which the male son born from the woman shall rule or feed all nations.

727. That a rod and staff signify power, and indeed the power of divine truth, arises especially from their being branches or boughs of trees, which signify the knowledges of truth and good, which are the truths of the natural man; and whereas they also support the body, they signify power; this is still more the case with a rod of iron, because iron, in like manner, signifies the truth of the natural man, and, by virtue of its hardness, it signifies power which cannot be resisted. It is from correspondence that rods and staffs hence derive the signification of the power of divine truth; it is from this circumstance that the use of staffs, in the spiritual world, where all things which appear are correspondences, is representative of the power of the inhabitants; in like manner in the Jewish church, which, like the ancient churches, was a representative church; hence it is, that miracles and signs were performed in Egypt, and afterwards in the wilderness, by Moses, by the stretching forth of his staff; as that "The waters being smitten by the staff were turned into blood" (Exod. vii. 1, 21); that "Frogs came up from the rivers and ponds, over which the staff was stretched forth" (Exod. viii. 1); and following: "That from the dust smitten with the staff there came forth lice" (Exod. viii. 16, 17); "That the staff being stretched out to heaven there came thunders and hail" (Exod. ix. 23); "That locusts were thereby produced" (Exod. x. 12); "That the sea Suph, the staff being extended upon it, was divided and afterwards returned" (Exod. xiv. 16, 21, 26): "That from the rock in Horeb, being smitten with the staff, waters issued forth" (Exod. xvii. 5; Numb. xx. 7–13); "That Joshua prevailed against Amalek when Moses lifted up his hand with the staff, and that Amalek prevailed when Moses let it down" (Exod xvii. 9–12); likewise, "That fire issued out of the rock, and consumed the flesh and the unleavened cakes which Gideon offered, when the angel of Jehovah touched it with the end of his staff" (Judg. vi. 21). The reason why those miracles were performed by the stretching out of the staff was, be-

cause the staff, from correspondence, signified the power of the Lord by divine truth, which power was treated of in the preceding article. That divine truth as to power is also signified in other parts of the Word by rods and staves, may appear from the following passages; thus in David : " Also when I walk in the shady valley, I will fear no evil, Thy rod and Thy staff shall console me ; Thou shalt set before me a table before mine enemies ; and Thou shalt make fat my head with oil, my cup shall abound" (Psalm xxiii. 4, 5). To walk in a shady valley, in the spiritual sense, signifies obscurity of the understanding, in which truths do not appear in their light ; Thy rod and Thy staff shall console me, signifies, that divine truth spiritual, together with divine truth natural, shall protect, because power is in them : the rod is divine truth spiritual, the staff divine truth natural, both together as to the power of protecting, for to console is to protect : inasmuch as a rod and staff signify divine truth as to power, therefore it follows, Thou shalt set before me a table, Thou shalt make fat my head with oil, my cup shall abound, by which is signified spiritual nourishment by divine truth ; for by setting a table is signified to be spiritually nourished, by making fat the head with oil, is signified by the good of love, and by the cup is signified by the truth of doctrine from the Word ; the cup being there substituted for wine. And in Ezekiel : " Thy mother was a vine planted near the waters : whence she had rods of strength, for sceptres of them that rule ; but she lifted herself up in her stature, among the intwisted branches, wherefore she is overturned in anger, she is thrown to the ground, and the east wind hath dried up her fruit ; the rods of her strength are torn off and withered, the fire hath devoured them all ; now she is planted in the wilderness, in a land of drought and thirst ; a fire hath issued from the rod of her branches, and hath devoured her fruit, that there is not in her a rod of strength, a sceptre of them that rule" (xix. 10–14). By these words is described the desolation of all truth in the Jewish church ; the princes, against whom the lamentation is taken up, signify truths, and the mother, who was made a lioness signifies the church ; these things are said concerning the latter and the former ; thy mother was a vine planted near the waters, signifies that the spiritual church, from its establishment, was instructed in truths, mother denotes the church in general, a vine the spiritual church specifically, waters denoting truths, and to be planted denoting to be established ; whence she had rods of strength for sceptres of them that rule, signifies divine truth in its power, and thence dominion over the falses of evil which are from hell, rods of strength denoting divine truth as to power, and sceptres divine truth as to dominion, for the sceptres of kings were short staves, from a significative tree, in the present case, from the vine ; but she hath lifted up herself in her stature amongst the intwisted branches, signifies the pride of self-derived intelligence from the scientifics of the natural man, that pride is signified by lifting up herself in her stature, and the scientifics of the natural man are signified by the entwisted branches ; she is overturned in anger, thrown to the ground, signifies the destruction thereof by falses of evil; the east wind hath dried up her fruit, signifies the destruction of the good thereof, the east wind denoting destruction, and fruit denoting good, which, with those who are in falses of evil, is the good of remains from the Word, the destruction whereof is signified by the drying up the fruit by an east wind; the rods of her strength are torn off and withered, signifies, that all divine truth is dissipated, whence the church has no power against the hells; a fire hath devoured them all, signifies pride originating in the love of self, which destroyed; now she is planted in a wilderness, in a land of drought and thirst, signifies desolation, until there is not any good of truth and truth of good remaining; a fire hath issued from the rod of her branches, signifies pride in singular the things thereof; hath devoured her fruit, signifies the consumption of good; so that there is not in her a rod of strength, a sceptre of them that rule, signifies the desolation of divine truth as to power and as to dominion, as above. And in Jeremiah: "Say ye how is the staff of strength broken, the staff of gracefulness; come down from thy glory and sit in thirst, O inhabitress, daughter of Dibon, for the waster of Moab cometh up against thee, and hath destroyed thy strong holds" (xlviii. 17, 18). By the daughter of Dibon is signified the external of the church, and thence the external of the Word, which is the literal sense thereof; and the waster of Moab signifies the adulteration thereof; hence it is evident what is signified by the staff of strength being broken, the staff of gracefulness, namely, that they had no longer divine truth in its power, which, as it is in the natural sense of the Word, is signified by the staff of strength, and in the spiritual sense by the staff of gracefulness; come down from thy glory, and sit in thirst, O inhabitress daughter of Dibon, signifies the deprivation and deficiency of divine truth, to descend from glory denoting the deprivation thereof, for glory is divine truth in light, and thirst denoting the deficiency or want thereof; for the waster of Moab cometh up against thee, signifies the adulteration of the Word as to the literal sense; and hath destroyed thy strong holds, signifies the taking away of defence, a strong hold or fortification denoting defence against falses and evils, and the literal sense of the Word being that defence. And in David: "Jehovah shall send the staff of thy strength out of Zion" (Psalm cx. 2). By the staff of strength here also is signified divine truth in its power, and by Zion the church which is in love to the Lord, and is thence called the celestial church. And in Micah: "Feed [or rule] thy people with thy rod, the flock of thine inheritance they shall feed in Bashan and Gilead according to the days of an age" (vii. 14). Feed [or rule] thy people with thy rod, signifies the instruction of those who are of the church in divine truths from the Word, to feed [or rule] signifies to instruct, people are those who are of the church in truths, and the rod there is the Word, because it is divine truth; by the flock of the heritage are signified those of the church who are in the spiritual things of the Word, which are the truths of the internal sense thereof: they shall feed in Bashan and Gilead, signifies instruction in the goods of the church and in the truths thereof from the natural sense of the Word.

And in Isaiah: "He shall smite the earth with the rod of his mouth, and with the spirit of His lips He shall slay the impious" (xi. 4); where also by the rod of the mouth of Jehovah is signified divine truth or the Word in the natural sense; and by the spirit of of his lips, is signified divine truth or the Word in the spiritual sense, both destroying the false of evil in the church, which is signified by smiting the earth and slaying the impious. The like is signified by smiting with a rod in the same prophet (chap. iv. 14); and by perforating with their staffs the head of the unfaithful" (Habak. iii. 14). And in Moses: "Israel sang a song concerning the fountain in Beer: O fountain, the princes digged, the chiefs of the people digged out, by the legislator with their staves" (Numb. xxi. 17, 18). By the fountain in Beer is here signified doctrine from the Word, Beer also, in the original tongue, signifies a fountain; by the princes who digged, and by the chiefs of the people who digged, are signified they who are intelligent and they who are wise from the Lord, who is there the legislator; by the staves by which they digged and digged out, is signified the understanding illustrated in divine truths. And in Zechariah: "As yet shall old males and old women dwell in the streets of Jerusalem, and the man in whose hand is a walking staff by reason of the multitude of days" (viii. 4). By old males and old women are signified they who are intelligent from doctrine and from the affection of truth; by the man in whose hand is a walking staff by reason of the multitude of days, are signified the wise who trust not to themselves but to the Lord alone; that these will be in the church, where there is the doctrine of genuine truth, is signified by, in the streets of Jerusalem, Jerusalem denoting the church as to doctrine, and streets the truths of doctrine, in this case genuine truths. And in Jeremiah: " Every man is become foolish by science, every founder is made ashamed by his graven image; the part of Jacob is not like them, but He is the Former of all, and Israel is the staff of His heritage, Jehovah Zebaoth is His name" (x. 14, 16; chap. li. 19). Every man is become foolish by science, signifies, by the scientifics of the natural man separate from the spiritual; every founder is made ashamed by his graven image, signifies, by the falses originating in self-derived intelligence; but He is the Former of all, signifies the Lord from whom is all intelligence of truth; Israel is the staff of his heritage, signifies the church in which is divine truth, and the power thereof against falses: and whereas the subject here treated of is concerning intelligence by divine truth, it is added, Jehovah Zebaoth is His name, the Lord being called Jehovah Zebaoth from divine truths in every complex, for Zebaoth signifies armies, and armies signify all the truths and goods of heaven and the church. When the sons of Israel murmured in the wilderness against Moses and Aaron on account of Korah, Dathan, and Abiram, because they were swallowed up by the earth, it was commanded that " The princes of the twelve tribes should place their staves in the tent of assembly, before the testimony; which being done, the staff of Aaron blossomed, and produced almonds" (Numb. xvii. 17-25). This was done, because they murmured against Jehovah, that is, against the Lord, and indeed against divine truth, which is from Him ; for Moses and Aaron represented the Lord as to the law, which is the Word ; on this account it was commanded, that the princes of the twelve tribes should place their staves in the tent of assembly before the testimony ; for by the twelve tribes, and specifically by their princes, were signified the truths of the church in every complex, and so likewise by their twelve staves ; and by the tent of assembly was represented and thence signified heaven, whence are the truths of the church, and by the testimony, the Lord himself ; the reason why the staff of Aaron blossomed and produced almonds, was, because his staff represented and thence signified truth from the good of love ; and inasmuch as it is truth from the good of love only which produces fruit, which is the good of charity, therefore his staff blossomed, and produced almonds, almonds signifying that good, in like manner as the tribe of Levi, concerning which see above, n. 444 : it is to be observed that tribe is expressed by the same word as a staff, as in Numb. i. 16 ; chap. ii. 5, 7 : hence by the twelve staves are signified the same as by the twelve tribes, viz. the divine truths of the church in every complex, concerning which see above, n. 39, 430, 431, 657.   Inasmuch as a staff signifies the power of divine truth, it also signifies the power of resisting evils and falses ; as in Isaiah : " Behold the Lord Jehovah Zebaoth, removing from Jerusalem and from Judah the staff and the stay, all the staff of bread, and all the staff of water, the mighty man and the man of war, the judge and the prophet" (iii. 1, 2).   By removing all the staff of bread and all the staff of water, is here signified, to take away all the good and truth of the church, which being taken away, there is no more any power of resisting evils and falses, to prevent their free entrance ; bread signifies the good of the church, water the truth thereof, and staff the same as to the power of resisting evils and falses ; hence it follows, the mighty man, and the man of war, the judge and the prophet, who shall also be removed, and by the mighty man and the man of war is signified truth combating against the evil and false, and by the judge and prophet the doctrine of good and truth.   And in Ezekiel : " Behold I break the staff of bread in Jerusalem, that they shall eat bread in weight and solicitude, and they shall drink waters in measure and astonishment" (iv. 16).   By breaking the staff of bread is signified that good and truth shall fail in the church, for bread here signifies both, wherefore it follows, that they shall eat bread by weight and in solicitude, and drink waters by measure, by which is signified a deficiency of good and truth, and thence of the power of resisting evils and falses. Similar things are signified by " breaking the staff of bread and of water" (Ezek. ch. v. 16 ; ch. xiv. 13 ; Psalm cv. 16 ; Levit. xxvi. 26). Whereas a rod and a staff signify the power of divine truth, and thence divine truth as to power, therefore they also signify, in the opposite sense, the power of the infernal false, and thence the infernal false as to power ; in this sense they are mentioned in the following passages ; thus in Isaiah : " Jehovah brake the staff of the impious, the rod of them that rule" (xiv. 5).   By breaking the staff of the impious is signified to destroy the power of the false from evil; and by breaking the rod of them that rule, is signified the rule of the false.   And in David: " The staff of impiety shall not rest upon the lot of the just, that the just may not put forth their hands to perversity" (Psalm cxxv. 3).   The staff of impiety signifies the power of the false from evil; upon the lot of the just signifies over truths from good, which are with the faithful, and especially with those who are in love to the Lord, for these, in the Word, are called the just; lest the just put forth their hands to perversities, signifies lest they falsify truths.   And in Lamentations: " I am the man who hath seen misery by the rod of his fury; he hath led me and brought me in darkness, and not into light" (iii. 1, 2).   These words were spoken concerning the devastation of the church; and by the rod of fury is signified the rule of the infernal false; he hath led me and brought me in darkness and not into light, signifies into mere falses and thus not into truths.   And in Isaiah: " Thou hast broken the yoke of his burden, and the staff of his shoulder, the rod of his ex-actor" (ix. 3); treating of the gentiles or nations who were in falses from ignorance, because they had not the Word, and to whom the Lord consequently was not known; the evil with which they were burdened, and the falses whereby they were infested, are signified by the yoke of the burden, the staff of the shoulder, and the rod of the exactor; the destruction thereof is signified by breaking them, for to break is predicated of a yoke, a staff, and a rod, and to destroy is predicated of evil and the false, which heavily oppress, power-fully persuade, and compel to obedience.   Again, in the same pro-phet: " At the voice of Jehovah, Ashur shall be amazed, he shall be smitten with a staff: then shall every passage of the rod of the foundation, upon which Jehovah shall cause to rest, be with timbrels and harps" (xxx. 31, 32); treating concerning the last judgment, when a new church shall take place; by Ashur who shall be amazed at the voice of Jehovah, and shall be smitten with a staff, is signi-fied ratiocination from falses, which shall be dissipated by divine truth; that then the truths of the literal sense of the Word shall be understood and received with joy, is signified by the passage of the rod of the foundation being then with timbrels and harps, passage signifying opening and free reception, and timbrels and harps sig-nifying the delights of the affection of truth; the reason why the truths of the literal sense of the Word are signified by the rod of the foundation, is, because that sense is a foundation to the truths of the spiritual sense; and whereas the latter rests upon the former, it is said, upon which Jehovah causeth to rest.   And in Zechariah: " The pride of Ashur shall be cast down, and the staff of Egypt shall recede" (x. 11).   By the pride of Ashur is signified the pride of self-derived intelligence, and by the staff of Egypt is signified the power arising from the confirmation of the falses thereof by the sci-entifics of the natural man.   Again, in Isaiah: " Woe to Ashur, the rod of Mine anger and the staff, which is in their hand, of Mine in-dignation: O My people inhabitants of Zion, be not afraid of Ashur, that he smite thee with a rod, and lift up upon thee the staff in the way of Egypt" (x. 5, 25, 26). By Ashur here also are signified ratiocinations from self-derived intelligence, by which truths are perverted and falsified; the falses thence derived, and the perversions of truth, are signified by the rod of mine anger, and by the staff of mine indignation which is in their hand; that truths shall not be perverted with those of the church who are in celestial love and in truths thence derived, is signified by, fear not O inhabitant of Zion; that the false presses and excites, and attempts to pervert by such things as appertain to the natural man, is signified by, that he smite thee with a rod, and lift up a staff upon thee in the way of Egypt, the way of Egypt denoting the scientifics of the natural man, from which come ratiocinations. Inasmuch as Egypt signifies the natural man with the things which are therein, and the natural man separate from the spiritual is in mere falses, therefore, " Egypt is called the staff of a bruised reed, which entereth and pierceth the hand, when one leaneth upon it" (Isaiah xxix. 6, 7; chap. xxxvi. 6); which may be seen explained above, n. 627. Again, in Isaiah: " Rejoice not thou, Philisthea, that the rod which smiteth thee is broken, for out of the root of the serpent shall go forth a basilisk, whose fruit is a fiery flying serpent" (xiv. 29). That by Philisthea is signified religion concerning faith separate from charity, by the root of the serpent that false principle, by the basilisk the destruction of the good and truth of the church, and by the fiery flying serpent, ratiocinations from the falses of evil, may be seen above, n. 386; thus similar things are signified by these serpents as by the dragon in this chapter of the Apocolypse; that Philisthea should not be glad that the rod which smiteth her is broken, signifies, that she should not glory that the dominion of that false is not yet destroyed. And in Hosea: " My people interrogate wood, and the staff thereof answereth them, because the spirit of whoredoms hath seduced them, and they have committed whoredom under their god" (iv. 12); treating of the falsification of the Word: by interrogating wood, or an idol of wood, is signified to consult intelligence grounded in the proprium which favors the loves thereof; by the staff answering them, is signified the false [principle], in which they confide, for when the proprium is consulted, the false answers, the proprium being of the will, thus of the love, and the false being of the understanding thence derived, thus of the thought; by the spirit of whoredoms which has seduced them, is signified the cupidity of falsifying; by committing whoredom under their god, is signified to falsify the truths of the Word. From these considerations, it may now appear what is signified by a rod and by a staff in each sense, and hence also it may be known what is understood by " the rod of iron, with which the male son should rule all nations;" and likewise by these words in the Apocalypse: " From the mouth of Him who sat upon the white horse went forth a sharp two-edged sword, that by it He may smite the nations, and He shall rule them with a rod of iron" (xix. 13); also by those words above, " To him that overcometh, will I give power over the nations, and he shall rule them with a rod of iron, as the vessels of a potter shall they be bruised" (ii. 26,

27; the explication of which may be seen above, n. 176; similar things therefore are signified by these Words in David: "Thou shalt bruise them with a rod of iron, as the vessel of a potter thou shalt disperse them" (Psalm ii. 9).

728. " And her child was caught up to God and his throne"— That hereby is signified the protection of the doctrine by the Lord, because for the new church, appears from the signification of the child or male son, which the woman encompassed with the sun, under whose feet was the moon, and on whose head was a crown of twelve stars, brought forth, as denoting doctrine from the Word, and indeed the doctrine of truth, that is, the doctrine of love to the Lord and of charity towards the neighbor, and lastly of faith; and from the signification of being caught up unto God and His throne, as denoting protection by the Lord from the dragon, which stood near the woman about to bring forth, with the intent and cupidity of devouring the birth: thus by these words is signified that protection by the Lord from those who are understood by the dragon; and whereas that doctrine was to be the doctrine of the church, which is called the New Jerusalem, therefore it is said, protection because for the new church: it is said, caught up to God and His throne, and by God is understood the Lord, and by His throne heaven; and the reason why it is to the Lord and to heaven, is, because the doctrine is from the Lord, and heaven is in that doctrine. The same as is here said concerning the child born of the woman, that it was caught up to God, is also said concerning Enoch the son of Jared, but of the latter in these words: " Enoch walked with God, and was no more, because God took him" (Gen. v. 24): who they are that are here understood by Enoch, and what is signified by these words, has been disclosed to me from heaven, namely, that they were those of the most ancient church who collected together the representatives and correspondences of natural things with spiritual; for the men of the most ancient church were in the spiritual understanding and perception of all things which they saw with their eyes, and thence from the objects in the world they perceived the spiritual things to which they correspond; and whereas the Lord foresaw that this spiritual perception would perish with their posterity, and with that perception also the knowledge of correspondences, by which mankind have conjunction with heaven, therefore the Lord provided, that some of those who lived with the most ancient people should collect the correspondences into one, and bring them together into a code; these persons are understood by Enoch, and this code is what is there signified, for this code, inasmuch as it was to serve the churches to come, which were to be established by the Lord after the deluge, for the science and knowledge of spiritual things in natural, was preserved by the Lord for their use, and also protected, lest the last posterity of the most ancient church, which was evil, should offer injury to it: this therefore is what is signified, in the spiritual sense, by Enoch being no more, because God took him. From these considerations it may

appear, what is signified by the child of the woman being caught up unto God and to His throne.

729. Verse 6. " And the woman fled into the wilderness, where she hath a place prepared of God, that they might nourish her there a thousand two hundred and sixty days."—" And the woman fled into the wilderness," signifies the church amongst a few, because with those who are not in good, and thence neither in truths: " where she hath a place prepared of God," signifies the state thereof, that in the mean time provision may be made [for its increase] amongst many : " that they may nourish her there a thousand two hundred and sixty days," signifies until it grows to its full state.

730. " And the woman fled into the wilderness"—That hereby is signified the church amongst a few, because with those who are not in good, and thence not in truths, appears from the signification of the woman, as denoting the church, concerning which see above, n. 707; and from the signification of the wilderness, as denoting where there are not truths because there is not good, concerning which we shall speak presently; and from the signification of flying thither, as denoting to abide amongst those who are not in truths, because not in good; and whereas, in the end of the church, there are but few who are in truths from good, therefore its abiding with a few is also signified : hence it may appear what these words involve, namely, that the new church, which is called the holy Jerusalem, and is signified by the woman, cannot as yet be instituted, except with few, by reason that the former church is become a wilderness; and the church is called a wilderness when there is no longer any good, and where there is no good there are no truths; and when the church is of such a quality, then evils and falses reign, which hinder the reception of its doctrine, which is the doctrine of love to the Lord and of charity towards the neighbor, with the truths thereto appertaining; and when doctrine is not received, the church is not, for the church is from doctrine.   Something shall first be said concerning there being no truths where there is no good : by good is understood good of the life according to truths of doctrine from the Word, the reason is, because the Lord never flows immediately into truths with man, but mediately by his good; for good is of the will, and the will is the man himself, the understanding being thence produced and formed; for the understanding is so adjoined to the will, that what the will loves, the understanding sees, and also brings forth into light, wherefore if the will is not in good, but in evil, then the influx of truth from the Lord into the understanding avails nothing, for it is dissipated, because it is not loved, yea, it is perverted, and the truth is falsified : hence it is manifest, why the Lord does not immediately flow into the understanding of man, except so far as the will is in good : the Lord can illustrate the understanding with every man, and so flow-in with divine truths, inasmuch as the faculty of understanding truth is given to every man, and this for the sake of his reformation; but still the Lord does not so flow-in, because truths do not remain, but in proportion as the will is re-

formed : to illustrate the understanding in truths even to faith, except in proportion as the will acts as one with it, would also be
dangerous, for man can then pervert, adulterate, and profane truths,
which exposes him to the worst condemnation : moreover, truths,
howsoever they are known and understood, if they are not at the
same time lived, are nothing but inanimate truths, and truths inanimate are as it were statues which are without life : from these considerations it may appear, whence it is, that there are no ,truths
where there is no good, unless as to form and not as to essence.
The reason why the man of the church is of such a quality at the end
of the church, is, because he then loves such things as are of the
body and the world above all things, and when these are loved
above all things, then the things which are of the Lord and of heaven are not loved, for no one can at the same time serve two masters,
but he will love the one and hate the other, for they are opposites :
for from the love of the body, which is the love of self, and from the
love of the world, which is the love of riches, when they are loved
above all things, evils of every kind flow forth, and from evils falses,
which are opposite to goods and truths, which flow from love to the
Lord, and from charity towards our neighbor : from these few observations it may appear whence it is that the woman is said to have
· fled into the wilderness, that is, amongst a few, because with those
who are not in good, and thence not in truths. In the Word frequent mention is made of a wilderness, and also of a desert and
waste, and thereby is signified the state of the church when there
is no longer any truth therein because there is no good ; the reason
why this state of the church is called a wilderness, is, because, in
the spiritual world, where they dwell who are not in truths, because
not in good, there is a wilderness, where there is no verdure in the'
plains, nor harvest in the field, nor fruit trees in the gardens, but a
barren, arid, and dry land : moveover by wilderness, in the Word,
is signified the state of the church with the gentiles who are in ignorance of truth, and yet in the good of life according to their religion,
from which they desire truths : it also signifies the state of those
who are in temptations, because in temptations goods and truths are
shut in by the evils and falses which emerge and are presented to
the mind.   That the former and the latter things are signified by
wilderness in the Word, may appear from the passages therein
where mention is made of wilderness. With respect to the 1st,
namely, that by wilderness is understood the state of the church,
when there is no more any truth therein, because there is no good,
it appears from the following passages. Thus in Isaiah : " Is this
the man that moveth the earth, that maketh the kingdoms tremble,
that laid the world into a wilderness, and destroyed the cities
thereof " (xiv. 16, 17) : speaking concerning Lucifer, by whom is
understood Babel : and by moving the earth, making the kingdoms
tremble, and laying the world into a wilderness, is signified to destroy all the truths and goods of the church, the earth denoting the
church, the kingdoms the truths thereof, world the goods thereof,
and wilderness where these are no longer ; by the cities which are

destroyed are signified doctrinals, a city denoting doctrine; and the adulteration of the Word, whereby doctrine and thence the church is destroyed is here signified by Babel. Again: "Upon the land of my people shall come up the thorn of the briar, because upon all the houses of gladness in the merry city; for the palace shall be a wilderness, the multitude of the city forsaken: it shall be a cliff and a beacon upon dens for ever, a joy of wild asses, a pasture of flocks" (xxxii. 13, 14): upon the land of my people shall come up the thorn of the briar, signifies the false of evil in the church, the thorn of the briar denoting the false of evil, and land or earth denoting the church; upon all the houses of gladness in the merry city, signifies, where the goods and truths of doctrine from the Word were received with affection; but what is signified by the palace being a wilderness, the multitude of the city forsaken, the cliff and beacon upon the dens, the joy of wild asses, and pasture of flocks, may be seen above, n. 410, where they are explained. Again: "By my rebuke I dry up the sea, I lay the rivers into a wilderness, the fish thereof shall stink, because there is no water, and shall die with thirst" (l. 2). By laying the rivers into a wilderness is signified to deprive the understanding of truths, consequently to deprive man of intelligence; the rest may be seen explained above, n. 342. And in Jeremiah: "I saw, when lo! Carmel was a wilderness, and all the cities were desolated before Jehovah; the whole earth shall be wasteness" (iv. 26, 27). By Carmel is signified the spiritual church which is in truths from good; its being a wilderness, signifies there being in it no truths from good; by the cities which are desolated are signified doctrinals without truths; by the whole earth being a wasteness is signified the church being destitute of good and thence destitute of truths. Again: "Many shepherds have destroyed My vineyard, they have trodden under foot my field, they have reduced the field of My desire to a wilderness of a desert; upon all the hills in the wilderness the wasters came, because the sword of Jehovah devoureth from the end of the earth to the end thereof" (xii. 10, 12). That the truths of the church were altogether destroyed by falses from evil, is signified by destroying the vineyard, treading under foot the field, reducing the field of desire to a wilderness of a desert, and by the wasters coming upon all the hills of the wilderness, because the sword of Jehovah devoureth; the vineyard and the field signify the church as to truth and good, the field of desire the same as to doctrine, and a wilderness of a desert signifies where those things are not; the wasters in the wilderness signify evils in consequence of not having truths; the sword of Jehovah devouring signifies the false destroying; from the end of the earth to the end of the earth signifies all things of the church. And in Lamentations: "With the danger of our souls we bring our bread, by reason of the sword of the wilderness" (v. 9). To bring bread with danger of their souls, signifies the difficulty and danger of procuring for themselves truths of life from the Word; by reason of the sword of the wilderness, signifies by reason of the false of evil reigning in the church falsifying truths, and thereby destroying them. And in Ezekiel:

" The vine is now planted in the wilderness, in a land of drought
and thirst" (xix. 13). By vine is signified the church, which in the
beginning of the chapter is called a mother who became a lioness;
it is said to be planted in a wilderness when there is no longer any
truth therein, because no good; a land of drought is where there is
no good but instead thereof evil, and a land of thirst is where there is
no truth, but instead thereof the false. And in Hosea : " Contend
with your mother, that she may remove her whoredoms from her
faces, lest peradventure I strip her naked and set her according to
the day of her birth, and set her as a wilderness, and dispose her as
a land of drought, and slay her by thirst" (ii. 2, 3) : treating of the
church which falsify the truths of the Word : mother denotes the
church, and her whoredoms the falsifications of truth ; the deprivation of all truth as before reformation took place, is signified by
stripping naked, and setting her according to the day of her birth;
the church without good is signified by a wilderness and land of
drought, and the deprivation of truth by slaying with thirst ; thirst
is predicated of truths, because water, which is thirsted for, signifies
truth, and drought is predicated of the want of good, because it is
from scorching. Again : " He amongst the brethren is fierce, the
east wind, the wind of Jehovah, shall come, ascending from the wilderness, and his spring shall become dry, and his fountain shall be
dried up" (xiii. 15) : treating of Ephraim, by whom is understood
the understanding of the Word, which is called fierce amongst the
brethren when it defends falses with animosity, and combats for
them against truths ; by the east wind, the wind of Jehovah, is signified the ardor of cupidity arising from the love and pride of destroying truths, which is said to ascend from the wilderness, when
from an understanding in which there are not any truths from good
but falses from evil, such an understanding is a wilderness because
it is empty and void ; that from such ardor and pride the all of doctrine and of the Word is destroyed, is signified by his spring shall
become dry, and his fountain shall be dried up, a spring signifying
doctrine, and a fountain the Word. And in Joel : " Unto thee, O
Jehovah, do I cry, because the fire hath devoured the dwellings of
the wilderness and the flame hath burnt down all the trees of the
field ; because the beasts of the field make their cry unto thee, because the brooks of waters are dried up, and the fire hath devoured
the dwellings of the wilderness" (i. 19, 20). The fire hath devoured
the dwellings of the wilderness and the flame hath burnt down all
the trees of the field, signifies, that the love of self and the conceit of
self intelligence has consumed all perception of good, and all understanding of the truth of doctrine derived from the literal sense of the
Word ; fire signifies the love of self, and flame the conceit of self-
derived intelligence ; the dwellings of the wilderness signify the
goods of doctrine from the literal sense of the Word, and the trees
of the field the knowledges of the truth thereof ; the literal sense of
the Word is called a wilderness when it is understood only naturally,
thus according to appearances, and not at the same time spiritually,
or according to the genuine sense; the beasts of the field make their

cry unto Thee, signifies, the lamentations of those who are natural, and still desire truths; that beasts signify the affections of the natural man may be seen above, n. 650; because the brooks of waters are dried up, and the fire hath devoured the dwellings of the wilderness, signifies that there are thence no longer any truths and goods of life. Again: "The day of Jehovah cometh; before Him a fire devoureth, and behind Him a flame rageth; as the garden of Eden is the land before Him, but behind Him a wilderness of wasteness, and there is nothing that is escaped for Him" (ii. 3). By the day of Jehovah is understood the end of the church, which is called the consummation of the age, and then the advent of the Lord; that in the end of the church the love of self and thence the conceit of self-derived intelligence consumes all the goods and truths of the church, is signified by, a fire devoureth before Him, and behind Him a flame rageth, fire signifying the love of self, and flame the conceit of self-derived intelligence, as above; as the garden of Eden is the land before him, but behind Him a wilderness of wasteness, signifies, that in the beginning, when that church was established with the ancients, there was the understanding of truth from good, but at its end, the false from evil, the garden of Eden denoting the understanding of truth from good, and thence wisdom, and a wilderness of wasteness denoting no understanding of truth from good, and thence insanity from falses which are from evil; by nothing escaping for him, is signified, that there is not the least of truth from good. And in Isaiah: "The earth mourneth and languisheth, Lebanon is ashamed and hath withered, Sharon is become as a wilderness, Bashan is shaken, and Carmel" (xxxiii. 9). By these words also is described the devastation of good and desolation of truth in the church: by Lebanon is signified the church as to the rational understanding of good and truth; by Sharon, Bashan, and Carmel, the same as to the knowledges of good and truth from the natural sense of the Word, the devastation and desolation of which is signified by mourning, languishing, and withering, and becoming as a wilderness, wilderness denoting where there is no truth, because no good. And in Jeremiah: "Because the earth is full of adulteries, because of the curse the earth mourneth, the pastures of the wilderness have become dry" (xxiii. 10). By the earth full of adulteries is signified the church in which the goods and truths thereof from the Word are adulterated; by the curse, on account of which the land mourneth, is signified all evil of the life and false of doctrine; and by the pastures of the wilderness, which have become dry, are signified the knowledges of good and truth from the Word, pastures denoting those knowledges because they feed the mind, and wilderness denoting the Word, when it is adulterated. And in David: "Jehovah layeth the rivers into a wilderness, and the going forth of waters into drought, a land of fruit into saltness, for the wickedness of them that dwell therein" (Psalm cvii. 33, 34). By the rivers which are laid into a wilderness, is signified intelligence from the understanding of truth, and also of the Word as to its interior sense, devastated by falses from evil, rivers denoting such things as are of intelligence, and a wilderness where those things are not, but instead thereof falses from evil; by the going forth of waters which are laid into drought, is signified, that the ultimate things of the understanding, which are called the knowledges of truth and good, are without all light and spiritual affection of truth, waters denoting truths, drought the deprivation thereof by reason of there being no light and affection, and the going forth denoting the ultimates thereof, such as are the truths of the literal sense of the Word; by the land of fruit which shall be laid into saltness, is signified the good of love and of life deeply vastated by falses, saltness denoting the devastation of truth by falses; and whereas all devastation by falses is from the evil of the life, it is therefore added, for the wickedness of them that dwell therein. And in Jeremiah: "Lift up thine eyes unto the hills, and see where thou hast committed fornication; upon the ways hast thou sat as an Arab in the wilderness, whence thou hast profaned the land with thy whoredoms and thy wickedness" (iii. 2). By these words also is described the adulteration and falsification of the Word, which are signified by committing fornication and whoredom; hence, lift up thine eyes to the hills and see where thou hast committed fornication, signifies, to animadvert to the knowledges of truth and good in the Word, that they are adulterated; to lift up the eyes signifies to animadvert, hills signify those knowledges by reason of the trees and groves which are upon them, whereby they are signified; by hills also are signified the goods of charity which are so destroyed; upon the ways hast thou sat as an Arab in the wilderness, signifies, to lie in wait lest any truth should come forth and be received, ways denote the truths of the church, to sit in them, denotes to lie in wait, and an Arab in the wilderness denotes as a robber in the wilderness slays and deprives; thou hast profaned the land with thy whoredoms and wickedness, signifies the falsification of the truths of the Word from evils which are made of the life. Again: "O generation see ye the Word of Jehovah; have I been a wilderness to Israel, have I been a land of darkness (ii. 31); that all good of life and truth of doctrine is taught in the Word, and not evil of life and false of doctrine, is understood by, see ye the Word of Jehovah, have I been a wilderness to Israel, have I been a land of darkness. And in Joel: "Egypt shall be a wasteness, and Edom a wilderness of wasteness, for the violence of the sons of Judah, whose innocent blood they have shed in their land" (iv. 19). By Egypt and by Edom is signified the natural man, which had perverted the truths and goods of the Word; that it shall be destroyed, so as to see only such things as serve for confirmation, is signified by, Egypt shall be a wasteness, and Edom a wilderness of wasteness; that this is on account of the adulteration of all the good and truth in the Word, is signified by, for the violence of the sons of Judah, whose innocent blood they have shed, the violence of the sons of Judah denoting the adulteration of the Word as to good, and the shedding of innocent blood the adulteration of the Word as to the truths thereof; that Judah signifies the celestial church, and also the Word, may be seen above, n. 211,

433; and that to shed innocent blood, signifies to offer violence to divine truth, thus to adulterate the truth of the Word, n. 329; the adulteration of the Word is effected by the scientifics of the natural man, when these are applied to confirm falses and evils, and this man becomes a wasteness and a wilderness, when his scientifics become confirmations of the false and of evil; Egypt signifies those scientifics, and Edom the conceit which thereby falsifies. And in Malachi: "Esau have I hated, and I have laid his mountains a waste, and his heritage to the dragons of the wilderness" (i. 3). By Esau is signified the love of the natural man: by his mountains are signified the evils from that love, and by his heritage the falses from those evils, and by the dragons of the wilderness are signified mere falsifications from which those falses exist. Inasmuch as with the Jewish nation all things of the Word were adulterated, and there was no longer any truth with them, because no good, therefore John the Baptist was in the wilderness, whereby the state of that church was represented; thus it is written in the Evangelist, "John the Baptist was in the wilderness, until the days of his appearing unto Israel" (Luke i. 80); "That he preached in the wilderness of Judea" (Matt. iii. 1, 2, 3; Mark i. 2, 3, 4; Luke iii. 2, 4, 5); and in Isaiah: "The voice of one crying in the wilderness, prepare the way of Jehovah, make plain in the desert a path for our God" (xi. 3). Hence also the Lord says concerning Jerusalem, whereby is understood the church as to doctrine, "your house shall be left deserted" (Luke xiii. 35); a house deserted signifies the church without truths because without good. And in Matthew: "If they say to you, lo Christ is in the wilderness, go not forth, if in the secret chambers, believe not" (xxiv. 26); but these words may be seen explained in the A. C. n. 3900; for by Christ is understood the Lord as to divine truth, consequently as to the Word and as to doctrine from the Word, and by false Christs, concerning whom those things are said, are signified falses of doctrine from the truths of the Word falsified. From the passages which have been now adduced from the Word it may appear, that by a wilderness is understood the church where there are no truths because no good, consequently where the false is because there is evil; for where truth and good is not, there is the false and evil; both cannot exist together, which is understood by the words of the Lord, that no man can serve two masters. II. That by a wilderness is also signified the state of the church with the gentiles or nations which were in ignorance of truth, and yet in the good of life, according to their religion, from which they desired truths, may likewise appear from the passages in the Word, where the church to be established with the gentiles is treated of; as in Isaiah: "The spirit shall be poured out upon you from on high, then the wilderness shall be a fruitful field, and the fruitful field shall be counted for a forest; judgment shall dwell in the wilderness, and justice shall remain in the fruitful field" (xxxii. 15, 16); treating of those who are in natural good, and are reforming; the influx out of heaven into them is signified by, the spirit shall be poured out upon you from on high: that then truth from a spiritual origin

shall be implanted in them, is signified by, the wilderness shall be a
fruitful field, a wilderness denoting the natural man destitute of
truths, and the fruitful field, or land of corn, denoting the natural
man fructified with truths; that he has thence the science of the
knowledges of truth and good, is signified by, the fruitful field shall
be counted for a forest, forest being predicated of the natural man as
a garden is of the spiritual, wherefore by a forest is signified science
and by a garden intelligence; that what is right and just is thence in
him, is signified by, judgment shall dwell in the wilderness, and justice
shall reside in the fruitful field; judgment and justice, in the spiritual
sense, signify truth and good, but, in the natural sense, what is right
and just. Again: "I will open rivers upon the cliffs, and fountains in
the midst of the valleys; I will make the wilderness into a lake of
waters, and the dry land into springs of waters; I will give in the
wilderness the cedar of Shittah, the myrtle and the tree of oil; I
will set in the desert the fir, the pine, and the box" (xli. 18, 19);
treating also of the reformation and illustration of the gentiles or nations; and by opening rivers upon the cliffs, and setting fountains
in the midst of the valleys, is signified to give intelligence from spiritual truth, and from natural truths, rivers upon the cliffs signifying
intelligence from spiritual truths, and fountains in the midst of valleys intelligence from natural truths; by making the wilderness into
a lake of waters, and the dry land into springs of waters, is signified
to fill with truths the spiritual man and the natural, where before
there were not any truths; the spiritual man in which there was
not before any truth is understood by a wilderness, and the natural
man into which there was not before any spiritual influx is understood by the dry land; truths in abundance appertaining to the spiritual man are understood by the lake of waters, and truths in abundance appertaining to the natural man by the springs of waters; by
setting in the wilderness the cedar of Shittah, the myrtle, and the
tree of oil, is signified to give rational truths and the perception
thereof; and by setting in the desert the fir, the pine, and the box,
are signified, in like manner, natural truths, which are scientifics
and knowledges, with the understanding thereof; the cedar denotes
rational truth of a superior order, the myrtle, rational truth of an inferior order, and the tree of oil, the perception of good and thence of
truth; the fir denotes natural truth of a superior order, the pine natural truth of an inferior order, and the box the understanding of
good and truth in the natural principle. And in David: "He layeth the wilderness into a lake of waters, and the dry land into the
going forth of waters; and there he maketh the hungry to dwell,
that they may erect a city of habitation" (Psalm cvii. 35, 36). Here
also the illustration of the gentiles is treated of; and by making the
wilderness a lake of waters, are signified similar things as above;
and there he maketh the hungry to dwell, signifies, for those who
desire truths, these being understood by the hungry in the Word;
that they may erect a city of habitation, signifies, that from those
truths they may make for themselves doctrine of life, a city
denoting doctrine, and to inhabit, denoting to live. And in

Isaiah: "Behold I make a new thing, now it shall spring forth, I will also make a way in the wilderness, rivers in the desert; the wild beasts of the field shall honor me, the dragons and the daughters of the owl, because I will give waters in the wilderness, rivers in the desert, to give drink to my people, my elect" (xliii. 19, 20). These things are also said concerning the new church to be established by the Lord with the gentiles; and by wilderness is signified the state of the church with those who are in ignorance of truth, and yet in the desire of knowing it; but what each particular signifies in the spiritual sense, may be seen explained above, n. 518. Again: "Jehovah shall console Zion, He shall console all her wastes, and He shall make her wilderness as Eden, and her desert as the garden of Jehovah; gladness and joy shall be found in her, confession and the voice of singing" (li. 3); likewise treating of the new church with the gentiles which should acknowledge the Lord: that church is understood by Zion, and the establishment thereof and their reformation by being consoled; by the wilderness, which shall be made as Eden, and by the desert as the garden of Jehovah, is signified wisdom and intelligence from love to the Lord, which is given to those who before were in no understanding of truth, and in no perception of good; but these things also may be seen explained above, n. 721. And in David: "The habitations of the willderness drop, and the hills gird themselves with exultation; the meadows are clothed with flocks, and the valleys are covered with corn" (Psalm lxv. 13, 14); also treating of the church with the gentiles; and by the dwellings of the wilderness dropping, is signified, that their minds, which before were in ignorance of truth, acknowledge and receive truths, to drop being predicated of the influx, acknowledgment, and reception of truth, dwellings of the interiors of man, which are of his mind, and wilderness of the state of ignorance of truth; the hills girding themselves with exultation, signifies, that goods with them receive truths with joy of heart; the meadows being clothed with flocks, and the valleys covered with corn, signifies that both minds, the spiritual and the natural, receive truths suitable to themselves, meadows denoting those things which are of the spiritual mind, and thence of the rational, and valleys those which are of the natural mind, and flocks spiritual truth, and corn natural truth. And in Isaiah: "Let them sing praise, the extremity of the earth, they who go down unto the sea, and the fulness thereof, the islands and the inhabitants of them: let the wilderness and the cities thereof lift up the voice, the villages which Arabia inhabiteth; let the dwellers of the rock sing, let them shout from the top of the mountains" (xlii. 10, 11); treating of the church with those who were remote from the truths of the church, being natural and sensual: their state of ignorance is understood by the wilderness, and their joy from the preaching and knowledge of truth, by singing praise and lifting up the voice; the rest may be seen explained above, n. 406. Inasmuch as the state of ignorance of truth, in which the gentiles were, is signified by a wilderness, and the desire of truth by hunger, and instruction from the Lord by feeding, therefore it came to pass that

the Lord retired into a wilderness, and there taught the multitude
which sought him, and afterwards fed them; that this took place in
wildernesses, may appear in Matthew chap. xiv. 13–22; chap.
xv. 32–38; Mark vi. 31–34; chap. viii. 1–9; Luke ix. 12–17); for
all things which were done by the Lord, and also which were with
the Lord, were representative, because they were correspondences,
thus also the things above; from which, and the passages that have
been adduced above, it is evident that a wilderness signifies such a
state with man as is not cultivated and inhabited, thus which is not
yet made vital from a spiritual principle, consequently, when applied
to the church, it signifies a state not vivified by truths, and thus the
religion of the gentiles, which was almost empty and void, inasmuch
as they had not the Word, where truths are, and thence knew not
the Lord, who teaches them; and whereas they had not truths,
therefore neither could their good be any other than according to the
quality of truth with them, for good is of a similar quality to its
truth, the one being of the other. From these considerations it may
appear that by a wilderness, where the gentiles are treated of, is
signified their ignorance of truth, and yet desire for it, to vivify their
goods. III. That by wilderness is also signified the state of those
who are in temptations, because in them truths and goods are shut in
by falses and evils, which emerge and agitate the mind, may appear
from the wandering of the sons of Israel forty years in the wilderness; for thereby was represented every state of temptations into
which they come, who are regenerating, and of whom a church is
about to be formed : every man is born natural, and also lives natural, until he becomes rational, and when he is become rational, then
he can be led of the Lord, and become spiritual, which is effected by
the implantation of the knowledges of truth from the Word, and then,
at the same time, by the opening of the spiritual mind, which receives
those things which are of heaven, and by the calling forth and elevation of those knowledges out of the natural man, and the conjunction thereof with the spiritual affection of truth : this opening and
conjunction cannot be otherwise given than by temptations, because
therein man combats inwardly against the falses and evils which are
in the natural man : in a word, man is introduced into the church,
and becomes a church, by temptations. These things were represented by the wandering and leading about of the sons of Israel in
the wilderness; the state of the natural man before he is regenerated,
was represented by their tarrying in the land of Egypt, for the land
of Egypt signified the natural man, with the scientifics and knowledges, together with the cupidities and appetites, which reside in
him, as may appear from what was said and shown above concerning Egypt, n. 654: but the spiritual state, which is the state of the
church with man, was represented by the introduction of the sons
of Israel into the land of Canaan, for the land of Canaan signified
the church with its truths and goods, together with the affections
and delights thereof, which reside in the spiritual man; but the reformation and regeneration of man, before from natural he becomes
spiritual, and thereby a church, was represented by their errors and'

wanderings in the wilderness forty years. That this is the case, and that that wilderness signified a state of temptations, may appear from the following passages in Moses : " Thou shalt remember all the way in which Jehovah thy God led thee these forty years in the wilderness, that He might afflict thee, and try thee, and know what was in thine heart, whether thou wouldest keep His precepts or no ; and He afflicted thee and made thee to hunger, and fed thee with manna, which thou knewest not, neither have thy fathers known, and that He might teach thee, that man doth not live by bread alone, but by every word that proceedeth out of the mouth of Jehovah doth man live : thy raiment waxed not old upon thee, and thy foot swelled not, these forty years" (Deut. viii. 2, 3, 4); " In the wilderness which thou sawest, Jehovah thy God carried thee, as a man carrieth his son, He went before you in the way to search out a place for you, in which ye might be encamped, in a fire by night to show you the way, and in a cloud by day" (Deut. i. 31, 33); " Jehovah who led thee through the wilderness great and formidable, of the serpent, of the fiery flying serpent, and of the scorpion, and of drought, where there were no waters ; who brought forth waters for thee out of the rock of flint, and fed thee with manna in the wilderness, that He might afflict and try thee, to do thee good in thy latter end" (Deut. viii. 15, 16). Again : " Jehovah found Jacob in a land of wilderness, in emptiness, in howling in the desert; He led him about, He instructed him, He guarded him as the pu   of the eye" (Deut. xxxii. 10). By all these particulars, and by all that are related in the book of Exodus concerning the journeyings of the sons of Israel in the wilderness from their going forth from Egypt to their entrance into the land of Canaan, are described the temptations in which the faithful are, before they become spiritual, thus before the goods of love and charity, with their truths, are implanted, which constitute the church with man. He who knows what spiritual temptations are, knows that man when he is in them, is infested by evils and falses, insomuch that he scarce knows otherwise than that he is in hell ; likewise that the Lord fights in man against them, from an interior principle ; as also that in the mean time he sustains him with spiritual meat and drink, which are the goods and truths of Heaven ; that the natural man loathes these things ; that the natural is nevertheless thus subdued, until it as it were dies with its concupiscences ; and that hereby he is subjected to the spiritual man ; and that thus man is reformed and regenerated, and introduced into the church ; these things are what are involved in all the circumstances related concerning the sons of Israel in the wilderness. But in order to make this more evident, a general explication shall be given of the passages here adduced : 1. That man in temptations is infested by evils and falses, insomuch that he scarce knows otherwise than that he is in hell, is understood by " Jehovah led thee through the wilderness, great and formidable, of the serpent, of the fiery flying serpent, of the scorpion, and of drought where there were no waters :" by the wilderness great and formidable are signified grievous temptations ; by the serpent, the fiery flying serpent, and the scorpion, are signified evils and falses with their persuasions emerging from the sensual and natural man, serpents denoting evils thence, fiery flying serpents, the falses thence derived, and scorpions persuasions ; by drought where there were no waters, is signified the deficiency and shutting in of truth. Those things are also understood by its being said, that Jehovah might afflict thee, and try thee, and know what was in thine heart. 2. That the Lord fights in man against evils and falses which are from hell, is signified by " Jehovah found Jacob in a wilderness, in emptiness, in howling in a desert, He guarded him as the pupil of His eye ;" likewise by His carrying him as a man carrieth his son ; and by going before them in a fire by night and in a cloud by day. 3. That the Lord in the mean time sustains man with spiritual meat and drink, which are the goods and truths of heaven, is signified by feeding them with manna, bringing forth waters for them out of the rock of flint, and by leading and instructing them ; by manna is understood the good of celestial love, and by waters out of the rock of flint are understood the truths of that good from the Lord. 4. That in temptations the natural man loathes these things, is understood by the sons of Israel so often complaining of the manna, and lusting after the food of Egypt ; wherefore it is here said, and Jehovah afflicted thee and caused thee to hunger, and fed thee with manna. 5. That still the natural man is subdued, and as it were dies with its concupiscences, and is subject to the spiritual man, was represented by all those having died in the wilderness who went forth out of Egyyt, and desired to return thither, refusing to enter into the land of Canaan ; and by their children being introduced into that land : that such things were represented and signified by those circumstances, can only be known and seen from the spiritual sense of the Word. 6. That man after the temptations becomes spiritual, and is introduced into the church, and by the church into heaven, was represented by their introduction into the land of Canaan, for the land of Canaan signified the church, and also heaven : and this is what was signified by these words : " That Jehovah might afflict thee, and try thee, to do thee good at thy latter end :" their spiritual life is described by Jehovah teaching them that man doth not live by bread alone, but by every word that proceeds out of the mouth of Jehovah. By their raiment not waxing old, and their feet not swelling, was signified that the natural man is not hurt by those afflictions, for garments signify the truths of the natural man, and the feet the natural man himself. Moreover by the number forty, whether years or days, is signified the entire duration of temptations, as may be seen above, n. 633. Similar things are involved in these words in David : " They wandered in the wilderness a desert life, they found not a city of habitation, hungry and thirsty ; when their soul fainted in the way, they cried unto Jehovah, He led them in the way of right that they might go to a city of habitation" (Psalm cvii. 4, 5, 6, 7). These words are spoken in general concerning those who are redeemed, specifically concerning the sons of Israel in the wilderness, and thereby are described the temptations of such as are regenerating by the Lord ; by the city of habitation which they found not, is signified the doctrine of life which constitutes the church in man; and inasmuch as the church is formed in man by a life according to doctrine, through the means of temptations, it is said that Jehovah led them in the way of right, that they might go to a city of habitation : the defect or want of truth even to despair, and yet a desire for it, is signified by their being hungry and thirsty, and their soul fainting in the way. And in Jeremiah : " I remembered thy youth, the love of thine espousals, when thou wentest after Me in the wilderness : they said not, where is Jehovah, who caused us to come up out of the land of Egypt, who led us in the wilderness, in a land of desert and of the pit, in a land of drought and of dense shade, in a land through which no man passed, and where no man dwelt; and I led you into a land of corn, to eat the fruit thereof and the good thereof" (ii. 2, 6, 7). By the youth and love of espousals, which Jehovah remembered, is signified the state of the reformation and regeneration of man, whilst from natural he becomes spiritual; inasmuch as man is thereby conjoined to the Lord, and as it were espoused to Him, this is what is understood by the love of espousals; and inasmuch as this is effected by temptations it is said, when thou wentest after Me in the wilderness; the state of temptations is described by, he led me in the wilderness, in a land of desert and the pit, in a land of drought and dense shade, a wilderness denoting that state, a land of desert and the pit denoting the same as to evils and falses which emerge, and a land of drought and dense shade denoting the perception of good and understanding of truth obscured; the state of man after temptations is described by, I led you into a land of corn, that ye might eat the fruit thereof and the good thereof, by which is signified introduction into the church in which are truths of doctrine, whereby there is an appropriation of the good of love and of charity, land signifying the church, land of corn denoting the church as to truths of doctrine, to eat denoting to appropriate, fruit the good of love, and good the good of charity and of life. And in Ezekiel : " I will bring you out from the peoples, and I will gather you from the lands, and I will lead you into a wilderness of peoples, and I will plead with you there face to face, even as I pleaded with your fathers in the wilderness of the land of Egypt; then will I cause you to pass under the rod, and I will bring you into the bond of the covenant" (xx. 34, 35, 36, 37). Here also the wilderness denotes a state of temptations, which state is called a wilderness of peoples and also the wilderness of the land of Egypt, because the state of the natural man before regeneration is understood, which, by reason that there are then no goods and truths, but evils and falses, is a wilderness and a desert, but when falses and evils are exterminated thence, and truths and good implanted in their place, from a wilderness he then becomes Lebanon and a garden, to plead with them in the wilderness face to face, signifies, to show them to the life and to acknowledgment of what quality they are, for in temptations the evils and falses of man emerge and appear; face to face denotes to the life and to acknowledgment; that after man has suffered hard things, conjunction is effected with the Lord, which is reformation, is signified by, then will I cause you to pass under the rod, and I will bring you into the bonds of the covenant, to pass under the rod denoting to suffer hard things, and the bond of the covenant denoting conjunction with the Lord. And in Hosea : " I will visit upon her the days of Baalim, in which she went after her paramours; wherefore behold I will bring you into the wilderness, and afterwards I will speak upon her heart, and I will give her her vineyards thence, and the valley of Achor for a door of hope, and she shall answer thither according to the days of her youth, and according to the days of her coming up out of the land of Egypt; and in that day thou shalt call me my husband, and shalt no more call me my Baal" (ii. 13–16). By Baalim and the paramours, after whom she went, are signified such things as appertain to the natural man, and are loved, namely, cupidities and the falsities thence derived; that these are to be removed by temptations, is signified by, I will bring you into the wilderness; that consolation will follow, is signified by, afterwards I will speak upon her heart; that then they will have truths spiritual and natural, is signified by, I will give her her vineyards thence and the valley of Achor; that afterwards the influx of good from heaven and joy thence derived shall be as with those who were of the ancient churches, and from natural became spiritual, is signified by, she shall answer or sing thither according to the days of her youth, and according to the days of her coming up out of the land of Egypt, the days of youth signifying the times of the ancient church, and the days of her coming up out of the land of Egypt, signifying when from natural they became spiritual; conjunction in such case with the Lord by the affections of truth, the cupidities from the natural man being rejected, is signified by, in that day thou shalt call me my husband, and thou shalt no more call me my Baal. Forasmuch as a wilderness signifies a state of temptations, and the number forty, whether years or days, the whole duration thereof from beginning to end, therefore the temptations of the Lord, which were the most cruel of all, and which He sustained from childhood to the passion of the cross, are understood by the temptations of forty days in the wilderness, concerning which it is thus written in the Evangelist: " Jesus was led by the spirit into the wilderness, that He might be tempted of the devil; and when He had fasted forty days, and forty nights, He afterwards hungered; and the tempter drew near unto him" (Matt. iv. 1, 2, 3; Luke iv. 1, 2, 3). " The spirit impelling Jesus caused Him to go out into the wilderness, and He was in the wilderness forty days, being tempted, and was with the beasts" (Mark i. 12, 13). By which it is not understood that the Lord was only forty days, and at the end thereof tempted by the devil, but that He was tempted through His whole life even to the last moment, as in the cruel anxiety of heart which He suffered in Gethsemane, and in the direful passion of the cross; for the Lord, by temptations admitted into the humanity which He had from the mother, subjugated all the hells, and at the same time glorified His Human [principle]; but concerning these temptations of the Lord, see what is related in the A. C. and what is thence collected into the D. of the N. J. n. 201; all those temptations of the Lord are signified by the temptations in the wilderness forty days and forty nights, inasmuch as wilderness signifies a state of temptation, and forty days and forty nights all the duration thereof: the reason why no more is said concerning them by the Evangelists, is, because there was no more revealed concerning them; but still in the prophets, and especially in the Psalms of David, they are described at large: by the beasts with which the Lord is said to have been, are signified the infernal societies; and by fasting is there signified affliction, such as takes place in the combats of temptations. IV. That by a wilderness is also signified hell. The reason is, because it is called a wilderness where there are no corn fields nor habitations, likewise where there are wild beasts, serpents, and dragons, by which is signified, where there is no truth of doctrine, nor good of life, consequently where there are concupiscences arising from evil loves, and thence falsities of every kind; and inasmuch as the latter things are in hell, and the former things in a wilderness, therefore from correspondences a wilderness also signifies hell. Moreover the natural man with every one, so long as it is separate from the spiritual, as is the case before regeneration, is hell, by reason that all the hereditary evil into which man is born resides in his natural man, and is not cast out thence, that is, removed, except by the influx of divine truth through heaven from the Lord; and this influx is not given into the natural man, except through the spiritual, for the natural man is in the world, and the spiritual man is in heaven, wherefore the spiritual man must first be opened, before hell, which is in the natural man, can be removed by the Lord out of heaven. How this removal is effected, was represented by the he-goat, called Asasel or the scape-goat, being cast out into the wilderness; for by the he-goat from correspondence is signified the natural man, as to his affections and knowledges, and, in the opposite sense, as to his cupidities and falsities: concerning this he-goat it is thus written in Moses: "Aaron shall take two he-goats, and give lots upon them, one for the he-goat to be sacrificed, the other for Asasel; and after that he hath expiated the tent of the assembly and the altar by the blood of the sacrificed bullock and of the sacrificed he-goat, he shall lay his hands upon the head of the he-goat Asasel, and confess upon it the iniquities and sins of the sons of Israel, which he shall give upon the head of the he-goat, and afterwards send him by the hand of a man appointed into the wilderness. So the he-goat shall bear upon himself all the iniquities of the sons of Israel into the land of excision and the wilderness, and also the flesh, the skin and the dung, of the bullock and the he-goat of sacrifice, shall be burned in the wilderness, and they should be expiated and cleansed from all their sins" (Lev. xvi. 5–29). These things were commanded in order that expiation might thereby be represented, that is, purification from evils and falses: the reason why two he-goats were taken to represent this, was, because the he-goat, from correspondence, signified the

natural man, the he-goat which was to be sacrificed, the natural
man as to the part purified, and the he-goat which was to be sent
into the wilderness, the natural man not purified; and whereas this
latter abounds with cupidities and uncleannesses of every kind, as
was said above, therefore that he-goat was sent out of the camp into
the land of excision and the wilderness, that he might carry off the
iniquities and sins of all in that church; by the land of excision and
the wilderness is signified hell; the laying on of hands by Aaron
upon his head, and the confession of sins, represented communication and translation; for thus it comes to pass when man is purified
or expiated from sins, for the sins are then remitted to hell, and the
affections of good and truth are implanted in their place; these as
to a part were represented by the fat, which was sacrificed from the
bullock and from the other he-goat, also by their blood, and especially by the burnt-offering from the ram, concerning which see
verse 5–24, in the same chapter, for the ram, from correspondence,
signifies the natural man as to the good of charity: it is however to
be observed, that by these things the people were not in the least
purified from their sins, but that they were representative only of
the purification of the natural man, whilst it is regenerating; all
things appertaining to the regeneration of man were represented by
such external things, especially by sacrifices, and this for the sake
of the conjunction of heaven with the church by those externals of
worship, the internals whereof, which were represented, were regarded in the heavens; who cannot see, that the sins of a whole
assembly could not be transmitted into the he-goat, and carried by
him to hell? From these considerations it may now fully appear,
what is signified by a wilderness in its various senses.

731. "Where she hath a place prepared of God"—That hereby
is signified its state, that in the mean time provision may be made
[for its increase] amongst many, appears from the signification of
place, as denoting state, concerning which we shall speak presently;
and from the signification of being prepared of God, as denoting to
be provided of the Lord, for what is done by man is prepared, but
what is done by the Lord is provided; to be provided is also predicated of state, which is signified by place, whilst to be prepared is
predicated of place: the reason why it is signified that the state in
the mean time may be provided with more, is, because by the woman flying into the wilderness, is signified that the church is as yet
amongst few, because amongst those who are not in good, and thence
not in truths, as may be seen in the preceding article, n. 730; hence
it follows, that by these words, namely, where the woman hath a
place prepared of God, is signified the state of the church, that in
the mean time provision may be made [for its increase] amongst
more; and that by the words following, namely, that they may nourish
her a thousand two hundred and sixty days, is signified, until it
grows to a full state, concerning which see below, n. 732. But
this state of the church which is understood by the place of the woman in the wilderness is more largely treated of in the following
parts of this chapter, for it is said that to the woman were given two

wings of a great eagle that she might fly into the wilderness to her place, where she should be nourished a time and times and half a time from the face of the dragon; besides other circumstances. The reason why place signifies state, is, because spaces, places, and distances, in the spiritual world, are, in their origin, states of life; they appear indeed altogether as in this world, but still they differ in this respect, that the quality of every one is known from the place where he dwells, as on the other hand the place where he dwells is known from his quality; thus it is in general as to the places of all according to the quarters, and in particular as to their places in societies, and also in singular as to their places in houses, yea, in their chambers, hence it is evident, that the place and quality of state make one, and this by reason that all things which are in the spiritual world, which appear before the eyes, even as to the earths themselves, are correspondences of things spiritual, and hence it is that place signifies state; that spaces, places, and distances, are in their origin, states, and thence, in the Word, signify states, may be seen in the work concerning H. & H. n. 191–199, under the article concerning space in heaven: hence also it is that it is customary in our world to express state by place, as to be set in a high place, in an eminent place, and in an illustrious place, for a high, eminent, and illustrious state.   From these considerations it may appear what is understood by the Lord's saying to His disciples, "That in His father's house there are many mansions, and that He should go to prepare a place for them, and if He went and prepared a place, that he should come and take them to himself" (John xiv. 2, 3).   By preparing a place for them is signified to provide heaven for every one according to the state of his life, for by the disciples are understood all who were to be of his church.   And in Luke: "When the unclean spirit is gone out of a man, he wandereth through dry places seeking rest" (xi. 24).   By the unclean spirit going out of a man is signified the removal of evils and falses thence derived from man when he performs repentance; by the dry places through which he wanders seeking rest, are signified the states of evil and the false which are of his life.   So in other parts of the Word where place and places are mentioned.

732. " That they may nourish her a thousand and two hundred and sixty days"—That hereby is signified, whilst it grows to the full, appears from the signification of a thousand two hundred and sixty days, as denoting from beginning to end, and thus what is full, concerning which see above, n. 636; for that number involves three and a half years, and three and a half, whether years or days, signify such as is full, as may be seen above, n. 532, 658: the reason why these words, that they may nourish her so many days, signify whilst it grows to the full, is, because this signification follows as a consequence from that of the words preceding, which are that the woman fled into the wilderness, where she has a place prepared of God; whereby is signified, that the New Church, which is understood by the woman, is first amongst a few, and in the mean time is provided amongst greater numbers, whence it now follows, until it grows to

the full; moreover by nourishing is signified to sustain life and grow. The causes why the New Church, which is called the Holy Jerusalem, is first to commence with a few, afterwards with greater numbers, and so at last to arrive to its full state, are several ; the first is, that its doctrine, which is the doctrine of love to the Lord and charity towards the neighbor, cannot be acknowledged and thence received, except by those who are interiorly affected with truths, and no others are interiorly affected with truths but they who see them, and they only see them who have cultivated their intellectual faculty, and have not destroyed it in themselves by the loves of self and of the world. Another cause is, that the doctrine of that church cannot be acknowledged, nor consequently received, except by those who have not confirmed themselves in doctrine, and at the same time in life, in faith alone ; confirmation in doctrine only, does not hinder reception, but if it be at the same time in life, it does hinder, for such persons do not know what love to the Lord is, nor what neighborly love or charity is, neither are they willing to know. The third cause is, that the New Church on earth increases according to its increase in the world of spirits, for spirits from thence are with men, and they are from those who were in the faith of their church, whilst they lived on earth, and no others of them receive the doctrine, but those who were in the spiritual affection of truth; such only are conjoined to heaven where that doctrine is, and conjoin heaven to man : the number of those in the spiritual world now increases daily, wherefore according to their increase, the church which is called the New Jerusalem increases on earth.   These also were the causes, why the Christian church, after the Lord left the world, increased so slow in Europe, and did not arrive to its full until an age had elapsed.

733. Verses 7, 8. "And there was war in heaven, Michael and his angels fought with the dragon, and the dragon fought and his angels.   And they prevailed not, and their place was not found any more in heaven."—" And there was war in heaven" signifies combat of the false against truth, and of truth against the false : "Michael and his angels fought with the dragon, and the dragon fought and his angels," signifies combat amongst those who are in favor of the life of love and charity, and who are in favor of the Divine [principle] of the Lord in His Human, against those who are in favor of faith alone or separate from charity, who are against the Divine [principle] of the Lord in His Human: "and they prevailed not, and their place was not found any more in heaven," signifies that they yielded, and that no where in the heavens hereafter is there given a place, corresponding to the state of their life, which is a state of thought alone, and of no affection of good and truth.

734. "And there was war in heaven"—That hereby is signified combat of the false against truth, and of truth against the false, appears from the signification of war in heaven, as denoting the combat of the false against truth and of truth against the false, concerning which we shall speak presently : by the false is here understood the false from evil, and by truth is understood truth from good; for

there exist falses of various kinds, but those only which are from
evil combat against truths from good, by reason that evil is opposed
to good, and all truth is of good.   All those are in the falses of evil,
who have thought nothing concerning heaven and concerning the
Lord in their life, but only concerning themselves and the world:
to think concerning heaven and the Lord, in the life, is to think of
acting in such or such a manner, because the Word so teaches and
commands, and they who so think and act, inasmuch as they live
from the Word, live from the Lord and heaven ; but to think only
concerning themselves and the world, is to think of acting in this
or that manner on account of the laws of the kingdom, and for the
sake of fame, honor, and gain, and such persons do not live to the
Lord and heaven, but to themselves and the world: these are they
who as to life are in evil, and from evil in falses ; and they who are
in falses from this origin combat against truths.   But their combating
is not against the Word, for this they call holy and divine, but it is
against the genuine truths of the Word, for they confirm their falses
from the Word understood as to the letter only, which in some passages is of such a nature that it may be interpreted to confirm the
most heretical principles, by reason that in that sense it is according
to the apprehension of children and the simple, who for the most
part are sensual, and receive only such things as appear before the
eyes ; and whereas the Word is such in the letter, therefore they
who are in falses from evil of life confirm their falses from the Word,
and so falsify the Word: thus also do they falsify the Word who
separate faith from charity ; as for example, wherever mention is
made of doing, or of deeds and works, they explain all such passages, of which there are thousands, as if nothing of deeds or works
were meant, but only believing and faith ; and so in other cases.
These observations are made in order that it may be known who
are meant by those who are in falses from evil, and who make war
with Michael and his angels, as treated of in the following article.
That war, in the Word, signifies spiritual war, which is of the false
from evil against truth from good, and vice versa, or what is the
same, which is waged by those who are in falses from evil against
those who are in truths from good, may appear from a number of
passages in the Word, of which we shall only adduce the following:
thus in Isaiah : " Many people shall go and say, go and let us ascend
to the mountain of Jehovah to the house of the God of Jacob, who
shall teach us of His ways, that we may go in His paths ; for out of
Zion shall go forth the law, and the Word of Jehovah from Jerusalem, that He may judge among the nations, and rebuke the people,
who shall beat their swords into plough-shares, and their spears into
pruning-hooks ; nation shall not lift up the sword against nation,
neither shall they learn war any more ; O house of Jacob, go ye,
and we will go, in the light of Jehovah" (ii. 3, 4, 5 ; Micah iv. 3).
These things are spoken concerning the advent of the Lord, and
that they who will be of his new church are to be instructed in
truths, whereby they will be led to heaven: by the mountain of Jehovah and the house of Jacob, is signified the church in which is

love to the Lord and worship from that love; convocation to that church, and thereby to the Lord, is signified by many people going and saying, go and let us ascend to that mountain; that they will be instructed in truths, by which they will be led, is signified by, He will teach us concerning His ways, that we may go in His paths, ways denoting truths, and paths the precepts of life; that they will be taught by the doctrine of the good of love, and by the doctrine of truth from that good, which are for the church out of heaven from the Lord, is signified by, out of Zion shall go forth the law, and the Word from Jerusalem, the law out of Zion denoting the doctrine of the good of love, and the Word from Jerusalem truth from that good; that then evils of life and falses of doctrine shall be dissipated, is signified by, He shall judge among the nations and rebuke the people, nations denoting those who are in evils, and people those who are in falses, thus, abstractedly, evils of life and falses of doctrine; that then, by the consent of all, combats shall cease, is signified by, they shall beat their swords into plough-shares and their spears into pruning-hooks, swords and spears denoting falses from evil combating against truths from good, and vice versa; plough-shares denote the goods of the church cultivated by truths, for a field which is tilled by the plough denotes the church as to the good of life, and pruning-hooks denote truths of doctrine, by reason that trees in gardens signify perceptions and knowledges of truth; similar things are signified by, nation shall not lift the sword against nation, neither shall they learn war any more, war signifying combats in every complex; that they shall live a life of wisdom, is signified by, go ye, and we will go, in the light of Jehovah, the light of Jehovah denoting the divine truth, and to go in it denoting to live according thereto, thus in a life of wisdom: that war here signifies spiritual war, which is of falses against truths and goods, and vice versa, and that swords and spears, which are arms of war, signify such things as are used in spiritual combats, appears manifestly, for the subject treated of is concerning the Lord and concerning the church to be established by Him, also concerning the doctrine for that church, wherefore it is said, He shall teach us concerning His ways, that we may go in His paths; likewise, go ye, and we will go, in the light of Jehovah.   And in Hosea: "I will make for them a covenant in that day with the wild beast of the field, and with the bird of the heavens, and the reptile of the earth; and the bow, and the sword, and the war, will I break from the earth, and I will cause them to lie down securely" (ii. 18).   What is signified by the wild beast of the field, the bird of the heavens, and the reptile of the earth, with which it is said Jehovah in that day will make a covenant, may be seen above, n. 388, 701, where it is also shown, that by breaking the bow, the sword, and the war, is signified cessation from all combat of the false and truth, wherefore it is added, and I will make them to lie down securely, whereby is meant security from the infestations of evils and falses which are from hell.   And in Zechariah : "I will cut off the chariot from Ephraim, and the horse from Jerusalem, and the bow of war shall be cut off; on the other hand he will speak peace to the nations" (ix. 10). These words also may be seen explained above, n. 357, from which it is evident that by the bow of war is signified the doctrine of truth combating against falses, for these things are said concerning the Lord. And in David: "Jehovah who setteth waste in the earth, who maketh wars to cease even to the extremity of the earth, who breaketh the bow, and cutteth the spear in sunder, who burneth the chariot in the fire" (Psalm xlvi. 9, 10). Here also by Jehovah making wars to cease to the extremity of the earth, is signified, that he makes combats to cease as understood in the spiritual sense, which are combats of falses against the truths and goods of the church, as may be seen above, n. 357. Again: "God breaketh the sparks of the bow, the shield, and the sword, and the war" (Psalm lxxvi. 4); for the explanation of which see above, n. 357, 365. And in Isaiah: "Before the swords shall they wander, before the drawn sword and before the bended bow, by reason of the grievousness of the war" (xxi. 5). What these words signify may be seen above, n. 131, 357, and that by the grievousness of the war, is signified, on account of the strong assault of the falsities against the knowledges of good, which are there signified by Arabia or Kedar. Again, in David: "Jehovah who teacheth my hands war, so that a bow of brass letteth itself down upon his arms" (Psalm xviii. 35). By teaching the hands war is not understood war against enemies in this world, but against enemies in hell, which is effected by combats of truth against falses and against evils; it appears indeed as if war was there understood, such as David waged against his enemies, and so that Jehovah teaches that war, and how to let down a bow of brass upon the arms, but still spiritual war is understood, and also a spiritual bow, which is the doctrine of truth, and a bow of brass, the doctrine of the good of life, and this because the Word, viewed in its essence, is spiritual; but concerning these words also see above, n. 357. Again, in David: "Jehovah strive with them that strive with me, fight against them that fight against me, take hold of shield and buckler and arise to my aid, draw out also the spear, and intervene against my persecutors; say unto my soul, I am thy salvation" (Psalm xxxv. 1, 2, 3). That in this passage by fighting, taking hold of shield and buckler, and drawing out the spear, is not signified to use those arms of war, is evident, inasmuch as they are spoken concerning Jehovah, but it is so said, because all the arms of war signify such things as appertain to spiritual war; by a shield, inasmuch as it defends the head, is signified defence against falses which destroy the understanding of truth; by a buckler, inasmuch as it defends the breast, is signified defence against the falses which destroy charity, which is the will of good; and by a spear, inasmuch as it defends all parts of the body, is signified defence in general; by reason of such things being signified it is added, say to my soul, I am thy salvation. Forasmuch as Jehovah, that is, the Lord, defends man from the hells, that is, from the evils and falses which thence continually arise, therefore He is called Jehovah Zebaoth, that is, Jehovah of armies, and by armies are signified the truths and goods of heaven, and thence of the church, in every complex, whereby the Lord removes the hells in general, and with every one in particular; hence it is that it is attributed to Jehovah, that He fights and maintains warfare as a hero and man of war in battles, as may appear from the following passages : thus in Isaiah : " Jehovah Zebaoth descendeth to fight upon Mount Zion, and upon the hill thereof" (xxx. 4): and in Zechariah : " Jehovah shall go forth and fight against the nations, according to the day of His fighting in the day of battle" (xiv. 3) : and in Isaiah : " Jehovah shall go forth as a hero, as a man of war He shall stir up zeal, He shall prevail over His enemies" (xlii. 13): and in Moses: " The war of Jehovah against Amalek from generation to generation" (Exod. xvii. 16). These things are said, because by Amalek are signified those falses of evil which continually infest the truths and goods of the church. Moreover by wars, in the historical parts of the Word, as well those which are related in the books of Moses, as those in the books of Joshua, Judges, Samuel, and the Kings, are also signified spiritual wars; as the wars against the Assyrians, Syrians, Egyptians, Philistines, and, in the beginning, against the idolatrous nations in the land of Canaan beyond and on this side Jordan ; but what they signify in particular can only be known from a particular knowledge of the quality of evil and the false signified by the Assyrians, the Babylonians, the Chaldæns, also by the Egyptians, Syrians, Philistines, and the rest: for all the people and nations who waged war with the sons of Israel, represented the hells, which were desirous to offer violence to the church represented by the sons of Israel : nevertheless the wars actually took place as they are described, but still they represented, and thence signified, spiritual wars, inasmuch as there is nothing said in the Word which is not inwardly spiritual, for the Word is divine, and what proceeds from the Divine is spiritual, and is terminated in what is natural.   That the ancients also had a Word both prophetical and historical, which is now lost, appears in Moses, Numb. xxi. where the prophetical parts thereof are mentioned, which are there called Enunciations, and the historical parts also, which are called the Wars of Jehovah, verses 14 and 27; those histories are called the wars of Jehovah, because thereby are signified the wars of the Lord with the hells, as is the case also with the wars in the histories of our Word.   Hence now it is that enemies, adversaries, opposers, persecutors, insurgents, and moreover all arms of war, as the spear, the buckler, the shield, the sword, the bow, arrows, the chariot, and others mentioned in the Word, signify such things as appertain to combat and defence against the hells. Thus again in Moses : " When thou goest out to war against the enemy, and seest the horse and the chariot, many people more than thou, thou shalt not be afraid of them, because Jehovah thy God is with thee.   The priest shall say to them, when they draw near to the battle, ye approach this day to the battle against your enemies, let not your heart soften, neither fear ye, neither tremble, nor be dismayed before them, for Jehovah your God goeth with you, to fight for you with your enemies, and to keep you" (Deut. xx. 1, 2,

3, 4). He who does not know that there is a spiritual sense in every part of the Word may suppose that nothing of a more interior nature is here understood than what appears in the letter; howbeit, by war, as well in this as other passages, is signified spiritual war, and hence by horse, chariot, and much people, are signified the falses of religion in which they confide, and from which they fight against the truths of the church; by horse, are signified the falses of the understanding and reasonings thence derived, by chariot, falses of doctrine, and by much people, falses in general; whether we say falses, or those who are principled in falses, it amounts to the same: that they shall not be afraid of them, nor tremble, because they are in the truths of the church from the Lord, and because the Lord is in these truths with man, and so from them fights for man against the hells, which are understood by enemies in the spiritual sense, therefore it is said, because Jehovah God is with you, and goeth with you to fight for you with your enemies, and to keep you: these two senses, namely, the natural and the spiritual, make one by the correspondences which exist between all things of the world and all things of heaven, whence there is a conjunction of heaven with man by the Word: but the spiritual sense which is latent in the historical parts of the Word, is more difficult to be seen than that in the prophetical parts, by reason that the historical circumstances keep the mind fixed in themselves, and thence withdraw it from thinking of any other sense than what appears in the letter, but still all the histories of the Word are representative of heavenly things and the words themselves are significative. That all those who are in truths of doctrine, and thence made spiritual, or men of the church, shall fight, and not they who are not yet made spiritual, is signified by the following words in the same chapter: " Afterwards the moderator shall speak to the people, saying, what man is there who hath built a new house, and hath not initiated it? let him go and return to his house, lest peradventure he die in the war, and another man initiate it. Or what man is there who hath planted a vineyard, and hath not perfected and gathered the fruits of it? let him go and return to his house, lest peradventure he die in the war, and another man perfect and reap the fruits of it. Or what man is there who hath betrothed a wife, and hath not taken her? let him go and return to his house, lest he die in the war, and another man take her. What man is timid and faint in heart? let him go and return to his house, that the heart of his brethren may not faint as his heart" (Deut. xx. 5, 6, 7, 8). That they who had built new houses, and had not yet initiated them, and who had planted vineyards, and not yet reaped the fruits of them, and who had betrothed wives, and not. yet taken them, should remain at home, lest they should die in the war, and other men should initiate their houses, gather the fruits of their vineyards, and take their wives, was commanded and sanctioned from causes existing in the spiritual world, which no one can see except he knows what is signified by building a house, planting a vineyard, and taking a wife, likewise by dying in war: by building a house is signified to establish the church, and so likewise by planting a vineyard, but by a house is signified the church as to good, and by a vineyard the church as to truth, for both good and truth must be implanted in man, in order that the church may be in him; the conjunction of both these, viz. of good and truth, is signified by betrothing and taking a wife; and by war is signified spiritual war, which is a state of combat against evils and falses from hell; and by dying in the war, is signified to yield, before the church, by those things is implanted, this also being effected by temptations, which are likewise signified by wars in the Word: from these considerations it may be concluded, what is signified by those statutes in the spiritual sense; viz. that the men of the church, that is, men in whom the church is, who are signified by the sons of Israel going out to the war, shall fight against the enemies, which are the hells, and not they who are not yet made men of the church, or in whom the church as yet is not; wherefore it is said that they shall not go out to the war, who have built houses, and not yet initiated them, likewise who have planted vineyards, and not yet gathered the fruits of them, as also who have betrothed wives, and have not yet taken or married them, for by all these are signified those in whom the church is not yet implanted, that is, who are not yet made men of the church; and it is said that they should depart and return to their house, lest they should die in the war, whereby is understood, that they should not prevail over their enemies, but the enemies over them, since they alone prevail over their spiritual enemies who are in truths from good, or with whom truth is conjoined with good; it is said also, lest another man initiate the house, gather the fruit of the vineyard, and take the wife, by which is signified, lest falses and evils conjoin themselves with good, or truth of another kind with the affection of good; for by another man (vir) is signified the false, and also other truth, thus truth not concordant; that the timid and faint in heart should also return home, signified those who were not yet in the goods and truths of the church and thereby in confidence in the Lord, for these fear the evil, and also cause others to fear them, which is signified by, lest the heart of their brethren should melt: these now are the interior causes, or causes from the spiritual world, why those things were commanded. That war signifies spiritual war, which is against things infernal, appears manifestly from this circumstance, that the offices and ministries of the Levites about the tent of the assembly were called a warfare, as is evident from these words of Moses: "It was commanded Moses that the Levites should be numbered from a son of thirty years to a son of fifty years, to exercise warfare, to do the work in the tent of the assembly" (Numb. iv. 23, 35, 39, 43, 47): and in another place: "This is the office of the Levites; from a son of twenty-five years and upwards he shall come to serve the warfare in the ministry of the tent of the assembly, but from a son of fifty years he shall depart from the warfare of the ministry, neither shall he minister any more" (Numb. viii. 24, 25). The reason why the labors and ministry of the Levites about the tent of the assembly are called warfare, is, because the Levites represented the truths of the church, and Aaron, to whom the Levites were given and allotted for service, represented the Lord as to the good of love, and as to the work of salvation, and whereas the Lord from the good of love by truths from the Word regenerates and saves men, and also removes evils and falses which are from hell, against which he continually fights, therefore the offices and ministries of the Levites were called a warfare; it is further evident from this consideration, that they were so called although the Levites did not go out to war against the enemies of the land : hence it is evident that the priesthood is a warfare, but a warfare against evils and falses : it is for the same reason that the church at this day is called a church militant or combating. Again, in Isaiah : " The voice of a multitude in the mountains, like as of a great people, the voice of the tumult of the kingdoms of the nations gathered together : Jehovah Zebaoth numbereth the army of the war" (xiii. 4). These words may be seen explained above, n. 453; and that by numbering the army of the war, is signified to arrange truths from good against falses from evil, which are signified by the kingdoms of the nations gathered together. Again, in the same prophet : " In that day Jehovah shall be for a spirit of judgment to him that sitteth upon judgment, and for fortitude (to those) who repel war from the gate" (xxviii. 6). These things are said concerning those who are not in the conceit of self-derived intelligence, which is treated of in that chapter, and is understood in verse 1, by the crown of pride, the drunkards of Ephraim : that they who are not in that conceit shall be in intelligence from the Lord, is signified by, Jehovah shall be for a spirit of judgment, to him that sitteth in judgment, judgment denoting the understanding of truth, thus intelligence ; Jehovah shall be for fortitude to those who repel war from the gate, signifies, that the Lord gives power to those who defend the Word and doctrine from the Word, and who endeavor to preserve them from being violated, a city denoting doctrine, and the gate which gives entrance thereto denoting natural truths ; hence it was that the elders sat to judge in the gates of the city.   And in Jeremiah : " Sanctify ye war against the daughter of Zion, arise and let us go up at noon, arise and let us go up in the night, and destroy her palaces : pour against Jerusalem the trench. Behold a people cometh from the land of the north, a cruel people, and they have no mercy ; their voice resoundeth as the sea, they ride upon horses, prepared as a man for war, against thee, O daughter of Zion" (vi. 3, 4, 5, 6, 22, 23).   The subject there treated of is concerning the falsification of the Word by those who are in self-derived intelligence, and who are understood by the people coming from the land of the north, for such persons in the spiritual world dwell in the north because in things falsified, from which they cannot see truths; but the church which is in genuine truths, is understood by the daughter of Zion; the assault of truth and destruction of the church by them, is signified by, sanctify ye war against the daughter of Zion, and pour against Jerusalem the trench, Jerusalem denoting the church, as to doctrine, and thence the doctrine of the church; the effort of destroying truths openly is signified by, arise, let us go up at noon ; and the effort of destroying them clandestinely, is signified by, arise, let us go up in the night; the endeavor to destroy the understanding of truth is signified by, let us destroy her palaces; their being altogether without any love of truth, and entirely in the love of the false, is signified by a cruel people, and having no mercy; that they reason from sciences, and from self-derived intelligence, is signified by, their voice resoundeth as the sea, they ride upon horses; their assaulting and fighting against truth, is signified by being prepared as a man for war. Again, in David: "Deliver me from the evil man, and from the man of violences save me, who think evils in the heart, all the day they gather together to war, they sharpen their tongue as serpents" (Psalm cxl. 2, 3, 4). By the evil man and the man of violences, are signified those who pervert the truths of the Word, for he is called a man of violences who from a wicked intention offers violence to the truths of the Word, by perverting them; such wicked intention is further described by thinking evils in the heart, and the perversion of the truths of the Word by gathering themselves together all the day for war; the ratiocinations by which they prevail, are signified by wars, wherefore it is also added, they sharpen their tongues as serpents. And in Zechariah: "They shall be as the mighty treading under foot the mire of the streets in the war, and they shall engage in battle, because Jehovah is in them, and the riders upon horses shall be made ashamed" (x. 5). The subject there treated of is concerning the advent of the Lord, and concerning those who are in truths from good from Him, concerning whom it is said, that they shall be as the mighty treading under the foot the mire of the streets in the war, whereby is signified that they shall dissipate and altogether destroy the falses of doctrine, the mire of the streets denoting that false, because a city signifies doctrine, the streets of a city its truths, and the mire therein what is false originating in falsified truth; and they shall engage in battle because Jehovah is with them, signifies, that they shall assault and overcome those falses by power from the Lord; and the riders upon horses shall be made ashamed, signifies, that every thing of self-derived intelligence shall yield, to be made ashamed denoting to yield, because it is said of those who are conquered, and to ride upon horses denoting to trust to self-derived intelligence. And in Hosea: "I will have compassion on the house of Judah, and I will save them by Jehovah their God; and I will not save them by the bow, and the sword, and by war, and by horses, and horsemen" (i. 7). By the house of Judah is signified the celestial church; by having compassion on and saving them by Jehovah their God, is signified salvation from the Lord; I will not save them by the bow, the sword, the war, horses and horsemen, signifies, not by such things as are of self-derived intelligence; what is signified by the bow, the sword, horses and horsemen, in particular, has been shown above in various places; war signifies combat from such things. And in Ezekiel: "Ye have not gone up into the breaches, neither have ye made up the hedge for the house of Israel, that ye might stand in the war in the day of Jehovah" (xiii. 5); speaking of the foolish prophets, by whom are signified falses of doctrine from the Word falsified; that they are not able to repair the lapses of the church, or amend any thing thereof, is signified by, ye have not gone up into the breaches, nor made up the hedge for the house of Israel, the breaches of the house of Israel denoting the lapses of the church, and the hedge thereof what defends from the irruption of the false, and thereby amends; not to stand in the war in the day of Jehovah, signifies not to combat against falses from evil, which are from hell in the day of the last judgment. And in Jeremiah : "How is the city of glory not left, the city of my joy ; wherefore her young men shall fall in the streets, and all the men of war shall be cut off in that day" (xlix. 25, 26 ; chap. l. 30). The doctrine of truth from the Word is understood by the city of glory, and by the city of the joy of Jehovah ; that this is turned into a doctrine of the false by falsifications of truth, is signified by being left or forsaken ; that all understanding of truth, and thereby all intelligence, would perish, is signified by, her young men shall fall in her streets, young men denoting the understanding of truth, and the streets of that city denoting falses of doctrine ; that there will no longer remain any truths combating against falses, is signified by, all the men of war shall be cut off, the men of war denoting those who are in truths, and combat from them against falses, and, abstractedly, truths themselves combating. And, in Isaiah : "Thy slain are not slain with the sword, neither killed in the war" (xxii. 2); treating of the valley of vision, whereby is signified the sensual man, who sees all things from the fallacies of the bodily senses ; and inasmuch as he does not understand truths, and thence in the place thereof seizes upon falses, therefore it is said, thy slain are not slain with the sword, neither killed in the war, whereby is signified that truths are not destroyed by ratiocinations from falses, neither by any combats of the false against truths, but from themselves, because from fallacies, by reason whereof truths do not appear. Again, in the same prophet: "I will commix Egypt against Egypt, and a man shall fight against his brother, and a man against his companion, city against city, kingdom against kingdom" (xix. 2). These things are said concerning the natural man separate from the spiritual, which is signified by Egypt ; the crowd of falses appertaining to that man reasoning and combating against the truths and goods of the spiritual man, is signified by, I will commix Egypt against Egypt, and a man shall fight against his brother, and a man against his companion : a man and brother signify truth and good, and, in the opposite sense, the false and evil, and a man and his companion signify truths amongst themselves, and, in the opposite sense, falses amongst themselves ; this dissension, and this combat, takes place when falses reign, inasmuch as falses continually dispute with falses, but not truths with truths ; that like contentions of the doctrines among themselves, or of the churches amongst themselves, will take place, is signified by, city shall fight against city, and kingdom against kingdom, city denoting doctrine, and kingdom the church thence derived. From these considerations it may appear what is signified by the words of

the Lord in the Evangelists : " Many shall come in My name, saying, I am Christ, and shall seduce many; but when ye shall hear of
wars and rumors of wars, see that ye be not troubled ; for nation
shall rise up against nation and kingdom against kingdom, and there
shall be famines, and pestilences, and earthquakes" (Matt. xxiv. 6,
7, 8; Mark xiii. 8, 9 ; Luke xxi. 9, 10, 11). These things were
said by the Lord to the disciples concerning the consummation of
the age, by which is signified the state of the church as to its ultimate, which is described in those chapters, wherefore also the successive perversion and falsification of the truth and good of the
Word, until there remains nothing but what is false and evil thence
derived, is there understood : by those who shall come in His name
and call themselves Christ, and seduce many, are signified those
who shall say that what they teach is divine truth, when yet it is
truth falsified, which in itself is the false, for by Christ is understood the Lord as to divine truth, but there, in the opposite sense,
truth falsified ; by wars and rumors of wars, which they shall hear,
are signified disputings and contentions concerning truths, and thence
falsifications ; by nation being stirred up against nation, and kingdom against kingdom, is signified, that evil shall combat with evil,
and false with false, for evils never agree amongst themselves, nor
falses amongst themselves, which is the cause of so many divisions
taking place in the church, and so many heresies being produced;
nation signifies those who are in evils, and kingdom those who are
in falses, of whom the church consists; and there shall be famines
and pestilences and earthquakes, signifies that there will be no longer
any knowledges of truth and good, and that by reason of the infection arising from falses, the state of the church will be changed,
famine denoting the privation of the knowledges of truth and good,
pestilences, infections from falses, and earthquakes, the changes of
the church.   Forasmuch as wars, in the Word, signify spiritual wars,
which are combats of the false against truth, and of truth against
the false, therefore those combats are described by " the war between the king of the north and the king of the south ; and by the
battle of the he-goat against the ram" in Daniel describing the war
between the king of the north and the king of the south, chap. xi.;
and describing the combat of the he-goat against the ram, chap. viii.,
and by the king of the north are there understood those who are in
falses, and by the king of the south those who are in truths ; and
by the he-goat are signified those who are in falses of doctrine, because in evil of life, and by the ram those who are in truths of doctrine, because in good of life.   Hence also it may appear what is
signified by war in other passages of the Apocalypse; as in the following : " When the witnesses shall have finished their testimony,
the beast, which cometh up from the abyss, shall make war with
them, and conquer them, and slay them" (xi. 7); again : " The spirits of demons making signs to go forth unto the kings of the earth
and of the whole orb of earths, to gather them together to the war
of that great day of God Almighty" (xvi. 14); and again : "Satan
shall go forth to seduce the nations, Gog and Magog, that he might

gather them together to war" (xxi. 8).   By war, in these passages also, is signified spiritual war, which is of the false against the truth and of truth against the false ; it is called war of the false against the truth and of truth against the false, but it is to be observed, that it is they who are in falses that combat against truths, but not so they who are in truths against falses, for they who are in falses always assault, but they who are in truths only defend ; and as to the Lord, He doth not ever fight again, but only defends truths ; but upon this subject we shall have occasion to speak elsewhere.

735. " Michael and his angels fought with the dragon, and the dragon fought and his angels"—That hereby is signified combat between those who are in favor of the life of love and charity, and in favor of the divine [principle] of the Lord in his human, against those who are in favor of faith alone and separate from charity, and who are against the Divine [principle] of the Lord in his human, appears from the signification of Michael and his angels, as denoting those who are in favor of the divine [principle] of the Lord in his human, and in favor of the life of love and charity, concerning which we shall speak presently ; and from the signification of the dragon, as denoting those who are in favor of faith alone and separate from the life of love and charity, and also against the divine of the Lord in his human ; that they who are in faith separate from charity, which is called faith alone, are understood by the dragon, was shown above, n. 714, 715, 716.   The reason why the same are also against the divine [principle] of the Lord in his human, that is, against the divine human, is, because most of those who have confirmed themselves in faith alone, are merely natural and sensual, and the natural and sensual man, separate from the spiritual, cannot have any idea of the divine [principle] in the human, for they think naturally and sensually concerning the human of the Lord, and not at the same time from any spiritual idea ; hence it is that they think of the Lord as of a common man altogether like themselves, which they also teach ; hence also it is that in the idea of their thought they place the divine [principle] of the Lord above his human, and thus separate them altogether, and this notwithstanding they are taught otherwise in their doctrine, which is the doctrine of Athanasius, concerning the Trinity, for this teaches, that the divine and human [principle] are in one person like the soul and body : let any one consult with himself, and he will perceive, that their idea concerning the Lord is as above described.   From these considerations it may appear what is understood by Michael and his angels who fought with the dragon, namely, they who acknowledge the divine human [principle] of the Lord and are in favor of the life of love and charity, for such cannot do otherwise than acknowledge the divine human [principle] of the Lord, by reason that otherwise they cannot be in any love to the Lord, nor thence in any charity towards their neighbor, inasmuch as this love and charity are solely from the Lord's divine human [principle], and not from the divine [principle] separate from His human, nor from the human separate from divine ; wherefore also, after the dragon was cast down to th

with his angels, a voice said out of heaven, "Now is come salvation, and power, and the kingdom of our God, and the power of
His Christ" (verse 10). From these considerations it may appear
what is meant by Michael and his angels. As to what respects Michael in particular, it is believed, from the sense of the letter, that
he is one of the archangels, whereas there is not any archangel in
the heavens; there are indeed angels superior and inferior, likewise
more or less wise, and also, in the societies of angels, there are moderators who are set over the rest, but still there are not any archangels who exercise any arbitrary authority, such government not
existing in the heavens, for there no one in his heart acknowledges
any above himself but the Lord alone, which is understood by these
words of the Lord in Matthew : "Be not ye called teacher, for one
is your teacher, Christ, but all ye are brethren; and call no man
your father on earth, for one is your father, who is in the heavens.
Neither be ye called master, for one is your master, Christ. He who
is greatest among you shall be your minister" (xxiii. 8–11); but by
those angels who are mentioned in the Word, as by Michael and
Raphael, are understood administrations and functions, and, in general, certain and determined parts of the administration and function
of all the angels; wherefore here by Michael is understood that part
of angelic function which was spoken of above, namely, the defending of that part of doctrine from the Word which teaches that the
human [principle] of the Lord is divine, and that man must live a
life of love to the Lord and of charity towards his neighbor in order
to obtain salvation from the Lord; consequently that part of the angelic function is understood, which combats against those who separate the divine [principle] from the human of the Lord, and who
separate faith from the life of love and charity, who also profess
charity in the mouth but not in the life. Moreover by angels, in the
Word, in the spiritual sense, are not understood angels, but divine
truths from the Lord, as may be seen above, n. 130, 302 : by reason
that the angels are not angels from their own proprium, but from the
reception of divine truth from the Lord; so likewise with respect to
archangels, who signify that divine truth which was mentioned
above. The angels in the heavens have also names as well as men
on earth, but their names are expressive of their functions, and in
general, every angel has a name given to him according to his quality, whence it is that name, in the Word, signifies the quality of a
thing and state. The name Michael, from its derivation in the Hebrew tongue, signified, who is as God? wherefore by Michael is signified the Lord as to that divine truth that the Lord is God also as to
the human [principle], and that man must live from Him, that is, in
love to Him from Him, and in love towards his neighbor. Michael
is also mentioned in Daniel, chap. x. 13, 21; xii. 1 : and in those
passages by him is signified the genuine truth from the Word, which
will be for those who will belong to the new church to be established
by the Lord, in like manner as in the present case, for by Michael
are understood those who will be in favor of the doctrine of the New
Jerusalem, the two essentials of which are, that the human [princi-

ple] of the Lord is divine, and that a life of love and charity ought to be lived. Michael is also mentioned in the Epistle of Jude, in these words: " Michael the archangel, when disputing with the devil, he reproved him concerning the body of Moses, durst not utter a sentence of blasphemy, but said, the Lord rebuke thee" (verse 9). These words were adduced by the apostle Jude from the ancient books which were written by correspondences, and in which by Moses was understood the Word, and by his body, the literal sense of the Word; and whereas they are understood by the devil, who are here in the Apocalypse understood by the dragon, who is also called the devil and satan, it is evident what is signified by Michael disputing with and reproving the devil concerning the body of Moses, viz. that they falsified the literal sense of the Word; and whereas the literal sense of the Word is such, that it can be warped by the evil from its genuine sense, and yet be received by the good according to the true understanding thereof, therefore it was said by the ancients, from whom those words of Jude were taken, that Michael durst not utter a sentence of blasphemy. That Moses in the spiritual sense, signifies the law, thus the Word, may be seen in the A. C. n. 4859, 5922, 6723, 6752, 6827, 7010, 7014, 7089, 7382, 8787, 8805, 9372, 9414, 9419, 9439, 10,234, 10,563, 10,571, 10,607, 10,614.

736. " And prevailed not, and their place was not found any more in heaven"—That hereby is signified that they yielded, and that no where in the heavens is there hereafter given a place corresponding to the state of their life, which is a state of thought alone, and of no affection of good and truth, appears from the signification of they prevailed not, as denoting that they yielded in combat; and from the signification of their place not being found any more in heaven, as denoting that hereafter there is not given in the heavens a place corresponding to the state of their life, concerning which we shall treat presently. The reason why this is not given hereafter, is, because the state of their life, which is understood by the dragon and his angels, is a state of thought alone, and of no affection of good and truth; for they who place the all of the church and thence the all of salvation in faith alone, cannot be in any affection of good and truth, these being of the life; for every man has two faculties of life, which are called understanding and will, and the understanding is that which thinks and the will is that which is affected, consequently the thought is of the understanding and the affection of the will; they therefore who separate faith from the life, think only concerning the truths of faith that they are so, and by so thinking, and on account thereof, they say that they shall be saved: and whereas they separate life from faith, they cannot be in any other affection than what is natural, which is of the love of self and of the world; hence it is that they conjoin the affections of these loves to those things which are of their faith, which conjunction does not constitute the heavenly marriage, which is heaven, but adultery, which is hell, for it is a conjunction of truth with the affection of evil, and this adultery corresponds to the adultery of a son with a

mother, as is evident from correspondences known in the spiritual world : but still, lest there should be a conjunction of truth with evil, it is provided by the Lord, that they should not have any genu-ine truths, but truths falsified, which in themselves are falses ; and whereas such a conjunction appertains to a faith separate, viz. of the false with evil, therefore the dragon, by whom they who are in such a faith are understood, is called satan and the devil, satan from the false, and devil from evil, for, as has been said above, the con-junction of truth and good constitutes heaven with man, but the con-junction of the false and evil constitutes hell with him.   The reason why they have not any genuine truths, is, because they derive all things of their faith from the literal sense of the Word, and do not consider that the truths which are in that sense, are appearances of truth, and that to assume and defend them for truths themselves, is to falsify the Word, according to what has been shown above, n. 719, 715, 720.   Hence now it is that the dragon with his angels was cast out of heaven to the earth.   The reason why their place not being found any more in heaven, signifies that hereafter there is not given a place in the heavens corresponding to the state of their life, is, be-cause all places in the heavens correspond to the life of the angels, whence it is that place signifies the state of the life, as was said above, n. 731 ; and whereas the life of all the angels in the heavens is the life of the affection of good and truth, and they who are in faith alone, and are understood by the dragon and his angels, have not this affection, therefore there is not given a place in the heavens corresponding to the state of their life.   Moreover all the angels in the heavens are spiritual affections, and every one of them thinks from his own affection, and according to it, whence it follows, that they who place the all of the church and thence of heaven in think-ing, and not in living, when they become spirits, think from their own affections, which are affections of what is evil and false, as was said above, consequently that their faith, which they made of the thought alone and not of the life, is exterminated and dissipated. In a word, no one can have any spiritual affection, which is of good and truth, except from the life of faith, which is charity : charity itself is the affection of good, and faith is the affection of truth, and both conjoined together into one, is the affection of good and truth.

737. In verse 3 it is said, that the dragon was seen in heaven ; and now, that war was made with him in heaven ; and afterwards, that the place of him and his angels was not found any more in hea-ven ; and yet notwithstanding, in verse 9, he is called the old ser-pent, also the devil and satan : hence it may be a matter of wonder to some, how the dragon, who is the devil, could be in heaven, and have any place there previous to his being cast down, when not-withstanding there could never be a place in heaven for the devil, but in hell only : it shall therefore be explained how this is : by the dragon are not understood those who have denied God and the Lord, and have rejected the Word, and made no account of the church and its doctrine, for such persons are cast into hell immediately after death, and never appear in heaven, much less have any place there ;

·herefore by the dragon and his angels are understood those who know God and the Lord, and say that the Word is holy, and also stand up for the church and its doctrine, but this only with the mouth and not with the heart; the reason why it is not with the heart, is, because they make no account of the life, and they who make no account of the life, are inwardly devils, however they may outwardly appear as angels: hence it may be manifest, that by the acknowledgment of God and the Lord, and by the reading and preaching of the Word, they were outwardly conjoined with heaven, but whereas they had no respect to the Lord and the Word in their lives, they were inwardly conjoined with hell: these are called the devil and satan, because they defiled the truths of the Word by the life of the love of self and the world, and by the evils which flow from those loves, as streams from their fountains, also because they applied the literal sense of the Word to confirm such a life, whence such persons become serpents above all others, being more noxious than others, for they are thereby enabled to draw over the simple good, who are in the ultimate heaven, to their side, especially by such things as they extract from the letter of the Word, and pervert to their purposes. The reason why it is said, that they were seen in heaven, and there fought with Michael and his angels, is, because the Word conjoined them with the heavens; for the conjunction of men with the heavens is by the Word; when however it was observed that they were in other affections than such as are heavenly, they were cast down from heaven. Nevertheless, since the accomplishment of the last judgment, it has been provided and ordained by the Lord that none hereafter should have conjunction with heaven but those who are in spiritual faith, and spiritual faith is procured by a life according to the truths of the Word, which life is called charity. This then is what is signified by the dragon with his angels being cast to the earth, and their place not being found any more in heaven.

738. Verse 9. " And that great dragon was cast down, that old serpent, called the devil and satan, which seduceth the world: he was cast down into the earth, and his angels were cast down with him." —"And that great dragon was cast down, that old serpent," signifies, that they were separated from heaven, and cast down into hell, who were in evils of life, and were thence become sensual, and by whom all things of the Word and thereby of the church were perverted: " called the devil and satan," signifies, because inwardly they were in evils and falses which are from hell : " which seduceth the whole world," signifies, which pervert all things of the church: " he was cast down into the earth, and his angels were cast down with him," signifies, that those evils and falses were thence condemned to hell.

739. " And that great dragon was cast down, that old serpent"— That hereby is signified that they were separated from heaven, and cast down into hell, who were in evils of life, and were thence become sensual, and by whom all things of the Word, and thereby of the church, were perverted, appears from the signification of being cast down, when predicated of the dragon, as denoting to be

separated from heaven and cast down to hell; that they were conjoined to heaven, but afterwards separated, may be seen in the preceding arti-cle, n. 737; that they were cast down and condemned to hell, is under-stood by being cast down to the earth, concerning which we shall speak presently; and from the signification of the great dragon, as deno-ting those who are in evils of life, and yet with their mouth confess God and the Lord, who also call the Word holy, and speak in favor of the church; that these are understood by the dragon may be seen above, n. 714, 715, 716, 718, 737; hence also he .is called a great dragon, for great, in the Word, is predicated of good, and, in the opposite sense, as in this case, of evil; but their falses are signified by his angels, concerning which we shall speak presently; and from the signification of the old serpent, as denoting those who are sensual, in this case that they became sensual by whom all things of the Word and of the church are perverted; that the sensual princi-ple is signified by the serpent may be seen above, n. 581, 715, and he is here called the old serpent, because there were such also for-merly, who perverted all things of the Word and the church. Ac-cording to the historical sense of the letter, by the old serpent is understood the serpent which seduced Adam and Eve in paradise, but by that serpent, as well as by this, are understood all those who are of such a nature and quality, and who seduce the whole world, as may appear from what follows in this paragraph. From these considerations it may appear, that by the great dragon, that old ser-pent, being cast down, is signified, that they were separated from heaven and cast down into hell who were in evils of life, and by whom all things of the Word and thereby of the church were per-verted. That all who are in evils of live become sensual, and that they who so become sensual pervert all things of the church, may appear from this consideration, that with men there are three degrees of life, an inmost, a middle, and an ultimate, and that these degrees in man are successively opened, as he becomes wise: every man is born altogether sensual, insomuch that even the five senses of the body are to be opened by use: after that he becomes sensual as to thought, for he thinks from the objects which have entered by the bodily senses; and afterwards he becomes interiorly sensual: but in pro-portion as by visual experiences, by the sciences, and especially by the uses of moral life, he procures for himself a natural lumen, in the same proportion he becomes interiorly natural; and this is the first or ultimate degree of the life of man. Forasmuch as in this state he imbibes from parents, masters, and preachers, and also read-ing the Word and other books, the knowledges of spiritual good and truth, and commits them to the memory, as other scientifics, the foundation of the church is then laid in him; but still if he does not advance farther, he remains natural, whereas if he does advance farther, viz., if he does live according to those knowledges from the Word, the interior degree is opened in him, and he becomes spirit-ual, but this only in proportion as he is affected with truths, under-stands them, wills them and does them; the reason is, because evils, and the falses thence derived, which hereditarily reside in the natural and sensual man, are removed, and as it were shaken off, in no other manner; for the spiritual man is in heaven, and the natural in the world, and in proportion as heaven can flow-in, that is, the Lord by heaven, through the spiritual man into the natural, in the same proportion evils, and the falses thence derived, are removed, which, as was said, reside in the natural man, for the Lord removes them, as he removes hell from heaven : the reason why the interior degree with man cannot otherwise be opened, is, because the evils and falses, which are in the natural man, keep it shut : for the spiritual degree, or spiritual mind, contracts itself at evil and the false of evil of whatever kind, as a fibril of the body at the sharp point of a needle, for it is known that the fibres of the body contract themselves at all hardness of touch whatever ; the case is similar with the interior mind of man, which is called the spiritual mind, at the touch or blast of evil and the false thence derived : but, on the other hand, when things homogeneous, which are divine truths from the Word, and which derive their essence from good, approach to that mind, it then opens itself ; but the opening is no otherwise effected, than by the reception of the good of love flowing in through heaven from the Lord, and by the conjunction thereof with the truths which man has committed to memory, and this is only effected by a life according to the divine truths in the Word, for when those truths become of the life, they are then called goods : hence it may appear how the second or middle degree is opened.   But the third or inmost degree is opened with those who immediately apply divine truths to life, and do not first reason concerning them from the memory, and thereby bring them into doubt; this is called the celestial degree. Inasmuch as these three degrees of life are with every man, but yet are opened in different manners, hence there are three heavens ; in the third or inmost heaven are those with whom the third degree is opened ; in the second or middle heaven are those with whom the second degree only is opened ; and in the first or ultimate heaven are those with whom the interior natural man, which is also called the rational man, is opened, for this man, if he is truly rational, receives influx from the Lord through heaven : all these come into heaven : but they who have received divine truths only in the memory, and not at the same time in the life, remain natural, yea, become sensual ; the reason is, because the evils into which man is born, reside, as was said above, in the natural and sensual man, and are not removed, and as it were shaken off, by the influx of good from the Lord, and by the reception thereof by man ; hence it is that the loves of the body reign in them, which, in general, are the love of self and the love of the world, and thence the love and conceit of self-derived intelligence, and these loves, with the evils and falses flowing from them, fill the interiors of the natural mind, which notwithstanding are covered over by appearances of honesty and decorum appertaining to moral life, on account of the world and of the laws therein published for the government of the external man : such persons, although they have filled the memory with knowledges

from the Word, from the dogmas of their several religions, and from
the sciences, are still natural, yea, sensual, for the interiors of the
natural mind, which are nearest to the spiritual mind, are closed
with them, by confirmations, even from the Word, against the
spiritual life, which is a life according to divine truths, and is called
charity towards the neighbor : these then, inasmuch they are sensual, are the dragon, and are called serpents, for serpent signifies
the sensual principle, by reason that the sensual is the lowest principle of man's life, and as it were creeps upon the ground, and licks
the dust, like a serpent.   In the way of illustration of this subject,
we will here adduce what is written in Genesis concerning the old
serpent which seduced Eve and Adam, and explain' the same according to the spiritual sense : the words are these : " Jehovah God
caused to grow out of the ground every tree that is pleasant to the
sight and good for food, and the tree of lives in the midst of the
garden, and the tree of science of good and evil.   And Jehovah God
commanded the man, saying, of every tree of the garden eating thou
mayest eat, but of the tree of the science of good and evil thou
mayest not eat, because in the day thou eatest thereof, dying thou
wilt die.   And the serpent was more subtle than any wild beast of
the field which Jehovah God made : and he said unto the woman,
yea, hath God said, ye shall not eat of every tree of the garden?
And the woman said unto the serpent, we may eat of the fruit of the
trees of the garden, but of the fruit of the tree which is in the midst
of the garden, God hath said, ye shall not eat of it, neither shall ye
touch it, lest ye die.   And the serpent said unto the woman, ye
shall not surely die, for God doth know that in the day ye eat
thereof, then y̌ ur eyes shall be opened, and ye shall be as God,
knowing good œand evil.   And the woman saw that the tree was
good for food, and that it was pleasant to the eyes, and a tree
to be desired to give intelligence, and she took of the fruit
thereof, and did eat, and she gave also to her man with her,
and he did eat : and the eyes of both were opened, and they
knew that they were naked, and they sewed fig leaves together
and made themselves girdles.   And Jehovah said unto the serpent,
because thou hast done this, cursed art thou above all cattle, and
above every wild beast of the field ; upon thy belly shalt thou walk,
and dust shalt thou eat, all the days of thy life : and I will put enmity between thee and between the woman, and between thy seed
and her seed ; he shall tread upon thy head, and thou shalt hurt his
heel.   And Jehovah God sent out the man from the garden of Eden,
and placed cherubs at the garden of Eden from the east, and the
flame of a sword turning itself to guard the way of the tree of lives"
(Genesis ii. 8, 9, 16, 17 ; chap. iii. 1–7, 14, 15, 24).   How the historical particulars concerning the creation of heaven and earth, which
are contained from the first chapter of Genesis to the account of the
deluge, are to be understood, cannot possibly be known, except
from the spiritual sense, which lies concealed in every part of the
literal sense of the Word : for those historical particulars concerning
the creation of heaven and earth, likewise concerning the garden in
Eden, and the posterity of Adam, even to the deluge, are historical

particulars so made, but nevertheless are most holy, because all the particulars of that sense, and the particular expressions thereof, are correspondences, and thence signify things spiritual : this may be discovered by any one who has any discernment, from the history of the creation in the first chapter, which began from light, when the sun did not yet exist, and from various other circumstances there related ; likewise from the creation of Eve the wife of Adam out of one of his ribs; as also from the account of the two trees in paradise, and the prohibition from eating of the tree of science of good and evil, notwithstanding which, and their being the most wise of all people, they did eat, being seduced by the serpent; moreover from the circumstance of the Lord placing such trees in the midst of the garden, and suffering them to be seduced by the serpent to eat of the forbidden tree, which notwithstanding He might have averted ; also from the whole human race being judged to eternal death, from the eating of that tree alone : who cannot see, that these things, with other things of a like nature which a short sighted understanding might in simplicity believe, would be contrary to the divine love and contrary to the divine providence and foresight? howbeit it is not hurtful that those things are believed according to the historical letter by the simple minded and by children, inasmuch as they serve, as well as the rest of the Word, to conjoin human minds to angelic minds, for angels are in the spiritual sense, when men are in the natural sense.   But what those historical circumstances involve in the spiritual sense, shall be briefly explained.   The subject treated of in the first chapter is concerning the new creation or establishment of the church, which was the most ancient church in this earth, and also the most excellent of all, for it was a celestial church, because principled in love to the Lord, whence the men of that church were the most wise, having almost immediate communication with the angels of heaven, by whom they derived wisdom from the Lord; and whereas they were in love to the Lord, and had revelations from heaven, and immediately committed to life the divine truths revealed, hence they were in a similar state with the angels of the third heaven; wherefore this heaven chiefly consists of the men of that church : this church is understood by Adam and his wife : but by the garden in Eden is signified their intelligence and wisdom, which is also described, in the spiritual sense, by all things that are mentioned concerning that garden ; and how wisdom was lost in their posterity, is described by the eating of the tree of science : for by the two trees placed in the midst of the garden, is understood perception from the Lord, and perception from the world; by the tree of lives, perception from the Lord, and by the tree of the science of good and evil, perception from the world, which, however, in itself is only knowledge and science : but by the serpent, which seduced them, is signified the sensual principle of man, which immediately communicates with the world, wherefore by their being seduced by the serpent is understood, the being seduced by the sensual principle, which derives all it has from the world, and nothing from heaven : for the men of the celestial church are such, that they perceive all the truths and goods of heaven from the Lord by influx into their interiors, whence they see goods and truths inwardly in themselves, as implanted, and have no need to learn them by a posterior way, or to treasure them up in their memory; hence neither do they reason concerning truths, whether they be so or not; for they who see truths in themselves, do not reason, inasmuch as this involves a doubting concerning their reality, which is also the cause that they never make mention of faith, for faith involves what is un- known, which is still to be believed although it is not seen. That the men of the most ancient church were of such a nature and qua- lity as is above described, has been revealed to me from heaven, for it was given me to discourse with them, and to be informed, as may appear from the various things related concerning the men of that church in the A. C. It is however to be observed, that it was never forbidden them to procure for themselves knowledges from heaven concerning good and evil, for thereby their intelligence and wisdom was perfected; neither was it forbidden to procure to themselves knowledges of good and evil from the world, for thence was the science of their natural man; but it was forbidden to view these knowledges by a posterior way, inasmuch as it was given them to see all things which appeared before their eyes in their world, by a prior way: to view the world and all things therein by a prior way, and thence to imbibe knowledges, is to view them from the light of heaven, and thereby to know their quality; wherefore also, by knowledges from the world, they were able to confirm things ce- lestial, and so to corroborate their wisdom: but it was forbidden them to view knowledges from the world by a posterior way, as is the case when conclusions are drawn from them concerning things celestial, and thus in an inverse order, which is called, by the learned, the order of physical or natural influx, which cannot by any means be given into things celestial: such did the men of the ancient church become, when they began to love worldly things above ce- lestial, and to be self elated and to glory on account of their wisdom, whence their posterity became sensual, and then their sensual prin- ciple, which is understood by the serpent, seduced them; and the sensual principle is not willing to advance by any other than a posterior way: this therefore is what is signified by the tree of the science of good and evil, of which it was forbidden them to eat. That it was allowable for them to procure for themselves know- ledges from the world, and to view them by a prior way, is signified by Jehovah God causing to grow out of the ground every tree de- sirable to the sight, and good for food; for by trees are signified knowledges and perceptions, by desirable to the sight is signified desirable to the understanding, and by good for food is signified what conduces to the nourishment of the mind: the knowledges of good and evil from the Lord, from which wisdom is derived, and the knowledges of good and evil from the world, from which science is derived, were represented by the tree of lives, and by the tree of the science of good and evil in the midst of the garden: that it was allowed them to appropriate to themselves knowledges from whatever source, as well from heaven as from the world, only that they should not proceed in an inverse order, by reasoning from them concerning things celestial, instead of thinking from things celestial concerning things worldly, is signified by Jehovah God commanding them to eat of every tree of the garden, but not of the tree of the science of good and evil; that otherwise celestial wisdom and the church would perish with them, is signified by, in the day that thou eatest thereof, dying thou wilt die, to eat, in the spiritual sense, signifying to appropriate to themselves : that the sensual principle seduced them, because it is proximately extant to the world, and thence feels whatever is pleasurable and delightful from the world, from which it is in fallacies, whilst it is ignorant of, and also rejects, celestial things, is signified by the serpent, the serpent denoting the sensual principle, and no other sensual principle than what was of themselves : the reason why the serpent is the devil and satan, is, because the sensual principle communicates with hell and makes one therewith, for in it resides all the evil of man in the complex; and whereas man from the sensual principle reasons from fallacies and from the delights of the loves of the world and of the body, and this with much readiness and subtlety, therefore the serpent is said to be more subtle than any wild beast of the field which Jehovah God made, the wild beast of the field, in the spiritual sense, signifying the affection of the natural man : inasmuch as the sensual principle supposes that wisdom is procured by knowledges from the world and by the natural sciences, and not by any influx out of heaven from the Lord, therefore from that ignorance and fallacy the serpent said unto the woman, ye shall not die, for God does know that in the day ye eat thereof, then your eyes shall be opened, and ye shall be as God, knowing good and evil; for the sensual man believes that he knows all things and that nothing is concealed from him; far different to the celestial man, who knows that he knows nothing from himself but from the Lord, and that what he does know is so little, as to be scarce anything respectively to what he does not know; yea, their posterity believed that they were gods, and that they knew all good and all evil, whereas from evil it is not possible to know celestial good, but only terrestrial and corporeal good, which, notwithstanding, in itself is not good, but from celestial good, man can know what is evil : that the affection of the natural man persuaded by the sensual principle, supposed that intelligence concerning the things of heaven and the church was to be acquired by the science of knowledges derived from the world, is signified by the woman seeing that the tree was good for food, also pleasant to the eyes, and desirable to give intelligence, for by the woman is here signified the natural affection of man, which derives its desires from the sensual principle, and that affection is of such a nature : that that affection also seduced the rational [principle] is signified by the woman taking of the fruit of that tree and eating, and giving to her man with her, and his eating thereof, for by the man of the woman is signified the rational principle; that they then saw themselves to be without truths and goods is signified by the eyes of both being

opened, and their knowing that they were naked, nakedness which
is ashamed signifying the deprivation of celestial love, and thence
of good and truth; and that they then clothed themselves with natural truths, lest they should appear deprived of celestial truths, is
signified by their sewing fig leaves together and making themselves
girdles, the fig tree signifying the natural man, and the leaf thereof
scientific truth : afterwards their sensual principle is described of
what quality it became, viz. that it altogether averted itself from
heaven, and turned itself to the world, and so did not receive anything divine : this was described by the curse of the serpent; for the
sensual principle of man cannot be reformed, wherefore it is only
removed when man is reforming, inasmuch as it adheres to the body
and is extant to the world, and therefore the delights which it thence
feels it calls goods : hence it is that it is said that the seed of the woman shall bruise its head, and that it shall hurt his heel; by the seed of
the woman is understood the Lord, by the head of the serpent, all evil,
and by the heel of the Lord is signified divine truth in ultimates,
which, with us, is the literal sense of the Word, and this the sensual man, or sensual principle of man, perverts and falsifies, and
thereby hurts : that the literal sense of the Word is a defence, that
the Lord may be approached only by appearances of truth, and not
by genuine truths, by those who are in evils, is signified by the
cherubs, which, with the flame of a sword turning itself, were placed
at the garden of Eden to guard the way of the tree of lives : but
these and other particulars contained in those chapters may be seen
explained in the A. C.

740. " Called the devil and Satan"—That hereby is signified, because inwardly they are in evils and in falses, which are from hell,
appears from the signification of the devil and Satan, as denoting hell
as to evils and as to falses, concerning which we shall speak presently; the reason why they are denoted who are inwardly in evils
and in falses thence derived, is, because they who are here understood by the dragon, and are called the devil and Satan, are not outwardly such, but inwardly, for outwardly they speak as men of the
church, and some as angels of heaven, concerning God, concerning
the Lord, concerning faith and love to Him, and concerning heaven
and hell, and deduce many things from the Word by which they confirm their dogmas; hence it is, that by these exteriors that they are
conjoined to heaven, whilst notwithstanding they are not inwardly
affected with them, much less delighted, being affected and delighted
only with corporeal and worldly things, insomuch that they consider
heavenly things as respectively of no account; in a word, they love
corporeal and worldly things above all, but heavenly things only as
things of service, so that the things which appertain to the body and
to the world are made the head, and things celestial or heavenly the
feet; they are such because they make no account of the life, saying
that faith alone saves, and not any good of life; and hence it is,
that they are devils and satans, for the real nature and quality of
man is such as he is interiorly, and not such as he is outwardly alone,
unless he speak and act outwardly from the interior; such also he

remains after death; for such as is the quality of man interiorly, such he is also as to the spirit, and the spirit of man is the affection, from which is derived the will and thence the life; hence it follows that they who make no account of the life are inwardly devils and satans, and also become such when they become spirits at their departure out of the world. The reason why they are called the devil and Satan, is, because by the devil is signified hell, and in like manner by Satan, but by the devil is signified the hell whence come evils, and by Satan the hell whence come falses; the reason why the latter hell is called Satan, is, because all who are there are called satans; and the reason why the former is called the devil, is because all who are there are called devils: that there was not any devil or Satan before the creation of the world who was an angel of light, and afterwards cast down with his crew into hell, may appear from what has been said in the work concerning H. & H. n. 311–316, under the article "that heaven and hell are from the human race." It is to be observed that there are two kingdoms into which the heavens are distinguished, viz. the celestial kingdom and the spiritual kingdom, concerning which also see the work concerning H. & H. n. 20–28: to these two kingdoms oppositely correspond two kingdoms, into which the hells are distinguished; to the celestial kingdom corresponds, in opposition, the infernal kingdom which consists of devils; and is thence called the devil; and to the spiritual kingdom corresponds, in opposition, the infernal kingdom which consists of satans, and is thence called Satan; and whereas the celestial kingdom consists of angels who are principled in love to the Lord, so the infernal kingdom corresponding in opposition to the celestial kingdom, consists of devils, who are principled in the love of self, and hence it is that from that hell there is an efflux of evils of every kind; and whereas the spiritual kingdom consists of angels who are principled in charity towards the neighbor, so the infernal kingdom which corresponds in opposition to the spiritual kingdom, consists of satans, who are principled in falses from the love of the world, and hence from that hell there is an efflux of falses of every kind. From these considerations it may appear, what the devil and Satan signify in the following passages in the Evangelists: "Jesus was brought into the wilderness that He might be tempted of the devil" (Matt. iv. 1, and following; Luke iv. 2–13). What is signified by the wilderness, and by the temptations of the Lord for forty days and forty nights, may be seen above, n. 730; His being tempted by the devil, signifies his being tempted by the hells whence come evils, thus by the worst of the hells; for those hells chiefly fought against the divine love of the Lord, the love reigning in those hells being the love of self, and this love is opposite to the Lord's love, and thus to the love which is from the Lord. And in Matthew: "The tares are the sons of the evil [one], the enemy who soweth them is the devil" (xiii. 38, 39). Tares signify falses of doctrine, of religion and worship, which are from evil, wherefore also they are called the sons of the evil one; and whereas evil produces them, it is said that it is the devil who soweth them. And in Luke: "Those

upon the way are they who hear, and afterwards cometh the devil,
and taketh away the word out of their heart, that they may not believe and be saved" (viii. 12); and in Mark: "These are they who
are upon the*way, where the Word is sown; and when they have
heard, immediately Satan cometh and taketh away the word sown in
their hearts" (iv. 15). Upon this occasion the devil is mentioned in
Luke, and Satan in Mark, the reason of which is, because by the
seed which fell upon the way, is signified truth from the Word, which
is received in the memory only and not in the life, and as this is
taken away both by the evil and the false, therefore the devil and
Satan are both mentioned, the former in Luke and the latter in Mark.
And in Matthew: "The king shall say to them at the left hand,
depart from me ye cursed into eternal fire prepared for the devil and
his angels" (xxv. 41). The reason why it is here said the devil, is,
because the words are spoken concerning those who did not perform
good works, and therefore performed evil works, for they who do
not the one, must do the other, and the works which they did not
do are recounted in the preceding verses, for when goods are lightly.
esteemed, evils are loved. And in John: "Judas Iscariot is called
by the Lord a devil" (vi. 70); and it is said, "that the devil injected
into his heart" (John xiii. 2); and "that after he had taken the sop
Satan entered into him" (John xiii. 27; Luke xxii. 3). The reason
why it is thus said, is, because by Judas Iscariot the Jews were
represented, who were in falses from evil, wherefore from evil he is
called a devil, and from falses Satan; hence it is said that the devil
injected into his heart, to inject into the heart denoting into the love,
which is of the will; also that after he had taken the sop, Satan entered into him, to enter into him with the sop denoting to enter into
the belly, which signifies into the thought, and falses from evil are
of the thought. Again, in John: "Jesus said unto the Jews, ye
are of your father the devil, and the desires of your father ye will
do; he was a murderer from the beginning, and stood not in the
truth, because the truth was not in him; when he speaketh a lie, he
speaketh from his own" (viii. 44). The Jewish nation is here described as to what it was from the beginning, viz. that it was in evil
and thence in falses; by their father the devil is understood evil from
hell, in which their fathers were in Egypt and afterwards in the wilderness; that they were desirous to remain in the evils of their own
cupidities is signified by, the desires of your father ye will do; that they
destroyed all the truth of the understanding, is signified by, he was
a murderer from the beginning, and stood not in the truth, because
the truth was not in him, man denoting the truth of intelligence,
whence man-slaughter or murder is the destruction thereof; their
falses from evil are signified by, when he speaketh a lie, he speaketh
from his own, his own or the proprium signifying the evil of the will,
and a lie the false thence derived. And in Matthew: "The Pharisees said concerning Jesus, He doth not cast out demons but by
Beelzebub the prince of the demons; Jesus, knowing their thoughts,
said to them, if Satan cast out Satan, he is divided against himself;
who then shall his kingdom stand? if I in the spirit of God cast out

demons, then is the kingdom of God come unto you" (xii. 24, 26, 28). The reason why it is here said Satan, and not the devil, is, because by Beelzebub, who was the god of Ekron, is understood the god of all falses, for Beelzebub, being intepreted, is the Lord of flies, and flies signify the falses of the sensual man, thus falses of every kind : hence it is that Beezebub is called Satan, wherefore also the Lord said, if I in the spirit of God cast out demons, then is the kingdom of God come unto you, for by the spirit of God is understood divine truth proceeding from the Lord, and by the kingdom of God thence is signified heaven and the church which is in divine truths. Again : " Peter rebuking Jesus for desiring to suffer, Jesus turned and said to Peter, get thee behind me Satan, thou art an offence, because thou savorest not of the things which are of God, but the things which are of men" (Matthew xvi. 22, 23; Mark viii. 33). The reason why the Lord spake these words to Peter, is, because Peter, in the representative sense, signified faith, and whereas faith is of truth, and also of the false, as in the present case, therefore Peter is called Satan, for, as was said, Satan denotes the hell whence falses arise; Peter represented faith in both senses, viz. faith from · charity, and faith without charity, and faith without charity is the faith of what is false; they also who are in faith without charity, take offence at the Lord's suffering Himself to be crucified, whence it is also called an offence; inasmuch as the passion of the cross was the last temptation which the Lord suffered, and was the full victory over all the hells, and also the full union of His divine [principle] with the divine human, and they who are in the faith of the false are ignorant of this, therefore the Lord said, thou savorest not the things which are of God but which are of men. And in Luke: "Jesus said to Simon, lo Satan hath earnestly desired you, that he might sift you as wheat; but I have prayed for thee, that thy faith fail not; thou therefore, when thoŭ shalt be converted, confirm thy brethren" (xxii. 31, 32). Here also Peter represents faith without charity, which faith is a faith of the false, for these things were said to him by the Lord, just before He denied Him thrice; because he represented faith, therefore the Lord says, I have prayed for thee, that · thy faith fail not; that he also then represented the faith of the false, appears from the Lord saying to him, thou, therefore, when thou shalt be converted, confirm thy brethren; inasmuch as the faith of the false is as chaff before the wind, therefore it is said that Satan earnestly desired them, that he might sift them as wheat, wheat denoting the good of charity separate from the chaff; hence it is evident why the name of Satan is here used. Again : "I saw Satan as lightning falling from heaven" (x. 18); where by Satan is signified the same as by the dragon here treated of, who was also seen in heaven, and was cast down from heaven; but the dragon is what is properly understood by the devil, and his angels are those who are understood by Satan; that by the angels of the dragon are understood the falses of evil, will be seen in the subsequent paragraph; by Satan falling down from heaven, in the above passage, is signified, that the Lord, by divine truth, which He then was, expelled out of heaven all falses, and that He subjugated those hells which are called Satan, in like manner as by Michael's casting down the dragon and his angels, concerning which see above, n. 737. And in Job: "There was a day when the sons of God came to stand near Jehovah, and Satan came in the midst of them; and Jehovah said unto Satan, whence comest thou? and Satan answered Jehovah, from wandering up and down the earth, and from walking through it. And Jehovah gave into the hand of Satan all things belonging to Job, but upon himself he was not to put forth his hand; and afterwards He gave him to touch his bone and his flesh" (i. 6–12; chap. ii. 1–7). That the things related concerning Job are historical particulars so made, may appear from the whole of that book; for the book of Job is a book of the ancient church, full of correspondences, according to the mode of writing at that time, but still it is a book of great excellence and use; the angels, at that time, were called the sons of God, because, by the sons of God, equally as by the angels, are understood divine truths, and by Satan, infernal falses; and whereas the hells tempt man by falses, as was afterwards the case with Job, and infernal falses are shaken off by divine truths, therefore it is said that Satan stood in the midst of the sons of God; what the other particulars signify we shall not explain at present, as it would be necessary to illustrate them in their series. And in David: "They lay upon me evil for good, and hatred for my love; set thou a wicked one over him, and let Satan stand at his right hand" (Ps. cix. 5, 6). This, like most other things in the Psalms of David, is a prophecy concerning the Lord, and concerning His temptations, and of the most cruel of all which He sustained; and whereas the Lord, in his temptations, fought from divine love against the hells, which were most hostile to Him, it is said, they lay upon me evil for good, and hatred for my love; and whereas the most infernal evil and false prevail with those hells, it is said, set thou a wicked one over him, and let Satan stand at his right hand, to stand at the right hand signifying to be altogether possessed, and Satan signifying the infernal false with which he was to be possessed. And in Zechariah: "Afterwards he showed me Joshua the high priest, standing before the angel of Jehovah, and Satan standing at his right hand to resist Him; and Jehovah said unto Satan, Jehovah rebuke thee, even He who chooseth Jerusalem: is it not a brand plucked out of the fire? and Joshua was clothed in polluted garments, and so was standing before the angel" (iii. 1, 2, 3). What is involved in these words can only appear from the series of things which precede and follow; and from thence it may appear, that it was thereby represented in what manner the Word was falsified. By Joshua, the high priest, was there signified the law or the Word, and the falsification thereof by his standing before the angel in polluted garments; hence it is evident, that by Satan is there understood the false of doctrine from the Word falsified; and whereas this began to prevail at that time, therefore Satan was seen by Zechariah standing at his right hand, and to stand at the right hand, signifies to combat against divine truth; inasmuch as the literal sense of the Word only can be falsified, by reason that in that sense there are truths only apparently, and they who interpret the Word according to the letter can hardly be convinced of falses, therefore Jehovah said, Jehovah rebuke thee, in like manner as above, n. 735, where it is explained what is signified by Michael disputing with the devil concerning the body of Moses, and saying to the devil, "the Lord rebuke thee" (Jude verse 9). Inasmuch as the truth of doctrine from the Word is understood, and the falsification thereof, it is therefore said, Jehovah who chooseth Jerusalem, is it not a brand plucked out of the fire? Jerusalem signifying the doctrine of the church, and by a brand plucked out of the fire is signified that there was but little of the truth remaining. In these passages in the Old Testament, Satan only is mentioned, and no where the devil, but instead of the latter the terms foe, enemy, hater, adversary, accuser, demon, likewise death and hell are made use of. From these considerations it may appear, that by the devil is signified the hell whence evils arise, and by Satan the hell whence falses arise; as also in the following passage in the Apocalypse: "Afterwards I saw an angel coming down from heaven who had the key of the abyss, and a great chain upon·his hand, and he laid hold of the dragon, the old serpent, which is the devil and Satan, and bound him a thousand years; and when the thousand years are consummated, Satan shall be loosened out of his prison, and shall seduce the nations; and the devil who seduced them was cast in a lake of fire and sulphur" (xx. 1, 2, 7, 8, 10). But what demons, demoniacs, and spirits of demons, signify, may be seen above, n. 586.

741. "Who seduceth the whole world"—That hereby is signified, which pervert all things of the church, appears from the signification of the whole world, as denoting all things of the church, concerning which we shall speak presently; and whereas all things of the church are signified by the whole world, therefore to seduce it signifies to pervert those things; for all things of the church are perverted, when the good of charity, which is the good of life, is separated from faith, and removed as not conducing or contributing anything to salvation; hence all things of the Word are falsified, and consequently all things of the church; for it is said by the Lord, that the law and the prophets, hang on those two commandments, to love God above all things, and our neighbor as ourselves, and these two commandments signify to live and act according to the precepts of the Word; for to love is to will and to do, inasmuch as what a man interiorly loves, this he wills, and what he wills, this he does; by the law and the prophets, are signified all things of the Word. There are two principles of evil and the false into which the church successively falls, viz. into the love of dominion over all things of the church and of heaven, which dominion is understood in the Word by Babel or Babylon; into this the church falls in consequence of evil; the other is the separation of faith from charity, by reason whereof all the good of life perishes; this is understood in the Word by Philistea, and is signified by the he-goat in Daniel, and by the dragon in the Apocalypse; into this the church falls in

consequence of the false.   But inasmuch as the subject treated of in
this chapter is concerning the dragon, by which is chiefly signified,
the religion of faith separate from charity, we will here adduce some
of the methods whereby the defenders of faith separate from charity
seduce the world : this they do especially by teaching, that because
no one can do good, which in itself is good, from himself, and without placing merit therein, therefore good works cannot contribute
anything to salvation ; but that still goods are to be done, on account
of the public good, and that these are the goods understood in the
Word, and in the preachings thence derived, and in some of the
prayers of the church ; but how they err in this matter shall now be
explained : when man does good from the Word, that is, because it
is commanded by the Lord in the Word, he does not then do it from
himself, but from the Lord, for the Lord is the Word (John i. 1, 14),
and is in those things which are from the Word with man, as He
also teaches in these words in John : " He who keepeth My word, I
will come unto him, and will make my abode with him" (xiv. 23):
hence it is that the Lord so often commands that we should do his
words and precepts, and that they who do them shall have life eternal, likewise that every one shall be judged according to his works :
hence now it follows, that they who do good from the Word, do it
from the Lord, and good from the Lord is truly good, and so far as
it is from the Lord, so far merit is not placed in it. ·That good done
from the Word, thus from the Lord, is truly good, appears also from
these words in the Apocalypse : " Behold I stand at the door, and
knock, if any one hear My voice, and open the door, I will enter in
unto him, and will sup with him, and he with Me" (iii. 20).   Hence
it is evident, that the Lord is every instant and continually present,
and gives the effort of doing good, but that man is to open the door,
that is, to receive the Lord, and he then receives Him when He does
good from His Word ; this, although it appears to man to be done
as from himself, yet nevertheless it is not of man, but of the Lord
with him ; the reason why it so appears to man, is, because he does
not feel otherwise than that he thinks from himself, and acts from
himself, when, notwithstanding, whilst he thinks and acts from the
Word, it is only as of himself, but from the Lord, wherefore he then
also believes this.   From these considerations it may be seen, that
the good which man does from the Word, is spiritual good, and that
it conjoins man to the Lord and to heaven ; but the good which man
does for the sake of the world and for the sake of societies in the
world, which is called civil and moral good, conjoins him to the
world and not to heaven ; and moreover the conjunction of the truth
of faith is with spiritual good, which is the good of neighborly love
or charity, by reason that faith in itself is spiritual, and what is spiritual cannot be conjoined with any other good than what is alike
spiritual ; but civil and moral good, separate from spiritual good, is
.not good in itself, because it is from man, yea, so far as a regard to
self and the world lies concealed in it, so far it is evil, wherefore this
cannot be conjoined with faith, and if it should be conjoined faith
would thereby be dissipated.   The reason why to seduce the whole

world, signifies to pervert all things of the church, is, because by world in general is signified the church as to all things appertaining thereto, as well goods as truths, but specifically it signifies the church as to good, as is the case more especially when the earth is mentioned at the same time; that by the earth, in the Word, is signified the church, was shown above, n. 304, 697: but when the world is mentioned at the same time, then by the earth is signified the church as to truth; for there are two things which constitute the church, viz. truth and good, and these two are signified by the earth and world in the following passages: thus in Isaiah: " With my soul have I desired thee in the night; with my spirit also in the midst of me have I expected Thee in the morning; for when Thou teachest the earth Thy judgments, the inhabitants of the world learn justice" (xxvi. 9). By night is signified the state when there is not the light of truth, and by morning is signified the state when there is the light of truth, the latter state is from love, but the former is when as yet there is not love, wherefore by the soul which hath desired Jehovah in the night, is signified the life which is not yet in the light of truth, and by the spirit in the midst of him, with which he expected Jehovah in the morning, is signified the life which is in the light of truth; hence it there follows, for when thou teachest the earth Thy judgments, the inhabitants of the world learn justice, whereby is signified that the church is in truths from the Lord, and by truths in good; the earth signifies the church as to truths, and the world the church as to good, for judgment, in the Word, is predicated of truth and justice of good, and inhabitants also signify the men of the church, who are in goods of doctrine and thence of life; that judgment, in the Word, is predicated of truth, and justice of good, may be seen in the A. C. n. 2235, 9857; and that to dwell or inhabit signifies to live, and thence dwellers or inhabitants those who are in the good of doctrine and thence of life, may be seen above, n. 133, 479, 662. And in Lamentations: " The kings of the earth believed not, and all the inhabitants of the world, that the enemy and the foe would come into the gates of Jerusalem" (iv. 12). By the kings of the earth are signified the men of the church who are in truths, and by the inhabitants of the world, the men of the church who are in good; that kings signify those who are in truths, may be seen above, n. 31, 553, 625; and that inhabitants signify those who are in good, was shown just above; hence it is evident that the earth signifies the church as to truths, and the world the church as to good; and whereas all things of the doctrine of the church were destroyed by falses and evils, it is said that they believed not that the enemy and foe would come into the gates of Jerusalem, the enemy denoting the falses which destroyed the truths of the church, which are meant by the kings of the earth, and the foe denoting the evils which destroyed the goods of the church, which are understood by the inhabitants of the world, and Jerusalem denoting the church as to doctrine. And in David: " Let all the earth fear Jehovah, let all the inhabitants of the world stand in awe of him" (Psalm xxxiii. 8). Here also by the earth, are signified those who are in the truths of

the church, and by the inhabitants of the world, those who are in
the goods of the church. Again: "The earth is Jehovah's, and
the fulness thereof, the world and they that dwell therein ; He hath
founded it upon the seas, and established it upon the floods" (Psalm
xxiv. 1, 2). By the earth here also is signified the church as to
truth, and the fulness thereof signifies all truths in the complex;
and by the world is signified the church as to good, and by the inhabitants thereof goods in the complex : what is signified by founding it upon the seas and establishing it upon the floods, may be seen
above, n. 275, 518. And in Isaiah: "We have conceived, we
have travailed in birth, we have as it were brought forth wind : we
have not made salvations to the earth, and the inhabitants of the
world have fallen" (xxvi. 18) : where also the earth denotes the
church as to truths, and the world the church as to goods : the rest
may be seen explained above, n. 721. Again: "Draw near, ye
nations, to hear, and hearken ye people ; let the earth hear and the
fulness thereof, the world and all its offspring" (xxxiv. 1). That by
nations are understood those who are in goods, and by people those
who are in truths, may be seen above, n. 175, 331, 625; wherefore
also it is said, let the earth hear, and the fulness thereof, the world
and all its offspring, for by the earth and the fulness thereof is signified the church as to all truths, and by the world and all its offspring, the church as to all goods. Again: "All the dwellers of
the world and inhabitants of the earth, when the sign of the mountains is lifted up, behold ye ; and when the trumpet is sounded, hear
ye" (xviii. 3). By the dwellers of the world and inhabitants of the
earth, are signified all in the church who are in goods and truths, as
above ; the coming of the Lord is signified by, when the signs of the
mountains shall be lifted up, behold ye, and when the trumpet shall
be sounded, hear ye, the sign upon the mountains and the sounding
of the trumpet signifying convocation to the church. Again, in David : "Before Jehovah because He cometh, because He cometh to
judge the earth ; He shall judge the world in justice, and the people
in verity" (Psalm xcvi. 13 ; Psalm xcviii. 9) : treating concerning
the coming of the Lord, and the last judgment then to take place :
inasmuch as by the world are signified those of the church who are
in good, and by people those who are in truths, therefore it is said,
that he shall judge the world in justice, and the people in verity,
justice being predicated of good, in like manner as the world.
Again: "Before the mountains were born, and the earth was formed,
and the world, from eternity and even to eternity, Thou art God"
(Psalm xc. 2). By the mountains are signified those who dwell
upon mountains in the heavens, who are those that are in celestial
good, but by the earth and the world is signified the church from
those who are in truths and in goods. Again: "Jehovah reigneth,
He hath clothed Himself with majesty, Jehovah hath clothed
Himself with strength, He hath girded Himself; the world also
shall be established, that it shall not be moved; Thy throne
is strengthened from that time, Thou art from eternity" (Psalm
xciii. 1, 2). These things are said concerning the Lord about

to come into the world : and whereas He has glory and power from the Human [principle] which He united to His Divine, it is said, that He put on majesty and strength, and that He girded Himself; for the Lord assumed the Human [principle] that He might be in the potency of subjugating the hells; the church which He was about to establish, and to defend for ever, is signified by the world which shall be established, and shall not be moved, and by the throne which shall be strengthened, for by the world is signified heaven and the church as to the reception of divine good, and by the throne, heaven and the church as to the reception of divine truth.   Again : "Say amongst the nations, Jehovah reigneth ; the world also shall be established, neither shall it be removed ; He shall judge the people in uprightnesses, the heavens shall be glad, and the earth shall rejoice" (Psalm cvi. 10, 11): treating also concerning the Lord's advent, and concerning the church to be established by Him, and defended to eternity, which is signified by the world which shall be established and shall not be removed, according to what was explained above; and whereas by the world is signified the church as to good, therefore it is also said concerning the people whom He shall judge in uprightnesses, for by the people are signified those who are in the truths of the church, in like manner as by the earth, wherefore they are called people of the earth, and inhabitants of the world, and uprightnesses denote truths; their joy who are in the church in the heavens and in the church in the earths, is signified by the heavens shall be glad, and the earth shall rejoice.   Again : "Jehovah shall judge the world in justice, He shall judge the people in uprightnesses" (Psalm ix. 9).   Inasmuch as by the world is understood the church as to good, and justice is predicated of good, therefore it is said, Jehovah shall judge the world in justice ; and inasmuch as they are called people who are in truths, and uprightnesses are truths, therefore it is was said, he shall judge the people in uprightnesses.   And in Jeremiah : "Jehovah maketh the earth by His power, and prepareth the world by His wisdom, and by His intelligence He stretcheth out the heavens" (x. 12 ; chap. li. 15).   Jehovah maketh the earth by His power, signifies, that the Lord establishes the church by the power of divine truth ; He prepareth the world by His wisdom, signifies, that the church which is in good, He formeth from divine good by divine truth ; by His intelligence He stretcheth out the heavens, signifies, that so He enlarges the heavens.   Again, in David : "The heavens are Thine, the earth is Thine, the world and the fulness thereof thou hast founded" (Psalm lxxxix. 12).   By the heavens and the earth is signified the church in the heavens and in the earths, each as to truths ; and by the world and the fulness thereof is signified the church in the heavens and in the earths, each as to goods, fulness denoting goods and truths in their whole complex.   Again : "If I should be hungry, I would not tell thee, for the world is Mine, and the fulness thereof" (Psalm l. 12).   These things are said concerning sacrifices, that the Lord does not delight in them, but in confession and works, for it follows, will I eat the flesh of the robust, or drink the blood of goats sacrifice to God confession, and pay thy vows to the Most High; wherefore by, if I should be hungry, is signified, if I should desire sacrifices; but whereas the Lord desires worship from goods and truths, it is said, for the world is Mine and the fulness thereof, fulness signifying goods and truths in their whole complex as above; this is said indeed concerning the beasts which should be sacrificed, but by them, in the spiritual sense, are signified various kinds of good and truth. And in Matthew it is written, " This Gospel of the kingdom shall be preached in the whole world, for a testimony to all nations, and then shall the end come" (xxiv. 14). Inasmuch as by the world is signified the church as to good, therefore it is said that that Gospel shall be preached to all nations, for by the nations who will hear and receive, are signified all who are in good, but by nations, in the opposite sense, are also signified all who are in evils, who also will hear, but in this case by the world is signified the universal church when fallen into evils, whence it is also said that then shall the end come. Again, in 1 Samuel: " Jehovah raiseth up the depressed out of the dust, He raiseth the needy from the dunghill, to cause them to sit with princes, and He maketh them to inherit a throne of glory, for the bases of the earth are Jehovah's and He setteth the world upon them" (ii. 8). This is the prophecy of Hannah the mother of Samuel: and by raising up the depressed out of the dust, and the needy from the dunghill, is signified the instruction of the gentiles or nations, and illustration in interior truths, which should be revealed from the Lord, consequently also removal from evils and falses; by the bases of the earth are signified exterior truths, such as are those of the literal sense of the Word, for upon these interior truths are founded, wherefore, by the world which he set upon them, is signified, the church as to all the goods and truths thereof: but for a more particular explication of these things see above, n. 253, 304. Again, in Isaiah: Jacob shall cause them who are to come to take root, Israel shall blossom and flourish, so that the faces of the world shall be filled with the produce" (xxvii. 6). By Jacob is understood the external church, and by Israel the internal church; and whereas the internal of the church is founded upon the externals thereof, and the internals are thence multiplied and fructified, it is said that Jacob shall cause them that are to come to take root, and that Israel shall blossom and flourish; the fructification of the church thence is signified by, the faces of the world shall be filled with the produce. Again, in the same prophet: " Is this the man that putteth the earth in commotion, that maketh the kingdoms tremble, that hath laid the world into a wilderness and destroyed the cities thereof? prepare the slaughter for his sons, for the iniquity of their fathers, that they rise not again and possess the earth, and fill the faces of the world with cities" (xiv. 16, 17, 21): treating of Lucifer, by whom is understood Babel, that is, the love of ruling over heaven and over earth; wherefore by putting the earth in commotion, making the kingdoms tremble, laying the world into a wilderness and destroying the cities thereof, is signified, to destroy all things of the church, the earth denotes the church as to truth, kingdoms denote the churches distinguished according to truths, the world denotes the church as to good, and the cities denote doctrinals; by preparing slaughter for the sons for the iniquities of their fathers, is signified the destruction of the falses arising from their evils; lest they possess the earth, and fill the faces of the world with cities, signifies, lest the falses and evils, and the doctrinals derived from them, occupy the universal church. Again, in the same prophet: "The earth shall mourn and be confounded, the world shall languish and be confounded, the loftiness of the people of the earth shall languish, and the earth itself shall be profaned under its inhabitants" (xxiv. 4, 5). In these words is described the desolation of the church as to the truths and goods thereof, by reason of the conceit of self-derived intelligence, and the profanation of truths from good; the desolation is described by mourning, being confounded, and languishing; the church as to truths and as to goods, is signified by the earth and by the world; the conceit of self-derived intelligence by the loftiness of the people of the earth, and the profanation of truths which are from good by the earth being profaned under its inhabitants. And in Nahum: "The mountains shall tremble before Him, and the hills shall melt; the earth shall be burnt up before Him, and the world, and all that dwell therein" (i. 5): what is signified by the mountains which shall tremble, and by the hills which shall melt, may be seen above, n. 400, 405; but by the earth being burnt up, and the world, and all that dwell therein, is signified, that the church as to all truths and goods thereof will perish by infernal love. Again, in David: "The channels of the waters appeared, and the foundations of the world were discovered, at Thy rebuke, O Jehovah, at the blast of the breath of Thy nostrils" (Psalm xviii. 16; 1 Sam. xxii. 16). That all things of the church as to the truths and as to the goods thereof were utterly overturned, is signified by, the channels of the waters appeared, and the foundations of the world were discovered, the channels of the waters denoting the truths, and the foundations of the world the goods thereof, and to appear and be discovered denoting to be utterly overturned; that this destruction is from the hatred and fury of the evil against things divine, is signified by, at Thy rebuke, O Jehovah, at the blast of the breath of Thy nostrils, for by the rebuke and the breath of the nostrils of Jehovah is signified the same as by His anger and wrath, elsewhere mentioned in the Word; but whereas there does not exist any anger or wrath in the Lord against the evil, but in the evil against the Lord, and these appear to them, when they perish, as from the Lord, therefore it is so said according to appearance; by the blast of the breath of the nostrils of Jehovah, is also understood the east wind, which destroys by drought, and by its penetrating power overturns. Again: "The voice of Thy thunder in the world, Thy lightning enlightened the world, the earth trembled and was put in commotion" (Psalm lxxvii. 19). Again: "His lightnings shall enlighten the world, the earth shall see and fear, the mountains shall melt as wax before Jehovah, before the Lord of the whole earth" (Psalm xcvii. 4, 5). By these words is described the state of the impious from the presence of the

Lord in His divine truth, which state is similar to that of the sons of Israel when the Lord appeared to them upon mount Sinai; that they then heard thunderings, saw lightnings, and that the mountain appeared in a consuming fire as of a furnace, and that they were exceedingly afraid, is known from the Word, and the reason of this was, because they were evil in heart; for the Lord appears to every one according to his quality, to the good as a recreating fire, and to the evil as a consuming fire; hence it is evident, what is signified by the voice of thy thunder in the world, by the lightnings enlightning the world, by the earth being put in commotion and trembling, and by the mountains melting before Jehovah, the Lord of the whole earth; by the world are understood all of the church who are in goods, but here, those who are in evils, and by the earth are understood all of the church who are in truths, but here, those who are in falses. Again, in Isaiah: "I will visit upon the world its wickedness, and upon the impious their iniquity" (xiii. 11). By the world here also are understood those of the church who are in evils, and by the impious those who are in falses, wherefore it is said, I will visit upon the world its wickedness, and upon the impious their iniquity, wickedness denoting evil, and iniquity being predicated of falses. And in Job: "They shall drive him from the light into darkness, and excommunicate him from the world" (xviii. 18). Inasmuch as by light is signified truth, and by the world the good of the church, and the impious, when he departs from truth into the false, also casts himself from good into evil, therefore it is said, they shall drive him from the light into darkness, and shall excommunicate him from the world, darkness denoting falses, and to be excommunicated from the world denoting to be cast out from the good of the church. Thus also in Luke: "Men being half dead through fear and expectation of those things which shall come upon the world of earths, for the powers of the heavens shall be put in commotion, and then shall they see the Son of Man, coming in a cloud of the heavens with power and much glory" (xxi. 26, 27). These things are said concerning the consummation of the age, which is the last time of the church, when there is no more any truth, because no good; the state of heaven at that time is described by those words, viz. that men shall be half dead through fear and expectation of those things which shall come upon the world of earths, whereby is described, the fear of those who are in the heavens, lest everything appertaining to the church should perish as to the good and thence as to the truths thereof, and the expectation of help from the Lord; the potency of divine truth being ready to fail, is signified by the commotion of the powers of the heavens, the powers of the heavens denoting divine truth as to potency; that the Lord will then manifest divine truth, which shall have potency, and from which intelligence shall be given, is signified by, then shall they see the Son of Man coming in a cloud of the heavens with power and much glory. Similar things are signified by the earth and by the world in the following words in the Apocalypse: "They are the spirits of demons making signs to go forth unto the kings of the earth, and of the whole world of earths, to gather them together to war" (xvi. 14). It is said unto the kings of the earth, and of the whole world of earths, because one principle of the church is signified by the earth, and another by the world. Inasmuch as by the world is signified the church as to good, therefore it also signifies all things of the church, for the essential of the church is good, wherefore where there is good, there also is truth, for all good desires truth, and wills to be conjoined with truths, and from them to be spiritually nourished, thus also reciprocally.

742. "Was cast down to the earth, and his angels were cast down with him"—That hereby is signified, that those evils and the falses thence derived were condemned to hell, appears from the signification of being cast down to the earth, as denoting to be separated from heaven and to be condemned to hell, concerning which we shall speak presently; and from the signification of the angels of the dragon, as denoting falses from evil, which evil is signified by the dragon: for by the angels of heaven, in the Word, are signified divine truths, inasmuch as they are receptions thereof, as may be seen above, n. 103, 302; whence by the angels of the dragon are signified the infernal falses which proceed from the evil which is signified by the dragon; those falses are for the most part truths falsified, which in themselves are falses, according to what was said above. The reason why to be cast to the earth is to be condemned to hell, is, because this is signified when mention is made of being cast forth from heaven: in the spiritual world there are earths as in the natural world, full of mountains and hills, likewise of valleys and rivers, and when these taken together are called the earth, then by the earth is signified the church; but when the lowest parts of the earth are understood, as is the case when mention is made of being cast down from heaven to the earth, then by the earth is signified what is damned, because under those lowest parts are the hells, and in the hells also there are earths, but such as are damned: it is for this reason that it is not usual for any angel to go with the head prone or inclining, and to look on the earth, nor indeed to lie upon it, in the lowest parts thereof, nor to take up any of the dust thereof; hence it came to pass, that they who in the world condemned others to hell, used to cast dust taken from the earth upon them, for this corresponded to the condemning them; for similar reasons also it is not allowable for any one to walk with naked feet upon those earths in the spiritual world: the earths there which are damned are readily known from those which are not damned, because the former are altogether barren and merely dust, excepting the thorns and briars which are here and there planted, whereas the latter are fertile, full of herbs, shrubs, trees, and corn fields. Hence it was a customary rite, in the Jewish representative church, to cast themselves to the earth, to roll themselves upon it, and to sprinkle dust thence upon their heads, when they were in great mourning on account of being defeated by their enemies, and on account of violence offered to their sanctuaries; by which they represented, that they acknowledged themselves to be of themselves accursed, and thus in the most hu-

miliating posture solicited that their sins might be remitted. That they who are understood by the dragon and his angels, were separated from heaven and condemned to hell, whilst the last judgment was performed, and also afterwards, was granted me to see, as an eye witness, concerning which more will be said at the end of this work. From these considerations it may appear, that by being cast out of heaven to the earth is signified to be condemned to hell.

743. Verses 10, 11, 12. " And I heard a great voice saying in heaven, now is come the safety, and the power, and the kingdom of our God, and the authority of His Christ; because the accuser of our brethren is cast down, that accuseth them before our God day and night. And they conquered him through the blood of the Lamb, and through the Word of their testimony : and they loved not their soul even to death. Therefore, rejoice ye 'heavens, and ye that dwell in them : woe to the inhabitants of the earth and of the sea, for the devil is come down unto you having great anger, knowing that he hath but a little time."—" And I heard a great voice saying in heaven," signifies the joy of the angels of heaven from the light and wisdom then appertaining to them ; " now is come the safety, and the power, and the kingdom of our God, and the authority of His Christ," signifies, that now the Lord has the power, by His divine truth, of saving those who are of His church, who receive it in heart and soul : "because the accuser of our brethren is cast down" signifies, after that they were separated from heaven, and condemned to hell, who fought against, or assaulted, the life of faith, which is charity : "that accuseth them before our God day and night" signifies, and reproved them and disputed with them continually from the Word : "and they conquered him by the blood of the Lamb," signifies resistance and victory by divine truth proceeding from the Divine Human [principle] of the Lord : "and by the Word of their testimony, signifies, and by the confession and acknowledgment of the Divine [principle] in His Human : "and they loved not their soul even to death," signifies the faithful, who, on account of those truths, suffered temptations, and made the life of the world of no account compared with the life of heaven : " wherefore rejoice ye heavens, and ye who dwell in them," signifies the salvation and thence the joy of those who become spiritual by the reception of divine truth : " woe to the inhabitants of the earth and sea," signifies, lamentation over those who become merely natural and sensual : " because the devil is come down unto you," signifies, because they receive evils from hell: " having great anger," signifies, hatred against spiritual truths and goods, which are of faith and life from the Word, consequently against those who are in them: " knowing that he hath a little time," signifies, because the state is changed.

744. " And I heard a great voice, saying in heaven"—That hereby is signified the joy of the angels of heaven from the light and wisdom then appertaining to them, appears from the signification of a great voice saying, as denoting testification of joy from the heart, concerning which we shall speak presently ; and from the significa-

tion of in heaven, as denoting with the angels of heaven. That the joy of the angels is from the light and wisdom then appertaining to them, follows of consequence; for when the dragons, by whom are understood those who are indeed in some science of the knowledges of truth and good from the Word, but still not in truths and goods, because not in the life thereof, were cast down, and so were no longer in conjunction with heaven, then the angels came into light and wisdom, whence their joy is expressed; the reason why the angels then came into light and wisdom, was, because there is a connection of all in the heavens, from the first of them to the last, that is, from the first, who are in the inmost or third heaven, to the last, who are in the ultimate or first heaven; for the Lord flows in through the third heaven into the ultimate, and by influx conjoins the heavens; hence it is that the universal heaven, in the sight of the Lord, is as one man; when, therefore, the ultimates of the heavens have connection with such as are conjoined to hell, thus with those who are signified by the dragon and his angels, then, according to the degree of that conjunction of the ultimate heaven, the light and intelligence of the angels is diminished : the case is similar as with the ultimates in man, which are the outermost skins, which invest the body in general and in particular, likewise the muscles within those skins, and also the nerves in their ultimates, from which ligatures and membranes are spread over the interiors; if those extremes or outermost parts are injured, or by any means infected, or if they become too much stretched, then in the same degree the life of feeling and acting perishes in the interiors, which are invested and included by those extremes; hence it is evident, that the health of the body depends upon the state of the extremes, as a house upon its foundation : this may especially admit of comparison with men worn down with age, with whom the extremes first harden, whence they are deprived of the faculty of feeling and acting, and by degrees the same takes place in the interiors, whence their death follows: the like reasoning holds good with the heavens, which are as one man in the sight of the Lord, when the postremes or ultimates as it were grow hard or callous, as is the case when those ultimates have conjunction with the hells; thus it was with the heavens, so long as the dragons were seen there, for the dragons, as was before observed, had conjunction with the ultimates of heaven, as to externals, but with the hells as to their internals; for this reason it was said that the dragon was seen in heaven, and that Michael fought with him in heaven, and afterwards that he was cast out of heaven; by which is signified, that he was separated. Hence now it is, that by a great voice heard in heaven, is signified testification of joy from the heart with the angels of heaven; that the joy was from the light and wisdom then appertaining to them, follows from what has been said, namely, that as man is in his active and sensitive life from the interiors, whilst the extremes are in their integrity, thus also the inferior and superior heavens are in their intelligence and wisdom, and thence in the joy of their heart; wherefore by the same words is understood, that the angels had joy from the light and wisdom then appertaining to them.

745. " Now is come the safety and the power and the kingdom of our God, and the authority of His Christ"—That hereby is signified, that now the Lord has the power of saving those who are of His church, by His divine truth, who receive it in heart and soul, appears from the signification of safety, as denoting salvation; and from the signification of power, as denoting the being able, thus possibility, of which we shall speak presently; and from the signification of kingdom, as denoting heaven and the church, concerning which see above, n. 48, 684; and from the signification of our God, as denoting the Lord in respect to His divine [principle]; and from the signification of the authority of His Christ, as denoting the efficacy of divine truth. That authority, or power, when predicated of the Lord, signifies the salvation of the human race, may be seen above, n. 293; and that the Lord has the power of saving by His divine truth, n. 333, 726; and whereas the Lord cannot save any others than those who receive divine truth from Him in the heart and soul, therefore this also is signified: hence it may appear, that by now is come the safety and the power and the kingdom of our God, and the authority of His Christ, is signified, that now the Lord has the power of saving, by His divine truth, those who are of His church, who receive it in heart and soul; it is said in the heart and soul, and thereby is understood in love and faith, likewise in will and understanding; for by soul, in the Word, where soul and heart are both mentioned, is signified faith, likewise understanding, and by heart is signified love, likewise will; for by soul, in the ultimate sense, is understood the respiration of man, which is also called his spirit, wherefore it is usual to say animation for the respiration, likewise, that man emits the spirit or soul when he dies; that soul likewise signifies faith, as also understanding, and the heart love, as also the will, is from correspondence; for faith and understanding correspond to the animation or respiration of the lungs, and the love and will correspond to the motion and pulse of the heart, concerning which correspondence see above, n. 167, and the A. C. n. 2930, 3883–3896, 9050. The reason why these words, now is come the safety and the power of our God, signify that the Lord can now save, thus that power there signifies the being able, thus possibility, is, because the Lord could not save those who were of His church, before the dragon with his angels was driven out, that is, separated from heaven: he who does not know the laws of divine order, may suppose that the Lord can save any whomsoever, thus the evil as well as the good, whence it is the opinion of some, that in the end all who are in hell will also be saved; but that no one can be saved from immediate mercy, but from mediate, and that still it is from pure mercy that they are saved who receive divine truth from the Lord in heart and soul, may be seen in the work concerning H. & H. n. 521–527. This also is understood by those words in John: " His own received Him not; but as many as received Him to them

gave He power to become the sons of God, believing in His name, who were born not of bloods, neither of the will of the flesh, nor of the will of man, but of God" (i. 11, 12, 13). By His own who received Him not are understood those who are of the church where the Word is, and to whom the Lord could thereby be known, wherefore those who were of the Jewish church are there understood by His own; by the Lord giving power to those who believe in His name to become the sons of God, is signified, to give heaven to those who receive divine truths from Him in the soul and heart, or in faith and life, to believe in His name denoting to receive the Lord in faith and life, for by the name of the Lord is signified all that by which He is worshiped; by the sons of God are understood those who are regenerated by the Lord; who are born not of bloods, signifies, who have not falsified and adulterated the Word; nor of the will of the flesh, signifies, who are not in evils from their proprium; nor of the will of man, signifies, who are not in falses from their proprium, for the will signifies man's proprium, flesh signifies evil, and man [vir] signifies the false; but born of God signifies who are regenerated by truths from the Word and by a life according thereto. From these considerations it may appear that they cannot be saved, who are not willing to be reformed and regenerated by the Lord, which is effected by the reception of divine truth in faith and life.

746. "Because the accuser of our brethren is cast down"—That hereby is signified, that after they were separated from heaven and condemned to hell, who assaulted the life of faith, which is charity, appears from the signification of being cast down, when predicated of the dragon, as denoting that they who are understood by the dragon were separated from heaven and condemned to hell, concerning which see above, n. 739, 742; and from the signification of the accuser of our brethren, as denoting those who assaulted the life of faith, which is charity; for by an accuser is signified one who assaults, chides, and rebukes, for he who accuses also assaults, chides, and rebukes; the same expression also, in the original tongue, signifying an adversary and rebuker; and what is wonderful, they who are dragons, although they make no account of the life, yet accuse the faithful in the spiritual world, if they observe in them any evil of ignorance, for they inquire into their life in order that they may reproach and condemn, and hence they are called accusers; but by the brethren whom they accuse, are understood all who are in the heavens, likewise all in the earths who are in the good of charity; the reason why they are called brethren, is, because they have all one father, viz. the Lord, and they who are in the good of love to the Lord, and in the good of charity towards their neighbor, are His sons, and are also called sons of God, sons of the kingdom, and heirs, whence it follows, that, inasmuch as they are the sons of one Father, they are also brethen; it was also the principal command of the Lord the Father, that they should love each other mutually, whence it is from love that they become brethren; love also is spiritual conjunction : hence it was, that in the churches with the ancients, in which charity was the essential, all were called brethren;

in like manner in our Christian church at its beginning; hence also
it is, that brother, in the spiritual sense, signifies charity. That for-
merly all who were of one church called themselves brethren, and
that the Lord names those brethren who are in love to Him and in
charity towards their neighbor, may appear from many passages in
the Word; but in order that it may distinctly be perceived what is
signified by brother, it shall be illustrated from the Word.   I. That
all who were of the Israelitish church called themselves brethren,
appears from the following passages; thus in Isaiah: " Then shall
they bring all your brethren, from all nations, a gift to Jehovah"
(lxvi. 20); and in Jeremiah : " No one shall cause a Jew his brother to serve" (xxxiv. 9); and in Ezekiel: " Son of Man, thy brethren, thy brethen, the sons of thy kindred and the whole house of
Israel" (xi. 15); and in Micah : " Until the remnant of his brethren
shall return unto the sons of Israel" (v. 2); and in Moses : " Moses
went out to his brethren, that he might see their burdens" (Exod.
ii. 16); " Moses said unto Jethro his father-in-law, I will return to
my brethren, who are in Egypt" (Exod. iv. 18); " When thy brother shall be impoverished" (Levit. xxv. 25, 35, 47); " But as to
your brethren, the sons of Israel, a man shall not rule over his brother with rigor" (Levit. xxv. 46); " Would to God that we had
died when our brethren died before Jehovah" (Numb. xx. 3); " Behold a man of the sons of Israel came and brought unto his brethren
a Midianitish woman" (Numb. xxv. 6): " Thou shalt open thine
hand to thy brother; when thy brother, a Hebrew man or Hebrew
woman, shall be sold to thee, he shall serve thee six years" (Deut.
xv. 11, 12); " If any one shall steal the soul of his brethren, and
shall make gain thereof" (Deut. xxiv. 6); " Forty times shalt thou
strike him, and not exceed, lest thy brother be accounted vile in
thine eyes" (Deut. xxv. 13).; and elsewhere. From these passages
it may appear, that the sons of Israel were all called brethren
amongst each other; the proximate cause of their being so called,
was their being all descended from Jacob, who was their common
father; but the remote cause was, because brother signifies the good
of charity, which good, inasmuch as it is the essential of the church,
also conjoins all after a spiritual manner; likewise because Israel,
in the supreme sense, signifies the Lord, and thence the sons of Israel the church.   II. That they also called themselves man and brother, likewise companion and brother; as in the following passages;
thus in Isaiah : " The land is darkened and the people are become
as fuel for the fire, they shall not spare a man his brother, they shall
eat every man the flesh of his own arm, Menasseh Ephraim, and
Ephraim Menasseh" (ix. 18, 20). By a man and brother is signified
truth and good, and, in the opposite sense, the false and evil, wherefore it is also said, Menasseh shall eat Ephraim, and Ephraim Menasseh, for by Menasseh is signified voluntary good, and by Ephraim
intellectual truth, both of the external church, and, in the opposite
sense, the evil and the false ; but these words may be seen explained
above, n. 386, 440, 600, 617.   Again : " I will commix Egypt with
Egypt, and they shall fight a man against his brother, and a man

against his companion, city against city, and kingdom against kingdom" (xix. 2). By Egypt here is signified the natural man separate from the spiritual, which, inasmuch as he is in no light of truth, disputes continually concerning good and evil, and concerning truth and the false, and that disputation is signified by, I will commix Egypt with Egypt, and they shall fight a man against his brother, and a man against his companion; by brother and companion is signified good from which is truth, and truth from good, and in the opposite sense, evil from which is the false, and the false from evil; wherefore it is also said, city against city, and kingdom against kingdom, city denoting doctrine, and kingdom the church from it, which, in like manner, were about to combat with each other. Again: "They shall help a man his companion, and shall say to his brother, be of good courage" (xli. 6). Similar things are here signified by companion and brother as were explained above. And in Jeremiah: "Take ye heed a man of his companion, and confide not upon any brother; for every brother supplanteth, and every companion calumniates" (ix. 3); again : "I will disperse them, a man with his brother" (xiii. 14); again: "Thus shall ye say a man to his companion, and a man to his brother, what doth Jehovah answer" (xxiii. 25); again: "Ye have not obeyed Me, by proclaiming liberty a man to his brother, and a man to his companion" (xxxiv. 9, 17); and in Ezekiel : "The sword of a man shall be against his brother" (xxxviii. 24); and in Joel : "They shall not drive forward a man his brother" (ii. 8); and in Micah : "They all lie in wait for bloods, they hunt a man his brother in a net" (vii. 2); and in Zechariah : "Show mercy and compassion every one to his brother" (vii. 9); and in Malachi : "Wherefore do we act perfidiously a man against his brother" (ii. 10); and in Moses : "There was a thick darkness of darkness over all the land of Egypt, a man saw not his brother" (Exod. x. 23); again : "At the end of seven years every creditor shall withhold his hand for what he hath credited his companion, neither shall he urge his companion, nor his brother" (Deut. xv. 1, 2); and elsewhere. In the proximate sense by man [vir] is understood every one, and by brother he who is of the same tribe, because in kindred, and by companion he who is of another tribe, because only in affinity; but in the spiritual sense by man [vir] is signified every one who is in truths, and, in the opposite sense, who is in falses; by brother is signified every one who is in the good of charity, and, abstractedly, that good itself; and by companion, every one principled in truth from that good, and, abstractedly, that truth itself; and, in the opposite sense, they signify the evil opposite to the good of charity, and the false opposite to the truth from that good; the reason why mention is made of brother and companion, is, because there are two things which constitute the church, viz. charity and faith, as there are two constituents of the life of man, will and understanding; hence also there are in man two parts which act as one, as the two eyes, two ears, two nostrils, two hands and feet, two lobes of the lungs, two chambers or ventricles of the heart, two hemispheres of the brain, and so on, of which one has reference to good from which is truth, and the other to truth from good; hence it is that it is said, brother and companion, and that brother signifies good, and companion the truth thereof. III. That the Lord calleth those of His church brethren, who are in the good of charity, appears from the following passages: "Jesus stretching out His hand over His disciples, said, behold My mother and My brethren; whosoever doth the will of My father, he is My brother and sister and mother" (Matt. xii. 49; Mark iii. 33, 34, 35). By the disciples over whom the Lord stretched out His hand are signified all who are of His church; by His brethren are signified those who are in the good of charity from Him; by sisters, those who are in truth from that good; and by mother is signified the church from them. And in Matthew: "Jesus said to Mary Magdalen, and the other Mary, be not afraid, go ye, tell My brethren to go into Galilee, and there they shall see Me" (xxviii. 10); where also by brethren are meant the disciples, by whom are signified all of the church, who are in the good of charity. And in John: "Jesus said to Mary, go to My brethren, and say to them, I ascend to My Father" (xx. 17). Here likewise the disciples are called brethren, because by the disciples, equally as by brethren, are signified all who are of His church in the good of charity. And in Matthew: "The king answering will say unto them, I say unto you, inasmuch as ye have done it to one of the least of these My brethren, ye have done it unto Me" (xxv. 40): that they who perform good works of charity are here called by the Lord brethren, appears from the words preceding; it is however to be observed, that the Lord, although He is their Father, still calls them brethren, but He is their Father from the divine love, but brother from the divine [principle] which proceeds from Him; the reason is, because all in the heavens are receptions of the divine [principle] which proceeds from Him, and the divine [principle] which proceeds from the Lord, of which they are receptions, is the Lord in heaven and also in the church; and this is not of angel or of man, but of the Lord with them, wherefore the good of charity itself with them, which is the Lord's own, He calls brother, consequently also angels and men, inasmuch as they are the recipient subjects of that good; in a word, the divine proceeding, which is the divine [principle] of the Lord in the heavens, is the divine [principle] born from the Lord in heaven, wherefore, from that divine [principle], that angels, who are recipients thereof, are called Sons of God, and inasmuch as these, by virtue of the divine [principle] received in themselves, are brethren, it is the Lord in them who says brother, for the angels do not speak from themselves, but from the Lord, whilst they speak from the good of charity, and hence it is that the Lord says, inasmuch as ye have done it to one of the least of these, My brethren, ye have done it unto Me; the goods of charity, therefore, which are enumerated in the verses preceding, are what, in the spiritual sense, are the brethren of the Lord, and which, for the reason before mentioned, are called by the Lord brethren; by the king, also, who thus calls them, is signified the divine proceeding, which in one word is called divine truth or the divine spiritual [principle], which in its essence is the good of charity. It is, therefore, to be well attended to, that the Lord did not call 'them brethren from the circumstance of His being a man like them, according to the opinion received in the Christian world ; and hence it follows, that it is not on this account allowable for any man to call the Lord brother, for he is God also as to the human principle and God is not a brother, but a Father ; the reason why the Lord is called brother in the church on earth, is, because they have conceived no other idea of His human [principle] than as of the human [principle] of another man, when notwithstanding, the human [principle] of the Lord is divine. Inasmuch as kings formerly represented the Lord as to divine truth, and the divine truth, received by the angels in the spiritual kingdom of the Lord, is the same with divine good spiritual, and good spiritual is the good of charity, therefore also the kings appointed over the sons of Israel called their subjects brethren, although it was not lawful, on the other hand, for the subjects to call their king brother, much less is it lawful thus to call the Lord, who is King of kings and Lord of lords ; thus it is written in David : "I will declare Thy name to my brethren, in the midst of the congregation will I praise thee" (Psalm xxii. 23) ; again : " I am become an alien to my brethren, and a stranger to the sons of my mother" (Psalm lxix. 9) ; again : " For my brethren and companions' sake, I will speak peace unto thee" (Psalm cxxii. 8). David spake these things as concerning himself, but still by David, in the representative spiritual sense, is there understood the Lord. And in Moses : " Thou shalt set over them a king from the midst of thy brethren, thou canst not set over them a man a stranger, who is not thy brother ; but let him not lift up his heart above his brethren" (Deut. xvii. 15, 20). By the brethren from whom he should set a king over them, are signified all who are of the church, for it is said thou canst not set over them a man a stranger, a stranger signifying one who is not of the church. Again : " Jehovah thy God shall raise up to thee a prophet out of the midst of thee, of thy brethren, like unto me, him shall ye obey" (Deut. xviii. 15, 18). This is a prophecy concerning the Lord, who is understood by the prophet whom Jehovah God shall raise up of the brethren ; it is said, of thy brethren, that is, of the brethren of Moses, because by Moses, in the representative sense, is understood the Lord as to the Word, and by a prophet, one who teaches the Word, thus also the Word and doctrine from the Word, and hence it is said, like unto Me : that Moses represented the Lord as to the law, thus as to the Word, may be seen in the A. C. n. 4859, 5922, 6723, 6752, 6771, 6827, 7010, 7014, 7089, 7382, 9372, 10,234. IV. That all those are called brethren by the Lord, who acknowledge Him, and are in the good of charity from Him, follows from this consideration, that the Lord is the Father of all and the teacher of all, and from Him, as a Father, is all the good of charity, and from Him as a teacher, all the truth of that good ; wherefore the Lord says in Matthew : " Be not ye willing to be called teacher, for one is your teacher, Christ, but all ye are brethren. And call no one your father

upon earth, for one is your father who is in the heavens" (xxiii.
8, 9). From hence it manifestly appears that the words of the Lord
are to be spiritually understood; for who that is a teacher might not
be called a teacher? or what father is not called a father? but
whereas by father is signified good, and by the Father in the heavens the divine good, and whereas by teacher or Rabbi, is signified
truth, and by the teacher Christ, the divine truth, therefore, on account of the spiritual sense in all things of the Word, it is said, call
no man your father on earth, nor any one teacher, viz. in the spiritual sense, but not in the natural sense; for in the natural sense,
they may be called fathers and teachers, but representatively, viz.
that the teachers in the world do indeed teach truths, but not from
themselves but from the Lord, and that fathers in the world are indeed good, and lead their children to good, but not of themselves,
but from the Lord; hence it follows, that although they are called
teachers and fathers, still they are not teachers and fathers, but the
Lord alone; to call also and to call by a name, signifies, in the
Word, to acknowledge the quality of any one: inasmuch as all in
heaven and in the church are disciples and sons of the Lord as a
teacher and as a father, therefore the Lord says, all ye are brethren;
for the Lord calls all in heaven and in the church sons and heirs,
from their consociation by love from Him, and thence by mutual
love which is charity; hence it is that they are called by the Lord
brethren; thus is to be understood what is usually said that all are
brethren in the Lord. From these considerations also it may appear, who they are that are meant by the Lord by brethren, namely,
all who acknowledge Him, and are in the good of charity from Him,
consequently who are of His church. These also are understood by
brethren in the following passages: "Jesus said unto Peter, thou
when thou shalt be converted, confirm thy brethren" (Luke xxii.
32). By brethren here are not understood the Jews, but all those
who acknowledge the Lord, and are in good from charity and faith,
thus all who should receive the gospel by Peter, as well Jews as
gentiles, for by Peter, in the Word of the evangelists, is understood
truth from good, consequently also, faith from charity; but there by
Peter is understood faith separate from charity, for just before it is
said concerning him, "Simon, lo Satan has earnestly desired you,
that he might sift you as wheat, but I have prayed for thee, that thy
faith fail not;" and afterwards it is said to him, "I say unto thee,
Peter, the cock shall not crow this day before thou hast thrice denied that thou knowest Me:" such also is faith without charity; but
by Peter converted is signified truth from good, which is from the
Lord, or faith from charity, which is from the Lord; therefore it is
said, thou, when thou art converted, confirm thy brethren. And in
Matthew: "Peter said, Lord, how oft shall my brother sin against
me, and I forgive him" (xviii. 21); and again: "So also will my
heavenly Father do to you, if ye forgive not ever one his brother
from your hearts their trespasses" (xviii. 35); and again: "If thy
brother hath sinned against thee, go and reprove him, between him
and thee alone; if he hear thee, thou hast gained thy brother"

(xviii. 15). In this passage by brother is understood the neighbor in general, thus every man, but especially those who are in the good of charity and thence in faith from the Lord, whoever they may be; for the subject treated of in those passages is concerning the good of charity, for forgiveness is of charity, and it is likewise said, if he hear, thou hast gained thy brother, by which is signified, if he acknowledge his trespasses, and be converted. Again, in Matthew: "Why discernest thou the mote which is in thy brother's eye, but observest not the beam which is in thine own eye? or how wilt thou say to thy brother, let me cast out the mote out of thine eye, when yet there is a beam in thine own eye? thou hypocrite, cast out first the beam out of thine own eye, and then shalt thou see clearly to cast out the mote out of thy brother's eye" (vii. 3, 4, 5). Here also the term brother is used, because the subject treated of is concerning charity, for by casting out the mote out of a brother's eye, is signified to inform concerning what is false and evil, and to reform: the reason why it is said by the Lord, a mote out of thy brother's eye, and a beam out of thine own eye, is on account of the spiritual sense contained in singular the things which the Lord spake, for, without that sense, what could be meant by seeing a mote in the eye of another, and not observing a beam in his own, also by casting a beam out of his own eye, before he casts a mote out of the eye of another? for by the mote is signified a slight false of evil, and by the beam a great false of evil, and by the eye is signified the understanding and also faith; the reason why the mote and the beam signify the false of evil, is, because by wood is signified good, and thence by beam the truth, of good, and, in the opposite sense, the false of evil, and by the eye is signified the understanding and faith; hence it is evident what is signified by seeing the mote and the beam, and by casting them out of the eye; that wood signifies good, and, in the opposite sense, evil, may be seen in the A. C. n. 643, 3720, 4943, 8354, 8740; and that the eye signifies the understanding, and also faith, n. 2701, 4403–4421, 4523–4534, 9051, 10,569, and also above, n. 37, 152; mention is made of a beam also in some other passages, where it signifies the false of evil, as in Gen. xix. 8; 2 Kings vi. 2, 5, 6; Habak. ii. 11; Cant. i. 17. Again, in Matthew: "He who doeth and teacheth, shall be called great in the kingdom of the heavens: I say unto you, unless your justice shall exceed the justice of the scribes and Pharisees, ye shall not enter into the kingdom of the heavens: ye have heard that it was said to them of old time, thou shalt not kill, but whosoever shall kill shall be liable to the judgment; but I say unto you that whosoever is angry with his brother rashly shall be in danger of the judgment; but whosoever shall say to his brother, raca, shall be in danger of the council; but whosoever shall say, thou fool, shall be in danger of hell fire. If thou offer thy gift upon the altar, and there remember that thy brother hath ought against thee, leave there thy gift before the altar, and go thy way, first be reconciled to thy brother, and then come and offer thy gift" (v. 19–24); in the whole of that chapter the subject treated of is concerning the interior life of man, which is of his soul, consequently of his will

and thought thence derived, thus concerning the life of charity,
which is the spiritual moral life: of this life the sons of Jacob were
altogether ignorant, by reason that they still continued from their
fathers to be external men; on this account also they were kept in
the observance of external worship, according to the statutes, which
were things external representing the internal things of worship and
of the church; but the Lord teaches in this chapter, that the interior
things of the church were not only to be represented by such external acts, but were also to be loved and done from the heart and soul;
wherefore that he shall be saved who from interior life teaches and
does the external things of the church, is signified by, he who teacheth and doeth shall be called great in the kingdom of the heavens:
that unless the life be internal and thence external, heaven is not in
man, and consequently he is not received in heaven, is signified by,
unless your justice shall exceed the justice of the scribes and Pharisees ye shall not enter into the kingdom of the heavens; by justice
is signified the good of life from the good of charity, and by exceeding that of the scribes and Pharisees, is signified, that the life must
be internal and not external without internal; the scribes and Pharisees were only in representative externals, and not in internals;
the external life from the internal is taught in the precept of the decalogue, thou shalt not kill, but they did not know that the desire
to kill a man is the same as to kill him, wherefore it is first said, ye
have heard that it was said to them of old time, thou shalt not kill,
and whosoever shall kill shall be liable to judgment; for an opinion
prevailed with the Jews from ancient time, that it was lawful to kill
on account of injuries done to themselves, especially the gentiles,
and that they should only be punished for it lightly or grievously
according to circumstances as to the state of the enmity, consequently
as to the body only, and not as to the soul; this is understood by
being liable to judgment; that he who without proper reason thinks
ill of his neighbor, and averts himself from the good of charity, shall
be punished lightly as to the soul, is signified by, whosoever is angry
with his brother rashly shall be liable to judgment, to be angry, denoting to think ill, for it is distinguished from saying raca, and saying thou fool; brother denoting the neighbor, and also the good of
charity, and to be liable to judgment denoting inquisition and punishment according to circumstances; that he who from ill or depraved thought heaps abuse on his neighbor, thus who contemns the
good of charity as vile, shall be grievously punished, is signified by,
whoever shall say to his brother, raca, shall be liable to the council,
for by saying raca is signified from ill or depraved thought to treat
with contumely the neighbor, thus, to account the good of charity
vile, to say raca denoting to account as nothing or vile, and brother
denoting the good of charity; that he who hates his neighbor, thus
who is altogether averse to the good of charity, is condemned to hell,
is signified by, whoever shall say, thou fool, shall be liable to hell
fire, to say thou fool denoting entire aversion, brother denoting the
good of charity, and hell fire denoting the hell where they are who
hate that good and thence their neighbor: there are three degrees of

hatred here described, the first is of an ill thought, which is to be angry, the second is of an ill intention thence derived, which is to say raca, and the third is of an ill will, which is to say thou fool, all these are degrees of hatred against the good of charity, for hatred is opposite to this good; and the three degrees of punishment are signified by the judgment, the council, and the gehenna of fire, punishments for the evils of a lighter kind being signified by the judgment, punishments for those of a more grievous kind, by the council, and for the most grievous of all, by the gehenna of fire. Forasmuch as the universal heaven is in the good of charity towards the neighbor, and the universal hell is in anger, enmity and hatred against the neighbor, and hence these are in opposition to that good; and whereas the worship of the Lord is worship from heaven, which is internal, but is no worship if anything thereof be from hell, and yet external worship without internal is from thence; therefore it is said, if thou offer thy gift upon the altar, and there remember that thy brother hath aught against thee, go thy way, first be reconciled to thy brother, and then come and offer thy gift: by the gift upon the altar is signified the worship of the Lord from love and charity, by brother is understood the neighbor, and abstractedly, the good of charity, and by having aught against thee, is signified anger, enmity, or hatred, and by being reconciled, is signified the dissipation thereof, and consequent conjunction by love. From these considerations it may appear, that by brother is understood by the Lord the same as by neighbor, and by neighbor, in the spiritual sense, is signified good in every complex, and good in every complex is the good of charity. The same is understood by brother in many passages in the Old Testament, in the spiritual sense; as in Moses, " Thou shalt not hate thy brother in thy heart" (Levit. xix. 17): and in David : " Behold how good and pleasant it is for brethren to dwell together in unity" (Psalm cxxxiii. 1). In this sense also, " Lot called the inhabitants of Sodom, brethren" (Gen. xix. 7): and it is also understood by " the covenant of brethren between the sons of Israel and Edom" (Amos i. 9): and by "the brotherhood between Judah and Israel" (Zech. xi. 4). For by the sons of Israel and Edom, likewise by Judah and Israel, in the spiritual sense, are not understood Israel and Edom and Judah, but the goods and truths of heaven and the church, which are all conjoined with each other.

747. " That accuseth them before God days and nights"—That hereby is signified, and reproved them and disputed with them from the Word continually, appears from the signification of accusing, as denoting to assault, concerning which see above, n. 746; whence it follows, that it also denotes to reprove and to dispute with, for he who accuses also disputes and reproaches; and from the signification of before God, as denoting from the Word, concerning which we shall speak presently; and from the signification of days and nights, as denoting continually and without intermission; for by days and nights are signified all states of the life, by day the state of the life when the mind is in a clear idea, and by night when the mind is in an obscure idea; the reason why by

these two states of life is signified continually, is, because, in the
spiritual world, there is not any distinction of times into years,
months, weeks, days, and hours, but instead thereof are changes of
state, for there angels and spirits are sometimes in a clear idea, and
sometimes in an obscure idea; that angels and spirits are alternately
in a state of clear perception, and in a state of obscure perception,
may be seen in the work concerning H. & H. n. 154–161: but in
particular their states succeed each other variously, as from one
affection into another, and it is these states from which angels and
spirits number their times, and which are thus in the place of such
times as are in the world, which are years, months, weeks, days,
nights, and hours; inasmuch now as their states of life in general
are changed as to the clearness or obscurity of the intellect, and thus
are in a continual succession, hence by days and nights is signified
continually. The reason why to accuse before God signifies to
rebuke and dispute from the Word, is, because they who are meant
by the dragon, or who separate faith from life, argue and dispute
from the Word, and to dispute from the Word is to dispute before
God, for God is in the Word, inasmuch as the Word is from God,
and is divine truth proceeding from the Lord; hence it is said in
John, "In the beginning was the Word, and the Word was with
God, and God was the Word" (i. 1). The reason why they dispute
for faith separate from the life of charity, is, because they confirm
their heresy from certain passages in the Word understood only according to the letter, and when they have thus confirmed it, they
believe it to be the essential truth of the church although it is false.
In general by accusing days and nights is signified the continual
influx of the false from those who are understood by the dragon, and
whereas their falses are from the Word falsified, hence this is signified by accusing before God.

748. "And they conquered him through the blood of the Lamb"—
That hereby is signified resistance and victory through divine truth
proceeding from the Divine Human [principle] of the Lord, appears
from the signification of blood, when predicated of the Lord, as denoting the divine truth proceeding from Him, concerning which see
above, n. 328, 329; and from the signification of the Lamb, as denoting the Lord as to the Divine Human [principle], concerning
which also see above n. 314; from which it must appear, that by
conquering the dragon through the blood of the Lamb, is signified
to conquer him, that is, those who are signified by the dragon and
his angels, by divine truth proceeding from the Divine Human [prin-
ciple] of the Lord. It is said, the divine truth proceeding from the
Divine Human [principle] of the Lord, by reason that all divine
truth which fills the heavens, and constitutes the wisdom of the angels in the heavens, thence proceeds; for the Divine Human [prin-
ciple] of the Lord is united with the Divine [principle] itself,
which was in him from conception, so that they are one; the
Divine [principle] itself, which was in him from conception,
is what He called Father, and this is united with His Human
[principle] as soul and body are united; hence it is that the Lord

says that He is one with the Father (John x. 30, 38); and that He is in the Father and the Father in Him (John xiv. 7–11); and whereas there is such a union, therefore the divine truth, after the glorification of His Human [principle], proceeds from His Divine Human [principle] : the divine truth proceeding from the Divine Human [principle] of the Lord, is what is called the Holy Spirit, and that this proceeds from the Human [principle] of the Lord glorified, He Himself teaches in John : " The Holy Spirit was not yet, because Jesus was not yet glorified" (vii. 39) : the Human [principle] glorified is the Divine Human [principle] : but more may be seen upon this subject in the D. of the N. J. n. 280–310; likewise in the work concerning H. & H. from beginning to end ; and that by the blood of the Lamb is understood the Divine [principle] which proceeds from the Divine Human [principle] of the Lord, may be seen above, n. 476. From these observations it may be seen how much the literal sense of the Word differs from the spiritual sense ; likewise, how the Word is falsified, if it is viewed outwardly only, and not at the same time inwardly : the difference between these senses may appear from this consideration, that by the blood of the Lamb, in the literal sense, is understood the Lord's passion of the cross, but in the spiritual sense, the divine truth proceeding from the Lord's Divine Human [principle] ; wherefore if it should be assumed for the real truth that Michael conquered the dragon by the Lord's passion of the cross, it would hence follow that the Lord thereby took away all the sins of the world, and also thereby moved His Father to compassion for mankind, when notwithstanding these ideas do not agree with divine truth, which is with the angels in heaven, nor with the genuine understanding of truth : who can ever understand that the Lord by the passion of the cross took away all the sins of the world, when notwithstanding every man's quality after death is according to what his life was in the world, and they who do evil come into hell, and they who do good into heaven? who can also understand that God the Father was moved to compassion or mercy from the blood of His Son on the cross, and that He had any need of such means, when notwithstanding He is in Himself mercy itself, love itself, and goodness itself? from these considerations it is evident, that the Word in this passage, and in a thousand others, must be falsified, if it is viewed outwardly only and not at the same time inwardly ; to view it outwardly is to view it from the letter, but to view it inwardly is to view it from the doctrine of genuine truth : if, therefore it is believed from doctrine that the Lord subjugated the hells, and at the same time glorified His Human [principle], by temptations, and that the passion of the cross was the last temptation and full victory, by which He subjugated the hells, and at the same time glorified His Human [principle], it falls under the understanding and thence into the faith, and the result is this, that it is an apparent truth that Michael conquered by the passion of the cross, but a real truth that He conquered by divine truth proceeding from the Divine Human [principle] of the Lord : but if the apparent truth be taken instead of the real truth, and confirmed, the Word is then falsified, according to what was adduced above, n. 719, by way of illustration.

749. " And by the word of their testimony"—That hereby is
signified, and by the confession and acknowledgment of the Divine
[principle] in His Human, appears from the signification of the word
of testimony, as denoting the confession of the Lord, and the acknowledgment of the Divine [principle] in His Human, concerning which
see above, n. 392, 635, 649 : that this is the word of testimony, is
evident from the following passages in the Apocalypse : " The angel
said unto John, I am thy fellow-servant, and of thy brethren who
have the testimony of Jesus : adore God, for the testimony of Jesus
is the spirit of prophecy" (xix. 10) : and after the angel had so said,
there appeared a white horse, and one sitting thereon, who was
called the Word of God, likewise King of kings and Lord of lords,
verses 13, 16 : hence it may appear, that by the word of their testimony is signified the confession and acknowledgment of the Divine
[principle] in the Human of the Lord : they who are in that acknowledgment are also in the acknowledgment that the Human [princi-
ple] of the Lord is Divine, for the Essential Divine [principle] cannot dwell elsewhere than in the Divine [principle] which is from
itself : but whereas the learned amongst us find some difficulty in
comprehending this, therefore in their thought they separate the
Divine [principle] from the Human of the Lord, and place the Divine
without or above it, which, notwithstanding, is contrary to the Christian doctrine concerning the trinity which is called the Athanasian
or Nicene confession, wherein it is taught, that the Divine [princi-
ple] assumed to itself the Human, and that they are not two but a
united person, altogether as soul and body.

750. " And they loved not their soul even to death"—That hereby
are signified the faithful who on account of those truths suffered
temptations, and made no account of the life of the world compared
with the life of heaven, appears from the signification of not loving
the soul, as denoting to make light of the life of the world in comparison with the life of heaven, concerning which we shall speak
presently ; and from the signification of even to death, as denoting
to suffer temptations : for they who are in combats of temptations,
make no account of the life of the world compared with the life of
heaven, nor, consequently, of the death of the body compared with
the life of the soul, as may appear from those who suffered martyr-
dom ; the reason is, because they know that the life in the world,
which is only for some years, is nothing respectively to the life in
heaven, which is eternal life, neither indeed is there any proportion
given between the times of the life of men in the world, and the life
in heaven which endures to eternity : let any one think, whether
there can be any proportion between a hundred thousand years, and
eternity, and he will find that there is not : such considerations, with
many others, flow-in from heaven with those who suffer spiritual
temptations, wherefore they do not love their soul, that is, their life
in the world, even to death.   What is understood by the soul is but
little known in the world, by reason that the learned have delivered
various hypotheses concerning the seat thereof in the body, likewise
concerning its essence, and also its influx and operation in the body ;

and from the ideas thence conceived concerning its immortality; hence it has come to be believed, that the soul has a sort of cogitative principle, ethereal in its essence, and that, when separated from the body, it is without organs of motion and of sense, such as it enjoyed in the world, until it is again conjoined to the body, which they say will take place at the time of the last judgment: inasmuch as an incongruous idea is hence conceived in the learned world concerning the soul of man, it is of importance to illustrate, from the Word, what is understood by the soul. By the soul, in general, is understood man, and, specifically, the life of man; and whereas in every man there are three degrees of life, there are also as many degrees of the soul. But whereas all the life of man resides in his two faculties, which are called will and understanding, whence sometimes, in the Word, they are called lives, in the plural, and whereas by the soul is understood the life, it follows, that there is a soul of the will, and a soul of the understanding, and that the soul of the will is the affection which is of love, and the soul of the understanding is the thought thence derived. But by soul, in the Word, is properly understood the life of the understanding of man, which is thought, and by the heart is understood the life of the will, which is affection, and whereas the respiration of the lungs corresponds to the life of the understanding which is thought, and the pulse of the heart corresponds to the life of the will which is affection, therefore by the soul, in the lowest natural sense, is understood the life of respiration; hence it is usual to say of those who are about to die, that they emit the soul or spirit, likewise, that they have no longer animation, or that no breathing from the mouth is sensibly perceived. That such things are meant by soul in the Word, may appear from the passages where it is mentioned, which shall now be adduced. I. That soul in general signifies man, appears from the following passages: thus in Moses: "Abram took every soul which they had gained in Haran, and they departed into the land of Canaan" (Gen. xii. 4): "The king of Sodom said unto Abraham, give me the souls and take the substance to thyself" (Gen. xiv. 21): "All the souls of the sons and daughters of Leah, were thirty and three" (Gen. xlvi. 15): "The sons of Joseph were two souls, every soul of the house of Jacob which came into Egypt, seventy" (Gen. xlvi. 27): "Every soul which hath eaten of a carcase, or what is torn, shall be unclean until the evening" (Levit. xvii. 15): "Thou shalt not keep any soul alive of the cities of the people" (Deut. xx. 16): "If a man steal the soul of his brethren, and make gain thereof" (Deut. xxiv. 6): "The soul which shall eat the fat and the blood shall be cut off" (Lev. vii. 27): "The soul which is not circumcised shall be cut off from the people" (Lev. xvii. 15): besides other passages in which soul signifies man. II. That the soul specifically signifies the life of the body, appears from these passages: thus in Luke: "The rich man thought with himself I will say to my soul, soul thou hast many goods laid up for many years, take thine ease, eat, drink, and be merry: but God said to him, thou unwise one, this night shall thy soul be required of thee" (xii. 19, 20): and in Moses:

"When the soul of Rachel was departing, she called his name Be-
noni" (Gen. xxxiv. 18): "All the men are dead which sought thy
soul" (Exod. iv. 19): "By the hand of them that seek thy soul"
(Jer. xix. 7, 9; chap. xxiv. 21): "He who departeth to the Chaldeans, shall live, and his soul shall be to him for spoil" (Jerem.
xxi. 9): "I will give thy soul for a prey" (Jerem. xlv. 5): ·
"Is this the fast which I choose, a day for a man to afflict his
soul" (Isaiah lviii. 5): "Reuben said to his brethren concerning
Joseph, let us not smite him in the soul" (Gen. xxxvii. 21): "Soul
for soul, eye for eye, tooth for tooth" (Deut. xix. 21): "Thou shalt
not take the upper or nether mill stone for a pledge, for he receiveth
the soul for a pledge" (Deut. xxiv. 6): "Samson said, let my soul
die with with the Philistines" (Judges xvi. 30): "Jezabel said to
Elias, that to-morrow she would make his soul as the soul of one of
them : and Elias departed for his soul" (1 Kings xix. 2, 3): "Peter
said, I will lay down my soul for Thee : Jesus answered, wilt thou
lay down thy soul for Me? verily I say, the cock shall not crow
until thou hast denied Me thrice" (John xiii. 37, 38): in those passages soul signifies the life of the body; as likewise where the Lord
speaks concerning the life of His body : "As the Son of Man came
not to be ministered unto, but to minister, and to give His soul a redemption for many" (Matt. xx. 28; Mark x. 45): "Behold I love
thee, therefore I will give man for thee, and people for thy soul"
(Isaiah xliii. 4): "Jesus said, greater love than this hath no man,
that a man lay down his soul for his friends" (John xv. 13): Jesus
said, I am the good shepherd, the good shepherd layeth down his
soul for the sheep. I lay down My soul, and I will take it again,
no man taketh it from Me, but I lay it down of Myself; I have
power to lay it down, and I have power to take it again" (John x.
11, 12, 15, 17, 18). III. That the soul signifies the life of the spirit
of man, which is called his spiritual life, appears from the following
passages : thus in the Evangelists : "Jesus said, fear not them who
can kill the body, but cannot kill the soul: rather fear Him who
can destroy both soul and body in hell" (Matt. x. 28; Luke xii. 4, 5):
"Whosoever would find his soul, shall lose it; and whosoever would
lose his soul for My sake, shall find it" (Matt. x. 39; Luke xvii.
33): "He who loveth his soul shall lose it,-but he who hateth his
soul in this world, shall keep it-to the life eternal" (John xii. 25):
"Jesus said, whosoever wilt come after Me, let him deny himself,
take up his cross, and follow me : he who desireth to keep his soul
shall lose it, but he who would lose it for My sake shall find it :
what will it profit a man, if he should gain the whole world, but lose
his soul; or what will a man give a sufficient price for the redemption of his soul" (Matt. xvi. 24, 25; Mark viii. 35, 36, 37; Luke
ix. 24, 25): "Jesus said, I came not to destroy souls, but to save
them" (Luke ix. 56): Mary said unto Elizabeth, "My soul doth
magnify the Lord" (Luke i. 46): "Simeon said unto Mary, concerning the infant Jesus, a dagger shall also pierce through thine own
soul, that the thoughts of many hearts may be revealed" (Luke ii.
35): "Jesus said, concerning the last times, in patience possess ye
your souls" (Luke xxi. 39): "The foundations have been bruised.

all are making gain with the deep parts of the soul" (Isaiah xix. 9, 10) : " With the danger of our souls we bring our bread, by reason of the sword of the wilderness" (Lament. v. 9) : " They have digged a pit for my soul" (Jerem. xviii. 20): " Their soul become as a watered garden" (Jerem. xxxi. 12) : " I will water the wearied soul, and every soul which grieveth I will fill" (Jer. xxxi. 25) : " Woe to them that sew pillows under all the arm pits of My hands, and that make kerchiefs upon the head of every stature, to hunt souls; will ye hunt the souls of My people, that ye may make souls alive to you ; thou hast profaned Me with My people, to slay the souls which ought not to die, and to vivify the souls which ought not to live" (Ezek. xiii. 18, 19): " Behold all souls are Mine, as the soul of the father, so the soul of the son, they are Mine; the soul which sinneth, it shall die" (Ezek. xviii. 4, 20): "I will go softly for the bitterness of my soul" (Isaiah xxxviii. 15) : " The waters compassed me about even to the soul" (Jonah ii. 6): " The waters came even unto the soul, I am sunk in deep mire" (Psalm lxix. 2): " They afflicted my foot with fetters, my soul came to the earth" (Psalm cv. 18): " Bring my soul out of prison" (Psalm cxlii. 8) : " Thou hast delivered my soul from death" (Psalm lvi. 14): " To rescue their soul from death, and to make them alive in famine" (Psalm xxxiii. 19): "Deliver me not to the soul of mine enemies" (Psalm xxvii. 12; xli. 3): "I afflicted my soul with hunger, lest they should say in their hearts, alas for his soul" (Psalm xxxv. 13, 25): " Thou wilt not leave my soul in hell, nor wilt thou give thine Holy one to see corruption" (Psalm xvi. 10): " The man who feareth Jehovah, he shall teach him the way which he shall choose, his soul shall pass the night in good" (Psalm xxv. 12, 13): " He that hath clean hands and a pure heart, who hath not lifted up his soul to vanity" (Psalm xxiv. 4): " He will keep the souls of the needy, He will redeem their soul from deceit and violence" (Psalm lxxii. 13, 14): " Bless Jehovah, O my soul" (Psalm ciii. 1, 22): "Let every soul praise Jah" (Psalm cl. 6): " They shall ask food for their soul" (Psalm lxxviii. 18): "Jehovah breathed into the nostrils of man the breath of lives, and man became a living soul" (Gen. ii. 7): in these passages soul is used to denote the life of the spirit of man, which is called his spiritual life. IV. Forasmuch as man has two faculties of life, viz. the faculty of understanding and the faculty of willing, and both these faculties constitute the spiritual life of man, it may appear from some of the passages above adduced, and likewise from the following, that the soul signifies that faculty which is called the life of the understanding of man : as in Moses : " Thou shalt love Jehovah God from thy whole heart, from thy whole soul, and from all thy strength" (Deut. vi. 5; chap. x. 12; chap. xi. 13; chap. xxvi. 16); and in the Evangelists : "Jesus said, thou shalt love the Lord thy God from thy whole heart, and from thy whole soul, and from thy whole mind" (Matt. xxii. 35; Mark xii. 33, 38; Luke x. 27). By loving Jehovah God with the whole heart and with the whole soul, is understood, with all the will and all the understanding, likewise, with all the love and all the faith, for the heart signifies the love and the will, and the soul signifies the faith and the understanding; the reason why the two former are signified by the heart, is, because the love of man is of his will; and the reason why the two latter are signified by the soul, is, because faith is of the understanding: this signification of the heart and the soul, is derived from correspondence; for the heart of man corresponds to the good of love, which is of his will, and the soul, or breath of the lungs, corresponds to the truth of faith, which is of the understanding : with all the strength and all the mind, signifies above all things. And in Ezekiel: "Their silver and their gold shall not be able to deliver them in the day of the anger of Jehovah, they shall not saturate their soul, neither shall they fill their bowels" (vii.19): here also the soul is put for the understanding of truth, which is said not to be saturated when there is no truth in the church, and the bowels for the will of good which are said not to be filled when there is no good in the church : inasmuch as silver, from correspondence, signifies truth, and, in the opposite sense, the false, and gold signifies good, and, in the opposite sense, evil, therefore it is said, their silver and their gold shall not be able to deliver them in the day of the anger of Jehovah, the silver and gold there denoting what is not true and what is not good, also what is false and evil, and the day of anger denoting the day of judgment. And in Isaiah : "The light of Israel shall be for a fire, and his Holy One for a flame, which shall set on fire and devour the glory of his forest and Carmel, it shall consume from the soul even to the flesh" (x. 17, 18). By the light of Israel and by His Holy One, which shall be for a fire and a flame, is understood the Lord as to the last judgment; by the fire and flame is signified the destruction of those who are in falses of evil : by the glory of the forest and Carmel, which the fire and flame shall devour and consume, is signified the truth and good of truth appertaining to the church, which, being turned into falses and evils of the false, will be destroyed; from the soul even to the flesh, signifies even from the understanding thereof to the will thereof, the soul denoting the understanding of truth, and flesh the will of good. Again: "The fool speaketh foolishness, to make empty the soul of the hungry, and he will cause the drink of the thirsty to fail" (xxxii. 6). Here also by the soul is signified man as to the understanding of good and truth, by the soul of the hungry the understanding of good, and by the drink of the thirsty the understanding of truth; that the man who is in falses of evil will endeavor to deprive thereof him who is in truth from good, is signified by, the fool speaketh foolishness, to make empty the soul, and to cause it to fail. Again: "It shall be as when a hungry man dreameth, as if he were eating, but when he awaketh, his soul is fasting ; and when a thirsty man dreameth, as if he were drinking, but when he waketh, behold he is faint, and his soul hath appetite; so shall be the multitude of all nations that fight against mount Zion" (xxix. 8). These things are said concerning those who are in falses from evil, and yet suppose them to be truths from good ; the falses from evil combating against the goods of the church, are signified by the multitude of all nations fighting against Mount Zion, multitude being predicated of truths, nations signifying evils, and Mount Zion the church as to the good of love; the belief that evils are good, when notwithstanding they are evils of the false, is signified by, it shall be as when a hungry man dreameth, as if he were eating, but when he awaketh, his soul is fasting: the hungry dreaming as if he were eating, signifies the opinion and erroneous faith concerning good, to dream, denoting such opinion and erroneous faith, and to be hungry, and as if he were eating, denoting as it were a desire for good and to be nourished thereby; but when he awaketh, signifies, when it is discovered what good is; his soul is fasting, signifies, that there is no understanding of good: similar things are said concerning truth, which are signified by, "when the thirsty man dreameth, as if he were drinking, but when he awaketh, behold he is faint, and his soul hath appetite;" to be thirsty and as if he were drinking whilst he dreameth, signifying the opinion and faith as it were of truth; but when he awaketh behold he is faint, and his soul hath appetite, signifies, that still it is not truth but the false, the soul there signifying the faith of the false, by reason of truth not being understood, for both evil and the false, as well as good and truth, are predicated of faith and understanding, when they are of the thought alone; for man can think so as it were to understand and thence believe that evil is good, as well as that the false is true; such are all those who are in falses of doctrine, and have faith only in their masters and books, and never think whether what they are taught may not be falses and evils, but believe them to be truths and goods because they can be confirmed, not knowing that false and evil may be equally confirmed as truth and good. Again, in the same prophet: "If thou press out thy soul to the hungry, and saturate the afflicted soul, thy light shall arise in darkness, and thy thick darkness be as the noon day" (lviii. 10). To press out the soul to the hungry, and to saturate the afflicted soul, signifies, to teach him what is good and what is true who desires it; by the hungry are signified those who desire good, and by the afflicted those who desire truth, and by pressing out the soul to them is signified to teach them good and truth, thus from the understanding doctrine and faith; that to those who are in ignorance, but still in the desire of truth and good, shall be given the understanding thereof, is signified by, thy light shall arise in darkness, and thy thick darkness be as the noonday; darkness and thick darkness denoting ignorance of truth and good, and the light and the noon day denoting the understanding thereof. And in Lamentations: "All the people sigh, they seek bread, they have given their desirable things for food to recreate their soul. He is far from me that comforteth, that recreateth my soul, my sons are become devastated, in that the enemy hath prevailed. My priests and my elders have expired in the city, because they sought food for themselves with which they might recreate their soul" (i. 11, 16, 19). These things are said concerning the church in which there is no more any truth and good of doctrine, whence the men thereof who are desirous of those things faint; the defect of good and truth in doctrine, and the desire for them to nourish the life of faith and of the understanding, is signified by, all the people sigh, they seek bread, they have given their desirable things for food to recreate their scul ; the defect or want is signified by their sighing, the desire for good by seeking bread, the desire for truth by giving their desirable things for food, and for the nourishment of faith and understanding, is signified by to recreate their soul; that there is not any nourishment of faith and understanding, because there are no longer truths by reason of evils of the life, is signified by, He is far from me that comforteth, that recreateth my soul, my sons are become devasted in that the enemy hath prevailed, the sons being devastated signifies truths being no more, and the enemy who hath prevailed signifies evil from hell, thus evil of the life ; that there are no longer any who teach good and truth, is signified by, my priests and my elders have expired in the city, the priests signifying those who teach good, and the elders those who teach truths, and the city signifying doctrine, and to expire denoting that they are no more ; there being no spiritual nourishment for them is signified by, when they sought food for themselves wherewith they might recreate their souls.   Again, in Lamentations : "They say to their mothers, where is the corn and the wine ? when they faint as the slain in the streets of the city, when their soul is poured out upon the bosom of their mothers" (ii. 12).   By these words are signified similar things as above, viz. that such is the desolation of the church from the defect of good and truth in doctrine, that the spiritual life therein faints and perishes: by mothers are signified the truths of the church ; by saying to them, where is the corn and the wine, is signified, where is now the good of doctrine and the truth thereof; by pouring out their soul upon the bosom of their mothers, is signified the fainting and perishing of spiritual life by reason of the desolation arising from the defect and want of truths; whereas by the soul is understood the life of faith, and the understanding of good and truth, which is the spiritual life of man, it is said that they faint as the slain in the street of the city, the slain denoting those who perish by falses, and the street of the city denoting the truth of doctrine.   And in Jonah : "When my soul fainted over me" (ii. 8).   Where the subject treated of is concerning temptations ; and by his soul fainting over him is signified the fainting of truth in faith and understanding.   And in David: "Mine eye is consumed by reason of indignity, my soul and my belly" (Psalm xxxi. 10) ; and again : "My soul is bowed down to the dust, my belly cleaveth to the earth" (Psalm xliv. 26).   By these words also is described a state of temptations : by the eye is signified the understanding, by the soul, the faith and understanding of truth, and by the belly, the faith and understanding of good : the reason why this is signified by the belly, is, because the belly receives the food, and by food and bread is signified good which nourishes, in the present case the understanding and faith ; the defect thereof in temptations is signified by consuming for indignity, bowing down to the dust, and cleaving to the earth.   And in Moses : "They said, now is our soul dry, there is nothing but this manna before our eyes" (Numb. xi. 6).   Inasmuch as by manna is signified spiritual nourishment, it also denotes the faith and understanding, or intelligence, of man, which are spiritually nourished; and whereas the sons of Israel were without natural nourishment, which yet they desired, therefore they said, our soul is dry, there is nothing else but manna before our eyes; by the soul being dry, is signified the life of faith and of the understanding fainting when there was not natural nourishment at the same time; by there is nothing else but manna before our eyes, is signified, that there was only spiritual nourishment; and because they loathed this, the flesh of quails or selav was given to them, by which is signified natural nourishment. And in Samuel: "Hannah said unto Eli, I have poured out my soul before Jehovah" (i. 15); where by pouring out the soul before Jehovah, is signified to press out or express the thoughts of her mind and heart. And in the Evangelists also it is written, "Be ye not solicitous for your soul, what ye shall eat, and what ye shall drink, nor for your body, what ye shall put on; is not the soul more than meat, and the body more than raiment?" (Matt. vi. 25; Luke xii. 22, 23.) These words, although they are spoken of the life of the body, still signify such things as are of the life of the spirit, for all things of the literal sense of the Word, which is natural, contain within them an internal sense, which is spiritual; in this sense by eating, drinking, and by meat, is signified spiritual nourishment, which is the nourishment of faith and therewith of the understanding, whence comes intelligence in things spiritual; hence it is said, be not ye solicitous for your soul what ye shall eat and what ye shall drink, is not the soul more than meat, to eat denoting to perceive good intellectually, thus spiritually, to drink denoting to perceive truth in the same manner, and meat denoting the good and truth from which is spiritual nourishment; by clothing the body and by raiment, is signified truth investing the good of love and of the will, raiment denoting that truth, and the body the good of love which is the good of the will. Again, in David: "O my soul, I lie in the midst of lions, the sons of men are set on fire" (Psalm lvii. 5). By the soul here also is signified the spiritual life, which is the life of faith, thus also the life of the understanding, for the understanding is formed from truths, and consists of them, as also faith; inasmuch as these things are signified by the soul, and the subject there treated of is concerning the vastation of truth, therefore it is said, I lie in the midst of lions, for by lions are there signified falses destroying the truths of the church; it is also said, the sons of men are set on fire, the sons of men signifying the truths of doctrine and of the church, which, when they are possessed from a corporeal love, and thereby perish, are said to be set on fire. Again, in Moses: "Abraham spake with the sons of Heth, if it is with your soul that I bury my dead" (Gen. xxiii. 8). Soul there signifies thought from truth; but these words are explained in the A. C. n. 2930. Again, in Jeremiah: "Thy lovers shall abhor thee, they shall seek thy soul" (iv. 30). By the lovers there mentioned are understood those who are in the love of evil: by seeking the soul is signified, to will to destroy the faith and understanding of truth by the falses of evil. And in Ezekiel: "Javan and Tubal, with the soul of man and vessels of brass they gave thy trading" (xxvii. 13); speaking of Tyre, whereby is signified the church as to the knowleges of truth and good : by trading is signified the acquisition and communication thereof: by Javan and Tubal is signified external representative worship; and by the soul of man and vessels of brass, are signified the science of truth and science of good in the natural man : the science of truth appertaining to the natural man, is also signified by souls of men" (Apoc. xviii. 13). The souls of men in these passages properly denote slaves or servants, by whom also, in the spiritual sense, are signified scientific truths of the natural man, which are things of service to the spiritual. V. Forasmuch as the life of faith, and also the life of the understanding of man, is from divine truth, therefore divine truth is also signified by soul; as in the following passages; thus in Jeremiah : "I will plant them in this land in verity, in my whole heart, and in my whole soul" (xxxii. 41). Inasmuch as there are two things which proceed from the Lord, divine good and divine truth, and these, being received by the angels of heaven and the men of the church, constitute heavenly life with them, it may thence appear what is signified by planting them in the whole heart and in the whole soul, viz. in his own divine good and divine truth, for the heart signifies the divine good of the divine love, and the soul the divine truth. Again, in the same prophet: "Jehovah sware by His soul" (li. 14; Amos vi. 8). Jehovah is said to swear by His soul, when He confirms by His divine truth, for to swear signifies to confirm, and the soul of Jehovah the divine truth. And in David : "Jehovah proveth the just; the impious, and him that loveth violence, His soul hateth" (Psalm xi. 5); where also by the soul of Jehovah is signified the divine truth, for by the violent, in the Word, is signified one who offers violence to divine truth, which being done by the falses of evil, therefore this is signified by the impious and him that loveth violence. And in Isaiah: "Mine elect in whom My soul is well pleased, I have given My spirit upon him" (xlii. 1); treating of the Lord, who is understood by the elect of Jehovah ; and whereas by the spirit of Jehovah, which was given upon Him, is signified the proceeding Divine [principle], therefore by the soul of Jehovah, which was well pleased in Him, is signified the divine truth; for in this Divine [principle] the Lord was as to His Humanity in the world. And in Jeremiah : "Jehovah said, though Moses and Samuel stood before Me, My soul [could] not [be] towards this people" (xv. 1). By Moses and Samuel, in the representative sense, is signified the Word ; and whereas the Word is divine truth, and by the people there mentioned are understood the sons of Israel, with whom there was not any divine truth but what was falsified and adulterated, it is said, My soul could not be towards this people. Again, in the same prophet: "Shall not my soul be avenged" (v. 9, 29). Here also by the soul of Jehovah is understood the divine truth, and hence, when the Lord executes judgment, it is said that His soul is avenged : the like is signified by the Son of Man coming to judgment, the Son of Man also denoting

the Lord, as to divine truth. Again : " Admit chastisement, O Jerusalem, lest my soul be disjointed from thee, and I reduce thee to
wasteness" (vi. 8). By Jerusalem is signified the church as to doctrine ; by admitting chastisement is signified to receive discipline ;
by, lest my soul be disjointed from thee, is signified, lest divine truth
should recede from them ; and by reducing to wasteness, is signified,
lest the church be desolated as to all truth. Again, in Isaiah : " Jehovah giveth soul to the people upon the earth, and spirit to them
that walk therein" (xlii. 5).   By the soul which Jehovah giveth to
the people upon the earth is signified divine truth from the Lord to
those who will be of His church.   By the spirit which Jehovah will
give to them that walk therein, is signified life according to divine
truth, to walk denoting to live. VI. Forasmuch as by soul, where
the Lord is treated of, is signified divine truth, hence spiritual life,
which is from truth, is also thereby signified ; as in Moses : " The
soul of all flesh is the blood" (Levit. xvii. 14).   Inasmuch as the ultimate life of man, which is the life of his body, consists in the blood,
therefore it is said that the soul of all flesh, that is the life thereof,
is its blood ; but whereas in every particular of the Word there is a
spiritual sense, and in that sense by blood is signified the truth of
doctrine from the Word, which is divine truth, therefore this also is
signified by the soul of all flesh ; that blood signifies the truth of doctrine from the Word, which is divine truth, may be seen above, n.
328, 329, 476 : inasmuch as this was signified by blood, therefore it
was forbidden the sons of Israel to eat blood, and therefore the blood
of the burnt-offerings and sacrifices was sprinkled about the altar,
and by blood, sanctifications and also inaugurations were performed,
likewise also by blood, the covenant of the God of Israel was entered
into, that is, of the Lord with the people ; the case is also the same
with the new covenant entered into by the Lord with the church at
this day, wherefore the blood of the Lord is called the blood of the
covenant, that is, of conjunction with the Lord, and this because the
divine truth proceeding from the Lord is what conjoins. From these
considerations it is now evident, why blood is called soul : it was
on account of this signification of blood that from the most ancient
time it was forbidden to eat blood, as may appear in Moses : " Every
creeping thing that liveth, to you it shall be for meat, but the flesh
with the soul thereof, the blood thereof, ye shall not eat" (Gen. ix.
4).   Here also it is said, that the blood is the soul of the flesh, which
it was forbid to eat, because by the eating of the blood was signified
the profanation of truth.   Again : " Whosoever shall eat any blood,
I will give My faces against the soul that eateth blood, that I may
cut off that soul from the midst of its people ; for the soul of the
flesh is in the blood ; therefore I have given it upon the altar to ex-
pate your souls, for it is the blood that expiateth for the soul"
(Levit. xvii. 10, 11).   Inasmuch as soul, like blood, signifies truth
from the Word, which is divine truth proceeding from the Lord, and
inasmuch as all worship of the Lord is performed by divine truth, it
is for this reason said, for the soul of the flesh is in the blood, therefore have I given it upon the altar, to give the blood upon the altar,

signifying worship from divine truth ; and inasmuch as all liberation from evils and falses, which is expiation, is effected by divine truth and by a life according thereto, therefore it is said, to expiate your souls, for it is the blood which expiateth for the soul. Again: " Surely the blood of your souls will I require, of the hand of every wild beast will I require it, especially of the hand of man [homo], of the hand of a man [vir] his brother, will I require the soul of man" (Gen. ix. 5). That by blood, and also by soul, is here understood the spiritual life of man, which is a life according to divine truth, may appear from this consideration, that whosoever extinguishes that life perishes in eternal death ; for no other can extinguish it, but he who is in infernal evil and false ; but these things may be seen explained in the A. C. VII. That by living soul is signified · life in general, may appear from the passages where beasts, birds, reptiles, and fish, are called living souls ; as in the following : " God said, let the waters bring forth abundantly the reptile, the living soul. God created great whales, and every living soul that creep-eth, which the waters brought forth" (Gen. i. 20, 21). "God said, let the earth produce the living soul, according to their kind, beast and wild beast" (Gen. i. 24); " Jehovah brought unto the man every beast of the field, and every bird of the heavens, to see what he would call it; and whatsoever the man called it, the living soul, that was its name" (Gen. ii. 19); " Every living soul which swim-meth, whithersoever the rivers come, shall live, whence there shall be much fish" (Ezek. xlvii. 9); and in the Apocalypse : " Every living soul in the sea died" (xvi. 3). By all animals, in the spiritual sense, are signified things appertaining to the natural man and his life ; and whereas by the life of the natural man, which is life in ulti-mates, is signified life in every complex, hence it is that they are called living souls. From these considerations it may now appear, what is signified in the Word by soul, viz. that it signifies the life of man both natural and spiritual, thus both of his body and spirit: hence it may be seen how perverse the idea is which is conceived by the learned, and thence by the vulgar, concerning the soul of man, viz., that it is a sort of individual being residing in some place of the body, either in the brain, or in the heart, or elsewhere, and that on being loosed from man by death, it is without any body, and without the powers of sense and motion, such as appertain to body, and that these are to be added to it at the day of the last judg-ment ; likewise, that in the meantime it is a somewhat flying in the ether, or remaining in a sort of limbo, where it waits for its access-ary partner, which is the body ; this now is the idea which is enter-tained in the world concerning the soul of man, when notwithstand-ing no such thing is thereby understood in the Word ; but it there signifies the life of man, which never can have any existence sepa-rate from a body, but in a body, for the body is the external form of that life which is called the soul, effecting its arbitrations and dis-posals in both worlds, as well the natural, in which man lives, as the spiritual, in which spirits and angels live; and whereas the divine [principle] proceeding from the Lord constitutes the life of all, therefore this is signified by soul in the celestial sense. Inasmuch as the proceeding divine [principle] wherever it comes, forms an image of the Lord, thus also forms angels and spirits, so that they become human forms according to reception, hence then it follows that by the soul which lives after death is to be understood the spirit of man, which is a man with both soul and body, with a soul which rules over the body, and with a body whereby it effects its arbitrations and disposals in the world in which it resides.

751. "Wherefore rejoice, ye heavens, and they who dwell therein"—That hereby is signified the salvation and thence the joy of those who become spiritual by the reception of divine truth, appears from the signification of rejoicing, as denoting joy on account of salvation ; and from the signification of the heavens, as denoting the spiritual, concerning which we shall speak presently ; and from the signification of they who dwell therein, as denoting those who live, in this case, spiritually ; that to dwell signifies to live, may be seen above, n. 133, 479, 662. The reason why the heavens signify the spiritual, is, because all who are in the heavens are spiritual, and because men who are become spiritual are likewise in the heavens, although in the world as to the body, wherefore by they who dwell in the heavens are not only understood the angels, but also men, for every man with whom the interior mind, which is called the spiritual mind is opened, is in the heavens, yea, he also som014etimes appears amongst the angels there : that this is the case, has been hitherto unknown in the world ; wherefore it is to be observed, that man as to his spirit is amongst spirits and angels, and indeed in that society of them into which he is to come after death ; the reason is, because the spiritual mind of man is altogether formed to the image of heaven, insomuch that it is heaven in its least form, wherefore it cannot but be where its form is, and this although the mind itself be as yet in the body ; but these things are better illustrated in the work concerning H. & H. n. 51–58, where it is shown that every angel, and also every man as to his interiors, if he be spiritual, is a heaven in its least form, corresponding to heaven in its greatest or grand form. Hence it is that, in the Word, when the creation of heaven and earth is treated of, the internal and external of the church is thereby understood in general, and, in particular, the internal and external, or spiritual and natural man. From these considerations it may appear, that by the heavens and they who dwell in them are signified all who are there, and likewise men who become spiritual by the reception of divine truth in doctrine and life.

752. "Woe to the inhabitants of the earth and of the sea"—That hereby is signified lamentation over those who become merely natural and sensual, appears from the signification of woe, as denoting lamentation, concerning which see above, n. 532 ; and from the signification of the inhabitants of the earth and of the sea, as denoting the merely natural and sensual ; for when by those who dwell in the heavens are signified the spiritual, by the inhabitants of the earth and of the sea are signified the natural and sensual, for the natural and sensual mind is beneath the spiritual mind, as the earth

and sea are beneath the heavens : in the spiritual world the heavens
also appear on high, and far off beneath them appear earths and
seas, and in the heavens dwell the spiritual, and upon the earths
afar off beneath them dwell the natural, and in the seas the sensual;
for every one dwells high above, or deep below, according as his
interiors, which are called the interiors of the mind, are opened or
closed; hence it is, that by heaven and earth, in certain passages of
the Word, is signified the church internal and external, or spiritual
and natural; likewise, in particular, the spiritual and natural man,
by reason that the church is in man, and hence the man who is spiritual is in the church.   The reason why by the earth and the sea
are here signified the merely natural and sensual, is, because by the
earth here mentioned is understood that earth to which the dragon
was cast down, and to which the devil is said to come down, as will
be seen in what follows; and the merely natural or external man is
there, for the natural man without the spiritual, or the external man
without the internal, is upon damned earth, under which is hell; for
man is born sensual and natural, thus as in hell, because into evils
of every kind, but by regeneration he becomes spiritual, and is
thereby drawn out of hell, and elevated into heaven, by the Lord;
hence it is, that this lamentation is over those who are merely natural and sensual.   The reason of such lamentations over them, is because they are meant who are in faith separate from charity, thus
who say that they are in the faith, although they are in no light of
faith ; and that such become merely natural and sensual, was shown
above, n. 714, 739 : such are also meant by the dragon and his angels, and by the old serpent, but in the present case are meant those
who suffer themselves to be easily seduced by the dragon and his
angels : it is these therefore, concerning whom it is said, Woe to
the inhabitants of the earth and the sea.   That by heaven and earth
is signified the internal church, which is spiritual, and the external
church, which is natural, may be seen above, n. 304; that by the
earth is also signified damnation, n. 742; that by seas are signified
the extreme parts or principles of the life of man, which are called
sensual, n. 275, 342, 511; that they also signify the hells, n. 537,
538.

753. " Because the devil is come down unto you"—That hereby
is signified, because they receive evils from hell, appears from the
signification of the devil, as denoting the hell from whence come
evils, concerning which see above, n. 740; and from the signification of coming down unto them, when predicated of the devil, as
denoting to be amongst them, to seduce them, and to be received by
them : by those unto whom the devil is here said to come down, are
understood the inhabitants of the earth and the sea, by whom are
signified the merely natural and sensual, who became such by reason of their rejecting the life of faith, which is called charity ; and
they who reject this from their religion, believing and saying in their
heart that they contribute nothing to salvation, but faith alone, and
piety in worship, remain natural, and also become sensual, so far as
they reject goods in act or deed, and give up themselves to the plea-

sures arising from the loves of self and of the world : these, inasmuch as they remain natural, yea, become sensual, receive with delight the evils which ascend out of hell, for the natural man is in those evils from his birth, and unless he becomes also spiritual, he remains in them ; for when man becomes spiritual, he communicates with the heavens, and thence receives goods, and the goods communicated through heaven from the Lord remove evils, which can only be effected by a life according to precepts from the Word.

754. "Having great anger"—That hereby is signified hatred against spiritual truths and goods, which are of faith and life from the Word, consequently against those who are in them, appears from the signification of great anger, when predicated of the devil, as denoting hatred ; for anger, when predicated of the Lord, signifies zeal, in which however inwardly is heaven, but when predicated of the devil it denotes hatred, in which inwardly is hell : that these, and various other things of a like nature, are signified by anger and wrath, may be seen above, n. 413, 481 at the end, 647, 643. The reason why the hatred of the devil is against spiritual truths and goods, is, because truths and goods merely natural are altogether opposite to them ; for truths and goods merely natural, are, in their essence, falses and evils, although before those who are merely natural and sensual they appear as truths and goods, because their goods are pleasures and delights flowing from the loves of self and the world, and their truths are what favor those goods ; and whereas the loves of self and of the world are from hell, therefore in their essence, they are evils and falses ; but spiritual truths and goods are in their essence truths and goods, because the goods are delights flowing from love to the Lord, and from love towards the neighbor, and the truths are what teach those goods ; and whereas these truths and goods are through heaven from the Lord, therefore they are called spiritual, for everything which proceeds from the Lord, is called spiritual ; and inasmuch as man cannot receive these truths and goods unless he believes them and does them, therefore it is added, which are of faith and life from the Word ; to live from the Word, is to live from the Lord, for the Lord is in the Word, yea is the Word. Now whereas truths and goods merely natural, which, in their essence, are falses and evils, are altogether opposite to truths and goods spiritual, which, in their essence, are truths and goods, therefore the devil, by whom is meant hell, is continually in hatred against them : hence it is, that from the hells there continually ascend hatreds of various kinds, and, on the other hand, from the heavens descend spiritual loves, also of various kinds, and that between the hatreds of the hells, and the loves of the heavens, there is an equilibrium, in which men in the world are held, in order that they may act from liberty according to reason ; wherefore they who do not live from the Word, but from the world, inasmuch as they remain natural, receive evils and thence falses from hell, and conceive from them hatred against spiritual truths and goods : their hatred does not indeed appear in the world, because it lies inwardly concealed in their spirit, but it is manifested after death, when they become spi-

rits; then, against those who are in spiritual truths and goods, they burn with so great hatred, that it cannot be described; it is indeed a deadly hatred; for as soon as they see an angel, who is in those truths and goods, yea, if they only hear them name the Lord, from whom they are derived, they immediately rush into the rage of hatred, and perceive nothing more delightful than to persecute them, and to do evil to them; and because they are not able to kill their body, they attempt with a burning heart to kill their soul. The reason why it is said, woe to the inhabitants of the earth and of the sea, because the devil comes down unto you having great anger, is, because, after the last judgment the state of the spiritual world was altogether changed; before the last judgment it was permitted those who could act a civil and moral life in externals, although they were not spiritual, to form to themselves as it were heavens, and there to enjoy such pleasures as they delighted in, in the world; but since the last judgment was accomplished, this is no longer permitted, for now every one is carried away according to his life, he who is merely natural to hell, and he who is spiritual to heaven: this also is what is signified by the dragon and his angels being cast out of heaven to the earth, viz. that before it was granted them to have conjunction with the angels who were in the ultimate heavens, and by reason thereof to form to themselves such heavens, but that it was no longer granted. This therefore is what is specifically understood by hatred against those who are in spiritual truths and goods, which hatred is signified by the great anger which the devil has against the inhabitants of the earth and sea.

755. "Knowing that he hath but little time"—That hereby is signified because the state is changed, appears from the signification of time, as denoting the proceeding state of life, concerning which see above, n. 571, 610, 664, 673: hence by having a little time is signified, that the former state was changed; for the former state is described by the dragon and his angels being seen in heaven, but the latter state is described by their being cast to the earth after the battle with Michael and his angels; the quality of this state was briefly shown in the preceding article; but a more full description thereof will be given after the conclusion of this work.

756. Verses 13, 14. "And when the dragon saw that he was cast into the earth, he persecuted the woman, who brought forth the male child. And there were given to the woman two wings of a great eagle, that she might fly into the wilderness to her place, where she should be nourished a time, and times, and half a time, from the face of the serpent."—"And when the dragon saw that he was cast to the earth," signifies, when the religion of faith alone separate from the life of charity was not acknowledged but accounted vile: "he persecuted the woman who brought forth the male child," signifies, that they who are understood by the dragon, from hatred and enmity would reject and calumniate the church, which is the New Jerusalem, because it maintains the doctrine of life: "and there were given to the woman two wings of a great eagle," signifies spiritual intelligence and circumspection, which is given by the Lord to those who

are of that church: "that she might fly into the wilderness to her place," signifies, as yet with but few, because amongst those who are not in the life of charity, and thence neither in truths: "that she might be nourished there a time, and times, and half a time, from the face of the serpent," signifies, until the church grows and comes to its fulness.

757. "And when the dragon saw he was cast to the earth"— That hereby is signified when the religion of faith alone separate from the life of charity was not acknowledged but accounted as vile, appears from the signification of seeing, as denoting to animadvert and perceive; and from the signification of the dragon, as denoting those in the church who make no account of the life; and whereas this is especially the case with those who hold the doctrine that faith alone justifies and not at all the life of faith which is charity, concerning which see above, n. 714, 715, 716, 718, 737; hence by the dragon is here signified the religion of faith alone separate from the life of charity; and from the signification of being cast to the earth, as denoting to be separated from heaven and condemned to hell, concerning which see above, n. 739, 742, 746. The reason why by being cast to the earth is here signified, that that religion was not acknowledged but accounted vile, is, because when anything appertaining to religion or to doctrine does not agree with truth and good, it is then separated from heaven, and is no longer acknowledged but accounted vile; this takes place first in the spiritual world, and afterwards in the natural world; for in such things as appertain to heaven and the church, both worlds act as one; for man, who lives in the natural world, cannot think otherwise concerning things spiritual, than as the spirits and angels think who are attendant upon him, inasmuch as things spiritual are above the natural thought of man, and the things which are above depend upon influx; this influx however is received only by those who are inwardly spiritual, such as are those who are in the affection of truth for the sake of truth, and who also live according to truths; by these the religion of faith separate from the life of charity is not acknowledged, but is accounted vile; the case is otherwise with those who are not affected with truths, except for the sake of fame, honor, and gain, consequently who make no account of the life of charity; these do not receive any influx from heaven, wherefore they make one with hell; these are they who are signified by the dragon.

758. "He persecuted the woman who brought forth the male child"—That hereby is signified that they who are understood by the dragon, from hatred and enmity would reject and calumniate the church, which is the New Jerusalem, because it holds the doctrine of life, appears from the signification of persecuting, when predicated of those who are understood by the dragon, as denoting from hatred and enmity to reject and calumniate, concerning which we shall speak presently; and from the signification of the woman, as denoting the church which is called the New Jerusalem, concerning which see above, n. 707, 721, 730; and from the signification of the male child, as denoting the doctrine of that church, which is the

doctrine of life, concerning which see above, n. 724, 725; hence it may appear that the dragon persecuting the woman who brought forth the male child, signifies that they who are understood by the dragon, will, from hatred and enmity, reject and calumniate the church, which is the New Jerusalem, because it holds the doctrine of life. That to persecute here signifies from hatred and enmity, to reject and calumniate, follows as a consequence from what precedes concerning the dragon; as that he stood near the woman about to bring forth, that he might devour her child; likewise, that he fought with Michael and his angels; and that, when he was cast to the earth he had great anger, and that from this anger, by which is signified hatred, he persecuted the woman; that by his anger is signified hatred, see above, n. 754; his hatred is moreover described in what follows, by his casting out of his mouth water as it were a flood after the woman, that it might swallow her up; and at last, when all attempts were in vain, that, being full of anger, he went to make war with the rest of her seed. The reason why they who are understood by the dragon are described as having such hatred again those who are signified by the woman, is, because they who are in faith separate from charity have such hatred against those who are in charity; and whereas they who are in such separate faith have conjunction with the hells, hence their hatred is like that of the hells against the heavens: whence this hatred is, shall here be briefly explained: all who are in the hells are in the loves of self and the world, but all who are in the heavens are in love to the Lord and towards their neighbor; and these loves are altogether opposite to each other: they who are in the loves of self and of the world, love nothing but their own proprium, and the proprium of man is mere evil; but they who are in love towards the Lord and towards their neighbor, do not love their own proprium, for they love the Lord above themselves, and their neighbor out of or without themselves; they are also withheld from their own proprium, and are held in the proprium of the Lord, which is divine: moreover all the delights of the life are delights of the loves: the delights of the loves of self and of the world are the delights of hatred of various kinds, but the delights of love towards the Lord and towards the neighbor are the delights of charity of various kinds, and these are diametrically opposite to each other; and whereas they who are in the hells act in all cases from the delights of their loves, which, as was said, are delights of hatred of various kinds, hence it is evident whence the dragon has such hatred against the woman; for by the dragon are understood those who are in the love of self, wherefore he is called the great red dragon, great and red being predicated of that love; he is also called the devil and Satan, the devil signifying all evil which is from hell, and Satan all the false thence derived, and evil is in hatred against good, and the false is in hatred against truth; he is also called the old serpent, whereby is understood the sensual principle, which is the ultimate principle of man's life, and wherein all such hatred resides. Similar is the hatred which they who are in faith separate from charity have against those who are in charity, which hatred is not manifested in this world, but in the spiritual world, when they become spirits; that this hatred is of a deadly kind, and that it is the essential delight of the life of evil spirits, may be seen above, n. 754; but that such delight is turned into what is direfully infernal, may be seen in the work concerning H. & H. n. 485–490.

759. "And there were given to the woman two wings of a great eagle"—That hereby are signified the spiritual intelligence and circumspection which are given by the Lord to those who are of that church, appears from the signification of the woman, as denoting the church which is called New Jerusalem, treated of above, and, consequently, the men of that church; and from the signification of wings, as denoting things spiritual, concerning which also see above, n. 282, 283, 529; and from the signification of an eagle, as denoting intelligence and circumspection, concerning which also see above, n. 282; hence it follows, that by the two wings of a great eagle being given to the woman, are signified the spiritual intelligence and circumspection which are given from the Lord to those who are of that church. How these things are to be understood, shall also be explained. Inasmuch as all who are understood by the dragon and his angels are natural, yea, sensual, as was shown above, and all such reason from appearances, which for the most part are fallacies, and thereby seduce the simple, therefore it is given to the men of the new church, which is called the Holy Jerusalem, to view the divine truths which are in the Word not sensually, that is, according to appearances, but spiritually, that is, according to their essences, and therefore the internal sense of the . Word is disclosed, which is spiritual, and solely for those who will be of that church; from that sense divine truth appears according to the real quality thereof in its own spiritual light, and, by virtue of this light, according to the quality thereof in its own natural light: the divine truth is the Word, and they who are of that church are illustrated from the spiritual light of the Word by influx out of heaven from the Lord, and this by reason that they acknowledge the divine [principle] in the human of the Lord, and from Him are in the spiritual affection of truth: by these and no others is spiritual light received, which continually flows in through heaven from the Lord with all who read the Word; hence is their illustration. How illustration is effected shall also be explained: every man, as to his thoughts and affections, is in the spiritual world, consequently he is there as to his spirit, for it is the spirit of man which thinks and which is affected: he who is made spiritual by regeneration from the Lord, is as to his spirit in a heavenly society, but the natural man, or one who is not regenerated, is as to his spirit in an infernal society: with the latter, evils continually flow in from hell, and are also received with delight; but with the former, goods continually flow in from heaven, and are also received; and whereas goods flow-in into his affection, and by means of the affection into the thought, hence he has illustration: this illustration is what is understood by the spiritual intelligence and circumspection which are signified by the wings of the eagle given to the wo-

man, with which she fled into the wilderness : these latter, viz. the
spiritual, are also, comparatively, as eagles flying aloft, whereas
they who are merely natural, are, comparatively as serpents, who
creep on the ground, and see the eagles above themselves, wherefore also in the verse presently following, the dragon is called a serpent.   Moreover by the wings of the eagle, which were given to
the woman, is signified the understanding, of truth ; for all who are
of that church, have the understanding enlightened, by virtue
whereof they are enabled to see truth from the light of truth, that
is, whether a thing be true or not true ; and inasmuch as they thus
see truth, they acknowledge it, and receive it in affection which
is of the will, whence truths with them become spiritual, consequently the spiritual mind, which is above the natural mind, with
them is opened, and this being opened receives angelic sight, which
is the sight of truth itself from the light thereof ; but on the other
hand they who are not of that church, who are such as do not acknowledge the divine [principle] in the Lord's human, and who do
not love truth spiritually, or because it is truth, cannot have the
understanding illustrated so as by virtue thereof to see whether a
thing be true or not, but they see appearances of truth as genuine
truths, and confirm them as genuine from the literal sense of the
Word, notwithstanding most things in that sense are appearances,
which, if confirmed as genuine truths, are falsified, and falsified
truths are falses ; these latter, inasmuch as they cannot see truths
from the light of truth, and so apprehend them in the understanding,
are in an obscure, yea, in a blind faith concerning things to be believed, and a blind faith is like an eye which can see little or nothing ; yea, a blind faith is not faith, but only a persuasion, and
whereas such a persuasion is from another, either from some master
or preacher, or from the Word not understood, it is an historical
faith, which is natural and not spiritual : such persons also, inasmuch as they do not see truths, are not willing that the doctrinals
of the church should be approached and viewed from any principle
of understanding, but say that they are to be received from a principle of obedience, which is called the obedience of faith, and the
things which are received from such a blind obedience are not
known whether they be true or false ; neither can such things open
the way to heaven, for in heaven nothing is acknowledged as truth
except what is seen, that is, understood ; the light of heaven also is
such, that by virtue thereof, truths appear before the understanding
of the mind, as objects of the world appear before the sight of the
eye ; wherefore they in the world who have seen truths no otherwise than from a blind sight of faith, when they are carried into heaven to the angels see nothing at all, not even the angels there, and
much less the magnificent things about them, and then also they become stupid as to the understanding, and their eyes are darkened,
and so they depart.   It is however to be observed, that all those
are here meant who have separated faith from charity, and not those
who have lived the life of faith which is called charity, and so have
not separated them, for all such are in the desire of seeing truths,

wherefore when they come into the spiritual world, which is immediately after their departure from this, it is given them to see truths, according to their desire; the reason is, because with them the spiritual mind is opened, and hence they are in the light of heaven, into which they are actually let after their departure from the natural world. From these considerations it may appear, what is signified by the wings of the eagle, viz. the understanding of truth; and whereas by the woman is understood the New Jerusalem, therefore by the wings being given to her, is signified, that the understanding· of truth is given, and will be given, to those who will be of that church.

760. " That she might fly into the wilderness to her place"—That hereby is signified as yet amongst a few, because amongst those who are not in the life of charity, that the church in the mean time might be provided amongst greater numbers, appears from the things which have been explained above, n. 730, 731, where the same things are expressed, only with this difference, that it is there said of the woman, that she fled into the wilderness, where she hath a place prepared of God, but here that she fled into the wilderness into her place.   ·

761. " That she might be nourished there a time, and times, and half a time, from the face of the serpent"—That hereby is signified, until the church grows and comes to its fulness, appears from the signification of being nourished, as denoting to be sustained, and in the mean time to grow; and from the signification of a time, and times, and half a time, as denoting the state of the increase of the church even to its fulness, for the same is hereby signified, as above, in verse 6, by a thousand two hundred and sixty days, the like being there said concerning the woman, viz. that she fled into the wilderness, where she hath a place prepared of God, that they may nourish her there a thousand two hundred and sixty days; that by this number is signified the same as by the number three and a half, likewise as by the number seven, viz. until it grows to the full, may be seen above, n. 732; but the reason why it is here said a time, times, and half a time, is, because the above-named numbers, in their places, also signify times, and by times are signified states of life which proceed, as may be seen above, n. 571, 610, 664, 673, 747, here, therefore, which proceed and grow even to the full: the reason why it is said a time, times, and half a time, is, because time, in the singular, signifies the state of good, times, in the. plural, the state of truth, both as to their implantation, and the half of time signifies the holy state of the church: the reason of such a signification is, because a thing in the singular number involves good, in the plural, truths, and the half what is holy, and the reason why the half involves what is holy, is, because three signify what is full, and in like manner three and a half and seven, but seven signifies what is full when predicated of things holy, or where things holy are treated of, and hence the half after three has a like signification, because it fills and makes up the half of that number, for three and a half doubled makes seven, and a number doubled or multiplied signifies the

same as the number which is doubled or multiplied, as in the present case with respect to seven and three and a half: that seven signify what is full, and whole or complete, and is predicated of things holy, may be seen above, n. 20, 24, 257. That such things are signified by a time, times, and half a time, may appear from these words in Daniel: "A man [vir] clothed in linen, lifted up his right hand and his left hand to the heavens, and sware by Him who liveth for ever that it shall be for a time appointed, of times appointed, and a half, and when they shall be accomplished to disperse the hand of the people of holiness, all these things shall be consummated" (xii. 7); from which it is evident that by those times is signified consummation, for it is said, until all these things shall be consummated, and by consummation is understood impletion, or fulfilment, thus a full state.

762. Verses 15, 16. "And the serpent cast out of his mouth water as a flood after the woman, that he might make her be carried away by the flood. And the earth helped the woman, and the earth opened her mouth, and swallowed up the flood, which the dragon cast out of his mouth."—"And the serpent cast out of his mouth water as a flood after the woman" signifies subtle reasonings in abundance concerning justification by faith alone from those who think sensually and not spiritually: "that he might cause her to be carried away by the flood," signifies, that that church might be blinded and dissipated by reasonings: "and the earth helped the woman, and the earth opened her mouth, and swallowed up the flood which the dragon cast out of his mouth," signifies, that they who are of the church which is not in truths afforded assistance, and received not the reasonings of those who were principled in faith separate from charity.

763. "And the serpent cast out of his mouth water as a flood after the woman"—That hereby are signified subtle reasonings in abundance concerning justification by faith alone from those who think sensually and not spiritually, appears from the signification of the serpent, as denoting the sensual, and, abstractedly, the sensual principle, which is the ultimate of the natural principle with man, concerning which see above, n. 70, 581, 739; that dragons also denote the sensual may be seen above, n. 714; and from the signification of the woman, as denoting the church, which will be the New Jerusalem, which is treated of above; and from the signification of mouth, as denoting thought, whence flows speech, concerning which also see above, n. 580; and from the signification of water, as denoting the truth of faith, and, in the opposite sense, the false, concerning which see above, n. 483, 518, 537, 538; and from the signification of a flood or stream, as denoting intelligence from the understanding of truth, and, in the opposite sense, reasoning from falses, concerning which also see above, n. 518: hence by the casting out water as a flood is signified reasoning from falses in abundance. The reason why they are subtle reasonings concerning justification by faith alone from those who think sensually and not spiritually, is, because by the dragon are understood those who defend

such justification, and who are sensual, and thence think and reason sensually and not spiritually : that such are signified by the dragon may be seen above, n. 714; and whereas by dragons and serpents are signified the sensual, and sensual men are subtle above others, and reason sharply from fallacies and falses, that therefore by the dragon and serpent, in the abstract sense, is signified subtlety, may be seen above, n. 715, 739, 581.   From these considerations then it is evident what is signified by the dragon casting out of his mouth water as a flood after the woman.   Inasmuch as such things are here signified, something shall also be said respecting their subtle reasonings in favor of justification by faith alone; their leading dogma is this, that man is justified and saved by faith alone without the works of the law, which are the goods of charity; but whereas in the Word of both Testaments they see works and deeds so often mentioned, and that man is to love and be active in good works, they cannot do otherwise than affirm that he ought to live well, but, inasmuch as they have separated works or deeds from faith, as not justifying or saving, they contrive with much subtlety to conjoin them with faith, but still in such a manner, that they rather separate than conjoin; but forasmuch as their reasonings are in such abundance, and contrived with so much subtlety, that they cannot be expressed in a small compass, therefore they shall be particularly disclosed in a small work upon Spiritual Faith, and be presented to view accommodated to the apprehension of the most simple.   It is believed in common, and they themselves who defend that doctrine also believe, that they think and reason spiritually because with expertness and subtlety; but let it be observed, that no one can think and reason spiritually, but he who is in illustration from the Lord, and thence in the spiritual affection of truth, for such only are in the light of truth, and the light of truth is the light of heaven, from which the angels have intelligence and wisdom; that light is what is called spiritual light, and consequently they who are in it are spiritual; but they who are in falses, however acutely and subtlely they may think and reason, are not spiritual, but natural, yea, sensual, for their thoughts, and the reasonings thence derived, are, for the most part, from the fallacies of the senses, which some adorn with eloquence, and embellish with the flowers of rhetoric, and also confirm by appearances from nature; some likewise adapt certain scientifics to their reasonings, which they pronounce from a fire of self-love and pride of self-derived intelligence therein originating, and thus with a sound as of the affection of truth : in such things consists their subtlety, which appears as wisdom before those who cannot or dare not enter from any understanding into such things as are of the church and of the Word : the reason why sensual men can think, speak, and act, with so much subtlety, is, because all evil resides in the sensual principle of man, and malignity in that man abounds in proportion to intelligence in the spiritual man ; this has been made evident to me from the malignity of the infernals, which is of such a nature and so great, as cannot possibly be described, and all who are in the hells are sensual; this is understood by the Lord's words in

Luke: "The sons of this age are more prudent in their generation than the sons of light" (xvi. 8); and by these words concerning the serpent in Moses: "The serpent was more subtle than every wild beast of the field, which Jehovah God made" (Gen. iii. 1): by the serpent is signified the sensual principle of man.

764. "And the earth helped the woman, and the earth opened her mouth, and swallowed up the flood which the dragon cast out of his mouth"—That hereby is signified that they who are of the church which is not in truths afforded assistance, and received not the subtle reasonings of those who were principled in faith separate from charity, appears from the signification of the earth which helped the woman, as denoting the church which is not in truths, for by the earth here is understood the earth of the wilderness, into which the woman fled, and where she had a place prepared of God; that the earth of the wilderness signifies the church which is not in truths because not in good, appears from the signification of the earth, as denoting the church, concerning which see above, n. 29, 304, 417, 697, 741, 742, 752; and from the signification of the wilderness, as denoting where there is no truth, concerning which also see above, n. 730; and from the signification of helping the woman, as denoting to afford assistance to the New Church, which is called the holy Jerusalem; and from the signification of opening her mouth, and swallowing up the flood, which the dragon cast out of his mouth, as denoting not to receive the subtle reasonings of those who were principled in faith separate from charity; for the flood of waters which the dragon cast out of his mouth, signifies subtle reasonings from falses, as is evident from the two preceding articles, and to open the mouth and swallow, when predicated of the church which is signified by the earth, signifies to take away, and whereas a thing is taken away when it is not received, it signifies not to receive. These things are thus to be understood: it is said above, that the woman fled into the wilderness where she hath a place prepared of God, and afterwards that she got the wings of an eagle, and flew to her own place, by which is signified, that the church which is called the New Jerusalem, is to tarry amongst those who are in the doctrine of faith separate from charity, whilst it grows to the full, until provision is made for its reception amongst greater numbers; but in that church there are dragons who separate faith from good works, not only in doctrine but also in life, whereas the rest in the same church, who live the life of faith, which is charity, are not dragons, although amongst them, for they know no other than that it is agreeable to doctrine that faith produces the fruits, which are good works, and that the faith which justifies and saves is to believe those things which are in the Word, and to do them; but the dragons are altogether of another way of thinking; but what the sentiments of these latter are, the former do not comprehend, and whereas they do not comprehend, neither do they receive; from which consideration it is manifest, that the church consisting of those who are not dragons, is understood by the earth which helped the woman, and swallowed up the stream which the dragon cast out of

his mouth. But what is the nature and quality of the reasonings, which are meant by the dragon, concerning the separation of faith from good works, and concerning their conjunction, and how subtle, and at the same time pernicious, those reasonings are, will be revealed, the Lord willing, in another place, likewise, that those reasonings have place only with the learned rulers of the church, and are not known to, because not understood by, the people of the church, and that hence it is that the New Church, which is called the Holy Jerusalem, is helped by these latter and also increases.

766. Verse 17. "And the dragon was angry against the woman, and went to make war with the rest of her seed, who keep the commandments of God, and have the testimony of Jesus Christ."—"And the dragon was angry against the woman," signifies the hatred of those who are understood by the dragon, against the church which is the New Jerusalem, incensed from the perception of its being favored by greater numbers: "and he went to make war with the rest of her seed," signifies, and thence an ardent effort originating in the life of evil to assault the truths of the doctrine of that church: "who keep the commandments of God," signifies, with those who live the life of faith, which is charity: "and who have the testimony of Jesus Christ," signifies, and who acknowledge the divine [principle] in the Lord's human.

767. "And the dragon was angry against the woman"—That hereby is signified the hatred of those who are understood by the dragon, against the church which is the New Jerusalem, incensed from the perception of its being favored by greater numbers, appears from the signification of anger, when predicated of the dragon, as denoting hatred, concerning which see above, n. 754, 758, whence to be angry denotes to be in hatred; that it is a grievous hatred incensed from the perception of that church being favored by greater numbers, follows as a consequence from what precedes and from what follows; from what precedes in that the earth opened her mouth, and helped the woman, and swallowed up the flood which the dragon cast out of his mouth, by which is signified, that the church in which the dragons also are, afforded assistance, and received not their subtle reasonings concerning faith alone; and from what follows, in that the dragon went to make war with the rest of her seed, by which is signified an ardent effort, arising from that hatred, to assault the truths of the doctrine of that church; whence it is that by the anger of the dragon is here signified such hatred incensed from the perception of the church increasing in favor; for, as was said above, by the woman flying into the wilderness to the place prepared of God, is signified, that the church, which is the New Jerusalem, was yet amongst a few, whilst provision was making for it amongst greater numbers, and for its growing to the full.

768. "And went to make war with the rest of her seed"—That hereby is signified, and thence an ardent effort, arising from a life of evil, to assault the truths of the doctrine of that church, appears from the signification of going, as denoting an ardent effort arising from a life of evil, concerning which we shall speak presently; and

from the signification of making war, as denoting to assault and desire to destroy, concerning which see above, n. 573, 734; and from
the signification of her seed, as denoting the truths of the doctrine
of the church, concerning which also we shall speak presently : the
reason why it is said the rest of her seed, is, because they are understood who are in those truths, and, in the abstract sense, the truths
themselves of that church, which they suppose themselves able to
assault and destroy.   The reason why to go, here signifies an ardent
effort from a life of evil, is, because to go, in the spiritual sense,
signifies to live, whence, in the Word, mention is frequently made
of going with the Lord, and of walking with him and after Him,
whereby is signified to live from the Lord; but when to go, is predicated of the dragon, whose life is a life of evil, it signifies to make
an effort from that life, and whereas that effort is an effort arising
from hatred, which is signified by his anger, see above, n. 754, 758,
hence an ardent effort is signified, because he who makes an effort
from hatred, makes an ardent effort.   Inasmuch as the hatred of
those who are understood by the dragon is a hatred against those
who are in the truths of the doctrine of that church, which is the
New Jerusalem, therefore it is a hatred against the truths of doctrine which appertain to them; for they who are in love towards
any one, also they who are in hatred against any one, are indeed in
love or hatred towards or against the person with whom those things
are which they love or hate, and these, in the present case, are the
truths of doctrine appertaining to them, wherefore the truths of doctrine are what are signified by the rest of her seed : hence it may
appear, that, in the spiritual sense of the Word, person is not regarded, but the thing abstracted from person, as, in the present case,
the thing which appertains to the person : this may be still farther
illustrated by the following consideration; it is said in the Word,
that the neighbor is to be loved as a man loves himself, but in the
spiritual sense it is not understood that the neighbor is thus to be
loved as to the person, but that those things are to be loved which
appertain to the person from the Lord; for a person is not actually
loved by reason of his being a person or man, but by reason of his
being of such or such a quality, and thus the person is loved from
his quality, wherefore that quality is what is understood by neighbor, and which therefore is the spiritual neighbor, or the neighbor
who is to be loved in the spiritual sense : this quality or neighbor
with those who are of the church of the Lord, is all that which proceeds from the Lord, which in general has reference to all good
both spiritual, moral, and civil, wherefore they who are in these
goods love those who are in the same ; this therefore is to love their
neighbor as themselves.   From these considerations it may appear,
that by the rest of her seed, viz. of the woman, by whom is signified
the church, are meant those who are in the truths of the doctrine of
that church, and, in the sense abstracted from persons, which is the
genuine spiritual sense, the truths of doctrine themselves : so likewise in other passages of the Word ; as in the following in Moses :
" I will put enmity between thee and the woman, and between thy

seed and her seed; He shall tread upon thy head, and thou shalt hurt his heel" (Gen. iii. 15). This is a prophecy concerning the Lord: by the serpent is there signified the sensual principle of man, where his proprium resides, which in itself is nothing but evil, and by the woman is signified the spiritual church, or the church which is in divine truths; and whereas the sensual principle of man was destroyed, and the man of the church is elevated from it when he becomes spiritual, hence it is said, I will put enmity between thee and the woman; by the seed of the serpent is signified all the false derived from evil, and by the seed of the woman all truth derived from good, and, in the supreme degree, divine truth: and whereas all divine truth is from the Lord, and the Lord thereby destroyed the false from evil, therefore it is said, He shall tread upon thy head; He, signifies the Lord, and head, all the false from evil; that still the sensual principle would do hurt to divine truth in its ultimates, which is the Word in the sense of the letter, is signified by, thou shalt hurt his heel, the heel denoting that ultimate of divine truth and that sense of the Word: that these do still suffer hurt, and have suffered hurt, from the sensual principle, is evident from this single example, viz. that the Roman Catholics by the woman here mentioned understand Mary, and the worship of her, wherefore in their Bibles they do not read *He* but *it* and *her;* thus also in a thousand other passages. And in Jeremiah: "Behold the days shall come in which I will sow the house of Israel and the house of Judah with the seed of man and the seed of beast" (xxx. 27): treating concerning the Lord, and concerning the New Church from Him: His advent is signified by, behold the days shall come; by sowing the house of Israel and the house of Judah, is signified, to reform those who will be of that church, the house of Israel denoting the spiritual church, and the house of Judah the celestial church; and whereas reformation is effected by spiritual truths and by natural truths thence derived, it is said, with the seed of man and the seed of beast, the seed of man denoting spiritual truth, from which man has intelligence, and the seed of beast natural truth, from which man has science, both from the affection of good, also a life according thereto; that man [homo] signifies the affection of spiritual truth and good, may be seen above, n. 280; and that beast signifies the natural affection, n. 650; thus the seed of man and seed of beast signify the truths of those affections. And in Malachi: "There is not one who doeth [this] who hath the spirit; is there one that seeketh the seed of God" (ii. 15): signifying that no one seeks divine truth; that the seed of God here signifies divine truth is evident; hence by the born of God are understood those who are regenerated of the Lord by divine truth, and by a life according thereto. And in Isaiah: "Jehovah willeth to bruise him, He hath weakened [him]: if Thou makest his soul guilt, he shall see seed, he shall prolong days, and the will of Jehovah shall prosper by his hand" (liii. 10). The subject treated of in the whole of this chapter is concerning the Lord, and concerning His temptations, by which He subjugated the hells; the increasing grievousness of His temptations is described by Jehovah's willing to bruise Him, and weakening Him, and the most grievous of all, which was the passion of the cross, is signified by making His soul guilt; by making His soul guilt is signified, the last temptation, whereby He fully subjugated the hells, and fully glorified His Human [principle], whence comes redemption; the divine truth which afterwards proceeded from His Divine Human [principle], and the salvation of all who receive divine truth from Him, is signified by, He shall see seed; the eternal duration thereof is signified by, He shall prolong days, to prolong, when predicated of the Lord, signifying eternal duration, and days signifying states of light, which are states of illustration of all by divine truth; that this is from His Divine [principle] for the salvation of mankind, is signified by, the will of Jehovah shall prosper by his hand. Again, in the same prophet: "Fear not, because I am with thee; from the east I will bring thy seed, and from the west I will gather thee; I will say to the north give, and to the south, keep not back, bring my sons from afar, my daughters from the extremity of the earth" (xliii. 5, 6). It is supposed that these words have reference to the bringing back of the sons of Israel into the land of Canaan; this however is not there meant, but salvation by the Lord of all who receive divine truth from Him, and of whom a new church is formed: this is what is signified by His seed which shall be brought from the east and gathered from the west, and which the north shall give and the south shall not prohibit; wherefore it also follows, bring my sons from afar, and my daughters from the extremity of the earth, sons denoting those who are in the truths of the church, and daughters those who are in the goods thereof: but these words may be seen more particularly explained above, n. 422, 704. Again: "Thou shall break forth to the right hand and to the left, and Thy seed shall inherit the nations, and make the desolate cities to be inhabited" (liv. 3). Treating concerning the church to be established by the Lord with the nations or gentiles, which church is there understood by the barren woman, who bare not, and who should have many sons, ver. 1: by the seed which shall inherit the nations, is signified the divine truth which shall be given to the nations; by breaking forth to the right hand and to the left, is signified extension and multiplication; by the right hand is signified truth which is in light, and by the left hand truth which is in shade, the reason of which signification is, because, in the spiritual world, to the right hand is the south, where they are who are in a clear light of truth, and to the left is the north, where they are who are in an obscure light of truth; by making the desolate cities to be inhabited, is signified their life according to divine truths, which before this were destroyed, cities denote the truths of doctrine from the Word, to be inhabited signifies a life according to them, and desolate cities signifies those truths heretofore destroyed, viz. with the Jewish nation. Again: "Their seed shall become known in the nations, and their offspring in the midst of the people; all that see them shall acknowledge them, that they are the seed which Jehovah hath blessed" (lxi. 9). These words also are spoken concerning the church to be established

by the Lord : and by the seed which shall become known in the
nations, is signified the divine truth, which will be received by those
who are in the good of life; and by the offspring in the midst of the
people, is signified life according thereto; by those who see them
acknowledging that they are the seed, is signified illustration that it
is genuine truth which they receive; which Jehovah hath blessed,
signifies that it is from the Lord : such is the signification of the
words in the sense abstracted from persons, but in the strict sense
they are understood who will receive divine truth from the Lord.
Again : "They are the seed of the blessed of Jehovah and their
offspring with them" (lxv. 23). Also treating concerning the church
from the Lord; and by the seed of the blessed of Jehovah are understood those who will receive divine truth from the Lord; and by
their offspring are understood those who live according thereto, but,
in the sense abstracted from persons, which is the genuine spiritual
sense, by seed is understood divine truth, and by offspring a life according thereto, according to what was shown above; the reason
why by offspring are understood those who live according to divine
truth, and, in the abstract sense, that life itself, is, because, in the
original tongue, the expression offspring [prognatus] is derived from
a word which signifies to go forth and to proceed, and that which
goes forth and proceeds from the divine truth received, is a life according to it. Again : "Even as the new heaven and the new
earth, which I am about to make, shall stand before Me, so shall
your seed stand and your name" (lxvi. 22): in like manner speaking of the Lord, and of the salvation of the faithful by Him : the
new church from Him is understood by the new heavens and new
earth, by the new heavens the church internal, and by the new earth,
the church external; that divine truth and its quality shall continue, is
signified by, your seed shall stand and your name, seed denoting
divine truth, which also is the truth of doctrine from the Word, and
name denoting the quality thereof; that by name is signified the
quality of a thing and state, may be seen above, n. 148. And in
David : Thou hast founded the earth, and the heavens are the work
of Thy hands; they shall perish, and Thou shalt continue: they
shall all wax old as a garment, as a garment shalt Thou change
them, and they shall be changed; but thou art the same, and Thy
years shall not be consumed: the sons of Thy servants shall dwell,
and their seed shall be established before Thee" (Psalm cii. 26, 27,
28, 29). By the earth which God hath formed, and by the heavens the
work of His hands, which shall perish, are signified the same as by the
former heaven and former earth which passed away, see Apoc. xxi.
1; and whereas the face of the earth and heavens in the spiritual
world will be altogether changed at the day of the last judgment,
and there will be a new earth and new heavens in the place of the
former, therefore it is said, that they shall all wax old as a garment,
as a garment shalt thou change them, and they shall be changed;
they are compared to garments, because garments signify external
truths, such as appertain to those who are in the former heavens and
former earth, which heaven and earth do not continue or endure,

because they are not in internal truths; the state of divine truth which shall endure from the Lord to eternity, is signified by, Thou shalt continue, and Thou art the same, and Thy years shall not be consumed, the years of God signifying states of divine truth; the sons of Thy servants shall dwell, and their seed shall be established before Thee, signifies, that angels and the men who are receptions of divine truth, shall have eternal life, and that the truths of doctrine with them shall endure to eternity, sons of the servants of God denoting angels and the men who are receptions of divine truth, and their seed denoting the truths of doctrine. Again: "The seed which shall serve Him shall be numbered to the Lord for a generation" (Psalm xxii. 31): treating also concerning the Lord; and by the seed which shall serve Him are meant those who are in truths of doctrine from the Word; and by, it shall be numbered to the Lord for a generation, is signified, that they shall be His to eternity, to be numbered denoting to be arranged and disposed in order, in the present case to be adnumerated or added to, thus to be His. In various parts of the Word mention is made of the seed of Abraham, Isaac, and Jacob, likewise of the seed of Israel, and thereby, in the historical sense of the letter, is understood their posterity, but, in the spiritual sense, divine truth is understood, and the truth of doctrine from the Word; the reason whereof is, because by Abraham, Isaac, and Jacob, and by Israel, in this sense, is understood the Lord, as may appear from the passages in the Word, where they are mentioned; as where it is said, that they shall come from the east and the west, and shall sit down with Abraham, Isaac, and Jacob, in the kingdom of the heavens (Matt. viii. 11); whereby is understood the fruition of celestial good from the Lord; the case is similar in other passages; and whereas the Lord is signified by them in the internal sense, therefore by their seed is signified the divine truth which is from the Lord, consequently also the truth of doctrine from the Word; as in these passages: thus in Moses: "Jehovah said to Abram, all the land which thou seest will I give to thee and to thy seed for ever: and I will make thy seed as the dust of the earth" (Gen. xiii. 15, 16). Again: "Look up towards the heavens and number the stars, so shall thy seed be" (Gen. xv. 15). "In thy seed shall all nations be blessed" (Gen. xxii. 18): unto Isaac: "To thee and to thy seed will I give all these lands, and I will multiply thy seed as the stars of heaven; and in thy seed shall all the nations of the earth be blessed" (Gen. xxvi. 3, 4, 5): unto Jacob: "Unto thy seed after thee will I give this land" (Gen. xxxv. 12). "The land given to Abraham, to Isaac, and Jacob, and to their seed after them" (Deut. i. 8). "The seed of your fathers, Abraham, Isaac, and Jacob" (Deut. iv. 37; chap. x. 15; chap. xi. 9): inasmuch as by Abraham, Isaac, and Jacob, as was said, is understood the Lord, by Abraham the Lord as to the Divine Celestial [principle] of the church, by Isaac as to the Divine Spiritual [principle] of the church, and by Jacob as to the Divine Natural [principle] of the church, therefore by their seed is signified the divine truth proceeding from the Lord, by the seed of Abraham, divine truth celestial, by the seed of Isaac, divine truth spiritual, and by the seed of Jacob, divine truth natural; consequently they who are in divine truth from the Lord are also understood; but by the land which the Lord will give to them, is understood the church, which is in divine truth from Him : hence it may be known what is signified by all nations being blessed in their seed; for they could not be blessed in their posterity, viz. in the Jewish and Israelitish nation, but in the Lord and from the Lord by the reception of divine truth from Him. That the Jews are not understood by the seed of Abraham, appears from the words of the Lord in John : "The Jews answered, we are the seed of Abraham and have never been servants to any man : Jesus answered, I know that ye are the seed of Abraham, but ye seek to kill Me, because My word hath no place in you; ye are of your father the devil" (John viii. 33, 37, 44): from which it is evident that they are not understood by the seed of Abraham, but that by Abraham is understood the Lord, and by the seed of Abraham, the divine truth from the Lord, which is the Word, for it is said, I know that ye are the seed of Abraham, but ye seek to kill Me, because My Word hath no place in you ; by the Lord's saying I know that ye are the seed of Abraham, is signified that He knew the truth of the church, which is the Word, was with them ; but that still they rejected the Lord, is signified by, ye seek to kill Me; and that they were not in divine truth from the Lord, is signified by, because My Word hath no place in you; and that there was nothing but evil and the false thence derived with them, is signified by, ye are of your father the devil and the truth is not in him; and afterwards, when he speaketh a lie he speaketh from his own, where by a lie is signified divine truth or the Word adulterated; that the Lord's saying, I know that ye are the seed of Abraham, was also because by Judah is signified the Lord as to the Word, may be seen above, n. 119, 433. And in David, "I will make them to fall in the wilderness, and I will make their seed to fall among the nations, and will scatter them in the lands" (Psalm cvi. 26, 27). By making their seed to fall among the nations, and by scattering them in the lands, is signified that divine truth would perish with them by evils and falses. The like is signified by the seed of Israel in these passages : "Thou Israel My servant, Jacob whom I have chosen, the seed of Abraham My friend, whom I have taken from the ends of the earth" (Isaiah xli. 8, 9). I will pour out My spirit upon the seed of Israel and Jacob, and My blessing upon their offspring" (Isaiah xlv. 25): "Jehovah liveth, who brought up and who led the seed of the house of Israel out of the land towards the north, and out of all the lands whither I have driven them, that they may dwell upon their own land" (Jer. xxxiii. 8). By Israel, in the supreme sense, is understood the Lord as to the internal of the church, wherefore by the seed of Israel likewise is signified the divine truth which is with those who are of the church signified by him ; for by Israel is also understood the church with those who are interiorly natural, and in truths there from a spiritual origin, wherefore the church which is spiritual natural is also thereby signified. Inasmuch as by David, in the Word, is understood the

Lord as to His royalty or kingly office, and by the royalty of the Lord is signified the divine truth in the church, hence also by his seed are understood those who are in the truths of the church from the Word, who are also called sons of the king, and sons of the kingdom, consequently also divine truths appertaining to them is also signified; as in the following passages: "As the army of the heavens cannot be numbered, nor the sand of the sea be measured, so will I multiply the seed of David and the Levites My ministers" (Jerem. xxxiii. 22): "I have made a covenant with Mine elect, I have sworn to David My servant, even to eternity will I establish thy seed, and I will build up thy throne for generation and generation. His seed will I set for ever, and His throne as the days of the heavens. His seed shall be to eternity and His throne as the sun before Me" (Psalm lxxxix. 4, 5, 30, 37). That by David, in the Word, is understood the Lord as to His royalty, which is the divine truth in the Lord's spiritual kingdom, may be seen above, n. 295; hence by his seed is signified that divine truth appertaining to those who are in truths from good, thus also who are in truths of doctrine from the Word, for the truths of doctrine from the Word, or the truths of the Word, are all derived from good; and whereas they are understood by the seed of David, therefore, in the abstract sense, the truth of the Word is also thereby understood, or the truth of doctrine from the Word; that by the seed of David are not understood his posterity, any one may see, for it is said that his seed shall be multiplied as the army of the heavens and the sand of the sea, and that it shall be established and endure to eternity, also that his throne shall be built up to generation and generation, and shall be as the days of the heavens and as the sun, which things cannot at all be said of the seed of David, that is, of his posterity, and of his throne, for where now are these to be found? but all those things coincide, when by David is understood the Lord, by his throne, heaven and the church, and by his seed the truth of heaven and the church. Again, in Jeremiah: "If my covenant [be] not of the day and the night, if I have not appointed the statutes of heaven and of the earth, then will I reprobate the seed of Jacob and of David My servant, that I will not take of his seed to rule over the seed of Abraham, Isaac, and Jacob; and I will cause their captivity to return, and have mercy upon them" (xxxiii. 25, 26). Again: "Thus saith Jehovah who giveth the sun for a light by day, the statutes of the moon and the stars for a light by night; if these statutes shall depart from before Me, the seed of Israel also shall cease from being a nation before Me for ever" (xxxi. 35, 36). In these passages by the seed of Jacob and David, likewise by the seed of Israel, are also understood those who are in divine truths, but by the seed of Jacob those who are in divine truth natural, by the seed of David those who are in divine truth spiritual, and by the seed of Israel, those who are in divine truth natural-spiritual, which is mediate between divine truth natural and spiritual; for there are degrees of divine truth as there are degrees of the reception thereof by the angels in the three heavens, and in the church; by the covenant of the day and the night, and by the statutes of heaven and earth, is signified the conjunction of the Lord with those who are in divine truths in the heavens, and who are in divine truths in the earths; by covenant is signified conjunction; by statutes the laws of conjunction, which are also the laws of order, and the laws of order are divine truths; by day is signified the light of truth such as it is with the angels in the heavens; and by night the light of truth such as it is with men on the earths, and likewise such as it is with those, both in the heavens and on the earths, who are under the Lord as a moon, wherefore also it is said, who giveth the sun for the light of the day, and the statutes of the moon and the stars for the light of the night; but by the seed of Abraham, Isaac, and Jacob, are here understood all who are of the church of the Lord in every degree, concerning whom, and the seed of Jacob and David, it is said, that if they acknowledge not the Lord, and received not divine truth from Him, the Lord will not reign over them.   Again, in the same Prophet : " No one of his seed shall prosper, who sitteth upon the throne of David, and ruleth any more in Judah" (xxii. 30). These things are said concerning Coniah, king of Judah, who is there called a despised and abject idol, and concerning whom it is said, that he and his seed shall be taken away and cast to the earth, verse 28 of the same chapter ; by which king is signified the same as by Satan, and by his seed the infernal false ; that this shall not rule in the church of the Lord, in which is divine truth celestial, is signified by, no one of his seed shall sit upon the throne of David nor rule any more in Judah, Judah there denoting the celestial church in which the Lord reigns. As by David was represented the royalty of the Lord, so by Aaron was represented His priesthood, wherefore by the seed of Aaron are understood those who are in the affection of genuine truth which is from celestial good; by reason of such representation the following statute was given for Aaron : "The great priest shall not take for a wife a widow, or a divorced woman, or a corrupt harlot, but he shall take a virgin of his own people to wife, lest he profane his seed amongst this people ; I Jehovah do sanctify him" (Leviticus xxi. 14, 15); whereas by man and wife, in the Word, in the spiritual sense thereof, is signified the understanding of truth and the will of good, and whereas thought is of the understanding and affection is of the will, therefore by man and wife is also signified the thought of truth and affection of good, likewise truth and good, whence it may appear what is signified by a widow, by one divorced, and by one corrupt and a harlot; by a widow is signified good without truth, because left by truth, which is the man ; by a woman divorced is signified good rejected by truth, thus such as is discordant; and by a corrupted harlot is signified good adulterated by falses, which is no longer good but evil ; on account of such things being signified by those women, the great priest was forbidden to take any of them to wife, because he represented the Lord as to the priesthood, whereby was signified the divine good ; and whereas by a virgin is signified the will or affection of genuine truth, and

genuine truth makes one and agrees with divine good, and these
two are conjoined in heaven and in the church, and being conjoined
are called the heavenly marriage, therefore it was enacted, that the
great priest should take a virgin to wife; and whereas from this
marriage is produced the truth of doctrine, but from a marriage with
such as are signified by a widow, a woman divorced, and a corrupted
harlot, is produced the false of doctrine, therefore it is said, lest he
profane his seed among his people: by seed is signified the genuine
truth of doctrine, and thence also the doctrine of genuine truth from
the good of celestial love, and by his people are signified those who
are of the church in which is the doctrine of genuine truth from the
Word; and whereas the marriage of the priest was representative
of the heavenly marriage, which is of the Lord with the church,
therefore it is said, I Jehovah do sanctify him. Inasmuch as the
great priest represented the Lord as to divine good, and by his seed
was signified divine truth, which is the same with the genuine truth
of doctrine, therefore it was also made a statute, " That a man a
stranger, who was not of the seed of Aaron, should not come near
to burn incense before Jehovah" (Numb. xviii. 5). By a man a
stranger is signified the false of doctrine, and by burning incense is
signified worship from spiritual good, which, in its essence, is genuine truth; and by the seed of the great priest is signified divine
truth from a celestial origin; on this account it was enacted that no
stranger who was not of the seed of Aaron, should offer incense in
the tent of the assembly before Jehovah. When it is known what
principle of heaven and the church was represented by other persons
also mentioned in the Word, it may also be known what is signified
by their seed, as by the seed of Noah, Ephraim, and Caleb, in the
following passages; concerning Noah: " I will set up my covenant with you, and with your seed after you" (Gen. ix. 9); " Israel said of Ephraim, his seed shall be the fulness of the earth"
(Gen. xlviii. 19); " And Jehovah said of Caleb, his seed shall
inherit the earth" (Numb. xiv. 24). What Noah and Ephraim
represented and signified may be seen explained in the A. C.;
but by Caleb were represented those who were to be introduced
into the church, whence by their seed also is signified the truth
of the doctrine of the church. The same as is signified by the
seed of man is also signified by the seed of the field, by reason that
a field also signifies the church, equally as man, and hence, in some
passages, seed and sowing are predicated of the people of the earth,
the same as of a field; as in the following; thus in Jeremiah: " I
had planted thee a noble vine, a seed of truth, how art thou converted into branches of a strange vine to Me" (ii. 21); and in David: " Their fruit will I destroy from the earth, and their seed from
the sons of man" (Psalm xxi. 11); and in Hosea: " I will sow Israel to Me in the earth" (ii. 23); and in Zechariah: " I will sow
Judah and Joseph amongst the people, and in places remote they
shall remember Me" (x. 9); and in Ezekiel: " I will look again to
you, that ye may be tilled and sown, then will I multiply upon you

man, all the house of Israel the whole of it" (**xxxvi. 9**); and in Jeremiah: " Behold the day is come in which I will sow the house of Israel and the house of Judah with the seed of man, and the seed ot beast" (**xxxi. 27**); " The seed sown are the sons of the kingdom" (**Matt. xiii. 38**). But that the seed of the field has a similar signification with the seed of man, it is not necessary in this place to exemplify, our present purpose being only to explain and confirm from the Word, what is signified by the seed of the woman which is here treated of. Inasmuch as by seed is signified the truth of doctrine from the Word, and, in the supreme sense, divine truth, hence, in the opposite sense, by seed is signified the false of doctrine, and the infernal false ; as in Isaiah : " Draw ye near hither, ye sons of the sorceress, the seed of the adulterer and the whore ; against whom do ye sport yourselves, against whom do ye dilate the mouth and lengthen out the tongue ? are ye not the children of prevarication, the seed of a lie" (**lvii. 3, 4**). By sons of the sorceress and the seed of the adulterer, are signified falses from the Word falsified and adulterated, by the sons of the sorceress, falses from the falsification of the Word, and by the seed of the adulterer, falses from the adulteration thereof; the Word is said to be falsified when the truths thereof are perverted, and to be adulterated when the goods thereof are in like manner perverted, likewise, when the truths are applied to the loves of self; by children of prevarication and the seed of a lie are signified the falses flowing from those former falses ; by sporting themselves is signified the delight derived from falsification; by dilating the mouth, is signified the delight of the thoughts therein originating, and by lengthening out the tongue, the delight of teaching and propagating them. And in Isaiah : " Woe to the sinful nation, a people laden with iniquity, a seed of evil [doers] sons [that are] corrupters ; they have forsaken Jehovah, they have provoked the Holy One of Israel, they have gone away backwards" (**i. 4**). By the sinful nation are signified those who are in evils, and by a people laden with iniquity, are signified those who are in falses thence derived, for nation, in the Word, is predicated of evils, and people of falses, as may be seen above, n. 175, 331, 625 ; the false of those who are principled in evils is signified by the seed of evil doers, and the falses of those who are principled in the falses from that evil are signified by the sons who are corrupters ; that sons signify those who are in truths, and, in the opposite sense, those who are in falses, and, abstractedly, truths and falses, may be seen above, n. 724; by, they have forsaken Jehovah and provoked the Holy One of Israel, is signified, that they have rejected divine good and divine truth, Jehovah denoting the Lord as to divine good, and the Holy One of Israel the Lord as to divine truth ; by their going away backwards is signified that they altogether receded from them, and went away to infernal evil and the false thence derived, for they who are in evils and falses in the spiritual world turn themselves backwards from the Lord, concerning which see the treatise on H. & H. n. 123. Again, in the same prophet: " Thou shalt not be united with them in the sepulchre, for Thou hast destroyed Thy land, Thou hast slain Thy people ; the seed of the malicious shall not be named for ever" (xiv. 20); speaking of Lucifer, by whom is understood Babel, and by the seed of the malicious which shall not be named for ever, is signified the dire false of evil which is from hell ; the rest may be seen explained above, n. 589, 659, 697. And in Moses : "He who giveth his seed to Molech, dying shall die, the people of the land shall stone him with stones : I will set my faces against this man, and I will cut him off from the midst of his people, because he hath given his seed to Molech, to pollute My sanctuary, and to profane the name of my holiness" (Levit. xx. 3 ; chap. xviii. 21). By giving of his seed to Molech, is signified to destroy the truth of the Word, and thence of the doctrine of the church, by application to the filthy loves of the body, as to murders, hatreds, revenges, adulteries, and the like, whence infernal falses are accepted instead of things divine, which are signified by the seed given to Molech ; Molech was the god of the sons of Ammon, (1 Kings xi. 7); and was set in the valley of Hinnom, which was called Tophet, where they offered up their sons and daughters in the fire (2 Kings xxiii. 10) ; the loves above mentioned being signified by that fire ; and whereas by seed given to Molech is signified such infernal false, and stoning was a punishment of death for the injury and destruction of the truth of the Word, and of doctrine thence derived, therefore it is said, that the man, who giveth of his seed to Molech, dying shall die, and the people of the land shall stone him with stones : that stoning was the punishment for injuring or destroying truth, may be seen above, n. 655 ; that that false is destructive of all the good of the Word and of the church, is signified by, I will set My faces against this man, and I will cut him off from the midst of his people, because he hath polluted My sanctuary, and profaned the name of My holiness ; by sanctuary is signified the truth of heaven and the church, and by the name of holiness is signified all the quality thereof. From the passages which have been adduced it may now appear, that by seed, in the supreme sense, is understood divine truth which is from the Lord, and consequently the truth of the Word and of the doctrine of the church which is from the Word ; and, in the opposite or bad sense, the infernal false opposite to that truth.

769. "Who keep the commandments of God"—That hereby is signified with those who live the life of faith, which is charity, appears from the signification of keeping the commandments of God, as denoting to live according to the precepts contained in the Word ; and whereas that life is the life of faith, and the life of faith is charity, therefore by keeping the commandments of God is signified to live the life of faith, which is charity : the reason why the life of faith denotes charity towards the neighbor, is, because by faith is understood the faith which is of the Word, thus the faith of truth in the Word and from the Word, and by charity is signified the love of good and truth, spiritual, moral, and civil ; and whereas that which a man loves he also wills, and what he wills, this he does, hence by keeping the commandments of God is signified to live the life of

faith, which is charity. From these considerations it may appear, that all they who separate faith from charity, are entirely ignorant of the true nature both of faith and charity, for concerning faith they have no other idea than as of any other thing of the memory, which is believed only in consequence of being heard from men of erudition; such faith however is merely an historical faith, for they do not see whether the thing be so any otherwise than because another has declared it, and what is seen only from another, may be confirmed both from the literal sense of the Word not understood and from reasonings grounded in appearances and scientifics, although, at the same time, it may be false, and in direct opposition to the truth; and when it is confirmed, it becomes a faith of persuasion; but neither this faith nor historical faith, is spiritual faith, nor, consequently, saving faith, for they have not as yet any life in them from the Lord; but to the end that man may receive this life, he must live according to the Lord's precepts in the Word, which is the same thing as to live from the Lord, because the Lord is the Word and in the Word, and this life is the life of faith, which is charity, and in this case his affection becomes charity, and the thought derived from that affection becomes faith; for all the thought of man derives its life from affection, inasmuch as without affection it is not possible for any one to think, wherefore when the affection of man becomes spiritual his thought also becomes spiritual; consequently, according to the quality of charity with man, such is his faith; hence it may appear that charity and faith act as one like affection and thought, or what is the same, like will and understanding, for affection is of the will, and thought is of the understanding, consequently they make one in act, as good and truth; hence it is evident that to live according to the precepts of the Lord from the Word, or to keep the commandments of God, is to live the life of faith, which is charity.

770. "And have the testimony of Jesus Christ"—That hereby is signified, and who acknowledge the divine [principle] in the Lord's human, appears from the signification of the testimony of Jesus Christ, as denoting the confession and acknowledgment of the divine [principle] of the Lord in His human, concerning which see above, n. 392, 635, 649, 749.

771. Ver. 18. "And I stood upon the sand of the sea"—That hereby is signified the continuation of the state of them who are signified by the dragon, appears from the signification of standing upon the sand of the sea, as denoting to see as yet the quality of those who are understood by the dragon, for it follows that he saw a beast ascending from the sea, to which the dragon gave his might, and his throne, and his power; and afterwards that he saw a beast ascending from the earth, which spake as a dragon, and several other things of a like nature; and whereas by the description of those beasts is continued the description of the state of those who are dragons, therefore this is what is signified by standing upon the sand of the sea. Moreover, by the sand of the sea is signified sterility, such as has place with those who think indeed concerning faith, but not

concerning the life of faith, which is charity, for where such dwell in the spiritual world, there appears nothing but heaps of stones and sand, and very rarely any grass or shrub ; hence also it is, that by the sand of the sea is signified the state of those who are understood by the dragon.

END OF TWELFTH CHAPTER AND THIRD VOLUME.